Age	Milestone	Age	Milestone
13 months	Pats toy in imitation Vocalizes four different vowel-consonant combinations Stands alone Walks alone	31 months	Builds tower of eight cubes Swings leg to kick ball Jumps distance of 4 inches
16 months	Scribbles spontaneously Imitates single words Walks alone with good coordination Throws ball while standing	34 months	Imitates vertical and horizontal strokes Poses question Walks on tiptoe for four steps
19 months	Builds tower of two cubes Uses word(s) to make wants known Walks up stairs or down stairs with help	37 months	Understands concept of one Understands two prepositions Walks up stairs, alternating feet
22 months	Combines word(s) and gesture(s) Points to three of doll's body parts Stands on right foot or left foot with help	42 months	Names four colors Understands four prepositions Copies a circle, a plus sign, or a square
25 months	Uses a two-word utterance Imitates a two-word sentence Runs with coordination	48 months	Goes to toilet alone Hops on one foot Throws ball overhand Climbs well
28 months	Builds tower of six cubes Uses a three-word sentence Walks up stairs or down stairs alone, placing both feet on each step	60 months	Skips Ties shoes Follows three commands Dresses and undresses self

Source: Ages 1 month through 42 months from N. Bayley (1993), *Bayley Scales of Infant Development,* Copyright © 1993 by The Psychological Corporation, a Harcourt Assessment Company. Adapted and reproduced by permission. All rights reserved. "Bayley Scales of Infant Development" is a trademark of The Psychological Corporation. Ages 48 months and 60 months from Lewis (1991), Northern and Downs (1991), and Shapiro (1991).

Assessment of Children
Behavioral and Clinical Applications
Fourth Edition

Jerome M. Sattler
San Diego State University

Jerome M. Sattler, Publisher, Inc.
San Diego

Editorial Services: Sally Lifland and Denise Throckmorton, Lifland et al., Bookmakers
Interior Design: Jerome M. Sattler and Sally Lifland
Cover Design: Jennifer Mathews and Jerome M. Sattler
Proofreaders: Gail Magin, Jane Hoover, Madge Schworer, and David N. Sattler
Indexers: Jeanne Yost and Susan Patt
Production Coordinators: Sally Lifland and Jerome M. Sattler
Compositor: Omegatype Typography, Inc., Champaign, Illinois
Cover Printer: Phoenix Color
Printer and Binder: Maple-Vail Book Manufacturing Group

This text was set in Times Roman and Helvetica, printed on Highland Book, Smyth sewn, with post
embossed Type 2 cover stock. The finish is matte polyester with spot gloss UV.

Cover: Wassily Kandinsky, *Spitzen im Bogen,* 1927

Library of Congress Catalog Card Number: 2001117982

ISBN 0-9618209-8-5

16 15 14 13 12 11 10 9 8 7 6 5 4 3 2 1   13 12 11 10 09 08 07 06 05 04 03 02 01

Printed in the United States of America

To the memory of

my parents,
Nathan and Pearl Sattler

my brother,
Paul Sattler

my father-in-law,
Richard McIntyre

my mother-in-law,
Marjorie McIntyre

my friend,
Victor Menache

for their love and affection will always endure

BRIEF CONTENTS

CONTENTS

LIST OF TABLES

LIST OF FIGURES

LIST OF EXHIBITS

PREFACE

A person who is severely impaired never knows his hidden sources of strength until he is treated like a normal human being and encouraged to shape his own life.
—Helen Keller

The fourth edition of *Assessment of Children: Behavioral and Clinical Applications* is a companion volume to *Assessment of Children: Cognitive Applications*. It is designed to be used as an independent text in such courses as personality assessment, behavioral assessment, and child clinical assessment. It can also be used together with *Assessment of Children: Cognitive Applications* to provide in-depth coverage of assessment of children. The text generally follows the format of the behavioral and clinical-psychoeducational sections of *Assessment of Children, Third Edition*.

Like former editions, the fourth edition of *Assessment of Children: Behavioral and Clinical Applications* is designed not only as a teaching text but also as a reference book for students and professionals. The revision is a major one. Every chapter has been rewritten to make the text more comprehensive, relevant, readable, up to date, and informative. The book contains new chapters on objective personality tests and functional behavioral assessment and new material on self-monitoring and school violence. Topics receiving expanded coverage include interviewing and behavioral observations, adaptive behavior, dynamic assessment, and assessment of children with attention-deficit/hyperactivity disorder, children with learning disabilities, children with mental retardation, children who are gifted, children with visual impairments, children with hearing impairments, children with an autistic disorder, and children with brain injury.

Assessment of Children: Behavioral and Clinical Applications, Fourth Edition contains several useful assessment aids and intervention guidelines. These include the following:

- Three detailed questionnaires—a Background Questionnaire, a Personal Data Questionnaire, and a School Referral Questionnaire—to assist in obtaining information about the referred child from a parent, from the child himself or herself, and from a teacher
- Eleven semistructured interviews designed for children with special needs, their parents, and their teachers
- Forms for conducting systematic behavioral observations
- Self-monitoring forms
- Functional behavioral assessment recording forms
- Tables showing developmental trends in cognitive development, language acquisition, concept of self, person percep-

tion, moral judgment, temporal concepts, and recognition of emotions
- Observation procedures for children who may have attention-deficit/hyperactivity disorder or autistic disorder
- Informal measures of phonological ability
- IQ–achievement discrepancy scores necessary to establish a significant difference in cases of learning disability
- Detailed intervention guidelines for helping children with attention-deficit/hyperactivity disorder, learning disabilities, mental retardation, autistic disorder, or brain injury

Assessment of Children: Behavioral and Clinical Applications, Fourth Edition contains several useful learning aids. These include the following:

- At the beginning of each chapter, lists of major headings and goals and objectives
- At the end of each chapter, a Thinking Through the Issues section, a summary of each major topic area, a list of key terms, concepts, and names, each linked to the page on which it appears, and a series of study questions
- In several chapters, exercises to help with mastery of the material
- A checklist for evaluating an examiner's interview techniques
- Glossaries of key terms used in the fields of learning disabilities and brain injury
- A checklist for identifying creativity
- Checklists for arriving at DSM-IV–TR diagnoses for attention-deficit/hyperactivity disorder and autistic disorder

The text also includes an extensive collection of cartoons touching on assessment, psychology, and education. The cartoons provide relief through humor and serve as a teaching and learning tool.

This book is based on the philosophy that a person cannot be a competent clinical assessor unless he or she has the relevant information about the child's presenting problem, the child's assets and limitations, the child's family, the child's classroom, and the child's environment, as well as knowledge of the interventions that might help the child and family. Therefore, in this text, you will find information both about the major problem areas encountered by children and about interventions. You should consult additional references about the child's problem areas, as needed.

As we enter the 21st century, we must be mindful of the prominent place that litigation occupies in American society. Assessment results, and the decisions reached on the basis of assessment results, may be questioned by those who seek legal recourse to change a diagnosis or recommendation.

Therefore, I strongly urge you to assume that everything you do has potential legal consequences. The best strategy is to be prepared. You can do this by (a) using the most appropriate assessment techniques and instruments, (b) maintaining accurate and complete records, and (c) keeping up with the research and clinical literature in your field.

Underlying all assessments are a respect for children and their families and a desire to help children. A thorough assessment should allow us to learn something about the child that we could not learn from simply talking to others about the child, observing the child, or reviewing the child's records. Assessment makes a difference in the lives of children and their families, as well as in the actions of the professionals, including educators, who work with children and their families.

Note to instructors: An *Instructor's Manual* accompanies *Assessment of Children: Behavioral and Clinical Applications, Fourth Edition.* The manual contains multiple-choice questions useful for objective examinations.

ACKNOWLEDGMENTS

No Passion on Earth
No Love or Hate
Is Equal to the Passion to Change
Someone Else's Draft.

—H. G. Wells

I wish to acknowledge the contributions of numerous individuals who have written original material for the book or who have assisted in updating various parts of the book:

Dr. William Reynolds, who is co-author of the chapter on assessment of behavioral, social, and emotional competencies

Dr. Lisa Weyandt, who is co-author of the chapters on learning disabilities and attention-deficit/hyperactivity disorder

Dr. Mary Ann Roberts, who is co-author of the chapter on attention-deficit/hyperactivity disorder

Carol Evans, MA, who is co-author of the chapter on visual impairments

Steven Hardy-Braz, Psy.S., who is co-author of the chapter on hearing impairments

Dr. Rik D'Amato, who is co-author of the chapters on brain injury

I also have been fortunate in receiving the wisdom, guidance, and suggestions of several individuals who willingly gave of their time and energy to read all or most of the manuscript. I wish to express my thanks and appreciation to

Dr. Vincent C. Alfonso, Fordham University
Dr. Ron Dumont, Fairleigh Dickenson University
Dr. William A. Hillix, San Diego State University
Dr. Nancy Mather, University of Arizona
Dr. Anne Owen, University of Kansas
Dr. Anthony W. Paolitto, James Madison University
Bonnie J. Sattler, MA, Kaiser Permanente, San Diego
Dr. David N. Sattler, Western Washington University
Dr. Lisa Weyandt, Central Washington University
Darlene Wheeler, MA, Riverside Public Schools
Dr. John O. Willis, Rivier College

The following individuals read one or more chapters of the manuscript. Their excellent feedback was extremely helpful in making the manuscript more scholarly and accurate.

Dr. Galen Aliesi, Western Michigan State University
Dr. Randy Borum, University of South Florida
Robert J. Clark, Ed.S., Topeka Public Schools

Dr. Michael L. Dimitroff, Governor State University
Dr. Robert A. Fein, National Threat Assessment Center
Dr. Vanessa Malcarne, San Diego State University
Dr. Guy McBride, Burke County Public Schools
Dr. Carl Meyers, Western Kentucky University
Dr. Jeff Miller, Duquesne University
Dr. Mary Ann Roberts, University of Iowa
Dr. Jian Jun Zhu, The Psychological Corporation

My able assistant, Kadir Samuel, helped me in numerous ways in getting the manuscript and book into production. Kadir, thanks for being so special. Your dependability and dedication to getting this book published are much appreciated.

Brenda Pinedo and Sharon Drum, at Jerome M. Sattler, Publisher, Inc., have been exceptional staff members. Thanks, Brenda and Sharon, for keeping the company office going and helping with the various details involved in getting this book into production.

I would like to thank the staff at the San Diego State Library for their assistance in obtaining books and reprints of articles. James F. Edwards, Steve Isachsen, and Rob Drake, from Instructional Technology Services at San Diego State University, and Adam D. Royce, James B. Varnel, Steve Bednarik, Larry "Matt" Matthews, and Robert Hilchey, from the College of Sciences Computing and Electronic Center at San Diego State University, were invaluable in helping me with the computer. Thank you all for your knowledge and expertise. It is comforting to know that you are available when I get into trouble with the computer, which seems to be a weekly occurrence. Lori Palmer, from Instructional Technology Services at San Diego State University, composed the figures that are in the book. Thank you, Lori.

I wish to thank the able secretarial staff of the Psychology Department at San Diego State University for relaying messages, notifying me of faxes, and helping me in innumerable other ways. Thank you, Darlene Pickrel, Linda Corio, and Sheryl Field.

I want to acknowledge Roy A. Wallace, West Coast representative from Maple-Vail Book Manufacturing Group. Roy, thank you for your help in getting this book printed. It has always been a pleasure working with you.

My family has been supportive throughout this 8-year project. Thank you, Bonnie, Heidi, David, Deborah, Keith, Walter, Nicole, and Justin, for your encouragement and support.

I have been fortunate in having a superb copyediting and production staff help get this book ready for publication. The folks at Lifland et al., Bookmakers are craftpersons and, as the title of their firm indicates, truly "bookmakers." Thank you, Sally Lifland, Denise Throckmorton, and Gail Magin, for your patience and tolerance and for working with me during a 10-month period to make the manuscript clear and readable, grammatically correct, organized, coherent, as free from error as possible, and a work that we can be proud of.

I want to thank Yoram Mizrahi and the staff at Omegatype for putting my galleys into pages with exceptional expertise. Thank you, Yoram, for doing such an excellent job.

Finally, I wish to acknowledge the role that San Diego State University has played in my life. For 36 years, this great university has given me the support and academic freedom needed to pursue my interests in teaching, research, writing, and consultation. Thank you, San Diego State University, for all that you have given me. I hope that in my small way I have returned something to my students and to the university community at large.

ABOUT THE AUTHOR

I grew up in the East Bronx of New York City during the 1930s and 1940s. Both of my parents came to the United States from villages in Poland in the early 1920s. I began my study of psychology at the City College of New York, obtaining my BA in 1952. I received my master's degree in 1953 and my Ph.D. in 1959 from the University of Kansas (KU). While at KU, I was introduced to gestalt and existential psychology and participated in the Veterans Administration clinical psychology training program. My mentors at KU, Fritz Heider and John Chotlos, were extraordinarily gifted and creative psychologists and teachers. In 1954, I was drafted into the U.S. Army and worked as a psychologist in an outpatient mental health clinic.

After graduation, I taught and worked in a child guidance clinic at Fort Hays Kansas State College. In 1961, I accepted a position at the University of North Dakota. In 1965, I joined the staff at San Diego State University (SDSU), where I taught for 29 years. I retired from SDSU in 1994. I am now a Professor Emeritus and Adjunct Professor at SDSU. Also, I am a Diplomate in Clinical Psychology and a Fellow of the American Psychological Association. In 1998, I received the Senior Scientist Award from the Division of School Psychology (Division 16) of the American Psychological Association. Finally, I am the author of *Clinical and Forensic Interviewing of Children and Families: Guidelines for the Mental Health, Education, Pediatric, and Child Maltreatment Fields* and one of the co-authors of the *Stanford-Binet Intelligence Scale: Fourth Edition.*

I had three excellent international experiences. The first was as a Fulbright lecturer at the University of Kebangsaan in Kuala Lumpur, Malaysia, in 1972. The second was as an exchange professor at Katholieke Universiteit in Nijmegen, The Netherlands, in 1983. And the third was as an exchange professor at University College Cork, in Cork, Ireland, in 1989.

When I am not working on a book, I enjoy ballroom dancing, walking, listening to jazz, watching movies, reading, and spending time with my family, including my two grandchildren.

I feel fortunate in having chosen a career that has allowed me the freedom and opportunity to write, teach, conduct research, travel, study, and interact with remarkable students and colleagues. Little did I realize when I started out 42 years ago that *Assessment of Children* would consume a good part of my professional and personal life. And little did I realize that the book would go through four editions, train over 200,000 students and professionals since its initial publication in 1973, be referred to as "the bible" of assessment, be translated into Spanish three times, and be rated by my fellow psychologists as one of the 50 great books in psychology. I am honored, gratified, and humbled by the recognition that *Assessment of Children* has received over the past 28 years.

ASSESSMENT OF BEHAVIOR BY INTERVIEW METHODS: GENERAL CONSIDERATIONS

A question rightly asked is half answered.

—C. G. J. Jacobi

An answer is invariably the parent of a great family of new questions.

—John Steinbeck

Goals and Objectives

This chapter is designed to enable you to do the following:

- Describe how a clinical assessment interview differs from a conversation, a psychotherapeutic interview, and a survey research interview

- Understand the strengths and weaknesses of the clinical assessment interview

- Compare unstructured, semistructured, and structured clinical assessment interviews

- Develop effective listening skills

- Develop rapport with the interviewee

- Time questions and change topics appropriately

- Formulate appropriate questions

- Avoid ineffective questions

- Use probing techniques

- Use structuring statements

- Encourage appropriate replies

- Deal with difficult situations in the interview

- Recognize your emotions

- Record information and schedule appointments

This is the first of three chapters on the clinical assessment interview; it focuses on general principles of interviewing. The second chapter discusses strategies particularly useful for interviewing children, parents, teachers, and families. The third chapter deals with the post-assessment interview, the reliability and validity of the interview, and other issues related to interviewing. It is important to realize that the interviewing guidelines in this section cannot cover every possible situation that may arise in the interview. However, after you master the material in this section, you should be able to handle many different situations. We will use the term *interviewer* instead of *examiner* and *interviewee* instead of *examinee* in this and the next two chapters, because parents and teachers, as well as children, often are interviewed as part of the case study.

The primary goal of the *clinical assessment interview* is to obtain relevant, reliable, and valid information about interviewees and their problems. This includes information about their personality, temperament, motor skills, cognitive skills, communication skills, study habits, work habits, interpersonal behavior, interests, daily living skills and difficulties, and perception of the referral problem. Important sources of information are the *content of the interview* (i.e., what the interviewee tells you) and the *interviewee's style* (i.e., how the interviewee speaks, behaves, and relates to you). The information you obtain will depend on how interviewees perceive you, the atmosphere you establish, your interviewing style, and—with children or clients with special needs—your success in gearing the interview to their abilities or developmental level.

CLINICAL ASSESSMENT INTERVIEWS VERSUS ORDINARY CONVERSATIONS AND OTHER TYPES OF INTERVIEWS

Clinical Assessment Interviews and Ordinary Conversations

There are several key differences between clinical assessment interviews and *ordinary conversation* (Kadushin, 1983). Let's compare the main characteristics of a clinical assessment interview to those of an ordinary conversation.

1. The clinical assessment interview is usually a formally arranged meeting; a conversation may occur spontaneously.
2. The interviewer is usually obliged to accept the interviewee's request for an interview, and sometimes children and parents also are obliged to come for an interview; there is usually no obligation to continue a conversation, and one of the parties may end it abruptly.
3. The clinical assessment interview has a definite purpose; a conversation may cover topics randomly, with no specific purpose.
4. The interviewer and interviewee have a well-defined and structured relationship in which the interviewer questions and the interviewee answers; a conversation usually involves a mutual exchange of ideas.

5. The interviewer plans and organizes his or her behavior; no planning is necessary for a conversation.
6. The interviewer attempts to direct the interaction and choose the content of the interview; a conversation usually flows.
7. The interviewer must focus on the interviewer-interviewee interaction; little or no attention may be given to the details of the interaction during a conversation.
8. The interviewer does not outwardly react to unpleasant facts and feelings that the interviewee reveals; parties may react emotionally or judgmentally during a conversation.
9. The interviewer clarifies questions and does not presume understanding; during a conversation, much may be left unstated or misunderstood.
10. The interviewer follows guidelines concerning confidentiality and privileged communication; parties to a conversation are under no legal or ethical obligation to keep the information discussed confidential.

In summary, ordinary conversation is more spontaneous, less formal, and less structured than clinical assessment interviews and has few of the characteristics associated with formal interviews. A clinical assessment interview is different from an ordinary conversation in that *the interview involves an interpersonal interaction that has a mutually accepted purpose, with formal, clearly defined roles and a set of norms governing the interaction.*

Clinical Assessment Interviews and Psychotherapeutic Interviews

Clinical assessment interviews and *psychotherapeutic interviews* are part of an ongoing assessment process. There is continuity between the two types of interviews, with changing and evolving goals rather than different ones. Still, there are important differences. Some of the main differences between clinical assessment interviews and psychotherapeutic interviews follow:

1. *Goals.* The purpose of the clinical assessment interview is to obtain relevant information in order to make an informed decision about the interviewee—for example, whether there is a problem and what types of treatment, interventions, or services the interviewee may need. The clinical assessment interview is not an open-ended, client-centered counseling session; there is an agenda to be covered. The function of the psychotherapeutic interview, in contrast, is to relieve the emotional distress of the client, foster insight, and enable changes in behavior and life situations.

2. *Direction and structure.* In the clinical assessment interview, the interviewer may cover a specific set of topics or questions in order to obtain developmental, medical, and social histories; formulate a detailed description of a specific problem; or conduct a mental status evaluation. The interviewer uses probing techniques to obtain detailed and accurate information. In the psychotherapeutic interview, the interviewer uses

specialized techniques to achieve therapeutic goals. The focus may be on problem solving, cognitive restructuring, or increasing awareness and expression of feelings.

3. *Contact time.* The length of a clinical assessment interview varies. Often, there is no expectation that the interviewer will see the interviewee again, except for the formal testing and possibly a post-assessment interview. Psychotherapeutic interview sessions, in contrast, usually last 50 minutes, and there is an expectation that the therapist will see the client for at least several interviews.

Despite the differences between clinical assessment interviews and psychotherapeutic interviews, they overlap in several ways. For instance, in psychotherapeutic interviews, you should continually assess the interviewee; and in clinical assessment interviews, you should use psychotherapeutic strategies to deal with interviewee reactions such as emotional upsets during the interview.

Some of the similarities between the two types of interviews follow:

1. *Rapport.* Interviewers and therapists must establish an accepting atmosphere in which interviewees/clients feel comfortable talking about themselves. This requires interviewers and therapists to be respectful, genuine, and empathic.

2. *Skills.* Interviewers and therapists must have a sound knowledge of child development and psychopathology and effective listening skills.

3. *Goals.* Interviewers and therapists must gather information and continuously assess their interviewees' and clients' thinking, affect, perceptions, and attributions.

See Figure 1-1 for an outline of objectives of the two types of interviews.

Clinical Assessment Interviews and Survey Research Interviews

Survey research interviews usually focus on interviewees' opinions or preferences with respect to various topics. To obtain this information, techniques similar to those used in clinical assessment interviews are used. There are, however, major differences between the two types of interviews. In survey research, interviewers usually initiate the interviews in order to obtain the interviewees' opinions about particular topics. Interviewees are encouraged to give brief responses or to choose one from a list of answers offered by the interviewer (e.g., "disagree," "somewhat agree," or "strongly agree"). What interviewees share in a survey research interview has few or no direct consequences for them personally; responses are used for survey purposes, not for making decisions about the interviewees' personal lives. In contrast, clinical assessment interviews are initiated by interviewees or their families because they are motivated to address problems, relieve symptoms, or seek changes. Interviewees are encouraged to provide in-depth

CLINICAL ASSESSMENT INTERVIEW OBJECTIVES

1. To obtain relevant information and to arrive at a decision (for example, diagnosis, need for referral, type of treatment or remediation needed)
2. To cover specific content areas (for example, developmental history, social history, mental status evaluation, analysis of problem behavior)
3. To limit contact—usually to one or two sessions

COMMON OBJECTIVES

1. To establish rapport
2. To facilitate communication
3. To communicate respect, genuineness, and empathy
4. To attend, listen, and reflect feelings and content
5. To gather information
6. To allow interviewee to reveal concerns and preoccupations
7. To assess interviewee's verbal and nonverbal communications

PSYCHOTHERAPEUTIC INTERVIEW OBJECTIVES

1. To foster behavioral, cognitive, and affective change
2. To use approaches geared to therapeutic goals (for example, insight, cognitive restructuring, reduction of distress)
3. To limit contact to the time required to achieve therapeutic goals—varies widely (with therapy and problem) from weeks to months or years

Figure 1-1. Differences and similarities between clinical assessment interviews and psychotherapeutic interviews.

responses, and the focus is on personal experiences and behavior. Furthermore, *the consequences of the clinical assessment interview are significant to the interviewee, no matter who initiates the interview*—a diagnosis may be made, an intervention plan formulated, or a recommendation made for placement in a special education program.

STRENGTHS AND WEAKNESSES OF THE CLINICAL ASSESSMENT INTERVIEW

Strengths of the Clinical Assessment Interview

The clinical assessment interview serves several functions for children and their families (Edelbrock & Costello, 1988; Gorden, 1975; Gresham, 1984). It allows the interviewer to do the following:

- Communicate and clarify the nature and goals of the assessment process to the child and parents
- Understand the child's and parents' expectations regarding the assessment
- Obtain information about the family's past and current life events
- Document the context, severity, and chronicity of the child's problem behaviors
- Use flexible procedures to ask the child and parents questions
- Resolve ambiguous responses
- Clarify misunderstandings that the child or parents may have
- Compare the child's and parents' verbal and nonverbal behaviors
- Verify previously collected information about the child and family
- Formulate hypotheses about the child and family that can be tested using other assessment procedures
- Learn about the child's perception and understanding of his or her problem
- Learn about the beliefs, values, and expectations held by parents and other adults (e.g., teachers) about the child's behavior
- Assess the child's and parents' receptivity to various intervention strategies and their willingness to follow recommendations

The interview, as previously noted, is a flexible assessment procedure, useful in generating and explaining hypotheses, as the focus of the discussion can be changed as needed. The interviewee's verbal responses and nonverbal behavior (e.g., posture, gestures, facial expressions, and voice inflection) can serve as valuable guides for understanding and evaluating the interviewee. Sometimes, the interview may be the only direct means of obtaining information from children or parents, particularly those who are illiterate, severely depressed, or unwilling to provide information by other means.

Overall, the interview is one of the most useful techniques for obtaining information, because it allows interviewees to express, in their own terms, their views about themselves and relevant life events. The interview allows great latitude for the interviewee's expression of concerns, thoughts, feelings, and reactions, with a minimum of structure and redirection on the part of the interviewer.

Weaknesses of the Clinical Assessment Interview

As an assessment tool, though, the clinical assessment interview has several weaknesses:

- Reliability and validity may be difficult to establish (see Chapter 4 in this text for information about reliability and validity).
- The freedom and versatility offered by the interview can result in lack of comparability across interviews.
- The information obtained by one interviewer may differ from that obtained by another interviewer.
- Interviewers may fail to elicit important data.
- Interviewers may fail to interpret the data accurately.
- Interviewees may provide inaccurate information (e.g., their long-term memory may be fallible; they may distort replies, be reluctant to reveal information, deliberately conceal information, or be unable to answer the queries).
- Interviewees, especially young children, may be limited in their language skills and hence have difficulty describing events or their thoughts and feelings.
- Interviewees may feel threatened, inadequate, or hurried and thus fail to respond adequately and accurately.
- Interviewees may be susceptible to subtle, unintended cues from the interviewer that may influence their replies.
- Interviewees and interviewers may have personal biases that result in selective attention and recall, inaccurate associations, and faulty conclusions.

PURPOSES OF CLINICAL ASSESSMENT INTERVIEWS

The purpose of a clinical assessment interview depends on whether it is an initial interview, a post-assessment interview, or a follow-up interview.

Initial Interview

The *initial interview* is designed to inform the interviewee about the assessment process and to obtain information relevant to diagnosis, treatment, remediation, or placement in special programs. The initial interview may be part of an assessment process that includes standardized psychological testing, or it may be the sole assessment procedure. When psychologists administer tests, an initial interview usually precedes the testing.

During the initial interview, you will form impressions of the interviewee's general attitude, attitude toward answering questions, attitude toward herself or himself, need for reassurance, and ability to establish a relationship with you, the interviewer. You will, of course, form other impressions that will be tested and evaluated as the interview progresses. You will want to obtain as much information as possible during the initial interview, not only because your workload may impose time constraints but also because the interviewee may not be available for further questioning. The goal is to gather information that will help you (a) develop hypotheses, (b) select and administer appropriate tests, (c) arrive at a valid evaluation of the child and her or his family, and (d) design effective interventions.

Post-Assessment Interview

The *post-assessment interview* (also known as the *exit interview*) is designed to discuss the assessment findings and recommendations with the interviewee's parents and, often, the interviewee. Sometimes exit interviews are held with the interviewee's teachers or the referral source. The post-assessment interview is covered more fully in Chapter 3.

Follow-Up Interview

The *follow-up interview* is designed to assess outcomes of treatment or interventions and to gauge the appropriateness of the assessment findings and recommendations. The treatment or intervention plan will need to be altered if it is not effective. Techniques appropriate for the initial interview and post-assessment interview also are useful for the follow-up interview (see Chapter 3).

DEGREES OF STRUCTURE IN INITIAL CLINICAL ASSESSMENT INTERVIEWS

Initial clinical assessment interviews vary in type; we will focus on three types—unstructured interviews, semistructured interviews, and structured interviews (Edelbrock & Costello, 1988). In unstructured interviews, the interview process is allowed to unfold without specific guidelines. Semistructured interviews are based on general and flexible guidelines. In structured interviews, the exact order and wording of each question is specified, with little opportunity for follow-up questions not directly related to the specified questions.

Within these categories, interviews can vary in degree of structure, scope, and depth. Unstructured interviews may cover one area in depth (e.g., school performance) or superficially touch on several areas (e.g., school, home). Similarly, semistructured interviews may be tailored to a single area (e.g., family relationships) or cover several areas. And structured interviews may differ in the coverage given to a partic-

ular area. Let's now look more closely at these three forms of initial interviews.

Unstructured Interviews

Unstructured interviews place a premium on allowing interviewees to tell their stories with minimal guidance. "Unstructured" doesn't mean, however, that there is no agenda. You will still need to guide interviewees to talk about issues and concerns relevant to the referral problem, and such guidance requires that your clinical skills be honed. Unstructured interviews are more versatile than either semistructured or structured interviews. You are free to follow up leads as needed and to tailor the interview to the specific interviewee. You can ask parents, teachers, friends, neighbors, and interviewees different questions, depending on their relationship to the child (and the contribution they can make to the assessment task). You also can use unstructured interviews to identify general problem areas, after which you can follow up with a semistructured or structured interview.

Semistructured Interviews

Semistructured interviews are likewise designed for clinically sophisticated interviewers. Although there are guidelines to follow, these types of interviews allow latitude in phrasing questions, pursuing alternative lines of inquiry, and interpreting responses. They are especially useful when you want to obtain detailed information about specific psychological concerns or physical problems. Appendix B contains several semistructured interviews, including interviews for children, parents, families, and teachers, as well as a mental status evaluation (see Sattler, 1998, for additional semistructured interviews). The semistructured interviews presented in Appendix B orient you to areas that you may want to cover. They are meant to be used as flexible guides, not as rigid rules. Use only those portions you think you need, and feel free to modify the wording and order of questions to fit the situation. Be sure to follow up leads and hypotheses. Each semistructured interview will help you target specific areas needing further inquiry.

The Semistructured Clinical Interview for Children and Adolescents Aged 6–19 (SCICA; McConaughy & Achenbach, 1994) provides a flexible procedure for interviewing children. After the interview is completed, the interviewer rates the symptoms reported by the interviewee on a 4-point scale (no occurrence, very slight or ambiguous occurrence, definite occurrence of mild to moderate intensity, and definite occurrence of severe intensity). The resulting scores are plotted on a profile that provides standardized scores for the following areas: anxious/depressed, anxious, family relations, withdrawn, aggressive behavior, attention problems, strange, and resistant. McConaughy and Achenbach (1994) emphasize that the SCICA should be used together with other assessment procedures. This advice is important, because reliability studies in the SCICA Manual indicate that neither its interrater reliability (the extent to which information obtained from one rater is comparable to that obtained from another rater) nor its test-retest reliability (the extent to which a person's score on the test on one occasion is comparable to that person's score on re-test) reaches an acceptable level for making diagnostic decisions about children. This should not be surprising, given the weaknesses of clinical assessment interviews pointed out earlier in the chapter.

As in all types of interviews, your focus during the semistructured interview must always be on the interviewee. This focus is needed because the interviewee (a) may not want to talk to you, (b) may be hesitant to discuss some topics, (c) may speak so quietly or quickly that you will have difficulty understanding him or her, (d) may be upset over some remark made, (e) may be unable to recall some details because of memory difficulties or other reasons, (f) may be physically sick and unable to concentrate on the questions, or (g) may be recovering from an illness that interferes with the ability to converse. In each case, you should deviate from the suggested list of questions as needed to handle the problem. Also deviate from the suggested list of questions when you need to probe, follow up leads, or check some point of interest.

Structured Interviews

Structured interviews are designed to increase the reliability and validity of traditional child diagnostic procedures. Such interviews are usually available for both children and parents. Structured interviews differ in the types of information they provide. Most yield information about the presence, absence, severity, onset, and duration of symptoms, but others yield quantitative scores in symptom areas or global indices of psychopathology. They minimize the role of interview bias and clinical inference in the interview process. Although these interviews require specialized training to administer, even individuals without professional degrees can be given this specialized training.

The following are some structured interviews:

1. Child and Adolescent Psychiatric Assessment (CAPA): Version 4.2–Child Version (Angold, Cox, Rutter, & Simonoff, 1996)
2. Child Adolescent Schedule (CAS) (Hodges, 1997)
3. Diagnostic Interview for Children and Adolescents–Revised (DICA–R) 8.0 (Reich, 1996)
4. Diagnostic Interview Schedule for Children (DISC–IV) (Shaffer, 1996)
5. Schedule for Affective Disorders and Schizophrenia for School-Age Children (K-SADS–IVR) (Ambrosini & Dixon, 1996)
6. Revised Schedule for Affective Disorders and Schizophrenia for School-Age Children: Present and Lifetime Version (K-SADS–PL) (Kaufman, Birmaher, Brent, Rao, & Ryan, 1996)

7. Schedule for Affective Disorders and Schizophrenia for School-Age Children: Epidemiological Version 5 (K-SADS–E5) (Orvaschel, 1995)

All of these structured interviews can be used for children with psychological disorders, and most can be used as survey interviews. All of the structured interviews have either parent versions or parent and child versions contained within the same interview. Table C-1 in Appendix C lists sources for these interviews. Structured interviews are continually being revised to conform to changes in accepted diagnostic systems, such as those reported in the most recent edition of the *Diagnostic and Statistic Manual of Mental Disorders (DSM)*. To incorporate advances in psychology and psychiatry, to conform with the nosology of colleagues, and to facilitate billing, use the latest version of *DSM* and the structured interviews associated with it.

Structured interviews generally use the same questions for each interviewee. This standardized procedure is particularly valuable when the primary goal is to make a psychiatric diagnosis or to obtain research data. In addition to assuring that each interviewee is asked the same questions (unless their responses require follow-up questions asked of some but not all interviewees), the standardization provided by structured interviews ensures that no topics are overlooked.

Hodges (1993), in her review of the available literature, offered the following conclusions about structured interviews for children and parents:

1. Children are able to answer questions about their mental status.
2. Asking direct questions about their mental status has no negative effects on children.
3. The reports of the parent and child "cannot be considered interchangeable, nor can the parent report be considered the 'gold standard' to which the child's report is compared" (p. 50).
4. In research studies, diagnostic interviews need to be supplemented with measures that evaluate children's level of functioning and degree of impairment.
5. Interviewers, even professionals, need to be trained to use structured interview schedules reliably.
6. Continued research is needed to evaluate the reliability and validity of structured interviews for children.

Potential difficulties with structured interviews. Structured interviews have several disadvantages (Kleinmuntz, 1982). Their rigid format may interfere with the establishment of rapport. Answers may be short and supply minimal information, making meaningful leads difficult to follow up. Structured interviews primarily indicate whether a disorder is present and are designed to produce diagnoses listed in *DSM* (Mash & Terdal, 1988). They neither address the specific family or individual dynamics that are necessary considerations in any intervention program nor focus on a functional analysis of behavior problems. And, unless they are revised, they become obsolete when the diagnostic system on which they are based is revised.

Reliability also may be a problem with structured interviews (McConaughy, 1996). First, young children may not be reliable informants. Second, reliability fluctuates, depending on the diagnosis. Third, scoring on a present-versus-absent format (i.e., whether a problem is or is not present) may be difficult because of subtle gradations of symptoms. Fourth, agreement between the responses of children and parents may be poor. Finally, lengthy interviews may challenge children's attention span, and consequently, the information obtained may not be valid.

The use of a structured interview does not guarantee that the interview will be conducted in a standardized way or that all interviewees and their parents will understand the questions in the same way. First, interviewers ask questions in different ways, using various vocal inflections, intonations, rhythms, and pauses. Second, interviewers engage in unique nonverbal behaviors and vocalizations (e.g., clearing the throat, making guttural sounds), use idiosyncratic words and phrases (e.g., "you know," "like," "that's fine"), and make clarifying remarks (e.g., "Can you repeat what you said?"). Third, interviewers may follow up responses differently, depending on their interpretation of the interviewees' statements. Fourth, interviewees and their parents may not understand the questions or may interpret the same question in different ways. For example, research shows that some children and mothers will have difficulty understanding questions related to obsessive and compulsive symptoms and to delusions (Breslau, 1987). Fifth, interviewees' parents' levels of anxiety or distress may be related to the number of symptoms they report. For example, research shows that mothers who were highly anxious or distressed reported more symptoms on the part of their children than did mothers who were less anxious or distressed (Frick, Silverthorn, & Evans, 1994). Finally, interviewers and interviewees give subtle unintended cues to each other that can be associated with language and communication patterns, attitudes, prejudices and stereotypes, cultural practices, social and interpersonal patterns of relating, and personal likes and dislikes. One or several of these may affect the interaction. These are only some of the ways variability is introduced into the interview, even when interviewers use a set of standard questions.

We recommend that you study one or more structured interviews. Not only are they valuable in and of themselves, but they also provide questions that you can incorporate into the traditional unstructured or semistructured assessment interview.

Computer-generated interviews. The ultimate in structured interviewing may be *computer-generated interviewing.* Computers present the same questions to all interviewees who are assigned to a particular interview schedule, deliver every question in the same manner, never fail to ask a question, and—for some interviewees—may make the interview more comfortable and less embarrassing. However, computers are impersonal and usually do not ask substitute questions or follow up meaningful leads; they cannot use clinical judgment to introduce questions or make inferences about the interviewee's nonverbal behavior.

Computers will miss subtle verbal and nonverbal cues and reactions that are noticeable to an interviewer. To be maximally effective, computer programs must adjust to the age and ability of the interviewee. As the fields of artificial intelligence and expert systems advance, computers are gaining flexibility. Computer interviewing may be the trend of the future. In fact, computers are already being used by some agencies as a preliminary assessment tool, followed by an interview with an interviewer who interprets the computer-generated data and explores areas needing further study.

Comparison of Unstructured, Semistructured, and Structured Interviews

All three types of interviews are valuable and play a role in the clinical assessment process. Unstructured interviews are preferred in some types of situations—especially crises, when the interviewee's concerns must be dealt with or an immediate decision made about the interviewee. Semistructured interviews can be tailored to nearly any problem area or situation and can elicit spontaneous information. Structured interviews are valuable when you want to cover several clinical areas systematically. It is best to view unstructured, semistructured, and structured interviews as complementary techniques that can be used independently or together.

> *The term* interview *was derived from the French* entrevoir, *to have a glimpse of, and* s'entrevoir, *to see each other.*
> —Arthur M. Wiens

INTRODUCTION TO INTERVIEWING GUIDELINES

Successful interviewing requires the ability to communicate clearly and the ability to understand the communications of interviewees, whether children or adults. Even if your clinical focus is on children, you will interview many adults as well, because a thorough assessment of children's problems will require you to interview parents, caregivers, and teachers. Although this section emphasizes interviewing children, much of the material also applies to interviewing adults.

During the interview, you will ask questions, follow up and probe responses, move from topic to topic, encourage replies, answer questions, gauge the pace of the interview, and formulate impressions of the interviewee. Following are important guidelines for conducting the interview, many of which are further described in this chapter (Gratus, 1988, adapted from pp. 91–93).

1. Prepare for the interview by considering the purpose of the interview, the physical setting, the structure of the interview, and the issues that may arise.
2. Decide whether you want to conduct a structured, semistructured, or unstructured interview or some combination of these different types of interviews.
3. If you decide on a semistructured or unstructured interview, know what information you want to obtain and frame your questions accordingly.
4. Learn as much as you can about the interviewee *before* the interview. Consider how the interviewee's health and situational factors may affect the interview. The more you know about the interviewee beforehand, the better position you will be in to conduct the interview and anticipate problems.
5. Be sure that any equipment you plan to use is in good working order.
6. If necessary, schedule the interview room in advance.
7. Make arrangements to decrease the likelihood of interruptions and distractions during the interview.
8. Consider the interviewee's cognitive and developmental levels and his or her ability to report factual information and feelings in the interview.
9. Greet the interviewee in a friendly, polite, open manner and speak clearly, using a reassuring tone.
10. Be prepared to explain confidentiality, and have the interviewee sign any necessary consent forms.
11. Establish rapport and try to put the interviewee at ease.
12. Recognize that you may have difficulty obtaining information when interviewees are anxious, upset, resistant, or unable to concentrate. Adjust your techniques to overcome their problems.
13. Be prepared to explain or expand on the questions you ask. Children, in particular, may not understand every question the first time you ask.
14. Develop the art of good listening. This means concentrating on what interviewees say, showing them that you are doing so, and "hearing" what they convey by their gestures and expressions. Remind yourself to *listen*.
15. Answer the interviewee's questions as clearly and directly as possible.
16. Periodically assess how the interview is proceeding, and make adjustments as needed.
17. Do not be frightened of silences. Pauses between questions may indicate that interviewees have more to say. Do not rush them. Give them the chance to answer you completely.
18. Check periodically to see that your understanding of the interviewee's problems is correct by offering a concise summary of the essential details.
19. Summarize, toward the end of the interview, the salient aspects of the information you have obtained.
20. Remember to ask open questions, to follow up and clarify ambiguous responses, and to probe carefully.
21. Record the information you obtain accurately, either during the interview proper or shortly thereafter. This is necessary because memory is unreliable. Keep your notes brief, and try not to lose eye contact with the interviewee for too long if you take notes during the interview.
22. Evaluate the information you obtain and decide whether you will need follow-up interviews.
23. Conclude the interview in the same friendly manner in which it began, and, no matter what the nature of the interview, always try to leave the interviewee with his or her dignity and self-esteem intact.
24. At the end of the interview, give the interviewee an opportunity to ask you any questions that he or she may have.

No matter how well you have planned the interview, each interviewee will present a new challenge. No individual is predictable. Even the most carefully laid plans may need to be changed. You must be flexible and prepared to deal with unanticipated problems. Recognize that there is no one absolute way to conduct the interview; alternative ways of asking questions can be equally effective in soliciting information.

Listen carefully to what the interviewee says. Interpret and assess what is significant, but do not accept everything as literal truth; remember, however, that it may be the interviewee's truth (Stevenson, 1960). Let the interviewee's values, culture, attitudes, and developmental level guide your interpretations.

Sometimes the interviewee's words are congruent with her or his emotions and sometimes they are not. *What* interviewees say is important, but *how* they act and speak are equally important. Consequently, you will need to attend to the interviewee's verbal and nonverbal communications. For more information on verbal-nonverbal discrepancies, see Cormier and Cormier (1998).

You will have difficulties as an interviewer if you fail to (a) express interest and warmth, (b) uncover the anxieties of the interviewee, (c) recognize when the anxieties of the interviewee are being exposed too rapidly, or (d) understand the cognitive level and culture of the interviewee. *However, failures are more likely to arise from a negative attitude than from technical difficulties* (Stevenson, 1960). Interviewees usually are forgiving of interviewers' mistakes, but not of interviewers' lack of interest or lack of kindness.

To be successful as an interviewer, you must know yourself, trust your ideas, be willing to make mistakes, and, above all, have a genuine desire to help the interviewee (Benjamin, 1981). You must be careful not to present yourself as all-knowing; instead, reveal your humanness to the interviewee. This means being honest with the interviewee and with yourself. Let the interviewee know that you do not have all the answers and that solutions may be difficult to find.

A good interview takes careful planning, skillful execution, and good organization; it is purposeful and goal-oriented. The success of the interview ultimately rests on your ability to guide the interview successfully. To acquire this skill, you will need practice, which is best acquired by interviewing volunteer children and adults before interviewing actual clients. Videotape and study yourself conducting these practice interviews. Ask skilled interviewers to review the videotapes and provide feedback on your interviewing techniques. Role-play various types of interviews. If possible, observe how skilled interviewers conduct interviews, and study their techniques. These activities will help you develop good interviewing skills.

The interview is affected by interviewer and interviewee characteristics (e.g., physical, cognitive, and affective factors), message components (e.g., language, nonverbal cues, and sensory cues), and interview climate (e.g., physical, social, temporal, and psychological factors). Your task is to be aware of these factors while you conduct the interview and to determine after the interview how these factors may have influenced the information you obtained.

EXTERNAL FACTORS AND ATMOSPHERE

Conduct the interview in a private, quiet room that is free from distractions. Select furniture that is appropriate for the interviewee. For example, use a low chair and table for a young child, and arrange the space so that there is no barrier between you and the child. For an older child or adult, you can use standard office equipment. You will, of course, need to use suitable furniture for those with special needs, such as interviewees with physical disabilities.

Keep interruptions to a minimum if you cannot avoid them entirely. Because telephone interruptions are particularly troublesome, arrange to have calls answered by the receptionist or sent directly to your voice mail. Another option is simply to unplug your telephone. If you must answer the telephone, inform the caller that you are busy and will call back. Obviously, you should not be glancing at your mail, working on other projects, eating lunch, or frequently looking at your watch during the interview.

Begin the interview at the scheduled time. If you need another session to complete the interview, tell the interviewee. You might say, "Mrs. Smith, we have about 5 minutes left. Because we need more time, let's schedule another meeting for next Tuesday at the same time, if that's convenient for you."

Interview the parent(s) without small children in the room. Small children can be distracting, and you need to have the complete attention of the parent. Ask the parent(s) to arrange for child care, or, as a last resort, arrange for someone to watch the child while you interview the parent.

FORMING IMPRESSIONS

When you and the interviewee first meet, both of you will form initial impressions. These impressions will change as the interview progresses. Be aware of signs of psychological disturbance (e.g., depression, severe anxiety, delusions) and signs of psychological health (e.g., good coping skills, good memory, fluent and expressive language). Also be aware of how the interviewee affects you (e.g., brings out compassion, pity, attraction, irritation, or discomfort). Recognizing these factors will help you regulate the pace of the interview and give you some appreciation of how the interviewee affects others. Remember, however, that your impressions can be subjective; to form accurate impressions of the interviewee, try to remain objective and rely on your good listening and observation skills.

LISTENING

Good listening skills are difficult to acquire and difficult to implement. Sometimes the interviewer becomes so preoccupied with what should be asked next that he or she fails to listen to what the interviewee is saying. This is especially true of novice interviewers. Effective listening is hampered when the interviewer (a) prematurely evaluates and judges everything the interviewee says, (b) interrupts the interviewee before he or she has enough time to develop an idea, (c) is preoccupied and fails to respond to the interviewee's concerns, and (d) is uncomfortable with silence (Downs, Smeyak, & Martin, 1980).

The following are some steps you can take to improve your listening skills:

1. Make sure that you have no hearing or visual problems that will interfere with your ability to conduct an interview.
2. Attend to your personal needs, such as eating and drinking and going to the restroom, before the interview begins.
3. Maintain interest in and involvement with the interviewee by following the interviewee's thoughts, paraphrasing, reflecting feelings, and probing for important details.
4. Attend to the interviewee's nonverbal communications.
5. Summarize information shared by the interviewee at various points in the interview so as to form a complete picture.

Here are some characteristics of effective listeners and ineffective listeners (adapted from Gratus, 1988).

EFFECTIVE LISTENERS

1. They have sufficient empathy to create the best surroundings, which permits the interviewees to give their best.
2. They are so well prepared that they have the freedom and confidence to truly listen to what is being said by the interviewee rather than worry about whether they are asking the right questions.
3. They decide in advance which questions to ask—and when to ask them—so that the interview will be structured to optimize the interviewee's ability to respond and feel at ease.
4. They have cultivated the ability to listen behind the words to catch the slightest nuance of meaning, emphasis, hesitation, uncertainty, omission, or inconsistency.

5. They have the persistence and patience to continue asking questions, even when interviewees omit or avoid giving information; they clearly communicate their expectations for cooperation and are patient but firm in enforcing them.

6. They strive to remain objective when listening; they also recognize that the events and experiences they are hearing about have been subjectively interpreted by the interviewee.

7. They are sparing with words and generous with concentration, and they find ways to communicate their interest nonverbally.

INEFFECTIVE LISTENERS

1. They hear what they want to hear, not what the interviewee is saying.

2. They listen only to those details that interest them and do not pay attention to the rest.

3. They are unable to put themselves in the interviewee's shoes and cannot really understand the feelings the interviewee is expressing.

4. They are too sympathetic to the interviewee's point of view to be able to listen objectively to what the interviewee is saying.

5. They are too involved with their own thoughts and problems to concentrate on those of the interviewee.

6. They are unprepared for the interview, so they are thinking of the next question to ask when they should instead be listening.

7. They are easily distracted by the interviewee's mannerisms, appearance, accent, and so on.

8. They are uncomfortable with silence, lack patience, and will not let the interviewee complete her or his thoughts.

Listening to the Interviewee

Much of the art of interviewing lies in the ability to listen creatively and empathically and to probe skillfully beneath the surface of the communication. *The ability to listen is the key factor in the interview* (Benjamin, 1981). Being a good listener means being free of preoccupations and giving interviewees your full attention. A good listener is attentive not only to *what* the interviewee says but also to *how* he or she says it—that is, to the interviewee's tones, expressions, and gestures, as well as physiological cues, such as pupil dilation, tremors, and blushing. A good listener is aware of what is *not* said, the feelings or facts lurking behind what is spoken. This requires use of the "inner ear" as well as the outer one. A good listener also uses empathic skills to judge when to say something that will relieve the interviewee's discomfort.

Listening to Yourself

Being a good listener also means listening to yourself. Become attuned to your thoughts, feelings, and actions, and learn how to deal with them appropriately during the inter-

view. Often you will need to suppress your reactions so that you can remain objective. If you have videotaped an interview, study the videotape to see how your needs, values, and standards emerged during the interview and how they affected your interview techniques and the hypotheses you formed about the interviewee.

Following are some questions you might ask yourself about your role as an interviewer:

• Do you recognize how your standards affect the judgments you make? For example, do you think that it is acceptable for an adolescent to be lazy because you were lazy as a 12-year-old? If so, do you say to yourself, "Why can't these parents be like my parents and leave her alone?"

• Can you determine the basis for your hypotheses? For example, if you hypothesize that a mother is hiding some facts about an issue, is your hypothesis based on something she said, the way she looked when she said it, the way she reacted to your questions, or a combination of these factors?

• Are you aware of the style or tone of your communications? For example, if you are speaking more rapidly with one interviewee than with others, why are you doing so? Or, if you are speaking in a condescending manner to an interviewee, why are you doing so?

• Are you aware of your emotional blindspots, such as sensitive words or concepts that may distract you from listening in an unbiased manner? For example, do you flinch when you hear the term *homosexual?* Do you panic when you hear the word *rape* because you were raped? What can you do about these reactions so that they don't interfere with your ability to listen effectively?

• If both parents are present, do you speak differently to one than the other? Do you listen more effectively to the mother or to the father? Why are you doing so?

> *A good listener is not only popular everywhere, but after a while he knows something.*
>
> —Wilson Mizner

ANALYTICAL LISTENING

The ability to analyze the responses of the interviewee critically *as* you listen—termed *analytical listening*—is an important interviewing skill. Your questions should be designed to obtain information from the interviewee. As the interviewee gives a response, immediately evaluate it and follow it up with an appropriate comment or question. For example, your evaluation may tell you that the interviewee's response was incomplete, irrelevant, inadequate, minimally appropriate, or appropriate. Based on your evaluation, you decide what to say next. The sequence is

*questioning → listening → analyzing →
further questioning or clarifying*

Purposes Served by Analytical Listening

Analytical listening serves several purposes (Downs et al., 1980). It will help you (a) understand the frame of reference of the interviewee, (b) reduce the interviewee's emotional tension, (c) convey to the interviewee a sense of his or her importance, (d) give the interviewee time to refine his or her thoughts, and (e) relate effectively to the interviewee. Good analytical listening skills include getting the main ideas, facts, and details; understanding the connotative meanings of words; identifying affect and attitudes appropriately; discriminating between fact and imagination; recognizing discrepancies; judging the relevancy of communications; and making valid inferences.

Recognizing Interviewees' Response Sets

Interviewees have certain ways or patterns of answering questions, called *response sets* (or *response styles*). Some response sets simply reflect the interviewee's preferred style of responding, such as giving brief answers, giving elaborate answers, giving answers only when certain of them, or answering only questions that are fully understood. These styles usually do not affect the accuracy of the information.

Other response sets, however, affect the accuracy of the information. Examples include the following:

- *Acquiescent response style* (usually saying "yes" to yes-no questions)
- Disagreeing with all or most questions (usually saying "no" to yes-no questions)
- Choosing the last or first alternative when presented with alternatives
- Slanting answers in a negative or positive direction
- Answering in a socially desirable or undesirable manner
- Giving answers even when uncertain of them in order to please the interviewer
- Answering questions even when the questions are not understood in order to please the interviewer
- Answering questions impulsively and then recanting the answers

You will need to be cognizant of the interviewee's response set. When you have a hunch that the interviewee's response set may be affecting the accuracy of her or his replies, introduce questions that will help you determine whether this is so. Here are some suggestions (Horton & Kochurka, 1995):

1. If the interviewee always answers "yes" to yes-no questions, introduce questions for which you know that "yes" is the wrong answer. For example, ask, "Do both your parents live at home?" when only one parent lives at home, or ask, "Do you have a sister?" when the interviewee has one brother.
2. If the interviewee always selects the last alternative in a series of alternatives, frame questions with an incorrect response as the last alternative. For example, if you know

the interviewee is *not* studying biology in school, ask, "Are you studying history, Spanish, or biology this semester?" or after the interviewee says a man touched her but she can't say where and you know she was touched on her buttocks, ask, "Did he touch you on your bottom, your back, or your arm?"

Be wary of interviewees' replies when they always select the same response alternative. When you interview children with developmental disabilities, be particularly alert to response sets that may affect the accuracy of the information. Children with developmental disabilities may be deficient in assertiveness skills and thus may be more prone to acquiesce by answering "yes" to yes-no questions (Horton & Kochurka, 1995).

Evaluating Whether You Have Gathered All the Information

You must judge whether you have obtained all the information the interviewee is willing to share with you and whether that amount is sufficient (Gorden, 1975). For example, if you ask an interviewee to tell you about his family and he simply says, "They're okay," you might want to probe further: "Well, tell me about how you get along with them" or "Describe your relationship with your parents." During most interviews, you will need to ask follow-up questions.

The following example illustrates the importance of flexibility in the interview. The interviewer tried to learn about the interviewee's ability to concentrate but appeared to reach a dead end. However, by shifting focus, the interviewer learned some useful information (Mannuzza, Fyer, & Klein, 1993, pp. 160–161, with changes in notation).

IR: What has your concentration been like recently?
IE: I don't understand what you're asking.
IR: Can you read an article in the paper or watch a TV program right through?
IE: I don't read the papers, and my television has been broken for several months.
IR: Do your thoughts drift off so that you don't take things in?
IE: Take things in? Maybe. I'm not sure if I know what you mean.
IR: Well, let's turn to something else. What do you do in your spare time?
IE: I play a lot of baseball.
IR: What position?
IE: Left field.
IR: Do you ever have difficulty focusing on the ball as it's coming toward you?
IE: Not too often.
IR: How often do you drop the ball or let it get past you?
IE: Well, that happens a lot. It's usually because I'm thinking about other things when I'm out in the field.
IR: Do you have any problem keeping your mind on the game or remembering the score from one inning to the next?
IE: Yes. I have to keep on looking at the score board. My teammates always complain that I'm not paying attention. They think that I don't care about the game, but that's not true.

Interviewees must recognize that you are evaluating their communications and organizing them into some coherent theme. By conveying an attitude of critical evaluation—interest in precise facts, correct inferences, and an accurate sequence of events—you show interviewees that you want to get beneath the surface of the communications and away from vague, superficial, and incomplete responses.

Staying Attuned

Toward the end of the interview, you can (a) ask about important areas you did not discuss, (b) clarify previously discussed material, (c) make other necessary comments, or (d) invite questions that the interviewee might have. Listening analytically will help you recognize the need for more information. For example, when interviewing recent immigrant parents, you may realize that you didn't ask whether the referred child was born in the United States or how old the referred child was when the family arrived in the United States. To know what information is missing, you need to be attuned to what you learned during the interview, and what information you still need to obtain. Do not wait until the interview is over to evaluate the information, or you will miss a chance to get the important information you are lacking. It is critical that you continuously evaluate the information you obtain.

> *Treat every word as having the potential of unlocking the mystery of the subject's way of viewing the world.*
> —Robert C. Bogdan and Sari K. Biklen

ESTABLISHING RAPPORT

The success of an interview, like that of any other assessment procedure, depends on the rapport you establish with the interviewee. Your aim is to create a comfortable and safe atmosphere that will allow the interviewee to talk openly and without fear of judgment or criticism. *Rapport is based on mutual confidence, respect, and acceptance.* It is your responsibility to engage the interviewee and to foster his or her impression of you as a trustworthy and helping person.

The climate you establish should ensure that the interviewee feels free to give information and express feelings. You must show the interviewee that you are willing to accept whatever information he or she wants to give, within the aims and goals of the interview. Establishing an appropriate climate is not a matter of attending only to the opening minutes of the interview. Because shifts in feelings and attitudes occur throughout the interview, you will need to stay keenly aware of how the interviewee responds to you and adjust your techniques accordingly to maintain an open and trusting climate.

Facilitating Rapport

You can facilitate rapport by doing the following:

- Make the interview a joint undertaking between you and the interviewee.
- Give the interviewee your undivided attention.
- Convey to the interviewee that you want to listen and can be trusted.
- Give the interviewee reassurance and support.
- Listen to the interviewee openly and nonjudgmentally.
- Speak slowly and clearly in a calm, matter-of-fact, friendly, and accepting manner.
- Interrupt the interviewee only when necessary.
- Use a warm and expressive tone.
- Maintain a natural, relaxed, and attentive posture.
- Maintain appropriate eye contact.
- Ask tactful questions.
- Time questions and comments appropriately.
- Ask the interviewee which name she or he prefers to use if the interviewee has several names.
- Ask the interviewee to help you pronounce her or his name if you have difficulty pronouncing it.
- Dress appropriately, particularly if you know that the interviewee expects a certain level of formality in appearance.

All these actions convey your interest in and respect for the interviewee.

Attending to Actions That May Diminish Rapport

The following is a list of actions to avoid if you want to establish rapport. We all engage in these actions at times, but as an interviewer, you should attempt to reduce their occurrence.

- Don't tell the interviewee about former clients or about the important people who refer cases to you. It is all right, however, to say that you talk to other kids.
- Don't be flippant or sarcastic about statements made by the interviewee.
- Don't use stereotyped phrases or overworked expressions such as "um," "you know," "like I said," "well," "alright then," or "whatever."
- Don't tune in only to the things that interest you.
- Don't disagree or argue with the interviewee.
- Don't verbally attack or belittle the interviewee.
- Don't try to influence the interviewee to accept your values.
- Don't register shock at life styles that differ from yours.
- Don't lecture the interviewee about waiting too long to come to see you or being wise to have come now.
- Don't interrupt the interviewee (unless the interviewee wanders off aimlessly).
- Don't be distracted by the interviewee's mannerisms, dress, accent, and so forth.
- Don't concentrate so much on making a good impression that you lose focus on the interviewee.

- Don't concentrate on the next question you intend to ask to the exclusion of the interviewee's answer to your current question.
- Don't suggest answers or complete the interviewee's sentence if he or she hesitates.
- Don't tell the interviewee how others answered the question.
- Don't engage in nonverbal behaviors that send negative messages (see Table 7-1 on page 185 of *Assessment of Children: Cognitive Applications*).
- Don't tell the interviewee that you can solve all of his or her problems.
- Don't give the interviewee inappropriate reassurance by saying that there is no cause to worry.
- Don't superficially listen to the interviewee, wait for the interviewee to finish speaking, and then try to make your point by telling the interviewee the way it "really" is.
- Don't minimize the depth of the interviewee's feelings.
- Don't tell the interviewee that you also have worries and problems.
- Don't be judgmental or accusatory.

Because the clinical assessment interview is a formal, professional interaction, the interviewee should not have to deal with your personal concerns. Disturbed or moved by some remark made by the interviewee, most of us as interviewers will occasionally let our attention wander to our own life and situation. When you have such reactions, redirect your attention to the interviewee. Gratus (1988) offers the following advice to interviewers who have lost their train of thought during the interview:

Return to the point where things started to go wrong, and no harm or loss of face will come from admitting the problem to the interviewee: "I'm sorry, I seem to have lost my train of thought. Now, where was I? Could we go back to ___?" In fact, the interviewee might even appreciate your admission, because it will make you appear more human and approachable.

You may not wish to go back but to proceed with the interview, in which case you should summarize before asking the next question. Summing up or paraphrasing has the immediate effect of getting you back into the flow of the interview, and at the same time reinforces what the interviewee has already told you. (adapted from p. 84)

Rapport may be difficult to establish when the interviewee does not want to be interviewed or to have the information from the interview shared with anyone else. In such cases, explain to the interviewee what will be gained by cooperating with you.

Getting Started

Interviewees are likely to be anxious to tell you their story as soon as possible. Therefore, it may not be necessary to engage in small talk—about the weather, baseball, or current news—to establish rapport with the interviewee. Sometimes a general opening question such as "How are you today?" may be all that you need to ask. This type of question gives interviewees an opportunity to talk about themselves and helps build rapport.

As soon as possible, focus on topics related to the referral question, to the interviewee's concerns, or to your concerns. Remember, however, that you may have to take a slight detour at times. For example, if the interviewee is anxious and you know about her or his interest in sports or movies, you might want to talk about one of these topics early in the interview. Although such talk seems tangential, it may help the shy, anxious, or inhibited interviewee relax enough to discuss more relevant issues.

Showing Interest

Showing interest in the information given to you by the interviewee is crucial in establishing rapport. Interviewees need to sense that you want to understand how they see the world; that you appreciate their experiences; that you share in their struggle to recall, organize, and express their experiences; that you appreciate their difficulties in discussing personal material; and that you want to reflect accurately their opinions, feelings, and beliefs (Gorden, 1975). You can show your interest by the things you say, by the way you say them, and by your actions. You need to be responsive, empathic, and sensitive.

Handling Anxiety

You will need to reassure anxious interviewees. For example, some children or parents may be too embarrassed to discuss their reasons for being at the interview. Older children may wonder what will happen to them because of the assessment. And most parents will be anxious to learn how severe their child's problems are and what can be done about them.

Interviewees may express their anxiety both verbally and nonverbally. Verbal indications of anxiety include sentence corrections, slips of the tongue, repetitions, stuttering, intruding or incoherent sounds, omissions, and frequent use of "uh" expressions. Nonverbal indications of anxiety include sweating, trembling, fidgeting, restlessness, hand clenching, twitching, scowling, and forced smiling.

When you sense that the interviewee's anxiety is interfering with rapport, encourage him or her to talk about it. Following are some possible leads (Kanfer, Eyberg, & Krahn, 1992; Shea, 1988; Stevenson, 1974):

- "Bill, I know that it's difficult to talk at first. I'm wondering what some of your concerns are about being here today."
- "Bill, it's hard to talk about personal feelings. Is there anything I can do to make things easier for you?"
- "This one is tough, isn't it, Bill?"
- "Something makes it hard for you to talk about this matter; would you tell me what it is that makes it hard?"

- "I know it's difficult to talk to a stranger, and it may take time for you to trust me. That's natural. I don't expect you to say anything that makes you uncomfortable unless you're ready."
- "It's all right if you don't feel like talking about that yet." This last lead gives the interviewee permission to wait but also establishes the expectation that the interviewee will be ready to discuss the topic later and that you will inquire about the topic again.

When all else fails and the interviewee still will not talk with you, you may need to gently point out the responsibilities of an interviewee: "We have to work together; we can't accomplish very much unless you tell me more about yourself." When interviewees are still not ready to discuss sensitive or anxiety-provoking material, return to the topic at a more opportune time. By being attentive to the interviewee's distress, you can help her or him experience what a therapeutic relationship with you or with another psychologist might be like. This knowledge might serve as a valuable precursor to or introduction to therapeutic interventions, if they are needed.

Young children may not understand that you expect them to share information with you or even that they have a problem. In such cases, be patient and encourage them to talk with you by playing games or doing other activities (see Chapter 2).

If you sense that the interviewee is anxious about some material that he or she has shared with you, you can probably reduce the anxiety by asking "What's it been like for you to share these experiences with me?" You also can compliment the interviewee for sharing. For example, you might say, "You've done an excellent job of sharing difficult material. It's really helping me to understand what you've been experiencing" (Shea, 1988, adapted from p. 47). Phrase your compliment so that it focuses on the interviewee's *sharing,* not on the content of the statement. You do not want to reinforce certain responses or to hint that certain responses are either right or wrong.

Handling Agitation and Crying

Interviewees may become agitated during the interview, especially when they have recently faced a traumatic experience. As they relive the experience, they may cry or express deep personal feelings. Acknowledge their feelings, and give them time to work through them; this should help make a difficult situation easier.

An interviewee who is sad and on the verge of tears may feel especially vulnerable. You might say, "You seem sad now" or "Are you trying not to cry?" or "It's all right to cry. We all cry at times. It's our body's way of telling us we're hurting. [Pause] Maybe you can tell me a little more about what is hurting you" (Shea, 1988, p. 259). However, if an adult's crying is excessive, you may have to be more firm and say, for instance, "Mr. Jones, this is obviously very upsetting and would be to most people. Take a moment to collect yourself. It's important

for us to talk more about what is bothering you" (Shea, 1988, p. 259, with change in notation). This comment, though firm, still should be said gently. Also, always have a box of tissues within easy reach of the interviewee.

Facilitating Communication

Use language suitable to the age, gender, and education of the interviewee. Be sure that your questions are concrete and easily understood and that you do not unintentionally bias interviewees toward a particular response (Gorden, 1975). You do not want to say, for example, "School isn't that bad, so why don't you like going to school?" Avoid ambiguous words, psychological jargon, and repeating the interviewee's slang or idioms that are unnatural to you. When interviewing children about parts of the body, *always* use their words for the body parts (and become comfortable using these sometimes uncomfortable-to-use words). Recognize when the interviewee's speech is figurative, and do not respond to it as the literal truth. For instance, if an interviewee says, "I feel like my insides are coming out," you do not want to say "Show me where they're coming out." Use of an appropriate vocabulary, especially a developmentally appropriate vocabulary, will also facilitate rapport.

TIMING QUESTIONS APPROPRIATELY

The initial part of the assessment should focus on areas that are not anxiety provoking or excessively sensitive. Premature or poorly timed questions may impede the progress of the assessment and discourage disclosure of vital information. The way the relationship with the interviewee unfolds should guide you in timing questions and discussing sensitive topics. As you and the interviewee develop a more trusting relationship, you can broach topics that you avoided earlier. Time your comments and questions so that they harmonize with the interviewee's flow of thoughts, while moving the assessment toward areas you want to explore.

The following are suggestions on how to pace the assessment properly (Gratus, 1988):

1. Have a good idea of the topics you want to cover.
2. Have a strategy, but be prepared to be flexible.
3. Focus on one topic at a time and then move on.
4. Keep the interviewee interested.
5. Know approximately how much time has elapsed (or remains) in the assessment.

The pace of the assessment should be rapid enough to keep the interest of the interviewee, but slow enough to allow the interviewee to formulate good answers. In addition, the assessment interview should not be too long or have many lapses. For preschool-aged children, 20 to 30 minutes may be sufficient; for school-aged children, 30 to 45 minutes might be appropriate; and for parents or caregivers, 50 to 75 minutes is suggested. But you are the one who must determine the time needed for each interviewee.

CHANGING TOPICS

Ideally, as noted above, you should proceed in an orderly manner and finish one area before going on to the next. However, if you find yourself needing to ask about a previous topic, do so. Introduce the question with an appropriate explanation at a convenient time, such as when the interviewee completes a topic. When you first think about it, you may want to make a note of what you want to ask.

It will take practice and sensitivity to judge when you have exhausted one topic and need to move to another. Continuously evaluate how the interview is progressing and how much shifting you believe the interviewee can tolerate. Some interviewees are disturbed by sudden shifts, whereas others become bored with a planned sequence of topics. As a rule, move on to another topic when the interviewee has adequately answered the previous one. Avoid abrupt shifts that may be puzzling to the interviewee. Transitional statements such as "Let's move on to…" or "Now I'd like to discuss…" or "We've covered this topic pretty thoroughly; now let's turn to another topic that may relate to your concerns" are useful in moving the assessment forward at a steady pace.

When the interviewee introduces a topic unrelated to the one under discussion, you must decide whether to explore the new topic (and risk losing continuity) or stay with the previous topic (and risk losing additional information). Sometimes the interviewee will change topics to avoid sensitive but relevant material. If this happens, you may want to note that the original topic was evaded and return to it later.

FORMULATING APPROPRIATE QUESTIONS

Questions form the heart of the interview. They direct the interviewee toward your concerns and elicit the information needed for the assessment. Good questions encourage the interviewee to answer freely and honestly about the topic at hand, whereas poor questions inhibit the interviewee or lead to distorted replies (Gratus, 1988). Questions serve many purposes, including (a) drawing out information, (b) amplifying statements, (c) guiding the discussion, (d) bringing out distinctions and similarities, (e) introducing a point needing further discussion, (f) encouraging opinions, (g) encouraging relaxation, and (h) clarifying your understanding.

The way you ask questions is as important as what you ask. Speak clearly and audibly at a moderate pace. When you speak, look at the interviewee. If you find yourself talking too fast, "Stop, take a deep breath and let the interviewee take over the talking again, prompted, of course, by a good question from you" (Gratus, 1988, p. 84). The tone of your voice

should convey a sense of assurance and confidence and vary to suit the circumstances of the topic.

Recognize that the way you ask questions can imply the answers you expect (Foddy, 1993):

- "Are you going to do _____?" implies an expectation.
- "You *are* going to do _____, aren't you?" implies a positive expectation—that is, a yes answer.
- "You're not you going to do _____, are you?" implies a negative expectation.
- "You are going to do _____, *aren't you?*" implies a doubtful expectation.

The words you stress can determine the meaning of what you say (Foddy, 1993). For example, the meaning of the question "How come you went to that friend's house after school?" depends on which words are stressed. Stressing "how come" conveys surprise or disapproval; stressing "that" implies a particular friend rather than any friend; stressing "house" conveys a request for an explanation (e.g., for going to the friend's house rather than to another place); and stressing "after school" implies a request for an explanation (e.g., why the activity was done after school rather than at another time).

When you formulate a question, the interviewee must understand your words in the same way you intend them. The most accurate communication comes about when the speaker (interviewee or interviewer) says what she or he *intends to say* and the listener (interviewee or interviewer) *understands what the speaker means to say* (Clark, 1985). However, speakers may mean more than they say, and listeners may read too much into what a speaker says. Speakers' communications will be more accurately understood when the communications are informative, truthful, relevant, unambiguous, and concise. It is only through cooperation between speakers and listeners that speakers' meanings are clearly understood. When a listener misinterprets (or overinterprets) what a speaker says, the meanings attributed to the speaker may be more a function of the listener's interpretation than the intention of the speaker.

Men may be read, as well as books, too much.
—Alexander Pope

A Continuum from Open-Ended to Closed-Ended Questions

Questions vary as to their degree of openness.

1. *Minimally focused questions.* At one end of the continuum are *minimally focused,* or *open-ended, questions;* these have a broad focus ("Tell me about what brings you here today").

2. *Moderately focused questions.* Toward the middle part of the continuum are *moderately focused questions;* these focus on a specific topic but give some latitude to the interviewee ("Tell me about how you get along with your mother").

3. *Highly focused questions.* At the other end of the continuum are *highly focused,* or *closed-ended, questions;* these allow little latitude ("What subjects does your son like in school?") and may require a yes-no answer ("Do you like school?") or the selection of one of two alternatives presented ("Do you believe that it would be better for you to remain in your regular class, or would you like to be placed in a special class?"). Closed-ended questions of the latter type are called *bipolar questions.*

Open-ended questions are usually preferable, especially at the start of the assessment, because they give the interviewee some responsibility for sharing her or his concerns and they cannot be answered by a simple yes or no. Open-ended questions give the interviewee the opportunity to describe events in her or his own words and may help you appreciate the interviewee's perspective. One good open-ended question can result in a response you could not obtain with numerous closed-ended questions.

Moderately focused questions are more directive than open-ended questions and are valuable as the assessment proceeds. You will formulate these questions in part in response to the interviewee's answers to your open-ended questions. Moderately focused questions (and closed-ended questions) are more efficient than open-ended questions in eliciting specific information and in speeding up the pace of the assessment. You also can formulate moderately focused questions to obtain clarification of a response previously given by the interviewee.

Bipolar questions are not as constraining as yes-no questions, but they still limit the interviewee's responses. Bipolar questions do not allow the interviewee to express degrees of liking or opinions, can lead to oversimplified responses, and are not suitable for the interviewee who has no opinion at all. However, bipolar questions are useful when you want to find out what the interviewee thinks or feels about specific alternatives related to an issue or when you need to help a reluctant interviewee express his or her thoughts and feelings. After the interviewee chooses one option, you can then say, "Tell me about your choice."

All these questions have their place in the assessment. It is only when you rely on one type or use them inappropriately or prematurely that they bias the assessment. For example, a question like "What's the name of the teacher who showed you pictures of naked children?" is specific and directive and may bias the assessment if used as the initial question in the assessment or topic area. It assumes that someone—a teacher—showed the child pictures of naked children. In legal settings, questions like this one are called leading questions. Responses to leading questions are often disallowed by the court. However, if the child spontaneously—or in response to an open-ended or moderately focused question—says, "My teacher showed us pictures of naked children," then a follow-up question like "What's the name of the teacher who showed you pictures of naked children?" would be appropriate. Table 1-1 shows the benefits and limitations

of open-ended and closed-ended questions. Leading questions are discussed in more detail later in the chapter.

Asking Direct Questions

Phrase questions positively and confidently. For example, say, "Tell me about …" or "I would like you to tell me about …" rather than "I wonder if you would be willing to tell me about …" or "Perhaps you might be willing to tell me about …." Also, state your questions clearly. You do not want to start a question, qualify part of it, then go back and reframe it, and in the process confuse the interviewee. For example, instead of asking "How old was your child when you began to teach him habits of—uh, well, letting him know that he should go to the bathroom—you know, control his bladder?" ask, "When did you begin Eddie's toilet training?" (Darley, 1978, p. 45).

The following are useful questions or statements for inquiring about a symptom, problem, or concern.

*   Tell me about _____.
*   How often does it happen?
*   When does it occur?
*   What happens when you feel that way?
*   What is it like to feel that way?
*   What was it like?
*   How old were you the first time you _____?
*   When was the last time you _____?
*   When you _____, how does it affect your school work?
*   Describe what it was like when _____.

> *Animal, vegetable, or mineral?*
> *That's usually the opening question in the game called "Twenty Questions." Then by narrowing down the scope of your questions, you're supposed to determine the object that someone has in mind.*
> *It isn't guesswork that leads to the right answer. It's using the right questions.*
> —Research Institute of America

AVOIDING CERTAIN TYPES OF QUESTIONS

The major types of questions to avoid are (a) yes-no questions, (b) double-barreled questions, (c) long, multiple questions, (d) leading questions, (e) random probing questions, (f) coercive questions, (g) embarrassing or accusatory questions, and (h) why questions. Let's now consider each of these types of questions and the reasons they should be avoided.

Avoiding Yes-No Questions

To avoid creating a climate of interrogation, do not formulate questions so that a simple yes or no will suffice, unless you

Table 1-1
Benefits and Limitations of Open-Ended and Closed-Ended Questions

Open-ended question (Asks for broad or general information)		Closed-ended question (Asks for specific information)	
Benefits	Limitations	Benefits	Limitations
Helps you discover interviewee's priorities	Consumes time and energy	Saves time and energy	Does not allow you to learn how much information interviewee has
Helps you discover interviewee's frame of reference	Makes it difficult to control interview	Helps when you have many questions and limited time	Does not allow you to learn how strongly interviewee feels about topics
Allows interviewee to talk through ideas	Makes it difficult to record responses, especially long, rambling responses	Allows you to guide interview	Does not allow you to learn about interviewee's thoughts on the topic
Gives interviewee freedom to structure an answer	Makes it difficult for interviewee to know how much detail you want	Allows you to focus on many specific areas	Thwarts interviewee's need to explain or talk about answers
Encourages catharsis (the relaxation of emotional tension and anxiety through any kind of expressive reaction)		Allows you to train other interviewers quickly	Allows interviewee to falsify answers easily
Reveals interviewee's emotional state		Helps interviewee reconstruct an event	
Reveals facts about interviewee		Motivates shy and reluctant interviewees	
Reveals how articulate interviewee is		Suffices when you need only brief answers without explanations	
Reveals depth of interviewee's knowledge			

Source: Adapted from Downs, Smeyak, and Martin (1980).

Calvin and Hobbes   by Bill Watterson

need to ask about a fact (such as whether a child has received help for a particular problem). For example, instead of asking "Do you like arithmetic?" or "Are your headaches severe?" ask, "What do you think about arithmetic?" or "Tell me about your headaches." The questions "Do you like arithmetic?" and "Are your headaches severe?" may bring the conversation to a halt because the interviewee can say "yes" or "no" and then remain silent. The question "What do you think about arithmetic?" and the statement "Tell me about your headaches" invite a longer reply, giving the interviewee an opportunity to answer more freely and allowing you to obtain more information.

Another disadvantage of yes-no questions is that they may require you to ask additional questions (Darley, 1978). For example, "What illnesses has Luanne had?" is a more effective question than "Has Luanne been sick much?" A yes answer to the last question would require a follow-up question to obtain the needed information. What, when, and how questions are likely to lead to more open and complete replies than yes-no questions. Frame your questions so that there is a good chance of getting the information you want directly. For example, instead of asking "Do you like your teacher?" ask, "What do you think about your teacher?" or "How do you feel about your teacher?" Using what, when, and how questions is usually a good strategy to encourage the interviewee to describe a problem, symptom, or situation.

Similarly, avoid questions that present only one alternative—for example, "Do you get frustrated when you are tired?"—because these questions, which are restrictive and may be leading, are likely to result in invalid replies. It is better to ask "When do you get frustrated?" or "How do you feel when you are tired?"

Avoiding Double-Barreled Questions

Double-barreled questions detract from the assessment because they confront the interviewee with two questions at once. Here are several examples of double-barreled questions and the dilemmas they cause:

1. "How do you feel about your mother and your teacher?" The interviewee might have trouble deciding which part of the question to answer first.
2. "What are the advantages and disadvantages of being in Miss Smith's class?" The interviewee might answer only one part of the question.
3. "At home, do you do any chores, and do you like doing them?" A "no" response will be difficult to interpret because there is no way of knowing to what part of the question the reply refers.

Avoiding Long, Multiple Questions

Avoid asking three- or four-part questions, as interviewees may answer part of a *long, multiple question* and avoid the

rest of the question. Examples of such questions include "Tell me about your parents, your teacher, and your brothers and sisters" and "When did you first notice that you were having trouble with David? Was it before or after you moved to your present neighborhood? And what have you been doing to help David?" Although all the questions in the latter example may be valuable and in the correct sequence, you should ask each separately, giving the interviewee time to respond after each question.

Avoiding Leading Questions

Leading questions—questions formulated to direct or control a response—tempt the interviewee to respond the way you want. The *way* you ask questions, as noted earlier, also may persuade the interviewee to give the desired response. Because leading questions may bias what the interviewee says, avoid using them. Here are five forms that leading (or suggestive) questions may take:

1. *Hinting at the expected response.* Examples: "He forced you to do that, didn't he?" directs the interviewee to agree with the response expected by the interviewer. "What else did she do?" implies that the person did something else.
2. *Identifying the response you expect from the interviewee in your question.* Example: "Don't you think Mr. Smith is a good teacher?"
3. *Using prior statements to cue the interviewee to respond in a certain way.* Example: "It's generally been found that rewarding children for their efforts is helpful in developing good habits. Do you reward Jill often?"
4. *Persuading the interviewee to agree with your recommendation.* Examples: "To aid Johnny's emotional development, we need to place him in a therapeutic program. Surely you wouldn't want to hold back his progress?" "Miss Jones is an exceptionally fine teacher, and I'm sure you'll give your consent to allow Maria to attend her class for special children."
5. *Assuming details that were not revealed by the interviewee.* Examples: "When was the first time it happened?" when the interviewee has not mentioned that it happened more than once; "So after the last time you were touched, whom did you tell?" when the interviewee has never mentioned that he or she told anybody; "That was scary, wasn't it?" when the interviewee has not described any feelings about the incident.

Avoiding Random Probing Questions

Do not use random, hit-or-miss questions (Gilmore, 1973). Using *random probing questions* is like throwing lots of bait in a stream and hoping you will catch a fish. Interviewers tend to use random probing when they do not know what to ask. For example, after a child admits to getting along well in school, the interviewer might say, "There must be something that you don't like or that causes you difficulty. How about some of the teachers … or other students … or recess periods … or tests?" When you have mastered the techniques of interviewing, you are less likely to resort to random probing.

Avoiding Coercive Questions

Interviewers may use *coercive questions* to try to force interviewees to see things as they see them. Two examples are "You'll agree with me that your teacher has some good points, right?" and "Why do you always find fault with your son when he seems to have so many good points?" Coercive questions are unprofessional and inhibit communication. Do not force your opinions on the interviewee.

Avoiding Embarrassing or Accusatory Questions

Formulate questions so that they do not embarrass, offend, or put the interviewee on the defensive. For example, instead of asking "How many times have you been expelled from school?" ask, "What difficulties have you had staying in school?" Likewise, for the question "In what school subjects have you received a failing grade?" you might substitute "What school subjects are difficult for you?" Finally, instead of the question "Are you telling me the truth?" you can use, "Is it possible that other people believe something different?" In these examples, the rephrased questions are potentially less embarrassing than the original questions because of their softened tone, yet they still might elicit the desired information.

Avoiding Why Questions

You should avoid questions that begin with *why,* particularly when they are directed at the child's actions. Children may react defensively to *why questions,* perceiving them as a request "to account for or justify their behavior rather than to describe what led up to the behavior" (Boggs & Eyberg, 1990, p. 93). The question "Why don't you help around the house?" can be rephrased as "What do you do to help around the house?" followed by "What don't you like to do around the house?" Both children and adults will likely respond better to the alternative wording. In addition, not using why questions can help to build rapport.

Similarly, a question such as "Why do you drink alcohol?" might cause interviewees to think that you are judging them. Suitable questions are "When do you drink alcohol?" and "How do you feel after you drink?" and "What thoughts do you have when you really want to drink?" Instead of asking "Why are you anxious?" you might ask, "What makes you anxious?" or "What do you do when you are anxious?" or "How long does the anxiety last before it goes away?"

There are times, however, when carefully asked why questions can be helpful and diagnostic. For example, "Why do you think Daddy said that?" might be useful in a case of alleged child maltreatment.

> *In assessments, as elsewhere, the value of the answer depends on the quality of the question.*
>
> —John Courtis

PROBING EFFECTIVELY

Probing is a key to successful interviewing. You need to probe because the interviewee is not likely to respond fully to your questions. Listening analytically can help you identify responses that are inadequate (e.g., incomplete, inconsistent, irrelevant, poorly organized, or ambiguous) or absent altogether.

Frank and Ernest

© 1991 Thaves / Reprinted with permission. Newspaper dist. by NEA, Inc.

An interviewee may give an inadequate response for various reasons (Downs et al., 1980, adapted from p. 88). For example, inadequate responses can occur when the interviewee

- does not understand the purpose of the question
- does not understand how you might use the information
- does not understand the kind of answer you want
- is uncertain about how much of an answer to give
- does not understand the language in the question
- is unwilling to give information that is personal, threatening, or endangering to self
- may not know the answer
- may not remember what happened
- finds it difficult to articulate feelings
- thinks that you will not accept or understand the answer
- does not care about you and therefore chooses not to cooperate fully
- does not care about the assessment and therefore chooses not to cooperate fully
- fears the results of giving an answer
- has competing thoughts, so his or her concentration lags

If you recognize the possible reason for the inadequate response, you may be able to determine the kinds of follow-up questions needed.

Probing Techniques

There are many types of probing questions and comments that you can use (see Table 1-2). We will examine 10 probing techniques: elaboration, clarification, repetition, challenging, silence, neutral phrases, reflective statements, periodic summaries, checking the interviewee's understanding, and miscellaneous probing statements (Downs et al., 1980).

Elaboration.   Use *elaboration* when you want the interviewee to provide additional information. Following are examples of comments you might use:

- "Tell me more about that."
- "Is there anything else?"
- "Please go on."
- "What happened then?"
- "Please expand on that."
- "What happened before the incident?"
- "What happened after the incident?"
- "How did you feel about that?"
- "What were you thinking then?"
- "Other reasons?"

Clarification.   Use *clarification* when you do not understand what the interviewee is saying or when you are puzzled by some details. Because you are responsible for maintaining effective communication, you need to clarify ambiguous communications as they occur. You do not want to risk getting the meaning wrong by guessing at what the interviewee means. For example, if a girl says, "I study a little every day,"

find out what she means by "a little." Do not take for granted that your understanding of "a little" is the same as hers.

Here are other examples of how an interviewer clarified ambiguous statements made by an interviewee:

IE: When my son was 12 years old, he had a bad attack of nerves.
IR: What do you mean by a "bad attack of nerves"?

IE: My son is not doing well.
IR: How is he not doing well?

IE: I'm doing OK in my history class.
IR: Tell me more about how you're doing.

Sometimes an interviewer can help the interviewee clarify and describe an indefinite communication (Stevenson, 1960):

IE: When I was younger, I had a nervous breakdown.
IR: Tell me about the nervous breakdown.
IE: I was just nervous then. It was terrible.
IR: Well, tell me exactly how you felt.
IE: I was weak all over, and I couldn't concentrate. I felt panicky and would go to bed for hours at a time, and ….

Following are examples of probing comments useful for clarifying communications:

- "So what you're saying is …."
- "Tell me what you mean by that."
- "I'm not sure what you mean. Tell me more about that."
- "Give me some examples."
- "I seem to have lost your point. I'm not sure what you meant by …."
- "Did that seem to make a difference to you?"
- "You mentioned that you can't sleep at night. What do you do when you can't sleep at night?"
- "How did you go about toilet training Sally?"
- "Which subjects do you like best?"
- "You mentioned that you like sports. Tell me what kinds of sports you like."
- "You said that you have trouble making friends. What kind of trouble are you having?"
- "Horrible? Tell me about how she is horrible."
- "When did your son do that?"
- "What is it about talking about _____ that makes you anxious?"
- "What were you thinking about when you were crying just now?"
- "Tell me what it is about _____ that makes you angry."

When interviewees tell you about their medical or psychological symptoms, ask them to describe the symptoms in more detail, especially when the symptoms are ambiguous or vague. Examples of ambiguous symptoms include *spells, blackouts, dizziness, weakness, nervous breakdown, nervousness, tension, anxiety, depression, voices in the head, peculiar thoughts,* and *strange feelings.* Also clarify any terms or phrases that are unfamiliar to you. Finally, ask about terms that may have multiple or unique connotations, such as *touching,*

Table 1-2
Types of Probing Techniques

Technique	Purpose	Example
Elaboration	To encourage the interviewee to provide additional information	"Tell me more about your family."
Clarification	To encourage the interviewee to clarify details that are not clear to you	"What do you mean by that?"
Repetition	To encourage the interviewee to respond when he or she has not answered your question	"Tell me again about things that you get angry about."
Challenging	To encourage the interviewee to clarify an incongruence in her or his communication	"Just a few minutes ago you said that you didn't like school, but just now you said that the art teacher was nice. How do you explain these different feelings?"
Silence	To encourage the interviewee to think or reflect about a topic or feeling	Appearing interested in the interviewee or nodding your head
Neutral phrases	To encourage the interviewee to keep talking	"Uh huh," "I see," or "OK"
Reflective statements	To encourage the interviewee to tell you more about a topic	"You seem to be saying that it's very difficult for you to talk with your father."
Periodic summaries	To encourage the interviewee to comment on the adequacy of your understanding and interpretation, to inform the interviewee that what he or she said was what he or she intended to say, to inform the interviewee that you have been listening, to build transitions from one topic to the next and give direction to the interview, to signal that you are at the end of the interview, and to sum up and clarify what you have covered	"Let's see if I understand what is going on at school...."
Checking the interviewee's understanding	To encourage the interviewee to rephrase your interpretations of her or his situation	"What do you think about what I just said about your family?"
Miscellaneous probing statements	To encourage the interviewee to discuss a topic more fully	Echoing the interviewee's last words (e.g., "You are really angry with your mother"), pausing expectantly, or repeating the interviewee's reply and then pausing

stroking, physical contact, punished, caressed, hurt, thing, da da, and *wee wee.* Your goal is to understand the interviewees' meaning, *not* to change or reject their language.

Repetition. Use *repetition* when the interviewee has not answered your question. You can repeat the question in the same words or with slight modification. Here are two examples in which the interviewer uses repetition:

IR: How are you doing in school?
IE: I'm taking five subjects.
IR: Tell me how you're doing in these subjects.

IR: What games do you like to play?
IE: I like lots of games.
IR: What are the names of some of the games you like?

Challenging. Use *challenging* (also referred to as *confrontation*) to clarify incongruencies in the interviewee's communications. For example, if the interviewee makes contradictory statements—"I hate school" and "I really enjoy woodshop"—you might want to call the inconsistency to his or her attention. You might say, "Before, you said that you hate school; now you say you enjoy one of your classes. Can you tell me about what you said?" or "Well, I may have misunderstood what you said about hating school." By exploring inconsistencies, contradictions, or omissions with tact, you may learn that the interviewee had forgotten some important fact, made a mistake, or needed the additional questioning to reveal potentially embarrassing material. Challenging may elicit more complete information or give the interviewee an opportunity to elaborate or change statements. Although challenging is potentially unpleasant to the interviewee (and to the interviewer-in-training), it can sometimes be helpful, especially when the interviewee is unaware of her or his inconsistency.

When you observe marked discrepancies between the verbal and nonverbal communications of the interviewee, challenging requires particular skill and sensitivity. Incongruence between verbal and nonverbal behaviors suggests that the interviewee may be experiencing conflict or ambivalent feelings. For example, an interviewee may reveal discomfort by tapping his or her feet and clasping hands while saying extremely pleasant things. Without knowing whether the interviewee is aware of the inconsistency, you must judge whether to call attention to discrepant communications. If you decide to do so, be cautious, because the interviewee may believe that you are being critical. When the relationship is on a firm basis and an accepting climate has been created, the interviewee may accept challenging more readily.

Challenging also can be used with interviewees who are defensive or malingering or who are disengaged from the assessment. In these cases, challenging is designed to get information about their motivation. When you challenge the interviewee with discrepancies, do so nonthreateningly and prepare to explore her or his feelings. Do not challenge to punish, accuse, or judge the interviewee.

The following questions, designed primarily for adolescents and older individuals, give interviewees an opportunity to address ambiguities and incongruities that arise within the assessment (adapted from Rogers, 1988, pp. 302–303).

Interviewees who are defensive.   If interviewees are unwilling to share relevant material with you because of shyness, lack of trust, guilt, or embarrassment, one of these comments may help them disclose more:

- "Although you're telling me that everything is going fine, when I hear about [description of current problems] I have some trouble understanding this. Could you help me to understand?"
- "I know how much you want me to believe that you have your problems well under control, but when I see your [clinical observations of the interviewee] I wonder if this is the case. What do you think?"
- "Life is not all black and white. Whenever someone tells me only good things, I wonder whether anything is being left out...."
- "According to you, you're having no difficulty handling [describe a specific problem], but according to [a reliable informant], it appears that _____. How do you explain the difference of opinion?"

Interviewees who may be malingering.   Interviewees may pretend that they cannot do something or do not know something when they are trying to feign illness, cover up material, or lie. In such cases, the following comments may prove useful:

- "Some problems you describe are rarely seen in teenagers with psychological problems. I'm worried that you might see things as worse than they are."
- "Earlier in the evaluation you told me _____; now you're telling me _____. I'm having trouble putting this together."
- "Although you have told me about [description of current problems], to me you haven't appeared _____."
- "I haven't been able to understand how things are quite as bad as you tell me they are."
- "According to you, you have [current problems], but according to [a reliable informant], you are _____. Can you help me understand this?"

Interviewees who are disengaged.   If interviewees fail to cooperate with you, do not seem to care about their responses, or seem remote, you might try one of the following:

- "I don't think we got off on the right foot. Can we start over? Tell me in your words what you see as your problems."
- "It seems as if you're not listening to what I have to say, and I know that you're not particularly pleased about being here. How can we make sure that this isn't a waste of time for you?"
- "I know you took these [psychological tests] for me, but I get the impression that you didn't pay much attention to how you answered them. What about [specific test items], to which you gave different answers at different times?"

The following excerpt shows how an interviewer called the attention of a 9-year-old boy to a discrepant communication (Reisman, 1973, adapted from pp. 60–61):

IR: You seem to feel very angry.
IE: (Nods, but says nothing)
IR: Can you tell me about your being angry?
IE: The kids at school make fun of me.
IR: Oh, in what way?
IE: They say I don't try in sports, and that I'm no good in baseball.
IR: And this makes you feel angry with them.
IE: No, I don't care. They're not my friends so I don't care what they say.
IR: (Pause) Well, then I wonder about why you would like help.
IE: (Pause) I'd like to have more friends in school.
IR: (Pause) On the one hand, you're saying you don't care about them, and on the other, you're saying you would like them to be your friends.
IE: (Begins to cry quietly) I do want them to be my friends.

Silence.   Use *silence* to allow the interviewee more time to reflect or think. Silence expresses that you are willing to wait for him or her to tell you more about the topic. Occasionally, silence will increase the interviewee's anxiety and lead the interviewee to talk more. You can accompany your silence with nonverbal expressions, such as a nod of your head. Silence is discussed in more detail later in the chapter.

Neutral phrases. Use *neutral phrases*—such as "uh huh," "I see," or "okay"—to encourage the interviewee to keep talking and to show that you are being attentive.

Reflective statements. Use *reflective statements,* in which you paraphrase a statement made by the interviewee, to get the interviewee to tell you more about a topic. Useful phrases with which to begin reflective restatements include

- "You feel that …."
- "It seems to you that …."
- "In other words, …."
- "As you see it, …."
- "What you seem to be saying is that …."
- "You believe …."
- "You think …."
- "I gather that …."
- "It sounds as if …."
- "From what I hear you saying, …."
- "If I'm hearing you correctly, …."

Reflection is a useful technique for guiding the interviewee; however, do not restate comments so frequently that you disturb the flow of conversation. Where possible, restatements should be in your words. Reflect the content, thoughts, and feelings of the interviewee, but do not parrot.

The following dialogue illustrates the use of a reflective statement in an assessment with a 12-year-old boy:

IE: My teacher doesn't want to help me. In fact, I think she's got something against me.
IR: You feel she doesn't like you.
IE: Well, she's very unfriendly, ever since I got into trouble last year.
IR: She hasn't liked you since last year?
IE: Yes, well, I think so. When I got into trouble last year, she ….

Additional uses of reflection. Reflection and feedback also serve other purposes. By occasionally reflecting and paraphrasing the communications of interviewees, you (a) provide them with valuable feedback, (b) let them know that you understand them, and (c) help them verbalize other feelings and concerns more clearly. A statement such as "So you felt that you had no one to turn to" conveys that you are attentive. Additionally, if your understanding of a statement is inaccurate, interviewees can correct your interpretation. Reflection also can help you when you are not sure what question to ask or in what direction you want the assessment to go. Reflection not only will buy you some time but may aid interviewees as well. It changes the focus from questioning and probing to a more personal approach. Finally, you can use reflection when interviewees use jargon or terms you believe they do not understand. By repeating their words, you pro-

vide a prompt that may lead them to clarify their comments (Boggs & Eyberg, 1990).

Reflection of both content and nonverbal behavior. You can use reflection both with the content of the interviewees' communications and with their nonverbal behavior. In reflecting the content of an interviewee's communication, paraphrase the main ideas of the communication without parroting the communication. For example, after an interviewee's lengthy description of a fight at school, you might make the following summary statement: "What you're saying is that you couldn't go back to school after the fight because everybody would look at you."

Interviewees' nonverbal behavior includes affect, gestures, posture, tone of voice, and facial expressions. By reflecting the interviewee's affect, you not only show understanding but also implicitly give him or her permission to experience the emotion. For example, when the interviewee is crying, you might say, "I can see that it makes you sad to talk about this" (Stevenson, 1974). Such remarks may help interviewees experience strong emotions or relive events during the assessment. But you must be cautious; otherwise, interviewees may become more focused on their feelings than on providing the requested information. Supplement your reflection of feelings with nonverbal behaviors of acceptance, such as smiling or nodding your head.

When an interviewee's nonverbal behavior expresses something that she or he has not yet verbalized, consider making a comment. You might say, for example, "You seem to be fidgety," "You looked frightened when you said that," or "Your fists were clenched when you were talking just now." The interviewee's nonverbal behavior also may be expressing something about you, the interviewer—"You bore me"—or some need—"I have to go to the bathroom." Reflecting nonverbal behavior may be especially useful when there is an impasse during the assessment. However, this technique may make interviewees self-conscious and hinder their communication, so use it with caution.

Rigid and reflecting interviewer styles. The rigid style of interviewing yields information, but often makes the interviewer appear to be distant and aloof. The reflective style of interviewing, in contrast, not only yields information but also gives interviewees a sense that the interviewer is "with" them and thus facilitates a smooth flow of information.

Let's look at an example of a rigid interviewing style followed by an example of a reflective interviewing style (Shea, 1988, pp. 105–107, with changes in notation).

RIGID STYLE OF INTERVIEWING

IE: The pressures at home have really reached a crisis point. I'm not certain where it will all lead; I only know I'm feeling the heat.
IR: What's your appetite like?
IE: I guess it's okay.…

IR: What's your sleep like?
IE: Not too good. I have a hard time falling asleep. My days are such a blur. I never feel balanced, even when I try to fall asleep. I can't concentrate enough to even read.
IR: What about your ability to concentrate?
IE: What do you mean?
IR: Have you noticed any changes in how you study?
IE: Maybe a little.
IR: In what direction?
IE: I guess I can't study as well.
IR: And what about your energy level? How has it been?
IE: Fairly uneven. It's hard to explain; but sometimes I don't feel like doing anything.

REFLECTIVE STYLE OF INTERVIEWING

IE: The pressures at home have really reached a crisis point. I'm not certain where it will all lead; I only know I'm feeling the heat.
IR: Sounds like you've been going through a lot. How has it affected the way you feel in general?
IE: I always feel drained. I'm simply tired. Life seems like one giant chore. And I can't sleep well.
IR: Tell me about the problems you're having with your sleep.
IE: I can't fall asleep. It takes several hours just to get to sleep. I'm wired. I'm wired even in the day. And I'm so agitated I can't concentrate, even enough to read to put myself to sleep.
IR: Once you're asleep, do you stay asleep?
IE: Never; I bet I wake up four or five times a night. And about 5 A.M. I'm awake, as if someone slapped me.
IR: How do you mean?
IE: It's like an alarm went off, and no matter how hard I try, I can't get back to sleep.
IR: What do you do instead?
IE: Worry…. I'm not kidding…. My mind fills with all sorts of worthless junk.
IR: You mentioned earlier that you have problems with concentration. Tell me a little more about that.
IE: Just simply can't function like I used to. Reading, doing homework, all those things take much longer than usual. It really disturbs me. My system seems out of whack.
IR: Do you think your appetite has been affected as well?
IE: No question. My appetite is way down. Food tastes like paste; really very little taste at all. I've even lost weight.
IR: About how much?
IE: Oh, about five pounds.
IR: Over how long a time?
IE: Maybe over a month or two.

Periodic summaries.   Use *periodic summaries* to (a) convey your understanding of the problem, (b) allow the interviewee to comment on the adequacy of your interpretation, (c) inform the interviewee that you have been listening, (d) build transitions from one topic to the next and give direction to the assessment, (e) signal that you are at the end of the assessment, and (f) sum up and clarify what you have covered (Downs et al., 1980).

You can use different methods to begin a summary, such as "Let's see if I understand what's going on at home" or "Let me see, as I understand things so far, …. Is that right?"

or "If I understand you correctly, you're saying …. Have I got it right?" Here is an example of a summary statement to an adolescent: "So, you're concerned about your relationship with your father and how this stress is affecting your school work. I also heard you say that you're trying to find some help for your problem."

Checking the interviewee's understanding.   Use a *check of the interviewee's understanding* to learn about the clarity of your communications. Here is an example: "It would help me if you could tell me what I just said about the ways we can help Jim. Then I can be sure that I said what I meant to say." By putting this request in the context of helping you, rather than determining whether the interviewee was listening to you or understanding what you said, you may reduce pressure on him or her.

Miscellaneous probing statements.   Other types of probing questions or techniques can be used to encourage the interviewee to discuss a topic more fully. Examples are echoing the last words of the interviewee; pausing expectantly, with a questioning facial expression; and repeating the reply of the interviewee and then pausing. An example of echoing can be found in the following exchange:

IR: How are you getting along in school?
IE: I'm not getting along too well.
IR: Not too well?

Do not confuse echoing with parroting. Echoing is a probing technique in which you rephrase the interviewee's statement in the form of a question to get the interviewee to expand on her or his remark. In contrast, parroting involves merely repeating the interviewee's statement verbatim and, as noted, is *not* a preferred technique.

Guidelines for Probing

Decide on what statements to probe by keeping in mind your assessment goals. For example, if statements made by the interviewee convey two or more possible leads, consider your goals before choosing which lead to follow up.

IE: I'm really mad at my teacher. She never gives us a clear assignment. I'm about ready to explode.
IR-1: How are the assignments unclear?
IR-2: You're really upset about this.

Either response is good. The first response would be appropriate to keep the conversation at an informational level. The second response would be useful for exploring the feelings of the interviewee. You also have the option of using both responses by first discussing content and then discussing feelings (or vice versa). For example, if you initially asked about how the assignments were unclear but also wanted to explore the interviewee's feelings about the assignments, you could say, "A while ago, you said that you were ready to explode about the way your teacher hands out assignments. Tell me more about the way you feel."

We have seen that probing comments allow you to direct, organize, and focus the assessment. You will want to consider the needs of the interviewee when you use such comments. Some interviewees may need to (a) know your reasons for asking certain questions, (b) see that you are willing to listen when they express feelings, or (c) have help in expressing feelings. In any event, be sensitive to the needs of interviewees as well as to your assessment goals.

The following example illustrates several options available for responding to statements made by an 11-year-old girl. Each option is followed by a brief comment. Note that some options are preferable to others.

IR: I know you're having problems at home, Sara. Tell me about them.

IE: Yes, I am. I'm planning to leave home and go and live with my aunt. It's impossible to live with my mother.

IR-1:   What kinds of problems are you having? (This is an open-ended question that essentially repeats the original question. It could be useful because it gives the interviewee a chance to be more specific.)

IR-2:   So you're having trouble with your mother. I'm interested in hearing about the kinds of problems you're having at home. (This comment is similar to the probing question by IR-1 but contains an empathic introductory comment as well.)

IR-3:   Is your aunt's house a better place to live? (This closed-ended question is tangential and a poor choice, especially when you want to find out about the problems the interviewee is facing at home.)

IR-4:   In what way is your mother impossible to live with? (This is a focused question asking about the interviewee's feelings about her mother.)

IR-5:   It sounds as if you've reached your limits at home. (This is a reflective comment, but it may be premature. It is, nevertheless, a useful option because it may reflect the interviewee's feelings about her situation.)

IR-6:   Don't you like it at home? (This closed-ended question is a poor choice. Obviously the interviewee doesn't like it at home. There is little reason to ask this question.)

IR-7:   When do you plan to leave home? (This is a closed-ended question that asks for useful information. However, it is premature at this point in the assessment. It assumes that the decision of the interviewee is final, which it may not be. Also, it directs the interviewee away from the original question.)

> *"Then you should say what you mean," the March Hare went on.*
>
> *"I do," Alice hastily replied; "at least—at least I mean what I say—that's the same thing, you know."*
>
> *"Not the same thing a bit!" said the Hatter; "why, you might just as well say that 'I see what I eat' is the same thing as 'I eat what I see!'"*
>
> —Lewis Carroll

USING STRUCTURING STATEMENTS

Structuring statements guide the interviewee in talking about a topic. At the beginning of the assessment, they may serve to reduce the interviewee's anxiety. Valuable at any time during the evaluation, they are particularly appropriate to begin or end a phase of the assessment, to set an objective, or to provide information about the direction of the assessment.

Examples of Structuring Statements Early in the Interview

The following two examples demonstrate different ways to provide structuring statements early in an interview.

- "The purpose of this assessment is to find ways to help your son Wayne with his temper. I'm interested in anything you

Non Sequitur   by Wiley

can tell me about him." This structuring statement made early in the interview directs parents to discuss their son, who has a problem with his temper. It acknowledges that parents can give useful information and enlists their cooperation. It also gives the parents an opportunity to discuss relevant material.

- "We have about an hour to talk, so perhaps we could begin with your telling me what brought you to see me today." This structuring statement provides a time frame for the interview, focuses on the perceptions of the interviewee, and invites the interviewee to discuss those perceptions.

Examples of Structuring Statements Later in the Interview

The following three examples illustrate reasons for using structuring statements later in the interview.

- "Perhaps we can come back to what you're talking about later. But since our time is limited, can you tell me about Jane's…?" This structuring statement can guide a parent to focus on the child's problem rather than on the parent's own problem.
- "You said that Fred has problems in several different areas. Perhaps we could talk about each in detail. How does that sound to you?" This structuring statement can guide a parent to discuss specific problems.
- "During the last week…" or "Since your headaches began…" or "When you were living with your father …." These structuring statements can guide the interviewee to discuss the precise time, place, or situation that you are interested in.

ENCOURAGING APPROPRIATE REPLIES

The following techniques will help you convey your interest to the interviewee, encourage the interviewee to elaborate on her or his response, or ease the interviewee's anxiety (Stevenson, 1974).

1. Nod your head.
2. Give a verbal prompt such as "uh-huh" and lean forward expectantly.
3. Repeat, in a questioning manner, the last word or phrase of something the interviewee has said.
4. Use gentle urging, such as "What happened then?" or "Go ahead, you're doing fine" or "I'd like to hear more about that."
5. Use the name of the interviewee frequently.
6. Maintain eye contact.
7. Maintain a friendly attitude, gentle speech, and a kind expression.
8. Express signs of understanding and empathy by saying, for example, "I can understand how difficult that must have been for you," "That probably made you feel better," "Surely," or "Naturally."

DEALING WITH DIFFICULT SITUATIONS

Some interviewees will be more challenging than others. For example, blocks in the assessment will arise when interviewees are uncommunicative, impatient, closed-minded, extremely hyperactive, dogmatic, argumentative, passive-aggressive, excessively anxious, opinionated, hostile, angry, uncooperative, highly agitated, disoriented, extremely depressed, or confused. (Table 1-3 offers information on additional interviewee styles that may create problems during the assessment.) The material in this section will help you deal with these and other difficult assessment situations.

Handling Interviewees Who Try to Take Control

When you lack confidence, feel intimidated by interviewees, or are poorly prepared for the assessment, interviewees might try to take control of the assessment (Gratus, 1988). Interviewees may sense that you are not in control during the opening minutes of the assessment or, for that matter, at any time during the evaluation. If you show confidence and appear friendly, helpful, and encouraging, they are less likely to try to assume control. If they still try to control the assessment despite all your best efforts, remain calm, detached, and objective; evaluate where the assessment has strayed; and refocus on the area of concern. Interviewees also might try to control the assessment because they want to avoid certain topics, because they are domineering, or because they have an agenda to cover. In these cases, help the interviewees understand that you need to cover certain topics in order to perform a thorough and meaningful assessment.

Handling Difficult Behavior

Interviewees may behave in ways that make you uncomfortable. Let's now look at some of these ways.

Interviewees who have emotional upsets. When interviewees become emotionally upset, do not stop their behavior prematurely. They may need time to work through their discomfort. By giving them time, you can learn more about their behavior. Dealing with such situations, of course, requires clinical judgment. You do not want to allow a situation to arise in which an interviewee becomes too disorganized, frightened, or aggressive. You must develop some tolerance for anxiety-provoking behavior, yet know when to step in to reduce or change the behavior if it becomes too intense or is on the verge of becoming out of control.

When interviewees show strong emotions, remain calm, objective, and detached. You should *not* show excessive sympathy and concern, react critically or judgmentally, or pry too deeply. As a clinical assessment interviewer, you want to obtain information, not uncover traumas. If you believe that uncovering the trauma will be useful, refer the interviewee to

Table 1-3
Difficult Interviewee Styles

Interviewee style	Description	Suggestions
Apprehensive	Has unsteady voice, has anxious gestures, constantly shifts body, has frozen facial expressions	Help interviewee see that fears about you are unfounded, give constant reassurance, smile and nod frequently, be calm and relaxed, don't rush questions
Arrogant	Answers each question as concisely and sharply as possible, acts insolent or cute, gives impression that the interview is beneath him or her	Help interviewee see how answering your questions will benefit him or her or someone else who is close to interviewee, probe with increasing directness
Crafty	Acts as if she or he has something to hide, tries to play games with you or outwit you	Let interviewee know that her or his ploy is not working, confront interviewee
Defensive	Says "I don't know," is hesitant, exaggerates or conceals unfavorable facts	Don't hurry interviewee; praise honest responses; ask simple, narrow questions at first
Disorganized	Seems confused or distracted	Be patient, use short directed questions, summarize frequently
Hostile	Appears angry, will not cooperate, withholds information, presents information hurriedly	Remain calm and interested, reassure interviewee that cooperation can be rewarding, touch on neutral topics at first
Nontalkative	Gives one- or two-word answers, provides little or no elaboration	Help interviewee explore reason for silence; spend more time developing rapport; ask easy questions and open-ended questions; relate anecdotes about similar experiences; convey interest by a nod, an encouraging smile, and a voice that indicates interest
Overeager	Talks too much because of a desire to aid you as much as possible	Help interviewee realize that you want an accurate and complete answer, don't be too flattered by interviewee's willingness to talk
Stolid	Appears impassive, unemotional, or slow	Ask questions slowly, be patient, help interviewee dig out facts, use ingenuity and perseverance
Tenacious	Doesn't admit the possibility of error; is bold, aggressive, or stubborn	Use polite, indirect, and tactful approaches; don't lose patience
Too talkative	Says too much; gives roundabout, long-winded answers	Phrase questions in a way that limits the scope of the response, tactfully bring interviewee back to topic

Source: Adapted from Donaghy (1984) and Zima (1983).

another source or address the trauma in a separate therapy session. Often, however, interviewees will feel better simply from talking to someone who is caring and is willing to listen to them. Interviewees who break down during the assessment are likely to feel embarrassed and awkward. When this happens, reassure them—through your words, facial expressions, and gestures—that it is acceptable for them to show their feelings and that you are interested in understanding how they feel. However, once they recover their composure, continue the assessment in the direction you had planned.

Occasionally, interviewees may inundate you with their innermost feelings and concerns. When this occurs, you may not grasp everything they say. In such cases, make a mental or written note of the areas to which you might want to return. Keep in mind that, at the end of the interview, it might be appropriate to refer the interviewee to a therapist with whom she or he can further discuss these feelings or problems.

Interviewees who make derogatory remarks about you. In extreme cases, interviewees may become abusive. They may disparage your training, gender, ethnicity, or other personal qualities. When this happens, consider possible reasons for their comments, such as a thought disorder or simple fright. Although verbally abusive comments may make you anxious and angry, do not respond in kind. You must rise above your personal feelings and help the interviewee calm down and return to the task at hand. To do so, you must remain calm, objective, and detached. At this point you have two options: you can ignore the comment or you can use the opportunity to set limits and boundaries. For example, if an adolescent calls you an "idiot" or a "stupid asshole," you might respond with "I realize you're angry about being here right now. But it's important that we treat each other with respect, which includes not calling each other names. Now, I'd like to hear more about …."

Interviewees who make derogatory remarks about other people.

Occasionally, interviewees may upset you by making racist comments, belittling groups, or making other insulting remarks. In such situations, you must control your reactions. Remind yourself that the purpose of interviews is to learn about interviewees, not to instruct them or confront them about your feelings. Although you may have value conflicts with the views you hear, you want to encourage interviewees to tell you what they feel, think, and believe. You are not there to change their views, but to learn what their views are and, if possible, how they developed (Bogdan & Biklen, 1982).

Interviewees who are uncooperative.

Interviewees may be uncooperative because (a) they were coerced to come to the assessment; (b) they are shy; (c) they resent you because of your ethnicity, gender, or some other factor; or (d) they are unable to attend to or concentrate on your questions. Uncooperative interviewees may maintain silence, show anger or hostility, give superficial answers, or attempt to end the session early. Although you should make every effort to establish rapport and reduce interviewees' stress or anger, your efforts may not always be successful. Also, remember that interviewees may not understand their role in the interview process. For example, interviewees may appear oppositional when, in reality, they do not have the social orientation or the cognitive maturity to know what is expected of them.

Interviewees who are violent.

Interviewees sometimes can become violent, particularly in emergency wards of mental hospitals or clinics. (This section is adapted from Shea, 1988.) Usually, the signs of imminent violent behavior are nonverbal, but they also can be verbal.

Interviewees may be exhibiting a sign of potentially violent behavior when they do any of the following:

- Begin to speak more quickly in a subtly angry tone of voice
- Make statements such as "You think you're a big shot, don't you?"
- Pace and refuse to sit down
- Make rapid and jerking gestures, such as pointing a finger at the interviewer
- Stare with increased intensity
- Show signs of paranoia, disorganization, or other psychotic processes

- Clench fists or grasp an object in a way that causes knuckles to whiten
- Snarl with lips pulled back, showing front teeth
- Raise a closed fist over the head
- Shake a fist
- Assume a boxing stance
- Gesture as if strangling an opponent
- Pound a fist into the opposite palm
- Make verbal threats that they are about to strike

Here are some suggestions for dealing with and defusing potentially violent behavior (Shea, 1988):

1. Consider taking precautionary measures, such as having help available and having a buzzer signal for emergencies.
2. Arrange chairs so that you have an unobstructed path to the doorway, especially with an interviewee you do not know.
3. Gently request that the interviewee return to his or her seat when the interviewee paces: "It might help you to relax if you sit there" or "I'd like you to sit over there so we can talk." You may quietly add a comment such as "It's difficult to have to keep staring up. I think things will go more smoothly if you sit over there."
4. Compliment the interviewee when he or she says something positive.
5. Change to a more neutral topic if the topic under discussion is too stressful.
6. Avoid the appearance of aggressive actions. You don't want to raise your voice, speed up your movements, make angry remarks, or do anything that may increase the interviewee's level of agitation. Instead, you want to appear calm in order to help an angry or frightened interviewee calm down. Speak in a normal and unhurried voice.
7. Assume a submissive posture: Decrease eye contact, avoid raising your hands in any gesture that may signify attack, avoid placing your hands behind your back (as this may arouse suspicion that a weapon is being hidden), avoid pulling your shoulders back and appearing powerful and confrontational, and remain in front of the interviewee (as an approach from behind or the side may startle him or her).
8. Give the interviewee sufficient space—getting too close may result in your being assaulted.
9. Be prepared to seek help if your actions fail. If you become fearful, consider leaving the room and returning with another staff member or a security guard. You can say, "I want to help you, but I will need some help. Please excuse me for a few minutes."

Confronting violent behavior is a frightening experience. Recognizing signs of possible violence and implementing strategies to prevent it will help you deal more effectively with this most difficult situation. You will need to use your clinical skills to help the interviewee regain a sense of control.

You also should consider your personal safety when you interview children and parents in their homes, particularly if you are in an unfamiliar location or dangerous neighborhood.

Consider notifying a friend or colleague of your location and what time you expect to return, carry a cell phone, or have a colleague accompany you. Work closely with law enforcement personnel or social services when your visit involves interviewing the family about possible child maltreatment.

Handling Sensitive Topics

You can introduce a potentially sensitive topic by pointing out that the problem is not a unique one. For example, if the referral question or reports from others lead you to suspect that the interviewee has a problem controlling her or his temper, you might say, "Sometimes people have difficulty controlling their tempers. Have you ever lost your temper?" If the answer is affirmative, you might follow it up by asking for examples. You also could ask, "Have you ever done anything you regretted when you lost your temper?"

With a parent who may have difficulty restraining his or her own aggressive behavior, you might say, "Sometimes parents can be pushed to their limit, and they're so upset they just feel like hitting their kid if the kid acts out one more time. Have you ever felt like that yourself?" (Shea, 1988, p. 323, with changes in notation).

If the interviewee is extremely reluctant to talk about a sensitive topic, such as sexual difficulties, you have several options. You can (a) ask a same-sex interviewer to conduct the assessment, (b) allow the interviewee to write out her or his concerns, or (c) ask a person whom the interviewee trusts to get the needed information.

Handling Inadequate Answers

It will not always be easy to learn why interviewees give inadequate answers or why they do not talk much. For example, interviewees may be shy, embarrassed to talk about themselves, or frightened about the outcome of the assessment; or they may not like the way you are conducting the interview. Try to find out why they are not responding and what you can do to make the situation more comfortable for them. You may have to redouble your efforts to establish rapport—be even more friendly, encouraging, warm, accepting, and nonjudgmental. You want to convey to the interviewee that you both are engaged in a cooperative enterprise from which he or she is likely to benefit.

If the interviewee still fails to respond after your attempts to be supportive, examine your behavior with the aid of the following questions:

1. Are your questions like interrogations, or are they open-ended questions designed to allow the interviewee to talk freely?
2. Are you asking questions too rapidly?
3. Are your questions too leading?
4. Do you convey the impression that you are in a hurry to complete the assessment?

5. Are you speaking in a dull, plodding manner that bores the interviewee?
6. Are you asking questions that the interviewee has already answered?
7. Did you establish rapport before exploring intimate topics?
8. Does the interviewee understand your questions?

Handling Memory Difficulties

An interviewee may have memory difficulties because (a) the events occurred in the remote past and were not particularly meaningful, (b) the events are too painful to recall, or (c) the interviewee has amnesia associated with neurological deficits or acute trauma. Memory lapses also may serve defensive purposes, such as protection against further pain. The pressure to recall by itself may be a barrier to recall. To help interviewees recall information, (a) give them time to think without pressure, (b) switch topics and then come back to the topic later in the assessment, or (c) ask direct questions about the topic to help them structure the sequence of events (Downs et al., 1980).

Handling Silences

Occasionally, conversation will halt. Learn to recognize different silences. A pause may mean one of several things. Maybe the interviewee has finished giving information about the topic, needs time to recall more information or consolidate thoughts, senses that she or he has been misunderstood, recognizes that you have touched on a sensitive area, or doesn't know what else to say.

Silence also may be a sign of mourning or deep reflection over some past tragedy; in such cases, do not feel compelled to say something to get the interviewee to talk. An empathic smile or a nod of the head is all that may be needed to show that you understand and are waiting for the interviewee to continue. If you do decide to speak, you might say, "Do you want to just be quiet for a while? That's fine."

Note the interviewee's posture for possible clues about what the silence might mean, but be sure to check them out. For example, crossed arms often suggest resistance, but they may just mean that the interviewee is cold. (The following discussion of extreme silences pertains particularly to older children and adults. Chapter 2 discusses the implications of silence for younger children.)

Statements to make when silence is extreme.
When progress is stifled or when the interviewee is extremely reluctant to continue, you might try discussing the difficulty. Following are useful statements to make at these times (Stevenson, 1960):

- "During the last few minutes, you've become pretty quiet. I'm wondering what you are feeling."
- "It's hard to go on talking about this, isn't it?"

- "It seems hard for you to talk to me about yourself. Is there anything I can do to make it easier for you?"
- "What are you thinking about right now?"
- "Something seems to be preventing you from talking. Could you tell me a little about what it is?"
- "I've been wondering if the difficulty you're having in talking comes from your wondering how I'll react to what you tell me."
- "We do not seem to have made much progress. Tell me what we can do differently."
- "We don't seem to be making a lot of progress. What do you think is the reason?"

Statements and questions such as these will likely cause the interviewee to respond with renewed interest. If they do not, think about why the interviewee might still be irritated or anxious. Interviewees may be reluctant to talk because of distrust or dislike of you, fear of you, fear of their own emotions, fear of examining themselves too closely, or uncertainty about the confidentiality of the assessment (Stevenson, 1960). Do not pressure interviewees to talk, and do not get into an argument about their silence. Instead, deal with their concerns sensitively and reassuringly.

Statements to make when silence suggests guilt. If you believe that the silence may be associated with guilt, you might say, "I can see that this is something that is very difficult for you to talk about, but it's important that we talk about it sometime. Should we do it now or come back to it later?"

Interviewee resistance.   Silence can indicate resistance. When you judge this to be the case, the following techniques may be useful (Shea, 1988):

1. Follow up on topics when interviewees give the slightest hint that they want to discuss them.
2. Temporarily avoid sensitive topics, such as the use of drugs and alcohol, sexual matters, or suicidal thoughts.
3. Choose topics that are neutral ("Tell me about your neighborhood" or "Tell me about your hobbies"), topics that the interviewee may have a strong opinion about ("What are some things your father does that you think are unfair?"), or ones that are meaningful or important to the interviewee ("What important things are now happening in your life?").
4. Use phrases with gentle commands. For example, say, "Tell me about…" or "Let's discuss…" instead of "Can you tell me…" or "Would you tell me …." Interviewees might answer the latter phrases with even more silence, frowns, or simply "no."
5. Increase eye contact and positive verbal comments. Accompany comments like "You're doing fine," "Go on," or "That's fine" with positive nonverbal gestures such as head nodding. However, with hostile interviewees, these techniques may not be appropriate because they may be unwarranted or misinterpreted.
6. Avoid long pauses between your questions.

7. Allow interviewees to "save face" by accepting their decision not to talk to you and asking them to complete a form or checklist instead. For example, some interviewees who are not willing to talk to you may be willing to complete a checklist and then discuss their responses with you. In these cases, they may leave the examination convinced that they have won by not talking to you, yet they have provided valuable information.

Appreciating silence.   At first, silences may seem to be interminably long, but in time you will learn to appreciate them. Silences can give you some time to think, reduce the tempo of an assessment that is too intense, or press interviewees to assume responsibility for what they are discussing (Reisman, 1973). You will want to avoid silences, however, when they are causing stress for the interviewee.

Handling Irrelevant Material

Some interviewees have difficulty knowing when to stop talking and produce a stream of irrelevant material. When this happens, redirect them; otherwise, you will waste time and get useless information. Here are some techniques you can use to redirect interviewees who wander off course (Gratus, 1988; Shea, 1988):

1. Comment on what they said, then refocus the direction of the interview. Say, for example, "Yes, that's very interesting, and we may come back to it later, but right now I'd like to discuss …." This statement lets interviewees know that they might have a chance to get back to the topic at some later stage and that you're not dismissing them completely. It allows you to regain control.
2. Use narrower questions that require relatively short and pinpointed answers.
3. Avoid positive nonverbal gestures, such as head nodding or any other behaviors that reinforce the behavior of the interviewees.
4. Use structuring statements to introduce topics. Say, for example, "We need to discuss how you're doing at home. This is an important area, so let's focus on it for a few minutes."
5. Use structuring statements to inform interviewees about how you want to conduct the interview, if the above techniques fail. Say, for example, "We have a limited amount of time. Let's focus on one important area at a time, because I need to understand each area as clearly as possible."
6. Confront interviewees, if needed, with their behavior. Say, for example, "I notice that when I ask a question, we wander off the topic. What do you think is happening?"
7. Guide interviewees back to the topic as firmly as possible. Say, for example, "Let's focus on how you're doing in school this semester. Please don't discuss other things right now. It's important that I learn about how you're doing in school this semester. If we wander off, I'll bring you back to the topic. Okay? Let's start with how you're getting along with your teacher."

Handling Questions About Your Clinical Competence

Interviewees may occasionally wonder about your competence and may confront you with questions about your ability to help them (Anderson & Stewart, 1983). They may ask you questions about your professional qualifications and credentials—for example, "Are you a student?" or "What kind of professional training have you had?"

Challenges to the interviewer's competence usually arise out of interviewees' concern about whether the interviewer can help them, and out of mistaken notions of what qualities and qualifications a good interviewer should have. Some interviewees rely on advanced degrees, whereas others think that if the interviewer is similar to them in race, culture, gender, or other attributes, he or she will automatically be a better interviewer for them. Interviewers and interviewees alike often make the mistaken assumption that only an interviewer who has successfully negotiated all stages of marriage, parenthood, and life is qualified to assess other people's problems. (Anderson & Stewart, 1983, pp. 149–150, with changes in notation)

Other forms of challenges include "I need a medical doctor, not a psychologist" and "You can't help me because you're [too young, too old, African American, Euro American, Hispanic American, Asian American, Native American, male, female, married, single, childless, too problem-free, too different, too much like us]" (Anderson & Stewart, 1983). These remarks reflect resistance by the interviewees—that is, the interviewees may not be ready to reveal intimate details of their lives to you. Here are some suggestions on how to deal with challenges to your competence.

1. *Don't be defensive.* Recognize that it is perfectly acceptable for interviewees to wonder about your competence (Anderson & Stewart, 1983). Accept their concerns and, to help yourself become less defensive, focus on them. Find out exactly what their concerns are. As they see that you are interested, caring, and trustworthy, they may become less resistant. You can accept their concerns with such statements as "That's a good question" or "Your point is a good one, which is one of the reasons we are closely supervised in our work" (Shea, 1988, p. 527). If interviewees are concerned about your professional qualifications, you can briefly explain your background in psychology, counseling, psychiatry, or any other relevant field of training. You can say, "I'm a professional who works with children and their families." If you are licensed or certified, you also can mention this to the interviewee. What you do not want to do is engage in a power struggle. If you do, the interview process may fail.

2. *Be prepared.* Be aware of your own vulnerabilities and be prepared to deal with them. For example, if you are an interviewer-in-training or look very young, be prepared to discuss these issues with the interviewee (Anderson & Stewart, 1983).

3. *Evaluate the context.* Determine at what point during the interview the interviewee challenged your competence. Was it at the beginning of the session, or was it when a sensitive topic was being raised? Consider what the interviewee's challenge may mean, what you may have done to provoke it, and whether the interviewee was trying to turn the focus away from himself or herself to avoid answering questions.

4. *Answer the question.* Answer directly any questions interviewees have about your professional background and training; do not say, "Why do you ask?" Answering their questions directly in a nondefensive way shows interviewees that you take their concerns seriously and that you are not intimidated (Anderson & Stewart, 1983).

5. *Admit that differences may be a problem and appeal for the interviewee's help.* Interviewees may be caught off guard by an appeal for their help: "No, I've never had a child with a drug problem; in fact, I have no children. Do you think that's a problem?" (Anderson & Stewart, 1983, p. 136). The request for feedback about what you might be missing may enlist their cooperation.

6. *Use humor.* If you judge that the interviewee would respond favorably to banter, you might say, if your age is questioned, "I'm only 25, but some days I feel a lot older. Does that qualify?" (Anderson & Stewart, 1983, p. 138, with change in notation). Follow such a remark with an offer to discuss the issue seriously. However, be cautious: "The use of humor demands some skill in knowing when it will be effective and appropriate rather than offensive.... A good rule is, 'When in doubt, don't'" (Anderson & Stewart, 1983, p. 138).

7. *Use the team approach.* Those of you who are in training can say, for example, "Yes, I'm a first-year psychology graduate student. My work here will be supervised by Dr. Smith, one of the members of the staff." You also can introduce the supervisor to the interviewee, stressing that the supervisor will be reviewing the assessment findings and interpretation.

8. *Admit that you will never know the depth of the interviewee's distress.* When interviewees have faced a severe crisis and say that you cannot understand them, admit that you do not know what they have experienced. However, reassure them that you want to listen to them and to understand how they are feeling. By listening carefully to what they have experienced, you will be establishing rapport.

Handling Self-Disclosure

Interviewees may ask you questions about yourself. Be tactful in responding to such questions. However, don't allow a situation to develop in which you are doing most of the talking and the interviewees are doing most of the questioning. Although some self-disclosure may be helpful, keep it to a minimum.

Handling Requests for Your Opinion

Interviewees may try to elicit your opinion about some personal matter or may try to get you to side with them. For example, they might ask you if you support their position.

Remain neutral in such situations. Simply reflect what they have told you and ask for further information, as needed.

IE: Mrs. Brown shouldn't have placed me on probation. Don't you agree with me?

IR: You seem to feel that she made the wrong decision. How come?

Occasionally, interviewees become more persistent.

IE: It seems that physical punishment is the only way I can get Darryl to mind. Now what's wrong with hitting him once in a while?

IR: You seem to be uncertain about whether physical punishment is okay.

IE: Well, that's not what I asked you. What do you think of physical punishment?

IR: What would you like me to say?

IE: I want you to agree with me.

IR: I'm not sure how my agreeing with you would help you. Have you found much support from your husband?

IE: Not too much. I don't get much support from anyone.

In the above incident, the interviewer tried to sidetrack the interviewee but was not successful. After the interviewer directly confronted the interviewee's question, the interviewee began talking about her feelings.

REMAINING OBJECTIVE

Distinguishing Between Acceptance and Endorsement

Consider the distinction between accepting the communications of interviewees and endorsing their communications. *Accepting* their communications means that you acknowledge and appreciate their point of view; it does not mean that you agree with or approve of it. *Endorsing* their communications means that you agree that their perspective is accurate. Accept an interviewee's viewpoint but do not endorse it. For example, if an interviewee tells you how angry he is about what another child did, you can acknowledge his feeling by saying "You were hurt when he did that." However, it would be inappropriate to say "That was an awful thing he did to you." The goal in such a situation is to express that you appreciate the interviewee's point of view, without endorsing it.

Recognizing Your Emotions and Keeping Them Under Control

Every assessment represents a unique interpersonal encounter. Your ability to conduct an effective assessment will be determined not only by your interviewing skills but also by personal factors in your life. You must be sensitive to how you are feeling as the interview begins. Do you have any personal concerns that might interfere with your ability to con-

duct the interview? Did anything happen shortly before the interview to make you anxious (e.g., a death in the family, too little sleep, recovery from an illness, a harrowing experience on the ward, confrontation with an angry interviewee)? Do you feel tired, rushed, angry, or depressed? You must ensure that these and similar feelings do not interfere with the assessment process.

During the interview, you will react to many things the interviewee says. You may feel sorrow, disgust, embarrassment, anger, pleasure, or humor. Recognize these feelings, but keep them under control. Again, you do not want them to interfere with the assessment. You do not have the latitude you have in personal relationships to respond to disagreement or anger in kind. If you express anger or disgust, for example, you might inhibit interviewees from talking further about intimate details of their lives. If something is humorous, you can laugh *with* the interviewee, but never *at* him or her!

If you believe that your feelings hampered the interview, look for the source of the difficulty. For example, were you too sympathetic, indifferent, cold, or overprotective; angry when the interviewee was rude or uncooperative because of your need to be liked; too reassuring because the interviewee's problems reminded you of your own problems; or too talkative in an effort to impress the interviewee with your knowledge? *Self-awareness is an important step in becoming an effective interviewer.*

RECORDING INFORMATION AND SCHEDULING

Recording Information

It is important to record what the interviewee says. However, it is difficult, if not impossible, to record every word unless you are skilled at shorthand or use a tape recorder or video camera. Therefore, if you merely take notes, jot down only the most important remarks made by the interviewee. You can paraphrase the communications of the interviewee or use various formal or informal shorthand techniques. Notes serve as a way of keeping records. If your notes are subpoenaed, you may have to make them available to an attorney. You can make note taking easier by telling the interviewee, "I'm taking notes so that I can remember important things you say, because what you say is important."

Student clinicians frequently use video or audio recordings during training. Audiotape recorders also are used by skilled interviewers, and videotape recording is highly recommended, if not a necessity, in child maltreatment cases. Be sure that you have the *written consent* of adult interviewees to use an audio or video recorder. With children, written consent of the parent may not be necessary in all circumstances, especially if the parent is suspected of child maltreatment. In child maltreatment cases, some agencies routinely tell children about the video recording, whereas others do not unless the children ask. Realize, however, that the presence of an audio or video recorder may affect an interviewee's comfort level and responses.

If you take notes, do not let note taking interfere with your listening. Do not hide behind your notes ("Let me see my notes about that matter") or use them in a secretive way. Also, maintain eye contact with the interviewee. If the interviewee speaks too quickly and this interferes with your note taking, you might say, "Please talk more slowly so that I can write down your important ideas." A remark like this, however, may interfere with the flow of conversation.

Scheduling Appointments

If you have a heavy assessment schedule, take a few minutes between sessions to write notes and relax. Unless there is a break, you may be thinking about the previous interview when you should be thinking about the present one.

Second Interviews

Occasionally, you may need more than one session to obtain the needed information. In such cases, schedule additional sessions. Here are some suggestions for ways to begin the second interview (Stevenson, 1960):

- "How have you been since our last meeting?"
- "What's been happening since we last met?"
- "Last time, we had to stop before we covered everything. Perhaps we can pick up where we left off."
- "You may have thought of some things that you didn't have a chance to say last time. Let's talk about those things now."

If these inquiries are not productive, you can turn to specific areas of the interviewee's history or current situation that you need to inquire about. If you administered psychological tests and the second interview occurs after you have completed the formal testing, you can ask questions related to the testing *and* to the interview. For example, you can ask questions about particular responses to test items, pursue unclear details that came up in the interview, and resolve any incongruities in the inter-

view, observations, or test findings. Also, if you gave the interviewee a self-monitoring task, you can look over the self-monitoring record and discuss it (see Chapter 5). Finally, you may want to give a brief summary of what you covered or learned during the prior interview.

THINKING THROUGH THE ISSUES

1. How easy might it be for you to forget that you are conducting a clinical assessment interview and fall back into your ordinary mode of conversation?
2. To what extent will the disadvantages associated with the clinical assessment interview affect the information you obtain?
3. When do you think you would use an unstructured interview, a semistructured interview, and a structured interview?
4. How would you prepare for an interview?
5. What do you see as the role for computer-generated interviewing? What are some advantages and disadvantages of computerized interviewing? Will computerized interviewing replace interviewers in clinical assessment? What are the ethical issues involved in using computers for interviewing?
6. During an interview, what clues might you use to guide you in evaluating the extent to which the interviewee is being open and honest?
7. How might the interviewee judge your openness and honesty?
8. Why might you have difficulty establishing rapport in an interview?
9. How will you know when your questions are effective?
10. Which probing techniques do you think you will use most frequently as a clinician? Why did you make these choices?
11. To what extent does the use of probing techniques reflect an invasion of privacy?
12. How can you determine whether silence reflects a mere pause or an impasse in the assessment?
13. How would you deal with interviewees who become emotionally upset?
14. If your emotions interfered with the flow of the interview, what steps would you take to regain control?
15. Imagine that you were an interviewee. How would you know whether the clinician liked you, understood you, and respected you? What would the clinician have to do to convey this information to you?

PEANUTS reprinted by permission of United Feature Syndicate, Inc.

SUMMARY

1. The primary goal of the clinical assessment interview is to obtain relevant, reliable, and valid information about the interviewees and their problems.
2. Information should be obtained about interviewees' personality, temperament, motor skills, cognitive skills, communication skills, study habits, work habits, interpersonal behavior, interests, daily living skills and difficulties, and perception of the referral problem.

Clinical Assessment Interviews versus Ordinary Conversations and Other Types of Interviews

3. A clinical assessment interview is different from an ordinary conversation in that the interview involves an interpersonal interaction that has a mutually accepted purpose, with formal, clearly defined roles and a set of norms governing the interaction.
4. There is continuity between clinical assessment interviews and psychotherapeutic interviews, with changing and evolving goals rather than different ones.
5. In psychotherapeutic interviews, you should continually assess the interviewee; and in clinical assessment interviews, you should use psychotherapeutic strategies to deal with interviewee reactions such as emotional upsets during the interview.
6. Survey research interviews usually focus on interviewees' opinions or preferences with respect to various topics.

Strengths and Weaknesses of the Clinical Assessment Interview

7. Overall, the interview is one of the most useful techniques for obtaining information, because it allows interviewees to express, in their own terms, their views about themselves and relevant life events.
8. The interview allows great latitude for the interviewee's expression of concerns, thoughts, feelings, and reactions, with a minimum of structure and redirection on the part of the interviewer.
9. The interview also has several weaknesses as an assessment tool.

Purposes of Clinical Assessment Interviews

10. The purpose of a clinical assessment interview depends on whether it is an initial interview, a post-assessment interview, or a follow-up interview.
11. The initial interview is designed to inform the interviewee about the assessment process and to obtain information relevant to diagnosis, treatment, remediation, or placement in special programs.
12. The post-assessment interview (also known as the exit interview) is designed to discuss the assessment findings and recommendations with the interviewee's parents and, often, the interviewee.
13. The follow-up interview is designed to assess outcomes of treatment or interventions and to gauge the appropriateness of the assessment findings and recommendations.

Degrees of Structure in Initial Clinical Assessment Interviews

14. Types of initial clinical assessment interviews include unstructured interviews, semistructured interviews, and structured interviews.
15. In unstructured interviews, the interview process is allowed to unfold without specific guidelines.
16. Semistructured interviews are based on general and flexible guidelines.
17. In structured interviews, the exact order and wording of each question is specified, with little opportunity for follow-up questions not directly related to the specified questions.

Introduction to Interviewing Guidelines

18. Successful interviewing requires the ability to communicate clearly and the ability to understand the communications of interviewees, whether children or adults.
19. During the interview, you will ask questions, follow up and probe responses, move from topic to topic, encourage replies, answer questions, gauge the pace of the interview, and formulate impressions of the interviewee.
20. No matter how well you have planned the interview, each interviewee will present a new challenge. No individual is predictable.
21. Listen carefully to what the interviewee says.
22. Interpret and assess what is significant, but do not accept everything as literal truth; remember, however, that it may be the interviewee's truth.
23. Let the interviewee's values, culture, attitudes, and developmental level guide your interpretations.
24. To be successful as an interviewer, you must know yourself, trust your ideas, be willing to make mistakes, and, above all, have a genuine desire to help the interviewee.
25. A good interview takes careful planning, skillful execution, and good organization; it is purposeful and goal-oriented.
26. The interview is affected by interviewer and interviewee characteristics (e.g., physical, cognitive, and affective factors), message components (e.g., language, nonverbal cues, and sensory cues), and interview climate (e.g., physical, social, temporal, and psychological factors).

External Factors and Atmosphere

27. Conduct the interview in a private, quiet room that is free from distractions.
28. Keep interruptions to a minimum if you cannot avoid them entirely.
29. Begin the interview at the scheduled time.
30. Interview the parent(s) without small children in the room.

Forming Impressions

31. When you and the interviewee first meet, both of you will form initial impressions. These impressions will change as the interview progresses.
32. Be aware of signs of psychological disturbance and signs of psychological health.

Listening

33. The ability to listen is the key factor in the interview.
34. Being a good listener means being free of preoccupations, giving interviewees your full attention, and listening to yourself.

Analytical Listening

35. The ability to analyze the responses of the interviewee critically as you listen—termed analytical listening—is an important interviewing skill.

36. Good analytical listening skills include getting the main ideas, facts, and details; understanding the connotative meanings of words; identifying affect and attitudes appropriately; discriminating between fact and imagination; recognizing discrepancies; judging the relevancy of communications; and making valid inferences.

37. Interviewees have certain ways or patterns of answering questions, called response sets (or response styles); you will need to be cognizant of their response sets.

38. You must judge whether you have obtained all the information the interviewee is willing to share with you and whether that amount is sufficient.

39. Interviewees must recognize that you are evaluating their communications and organizing them into some coherent theme.

40. Toward the end of the interview, you can (a) ask about important areas you did not discuss, (b) clarify previously discussed material, (c) make other necessary comments, or (d) invite questions that the interviewee might have.

Establishing Rapport

41. The success of an interview, like that of any other assessment procedure, depends on the rapport you establish with the interviewee.

42. Rapport is based on mutual confidence, respect, and acceptance.

43. Because the clinical assessment interview is a formal, professional interaction, the interviewee should not have to deal with your personal concerns.

44. Rapport may be difficult to establish when the interviewee does not want to be interviewed or have the information from the interview shared with anyone else.

45. Showing interest in the information given to you by the interviewee is crucial in establishing rapport.

46. Reassure anxious interviewees.

47. Interviewees may express their anxiety either verbally or nonverbally.

48. When you sense that the interviewee's anxiety is interfering with rapport, encourage him or her to talk about it.

49. When all else fails and the interviewee still will not talk with you, you may need to gently point out the responsibilities of an interviewee.

50. Compliment the interviewee's sharing.

51. Use language suitable to the age, gender, and education of the interviewee.

Timing Questions Appropriately

52. The initial part of the assessment should focus on areas that are not anxiety-provoking or excessively sensitive.

53. Premature or poorly timed questions may impede the progress of the assessment and discourage disclosure of vital information.

54. The pace of the assessment should be rapid enough to keep the interest of the interviewee, but slow enough to allow the interviewee to formulate good answers.

Changing Topics

55. Proceed in an orderly manner, and finish one area before going on to the next.

56. It will take practice and sensitivity to judge when you have exhausted one topic and need to move to another.

Formulating Appropriate Questions

57. Questions form the heart of the interview. They direct the interviewee toward your concerns and elicit the information needed for the assessment.

58. The way you ask questions is as important as what you ask. Speak clearly and audibly at a moderate pace.

59. The words you stress can determine the meaning of what you say.

60. When you formulate a question, the interviewee must understand your words in the same way you intend them.

61. Questions vary as to their degree of openness and include minimally focused questions, moderately focused questions, and highly focused questions.

62. Open-ended questions are usually preferable, especially at the start of the assessment, because they give the interviewee some responsibility for sharing her or his concerns.

63. Moderately focused questions are more directive than open-ended questions and are valuable as the assessment proceeds.

64. All types of questions have their place in the assessment.

65. Phrase questions positively and confidently.

Avoiding Certain Types of Questions

66. The major types of questions to avoid are yes-no questions; double-barreled questions; long, multiple questions; leading questions; random probing questions; coercive questions; embarrassing or accusatory questions; and why questions.

Probing Effectively

67. Probing is a key to successful interviewing.

68. By recognizing the possible reason for an inadequate response, you can probably determine the kinds of follow-up questions needed.

69. Types of probing questions and comments include elaboration, clarification, repetition, challenging, silence, neutral phrases, reflective statements, periodic summaries, checking the interviewee's understanding, and miscellaneous probing statements.

70. Use elaboration when you want the interviewee to provide additional information.

71. Use clarification when you do not understand what the interviewee is saying or when you are puzzled by some details.

72. Use repetition when the interviewee has not answered your question.

73. Use challenging (also referred to as confrontation) to clarify incongruencies in the interviewee's communications.

74. Use silence to allow the interviewee more time to reflect or think.

75. Use neutral phrases—such as "uh huh," "I see," or "okay"— to encourage the interviewee to keep talking and to show that you are being attentive.

76. Use reflective statements to get the interviewee to tell you more about a topic.

77. Use periodic summaries to convey your understanding of the problem, allow the interviewee to comment on the adequacy of your interpretation, inform the interviewee that you have been listening, build transitions from one topic to the next and give direction to the assessment, signal that you are at the end of the assessment, and sum up and clarify what you have covered.

78. Use a check of the interviewee's understanding to learn about the clarity of your communications.

79. Other types of probing questions or techniques can be used to encourage the interviewee to discuss a topic more fully.

80. Decide on what statements to probe by keeping in mind your assessment goals.

Using Structuring Statements

81. Structuring statements guide the interviewee in talking about a topic.

Encouraging Appropriate Replies

82. Several techniques can be used to help you convey your interest to the interviewee, encourage the interviewee to elaborate on her or his response, or ease the interviewee's anxiety.

Dealing with Difficult Situations

83. When interviewees become emotionally upset, do not stop their behavior prematurely.

84. When interviewees show strong emotions, remain calm, objective, and detached.

85. When interviewees make derogatory remarks about you, try to determine possible reasons for their comments.

86. When interviewees make derogatory remarks about other people, control your reactions.

87. When interviewees are uncooperative, there may be little that you can do to establish rapport.

88. When interviewees appear to be violent, try to defuse their potentially violent behavior.

89. Consider your personal safety when you interview children and parents in their homes, particularly if you are in an unfamiliar location or dangerous neighborhood.

90. You can introduce a potentially sensitive topic by pointing out that the problem is not a unique one.

91. It will not always be easy to learn why interviewees give inadequate answers or why they do not talk much.

92. Memory difficulties may occur because the events were not particularly meaningful, the events are too painful to recall, or the interviewee has amnesia.

93. Learn to recognize different silences.

94. Several techniques can be used to redirect interviewees who introduce irrelevant material.

95. There are several ways to deal with questions about your clinical competence: do not be defensive, be prepared to make a response, evaluate the context, answer the question, admit that differences may be a problem, use humor, use the team approach, and admit that you will never know the depth of the interviewee's distress.

96. Be tactful in responding to questions about yourself.

97. Remain neutral when interviewees try to get you to side with them.

Remaining Objective

98. Accepting the communications of interviewees means that you acknowledge and appreciate their point of view; it does not mean that you agree with or approve of it.

99. Endorsing the communications of interviewees would mean that you agree that their perspective is accurate.

100. Your ability to conduct an effective assessment will be determined not only by your interviewing skills but also by personal factors in your life. You must be sensitive to how you are feeling as the interview begins.

Recording Information and Scheduling

101. It is important to record what the interviewee says.

102. If you have a heavy assessment schedule, take a few minutes between sessions to write notes and relax.

KEY TERMS, CONCEPTS, AND NAMES

Clinical assessment interview (p. 2)
Ordinary conversation (p. 2)
Psychotherapeutic interview (p. 2)
Survey research interview (p. 3)
Strengths and weaknesses of the clinical assessment interview (p. 4)
Purposes of the clinical assessment interview (p. 4)
Initial interview (p. 4)
Post-assessment interview (exit interview) (p. 5)
Follow-up interview (p. 5)
Unstructured interview (p. 5)
Semistructured interview (p. 5)
Structured interview (p. 6)
Computer-generated interview (p. 7)
External factors and atmosphere (p. 9)
Forming impressions (p. 9)
Listening (p. 9)
Analytical listening (p. 10)
Response sets (response styles) (p. 11)
Acquiescent response style (p. 11)
Establishing rapport (p. 12)
Timing questions appropriately (p. 14)
Changing topics (p. 15)
Formulating appropriate questions (p. 15)
Continuum from open-ended to closed-ended questions (p. 15)
Minimally focused questions (p. 15)
Open-ended questions (p. 15)
Moderately focused questions (p. 15)
Highly focused questions (p. 16)
Closed-ended questions (p. 16)
Bipolar questions (p. 16)
Avoiding certain types of questions (p. 16)
Yes-no questions (p. 16)
Double-barreled questions (p. 18)
Long, multiple questions (p. 18)
Leading questions (p. 18)
Random probing questions (p. 18)
Coercive questions (p. 19)
Embarrassing or accusatory questions (p. 19)
Why questions (p. 19)
Probing effectively (p. 19)
Elaboration (p. 20)
Clarification (p. 20)
Repetition (p. 21)
Challenging (p. 21)
Silence (p. 22)
Neutral phrases (p. 23)
Reflective statements (p. 23)
Periodic summaries (p. 24)
Checking the interviewee's understanding (p. 24)

Miscellaneous probing statements (p. 24)
Using structuring statements (p. 25)
Encouraging appropriate replies (p. 26)
Dealing with difficult situations (p. 26)
Handling interviewees who try to take control (p. 26)
Handling difficult behavior (p. 26)
Handling sensitive topics (p. 29)
Handling inadequate answers (p. 29)
Handling memory difficulties (p. 29)
Handling silences (p. 29)
Handling irrelevant material (p. 30)
Handling questions about your clinical competence (p. 31)
Handling self-disclosure (p. 31)
Handling requests for your opinion (p. 31)
Remaining objective (p. 32)
Acceptance of communication (p. 32)
Endorsement of communication (p. 32)
Recording information (p. 32)
Scheduling appointments (p. 33)
Second interviews (p. 33)

STUDY QUESTIONS

1. Discuss the similarities and differences between a clinical assessment interview and an ordinary conversation.
2. Discuss the similarities and differences between a clinical assessment interview and a psychotherapeutic interview.
3. Discuss the similarities and differences between a clinical assessment interview and a survey research interview.
4. What are the strengths and weaknesses of the clinical assessment interview?
5. Compare and contrast the initial interview, the post-assessment interview, and the follow-up interview.
6. Compare unstructured, semistructured, and structured interviews. Comment on the advantages and disadvantages of each.
7. Discuss the benefits and limitations of computer-generated interviewing.
8. Suppose that you were asked to prepare a lecture on 10 important guidelines for conducting clinical assessment interviews. What guidelines would you present?
9. What factors may influence an interview? In your answer, discuss interviewer and interviewee characteristics, components of the message, and the climate of the interview.
10. Characterize an effective listener and an ineffective listener.
11. Discuss the concept of analytical listening. Include in your discussion the various purposes served by analytical reasoning, response sets, and obtaining relevant information.
12. What are some important factors to consider in establishing rapport in an interview?
13. What are some important factors to consider in timing questions?
14. What are some factors to consider in changing topics?
15. What are some factors to consider in formulating appropriate questions?
16. Discuss the major types of questions to avoid in an interview.
17. What are some factors to consider in probing effectively? Include in your discussion several useful probing techniques.
18. Discuss the use of structuring statements and give some examples.
19. How would you go about encouraging appropriate replies?
20. Describe at least four difficult situations that you may encounter in an interview and give suggestions for dealing with them.
21. Distinguish between acceptance and endorsement of an interviewee's communications.
22. Discuss some of the issues involved in recording information and scheduling.

2

INTERVIEWING CHILDREN, PARENTS, TEACHERS, AND FAMILIES

Children live in a world of imagination and feeling.... They invest the most insignificant object with any form they please, and see in it whatever they wish to see.

—Adam G. Oehlenschlager

It is the supreme art of the teacher to awaken joy in creative expression and knowledge.

—Albert Einstein

No matter how many communes anybody invents, the family always creeps back.

—Margaret Mead

Goals and Objectives

This chapter is designed to enable you to do the following:

- Identify the goals of the initial assessment interview with children

- Develop interviewing strategies that are age appropriate

- Use specialized interview techniques that are effective with children

- Understand techniques for interviewing parents

- Understand techniques for interviewing teachers

- Understand techniques for interviewing families

- Become familiar with techniques for closing the initial interview

- Evaluate the initial interview findings

- Evaluate your role as an interviewer

GENERAL CONSIDERATIONS IN AN INITIAL INTERVIEW WITH CHILDREN

Interviews with children will give you information about their perceptions of problems, their thoughts and feelings about themselves, and their impressions of their situation and their relationships. How you obtain this information depends on children's developmental level and their linguistic and conceptual abilities (Bierman, 1983). You will need to encourage children to reveal their thoughts and feelings to you.

Children are sometimes more difficult to interview than adults because of limitations in language comprehension, language expression, conceptual ability, and memory. They may not know the words to describe their symptoms, particularly the subjective experience associated with their feelings. For example, because of their limited vocabulary, they may have difficulty distinguishing a *throbbing* pain from a *dull* one. They may identify an emotion as a physical sensation: Feeling anxious may be described as a stomachache. They also can be led to make inaccurate statements by poorly worded questions, so you must be particularly careful about how you word questions with children.

Keep in mind that children may not be aware that they have problems. If they come to see you, it will usually be because someone told them to or because someone brought them to you. If they come under protest, you must gain their trust. With older children, a sentence or two describing the reason for the interview may help establish rapport and trust. With younger children, you will have to find a way to help them relax. Suggestions for working with reticent children are provided later in this chapter.

Children may give you hints concerning troubling information, such as their having been maltreated. In such cases, convey to them that you are interested in what they might want to tell you. *You want them to know that you can accept them no matter what they tell you.* If you disregard or dismiss their hints about maltreatment or other problems, they probably will not volunteer more information.

When conducting an interview, always consider the child's age, experiences, level of cognitive development, and ability to express himself or herself, as well as the extensiveness of any psychological disturbance. Each of these factors will affect the interview, and some may not become apparent until after the interview has begun. You also want to be aware of the child's attention, concentration, and level of distractibility, as well as any physical impediments that might affect the interview. Several interviewing techniques discussed in the previous chapter also are discussed in this chapter, with particular emphasis on their application to children.

We cannot emphasize enough the importance of considering the child's level of linguistic and conceptual development. Suppose an interviewer asked an 8-year-old girl if she ever had any delusions. The child, not understanding what the word meant but wanting to please the interviewer, might say, "Yes, all the time." If the interviewer recorded the response and continued the interview, he or she might well reach a tentative diagnosis of a thought disorder. Such a situation can be avoided by telling the child the ground rules, such as "Say 'I don't understand' when you don't understand a word or question and I'll try to explain or ask it better," and by explaining sophisticated vocabulary and concepts.

Children are more dependent on their immediate environments than adults are, as they have less power to shape them. Children have little first-hand knowledge about the opportunities that exist beyond their immediate familial and physical environments. Because of restricted resources, they are less able than adults to make significant changes in their surroundings that might help them reduce stress.

Children also differ from adults in that they are in a process of rapid intellectual, emotional, and behavioral development. Compared with adults, they are more open to new ways of behaving, thinking, and feeling, and their personality patterns are less rigid or set. They also may be more open in expressing their feelings, thoughts, and concerns.

Strangeness of the Interview Situation

Because the interview setting is unfamiliar and because the interviewer is a stranger, children's behavior in the interview may not be typical of their behavior in other settings (Bierman, 1990). Even so, there is still a good chance that you can establish rapport and learn about their feelings, beliefs, and concerns. The first 10 or 15 minutes of the interview may give you useful information about their initial reactions to new and stressful situations. Information obtained from children can be followed up in interviews with their parents and teachers.

Interviewer-Initiated Interviews

In school settings, and particularly in juvenile detention settings, you may initiate interviews when neither the children nor the parents have sought help for a problem. In these cases, you must exercise special care on first contact with the children. Inform them simply and directly why you asked them to come to see you. Be prepared to spend additional time establishing rapport. With parents who have not initiated the interview, be prepared to work harder to gain their trust by responding understandingly to their concerns.

Goals of the Initial Interview with Children

The goals of the initial interview with a child will depend on the referral question, as well as on the child's age and communication skills. Generally, the initial interview with a child is designed to do the following:

1. Obtain informed consent to conduct the interview (for older children) or agreement to be at the interview (for younger children)
2. Evaluate the child's understanding of the reason for the interview and her or his feelings about being at the interview

3. Gather information about the child's perception of the situation that led to the interview

4. Identify antecedent and consequent events, including potentially reinforcing events, related to the child's problems

5. Estimate the frequency, magnitude, duration, intensity, and pervasiveness of the child's problems

6. Identify the circumstances in which the problems are most or least likely to occur

7. Identify factors associated with the parents, school, and environment that may contribute to the problems

8. Gather information about the child's perceptions of his or her parents, teachers, peers, and other significant individuals in his or her life

9. Assess the child's strengths, motivations, and resources for change

10. Evaluate the child's ability and willingness to participate in the assessment process

11. Estimate what the child's level of functioning was *before* an injury

12. Discuss the assessment procedures and possible follow-up procedures

TECHNIQUES FOR INTERVIEWING CHILDREN

General Techniques

The most common way to help young children remember, think, and tell you about themselves is to ask them questions. Unskilled use of questions, however, may inhibit their responses. If you use questions extensively and employ relatively few acknowledging or accepting statements (such as "I see," "Oh," or "Really"), children are more likely to give brief replies. Continual questioning also may inhibit children from volunteering information or asking questions themselves.

Recognize that in asking a question, you are making a demand—you are directing the attention of the child to memories or ideas that he or she might not have otherwise considered. Children generally need more time than adults to think about the questions and to think about their answers. If you want to obtain only specific information from children and are confident that they understand the questions, a direct question-and-answer format may be acceptable. However, you should avoid a strict question-and-answer format (a) if you are unsure of exactly what information you want and need; (b) if you want the child to take an active, constructive role in the interview; or (c) if you are unsure whether the child understands your questions. In these cases, use a more conversational style.

You can become a more effective interviewer of children by learning about their current interests. Look at Saturday morning television programs, talk with parents, visit toy stores, look at children's books, and visit day care centers and schools to observe children in their natural environments. Familiarity with children's interests will help you establish rapport with children and may give you insight about them.

Chapter 1 in this text presented general suggestions for conducting interviews. This chapter focuses on interview strategies particularly useful in establishing rapport with and maintaining the cooperation of children. You will need to adjust your interviewing strategy depending on how children respond (Bierman & Schwartz, 1986). Following is an amusing example of how the interviewer heard the adolescent's response but ignored the implications of the response.

IR: Do you have any fears?
IE: I have a terrible fear of deadlines.
IR: Tell me everything about your fear of deadlines. You have until 10:50.

Specific Techniques

Here are 22 techniques that are useful in interviewing children.

1. *Consider the child's age and needs in setting the tempo and length of the interview.* You need to be alert to how tired the child is becoming. Take short breaks of about 5 minutes each during a lengthy interview (e.g., 50 minutes or more). Provide a brief period of free play or nonintense activity at any time, if needed. Leave some time toward the end of the interview to allow the child to regain composure, especially if the child reveals strong feelings during the interview.

2. *Formulate appropriate opening statements.* The opening statement that will help put the child at ease will depend on the child's age, ability level, and behavior and the reason for the referral. After introducing yourself and establishing rapport, you might say,

- "This is a place where moms and dads and kids come to talk with a helper like me. Sometimes they tell me they wish things could go better at home or at school. I help them figure things out so that they can feel better" (Bierman, 1990, p. 212).

or

- "Your teacher has told me about some problems you've been having, but I'd like to hear about them from you."

or

- "I understand that you're having some problems at home."

To an older child, it may be useful to say,

- "What brings you here today?"

or

- "We could begin by your letting me know what's bothering you."

To a child in school, an appropriate comment might be

- "I'm Ms. Smith, the school psychologist. I understand from Mr. Jones that you're not doing too well in school. I'd like to hear what you think about how you're doing."

To a child in a juvenile detention center, you might say,

- "I'm Dr. Brown, a staff psychologist here at the center. I'd like to talk to you about why you're here at the center."

3. *Use appropriate language and intonation.* Use simple vocabulary and short sentences tailored to the developmental and cognitive levels of the child. For example, instead of saying "What things are reinforcing for you?" say, "What things do you like?" Be sure that the child understands the questions. Use simple terms in exploring the child's feelings. For example, use *sad* instead of *depressed,* and *happy* instead of *enthusiastic.* Be friendly, and show interest in the child.

4. *Avoid leading questions.* You especially want to avoid leading the child to give a particular response. For example, in a case of alleged child maltreatment, do not tell the child that the alleged offender is bad or that the child should tell you the bad things the offender has done. Similarly, phrase your questions so that the child does not receive any hint that one response is more acceptable than another. Be sure that the manner and tone of your voice do not reveal any personal biases.

5. *Ask for examples.* Ask the child to give examples of how she or he behaves or how other people behave when they are feeling a certain way (e.g., how they behave when they are sad).

6. *Be open to what the child tells you.* You want to convey to the child that you are open and accepting of what he or she wants to tell you. This means that you must not ignore information that does not support your expectations or beliefs. You want to take a more active role with children than you necessarily would with adults. Gather as complete a story as possible from the child, but do not *interpret* what happened to him or her.

7. *Make descriptive comments.* When you comment on the child's appearance, behavior, or demeanor, you are making a descriptive comment (Kanfer et al., 1983; 1992). Descriptive comments provide a simple way of giving attention to the child and encouraging the child to continue with appropriate behavior. An added benefit of descriptive comments is that you can use them to maintain communication with the child while you are formulating other questions. Examples of descriptive comments include "I see that you're feeding the doll" and "You look cheerful today." Descriptive comments are nonthreatening, focus the child's attention, and encourage the child to elaborate further (Boggs & Eyberg, 1990).

8. *Use reflection.* Reflective statements rephrase what the child has said or done, retaining the essential meaning of the communication or behavior (Kanfer et al., 1992). These statements provide clarity and help organize the child's behavior. For example, in response to the statement "My brother is a brat," you might say, "So you're saying that your brother doesn't act the way you want him to, is that right?"

9. *Give praise frequently.* Praise and support serve to guide the child to talk about areas that you consider important (Kanfer et al., 1983). Younger children typically will need more praise than older children. Examples of praise are "I'm glad you can tell me about these things" and "Some of these things are hard to talk about, but you're doing fine." *Praise children's efforts, not what they say.* For example, do not reward a child for making responses that she or he thinks you want to hear. Similarly, do not use coercion, pressure, or threats—such as telling the child that she or he cannot play with toys, go to the bathroom, go home, or get to see her or his parents soon—to get the child to respond in the way you would like.

10. *Avoid critical statements.* Criticism is likely to generate anger, hostility, resentment, or frustration—reactions that will interfere with your ability to establish and maintain rapport (Kanfer et al., 1992). Examples of critical statements are "You're not trying very hard" and "Stop tearing the paper." When the child is behaving negatively, focus on more appropriate behavior to turn the attention of the child away from the negative behavior. You also can invoke rules that govern the playroom or office. For example, when a child is throwing blocks, say, "Let's throw the ball," or when a child is tearing paper inappropriately, say, "One of the rules is that you can't tear this paper." If you are forewarned, you can have available paper that the child can tear. In that case, you can say, "One of the rules is that you can only tear this paper." This may help establish limits and redirect the child's inappropriate behavior. Sometimes you can ignore inappropriate behavior, make a mental note to watch for positive behavior, and reinforce the positive behavior. Here are two examples of how this can be done (Kanfer et al., 1992, adapted from pp. 52–53):

IE: (Climbs on table)
IR: (Ignores climbing)
IE: (Gets off table)
IR: It's safer when you stand on the floor.

IR: Tell me a story about this picture.
IE: I can't think of anything.
IR: (Ignores statement) What is this girl doing?
IE: She's sitting.
IR: She is sitting. I'm glad you told me about part of the picture. What else is going on in the picture?

11. *Use simple questions and concrete referents.* You can increase the child's responsiveness and elicit more coherent and complete responses by simplifying the questions, adding concrete referents, and simplifying the responses required (Bierman, 1983). For example, you can say, "Tell me one thing that you like about your teacher," "What was happening the last time you felt that way?" or "What happened yesterday morning when you woke up?" Following are techniques that use concrete referents to help children talk about their feelings. These techniques are especially useful with children who are reluctant to talk about themselves.

a. *Ask for affect labels.* Show the child simple line drawings that depict faces expressing emotions such as happiness, sadness, and anger (Bierman, 1990; see Figure 2-1). First, point to each face and say, "Tell me how this face looks." Then, ask a series of questions such as "How do you look when you go to school?" "How do you look when you go to bed?" and "How do you look when your daddy (or mommy) comes home?" After each question, ask the child to point to a face. The pointing technique is especially useful

Figure 2-1. Line drawings depicting three emotional expressions.

for young children because they do not have to make a verbal response.

If the child is reluctant to tell you about the faces, consider saying "How would a child feel if he [she] had a time out? Point to a picture that shows how he [she] would feel." If the child points correctly, say, "That's right, a child would feel sad [angry] if he [she] was punished. What do you think he [she] did to get punished?" Follow up by asking "Who punished him [her]?" and "What was the punishment?" To learn the child's feelings, for example, about a positive event and about an aggressive event, you first might say, "How would a child feel if he [she] got a special toy? Point to a picture that shows how he [she] would feel." Follow up with appropriate questions. You then might say, "How would a child feel if he [she] had a fight with another child? Point to a picture that shows how he [she] would feel." Again, follow up with appropriate questions.

A more difficult version of this procedure is to point to each face in turn and say, "Tell me something that makes you feel like this" (Bierman, 1990, p. 213). With children who are willing to talk about their feelings, you can then probe their response to the faces. For example, if a boy says that he is angry when he fights with his brother, you can ask, "What about fighting with your brother makes you angry?" You can follow up with "What do you do when you fight with your brother?" If the child seems threatened by the questions or simply refuses to answer, stop probing. (See Bierman, 1990, for a discussion of other techniques useful in eliciting affect-laden material.)

b. *Use the picture-question technique.* From a magazine, book, or other source, select pictures that you think will engage the child. Show the child the pictures one at time, and ask the child to tell a story about each picture. The picture-question technique, although similar to thematic projective techniques, is not used as a personality or projective test (Bierman, 1990). Rather, it is simply a way to encourage children to talk about their feelings. Pictures, as opposed to questions, may serve as a less intrusive and more concrete way of gathering information about children's feelings.

You may select pictures that relate to specific themes in the child's life. For example, if you want to find out about how a girl feels about a new baby in the family, show her a picture that contains a girl, a mother, and a baby. First ask,

"What do you think is happening?" Then say, "How does the girl feel about the baby?" Then ask, "What's going to happen?" If you want to learn about a boy's feelings about his parents' divorce, show him a picture of a boy about his age, a mother, and a father. You might say, "Here are a mom and dad and a boy about your age. The mom and dad are divorced. What do you think happened?… What did the mom say?…What did the dad say?… What did the boy say?… How did the mom feel?… How did the dad feel?… How did the boy feel?… What will happen next?… Did that ever happen to you?… What did you do?… How did you feel?" (Bierman, 1983, p. 234, with changes in notation).

Use of the picture-question technique might affect how the child responds to a projective story-telling test, like the Children's Apperception Test, if the test is to be administered later. Therefore, you should weigh the advantages and disadvantages of using the picture-question procedure. To encourage a reluctant child to talk to you, you might want to try other techniques before the picture-question technique, especially if you plan to administer a story-telling test.

c. *Have the child draw a picture and tell about it.* Ask the child to draw a picture of a child or an adult, and then ask about the picture (Bierman, 1983). Following is a brief list of questions that you might ask as you point to the picture; add additional questions as needed.

- "What an interesting drawing. Now we're going to do something special. Tell me three things that this child likes to do."
- "Tell me three things that this child doesn't like to do."
- "What does this child like about school?"
- "What doesn't this child like about school?"
- "What does this child like about her family?"
- "What doesn't this child like about her family?"
- "What are this child's favorite things to do after school?"
- "What does this child do that gets her into trouble?"
- "What makes this child happy?"
- "What makes this child sad?"
- "What does this child like best about himself [herself]?"
- "What makes this child angry?"
- "What games does this child like to play?"
- "What makes this child frightened?"
- "How do other children feel about this child?"

You can repeat the procedure by asking the child to draw a picture of an adult, substituting "woman" or "man" for "child" in the above questions. The drawing-a-picture technique allows you to encourage and praise the child for his or her efforts and gives the child a way of expressing hopes, fears, and frustrations (Bierman, 1983).

d. *Use the story-completion technique.* First, ask the child to complete sentence stems that you have constructed about the child's life situation. Here is one way of introducing the task (Bierman & Schwartz, 1986):

Okay, now I have this story that we're supposed to fill out together. I'll read the story, and then you think of an answer to fill in the blanks, okay? This first story is about the way kids act at school. At

"You must be Mr. and Mrs. Smith.
I'd recognize you anywhere from Henry's drawings."

Courtesy of Jeff Bryson and Jerome M. Sattler.

school, some kids act really _____. How should I say they act? (Child replies, "mean.") OK, good answer! One mean thing that they do is _____. (Child replies, "fight.") Fight, yeah, that's a mean thing. Another mean thing they do is _____. (p. 271)

As the child becomes more comfortable answering these structured sentence completions, the interviewer can interject probing questions like "Wow, do kids do that in your school, too?" or "Has that ever happened to anyone you know?" Using this flexible story-completion approach, the interviewer can get a basic sense of the social perceptions and reasoning level of the child and, depending on the child's responsiveness, can also pursue themes of personal relevance to the child (Bierman & Schwartz, 1986).

e.   *Have the child respond to a hypothetical problem.* Ask the child to respond to a hypothetical problem that addresses relevant issues. For example, you might say (Bierman & Schwartz, 1986),

I know of a girl who has a problem that you might be able to help with. Her parents have been talking about getting a divorce, and she's scared about it. She doesn't really know what it will be like, or how she will feel, or what she can do about it. What do you think I can say to help her? (p. 272, with changes in notation)

This technique may be less anxiety-provoking than open-ended questions would be. It also makes fewer demands on the child's conceptual and verbal skills.

f.   *Model the interview after a school-type task.* Sometimes it is helpful to make the interview resemble a more familiar school-type task (Bierman & Schwartz, 1986):

The interviewer might introduce some papers with a comment such as "There are some questions I need to ask you," and go on to write notes periodically during the interview. This approach enables the interviewer to become an ally of the child—working with the child to obtain the necessary answers. Interviewer comments such as "Oh, here's a tough one—see what you think of this one" can soften the im-

pact of difficult questions, and praise can be directed toward the child's task mastery attempts (e.g., "Neat answer! That one seemed kind of hard to me, but you've clearly thought about it"). Additionally, focusing on the paper enables the interviewer to avoid extended, intensive eye contact with the child. (p. 270, with changes in notation)

12.   *Formulate questions in the subjunctive mood (hypothetical) when necessary.* Questions formulated in the subjunctive mood (i.e., hypothetical questions) may encourage a reticent child to speak. Useful leads that employ a subjunctive mood include "Suppose you were…," "Imagine…," "What if you…," and "Let's pretend that …." For example, you might say, "Suppose you were to take a friend to your house. Suppose you were going to show your friend some things there— what kinds of things might your friend see?" Hypothetical questions allow "the child some degree of emotional distance by adding a game-like quality to the question" (Goodman & Sours, 1967, p. 29). For some children, this type of question is preferable to a question such as "What is your family like?"

13.   *Be tactful.* Phrase questions tactfully to avoid causing children anxiety or embarrassment. An ineptly worded question may lead to discomfort. For example, after a child complained about a teacher, it would be tactless to ask, "Do you always have trouble with teachers?" You might get a more responsive answer if you asked, "Have you found other teachers as upsetting as this one?" or if you simply acknowledged the child's feelings about his or her teacher. Similarly, instead of asking "Did you quit school?"—which may require an admission of having done so—ask, "What was the last grade you were in?"

14.   *Recognize the child's discomfort.* When a child is uncomfortable, it is important to recognize that fact and make the situation as stress-free as possible. You must realize that a child may have additional discomfort if, for instance, family members are actively responsible for her or his problems. Be ready to change topics if the child becomes too distressed.

15.   *Use props, crayons, clay, or toys to help a young child talk.* You will need special skills to help a young child talk. Props can be particularly valuable when the child seems unable to converse freely:

A common method is the use of props to stimulate memory, to supplement language ability, or to facilitate communication in the interview setting. Props can be used to re-create the setting of an event, permitting the child to reenact the event itself. A doll house and dolls, for instance, can be used to help describe a domestic event that is either too complex or too traumatic to describe in words. Pretending to talk on the telephone may act as a vehicle for talking with the interviewer. It may also help the child feel a sense of control over the interview, since he or she can stop the conversation at any time by hanging up. (Garbarino & Stott, 1989, p. 191, with changes in notation)

Another method for reducing the child's self-consciousness is to allow the child to use crayons or clay while he or she talks to you. Do not allow the use of crayons or clay to become a convenient escape from talking, however. The young child also can be allowed to express himself or herself with toys. Carefully observe the child's play—including motor, language, and fantasy elements.

16. *Use a sentence-completion technique.* A way to elicit information from preteens and adolescents who are reticent to talk with you is to use a sentence-completion technique. Interpret the results cautiously, however, using the information obtained to establish hypotheses rather than reach firm conclusions. The technique consists of giving sentence stems orally and then recording the preteen or adolescent's answers. Or, if the preteen or adolescent's reading and writing skills are sufficiently developed, she or he may be willing to read the sentence stems and write her or his responses. You then can use these responses to probe further about an area. Table 2-1 shows examples of sentence stems that you can use.

17. *Use fantasy techniques.* For preteens and adolescents who are reluctant to speak with you, consider using fantasy techniques, such as the three wishes technique or the desert island technique (Barker, 1990). As with the sentence-completion technique, results must be interpreted cautiously, with the information obtained used to generate hypotheses rather than reach firm conclusions.

a. *Three wishes technique.* To use the three wishes technique, say, "If you could have any three wishes, what would they be?" Alternative phrasing is "If you could wish for any three things to happen, what would they be?" Listen carefully to what the preteen or adolescent says. The wishes expressed may give you some indication of feelings about his or her parents, siblings, friends, insecurities, and so forth. You can then follow up on the answers. The three wishes technique may not be appropriate for younger children because they are likely to come up with concrete wishes, such as a bike, a toy, or something to eat.

b. *Desert island technique.* To use the desert island technique, ask the preteen or adolescent whom she or he would like to be with on a desert island. Say, "Here's a pretend question. Imagine you were shipwrecked on a desert island. There's no one else there, but you've got plenty of food to eat and water to drink. If you could have just one person to be with you on the island—anyone in the whole world—whom would you most want to have?" (Barker, 1990, p. 66, with changes in notation).

After the preteen or adolescent has selected someone, say, "Now if you could have another person—[the person first named] and somebody else—whom would you choose next?" Then ask, "And if you could have one more—and this would be the last one you could have—whom would you choose for your third person?" You also can ask two or three additional questions, such as "Is there anyone you wouldn't want to have on the island with you?" If the preteen or adolescent says "Yes," say, "Who would that be?" Follow up with "Tell me the reason for each of your choices."

18. *Help the child express his or her thoughts and feelings.* You can help the child express his or her thoughts and feelings in several ways. First, let the child speak in whatever words he or she chooses. Second, encourage the child to speak freely and openly, and follow up leads that he or she gives you. Third, convey to the child that you are willing to listen to any of his or her feelings and thoughts, even those that may be culturally unacceptable.

The following techniques may help children talk about difficult issues (Yarrow, 1960, adapted from p. 580, with additions from Bierman & Schwartz, 1986, p. 271).

a. *Present two alternatives.* Examples:

- "If your little brother writes on the wall, do you punish him so he won't do it again, or do you see that your mother finds out about it?"
- "Do you ever wish that you could be someone else, or are you happy being yourself?"
- "Do you ever wish that your dad spent more time with you, or do you think he spends enough time with you?"

You can follow up the child's response to each question. To follow up the first question, you might say, "How would you punish him?" or "What would your mother do when she found out?" A follow-up to the second question might be

---

Table 2-1
Sentence-Completion Technique

Directions: Say to the child "I'm going to start a sentence. I'd like you to finish it any way you want. Here is an example. If I say 'A car …,' you can say 'is fun to go in,' 'is nice to have,' 'is good when it works,' 'costs a lot of money,' or anything else that you can think of. OK? Let's try the first one."

1. My favorite TV show _____.
2. At night _____.
3. My teacher _____.
4. The scariest thing is when _____ .
5. Mothers _____.
6. At school, I usually feel _____.
7. I hate it when _____.
8. When I wake up, I usually _____.
9. I dislike _____.
10. Fathers _____.
11. I am happiest when _____.
12. My favorite subjects are _____.
13. I worry about _____.
14. My friends _____.
15. I need _____.
16. My life would be better if _____.
17. I feel angry when _____.
18. My neighborhood is _____.
19. Animals are _____.
20. It is wrong to _____.
21. The best thing about being me is _____.
22. I like _____.
23. The saddest time is when _____.
24. The best thing about my home is _____.
25. My favorite book is _____.
26. I feel ashamed when _____.
27. My worst subjects are _____.
28. I am proud of _____.
29. If I could change one thing about my family, it would be _____.
30. (If appropriate) My sister(s) _____.
31. (If appropriate) My brother(s) _____.

"Who would you like to be?" or "What makes you happy about yourself?" After any response to the third question, you could ask, "How much time does he spend with you?"

b. *Give children an opportunity to express a positive response before presenting a question that will require a negative response.* Examples:

- "What things do you like best about school?" After the child responds, say, "What things aren't so good about school?"
- "What is one thing that you like best about your sister?" After the child responds, say, "What is something your sister does that you don't like very much?"

You can extend these techniques with specific probing comments.

Follow-up comments that provide concrete structure are usually more effective in helping the child expand his or her answers to initial questions. For example, a child might respond to the question "What kinds of things don't you like about school?" with a one-word answer or "I don't know." A structured probe might be "Well, let's just try to think about one thing first. Tell me one thing you don't like at school." If the child simply answers "Math," a structured probing question might be "What happens in math that you don't like very much?" Or, if that does not work, you could offer a choice: "Well, is it more the work you don't like or the teacher?" These focused questions are all preferable to vague questions such as "Can you tell me anything else?" This almost invariably receives a negative response. (Bierman, 1983, p. 235, with changes in notation)

19. *Clarify an episode of misbehavior by recounting it.* When you want to obtain further information from a child about an episode of misbehavior, ask the child to recount the details of the episode, as illustrated in the following dialogue (Karoly, 1981, adapted from p. 102):

IR: Your teacher tells me that yesterday a bunch of kids in your class "went wild" with paints, throwing them around the room and at other kids.
IE: Yeah.
IR: That really happened?
IE: Yeah. So?
IR: What led up to it?
IE: The kids were bored.
IR: Were you bored?
IE: Yeah, I guess.
IR: Did you throw the paints too?
IE: Yeah.
IR: Did you enjoy throwing the paints?
IE: What do you mean?
IR: Was it a way to be less bored?
IE: Sure…for a while.
IR: Then what happened?
IE: We had to clean the place up. It took all afternoon.
IR: Did you think you would have to clean up?
IE: I don't know.
IR: Was it unfair for her to make you clean up?
IE: The janitor should do it.
IR: But the kids made the mess.
IE: Mrs. Masters [the teacher] is supposed to give us stuff to do.

In this case, the recounting technique brought to light the child's perception that the teacher is responsible for keeping the students occupied.

20. *Clarify interview procedures for children who are minimally communicative.* Some children may respond to your questions with "Yes," "No," "I don't know," or "I guess." It is best to handle these responses with comments like the following:

- "What I'd like to have you do rather than just saying 'Yes' or 'No' is to try to tell me as much as you can about what I ask you."
- "Sometimes it's hard to talk about things. But I'd really like you to try. It will help me get to know you better."

On the rare occasions when a child simply refuses to participate in the initial interview, it probably is best to reschedule the interview, as illustrated in the following case (Reisman, 1973).

Suzie, a 7-year-old girl, had refused to attend school. When first seen by the interviewer, she was clutching tightly to her mother and refused to accompany the interviewer to his office. When brought to the office by her mother, she began kicking and biting her mother, crying and screaming because her mother wanted to leave to go to her own appointment. After her mother left, Suzie retreated to a corner, where she wept angrily, hurling curses at the interviewer, demanding to see her mother, and refusing to cooperate. In such cases, it may be best to go along with the child's behavior and allow the behavior to run its course. Arrange to see the child again for another meeting. It may take a few sessions before you obtain the child's trust, acceptance, and cooperation.

21. *Understand and use silence.* Because clinical assessment interviews depend primarily on conversation, children who are silent are a challenge. Possible reasons for children's silence are (a) they resent being at the interview, (b) they are frightened, (c) they want to talk but don't know what to say, (d) they prefer to sit quietly and do nothing else, and (e) they need time to collect their ideas in order to express them (Reisman, 1973). Chapter 1 presents other possible reasons for silence. Determine which possibility is most applicable, because what you decide will have a direct bearing on how you proceed. For some children, silence is comfortable at first but can become stressful. Other children find silence stressful from the beginning but do not know how to break it. Children under 5 or 6 years of age usually have more difficulty with silence than older children do. If silence leads to resistance, it can be detrimental to the interview. Therefore, try to keep silences to a minimum with young children.

There are several ways that you can cope with children's silences. Children who are angry about coming for the interview may be silent initially, but they will likely start to talk to you once they begin to accept you and understand the purpose of the interview. If they wish to remain silent, you should accept their decision. When young children or preteens are silent, point out that they can play with the toys and play materials if they would like. If the silence continues, you can comment from time to time about what they are doing and how much time is left. You also can play with some toys as they play. These activities may serve as a way to break the silence and build rapport.

What you don't want to do is to assume that children's silence (or failure to respond to questions) means that they are ashamed of talking about the topic. Failure to respond may simply mean that they have nothing to say about the question, that the situation is strange, or that other unknown factors are operating.

22. *Handle resistance and anxiety by giving support and reassurance.* Older children may be reluctant to reveal their feelings and thoughts to a stranger, especially when they are concerned about the reason for and outcome of the evaluation. They may show their anxiety through hesitancy in speech, sadness, hostility, or other means (Jennings, 1982).

If you observe that a child is anxious, you may want to help the child express his or her anxiety directly. You could say, "How do you feel about being here today?" or "You look a little nervous about talking to me." You might want to respond to the child's answers with (a) encouragement or support, (b) a statement that asks for further exploration, or (c) a comment that acknowledges his or her feelings (Jennings, 1982). Matter-of-factly accepting everything the child says, helping the child understand the reasons for the evaluation, and helping the child work through his or her feelings also may help reduce anxiety. Following are things you might say to reluctant children:

- "Many children feel as you do at the beginning. But in a little while, most feel more relaxed. You probably will too."
- "I'd like to understand why you don't want to talk."
- "You seem to feel hesitant about talking with me."

AREAS COVERED IN THE INITIAL INTERVIEW WITH CHILDREN

The typical sequence in an interview with a child is as follows:

1. Introduce yourself to the parent (or caregiver or guardian) and to the child by giving your name and professional title.
2. Greet the child.
3. Open the interview with an introductory statement.
4. Continue the interview as appropriate.
5. Review the referral issues with the child.
6. Describe what will happen to the child after you complete the interview.
7. Express appreciation for the child's effort and cooperation.
8. Close the interview.

Following are typical areas covered in the initial interview with children:

- Reasons for coming
- Confidentiality and other possible ethical concerns
- School (including perception of teachers, peer group, and school environment)
- Home (including perception of parents, siblings, and home environment)
- Interests (including leisure time activities, hobbies, recreation, clubs, and sports)
- Friends
- Moods and feelings
- Fears and worries
- Self-concept
- Somatic concerns
- Obsessions and compulsions
- Thought disorders
- Memories or fantasies (their own recollections, as well as what their parents told them about their infancy and early childhood, including developmental milestones)
- Aspirations (including career possibilities)
- Other information voluntarily supplied by the children

During the initial interview with adolescents, these additional areas could be covered:

- Jobs
- Sexual relations (including sexual identity and peer relationships)
- Eating habits
- Drug and alcohol use (including frequency of use and type of drug)
- Pregnancy (for females)
- Impregnation of a female (for males)

In discussing these areas, attend to the child's (a) ability to relate to you, (b) ability to discuss relevant information, (c) thought processes, (d) language, (e) affect, (f) nonverbal behaviors, and (g) temperament and personality, as well as any indications of possible psychological disturbances. The questions presented in Table B-1 in Appendix B will aid you in obtaining information about the areas noted. The questions in Table B-1 are only sample questions, meant to illustrate the areas most frequently covered in interviews with children; do not use the questions mechanically. Include follow-up and probing questions and reassuring comments as needed. You may need to alter the wording of some questions in Table B-1, depending on the child's age. See Chapter 1 for more information about flexibility in interviewing.

Reinforcers

In some situations (such as when you are planning a therapeutic behavioral intervention), you may want to identify, during the interview, reinforcers important to the children. The positive reinforcement sentence-completion technique shown in Table 2-2 is useful for this purpose.

Children's Environment

If you believe that the physical layout of the child's home may be contributing to the difficulties, you can ask the child to draw a picture of her or his room and any other relevant

SCHOOLIES © 2000 by John P. Wood

I couldn't get any help with my homework last night. My mom was at the parent involvement meeting.

Copyright © 2000 by John P. Wood. Reprinted with permission.

rooms in the house. Then ask the child to tell you about each room. This technique also is helpful in establishing rapport and getting children used to the question-and-answer flow of the interview. You should not assume that what the child draws is a valid representation of the home; therefore, you might want to verify details about the home with the parents.

Mental Status Evaluation

As part of the initial interview with children, you may want to conduct a mental status evaluation. A mental status evaluation may be particularly helpful (a) in cases of brain injury, (b) when children appear confused, or (c) when you want to obtain an overall sense of their general mental functioning. Table B-2 in Appendix B offers a brief mental status examination for older children. This type of evaluation is especially important when children appear to have problems in orientation to time, place, or person; memory or attention; or the ability to think clearly. Interpret all areas in a mental status evaluation within a developmental framework, using age-appropriate norms or age-appropriate expectations.

INTERVIEWING PARENTS

The interview with parents is an important part of the assessment process. Parents have a wealth of knowledge about their children. A well-conducted parent interview will (a) establish rapport and a positive working relationship with the par-

Table 2-2
Positive Reinforcement Sentence Completion for School-Aged Children

Directions: Read all the sentence stems to the child, following up on the child's responses as necessary. Then state all the reinforcers named by the child, and ask the child to rank them in order of their importance.

1. My favorite grown-up is _____.
2. My favorite thing to do with him (her) is _____.
3. The best reward anybody can give me is _____.
4. The two things I like best to do are _____.
5. My favorite adult at school is _____.
6. When I do something well, what my mother does is _____.
7. I feel terrific when _____.
8. When I have money, I like to _____.
9. Something I really want is _____.
10. The person I would like most to reward me is _____.
11. I would like [person's name] to reward me by _____.
12. The thing I like best to do with my mother is _____.
13. On Saturday or Sunday, my favorite thing to do is _____.
14. The thing I like to do most is _____.
15. My two favorite TV programs are _____.
16. The thing I like best to do with my father is _____.
17. My favorite music to listen to is _____.

Child's Ranking of Reinforcers

_____
_____
_____
_____
_____
_____

Source: Adapted from Tharp and Wetzel (1969).

ents, (b) focus the attention of the parents on the issues, (c) serve as a valuable source of information about the child and family, (d) help the parents organize and reflect on the information, (e) contribute to the formulation of a diagnosis, (f) provide a basis for decisions about treatment and further investigation, and (g) lay the groundwork for parental efforts to be a part of intervention efforts (Barkley, 1981a; Canino, 1985; La Greca, 1983).

You want the parents to participate actively in the interview. To encourage them to do so, you need to treat them with respect and honesty. Consider their cultural and ethnic backgrounds and practices and use the language they understand. Strive to establish a collaborative working relationship with them. Make sure they understand the limits of confidentiality (see Chapter 3).

Parents not only serve as an important source of information but also will play a key role in any proposed intervention. If invasive or demanding questions and unempathic responses cause them to feel threatened by the initial interview, they may prematurely terminate contact with you and find excuses to avoid coming for further help. They may say that they have transportation difficulties, babysitting problems, or problems in scheduling appointments; sometimes, however, these may be legitimate concerns. You want to lessen any anxiety parents have and make every effort to show them that you are interested in them and concerned about what is in the best interest of their child.

Recognize that not all parents will be reliable informants. Expect to find some distortions, biases, and memory lags in the information you collect from them. Developmental milestones are difficult to remember, and relating particular events to particular behavioral responses may be even more difficult. Research on the accuracy of parental reports suggests the following (Canino, 1985):

- Variables such as the child's weight, height, and health are recalled more accurately by parents than information about the child's personality and temperament.
- Discrete symptoms that the child had (such as nightmares, stuttering, bedwetting, stealing, and temper tantrums) are recalled better than less well-defined symptoms (such as the child's activity level, feeling states, and social relationships).
- Major events in the family (such as deaths, weddings, moves, financial reversals, and births) and their dates are recalled relatively accurately.
- Mothers are usually more reliable informants about the child's development than are fathers.

Courtesy Herman Zilinski.

Goals of the Initial Interview with Parents

Following are the main goals of the initial clinical assessment interview with parents (Mash & Terdal, 1981):

1. To gather information about parental concerns and goals
2. To obtain informed consent from the parents to conduct an assessment of the child
3. To discuss the assessment procedures that may be used with the child
4. To assess parental perceptions of the strengths and weaknesses of the child
5. To obtain a case history of the child, including the child's medical, developmental, educational, and social histories
6. To identify the child's problems and related antecedent and consequent events
7. To determine how the parents have dealt with the problem(s) in the past (including whether they sought prior treatment and, if so, who provided the treatment and the dates and outcomes of the treatment) and to obtain permission to obtain records from any previous treatment
8. To identify events that reinforced the problem(s) for both the child and the parents
9. To obtain a family history (where relevant)
10. To assess the parents' motivation and resources for change and their expectations for the child's treatment
11. To discuss what follow-up contacts they and their child may need

If all these goals are reached, you can probably develop some preliminary hypotheses about the child's difficulties, strengths, and weaknesses and about the parents' reactions, concerns, coping abilities, strengths, and weaknesses. You can also construct a picture of the family's life style and its prevailing values, mores, and concerns. In order to meet these goals, you will need to use the effective interviewing skills described in Chapter 1. These include rapport-building skills, communication skills, and listening skills.

Age of the Child

The age of the child will, in part, determine the content of the interview with the parents. If you are interviewing the parents of a toddler or preschooler, the focus will be on the mother's pregnancy and delivery, the child's early developmental milestones, and the nature of the problem. With parents of elementary school-age children, you also will need to ask about language and motor skills, peer and social relations, and educational progress. With parents of adolescents, you will want to inquire about all of these, as well as the adolescent's peer group, sexual activity, academic progress, vocational plans, interests, and use of alcohol, drugs, and tobacco.

Concerns of Parents

Parents may be apprehensive about their child's evaluation. Depending on the type and severity of the child's problems, their cultural subgroup and ethnicity, and their religious affiliation, they may be concerned about any of the following issues:

1. *Etiology.* What is the cause of the child's problem? How serious is the child's problem?

2. *Interventions.* What can they do about the child's problem? What treatment is needed, and will the treatment cure the problem? Where can the child get treatment? How long will the treatment last? How much will it cost? Will their insurance cover the cost of treatment (if they are insured)? What special services will their child need? Will they also need to be seen for treatment? What can they do at home to help their child? Where can they get more information about their child's condition? Will the authorities try to remove the child from their home?

3. *Family issues.* Will other children in the family also have these problems? What should they tell their other children about their sibling's condition? How will the other children in the family react to their sibling's being seen by a mental health professional? What secrets will the child reveal about the family? Will telling these secrets damage the family in any way?

4. *Parental responsibility.* Are they responsible for their child's problems? Have they exaggerated the problem or put ideas into their child's head? Will other people think that they are incapable of taking care of their child? Is it one parent's fault more than the other's?

5. *Stigma.* Will their child resent them for taking him or her to a mental health professional? What will it mean that their child has a record of visiting a "shrink"? Will other people think that their family is crazy? What will relatives, neighbors, friends, the child's peers, the peers' parents, and the child's teachers think about the child's going to see a mental health professional?

6. *Results.* Will they receive a report? When will they receive the final results and recommendations? Who will have access to the findings?

Parents may ask you how to prepare their child for the interview. Tell them to be straightforward. Suggest that they tell the child (a) who is going to be seen, (b) the reason for the appointment, and (c) what will happen. Explanations should, of course, be consistent with the child's level of comprehension. With children between ages 3 and 6 years, parents should emphasize that there will be toys to play with in the office and that the child will be talking with someone. With children between ages 6 and 10 years, parents should emphasize that the child will be talking with someone and possibly playing some games. With children older than 10 years, parents should emphasize that the interviewer is someone who knows how to help children (or teenagers) and families, that the child (or adolescent) will be talking with that person, and that it often helps to obtain the advice of someone outside the family.

Potential Negative Feelings of Parents

By the time parents seek an evaluation for a school-age child (and sometimes for a preschool child as well), they may have already experienced much frustration and anguish. Although they may have seen other professionals, they still may be seeking a magic solution. They may know that their child has a problem but be tired of feeling that they are to blame. If they feel this way, they may displace on you the anger that has developed from prior encounters with medical and mental health professionals. Because parents may feel inadequate—as a result of their inability to work with their child and their impatience and irritability with her or him—they also may have feelings of guilt and a diminished sense of self-esteem.

Parents sometimes deny that there is a problem and react angrily to being interviewed. At a school-initiated interview, for example, they may make the following types of comments:

• *Comments reflecting anger or denial.* "We didn't know she was having any problems. No one told us before." "We don't see any problems like that at home."

• *Comments implying blame.* "Do you think it's because my wife works?" "Do you think it's because my husband spends so little time with him?"

• *Comments reflecting rationalization.* "Perhaps it's because his older brother is like that." "You know, we're divorced. That could be the reason."

• *Comments reflecting disbelief.* "How can you tell from just a few weeks in class?" "Aren't all children his age like that?"

• *Comments that point to the school's responsibility.* "If you would give her special help, it would help the problem." "I think he should see a counselor. That will straighten everything out." "You found it. You fix it."

Address any negative feelings the parents have about themselves or others during your initial contact with them; otherwise, their feelings may interfere with the interview. Give them an opportunity to talk about their feelings. Help the parents recognize that you can work together to understand and improve the behavior and functioning of their child. Tell them that you are aware of the discomfort they feel in discussing personal topics and that you welcome their questions. *Keep in mind, however, that the focus of the interview is the child, not the parents.*

Occasionally, you will find that the parents have problems such as depression, stress, marital conflict, or substance abuse. If so, refer them for appropriate treatment services and be sure to give them referral names and telephone numbers. In many clinics, children will not be seen for treatment unless their parents also are involved in treatment.

Background Questionnaire

Another way to obtain information about the child and family is to have the parents complete a background questionnaire before the interview (see Table A-1 in Appendix A for an example of a background questionnaire). A background questionnaire is useful in obtaining a detailed account of the child's developmental, social, medical, and educational history, as well as information about the family. You can send the background questionnaire to the parents a week or two before the scheduled interview and ask them to send it back a few days before the interview. If necessary, they can bring it with them to the interview, but it is beneficial to have the questionnaire returned before the interview so that you can review it. Be sure to provide your telephone number so that they can contact you if they have questions.

Sometimes you may want to complete the background questionnaire jointly with the parents, especially if they have reading or writing difficulties or cannot complete it for some other reason. Filling out the background questionnaire together serves as a type of structured interview. Time constraints or agency policy, however, may not allow you to complete the background questionnaire in an interview format.

Useful Interview Formats with Parents

Three useful formats for interviewing parents are the unstructured (open-ended) interview, the semistructured interview, and the structured interview. When parents are extremely anxious or resistant, it is best to use an open-ended format at the initial stage of the interview before moving on to a semistructured interview, a structured interview, or another interview format (see Chapter 1 for a discussion of the three types of interviews).

During any type of interview, when parents have difficulty recalling the child's developmental milestones, you can provide a time frame to help them (Rudel, 1988):

"Was he walking on his first birthday?" If this fails, you can discuss family history (moves from one place of residence to another, holidays, family celebrations, or visits to relatives) and, by estimating the child's age on these occasions, can relate developmental data to these events. "Was he toilet-trained when you visited your in-laws? Did you have to change diapers en route? Did he speak to your mother when he met her? Do you recall what they said? Was your mother surprised that he was not talking in sentences at that time?" By providing an event-related context, you sometimes can obtain a more reliable estimate of the child's developmental history. (p. 90, with changes in notation)

If parents cannot recall developmental events, this may mean that the child's development was normal; the parents would likely remember unusual or deviant behavior (Rudel, 1988). In rare cases, it could mean that the child was neglected.

Semistructured interview. A semistructured interview is useful in assessing (a) what is important to the parents, (b) what they hope to accomplish from the evaluation, (c) their concerns, and (d) how they view their own role in helping the child. The semistructured interview allows parents the leeway to discuss anything they believe is relevant.

Three common types of semistructured interviews with parents are the developmental history interview, the screening interview with parents of preschool children, and the typical-day interview.

1. *Developmental history interview.* If the parents do not complete a background questionnaire, you will need to obtain a history of the child's development. The history should provide background information, some perspective on the current situation of the child, what interventions have been tried and with what success, and clues to what might benefit the child in the future. Following are typical areas covered in a developmental history interview (Nay, 1979):

- *Description of child's birth and events related to the birth* (including mother's health; mother's use of drugs, alcohol, or cigarettes during pregnancy; and pregnancy and birth complications)
- *Child's developmental history* (including important developmental milestones such as age at sitting, standing, walking, use of functional language, and bladder and bowel control; self-help skills; and personal-social relationships)
- *Child's medical history* (including types and dates of injuries, accidents, operations, and significant illnesses, as well as prescribed medications)
- *Characteristics of family and family history* (including age, ordinal position, sex, occupation, employment status, and marital status of family members and significant medical, educational, and mental health history of siblings and parents)
- *Child's cognitive level, personality, and temperament* (including the child's cognitive level of functioning, reasoning, memory, flexibility, degree of organization, ability to plan, ability to attend and concentrate, and ability to inhibit responses)
- *Child's interpersonal skills* (including child's ability to form friendships and relationships with others, child's play activities, and how other children and adults relate to the child)
- *Child's educational history* (including schools attended, grades, attitude toward schooling, relationships with teachers and peers, and special education services received)
- *Child's sexual behaviors* (including relationships with those of the same and opposite sex)
- *Child's occupational history, if any* (including types and dates of employment, attitude toward work, and occupational goals)
- *Description of presenting problem* (including a detailed description of the problem, antecedent events, consequences, and how the parents have dealt with the problem)
- *Parental expectations* (including the parents' expectations and goals for treatment of their child and, if appropriate, themselves)

Table B-5 in Appendix B provides a semistructured interview for obtaining a detailed case history from parents. The parents are asked to describe the child's problem behavior, home environment, neighborhood, sibling relations, peer relations, relationship with the parents, interests and hobbies, daily activities, cognitive functioning, academic functioning, biological functioning, affective life, and abilities in comparison with those of siblings, as well as their own concerns and related issues.

2. *Screening interview with parents of preschool children.* Table B-7 in Appendix B provides a brief semistructured

screening interview for use with parents of preschool children. It focuses on the parents' concerns about their child's development. It is useful when you want an overview of how a preschool child is functioning.

3. *Typical-day interview.* Sometimes you will want to ask a parent or caregiver about how his or her preschool- or elementary school–aged child spends a typical day (see the semistructured interview in Table B-8 in Appendix B). This information can help you better understand how the child functions in his or her family and social and interpersonal environments. For preschool-aged children who are not attending school, you might ask about any day of the week. For preschoolers who are attending school and for school-aged children, you should ask about a typical Saturday or Sunday if you want to know about a full day at home or any weekday if you want to know about a school day. Or, you might ask about both a typical school day and a typical weekend day.

These three types of interviews will not gather biographical information from the parents. You must obtain this information by having the parents complete an information form or questionnaire that asks them to give their name, address, and phone number; the child's teacher's name; and other important identifying information. The background questionnaire shown in Table A-1 in Appendix A has a section for obtaining biographical information.

Structured interview. In a structured interview, the questions are designed to cover various areas of psychopathology systematically. Chapter 1 in this text describes several structured interviews. They are useful when you need to arrive at a specific diagnosis.

Major Components of the Initial Interview with Parents

The major components of an initial interview with parents are as follows:

1. *Greet the parents.*
2. *Give your name and professional title.*
3. *Open the interview with an introductory statement.* Useful introductory statements include the following (Lichtenstein & Ireton, 1984):

- "Tell me what brings you here today."
- "How can I help you?"
- "Tell me about your child."
- "Please tell me your concerns about your child."
- "Please tell me what [child's name] has been doing lately."
- "How well do you think your child is doing?"
- "How do you get along with your child?"
- "I understand that your son [daughter] is having some difficulties in school. I'd like to discuss these difficulties with you and see whether we can work together to develop a plan to help him [her]."

4. *Ask parents about items on the background questionnaire.* If the parents have completed a background questionnaire, you will not have to go over most of the areas covered in a developmental history interview. Nevertheless, allow them to describe in their own words their concerns about their child. Also ask the parents about any items on the background questionnaire that need to be clarified—for example, "I see that John is having problems at home. Would you tell me more about these problems?" If the parents have not completed a questionnaire, ask them about the typical areas covered in a developmental history. As previously noted, you might want to use the semistructured interview in Table B-5 in Appendix B.

5. *Review problems.* Review the child's problems as presented by the parents, and ask the parents whether they would like to comment further on any problem.

6. *Describe the assessment procedure.* If psychological tests will be administered to the child, explain the purposes of the tests and why they will be administered. Inform the parents about who will have access to the assessment information and how the information will be used. Discuss confidentiality of the assessment results, including the conditions under which confidentiality will need to be broken. (See Chapter 3 for further discussion of confidentiality.) In some cases, this also would be an appropriate time to offer the parents information on services available through the clinic, school, or hospital. Otherwise, you may want to offer this information in the post-assessment interview.

7. *Arrange for a post-assessment interview.* Arrange to discuss the results of the assessment with the parents. In some cases, the results will be presented to the parents at an interdisciplinary staff conference. In other cases, one interviewer may present the overall results of the assessment based on reports provided by all the professionals involved in the case. In still other cases, only the interviewer who conducted the evaluation will present his or her results to the parents.

8. *Close the interview.* Escort the parents from the room and make appropriate closing remarks, such as "Thank you for coming. In case you have any other questions, here is my phone number."

Guidelines for Interviewing Parents

Following are 20 guidelines for interviewing parents:

1. Listen carefully to the parents' concerns.
2. Explain what lies ahead, what may be involved in the assessment process, and what interventions are possible.
3. Adopt a calm, nonjudgmental approach to reduce the parents' stress.
4. Help the parents understand that many children have problems at times and that emotional problems or physical problems may develop in a child because of events beyond the parents' control.
5. Reassure parents that the records will be kept confidential, unless the law requires that the records be disclosed

or agency policy requires that the records be shared with others.

6. Help parents who are having problems in managing their child understand that child rearing is a complex and difficult activity and that a child with special needs may be especially difficult to cope with.

7. Take special care to convey respect for the parents' feelings.

8. Avoid any suggestion that the parents are to blame for their child's difficulties. (This and the following two points do not apply when the parents have maltreated their child or are alleged to have done so.)

9. Emphasize their constructive and helpful parenting skills rather than their destructive or harmful approaches.

10. Enlist their cooperation in the diagnostic and remediation program; do not be authoritarian.

11. Schedule more than one meeting if parents are uncooperative or if the information provided is complex.

12. If working with a two-parent family, try to get both parents to come to the interview. Having both parents at the interview will help you gain a more complete picture of the family.

13. Consider interviewing parents separately, especially in cases of custody evaluations, child maltreatment, or domestic violence or when the parents are hostile.

14. Help the parents clarify vague, ambiguous, or incomplete statements.

15. Encourage the parents to discuss their child's problem fully and how the problem affects the family.

16. Use follow-up and probing questions to learn about the specific conditions that may serve to instigate, maintain, or limit the child's behavior and about the child's and parents' resources and motivation to change.

17. Determine the areas in which the parents agree and disagree about child management.

18. Appropriately and gently guide the parents back to the topic if they give many irrelevant details.

19. Ask the parents to check their recollections against baby books, medical and school records, and other formal and informal records if their memory of important events or their dates is hazy.

20. If you schedule a second interview, ask the parents to keep a record of the occurrences of the problem if you believe that such a record would be helpful. The record should include where the problematic event occurred, when it occurred, what preceded it, what followed it, their reactions to it, their manner of dealing with it, and who else was involved. You can use a form similar to the one shown in Table 5-9 in Chapter 5, deleting the term *self-monitoring* from the heading.

> *Before I got married, I had six theories about bringing up children; now I have six children and no theories.*
>
> —John Wilmot

Courtesy of Herman Zilinski.

INTERVIEWING TEACHERS

During the initial interview with teachers, you can cover many of the same topics that you cover with parents. The focus, however, is somewhat different. When you interview a teacher, your concern is not only with the teacher's perception of the problem, the antecedents and consequences of the problem behavior, and what the teacher has done to alleviate the problem, but also with how other children and teachers react to the child and how the child performs academically. If the child's problem occurs in a specific situation or setting, discover what the teacher considers appropriate behavior in that situation or setting. For help with interviewing teachers, see Table B-11 in Appendix B.

You also can use a teacher-completed questionnaire (School Referral Questionnaire) as part of the assessment (see Table A-3 in Appendix A). Ask the teacher to complete it before the interview, and then review it before you meet with her or him. Like the parent background questionnaire, it may give you some useful leads for further inquiry during the interview proper.

Areas Covered in the Initial Interview with Teachers

Areas covered in the initial interview with teachers include the teacher's perception of the child's problem behavior, reactions to the child's problem behavior, opinion of the child's relationship with peers, assessment of the child's academic performance, assessment of the child's strengths and weaknesses, view of the child's family, expectations for the child, and suggestions for helping the child.

Two Examples of What to Ask in an Initial Interview with Teachers

The following two examples illustrate the types of questions you might ask in an initial interview with a teacher. The examples show how you can use the interview to develop a plan for obtaining further information about the child's problem. (The examples are adapted from Bergan, 1977, pp. 97–99; used with permission of the author.)

CHILD WITH BEHAVIOR PROBLEM

"Tell me about Alice's problem in the classroom."

"What does Alice do when she annoys you?"

"How often during the week does she talk out of turn?"

"You've said that Alice talks without permission. She does this about four times a day. Is that right?"

"What is generally going on right before Alice talks out of turn?"

"What are you usually doing just before Alice talks out of turn?"

"What do you do when Alice talks out of turn?"

"When does she talk out of turn during the day?"

"On what days of the week does she talk out of turn?"

SCHOOLIES © 1998 by John P. Wood

I got punished for skipping the workshop on non-coercive discipline.

Copyright © 1998 by John P. Wood. Reprinted with permission.

"You've said that Alice usually talks out of turn when your back is turned and you're writing on the blackboard. Is that right?"

"Afterwards, the other kids giggle and laugh and sometimes treat her as though she had really done something great. Is that correct?"

"Will you be able to record when Alice talks out of turn?"

"The record will help us to establish a baseline against which to evaluate the success of our intervention plan."

"Throughout the rest of this week, would you record on this form the number of times Alice talks out of turn?"

"If you have the time to do it, you also could make a note of what happens before and after she talks out of turn."

"Do these suggestions meet with your approval?"

"We agreed that you would record the number of times that Alice talks out of turn during the rest of this week."

"You're going to use this form."

"If you have a chance, please note what happens before and after she talks out of turn."

"Did I summarize our recording plans accurately?"

"Could we meet Monday or Tuesday of next week?"

"Shall we meet in the teacher's lounge or in your classroom?"

"If it's okay, I'll give you a call sometime this week to see how the data collection is going."

CHILD WITH READING PROBLEM

"Tell me about Ted's reading problem."

"Give me some other examples of Ted's reading difficulties."

"About how many errors does Ted make during an oral reading session?"

"You said that Ted continually misreads and omits words during oral reading. Is that correct?"

"How do you introduce oral reading?"

"How do the other children react when Ted makes errors while reading?"

"What is the sequence of steps that you go through in teaching reading in the oral reading groups?"

"You said that when you call on Ted to read, he reads eagerly and that after he has finished, you always go over all of his mistakes with him. You pronounce the words for him and have him say the words correctly. Is that an accurate review of what happens?"

"If you could record the number of errors that Ted makes during reading for the rest of the week, it would help us to establish a baseline against which we can measure improvement in his reading."

"You could use this form for recording."

"And if you have a chance, note the other children's reactions and your own reactions when Ted makes a mistake."

"Would these plans be okay with you?"

"To summarize, we said that you would use this form to record the number of errors that Ted makes during oral reading for the rest of the week and that, if you have the chance, you'll note your own reactions and those of the other children to Ted's mistakes. Is that right?"

"Could we meet Monday or Tuesday of next week?"

"Shall we meet in the teacher's lounge or in your classroom?"

"If it's okay, I'll give you a call sometime this week to see how the data collection is going."

Working with the Teacher

Allay the teacher's anxiety about his or her responsibility for the child's problem behaviors. Inform the teacher that children's problems likely stem from a variety of factors. Tell the teacher when the assessment results will be ready, and do not leave the impression that immediate changes for the better will occur. If you want to observe the child in the classroom, follow the procedures discussed in Chapter 5.

Based on your interview with the teacher (and on classroom observations and interviews with the child and parents), you can probably come to some understanding about the following matters:

1. What does the teacher see as the major problem(s)?
2. How effective are the teacher's teaching skills and behavior management skills?
3. Is the child's class placement appropriate?
4. If a placement change is needed for the child, what might be more appropriate?
5. What insights does the teacher have about the child?
6. What techniques have been successful (or partially successful) in helping the child?
7. What techniques have been unsuccessful in helping the child?
8. How do other children contribute to the problem?

9. What stressors exist in the classroom?
10. If stressors are present in the classroom, how can they be diminished?
11. How does the teacher's account of the child's problem(s) agree with those of the parents and the child?
12. What are the teacher's recommendations for interventions?

> *Children need models rather than critics.*
>
> —Joseph Joubert

INTERVIEWING THE FAMILY

Goals of the Initial Family Interview

The goals of the initial family interview are to obtain historical and current details of family life relevant to the problems of the child and to observe patterns of family interaction. The family's strengths and weaknesses also should be noted.

A family interview is valuable for the following reasons (Kinsbourne & Caplan, 1979):

- It informs the child and the parents that you prefer to be open about the problem and that it is important to include the child in the interview.
- It allows you to observe how the parents and child interact when discussing the problem and other matters.
- It allows you to gather information about (a) the child's problem, (b) the family's understanding of the child's problem, (c) family dynamics, communication patterns, and social and cultural values, (d) how well the family accepts the child, (e) what impact the child's difficulties have on the

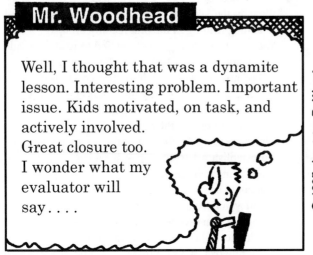

Mr. Woodhead

Well, I thought that was a dynamite lesson. Interesting problem. Important issue. Kids motivated, on task, and actively involved.
Great closure too.
I wonder what my evaluator will say. . . .

© 1997 by John P. Wood

You talk to the left side of the room too much.

family, on the parents' relationship, and on other family members, and (f) the extent to which the family is using functional or dysfunctional strategies to cope with the child's problems.

- It will help you clarify the family structure, along with details of the family's makeup, such as names, ages, relationships, and occupations of members (or a parent may supply this information on a questionnaire).
- It will help you evaluate the family's motivation to help the child and determine what interventions are possible given the family's resources.

This interview may be the family's first attempt as a family unit to discuss the perceived problem. It may be a turning point in the child's life when you say to the family, "Let's all go into my office and discuss why you're here today."

The following represent *functional family strategies*—positive strategies that families may use to cope with a child with a psychological or medical disorder (DePompei, Blosser, & Zarski, 1989):

1. *Reacting.* Family members have initial reactions of grief, anger, disappointment, guilt, anxiety, frustration, and a sense of loss.

2. *Mobilizing.* Family members draw on internal and external support systems to respond to the needs of the child.

3. *Recognition.* Family members perceive the strengths and weaknesses of the child in a realistic light.

4. *Understanding.* Family members gain an understanding of what the interventions might accomplish.

5. *Continuing.* Family members continue with other aspects of their lives.

6. *Hoping.* Family members maintain hope for the future for the child and for themselves.

7. *Appreciating.* Family members develop a new appreciation for many aspects of life for themselves and for their child.

8. *Reasoning.* Family members engage in adequate reasoning and do not make faulty assumptions.

The following represent *dysfunctional family strategies*—negative strategies that families may use to cope with a child with a psychological or medical disorder (DePompei et al., 1989):

1. *Blaming.* Family members criticize actions of the child, threaten the child, accuse the child of acting to embarrass them, and blame the child for unrelated family problems. Parents also may blame each other or themselves for the child's problems.

2. *Taking over.* Family members assume responsibility for the child by speaking for the child and by performing tasks that the child could or should do.

3. *Employing power.* Family members use authority to direct the behaviors of the child or rely heavily on the use of guilt to maintain their position and authority.

4. *Avoiding.* Family members use work, medications, food, and blaming the child to remove themselves from di-

rect involvement in the family; they also fail to accept responsibility for family disharmony.

5. *Denying.* Family members seek to maintain the status quo, failing to recognize that the child's disability has changed the family's patterns of functioning.

6. *Controlling.* Family members select what the child should do rather than allowing the child to choose for himself or herself.

7. *Rescuing.* Family members remove the child from situations that the child created so that the child does not have to suffer the consequences of her or his actions.

8. *Faulty reasoning.* Family members engage in rationalizing—if the child could just come home from the hospital or clinic and return to school or work, everything would return to normal—and assume that the child has behavioral controls that the child does not have.

Families may cope with stress in adaptive or maladaptive ways or in some combination of the two (Turk & Kerns, 1985). A key factor in coping with stress—whether the stress is psychological, environmental, or physical—is how the family was functioning *before* the stress occurred. A family that was functioning well before the stress occurred may continue to function adequately, although with some problems. The family may handle the stress, protect its members, adjust to role changes within the family, and continue to carry out its functions. A family that was not functioning well before the stress may break down in the face of stress, which, in turn, may lead to maladaptive behavior or illness on the part of its members.

When you interview the family, a healthy sibling also may be present. In such cases, you may find that the healthy child who has a sibling with a psychological or medical disorder is also under stress. Healthy siblings may dislike their increased responsibilities at home, be unhappy about decreased parental attention and increased parental tension, feel guilt and shame, be upset about having to deal with the negative reactions of those outside the family, resent the sibling with a psychological or medical disorder, and be concerned and worried about their sibling. Be prepared to deal with these and similar issues and reactions.

The family interview, like the interview with the child or parents alone, may be the first encounter the family has with a mental health professional and may serve as the beginning of a family therapy intervention program.

Necessity of Individual Interviews

It is important to note that the family interview is not a substitute for individual interviews—you should still see the child and the parents separately. You may also have to meet with each parent separately. Parents and children may be more open in an individual interview than in a family interview. Observing how they behave in both an individual and a family interview may be helpful. If you begin the assessment with a family interview, obtain the child's developmental history from the parents during their interview without the child.

Guidelines for Conducting the Family Interview

You want to create a setting in which the family members can risk sharing their feelings and problems and can seek information about the referred child's problems and their problems as they relate to the child. Help every family member feel at ease and involved. You want family members to interact freely, to contribute ideas about the problem, to describe the conditions that they find most troublesome, and to discuss what changes they would like to see and what might be done to resolve the problem. *Recognize that your questions may result in painful confrontations among family members and may elicit feelings that have not been previously articulated.* When confrontations occur, offer support to the family members who need it.

Before beginning the family interview, consider who referred the family to you, the reason for the referral, and whether the family came voluntarily or under coercion (e.g., at the insistence of the court, the school, or one family member). Following are useful guidelines for conducting the family interview (Kinston & Loader, 1984):

1. Encourage open discussion among the family members.
2. Lower the parents' and child's stress levels as much as possible.
3. Reduce the family's anxiety and fear of negative evaluations.
4. Support any family member who is on the "hot seat."
5. Do not create guilt or loss of face for any family member.
6. Create a safe and supportive atmosphere and a sense of trust so that family members can interact comfortably and naturally.
7. Use praise, approval, and reflection of feeling to ease family members' acceptance of the interview.
8. Help family members see that you are interested in each member's point of view and that you want to understand them. Do not take sides.
9. Help family members clarify their thoughts.
10. Be objective and understanding in your evaluation of family members.
11. Maintain a balance between formality and informality, while promoting informality among the family members.
12. Encourage those family members who are children to participate in the discussion.
13. Encourage family members to give specific examples of concerns and problems.
14. Do not provoke family members. Ask, for example, "How do arguments arise?" rather than "Who's the troublemaker in the family?"
15. Be aware of the dynamics among the family members.

If you follow these guidelines, the family members may be more willing to engage in a free discussion of the personal and intimate details of their lives.

Table 2-3 presents some guidelines for observing the family. Note, for example, which members talk, in what sequence, at whom each member looks, and who speaks first, interrupts, clarifies, registers surprise, remains silent, disagrees, assumes a leadership role, expresses emotional warmth, and accepts responsibility. In addition, observe whether the child misbehaves and, if so, how the parents discipline the child. Also note how the parents view the child and her or his problems, how the family resolves anger, if members are encouraged to speak, whether they support and cooperate with each other, and if they make physical contact.

If you touch upon an emotionally charged area that upsets family members and makes it difficult to continue the interview, consider moving on to a more neutral subject. You can schedule a second session, if needed, to explore sensitive areas. You want to obtain as much information as possible during the initial evaluation, but you do not want to cause undue anxiety. In crises, instead of conducting a standard intake assessment interview, you might need to focus on what can be done immediately about the problem. For more information on crisis interviewing, see Sattler (1998).

When a child at the family interview seems unable to answer a question and appears uncomfortable, do not prolong the discomfort. It is best to take the child off the hook (Karpel & Strauss, 1983). Consider rephrasing the question, switching to another topic, or questioning another family member. You might even consider saying that the question was "too fuzzy," as a way of reassuring the child. Finally, you can "encourage the child to bring up the topic later if he or she gets any new ideas" (Karpel & Strauss, 1983, p. 204).

You want to be aware of how the family members perceive you. For example, note at what points they ask you to give your opinion, to intercede, to solve problems, or to give them support. Key interviewing skills are listening to one family member while simultaneously observing other family members, being aware of your role in the interactions, and being aware of your reactions to the family members.

Table B-10 in Appendix B provides an example of a semistructured family interview. It covers the presenting problem and issues related to the family's image, perceptions of its members, organization, communication patterns, relationships, activities, conflicts, and decision-making style.

Strategies for Working with Resistant Families

When you meet family members who have *not* come to see you voluntarily, you may have to clarify your role by informing them of your goals. Tell the family that you need to obtain information to make the most appropriate recommendations. One way to begin is to say, "The school [or other referral source] has asked me to meet with you. I understand that Bill is [describe problem]. I'm here to help you and Bill with the problem." Interviewing a family ordered to come to see you will require patience.

You will also meet family members who will deny the problem or resist your efforts to obtain information. Your

Table 2-3
Guidelines for Observing the Family

Early Moments of the Interview
1. How did the family enter the room?
2. Were the family members resistant or cooperative?
3. If the child was resistant, how did the parents deal with him or her?
4. How were the family members dressed?
5. How did they seat themselves?
6. Who replied first to the interviewer's initial comment?
7. What was the tone of voice of each family member?
8. What was the demeanor of each family member? (For example, did they appear anxious, distressed, or comfortable during the early moments of the interview?)

Intrafamily Relations
9. How did the parents treat the referred child?
10. How did the parents treat the other children (if present)?
11. Were all the children treated similarly (if more than one child was present)?
12. How did the children treat their parents?
13. What pairings occurred between family members?
14. Who talked to whom and in what manner?
15. What was the sequence of talking?
16. Were the family members protective of one another?
17. Did one family member speak for another member without taking into account the latter's feelings?
18. Did one family member ask another member about what a third member said in the presence of the third member?
19. Did family members interrupt each other?
20. Did one family member attempt to control, silence, or intimidate other family members?
21. Did two family members engage in nonverbal activities together? (For example, did they cry together, laugh together, roll eyes together, or make certain facial expressions together?)
22. Were there times when there was a chain reaction between pairs of family members that distracted them from their task?

23. Did one family member disregard other members' feelings?
24. Did the family members describe each other in clear terms?
25. Did one family member intercede in a dialogue between two other members? If so, how did the pair accept the intercession?

Affect Displayed by Family Members
26. What type of affect was displayed by the family members during most of the interview? (For example, were the family members anxious, depressed, angry, sullen, calm, happy, upbeat, or hopeful?)
27. What degree of receptivity did the family members show about the problem and its possible resolutions?

Relationship with the Interviewer
28. How did the family members relate to you? (For example, did one member try to get too close to you? Were the members distant and aloof from you?)

Background Factors
29. What was happening in the family that might be contributing to the child's problem?
30. Was there someone missing from the interview who might add important information about the problem?
31. Who in the family thought it was a good idea to come to see you, and who did not think so?
32. What did the family expect from the interview?
33. Did the parents share the same view of the child's behavior and problem? If not, how did the parents' views differ?

Causes and Interventions
34. What did the parents think is the cause of the problem?
35. What did the child think is the cause of his or her problem?
36. What can be done to change the situation?
37. What did the parents want to do about the problem?
38. What did the child want to do about the problem?

---

patience will be tried when this happens. Be patient, however; show the family that you are a good listener, are genuinely interested in its problems, and are willing to wait until the reluctant members are willing to participate.

Here are some useful strategies for handling various types of resistance in the family interview (Anderson & Stewart, 1983):

1. *The parents say that the child is the problem, not themselves or the family.* Continue to focus on the child, at least initially. If the child is old enough and mature enough to handle the confrontation, ask the child whether the parents' position is accurate: "Is what they are saying about you really true?"

2. *The family denies there is a problem.* Be supportive of the family so that family members may come to trust you. Allow the family members to say that they are there because of someone else's referral ("We're doing this only because the doctor told us to come").

3. *One member dominates the discussion.* Attend to the family member who is talking, but move on to other family members. Inform them that the family member who is doing

all the talking is getting the other members off the hook. Tell the family member who is talking that what he or she is saying is important, but that you want to hear from everyone.

4. *The child will not talk.* One strategy is to inform the family of the importance of having everyone talk: "I really need to hear what everyone thinks of all this" or "It will help me to understand what's going on in this family if each of you tells me what you think." A second strategy is to give the child permission to be silent: "Okay, Henry, it's okay if you don't want to be here and even if you don't want to talk. Maybe if you just listen while your parents and I talk, it will be helpful. If you change your mind and want to join in, let us know." A third strategy is to take the avenue of least resistance and focus on those members who will speak. As the child sees that you listen and are fair, he or she may begin to talk.

5. *The family insists that the focus be only on historical information.* Ask the family why the information is relevant: "Okay, so Helen was 5 when she entered kindergarten and had two teachers. How's that going to help us now?"

6. *The family refuses to focus on historical information.* Provide the family with a rationale for what you want to learn: "I think it's important to get a picture of the family members' health and illnesses, both physical and psychological" or "We don't want to make any assumptions about what the problem is until we look at your history so that we can get a good perspective on what's happening now."

7. *The family cannot find a time for all members to meet.* Be flexible in scheduling appointments, because some families can meet only in the evenings or on weekends. You can give the family members the job of finding available times, you can make a home visit, or you can arrange for transportation.

8. *The family disagrees about the problem.* Find a new definition of the problem that everyone can agree with. Inform the family that everybody's feelings are important and legitimate in exploring what the problem might be.

Opening Phase of the Family Interview

Here are some techniques you can use during the opening phase of the family interview.

1. After introducing yourself, you might say, "We are all here today to work out the problems you're having as a family. I'd like to hear from each of you about what is going on." Then you might say, "Who would like to begin the discussion?"
2. Or, looking at no one in particular but addressing the family as a whole, you might say, "Would you like to tell me why you're here today?" or "How can I help you?"
3. Another possibility is to say, "I asked you all to come here today so that I can find out how you all feel about your family." Then pause and see whether anyone begins to speak. If you need to, you can say, "Perhaps you all can tell me what you see as the problems you're having as a family."
4. Encourage reluctant members to speak in the interest of being helpful.
5. Foreclose lengthy or excessive responses with such comments as "We have a lot of ground to cover. Let's hear what Mr. Smith thinks."
6. In working with families that have been directed to see you because their child has misbehaved, you might say to the family early in the interview, "You know, raising a child is difficult for many families today. How has it been for you?" This comment recognizes that the family is struggling with issues common to many families with children and invites their participation.
7. In cases of a court or school referral, you also might consider saying, "I know that the [court, school, etc.] has asked all of you to come to see me. But I also believe, [say the child's name and look at him or her], that your parents care about what happens to you and that you also care about what happens to you. I'm interested in how I can help all of you [looking at the entire family] get through this." By acknowledging that the parents have complied with an order or referral, these comments may help reduce the family's defensiveness (Oster, Caro, Eagen, & Lillo, 1988).

8. Pay special attention to the way each family member perceives and describes the problem.

Middle Phase of the Family Interview

After each family member has had time to share her or his views about the presenting problems (say, for a total of 15 to 20 minutes), you can turn to a discussion of the family (see questions 15 through 54 in Table B-10 in Appendix B). In addition to what the family members report, be alert to the nonverbal cues that they give (e.g., knowing glances, fidgeting), how they speak to each other (e.g., friendly, hostile, neutral), power maneuvers (e.g., who tries to control the discussion), provocative behaviors (e.g., who tries to start an argument), and their ability to send and receive messages (e.g., clarity of communications, clarity of responses). Encourage all family members to participate in the discussions.

Family assessment tasks. To study family interaction patterns, you might want to give the family one or more of the tasks described below. The middle phase of the interview may be the most appropriate time to give one of these tasks, but you can do so in any phase of the interview. Tasks 1, 2, and 3 are from Szapocznik and Kurtines (1989, adapted from p. 35), and Task 9 is from Olson and Portner (1983).

Task 1. Planning a Menu

"Suppose all of you had to work out a menu for dinner tonight and would like to have your favorite foods for dinner. But you can only have one main dish, one vegetable, one drink, and one dessert. Discuss this together; however, you must choose one meal you would all enjoy that consists of one main dish, one vegetable, one drink, and one dessert. Go ahead."

Task 2. Commenting on Things Others Do in the Family That Please or Displease the Members

"Each of you tell about one thing each person in the family does that pleases you the most and makes you feel good, and one thing each one does that makes you unhappy or mad. Everyone try to give his or her own ideas about this. Go ahead."

Task 3. Discussing a Family Argument

"In every family, things happen that create a fuss now and then. Together, discuss an argument you have had—a fight or argument at home. Discuss what started it, who was part of it, what happened, and how it ended. See if you can remember what it was all about. Go ahead."

Task 4. Planning a Family Vacation

"What would your family like to do for a vacation? Discuss this together. However, you must all agree on the final choice. Go ahead."

Task 5. Allocating Lottery Winnings

"If a member of your family won $500,000 in a lottery, what would your family do with it? Discuss this together. However, you must all agree on the way the money will be handled. Go ahead."

Task 6. Planning an Activity

"Plan something to do together as a family. The plan you come up with should be one with which everyone agrees. Go ahead."

Task 7. Using Descriptive Phrases to Characterize the Family

"Come up with as many phrases as you can that describe your family as a group. Select one member to record your answers. All of you must agree with the phrases that describe your family before they are written down. Go ahead."

Task 8. Making Up a Story

(Select a picture from a magazine or from some other source that you think would be useful for this task.) "Here's a picture. Make up a story about the picture. Select one member to record the story. The story should be one with which you all agree. In the story, tell what is happening in the picture. Include a beginning, a middle, and an end to the story. Go ahead."

Task 9. Discussing Specific Issues

With a family that is shy or hesitant to discuss issues or with a family that needs more structuring, consider using the following procedure. Say, "I'm going to name some issues, one at a time. I'd like you to tell me whether the issue is or is not a problem in your family. OK? Here's the first one." You can then name each of the following issues or select only the ones you believe are most pertinent for the family: money, communication, sharing feelings, expressing feelings, physical intimacy, recreation, friends, alcohol, drugs, raising the children, handling parental responsibility, sharing responsibilities for raising the children, jealousy, personal habits, resolving conflicts, taking disagreements seriously, leisure time, vacations, making decisions, time spent away from home, careers, moving to a new place, sharing household duties, putting clothing away, and having time to be alone. Explore any problem area mentioned by the family: "In what way is _____ a problem?" Try to get each member to respond. If there are disagreements, say, "It seems that you have different ideas about whether _____ is a problem. Let's discuss why you have different ideas."

Task 10. Participating in Miscellaneous Activities

Request that a parent ask the child to perform some action, such as writing a sentence, doing an arithmetic problem, or solving a puzzle. Observe how the parent asks the child to perform the task, how the child does it, how other members react as the child performs the task, and how the child presents the finished task. (Also see Chapter 4 for guidelines for observing parent-child interactions.)

Any of these 10 tasks will help you learn about the family's negotiation style; ways of resolving conflicts; pattern of alliances; decision-making style; patterns of parent-child, parent-parent, sibling-sibling, and parent-sibling interactions; roles; communication and language patterns; beliefs and expectations; and affective reactions. Be prepared, though, if a task becomes too stressful, to move on to something less threatening.

Additional areas to probe in a family interview. In addition to asking the questions in Table B-10 in Appendix B and assigning the family assessment tasks, you also might want to explore several areas of family life. These include the layout of the home; a typical day in the life of the family; rules, regulations, and limit setting within the family; alliances and coalitions with the family; family disagreements; changes that the family members want to make; and previous family crises and how they were resolved. We now consider each of these areas in more detail. (Sample instructions are from Karpel and Strauss, 1983, adapted from pp. 137–147.)

1. *Layout of the home.* After the initial discussion of the problem, a useful way to get family members to talk is to ask them about the layout of the home: "I want to take a little bit of time to pull back from discussing the immediate problem, just to get a better idea about your family. You've mentioned some things already, but maybe one way to start would be for you to give me a description of your home, the layout of the rooms, who sleeps where, and anything you want to tell me about your home." Ask follow-up questions as needed.

2. *A typical day.* A useful probing question for this area is "I also want to get a description from all of you of what a typical day consists of for your family. Start from the first thing in the morning, beginning with who gets up first. Go ahead." If the family tells you about an atypical day, redirect them to discuss a typical day, usually a weekday. You also can ask them how they spend a typical weekend day. You may want to ask about the following issues (Karpel & Strauss, 1983, adapted from p. 139):

- Do any family members have breakfast at home?
- (If yes) Do they eat together?
- Which members, if any, are home during the day or come home for lunch?
- At what time do different family members arrive home from school or work?
- Who usually prepares dinner?
- Who is usually home for dinner?
- Does the family eat together?
  (If yes, consider the next four questions; if no, go to the fifth question.)

- Do they have an established seating arrangement at a table for dinner?
- What is the atmosphere around the table at a typical family dinner?
- Are things quiet or noisy at dinner?
- If noisy, is the noise from animated conversations and joking or from petty arguments or major conflicts?
- How does each family member spend the evening?
- When does each family member usually go to bed?

3. *Rules, regulations, and limit setting.* A useful question for this area of family life is "All families have certain rules and regulations for people in the family—chores, curfews, and that kind of thing. What are some of the rules and regulations in your family?" Valuable follow-up questions might cover what happens if chores are not done; how discipline is managed by the parents; whether both parents play active roles in discipline; whether the parents work together, independently, or at cross-purposes in using discipline; what role each parent plays in disciplining the children; and whether the discipline is appropriate for the children's behavior and age.

4. *Alliances and coalitions.* Several different probing statements may easily reveal the family's alliances and coalitions. For example, you might say, "I'd like to get a better idea of who spends time with each other in the family." After they discuss this, you can say, "I'd like to know who you're most likely to talk to when something is on your mind." You can direct these questions to each member of the family. Other useful questions are "Who sticks up for whom?" and "Who worries about whom in the family?" and "Whom do you worry about the most?"

5. *Family disagreements.* One useful approach (as you look at each family member) is "Every family has areas they frequently disagree about, but these areas differ from one family to another. I wonder if you could tell me about the kinds of disagreements your family has most often." Another version is "Most families have some kind of disagreement about something or some gripes about something every once in a while. What types of gripes have there been from time to time in your family?" After someone describes an event, obtain more detailed information by asking follow-up questions such as "What was said first?" "What happened next?" "What was everyone doing at the time?" "How did it end?"

6. *Desired changes.* Useful questions are "Can any of you think of any changes you'd like to see made in your family?" "If you could change anything you wanted about your family or about life in the family, what kinds of changes would you make?" and, directed at the children, "If you had magic powers and could change anything you wanted, what would you change about your family?"

7. *Previous family crises.* A useful statement is "It will help us in dealing with the present problem to learn something about any previous problems that your family has experienced or that any members of the family have gone through. Any past situation that has been especially upsetting to the family or put stress on it would help me better understand your family, as would any previous problems that required professional help." Or you can substitute for the second sentence "Have there ever been times that have been really rough for the family?" Ask follow-up questions as needed. The way the family managed past crises may help you learn about the family's organization, judgment, flexibility, mutual trust, and internal resources.

Closing Phase of the Family Interview

Toward the end of the interview, summarize the salient points, including comments on the family dynamics related to the child's problem. Then ask the family members to respond to your formulation. After that, give your initial recommendations and ask the family members what they think about them. Gauge the family's willingness to change and the suitability of its members for treatment.

It also may be useful toward the end of the family interview to ask whether there is anything else you should know about how the family is functioning. Ask about any recent changes, problems, or stressors that the family members think are noteworthy.

What you achieve in the initial family interview will be a function of your interview style and the idiosyncrasies of each family. You may not obtain all the information you want, but do your best to evaluate the family. When you review the information obtained in the family interview, consider such questions as the following:

1. Who referred the family?
2. What is the composition of the family?
3. Who was present at and who was absent from the interview?
4. How does the family provide models for its members; handle its successes and failures; recognize the talents, skills, and interests of its members; and use resources in the community?
5. Overall, what are the strengths and weaknesses of the family?
6. What prior interventions has the family received, and with what result?
7. What are the family's resources?
8. What types of services does the family need?
9. What short-term and long-term goals can be formulated?

For more information about family assessment, see Beavers and Hampson (1990). Also see Sattler (1998) for checklists useful for evaluating the family.

Tasks in Preparation for a Second Family Interview

If you plan to ask the family to return for a second interview, you may want the family to record information about a problem area in the interim. This information may help both you and the family understand the problem better. For example, you might give each member the same task, such as recording disagreements that occur between family members, recording positive statements, or both. When they bring this information to the second session, you can review (a) the types of disagreements that occurred or positive statements that were made, (b) the extent to which the family members agree and disagree about what happened during the week, (c) whether there is more agreement between the child and one parent than between the child and the other parent, and (d) whether there is more agreement about certain types of behaviors than others (e.g., pleasing versus displeasing behaviors, passive versus active behaviors, cognitive versus affective behaviors). Chapter 4 in this text describes procedures for conducting a home observation.

A family was seated in a restaurant. The waitress took the order of the adults and then turned to their young son. "What will you have, sonny?" she asked. The boy said timidly, "I want a hot dog." Before the waitress could write down the order, the mother interrupted. "No hot dog," she said. "Give him potatoes, beef and some carrots." But the waitress ignored her completely. "Do you want some ketchup or mustard on your hot dog?" she asked of the boy. "Ketchup," he replied with a happy smile on his face. "Coming up," the waitress said, starting for the kitchen. There was a stunned silence upon her departure. Finally, the boy turned to his parents. "Know what?" he said. "She thinks I'm real."

—Bill Adler

"Now that Mommy and I have started investing for your college education, we thought this would be a good time to discuss your retirement options."

THINKING THROUGH THE ISSUES

1. How do interviews with children differ from interviews with adults?
2. What difficulties may arise when you interview young children?
3. Do you think that you can evaluate the psychological framework of a young child?
4. How accurate are the reports of young children?
5. What other types of problems might you encounter in interviewing children, besides those discussed in the text?
6. How would you handle a situation in which the information given by the child and parents, or child and teacher, or parents and teacher differed?
7. With which type of interview—individual or family—will you be more comfortable, or will you be equally comfortable with both? Explain the basis for your answer.
8. What stresses will family interviews place on you that are different from those occuring in individual interviews?
9. What problems do you foresee in handling the group dynamics of the family interview?
10. Does the family interview simply involve interviewing individuals in a group, or does it have its own dynamics? What is the basis for your answer?
11. What do you think you can learn in a family interview that you cannot learn in individual interviews with each family member?
12. How are you going to deal with a family member who wants to dominate the family interview?
13. How would you bring a family together for an interview if the members did not want to be together?
14. How have your beliefs about your family changed throughout the years?
15. How have you adopted or assimilated values that differ from those of your family?

SUMMARY

General Considerations in an Initial Interview with Children

1. Interviews with children will give you information about children's perceptions of problems, their thoughts and feelings about themselves, and their impressions of their situation and their relationships.
2. Children are sometimes more difficult to interview than adults because of limitations in language comprehension, language expression, conceptual ability, and memory.
3. Keep in mind that children may not be aware that they have problems. When conducting an interview, always consider the child's age, experiences, level of cognitive development, and ability to express himself or herself, as well as the extensiveness of any psychological disturbance.
4. Children are more dependent on their immediate environments than adults are, as they have less power to shape them.
5. Children also differ from adults in that they are in a process of rapid intellectual, emotional, and behavioral development.
6. Because the interview setting is unfamiliar and because the interviewer is a stranger, children's behavior in the interview may not be typical of their behavior in other settings.
7. In school settings, and particularly in juvenile detention settings, you may initiate interviews when neither the children nor the parents have sought help for a problem.

8. The goals of the initial interview with a child will depend on the referral question, as well as on the child's age and communication skills.

Techniques for Interviewing Children

9. The most common way to help young children remember, think, and tell you about themselves is to ask them questions.

10. Recognize that in asking a question, you are making a demand—you are directing the attention of the child to memories or ideas that he or she might not have otherwise considered.

11. Children generally need more time than adults to think about questions and to think about their answers.

12. You can become a more effective interviewer of children by learning about their current interests.

13. The following are 22 useful techniques for interviewing children: Consider the child's age and needs in setting the tempo and length of the interview. Formulate appropriate opening statements. Use appropriate language and intonation. Avoid leading questions. Ask for examples. Be open to what the child tells you. Make descriptive comments. Use reflection. Give praise frequently. Avoid critical statements. Use simple questions and concrete referents. Formulate questions in the subjunctive mood when necessary. Be tactful. Recognize the child's discomfort. Use props, crayons, clay, or toys to help a young child talk. Use a sentence-completion technique. Use fantasy techniques. Help the child express his or her thoughts and feelings. Clarify an episode of misbehavior by recounting it. Clarify interview procedures for children who are minimally communicative. Understand and use silence. Handle resistance and anxiety by giving support and reassurance.

Areas Covered in the Initial Interview with Children

14. The typical sequence in interviewing a child is to introduce yourself to the parent (or caregiver or guardian) and to the child by giving your name and professional title, greet the child, open the interview with an introductory statement, continue the interview as appropriate, review the referral issues with the child, describe what will happen to the child after you complete the interview, express appreciation for the child's effort and cooperation, and close the interview.

15. Typical areas covered in the initial interview with children include reasons for coming to the interview, confidentiality, school, home, interests, friends, moods and feelings, fears and worries, self-concept, somatic concerns, obsessions and compulsions, thought disorders, memories or fantasies, aspirations, and other information voluntarily supplied by the children. In addition, for adolescents, typical areas include jobs, sexual relations, eating habits, possible drug and alcohol use, and pregnancy or impregnation.

16. You may want to ask about reinforcers important to the children if you are planning a therapeutic behavioral intervention.

17. If you believe that the physical layout of the child's home may be contributing to the difficulties, you can ask the child to draw a picture of her or his room and any other relevant rooms in the house.

18. As part of the initial interview with children, you may want to conduct a mental status evaluation.

Interviewing Parents

19. A well-conducted parent interview will establish rapport and a positive working relationship with the parents, focus the attention of the parents on the issues, serve as valuable information about the child and family, help the parents organize and reflect on the information, contribute to the formulation of a diagnosis, provide a basis for decisions about treatment and further investigation, and lay the groundwork for parental efforts to be a part of intervention efforts.

20. You want the parents to participate actively in the interview.

21. Parents serve as an important source of information and will play a key role in any proposed intervention.

22. Recognize that not all parents will be reliable informants. Expect to find some distortions, biases, and memory lags in the information you collect from them.

23. If you conduct an appropriate interview with parents, you should be able to develop some preliminary hypotheses about the child's difficulties, strengths, and weaknesses and about the parents' reactions, concerns, coping abilities, strengths, and weaknesses. You can also construct a picture of the family's life style and its prevailing values, mores, and concerns.

24. The age of the child will, in part, determine the content of the interview with the parents.

25. Parents may be apprehensive about their child's evaluation.

26. Depending on the type and severity of the child's problems, their cultural subgroup and ethnicity, and their religious affiliation, they may be concerned about the etiology of their child's problem, possible interventions, family issues, their responsibility, possible stigma associated with coming to a mental health professional, and the results.

27. If parents ask you what they should say to their child about coming to see you, advise them to be straightforward with their child.

28. By the time parents seek an evaluation for a school-age child (and sometimes for a preschool child as well), they may have already experienced much frustration and anguish. Expect some negative feelings from the parents and deal with these feelings during your initial contact.

29. Another way to obtain information about the child and family is to have the parents complete a background questionnaire before the interview.

30. Three useful formats for interviewing parents are the unstructured (open-ended) interview, the semistructured interview, and the structured interview.

31. When parents are extremely anxious or resistant, it is best to use an open-ended format at the initial stage of the interview before moving on to a semistructured interview, a structured interview, or another interview format.

32. A semistructured interview is useful in assessing what is important to the parents, what they hope to accomplish from the evaluation, their concerns, and how they view their own role in helping the child.

33. A structured interview is useful when you want to cover various areas of psychopathology systematically.

34. The major components of the initial interview with parents include greeting the parents, giving your name and professional title, opening the interview with an introductory statement, asking the parents about items on the background questionnaire that are of interest (if they have completed a background questionnaire) or covering similar content areas, reviewing problems, describing the assessment procedure, arranging for a post-assessment interview, and closing the interview.

35. Following specific guidelines for interviewing parents will allow you to obtain the needed information.

Interviewing Teachers

36. When you interview a teacher, your concern is not only with the teacher's perception of the problem, the antecedents and consequences of the problem behavior, and what the teacher has done to alleviate the problem, but also with how other children and teachers react to the child and how the child performs academically.
37. You also can use a teacher-completed questionnaire (School Referral Questionnaire) as part of the assessment.
38. Areas covered in the initial interview with teachers include the teacher's perception of the child's problem behavior, reactions to the child's problem behavior, opinion of the child's relationship with peers, assessment of the child's academic performance, assessment of the child's strengths and weaknesses, view of the child's family, expectations for the child, and suggestions for helping the child.
39. Allay the teacher's anxiety about his or her responsibility for the child's problem behaviors.

Interviewing the Family

40. The goals of the initial family interview are to obtain historical and current details of family life relevant to the problems of the child, to observe patterns of family interaction, and to note the family's strengths and weaknesses.
41. This interview may be the family's first attempt as a family unit to discuss the perceived problem.
42. Families may have functional or dysfunctional strategies to cope with their child's psychological or medical disorder.
43. The family interview, like the interview with the child or parents alone, may be the first encounter the family has with a mental health professional and may serve as the beginning of a family therapy intervention program.
44. You can use different strategies during the three phases of the family interview. In the opening phase, encourage the family members to talk about their concerns. During the middle phase, focus on general family dynamics and issues. In the closing phase, summarize the salient points of the interview.
45. There are several family assessment tasks you can use to study family interaction patterns. These include planning a menu, commenting on things others do in the family that please or displease the members, discussing a family argument, planning a family vacation, allocating lottery winnings, planning an activity, using descriptive phrases to characterize the family, making up a story, discussing specific issues, and participating in miscellaneous activities. Any of these 10 tasks will help you learn about the family's negotiation style; ways of resolving conflicts; pattern of alliances; decision-making style; patterns of parent-child, parent-parent, sibling-sibling, and parent-sibling interactions; roles; communication and language patterns; beliefs and expectations; and affective reactions.
46. Other areas of family life that you might want to explore include the layout of the home; a typical day in the life of the family; rules, regulations, and limit setting within the family; alliances and coalitions with the family; family disagreements; changes that the family members want to make; and previous family crises.
47. Toward the end of the interview, summarize the salient points, including comments on the family dynamics related to the child's problem. Then ask the family members to respond to your formulation. After that, give your initial recommendations and ask the family members what they think about them. Gauge the family's willingness to change and the suitability of its members for treatment.
48. What you achieve in the initial family interview will be a function of your interview style and the idiosyncrasies of each family.
49. If you plan to ask the family to return for a second interview, you may want the family to record information about a problem area in the interim.

KEY TERMS, CONCEPTS, AND NAMES

Techniques for interviewing children (p. 40)
Descriptive comments (p. 41)
Reflection (p. 41)
Concrete referents (p. 41)
Affect labels (p. 41)
Picture-question technique (p. 42)
Drawing-a-picture technique (p. 42)
Story-completion technique (p. 42)
Responding to a hypothetical problem (p. 43)
Modeling the interview after a school-type task (p. 43)
Formulating questions in the subjunctive mood (p. 43)
Use of props, crayons, clay, or toys (p. 43)
Sentence-completion technique (p. 44)
Fantasy techniques (p. 44)
Three wishes technique (p. 44)
Desert island technique (p. 44)
Handling resistance by giving support and reassurance (p. 46)
Areas covered in the initial interview with children (p. 46)
Reinforcers (p. 46)
Children's environment (p. 46)
Mental status evaluation (p. 47)
Goals of the initial interview with parents (p. 48)
Concerns of parents (p. 48)
Potential negative feelings of parents (p. 49)
Background questionnaire (p. 49)
Interview formats with parents (p. 50)
Developmental history interview (p. 50)
Screening interview with parents of preschool children (p. 50)
Typical-day interview (p. 51)
Major components of initial interview with parents (p. 51)
Guidelines for interviewing parents (p. 51)
Areas covered in the initial interview with teachers (p. 52)
Goals of the initial family interview (p. 54)
Functional family strategies (p. 55)
Reacting (p. 55)
Mobilizing (p. 55)
Recognition (p. 55)
Understanding (p. 55)
Continuing (p. 55)
Hoping (p. 55)
Appreciating (p. 55)
Reasoning (p. 55)
Dysfunctional family strategies (p. 55)
Blaming (p. 55)
Taking over (p. 55)
Employing power (p. 55)
Avoiding (p. 55)
Denying (p. 55)
Controlling (p. 55)
Rescuing (p. 55)

Faulty reasoning (p. 55)
Strategies for working with resistant families (p. 56)
Opening phase of the family interview (p. 58)
Middle phase of the family interview (p. 58)
Family assessment tasks (p. 58)
Additional areas to probe in a family interview (p. 59)
Closing phase of the family interview (p. 60)
Tasks in preparation for a second family interview (p. 60)

STUDY QUESTIONS

1. Discuss some general considerations in interviewing children. In your discussion, include goals of the initial interview and why children can be more difficult to interview than adults.
2. Twenty-two specific techniques for interviewing children are discussed in the text. Describe seven of them.
3. What are the typical areas covered in the initial interview with children?
4. Discuss the mental status evaluation. In your discussion, comment on the areas typically covered in a mental status evaluation and some important factors to evaluate in each area.
5. Discuss some important factors to consider in interviewing parents. Include in your discussion some of the goals of the initial interview with parents.

6. What are some typical concerns parents may express in the interview?
7. How can you go about reducing parental resistance during the initial interview?
8. Discuss how a background questionnaire is a useful adjunct to the interview.
9. What are some useful formats for interviewing parents?
10. Describe the major components of the initial interview with parents.
11. Describe several guidelines for interviewing parents.
12. How would you go about interviewing teachers? Include in your discussion the typical areas covered in the initial interview with teachers.
13. Discuss the family interview. Include in your discussion the goals of the family interview, guidelines for conducting the family interview, strategies for working with resistant families, phases of the family interview, family assessment tasks, and evaluating the family interview.
14. Discuss some tasks that you might give the family in preparation for a second family interview.

3

OTHER CONSIDERATIONS RELATED TO THE INTERVIEW

Many individuals have, like uncut diamonds, shining qualities beneath a rough exterior.

—Juvenal

Closing the Initial Interview

The Post-Assessment Interview

The Follow-Up Interview

Reliability and Validity of the Interview

Evaluating Your Interview Techniques

Thinking Through the Issues

Summary

Goals and Objectives

This chapter is designed to enable you to do the following:

- Close the initial interview

- Evaluate the initial interview

- Describe the major components of the post-assessment interview

- Understand the reactions of parents who learn that their child has special needs

- Discuss the reliability and validity of the interview

This chapter covers a variety of topics related to the interview. Guidelines are provided on (a) closing the initial interview, (b) evaluating the initial interview, (c) conducting a post-assessment interview, (d) conducting a follow-up interview, and (e) evaluating the interview findings by considering issues of reliability and validity.

CLOSING THE INITIAL INTERVIEW

The final moments of the interview are as important as any other period in the interview. They give you a chance to summarize what you have learned, obtain feedback from the interviewee about whether you have understood him or her, ask lingering questions, inform the interviewee about additional assessments needed and about possible interventions, and give the interviewee time to share any remaining thoughts and feelings.

Do not rush the ending of the interview. Budget your time so that there is enough remaining to go over what you need to cover. You want the interviewee to leave feeling that she or he has made a contribution and that the experience was worthwhile. Be courteous and friendly; tell the interviewee what will happen next and what you will expect of her or him. You do not want the interviewee to feel dismissed or used for your own purposes. A comment such as "Thank you for coming" might be all that you need to say to convey a sense of respect. If you discuss possible interventions and a prognosis, be careful not to create false hopes or expectations. You want to be as realistic as possible, recognizing what the intervention program may or may not accomplish.

The method you use to close the interview is especially important when the interviewee is expressing some deeply felt emotion. Try not to end the interview abruptly; allow enough time for the interviewee to regain composure before he or she leaves. Allow an interviewee who is in the middle of a communication to finish. Gauge the time and, when necessary, provide some indication to the interviewee that the interview will soon be over (say, in 10 minutes). When the interviewee recognizes that the interview will soon be over, he or she may begin to move away from the subject at hand and regain composure.

What you say, of course, will depend on whether you plan to see the interviewee again. If you do not, you might say, "You have some deep feelings about _____. However, since our time together is about up, I would be glad to give you the names of some professionals you could contact. I'm sure they will be able to help you. I do appreciate your cooperation." If you plan to see the interviewee again, you might say, "I can see that this is extremely important to you, and we need to talk about it some more. But our time is just about up for today. We can continue next time." Then arrange another appointment, while continuing to express support, understanding, and confidence that you can help the interviewee find a solution.

Planning for Enough Time at the Close of the Interview

It is easy to continue the main body of the interview to a point where there is little time left to end it appropriately, especially if you are on a tight schedule. Be aware of how much time has passed, what important areas you need to discuss, and how much time the interviewee may need to discuss any remaining concerns. When you are first learning to conduct interviews, have a clock in a visible location so that you do not lose track of time (however, do not let the clock distract you). Before you begin the interview, make note of the areas you want to discuss, and budget your time so that you can cover them.

Issues to consider near the completion of the interview. Here are some issues you will want to consider near the close of the interview:

1. Have you covered everything you wanted to cover?
2. Does the interviewee understand why additional assessments are necessary?
3. Does the interviewee understand how she or he will obtain the results of the assessment?
4. Have you and the interviewee had the opportunity to correct any misperceptions?
5. Does the interviewee understand how you will use the assessment findings? (For example, will they be used to make recommendations, given to a court, or given to school officials?)
6. Is the interviewee aware of the clinic's, school's, or your policies regarding fees and procedures?
7. Have you treated the interviewee with respect and concern?

You also will want to consider these and similar issues when you reflect on the interview as a whole.

If you find that you cannot recall some important information that has been discussed, you can say, "I know you told me about [describe topic], but I didn't note it fully. Can you tell me more about [the topic]?" You can make this type of statement at any time during the interview.

Give the interviewee the opportunity to ask questions. Use the last minutes of the initial interview to summarize and evaluate what you have learned and to give the interviewee an opportunity to ask any remaining questions that he or she might have.

Recognize the interviewee's concerns. Toward the close of the interview, the interviewee may wonder how the interview went, how serious the problem is, whether you can be of help, what you thought of her or him, whether she or he has told all you need to know, and what will happen next. Be prepared to deal with these and similar concerns. Here are some useful questions to ask:

• "Is there anything else you would like to tell me?"

- "Is there anything else you think I should know?"
- "I've asked you a lot of questions. Are there any questions that you'd like to ask me?"

Following are some examples of interviewees' concerns and possible interviewer responses. The interviewer's response, of course, depends on the specific situation.

1. IE: Did I say the right things?
   IR-1: Yes, you did. There are no right or wrong answers. You told me about yourself, and that was helpful.
   IR-2: Your responses have been helpful, and I believe we can help you.

2. IE: Do you think you can help me?
   IR: Yes, I do, but it will take time to work things out.

3. IE: Well, am I crazy?
   IR-1: (If there is no evidence of psychosis) No, you're not crazy. Sometimes teenagers think that things are not under their control, but this is common.
   IR-2: (If there is evidence of psychosis) You seem to have some problems in your thinking, and that concerns you.

4. IE: Am I going to be sent away?
   IR-1: (If no such plans are being considered) No, you're not going to be sent away. You'll be going home when we finish.
   IR-2: (If you are not sure whether the child is going to be sent away) We should wait until all the results are in before we make any decisions. But whatever we decide, we'll let you know, and we'll always try to do what is best for you.

5. IE: So what happens now?
   IR: First, we need to study what we have learned about you and your family. Then, after all the results are in, we'll talk about how to make things better.

The Summary Statement

A summary statement should identify the main points of the problem for the interviewee's confirmation or correction. Following is an example of a summary statement from an interview with a teacher: "You believe that Helen's major problem is her inability to read. Emotionally, you see her as well adjusted. However, her frustration in learning how to read gets her down at times." Toward the close of the initial interview with a parent, you might say something like "We met today so that I could learn about Bill. Do you believe that I have most of the important information?" Or, you could say, "I think we've accomplished a great deal today. The information you have given me is very helpful. I appreciate your cooperation and look forward to seeing you again after we have completed the evaluation." These statements are not mutually exclusive; they can be used together at the close of the interview. Toward the end of an interview with a child, you

could say, "I know that you're having difficulties in school in reading and math. When we're finished with the evaluation, we'll make plans to help you." When necessary, make an appointment with the interviewee to discuss the assessment findings and recommendations.

Acknowledge your satisfaction with cooperative interviewees. It may be helpful, especially with children, to acknowledge their openness and willingness to share their problems, concerns, hopes, and expectations. Comments such as the following may be appropriate (Jennings, 1982):

- "I appreciate your sharing your concerns with me."
- "It took a lot of courage to talk to me about yourself, your family, and your school."
- "It took a lot of trust to tell me what you just did, and I'm proud of you for doing that."
- "You took this interview seriously, and that will help me do my best to help you."

Acknowledge your disappointment with uncooperative interviewees. When the interviewee has been uncooperative and you need to schedule another appointment, you might want to express your concern about how the interview went: "We didn't get too much accomplished today. Perhaps next time we can cover more ground."

THE POST-ASSESSMENT INTERVIEW

The post-assessment interview (also called the *interpretive interview*) with children and parents serves several purposes. These include presenting the findings, presenting possible interventions, helping children and parents understand the findings and interventions, allowing children and parents to express their concerns, and exploring any additional areas of concern. As in the initial interview, use understandable terminology and explanations.

When you plan the post-assessment interview, consider the information you want to discuss with the child and the parents, how much detail you expect to give, and the order in which you want to present the information. During the post-assessment interview, leave plenty of time for the child and parents to ask you questions. Encourage them to ask about any areas they do not understand, and answer them carefully. In your presentation, be sure to discuss the family's strengths and also its weaknesses. Like the initial interview, the post-assessment interview will be most successful when the child and parents see you as competent, trustworthy, understanding, and interested in helping them. We strongly recommend that you not conduct the post-assessment interview until the psychological report has been completed (see Chapter 21 in *Assessment of Children: Cognitive Applications*). Although this chapter focuses on the post-assessment interview with children and with parents, the procedures discussed are applicable to any post-assessment interview—with teachers, physicians, attorneys, or other interested parties.

Two cautions are in order about the post-assessment interview. Recognize that if you are discussing with the parents and child the results from examinations performed by other professionals, you might not be able to answer all of their questions about these results. Therefore, when needed, arrange to have the other professionals attend the meeting. Also remember that, as a clinical assessor, you will be making important decisions about children's lives. *You should never make a diagnosis, a recommendation concerning a child's treatment or placement, or a decision about whether an alleged event took place unless you are fully qualified to do so.*

Guidelines for the Post-Assessment Interview

We can look at the post-assessment interview with the child and parents as having five aspects—cognitive, interactive, affective, ethicoreligious, and ethnocultural.

1. The *cognitive aspect* refers to how the parents and child understand the information given to them.
2. The *interactive aspect* refers to the interaction between the interviewer and the parents and child, with the interviewer encouraging the parents and child to participate and helping them to understand and accept the results of the evaluation and the treatment recommendations.
3. The *affective aspect* refers to the feelings of the parents and child about the information presented.
4. The *ethicoreligious aspect* refers to how the parents' and child's ethical and religious views affect (a) their reactions to the information they receive, (b) their beliefs about their responsibility for the problem, and (c) their willingness to follow the treatment recommendations.
5. The *ethnocultural aspect* refers to how the parents' and child's ethnic background and cultural practices affect their reactions to the information they receive and their willingness to follow the treatment recommendations.

The parents and child need time to express their reactions to the information they receive. They may feel threatened by the results, have doubts about the accuracy of the results, or experience feelings such as anger, embarrassment, disappointment, or even relief and satisfaction. You will need to cope with their reactions.

When preparing to discuss your findings, experiment with terms that you feel comfortable with and that can be easily understood by children and parents. When presenting the findings, ask the family members if they understand what you have said and whether they would like to discuss any matters more fully. Questions such as "Is that clear?" or "Would you like me to go over that again?" or "Do you have any other questions?" are helpful.

Following are examples of ways to discuss technical concepts with older children and parents and other interested individuals involved in the case.

- *Statistical significance:* "Test scores can never be perfectly accurate. A statistically significant difference between scores is one that is large enough that it likely didn't occur by chance. Thus, there is probably a true difference between the abilities being measured."
- *Basal and ceiling levels:* "Most tests go from easy to difficult items. In addition, depending on the examinee's [student's] age, some tests have different beginning points. Some tests also have different ending points depending on how many items are passed and failed. These procedures help make the testing go more smoothly."
- *Percentile ranks:* "Percentile ranks tell the percent of children whom we would expect to score as high as this student. The 55th percentile rank means this student scored equal to or higher than 55% of children his age on this test."

As in the initial interview, in the post-assessment interview you will want to (a) actively listen to the child and parents; (b) be aware of their nonverbal behavior (e.g., shaking the head, scowling, frowning, sighing, whistling, raising eyebrows, or crying); (c) treat both the child and the parents with respect and dignity; (d) recognize family values, customs, beliefs, and cultural practices; (e) communicate openly and honestly with the child and parents; (f) build on their strengths; and (g) acknowledge and address their concerns and needs.

To older children and parents, be prepared to offer such comments as the following:

- "This is hard for you to hear."
- "It must be good to hear that the problems were not as bad as you expected."
- "This is a lot of information to understand, and it may be confusing for you."
- "Do you want to get another opinion?"
- "You may be thinking, 'Where do we go from here?'"
- "What would you like to do now?"
- "What do you think about what I've told you?"
- "Is that clear?"
- "Would you like me to go over that again?"
- "Are the results similar to what you expected?" (If not) "In what way are they different?"
- (If the child has been examined before) "How do these findings compare with what you've heard before?"
- "What do you think you should do, based on what I've just told you?"

In addition, to parents, you might say:

- "It's difficult to learn that your child is having these problems."
- "Perhaps you're wondering what can be done to help your child."

Keep the post-assessment interview to about 1 or 1½ hours in length. Longer sessions may tax the abilities of the child or parents to comprehend and integrate the information. If needed, schedule a second session. For example, you might discuss the results in one session and the intervention plan in a second session.

Confidentiality. A potentially troubling issue in the post-assessment interview with parents is the confidentiality of the information obtained from the child. Specifically, what role do children have in limiting the information their parents receive? Unfortunately, there are no clear legal guidelines about the extent to which information received from children is confidential; the courts and legislatures continue to define the rights of children and their parents. Although parents are responsible for their children, there is an increasing tendency toward protecting the rights of children to make their own decisions, especially when children can make competent ones (also see Chapter 3 in *Assessment of Children: Cognitive Applications*).

Release of information. It is preferable to request children's permission to release information to their parents, but you may not be legally required to do so. Obviously, you should consider the children's age and their ability to give the required permission. Any release of information must be in accordance with the laws of your state (also see Chapter 3 in *Assessment of Children: Cognitive Applications*).

Post-Assessment Interview with Children

Hold the post-assessment interview with the child as soon as possible after the evaluation has been completed—it may serve to allay his or her fears about the assessment. The assessment results are beneficial to children who can understand the information. Children need this information as much as anyone else because they make many important self-appraisals. For example, some children wrongly estimate their abilities, and a face-to-face conference may give them information they need for self-corrective or esteem-building purposes.

Post-Assessment Interview with Parents

In the post-assessment interview with the parents, your role is to (a) provide a thorough presentation of the child's learning or emotional problems (description, etiology, severity, and prognosis), (b) plan a specific program geared to the child's needs and capabilities, (c) recognize and deal with the personal problems of the parents as they affect the child or as they are affected by the child's condition, and (d) plan for future meetings as needed. Review the presenting problem, report and explain the assessment findings, and discuss the recommendations in a professional, caring, and thoughtful manner.

Four phases of the post-assessment interview with parents. Four phases characterize the post-assessment interview with parents: establishment of rapport, communication of results, discussion of recommendations, and termination.

FIRST PHASE: ESTABLISHING RAPPORT

(Note: You can do much to establish rapport before the interview even begins, as the first four recommendations attest.)

1. *Arrange to meet with the parents in a private setting, and avoid interruptions.*

2. *Allow enough time for the meeting.*

3. *Make every effort to have both parents at the interview.* This will help you obtain a more objective picture of their reactions and will enable them to share in the decisions that need to be made about their child. It will also relieve one parent of the burden of having to convey to the other parent the results of the evaluation.

4. *Find out whether the parents want to bring other people (such as a relative or an interpreter) to the meeting, and allow them to do so.*

5. *Greet the parents promptly, and provide your name.*

6. *Start the session by saying something positive about the child.*

7. *Show respect and appreciation.* Help the parents feel comfortable during the interview. Encourage them to talk and to ask questions freely. Recognize the frustration and hardship that have brought them to you and that they may still have to face in the future. Convey to them that they have something important to contribute to the discussion. Avoid making them feel defensive, avoid fault finding and accusations, and avoid pity and condescension. Point out how they have been helpful (e.g., bringing their child to the evaluation and participating themselves) and the positive qualities of the family and the child. Your respect for the parents and your appreciation of their problems will go a long way toward facilitating a successful post-assessment interview.

8. *Review what the parents have told you are their primary concerns, what they hope to learn from the evaluation, what they think are the causes of the problem, and what they think should be done about the problem.* If you have not seen the parents before the post-assessment interview, ask them to comment on each of these areas. Encourage the parents to take an active role in the interview.

9. *Never be afraid to say "I don't know."*

SECOND PHASE: COMMUNICATING THE ASSESSMENT RESULTS

1. *Summarize the assessment results and their implications as clearly as possible.* Be relaxed and unhurried in your presentation, and speak clearly, gently, and slowly. Explain your findings in a straightforward, detailed, and unambiguous manner.

2. *Focus the interview on the child.* Explain to the parents which of the child's problems are major and which are minor. Include information on the child's competencies in addition to limitations. Help the parents understand that children with psychological or medical disorders have the same needs as all children, along with some unique needs of their own. Stress the strengths and potentials of the child, keeping in mind, of course, the nature of the child's problems and the limitations associated with them. Parents especially need help so as not to be overwhelmed by their child's disorder. Inform the parents that your primary concern is the welfare and happiness of the child and that you want to work with them to achieve this goal. This focus might help reduce the personal frustration of the parents. If the parents discuss their personal problems, redirect the discussion to the child's

problems. It is not that the parents' problems are unimportant, but rather that your focus *now* should be on the child. You can refer them to another professional who can address their problems on another occasion.

3. *Be prepared, if the results suggest that the child has a serious problem, to deal with such parental reactions as anxiety, grief, disbelief, shock, denial, ambivalence, anger, disappointment, guilt, despair, and even relief.* Some parents may feel cheated because they did not produce a "perfect" child, and others may feel guilty or make self-deprecating remarks. Help the parents express their feelings, and acknowledge the feelings they express. You will need to be especially patient and understanding at these times. If the parents cry, tell them that it is okay and that many parents cry when they are given similar news.

4. *Raise the issue of etiology.* Parents are often concerned about the source of their child's problem, even if they do not ask about it. They may have misperceptions about what caused the child's problem and may feel guilty. Discussing the possible etiology gives you the opportunity to correct their misperceptions and relieve their guilt.

5. *Use the diagnostic findings to help the parents give up erroneous ideas and adopt a more realistic approach to the child's problems.* Give the parents copies of the reports, and discuss the assessment results. Some diagnoses are easier for parents to understand than others. A known genetic disorder such as phenylketonuria (PKU) that has predictable consequences may be easier to discuss than conditions that are not clear-cut, such as attention deficit/hyperactivity disorder (ADHD). Use labels cautiously whenever there is any doubt about the diagnosis. Help the parents understand that the problems are only one aspect of their child's life, that they need to deal with difficulties rather than avoid them, that they must set realistic expectations for their child, and that they have to shift their focus from searching for the cause of the problems to determining what they can do for the child. Encourage the parents to view their child as a unique individual with rights and potentials.

6. *Evaluate how the parents understand the results throughout this second phase.* Occasionally, you may have difficulty helping the parents understand the assessment findings and recommendations. This may happen, for example, because parents have feelings of guilt that interfere with their ability to accept the information, are embarrassed to admit that they do not understand the information, or are frustrated at not being able to solve the problem themselves and resent your interference. A calm, encouraging, and supporting manner should help parents to accept the results and recommendations more easily. Some parents may consider it impolite to interrupt you, to ask you questions, or to reveal that they did not understand what you said. You cannot be sure from their manner that they understood you. You should check the parents' understanding of their child's disorder by saying something like "Please tell me in your own words what you understand about your child's condition." Use follow-up comments as needed.

Parents who held erroneous beliefs about their child's condition before the interview will probably not change them after one interview. These beliefs may be protecting them from unpleasant consequences. Therefore, you may need several interviews with the parents. You also may want to visit their home in such cases.

7. *Be aware of your attitude toward the parents and the child.* You do not want to show pity or condescension. Instead, you want to be empathic and respectful and show an appreciation of the parents' and child's problems. Do not hide your feelings, because the parents will value them as indications of your concern and your humanity. Keep in mind that your reactions should be professional. For example, weeping uncontrollably would be inappropriate.

8. *Be aware of potential pitfalls in discussing the results.* You do not want to be hurried, lecture, get sidetracked by tangential issues, offer premature interpretations of the child's behavior or motivation, be vague and overgeneral, be definitive based on limited findings, ignore parents' views or become defensive when they challenge your views, criticize or blame the parents, show pity or sorrow, appear irritated at questions, or give too much or too little information.

THIRD PHASE: DISCUSSING THE RECOMMENDATIONS

1. *Try to let the parents formulate a plan of action.* Allow time for the parents to assimilate the findings. Help them plan how much information about the child to give to other individuals, such as siblings, grandparents, friends, and neighbors, and how to share this information with others. Do not try to bring about fundamental changes in the parents' child-rearing or educational philosophy. Instead, focus on the concrete issues at hand.

2. *Present your recommendations, and discuss possible alternative courses of action.* Develop the intervention plans with the parents, and ask for their opinions about any options. If you recommend additional diagnostic procedures, explain to the parents why the procedures are needed.

3. *If you recommend a treatment, be prepared to discuss possible treatment or remediation strategies, length of treatment, and costs.* Present possible intervention options, as needed. Give the parents all the options that could help their child. If appropriate, let them know that competent professionals are available to work with their child and with them. If the child needs special treatment, describe the benefits (and drawbacks, if any) of the treatment and how the treatment will contribute to the development of the child. Deal honestly and nondefensively with any concerns that the parents may have. If you (and the school team) recommend placement of their child in a special class, give the parents the opportunity to visit the class (or other facility) and to discuss the program with the teacher (or staff) before they make a placement decision.

4. *Encourage the parents to assume responsibility, not to be dependent.* Some parents may appear attentive, but in actuality not listen to what you have to say. They may fear the future and resist taking responsibility for addressing their child's problem. They may want to abdicate all their responsibility to you: "We're in your hands, doctor. Anything you say we'll do. You know best." They may attribute magic curative powers to you—as all-powerful and all-knowing. They may prefer that *you* deal with their child's problems. You

Reprinted with special permission of King Features Syndicate.

may feel flattered by their dependence on you, but this is not what they need. They need to assume responsibility and work through their dependency feelings.

5. *Give the parents the opportunity to ask questions about the recommendations.* Evaluate what the parents think and feel about the recommendations. Some parents simply want to hear that everything will work out well without their having to put forth any effort. Others fear that nothing will change and that the problems will continue. Help the parents see that you recognize their concerns, but be realistic.

6. *Carefully consider everything you know about the case before offering an opinion about prognosis, especially when dealing with young children.* Include appropriate precautions about the imprecision of any prognosis. You want to leave the parents with hope, even when their child is severely disabled; however, do not give them false expectations. Parents of a child with a disability need to know that their child will still grow and develop over time, albeit at a slower rate than would a child without disabilities. Focus on the most appropriate means to obtain short-term rehabilitation goals. This will give the parents direction and motivation.

7. *Inform the parents of their legal rights, and be sure they understand them.* Discuss their rights under applicable federal laws and relevant state and local policies (see Chapter 3 in *Assessment of Children: Cognitive Applications*).

8. *Recommend books, pamphlets, materials, and organizations that will help the parents and child.* Ask the parents if they are interested in reading about their child's disorder, illness, or condition. Also, ask them if they are interested in contacting local or national organizations to learn more about their child's problems or in joining a support group or an advocacy group. If they are, provide them with the necessary information.

FINAL PHASE: TERMINATING THE POST-ASSESSMENT INTERVIEW

1. *Evaluate the parents' understanding and feelings about the results and recommendations toward the end of the post-assessment interview.* You could say, for example, "We met today so that we could discuss the results of the evaluation. What is your understanding of the findings?… How do you feel about the recommendations?"

2. *Encourage the parents to ask any additional questions, especially if you believe that they still have some concerns about the results or recommendations.* They may ask about how to obtain a second opinion, who will have access to the

Copyright © 1998 by John P. Wood. Reprinted with permission.

assessment results, how long treatment may take, what role they will have in the intervention plan, what community resources are available, and the cost of treatment. Answer their questions to the best of your ability, and direct them to other sources of information if necessary.

3. *Inform the parents that you are available for later meetings.* Make it easy for them to arrange subsequent meetings. You want to have an open-door policy. Encourage them to contact you or other professionals any time they have questions—even weeks, months, or years after the initial diagnosis has been made.

4. *Convey to the parents your understanding of their difficulty, especially if they are unable to accept the results of the evaluation.* Describe referral services. Should they want other opinions, provide them with the names of other agencies or professionals.

5. *Find out what the parents want to do immediately after the interview is over.* Ask the parents what they would like to do, such as sit in the waiting room for a while, talk to another professional if one is available, or go home.

6. *Close the interview by giving the parents your business telephone number (if they don't already have it) and by inviting them to call you if they have further questions.* Again, you might want to compliment the parents on their participation in the assessment and encourage them to follow the recommendations. Escort the parents from the room, thank them for their cooperation, and say goodbye.

Evaluation of the post-assessment interview with parents. Questions to consider in the post-assessment interview with parents include the following:

1. How much information did the parents hear and absorb?

2. Did the parents understand the results?
3. Did they accept the results?
4. Did they understand the recommendations?
5. Did they accept the recommendations?
6. What areas of the evaluation and recommendations did they question, if any?
7. What type of interventions did they want?
8. Did they understand their rights under relevant federal and state laws and local policies?
9. Did they want a second evaluation of their child from an independent source?
10. What would they consider indications of successful treatment or remediation?
11. How willing are they to change their own expectations and behavior?
12. Are they willing to involve themselves in parent-training programs or in other skill programs?
13. What are their resources for making changes and for cooperating with the recommendations?
14. What resources do the parents have to hospitalize or institutionalize their child if it should become necessary?

When handled poorly, the initial diagnostic phase will remain as a bitter memory whose details linger in the minds of the parent for many years thereafter. When handled with sensitivity and technical skill, this experience can contribute to a strong foundation for productive family adaptation and for constructive parent-professional collaboration.

—Michael Thomasgard and Jack P. Shonkoff

Post-assessment interview with parents as a staff conference. In some settings—such as schools, mental health clinics, and hospitals—several professionals may evaluate the child and the family. In such settings, a staff conference may be helpful when each member of the team can make a unique contribution to the presentation or when it is important for the parents or child to hear the views of each professional. When the post-assessment interview with parents is in the form of a staff conference, the following guidelines complement those presented previously (Greenbaum, 1982):

1. *Prepare for the conference carefully.* The team leader (sometimes called the case manager) should review all case history information, medical reports, test results, and recommendations.

2. *Set specific goals for the conference.* Before the conference, team members should reach a unified position and the team leader should prepare a list of goals.

3. *Be organized.* The team leader should begin and end the conference on time, follow the agenda, and allow enough time to cover the agenda. Team members should introduce themselves. If each member presents his or her findings, the presentations should be organized and orderly.

4. *Individualize the conference.* Team members should focus on material relevant to the concerns of the child and family.

5. *Appear confident.* Team members should choose their words carefully and maintain their composure.

6. *Don't be defensive.* Team members should recognize that they do not have all the answers. They should not become involved in power struggles with the parents or with each other.

7. *Form an alliance with the parents.* Team members should see the parents as part of the team, help the parents to see themselves as part of the team, and encourage the parents to work with the team in carrying out the recommendations. Parents should be encouraged to address questions to any team member.

8. *Explore the needs of the parents.* Team members need to understand the feelings and reactions of the parents and switch from the agenda, if necessary, to help the parents work through their special concerns.

9. *Tell it like it is.* Team members should be direct and honest and avoid technical jargon. They should discuss public laws and state and local policies that pertain to the child and family (see Chapter 3 in *Assessment of Children: Cognitive Applications*).

10. *Explain the recommended interventions.* The team leader or another team member should explain the interventions. Parents should not be pressured to follow a plan they believe is inappropriate for their child.

11. *Make a closing statement.* The team leader should summarize the findings and decisions, arrange for future appointments, and tell the parents how they can reach each member of the team.

Holding a staff conference may not be the best way to conduct a post-assessment interview. Sitting at one end of a table watching six or seven professionals give reports is an intimidating experience for many parents. Other alternatives are to have a designated case manager who meets with the parents and summarizes the findings and recommendations of the staff and to have each professional meet individually with the parents.

Overview of the post-assessment interview with parents. The way in which each post-assessment interview unfolds will depend on the needs of the parents and on your orientation. *Always show warmth, understanding, and respect.* Children and parents are appreciative when they see that you are listening to them and understand their concerns. Help parents become less defensive by telling them that you appreciate the effort they are making to help their child. The crucial test of the effectiveness of the post-assessment interview is whether the parents act on what they have learned.

In working with families of children with special needs, recognize that the family has considerable influence on the ability of the child to deal with the problems and to profit from an intervention program. Help the family members understand how the child can cope with the problems so that they can cooperate in the intervention efforts and support the child at home.

Parents' reactions to the assessment will depend on the entire process—from the beginning of the initial interview to the end of the post-assessment interview. Parents are likely to resent professionals who fail to include them in the decision-making process, view them as objects, talk down to them, or fail to consider their needs (Boyer & Chesteen, 1992). Conversely, parents are likely to appreciate professionals who answer their questions honestly, give understandable explanations, respect their self-determination, solicit their participation, give them support, offer understandable and realistic recommendations, provide information about the best possible care, and are knowledgeable about community resources.

The post-assessment interview with parents requires sensitivity and understanding of their feelings, needs, and desires. It is not a matter of simply reciting results or reading a report. Rather, you should make every effort to enlist the parents' cooperation in working toward an effective intervention plan. You want to establish a collaborative partnership with the parents so that together you can come to a better understanding of the needs of the child and work toward solving the problems.

The post-assessment interview is an important part of the assessment procedure. It can be particularly rewarding because it allows you to present the results in a purposeful way. It also can be frustrating and even heartbreaking. Understanding your attitudes toward children with special needs is important in working with them and with their parents. By following the guidelines presented in this chapter, you can alleviate some of your anxieties about communicating the assessment results to parents and children.

Thank you for letting me know by your voice and your expression that you cared when you told me the diagnosis.
—Anonymous

THE FOLLOW-UP INTERVIEW

The three interview chapters in this section are focused primarily on the initial clinical assessment interview and the post-assessment interview, but much of the material that you have read regarding the post-assessment interview also applies to the follow-up interview. The follow-up interview is designed to obtain information about how the child and family are functioning and to evaluate the intervention efforts, where applicable. For example, follow-up interviews with parents may focus on the following areas (Krehbiel & Kroth, 1991):

• Changes in the child's functioning
• The child's performance at home
• The child's progress in school (where appropriate)
• The parents' concerns about whether they are doing the right thing for their child or are expecting too much or too little
• The family's adjustment to the child's problem
• The parents' efforts toward providing the child with normal experiences
• The family's needs that are not being met
• The family's stress level
• The family's social, emotional, and community supports
• The parents' attitudes toward professionals who are working with the child

PARENT-
TEACHER
CONFERENCES

Dave Carpenter.

" I SAID, 'YOUR SON DOESN'T SEEM TO LISTEN
VERY WELL."

Courtesy of Dave Carpenter.

• The parents' satisfaction with the intervention program(s)
• The family's plans for the future

During follow-up interviews, you may need to work on some of the following issues (Rollin, 1987):

1. Help the parents and other family members discover any areas of conflict that may interfere with healthy family functioning.
2. Help the parents and other family members understand the effects of the child's disability as a family issue and not as an issue that belongs to only one or two family members.
3. Encourage the parents and other family members to help the child with a disability use whatever rehabilitation services and assistive devices have been recommended.
4. Help each parent and family member understand her or his unique role within the family and how each can assist the child with a disability.
5. Help the parents and other family members make future plans for the child with a disability.
6. Recognize that the parents and other family members may have different attitudes about the recommended interventions and assistive devices; help them work through their differences.

When the parents show that they are taking adequate care of their child, you should acknowledge their progress. Such comments reinforce the parents' efforts in raising a child with special needs. Some examples follow (Krehbiel & Kroth, 1991, adapted from p. 118):

• "You've come a long way in learning medical terminology."
• "You have discovered the basis of Paul's refusal to maintain his diet. Tell me how you did that."
• "So things are still frustrating and difficult, but you now have the routine under control."
• "Sometimes new parents I see like to talk with other parents. Would you like to talk with some?"

RELIABILITY AND VALIDITY OF THE INTERVIEW

Obtaining reliable and valid information from the interviewee is critical in clinical assessment interviewing. Therefore, you must evaluate the interview—as you would any other assessment technique—for reliability and validity. Following are several types of reliability related to the interview (Mash & Terdal, 1981, adapted from p. 46):

• *Test-retest reliability*—the degree to which the information obtained from the interviewee on one occasion is comparable to the information that was or would have been obtained from the same interviewee on other occasions
• *Interinterviewee agreement*—the degree to which the information obtained from one interviewee agrees with the information obtained from another interviewee

Courtesy of Herman Zilinski.

- *Internal consistency*—the degree to which the information given by an interviewee is consistent with other information given by the interviewee in the same interview
- *Interinterviewer reliability, or method error*—the degree to which the information obtained by one interviewer is consistent with that obtained by another interviewer from the same interviewee

The two major types of validity related to the interview are concurrent and predictive validity (Mash & Terdal, 1981, p. 47, with changes in notation):

- *Concurrent validity*—the degree to which the information obtained in the interview corresponds to the information obtained through other methods
- *Predictive validity*—the degree to which information obtained in the interview predicts the treatment outcome

You are likely to find that children and parents differ in their reports and that younger children differ from older children in the reliability of their reports. Here are some findings.

1. Children and parents agree *least* often about covert and private symptoms such as anxiety, fear, and obsessions; they agree more often about overt, easily observable behaviors such as behavior problems and conduct problems (Edelbrock, Costello, Dulcan, Conover, & Kalas, 1986; Thompson, Merritt, Keith, Murphy, & Johndrow, 1993).
2. Agreement between children and parents is moderate for depressive symptoms (Klein, 1991).

3. Generally, parents are more reliable than children in reporting children's symptoms (Klein, 1991).
4. Adolescents are more reliable than younger school-aged children in reporting symptoms (Edelbrock, Costello, Dulcan, Kalas, & Conover, 1985; Schwab-Stone, Fallon, Briggs, & Crowther, 1994; Schwab-Stone, Fisher, Piacentini, Shaffer, Davies, & Briggs, 1993). Younger school-aged children have particular difficulties with questions about duration and onset of symptoms, but not with questions about fears.

Reports of symptoms by young children should be confirmed by other sources. Reports by adolescents are more reliable because their improved cognitive, memory, and language skills enable them to respond more accurately to questions that require self-awareness, perspective taking, recall, reasoning ability, and expressive skill. But even adolescents' reports may show poor agreement with parents' reports (Klein, 1991). *Whenever you get conflicting information, you need to inquire further.*

You may have difficulty determining the overall reliability and validity of an interview because interviews yield several types of information, including demographic, developmental, observational, and diagnostic data (Bellack & Hersen, 1980). Ideally, you should have independent estimates of the reliability and validity of each type of information. In addition, interviews are highly dependent on specific interviewer and interviewee characteristics, type of interview, and the conditions under which the interview takes place. These factors interact—not only among themselves, but also with the different types of information—to affect the reliability and validity of the information obtained. Despite these complexities, you need to evaluate the reliability and validity of information obtained in the interview as you would information obtained from other types of assessments. Chapter 4 in *Assessment of Children: Cognitive Assessment* discusses other aspects of reliability and validity that pertain to the interview.

Courtesy of Brendan Mulcahy.

EVALUATING YOUR INTERVIEW TECHNIQUES

This section has presented guidelines to help you become a successful clinical assessment interviewer. However, you should not follow the guidelines rigidly or expect them to cover every possible contingency. Human relationships are unique, and a "cookbook" of techniques is neither possible nor desirable. You must be the judge of how, when, and where to use a particular procedure.

You should carefully evaluate your interview techniques, particularly when you are first learning to interview or when you have not conducted an interview for some time. One way is simply to think about the interview and then evaluate your performance in the interview shortly after its completion. Or, you can record some interviews that you conduct on either audiotape or videotape (with proper consent) and then study the recordings. Both audiotapes and videotapes give you the opportunity to study your interview techniques and your diction, speech intensity, and other voice and speech characteristics. Videotapes, in addition, allow you to evaluate your eye contact, posture, gestures, and other nonverbal behaviors. If possible, review your tape recordings with a classmate or, better yet, with someone who has expertise in interviewing.

Questions to Consider in Your Self-Evaluation

You can evaluate your interview techniques by answering the questions in Table 3-1 and then rating the competencies shown in Table 3-2. During your training, you should answer the questions and complete the ratings after each interview. Table 3-2 also can be used by your supervisor to rate your interview techniques.

As you review your answers to the questions in Table 3-1 and Table 3-2, what themes emerge? What are the strengths and weaknesses of your interviewing style? What can you do to improve your interview techniques? After you conducted several interviews, did any pattern emerge in your interviewing style? Did you improve your skills in subsequent interviews?

If you have a rating of 4 or 5 ("poor demonstration of this skill" or "very poor demonstration of this skill") on any of the items in Table 3-2, determine why, when, and where the difficulty occurred and what you can do to improve your interview techniques. For example, if you daydreamed, try to determine why. During what part of the interview did the daydreaming occur? What content was being covered? Did you have other problems with similar content? Was the content of your daydream related to the communications of the interviewee in some way? Or if you conveyed to the interviewee such personal needs as wanting respect from her or him or wanting to be liked, determine whether these messages interfered with the relationship. The interviewee may have felt guilty if she or he did not satisfy your needs. Think about why it was necessary

for you to have these needs fulfilled in a professional relationship. Evaluate thoroughly every problem you find with your interview techniques. With colleagues, friends, and family, practice situations involving these problem areas.

Obtaining Feedback from the Interviewee

During your training (and even periodically during your career), you may want to obtain feedback from interviewees about your performance. If you decide to do so, you can use the checklist shown in Table 3-3. It contains 18 yes-no questions and space for additional comments.

Recognizing the Interviewee's Limitations

If you were unsuccessful in obtaining information from the interviewee, do not be too hard on yourself. There are children and parents who simply will not cooperate or will not disclose information for various reasons. Children with an autistic disorder, those with a severe conduct disorder, or those who are severely developmentally disabled, for example, may be uncooperative or unable to provide the desired information. Parents who have been coerced to come to the interview also may be uncooperative. In such cases, note their behavior and schedule another appointment. Your failure to obtain information may be related more to the problems of the interviewee than to your clinical skills. As your clinical skills improve, however, you may become more successful in interviewing challenging children and parents or children and parents who are in difficult situations.

THINKING THROUGH THE ISSUES

1. If you see that you are running out of time in the interview, what is the best strategy to follow? Explain your reasoning.
2. Under what conditions would you want to see the interviewee for a second interview?
3. What problems do you foresee in bringing an interview to an end?
4. What are the problems involved in explaining the results of clinical evaluations to children, parents, and others?
5. What steps could you take to handle informing children and parents about diagnoses that imply serious pathology?
6. In the post-assessment interview, how would your approach with children differ from your approach with parents?
7. What problems do you think you might have in explaining to children and parents the assessment results obtained by other professionals?
8. What could you do to improve the reliability and validity of the interview?
9. Do you think that you will be successful in interviewing all types of clients? If not, what can you do to improve your ability to interview clients from different age, cultural, and linguistic groups and with different types of temperaments and psychological disorders?

**Table 3-1
Evaluating Your Performance in the Interview**

Background Influences
1. What assumptions did you make as an interviewer?
2. Were any of your assumptions based on stereotypes?
3. Were your understanding and interpretations of what you saw, heard, and said biased? If so, in what way?

Factors Evident During the Interview
4. How did environmental conditions—such as degree of privacy and comfort, placement of furniture, noise level, and temperature—affect the interview?
5. Did you subtly influence the interviewee to give certain responses? If so, what did you do, and were you aware that you were doing it?
6. How were you affected by the interviewee's appearance, voice, audibility, articulation, projection of interest, rate of speech, pauses, facial expressions, and other characteristics?
7. Were you able to suspend judgment about the interviewee?
8. As the interview progressed, what thoughts did you have about your role and about how the interview developed?
9. What did the interviewee say or do that led you to form opinions of him or her?
10. What type of questions did you rely on (e.g., open-ended or closed-ended)?
11. Did you probe and follow up leads?
12. How did you begin the interview?
13. How did you end the interview?
14. How do you feel about the interviewee?
15. Were you aware of your verbal behavior? If so, what was it like?
16. Were you aware of your nonverbal behavior? If so, what was it like?
17. Did your nonverbal behavior change as the interview progressed? If so, in what way did it change?
18. What role did your appearance, eye contact, and facial expressions play in the interview?
19. How do you think the interviewee reacted to your appearance, voice, audibility, articulation, projection of interest, rate of speech, pauses, facial expressions, and other characteristics?
20. To what degree did your verbal and nonverbal behavior match?
21. Did your verbal behavior change as the interview progressed? If so, in what way did it change?
22. Were you distracted? If so, (a) what distracted you from listening more carefully, (b) what did you do to reduce the distractions and become a more effective listener, and (c) what can you do to prevent these distractions from occurring in interviews in the future?
23. Did you daydream, let your mind wander, or tune out the interviewee? If so, when during the interview did this happen, how often, and why do you think it happened?
24. How well did you understand the interviewee's verbal communications?
25. Were you aware of the interviewee's nonverbal behavior?
26. Were you aware of any changes in the interviewee's verbal and nonverbal behavior?
27. Were you a good listener?
28. How effectively were you able to listen to the interviewee when he or she presented a viewpoint that differed from your own?

29. How effective were you in spotting the major themes in the interviewee's communications?
30. How effective were you in noticing discrepancies between the interviewee's verbal and nonverbal communications?
31. How did you deal with any difficulties—for example, an interviewee who appeared to be exaggerating, who contradicted himself or herself, who misinterpreted situations, who held things back, or who felt extremely emotional?
32. How did you feel during silences?
33. How did you handle silences?
34. What communication problems developed in the interview?
35. Were any of the communication problems associated with you and the interviewee's assigning different meanings to the same words?
36. What role did "technical talk" or jargon play in communication difficulties?
37. How did you react to questions about you posed by the interviewee?
38. If there were any personal rebuffs, how did you handle them?
39. To what extent were you aware of your feelings about what was going on during the interview, including feelings about the interviewee and feelings about yourself?
40. Was there any material discussed by the interviewee that made you anxious or uncomfortable? If so, what was the material, and why did it make you anxious or uncomfortable?
41. What risks were involved in saying some of the things you said?
42. What did you achieve by saying some of the things you said?
43. What role did power and status play in the interview?
44. Did you have trouble formulating questions? If so, why and was it obvious to the interviewee?
45. How did you want the interviewee to perceive you?

Evaluation of the Interview
46. What did you learn about the interviewee?
47. How motivated to talk with you did the interviewee appear to be?
48. How easily was the interviewee able to recall information?
49. How accurate do you believe the interviewee was in recalling experiences?
50. How did the interviewee react to your questions?
51. How do you think the interviewee perceived you (e.g., trusting, accessible, understandable, competent, cold, distant, aloof, marginally competent)?
52. Do you think that the interviewee saw you as an effective interviewer?
53. Did you have clearly formulated goals and purposes upon beginning the interview?
54. Did you keep these goals and purposes in mind during the interview?
55. Did you accomplish your interview goals?
56. What did you learn about your interviewing techniques?
57. Which techniques were most successful?
58. How could you have been a more effective interviewer?
59. What would you do differently?
60. How satisfied were you with your overall performance in the interview?

Table 3-2
Interview Techniques Checklist

INTERVIEW TECHNIQUES CHECKLIST

Name of interviewer: _____   Date of interview: _____

Name of interviewee: _____   Rater's name: _____

Rating key:

1	2	3	4	5	NA
Very poor demonstration of this skill	Poor demonstration of this skill	Adequate demonstration of this skill	Good demonstration of this skill	Excellent demonstration of this skill	Not applicable

Skill		Rating				
1. Made a smooth transition from opening greeting to next topic	1	2	3	4	5	NA
2. Created a positive interview climate	1	2	3	4	5	NA
3. Showed respect for interviewee	1	2	3	4	5	NA
4. Gave undivided attention to interviewee	1	2	3	4	5	NA
5. Established an environment free from distractions	1	2	3	4	5	NA
6. Used good diction	1	2	3	4	5	NA
7. Spoke in a clear, audible voice with warmth	1	2	3	4	5	NA
8. Spoke in a modulated voice that reflected nuances of feeling	1	2	3	4	5	NA
9. Spoke at a moderate tempo	1	2	3	4	5	NA
10. Used appropriate vocabulary	1	2	3	4	5	NA
11. Formulated general questions	1	2	3	4	5	NA
12. Formulated open-ended questions	1	2	3	4	5	NA
13. Formulated follow-up questions to pursue issues	1	2	3	4	5	NA
14. Used nonleading questions	1	2	3	4	5	NA
15. Used relatively few yes-no questions	1	2	3	4	5	NA
16. Used few, if any, multiple-choice questions	1	2	3	4	5	NA
17. Used structuring statements	1	2	3	4	5	NA
18. Encouraged replies	1	2	3	4	5	NA
19. Used probes effectively	1	2	3	4	5	NA
20. Allowed interviewee to express feelings and thoughts in her or his own way	1	2	3	4	5	NA
21. Followed up leads	1	2	3	4	5	NA
22. Was attentive to interviewee's nonverbal behavior	1	2	3	4	5	NA
23. Conveyed to interviewee a desire to understand her or him	1	2	3	4	5	NA
24. Conveyed to interviewee an interest in obtaining relevant facts, not in confirming pre-existing hypotheses	1	2	3	4	5	NA
25. Rephrased questions	1	2	3	4	5	NA
26. Used reflection	1	2	3	4	5	NA
27. Used feedback	1	2	3	4	5	NA
28. Handled a minimally communicative interviewee	1	2	3	4	5	NA
29. Handled interviewee's resistance and anxiety	1	2	3	4	5	NA
30. Showed sensitivity to interviewee's emotional state	1	2	3	4	5	NA
31. Clarified areas of confusion in interviewee's statements	1	2	3	4	5	NA
32. Intervened when interviewee had difficulty expressing thoughts	1	2	3	4	5	NA
33. Handled rambling communications	1	2	3	4	5	NA
34. Dealt with difficult behavior	1	2	3	4	5	NA
35. Used props, crayons, clay, or toys	1	2	3	4	5	NA

(Continued)

Table 3-2 *(Continued)*

Skill	Rating					
36. Timed questions	1	2	3	4	5	NA
37. Handled silences	1	2	3	4	5	NA
38. Used periodic summaries	1	2	3	4	5	NA
39. Asked questions about all relevant areas without avoiding potentially stressful ones	1	2	3	4	5	NA
40. Provided appropriate support to interviewee to minimize effects of discussing stressful topics	1	2	3	4	5	NA
41. Made clear transitions	1	2	3	4	5	NA
42. Paced the interview	1	2	3	4	5	NA
43. Self-disclosed only when necessary	1	2	3	4	5	NA
44. Evidenced appropriate sensitivity to issues related to interviewee's cultural identity	1	2	3	4	5	NA
45. Established and maintained eye contact	1	2	3	4	5	NA
46. Maintained facial expressions relevant to content	1	2	3	4	5	NA
47. Used nonverbal behavior to further the interview	1	2	3	4	5	NA
48. Demonstrated consistency between nonverbal and verbal behavior	1	2	3	4	5	NA
49. Responded in nonjudgmental manner (without moralizing, advising prematurely, persuading, criticizing, or labeling)	1	2	3	4	5	NA
50. Resisted distractions	1	2	3	4	5	NA
51. Avoided overreacting	1	2	3	4	5	NA
52. Avoided arguments	1	2	3	4	5	NA
53. Handled interviewee's questions and concerns	1	2	3	4	5	NA
54. Allowed interviewee to express remaining thoughts and questions at close of interview	1	2	3	4	5	NA
55. Arranged for post-assessment interview	1	2	3	4	5	NA
56. Used summary statements as needed	1	2	3	4	5	NA
57. Used closing statements	1	2	3	4	5	NA

Comments: _____
_____
_____
_____

SUMMARY

Closing the Initial Interview

1. The final moments of the interview are as important as any other period in the interview; they give you a chance to summarize and evaluate what you have learned.
2. Do not rush the ending of the interview.
3. The method you use to close the interview is especially important when the interviewee is expressing some deeply felt emotion.
4. What you say at the conclusion of the initial interview will depend on whether you plan to see the interviewee again.
5. Be aware of how much time has passed, what important areas you need to discuss, and how much time the interviewee may need to discuss any remaining concerns.
6. Use the last minutes of the initial interview to summarize and evaluate what you have learned and to give the interviewee an opportunity to ask any remaining questions that he or she might have.
7. Be prepared to deal with the interviewee's concerns.
8. A summary statement should identify the main points of the problem for the interviewee's confirmation or correction.
9. It may be helpful, especially with children, to acknowledge their openness and willingness to share their problems, concerns, hopes, and expectations.

10. When the interviewee has been uncooperative and you need to schedule another appointment, you might want to express your concern about how the interview went.

The Post-Assessment Interview

11. The post-assessment interview (also called the interpretive interview) with children and parents serves several purposes, such as presenting the findings, presenting possible interventions, helping children and parents understand the findings and interventions, allowing children and parents to express their concerns, and exploring any additional areas of concern.
12. When you plan the post-assessment interview, consider the information you want to discuss with the child and the parents, how much detail you expect to give, and the order in which you want to present the information.
13. Recognize that if you are discussing with the parents and child the results from examinations performed by other professionals, you might not be able to answer all of their questions about these results.
14. Remember that, as clinical assessor, you will be making important decisions about children's lives.
15. You should never make a diagnosis, a recommendation concerning a child's treatment or placement, or a decision about

Table 3-3
Checklist for an Interviewee's Evaluation of an Interviewer

EVALUATING THE INTERVIEWER

Client's name: _____   Name of interviewer: _____

Date of interview: _____

Directions: Please rate the interviewer on each item. Use the following rating scale:

Y = Yes
N = No
? = Not sure

For each item, circle the choice that best describes your rating. Be sure to respond to each item. Thank you!

Item	Rating			Item	Rating		
1. The interviewer saw me at approximately the scheduled time.	Y	N	?	10. The interviewer asked about my feelings and responded appropriately to them.	Y	N	?
2. The interviewer put me at ease during the interview.	Y	N	?	11. I was able to talk about problems and issues that were important to me.	Y	N	?
3. The interviewer greeted me in a way that made me feel comfortable.	Y	N	?	12. The topics covered by the interviewer were appropriate.	Y	N	?
4. The interviewer appeared interested in me.	Y	N	?	13. The interviewer seemed organized during the interview.	Y	N	?
5. The interviewer appeared to be confident.	Y	N	?	14. The interviewer was thorough in asking me relevant questions.	Y	N	?
6. The interviewer spoke clearly and was easily understood.	Y	N	?	15. The interviewer summarized the problems as he or she saw them.	Y	N	?
7. The interviewer asked questions in a way that allowed me time to think about my answer.	Y	N	?	16. The time spent with the interviewer was adequate for my needs.	Y	N	?
8. The interviewer asked relevant questions about my personal and social life.	Y	N	?	17. I felt nervous during the interview.	Y	N	?
9. The interviewer seemed to understand me.	Y	N	?	18. Overall, I felt satisfied with the interview.	Y	N	?

Any other comments are welcome.

_____

_____

_____

Source: Adapted from Brockway (1978).

whether an alleged event took place unless you are fully qualified to do so.

16. We can look at the post-assessment interview with the child and parents as having five aspects—cognitive, interactive, affective, ethicoreligious, and ethnocultural.

17. You will need to cope with the reactions of children and parents to the information they receive.

18. When preparing to discuss your findings, experiment with terms that you feel comfortable with and that can be easily understood by children and parents.

19. As in the initial interview, in the post-assessment interview you will want to actively listen to the child and parents; be aware of their nonverbal behavior; treat both the child and the parents with respect and dignity; recognize family values, customs, be-

liefs, and cultural practices; communicate openly and honestly with the child and parents; build on their strengths; and acknowledge and address their concerns and needs.

20. Keep the post-assessment interview to about 1 or 1½ hours in length.

21. Although parents are responsible for their children, there is an increasing tendency toward protecting the rights of children to make their own decisions, especially when children can make competent ones.

22. Any release of information must be in accordance with the laws of your state.

23. Hold the post-assessment interview with the child as soon as possible after the evaluation has been completed—it may serve to allay his or her fears about the assessment.

24. In the post-assessment interview with the parents, your role is to provide a thorough presentation of the child's learning or emotional problems (description, etiology, severity, and prognosis), plan a specific program geared to the child's needs and capabilities, recognize and deal with the personal problems of the parents as they affect the child or as they are affected by the child's condition, and plan for future meetings as needed.

25. Four phases characterize the post-assessment interview with parents: establishment of rapport, communication of results, discussion of recommendations, and termination.

26. It is important to evaluate how the post-assessment interview with the parents went.

27. The post-assessment interview with parents may be held as a staff conference.

28. The way in which each post-assessment interview unfolds will depend on the needs of the parents and on your orientation. Always show warmth, understanding, and respect.

29. In working with families of children with special needs, recognize that the family has considerable influence on the ability of the child to deal with the problems and to profit from an intervention program.

30. Parents' reactions to the assessment will depend on the entire process—from the beginning of the initial interview to the end of the post-assessment interview.

31. The post-assessment interview with parents requires sensitivity and understanding of their feelings, needs, and desires.

32. The post-assessment interview represents an important part of the assessment procedure.

Follow-Up Interview

33. The follow-up interview is designed to obtain information about how the child and family are functioning and to evaluate the intervention efforts, where applicable.

34. When the parents show that they are taking adequate care of their child, you should acknowledge their progress. Such comments reinforce the parents' efforts in raising a child with special needs.

Reliability and Validity of the Interview

35. You must evaluate the interview—as you would any other assessment technique—for reliability and validity.

36. Types of reliability related to the interview are test-retest reliability, interinterviewee agreement, internal consistency, and interinterviewer reliability.

37. Types of validity related to the interview are concurrent and predictive validity.

38. Children and parents are likely to differ in their reports.

39. Adolescents are more reliable than younger school-aged children in reporting symptoms.

40. Reports of symptoms by young children should be confirmed by other sources.

41. You may have difficulty determining the overall reliability and validity of an interview because interviews yield several types of information, including demographic, developmental, observational, and diagnostic data.

Evaluating Your Interview Techniques

42. Do not follow the guidelines presented in the interview section rigidly or expect them to cover every possible contingency.

43. Human relationships are unique, and a "cookbook" of techniques is neither possible nor desirable.

44. You must be the judge of how, when, and where to use a particular procedure.

45. You should carefully evaluate your interview techniques, particularly when you are first learning to interview or when you have not conducted an interview for some time.

46. During your training (and even periodically during your career), you may want to obtain feedback from interviewees about your performance.

47. If you were unsuccessful in obtaining information from the interviewee, do not be too hard on yourself. There are children and parents who simply will not cooperate or who will not disclose information for various reasons.

48. As your clinical skills improve, you may become more successful in interviewing challenging children and parents or children and parents who are in difficult situations.

KEY TERMS, CONCEPTS, AND NAMES

Closing the initial interview (p. 66)
Recognizing the interviewee's concerns (p. 66)
Summary statement (p. 67)
Post-assessment interview (interpretive interview) (p. 67)
Cognitive aspect of the post-assessment interview (p. 68)
Interactive aspect of the post-assessment interview (p. 68)
Affective aspect of the post-assessment interview (p. 68)
Ethicoreligious aspect of the post-assessment interview (p. 68)
Ethnocultural aspect of the post-assessment interview (p. 68)
Confidentiality of information (p. 69)
Release of information (p. 69)
Four phases of the post-assessment interview with parents (p. 69)
Evaluation of the post-assessment interview with parents (p. 72)
Post-assessment interview with parents as a staff conference (p. 73)
Follow-up interview (p. 74)
Reliability and validity of the interview (p. 74)
Test-retest reliability (p. 74)
Interinterviewee agreement reliability (p. 74)
Internal consistency reliability (p. 75)
Interinterviewer reliability (p. 75)
Method error reliability (p. 75)
Concurrent validity (p. 75)
Predictive validity (p. 75)
Evaluating your interview techniques (p. 76)

STUDY QUESTIONS

1. Discuss the closing phase of the initial interview. What factors need to be considered at the close of the interview?

2. Discuss the post-assessment interview. Include in your discussion (a) the purposes of the post-assessment interview, (b) general guidelines, (c) the issue of confidentiality, (d) the post-assessment interview with children, and (e) the post-assessment interview with parents.

3. Discuss the four phases of the post-assessment interview with parents. In your discussion, focus on key points that should be attended to in each phase.

4. What are some important questions to consider in evaluating the post-assessment interview with parents?
5. Discuss the post-assessment interview as a staff conference.
6. Discuss the follow-up interview. Include in your discussion important areas to focus on and how you would acknowledge the progress of the child and parents (if appropriate).

7. What factors should you consider in evaluating your interview techniques?

4

ASSESSMENT OF BEHAVIOR BY OBSERVATIONAL METHODS: PART I

Observers, then, must be photographers of phenomena; their observations must accurately represent nature. We must observe without any preconceived idea; the observer's mind must be passive, that is, must hold its peace; it listens to nature and writes at nature's dictation.

—Claude Bernard

Goals and Objectives

This chapter is designed to enable you to do the following:

- Understand four major observational recording methods—narrative, event, interval, and ratings methods

- Compare and contrast these four observational recording methods

- Design an observational assessment

Observing the behavior of children in natural or specially designed settings contributes to the clinical and psychoeducational assessment. Observations add a personalized dimension to the assessment process, particularly when used in conjunction with objective tests, behavior checklists, questionnaires, interviews, personality inventories, projective tests, and other assessment procedures. Behavioral observations serve the following assessment functions:

1. They provide a picture of children's spontaneous behavior in everyday life settings, such as the classroom, playground, home, or hospital ward, or in specially designed settings, such as a clinic playroom.
2. They provide information about children's interpersonal behavior and learning style.
3. They provide a systematic record of children's behaviors and the behaviors of others, which can be used for evaluation, intervention planning, and monitoring changes associated with interventions.
4. They allow for verification of the accuracy of parental and teacher reports about children's behaviors.
5. They allow for comparisons between behavior in the test situation and behavior in naturalistic settings.
6. They provide information independent of children's ability or willingness to report information.
7. They provide information about young children and children with developmental disabilities who may not easily be evaluated with other procedures.
8. They permit functional behavioral assessment by providing a means of identifying the target behavior, documenting its antecedents and consequences, and evaluating the effects of interventions.

Observational systems are extremely versatile. They can be designed to quantify many different types of behaviors in almost any setting, and they can be uniquely tailored to the needs of an individual child. To be most useful, the systematic observation of behavior should have (a) a goal, (b) a focus, (c) a limit on the amount of data to be collected, and (d) a standardized recording method that has adequate reliability and validity.

The information you obtain from the observation of behavior will help you evaluate the concerns of the referral source, arrive at a diagnosis, provide feedback and suggestions for achieving behavioral change, and monitor the efficacy of interventions. Although observations give you valuable information about manifest (or observable) behavior, they do not tell you about the child's beliefs, perceptions, feelings, and attitudes about his or her past, present, or future behavior. To obtain this information, you will have to use interviews, self-report inventories, or perhaps projective instruments. Some of these techniques are covered in other chapters of this book (see Chapters 1, 2, and 6).

Let's look at an example of how behavioral observations can assist you in an assessment. Suppose a teacher has referred Bill to you because of his aggressive behavior in class. In addition to carrying out the psychometric assessment and interviews, you decide to visit the classroom a few times to observe Bill and the class. You observe that Bill's aggressive behavior occurs only after other children instigate some hostile act directed at him, such as taking away his pencil or kicking his chair. The psychometric and interview data allow you to rule out psychopathology, brain damage, and familial instability. With this information, you can help the teacher understand Bill's behavior. Perhaps simply moving Bill to a part of the room where the children are more supportive might help; or, you might suggest that Bill (or his peers) participate in a social skills training program.

USING OBSERVATIONAL METHODS

In the *systematic observation of behavior,* you observe a child's behavior in natural or specially designed settings, record or classify each behavior objectively as it occurs or shortly thereafter, ensure that the obtained data are reliable and valid, and convert the data into quantitative information. You may use behavioral observations to obtain global impressions, to rate and record various behaviors, or to focus on specific problematic behaviors (such as aggression, inattentiveness, or hyperactivity) that you identified earlier through general observations, interviews, checklists, or reports from others. Ideally, it would be useful to know how often the behaviors of interest naturally occur in the child's peer group and then compare the child's behavior with these norms.

Although the scientific principles on which we base systematic behavioral observation should ensure the highest possible degree of accuracy and precision, it is never possible to capture all of the behaviors exhibited by a child during the observation. Thus, you must make decisions about what behavior you want to observe and how you want to record it. The assumption behind the sampling of behavior is that the behaviors recorded over a period of time will constitute a representative sample of behavior.

To be a skilled observer, you need to be able to understand behavioral codes, distinguish one behavior from another, sustain attention, attend to detail, react quickly, compute rates of behavior, summarize behavior samples verbally, and recognize how your presence affects the child and others in the setting. *Sensitivity, acuity, and perceptiveness are keys to becoming a skilled observer.* An underlying assumption of all observational methods is that observers can identify important behaviors, note their occurrences, classify them, and judge their strength and degree of deviance. This and the following chapter cover the principles of behavioral observation and provide exercises to help you develop skills that you can apply to observing a wide range of human behavior in many settings.

Although all assessment procedures require diligence on the part of the clinician, observational assessments require a subtly different type of diligence because the stimuli are not controlled by the clinician and the scoring procedures are not as exact as those used in standardized tests. As you will read in Chapter 5, several procedures are used to increase observer reliability and validity, including applying well-defined observational codes that contain operational definitions of content categories and following precise methods of recording data.

Defining Observed Behaviors

You must first define the behaviors that you are going to observe—the *target behaviors*—in objective, clear, and complete terms. Your definitions (or those in the coding system that you use) should help you recognize when each behavior is occurring and distinguish the target behaviors from other similar behaviors. You want to record relevant behaviors and exclude irrelevant behaviors. The definitions, sometimes referred to as *operational definitions,* should be as explicit as possible so as to minimize inferences when you observe behavior. You accomplish this, in part, by specifying the precise operations that signal the appearance of the behavior as well as specifying the operations that do not reveal the behavior of interest. For example, the requirements for coding the behavior "inappropriate gross motor behavior—standing" may include "motor activity that results in the child's leaving his or her seat or standing on one or both legs (on the floor, chair, or desk) in an erect or semi-erect position; this code is not used when the child has permission to leave his or her seat or when the child must move in order to work on a task." (See Table D-1, Appendix D, category V, for a complete description of the criteria for coding this behavioral category.)

Here are some steps that you can follow in developing an operational definition of a target behavior:

1. Define the target behavior as clearly and precisely as possible.
2. List examples of the target behavior.
3. Revise the definition of the target behavior to include all of the examples.
4. List examples of behaviors that are similar to the target behavior, but yet do not qualify as reflecting the target behavior.
5. Revise the definition so that it does not include the nonqualifying examples.
6. Give the definition to untrained as well as trained observers and see if they can reliably record the occurrence and nonoccurrence of the target behavior. An observational videotape is useful for this step.

Some behaviors are easier to define than others. For example, crying, which can be defined as a vocal noise that is loud enough to be heard and does not involve recognizable words, is easier to define than sharing. Behaviors like sharing can be defined by focusing on the specific acts involved in sharing, such as giving a toy to another child, allowing another child to sit on the same mat, or giving a piece of candy to another child. Replacing imprecise or vague terms with exact words or descriptions will help you define the behaviors of interest. Your definitions should be precise and clear enough that another observer could replicate your findings.

Here are some examples of precise definitions of pain behavior (adapted from Paulsen & Altmaier, 1995, p. 105):

- *Guarding*—abnormally stiff, interrupted, or rigid movements while walking or moving from one position to another

- *Bracing*—a stationary position in which a fully extended limb supports and maintains an abnormal distribution of weight
- *Rubbing*—touching, rubbing, or holding the affected area of pain
- *Grimacing*—an obvious facial expression of pain, which may include furrowed brow, narrowed eyes, tightened lips, corners of mouth pulled back, and clenched teeth
- *Verbal complaints*—any audible language or nonlanguage sounds indicating pain
- *Sighing*—obvious exaggerated exhalation of air, usually accompanied by shoulders first rising and then falling; cheeks may be expanded

Conducting Observations in Sequence

In some situations, you may want to begin your observations by using global or general coding categories. This approach would be appropriate, for example, if someone asked you to observe a child who was "having problems" in school. After carefully observing the child's behavior during various classes and times of the day, you might note specific behaviors that you wanted to observe more closely. You would then direct your further observations to the specific behaviors of interest.

When you first observe a child referred for a specified behavior problem, do not focus exclusively on that behavior. At least during your initial observation, observe the child's overall behavior and that of other children and adults in the setting. This is important because it gives you the opportunity to observe other potentially important behaviors of the child and allows you to evaluate the referred child's behavior in the context of other individuals' behavior in that setting (Nay, 1979).

Timing Observation Periods

Once you have defined the target behaviors you want to observe, select an appropriate observation period in which the ongoing activity is compatible with the target behavior. If the child is participating in a stand-up spelling bee, for example, you will not be able to observe and record episodes of inappropriate out-of-seat behavior. If possible, observe the child at different times during the day and in several problematic settings, such as at home, on the playground, and in school. Select your observation times so that there is a chance that you will observe a representative sample of the behaviors of interest. If you do not obtain a representative sample of behavior, the observational results will not be valid.

Paying Attention to Special Occurrences

Even when you are concentrating on specific behaviors, be attuned to other events happening at the time of the observation. Fire drills, substitute teachers, new aides, special events, upcoming holidays, and other children's misbehavior are examples of events that may have a direct bearing on the referred child's behavior. You will, of course, want to note such events on your observational record.

Preparing for the Unexpected

No matter how carefully you prepare for your observational assessment, observations conducted in naturalistic settings are not under your control. For example, your plan to observe Joyce in a history class with her general education teacher may fall asunder when there is a fire drill, a field trip, an assembly, or a substitute teacher. Similarly, it is possible that on the day you select to visit Dwight's home to observe how he interacts with his parents, his father will be called away. Your scheduled observation of a patient in a hospital ward may be hampered because the patient needs to have an unexpected laboratory test and requires sedation. Or, just as you get attuned to listening and observing conversation on the ward, someone may turn on the TV set and people's voices will be drowned out. In naturalistic settings, you are at the mercy of events you cannot control; be aware of these limitations and be prepared to encounter them. Your tolerance for frustration will be tested, along with your flexibility and resourcefulness.

APPLICABILITY OF OBSERVATIONAL METHODS

Observational methods are particularly useful for (a) studying behaviors that have a relatively high frequency, (b) assessing global behaviors such as aggression, social withdrawal, sociability, and attention, and (c) evaluating a child's progress over time. Systematic observation in a naturalistic setting may *not* be the method of choice for some behaviors, particularly those that occur infrequently, covertly, or only in response to some specific stimuli. For example, it may not be possible to observe a child stealing or setting fires, for these behaviors may occur only three or four times a year and only when no one is watching. Similarly, responses to stress, outbursts of anger, and reactions to tragedy may be difficult to observe because they are rare events. And while naturalistic observation permits the recording of public behavior, it does not capture private behavior, such as thoughts or sexual behaviors. For such behaviors, self-monitoring techniques (see Chapter 5), planned incident procedures (setting up a contrived situation to evoke the target behavior), or role-play techniques may be preferable.

Planned Incident Procedure

A *planned incident procedure* (or controlled observation), which entails observing children in a specially contrived situation or setting, is the method of choice when you want to elicit specific behaviors. It gives you more control over the behaviors of interest. In a natural setting, you must wait for the behavior to occur; in the planned incident procedure, you can create conditions that may evoke the behavior of interest. You can do this by introducing special toys or furniture or by systematically varying how people in the setting react to the child. For example, if you want to study the effects of music or noise on the child's behavior, you can introduce different types of music or noise or different intensities of the same music or noise at specific times into the playroom. Planned incident procedures are also useful when you want to observe how different children react to the same stimulus conditions. Exhibit 4-1 describes a planned incident procedure.

The assumption underlying a planned incident procedure is that a contrived situation can bring out important behaviors more quickly and efficiently than a "natural" situation, saving valuable time. However, one disadvantage of contrived settings is that they do not allow unforeseen, possibly informative, events to occur. Another disadvantage is that the participants may not behave spontaneously because they recognize that the situation is contrived. In real-life settings, though, it may be difficult to sample the behaviors of interest, and other conditions may make the recording of the target behaviors difficult. Whichever procedure or procedures you decide to use (planned incident procedures and natural settings can be used together because they complement each other), recognize that each procedure has advantages and disadvantages and that both can contribute important information to the assessment.

Ecological Assessment

Assessment by observational methods is particularly valuable in *ecological assessment,* which focuses on the physical attributes and the psychological attributes of the setting in which behavior occurs. Physical attributes include spatial arrangements, seating arrangements, lighting, and noise; psychological attributes include familial, peer, and teacher relationships. The evaluation of settings is particularly important for answering such questions as "Which classroom is best for Jim, who has a behavior disorder?" "How can the home be modified to improve Helen's behavior?" or "What type of foster home would be best for Jamie?"

Following are examples of questions about a child's behavior problem from an ecological perspective:

- "Does the child engage in the problem behavior with one teacher but not with another?"
- "At school but not at home?"
- "When working independently but not when working in a small group?"
- "With one parent but not with the other?"
- "During the early morning hours but not evening hours?"
- "With one ward aide but not with others?"

Answers to these and similar questions will help you evaluate the settings that may be associated with the problem behavior (Alessi, 1988). If the child shows problem behaviors in some

Exhibit 4-1
Observing Preschool Children's Reactions to Specially Designed Situations

Zahn-Waxler, McKnew, Cummings, Davenport, and Radke-Yarrow (1984) designed a setting for observing preschool children's reactions to specially created incidents. The referred child, a familiar same-age playmate, parents of the two children, and staff members interact in the setting under various conditions intended to induce conflict, distress, frustration, and enjoyment. Aggression, altruism, and other emotions may be revealed.

The room in which the observations are conducted, preferably a living room–kitchenette area, should contain a standard set of toys (for example, rocking horse, ball, pull toy, toy telephone). The following conditions should be established (adapted from Zahn-Waxler et al., 1984, p. 237):

1. *A novel environment.* Initially, the children play in the novel room, with the mothers watching. (5 minutes)
2. *A background climate of affection and sharing.* Two female adults enter the adjoining kitchen. They greet the mothers and children and then cooperate with each other in a warm and friendly fashion while getting coffee for the mothers and juice for the children and straightening the kitchen. (5 minutes)
3. *A neutral context.* There are no experimental interventions. (5 minutes)
4. *A background climate of hostility, anger, and rejection.* The two women return and have a verbal argument while washing the dishes. Each accuses the other of not doing her share of work around the building. (5 minutes)
5. *A second neutral context.* (5 minutes)
6. *A reconciliation.* The adults return, greet each other with affection, and apologize for their behavior. (2 minutes)
7. *A friend's separation experience.* The mother of the referred child's friend is asked to leave the room. (1 minute)
8. *Separation from the mother.* The referred child's own mother is called from the room as well. (1 minute)
9. *Reunion with the mother.* Both mothers return to the room. (4 minutes)

Mothers should be asked not to initiate activities or to interrupt interactions between the children unless something makes them uncomfortable or appears to be dangerous. The above conditions can be modified to suit the specific room arrangements.

Suggested event observational recording codes are as follows (Zahn-Waxler et al., 1984):

1. *Aggression:* actions that have potential for causing physical or psychological harm
   a. Interpersonal physical aggression—hitting, kicking, pushing, or throwing things

   b. Object struggle—attempts to grab or take another's possession
   c. Undirected aggression—acts against the physical environment (e.g., banging on walls, throwing things on the floor, kicking toys)
   d. Intense aggression—acts that are violent or potentially dangerous
2. *Altruism or empathic intervention:* acts of kindness and caring directed toward others
   a. Child helps, cooperates, provides comfort, or sympathizes with other person (e.g., pats or hugs a crying person, kisses a hurt, says "It's OK" or "Be careful," provides a bottle)
   b. Child shares either objects or self (e.g., invites other to join in particular play activities)

A suggested scale for rating various forms of emotional expressiveness is as follows:

RATING SCALE

1	2	3	4	5
emotion absent	emotion expressed slightly	emotion expressed somewhat	emotion expressed moderately	emotion expressed frequently

Emotion	Rating
a. Positive emotion (laughter, smiling, happiness, excitement expressed facially, vocally, or bodily)	1 2 3 4 5
b. Anger (angry yelling, screaming, angry facial expressions, impassioned threats or complaints)	1 2 3 4 5
c. Distress (crying, crankiness, whining, concerned facial expressions)	1 2 3 4 5
d. Emotionality (combined scores for positive emotion, anger, and distress)	1 2 3 4 5

settings but not others, look for possible explanations. For example, if the problem behaviors occur in only some school settings, were there different teachers with different expectations or teaching methods or did the problem behaviors occur at a particular time of the day?

An ecological assessment may also focus on (a) how changes in one behavior affect other behaviors or (b) how changes in one part of the environment produce changes in other parts of the environment that, in turn, affect the child. You can use a three-component framework, described in

Table 4-1, to organize ecological assessment data along the following lines: *setting appearance and contents, setting operation,* and *setting opportunities* (Hiltonsmith & Keller, 1983).

Home Observations

When you visit a home, you may have the opportunity to observe family members interacting, environmental stressors, and the physical characteristics of the home. Do not visit a home without prior permission of, and scheduling with, the parents. In general, you will want to respect the parents' wishes if they do not want you to visit the home. However, there are exceptions to this guideline. For example, in cases of alleged child maltreatment, Child Protective Services workers may enter the home without the permission of a parent or caregiver to investigate the allegation (be familiar with your state laws). In such situations, a law enforcement officer may also be present. Law enforcement personnel can enter the home without the family's permission under certain circumstances, such as when they have obtained a warrant or when they have requisite knowledge that a child may be in danger. Case workers in social agencies can make unannounced visits to evaluate foster homes. Parental permission to enter a home is not needed when an agency has a court order to enter the home.

Overall, with a child of any age, you will want to observe whether the parent (a) can relax and be comfortable with her or his child, (b) is accepting and affectionate with her or his child, (c) is sensitive to the child's needs, wants, and desires, (d) seems able to take the child's perspective, (e) remains alert to issues of safety and protection while allowing the child freedom to explore the environment within the limits of her or his age and ability, and (f) helps the child acquire new skills. Similarly, you will want to observe how the child responds to the parent.

Advantages of observing a family at home include the following (Goldenberg, 1983):

1. Obtaining a picture of how the family functions naturally
2. Obtaining a good idea of how each family member functions in his or her everyday role
3. Reducing the chance that a family member will be absent, which is more likely in an office interview
4. Promoting recognition among family members that the entire family shares responsibility for making changes or improvements
5. Decreasing anxiety among family members because of the familiar surroundings and thus facilitating more open communication among the family members
6. Decreasing the impact of the common "doctor-patient" stereotypes

Family observations are useful in obtaining information about patterns of interaction among the members of the family, the emotional climate of the home, family conflicts, and patterns of resolution after a conflict.

Table 4-1
A Framework for Organizing Data on Home and School Settings

Component	Elements
A. *Setting appearance and contents* (observable, physical, and measurable aspects of the setting)	1. *Physical features*—spatial layout, size of room, type and arrangement of furniture, and related features 2. *Ambient features*—noise level, lighting, and temperature 3. *Setting contents*—presence or absence of television sets, books, interactive board games, computers, and similar items
B. *Setting operation* (how the setting works, including interpersonal interactions among people in the setting and in other settings and physical aspects of the setting)	1. *Organizational patterns*—who leads and follows and what reinforcers are present in the setting 2. *Communication patterns*—who initiates conversation and to whom the conversation is directed 3. *Ecological patterns*—how the setting is used by the individuals therein
C. *Setting opportunities* (how the setting provides for the needs of the individuals in the setting)	1. *Nurturance and sustenance*—how basic needs of the individuals are met (e.g., the needs for food, clothing, and shelter) 2. *Cognitive/linguistic stimulation*—the degree to which individuals receive stimulation for cognitive development 3. *Social/emotional stimulation*—the degree to which individuals receive stimulation for social/emotional growth and development

Source: Adapted from Hiltonsmith and Keller (1983).

Your observations should help you to answer such questions as the following (Besharov, 1990; Garbarino et al., 1987; Kropenske & Howard, 1994; Polansky, Borgman, & De Saix, 1972):

1. Is the home located in a safe neighborhood?
2. What is the condition of the home and home furnishings? For example, are there any observable safety or health hazards within the home (including those associated with the electrical system, gas lines, water supply, and sanitary facilities)? Also, what is the condition of the beds, chairs, and curtains?
3. Is the food supply adequate, both in quantity and in nutritional content?
4. What play equipment is present?
5. What are the sleeping arrangements?
6. What is the quality of the sleeping areas?
7. If there is a newborn child, what supplies do the parents have for the infant?
8. How are the children dressed and groomed?
9. What educational and recreational equipment and accessories are available?
10. Is there a telephone in the home?
11. Does the family have a car? If so, what condition is it in?
12. Does the family use public transportation?
13. Are inappropriately sexual or violent videos or other materials accessible to the children?
14. How do the children interact with the parents?
15. How do the parents interact with the children?
16. How do the children get along with each other?
17. How do the parents interact with each other?
18. Who is living in the home, and what are their relationships to the children?
19. What are the occupations of the people living in the home?
20. Is there evidence of domestic violence?
21. What type of discipline, if any, is used by the parents?

Conditions affecting home observations. Your ability to do a home observation may be influenced by the conditions you meet in the home. You may be fortunate and find parents who are cooperative and grateful for your help. If this is the case, you can spend adequate time with the family and complete your evaluation. On the other hand, you may find hostile parents who resent your presence, or you may find a filthy house and brutalized children. In such cases, you must exercise caution and good judgment, performing only a cursory inspection before you leave quickly and notify the appropriate authorities if you suspect that the children are being abused or neglected. *If you suspect that it is dangerous for you to visit a home because of conditions in the home or neighborhood, do not go to the house unless accompanied by a police officer.*

When evaluating the child's home, remember that poverty will affect the family's material possessions. For example, the fact that there is no telephone or car or the home lacks toys does not mean that the family is more dysfunctional than a family that can afford those things. *Poverty should not bias your observations about how the family functions.*

When children and parents know that they are being observed, their behavior may change; such changes in behavior are referred to as reactive effects. For example, they may feel conspicuous or anxious, sweat profusely, stammer, or speak more quickly than usual, or they may appear relaxed, speak more slowly and distinctly than usual, or censor swear words. It is safe to assume that when you observe children and their parents, reactive effects are present. However, unless the children or parents tell you that their behavior was atypical, you will have difficulty evaluating how representative the observed behaviors are.

Home visits have some disadvantages (Drotar & Crawford, 1987). First, they may not be accepted by families. Second, as noted above, what you observe may not be a representative sample of the family's behavior (see the discussion of reactivity in Chapter 5). Finally, home visits cost more than office visits. You will have to weigh the advantages of home visits against the disadvantages when deciding whether to arrange for a home or office visit.

Case illustration. The following case illustrates the advantage of a home visit (adapted from Drotar & Crawford, 1987, p. 344).

Johnny's mother was upset by her 2-year-old's sleep disturbance and behavior problems. She had become increasingly angry and frustrated by his difficult, noncompliant behavior, but during the interview she did not provide specific details concerning her interactions with her son. He was very active but much more competent than his mother had described him. A home visit clarified the nature of his interactions with his mother. As Johnny's mother pointed out the places where he had broken knickknacks and otherwise "left the living room in ruins," it became clear that she expected him to curb his age-appropriate curiosity completely. During the home visit, she misinterpreted Johnny's active, curious behavior as deliberate defiance and became angered when he did not immediately follow her commands. She was a single parent managing a job and child care. Johnny, therefore, anxious to have his mother's undivided attention, seemed to engage in negative behavior to get her attention. These observations stimulated a productive dialogue between the psychologist and Johnny's mother that helped her to begin to reappraise Johnny's behavior. She also was able to rearrange the home environment to avoid some of the negative confrontations with Johnny.

Tests and Interviews

When you administer tests and conduct interviews, you also can observe the child's behavior. Many of the principles discussed in this chapter apply to these activities as well.

DESIGNING AN OBSERVATIONAL ASSESSMENT

The key to obtaining meaningful descriptions of behavior is coming up with the right combination of an observational recording method and a coding system. There are several useful

"I'm Kevin's teacher and I came to meet the cruel
stepmother who won't let him do his homework . . . "

Reprinted with permission from Dave Carpenter.

recording methods, ranging from those that describe behavioral sequences to those that describe only one or two events. Coding systems specify the categories used in recording the observations. The categories, such as aggressive behavior and passive behavior or on-task behavior and off-task behavior, refer to the behavioral content of the observations. It is best to combine a recording method with a coding system to map the target behaviors. Coding systems not only highlight target behaviors but also may measure several important dimensions of the target behaviors (e.g., the frequency, duration, intensity, and latency of the behaviors), as well as how factors in the setting affect behavior.

The best system for a particular situation will depend on your assessment goals. You may want to (a) use a coding system designed by others, (b) combine categories of existing systems, (c) modify existing systems, or (d) design your own system. In selecting or designing a coding system, ask yourself what questions you want answered and how the coding system will help you answer these questions. Existing systems differ in the range of behaviors assessed and the level of inference required by the observational categories. If you find a system that is generally useful for your purposes, by all means use it, especially if the system has good target definitions, systematic coding guidelines, good reliability, and good validity. Designing your own observational system can

be time consuming. On some occasions, however, you may have to supplement an existing system with additional categories that have special relevance to the referral question. In such instances, you will need to define carefully any coding categories that you add. Although you will usually be interested in behaviors related to the problem, consider other behaviors that might be relevant to the problem or to the situation or setting in which the problem occurs.

Some behaviors occur frequently, others infrequently. Some are of long duration, others of short duration. Some are intense, others mild. Some occur immediately after a request, others are delayed. And some behaviors are consistent during an episode, whereas others are variable. In designing or selecting your recording method, consider the attributes of the target behaviors because they will determine what methods are most likely to ensure that you will observe the target behaviors.

The observational recording methods particularly useful for clinical and psychoeducational tasks are narrative recording, interval recording, event recording, and ratings recording. The following sections provide information on each of these recording methods, including a description, major uses, design considerations, quantitative data obtained, advantages, disadvantages, examples, and exercises to develop your skill in using the method.

NARRATIVE RECORDING

Narrative recording will help you formulate a comprehensive description of the child's (or group's) natural behavior. You, as well as parents, relatives, or even the child, can record descriptions of behavior. Narrative recordings are referred to as *anecdotal recordings* when they include anything that seems noteworthy to the observer; a specific time frame or specific codes or categories are not needed. When the observer attempts to record behavior as it occurs, we refer to the narrative recording as a *running record*. Narrative recordings describe events without using quantitative recording procedures.

Global, Semi-Global, and Narrow Descriptions of Behavior

Observations in a narrative recording can be global, semi-global, or narrow (Barker & Wright, 1954). *Global descriptions* (also referred to as *molar* or *broad descriptions*) focus on actions that reflect the child's behavior as a whole. They may incorporate different specific behaviors or require inferential judgments. *Semi-global descriptions* contain additional general details of the behaviors of interest. *Narrow descriptions* (also referred to as *molecular* or *fine descriptions*) reflect specific details of the child's behavior or the setting. For example, in each of the following pairs, description (a) is global and description (b) is narrow:

- (a) Hurrying to school. (b) Tripping when going up the school stairs.

- (a) Eating. (b) Chewing noisily.
- (a) Playing at school. (b) Jumping rope.

Here is another example of a global, a semi-global, and a narrow description (Barker & Wright, 1954):

- *Global description:* "George went berry picking for his mother." (This description identifies a complete episode. It tells us what George was observed to do, but relatively little about how George did the activity.)
- *Semi-global description:* "George took a basket from the kitchen table and walked outdoors, where he mounted his bicycle and went to pick berries for his mother." (This description provides more information than the first one, but it is still limited in information about how George's actions were performed.)
- *Narrow description:* "George, with his lips quivering, his brows knit, and the corners of his mouth turned down, took a basket from the kitchen table and, with the fingers of his left hand wound limply around the handle of the basket, his shoulders hunched, his chin sagging against his chest, and his feet dragging, walked outdoors, where he mounted his bicycle and, with his head still bent, went to pick berries for his mother." (This description gives us information about how George's actions were performed. The quivering lips, the knit brows, and the dragging feet suggest that George went to pick the berries unwillingly and unhappily. The information is useful because it tells about the "how" of what George did and gives important information about his disposition.)

A Continuum of Inferential Judgments

Narrative observations form a continuum from low inferential judgments to high inferential judgments. When you record directly observable behavior (e.g., actions, motor activity, and verbalizations), you are making low inferential judgments; when you record interpretations based on directly observable behaviors, you are making high inferential judgments. Examples of these two types of statements follow (Alessi, 1980). In each set, description (a) is a behavioral descriptive statement (low inferential), whereas description (b) is a behavioral inferential statement (high inferential).

- (a) He slams the book on the desk. (b) He is frustrated.
- (a) She hit Helen three times with a stick. (b) She is angry.
- (a) He achieved 100 percent accuracy on his mathematics test. (b) He is gifted in mathematics.
- (a) She says mostly positive things about herself. (b) She has a good self-concept.

Behavioral descriptive statements relate behaviors as they occur, without explanations. *Behavioral inferential statements* go beyond describing behaviors; they are attempts to integrate or theorize. In the early stages of your narrative recording, concentrate on making behavioral descriptive statements, keeping inferential statements to a minimum. In-terpret the observational recording data only after you have had an opportunity to study the data carefully and then integrate these observations with information obtained from other sources.

Major Uses of Narrative Recording

You can make narrative observations in various settings and time periods, to create an in-depth picture of the behavior of a child, a group, or a teacher. In clinical assessment, narrative recordings are particularly valuable as a precursor to more specific and quantifiable observations. A running account of the child's behavior may provide leads about behavioral and environmental events worthy of further analysis and suggest hypotheses about factors controlling the target behaviors.

Following are examples of situations or settings in which you might use narrative recordings.

Observing a child's social skills and communication skills. Narrative recording can help you to learn about a child's social skills and communication skills (Cohen, Stern, & Balaban, 1997; Gresham, 1983; Mattes & Omark, 1984). Carefully observe the child's interactions with others. For example:

- What are the child's facial expressions, gestures, and actions, as well as the body language and actions of others who communicate with the child?
- How does the child communicate with others (e.g., rarely initiates verbal interactions, often initiates verbal interactions, uses gestures instead of speech)?
- How do others respond to the child's communications (e.g., accept the communications, seem puzzled by the communications, withdraw from the child)?
- Does the child use positive verbalizations, such as *please, thank you,* and *excuse me?*
- How does the child show interest in other children in the setting (e.g., plays with other children, stares at other children)?
- How does the child make contact with other children (e.g., confidently, tentatively, aggressively)?
- What is the quality of the child's behavior with other children (e.g., sharing, friendly, bullying, impatient, aggressive, withdrawn)?
- How does the child respond when other children initiate interactions?
- What is the quality of the child's relationship with adults in the setting? Note how frequently the child makes contact with adults and in which situations, and observe whether the child is matter-of-fact, warmhearted, reserved, open, whining, belligerent, clinging, or hostile.
- How does the child gain attention from adults (e.g., politely or through excessive talking, tattling, sidling up and touching, or hanging on)?
- Does the child comply with teacher and parent requests to share?

- How does the child react to limits that are set by adults (e.g., accepts limits, defies them, slows but doesn't change present behavior)?
- How does the child react to criticism from adults and from other children (e.g., accepts it, cries, pouts)?
- What is the nature of the child's relationships with adults (e.g., dependent, respectful, disrespectful)?

Observing a family.   Narrative recording can help you evaluate family interactive patterns. Observe the content and style of the communications, such as what is discussed and how it is discussed; the roles assumed by family members, such as leadership and follower roles; the patterns of interaction, such as who communicates with whom; what coalitions exist; and which family members defend, protect, or attack other members. Also observe the affect displayed by the family members, such as the following (Hops, Biglan, Sherman, Arthur, Friedman, & Osteen, 1987):

- Happy affect (happiness, smiling, excitement, humorous tone)
- Caring affect (warmth, affection, supportiveness, liking of another)
- Neutral affect (even-tempered, conversational tone)
- Anxious affect (fear, anxiety, nervousness)
- Whiny affect (whiny voice, worry)
- Dysphoric affect (sadness, depression, fatigue, sullenness, crying)
- Aversive affect (anger, sarcasm toward or ridicule of another, cold detachment)
- Pain affect (any nonverbal expression of pain)

When observing a family, you will need to listen carefully to what the family members are saying. Also observe their facial expressions, gestures, actions, and body language.

Observing a group.   Narrative recordings are useful when you observe a group. Pay particular attention to the patterns of peer preference or attraction, indifference, antagonism, and influence. The following questions are useful when observing a group of children in a classroom or in other settings:

1. What is the group climate like?
2. What patterns of interaction are evident?
3. Who are the leaders and who are the followers?
4. What other roles seem to be represented in the group (e.g., facilitator, troublemaker, conciliator, criticizer)?
5. Which children participate in group activities, and which are on the fringes?
6. What patterns of relationships do you see (e.g., what subgroups are formed)?
7. What is the seating arrangement in the room?
8. Which children are accepted by the group, and which are rejected?
9. How does the group react to newcomers?
10. How does the group react when its leaders are absent?
11. How does the group react to different teachers?
12. How does the group react to new situations?

Observing a teacher.   When you visit a classroom, you will want to observe the teacher's method and style of teaching and classroom management. You will want to note the questions the teacher asks, the guidance the teacher provides, the information the teacher gives, how the teacher makes corrections, and the positive and negative reinforcements the teacher uses. You will also want to observe students' activities, such as whether their behavior is on-task or off-task and what their reactions to the lesson and to the teacher are. Be sensitive to environmental aspects such as noises associated with activities going on in the hallway or street and aromas coming from the cafeteria. Note the space allotted for various activities, the period of the day when the activities occur, the equipment used for the activities, the seating arrangements, the classroom displays, and the atmosphere in the room. Be sensitive to both verbal and nonverbal cues, patterns of interaction, group formations, and any other features that will help you understand how the classroom functions. Although you will probably not be able to observe everything alluded to in Table 4-2 during a short observation period, try to answer as many questions as possible.

Observing children in informal interactions.   It is sometimes helpful to observe the child informally in a situation that is a variant of a natural procedure combined with a planned incident procedure. For example, after you have finished testing, bring out some toys and ask the child's parent or sibling to play with the referred child. Leave the situation

"I expect you all to be independent, innovative, critical thinkers who will do exactly as I say."

Table 4-2
Questions for Observing a Teacher and Classroom

Description of Classroom

1. What grade are you observing?
2. How many children are in the classroom?
3. How many teacher's aides or other adults are in the classroom?
4. What are the pertinent classroom environmental variables (e.g., seating arrangements, accessibility for children with disabilities, amount of space, air quality, temperature, lighting, noise level, activity level, condition of the building and school grounds)?
5. What distractions, if any, are present inside and outside the classroom?
6. What is the schedule of activities (e.g., length of day, days per week, length of sessions, consistency in schedule, free time)?
7. Is the schedule followed?
8. What is the atmosphere in the classroom (e.g., organized, disorganized, pleasant, unpleasant, disciplined, undisciplined, quiet, noisy)?
9. What subject matter is being covered (e.g., reading, math, spelling, art, science, music, physical education)?
10. When is each subject taught, and how much time is devoted to it?
11. What are the transition routines between subjects and classes (e.g., rules for putting away materials, rules for getting out materials, rules for finishing assignments)?

Teacher Style and Effectiveness

12. What materials does the teacher use (e.g., books, worksheets, computer exercises)?
13. What are the resources of the classroom (e.g., computers, maps, books, audiovisual equipment, tutors)?
14. What instructional materials and techniques does the teacher use (e.g., verbal instructions, written instructions, physical demonstration, pictorial instructions, calculators, tape recorders, computers, multimethod presentations)?
15. What instructional methods are used (e.g., lectures, cooperative groups, learning centers, hands-on activities)?
16. What cuing systems are used (e.g., daily schedule on the bulletin board, lists of tasks on the blackboard, personal contracts, assignment sheets)?
17. How would you describe the teacher's lectures (e.g., presents clear and concrete messages, delivers lectures with enthusiasm, presents items in sequence and with sufficient repetition, presents material at a satisfactory pace, provides an overview of the content at the beginning of the lesson, reviews objectives of the lesson, outlines the content and signals transitions between parts of the lesson, calls attention to the main ideas of the lesson, summarizes parts of the lesson as they are completed, reviews the main ideas at the end of the lesson)?
18. What are the work expectations (e.g., length of assignments, time allotted for independent work, time allowed for group work, time allotted to complete assignments, time allotted for socialization, use of self-paced materials)?
19. What is the quality of the assignments (e.g., clearly stated, accompanied by objective and well-enforced criteria for completion)?
20. Do students have a choice in planning activities or in completing assignments?
21. If there are choices, are the students taught to be responsible for their choices and to accept the consequences of their choices or agreements?
22. Are the students placed in groups (e.g., are students who are low performers in the smallest group and students who are high performers in the largest group)? (If no, go to question 26.)
23. How does the teacher decide to place children in a specific group?
24. Do the groups serve their intended functions?
25. Do all the children in a group work on the same activity at the same time?
26. Do the students ask questions and participate in discussions? If so, how does the teacher respond to their comments and questions (e.g., encourage and accept ideas or discourage ideas)?
27. What type of assistance does the teacher give the students?
28. Does the teacher provide additional time for students who need help? If so, when is the time available (e.g., before first period, during recess, during lunch, after school, on Saturday)?
29. What assessment takes place (e.g., timed or untimed tests, multiple-choice tests, essay tests, open-book tests, take-home tests, oral presentations)?
30. Is sufficient time allotted for the tests?
31. How is the assessment information used (e.g., feedback to students)?
32. What grading methods are used by the teacher?
33. Are the lesson plans differentiated for different individuals or groups of students? If any children receive individualized instruction, how many?
34. Do the students seem to be attending to the lecture and involved in the assignments?
35. Do the students help each other?
36. What kinds of expectations are being transmitted by the teacher to the students about classroom behavior?
37. What kind of questions does the teacher ask (e.g., open-ended, forced-choice)?
38. How effective is classroom management (e.g., type of discipline, enforcement of classroom rules)?
39. How are the students' contributions—reports, tests, drawings, and other work—organized in the classroom (e.g., displayed in the room, kept in folders near the teacher's desk, kept by each student at his or her desk)?
40. What motivational variables are used by the teacher (e.g., tokens for achievement, self-recording or charting of academic progress, time in a game center or on a recreational activity, extra time for lunch or for a break)?
41. Does the teacher meet the needs of children with disabilities? If so, how (e.g., allows them to ask questions when they do not understand, photocopy other students' notes, tape-record lectures, take examinations orally, or obtain time-limit extensions on examinations)?

Source: Adapted from Boxer, Challen, and McCarthy (1991) and Ylvisaker, Hartwick, and Stevens (1991).

unstructured: You want to learn how the child expresses himself or herself in a more relaxed situation and how the child and parent (or sibling) interact. Three sets of specific guidelines for observing parent-child interactions follow. These guidelines are relevant for observing interactions either in a clinic play room or at home. The first is for observing parent-infant interactions (Baird, Haas, McCormick, Carruth, & Turner, 1992; Hirshberg, 1993); the second, for observing parent-toddler interactions (Hirshberg, 1993; Zahn-Waxler, Iannotti, Cummings, & Denham, 1990); and the third, for observing interactions between a parent and a school-aged child (Mahoney, Powell, & Finger, 1986; Stein, Gambrill, & Wiltse, 1978).

PARENT-INFANT INTERACTIONS

1. *Social interactions.* Do the parent and infant interact socially? For example, does the parent look and smile at the infant as the infant looks and smiles at the parent? How does the infant respond to physical contact with the parent?

2. *Responsiveness.* Does the parent respond to the infant's interpersonal signals? For example, does the parent take a toy offered by the infant? How does the infant respond to the parent's actions and presence? For example, does the infant take a toy offered by the parent?

3. *Directing.* Does the parent direct the infant in an attempt to lead the pace, content, or form of the infant's behavior? For example, does the parent tell an infant who is playing with beads to "Put them on your arm"? How does the infant respond to the parent's directions?

4. *Intrusiveness.* Does the parent's intrusiveness lead to breaks in the infant's attention? For example, does the parent offer a rattle to an infant who is playing with another toy? How does the infant respond to the parent's intrusions?

5. *Joining.* Does the parent join the infant's play? For example, does the parent touch an object similar to the one the infant touched? How does the infant respond when the parent joins her or him in play?

6. *Imitation.* Does the parent respond to a behavior initiated by the infant and vice versa? For example, does the parent kiss the infant after the infant kisses the parent or imitate the infant's coos? How does the infant respond to the parent's imitation?

7. *Affect and attitude.* What types of affect are displayed by the parent and the infant? For example, do the parent and infant show (a) pleasure, enjoyment, and a happy mood, (b) warmth, tenderness, and affection, (c) irritability, anger, impatience, or hostility, or (d) approval or disapproval? Does the parent (a) hold and comfort the infant, (b) use affectionate statements such as "You're Mommy's little sweetie," (c) make positive statements such as "That's great!" about the infant's behavior, or (d) display affection in expressions or behavior (e.g., smiling at, holding, or hugging the infant)? How does the infant respond to the parent? Does the infant hug the parent or show other signs of warmth and affection? Is affect appropriate to the situation?

8. *Safety and protection.* Is the parent alert to protecting the physical safety of the infant? For example, does the parent continuously monitor the infant's safety and take action to protect her or him when necessary? Is the parent appropriately vigilant and protective, overprotective and highly anxious about the baby's safety, or careless and lacking in awareness? Does the infant show excessive caution and timidity or recklessness? (Sample questions are adapted from Hirschberg, 1993, p. 183.)

9. *Physiological regulation.* Is the parent alert to the infant's needs for food, warmth, stimulation, elimination, and sleep? For example, does the parent recognize when the infant is hungry or when the stimulation should be reduced or increased? How does the infant respond to the parent's attempts at regulation?

10. *Teaching and learning.* Does the parent try to help the infant learn new skills? If so, how does the parent go about teaching the infant those skills? Does the parent show flexibility in helping the infant and in keeping the infant focused on the task? How does the infant respond to the parent's teaching?

11. *Power and control.* How does the parent present herself or himself to the infant? For example, is the parent calm, confident, and in control of herself or himself, of the infant, and of the situation, or does the parent appear passive, overwhelmed, disorganized, confused, tense, or potentially explosive? How does the infant respond to the parent's attempt to control (or failure to control) the situation?

PARENT-TODDLER INTERACTIONS

1. *Attunement to needs.* Is the parent attuned to the toddler's needs? For example, does the parent (a) simplify or provide more information when the toddler apparently does not understand, (b) show sensitivity to the toddler's visual perspective by moving objects into or out of the toddler's field of vision or by giving information about the location of objects, or (c) indicate awareness of the toddler's wants, needs, or feelings without the toddler's explicitly expressing these? Is the toddler attuned to the parent's needs? Does the toddler push the parent to his or her limits? Does the toddler recognize when the parent is happy, sad, tired, angry, and so forth? How does the toddler react? What does the toddler do?

2. *Promotion of prosocial behaviors.* Does the parent verbally encourage prosocial behavior? For example, does the parent (a) state "It's his turn" or something similar when the toddler is playing with another child or (b) share, help, or show compassion to the toddler or another child or adult who is present?

3. *Perspective-taking or self-awareness.* Does the parent encourage perspective-taking or self-awareness? For example, does the parent (a) direct the toddler's attention to the feelings of others in the room by making a comment such as "Why is John so sad?" (b) direct the toddler's attention to the toddler's own thoughts by saying "You thought that this was the big block" or something similar, or (c) use another person

as a point of reference by saying "It's the one in front of Sarah" or something similar?

4. *Affect and attitude.* What types of affect do the parent and the toddler display? For example, do the parent and toddler show (a) pleasure, enjoyment, and a happy mood, (b) warmth, tenderness, and affection, (c) irritability, anger, impatience, or hostility, or (d) approval or disapproval? Does the parent (a) use affectionate statements such as "You're Daddy's big girl," (b) make positive statements such as "That's great!" about the toddler's behavior, or (c) display affection in expressions or behavior (e.g., smiling at, holding, or hugging the toddler)? Does the toddler hug the parent or show other signs of warmth and affection? Is affect appropriate to the situation?

5. *Modulated control.* Does the parent modulate his or her behavior? For example, does the parent (a) use qualified commands or questions to direct the toddler's behavior, such as "Would you like to…," "Why don't you…," "How about if we…" "Maybe you could…" or (b) set limits or establish contingencies by saying "You can have juice as soon as you put your things in this box" or something similar?

6. *Power and control.* How does the parent present himself or herself to the toddler? For example, is the parent calm, confident, and in control of himself or herself, of the toddler, and of the situation, or does the parent appear passive, overwhelmed, disorganized, confused, tense, or potentially explosive? How does the parent manage the challenges the toddler presents during the observation, such as a refusal to clean up, frequent interruptions, or acting-out behavior? Does the parent use unqualified, power-assertive methods such as direct commands, prohibitions, shouting, or physical control methods? How does the toddler respond to the parent's attempt to control (or failure to control) the situation?

7. *Physiological regulation.* Is the parent alert to the toddler's needs for food, warmth, stimulation, elimination, and sleep? For example, does the parent recognize when the toddler is hungry or when stimulation should be reduced or increased? How does the toddler respond to the parent's attempts at regulation and nurturing?

8. *Teaching and learning.* Does the parent try to help the toddler learn new skills? If so, how does the parent go about teaching the toddler those skills? Does the parent show flexibility in helping the toddler and in keeping the toddler focused on the task? How does the toddler respond to the parent's teaching?

PARENT AND SCHOOL-AGED CHILD INTERACTIONS

1. *Affect and attitude.* What types of affect do the parent and the child display? For example, do the parent and child show (a) pleasure, enjoyment, and a happy mood, (b) warmth, tenderness, and affection, (c) irritability, anger, impatience, or hostility, or (d) approval or disapproval? Is the affect appropriate to the situation?

2. *Responsiveness to behavior.* Is the parent responsive to the child, and is the child responsive to the parent? For ex-

ample, does the parent (a) respond to the child's distress, (b) make suggestions to the child, or (c) respond to the child's questions with caring and sensitivity? How does the child respond to the parent's needs and requests?

3. *Responsiveness of affect.* How do the parent and child respond to each other's expressions of affect? For example, does the parent acknowledge and assist the child, if necessary, in the appropriate expression of feelings, such as affection or anger? How does the child respond when the parent is angry, hurt, or disappointed? Do parent and child comfort each other, or are they sarcastic or indifferent to expressions of affect?

4. *Stimulation of the child and parent.* Does the parent stimulate the child, and does the child stimulate the parent? For example, does the parent (a) provide toys for the child, (b) play with the child, (c) make physical contact with the child, (d) talk to the child, or (e) encourage the child? Does the child introduce new ideas to the parent? How does the parent respond to new ideas presented by the child (e.g., welcomes them, denies them, becomes angry)?

5. *Power and control.* Does the parent control the child's behavior, does the child control the parent's behavior, or is there flexibility in the interaction? For example, does the parent (a) protect the child, (b) control the child's play and behavior by ordering, demanding compliance, or making threats, (c) restrict the child's activities, or (d) criticize or punish the child? Does the child demand certain things from the parent or criticize the parent? How does the parent deal with issues of child management? For example:

- What behaviors evoke praise or punishment from the parent?
- How much time elapses before the parent responds to the child's behavior?
- What behavior does the parent ignore?
- How consistent is the parent in following through on promised rewards or punishments?
- What rewards or punishments are used by the parent (e.g., a hug or a positive statement, physical punishment or a demeaning statement)?
- How realistic is the promised punishment (e.g., "You can't go out for the next two months!")?
- Does the parent make threatening statements (e.g., "If you aren't good, I'll leave you" or "I won't love you anymore if you do that again")?
- Does the parent tell the child why the child is being punished?
- Does the parent deliver punishments and rewards uniformly to all the children involved in the behavior?
- Do verbal communications accompany punishments or rewards?
- In two-parent families, do both parents administer the punishments and rewards, and do the parents agree or disagree about the punishments and rewards?
- Does the parent bribe the child (e.g., "If you leave me alone, I'll give you candy later on")?

- Does the parent set limits for the child (e.g., "You may go as far as the street corner, but you cannot cross the street")?
- Does the parent appear to respect the child's viewpoint?

How to Design a Narrative Recording

In designing a narrative recording, you must decide on (a) the number of times you will observe the child, (b) the length of each observation period, (c) the time periods during which you will conduct the observations, (d) the type of narrative recording you will use, (e) the target behaviors you will observe, and (f) the method of recording data.

Frequency, length, and time of observation period.
The child's age, the setting, and the reason for the assessment will influence the number of times you will need to observe the child, the length of the observation period, and when you should conduct the observations. An observation session may last from 10 to 30 minutes or even longer. Time your observations so that they will yield representative data; if possible, observe the child more than once and at different times during the day. To find out when the target behavior is most likely to occur, consult with the referral source (e.g., the classroom teacher) about when and where the target behavior occurs most frequently, and observe at those times.

Type of narrative recording.
For clinical and psychoeducational assessment, anecdotal recordings are preferred. Usually, there are no restrictions on what you observe. In addition to the behavior of the referred child, fully describe the setting (e.g., the scene, the people in the setting, and the ongoing action). Report everything that the referred child says and does, everything that other people say and do to the referred child, and what other people say and do that is relevant to understanding the setting. Use everyday descriptive language in all of your narratives. The narrative should read like a newspaper article, telling when and how the behavior of concern occurred and what features of the environment served to alter or influence the behavior.

Target behaviors.
If you are conducting a preliminary observation, include general impressions of the child and the setting in your narrative recording. When you have identified the target behaviors, begin to concentrate on them along with their antecedent and consequent events.

Method of recording data.
You may write your narrative recording, type it into a portable computer, or record your comments on audiotape. You also may use narrative recording with other recording methods, such as videotaping. If you plan to videotape a child or to record his or her comments on tape, be sure to obtain parental permission and explain how the audiotape or videotape will be used. For behaviors of concern that occur frequently, an anecdotal

record form (see Table 4-3) is useful in recording specific observations at specified times.

Guidelines for Making a Narrative Recording

Some helpful suggestions for making a narrative recording include the following:

- Identify in advance the referred child, as well as other children and adults in the setting that you intend to observe.
- Note the setting and the time of day.
- Describe the referred child's behavior, that of other children and adults in the setting, and the factors that affect the referred child's and others' behavior.
- Consider how the setting—which includes the children, the adults, and the physical and spatial determinants—affects the behavior of the referred child and others.
- Record the referred child's and others' verbal and nonverbal behavior.
- Record the event (or anecdote) as soon as possible after you complete your observation.
- Record important verbalizations as precisely as possible, including direct quotations of the referred child and others.
- In your written description, preserve the sequence of the behaviors observed.
- Be as objective, accurate, and complete as possible in your written description.
- Use everyday language in your written description.
- Describe, rather than interpret, the referred child's behavior and the behavior of others.
- Record the reactions of others to the referred child's behavior.
- Recognize that your initial impressions of the referred child and others in the setting may change during the observation.
- Consider how your presence may have affected the referred child's behavior and that of others in the setting.
- Always consider your role in the assessment process, particularly how you are reacting and feeling.
- Do not allow your interest in specific behaviors to keep you from recording general impressions.
- When you interpret the referred child's behavior, consider possible reasons for it.
- Finally, integrate all sources of behavioral information, including interpretations of behavior, into a unified and coherent picture of the referred child's behavior.

Quantitative Data in Narrative Recordings

Although narrative recordings do not involve quantitative recording procedures, you can use your record to obtain quantitative data. For example, you may note the number of times the child performed a particular action or the number of times the child spoke. In addition, you can code the qualitative

Table 4-3
Observation Protocol Based on Anecdotal Record System

WESTERN MICHIGAN UNIVERSITY
CLASSROOM OBSERVATION RECORD PROTOCOL

Student: _____Mary_____	Comparison: _____C.J._____	Observer: _____School Psychologist (L.C.)_____
Age: _____6-10_____	Age: _____6-7_____	Other Observer: _____Social Worker_____
Grade: _____2nd_____		Class Size: _____26_____
School: _____Westwood_____		Class Type: _____Regular ed._____
Teacher: _____Mrs. Kaput_____		Time Stop: _____10:23_____
Date: _4_ / _3_ / _99_		Time Start: _____10:13_____
month day year		Total Time: _____:10_____

Reason for observation (What question do we want to answer?):

To explore reported discrepancy between Mary's behavior and that of her classroom peers.

Classroom activity and explicit rules in effect at time of observation:

Activity: Math. See notes below for details. Rules: 1. Follow teacher's directions; 2. work quietly; 3. complete work.

Description of observation techniques (interval or time sample and length):

30-second interval for Mary and comparison, 2-minute time sample for class scan check.

Behavior codes:	*Grouping codes:*	*Teacher/peer reaction codes:*	*Participants' codes:*
T = on-task	L = large group	AA = attention to all	Ma = Mary
V = verbal off-task	S = small group	A+ = positive attention to student	Te = teacher
M = motor off-task	O = one to one	A– = negative attention to student	
P = passive off-task	I = independent act	Ao = no attention to student	
=	F = free time	An = neutral attention to student	
=	=	=	

	Time	Student	Comparison	Class scan check	Anecdotal notes on behavior	Grouping	Teacher reaction	Peer reaction
1.	10:13	P	T		Ma not responding to teacher	L	An	Ao
2.		M	T		Standing up–other sitting	L	Ao	A+
3.	10:14	M	T		Te leads Ma back to desk	L	An	Ao
4.		M	T	80%	Standing up	L	Ao	A+
5.	10:15	P	T		Sitting staring at others	L	Ao	A+
6.		T	M		Looking at teacher	S	Ao	Ao
7.	10:16	T	M	76%	Sitting quietly and listening	S	Ao	Ao
8.		T	T		Working at desk	S	Ao	Ao
9.	10:17	P	T		Looking out window	L	Ao	Ao
10.		T	T	83%	Copying math problems	L	Ao	Ao
11.	10:18	P	T		Staring at board	L	Ao	Ao
12.		M	T		On floor getting pencil	L	Ao	Ao
13.	10:19	M	T	80%	On floor getting pencil	L	Ao	A+
14.		M	M		On floor poking other	L	Ao	A+
15.	10:20	P	T		In seat staring	L	Ao	Ao
16		P	T	88%	In seat staring	L	Ao	Ao
17.	10:21	T	T		Writing math	S	An	Ao
18.		T	T		Writing math	S	Ao	Ao
19.	10:22	M	T	80%	Walking around classroom	S	Ao	A+
20.		T	T		Writing math	S	Ao	Ao
Summary :		35% (7/20)	85% (17/20)	81%		L = 13; S = 7	Ao = 17; An = 3	Ao = 14; A+ = 6

Reliability = 83%

(Continued)

Table 4-3 *(Continued)*

Note. The top part of the protocol contains identifying information characteristic of any test protocol. Also included is space for noting the reason for referral, classroom activity and rules in effect during the observation period, and a description of the recording procedure used (e.g., 30-second interval). The mid-section of the protocol contains a coding system for noting various behaviors, situations, and teacher reactions during the observation session. The bottom half of the protocol contains 20 blank lines, each one representing either an interval for observation or a time sample frame. These are numbered from 1 to 20 down the left-hand side. Each blank line has a space to record the behavior of the referred and comparison students, anecdotal notes on the incident, the grouping situation at that time, and the teacher's reaction to the incident.

The recorded data are summarized at the bottom. In the sample case, the referred student was on-task during only 7 of the 20 intervals observed, whereas the comparison student was on-task during 17 of the same 20 intervals. Furthermore, the referred student's off-task behavior consisted entirely of motor and passive, as opposed to verbal, off-task responses. By contrast, the comparison student's off-task behavior was entirely motor. The teacher gave no attention to either student during 17 of 20 intervals observed, and neutral attention during the other three intervals. However, peers attended to the off-task behavior on 6 occasions.

Source: Reprinted and adapted with permission of the publisher and author from G. J. Alessi, "Behavioral Observation for the School Psychologist: Responsive-Discrepancy Model," *School Psychology Review*, 1980, 9, pp. 36–37. © National Association of School Psychologists.

information into various categories and then quantify the coding (see, for example, Barker & Wright, 1954).

Advantages of Narrative Recording

Narrative recording has the following advantages:

- It provides a record of the child's behavior and of your general impressions.
- It maintains the original sequence of events.
- It provides a means of gathering information and discovering critical behaviors.
- It allows you to assess progress.
- It provides a record of continuing difficulties.
- It requires little equipment.
- It is a valuable precursor to more systematic observational procedures.

Disadvantages of Narrative Recording

Narrative recording has the following disadvantages:

- It is not well suited to obtaining quantifiable data.
- It is difficult to validate.
- It may not describe fully some types of critical behaviors.
- It may produce findings with limited generalizability.
- It may vary from observer to observer.

Illustrations of Narrative Recording

The example below is a narrative record for a 4½-year-old boy at preschool (adapted from Cohen & Stern, 1970, p. 34). The record captures the child's mood and contains many qualifying details.

AN ANECDOTAL RECORDING

Winky points to the window and, with radiant face, calls in delight, "It's snowing cherry blossoms! First they are white, then green, then red, red, red! I want to paint!" He goes to the easel and quickly snatches up a smock. Sliding in beside Wayne, he whispers to him,

"Wayne, you want blue? I give it to you, okay? You give me red because I'm going to make cherries, lots of red cherries!"

After the boys exchange paint jars, Winky sits erect and, with a sigh of contentment, starts quickly but with clean strokes to ease his brush against the edge of the jar. He makes dots all around the outer part of the paper. His tongue licks his upper lip, his eyes shine, his body is quiet but intense. The red dots are big, well-rounded, full of color, and clearly separated. While working, Winky sings to himself, "Red cherries, big, round red cherries!" The first picture completed, he calls the teacher to hang it up to dry. The next picture starts as the first did, with dots at the outside edge, but soon filling the entire paper. He uses green too, but the colors do not overlap.

Still singing his little phrase, Winky paints a third and fourth picture, concentrating intently on his work.

The other children pick up his song, and Wayne starts to paint blue dots on his paper. Waving his brush, Winky asks, "Wayne, want to try my cherries?" Swiftly and jubilantly he swishes his brush across Wayne's chin. Laughing, he paints dots on his own hands. "My hands are full of cherries," he shouts. He runs into the adjoining room, calling excitedly to the children, "My hands are full of cherries!" He strides into the bathroom to wash his hands. Susie follows him in, calling, "Let's see, Winky." "Ha, I ate them all," he gloats as he shows his washed hands with a sweeping movement. He grabs a toy bottle from the shelf, fills it with water, and asks the teacher to put the nipple on. He lies down then on a mattress and sucks the bottle, his face softly smiling, his eyes big and gazing into space, his whole body relaxed.

The next example is a 4-minute narrative record for a 7-year, 4-month-old boy, beginning at the time he awoke on the morning of a school day (adapted from Barker & Wright, 1966, pp. 15–17). Notice that the recording describes the mother's statements, as well as her voice quality, and the child's facial expressions, glances, and actions, together with the quality of his behavior.

A RUNNING RECORD

7:00   Mrs. Birch said with pleasant casualness, "Raymond, wake up." With a little more urgency in her voice, she spoke again: "Son, are you going to school today?"

Raymond didn't respond immediately.

He screwed up his face and whimpered a little.

He lay still.

His mother repeated, "Raymond, wake up." This was said pleasantly; the mother was apparently in good spirits and was willing to put up with her son's reluctance.

Raymond whimpered again and kicked his feet rapidly in protest.

He squirmed around and rolled over crossways on the bed.

His mother removed the covers.

He again kicked his feet in protest.

He sat up and rubbed his eyes.

He glanced at me and smiled.

I smiled in return as I continued making notes.

7:01   Raymond picked up a sock and began tugging and pulling it on his left foot. As his mother watched him, she said kiddingly, "Can't you get your peepers open?"

Raymond stopped putting on his sock long enough to rub his eyes again. He appeared to be very sleepy.

He said "Mommie" plaintively and continued mumbling in an unintelligible way something about his undershirt.

7:02   His mother asked, "Do you want to put this undershirt on, or do you want to wear the one you have on?"

Raymond sleepily mumbled something in reply.

Raymond struggled out of the T-shirt that he had on.

He put on the clean striped T-shirt more easily.

7:03   He pulled on his right sock.

He picked up his left tennis shoe and put it on.

He laced his left shoe with deliberation, looking intently at the shoe as he worked steadily until he had it all laced.

7:04   He put on his right shoe.

He laced up his right shoe. Again he worked intently, looking at the shoe as he laced it.

His mother called, "Raymond, do you want an egg for breakfast?" in a pleasant, inquiring tone.

Raymond responded very sleepily, "No."

Raymond climbed back into bed.

Exercise 4-1.
Narrative Recording Exercises

1. With a co-observer, observe one child on a playground. Conduct an anecdotal recording for 5 minutes. If the playground is associated with a school, obtain permission from the administration before engaging in this activity.

Compare your record with that of your co-observer. How similar are the two recordings? What did your co-observer in-

clude that you did not, and vice versa? Consider the following questions in evaluating your narrative recording:

- How detailed is your recording of the child's behavior? Does the recording provide a visual picture of what was happening?
- What behaviors might you have missed?
- Why did you record some behaviors and not others?
- How did the setting influence the child's behavior?
- To what extent did the child's behavior represent that of his or her peer group?
- What biases, if any, may have affected your observations?
- Were your observations primarily of specific details or of general behaviors?
- What hypotheses did you develop about potential problem behaviors?
- What specific behaviors would you like to observe at another time?
- How might your presence have altered the child's behavior?
- What could you have done to minimize this influence?
- How did your narrative recording contribute to your understanding of the child?
- Which statements in your recording reflect high, medium, and low inferential judgments?

To answer the last question, construct a form with two column headings: (a) statement and (b) inference level (high, medium, low). Select 30 statements from your report—10 from the beginning, 10 from the middle, and 10 from the end. Statements may be complete sentences or sentence fragments. Thus, one sentence in your recording may generate more than one statement. Number each statement in your description, and place the numbered statements in the first column. Decide whether each statement reflects a high, medium, or low level of inference. Complete this same form for your co-observer's recording, and have your co-observer do the same for your recording. (Photocopying the two forms *after* the statements are typed but *before* the classifications are made will facilitate this process.) Determine the level of interobserver agreement for each statement by calculating the percentage agreement (number of agreements divided by number of statements, which in this case is 30). The chart below illustrates how the form would be completed for the first part of the narrative running record shown on pages 98 and 99.

Statement	Inference Level (high, medium, low)
1. Mrs. Birch said with pleasant casualness,	Medium
2. "Raymond, wake up."	Low
3. With a little more urgency in her voice, she spoke again:	Medium
4. "Son, are you going to school today?"	Low
5. Raymond didn't respond immediately.	Low
6. He screwed up his face	Low
7. and whimpered a little.	Low
8. He lay still.	Low

Write a one- or two-paragraph report describing your observation. Include information about (a) the child (age, gender, and other relevant characteristics), (b) the physical setting in which the observation took place, (c) the length of time you observed the child, (d) what you observed, (e) the level of agreement with your co-observer, and (f) the implications of the findings (for example, whether the behavior was appropriate or inappropriate).

2. With a co-observer, observe a group of children on a playground. Conduct a running record of the group's behavior for a 5-minute time period. Follow the guidelines given in Exercise 1 for evaluating a recording, but substitute *group* for *child* as the focus of your observation.

3. Compare the recordings obtained in Exercises 1 and 2. What are the differences between observing one child and observing a group? What information do you gain (or lose) in each type of recording? Write up your analysis in a one- or two-paragraph report.

4. Narrative recordings can also be used to observe specific types of behavior in various settings. Study the attachment behavior of 1- or 2-year-olds by observing their behavior when they are left at a day care center or at a nursery maintained by a church or synagogue during a religious service. Obtain approval from the center, church, or synagogue administration before engaging in this activity.

    With a co-observer, make an anecdotal record of (a) one child's behavior at the time her or his parent leaves, (b) the parent's reaction, (c) the caregiver's behavior, (d) the child's response to the caregiver, and (e) the child's behavior after the parent has left the room. If your observation takes place in a church or synagogue, also observe the child's and parent's reactions when the parent returns. (You should also observe these reactions at a full-time day care center if you can return at the end of the day.) Conduct the observation for at least a 30- to 60-minute period. If time permits, observe other children, but only one child at a time. Be sure that you and your co-observer agree on the child to be observed and the observation method to be used. Arrive early. Use the guidelines in Exercise 1 for evaluating your recording.

INTERVAL RECORDING

Interval recording (sometimes referred to as *time sampling, interval sampling,* or *interval time sampling*) focuses on selected aspects of behavior as they occur within specified intervals of time. The term *sampling* conveys the basic idea of interval recording—you sample behavior rather than recording every behavior as it occurs during the observational period. The observational period is divided into brief segments, or intervals (usually 5 to 30 seconds long, depending on the length of the observation), during which you note whether a behavior occurs. You tally the presence or absence of the predefined target behavior in each interval. Interval recording is especially suitable for controlled observations and laboratory studies. In cases where time sampling is distinguished from interval recording, *time sampling* implies that brief observations are made either at specified times during the day or at random times (such time sampling requires that the target behavior have a moderate to high frequency of occurrence), whereas *interval recording* indicates that a discrete observa-

"Good morning, children. I'm Ms. Givens. If you have any questions, you can reach me at www.msg.com."

Reprinted with permission from Art Bouthillier.

tional period—say, 15 or 30 minutes—is divided into a specified number of intervals.

    There are several interval recording procedures.

    1. *Partial-interval time sampling.* You record (score) a behavior *only once,* regardless of how long it lasts or how many times it occurs in the interval. This commonly used interval recording method (see Table 4-4) is particularly useful for behaviors that occur fleetingly, such as smiling. It reveals the consistency of behavior.

    2. *Whole-interval time sampling.* You score a behavior *only when it occurs at the beginning of the interval and lasts throughout the interval.* This method is particularly useful when you want to know which behaviors (such as out-of-seat behavior) the child performs continuously during an interval.

    3. *Point time interval sampling.* You score a behavior *only when it occurs at a specific time (or times) during the interval.* For example, you might record a specific behavior only if it occurs during the first 10 seconds of each hour, not when it occurs during the remaining 59 minutes and 50 seconds. This procedure allows you to observe behavior for brief periods at different times during the day. When you use this procedure with groups of children, you can set up a rotational system for observing each child in turn.

    4. *Momentary time interval sampling.* You score a behavior *only if it occurs at the moment the interval begins or ends.* For example, if the interval is 30 seconds, you score only behaviors observed at the end of the 30-second interval. You can use this procedure for observing groups of children. For example, with five children, you can set up a 50-second observation cycle, observing a different one of the five chil-

Table 4-4
Example of a Three-Minute Partial-Interval Time Sample Recording

Referred (R): ___Jim___
Comparison (C): ___Ted___
Date: ___March 2, 2001___

Class: ___Mrs. Jones___
Time: ___11:00 to 11:03 a.m.___

Behaviors	Tot.		1	2	3	4	5	6	7	8	9	10	11	12
Passive off-task	5	R	X	O	O	O	O	O	X	X	X	O	O	X
	1	C	O	O	O	O	O	O	X	O	O	O	O	O
Disruptive off-task	1	R	O	O	O	X	O	O	O	O	O	O	O	O
	0	C	O	O	O	O	O	O	O	O	O	O	O	O
On-task	6	R	O	X	X	O	X	X	O	O	O	X	X	O
	11	C	X	X	X	X	X	X	O	X	X	X	X	X

Note. Abbreviations are R = referred child, C = comparison child, X = behavior observed, O = behavior not observed, Tot. = Total. Each number reflects a 10-second observation period followed by a 5-second pause for recording data. Three types of behavior were recorded: passive off-task behavior, disruptive off-task behavior, and on-task behavior. Jim engaged in off-task behavior in 6 of the 12 intervals; 5 of the off-task behaviors were passive. Thus, in 50% of the intervals he showed some kind of off-task behavior. In contrast, Ted had only 1 interval with off-task behavior (passive).

dren at the end of each 10-second interval within the 50-second cycle. This variant is useful with behaviors that occur at moderate but steady rates (e.g., tics, hand movements, thumbsucking, stereotypic behavior, and facial expressions). A 30-second interval is useful for most behaviors (Kearns, Edwards, & Tingstrom, 1990).

5. *Variable interoccasion interval time sampling.* You score a behavior *only if it occurs during preselected random time intervals.* Instead of always recording behaviors during the first minute of each hour (a fixed interval), you might randomly designate, for instance, a 1-minute observation period for each observation hour (any 1-minute period between the 1st and the 60th minutes). For a 6-hour observation period, a random 1-minute observation schedule might be as follows:

- First hour—30th to 31st minute
- Second hour—12th to 13th minute
- Third hour—51st to 52nd minute
- Fourth hour—2nd to 3rd minute
- Fifth hour—8th to 9th minute
- Sixth hour—46th to 47th minute

This method is useful when you want to obtain a sample of behavior over an extended period of time and rule out temporal effects.

Major Uses of Interval Recording

Interval recording is useful for observing behaviors that (a) are overt, (b) do not always have a clearcut beginning and

ending, and (c) occur with moderate frequency, such as once every 10 to 15 seconds. Examples include reading, working, sitting, touching objects, roughhousing, conversing appropriately, shouting, screaming, hitting, playing with toys, making noise, smiling, lying down, and thumbsucking. Interval recording is not suitable, for example, for recording the exact frequency of behavior, the duration of behavior, or covert behaviors such as subtle bodily movements.

How to Design an Interval Recording

In designing an interval recording, you must decide on (a) the number of times you will observe the child, (b) the length of the observation period, (c) the time periods during which observations will be conducted, (d) the type of interval recording to be used, (e) the length of the observation interval, (f) the length of the recording interval (an interval devoted only to recording data), if needed, (g) the target behaviors you want to observe, and (h) the method of recording data.

Frequency, length, and time of observation period.
The child's age, the setting, and the reason for the assessment will influence the number of times you will need to observe the child, the length of the observation period, and when you should conduct the observations. An observation session may last from 10 to 30 minutes or even longer. Time your observations so that you can observe a representative sample of the target behaviors. Try to observe the child more than once and at different times during the day.

Type of interval recording. Select an interval recording method that will best give you the information that you need.

Length of the observation interval. The length of the observation interval will depend on the target behaviors. Gear the interval length to the onset and termination of the behaviors under observation. An appropriate interval length will minimize distortion of the behavioral sequences and frequencies. Short intervals are preferable for behaviors that last a short time, such as making excessive noise, pushing other children, mouthing objects, and self-stimulation. Long intervals are useful for behaviors that last a long time, such as arguing excessively or sleeping in the classroom.

Length of the recording interval. Include a recording interval whenever the scoring will interfere with the ongoing observations. If you use a recording interval, you need to have something to tell you when an interval begins and ends, such as a silent cuing device that signals the onset and offset of the observation and recording intervals. Although you can use various electronic devices, a simple method is to record on an audio cassette tape words that signal the observation and recording intervals and to listen to the tape via an earjack while observing. For a 10-second observation interval and 5-second recording interval, you could use the following sequence, with the words "first," "second," and "third" referring to the interval number: "First" (0 seconds), "Record" (10 seconds), "Second" (15 seconds), "Record" (25 seconds), "Third" (30 seconds), "Record" (40 seconds), and so forth. You can use a similar cuing system when you have only observation intervals. Whatever the cuing system, it should not interfere with the ongoing observations. A cuing system will help to ensure that you and another observer score the same numbered interval, which will result in greater interobserver agreement. If one observer skips an interval, agreement on all the remaining intervals may be lacking.

Target behaviors. Select target behaviors based on prior narrative recordings, interview information, referral questions, or the child's test behavior. When you use a predesigned (either published or unpublished) observational coding system (see Chapter 5), the coding system will specify the target behaviors.

Method of recording data. You can record data with pencil and paper or with an electronic recording device. Table 4-5 shows a standard recording form that you can use with various recording methods and coding systems.

Another approach is to use a system that allows you to automatically graph the data as you record them. When you finish your observations, you have a picture of the child's behavior that you can share immediately with the referral source. Table 4-6 shows a self-graphing data recording system in which minutes and days are used as the time intervals. You also can graph the collected data across days, as shown in Table 4-7.

When you use interval recording, you may record the score for the behavior(s) either during the interval or immediately afterward. If you record during the interval, there will be no break between intervals; the observation intervals will be successive. For a 10-second observation interval, the observation intervals would be as follows:

- Observation interval and recording (10 seconds)
- Observation interval and recording (10 seconds)
- Observation interval and recording (10 seconds) (Sequence continues)

If you record after the interval, the observation intervals will alternate with intervals for recording behavior. For example, the observation period might consist of a series of cycles in which a 10-second observation interval was followed by a 5-second recording interval. A typical sequence would be as follows:

- Observation interval (10 seconds)
- Recording interval (5 seconds)
- Observation interval (10 seconds)
- Recording interval (5 seconds) (Sequence repeats)

The second method is usually a necessity when you are recording several behaviors during an interval, for you must look away from the child to put notations in the appropriate spaces. The length of the observation interval—as well as the length of the recording interval, if used—should remain fixed across all observations to ensure uniformity of the observations.

To observe the referred child, the teacher, and the class, you might use a sequential procedure in which you observe first the child, then the teacher, and then the class. You could divide a 60-second observation period in the following way:

- Observe child (1–10 seconds)
- Observe teacher (11–20 seconds)
- Observe class (21–30 seconds)
- Observe child (31–40 seconds)
- Observe teacher (41–50 seconds)
- Observe class (51–60 seconds) (Sequence repeats)

If needed, intersperse recording intervals with observation periods. The following sequence consists of 7-second observation intervals and 3-second recording intervals:

- Observe child (1–7 seconds)
- Record behavior (8–10 seconds)
- Observe teacher (11–17 seconds)
- Record behavior (18–20 seconds)
- Observe class (21–27 seconds)
- Record behavior (28–30 seconds) (Sequence repeats)

Sequential observation procedures permit flexibility in recording the behavior of individuals and groups. You also can use them with different behavioral coding systems to fit particular assessment needs.

Table 4-5
General Recording Protocol

WESTERN MICHIGAN UNIVERSITY
CLASSROOM OBSERVATION RECORD PROTOCOL

Referred (R): Sue	Comparison (C): Andrea	Observer: Psychologist
Age: 8-6	Age: 8-5	Other Observer: Paraprofessional
Grade: 3rd		Class Size: 31
School: Pine Elementary		Class Type: Regular ed.
Teacher: Mrs. Graves		Time Stop: 11:16
Date: 10 / 6 / 99		Time Start: 11:09
month day year		Total Time: :07

Reason for observation (What question do we want to answer?):

To observe whether Sue's behavior during reading differs from that of another child.

Classroom activity and explicit rules in effect at time of observation:

Activity: Reading. Rules: 1. Work quietly; 2. sit at desks; 3. raise hand for help.

Grouping situation (G):
(circle one)
L = large group   (I) = independent act
S = small group   F = free time
O = one to one

Teacher (T)/peer (P) reaction codes:
AA = attention to all
A+ = positive attention to student
A– = negative attention to student
Ao = no attention to student
An = neutral attention to student

Observation recording method:
(a) interval size 15".
(b) time sample: size _____.
(c) event count
(d) duration
(e) latency

Behaviors*	Tot.		1 15	30	45	60	2 15	30	45	60	3 15	30	45	60	4 15	30	45	60
Verbal off-task	8	R	X	O	O	X	X	O	O	X	X	O	O	X	X	O	X	
	2	C	O	X	O	O	X	O	O	O	O	O	O	O	O	O	O	
		T	Ao	Ao		Ao	An			Ao	Ao			Ao	An		Ao	
		P																
		G																
1		Sc																
Motor off-task	4	R	X	O	X	O	O	O	O	O	O	X	X	O	O	O	O	
	1	C	O	O	O	O	O	O	O	O	O	O	O	X	O	O	O	
		T	Ao		Ao							Ao	An	Ao				
		P																
		G																
2		Sc																
Passive off-task	1	R	O	O	O	O	O	X	O	O	O	O	O	O	O	O	O	
	1	C	O	O	O	O	O	O	X	O	O	O	O	O	O	O	O	
		T							Ao	An								
		P																
		G																
3		Sc																
On-task	3	R	O	X	O	O	O	O	X	O	O	O	O	O	O	X	O	
	11	C	X	O	X	X	O	X	O	X	X	X	X	O	X	X	X	
		T	Ao	An	An	An		Ao		Ao	Ao	An	Ao		Ao	An	Ao	
		P																
		G																
4		Sc																
Out of seat (duration)	53"	R	14"	8"	22"	9"												
	6"	C	6"															
		T	A–	A–	An	A–												
		P																
		G																
5		Sc																

Were reliability data collected? (Yes) No.   If yes, interobserver % agreements = 83%. Sc = Scan check.
*Include specific behavior definitions on back, as well as comments (strengths, contextual observations, etc).

(Continued)

Table 4-5 *(Continued)*

Note. The form includes spaces for identifying information and spaces down the left side for writing in the behaviors being observed. Across the page are numbers with columns of boxes underneath. Each number can refer to successive (a) intervals, (b) behavior counts, (c) duration measures, or (d) latency measures. For interval and behavior measures, data would be recorded with an X (target behavior occurred) or an O (target behavior did not occur) in each block. For duration and latency measures, the actual elapsed time would be entered in the successive boxes (e.g., 14″/8″/22″/9″).

Each space for writing in a behavior category has six rows of boxes after it: R = referred student, C = comparison student, T = teacher's reaction, P = peer reaction, G = group reaction, and Sc = Scan check. Two spaces are provided for summarizing the data recorded in the blocks across the first two rows. Scan check refers to the percentage of children in the class who are performing the behavior.

The duration recording is entered in the same boxes as the interval data, but it does not refer to any specific intervals. In this example, there were four occasions during the session when the referred child was out of seat and one occasion when the comparison child was out of seat. The duration recording was made independently of the interval recording.

Source: Reprinted and adapted with permission of the publisher and author from G. J. Alessi, "Behavioral Observation for the School Psychologist: Responsive-Discrepancy Model," *School Psychology Review*, 1980, 9, pp. 36–37. © National Association of School Psychologists.

Quantitative Data in Interval Recording

The primary piece of quantitative data obtained in interval recording is the number of intervals in which the target behaviors did occur. Note that the frequency count reflects the number of *intervals* in which the behavior occurred, not the number of times the behavior occurred (see Event Recording below).

If you want information on the intensity of the behavior, you can build an intensity dimension into the behavioral code. For example, if you want to record the intensity of hyperactive behavior, you can include codes representing different degrees of intensity (e.g., mildly hyperactive, moderately hyperactive, and extremely hyperactive).

Advantages of Interval Recording

Interval recording has the following advantages (Kazdin, 1981; Nay, 1979):

- It may help to define important time-behavior relations.
- It facilitates checking for interobserver reliability.
- It helps to ensure that the predefined behaviors are observed under the same conditions each time.
- It uses time efficiently.
- It focuses the observer's attention on the child's behavior by structuring the observations.
- It permits the recording of virtually any observable behavior.
- It allows for the collection of a large number of observations in a short period of time.
- It requires minimal and inexpensive equipment.

Disadvantages of Interval Recording

Interval recording has the following disadvantages:

- It provides a somewhat artificial view of the behavior sequence because the time interval—not the behavior—dictates the recording framework.
- It may allow important behaviors related to the problem to be overlooked.

- It does not provide information about the quality of the behavior (i.e., how the behavior was performed) or about the situation (i.e., whether the child was agitated, paying attention, or sleeping while in his or her seat) unless such information is specifically coded into the recording system.
- It may not reveal the actual frequency or duration of the behavior (e.g., one 60-second continuous period of off-task behavior would be recorded as four separate events in a 10-second observation/5-second recording interval system).
- It may overestimate the frequency of low-rate behaviors or behaviors of short duration and underestimate the frequency of high-rate behaviors.
- It may require observers to undergo considerable training to learn the recording system.

Illustration of Interval Recording

The following example illustrates how an observer used interval recording in a classroom to observe the on- and off-task behaviors of children with mental retardation (adapted from Whitman, Scibak, Butler, Richter, & Johnson, 1982, pp. 557–558). In addition to the data on on- and off-task behaviors, the observer obtained data on the number of problems each child completed and solved. Chapter 5 discusses the interobserver reliability referred to in the illustration.

INTERVAL RECORDING: OBSERVING ON-TASK AND OFF-TASK BEHAVIOR

Students and Setting

Three students with attentional problems from a class for children identified as having mental retardation were the focus of the observation. The three children could follow simple instructions and were achieving at a first-grade level. When assigned an academic task to complete, they were generally off-task, frequently glancing up from assigned work, turning to watch other children, and playing with objects on their desks.

A fourth child was selected as a comparison student. Her teacher reported that she did not have attentional problems.

Table 4-6
Self-Graphing Data Recording System

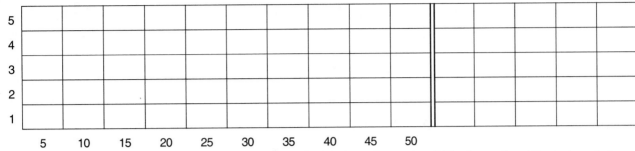

a. Graph paper with series of columns, each five blocks high. Double heavy line marks off 10 columns, for a 50-minute period.

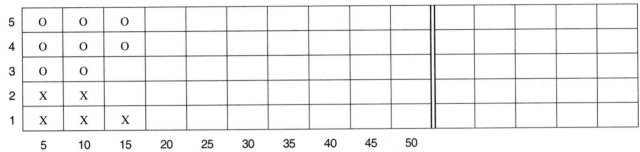

b. Chart after 13 minutes of monitoring student's behavior. First two columns are completed, and the third is partially completed. If the student behaves appropriately during the next (14th) minute, the observer will mark an X in the third column just above the other X. If the student misbehaves, the observer will mark an O in that column just under the other two Os.

	5	10	15	20	25	30	35	40	45	50					
5	O	O	O	O	O	O	O	O	O	O					
4	O	O	O	O	O	O	X	O	X	X					
3	O	O	O	X	O	X	X	X	X	X					
2	X	X	X	X	X	X	X	X	X	X					
1	X	X	X	X	X	X	X	X	X	X					

c. Chart after the observer has completed the 50-minute period.

Note. To create a self-graphing data recording system, begin with a piece of graph paper. Mark two heavy lines across the paper so that 5 blocks are between the lines. You have now a series of columns, all 5 blocks high. Each block will represent an interval (e.g., 1 minute) of observation time. Mark off the number of 5-block columns needed for the scheduled observation periods: a 50-minute period would need 10 columns of 5 blocks, a 30-minute period would need 6 columns, a 45-minute period would need 9 columns, and a 5-minute period would need only one column. For now, let's assume you have scheduled a 50-minute period for your observations, as shown in (a). You have marked off 10 columns on your paper, each 5 blocks high, for a total of 50 blocks: one block for each minute scheduled.

For each interval (minute) in which the on-task behavior occurs, you will place an X in a box. For each interval in which the behavior does not occur, you will place an O in a box. Start with the left column and work toward the right. In each column, work from the bottom up with the Xs and from the top down with the Os. When the Xs and Os meet in the middle, the column is filled. Move to the next column to the right and continue: Xs from the bottom up, Os from the top down, until they meet. As you move across the row of 5-block columns, the data recorded will automatically form a graph. With this method, trends in data across the session can be easily identified and shared with school personnel, referral sources, or parents. Focusing on the Xs in (c) shows that the amount of on-task behavior by the student is steadily increasing during the observation session (i.e., there are fewer Xs in the first columns and more Xs in the later columns).

Source: Reprinted and adapted with permission of the publisher and author from G. J. Alessi, "Behavioral Observation for the School Psychologist: Responsive-Discrepancy Model," *School Psychology Review*, 1980, *9*, pp. 39–40. © National Association of School Psychologists.

Table 4-7
Automatic Graphing Data Collection Procedures

Interval	1	2	3	4	5	6	7	8	9	10	11	12	13	14	15	16	17	18	19	20	21	22	23	24	25	26	27	28	29	30
19	O	O	O	O	O	O	O	O	O	O	O	O	O	O	O	O	O	O	O	O	O	O	O	O	O	O	O	O	O	O
18	O	O	O	O	O	O	O	O	O	O	O	O	O	O	O	O	O	O	O	O	O	O	O	O	O	O	O	O	O	O
17	O	O	O	O	O	O	O	O	O	O	O	O	O	O	O	O	O	O	O	O	O	O	O	O	O	O	O	O	O	O
16	O	O	O	O	O	O	O	O	O	O	O	O	O	O	O	O	O	O	O	O	O	O	O	O	O	O	O	O	O	O
15	O	O	O	O	O	O	O	O	O	O	O	O	O	O	O	O	O	O	O	O	O	O	O	O	O	O	O	O	O	O
14	O	O	X	O	O	O	O	O	O	O	O	O	O	O	O	O	O	O	O	O	O	O	O	O	O	O	O	O	O	O
13	X	O	X	X	O	O	O	O	O	O	O	O	O	O	O	O	O	O	O	O	O	O	O	O	O	O	O	O	O	O
12	X	X	X	X	O	O	O	O	O	O	O	O	O	O	O	O	O	O	O	O	O	O	O	O	O	O	O	O	O	O
11	X	X	X	X	O	O	O	O	O	O	O	O	O	O	O	O	O	O	O	O	O	O	O	O	O	O	O	O	O	O
10	X	X	X	X	O	O	O	O	O	O	O	O	O	O	O	O	O	O	O	O	O	O	O	O	O	O	O	O	O	O
9	X	X	X	X	O	O	O	O	O	O	O	O	O	O	O	O	O	O	O	O	O	O	O	O	O	O	O	O	O	O
8	X	X	X	X	X	O	O	O	O	O	O	O	O	O	O	O	O	O	O	O	O	O	O	O	O	O	O	O	O	O
7	X	X	X	X	X	X	X	O	O	O	O	O	O	O	O	O	O	O	O	O	O	O	O	O	O	O	O	O	O	O
6	X	X	X	X	X	X	X	X	O	O	O	X	O	O	O	O	O	O	O	O	O	O	O	O	O	O	O	O	O	O
5	X	X	X	X	X	X	X	X	O	O	O	X	O	O	O	O	O	O	O	O	O	O	O	O	O	O	O	O	O	O
4	X	X	X	X	X	X	X	X	X	X	O	X	O	O	O	O	O	O	O	O	O	O	O	O	O	O	O	O	O	O
3	X	X	X	X	X	X	X	X	X	X	X	X	X	O	O	O	O	X	O	O	O	O	O	O	O	O	O	O	O	O
2	X	X	X	X	X	X	X	X	X	X	X	X	X	X	X	X	X	O	X	O	X	O	O	O	O	O	O	O	O	O
1	X	X	X	X	X	X	X	X	X	X	X	X	X	X	X	X	X	X	X	X	X	X	X	O	X	X	O	X	O	O

Note. Days 1 through 30 are across the abcissa, and intervals 1 through 19 are up the ordinate. The heavy line between days 4 and 5 indicates the beginning of an intervention plan. Intervals with talk-outs are scored with Xs, and quiet intervals are scored with Os. By reading from left to right and focusing on the Xs, you can see a clear downward trend in the number of intervals scored for talking out over the 30-day period (more Xs in the earlier columns and fewer Xs in the later columns). There is a swift drop in the number of intervals scored for talking out just after the intervention was implemented (day 5), suggesting the effectiveness of this procedure.

Source: Reprinted and adapted with permission of the publisher and author from G. J. Alessi, "Behavioral Observation for the School Psychologist: Responsive-Discrepancy Model," *School Psychology Review*, 1980, *9*, p. 41. © National Association of School Psychologists.

The observation took place in the classroom during math and writing periods. There were 13 students in the class. The daily curriculum was aimed at developing basic math, writing, and reading. Special materials were constructed for the observation period. These materials, which would be used again after special training procedures were begun, consisted of sheets of simple one-digit math problems and spelling exercises. During each math session, 140 addition and subtraction problems were given to each child, considerably more than any of them had time to complete. The spelling exercises required children to copy three- and four-letter words. During each session, the students were asked to copy two pages of spelling words, each page containing 16 words.

Coding Categories

On-task behavior was defined as (a) the children's buttocks had to be touching the seat of the chair and (b) their eyes had to be oriented toward the task materials while (c) they interacted manually with the task materials. Two of the three referred children were observed simultaneously on an alternating basis—that is, every 5 minutes a different pair of children was observed. Thus, during each 30-minute session, each child was observed for a total of 20 minutes. These observations were made once a week. The comparison child was observed separately, once a week for 20 minutes.

A partial-interval rating system was used, with 10-second observation intervals. Any break in eye or manual contact with the task materials or incorrect posturing resulted in that interval's being scored as off-task. Other responses recorded included the percentage of 50 math problems completed, the percentage of attempted math problems correct, the percentage of 350 letters completed, and the percentage of completed words spelled correctly by each child.

Interobserver reliability was determined twice during each session by use of a second observer. Interobserver reliability for both occurrence and nonoccurrence of on-task behavior was computed on an interval-by-interval basis. The number of agreements across the two observers was divided by the number of agreements plus disagreements, and the result was multiplied by 100. The reliability of the performance measures was checked by percentage agreement.

In another study, momentary time interval sampling was used to evaluate the behavior of children in a classroom (Slate & Saudargas, 1987). A 20-minute observation period was divided into 15-second intervals. At the end of every 15-second interval, an observer recorded the occurrence of one of the following six target behaviors: *schoolwork* (student is doing assigned work while having head and eyes oriented toward the work materials or oriented toward the teacher during a lecture or discussion), *looking around* (student's eyes and ears are oriented away from the classroom activity), *out-of-seat* (student is out of her or his seat for any reason), *social interaction—child* (verbal or nonverbal interactions are taking place between target student and any other student while target student is seated), *social interaction—teacher* (target student and teacher are interacting verbally or nonverbally while target student is seated), and *other activity* (student is engaged in an activity not defined as schoolwork, such as preparing to begin work or doing math during reading time). Only one behavior was coded in any one interval because the six behaviors are mutually exclusive.

Exercise 4-2.
Interval Recording Exercises

1. With a co-observer, observe one child on a playground for 5 minutes. Select a child who appears to be engaged in play with another child. Use a partial-interval time sampling procedure, with 10 seconds for the observation interval and 5 seconds for the recording interval. Use a tape recorder, preferably with earphones, to signal the beginning and end of the observation and recording intervals. Use a two-category coding system: (a) aggressive behavior and (b) nonaggressive behavior. Aggressive behavior is defined in Exhibit 4-1. Mark an X for aggressive behavior and an O for nonaggressive behavior, using the recording protocol shown in Table 4-6.

    After you complete your recording, determine the level of interobserver agreement. Calculate the following interobserver agreement indices: (a) percentage agreement for occurrence of target behavior, (b) percentage agreement for nonoccurrence of target behavior, (c) percentage agreement for both categories, and (d) kappa. Formulas for obtaining these indices are covered in Chapter 5 in this text.

    Consider the following questions in evaluating your interval recording:

- How clearly was each behavior observed?
- To what extent might the time of day have affected the child's behavior?
- To what extent did the setting affect the child's behavior?
- Were the observational categories useful?
- How could the observational categories be improved?
- To what extent was the child's behavior similar to that of other children of the same age level?

- Did the coding categories reveal information that might have been missed if only a narrative recording had been used?
- What biases, if any, may have affected your observations?
- How might your presence have altered the child's behavior?
- What could you have done to minimize this influence?
- How did your interval recording contribute to your understanding of the child?

    Write a one- or two-paragraph report that describes your observation. Include information about (a) the child (age, gender, and other relevant characteristics), (b) the physical setting in which the observation took place, (c) the length of time you observed the child, (d) the number of intervals in which the target behavior occurred, (e) the level of agreement with your co-observer, (f) any difficulty in determining when the target behavior began and ended, (g) whether the definition of the target behavior was satisfactory and suggestions for improving the definition, and (h) the implications of the findings (e.g., whether the behavior was appropriate or inappropriate).

2. Follow the steps described in Exercise 1. Using a whole-interval time sampling procedure, observe a different child on the playground. Again, choose one who appears to be engaged in play with another child.

3. Compare the recordings obtained in Exercises 1 and 2. What are the differences between using a partial-interval and a whole-interval time sampling procedure? Which one gives you a more accurate picture of the child's behavior? Why? Write a one- or two-paragraph analysis of your findings.

EVENT RECORDING

In *event recording* (also called *event sampling*), you record each instance of a specific behavior or event as it occurs during the observation period. Like interval recording, event recording *samples behavior.* However, whereas the unit of measure in interval recording is the time interval imposed on the target behavior, the unit of measure in event recording is the behavior. In other words, you wait for the preselected behavior (the event) to occur and then record it. Like interval recording, event recording is especially useful for controlled observations and laboratory studies.

Major Uses of Event Recording

Event recording provides a continuous temporal record of the observed behaviors and thus is particularly appropriate for measuring discrete responses that have clearly defined beginnings and endings. Examples are spelling a word correctly, completing a problem, making a social response (e.g., saying "hello" or sharing a toy), pulling clothing, acting aggressively, getting out of a seat, using profanity, toileting, eating, asking a question, having a seizure, making a speech error, or arriving late to class. Behaviors that leave *permanent products* (such as number of words spelled correctly, number of problems completed, or number of drawings) are especially easy to measure by event recording. Additionally, if you use permanent products, you do not need to be present when the behavior occurs. The teacher or parent can collect the permanent products for you.

Event recording is less suitable for high-rate behaviors or for behaviors that vary in duration. For example, hand clapping is a behavior that may occur so frequently that separating each occurrence becomes difficult. Other behaviors that may occur too frequently for event recording include rocking movements; rapid jerks of the head, hands, or legs; running; and tapping objects. Responses that may extend over different periods and that will be difficult to record by event recording include thumbsucking, reading, listening, and aggressive interactions.

How to Design an Event Recording

In designing an event recording you must decide on (a) the number of times you will observe the child, (b) the length of the observation period, (c) the time periods during which you will conduct the observations, (d) the target behaviors you will observe, and (e) the method of recording data.

Frequency, length, and time of observation period.
The child's age, the setting, and the reason for the assessment will influence the number of times you will need to observe the child, the length of the observation period, and when you should conduct the observations. An observation session may last from 10 to 30 minutes or even longer. Time your observations so that you can observe a representative sample of the target behavior. If possible, observe the child more than once and at different times throughout the day.

Target behaviors.
As in interval recording, base the selection of target behaviors on prior narrative recordings, interview information, referral questions, or the child's test behavior. If you use a predesigned coding system, the system will specify target behaviors (see Chapter 5). Remember to select behaviors that have an easily discernible beginning and ending.

Method of recording data.
You can record responses in various ways, such as using a checklist, a wrist counter, a hand counter, an electromechanical counter, or another mechanical device or transferring small objects from one of your pockets to another. For paper-and-pencil recordings, you can use various methods to make tallies. One is the traditional stroke method:

$$| \quad || \quad ||| \quad |||| \quad ||||$$

Another is the dot-and-line method, which is often used when there is limited space on the recording protocol:

• •• •.• :•: ::: :|: :|: :|| ::|| □ ☒ ⊠

Table 4-8
Two Paper-and-Pencil Methods for Recording Frequency of Behavior

Behavior	Method — Dot and line	Method — Stroke	Frequency of behavior
Aggression	☒	||||| ||||	9
Cooperation	:· :·	||||	4
Crying	• •	||	2

Note. In the dot-and-line method, each dot represents one count and each line represents one count.

Table 4-8 illustrates these methods for making tallies.

You can also use the general recording protocol shown in Table 4-5 for event recording. For behaviors that occur frequently, a combination of event recording and 1-minute interval recording may be the best choice (see Table 4-9; Alessi, 1980).

To record the duration of a behavior, you can use a stopwatch, a wristwatch with a second hand, a time clock, a wall clock, or some other timing device. If you want to record the exact time a behavior occurred, you may want to use a handheld computer. There are also some counters that will record both the frequency of an event and its duration. For example, a counter panel that has several keys can be used, with one key assigned to each behavior. You simply hold the key down for the duration of the behavior, and the panel records the frequency and duration of the behavior.

Quantitative Data in Event Recording

The primary piece of quantitative data obtained in event recording is the *frequency count*—the number of occurrences of a behavior in a given time period. For example, an event recording might yield the information that "Chris used 10 profane words during a 20-minute observation period." In addition to the frequency of the behavior, you can measure several other behavioral dimensions in event recording, including the rate of the behavior, duration of the behavior, intensity of the behavior, and latency of the behavior. Let's consider each of these dimensions.

Rate of behavior. You obtain the rate at which a behavior occurs during the session by dividing the number of behaviors by the length of the observation period:

$$\text{Rate of behavior} = \frac{n}{t}$$

where n = number of behaviors
t = length of observation period

Table 4-9
Comparison of Event and Interval Records of Observation Conducted in 1-Minute Intervals

Behaviors	Tot.		1	2	3	4	5	6	7	8	9	10	11	12	13	14	15
Talk-outs by event record	76	R	⊡	⊠	⊡	⊠	⊡	⊡	⊡		∶	∶	⊡	∶	∶	·	·
	9	C		∷	·	·		·						∶			
1		T															
Talk-outs by interval record	14	R	X	X	X	X	X	X	X	O	X	X	X	X	X	X	X
	4	C	O	X	O	X	O	X	O	O	O	O	O	X	O	O	O
2		T															

Note. The top part shows event data for talking-out behavior within each interval. The bottom part shows the same data as scored by the interval-only method. The comparison illustrates that the interval record is not as sensitive to the dynamics of the high rate of behavior as the event-within-interval record is. With the event record (top), one can see a sudden decrease in rate of talking out after minute 7. The interval record is insensitive to this change. Likewise, the discrepancy between the two students' data is greater as measured by the event record; it is underestimated by the interval record. R = referred student, C = control student, T = teacher.

Source: Reprinted and adapted with permission of the publisher and author from G. J. Alessi, "Behavioral Observation for the School Psychologist: Responsive-Discrepancy Model," *School Psychology Review,* 1980, *9,* p. 39. © National Association of School Psychologists.

For example, if Jessica were observed to be out of her seat 40 times during a 10-minute observation period, her rate of behavior would be as follows:

$$\text{Rate of behavior} = \frac{n}{t} = \frac{40}{10} = \frac{4}{1}$$
$$= 4 \text{ occurrences per minute}$$

Jessica's rate of out-of-seat behavior was observed to be 4 times per minute. Rate of behavior is a useful index for noting changes in the child's behavior, especially across observation sessions of differing length.

Duration of behavior. You obtain the duration of behavior by noting how long each occurrence of the behavior lasts—the period between the beginning and the end of the behavior. You might use a duration measure, for example, to determine the duration of temper tantrums, crying episodes, arguments, verbal tirades, sustained conversations, on-task behavior, out-of-seat behavior, cooperative behavior, thumbsucking, off-task responding, or delays in returning home from school.

In addition to the duration measure, there are two other measures of the duration of behavior (Cone & Foster, 1982). One is the percentage of time the behavior occurs, and the other is the average duration of the behavior. The percentage of time the behavior occurs is computed by dividing the total duration of the behavior by the length of the observation period:

$$\text{Percentage of time behavior occurs} = \frac{d}{t} \times 100$$

where d = total duration of behavior (time spent responding)
t = length of observation period

The average duration of the behavior is computed by dividing the total duration of the behavior by the number of episodes of the behavior:

$$\text{Average duration of behavior} = \frac{d}{e}$$

where d = total duration of behavior (time spent responding)
e = number of episodes (or occurrences) of behavior

Suppose a child has two 3-minute tantrums (two episodes) during a 30-minute observation session on day 1 and six 1-minute tantrums (six episodes) during a 60-minute session on day 2. The total duration of the tantrums is 6 minutes on both days, but the response patterns differ.

Using the formula for the percentage of time spent having tantrums, we have

Day 1:

$$\text{Percentage of time having tantrums} = \frac{d}{t} \times 100 = \frac{6 \text{ min}}{30 \text{ min}} \times 100$$
$$= 20\% \text{ per session}$$

Day 2:

$$\text{Percentage of time having tantrums} = \frac{d}{t} \times 100 = \frac{6 \text{ min}}{60 \text{ min}} \times 100$$
$$= 10\% \text{ per session}$$

Using the formula for the average duration of each episode, we have

Day 1:

$$\text{Average duration of behavior} = \frac{d}{e} = \frac{6 \text{ min}}{2}$$
$$= 3 \text{ minutes per response}$$

Day 2:

$$\text{Average duration of behavior} = \frac{d}{e} = \frac{6 \text{ min}}{6}$$

$$= 1 \text{ minute per response}$$

The behavior occurred 20% of the time on day 1 and 10% of the time on day 2, and the average duration of an incident was 3 minutes per response on day 1 and 1 minute per response on day 2.

The first measure is preferable when you are interested in how much time a child spends in a particular activity relative to other activities (e.g., "academic engaged time") but care little about the duration of each instance of the behavior. This method masks the duration per response. The second method is useful when you are interested in the average duration of a response, such as when you are assessing the average duration of an appropriate behavior. This method ignores the length of the time interval over which the data are collected (Cone & Foster, 1982). If you prefer, you can report both measures.

Intensity of behavior.   You obtain the intensity of behavior by dividing the behavior into degrees of intensity, as in interval recording. For example, if you want to record intensities of aggressive behavior, categorize behaviors as slightly aggressive, moderately aggressive, and severely aggressive. If you are observing a student whose teacher has reported that he turns in all assignments but complains, you can create four categories, such as (1) hands in assignment on time with no complaints; (2) hands in assignment on time and complains; (3) hands in assignment late with no complaints; (4) hands in assignment late and complains (Cone & Foster, 1982). Record a separate frequency count for each category.

Latency of behavior.   You obtain the latency of behavior by noting the amount of time that elapses between a given cue (e.g., the initiation of a request) and the onset of the behavior; this tells you how long it took the child to begin the behavior. In place of the initiation of a request, you can use an event *known* to produce or facilitate the occurrence of a behavior, such as the ringing of a bell to signal the end of a class period. Latency is usually measured with a stopwatch, used to determine the time from the cue to the onset of the behavior. Latency measures are useful when you need to determine the time it takes a child to begin working after instructions have been given, to begin complying with a request (e.g., the time it takes a child to sit down, stand up, put away objects, or begin an assignment), or to stand up after an alarm rings (Sulzer-Azaroff & Reese, 1982). Latency measures are particularly useful when you are concerned about the child's ability to follow directions (Alessi, 1988).

Advantages of Event Recording

Event recording has the following advantages (Kazdin, 1981; Nay, 1979):

- It detects behaviors with low rates, particularly when observations are made by persons who are ordinarily in the setting.

- It facilitates the study of many different behaviors or events.
- It uses time and personnel efficiently, especially when observations are made by persons who are ordinarily in the setting.
- It can accommodate many different recording methods.
- It provides information about changes in behavior over time and the amount of behavior performed.

Disadvantages of Event Recording

Event recording has the following disadvantages:

- It provides a somewhat artificial view of the behavior sequence by separating the present event from conditions in the past that may have led up to it.
- It does not reveal sequences or temporal patterns, unless the time of the response is recorded.
- It breaks up the continuity of behavior by using limited categories.
- It is not suited to recording behaviors that are not discrete.
- It presents difficulties in establishing reliability across multiple observers.
- It requires observers to maintain an optimal level of attention over long periods of time, because few cues are used and responses may be relatively infrequent.
- It limits quantification of the *how* and *why* associated with the event, unless these also are recorded.
- It makes comparison across sessions difficult if the length of the observation period is not constant.

Illustrations of Event Recording

Table 4-10 illustrates how you can use event recording to compare two children's inappropriate talking.

In the example that follows, event recording and a duration measure are used in combination to examine one child's out-of-seat behavior (Whitman, Scibak, Butler, Richter, & Johnson, 1982). Notice that interobserver reliability was determined.

EVENT AND DURATION RECORDING: OBSERVING OUT-OF-SEAT BEHAVIOR

Linda is a 9-year-old girl who attended a primary-level special class for children with mental retardation in a public school system. Her teacher said that Linda functioned educationally at approximately the first-grade level and spent most of the day out of her seat. This behavior interfered with the completion of classroom work and distracted other children. Observations were made Monday through Friday from 9:00 a.m. to 9:20 a.m. during the math period in the child's classroom. The observation was designed so as not to interfere with regular classroom routines.

The observers sat against a wall in the classroom, approximately 10 feet from Linda. The target behavior was Linda's out-of-seat behavior. This behavior was recorded when the child's buttocks were not in contact with the chair seat. An event recording system was used to count out-of-seat behavior as defined. In addition, the total duration of each occurrence was recorded, using a stopwatch that was started and stopped at the beginning and end of the target behavior. Interobserver reliability was assessed with two observers us-

Table 4-10
Example of Event Recording of Inappropriate Talking to Another Child

Referred child: Jim   Date: March 1, 1996
Comparison child: Ted   Class: Mrs. Jones

Day	Time of day 9:00 to 9:30	11:00 to 11:30	2:00 to 2:30	Total (Jim/Ted)
Monday	4/1	3/0	2/0	9/1
Tuesday	3/0	2/0	0/0	5/0
Wednesday	4/1	4/1	1/0	9/2
Thursday	2/0	2/0	1/1	5/1
Friday	1/0	1/0	0/1	2/1
Total	14/2	12/1	4/2	30/5

*Note.*This record presents a summary of the observational records for two children: Jim, the referred child, and Ted, the comparison child. The values indicate the number of times Jim or Ted spoke with another child inappropriately. Numbers for Jim are to the left of the slash, and number for Ted are to the right of the slash. The record indicates that during the 7½ hours of observations, Jim spoke to another child six times more frequently than Ted. His inappropriate behavior occurred most frequently on Monday and Wednesday and at 9:00–9:30 and 11:00–11:30 A.M. The inappropriate behavior seldom occurred on Friday or at 2:00–2:30 P.M. Further investigation would be needed to determine what factors in the child's environment lead to increases and decreases in the inappropriate behavior. In addition, further observation should be made to determine the stability of the observed behavior pattern.

ing the rating system to record Linda's behavior (simultaneously but independently). These checks were made a minimum of two times per session. Interobserver agreement was calculated by (a) dividing the number of out-of-seat responses scored by the observer with the lower number of responses by the number of out-of-seat responses scored by the observer with the greater number of responses and (b) then multiplying by 100. Interobserver duration agreement was calculated in a similar manner.

Exercise 4-3.
Event Recording Exercises

1. With a co-observer, observe one child on a playground for 5 minutes. Using an event recording procedure, record each time the child engages in play (as a general category) with another child. Play with another child includes parallel, cooperative, and uncooperative play (see Table F-2 in Appendix F for definitions), but not solitary play. Use the dot-and-line method to record the target behavior.

    After you have completed your recording, determine the level of interobserver agreement by calculating percentage agreement (see the section on procedures for assessing reliability in Chapter 5). Also calculate the rate of the target behavior.

Consider the following questions in evaluating your event recording:

- How clearly was the target behavior observed?
- Did the target behavior occur with sufficient frequency to be observed?
- To what extent might the time of day have affected the child's behavior?
- To what extent did the setting affect the child's behavior?
- To what extent was the target behavior representative of the child's behavior during the observation?
- How could the definition of the observational category be improved?
- What could be done to improve the representativeness of the observations?
- To what extent was the child's behavior representative of that of his or her peers?
- What biases, if any, may have affected your observation?
- How might your presence have altered the child's behavior?
- What could you have done to minimize your influence?
- How did your event recording contribute to your understanding of the child?

Write a one- or two-paragraph report that describes your observation. Include information about (a) the child (age, gender, and other relevant characteristics), (b) the physical setting in which the observation took place, (c) the length of time you observed the child, (d) the frequency of the target behavior, (e) the level of agreement with your co-observer, (f) any difficulty of determining when the target behavior began and ended, (g) whether the definition of the target behavior was satisfactory and suggestions for improving the definition, and (h) the implications of the findings (for example, whether the behavior was appropriate or inappropriate).

2. Follow the same general procedure as described in Exercise 1. Now, however, observe three target behaviors: (a) solitary play, (b) parallel play, and (c) group play (see Table F-2 in Appendix F for definitions). Calculate the level of interobserver percentage agreement separately for each of the three target behaviors. Calculate the rate of behavior separately for each target behavior. Follow the guidelines in Exercise 1.

3. Follow the same general procedure as described in Exercise 1. Now, however, observe four subtypes of play—functional play, constructive play, dramatic play, and games-with-rules play—that fall within each type of play (solitary play, parallel play, and group play; see Table F-2 in Appendix F for definitions). Calculate the level of interobserver percentage agreement separately for each of the 12 target behaviors. Calculate the rate of behavior separately for each target behavior. Follow the guidelines in Exercise 1.

4. Compare the recordings obtained in Exercises 1, 2, and 3. What are the differences between observing play as a general category, as in Exercise 1, observing the three different types of play, as in Exercise 2, and observing the 12 subtypes of play, as in Exercise 3? What purposes does each type of recording serve? What information do you gain (or lose) with each type of recording? Which type of recording is more reliable, and why? Write up your analysis in a one- or two-paragraph report.

5. With a co-observer, observe a child in a preschool for a 30-minute period. Obtain permission from the school administration before beginning this activity. Select a child who appears to be engaging in inappropriate behavior (a target

behavior), such as fighting, temper tantrums, disruptive behavior, or uncooperative behavior. Record each time the inappropriate behavior occurs, using the dot-and-line method.

Observe whether the child's inappropriate behavior receives attention from an adult in the room (a target behavior). This information will provide some indication of the consequences of the behavior. Record each time the child receives attention, using the dot-and-line method. Your recording form should have spaces for recording the frequency of the child's inappropriate behavior and the frequency of the adult's attention.

Calculate the level of interobserver percentage agreement separately for the two target behaviors. Calculate the rate of behavior separately for the two target behaviors. Follow the guidelines in Exercise 1.

6. Follow the same general procedure as described in Exercise 1. Now, however, record the *duration* of the child's play with another child. Use a stopwatch or other device to record the elapsed time. Calculate the level of interobserver agreement, the average duration of the behavior, and the percentage of time spent on the behavior.

RATINGS RECORDING

With ratings recording, you rate behavior on a scale or checklist, usually at the end of the observation period. The scale is designed so that you can indicate the degree to which (a) you have observed the attribute (e.g., cooperativeness, aggression) or (b) you perceive the attribute to be present in the child. Thus, you must not only observe the child but also evaluate the degree to which the attribute being rated is present. The rating produces an ordinal score (see Chapter 4 in *Assessment of Children: Cognitive Applications*). Rating scales usually involve a greater degree of observer subjectivity than do other behavioral recording methods.

Major Uses of Ratings Recording

Ratings are useful for evaluating the more global aspects of behavior and for quantifying impressions (e.g., whether the examinee was motivated or hostile, whether the results were reliable). The Behavior and Attitude Checklist in Table 7-6 in Chapter 7 in *Assessment of Children: Cognitive Applications* is one such rating procedure that can be used to rate behavior when you administer tests. Rating scales are useful for assessing behaviors or products that are difficult to measure directly. For example, you can use a rating scale that ranges from very poor (1) to excellent (7) to rate the legibility of handwriting, the quality of arts and crafts products, the neatness of a room, or performance style during physical exercises or other activities. To provide judgments about the intensity of a behavior, ratings from not intense (1) to extremely intense (5) are useful. Because rating scales are easy to standardize, they can be used for many purposes in numerous settings.

You can compare results based on ratings with results obtained from more specific observational procedures, such as interval or event recording. These comparisons may reveal the consistency of the results across methods. Ratings are valuable in some assessment situations because they are less costly in time and personnel resources than are other methods. Ratings also allow you to (a) consider more subtle and unique clues, (b) overcome the fragmentation associated with behavioral counts, and (c) evaluate a quality and unity in the child's behavior that may be inaccessible with more detailed and objective coding systems. We sometimes de-

MR. WOODHEAD © 1999 by John P. Wood

scribe the quantitative dimension associated with ratings as "behavior as a whole."

How to Design a Ratings Recording

In designing a ratings recording, you must decide on (a) the number of times you will observe the child, (b) the length of the observation period, (c) the time periods during which you will conduct the observations, (d) the target behaviors you will observe, and (e) the method of recording data.

Frequency, length, and time of observation period.

As with other recording methods, the child's age, the setting, and the reason for the assessment will influence the number of times you will need to observe the child, the length of the observation period, and when you should conduct the observations. An observation session may last from 10 to 30 minutes or even longer. Time the observation period so that you obtain a representative sample of behavior. If possible, observe the child more than once and at different times during the day.

Target behaviors.

As in interval and event recording, base your selection of target behaviors on prior information from narrative recordings, interviews, referral questions, and test results.

Method of recording data.

Your ratings will usually be recorded on a scale that has five points. The points or numbers represent a behavioral continuum that should be defined as precisely as possible. Following are some typical formats for rating scales:

Example 1

Circle the most appropriate number:

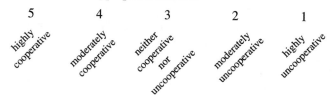

5   4   3   2   1

highly cooperative / moderately cooperative / neither cooperative nor uncooperative / moderately uncooperative / highly uncooperative

Example 2

Shares toys (circle one number):

5	4	3	2	1
always	frequently	sometimes	seldom	never

Example 3

How self-reliant was the child during the observation (circle one number)?

1	2	3	4	5
very dependent	usually dependent	somewhat self-reliant and somewhat dependent	usually self-reliant	very self-reliant

Example 4

Infant's visual attentiveness or alertness (circle one number):

5   Eyes closed all the time
4   Eyes open about one-quarter of the time
3   Eyes open about half the time
2   Eyes open about three-quarters of the time
1   Eyes open most or all of the time

Example 5

Infant's activity level (circle one number):

1   No gross activity and no small movements
2   Very small, occasional, or isolated movements
3   Occasional or intermittent movements
4   Relatively sustained movements
5   Sustained or continuous movements

Example 6

Place an X on the line that best reflects your rating.

anxious ___:___:___:___:___ not anxious

You can design rating systems to measure selected antecedents and consequences associated with the target behavior. For example, you might ask, "When situation Z occurs, how often does Mike do X?" or "After Mike does X, how often does [other person] react by doing Y?" Examples 7 and 8 below show rating scales for these questions.

Example 7

After Justin throws a temper tantrum, how often do his peers react by laughing? Circle one.

5	4	3	2	1
always	frequently	sometimes	seldom	never

Example 8

How does Helen's behavior this week compare with her behavior 4 weeks ago? Circle one.

1	2	3	4	5
much worse	worse	no different	better	much better

Example 9

How frequently does Veronica engage in positive behavior? Circle one.

5   Always
4   Frequently
3   Occasionally
2   Rarely
1   Never

Example 10

How confident are you that your ratings are accurate?

5   Definitely confident
4   Moderately confident
3   Confident
2   Not very confident
1   Definitely not confident

Notice that in Example 6 verbal descriptions are given only for the end points of the continuum and no numbers are used, whereas in the other examples each point on the continuum has a number coupled with a verbal description. You can, however, also convert each entry on the scale in Example 6 to a number (e.g., 5, 4, 3, 2, 1).

Quantitative Data in Ratings Recording

The prime source of data in ratings is the scale value (or number or score) on the rating scale. A major difficulty associated with ratings is that the assumptions underlying the scale values are not always clear; observers may therefore differ in their interpretation of the scale positions. For example, does *almost always* mean 99% to 100% of the time or 90% to 100% of the time? Does *often* mean the same on a 5-point scale as it does on a 7-point scale? Providing detailed examples of behaviors associated with each scale point will help you to apply consistent standards in interpreting scale values and will enhance interobserver reliability. Always make your ratings shortly after the completion of the observation session. If you wait too long, you may forget what you saw or your impression may become distorted.

You may improve a rating scale designed to obtain an estimate of frequency of occurrence by anchoring the frequency descriptions to percentages of time. Here is an example:

5   Almost always (86% to 100% of the time)
4   Frequently (66% to 85% of the time)
3   Occasionally (36% to 65% of the time)
2   Rarely (16% to 35% of the time)
1   Almost never (0% to 15% of the time)

Even though these percentages help to define more precisely the frequency descriptions ("almost always" to "almost never"), raters still must estimate how often the behaviors in question occurred.

Advantages of Ratings Recording

The ratings method has the following advantages:

- It provides a common frame of reference for comparing individuals.
- It is suited to recording many different behaviors.
- It can be used to rate the behaviors of many individuals or of a group as a whole.

- It records qualitative aspects of behavior.
- It generates data in a form suitable for statistical analyses.
- It is time efficient.
- It is a convenient method for recording the perceptions of multiple observers.

Disadvantages of Ratings Recording

The ratings method has the following disadvantages:

- It uses scale values that may be based on unclear assumptions.
- It may have low interobserver reliability because of complex or ambiguous terms, scale positions that are interpreted differently by different observers, a tendency among some observers to use the center of the rating scale and avoid extreme positions (central tendency error), and halo effects.
- It is not suited to recording important quantitative information, such as the frequency, duration, or latency of behavior.
- It is not suited to recording antecedent and consequent events, unless a method for doing so is built into the design of the ratings recording.
- It may be inaccurate if there is a time delay between the behavioral observations and the observer's ratings of the behavior.

Illustration of Ratings Recording

Table 4-11 shows a behavioral rating scale for assessing the presence of distress behaviors (pain and anxiety) in children undergoing a painful medical procedure—bone marrow aspiration treatment for cancer. Observers can complete the scale at various times during the procedure. The observers do not participate in the treatment procedure; they position themselves so that they are unobtrusive but have a clear view of the child as the child lies on the treatment table. Observers also can use this scale for rating children's reactions to other painful medical procedures.

Exercise 4-4.
Ratings Recording Exercises

1. With a co-observer, observe one child on a playground for a period of 5 minutes. After you observe the child, complete the following rating scales.

RATING SCALES
Directions: Place an X in the appropriate space.

1. cooperative ___:___:___:___:___ uncooperative
2. sad ___:___:___:___:___ happy
3. active ___:___:___:___:___ inactive
4. coordinated ___:___:___:___:___ uncoordinated
5. aggressive ___:___:___:___:___ passive

After you complete the scales, convert each rating to a number, assigning the number 1 to ratings in the left-most column and the number 5 to ratings in the right-most column. Determine the level of interobserver agreement by calculating (a) the percentage agreement (i.e., how many ratings were the same across the five scales; see Chapter 5 in this text) and (b) the product-moment correlation (see Chapter 4 in *Assessment of Children: Cognitive Applications*).

Consider the following questions in evaluating your ratings recording.

- How did the rating scales guide your observations?
- What additional scales would have been useful?
- To what extent might the time of day have affected the child's behavior?
- To what extent did the setting affect the child's behavior?
- To what extent were the dimensions covered in the scales representative of the child's general behavior?
- What could be done to improve the representativeness of the observations?
- To what extent was the child's behavior representative of that of her or his peers?
- Did the scales reveal information that might have been missed with a narrative recording?
- What biases, if any, may have affected your observations?
- How might your presence have altered the child's behavior?
- What could you have done to minimize this influence?
- How did your ratings recording contribute to your understanding of the child?

Write a one- or two-paragraph report that describes your observation. Include information about (a) the child (age, gender, and other relevant characteristics), (b) the physical setting in which the observation took place, (c) the length of time you observed the child, (d) the ratings you made, (e) the level of agreement with your co-observer, (f) the difficulties you had in using the rating scales and suggestions for improving the scales, and (g) the implications of the findings (for example, whether the behavior was appropriate or inappropriate).

2. Design your own ratings recording procedure for observing children in some setting. Develop five rating scales, different from those used in Exercise 1. With a co-observer, observe one child or a group of children, depending on the specific procedure developed, for a period of 5 minutes. Follow the procedures in Exercise 1 for evaluating your recording.

EVALUATIONS OF RECORDING METHODS

Interval, event, and ratings recording methods may not provide the breadth of information that narrative recordings do, but they allow you to (a) systematically evaluate specific behaviors of interest, (b) sample many children and various situations, (c) compare children and develop norms, and (d) generalize findings, all within a reasonable period. With both interval and event recording, it is relatively easy to tally

---

Table 4-11
Procedure Behavior Checklist

Directions: Rate each behavior using the following 5-point scale.

1	2	3	4	5
very mild	mild	neutral	intense	extremely intense

Circle one number for each behavior.

Behavior	Rating
1. Muscle tension	1 2 3 4 5
2. Screaming	1 2 3 4 5
3. Crying	1 2 3 4 5
4. Restraint used	1 2 3 4 5
5. Pain verbalized	1 2 3 4 5
6. Anxiety verbalized	1 2 3 4 5
7. Verbal stalling	1 2 3 4 5
8. Physical resistance	1 2 3 4 5

Note. Behaviors are defined as follows: (1) *Muscle tension*—contraction of any observable body part (e.g., shuts eyes tight, clenches jaw, stiffens body, clenches fists, or grits teeth); (2) *Screaming*—raises voice or yells with sounds or words; (3) *Crying*—displays tears or sobs; (4) *Restraint used*—is held down by someone or has heavy tape placed across legs onto table; (5) *Pain verbalized*—says "ow," or "ouch," or comments about hurting (e.g., "You're hurting me"); (6) *Anxiety verbalized*—says "I'm scared" or "I'm afraid"; (7) *Verbal stalling*—verbally expresses desire to delay ("Stop," "I'm not ready," "I want to tell you something," etc.); (8) *Physical resistance*—moves around, will not stay in position, or tries to climb off table.

See Katz, Kellerman, and Siegel (1980) for additional items.
Source: Adapted from LeBaron and Zeltzer (1984).

---

behaviors, particularly when they are clearly defined and observable. Both methods provide information about behavior during one time period and about changes in the child's behavior from one time period to another.

Narrative recording is more useful than the other recording methods for preserving the sequence of interactions so that dependencies among behaviors can be measured adequately. For example, with a narrative recording you are in a better position to answer questions such as "If this happens, what is likely to happen next?"

Interval recording is useful when you want to obtain information about behavior across time intervals (or temporal patterns of behavioral occurrences). Interval recording can answer questions such as "Did Tom's off-task behavior occur throughout the observation period or only during part of the observation period?" You can enhance your interval recording by making the length of the interval as close as possible to the duration of the behavior. Generally, interval recording provides a sample of behavior adequate for many clinical and psychoeducational purposes, particularly when your concern is the presence or absence of behavior. You have a reasonable chance of recording even infrequent momentary behaviors with interval recording if observation sessions are sufficiently long.

Event recording is more useful than interval recording when you want a measure of the number of times a behavior occurs. You will want this information when either an increase or a decrease in certain behaviors is desired (rather than the number of scored intervals) or when the characteristics of an event or behavior are of interest, such as the frequency of the behavior. Event recording, however, is not as useful as interval recording for behaviors that do not have a discrete beginning and ending or that occur rarely, such as temper tantrums.

Ratings may be especially useful because they provide information about the intensity of the behavior. They also are more useful than the other recording methods in quantifying global impressions of behavior.

THINKING THROUGH THE ISSUES

1. Why is it important to observe a child at school, at home, or at free play when you perform a clinical assessment? Discuss your answer.
2. What can you do to ensure that your observations are reliable and valid?
3. When would it be valuable to use four different recording methods (e.g., narrative, interval, event, and ratings) to observe a child, a family, or a class?
4. What are the basic requirements for an effective recording system?
5. What stresses might you face when you visit a child's home?
6. What conditions in a child's home would affect you, and how might you react to these conditions?

SUMMARY

1. Observing the behavior of children in natural or specially designed settings contributes to the clinical and psychoeducational assessment.
2. Behavioral observations provide a picture of children's spontaneous behavior in everyday life settings; provide information about children's interpersonal behavior and learning style; provide a systematic record of the children's behaviors and the behaviors of others, which can be used for evaluation, intervention planning, and monitoring changes; allow for verification of the accuracy of parental and teacher reports about children's behavior; allow for comparisons between behavior in the test situation and behavior in naturalistic settings; provide information independent of children's ability or willingness to report information; and provide information about young children and children with developmental disabilities who may not easily be evaluated with other procedures.
3. To be most useful, the systematic observation of behavior should have (a) a goal, (b) a focus, (c) a limit on the amount of data collected, and (d) a standardized recording method that has adequate reliability and validity.

Using Observational Methods

4. The assumption behind the sampling of behavior is that the behaviors recorded over a period of time will constitute a representative sample of behavior.
5. In observational assessments, the stimuli are not controlled by the clinician, and the scoring procedures are not as exact as those used in standardized tests.
6. In designing an observation, first define the behaviors that you are going to observe—the target behaviors—in objective, clear, and complete terms.
7. Your definitions (or those in the coding system that you use) should help you recognize when each behavior is occurring and distinguish the target behaviors from other similar behaviors. Definitions should be precise and clear enough that another observer could replicate your findings.
8. When you first observe a child referred for a specified behavior problem, do not focus exclusively on that behavior.
9. At least during your initial observation, observe the child's overall behavior and that of other children and adults in the setting.
10. Observe the child at different times during the day and in several settings.
11. Select an appropriate observation period in which the ongoing activity is compatible with the target behavior.
12. Select your observation times so that there is a chance that you will observe a representative sample of the behaviors of interest.
13. If you do not obtain a representative sample of behavior, the observation results will not be valid.

Applicability of Observational Methods

14. Observational methods are particularly useful for (a) studying behaviors that have a relatively high frequency, (b) assessing global behaviors such as aggression, social withdrawal, sociability, and attention, and (c) evaluating a child's progress over time.
15. Systematic observation in a naturalistic setting may not be the method of choice for some behaviors, particularly those that occur infrequently, covertly, or only in response to some specific stimuli.
16. A planned incident procedure (or controlled observation), which entails observing children in a specially contrived situation or setting, is the method of choice when you want to elicit specific behaviors.
17. Assessment by observational methods is particularly valuable in ecological assessment, which focuses on the physical attributes and the psychological attributes of the setting in which behavior occurs.
18. Physical attributes of the setting include spatial arrangements, seating arrangements, lighting, and noise; psychological attributes include familial, peer, and teacher relationships.
19. An ecological assessment may also focus on (a) how changes in one behavior affect other behaviors or (b) how changes in one part of the environment produce changes in other parts of the environment that, in turn, affect the child.
20. Advantages of observing a family at home include obtaining a picture of how the family functions naturally; obtaining a good idea of how each family member functions in his or her everyday role; reducing the chance that a family member will be absent, which is more likely in an office interview; promoting recognition among family members that the entire family shares responsibility for making changes or improvements;

decreasing anxiety among family members because of the familiar surroundings and thus facilitating more open communication among the family members; and decreasing the impact of the common "doctor-patient" stereotypes.

21. Family observations are useful in obtaining information about patterns of interaction among the members of the family, the emotional climate of the home, family conflicts, and patterns of resolution after a conflict.

Designing an Observational Assessment

22. The key to obtaining meaningful descriptions of behavior is coming up with the right combination of an observational recording method and a coding system.

23. Coding systems not only highlight target behaviors but also may measure several important dimensions of the target behaviors (e.g., the frequency, duration, intensity, and latency of the behaviors), as well as how factors in the setting affect behavior.

24. The observational recording methods particularly useful for clinical and psychoeducational tasks are narrative recording, interval recording, event recording, and ratings recording.

Narrative Recording

25. You, as well as parents, relatives, or even the child, can record descriptions of behavior.

26. Narrative recordings are referred to as anecdotal recordings when they include anything that seems noteworthy to the observer; a specific time frame or specific codes or categories are not needed.

27. When the observer attempts to record behavior as it occurs, we refer to the narrative recording as a running record.

28. Narrative recordings describe events without using quantitative recording procedures.

29. Observations in a narrative recording can be global, semi-global, or narrow.

30. Global descriptions (also referred to as molar or broad descriptions) focus on actions that reflect the child's behavior as a whole.

31. Semi-global descriptions contain additional general details of the behaviors of interest.

32. Narrow descriptions (also referred to as molecular or fine descriptions) reflect specific details of the child's behavior or the setting.

33. Narrative observations form a continuum from low inferential judgments to high inferential judgments.

34. When you record directly observable behavior (e.g., actions, motor activity, and verbalizations), you are making low inferential judgments.

35. When you record interpretations based on behaviors, you are making high inferential judgments.

36. Behavioral descriptive statements relate behaviors as they occur, without explanations.

37. Behavioral inferential statements go beyond describing behaviors; they are attempts to integrate or theorize.

38. You can make narrative observations in various settings and time periods, to create an in-depth picture of the behavior of a child, a group, or a teacher.

39. In clinical assessment, narrative recordings are particularly valuable as a precursor to more specific and quantifiable observations. A running account of the child's behavior may provide leads about behavioral and environmental events worthy of further analysis and suggest hypotheses about factors controlling the target behaviors.

40. Narrative recording can help you to learn about a child's social skills and communication skills and help you evaluate family interactive patterns.

41. Narrative recordings are useful when you observe a group.

42. In observing a group, pay particular attention to the patterns of peer preference or attraction, indifference, antagonism, and influence.

43. When you visit a classroom, you will want to observe the teacher's method and style of teaching and classroom management.

44. It is sometimes helpful to observe the child informally in a situation that you create, unrelated to the formal testing. This type of observation is a variant of a natural procedure combined with a planned incident procedure.

45. In designing a narrative recording (or an interval, event, or rating recording), you must decide on (a) the number of times you will observe the child, (b) the length of each observation period, (c) the time periods during which you will conduct the observations, (d) the type of recording you will use, (e) the target behaviors you will observe, and (f) the method of recording data.

46. The child's age, the setting, and the reason for the assessment will influence the number of times you will need to observe the child, the length of the observation period, and when you should conduct the observations.

47. Although narrative recordings do not involve quantitative recording procedures, you can use your record to obtain quantitative data.

48. Narrative recording has the advantages of providing a record of the child's behavior and of your general impressions, maintaining the original sequence of events, providing a means of gathering information and discovering critical behaviors, allowing you to assess progress, providing a record of continuing difficulties, requiring little equipment, and serving as a valuable precursor to more systematic observational procedures.

49. Narrative recording has the disadvantages of not being well suited to obtaining quantifiable data, being difficult to validate, not describing fully some types of critical behaviors, producing findings with limited generalizability, and varying from observer to observer.

Interval Recording

50. Interval recording (sometimes referred to as time sampling, interval sampling, or interval time sampling) focuses on selected aspects of behavior as they occur within specified intervals of time. The term *sampling* conveys the basic idea of interval recording—you sample behavior rather than recording every behavior as it occurs during the observational period.

51. Interval recording procedures include partial-interval time sampling, whole-interval time sampling, point time interval sampling, momentary time interval sampling, and variable interoccasion interval time sampling.

52. Interval recording is useful for observing behaviors that (a) are overt, (b) do not always have a clearcut beginning and ending, and (c) occur with moderate frequency, such as once every 10 to 15 seconds.

53. Select target behaviors based on prior narrative recordings, interview information, referral questions, or the child's test behavior.

54. The primary piece of quantitative data obtained in interval recording is the number of intervals in which the target behaviors did occur.
55. Interval recording has the advantages of helping to define important time-behavior relations, facilitating checking for interobserver reliability, helping to ensure that the predefined behaviors are observed under the same conditions each time, using time efficiently, focusing the observer's attention on the child's behavior by structuring the observations, permitting the recording of virtually any observable behavior, allowing for the collection of a large number of observations in a short period of time, and requiring minimal and inexpensive equipment.
56. Interval recording has the disadvantages of providing a somewhat artificial view of the behavior sequence because the time interval—not the behavior—dictates the recording framework, allowing important behaviors related to the problem to be overlooked, failing to provide information about the quality of the behavior (i.e., how the behavior was performed) or about the situation (i.e., whether the child was agitated, paying attention, or sleeping while in his or her seat) unless such information is specifically coded into the recording system, not revealing the actual frequency or duration of the behavior, overestimating the frequency of low-rate behaviors or behaviors of short duration, underestimating the frequency of high-rate behaviors, and requiring observers to undergo considerable training to learn the recording system.

Event Recording

57. In event recording (also called event sampling), you record each instance of a specific behavior or event as it occurs during the observation period.
58. Event recording provides a continuous temporal record of the observed behaviors and thus is particularly appropriate for measuring discrete responses that have clearly defined beginnings and endings.
59. You can record event recording responses in various ways, such as using a checklist, a wrist counter, a hand counter, an electromechanical counter, or another mechanical device or transferring small objects from one of your pockets to another.
60. The primary piece of quantitative data obtained in event recording is the frequency count—the number of occurrences of a behavior in a given time period.
61. Event recording has the advantages of detecting behaviors with low rates, particularly when observations are made by persons who are ordinarily in the setting; facilitating the study of many different behaviors or events; using time and personnel efficiently, especially when observations are made by persons who are ordinarily in the setting; accommodating many different recording methods; and providing information about changes in behavior over time and the amount of behavior performed.
62. Event recording has the disadvantages of providing a somewhat artificial view of the behavior sequence by separating the present event from conditions in the past that may have led up to it; not revealing sequences or temporal patterns, unless the time of the response is recorded; breaking up the continuity of behavior by using limited categories; not being suited to recording behaviors that are not discrete; presenting difficulties in establishing reliability across multiple observers; requiring observers to maintain an optimal level of attention over long periods of time, because few cues are used and responses may be

relatively infrequent; limiting quantification of the how and why associated with the event, unless these also are recorded; and making comparisons across sessions difficult if the length of the observation period is not constant.

Ratings Recording

63. With ratings recording, you rate behavior on a scale or checklist, usually at the end of the observation period.
64. Ratings are useful for evaluating the more global aspects of behavior and for quantifying impressions (e.g., whether the examinee was motivated or hostile, whether the results were reliable).
65. You can compare results based on ratings with results obtained from more specific observational procedures, such as interval or event recording.
66. Your ratings will usually be recorded on a scale that has five points.
67. The prime source of data in ratings is the scale value (or number or score) on the rating scale.
68. The ratings method has the advantages of providing a common frame of reference for comparing individuals, being suited to recording many different behaviors, being useful for rating the behaviors of many individuals or of a group as a whole, recording qualitative aspects of behavior, generating data in a form suitable for statistical analyses, being time efficient, and being a convenient method for recording the perceptions of multiple observers.
69. The ratings method has the disadvantages of using scale values that may be based on unclear assumptions, having low interobserver reliability, not being suited to recording important quantitative information, usually not being suited to recording antecedent and consequent events, and being inaccurate if there is a time delay between the behavioral observations and the observer's ratings of the behavior.

KEY TERMS, CONCEPTS, AND NAMES

Systematic observation of behavior (p. 84)
Target behaviors (p. 85)
Operational definitions (p. 85)
Planned incident procedures (p. 86)
Ecological assessment (p. 86)
Home observations (p. 88)
Designing an observational assessment (p. 89)
Narrative recording (p. 90)
Anecdotal recording (p. 90)
Running record (p. 90)
Global descriptions (p. 90)
Molar or board descriptions (p. 90)
Semi-global descriptions (p. 90)
Narrow descriptions (p. 90)
Molecular or fine descriptions (p. 90)
Continuum of inferential judgements (p. 91)
Behavioral descriptive statements (p. 91)
Behavioral inferential statements (p. 91)
Interval recording (p. 100)
Time sampling (p. 100)
Interval sampling (p. 100)

STUDY QUESTIONS

1. What are some purposes served by the direct observation of behavior?

2. Discuss an ecological assessment. Include in your discussion the assets and limitations of this type of assessment.

3. What are some of the key areas to consider in designing a systematic observation of behavior?

4. Discuss the narrative recording method. Include in your discussion types of narrative recordings, different levels of description, inferential judgments, major uses of the method, design considerations, and advantages and disadvantages.

5. Discuss the interval recording method. Include in your discussion the five different types of interval recording methods, major uses of the method, design considerations, quantitative data, and advantages and disadvantages.

6. Discuss the event recording method. Include in your discussion a description of the method, major uses of the method, design considerations, quantitative data, and advantages and disadvantages.

7. Discuss ratings recording. Include in your discussion a description of the method, major uses of the method, quantitative data, and advantages and disadvantages.

8. Indicate which type of recording method is preferred for observing each of the following and why: (a) use of slang words, (b) tics, (c) quality of a story, and (d) the event preceding an aggressive behavior (antecedent event).

9. Compare and contrast narrative recording, interval recording, event recording, and ratings recording.

5

ASSESSMENT OF BEHAVIOR BY OBSERVATIONAL METHODS: PART II

I assume that some people may find themselves temperamentally more suited to systematic observation than others. But I also assume that anybody can be trained to be a better questioner, a more careful methodologist, a more nuanced paraphraser, a more patient observer, a more subtle student of everyday life, a more complicated person capable of registering more of the complications in the world.

—Karl E. Weick

Observational Coding Systems

Recording Method and Coding System Combined

Guidelines for Designing or Selecting a Behavioral Observational Assessment

Sources of Unreliability

Procedures for Assessing Reliability

Procedures for Assessing Validity

Procedures for Reducing Errors in Observations

Cautions on the Use of Observations

Self-Monitoring Assessment

Reporting Behavioral Observations

Psychological Evaluation

Thinking Through the Issues

Summary

Goals and Objectives

This chapter is designed to enable you to do the following:

- Become familiar with ways to evaluate the reliability of observational methods

- Become familiar with ways to evaluate the validity of observational methods

- Understand self-monitoring assessment

- Prepare reports based on observational assessments

This chapter continues coverage of systematic behavioral observation. It will (a) familiarize you with several observational coding systems, (b) provide you with the tools with which to evaluate the reliability and validity of your observations, (c) help you reduce errors associated with behavioral observations, (d) help you use self-monitoring procedures, and (e) teach you how to report your observational findings.

OBSERVATIONAL CODING SYSTEMS

Observational coding systems are used to categorize behavioral observations. They usually consist of two or more categories that cover a range of behaviors, although, on occasion, a single category may be appropriate. Even when you are considering just one target behavior, you must also consider those times when it does *not* occur. Thus, though your focus is on one behavior, you can think of a one-category coding system used in interval or event recording as having two categories—the *presence* of the behavior and the *absence* of the behavior.

Before you use a coding system, carefully evaluate the following (Nay, 1979): (a) its rationale, (b) the setting(s) in which it is applicable, (c) definitions of the coding categories, (d) the description of how behavior is sampled, (e) rules governing the behavior of observers, such as a hierarchy of codes, (f) reliability, including overall reliability and the reliability of each coding category, (g) validity, and (h) positive and negative features (including potential problem areas).

How to Select an Observational Coding System

In selecting an observational coding system, consider the following:

- What questions do you want to answer with your observational assessment?
- What existing system best meets the assessment, treatment, or research goals?
- Are you interested in investigating global areas of behavior or just a few specific behaviors?
- How many behaviors do you want to observe?
- What aspects of the situation merit attention?
- Are the behaviors you want to observe easily identified?

Select the simplest possible coding system that will answer your questions. If your purpose is to obtain a general description of behavior, select a system that uses global categories. If you are interested in only a few behaviors related to the referral question, select a system that uses specific categories related to these behaviors. If you want to examine the relationship between a behavior and its environmental determinants, use a multidimensional system that includes relevant antecedent and consequent events. Finally, if you want to record sequential observational data, use a sequential observational procedure, such as one described by Bakeman and Gottman (1986).

When you want to measure a few behaviors, you should have little difficulty in selecting an adequate recording system. Avoid selecting a coding system that requires you to make multiple decisions and to use multiple categories, at least during your initial training period, because these systems are difficult to use. Memorize the coding system *before* the formal observation begins, but keep the code definitions handy in case you need to refresh your memory.

Observational coding systems have been developed to evaluate individual children, groups, and classes in different settings. Observational codes also can cover environmental responses to children's behavior. Table 5-1 lists several observational coding systems; recognize, however, that these are only a sample of the hundreds of systems that have been developed for different purposes. Tables 5-2, 5-3, and 5-4 (on pages 124, 125, and 127, respectively) illustrate coding systems for observing children, teachers, and classrooms, respectively. The systems illustrated require immediate, not retrospective, observation; observers must observe and record behavior as the behavior occurs, while keeping inferences to a minimum.

Use of Computers in Observational Recording

Computerized observational systems, which use a laptop computer, hand-held computer, or bar-code scanner, are available for collecting real-time observational data. In a review of 15 computerized systems, Kahng and Iwata (1998) provided ordering and pricing information. Capabilities of the various systems include (a) recording many different responses, (b) recording responses for different groups, (c) recording and calculating response frequency, duration of behavior, interval responses, latency of behavior, interresponse time, and discrete trials, (d) calculating measures of central tendency (mean and median), variability (range and frequency distribution), statistical significance, and reliability (interobserver agreement—overall occurrence, occurrence, and nonoccurrence—and kappa), and (e) graphing the data. Computerized systems are valuable in conducting systematic observations.

Coding Systems for Observing Children's Behavior

Table 5-2 shows several coding systems for observing children's behavior.

- The *two-category coding system* provides broad information about on-task and off-task behavior. It is particularly useful when the general climate of a classroom or other facility is the focus of assessment. You may have to make some inferences (i.e., make logical judgments from the observations) to distinguish between the two categories in the system.
- The *three-category coding system* is a refinement of the two-category system. It is useful for assessing passive and

Table 5-1
Examples of Observational Coding Systems

Authors	Title	Description
Atkins, Pelham, & Licht (1988)	Classroom Observations of Conduct and Attention Deficit Disorders (COCADD)	A 32-item behavioral observational coding system that includes 5 domains (positive, physical-social orientation, vocal activities, nonvocal activities, and play activities) organized into 7 composite variables for classroom observations (overactive, distracted, verbal disruptive, off-task verbal, verbal aggressive, physical aggressive, and stealing/cheating) and 5 composite variables for playground observations (verbal disruptive, verbal aggressive, physical aggressive, stealing/cheating, and highly active play).
Bradley (1994)	HOME Inventory	A home observational schedule useful for observing homes of normal children. Separate scales are available for infants, preschool children, and elementary school–aged children. For example, for preschool children there are 8 subscales—Learning Stimulation, Language Stimulation, Physical Environment, Warmth and Affection, Academic Stimulation, Modeling, Variety in Experience, and Acceptance. There also is a HOME Inventory for children with disabilities.
Bramlett & Barnett (1993)	Preschool Observation Code (POC)	A 20-item behavioral observational code—with 9 state categories, 5 event categories, and 6 teacher-child interaction categories—designed to record preschool children's behavior.
Dadds, Schwartz, & Sanders (1987)	Family Observation Schedule (FOS)	A 20-item behavioral observational code—including 13 categories of parent behaviors and 7 categories of child behaviors—useful for observing family interaction patterns.
Dumas (1987)	INTERACT	A computer-based 38-item coding system—with 10 natural behavior codes, 5 positive behavior codes, 5 aversive behavior codes, 8 response codes, and 10 setting codes—designed to measure family interactions in natural settings.
Gilbert & Christensen (1988)	Family Alliances Coding System (FACS)	A 20-item behavioral observational code—with 6 positive valence codes, 3 neutral valence codes, 8 negative valence codes, and 3 affect codes—designed to measure the interactional behaviors by which family members express their alliance relations with one another.
Guida (1987)	Naturalistic Observation of Academic Anxiety (NOAA)	A 5-item behavioral observational code for recording anxiety in a classroom.
Harms & Clifford (1998)	Early Childhood Environment Rating Scale (ECERS)	An objective rating scale for measuring the quality of the childcare environment, with 43 individual scales grouped into 6 areas.

(Continued)

Table 5-1 *(Continued)*		
Authors	*Title*	*Description*
Hops, Biglan, Sherman, Arthur, Friedman, & Osteen (1987)	Living in Family Environments (LIFE)	A 38-category home behavioral observational code, including 7 context codes, 8 affect codes, and 23 content codes.
Iverson & Segal (1992)	Behavior Observation Record (BOR)	A 35-item time/event sampling behavioral observational code designed to assess social behaviors and the quality or effectiveness of these behaviors on a playground. The items are grouped under 4 categories of social behaviors: child alone, child approaching others, child being approached, and child interacting with others.
Landesman (1987)	Home Observation Code (Modified)	A 79-item behavioral observational code, with items grouped into 8 areas, designed for use in residential settings for individuals with mental retardation.
Mash & Barkley (1986)	Response-Class Matrix (RCM)	A 13-item behavioral observational code—with 6 child behaviors and 7 maternal behaviors—designed to measure parent-child interactions in a clinic, laboratory, playroom, or home setting.
Mayes (1991)	Mayes Hyperactivity Observation System (MHOS)	A 7-item behavioral observational code designed to measure hyperactivity under standardized free-play conditions.
Pianta, Smith, & Reeve (1991)	Global Ratings of Mother-Child Interaction	An 8-item behavioral observational rating scale—including 5 child scales and 3 adult scales—designed to measure interactions between child and mother.
Saudargas & Lentz (1986)	State-Event Classroom Observation System (SECOS)	An 11-item classroom observational code with 8 state behaviors and 11 event behaviors, of which 5 are for students and 6 are for the teacher.
Shapiro (1996)	Behavior Observation of Students in Schools (BOSS)	A 6-category classroom code, 5 of which are for students and 1 of which is for teachers.
Stern, MacKain, Raduns, Hopper, Kaminsky, Evans, Shilling, Giraldo, Kaplan, Nachman, Trad, Polan, Barnard, & Spieker (1992)	Kiddie-Infant Descriptive Instrument for the Measurement of Affective States in Infancy and Early Childhood (KIDIES)	A 9-item behavioral observational rating system designed to evaluate affective states in infants and preschool children.
Tarbell, Cohen, & Marsh (1992)	Toddler-Preschooler Postoperative Pain Scale (TPPPS)	A 7-item behavioral observational code, divided among 3 pain behavior categories: vocal pain, facial pain, and bodily pain. It is designed to measure postoperative pain in children aged 1 through 5 years.
Wistedt, Rasmussen, Pedersen, Malm, Traskman-Bendz, Wakelin, & Bech (1990)	Social Dysfunction and Aggression Scale (SDAS)	An 11-item behavioral observational code designed for observing individuals in in-patient settings who may display socially disturbed or aggressive behavior.

Table 5-2
Four Examples of Coding Systems for Observing Children's Behavior

Coding system	Examples
I. Two Categories	
1. On-Task Behavior (appropriate behavior for the situation)	Putting hand up when he or she wants to say something, listening while teacher is talking, working quietly at desk, asking teacher for permission to leave desk, volunteering information, answering questions, following teacher's directions
2. Off-Task Behavior (inappropriate behavior for the situation)	a. Passive inappropriate actions (for example, staring into space, lack of perseverance, looking around room, working on wrong assignment) b. Active inappropriate actions (for example, talking to classmates, making noise, hitting, fighting, banging, being out of seat without permission, physical destructiveness, stealing, threatening others, setting fires)
II. Three Categories	
1. On-Task Behavior	See examples under I.1.
2. Passive Off-Task Behavior (passive behavior that is inappropriate but does not disrupt others)	See examples under I.2.a.
3. Disruptive Off-Task Behavior (inappropriate disruptive behavior)	See examples under I.2.b.
III. Four Categories	
1. On-Task Behavior	See examples under I.1.
2. Verbal Off-Task Behavior	Talking out, teasing
3. Motor Off-Task Behavior	Being out of seat, hitting others, throwing objects, playing with objects
4. Passive Off-Task Behavior	Daydreaming, sleeping, sulking
IV. Ten Categories	
1. Interference	Interrupting teacher or another student
2. Off-Task	Engaging in other than assigned work
3. Noncompliance	Failing to follow teacher's instructions
4. Minor Motor Movements	Moving buttocks, rocking
5. Gross Motor Movements	Leaving seat, standing without permission
6. Out-of-Chair Behavior	Remaining out of chair for a period of time
7. Physical Aggression	Kicking, hitting
8. Threat or Verbal Aggression	Making threatening gestures, bullying
9. Solicitation of Teacher	Raising hand, calling out to teacher
10. Absence of Behavior	Engaging in no inappropriate behavior as defined by the above categories

Note. The 10-category system is from Abikoff and Gittelman (1985) and can be found in Table D-1 in Appendix D.

Table 5-3
Three Examples of Coding Systems for Observing Teacher's Behavior

Coding system	Examples
I. Two Categories	
1. Verbal Approval Responses (comments that follow an on-task behavior)	"Bob, your spelling has improved considerably."
2. Verbal Disapproval Responses (comments that follow an off-task behavior)	"Class, stop making noise."
II. Three Categories	
1. Praise (verbalization indicating that the teacher was pleased with the student's behavior)	"John, your reading was excellent."
2. Prompts (verbalization conveying additional information or directing the student's attention to the task)	"The first step in solving the problem is to divide the sales price by the number of items purchased."
3. Criticism (verbalization indicating that the teacher was displeased with the student's behavior)	"Mary, do not talk during the reading assignment."
III. Six Categories	
1. Academic Approval	"Your score was much improved."
2. Academic Disapproval	"Your study habits are not satisfactory."
3. Social Approval	"I am pleased with your ability to work with Helen."
4. Social Disapproval	"Your relationship with your teammates is poor."
5. Mistake (inappropriate use of one of the above four behaviors)	Informing child that behavior was unsatisfactory when there was no evidence that it was
6. No Approval or Disapproval	Absence of behaviors that could be recorded as approval or disapproval

disruptive dimensions of inappropriate behavior. These two dimensions are similar to the internalizing (passive) and externalizing (disruptive) dimensions of child behavior found on many behavioral checklists. (See Chapter 6 for coverage of behavioral checklists.) You can use this three-category coding system for individuals as well as for an entire class.

- The *four-category coding system* is useful when you need information about whether the disruptive off-task behavior is verbal, motor, or passive. You can use this four-category coding system for observing individual children in a classroom.

- The *ten-category system* is a more extensive system for observing classroom behavior, with 9 of the 10 categories referring to inappropriate behavior. This system provides detailed information about a child's actions. Table D-1 in Appendix D shows the complete system with recording instructions; it is called the Classroom Observation Code: A Modification of the Stony Brook Code. The system is especially useful for recording children's hyperactive behavior.

Here is an example of a three-category system that is useful for observing children's social behavior (adapted from Whalen, Henker, Swanson, Granger, Kliewer, & Spencer, 1987, p. 189):

- *Appropriate social behavior* (e.g., conversing, initiating social contact, or participating in an ongoing game)
- *Negative social behavior* (e.g., rule-breaking, noncompliance, disruption, teasing, verbal or physical aggression)
- *Nonsocial behavior* (e.g., solitary play, daydreaming, bystanding)

The categories are mutually exclusive and allow for the monitoring of appropriate and inappropriate interpersonal behavior and social and nonsocial interpersonal behavior.

Appendixes E and F show other coding systems. Table F-2 in Appendix F is a coding system for observing children's play, with three global categories and four subcategories. Table F-3 in Appendix F is a 28-item behavioral observational system for observing the social competence of preschool children; it classifies behavior according to such dimensions as interest, apathy, cooperation, and anger.

Coding Systems for Observing Teachers' Behavior

Observational coding systems also are useful for studying the behavior of classroom teachers. Assessing the teacher's behavior is important because the teacher's behavior may affect the referred child's behavior and the classroom climate. The two-, three-, and six-category systems shown in Table 5-3 on page 125 provide a record of the teacher's interactions with a specific child or with the class as a whole.

Coding Systems for Observing Students, Teachers, and Classes

The separate coding systems designed for students and teachers can be combined to form a more complete coding system, and additional categories for entire classes can be added. Table 5-4 on page 127 illustrates one such combined coding system, which emphasizes appropriate as well as inappropriate behaviors. Eleven student behavior codes (six on-task behaviors, four off-task behaviors, and one neutral behavior) are included, along with four teacher codes and two class codes.

RECORDING METHOD AND CODING SYSTEM COMBINED

Exhibit 5-1 on page 128 shows event recording combined with a three-category coding system to examine aggressive behavior on the playground. Exhibit 5-2 on page 129 shows interval recording combined with a staff-resident interaction coding system to study efforts at rehabilitation of individuals with mental retardation. The detailed ward coding system allows for an analysis of staff-resident interactions, whereas the playground coding system focuses on aggressive behaviors only. You can expand the playground coding system, of course, to include other behavioral categories.

GUIDELINES FOR DESIGNING OR SELECTING A BEHAVIORAL OBSERVATIONAL ASSESSMENT

The following guidelines will assist you in designing or selecting a behavioral observational assessment:

- Design or select a coding system that represents the behaviors of concern.
- Use categories sparingly; do not overload the coding system.
- Use categories that are easily identifiable and clearly defined.
- Select the recording method that best fits the coding system. (Table 5-5 on page 130 summarizes the four major types of recording methods.)
- Select an interval length that matches the duration of the target behaviors.
- Select a length of time for the observations that is sufficient to reveal the most salient features of the target behavior without taxing your ability to record accurately.
- Schedule the observation period so that it coincides with the times of day when the target behavior is most likely to occur.
- Conduct observations across multiple settings and on multiple occasions, if possible.
- Design or select an appropriate recording sheet, with clearly labeled precoded categories and spaces for your entries.
- Conduct extensive general observations prior to formulating your specific observational strategy.
- Design or select a final assessment strategy likely to detect the target behaviors of interest, given their typical rate and duration.

SOURCES OF UNRELIABILITY

The data you obtain from behavioral observations, like the data you obtain from any other assessment procedure, must be reliable and valid. Establishing observer agreement will ensure that your observations are replicable and consistent (reliable), which in turn will help establish their accuracy (validity). In the observation of behavior, reliability and

Table 5-4
Coding System for Observing Students and Teachers in the Classroom

Student Code Summaries

Attending (AT)	The student must be (a) looking at the teacher when the teacher is talking, (b) looking at the materials in the classroom that have to do with the lesson, or (c) engaged in other looking behavior appropriate to the academic situation.
Working (WK)	The student is working on academic material without any overt verbal components, either in a group or in an individual seatwork situation.
Volunteering (VO)	By verbal or nonverbal means, the student responds to teacher requests by volunteering information of an academic nature.
Reading Aloud (RA)	The student is reading aloud, either individually or as part of a group recitation.
Appropriate Behavior (AB)	This is a broad category used to code appropriate behavior not otherwise specifically defined, including asking or answering questions, raising hand for help, and acquiring or distributing materials.
Interaction with Peer about Academic Materials (IP+)	The student is interacting with a peer or peers about academic materials and is not violating classroom rules. Verbal communications between peers (e.g., talking, handling materials, working together on academic materials) were coded IP+.
Interaction with Peer about Nonacademic Materials (IP−)	The student is interacting with a peer about academic materials inappropriate for the period in which the observation occurs (unless this has been approved by the teacher) or about nonacademic material. The interaction may be verbal or nonverbal.
Don't Know (DK)	The child indicates, in either a verbal or a nonverbal manner, that he or she does not know the answer.
Inappropriate Locale (IL)	The child, without the teacher's approval, is in a classroom area that is not appropriate for the academic activity that is occurring at the time.
Looking Around (LA)	The child is looking away from the appropriate academic task at hand.
Inappropriate Behavior (IB)	This is a second broad category, used to code inappropriate behaviors not otherwise defined. Behaviors include calling out an answer when a question is directed to another student and interrupting the teacher or another student who is talking.

Teacher Code Summaries

Approval (AP)	The teacher gives a clear verbal, gestural, or physical approval to the student or to the group of which the student is a member.
Disapproval (DI)	The teacher gives a clear verbal, gestural, or physical disapproval of the child's behavior, either individually or as part of a group.
No Response (NR)	The teacher does not respond to the student, either as part of the group or individually.
Verbal Interactions (VI)	Verbalizations that are not approvals or disapprovals are directed at the child or her or his group. Verbalizations may relate to instruction or management.

Class Code Summaries

Appropriate Behavior (AB)	The entire class (all students) is engaged in activities that are considered appropriate to the situation, as defined by the teacher's rules and the activity at hand.
Inappropriate Behavior (IB)	At least one student in the class is observed engaged in behaviors not considered appropriate according to the teacher's rules and the activity at hand.

Source: Reprinted and adapted with permission of the publisher and authors from C. R. Greenwood, H. Hops, H. M. Walker, J. J. Guild, J. Stokes, K. R. Young, K. S. Keleman, and M. Willardson, "Standardized Classroom Management Program: Social Validation and Replication Studies in Utah and Oregon," *Journal of Applied Behavior Analysis,* 1979, *12,* p. 240. © Society for the Experimental Analysis of Behavior, Inc.

MR. WOODHEAD © 2000 by John P. Wood

I don't get it. He sits up there staring at his computer, but he sees everything.

We can't get away with anything anymore.

Wait a minute — What's that on your head?!

Copyright © 2000 by John P. Wood.

Exhibit 5-1
Naturalistic Observational Recording of Children on a Playground: Recording Aggressiveness and Related Behaviors

Coding Categories
Three classes of problem behaviors were observed:

1. *Aggression*: Striking, slapping, tripping, kicking, pushing, or pulling others; "karate" moves ending within 1 foot of another person; doing anything that ends with another child's falling to the ground.
2. *Property abuse*: Taking another person's property without permission; throwing school books, lunches, or anyone else's property; throwing any object at passing or parked cars; digging holes in the ground with one's feet or hands; breaking pencils or pens or other objects.
3. *Rule violations*: Resisting or talking back to an aide; climbing more than 1 foot off the ground on a playground structure not meant for climbing; suspending one's self on a playground structure in any position that results in the head's not being 180 degrees above the feet.

The Playground Observation System
Based on the existing geography (e.g., building corners or edges of playground equipment), the playground was divided into three roughly equivalent "pie slices," which were the responsibility of separate observers. These slices were then halved (again, as defined by other permanent structures), and each half was monitored for alternate 15-second periods. Thus, an observer attended to only one-sixth of the playground at a time, and only half the playground was observed at any given moment.

Three observers stood in the middle of the playground facing their areas. A tape recording instructed them to start watching the left-hand portion of their section, at which time they began recording incidents with the aid of hand counters. After 15 seconds, the tape cued a "switch" to the remaining portion of the observers' area. This continued for 2 minutes, when a "stop" signaled that the cumulative frequency of incidents observed was to be entered on the data sheets. The entire process occurred in 10 iterations (i.e., observe left for 15 seconds, observe right for 15 seconds, and back left again, recording the totals every 2 minutes), from 8:20 to 8:40 A.M.

A particular inappropriate incident (e.g., kicking directed at one child by another child) was counted only once per 15-second interval. However, more than one incident was scored if one child inflicted several types of aggression on another (for example, one child's hitting and kicking another resulted in two incidents' being counted). If two children assaulted a third individual or one child assaulted two peers, two incidents were scored. The 15-second intervals were arbitrarily considered to be independent; thus, if two children were observed to be wrestling with one another for two intervals, four incidents were recorded.

Reliability
Reliability was determined by having interobserver checks on various days.

Source: Reprinted and adapted with permission of the publisher and authors from H. A. Murphy, J. M. Hutchison, and J. S. Bailey, "Behavioral School Psychology Goes Outdoors: The Effects of Organized Games on Playground Aggression," *Journal of Applied Behavior Analysis*, 1983, *16*, pp. 30–31. © Society for the Experimental Analysis of Behavior, Inc.

Exhibit 5-2
Naturalistic Observation in an Institution for Children with Mental Retardation:
Recording Staff and Residents' Efforts at Rehabilitation

Coding Categories

Behaviors of both staff and residents were recorded. The following coding categories were used for staff and resident behaviors:

STAFF BEHAVIORS

1. *No interaction*—no physical or verbal interaction between the staff member and any resident.
2. *Verbal instruction*—through standard language (i.e., either vocal or manual communication), staff instructs the resident to perform some activity and offers no physical assistance.
3. *Nonverbal instruction*—through a nonverbal gesture (not including manual communication), staff instructs the resident to perform some activity and offers no physical assistance.
4. *Verbal instruction with physical assistance*—through standard language (i.e., either vocal or manual communication), staff instructs the resident to perform some activity and provides physical assistance (e.g., guides resident through a self-dressing task with verbal aid).
5. *Nonverbal instruction with physical assistance*—through a nonverbal gesture (not including manual communication), staff instructs the resident to perform some activity and provides physical assistance (e.g., points to the door and guides resident to move toward the door).
6. *Physical assistance*—without prior verbal or nonverbal instruction, staff physically assists resident (e.g., staff helps resident put on his or her shoes).
7. *Social*—staff claps for, praises, hugs, etc., resident.
8. *Custodial guidance*—staff physically assists resident in a custodial manner in a non-task situation (e.g., ties shoes of resident in order to allow resident to move along quickly with other residents).

RESIDENT BEHAVIORS

1. *On-task*—resident emits a verbal or motoric response to a question, command, instruction, or nonverbal cue (e.g., a gesture by the staff) or complies without making an overt response when no overt response is necessary or appropriate (e.g., looking at pictures in a book).
2. *Off-task*—in the presence of a cue for responding, resident either does not respond, responds inappropriately, or does not look at relevant task stimuli.
3. *No programming*—nothing is being asked of the resident, being demonstrated to the resident, or being provided for the resident to do.
4. *Self-aggressive*—resident intentionally strikes, bites, slaps, hits, or kicks own body or causes his or her body and other objects to contact with force.

5. *Other aggressive*—resident intentionally strikes at, throws objects at, or verbally threatens others or in some other way threatens to harm another resident or a staff member.
6. *Self-stimulatory*—resident engages in solitary activity but actively manipulates some object(s) or is engaged in solitary, asocial, repetitive behavior (e.g., rocking, headweaving).

Recording Procedure

For 16 days, four observers each recorded for 250 minutes per day. Each person observed in one of five locations for about 50 minutes. Then the observer walked to another location and recorded for another 50 minutes. This procedure was followed from about 9:30 to 11:20 A.M. and 1:00 to 3:50 P.M. each day, until each observer had recorded in the five locations. Sites were rotated so that no observer was in a site more than once per day and so that each site was observed by each person about the same amount of time. Data were recorded at 6-second intervals, with the intervals being signaled through earplugs by a portable tape recorder. At the end of each interval, the observer marked any response category that had occurred within the 6-second interval.

There were three recording rules other than that of simply marking what had just occurred:

(a) After observation of a staff member, something had to be marked. If none of the seven response categories occurred, the observer marked the no interaction category.
(b) After each observation of a resident, on-task, off-task, or no programming had to be marked (the categories of aggression and self-stimulation were to be marked only if they had just occurred).
(c) If more than one resident or staff response occurred in the same interval, both could be marked (e.g., self-stimulatory and off-task responding).

Reliability

Interobserver agreement was assessed each day by randomly assigning a second observer to the various recording sites. This produced about 40 hours of reliability assessment. Observations were coordinated through a y-plug from the tape recorder that allowed each observer to hear the beginning of each successive interval. Because something was marked at the end of each 6-second interval and because the observers were 3 meters apart, the observations were quite independent. Interobserver agreement was calculated by dividing the number of intervals in which both observers agreed by the total number of intervals.

Source: Reprinted and adapted with permission of the publisher and authors from A. C. Repp and L. E. Barton, "Naturalistic Observations of Institutionalized Retarded Persons: A Comparison of Licensure Decisions and Behavioral Observations," *Journal of Applied Behavior Analysis*, 1980, *13*, pp. 335–337. © Society for the Experimental Analysis of Behavior, Inc.

Table 5-5
Observational Recording Methods

Recording method	Types	Applications	Data	Advantages	Disadvantages
Narrative recording: Behavior is comprehensively described.	*Anecdotal recording:* Anything that appears noteworthy is recorded. *Running record:* Observer makes an on-the-spot description of behaviors.	Is useful as a precursor to more specific and quantifiable observations Helps in the development of hypotheses about factors controlling target behaviors Provides an in-depth picture of behavior	No specific quantitative data, although the record can be analyzed for various occurrences of behavior	Provides a record of child's behavior and general impressions Maintains original sequence of events Facilitates discovering critical behaviors and noting continuing difficulties Requires a minimum of equipment	Is not well suited to obtaining quantifiable data Is costly in terms of time and person power Is difficult to validate May be insensitive to critical behaviors Produces findings with limited generalizability
Interval recording: Observational period is divided into brief segments or intervals; observer notes whether a behavior occurs in each interval.	*Partial-interval time sampling:* Behavior is scored only once during the interval, regardless of duration or frequency of occurrence. *Whole-interval time sampling:* Behavior is scored only when it lasts from the beginning to the end of the interval. *Point time interval sampling:* Behavior is scored only when it occurs at a designated time during the interval. *Momentary time interval sampling:* Behavior is scored only when it occurs at the end of the interval. *Variable interoccasion interval time sampling:* Behavior is scored only when it occurs during designated random time intervals.	Is useful for behaviors that are overt or easily observable, that are not clearly discrete, and that occur with reasonable frequency (for example, reading, working, roughhousing, smiling, playing with toys)	Number of intervals in which target behaviors did or did not occur	Defines important time-behavior relationships Facilitates checking interobserver reliability Maintains standard observation conditions in an economical way Enhances attention to specific behaviors Allows for flexibility in recording large numbers of behaviors	Provides a somewhat artificial view of behavior sequence May lead observer to overlook important behaviors Usually tells little about quality of behaviors or situation Provides numbers that are usually not related to frequency of behaviors Is not sensitive to very low frequency behaviors and, in point time sampling, behaviors of short duration

(Continued)

Table 5-5 *(Continued)*

Recording method	Types	Applications	Data	Advantages	Disadvantages
Event recording: Each instance of a specific behavior (event) is observed and recorded.	*Event:* Observer waits for preselected behavior to occur and then records its occurrence. *Duration:* Observer determines the amount of time that elapses between the beginning and the end of the behavior. *Intensity:* Behavior is divided into various degrees of intensity, and behavior of each degree is recorded separately. *Latency:* Observer determines the amount of time that elapses between the initiation of a request and the onset of behavior.	Is useful for behaviors that have clearly defined beginnings and endings, such as spelling words correctly, making rocking movements, asking questions, and making speech errors	Number of occurrences of the behavior—frequency count Also, in some cases, rate of behavior, duration of behavior (time), intensity of behavior (if built into code), and latency of behavior (time)	Facilitates detection of low-frequency behaviors Facilitates study of many different behaviors in an economical and flexible manner Provides information about the frequency with which behavior occurs and about changes in behavior over time	Provides artificial view of behavior sequence and breaks up continuity of behavior Is not suited to recording nondiscrete behaviors Presents difficulties in establishing reliability Limits quantification of the how and why associated with behavior Makes comparison across sessions difficult if the length of the observation period is not constant
Ratings recording: Behavior is observed and then rated on various scales.	*5-point scales* *7-point scales* *Other dimensional scales*	Is useful for evaluating more global aspects of behavior and for quantifying impressions	Scale value (or number or score) on rating scale	Allows for the recording of many different behaviors in an efficient manner Allows for the rating of many individuals and the group as a whole Permits rating of subtle aspects of behavior Facilitates statistical analyses	Uses scale values which may be based on unclear assumptions May have low reliability Does not allow for recording of important quantitative dimensions Does not allow for recording of antecedent and consequent events

validity are influenced by several factors, including (a) the observer, (b) the setting, (c) the coding system, (d) the child, parent, teacher, other target person, or group, and (e) the interactions among these sources (see Table 5-6). Although most of Table 5-6 requires no explanation, some observer errors and errors associated with the referred child (or group) warrant further comment.

Observer Differences

Observers will differ, for example, in their sensitivity to subtle social cues and to situational, gender, and ethnic factors that may play a role in influencing behavior. Observers may also differ in how they are affected by a sequence of behaviors (such as on- and off-task behaviors or aggressive and altruistic behaviors), and their response to the sequence may affect their subsequent observations.

Observer Bias

Observer bias refers to errors committed by the observer in the course of the observational assessment. The term encompasses anything an observer does that distorts the recording of behavior, such as allowing expectations to influence his or

Table 5-6
Sources and Types of Errors in Observations of Behavior

Source of error	Type of error
Personal qualities of the observer	*Central tendency*—Observer uses the middle category of a rating scale more frequently than the end categories and, in the process, tends to underestimate intense behaviors and overestimate weak behaviors. *Leniency or generosity*—Observer makes inflated judgments about the referred child. *Primacy effect*—Observer allows first impressions to have a distorting effect on later impressions or judgments. *Halo effect*—Observer makes judgments based on a general impression of the referred child or the child's most salient characteristic. *Personal theory*—Observer fits the observations to his or her personal theoretical assumptions. *Personal values*—Observer fits the observations to his or her personal expectations, values, and interests. *Overestimation of traits or behaviors that are barely self-acknowledged*—Observer overestimates in the referred child traits and behaviors that observer barely acknowledges in himself or herself. *Logical error*—Observer makes similar judgments on traits that seem to be logically related. *Contrast error*—On specific traits, observer judges others to be more different from himself or herself than they actually are. *Proximity error*—Observer judges specific traits as similar because the format of the judgments places them close together in time or space. *Personal effects*—Unbeknownst to the observer, his or her personal characteristics (such as age, sex, race, and status) affect the referred child's behavior. *Observer drift*—Over time, observer changes the criterion (or threshold) for judging the presence or absence of a behavior because of fatigue or learning or other variables. *Omission*—Observer fails to score behavior that has occurred. *Commission*—Observer miscodes behavior. *Expectancy effects*—Observer's expectations influence what he or she records, or observer expects something to happen and communicates these expectations to the child. *Observer reactivity*—Observer changes recording of behavior when he or she is aware of being observed. *Nonverbal cues*—Observer unintentionally cues the child nonverbally and by so doing reinforces certain behaviors.
Setting, codes, scales, and instruments	*Unrepresentative behavioral setting*—Observer selects only one setting or only one time period and thereby fails to sample representative behaviors adequately. *Coding complexity*—Observer cannot use codes accurately because there are (a) too many categories in the system, (b) too many categories scored on a given occasion, and/or (c) too many children observed on a given occasion. *Influence of extraneous cues*—Certain events in the environment influence observer to score the occurrence of a behavior when the behavior is not occurring. *Rating scales*—Observer inappropriately uses broad-category rating scales to classify behaviors and thereby loses fine distinctions. *Mechanical instruments*—Observer fails to check the accuracy of mechanical devices used for recording data (for example, stopwatch or counter).
The referred child (or children)	*Child reactivity*—Referred child's behavior changes as a result of the knowledge that he or she is being observed. *Role selection*—Referred child adopts a particular role as a result of the knowledge that he or she is being observed. *Measurement becomes an agent of change*—Referred child makes a significant change in his or her behavior or attitudes as a result of having behavior measured and observed. *Response set*—Referred child responds in a manner that conforms to cues from the observer. *Behavior drift*—Child's behavior continues, but in a form that drifts outside the range of definitions being used.
The sample (usually large samples or groups)	*Unrepresentative sample*—Observer fails to obtain a representative sample of the population. *Sample instability*—Observer fails to recognize population changes over time, making it difficult to compare present sample's results with those of previous samples. *Unrepresentative data*—Observer fails to recognize geographical and regional differences in behavior between samples.

Source: Adapted in part from Fassnacht (1982).

her observations, using certain categories or scale positions and neglecting others, showing leniency by not recognizing the severity of the observed behavior, having lapses in attention, or allowing the recording to be influenced by extraneous cues. Observers are susceptible to such influences as halo effects, prior information about the child, qualities of the setting, and expectations of others. A behavior that does not clearly fit a particular category is more susceptible to observer bias than is a behavior that fits a category clearly.

The following examples illustrate observer bias:

- Observers' expectations that the referred child will act aggressively influence them to record marginally aggressive acts as aggressive, whereas other observers without this expectation would record the same acts as nonaggressive.
- An extraneous cue, such as the teacher's praising the referred child for completing a previous assignment, leads observers to record on-task behavior in the observation interval, even though the referred child is not working on the current class assignment.
- Observers change the way they observe when they know that they are being observed by a supervisor or when they are told that their records will be compared with those of another observer. This tendency to be more careful, vigilant, and attentive to details when they know they are being evaluated is referred to as *observer reactivity*. Interestingly, when observers know they are being observed, their accuracy tends to increase (Foster & Cone, 1986).

Observer Drift

When observation continues over a long period, observers may show signs of forgetfulness, fatigue, and decreased motivation. For example, an observer may begin with one standard for scoring aggression, but over time change that standard. Observer drift may occur even when observers use specific definitions of behavior.

Difficulties in Coding Behavior

Global categories, such as *off-task behavior* or *inappropriate behavior,* require a higher level of inference than do specific categories, such as *hitting* or *out-of-seat behavior.* Reliability may be more difficult to achieve with global categories. Although you should attempt to define target behaviors precisely, some behaviors may be difficult to categorize. For example, how will you distinguish between a child who is staring into space and one who is thinking about a problem? Using observational codes often requires careful judgment.

Timing of Behavior

The timing of a sequence of events is not as simple as it appears. For example, when exactly does a child's refusal to eat begin and end? The time unit selected by the observer may not always be an exact mapping of the behavioral event.

Difficulties in Obtaining a Representative Sample of Behavior

You may not always be able to see or hear the child you are observing. For example, the child may wander out of view, turn his or her face away from you, whisper when you are trying to record what he or she is saying, or suddenly leave the room to go to the bathroom.

PROCEDURES FOR ASSESSING RELIABILITY

Three useful estimates of the reliability of observational coding are interobserver reliability, test-retest reliability, and internal consistency reliability. Interobserver reliability is the most important form of reliability for behavioral observations. Without interobserver reliability, the other forms of reliability have little meaning.

Interobserver Reliability

Estimates of interobserver reliability (also called *interobserver agreement*) are usually based on scores of two or more observers who record the same information while *simultaneously* and *independently* observing the same child or group (Nay, 1979). The data may be in the form of categorical judgments or interval scale ratings (see Chapter 4 in *Assessment of Children: Cognitive Applications*). Once you obtain these data, select and compute an appropriate statistical index of agreement. Several procedures are available for measuring interobserver reliability, including correlational coefficients (such as the product-moment correlation coefficient, or phi coefficient, and the intraclass correlation coefficient) and percentage agreement indices (such as kappa and uncorrected percentage agreement). These procedures measure different aspects of interobserver agreement and may yield different reliability estimates for the same set of data.

Product-moment correlation coefficient. If you are interested in the pattern of agreement among the observers' ratings, irrespective of the level of agreement, and you are using an interval scale of measurement, then the *product-moment correlation coefficient* is satisfactory (see Chapter 4 in *Assessment of Children: Cognitive Applications*). The product-moment correlation coefficient is sufficient when you simply want to establish whether one measure is linearly related to another measure. As an index of the agreement between observers, though, the product-moment correlation coefficient is usually not the method of choice, except with rating scale data. The *phi coefficient* is a particular version of the product-moment correlation coefficient used when the data are dichotomous—that is, in the form of 1 and 0. The phi coefficient is applicable to a 2×2 table only. See Table 4-3 in Chapter 4 in *Assessment of Children: Cognitive Applications* for the formula for computing the phi coefficient.

Intraclass correlation coefficient. When both the pattern of agreement and the level of agreement are important and you have an interval scale of measurement, you can use the *intraclass correlation coefficient* (McGraw & Wong, 1996; Shrout & Fleiss, 1979; Wong & McGraw, 1999). This correlation coefficient is useful when you have several sets of scores on one variable and no way of ordering the scores within a set. A computer program is available for computing four different intraclass correlation coefficient estimates (Strube, 1985).

Kappa. When the data form an ordinal scale and you are interested in correcting for chance agreement, *kappa* (κ) is a useful index of agreement (Cohen, 1960, 1968). Kappa considers both the occurrence and the nonoccurrence of behavior, corrected for chance agreement among observers. It is appropriate in situations where there are no independent criteria or bases for independent expert evaluation. Kappa measures the degree of consensus among observers; it evaluates precision, but not whether the observations are valid. Kappa is one of the preferred interrater reliability procedures and can be used for multiple observers and multiple categories. Exhibit 5-3 shows procedures for computing kappa. A computer program is available for computing kappa for multiple observers, multiple categories, and missing data (Oud & Sattler, 1984).

Kappa should not be used when the behaviors occur infrequently, because it has high variability in such situations (Shrout, Spitzer, & Fleiss, 1987). For example, kappa should not be used when there is a shift from high levels of the problem behavior (hits) during the preintervention baseline level to low levels of the problem behavior (few or no hits) during or after treatment. Kappa values of .75 or higher indicate excellent agreement, values of .40 to .69 indicate fair to good agreement, and values below .40 indicate poor agreement.

Percentage agreement. When you want a measure of the percentage agreement among two or more observers but are not concerned with correcting for chance agreement, you can use an uncorrected percentage agreement index. *Uncorrected percentage agreement,* which is simply the percentage of agreement of two or more observers, is susceptible to overestimating agreement when chance agreement is high. Although percentage agreement is not synonymous with reliability, it is useful as a preliminary check of the adequacy of your observational recordings because of its ease of computation and interpretation and its sensitivity to bias and systematic errors. In the material that follows, we will refer to uncorrected percentage agreement as *percentage agreement.*

Interval recording percentage agreement estimate. In interval recording, you can use several percentage agreement measures for determining interobserver agreement. Three such measures are (a) overall agreement, (b) agreement on the occurrence of the behavior, and (c) agreement on the nonoccurrence of the behavior. The key difference among the three measures is the specific interval used to determine the level of interobserver agreement. Let's use the data in Figure 5-1 to calculate these three interobserver percentage agreement measures.

Agreement on total observations. Overall agreement considers the total number of intervals and the occurrence or nonoccurrence of a behavior in each interval. We can define agreement as occurring when both observers score either the occurrence or the nonoccurrence of a behavior in a given interval. The procedure is as follows:

1. Considering all intervals, make two counts—one of the number of intervals in which the observers agreed on the occurrence or nonoccurrence of a behavior and one of the number of intervals in which they disagreed.
2. Divide the number of agreements by the total number of agreements plus disagreements and multiply by 100. The result is the percentage of interobserver agreement for the total number of intervals.

The formula for interobserver percentage agreement for the total number of intervals is as follows:

$$\%A_{\text{IR tot}} = \frac{A_{\text{tot}}}{A_{\text{tot}} + D} \times 100$$

where $\%A_{\text{IR tot}}$ = interval recording percentage agreement for the total number of intervals

A_{tot} = number of intervals in which Observer 1 and Observer 2 *agreed* on whether the behavior occurred or did not occur

D = number of intervals in which Observer 1 and Observer 2 *disagreed* on whether the behavior occurred or did not occur

Example: The two observers agreed that the target behavior occurred or did not occur in intervals 1, 2, 3, 5, 6, 7, and 10 (seven agreements), but disagreed about intervals 4, 8, and 9 (three disagreements). Therefore, there was a 70% rate of

	1	2	3	4	5	6	7	8	9	10
Observer 1	X	O	X	O	X	O	O	X	O	X
Observer 2	X	O	X	X	X	O	O	O	X	X

Note. X indicates occurrence of behavior; O indicates nonoccurrence of behavior.

Figure 5-1. Raw data for three interobserver percentage agreement measures.

Exhibit 5-3
Procedures for Computing Kappa (κ)

Kappa (κ) is a useful statistic for measuring interobserver reliability (or interobserver agreement) for categorical data. Kappa indicates the proportion of agreements, corrected for chance agreements. Like correlation coefficients, kappa ranges from +1.00 to −1.00. When kappa is positive, the proportion of observed agreement is *more than* would be expected by chance. When kappa is equal to zero, the proportion of observed agreement *equals* what would be expected by chance. When kappa is negative, the proportion of observed agreement is *less than* what would be expected by chance.

Suppose two observers scored one child over 100 intervals for the occurrence or nonoccurrence of a behavior. Observer 1 scored the occurrence of the behavior in 90 intervals, and Observer 2 scored the occurrence of the behavior in 80 intervals. In this situation, there must be some agreement because both observers scored more than 50 intervals. The figure shows that, for the two observers, the lowest possible number of overlapping occurrence intervals (that is, intervals scored identically by the two observers) is 70. This minimum overlap of 70 intervals occurs when 10 of the occurrence intervals scored by Observer 2 correspond to the 10 nonoccurrence intervals scored by Observer 1. In this case, the correction for chance agreement in the kappa formula is 72%. The procedure for obtaining the chance correction is discussed below.

Kappa can be used for multiple categories and multiple raters. Formulas are presented below for computing kappa for (a) two observers and multiple categories and (b) the special case of two observers and two categories (2 × 2 contingency table). Formulas for computing kappa for multiple categories as well as for multiple raters are found in Conger (1980) and Uebersax (1982). Uebersax presents a generalized kappa formula that is also appropriate for handling missing data.

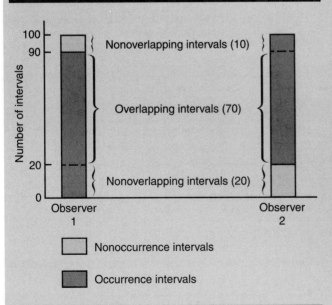

Nonoccurrence intervals

Occurrence intervals

Kappa for Two Observers and Multiple Categories
To introduce the general kappa formula for two observers and multiple categories, let us set up a 3 x 3 contingency table representing two observers and three recording categories. The designations for the contingency table are as follows:

		Observer 2			
		C_1	C_2	C_3	
	C_1	n_{11}	n_{12}	n_{13}	n_{1+}
Observer 1	C_2	n_{21}	n_{22}	n_{23}	n_{2+}
	C_3	n_{31}	n_{32}	n_{33}	n_{3+}
		n_{+1}	n_{+2}	n_{+3}	N

Each cell is designated by two subscripts. The first subscript refers to the row, the second to the column. Thus, n_{23} designates the cell in the second row, third column. The rows and columns correspond to the three different observation categories (C_1, C_2, C_3). The marginal totals for Observer 1 are designated by n_{1+}, n_{2+}, and n_{3+}, and those for Observer 2 are designated by n_{+1}, n_{+2}, and n_{+3}.

The general formula for kappa is

$$\kappa = \frac{p_o - p_c}{1 - p_c}$$

where p_o = the observed proportion of agreement
p_c = the proportion of agreement expected by chance alone

The computational formulas for p_o and p_c are

$$p_o = \frac{\sum_{i=1}^{C} n_{ii}}{N}$$

$$= \frac{(n_{11} + n_{22} + n_{33} + \cdots + n_{ii})}{N}$$

$$p_c = \frac{\sum_{i=1}^{C} (n_{i+})(n_{+i})}{N^2}$$

$$= \frac{(n_{1+} \times n_{+1}) + (n_{2+} \times n_{+2}) + (n_{3+} \times n_{+3}) + \cdots + (n_{i+} \times n_{+i})}{N^2}$$

where n_{ii} = total number of agreements for the ith category (main diagonal)
n_{i+} = marginal total for Observer 1 on the ith category
n_{+i} = marginal total for Observer 2 on the ith category
N = total number of observation periods (for example, intervals)

Let us apply this formula to some hypothetical data obtained by two observers who scored the same child over 10 intervals, using three observation categories. The three codes used by the two observers were verbal off-task (VO), motor off-task (MO), and on-task (OT). The data were as follows:

(Continued)

Exhibit 5-3 *(Continued)*

Interval	Observer 1	Observer 2
1	VO	MO
2	VO	VO
3	MO	MO
4	OT	OT
5	OT	OT
6	VO	VO
7	MO	MO
8	MO	VO
9	MO	MO
10	VO	VO

Placing these scores in a 3 × 3 contingency table gives us the following:

		Observer 2			
		VO	MO	OT	
	VO	3	1	0	4
Observer 1	MO	1	3	0	4
	OT	0	0	2	2
		4	4	2	10

To calculate kappa, we first obtain p_o and p_c:

$$p_o = \frac{n_{11} + n_{22} + n_{33} + \cdots + n_{ii}}{N}$$

$$= \frac{3 + 3 + 2}{10} = \frac{8}{10} = .80$$

$$p_c = \frac{(n_{1+} \times n_{+1}) + (n_{2+} \times n_{+2}) + (n_{3+} \times n_{+3}) + \cdots + (n_{i+} \times n_{+i})}{N^2}$$

$$= \frac{(4 \times 4) + (4 \times 4) + (2 \times 2)}{10^2} = \frac{16 + 16 + 4}{100}$$

$$= \frac{36}{100} = .36$$

Then we put the values of p_o and p_c into the formula for kappa:

$$\kappa = \frac{.80 - .36}{1 - .36} = \frac{.44}{.64} = .69$$

If a straight percentage agreement had been used, the level would have been 80% (or what p_o equals). Kappa gives us a co-efficient of .69, a somewhat lower level of agreement. A kappa of .70 is considered to indicate an acceptable level of agreement.

Kappa for a 2 × 2 Contingency Table

We now consider kappa for the special case of binary ratings, with two observers and two observation categories (e.g., occurrence/nonoccurrence or agreement/disagreement in a 2 × 2 contingency table).

The general formula for kappa, as we have seen, is

$$\kappa = \frac{p_o - p_c}{1 - p_c}$$

In a 2 × 2 contingency table, p_o is computed by dividing the two cells in which both observers agree by the total number of obser-

vation periods or intervals (N); p_c is computed by adding the products of the marginal frequencies and then dividing this value by the total number of observation periods or intervals squared. Thus, for the contingency table

		Observer 2		
		O	NO	Total
	O	a	b	$a + b$
Observer 1	NO	c	d	$c + d$
	Total	$a + c$	$b + d$	N

$$p_o = \frac{a + d}{N}$$

$$p_c = \frac{(a + b)(a + c) + (c + d)(b + d)}{N^2}$$

where p_o = observed proportion of agreement
p_c = proportion of agreement expected by chance alone
N = total number of observation periods

A computationally more convenient formula for computing kappa in a 2 × 2 contingency table is

$$\kappa = \frac{2(ad - bc)}{(a + b)(b + d) + (a + c)(c + d)}$$

where a = number of intervals in which Observer 1 and Observer 2 scored the behavior as occurring
b = number of intervals in which Observer 1 scored the behavior as occurring and Observer 2 scored the behavior as not occurring
c = number of intervals in which Observer 1 scored the behavior as not occurring and Observer 2 scored the behavior as occurring
d = number of intervals in which Observer 1 and Observer 2 scored the behavior as not occurring

The data for two observers who scored one child over 100 intervals are summarized as follows:

		Observer 2		
		O	NO	Total
	O	20	6	26
Observer 1	NO	2	72	74
	Total	22	78	100

$$\kappa = \frac{2(ad - bc)}{(a + b)(b + d) + (a + c)(c + d)}$$

$$= \frac{2[(20 \times 72) - (6 \times 2)]}{(26 \times 78) + (22 \times 74)} = \frac{2(1440 - 12)}{2028 + 1628}$$

$$= \frac{2(1428)}{3656} = \frac{2856}{3656} = 78$$

For the above data, p_o, the observed proportion of agreement, is

$$p_o = \frac{a + d}{N} = \frac{20 + 72}{100} = \frac{92}{100} = 92\%$$

(Continued)

Exhibit 5-3 *(Continued)*

and p_c, the proportion of agreement expected by chance alone, is

$$p_c = \frac{(a+b)(a+c)+(c+d)(b+d)}{N^2}$$

$$= \frac{(26 \times 22)+(74 \times 78)}{100^2}$$

$$= \frac{6344}{10,000} = 63\%$$

Again, a kappa of .78 is a more conservative estimate of inter-observer agreement than the 92% agreement rate, uncorrected for chance.

---

agreement in scoring the target behavior over the total number of intervals recorded:

$$\%A_{IR\,tot} = \frac{A_{tot}}{A_{tot}+D} \times 100$$

$$= \frac{7}{7+3} \times 100 = \frac{7}{10} \times 100 = 70\%$$

Agreement on occurrence observations. Agreement on the occurrence of the behavior considers only those intervals in which at least one of the two observers recorded the occurrence of a behavior. We define agreement as occurring when both observers score the occurrence of a behavior in a given interval. This procedure is similar to the one you use for total observations, except that you use only a portion of the intervals.

1. Considering only those intervals in which at least one of the two observers recorded the occurrence of a behavior, make two counts—one of the number of intervals in which the observers agreed on the occurrence of a behavior and one of the number of intervals in which the observers disagreed.
2. Divide the number of agreements by the total number of agreements plus disagreements and multiply by 100. The result is the percentage of interobserver agreement for those intervals in which at least one observer scored the behavior as occurring.

The formula for interobserver percentage agreement for behavior occurrence is a variant of the one used for overall percentage agreement:

$$\%A_{IR\,occ} = \frac{A_{occ}}{A_{occ}+D} \times 100$$

where $\%A_{IR\,occ}$ = interval recording percentage agreement for intervals in which occurrence of behavior is scored

A_{occ} = number of intervals in which both observers *agreed* that the behavior did occur

D = number of intervals in which the observers *disagreed* on whether the behavior occurred

Example: The two observers agreed that the target behavior occurred in intervals 1, 3, 5, and 10 (four agreements), but only one of the observers scored an occurrence of the behavior in intervals 4, 8, and 9 (three disagreements). Thus, there was a 57% level of agreement for scoring the target behavior as occurring:

$$\%A_{IR\,occ} = \frac{A_{occ}}{A_{occ}+D} \times 100$$

$$= \frac{4}{4+3} \times 100 = \frac{4}{7} \times 100 = 57\%$$

If neither observer records an instance of an occurrence of a target behavior, you cannot calculate a reliability index for this category.

Agreement on nonoccurrence observations. Agreement on the nonoccurrence of the behavior considers only those intervals in which either one or both observers recorded the nonoccurrence of a behavior. We define agreement as occurring when both observers score the nonoccurrence of a behavior in a given interval. This procedure is similar to the one described above.

1. Considering only those intervals in which at least one of the two observers recorded the nonoccurrence of a behavior, make two counts—one of the number of intervals in which the observers agreed on the nonoccurrence of a behavior and one of the number of intervals in which the observers disagreed.
2. Divide the number of agreements by the total number of agreements plus disagreements and multiply by 100. The result is the percentage of interobserver agreement for those intervals in which the observers scored the behavior as not occurring.

The formula for interobserver percentage agreement for behavior nonoccurrence is another variant of the one used for overall percentage agreement:

$$\%A_{IR\,non} = \frac{A_{non}}{A_{non}+D} \times 100$$

where $\%A_{\text{IR non}}$ = interval recording percentage agreement for intervals in which nonoccurrence of behavior is scored

A_{non} = number of intervals in which both observers *agreed* that the behavior did not occur

D = number of intervals in which the observers *disagreed* on whether the behavior did not occur

Example: The two observers agreed that the target behavior did not occur in intervals 2, 6, and 7 (three agreements). In intervals 4, 8, and 9, however, only one of the observers scored the nonoccurrence of the behavior (three disagreements). Thus, the level of agreement was 50% for scoring the target behavior as not occurring:

$$\%A_{\text{IR non}} = \frac{A_{\text{non}}}{A_{\text{non}} + D} \times 100$$

$$= \frac{3}{3+3} \times 100 = \frac{3}{6} \times 100 = 50\%$$

If neither observer records an instance of a nonoccurrence of a target behavior, you cannot calculate an agreement index for this category.

Comment on interval recording percentage agreement estimates.   When observers score the occurrence of a behavior in only a small proportion of the intervals, compute interobserver percentage agreement only for those intervals in which the observers scored an occurrence of the behavior; the use of total intervals might cause some distortion of the rate of agreement. For example, suppose that, in a 100-interval observation period, one observer scored the occurrence of the target behavior in three intervals and the other observer scored the occurrence of the behavior in one of those three intervals. The observers' rate of agreement in scoring the occurrence of the behavior is 33%. Use of the total intervals would result in an agreement rate of 98%. The 33% agreement figure more accurately represents the observers' ability to identify the target behavior when it occurs.

When observers score occurrence of a behavior in a large proportion of the intervals, you might want to study the rate of agreement in those intervals in which the observers scored the nonoccurrence of the behavior. In this case, you would use the third method discussed above.

When you use more than one category in an observation system, as is common, you must decide whether to evaluate interobserver agreement for the total observations, for the separate categories, or for both. We recommend that you compute interobserver agreement for each category as well as for the total observations. This will give you valuable information about where potential difficulties may lie, such as with the coding system or with the observers. *Consider a percentage agreement of 80% or above as satisfactory.*

Table 5-7 shows the three types of percentage agreement measures and kappa calculated for 10 sets of data. The table also has a column for chance agreement. It is evident that in some cases the four measures differ greatly. In cases 2, 4, 8, and 10, kappa gives a .00 coefficient, whereas the total percentage agreement measure ranges from 50% to 98%. Kappa thus provides a more conservative index of interobserver agreement. The table also shows that the value of kappa is significantly affected by chance agreement. In example 3, kappa is .66; a change in a single agreement in one interval causes the value of kappa to change to .00 in example 4. These examples, therefore, show that kappa for some data sets may be difficult to interpret.

Event recording percentage agreement estimate.
In event recording, you can estimate interobserver percentage agreement by dividing the number of occurrences of the event reported by the observer recording the lower frequency by the number of occurrences of the event reported by the other observer. The percentage agreement formula for event recording is as follows:

$$\%A_{\text{ER}} = \frac{f_{\text{l}}}{f_{\text{h}}} \times 100$$

Example: Two observers recorded out-of-seat behavior, the target event. During a 20-minute observation period, one observer recorded 5 occurrences of the behavior and the other observer recorded 8 occurrences. Substitute into the formula as follows:

$$\%A_{\text{ER}} = \frac{f_1}{f_2} \times 100$$

$$= \frac{5}{8} \times 100 = 62.5\%$$

There was 62.5% agreement between the two observers in the number of occurrences of the target behavior. This level of agreement does not mean that the observers recorded the same target behavior, however. It could be that there were 13 occurrences of the target behavior, 5 of which were recorded by one observer and 8 of which were recorded by the other. The level of agreement simply indicates that the ratio of events reported in common was 62.5%. Unless the observational recording procedure used specific intervals or times, there is no way of knowing whether the two observers *recorded the same events.*

Duration recording percentage agreement estimate.
The interobserver percentage agreement estimate for duration recording is similar to the one used for event recording. The percentage agreement formula for duration recording is as follows:

$$\%A_{\text{DR}} = \frac{t_{\text{l}}}{t_{\text{h}}} \times 100$$

Example: Two observers recorded the target event of a child's staring out the window. One observer clocked an

Table 5-7
Comparison of Four Observer Agreement Formulas for 10 Sets of Data

O_1 \ O_2 (a b / c d)	Chance percentage agreement on occurrence	Occurrence percentage agreement	Nonoccurrence percentage agreement	Total percentage agreement	Kappa
1. 50 0 / 0 0	100	100	—	100	1.00
2. 49 1 / 0 0	98	98	0	98	.00
3. 48 1 / 0 1	94	98	50	98	.66
4. 0 1 / 0 49	0	0	98	98	.00
5. 25 0 / 0 25	25	100	100	100	1.00
6. 24 1 / 0 25	24	96	96	98	.96
7. 20 10 / 0 20	24	67	67	80	.62
8. 9 16 / 9 16	18	26	39	50	.00
9. 1 24 / 24 1	25	2	2	4	−.92
10. 14 12 / 13 11	28	36	31	50	.00

Note. See text for computational formulas for each agreement index and kappa. The formula for chance percentage agreement on occurrence is $OC = \dfrac{(a+b)(a+c)}{N^2}$. In the 2 × 2 table (column one), O_1 = Observer 1, O_2 = Observer 2, O = occurrence, NO = nonoccurrence.

episode at 360 seconds; the other, at 365 seconds. Substitute into the formula as follows:

$$\%A_{DR} = \frac{t_1}{t_h} \times 100$$

$$= \frac{360}{365} \times 100 = 98\%$$

Thus, there was 98% agreement between the two observers in the duration of the staring-out-the-window behavior. This level of agreement does not mean that the observers recorded the duration of the same target behavior, however. It could be that the child stared out the window for a total of 400 seconds and the two observers recorded different times when the behavior occurred.

Ratings recording percentage agreement estimate. In ratings recording, you can estimate interobserver percentage agreement by determining whether the two observers gave the same rating on each scale. The percentage agreement formula for ratings recording is as follows:

$$\%A_{RR} = \frac{A_{rr}}{A_{rr} + D} \times 100$$

where $\%A_{RR}$ = ratings recording percentage agreement for the total number of scales

A_{rr} = number of scales in which both observers *agreed* on the rating

D = number of scales in which the observers *disagreed* on the rating

Example: After a 30-minute observation period, two observers completed ten 5-point rating scales. They agreed on ratings for 8 of the 10 scales. Substitute into the formula as follows:

$$\%A_{RR} = \frac{A_{rr}}{A_{rr} + D} \times 100$$

$$= \frac{8}{8 + 2} \times 100 = \frac{8}{10} \times 100 = 80\%$$

Thus, there was 80% agreement between the two observers in their ratings.

In ratings recording, a 7-point scale requires finer judgments than a 3-point or 5-point scale. Hence, the more categories you have in a rating scale, the lower the interobserver percentage agreement is likely to be. Normally, percentage agreement considers only the absolute level of agreement; that is, you count an agreement only when both observers give exactly the same rating. This agreement procedure does not consider the pattern of ratings. If one observer is consistently one scale position above (or below) the other observer, you will still count a disagreement for each scale. An alternative approach is to count an agreement when the two observers are no more than one scale position apart. This is a less stringent method but still provides information about the pattern of observer agreement. In ratings recording, you also may want to compute a product-moment correlation (or intraclass correlation coefficient) to determine the pattern of agreement between the two observers.

Comment on interobserver reliability. Do not confuse percentage agreement indices with product-moment correlation coefficients—they do not mean the same thing (Moore, 1987). For example, a percentage agreement of .60 does not express the same degree of interobserver reliability as $r = .60$. In fact, when the phenomenon of interest occurs in about 50% of the observations, a percentage agreement of .50 yields $r = .00$, a percentage agreement of .75 yields $r = .50$, and a percentage agreement of .95 yields $r = .90$. When the phenomenon of interest occurs rarely or frequently, the range of correlation coefficients associated with each percentage agreement rate is considerable. In the three cases just illustrated, a percentage agreement of .50 yields interobserver reliability correlation coefficients ranging from $r = -.12$ to $r = .02$, a percentage agreement of .75 yields interobserver reliability correlation coefficients ranging from $r = .23$ to $r = .50$, and a percentage agreement of .90 yields interobserver reliability correlation coefficients ranging from $r = .76$ to $r = .90$, depending on the relative frequency of occurrence of the phenomenon.

Obtaining satisfactory reliability between two observers does not ensure that the data are meaningful or accurate. High reliabilities may be associated with observation codes that are relatively insensitive to the occurrence of important or meaningful behaviors. Or behaviors may occur at levels beyond those included in the observation codes. Thus, high agreement between observers is no guarantee that the observational system provides accurate measurements of behaviors related to the problem. And after the observations are completed, inferences must be made and conclusions drawn. This is by no means a foolproof process. Different observers may draw different conclusions from the same set of observations. Such differences, then, are another source of unreliability in the observational report.

Test-Retest Reliability

The consistency of behavior over time and situations is another measure of the reliability of behavioral observations. You should strive to sample the target behaviors more than once and in more than one setting. You can use the percentage agreement interval recording formulas to evaluate test-retest reliability. You can also use various correlational procedures, depending on the scaling of the data. For example, you can assess intraindividual stability by correlating the frequency of each targeted behavior observed on one occasion with the frequency of each targeted behavior observed by the same observer on another occasion. The product-moment correlation coefficient that you obtain does not allow you to evaluate which of the behaviors show more or less stability, because you compute the correlation across all categories. By scanning the changes from the first to the second observation periods for each category, however, you can obtain some idea of which categories show the most change.

When instability occurs, it may be caused by changes in the child, the setting, the observer, the definitions of the behaviors used by the observer, or the methods used for the observation. Determine which factor or combination of factors is responsible for the instability by carefully studying all sources of data and the procedures you used in the observational assessment.

Internal Consistency Reliability

Internal consistency reliability reflects how consistent an assessment instrument is in measuring the same characteristics. One way of obtaining internal consistency estimates is to divide the observation measure into two equal parts (e.g., odd- and even-numbered items). Chapter 4 in *Assessment of Children: Cognitive Applications* describes formulas for measuring internal consistency reliability. You also can use factor analysis, discriminant function analysis, and various correlational procedures (depending on the scaling of the data) to evaluate the internal composition of items in observational coding systems.

PROCEDURES FOR ASSESSING VALIDITY

Validity, which refers to the extent to which procedures are measuring what they are supposed to measure (see Chapter 4 in *Assessment of Children: Cognitive Applications*), is evaluated by studying the meaningfulness and relevance of the behavioral measures. Carrying out valid behavioral observations is often problematic, because it is difficult to obtain an adequate and representative sample of behavior in a short time. Acquiring an adequate and representative sample of behavior would require sampling in many different types of situations, and this is rarely practical. Validation criteria include ratings from others familiar with the child and observations in controlled experimental situations. But these criteria are not absolute and do not offer proof of validity. A further difficulty arises when the two indices purporting to measure the same behavior are not in agreement. Which measure is valid or representative? Because behavior is variable, it is possible that both measures are accurate, even though the criterion measures show poor agreement.

Here is an example of how you might go about establishing the validity of an observational coding system designed to evaluate hyperactivity:

- For construct validity, establish whether the behaviors coded (e.g., fidgeting, out-of-chair movements) constitute a satisfactory and functional definition of hyperactivity.
- For content validity, establish whether the data reflect the nature and degree of hyperactivity displayed during the observation.
- For concurrent validity, establish whether the behavior under observation accurately reflects the child's reactions in other situations.
- For predictive validity, establish whether the behaviors coded predict other important criteria.

Establishing validity is no simple matter. However, if you can satisfy the above criteria, you can be fairly certain that you are measuring hyperactivity.

Representativeness and Generalizability of Findings

Two major factors affecting the validity of the observational assessment are the *representativeness* and the *generalizability* of the findings. For example, to what degree does the behavior observed during the time-sampling procedure reflect behavior in the total time period and behavior in other situa-

tions to which you want to generalize the findings? Or, to what degree is the narrative recording, event recording, or ratings recording representative of the referred child's behavior in similar settings? Consider these questions each time you evaluate your observational assessment.

Reactivity

A child's behavior under observation may be affected by the child's awareness that someone is observing him or her, by the child's prior interactions with the observer, or by the observer's personal characteristics. We refer to this effect as *reactivity* or the *guinea pig effect*. Reactivity, in this sense, refers to changes in the behavior of the observed child that are related to the presence of the observer. Ordinarily, these changes are unwanted, because they distort the child's usual pattern of behavior, which is of major interest to the observer. For example, a child who is usually aggressive may avoid aggressive behavior when an observer is present. Whether the child is conscious of being observed depends on several factors, including the child's age, degree of sophistication, familiarity with the observer, and previous experience with being observed; the setting; the number of children in the setting; the number of children being observed; and the conspicuousness of the observer.

To minimize reactivity, conduct your observations as unobtrusively as possible. As a general rule, do not assume that stable behavior during the observation period is necessarily typical behavior or that any changes you observe in the child's behavior would have occurred if you were not present. A child's reactivity to an observer presents a particular threat to the validity of the observational assessment. In some cases, it may be better to have an observer whom the child knows, whereas in other cases it may be better to have someone unfamiliar to the child. If you have a choice in selecting the observer, your knowledge of the case should guide you in deciding who the observer should be.

You can judge whether reactive effects have occurred by looking for (a) systematic changes in the child's behavior over time, some of which may be related to the presence of the observer, (b) increased variability in the child's behavior, (c) reports from the child that the child changed behavior as a result of being observed, and (d) discrepancies between different measures of the child's same behavior, when measures were obtained under different observation conditions (Haynes & Horn, 1982). Although these indices do not *prove* that reactive effects are present, they suggest that such effects may be operating.

Harris and Lahey (1982) believe that reactivity is often so powerful that it clouds the observational data. "Unless it has been well-documented that reactivity is not a factor in a given situation, observational data may be taken as a demonstration that a particular behavior is in a [child's] repertoire, but not that it is performed in the absence of observation" (p. 536).

Not everyone agrees, however, that reactivity is necessarily detrimental to observational assessment. Cone and Foster

(1982), for example, noted that reactivity may pose problems for some research and clinical objectives but not for others.

The important issue seems to be not whether observed individuals react differently under conditions of known observation but rather whether data collected under such conditions are less useful than those collected surreptitiously.

In this vein it is conceivable that reactive data may have even greater utility or social validity than nonreactive data in some circumstances. This could occur when [you wish] to generalize to situations involving similar levels of obtrusive observation. For example, in assessing the adequacy of vocal presentations before audiences, it is probably the case that data obtained from conditions in which the client is aware of being observed will correlate more highly with subsequent real-life presentations. Similarly, relatively reactive heterosocial skills assessment may evidence greater utility than less reactive assessment, given that most heterosocial interactions contain an evaluative component. Removing a significant portion of this component from the assessment process could lead to lower correlations with relevant criteria. As Barker and Wright (1954) pointed out long ago, interaction between an observer and a person observed is important in its own right, not just as a potential confounding element to be uniformly eliminated or controlled. (p. 343, with changes in notation)

Reactivity also is useful because it may suggest possible interventions (Galen Alessi, personal communication, March 2000). For example, a child who reacts positively to the mere presence of an observer clearly can control the behaviors of concern. In this situation, reactivity leads the observer to be optimistic about treatment.

PROCEDURES FOR REDUCING ERRORS IN OBSERVATIONS

Reducing Errors in Reliability

You can use several procedures to reduce errors in reliability. One method is to study the errors listed in Table 5-6 (see page 132) and then try to avoid or limit them when you perform behavioral observations. You can reduce or eliminate many of these errors simply by practicing. To eliminate others, you may need to further refine your recording procedures and rating scales. Some errors, such as those associated with your personal characteristics (e.g., gender, height, weight, skin color, voice) or with the reactions of the referred child, may be difficult to eliminate, but you can minimize their effects simply by being aware of their potential influence.

You can increase reliability by (a) having clear and precise definitions of behaviors, (b) following systematic and precise rules governing the observations, (c) becoming well trained in observational procedures, and (d) using observation periods that are not excessively long. Although observer drift is difficult to control, you can reduce it by making frequent checks of your recordings, becoming thoroughly familiar with the recording system beforehand, and making periodic calibrations during the observation session to check the consistency of your observations (e.g., determining whether you are using

the recording system in the same way as other observers, and whether your understanding of the definitions has changed during the course of the observation). These procedures also reduce other sources of observer bias.

You can further reduce errors by gaining an understanding of your decision criteria—such as the degree of certainty you must have to report that a behavior did or did not occur—and comparing your decision criteria with those of other observers. Signal detection approaches can be useful in achieving these goals (Lord, 1985). These approaches focus on an observer's ability to detect stimuli, considering the observer's response style (e.g., whether the observer uses liberal or conservative decision criteria). In some cases, using global categories to classify behavior (such as *sociable* vs. *unsociable* or *sensitive* vs. *insensitive*) may be unwise, because global categories—which require more inferences than narrow categories (such as *out-of-seat* vs. *in-seat*)—are more susceptible to observer bias. Thus, you can use global categories when they meet your assessment goals and are methodologically sound, but to reduce observer bias, use narrow categories when possible.

Comparing Observation Results with a Criterion

During your training, regularly compare your results with those of a highly trained observer or with standard criterion recordings. The agreement between an observer's recordings and standard criterion recordings is referred to as *criterion-related agreement*. Even trained observers should periodically compare their results with those of another observer or standard criterion recordings to evaluate their reliability.

Another method of checking the reliability of your ratings involves videotaping the behavior of a child (or class). After recording your observations in the setting in which the behaviors occur, rate the child's behavior again from the videotape. *Always obtain parental permission before making a videotape recording.* (As noted in Chapter 3 of *Assessment of Children: Cognitive Applications,* no assessment should be carried out without parental permission and without informing the child.) The level of agreement between the two recordings is a measure of the reliability of your ratings. This method is generally used only for training purposes, however, as your memory of the first observation may affect your second observation and you may overestimate reliability.

If possible, also compare your observation of the videotape with that of an expert and those of several peers. Thoroughly discuss any disagreements, and compute estimates of interobserver agreement. Low interobserver percentage agreement may mean that the categories are not clearly defined, that one (or more) of the observers does not understand them, or that other factors are interfering with agreement. You may be able to increase interobserver reliability by practicing observational assessment in environments similar to those in which you will work, whether during site visits or from videotaped recordings.

An acceptable level of interobserver agreement does not rule out observer error, however. You can have a high level of interobserver agreement and still have observer bias and observer drift if both observers have a similar bias or make similar errors. The level of agreement is even more likely to mask errors when you compare two of your own recordings.

Reducing Reactivity

Although reactivity may be useful in limited cases, you will most often want to minimize it. To this end, here are some suggestions (Nay, 1979):

- *Become as neutral a stimulus as possible.* Avoid making eye contact with or interacting with the referred child or any other children during the observation period. To provide a rationale for your presence in the classroom, the teacher might say to the class: "Ms. A is here today to see what we do." At the beginning of each school year, make a few short visits to each class so that the children become accustomed to seeing you.
- *Position yourself so that you are away from the ordinary paths of movement in the classroom and yet still have an unobstructed view of the child and setting.* A good position in the classroom is often to the rear or side of the room. You want, if possible, to have a clear view of everything occurring in the classroom.
- *Shift your attention from one child to another.* By so doing, you will avoid calling attention to any one individual child.
- *Limit your stimulus value.* Do not dress or act in a manner that attracts attention.
- *Follow all rules, regulations, and informal policies of the school, institution, or family.* Before going into a classroom, institution, or home, review your specific procedures with the teacher, administrative personnel, or the parents.
- *Enter the setting when your entrance will least disrupt the ongoing behavior.* For classroom observations, enter the classroom before class begins or at break time. If possible, try to be in the setting for a period of time *before* the formal observation begins. If the teacher or family or children become used to your presence, their behavior may be more natural, and less reactive, when the formal observation begins.

These suggestions will help you become a more natural part of the setting and diminish the child's awareness of your presence. Awareness by itself does not necessarily affect the child's behavior. It is only when the child's awareness of you leads to changes in her or his behavior that the validity of the observation is jeopardized. The reason for the assessment may determine how much influence your presence will have on the child's behavior. A child who knows that the results of the assessment will be used to determine her or his class placement may be more affected by your presence than a child who believes that the results will have little or no bearing on her or his status in school.

If you conduct the observations *prior* to interviewing or testing the child, the child is less likely to feel concerned about your being in the classroom. Additionally, when you do work with the child, the child may have a sense of familiarity with you from the beginning: "Oh, you're the lady who was in my class the other day." As noted previously, you will need to inform the child that he or she is being evaluated with the consent of his or her parents.

Establishing Informal Norms

Developing informal norms will help you place the child's behavior in a meaningful context. In a group setting, you might observe the behavior of the referred child and that of one or more peers (Alessi, 1980). The behavior of the child's peers can then serve as a norm (sometimes referred to as a "micronorm") against which you can compare the behavior of the referred child. The peers should be children of the same age and sex as the referred child, who have not been identified as experiencing behavior problems and who are as *representative* of the total peer group as possible. From this pool, you can randomly select one or more children for comparison.

Another procedure is to establish local norms for the entire class, using the scan check method. The scan check method involves scanning the entire class for, say, 2 seconds every 2 minutes (for a period of 8 to 10 minutes) and recording how many students are off-task. Still another procedure for establishing informal norms is to compare the child's present behavior with his or her past behavior, thereby using the child as his or her own norm, or standard.

Obtaining a peer or class rating permits you to measure the difference between the frequency with which the referred child engages in a particular behavior and the frequency with which the peer or class does. You can compute a discrepancy ratio to summarize the results of peer or class comparisons. The *discrepancy ratio* is the difference between the median level of the referred child's behavior and the median level of the peer's (or class's) behavior. You could describe the referred child who is off-task six times per minute while his or her peers are off-task three times per minute as "off-task twice as often as his or her peers."

Here is an example of how you can obtain informal norms (Alessi, 1980). Assume that a teacher referred Robert for his talking-out and out-of-seat behaviors in class. You observe Robert along with Todd, who has not been identified as talking out excessively and is considered an "average" child in this regard. Every few minutes, you also scan the class and note how many of the children are talking out or are out of their seats. Your results are as follows:

	Talking-out Behavior	*Out-of-seat Behavior*
Robert	20	10
Todd	2	1
Class (%) (6 scans)	3% (1/30)	6% (2/30)

These data suggest that Robert engages in more inappropriate behavior (as defined by the teacher) than does either the comparison child or the class as a whole. If you accept these data as reflecting approximate norms for behavior in this class, you can conclude that Robert's behavior deviates from the norm. In this example, both a comparison child and local class norms provide standards for interpreting the behavior of the referred child. Without these standards, it would be difficult to know whether the behavior of the referred child was deviant.

Some Potential Problems and Suggested Solutions

Following are some problems associated with classroom observations, along with suggestions for avoiding them (Alessi, 1980, 1988).

Problem 1. The observation occurs during a part of the day in which the child does not exhibit the problem behavior.

Suggestion: Confer with the teacher before you schedule your observations. For example, ask the teacher the following questions: "When does this behavior occur most often? At what times? Which day or days of the week? During which subjects? When is it best to observe the child to ensure that the behavior occurs? When is the behavior at its worst?" Then arrange your schedule to observe the child at a prime time. Whenever possible, spread your observation over three or four 10-minute sessions, rather than one 30-to-40-minute session, and across a week or two. Also, you may want to try to find out what else is different that day or part of the day to get leads on what may be contributing to the problem behavior and what might be an effective intervention. The fact that the referred child's inappropriate behavior did not occur during the observation is a positive sign because it indicates that the behavior may be under some voluntary control.

Problem 2. The comparison child whom you select or who is selected for you also has a behavioral problem.

Suggestion: You can control this potential difficulty by consulting with the teacher about selecting an "average" child or by selecting a different comparison child for each 10-minute observation period.

Problem 3. The critical behaviors that you need to observe are poorly defined.

Suggestion: Further discussion with the teacher about the child's problems may eliminate this potential source of difficulty. Here is an example: Although the teacher has referred the child for talking-out behavior, the teacher seems to be more concerned with the content of the child's outbursts than the frequency. On the few occasions on which the child talks out, the talking is laced with profanity. Learning of the teacher's true concern puts you in a better position to develop interventions.

Problem 4. The child has been referred for reasons other than those given, either because the teacher does not want to state the primary reason for the referral or because the teacher has a hidden agenda. For example, the teacher may want the child removed from the classroom for behavior problems but refer the child for poor academic performance.

Suggestion: This may be the most difficult problem to solve. Its solution depends on the teacher's willingness to openly discuss his or her feelings about the referred child with you. Teachers may not be aware of their own hidden agendas. Good consultation and interviewing skills (see Chapters 1 to 3) are especially important in this situation. Determining the teacher's standards can also be valuable. Some teachers have rigid standards; others have lenient standards. For example, some teachers want behaviors to be close to perfection, whereas others accept less perfect behavior without becoming too concerned.

Problem 5. The level of the child's problem behavior differs from task to task within the same class.

Suggestion: Examine the way each task is taught. It may be that different teaching practices are used for each task. Also consider the possibility that the child's ability or comfort level varies depending on the task, and that the child acts out when frustrated.

Problem 6. The interval recording method does not capture the changes in behavior.

Suggestion: Check to see how frequently the behavior is occurring and what kind of interval was selected for recording the behavior. For example, suppose the behavior occurs steadily about six times a minute, but the interval selected is a 1-minute interval. You will not be able to detect a change to one occurrence per minute because you record only one instance per interval. The solution is to use an interval short enough that the behavior in unlikely to occur more than once per interval.

General Guidelines for Conducting Reliable and Valid Observations

The following general guidelines will assist you in conducting reliable and valid behavioral observations:

- Understand thoroughly the recording techniques, rating scales, checklists, mechanical instruments, or computer program used for the observations. Be sure that the critical behaviors are highly specific and clearly defined.
- Check the accuracy of all mechanical instruments used for the data collection before beginning the observations.
- Use a timer that is silent. If your timing device beeps, modify it so that it does not beep while you conduct the observation.
- Train yourself to be a critical observer of behavior.
- Draw samples of behavior from various situations and at different times during the day, particularly when you are observing groups of children or developing norms.
- Discover what biases, faults, and weaknesses you may have that influence your observation of behavior. Develop self-understanding and critical self-evaluation skills.

- Develop a healthy skepticism toward previous reports about the referred child's behavior in order to be as objective as possible.
- Suppress assumptions and speculations about the meaning and implications of the child's behavior while you are recording data.
- Consider whether reactivity affected your findings and conclusions.
- Consider what factors precipitate and maintain the child's behavior and how other individuals in the child's setting respond to the behavior.
- Compare your observations periodically with those of an independent observer who is using the same scoring system.
- Recalibrate your recordings regularly by checking them against standard protocols.
- Keep abreast of observation research and theory.

You cannot avoid having beliefs and expectations; what you can and must avoid is prejudging what you find. Your observations will be affected by the child's behavior, the reasons for the referral, your decision criteria, your willingness to record a behavior as occurring or not occurring, your familiarity with the behavioral observational coding system, the amount of time you spend observing, your experience with children with special needs, and your familiarity with the referred child. All of these factors may also affect a co-observer's recordings. An understanding of these factors will help you obtain more reliable and valid recordings.

CAUTIONS ON THE USE OF OBSERVATIONS

Observational methods, like other assessment procedures, have their strengths and weaknesses (see Figure 5-2). The strengths of naturalistic observation also contribute to its weakness as a scientific procedure: It is difficult to standardize naturally occurring stimulus conditions, and human observers are fallible. These weaknesses must be considered when you conduct the observation and evaluate the results.

Although time-sampling procedures are useful, there are some disadvantages associated with observing just a single behavior or a few behaviors. First, you may be preconsciously tempted to identify behaviors according to how easily you can observe and record them. Second, the observation of a few behaviors may complicate detection of other behaviors—either positive or negative—that reveal important information about the child. Thus, when you focus on a single behavior, you should remain cognizant of the child's other behaviors as well. Third, as discussed earlier, consider the ecological validity of the findings. Is the behavior under observation representative of the child's usual behavior? Because observational data are so dependent on the judgments of the observer (perhaps even more so than in other assessment procedures), you must always consider to what extent your needs and expectancies may have affected the observation.

If you follow the procedures described in the previous section for reducing unreliable recordings, you will diminish some of these factors. Overall, observational data—whether obtained during the interview or during formal testing or in a natural or specially contrived setting—make an important contribution to the assessment process.

We have pointed out that the observation should be conducted unobtrusively. For example, when you are observing a child in a classroom, the child's classmates should not be aware that the child is the focus of your observations. Ask the teacher not to introduce you as "the person who is here to observe Harry" or "Harry's friend." In some settings, you can observe the referred child from a room that has a one-way mirror, from a classroom that overlooks the playground, or from a video monitor (if a camera is present in the setting).

The observation of certain behaviors, such as intimate conversations, may not be appropriate; in such cases, consider using self-reports. Additionally, parents, teachers, or aides may hide or refrain from engaging in socially undesirable behaviors, such as emotional abuse or excessive punishment, when they are aware of being observed. *Direct observation of behavior is always contraindicated when your presence could lead to undesirable side effects or unintended negative consequences or outcomes* (Cone & Foster, 1982). Going into a work setting to observe an adolescent who has been in an inpatient unit could cause the adolescent to be identified, labeled, and ostracized, for example. Therefore, always consider any possible unintended harmful consequences associated with your behavioral observations, and be sure to take appropriate steps to avoid such outcomes.

SELF-MONITORING ASSESSMENT

If your evaluation extends beyond one session, one way to obtain more information about a particular behavior (we use the term *behavior* to include the child's actions, thoughts, and feelings) is to ask the child to conduct a self-monitoring assessment. In a *self-monitoring assessment,* the child observes and records specific overt or covert aspects of her or his behavior and, sometimes, the circumstances associated with the behavior over a specified period. To perform a self-monitoring assessment, the child must discriminate the presence or absence of a particular response (e.g., a thought, an action performed by self, or an action performed by another) and record the response in a behavioral log or diary or use a golf counter, wrist counter, mechanical device, or hand-held computer. The appropriate procedure depends on the ease of detection of the target response, the response frequency, the age and intellectual ability of the child, and the ease of use of the procedure. The goal is to have the child make a systematic record of the behaviors of interest, gain awareness of her or his behavior, and participate in resolving the problem.

By requiring them to discriminate changes in their problems and to see how problems change over time and across

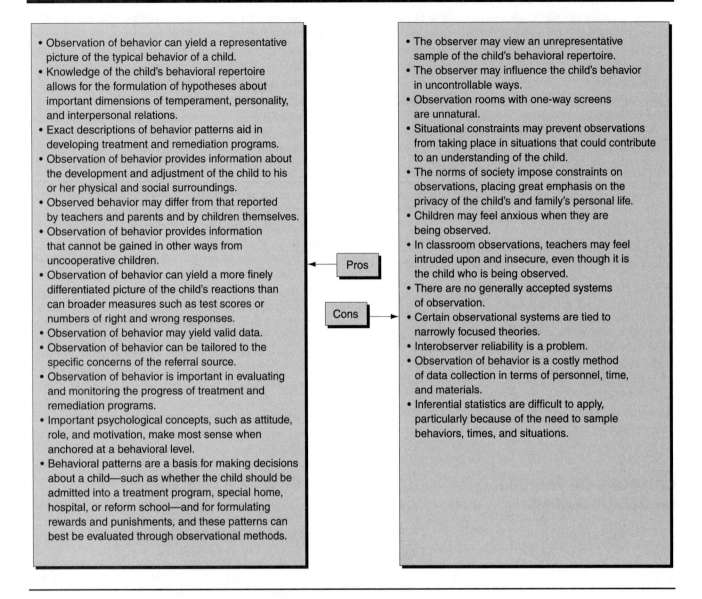

Figure 5-2. Observation of behavior as a measurement technique: Pros and cons.

situations, self-monitoring procedures may help children become better observers of their own behavior. Self-monitoring also enables children with problems to recognize that they are not helpless, but can do something constructive.

Self-monitoring of symptom changes, activity level, mood ratings, and situational contexts will give you information about the antecedent and consequent events associated with the child's symptoms. With this information, you are in a better position to formulate hypotheses about the relationship between environmental or situational variables and the child's problems. For example, you may find a relationship between different settings and the child's problems (e.g., problems appear at school but not at home) or a relationship between stressful events and problem expression (e.g., problems appear before a test but not before a picnic).

Self-monitoring assessment has several advantages (Bornstein, Hamilton, & Bornstein, 1986; Tunks & Billissimo, 1991):

1. It minimizes the use of retrospective reporting, thereby diminishing the chance of errors of memory or other distortions.

2. It can aid the child in answering questions about his or her behavior.

3. It may sensitize the child to his or her problem behavior and to the situations in which the problem behavior occurs.

4. It minimizes the child's reactions to being observed by someone else.

5. It provides information about the child's behavior in different settings and over a period of time.

behavioral observation or behavioral shaping?

Courtesy of Jerome M. Sattler.

6. It provides a relatively objective picture of the child's behavior, because it tends to minimize defensiveness and the withholding of information.
7. It is helpful in obtaining information about private activities (e.g., covert thoughts or feelings, levels of anxious or depressed feelings) or activities that are of low frequency (e.g., a self-inflicted wound, a panic attack, a seizure, a migraine headache, or an eating binge).
8. It can provide a baseline of the frequency, intensity, duration, latency, and other characteristics of the presenting problem before an intervention is begun.

(The remainder of this section on self-monitoring assessment is based in part on Bornstein et al., 1986.)

Rationales for Self-Monitoring Assessment

Following are some of the rationales supporting the use of self-monitoring assessment:

- Children have (or should have) control over their behavior.
- Children benefit from receiving feedback about their behavior in several settings.
- The procedure is portable and cost effective.

- The procedure provides an in-depth picture of the behaviors under study, including access to private data, at the time the behaviors are occurring.
- The procedure, depending on the task and the child's ability, often has good reliability and validity.
- The procedure reduces, but does not eliminate, reactive effects; these effects, as you have read, are the changes that children make in their behavior simply because they know that they are being observed or that their work will be looked at.

Setting Up a Self-Monitoring Assessment

Setting up a self-monitoring assessment involves selecting the appropriate target behaviors, identifying the variables that may relate to those behaviors, and choosing a recording procedure that is easy to use and provides adequate and accurate information. You may want the self-monitoring assessment to give you information about the following areas:

- Frequency of the behavior (e.g., 5 times a day)
- Onset of the behavior (e.g., at the beginning of the class)
- Quality of the behavior (e.g., depressive behavior)
- Intensity of the behavior (e.g., ranges from moderate to severe crying)

- Duration of the behavior (e.g., 3 minutes)
- Latency of the behavior (e.g., 1 hour after instructions are given)
- Situation in which the behavior occurs (e.g., on the playground)
- Antecedent events associated with the behavior (e.g., not chosen to be on a team)
- Consequent events associated with the behavior (e.g., sent to the vice-principal's office)

Following are examples of self-monitoring strategies that can be used for specific types of problems in children (Peterson & Tremblay, 1999; Shapiro & Cole, 1999):

- *Self-monitoring of on-task behavior:* reporting instances of paying attention to teacher or parent, cleaning up after an activity, or working on an activity
- *Self-monitoring of academic skills:* recording the number of problems completed on a worksheet, the number of correct answers to math problems, the number of words written in an essay, or the number of words spelled correctly
- *Self-monitoring of study methods and goals:* setting goals and then determining whether there is progress toward the goals and whether the goals are reached
- *Self-monitoring of social anxiety* (primarily for older children): recording the frequency and duration of contacts with others, the number of social interactions, or the rate of speech difficulty
- *Self-monitoring of asthma:* taking readings of breathing capacity, recording when medication is taken, and recording the severity of asthmatic attacks
- *Self-monitoring of other behavioral and nonacademic problems:* recording disruptive behaviors, compliance with teacher's daily expectations (e.g., bringing necessary materials to class, writing homework assignment in a notebook, completing class assignments, completing homework, completing classroom chores), social skills, stereotypical behaviors (e.g., number of hairs that are pulled out), or inappropriate verbalizations

Implementing a Self-Monitoring Assessment

In implementing a self-monitoring assessment, consider the child's age, motivation, and cognitive level and how these factors may affect her or his ability to do the recording. The child should understand fully how to use the recording procedure and how to recognize the target behaviors. Consider the following in implementing a self-monitoring procedure (Korotitsch & Nelson-Gray, 1999; Mace & Kratochwill, 1988).

1. *Give the child a clear and simple definition of the behavior to be monitored and recorded.* The child needs to know as clearly as possible what the target behavior is that he or she is to record. Define the behavior clearly and use illustrations as needed. The child needs to be able to distinguish the target behavior from other similar behaviors. You can write, use pictures, or invent other methods to present the definitions, depending on the child's level of functioning. When appropriate, include the definition on the recording form. If the self-monitoring form requires reading ability, be sure that the child can read at the required level.

2. *Provide clear and simple instructions on how to perform the self-monitoring task.* Inform the child about how to monitor the behavior. For example, give the following instructions to a child who needs to record the number of math problems completed correctly: "First, set the timer for 25 minutes [demonstrate]. Second, do as many math problems on the worksheet as you can until the timer rings. Third, when the timer rings, stop working and mark your answers as right or wrong, using the answer key. Fourth, count the number of problems you completed correctly. Fifth, write the number in the box next to today's date on the record form."

3. *Focus on a single target behavior.*

4. *Select a positive target behavior rather than a negative one, if possible.*

5. *Have the child record the target behavior as soon as possible after its occurrence.*

6. *Demonstrate the self-monitoring procedure, using the actual recording form or recording device.* Model the recording procedure for the child. Discuss with the child any potential problems. With some children, you may want to use mechanical recording means—such as counters or tokens and plastic boxes—instead of written records of behavior or computer recording. Label each step as you complete it.

7. *Give the child the instructions in writing or in picture form.*

8. *Ask the child to role-play the self-monitoring procedure, including defining the target behavior.*

9. *Ask the child if he or she has any questions about the procedure.*

10. *Conduct several trials to see whether the child understands and can carry out the procedure adequately.*

11. *Conduct accuracy checks randomly and inform the child that the checks will be made intermittently.*

12. *Arrange for the child to receive reinforcements contingent on recording accurate data.*

Self-monitoring assessment may cause the child to become anxious. For example, the child's anxiety level may increase when she or he records failures or lack of progress. Consequently, you will need to monitor whether the procedure induces anxiety. If you find that it does, alter it as needed. Or, you might reassure the child that this is an important first step in reducing the anxiety-provoking problem. For self-monitoring to be effective, the child's parents, teachers, and siblings and other significant persons in the child's environment must be supportive of the procedure and encourage the child to record the needed information.

The following case illustrates the use of a self-monitoring procedure to assess a problem behavior (adapted from Evans & Sullivan, 1993, pp. 79–80).

PAUL

Paul, a 12-year-old boy, was referred because of excessive thumbsucking. His dentist had informed his parents that this behavior was having a destructive effect upon his teeth. Paul and his parents said that his friends had begun to tease him more frequently about sucking his thumb. As part of the evaluation, the psychologist wanted to assess the frequency of thumbsucking and the antecedent events for this behavior. Paul was instructed to record the number of times he sucked his thumb before school, during morning time in school, during afternoon time in school, and after school. In addition, Paul recorded where he was and what he was doing when he sucked his thumb. To estimate the accuracy of Paul's self-recordings, his father recorded the number of times Paul sucked his thumb when Paul was at home.

Examples of Self-Monitoring Assessment Forms

Table 5-8 shows a self-monitoring form that you can give to older children to record stressful situations and other events.

Table 5-9 contains a daily exercise log. Table 5-10 shows a self-monitoring form that can be used by school-aged children to record whether they are attending to school work when a tone sounds. The students are given an audio device with earphones. When they hear a tone, they record whether or not they were attending to school work. The tones are presented randomly at intervals ranging from 15 to 90 seconds, with a tone emitted about every 30 seconds. The form can be used for several different types of behaviors.

Table 5-11 illustrates a diary form that can be used by older students to record events associated with problem behaviors. You can modify it to obtain the information you want the child to record. For example, the form might include a section covering positive behaviors, a section covering both negative and positive behaviors, or an instruction to record a particular behavior, such as the number of pages the child read in class or the number of times his or her attention wandered from the assigned task.

Table 5-12 shows a form that can be used to record the number of times a target behavior occurs. The target behavior can be any off-task or on-task behavior. Examples are "Was I out of my seat?" "Was I paying attention to the teacher?" "Was I disruptive (for example, I was out of my seat, I was touching others' property, I was making inappropriate

---

Table 5-8
Self-Monitoring Form for Recording Stressful Situations

SELF-MONITORING QUESTIONNAIRE

Name: _____

Directions: Complete the following items for each situation that made you unhappy.

Date	Describe situation	What happened before?	What happened after?	Who else was there?	How did you feel and think?	Stress rating[a]

[a]Rate how much stress you were feeling on a scale from 1 to 10, with 1 = the least intense stress and 10 = the most intense stress.
Note. This form can be expanded to include 7 days.

Table 5-9
Self-Monitoring Form for Recording Daily Exercise

EXERCISE LOG

Name: _____

Directions: Complete the following items about your daily exercise.

Date	What kinds of exercise did you do?	What time of day did you exercise?	How many minutes did you exercise?	Who else was there?	How much did you exert yourself?[a]	How much did you enjoy yourself?[b]	What problems did you have while exercising?

[a]Use a scale from 1 to 10, with 1 = No exertion and 10 = Completely exhausted.
[b]Use a scale from 1 to 10, with 1 = Did not enjoy at all and 10 = Really enjoyed.
Note. This form can be expanded to include 7 days.

Table 5-10
Self-Monitoring Form for Recording Attention

RECORDING FORM

Name: _____   Date: _____

Instructions: Circle **Yes** each time you were paying attention to the teacher when you heard the tone, and circle **No** if you weren't paying attention to the teacher when you heard the tone.

1. Yes No	6. Yes No	11. Yes No	16. Yes No
2. Yes No	7. Yes No	12. Yes No	17. Yes No
3. Yes No	8. Yes No	13. Yes No	18. Yes No
4. Yes No	9. Yes No	14. Yes No	19. Yes No
5. Yes No	10. Yes No	15. Yes No	20. Yes No

sounds, or I was hitting or pushing others)?" "Was I working on the lesson (that is, my eyes were on the work, I was not interrupting others, I stayed in my seat, I raised my hand if I had a question, I did not touch others' property, I did not talk unless I was called upon by the teacher)?"

Table 5-13 presents a form for recording intensity of reaction. Children are asked to record the time at which the recording was made and the intensity of the feeling. The hours shown are from 6 A.M. to 12 A.M. A five-point scale is used to record the intensity of the feeling; the intensity dimension can be changed to accommodate different feelings (or behaviors).

Table 5-14 shows a form to use with children who have trouble remembering their homework assignments. Sattler (1998) has other examples of self-monitoring forms for older children.

Two additional tables are useful with younger children. Table 5-15 shows a series of two faces (smiling and sad) that can be used to record whether children thought they were on-task or off-task. Table 5-16 shows a series of five faces, ranging from smiling to neutral to sad, that provide a finer scale for children to use in recording their thoughts about their behavior. In using any of these tables, present the task clearly to

Table 5-11
Student Diary Form

STUDENT DIARY

Name: _____   Date: _____

1. Did you have any problems today? (Circle one) Yes   No
   If you circled Yes, please complete the following items.
2. Describe the problem.
   _____
   _____

3. What happened before the problem began?
   _____
   _____

4. What happened after the problem began?
   _____
   _____

5. What did you do about the problem?
   _____
   _____

6. What did your teacher do about the problem?
   _____
   _____

7. What did the other students in the class do about the problem?
   _____
   _____

8. Why do you think the problem happened?
   _____
   _____

9. Describe anything else about the problem that you think is important.
   _____
   _____

Table 5-12
Self-Monitoring Form for Recording Target Behavior

RECORDING FORM

Name: _____   Date: _____

Behavior to record: Out-of-seat

Directions: Fill in one circle each time you were out of your seat when you were not supposed to be out of your seat.

Morning   O O O O O O O O O O O O O O O O O O O O O O O O O O O O O O O

Afternoon O O O O O O O O O O O O O O O O O O O O O O O O O O O O O O O

Note. The target behavior can be changed as needed. The form also can be changed to show specific time periods if needed.

Table 5-13
Self-Monitoring Form for Recording Intensity of Reaction

RECORDING FORM FOR FEELINGS

Name: _____

Directions: Three times each day—once in the morning, once in the afternoon, and once at night—complete the sadness graph. In the column that indicates the time when you record your answer, put an X in the square opposite the number that says how you feel. Use the following scale:

1 = I do not feel sad.
2 = I feel a little sad.
3 = I feel somewhat sad.
4 = I feel very sad.
5 = I feel extremely sad.

Day: _____   Date: _____

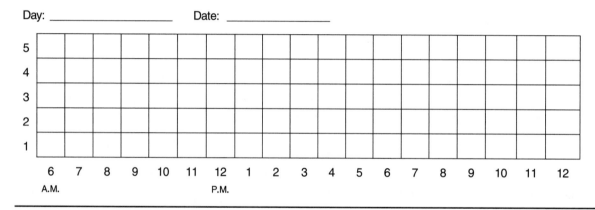

Note. This form can be used for any type of emotion or pain. Adapted from Allen and Matthews (1998).

the children. For example, when they hear a tone or bell, children can be asked to record such things as the following: Was I paying attention? Was I doing what I was supposed to be doing? Was I working hard? Was I in my seat?

Use of Computers in Self-Monitoring

Hand-held computers are another means of recording data. They can (a) prompt children at prescribed times during the day to record responses, (b) record responses at the actual time the responses are taking place, (c) check children's accuracy by examining inconsistencies and invalid responses, (d) summarize data in graphic or table form, which can then be downloaded to a desk-top computer, and (e) help children set goals and monitor their progress (Farrell, 1991; Haynes, 1998).

Problems in Self-Monitoring Assessment

Limitations associated with self-monitoring assessment include reactive effects and difficulty in keeping accurate records. Let's examine each of these in more detail.

Reactive effects in self-monitoring assessment. Reactive effects are possible with self-monitoring assessment because the children know that someone will be looking at their recording sheet and because their own attention has been drawn to selected behaviors. If children change their behavior because of reactive effects, the changes may distort or modify the behaviors being studied. Reactive effects may be beneficial, though, in intervention programs if they *reduce* the frequency of negative behaviors or *increase* the frequency of positive behaviors. You need to monitor reactive effects to learn whether they are interfering with the assessment.

Accuracy effects in self-monitoring assessment. The accuracy of the recordings may be affected by the following factors:

- The child's age
- The degree and type of psychopathology
- The child's degree of cooperativeness and interest
- The child's willingness to be objective and record negative behavior as well as positive behavior
- The type of behavior targeted (e.g., verbal or nonverbal, private or public, appropriate verbalization or inappropriate

Table 5-14
Self-Monitoring Form for Recording Homework Assignments

RECORDING FORM FOR HOMEWORK

Name: _____   Date: _____

Class: _____   Teacher: _____

Directions: Circle Y ("yes"), N ("no"), or NA ("not applicable") after each question.

Questions	Circle One		
1. Did you read the homework assignment sheet in class?	Y	N	NA
2. Did you put the homework assignment sheet in your notebook or write the homework assignment in your notebook in class?	Y	N	NA
3. Did you ask questions when you did not understand the homework assignment?	Y	N	NA
4. Did you take home the homework assignment sheet or your notes about the homework assignment?	Y	N	NA
5. Did you take home the books you needed to do the homework?	Y	N	NA
6. Did you complete the homework at home?	Y	N	NA
If you said "no" to question 6, leave questions 7 and 8 blank. If you said "yes" to question 6, go to question 7.			
7. If you completed the homework, did you bring it to class?	Y	N	NA
If you said "no" to question 7, leave question 8 blank. If you said "yes" to question 7, answer question 8 if you have a work folder in class.	Y	N	NA
8. If you brought the homework to class, did you file it in your work folder?	Y	N	NA

Source: Adapted from Trapani and Gettinger (1996).

verbalization, appropriate behavior or inappropriate behavior)

- The difficulty in discriminating on-task and off-task behavior
- The length of time it takes to record the behavior
- The valence of the behavior (e.g., positive, negative, neutral)
- The degree of effort required to record the behavior (e.g., the number of behaviors to be monitored and what needs to be done to record the behavior)
- The other activities occurring contemporaneously
- The setting in which the recording takes place (e.g., home, school, playground)
- The response of others in the setting (e.g., teachers, other students, parents, siblings, other relatives)
- The type of recording device (e.g., paper and pencil, mechanical device, computer)
- The presence of observers who also may be recording the child's behavior

Children who are not well motivated, for example, may not do recordings daily. In such cases, they should be encouraged to turn in their recordings every day and be rewarded for their efforts. Sometimes children will initially be well motivated and then lose interest. In such cases, you might want to change the cuing device (Shapiro, 1984). Sometimes children become so absorbed in their work that they forget to monitor their behavior.

Behaviors that are contrary to advice given by physicians, teachers, or parents are more likely to be misreported than behaviors that follow the advice. For example, eating forbidden foods is more likely not to be reported than eating acceptable foods. Children may be embarrassed to report inappropriate behavior and may "fake good."

Encourage children to be honest in their reports. Emphasize that they do not have to impress you with positive reports and that, by being honest, they allow you to help them better. Reassure them that they will not be punished for reporting negative behavior and that you simply want to get a better idea of how they behave in one or more settings. However, you should caution children that if you observe any behavior that may be dangerous to them, you must report it to their parents or to the authorities.

Children under 5 or 6 years of age will likely have difficulty making self-monitoring recordings (Shapiro, 1984). Therefore, limit the target behaviors to one or two behaviors and use a simple and clear recording procedure. Also use visual or verbal-auditory cues whenever possible to prompt the self-observation and recording. Finally, you may want to give children appropriate rewards for accurate recordings or establish a token economy for accurate recordings.

Even for older children, the procedure must be simple and readily comprehensible. You can enhance children's accuracy by giving immediate feedback about how their recording agreed with that of an external judge, carefully defining

Table 5-15
Self-Monitoring Form for Younger Children for Recording Behavior in Two Categories

RECORDING FORM

Name: _____ Date: _____

Directions:

If you were paying attention to your school work or teacher when the tone sounded, put an X on this face:

If you were *not* paying attention to your school work or teacher when the tone sounded, put an X on this face:

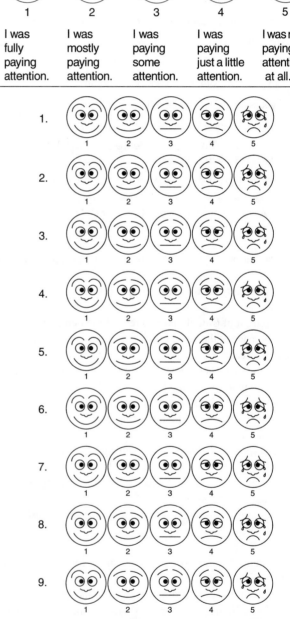

Note. This form can be used for any off-task behavior.

Table 5-16
Self-Monitoring Form for Younger Children for Recording Behavior in Five Categories

RECORDING FORM

Name: _____ Date: _____

Directions:

Put an X on the face that shows what you were doing when the tone sounded. Here is what the faces mean.

1	2	3	4	5
I was fully paying attention.	I was mostly paying attention.	I was paying some attention.	I was paying just a little attention.	I was not paying attention at all.

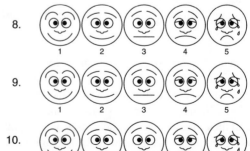

the target behaviors, providing examples, selecting behaviors that are readily discriminable, modeling the process, giving several trials, keeping the procedure short (e.g., less than 5 minutes), and having them record the behavior immediately after it occurs rather than waiting until the end of the day.

When children are completing a self-monitoring assessment for specific symptoms, prompts from parents or teachers at the appointed or critical times usually increase the children's compliance with the procedure. However, children may sometimes be engaged in activities that interfere with the self-monitoring. In such cases, accept the fact that the procedure will be less than perfect because of natural events that happen in the children's lives. You may want to evaluate the accuracy of the children's recordings by having an observer also record the children's behavior or by examining byproducts associated with the behavior of interest (e.g., the number of problems completed on an assignment sheet).

Comment on Self-Monitoring Assessment

In establishing a self-monitoring assessment, tailor the techniques and instructions to the comprehension level of the child. Consider role playing the self-monitoring procedure *before* you end the session. Obviously, self-monitoring assessment, like any self-report measure, is open to distortion if the children want to deny problems, exaggerate symptoms to gain attention, or withhold sensitive information. Make every effort to enlist the children's cooperation and interest in the procedure. Help them understand the purpose and value of the activity. The key to successful self-monitoring assessment is to do the following: (a) clearly define the behavior of interest, (b) ensure that the child understands the procedures, (c) make the recording procedure uncomplicated, (d) enlist the child's cooperation and the cooperation of significant others, and (e) minimize interference from others.

The cues used in a self-monitoring assessment should be randomly distributed to avoid a fixed interval (Shapiro & Cole, 1994). With a fixed interval, children may stop working until they hear the cue. For many behaviors, the cues should be given 10 to 90 seconds apart. To increase children's motivation, the cues can be an interesting sound, such as a bell, whistle, funny noise, or beep.

When self-monitoring assessment is part of an intervention program, you may use the data (a) as an index of change, (b) for evaluating improvement in self-regulation, (c) for evaluating the effectiveness of the intervention plan, and (d) for carrying out changes in the plan. Self-monitoring assessment also may help children focus on the behavior of interest and may help them understand the relationship among situational events, the occurrence of the behavior, and possible consequences associated with the behavior. For more information about self-monitoring, see issue Number 4 of *Psychological Assessment* (1999, Volume 11) and Shapiro and Cole (1994).

REPORTING BEHAVIORAL OBSERVATIONS

Following is a list of items generally included in a report of observational findings. Not all of the information will apply to every situation, of course.

1. *Personal data*—child's age, sex, physical characteristics, and other relevant characteristics
2. *Setting data*—date, time, place, length of observation, setting (including type of room, people, and significant others), recording method, and coding system (or behaviors observed)
3. *Reliability*—including reliability methods used, if appropriate
4. *Validity*—including validity methods used, if appropriate
5. *Intensity*—how much the problem behavior interfered with the child's other activities
6. *Severity*—the extent to which the problem behavior reflects psychopathology
7. *Duration*—the length of the episode of the problem behavior
8. *Frequency*—how often the problem behavior occurred
9. *Generality*—the number of situations in which the problem behavior occurred
10. *Norms*—how often the comparison child and the referred child's peer group (or class) engaged in the same behavior
11. *Antecedents of the problem behavior*—what the child was doing before the problem behavior occurred and what was happening in the setting at that time
12. *Consequences of the problem behavior*—what happened to the child after he or she engaged in the problem behavior (e.g., the child obtained relief by escaping or avoiding the task, or what is referred to as "negative reinforcement"; the child obtained a reward for the problem behavior, or what is referred to as "positive reinforcement"; or the child was disciplined for the problem behavior), how much the problem behavior disrupted the activities of the other children, and what responses were made by the teacher or parents or other children
13. *Peer group acceptance*—whether other children accepted the problem behavior
14. *Adult acceptance*—whether adults accepted the problem behavior
15. *Agreement with referral source*—whether the problem behavior agreed with the referral source's description
16. *Additional problem behaviors*—any other problems exhibited by the child
17. *Positive behaviors*—behaviors that may be useful for designing interventions
18. *Observational difficulties*—difficulties encountered in conducting the observation (e.g., problems in determining onset or termination of response, counting number of responses, defining target responses)
19. *Implications of the findings*—actions that should be taken as a result of the findings (e.g., whether the child would benefit from being transferred to another setting)

In describing the results of a systematic behavioral observation, you should evaluate how the setting, the people in the setting, and the environment as a whole may have affected the child's behavior. For example, if there were other people in the setting, how did they affect the child? If the child's behavior changed with changes in the setting, did the other children's behavior change as well?

As noted earlier (see page 143), it is helpful to compare and contrast the referred child's behavior with that of a comparison child. Use both the comparison child and other children in the group as an informal baseline for evaluating the behavior of the referred child. For example, if you say that a child's interaction with others was limited, also say something about how other children in the group interacted. Everything you observe should be stated in relation to the referred child.

When you write about people at a facility, refer to them the way the facility does, as *clients, patients, members,* or *students.* Keep the way you describe the examinee consistent throughout the report. Generally, it is good practice to refer to the examinee by her or his name. (If you are conducting a systematic behavioral observation for a practice class assignment and there is no referred child, select a child for the practice observation and make up a name for that child that you can use in the report.) Include information about the place of observation, day and time of observation, type of observation, length of the observation session(s), observational findings, and implications of the observational findings. If you present in the report information that comes from an agency brochure, agency staff member, or another source, give the origin of the information. If you do not, readers may think that the information was based on your observations.

In commenting about the teacher, a statement such as "Twelve percent of the time the teacher's comments were approving" is incomplete if it is not accompanied with another statement indicating what the teacher was doing the rest of the time. Including too many numbers can cloud the meaning of an observational report; instead, report averages and general findings.

Do not include in the report comments about what you were thinking as you were recording the information. The main focus should be on what you observed.

If you introduce a paragraph with a statement such as "Five methods were used .... The first was...," then begin your discussion of each of the other four methods with a phrase that implies the order of the five methods (e.g., "The second was ...."). In the summary of a systematic observational report, include a description of the referred child, the comparison child (but do not personally identify the comparison child), other people, the setting, and the major findings and conclusions.

Help the reader understand the reason for your conclusions. For example, the statement (made about a duration count) that "Fred's play with other children was infrequent, at the rate of only once every 36 seconds" may leave the reader wondering why the rate of once every 36 seconds was considered infrequent. Was this rate different from that of the other children playing?

Clearly describe the categories you used to observe behavior. The following sentence, for example, fails to do so: "The observers recorded the number of times Bill engaged in the following behaviors: attending, working, inappropriate locale, and don't know." Instead of writing "inappropriate locale," write "goes to an inappropriate locale"; instead of writing "don't know," write "says 'I don't know'."

When you report a percentage agreement or a reliability coefficient obtained for a systematic behavioral observation, follow it with a statement about whether the percentage agreement or reliability coefficient is satisfactory. You should not give statistics without explanation. Preferably, consider reliability in an all-or-none fashion—that is, report that it was or was not satisfactory rather than reporting that it was marginally satisfactory.

If reliability was too low, discuss the reasons. Also discuss the implications of all reliability indices. For example, does the low reliability of an observational method influence every section of the systematic behavioral observational results or just selected parts? If you say, for example, that there was 40% agreement on the five rating scales, explain to the reader what this level of agreement means. Do not leave a statement like this unexplained. Also, if reliability was not satisfactory, indicate that the findings must be viewed with caution or that they are not representative of the behaviors under observation.

Do not minimize the importance of low interrater reliability just because the behavior was infrequent. For example, if you have poor rater agreement when the behavior occurred once only (that is, one rater recorded it and the other one did not), do not write, "The percentage agreement for aggression was 0%. However, this figure is misleading because the behavior was seen only once." The 0% agreement is not misleading; it reflects what actually was recorded by the observers. If your findings differ from those of your co-observer, explain the possible reasons for the differences. You could write, "The percentage agreement for aggression was 0%. The child was observed to be aggressive on one occasion by one of the observers but not by the other one. This might mean that child's aggressive acts were surreptitious, that the observers did not agree on what would count as aggression, or that the aggressive acts were not clearcut and therefore were difficult to interpret."

When you report the reliability of a ratings observation, provide the percentage agreement as well as the absolute values of the ratings (e.g., 4.3 or 2.8) and what the values imply (e.g., extremely aggressive behavior or somewhat passive behavior). Explain the meaning of all statistical indices you present in the report. For example, does the percent agreement, correlation coefficient, or kappa indicate satisfactory or unsatisfactory observer agreement? Does the statistical index mean that the ratings were reliable or unreliable? And, as noted previously, if the ratings were unreliable, discuss what may have led to the poor reliability of the observational recordings. Chapter 21 in *Assessment of Children: Cognitive Applications* provides further guidelines for writing a psychological report.

PSYCHOLOGICAL EVALUATION

Exhibit 5-4 presents a psychological evaluation of an adolescent with mental retardation observed at a vocational training center. The evaluation is a case study involving systematic behavioral observation. In practice, you would typically choose one or two observational procedures, based on the reason for referral, previous psychometric assessment findings, and the frequency, duration, and type of behavior under observation. Because the purpose of this case study is to demonstrate the various observational approaches discussed in this chapter, it applies five observational techniques and shows the kinds of results each renders. The report presents a description of the adolescent, a detailed description of the observational methods used (including target behaviors and rating scales), and a statement about reliability and validity. The observational findings section integrates the findings from the five techniques used. A short summary, which highlights the observational findings, concludes the report.

THINKING THROUGH THE ISSUES

1. What are the basic requirements for an effective recording system?
2. Develop a recording system for some setting with which you are familiar, and include both positive and negative behaviors.
3. Reactivity is said to be the bane of observational recording. Do you agree or disagree? Why?
4. How could you use behavioral observations to confirm hypotheses generated from a child's performance on an individual intelligence test?
5. How useful is self-monitoring assessment? Describe several situations in which you believe self-monitoring might be helpful.

SUMMARY

Observational Coding Systems

1. Observational coding systems are used to categorize behavioral observations. They usually consist of two or more categories that cover a range of behaviors, although, on occasion, a single category may be appropriate.
2. Before you use a coding system, carefully evaluate (a) its rationale, (b) the setting(s) in which it is applicable, (c) definitions of the coding categories, (d) the description of how behavior is sampled, (e) rules governing the behavior of observers, such as a hierarchy of codes, (f) reliability, including overall reliability and the reliability of each coding category, (g) validity, and (h) positive and negative features (including potential problem areas).

3. When designing an observational coding system, select categories that best meet the assessment, treatment, or research goals.
4. Use the simplest possible coding system that will answer your questions.
5. Observational coding systems have been developed to evaluate individual children, groups, and classes in different settings.
6. Computerized systems, which use a laptop computer, hand-held computer, or bar-code scanner, are available for collecting real-time observational data.
7. Observational coding systems also are useful for studying the behavior of classroom teachers.

Sources of Unreliability

8. The data you obtain from behavioral observations, like the data you obtain from any other assessment procedure, must be reliable and valid.
9. Observers will differ, for example, in their sensitivity to subtle social cues and to situational, gender, and ethnic factors that may play a role in influencing behavior.
10. Observer bias refers to errors committed by the observer in the course of the observational assessment.
11. When observation continues over a long period, observers may show signs of observer drift, such as forgetfulness, fatigue, and decreased motivation.
12. Reliability may be more difficult to achieve with global categories.

Procedures for Assessing Reliability

13. Estimates of interobserver reliability (also called interobserver agreement) are usually based on scores of two or more observers who record the same information while simultaneously and independently observing the same child or group.
14. If you are interested in the pattern of agreement among the observers' ratings, irrespective of the level of agreement, and you are using an interval scale of measurement, then the product-moment correlation coefficient is a satisfactory measure of reliability.
15. When both the pattern of agreement and the level of agreement are important and you have an interval scale of measurement, you can use the intraclass correlation coefficient.
16. When the data form an ordinal scale and you are interested in correcting for chance agreement, kappa (κ) is a useful index of agreement.
17. When you want a measure of the percentage agreement among two or more observers but are not concerned with correcting for chance agreement, you can use an uncorrected percentage agreement index.
18. In interval recording, you can use several percentage agreement methods for determining interobserver agreement.
19. In event recording, you can estimate interobserver percentage agreement by dividing the number of occurrences of the event reported by the observer recording the lower frequency by the number of occurrences of the event reported by the other observer.
20. In ratings recording, you can estimate interobserver percentage agreement by determining whether the two observers gave the same rating on each scale.
21. Obtaining satisfactory reliability between two observers does not ensure that the data are meaningful or accurate, because high reliabilities may be associated with observation codes that

Exhibit 5-4
Psychological Evaluation: Behavioral Observation

Name: Andy Lopez

Date of birth: June 1, 1983

Chronological age: 16-11

Observer: Todd Johnson

Date of observation: May 1, 2000

Date of report: May 6, 2000

Co-observer: Jill Cole

Reason for Referral
Andy was observed at Path Services in order to evaluate his progress in a special training program for mentally retarded adolescents. The observation was conducted to fulfill a requirement for a graduate psychological assessment course at Blank State University.

Description of Client Observed and Setting
Andy was observed for a 1-hour period in a class at Path Services, a vocational training and placement center for mentally retarded individuals. The observation was conducted on May 1, 1986 from 8:30 A.M. to 9:30 A.M.

Andy is a black-haired, olive-complexioned male. He is 16 years 11 months of age, 5 feet 10 inches tall, and weighs 200 pounds. He wore a blue work shirt, blue work pants, and black calf-high work boots. He was neatly groomed. Andy was observed during a class lecture on window washing and a window-washing activity.

Observational Methods
Narrative, running record, event, interval, and rating observation techniques were used. For the purpose of assessing reliability, two observers simultaneously but independently observed Andy's behavior. During the 10-minute narrative recording, the entire class was observed. For the 5-minute running record, Andy's behavior was observed and recorded.

During the 10-minute event recording, the observers recorded the number of times Andy engaged in the following behaviors: touching his boot with his hand, tapping his foot on the floor, touching his face or head with his hand, yawning, and raising his hand or motioning with it for the purpose of gaining another person's attention.

For the interval recording, Andy was observed over the course of three time periods. The first, which lasted for 6 minutes and 40 seconds, consisted of 16 15-second observation intervals interspersed with 10-second recording intervals. During this time, the observers recorded whether Andy engaged in any of the following nine behaviors: attending, working, volunteering, reading aloud, displaying other appropriate behavior, interacting with a peer about academic materials, interacting with a peer about nonacademic materials, looking around, and displaying other inappropriate behavior.

The second and third interval recordings each lasted for 4 minutes, and consisted of 16 10-second observation intervals interspersed with 5-second recording intervals. The target behaviors for the second interval recording involved the following behaviors on the part of the teacher with respect to Andy or the entire class: approval, disapproval, no response, and verbal in-

teraction. The target behaviors for the third interval recording were appropriate behavior and inappropriate behavior of the class as a whole.

Andy was observed for approximately 45 minutes while the observers made narrative, running record, event, and interval recordings. An additional 10 minutes of observation time was used for narrative recording of the teacher's behavior in relation to Andy. After all of the observations were finished, the observers completed eight 7-point rating scales: on-task (always–never), verbal off-task (always–never), motor off-task (always–never), passive off-task (always–never), verbalization (clear–unclear), teacher verbal approval responses (frequent–absent), teacher verbal disapproval responses (frequent–absent), and class-appropriate behavior (always–never).

Several interobserver agreement indices were calculated from the event, interval, and rating observational data. These included overall percentage of agreement, percentages of agreement on occurrence and nonoccurrence of the behaviors, and kappa. Six reliability indices for the occurrence of particular behaviors could not be calculated because both observers agreed that the behavior had not occurred. Fifty-three of the 63 reliability indices calculated were satisfactory (at least 90% agreement). The 10 unsatisfactory indices were primarily in areas in which the behavior assessed was not discrete or the observers encountered difficulty with direct observation because their view was restricted. Overall, interrater reliability appears to be satisfactory. The results also appear to be valid.

Observational Findings
Andy predominantly engaged in appropriate class behavior. He did, however, occasionally exhibit inappropriate verbal and passive off-task behaviors. During the first 15 minutes of the lecture on window washing, Andy appeared tired, distracted, and restless. He sat in a slouched position, with his buttocks on the edge of the chair, legs outstretched, and upper back against the top of the chairback. He frequently closed his eyes or rubbed them in what looked like an attempt to wake up and coughed 11 times during the 10-minute event recording. When Andy heard noises or voices outside the classroom or when someone entered or left, he always turned around to look and he often waved. Andy occasionally bent over to untie and retie his boot laces. He frequently rubbed his head or the skin around his mouth and nose; during event recording, he did this at a rate of once every 40 seconds.

Andy demonstrated that his full attention was not on the teacher by asking "Do we have to go outside and clean up?" approximately 2 minutes after the teacher spoke to the class about that same issue. Andy failed to sign in when he entered the

(Continued)

Exhibit 5-4 *(Continued)*

room, and the teacher had to tell him to do so approximately 10 minutes into the class period. Upon approaching the sign-in sheet, Andy searched in his pockets for a pen. When he realized he did not have one, he turned toward his classmates and asked in a fairly loud voice if anybody had a pen that he could borrow. On three occasions during the first 5 minutes of the lecture, Andy spoke to another class member. Despite Andy's inappropriate behavior, he was not disruptive to the others in the classroom.

As the lecture progressed, Andy's boredom and restlessness decreased, and his attentiveness increased. Despite his seeming distractedness, he answered many of the teacher's questions appropriately. First, he eagerly and quickly sat up straight, raised his hand, and then waited for the teacher to call on him. However, on two occasions he shouted out an answer before called on by the teacher. For example, after a majority of the class members unsuccessfully guessed answers to a question, Andy answered with conviction, "I know what it is—water is minerals." However, at other times his behavior was quite appropriate, and he gave accurate answers after waiting to be recognized by the teacher. In response to the teacher's question about what supplies the window washer needs, Andy quickly said, "squeegee, bucket, spray bottle, and rags." When the teacher subsequently asked what the bucket was used for and why the rags were folded, Andy promptly supplied the correct reasons. When he was not called upon, Andy tended to look disappointed.

Andy exhibited the same eagerness during the window-washing activity. He pulled his chair close to the demonstration window, attended to the teacher, and enthusiastically volunteered to perform the task. Andy apparently understood the teacher's instructions, as he washed the window accordingly. He worked diligently and responded well to the teacher's questions. When Andy was done, for example, the teacher said, "Now what are you going to do?" Andy quickly and correctly replied, "Look for streaks." When Andy found spots on the window, he asked the teacher, "Want me to get paper towels?" When the teacher indicated yes, Andy promptly retrieved paper towels from the front of the classroom and wiped the spots off the window. Andy meticulously inspected the window and enthusiastically asked, "How does it look, Tim?" The teacher responded, "Good, I think,"

and Andy smiled. Andy's verbalizations were always clear and grammatically correct. Although he usually sat off to the side, rather than among his classmates, he appeared to be friendly with them.

The teacher interacted with the students throughout the observation period. Interaction was predominantly verbal—it included lecturing, asking questions, explaining how to wash the window, and commenting on the students' demonstrations. Most of the interaction was instructional; thus, approval and disapproval were infrequent. When approval was given, it was more frequently nonverbal (e.g., a smile or a nod of the head) than verbal. Andy received nonverbal approval on two occasions and verbal approval on one occasion. He appeared content when he was given either verbal or nonverbal approval. When the teacher used disapproval, it was in a firm but gentle manner. Andy did not receive disapproval for any of his actions. Overall, the teacher was patient and had good rapport with the students. Andy and his classmates, for the most part, were cooperative, respectful, and well behaved.

Summary and Impressions

This observation was conducted on the morning of May 1, 2000 at Path Services in order to fulfill a course requirement. Andy is a 16-year, 11-month-old male. At the beginning of the class on window-washing procedures, Andy appeared to be restless, distracted, and tired. When the teacher began to ask questions, however, Andy became more involved. His attention increased as he eagerly, correctly, and appropriately answered many of the teacher's questions. Andy's verbalizations were always clear and coherent, and he was eager and enthusiastic as he washed windows. He followed instructions and worked diligently and consistently. Andy's distractibility seemed to be caused by an over-alertness to the things happening in his environment. He appeared to be outgoing and amiable. Andy was attracted to both mental and physical stimulation. He seemed to enjoy the recognition he received through successful participation in the class activity.

(Signature)
_____
Todd Johnson, B.A., Observer

are relatively insensitive to the occurrence of important or meaningful behaviors.

22. The consistency of behavior over time and situations is another measure of the reliability of behavioral observations.

23. You should strive to sample the target behaviors more than once and in more than one setting.

24. Internal consistency reliability reflects how consistent an assessment instrument is in measuring the same characteristics.

Procedures for Assessing Validity

25. Validity, which refers to the extent to which procedures are measuring what they are supposed to measure, is evaluated by studying the meaningfulness and relevance of the behavioral measures.

26. Two major factors affecting the validity of the observational assessment are the representativeness and the generalizability of the findings.

27. A child's behavior under observation may be affected by the child's awareness that someone is observing him or her, by the child's prior interactions with the observer, or by the observer's personal characteristics. We refer to this effect as reactivity or the guinea pig effect.

28. To minimize reactivity, conduct your observations as unobtrusively as possible.

29. You can judge whether reactive effects have occurred by looking for (a) systematic changes in the child's behavior over time, some of which may be related to the presence of the observer, (b) increased variability in the child's behavior, (c) reports from

SNAPSHOTS by Jason Love

At Pisa Elementary School.

Reprinted with permission from Jason Love.

the child that he or she changed behavior as a result of being observed, and (d) discrepancies between different measures of the child's same behavior, when measures were obtained under different observation conditions.

Procedures for Reducing Errors in Observations

30. You can increase reliability by (a) having clear and precise definitions of behaviors, (b) following systematic and precise rules governing the observations, (c) becoming well trained in observational procedures, and (d) using observation periods that are not excessively long.
31. You can further reduce errors by gaining an understanding of your decision criteria—such as the degree of certainty you must have to report that a behavior did or did not occur—and comparing your decision criteria with those of other observers.
32. During your training, regularly compare your results with those of a highly trained observer or with standard criterion recordings.
33. The agreement between an observer's recordings and standard criterion recordings is referred to as criterion-related agreement.
34. Another method of checking the reliability of your ratings involves videotaping the behavior of a child (or class).
35. An acceptable level of interobserver agreement does not rule out observer error, however, because you can have a high level

of interobserver agreement and still have observer bias and observer drift if both observers have a similar bias or make similar errors.

36. To reduce reactivity, (a) become as neutral a stimulus as possible, (b) position yourself so that you are away from the ordinary paths of movement in the classroom and yet still have an unobstructed view of the child and setting, (c) shift your attention from one child to another, (d) limit your stimulus value, (e) follow all rules, regulations, and informal policies of the school, institution, or family, and (f) enter the setting when your entrance will least disrupt the ongoing behavior.
37. Developing informal norms will help you place the child's behavior in a meaningful context.
38. Another norming procedure is to establish local norms for the entire class, using the scan check method.
39. Obtaining a peer or class rating permits you to measure the difference between the frequency with which the referred child engages in a particular behavior and the frequency with which the peer or class does.
40. You cannot avoid having beliefs and expectations; what you can and must avoid is prejudging what you find.

Cautions on the Use of Observations

41. The strengths of naturalistic observation also contribute to its weakness as a scientific procedure: It is difficult to standardize naturally occurring stimulus conditions, and human observers are fallible.
42. The observation of certain behaviors, such as intimate conversations, may not be appropriate; in such cases, consider using self-reports.

Self-Monitoring Assessment

43. If your evaluation extends beyond one session, one way to obtain more information about a particular behavior is to ask the child to conduct a self-monitoring assessment.
44. In a self-monitoring assessment, the child observes and records specific overt or covert aspects of her or his behavior and, sometimes, the circumstances associated with the behavior over a specified period.
45. To perform a self-monitoring assessment, the child must discriminate the presence or absence of a particular response (e.g., a thought, an action performed by self, or an action performed by another) and record the response in a behavioral log or diary or use a golf counter, wrist counter, mechanical device, or handheld computer.
46. The appropriate procedure depends on the ease of detection of the target response, the response frequency, the age and intellectual ability of the child, and the ease of use of the procedure.
47. The goal is to have the child make a systematic record of the behaviors of interest, gain awareness of her or his behavior, and participate in resolving the problem.
48. By requiring them to discriminate changes in their problems and to see how problems change over time and across situations, self-monitoring procedures may help children become better observers of their own behavior.
49. Self-monitoring of symptom changes, activity level, mood ratings, and situational contexts will give you information about the antecedent and consequent events associated with the child's symptoms.

50. Setting up a self-monitoring assessment involves choosing the appropriate target behaviors, identifying the variables that may relate to those behaviors, and choosing a recording procedure that is easy to use and provides adequate and accurate information.

51. In implementing a self-monitoring assessment, consider the child's age, motivation, and cognitive level and how these factors may affect his or her ability to do the recording.

52. The child should understand fully how to use the recording procedure and how to recognize the target behaviors.

53. You will need to monitor whether the self-monitoring procedure induces anxiety.

54. Hand-held computers are one means of recording data.

55. Limitations associated with self-monitoring assessment include reactive effects and difficulty in keeping accurate records.

56. A child who is not well motivated may not do recordings daily.

57. Behaviors that are contrary to advice given by physicians, teachers, or parents are more likely to be misreported than behaviors that follow the advice.

58. Children under 5 or 6 years of age will likely have difficulty making self-monitoring recordings.

59. When children are completing a self-monitoring assessment for specific symptoms, prompts from parents or teachers at the appointed or critical times usually increase the children's compliance with the procedure.

60. In establishing a self-monitoring assessment, tailor the techniques and instructions to the comprehension level of the child.

61. The cues used in a self-monitoring assessment should be randomly distributed to avoid a fixed interval.

62. When self-monitoring assessment is part of an intervention program, you may use the data (a) as an index of change, (b) for evaluating improvement in self-regulation, (c) for evaluating the effectiveness of the intervention plan, and (d) for carrying out changes in the plan.

Reporting Behavioral Observations

63. In describing the results of a systematic behavioral observation, you should evaluate how the setting, the people in the setting, and the environment as a whole may have affected the child's behavior.

64. A preferred way to conduct a systematic behavioral observation is to compare and contrast the referred child's behavior with that of a comparison child.

65. Do not minimize the importance of low interrater reliability just because the behavior was infrequent.

66. Explain the meaning of all statistical indices you present in the report.

KEY TERMS, CONCEPTS, AND NAMES

Observational coding systems (p. 121)
Reliability of behavioral observations (p. 126)
Observer bias (p. 131)
Central tendency error (p. 132)
Leniency or generosity error (p. 132)
Primacy effect error (p. 132)
Halo effect error (p. 132)
Personal theory error (p. 132)
Personal values error (p. 132)
Logical error (p. 132)
Contrast error (p. 132)
Proximity error (p. 132)
Personal effects error (p. 132)
Observer drift (p. 132)
Omission error (p. 132)
Commission error (p. 132)
Expectancy effects (p. 132)
Observer reactivity (p. 132)
Nonverbal cues (p. 132)
Unrepresentative behavioral setting (p. 132)
Coding complexity (p. 132)
Child reactivity (p. 132)
Role selection (p. 132)
Response set (p. 132)
Behavior drift (p. 132)
Unrepresentative sample (p. 132)
Sample instability (p. 132)
Unrepresentative data (p. 132)
Interobserver reliability (p. 133)
Interobserver agreement (p. 133)
Product-moment correlation coefficient (p. 133)
Phi coefficient (p. 133)
Intraclass correlation coefficient (p. 134)
Kappa (κ) (p. 134)
Uncorrected percentage agreement (p. 134)
Percentage agreement (p. 134)
Agreement on total observations (p. 134)
Agreement on occurrence observations (p. 134)
Agreement on nonoccurrence observations (p. 137)
Event recording percentage agreement estimate (p. 138)
Duration recording percentage agreement estimate (p. 138)
Ratings recording percentage agreement estimate (p. 140)
Concurrent or interobserver reliability (p. 140)
Test-retest reliability (p. 140)
Internal consistency reliability (p. 140)
Validity of behavioral observations (p. 141)
Representativeness and generalizability
   of findings (p. 141)
Reactivity (the guinea pig effect) (p. 141)
Reducing errors in reliability (p. 142)
Criterion-related agreement (p. 142)
Reducing reactivity (p. 143)
Establishing informal norms (p. 143)
Discrepancy ratio (p. 143)
Self-monitoring assessment (p. 145)
Reporting behavioral observations (p. 155)

STUDY QUESTIONS

1. What factors should you consider when designing or selecting an observational coding system?

2. Discuss factors that may affect the reliability of behavioral observations.

3. Discuss the following measures of interobserver agreement: product-moment correlation coefficient, intraclass correlation coefficient, kappa, and percentage agreement.

4. What factors may affect the test-retest reliability and internal consistency of behavioral observations?

5. Discuss factors affecting the validity of behavioral observations.

6. Discuss reactivity in observational recordings. Explain why reactivity may not necessarily be detrimental, and suggest ways to reduce reactivity.

7. How would you go about reducing the number of errors that occur in your behavioral observations?

8. Discuss the strengths and limitations of observational methods.

9. Discuss self-monitoring observational procedures, including their strengths and weaknesses.

10. Present 10 guidelines for reporting behavioral observations in psychological reports.

6

ASSESSMENT OF BEHAVIORAL, SOCIAL, AND EMOTIONAL COMPETENCIES

by William M. Reynolds and Jerome M. Sattler

…the character which shapes our conduct is a definite and durable "something," and therefore it is reasonable to measure it.

—Sir Francis Galton

Goals and Objectives

This chapter is designed to enable you to do the following:

- Describe several self-report, parent report, and teacher report measures of behavioral, social, and emotional competencies in children and adolescents

- Compare and contrast multidimensional measures of child and adolescent behavioral, social, and emotional competencies

- Understand issues in the selection of measures for use in the evaluation of behavioral, social, and emotional competencies in children and adolescents

Measures of behavioral, social, and emotional competencies in children and adolescents are useful for several reasons:

- They help to identify the examinee's behavioral, social, and emotional strengths and deficiencies.
- They are relatively easy to administer and score and are helpful in describing clinically relevant dimensions of behavior.
- They provide an objective basis for evaluating the examinee's progress or the results of an intervention program.
- They permit comparison of the examinee's behavior in different settings, such as at home and at school.
- They facilitate comparison of information from different informants: (a) how the child and the parents view the child's problems, (b) how each parent views the child's problems, (c) how one parent's views of the child's problems compare with the other parent's views, (d) how teachers view the child's problems, and (e) how the parents' views of the child's problems compare with the teachers' views.
- They provide a standardized way of reporting information between and within organizations.
- They stimulate new intervention programs and research.

Such measures are greatly needed because, although nearly 20% of children and adolescents in the United States show symptoms of psychological disorders in any given year, most go unidentified and untreated (U.S. Department of Health and Human Services, 1999).

BACKGROUND CONSIDERATIONS

Objective Measures vs. Projective Measures

Most published measures of behavioral, social, and emotional competencies can be classified as objective (structured) or projective (unstructured). *Objective measures* contain items that are relatively clear and structured, require responses that are limited and relatively clear in meaning, and use scoring procedures that are precise and straightforward. The scores are based on the responses given by an examinee, parent, or teacher and can be quantified, normed, and profiled. Thus, the objectivity in objective measures lies both in the test material (item content and response format) and in the examiner (rigorous scoring methods leave little, if anything, to the examiner's judgment).

Projective measures contain ambiguous stimuli—such as inkblots or pictures of situations or people—that permit the examinee to project covert aspects of his or her personality onto the stimuli. The examinee's responses are then evaluated by use of an interpretive system associated with the projective measure. Projective measures may provide quantifiable scores, depending on the method used to interpret the responses.

Construction of Objective Measures

In objective measures of behavioral, social, and emotional competencies, various strategies are used to develop items and scales. These include factor analysis (placing in a factor items that cluster together), empirical keying (using selected items to distinguish one group from another), theoretical constructs (using selected items to measure the theoretical constructs underlying the construction of the test), and content analysis (using experts to select items to measure the trait or diagnostic category of interest).

Scores obtained from measures of behavioral, social, and emotional competencies reflect the complex interaction of several factors. Although some of the following factors play a more important role than others, each contributes to the final score or rating.

- The type of scale or checklist used (e.g., content of items, social desirability of items, scale values, wording of items, reading level required by items, standardization sample, date of standardization)

Frank and Ernest

© 1999 Thaves / Reprinted with permission. Newspaper dist. by NEA, Inc.

- The child (e.g., age, sex, ethnicity, type of disturbance, reading ability, degree of openness)
- The informant or rater (e.g., expectancies, recall ability, openness, comprehension of items, accuracy of observations, response bias)
- The examiner (e.g., sex, ethnicity, traits, status)
- The setting (e.g., school, home, playground, hospital, clinic, correctional facility)
- The reasons for the evaluation (e.g., screening, diagnosis, placement, intervention, program evaluation)

Scale Names

The same scale names in different measures of behavioral, social, and emotional competencies may cover the same or different behaviors, and, conversely, different scale names may cover different or similar behaviors. For example, some scales isolate hyperactive behavior, whereas others include hyperactive behavior under a conduct problem factor. Scale content may be based on expert systems such as *DSM-IV–TR* or on the results of statistical analyses, rather than on content specifications.

The Informant

When informants, such as parents or teachers, complete a measure of behavioral, social, and emotional competencies, they make judgments about a child's functioning. Because their judgments are subject to bias and distortion, informants' credibility must be carefully examined. If there are doubts about their credibility, the validity of the results must be questioned. In the process of completing a measure of behavioral, social, and emotional competencies, informants may reveal their own attitudes toward the child and toward the topics covered by the measure. Depending on the problem being evaluated, informants may or may not have had the opportunity to observe the behavior or know how the child is feeling. When there are multiple informants, consider the consistency of ratings across informants.

Different ratings among informants may mean one or more of the following:

- The child varies her or his behavior depending on the situation or setting.
- One or more of the informants is unreliable.
- The informants have different response styles (e.g., one informant is reluctant to report minor deviations, while another is willing to report the slightest deviation as a problem; one informant tends to use extremely high and low ratings, while another sticks closely to average ratings).
- Stress level among informants is high.
- The type of problem manifested by the child is difficult to observe (e.g., symptoms of an internalizing disorder are more difficult to observe than symptoms of an externalizing disorder).
- Other, unknown factors are contributing to the unreliability of the ratings.

Informants differ as to their familiarity with the child, sensitivity and tolerance for behavior problems, personality, expectations, comfort with various test formats, and willingness to use certain rating scale positions. In addition, informants may use different frames of reference or interpret similar behaviors in different ways, depending on whether the child is a clinic patient or is attending a public school. The child's ethnicity, socioeconomic status, appearance, and degree of psychopathology also may influence informants' judgments of the child's behavior.

The reliability and validity of ratings may be affected by the specificity of the rating task. For example, items that require ratings of specific behaviors (e.g., "Has the child fought with another child on at least three occasions during the last month?") may yield more reliable results than items requiring global judgments (e.g., "Is the child aggressive?").

Because parents and teachers are likely to see different aspects of a child, information from both sources is needed to obtain a comprehensive picture of the child. Parents are better able to rate behaviors that occur primarily at home (eating, sleeping, sibling relations, family relations, acting out), whereas teachers are more qualified to rate behaviors that occur primarily at school (academic performance, peer relations, attention, following directions). Teacher ratings have the advantage of being based on observations made in a relatively consistent setting (i.e., the classroom) and on direct comparisons with other children at the same developmental level as the referred child. Teachers may not be available during off-contact periods, however. Also, they may have to rely on a limited sample of behavior when they are asked to rate a child during the first few months of the school year or when they are asked to rate a behavior that occurs outside the classroom. Rating adolescent behaviors is particularly difficult for teachers because they have limited contact with junior and senior high school students. Parent ratings have the advantage of being based on observations of the child's behavior in different settings and over a long period. However, parents too usually have fewer opportunities to observe behavior as children grow older and become more independent.

Response Styles

One way of categorizing *response styles* (also referred to as *response sets*) is on the basis of the respondent's intentions. Respondents (examinees or informants) may deliberately or unknowingly slant their replies to create a certain picture. Some respondents and informants want to present a favorable picture (*faking-good response set*); others, an unfavorable picture (*faking-bad response set*); still others, a specific picture (self-assertive, extroverted). The faking-good response set may be used in an employment situation where the respondent wants to appear in the best possible light. The faking-bad response set may be used when the examinee wants to obtain special services or financial gain, remain in a setting rather than be discharged, or get attention or sympathy.

Another categorization of response style reflects the characteristic way individuals respond to items, regardless of

Copyright © 1999 by John P. Wood.

content. A respondent with an *acquiescence response set* has a tendency to agree with each item, while a respondent with a *deviance response set* has a tendency to respond in a deviant, unfavorable, uncommon, or unusual way. A respondent with a *social desirability response set* has a tendency to answer items in the right, appropriate, or most socially accepted way, regardless of whether the answers are true. Socially desirable answers commonly are given in an attempt to make the respondent look good, more acceptable, less deviant, or less idiosyncratic.

Test developers usually try to control for response styles by varying the item content (e.g., wording some items positively and some negatively), measuring the respondent's tendency to answer items in a socially desirable direction and then adjusting scores to take this tendency into account, using neutral items, or pairing items so that their social desirability is similar. You should routinely consider whether the respondent's responses reflect an underlying response style.

Weaknesses and Strengths of Objective Measures

Objective measures permit information to be obtained under standard conditions. Use of standard conditions allows for comparison of respondents' scores, provided various assumptions hold. These include that (a) the items have the same or similar meaning for all respondents, (b) informants can describe or rate the child adequately, (c) respondents report their behaviors, thoughts, and feelings openly and honestly or make their ratings openly and honestly, and (d) the measures have adequate reliability and validity.

Because these assumptions do not always hold, difficulties may be encountered with the use of objective measures. Items, no matter how clearly stated, may be misinterpreted. Some respondents cannot make appropriate ratings, particularly when they have serious psychological difficulties or when they are extremely defensive. Others, as noted previously, deliberately distort their replies. Still others have difficulty understanding the items, particularly in the context of mental retardation, inadequate reading skills, or visual or auditory impairments. Finally, objective measures may be influenced by situational factors, thus restricting the generalizability of the results. For example, a child with conduct problems may respond to the items based on his or her present situation rather than how he or she typically feels or thinks.

Measures of behavioral, social, and emotional competencies provide little information about the dynamics underlying a response. For example, although two respondents may agree with the statement "I have bad thoughts once in a while," their bases for agreeing with the statement may differ. In addition, "once in a while" is open to interpretation. And the fixed format (true/false) does not allow for explanations or clarifications. Finally, the same score for different examinees may be based on different patterns of behavior, needs, and cognitions.

In spite of their limitations, objective measures can be valuable. They are economical to use, can be scored objectively by hand (and often by computer), and in general have good reliability and validity. As with any assessment procedure, a knowledge of the strengths and limitations of measures of behavioral, social, and emotional competencies will help you in their proper use and application. You should study the test manual and technical information for each test that you use, and supplement this information with test reviews and research reports.

Comparison of Measures of Behavioral, Social, and Emotional Competencies with Direct Observation of Behavior

Behavior problems can be evaluated with direct observational methods (see Chapters 4 and 5) as well as with measures of behavioral, social, and emotional competencies. Unfortunately, these two methods do not always provide congruent data because they are based on different behavior samples. Measures of behavioral, social, and emotional competencies sample behaviors over an extended time, whereas direct observations of behavior focus on a limited segment of behavior. Because measures of behavioral, social, and emotional competencies and direct observational methods may be valid for different purposes and because each provides a different perspective on problem behaviors, both should be used to assess problem behavior.

Evaluating Measures of Behavioral, Social, and Emotional Competencies

Before using measures of behavioral, social, and emotional competencies, evaluate their applicability for the specific assessment task. As with any procedure, you will want to evaluate their psychometric properties (see Chapter 4 in *Assessment of Children: Cognitive Applications*). In addition, as noted previously, you will need to evaluate the credibility of the informants. Areas to consider include the following:

1. *Representativeness of the norm group.* Consider whether the norm group is representative of the population and whether total sample, age, and gender norms are provided.
2. *Reliability and validity of the measures.* Consider the internal consistency reliability, test-retest reliability, and validity of the measure.
3. *Reliability of informants.* Consider whether the informants make errors similar to those that occur with observational methods, such as halo effect errors, leniency errors, proximity errors, and social desirability effect errors (see Chapters 4 and 5). Situational factors also may affect informants' ratings. Informants may rate a child as more deviant on the initial assessment and less deviant at the end of an intervention simply to please the therapist or teacher. Take precautions to minimize the occurrence of such errors. Also consider interrater reliability.
4. *Scope.* Consider the scope of the measures, such as whether they address broad-based problems or narrow-based problems.
5. *Structure.* Consider the content of the items, domains covered by the items, number of items, number of response alternatives, number of points defined on the rating scale, time period covered by the items, and types of judgments required. Some measures have two response alternatives (e.g., yes, no), whereas others have three or more (e.g., never, seldom, often). Ratings may be based on a specific time period (e.g. "Rate how aggressive the child was during the past week") or on a nonspecific time period (e.g., "Rate how aggressive the child is").
6. *Clinical utility.* Consider whether the measures have good clinical utility. They should be easy to administer, provide useful clinical information, and be sensitive to the effects of interventions.

THE INTERNALIZING-EXTERNALIZING CONTINUUM

The internalizing-externalizing continuum is a useful way of viewing behavioral, social, and emotional disorders (Achenbach & McConaughy, 1992). Psychological disorders may be reflected in internalizing symptoms, externalizing symptoms, or both types of symptoms. The internalizing-externalizing continuum does not relate to the underlying psychological processes or causes of disorders; rather, it is oriented to the expression of symptoms.

Externalizing disorders of childhood and adolescence are characterized by overt behavioral excesses or disturbances. They are generally distressing to the child's parents, teachers, peers, and others. In *DSM-IV–TR,* externalizing disorders are represented by conduct disorder, attention-deficit/hyperactivity

disorder, and oppositional defiant disorder. Other problems such as aggression, excessive anger, and delinquency, although not formal disorders listed in *DSM-IV–TR,* nevertheless, may be of sufficient severity or frequency to cause significant adjustment difficulties for children in school and in the community.

Internalizing disorders usually are covert and not easily observable, and thus present evaluation and identification difficulties. Although they typically are distressing to the child or adolescent, they are less likely than externalizing disorders to come to the attention of parents and teachers. The severity of internalizing disorders is, in large part, a function of the child's subjective experience. For example, depressive symptoms might include suicidal ideation, fatigue, and feelings of low self-worth.

Children with multiple disorders are said to suffer from comorbidity. They may have two or more externalizing disorders, such as attention-deficit/hyperactivity disorder and conduct disorder, or two or more internalizing disorders, such as generalized anxiety disorder and post-traumatic stress disorder. Some children have both an internalizing and an externalizing disorder, such as conduct disorder and major depression.

MEASURES OF BEHAVIORAL, SOCIAL, AND EMOTIONAL COMPETENCIES

The measures of behavioral, social, and emotional competencies surveyed in this chapter are designed to assess internalizing and externalizing problems, as well as a broad range of other competencies. The primary sources of information for

Copyright © 1997 by John P. Wood.

these measures are parents, teachers, and the children themselves. In some cases, there may be multiple informants (see Table 6-1). This chapter does not cover single-domain measures of behavioral, social, and emotional competencies in children and adolescents. Examples of measures not covered include (a) self-concept measures, such as the Piers Harris Self-Concept Scale (Piers, 1984) and Self-Perception Profile for Adolescents (Harter, 1988), (b) depression measures, such as the Children's Depression Inventory (Kovacs, 1992), Reynolds Child Depression Scale (Reynolds, 1989), and Reynolds Adolescent Depression Scale (Reynolds, 1987), (c) social skills measures, such as the Social Skills Rating Scale (Gresham & Elliott, 1990), and (d) anxiety measures, such as the Revised Children's Manifest Anxiety Scale (Reynolds & Richmond, 1985) and State-Trait Anxiety Inventory for Children (Spielberger, 1973). Similarly, this book does not survey projective techniques (e.g., the Rorschach method), apperception and thematic methods (e.g., Children's Apperception Test), sentence completion methods, or drawing methods.

In evaluating the measures described in this chapter, keep in mind, first, that parents and teachers can evaluate externalizing disorders better than internalizing disorders because the former are more easily observable than the latter. Second, children and adolescents are better reporters of internalizing disorders than are parents and teachers, given the covert nature of these problems, so self-report measures are preferred for the assessment of internalizing disorders. Third, norms are best when there is a large, nationally stratified standardization sample that includes equal numbers of males and females and when gender and age norms are provided in addition to combined total sample norms. Lastly, it is critical that the child or adolescent or adult respondent have the reading level required for self-report measures. Note that a child's reading level may not be the same as her or his grade level; a child may read above or below her or his grade level.

Table 6-1
Summary Table of Behavioral, Social, and Emotional Measures by Informant Type

Informant					
Self		Teacher		Parent	
Measure	Ages	Measure	Ages	Measure	Ages
Adolescent Psychopathology Scale (APS; Reynolds, 1998a, b)	12–19 years	Behavior Assessment System for Children–Teacher Rating Scale (BASC–TRS; Reynolds & Kamphaus, 1992)	4–18 years	Behavior Assessment System for Children–Parent Rating Scale (BASC–PRS; Reynolds & Kamphaus, 1992)	4–18 years
Adolescent Psychopathology Scale–Short Form (APS–SF; Reynolds, 2000)	12–19 years	Conners' Teacher Rating Scale–Revised (CTRS–R; Conners, 1997)	3–17 years	Child Behavior Checklist (CBCL; Achenbach, 1991a)	4–18 years
Behavior Assessment System for Children–Self-Report of Personality (BASC–SRP; Reynolds & Kamphaus, 1992)	8–18 years	Devereux Scales of Mental Disorders (DSMD; Naglieri, LeBuffe, & Pfeiffer, 1994)	5–18 years	Conners' Parent Rating Scale–Revised (CPRS–R; Conners, 1997)	3–17 years
Conners-Wells' Adolescent Self-Report Scale (CASS; Conners, 1997)	12–17 years	Revised Behavior Problem Checklist (RBPC; Quay & Peterson, 1996)	5–18 years	Devereux Scales of Mental Disorders (DSMD; Naglieri, LeBuffe, & Pfeiffer, 1994)	5–18 years
Millon Adolescent Personality Inventory (MAPI; Millon, Green, & Meagher, 1982)	13–19 years	Student Behavior Survey (SBS; Lachar et al., 2000)	5–18 years	Personality Inventory for Children–Second Edition (PIC–2; Wirt et al., 2001)	5–19 years
Minnesota Multiphasic Personality Inventory–Adolescent (MMPI–A; Butcher et al., 1992)	14–18 years	Teacher's Report Form (TRF; Achenbach, 1991b)	5–18 years		
Personality Inventory for Youth (PIY; Lachar & Gruber, 1995a, b)	10–18 years				
Reynolds Adolescent Adjustment Screening Inventory (RAASI; Reynolds, 2001)	12–19 years				
Youth Self-Report (YSR; Achenbach, 1991c)	11–18 years				

ADOLESCENT PSYCHOPATHOLOGY SCALE AND ADOLESCENT PSYCHOPATHOLOGY SCALE– SHORT FORM

The 346-item Adolescent Psychopathology Scale (APS; Reynolds, 1998a, 1998b) and the 115-item Adolescent Psychopathology Scale–Short Form (APS–SF; Reynolds, 2000) are two separate but related measures that assess internalizing and externalizing disorders in adolescents. The APS is a comprehensive measure of 25 *DSM-IV–TR* disorders as well as other social and emotional problems, whereas the APS–SF is a brief form that assesses 12 critical areas of adolescent social and emotional competencies.

The APS is a self-report measure of adolescent psychopathology, personality, and psychosocial problems, developed for adolescents ages 12 to 19 years. It has 40 scales: (a) 20 clinical and 5 personality scales that evaluate symptoms associated with *DSM-IV–TR* disorders, (b) 11 psychosocial problem content scales that assess psychological problems, and (c) 4 response style scales that provide information on truthfulness, consistency, infrequency, and critical item endorsement (e.g., veracity of responses, random responding, or unusual or bizarre behaviors). The APS takes about 45 to 60 minutes to complete and requires a third-grade reading level. The scales in the APS are grouped into three broadbandwidth factors that provide scores for internalizing, externalizing, and personality problem domains (see Table 6-2).

The APS–SF is for situations requiring a brief form. Designed for ages 12 to 19 years, it takes about 15 to 20 minutes to administer, measures 12 clinical disorders, and has two validity scales that provide information on defensiveness and consistency in responding. The APS–SF includes an Academic Problems scale and an Anger/Violence Proneness scale that are not included on the APS, and it also has modified APS scales. Table 6-3 lists the 14 APS–SF scales and the corresponding APS scales.

Scores

Item response formats (both rating scale and time period) on both forms vary depending on the disorder. For example, the Conduct Disorder scale uses a two-point response format (true/false) for rating problem behaviors over the past 6 months, whereas the Major Depression scale uses a three-point response format (almost never, sometimes, nearly every day) for rating symptoms of depression over the past 2 weeks. The APS and APS–SF can be scored by a computer program, which provides raw scores and T scores ($M = 50$, $SD = 10$) for all scales and an interpretive report.

Standardization

The APS and APS–SF were standardized on a stratified sample of 1,827 adolescents, drawn from 1989 to 1991 from eight states, that closely matched the 1990 U.S. Census data

for age, gender, and ethnicity. In addition, there was a clinical sample of 506 adolescents from 31 psychiatric inpatient and outpatient settings in 22 states that represented a range of *DSM-IV–TR* disorders. An additional sample of 1,007 adolescents from school settings was used in reliability and validity studies.

Table 6-2
Domains and Scales on the Adolescent Psychopathology Scale

Domain	Scales
Clinical Disorders	Attention-Deficit/ Hyperactivity Disorder Conduct Disorder Oppositional Defiant Disorder Adjustment Disorder Substance Abuse Disorder Anorexia Nervosa Bulimia Nervosa Sleep Disorder Somatization Disorder Panic Disorder Obsessive Compulsive Disorder Generalized Anxiety Disorder Social Phobia Separation Anxiety Disorder Posttraumatic Stress Disorder Major Depression Dysthymic Disorder Mania Depersonalization Disorder Schizophrenia
Personality Disorders	Avoidant Personality Disorder Obsessive-Compulsive Personality Disorder Borderline Personality Disorder Schizotypal Personality Disorder Paranoid Personality Disorder
Psychosocial Problem Content	Self-Concept Scale Psychosocial Substance Use Difficulties Introversion Scale Alienation-Boredom Scale Anger Scale Aggression Scale Interpersonal Problem Scale Emotional Lability Scale Disorientation Scale Suicide Scale Social Adaptation Scale
Response Style Indicators	Lie Response Scale Consistency Response Scale Infrequency Response Scale Critical Item Endorsement
Factor Score	Internalizing Disorder Factor Score Scale Externalizing Disorder Factor Score Scale Personality Disorder Factor Score Scale

Table 6-3
Scales on the Adolescent Psychopathology Scale–Short Form Corresponding with Those on the Adolescent Psychopathology Scale

Adolescent Psychopathology Scale–Short Form	Adolescent Psychopathology Scale
Conduct Disorder	Conduct Disorder
Oppositional Defiant Disorder	Oppositional Defiant Disorder
Substance Abuse Disorder	Substance Abuse Disorder
Anger/Violence Proneness	Anger Scale /Aggression Scale
Academic Problems	Attention-Deficit/Hyperactivity Disorder
Generalized Anxiety Disorder	Generalized Anxiety Disorder
Posttraumatic Stress Disorder	Posttraumatic Stress Disorder
Major Depression	Major Depression
Eating Disturbance	Anorexia Nervosa/Bulimia Nervosa
Suicide Scale	Suicide Scale
Self-Concept Scale	Self-Concept Scale
Interpersonal Problems	Interpersonal Problem Scale
Defensiveness	Lie Response Scale
Consistency Response	Consistency Response Scale

Reliability

Internal consistency reliabilities for the APS in the school-based standardization sample range from .69 to .95 ($Mdn\ r_{xx}$ = .83) for the Clinical Disorder, Personality Disorder, and Psychosocial Problem Content scales. Median internal consistency reliabilities are .95 for the Internalizing Disorder factor, .86 for the Externalizing Disorder factor, and .86 for the Personality Disorder factor.

In the clinical sample, internal consistency reliabilities for the APS range from .70 to .95 ($Mdn\ r_{xx}$ = .84) for the Clinical Disorder, Personality Disorder, and Psychosocial Problem Content scales. Internal consistency reliabilities are .95 for the Internalizing Disorder factor, .82 for the Externalizing Disorder factor, and .88 for the Personality Disorder factor.

Test-retest reliabilities, obtained on a sample of 64 adolescents in a school setting over a 2-week retest interval, range from .76 to .89 ($Mdn\ r_{tt}$ = .84) for the Clinical Disorder, Personality Disorder, and Psychosocial Problem Content scales. Test-retest reliabilities are .82, .85, and .81 for the Internalizing Disorder factor, Externalizing Disorder factor, and Personality Disorder factor, respectively.

In the school-based standardization sample, internal consistency reliabilities for the APS–SF range from .80 to .91 ($Mdn\ r_{xx}$ = .84) for the 12 clinical scales. In the clinical sample, internal consistency reliabilities for the 12 clinical scales range from .82 to .91 ($Mdn\ r_{xx}$ = .86). Test-retest reliabilities,

obtained on a sample of 64 adolescents in a school setting over a 2-week retest interval, range from .76 to .91 ($Mdn\ r_{tt}$ = .84) for the 12 clinical scales.

Validity

The content validity of the APS and APS–SF is supported by strong correlations of items with the total scale and by findings from factor analyses. Construct validity is supported by factor analyses indicating that APS and APS–SF scales evaluate *DSM-IV–TR* disorders satisfactorily. Criterion-related validity is supported by satisfactory correlations between APS and Minnesota Multiphasic Personality Inventory scales and between the APS and other self-report and clinical measures. Discriminant validity is good, as noted by (a) low correlations between the APS scales and measures of social desirability and cognitive ability and (b) significant score differences between the standardization and clinical samples on all APS scales except the Consistency Response scale.

Comment on the APS and APS–SF

The APS provides for a comprehensive assessment of many *DSM-IV–TR* clinical and personality disorders, including disorders not evaluated by other measures. It has good reliability and validity and is easy to score using a computer program that also provides a detailed psychological report. The APS–SF also has good validity and reliability, and it provides for the assessment of important domains of adolescent psychopathology. It is easy to administer and score with a computer, and it serves as an alternative to the APS when time is at a premium. The Academic Problems and Anger/Violence Proneness scales make the APS–SF particularly useful in school settings.

BEHAVIOR ASSESSMENT SYSTEM FOR CHILDREN

The Behavior Assessment System for Children (BASC; Reynolds & Kamphaus, 1992) contains the Teacher Rating Scale, the Parent Rating Scale, and the Self-Report of Personality. The BASC is designed to evaluate psychological problems in children and adolescents. The Teacher Rating Scale and Parent Rating Scale each have three versions: Preschool (109 items for the Teacher Rating Scale and 105 items for the Parent Rating Scale, at ages 4 to 5 years), Child (148 items for the Teacher Rating Scale and 138 items for the Parent Rating Scale, at ages 6 to 11 years), and Adolescent (138 items for the Teacher Rating Scale and 126 items for the Parent Rating Scale, at ages 12 to 18 years). Each form requires about 10 to 20 minutes to complete. The Self-Report of Personality has two versions: Child (152 items, at ages 8 to 11 years) and Adolescent (186 items, at ages 12 to 18 years). Each version takes about 30 minutes to complete. Table 6-4 shows the composites in each scale.

Scores

The Teacher Rating Scale and the Parent Rating Scale both use a 4-point response format (never, sometimes, often, almost always), while the Self-Report of Personality uses a 2-point response format (true/false). The three scales provide T scores ($M = 50$, $SD = 10$) and percentile ranks. Scoring can be done with self-scoring carbonless answer sheets or by using a computer, although entering data into the scoring program can be difficult (Sandoval & Echandia, 1994).

Standardization

The standardization sample consisted of (a) 2,084 children ages 6 to 11 years and 1,090 adolescents ages 12 to 18 for the Parent Rating Scale, (b) 1,259 children ages 6 to 11 years and 809 adolescents ages 12 to 18 for the Teacher Rating Scale, and (c) 5,413 children ages 8 to 11 and 4,448 adolescents ages 12 to 18 for the Self-Report of Personality. The sample was drawn from 1988 to 1991 and closely matched the 1986 U.S. Census data with regard to age, gender, and ethnicity. Separate norms are presented for males, females, and clinical samples. About 70% of the clinical samples were males with a diagnosis of either conduct disorder or behavior disorder.

Reliability

Internal consistency reliabilities for the three scales in the school sample range from (a) .62 to .95 ($Mdn\ r_{xx} = .88$) for the Teacher Rating Scale, (b) .58 to .94 ($Mdn\ r_{xx} = .78$) for the Parent Rating Scale, and (c) .61 to .89 ($Mdn\ r_{xx} = .81$) for the Self-Report of Personality.

Interrater reliabilities for the Parent Rating Scale are generally low, ranging from .35 to .73 ($Mdn\ r_{rr} = .57$). Test-retest reliabilities for the Parent Rating Scale with several samples over a 2- to 8-week interval range from .41 to .94 ($Mdn\ r_{tt} = .85$).

Interrater reliabilities for the Teacher Rating Scale range from .29 to .70 ($Mdn\ r_{rr} = .63$) for preschool children and from .44 to .93 ($Mdn\ r_{rr} = .71$) for school-age children; no interrater reliability data were reported for adolescents. Test-retest reliabilities for the Teacher Rating Scale with several samples over a 2- to 8-week interval range from .59 to .95 ($Mdn\ r_{tt} = .89$).

Test-retest reliabilities for the Self-Report of Personality with a sample of 119 children and 104 adolescents from school and clinical settings retested over a 2- to 8-week interval range from .57 to .81 ($Mdn\ r_{tt} = .76$) for children and from .67 to .81 ($Mdn\ r_{tt} = .76$) for adolescents.

Validity

Construct validity for the internalizing and externalizing dimensions of the BASC scales is supported by results of factor and structural equation analyses. Criterion-related validity is satisfactory for the three scales, as shown by acceptable correlations with other similar measures. In addition, several studies (Doyle, Ostrander, Skare, Crosby, & August, 1997; Vaughn, Riccio, Hynd, & Hall, 1997) support the validity of the Parent Rating Scale and Teacher Rating Scale for the assessment and identification of children with attention-deficit/hyperactivity disorder. The Manual, however, reports few studies showing the ways in which clinical groups differ on the scales.

Comment on the BASC

The BASC is one of the few measures that provide for an integrative approach to the assessment of children and adolescents across multiple informants. Its strength is in the assessment of children ages 6 to 11 years, particularly in the evaluation of externalizing behavior problems. However, the BASC has several problems. For example, it measures a limited number of psychopathology and personality domains, its

Table 6-4
Informant Versions and Associated Scales on the Behavior Assessment System for Children

Parent Rating Scale		Teacher Rating Scale		Self-Report of Personality	
Scales and composites	Ages	Scales and composites	Ages	Scales and composites	Ages
Scale		**Scale**		**Scale**	
Adaptability	4–5; 6–11	Adaptability	4–5; 6–11	Anxiety	8–11; 12–18
Aggression	4–5; 6–11; 12–18	Aggression	4–5; 6–11; 12–18	Attitude to School	8–11; 12–18
Anxiety	4–5; 6–11; 12–18	Anxiety	4–5; 6–11; 12–18	Attitude to Teachers	8–11; 12–18
Attention Problems	4–5; 6–11; 12–18	Attention Problems	4–5; 6–11; 12–18	Atypicality	8–11; 12–18
Atypicality	4–5; 6–11; 12–18	Atypicality	4–5; 6–11; 12–18	Depression	8–11; 12–18
Conduct Problems	6–11; 12–18	Conduct Problems	6–11; 12–18	Interpersonal Relations	8–11; 12–18
Depression	4–5; 6–11; 12–18	Depression	4–5; 6–11; 12–18	Locus of Control	8–11; 12–18
Hyperactivity	4–5; 6–11; 12–18	Hyperactivity	4–5; 6–11; 12–18	Relations with Parents	8–11; 12–18
Leadership	6–11; 12–18	Leadership	6–11; 12–18	Self-Esteem	8–11; 12–18
Social Skills	4–5; 6–11; 12–18	Learning Problems	6–11; 12–18	Self-Reliance	8–11; 12–18
Somatization	4–5; 6–11; 12–18	Social Skills	4–5; 6–11; 12–18	Sensation Seeking	12–18
Withdrawal	4–5; 6–11; 12–18	Somatization	4–5; 6–11; 12–18	Sense of Inadequacy	8–11; 12–18
		Study Skills	6–11; 12–18	Social Stress	8–11; 12–18
		Withdrawal	4–5; 6–11; 12–18	Somatization	12–18
Composite		**Composite**		**Composite**	
Externalizing Problems	4–18	Externalizing Problems	4–18	School Maladjustment	8–18
Internalizing Problems	4–18	Internalizing Problems	4–18	Clinical Maladjustment	8–18
Adaptive Skills	4–12	Adaptive Skills	4–18	Personal Maladjustment	8–18
Behavioral Symptom Index	4–18	Behavioral Symptom Index	All ages	Emotional Symptoms Index	8–18
		School Problems	6–18		

structure makes comparison of child self-ratings with ratings from parents and teachers difficult, it has low reliabilities in several instances, it has limited validity information about its applicability for use with preschool children, and the readability level of the Self-Report of Personality may be too high (Sandoval & Echandia, 1994).

CHILD BEHAVIOR CHECKLIST, TEACHER'S REPORT FORM, AND YOUTH SELF-REPORT

The Child Behavior Checklist (CBCL; Achenbach, 1991a), Teacher's Report Form (TRF; Achenbach, 1991b), and Youth Self-Report (YSR; Achenbach, 1991c) measure internalizing-externalizing problems in children and adolescents. The Child Behavior Checklist, with 120 items in nine scales, is designed for parents of children and adolescents ages 4 to 18 years. The

Teacher's Report Form, with 120 items in eight scales, is designed for teachers of children and adolescents ages 6 to 18 years. The Youth Self-Report, with 119 items in nine scales, is designed for adolescents ages 11 to 18 years; it requires a fifth-grade reading level. Table 6-5 shows the scales in each measure. Internalizing, Externalizing, and Total scores are also obtained on each measure, with the Internalizing score the sum of Withdrawn, Somatic Complaints, and Anxious/Depressed scales and the Externalizing score the sum of Delinquent Behavior and Aggressive Behavior scales. All scales were developed on the basis of factor analysis. The CBCL and the TRF take approximately 10 to 15 minutes to complete, while the YSR takes approximately 30 minutes to complete.

Scores

Items are scored on a 3-point scale (not true, somewhat true or sometimes true, and very true or often true). Scoring tem-

SCHOOLIES © 1998 by John P. Wood

Tommy's failure to do this assignment is actually a victory in his never-ending struggle for self-directed learning and true educational freedom.

You've hired your own spin doctor?!

Copyright © 1998 by John P. Wood.

plates, scannable answer sheets, and computer scoring are available. The computer program provides a profile of the scores. *T* scores ($M = 50$, $SD = 10$) and percentile ranks are provided for all scales.

Standardization

The standardization sample for the Child Behavior Checklist consisted of 1,200 males and females ages 4 to 11 years and 1,168 males and females ages 12 to 18 years. The standardization sample was ethnically diverse, with 73% Euro American, 16% African American, 7% Hispanic American, and 3% other. Most of the raters (82%) were mothers.

The standardization sample for the Teacher's Report Form consisted of 713 males and females ages 5 to 11 years and 678 males and females ages 12 to 18 years. The standardization sample was ethnically diverse, with 76% Euro American, 14% African American, 7% Hispanic American, and 3% other.

The standardization sample for the Youth Self-Report consisted of 637 males and 678 females and was stratified by geographic area and parental socioeconomic level. The standardization sample was ethnically diverse, with 72% Euro American, 16% African American, 8% Hispanic American, and 4% other.

The standardization samples for all three scales were obtained in 1989. They represent a close ethnic match to the 1990 U.S. Census data.

Reliability

Internal consistency reliabilities for the Child Behavior Checklist range from .56 to .92 (*Mdn* r_{xx} = .78). Test-retest reliabilities for 80 children and adolescents retested over a 1-week interval range from .63 to .97 (*Mdn* r_{tt} = .86). Interrater reliability coefficients (mother and father ratings) range from .26 to .86 (*Mdn* r_{rr} = .72).

Internal consistency reliabilities for the Teacher's Report Form range from .63 to .96 (*Mdn* r_{xx} = .85). Test-retest reliabilities for 44 children retested over a 1- to 4-week interval range from .82 to .95 for males and from .43 to .99 for females. Interrater reliability coefficients (pairs of teachers) range from –.05 to .81 (*Mdn* r_{rr} = .55).

Internal consistency reliabilities for the Youth Self-Report range from .59 to .90 (*Mdn* r_{xx} = .78) for males and from .59 to .86 (*Mdn* r_{xx} = .76) for females. Test-retest reliabilities range from .47 to .81 (*Mdn* r_{tt} = .70) for 50 children ages 11 to 18 years retested over a 1-week interval and from .30 to .60 (*Mdn* r_{tt} = 48) for 111 children ages 11 to 14 years retested over a 7-month interval.

Validity

The validity of the 1991 version of the Child Behavior Checklist is in part inferred from research with previous versions. However, because there have been changes in the

Table 6-5
Scales on the Child Behavior Checklist, Teacher's Report Form, and Youth Self-Report

Scale	Form		
	CBCL	TRF	YSR
Withdrawn	All ages	All ages	All ages
Somatic Complaints	All ages	All ages	All ages
Anxious/Depressed	All ages	All ages	All ages
Social Problems	All ages	All ages	All ages
Thought Problems	All ages	All ages	All ages
Attention Problems	All ages	All ages	All ages
Delinquent Behavior	All ages	All ages	All ages
Aggressive Behavior	All ages	All ages	All ages
Sex Problems	Ages 4–11	—	—
Self-Destructive/ Identity Problems	—	—	Boys only

Note. Abbreviations are as follows:
CBCL = Child Behavior Checklist; TRF = Teacher's Report Form; YSR = Youth Self-Report.

content and construction of items, previous research is not a fully applicable basis for evaluating the validity of the 1991 version. Concurrent validity is satisfactory, as shown by acceptable correlations with the Conners' Parent Questionnaire and the Revised Behavior Problem Checklist. Acceptable discriminant validity is shown by significant differences in Child Behavior Checklist scores between referred and nonreferred samples of children and adolescents.

The Teacher's Report Form has satisfactory concurrent validity, as shown by high correlations with the Conners' Teacher Rating Scale and with a prior version of the Teacher's Report Form. Discriminant validity is satisfactory, as demonstrated by differences in scores between referred and nonreferred samples of children and adolescents.

The Youth Self-Report has satisfactory discriminant validity, as demonstrated by differences between referred and nonreferred samples on most scales. Concurrent validity is acceptable, as demonstrated by high correlations between the 1991 version and the prior version of the Youth Self-Report. No evidence for convergent or discriminant validity is reported in the Manual.

Research has yielded mixed results on the Youth Self-Report and Child Behavior Checklist as instruments for identifying children and adolescents at risk for psychological problems (Bird, Gould, Rubio-Stipec, & Staghezza, 1991; Casat, Norton, & Boyle-Whitesel, 1999; Drotar, Stein, & Perrin, 1995; Handwerk, Larzelere, Friman, & Soper, 1999; Jensen, Salzberg, Richter, & Watanabe, 1993; Jensen & Watanabe, 1999; Morgan & Cauce, 1999; Perrin, Stein, & Drotar, 1991; Song, Singh, & Singer, 1994; Thurber & Hollingsworth, 1992). In addition, the YSR does not provide validity scales for detecting response styles or inappropriate responding, although some items assess social desirability.

Comment on the CBCL, TRF, and YSF

A strength of the Child Behavior Checklist, Teacher's Report Form, and Youth Self-Report is that they support cross-informant assessment of children and adolescents. However, several of the scales show low levels of reliability, suggesting caution in their interpretation and application. The three forms should be considered as broad-based screening measures, not as precise measures of psychological disorders.

CONNERS' RATING SCALES–REVISED

The Conners' Rating Scales–Revised (CRS–R; Conners, 1997) provide for cross-informant assessment of behavior problems in children and adolescents, with a primary emphasis on externalizing problems. The parent and teacher versions are designed for rating children ages 3 to 17 years, whereas the self-report versions are designed for adolescents ages 12 to 17 years. The scales are revised and restandardized from previous versions.

Copyright © 2000 by John P. Wood.

The CRS–R has several forms (also see Table 6-6):

- Conners' Parent Rating Scale–Revised: Long Form (80 items)
- Conners' Parent Rating Scale–Revised: Short Form (27 items)
- Conners' Teacher Rating Scale–Revised: Long Form (59 items)
- Conners' Teacher Rating Scale–Revised: Short Form (28 items)
- Conners-Wells' Adolescent Self-Report Scale: Long Form (87 items)
- Conners-Wells' Adolescent Self-Report Scale: Short Form (27 items)

In addition, the CRS–R has separate auxiliary scales that are versions of the CRS–R scales. For example, the Conners' Global Index–Parent is the same as the well-known 10-item Conners' Hyperactivity Scale. The time required to complete each version varies with the length of the scale.

Scores

All versions use a 4-point rating scale (0 = not true at all, 1 = just a little true, 2 = pretty much true, 3 = very much true). Scoring is done with a self-scoring answer sheet or by using a computer program that allows the respondent (parent, teacher, or adolescent) to complete the CRS–R on a computer. The computer method provides a score and an interpretive report. Scannable fax-back forms can be sent to the publisher for computer scoring and interpretation. Raw scores are converted to T scores ($M = 50$, $SD = 10$).

**Table 6-6
Conners' Rating Scales—Revised Versions
and Subscales**

Scale	Subscales

Conners' Parent Rating Scale–Revised: Long Form (CPRS–R: L)	Oppositional
	Cognitive Problems
	Hyperactivity
	Anxious-Shy
	Perfectionism
	Social Problems
	Psychosomatic
	Conners' Global Index
	    Restless-Impulsive
	    Emotional Lability
	ADHD Index
	DSM-IV Symptom Subscale
	    DSM-IV Inattentive
	    DSM-IV Hyperactivity-
	      Impulsive

Conners' Parent Rating Scale–Revised: Short Form (CPRS–R: S)	Oppositional Cognitive Problems Hyperactivity ADHD Index

Conners' Teacher Rating Scale–Revised: Long Form (CTRS–R: L)	Oppositional
	Cognitive Problems
	Hyperactivity
	Anxious-Shy
	Perfectionism
	Social Problems
	Conners' Global Index
	    Restless-Impulsive
	    Emotional Lability
	ADHD Index
	DSM-IV Symptom Subscale
	    DSM-IV Inattentive
	    DSM-IV Hyperactivity-
	      Impulsive

Conners' Teacher Rating Scale–Revised: Short Form (CTRS–R: S)	Oppositional Cognitive Problems Hyperactivity ADHD Index

Conners-Wells' Adolescent Self-Report Scale: Long Form (CASS: L)	Family Problems
	Emotional Problems
	Conduct Problems
	Cognitive Problems
	Anger Control Problems
	Hyperactivity
	ADHD Index
	DSM-IV Symptom Subscale
	    DSM-IV Inattentive
	    DSM-IV Hyperactivity-
	      Impulsive

Conners-Wells' Adolescent Self-Report Scale: Short Form (CASS: S)	Conduct Problems Cognitive Problems Anger Control Problems Hyperactive-Impulsive ADHD Index

Standardization

The standardization sample consisted of over 8,000 individuals drawn from 1993 to 1996 from 45 U.S. states and 10 Canadian provinces. Norms are provided separately for males and females by age levels. The sample does not match U.S. Census data. For example, there is a higher proportion of Euro American children in the standardization sample than in the general population. In addition, there are substantial differences in ethnic composition across the forms.

Reliability

Internal consistency reliabilities for the Parent and Teacher Forms are acceptable, ranging from .73 to .96 ($Mdn\ r_{xx} = .90$). Internal consistency reliabilities for the Adolescent Self-Report Form are acceptable, ranging from .75 to .92 ($Mdn\ r_{xx} = .84$).

Test-retest reliabilities for the Parent and Teacher Forms with a sample of 49 children and adolescents over a 6- to 8-week retest interval are variable. They range from (a) .47 to .85 ($Mdn\ r_{tt} = .70$) for the Parent Long Form, (b) .62 to .85 ($Mdn\ r_{tt} = .73$) for the Parent Short Form, (c) .47 to .86 ($Mdn\ r_{tt} = .72$) for the Teacher Long Form, and (d) .72 to .92 ($Mdn\ r_{tt} = .83$) for the Teacher Short Form. Test-retest reliabilities with a sample of 50 children and adolescents retested over a 6- to 8-week interval range from .73 to .89 ($Mdn\ r_{tt} = .83$) for the Adolescent Self-Report Long Form and from .72 to .87 ($Mdn\ r_{tt} = .83$) for the Adolescent Self-Report Short Form.

Validity

Construct validity is satisfactory, based on the results of a factor analysis used to construct the scales. Convergent validity is good, as demonstrated by high correlations (range of .95 to .99) between long and short forms of the various scales. Criterion validity is good, as shown by high correlations between various versions of the scales. Convergent validity is satisfactory, as demonstrated by acceptable correlations between (a) similar scales on the Parent and Teacher Forms and (b) the Adolescent Self-Report and Parent Forms. Discriminant validity in the form of contrasted groups is good, as shown by significant differences in the Parent and Teacher Forms between clinical and nonclinical samples of children.

Comment on the CRS–R

The CRS–R scales are a significant improvement over previous versions. A useful addition is the Self-Report Scale. However, the sizes of the standardization samples are small (i.e., less than 100) for many age and gender groups. The CRS–R scales show adequate to good reliability and adequate validity, with the informant versions particularly strong in evaluating externalizing problems, such as those associated with ADHD. The Self-Report Scale is useful for measuring

MR. WOODHEAD © 2000 by John P. Wood

Before you grade my final exam, I must tell you something.

Remember all of the stress and frustration I've caused you?

Well, unless I pass, I'm asking for you as my teacher again next year.

general distress, but it is limited in its coverage of specific social and emotional problems.

DEVEREUX SCALES OF MENTAL DISORDERS

The Devereux Scales of Mental Disorders (DSMD; Naglieri, LeBuffe, & Pfeiffer, 1994) is a behavior rating scale for children ages 5 to 12 years (111 items) and adolescents ages 13 to 18 years (110 items) that can be completed by a parent or teacher in about 15 minutes. The DSMD has six scales, five of which are common to both age groups (see Table 6-7).

Table 6-7 Scales and Composites on the Devereux Scales of Mental Disorders	
Version	
Child	*Adolescent*
Scale	**Scale**
Conduct	Conduct
Attention	Delinquency
Anxiety	Anxiety
Depression	Depression
Autism	Autism
Acute Problems	Acute Problems
Composite	**Composite**
Externalizing	Externalizing
Internalizing	Internalizing
Critical Pathology	Critical Pathology

Scores

Items on the DSMD are scored on a 5-point scale (0 = never, 1 = rarely, 2 = occasionally, 3 = frequently, 4 = very frequently), according to the frequency of occurrence of the behavior over the past 4 weeks. Raw scores are converted to T scores ($M = 50$, $SD = 10$) and percentile ranks. Standard scores are provided for each scale and for three composites: Externalizing (Conduct and Attention/Delinquency), Internalizing (Anxiety and Depression), and Critical Pathology (Autism and Acute Problems).

Standardization

The DSMD was standardized on 2,042 children ages 5 to 12 years and 1,111 adolescents ages 13 to 18 years. The standardization sample was collected in 1991 from 17 states and closely matched the 1990 U.S. Census data. Norms for child and adolescent versions are provided separately by gender, based on teacher and parent ratings.

Reliability

Internal consistency reliabilities for the six DSMD scales range from .70 to .99 (*Mdn* r_{xx} = .87) for parents and from .76 to .98 (*Mdn* r_{xx} = .91) for teachers. Test-retest reliability was assessed on 30 children and adolescents rated by teachers and on 18 children and adolescents rated by staff in a clinical setting over a 1-day retest interval. Test-retest reliabilities range from .75 to .95 (*Mdn* r_{tt} = .81) for teacher ratings and from .41 to .79 (*Mdn* r_{tt} = .75) for staff ratings. Test-retest reliabilities for 99 children and 35 adolescents from several public schools over a 1-week retest interval range from .32 to .89 (*Mdn* r_{tt} = .87) for the children and from .40 to .83 (*Mdn* r_{tt}

= .61) for the adolescents. Interrater reliabilities based on 45 children and seven sets of teacher and teachers' aide ratings range from .44 to .66 ($Mdn\ r_{rr}$ = .54).

Validity

The DSMD was developed based on factor analysis. However, the placement of items appears to be somewhat peculiar. For example, items dealing with excessive eating are placed on the same factor as items dealing with having hallucinations and torturing animals. Discriminant validity in the form of contrasted groups is acceptable, as demonstrated by several studies of clinical and nonclinical samples that show significant differences between groups on all DSMD scales. The Manual provides no evidence of criterion-related validity or of concurrent validity. As on other instruments, parents and teachers differed significantly in their ratings of children and adolescents.

Comment on the DSMD

The DSMD is a parent and teacher rating scale that has good reliability, but limited validity. In addition, it is somewhat limited in its evaluation of psychopathology. Some items include content that is difficult for parents and teachers to evaluate. Although the Manual states that the DSMD is designed to reflect symptoms in *DSM-IV*, the scale fails to do so.

Copyright © 1997 by John P. Wood.

MILLON ADOLESCENT PERSONALITY INVENTORY

The Millon Adolescent Personality Inventory (MAPI; Millon, Green, & Meagher, 1982) is a 150-item self-report scale for use with adolescents ages 13 to 19 years. It has eight Personality Style scales, eight Expressed Concerns scales, and four Behavioral Correlates scales (see Table 6-8). The MAPI is based on Millon's perspective of personality, which proposes that personality is reflected in patterns of personality style (e.g., cooperative, acquiescent) and in patterns of personality attributes (e.g., sexual acceptance, peer security). The scale takes about 30 minutes to complete.

Scores

The MAPI uses a true/false answer format. Answer sheets can be scored by the publisher only. Raw scores are converted to specially created base-rate scores developed by Millon. These scores are not standard scores. They have a median of 50, but no standard deviation is reported. Several score report options are available from the publisher.

Standardization

The standardization sample consisted of 2,157 adolescents ages 13 to 19 years from public and parochial schools, with 92% between the ages of 14 and 17 years. Geographic location

Table 6-8
Domains and Scales on the Millon Adolescent Personality Inventory

Domain	Scales
Personality Styles	Introversive Inhibited Cooperative Sociable Confident Forceful Respectful Sensitive
Expressed Concerns	Self-Concept Personal Esteem Body Comfort Sexual Acceptance Peer Security Social Tolerance Family Rapport Academic Confidence
Behavioral Correlates	Impulse Control Societal Compliance Scholastic Achievement Attendance Consistency

is not specified. In addition, no date is given for the collection of the standardization data. The ethnic distribution of the sample—approximately 84% Euro American, 11% African American, 3% Hispanic American, and 2% other—was not matched to U.S. Census data. The clinical sample consisted of 430 adolescents, the majority from outpatient settings, who were seen for psychological assessment or were in therapy.

Reliability

Internal consistency reliabilities range from .67 to .84 (*Mdn* r_{xx} = .77) for an unspecified clinical sample. Test-retest reliabilities over a 5-month retest interval range from .53 to .82 (*Mdn* r_{tt} = .75) in a clinical sample of 105 children.

Validity

Construct validity receives marginal support from a factor analysis that resulted in four factors unrelated to Millon's personality theory. Concurrent validity also is marginal, as correlations between selected MAPI scales and scales on other personality measures yielded mixed results. Johnson, Archer, Sheaffer, and Miller (1992) found little agreement between MAPI results and clinical diagnoses in a sample of 199 adolescent psychiatric patients; the MAPI also was poor at diagnosing mood, adjustment, personality, and behavior disorders.

Comment on the MAPI

The MAPI was designed to reflect dimensions of personality postulated by Millon. However, the problematic scoring procedure, extensive item overlap across scales, limited evidence of validity, and complexities of interpretation suggest caution in using this instrument.

MINNESOTA MULTIPHASIC PERSONALITY INVENTORY–ADOLESCENT

The Minnesota Multiphasic Personality Inventory–Adolescent (MMPI–A; Butcher, Williams, Graham, Archer, Tellegen, Ben-Porath, & Kaemmer, 1992), designed for adolescents ages 14 to 18 years, draws on the long history of the MMPI, which was developed in the 1940s by Hathaway and McKinley. A majority of the 478 items on the MMPI–A were drawn from the MMPI. The MMPI–A has 10 basic scales, 7 validity scales, and 15 new content scales (see Table 6-9). The reading level varies by item, with a seventh-grade reading level recommended; however, many items require a higher reading level (Archer, 1997). The MMPI–A takes 60 to 90 minutes to complete.

Scores

The MMPI–A uses a true/false format. It can be scored by hand; by mail-in to the test publisher, which will provide a

Courtesy of Herman Zilinski.

variety of score and interpretive reports; or by computer software from other sources (Archer, 1999). Raw scores are transformed to *T* scores (*M* = 50, *SD* = 10).

Standardization

The standardization sample consisted of 805 males and 815 females drawn from 1985 to 1989 from eight states, with 85% of the sample from the Midwest and East Coast. Most of the adolescents (95%) were between the ages of 14 and 17 years. U.S. Census data for 1980 were used as a basis for matching the sample. The ethnic distribution was 76% Euro American, 12% African American, and 12% other. Over 60% of the sample came from families in which the parents had some college education. Norms are provided separately for males and females. A clinical sample of 713 adolescents from treatment settings in Minnesota, tested between 1985 and 1988, was used for additional norms.

Reliability

Internal consistency reliabilities in the school-based standardization sample range from .40 to .89 (*Mdn* r_{xx} = .67) for the basic scales and from .55 to .83 (*Mdn* r_{xx} = .75) for the content scales. Internal consistency reliabilities in the clinical sample range from .35 to .91 (*Mdn* r_{xx} = .66) for the basic scales and from .63 to .89 (*Mdn* r_{xx} = .78) for the content scales. Test-retest reliabilities, assessed on 154 adolescents in

Table 6-9
Scales on the Minnesota Multiphasic Personality Inventory–Adolescent (MMPI–A)

Type	Names
Validity Scales	Variable Response Inconsistency True Response Inconsistency Infrequency 1 Infrequency 2 Infrequency Lie Defensiveness
Basic Scales	Hypochondriasis Depression Hysteria Psychopathic Deviate Masculinity-Femininity Paranoia Psychasthenia Schizophrenia Hypomania Social Introversion
Content Scales	Anxiety Obsessiveness Depression Health Concerns Alienation Bizarre Mentation Anger Cynicism Conduct Problems Low Self-Esteem Low Aspiration Social Discomfort Family Problems School Problems Negative Treatment Indicators

a school setting over a 1-week retest interval, range from .65 to .84 ($Mdn\ r_{tt} = .80$) for the basic scales and from .62 to .82 ($Mdn\ r_{tt} = .72$) for the content scales.

Validity

Construct validity as reported in the Manual is limited. A factor analysis of the basic scales conducted separately for males and females in the school sample yielded four factors, with most scales loading on the first factor, and limited interpretability of factors. The factors did not differentiate between internalizing and externalizing problems. This difficulty may be due in part to the overlap in item content across the basic MMPI–A scales. Correlations between the basic scales and the Child Behavior Checklist and clinical information derived from records were low, with most in the .10 to .29 range. Other validation studies have yielded mixed results. Studying

99 males in a state correctional facility, Cashel, Rogers, Sewell, and Holliman (1998) compared diagnostic interview items and MMPI–A diagnoses. Agreement between MMPI–A and *DSM-IV* diagnoses ranged from 58% for conduct disorder to 83% for generalized anxiety disorder. Many of the MMPI–A scales did not show significant correlations with their counterpart items on the diagnostic interview.

Comment on the MMPI–A

The MMPI–A is a downward extension and revision of the MMPI, although much of the content of the original MMPI developed for adults in the 1940s remains in this revision. The MMPI–A has a limited age range, requires a reading level above that of many adolescents, and has moderate reliability and validity. The new content scales provide useful information on adolescent psychopathology. If you do use the MMPI–A, see books by Archer (1997), Butcher and Williams (1992), and Williams, Butcher, Ben-Porath, and Graham (1992) for help with interpretation.

PERSONALITY INVENTORY FOR CHILDREN–SECOND EDITION

The Personality Inventory for Children–Second Edition (PIC–2; Wirt, Lachar, Seat, & Broen, 2001) is a parent-completed survey of children's behavior. A revision of a scale originally published in 1977, the PIC–2 is designed for kindergarten to twelfth grade or children and adolescents from ages 5 to 19

years. The standard form contains 275 items, and the brief form (called the Behavioral Summary) contains 96 items. Items cover behavioral, emotional, cognitive, and interpersonal adjustment.

The PIC–2 has three validity scales, nine adjustment scales, and 21 adjustment subscales (see Table 6-10). To complete the PIC–2, parents (or caregivers) use an answer sheet provided by the test publisher. The survey can be scored by hand or mailed to the test publisher for computer scoring. The PIC–2 also can be administered and scored on a personal computer. The standard form takes about 40 min-

utes to complete; the Behavioral Summary takes about 15 minutes to complete. The Manual provides interpretive guidelines for all scales and subscales. There also is a Spanish-language version of the PIC–2.

Scores

Items are scored true or false. Raw scores are converted into T scores ($M = 50$, $SD = 10$) for all scales and subscales. The standard form has no section scores or total score. The Behavioral Summary has scores for the eight scales, as well as scores for the three composite scales and a total score (see Table 6-11). One set of norms is provided for males and females for all ages from 5 to 19 years.

Standardization

The PIC–2 was standardized during the period from 1995 to 2000 on a sample of 2,306 respondents. The sample was generally representative of the U.S. Census data. Stratification variables consisted of gender, age, ethnic background, geographic region, parents' education (as an index of SES), and guardianship status. Respondents participating in the standardization had children in 23 schools in 12 states. Respondents were mothers (82%), fathers (15%), and other caregivers (3%). The referred sample consisted of 1,551 cases obtained from 39 cities in 17 states.

Reliability

Internal consistency reliabilities for the nine adjustment scales range from .75 to .91 ($Mdn\ r_{xx} = .84$) in the standardization sample and from .81 to .95 ($Mdn\ r_{xx} = .89$) in the referred sample.

Table 6-10
Personality Inventory for Children–Second Edition Scales and Subscales

Scale	Subscales
Response Validity Scale Inconsistency	—
Dissimulation	—
Defensiveness	—
Adjustment Scale Cognitive Impairment	Inadequate Abilities Poor Achievement Developmental Delay
Impulsivity and Distractibility	Disruptive Behavior Fearlessness
Delinquency	Antisocial Behavior Dyscontrol Noncompliance
Family Dysfunction	Conflict Among Members Parent Maladjustment
Reality Distortion	Developmental Deviation Hallucinations and Delusions
Somatic Concern	Psychosomatic Preoccupation Muscular Tension and Anxiety
Psychological Discomfort	Fear and Worry Depression Sleep Disturbance/ Preoccupation with Death
Social Withdrawal	Social Introversion Isolation
Social Skill Deficits	Limited Peer Status Conflict with Peers

---

Table 6-11
Personality Inventory for Children–Second Edition Behavioral Summary Composite and Adjustment Scales

Composite scale	Adjustment scales
Externalizing Composite	Impulsivity and Distractibility–Short Delinquency–Short
Internalizing Composite	Reality Distortion–Short Somatic Concern–Short Psychological Discomfort–Short
Social Adjustment Composite	Social Withdrawal–Short Social Skill Deficits–Short
Total Score	Combination of the seven scales plus Family Dysfunction–Short

Internal consistency reliabilities for the 21 adjustment subscales range from .49 to .86 (*Mdn* r_{xx} = .74) in the standardization sample and from .68 to .92 (*Mdn* r_{xx} = .80) in the referred sample.

Internal consistency reliabilities for the eight Behavioral Summary adjustment scales range from .63 to .82 (*Mdn* r_{xx} = .72) in the standardization sample and from .73 to .89 (*Mdn* r_{xx} = .82) in the referred sample. Internal consistency reliabilities for the Behavioral Summary composite scales and total score range from .78 to .93 in the standardization sample and from .86 to .95 in the referred sample.

Test-retest reliabilities for the nine adjustment scales after one week (*N* = 110) range from .66 to .90 (*Mdn* r_{tt} = .82) in the standardization sample and from .88 to .94 (*Mdn* r_{tt} = .90) in the referred sample. Four of the 18 test-retest correlations are below .80, and one is below .70.

Test-retest reliabilities for the 21 adjustment subscales range from .63 to .87 (*Mdn* r_{tt} = .79) in the standardization sample and from .76 to .95 (*Mdn* r_{tt} = .88) in the referred sample.

Test-retest reliabilities for the eight Behavioral Summary adjustment scales range from .58 to .85 (*Mdn* r_{tt} = .78) in the standardization sample and from .85 to .89 (*Mdn* r_{tt} = .87) in the referred sample. Test-retest reliabilities for the Behavioral Summary composite scales and total score range from .71 to .85 in the standardization sample and are all at .89 in the referred sample.

Interrater reliabilities for the nine adjustment scales range from .54 to .90 (*Mdn* r_{rr} = .80) in the standardization sample for mothers and fathers who rated 60 children and from .67 to .88 (*Mdn* r_{rr} = .73) in the referred sample for mothers and fathers who rated 65 children.

Interrater reliabilities for the 21 adjustment subscales range from .49 to .89 (*Mdn* r_{rr} = .80) in the standardization sample and from .56 to .93 (*Mdn* r_{rr} = .71) in the referred sample.

Interrater reliabilities for the eight Behavioral Summary adjustment scales range from .54 to .82 (*Mdn* r_{rr} = .72) in the standardization sample range and from .61 to .82 (*Mdn* r_{rr} = .65) in the referred sample. Interrater reliabilities for the Behavioral Summary composite scales and total score range from .71 to .86 in the standardization sample and from .68 to .78 in the referred sample.

Validity

Content validity is satisfactory, as items generally correlate more highly with their home scale than with other scales. Construct validity is limited; a factor analysis of the scales with the referred sample resulted in five factors rather than the nine PIC–2 scales. The Manual does not report a factor analysis for the standardization sample. Convergent validity and discriminant validity are satisfactory, as the PIC–2 correlates more highly with similar measures than with different measures. The PIC–2 also discriminates between different types of groups.

Comment on the PIC–2

The PIC–2 has several strengths. First, it covers a range of psychological and adjustment problems. Second, the validity scales are potentially useful. Third, the interpretive guidelines are useful. Reliability of the PIC–2 is moderate to good for most of the scales, although low reliability is reported for some of the subscales. Higher reliabilities are found in the referred sample. More research is needed with the PIC–2 in order to evaluate it more fully.

PERSONALITY INVENTORY FOR YOUTH

The Personality Inventory for Youth (PIY; Lachar & Gruber, 1995a, 1995b), a 270-item self-report, is a companion measure to the Personality Inventory for Children (PIC), for use with children and adolescents from ages 10 to 18 years. Items are written at a third-grade reading level. The PIY has nine clinical scales and four validity scales. The nine clinical scales are further divided into two or three subscales (see Table 6-12). The PIY also has 87 items, designated as Critical Items, to help in the assessment of psychopathology. The PIY takes about 30 to 60 minutes to complete.

Scores

The PIY uses a true/false response format. It can be hand scored by the examiner, scored by personal computer, or computer scored by the test publisher. Both computer scoring procedures provide a comprehensive interpretive report. Raw scores are converted to T scores ($M = 50$, $SD = 10$). Norms are provided for males and females.

Standardization

The PIY was standardized in 1991 and 1992 on a stratified sample of 2,327 students from grades 4 to 12. The 1987 U.S. Census data were used to match the sample. The sample, drawn from five states, was 46% male and 54% female, with 74% Euro American. In addition, there was a clinical standardization sample of 1,178 adolescents.

Reliability

Internal consistency reliabilities for the nine clinical scales range from .71 to .90 ($Mdn \ r_{xx} = .82$) in the regular education sample and from .74 to .92 ($Mdn \ r_{xx} = .85$) in the clinical sample. Internal consistency reliabilities for the subscales range from .40 to .79 ($Mdn \ r_{xx} = .70$) in the regular education sample and from .44 to .84 ($Mdn \ r_{xx} = .73$) in the clinical sample. Test-retest reliabilities for the clinical scales ranged from .81 to .91 ($Mdn \ r_{tt} = .85$) in a sample of 129 adolescents in a school setting retested over a 7- to 10-day interval and from .76 to .91 ($Mdn \ r_{tt} = .82$) in a clinical sample of 86 adolescents retested over a 7-day interval.

Validity

Criterion-related validity is satisfactory to good, as demonstrated by low to moderate correlations between the PIY and

Table 6-12
Scales and Subscales on the Personality Inventory for Youth

Scale	Subscales
Cognitive Impairment	Poor Achievement and Memory Inadequate Abilities Learning Problems
Impulsivity and Distractibility	Brashness Distractibility Impulsivity
Delinquency	Antisocial Behavior Dyscontrol Noncompliance
Family Dysfunction	Parent-Child Conflict Parent Maladjustment Marital Discord
Reality Distortion	Feelings of Alienation Hallucinations and Delusions
Somatic Concern	Psychosomatic Syndrome Muscular Tension and Anxiety Preoccupation with Disease
Psychological Discomfort	Fear and Worry Depression Sleep Disturbance
Social Withdrawal	Social Introversion Isolation
Social Skills Deficits	Limited Peer Status Conflict with Peers
Validity	—
Inconsistency	—
Dissimulation	—
Defensiveness	—

the MMPI in a group of 152 adolescents from the clinical sample. Further evidence for acceptable criterion-related validity was provided by moderate correlations with other measures of adjustment in a clinical sample of 50 females and 29 males.

Comment on the PIY

The PIY evaluates a number of domains, such as Family Dysfunction, which are useful in understanding the problems of adolescents. Because the PIY scales were developed by "factor-guided" procedures, the content of each scale and subscale needs to be carefully examined to determine whether elevated scores were caused by items consistent with the scale description. Overall, reliability and validity are good. A comprehensive score and interpretive report are available.

STUDENT BEHAVIOR SURVEY

The Student Behavior Survey (SBS; Lachar, Wingenfeld, Kline, & Gruber, 2000) is a teacher-completed, 102-item survey of student behavior. The SBS is designed for kindergarten to twelfth grade or from ages 5 to 18 years. Items cover student achievement, academic and social skills, parent cooperation, and emotional and behavioral adjustment. The SBS contains three sections, with a total of 14 scales (see Table 6-13), and can be completed in about 15 minutes. To complete the SBS, teachers use an answer sheet provided by the test publisher. Scoring can be done by hand. The Manual provides interpretive guidelines for each scale. The SBS is designed to be used as a screening measure and not for making diagnostic decisions.

Scores

On 13 of the 14 scales, items are scored on a 4-point scale: 1 = never, 2 = seldom, 3 = sometimes, and 4 = usually. Academic Performance is scored on a 5-point scale: 1 = deficient, 2 = below average, 3 = average, 4 = above average, and 5 = superior. Raw scores are converted into T scores ($M = 50$, $SD = 10$) for all 14 scales. Norms are provided for males and females across two age bands (5 to 11 years and 12 to 18 years). There are no section scores or total score. High scores on the Academic Resources section indicate positive qualities, whereas high scores on the Adjustment Problems and Disruptive Behavior sections indicate negative qualities and

problematic behavior, suggesting that a more in-depth assessment is needed.

Standardization

The SBS was standardized from 1994 to 1999 on a regular education sample and on a clinically and educationally referred sample. The regular education sample consisted of 2,612 cases that were generally representative of the 1998 U.S. Census data. Stratification variables were gender, age, ethnic background, geographic region, and parents' education (as an index of SES). However, parents whose educational level was higher than that of the population were overrepresented in the sample (35.2% versus 26.9% in the 4 years or more of college category). Teachers participating in the standardization were from 22 schools in 11 states. The clinically and educationally referred sample consisted of 1,315 cases obtained from 41 cities in 17 states.

Reliability

In the regular education sample, internal consistency reliabilities range from .86 to .95 (Mdn $r_{xx} = .89$). In the clinically and educationally referred sample, they range from .85 to .95 (Mdn $r_{xx} = .89$).

Test-retest reliabilities for four samples retested over 28.5 weeks, 11.4 weeks, 1.7 weeks, and 2.1 weeks (N of 49, 56, 52, and 31, respectively) range from .29 to .94 (Mdn $r_{tt} = .80$). The Manual does not indicate whether the test-retest samples were from the regular education group or from the clinically and educationally referred group.

Interrater reliabilities range from .44 to .91 (Mdn $r_{rr} = .76$) for two teachers who rated 30 regular education students and from .56 to .93 (Mdn $r_{rr} = .74$) for two teachers who rated 30 special education students.

Validity

Content validity is satisfactory, as items generally correlate more highly with their home scale than with other scales. Construct validity receives some support from a factor analysis that yielded three factors with the clinically and educationally referred sample. The Manual, however, does not report a factor analysis for the regular education sample. Convergent validity and discriminant validity are satisfactory, as the SBS correlates more highly with similar measures than with different measures. The SBS also discriminates between different types of groups.

Comment on the SBS

The SBS must be used with caution until further research is reported. Some scales have low test-retest reliabilities and interrater reliabilities, and no information is provided about re-

Table 6-13
Student Behavior Survey Sections and Scales

Section	Scales
Academic Resources	Academic Performance Academic Habits Social Skills Parent Participation
Adjustment Problems	Health Concerns Emotional Distress Unusual Behavior Social Problems Verbal Aggression Physical Aggression Behavior Problems
Disruptive Behavior	Attention-Deficit/ Hyperactivity Oppositional Defiant Conduct Problems

liability for the individual age levels. However, validity is satisfactory.

REVISED BEHAVIOR PROBLEM CHECKLIST

The 89-item Revised Behavior Problem Checklist (RBPC; Quay & Peterson, 1996) is an updated and expanded version of the Behavior Problem Checklist (BPC). The RBPC has six scales: Conduct Disorder, Socialized Aggression, Attention Problems–Immaturity, Anxiety-Withdrawal, Psychotic Behavior, and Motor Tension–Excess. The RBPC is for use by parents and teachers of children and adolescents ages 5 to 18 years and requires about 15 to 20 minutes to complete.

Scores

Items are rated, based on the child's current problems, on a 3-point scale (0 = not a problem, 1 = mild problem, 2 = severe problem). Raw scores are converted to T scores ($M = 50$, $SD = 10$).

Standardization

The standardization group consisted of 972 students in kindergarten to eighth grade from schools in three states, plus 270 seriously emotionally disturbed students in kindergarten to twelfth grade from a school district in Florida. For the regular education sample, norms are provided by grade and gender, with relatively small sample sizes (e.g., N of 53 and 69 for the seventh- and eighth-grade norm groups, respectively). Similarly, there are low numbers of students with emotional disturbance in the older age group (Ns of 29 males and 22 females in the seventh to twelfth grades). The standardization sample is described as a "convenience" sample and was not matched to U.S. Census data. Although the date for the collection of standardization data is not provided, the data appear to have been collected in the early and mid 1980s. The school sample was estimated to be approximately 90% Euro American.

Reliability

Internal consistency reliabilities range from $r_{xx} = .68$ to .95 ($Mdn\ r_{xx} = .89$) for the six scales in a sample of 294 children in regular education. Interrater reliabilities in a sample of 172 developmentally delayed children rated by their teachers range from .53 to .85 ($Mdn\ r_{rr} = .58$). Interrater reliabilities between mothers and fathers for 70 children range from .55 to .93 ($Mdn\ r_{rr} = .72$). Test-retest reliabilities for 149 children in grades 1 to 6 rated by their teachers over a 2-month interval range from .49 to .83 ($Mdn\ r_{tt} = .66$).

Validity

Criterion validity is satisfactory, as noted by high correlations (range of .63 to .97) between the RBPC and similar scales.

Copyright © 1999 by John P. Wood.

Discriminant validity is satisfactory, as shown by significant differences between clinical and normal samples for males and females. Construct validity is supported by acceptable correlations between the RBPC and behavioral observations and between the RBPC and peer nominations of aggression, withdrawal, and likability in a sample of 34 children.

Comment on the RBPC

The RBPC is a major revision of the BPC, the latter being one of the first contemporary standardized rating scales for the assessment of behavior problems in children. The RBPC evaluates relevant problems of children and adolescents, although it does not provide specific diagnostic formulations and focuses primarily on externalizing problems, such as conduct disorder, aggression, attention, and motoric excesses. However, caution should be used in the interpretation of standard scores because they are based on small sample sizes for some groups. Although the instrument is presented as a parent and teacher rating scale, norms are provided for teachers only.

REYNOLDS ADOLESCENT ADJUSTMENT SCREENING INVENTORY

The Reynolds Adolescent Adjustment Screening Inventory (RAASI; Reynolds, 2001) is a 32-item rapid-screening self-report measure of adjustment, for use by adolescents ages 12 to 19 years. The RAASI provides scores for two externalizing problems and two internalizing problems, as well as total adjustment. It takes about 5 minutes to complete and requires a third-grade reading level. The RAASI has five scales: Antisocial Behavior, Anger Control Problems, Emotional Distress, Positive Self, and Adjustment Total.

Scores

The RAASI items use a 3-point scale (never or almost never, sometimes, nearly all the time). Scoring is with a self-scoring carbonless answer sheet. Raw scores are converted into T scores ($M = 50$, $SD = 10$) and percentile ranks. Norms are provided for the total sample and for gender and age groups (ages 12 to 14 years and ages 15 to 19 years).

Standardization

The RAASI was standardized on a stratified sample of 1,827 adolescents, ages 12 to 19 years. The sample was drawn from 1989 to 1991 from eight states and closely matched the 1990 U.S. Census data for age, gender, and ethnicity. In addition, there was a clinical sample of 506 adolescents from 31 psychiatric inpatient and outpatient settings in 22 states, representing a wide range of *DSM–IV–TR* disorders. An additional 1,007 adolescents from school settings were used in the RAASI reliability and validity studies.

Reliability

Internal consistency reliabilities for the first four scales range from .71 to .91 (Mdn $r_{xx} = .82$) in the school-based sample and from .68 to .91 (Mdn $r_{xx} = .83$) in the clinical sample. The internal consistency reliability is .91 for the Adjustment Total scale in both the school-based and the clinical sample. Test-retest reliabilities in a sample of 64 adolescents in a school setting retested over a 2-week interval range from .83 to .89 (Mdn $r_{tt} = .85$) for the first four scales. For the Adjustment Total scale, the test-retest reliability is .89.

Validity

Construct validity is satisfactory, as noted by a factor analysis that supports the internalizing and externalizing dimensions of the RAASI. Criterion-related validity is satisfactory, as noted by acceptable correlations between the RAASI and APS Clinical Disorder Scales, the MMPI, and various other self-report and clinical interview measures. Discriminant validity was supported by low correlations between the RAASI and measures of intelligence, achievement, and social desirability and by significant differences between the school and clinical samples.

Comment on the RAASI

The RAASI shows good reliability and validity, takes about 5 minutes to complete, and serves as a screening measure of adjustment problems in adolescents. It can be individually or group administered, and the results can be followed up with more in-depth measures as warranted.

THINKING THROUGH THE ISSUES

1. For what types of problems are parents or teachers a preferred source of assessment information, and for what types of problems are children or adolescents better reporters?
2. How does level of reading ability influence the selection of self-report measures?
3. How do measures of behavioral, social, and emotional competencies differ from measures of intelligence, achievement, and language?

SUMMARY

1. Measures of behavioral, social, and emotional competencies in children and adolescents are useful for school and mental health evaluations and for formulating and evaluating intervention programs.

Background Considerations

2. Objective measures contain items that are relatively clear and structured, require responses that are limited and relatively clear in meaning, and use scoring procedures that are precise and straightforward.
3. Projective measures contain ambiguous stimuli—such as inkblots or pictures of situations or people—that permit the examinee to project covert aspects of his or her personality onto the stimuli.
4. In objective measures of behavioral, social, and emotional competencies, various strategies are used to develop items and profiles. These include factor analysis, empirical keying, theoretical constructs, and content analysis.
5. Scores obtained from measures of behavioral, social, and emotional competencies reflect the complex interaction of several factors.
6. The same scale names in different measures of behavioral, social, and emotional competencies may cover the same or different behaviors, and, conversely, different scale names may cover different or similar behaviors.
7. When informants, such as parents or teachers, complete a measure of behavioral, social, and emotional competencies, they make judgments about a child's functioning.
8. Because their judgments are subject to bias and distortion, informants' credibility must be carefully examined.
9. Informants differ as to their familiarity with the child, sensitivity and tolerance for behavior problems, personality, expectations, comfort with various test formats, and willingness to use certain rating scale positions.
10. The reliability and validity of ratings may be affected by the specificity of the rating task.

11. Because parents and teachers are likely to see different aspects of a child, information from both sources is needed to obtain a comprehensive picture of the child.

12. Respondents (examinees or informants) may deliberately or unknowingly slant their replies to create a certain picture.

13. Test developers usually try to control for response styles by varying the item content, measuring the respondent's tendency to answer items in a socially desirable direction and then adjusting scores to take this tendency into account.

14. You should routinely consider whether the respondent's responses reflect an underlying response style.

15. Objective measures permit information to be obtained under standard conditions.

16. Difficulties may be encountered with the use of objective measures because items, no matter how clearly stated, may be misinterpreted.

17. Measures of behavioral, social, and emotional competencies provide little information about the dynamics underlying a response.

18. In spite of their limitations, objective measures can be valuable. They are economical to use, can be scored objectively by hand (and often computer), and in general have good reliability and validity.

19. Direct observational methods and measures of behavioral, social, and emotional competencies do not always provide congruent data because they are based on different behavior samples. However, both are useful assessment measures.

20. Before using a measure of behavioral, social, and emotional competencies, consider the representativeness of the norm group, reliability and validity of the measure, reliability of the informants, scope, structure, and clinical utility.

The Internalizing-Externalizing Continuum

21. The internalizing-externalizing continuum is a useful way of viewing behavioral, social, and emotional disorders.

22. Externalizing disorders of childhood and adolescence are characterized by overt behavioral excesses or disturbances and are generally distressing to the child's parents, teachers, peers, and others.

23. Internalizing disorders usually are covert and not easily observable, and thus present evaluation and identification difficulties. Although they typically are distressing to the child or adolescent, they are less likely than externalizing disorders to come to the attention of parents and teachers.

24. Children with multiple disorders are said to suffer from comorbidity (co-existing conditions).

Measures of Behavioral, Social, and Emotional Competencies

25. The measures of behavioral, social, and emotional competencies surveyed in this chapter are designed to assess internalizing and externalizing problems, as well as a broad range of other competencies.

26. The primary sources of information for these measures are parents, teachers, and the children themselves.

27. Parents and teachers can evaluate externalizing disorders better than internalizing disorders because the former are more easily observable than the latter.

28. Children and adolescents are better reporters of internalizing disorders than are parents and teachers, given the covert nature of these problems.

29. Norms are best when there is a large, nationally stratified standardization sample that includes equal numbers of males and females and when gender and age norms are provided in addition to combined total sample norms.

30. It is critical that the child or adolescent have the reading level required for self-report measures.

Adolescent Psychopathology Scale and Adolescent Psychopathology Scale–Short Form

31. The APS and the APS–SF are self-report measures that evaluate several *DSM-IV–TR* disorders, as well as other social and emotional problems, in children ages 12 to 19 years. A computer scoring program provides a detailed score report. Both forms require about a third-grade reading level. The APS takes about 45 to 60 minutes to complete, while the APS–SF takes about 15 to 20 minutes to complete. Both forms have good reliability and validity.

Behavior Assessment System for Children

32. The BASC is designed to evaluate psychological problems in children and adolescents ages 4 to 18 years. The Teacher and Parent forms each take about 10 to 20 minutes to complete, while the Self-Report form takes about 30 minutes to complete. It has moderate to good reliability and validity and provides for assessment of children and adolescents by multiple informants.

Child Behavior Checklist, Teacher's Report Form, and Youth Self-Report

33. The CBCL, which is designed for parents of children and adolescents ages 4 to 18 years, measures nine factorially derived scales and internalizing and externalizing factors. It takes about 10 to 15 minutes to complete, has variable reliability and validity, and is best suited as a screening measure to evaluate internalizing problems in children and adolescents.

34. The TRF, which is designed for teachers of children ages 6 to 18 years, has eight factorially derived scales and measures internalizing and externalizing factors. It takes about 10 to 15 minutes to complete, has variable reliability and validity, and is most appropriate in screening for externalizing problems in children and adolescents.

35. The YSR, which is designed for use with adolescents ages 11 to 18 years of age, requires a fifth-grade reading level. It has nine scales and provides internalizing and externalizing factor scores. It takes approximately 30 minutes to complete and has variable reliability and validity.

Conners' Rating Scales–Revised

36. The CRS–R includes parent, teacher, and self-report measures, with long and short forms available for each version. The parent and teacher versions cover children ages 3 to 17 years, while the self-report version covers ages 12 to 17 years. Most of the scales focus on externalizing problems and disorders. The time required to complete these measures varies with the version. All

forms show good reliability and adequate validity and are particularly useful in the evaluation of externalizing problems in children.

Devereux Scales of Mental Disorder

37. The DSMD is a behavior rating scale that can be completed by a parent or teacher. It is designed for ages 5 to 18 years. The DSMD covers six problem domains in children and adolescents. It takes about 15 minutes to complete and has good reliability but limited validity.

Millon Adolescent Personality Inventory

38. The MAPI is a self-report scale for use with adolescents ages 13 to 19 years. It has eight Personality Style scales, eight Expressed Concerns scales, and four Behavioral Correlates scales. It requires about 30 minutes to complete. The test has moderate reliability and weak validity.

Minnesota Multiphasic Personality Inventory-Adolescent

39. The MMPI–A is a revision and downward extension of the MMPI, but maintains most of the items from the original adult scale developed in the 1940s. It is designed for use with adolescents ages 14 to 18 years. It has 10 basic scales, 7 validity scales, and 15 content scales. It requires seventh-grade reading ability and takes about 60 to 90 minutes to complete. The test has moderate reliability and validity.

Personality Inventory for Children–Second Edition

40. The PIC–2 is a parent-completed measure of child and adolescent personality and psychopathology for children and adolescents ages 5 to 19 years. It provides scores on three validity scales, nine adjustment scales, and 21 adjustment subscales. It takes about 40 minutes to complete. It has variable reliability and adequate validity.

Personality Inventory for Youth

41. The PIY, a self-report, is a companion measure to the PIC for use with children and adolescents in grades 4 to 12. Items are written at a third-grade reading level. It has nine clinical scales, each with two or three subscales and four validity scales. It takes about 30 to 60 minutes to complete. The inventory has good reliability and validity.

Student Behavior Survey

42. The SBS is a teacher-completed, 102-item survey of student behavior for children and adolescents ages 5 to 18 years. It has three sections, with three, four, or seven scales associated with each section. It has variable reliability and adequate validity.

Revised Behavior Problem Checklist

43. The RBPC is an updated and expanded version of the BPC. It has six scales: Conduct Disorder, Socialized Aggression, Attention Problems–Immaturity, Anxiety-Withdrawal, Psychotic Behavior, and Motor Tension–Excess. The checklist is for use by parents and teachers of children and adolescents ages 5 to 18 years and requires about 15 to 20 minutes to complete. Reliability and validity are adequate.

Reynolds Adolescent Adjustment Screening Inventory

44. The RAASI is a rapid-screening self-report measure of adjustment, for use by adolescents ages 12 to 19 years. It measures two externalizing problems (Antisocial Behaviors and Anger Control Problems) and two internalizing problems (Emotional Distress and Positive Self), takes about 5 minutes to complete, and requires a third-grade reading level. It has good reliability and validity.

KEY TERMS, CONCEPTS, AND NAMES

Objective measures (p. 164)
Projective measures (p. 164)
Informant (p. 165)
Response styles (p. 165)
Response sets (p. 165)
Faking-good response set (p. 165)
Faking-bad response set (p. 165)
Acquiescence response set (p. 166)
Deviance response set (p. 166)
Social desirability response set (p. 166)
Representativeness of the norm group (p. 167)
Reliability and validity (p. 167)
Reliability of informants (p. 167)
Scope (p. 167)
Structure (p. 167)
Clinical utility (p. 167)
Externalizing disorders (p. 167)
Internalizing disorders (p. 167)
Adolescent Psychopathology Scale (p. 169)
Adolescent Psychopathology Scale–Short Form (p. 169)
Behavior Assessment System for Children (p. 169)
Child Behavior Checklist (p. 172)
Teacher Report Form (p. 172)
Youth Self-Report (p. 172)
Conners' Rating Scales–Revised (p. 174)
Devereux Scales of Mental Disorder (p. 176)
Millon Adolescent Personality Inventory (p. 177)
Minnesota Multiphasic Personality Inventory–Adolescent (p. 178)
Personality Inventory for Children–Second Edition (p. 179)
Personality Inventory for Youth (p. 182)
Student Behavior Survey (p. 183)
Revised Behavior Problem Checklist (p. 184)
Reynolds Adolescent Adjustment Screening Inventory (p. 184)

STUDY QUESTIONS

1. Discuss the differences between objective measures and projective measures.
2. Discuss the factors involved in the construction of objective measures of behavioral, social, and emotional competencies.

3. Discuss factors to consider in evaluating informants.
4. Describe some basic assumptions underlying objective measures of behavioral, social, and emotional competencies.
5. Describe several criteria used to evaluate objective measures of behavioral, social, and emotional competencies.
6. Discuss the distinction between internalizing and externalizing disorders.
7. Discuss each of the following measures. Include in your discussion a description of the measure, scales, scores, standardization, reliability, and validity, and provide an overall evaluation of the measure.

   Adolescent Psychopathology Scale
   Adolescent Psychopathology Scale–Short Form
   Behavior Assessment System for Children
   Child Behavior Checklist
   Teacher Report Form

   Youth Self-Report
   Conners' Rating Scales–Revised
   Devereux Scales of Mental Disorders
   Millon Adolescent Personality Inventory
   Minnesota Multiphasic Personality Inventory–Adolescent
   Personality Inventory for Children–Second Edition
   Personality Inventory for Youth
   Student Behavior Survey
   Revised Behavior Problem Checklist
   Reynolds Adolescent Adjustment Screening Inventory

8. Compare and contrast the following measures of psychopathology: Adolescent Psychopathology Scale, Youth Self-Report, Millon Adolescent Personality Inventory, Minnesota Multiphasic Personality Inventory–Adolescent, and Personality Inventory for Children–Second Edition.

7

ASSESSMENT OF ADAPTIVE BEHAVIOR

Talents are best nurtured in solitude: character is best formed in the stormy billows of the world.

—Goethe

Goals and Objectives

This chapter is designed to enable you to do the following:

- Understand the concept of adaptive behavior

- Describe and evaluate individual measures of adaptive behavior

Adaptive behavior scales assist clinicians in making diagnoses, formulating discharge plans, and developing interventions. Adaptive behavior scales play an important role in the assessment of children with developmental disabilities and children with mental retardation in particular. Before we review the major instruments designed to assess adaptive behavior in children and adults, we will look at the definition of adaptive behavior and some psychometric considerations involved in the measurement of adaptive behavior.

DEFINITION OF ADAPTIVE BEHAVIOR

The American Association on Mental Retardation (AAMR, 1992) defines *adaptive behavior* as the effectiveness with which individuals meet the standards of personal independence and social responsibility expected of individuals of their age and cultural group. The assessment of adaptive behavior focuses on two major issues: (a) the degree to which individuals are able to function and maintain themselves independently and (b) the degree to which they meet the culturally imposed demands of personal and social responsibility. Adaptive behavior, therefore, reflects a person's competence in meeting independent needs and satisfying the social demands of his or her environment. (See Chapter 13 for a discussion of adaptive behavior in relation to the definition of mental retardation.)

Adaptive behavior is best viewed as having a multifactorial structure, such as the following (Schalock, 1999):

- Motor or physical skills (e.g., skills in gross- and fine-motor behavior, ambulating, basic eating, toileting)
- Independent living skills (e.g., skills in performing household chores, dressing, bathing, preparing food, washing dishes)
- Cognitive, communication, and academic skills (e.g., skills in receptive and expressive language, reading and writing, handling money)
- Social competence skills (e.g., skills in establishing friendships, interacting with others, social reasoning, social comprehension)

Adaptive behavior is difficult to define for several reasons. First, adaptive behavior is not independent of intelligence. For example, a reasonable estimate of the correlation between adaptive behavior and intelligence would be in the .30s to .40s (Editorial Board, 1996; Harrison & Oakland, 2000). Both adaptive behavior and intelligence enable the individual to meet the natural and social demands of her or his environment (see Chapter 5 in *Assessment of Children: Cognitive Applications* for definitions of intelligence).

Second, the number of dimensions associated with adaptive behavior is unknown. The 10 areas proposed by the AAMR have not been shown to be independent factors (see Table 7-1 later in the chapter). Furthermore, several of the AAMR adaptive skill areas are not relevant to the assessment of adaptive behavior among preschool and young children.

Third, what is accepted as adaptive behavior at one age may not be acceptable at another age. Adaptive behavior, for

Copyright © 2000, John P. Wood. Reprinted with permission.

example, reflects maturation during preschool years, academic performance during school years, and social and economic independence during early adulthood.

Fourth, what constitutes adaptive behavior is variable, not absolute, and depends on the demands of a given environment. For example, a child may show acceptable adaptive behavior at school but not at home or when living in a small town but not when living in a metropolitan area.

Finally, different measures of adaptive behavior may give different results (Goldstein, Smith, Waldrep, & Inderbitzen, 1987; Middleton, Keene, & Brown, 1990). Even different forms of the same adaptive behavior measure may yield different results (Sholle-Martin & Alessi, 1988). Results vary because of differences in response formats, content and technical adequacy, standardization groups, times when the standardization was conducted, and raters.

An assessment of adaptive behavior must consider the child's physical skills, cognitive ability, affect, motivation, culture, socioeconomic status, family (including parents, siblings, extended family, and the expectations of family members), and environment. Consequently, adaptive behavior represents the interaction of personal, cognitive, social, and situational variables.

PSYCHOMETRIC CONSIDERATIONS

The measurement of adaptive behavior usually depends on information obtained from a parent, a teacher, or another informant. Informants, as noted in Chapter 6, differ as to their (a) familiarity with the child, (b) ability to provide reliable and valid information about the child, (c) sensitivity to and tolerance for behavior problems, (d) personality, (e) expectations, (f) tendency to agree or disagree with items, (g) preference for using extreme or intermediate positions on rating scales, and (h) frame of reference used to evaluate the child. Difficulties in any of these areas may yield invalid scores, especially when informants lack appropriate information or distort their responses.

Ratings of adaptive behavior depend on the informant's ability to observe the child's behavior. If the behavior is present in the child's repertoire but not observed by the informant, the child will not receive credit for that behavior.

Informants differ among themselves in their ratings of children, and informants' ratings differ from children's self-ratings. An analysis of 269 studies that compared informants' ratings on behavioral checklists with those of other informants and with children's self-ratings found the following relationships (Achenbach, 1993):

- A mean r of .60 between informants who occupied similar roles in relation to the child (e.g., caregivers versus caregivers, teachers versus teachers, mental health workers versus mental health workers)
- A mean r of .28 between informants who occupied different roles in relation to the child (e.g., parents versus teachers, parents versus mental health workers)
- A mean r of .22 between children's self-ratings and ratings by others (e.g., children versus parents, children versus teachers, children versus mental health workers)

The relatively low correlations between parent and teacher ratings of adaptive behavior suggest that there is considerable situational specificity in children's adaptive behavior. In other words, behavioral checklists yield relatively independent information about children's adaptive behavior in home and school settings. One implication of the low correlations between parent and teacher ratings of adaptive behavior is that proposed interventions may be inappropriate when information on adaptive behavior comes from a single source or setting. A second implication is that carrying out a complete assessment of adaptive behavior requires obtaining information from a parent *and* a teacher (or aide), as well as conducting systematic behavioral observations (see Chapters 4 and 5). In addition, where feasible, ratings should be obtained from the children themselves.

In evaluating measures of adaptive behavior, use the same criteria as you would for any psychometric measure (see Chapter 4 in *Assessment of Children: Cognitive Applications*). Essentially, you will want to consider (a) the representativeness of the norm group, (b) the measure's reliability, validity, scope, structure, and clinical utility, and (c) the reliability and validity of the informants' ratings and the children's self-ratings.

Following are some measurement concerns surrounding the assessment of adaptive behavior (Jenkinson, 1996):

1. How do the reliability and validity of part scores compare with the reliability and validity of global scores?
2. How did the American Association on Mental Retardation, in its definition of mental retardation, arrive at a criterion of *two deficits* in adaptive behavior rather than *three or more deficits* in adaptive behavior?
3. What do scores on measures of adaptive behavior tell us about the supports the person needs?
4. How much do scores on measures of adaptive behavior reflect how the person functions in a specific environment?
5. How much do scores on measures of adaptive behavior generalize to different environments?
6. How should measures of adaptive behavior be used if they have negatively skewed distributions (i.e., scores drop off sharply at the positive end of the distribution and cluster at the negative end of the distribution)?
7. What is meant by *high* adaptive behavior, particularly in older adolescents and adults?

Jenkinson (1996) concluded that "we should stop treating adaptive behavior as though it is distributed in the same way as intelligence. No amount of technical refinement will compensate for an inadequate or inappropriate theoretical construct" (p. 101). Instead, he proposed that we use a needs-based assessment focusing on "the extent of support required by the individual, rather than the absence of skills and competencies quantified in terms of a standard score" (p. 101).

INFORMAL ASSESSMENT OF ADAPTIVE BEHAVIOR

Table 7-1 provides an informal checklist to assist you in evaluating the 10 adaptive skill areas delineated in the AAMR definition of adaptive behavior. You must consider the child's age in evaluating the skills needed in each adaptive skill area.

VINELAND ADAPTIVE BEHAVIOR SCALES

The Vineland Adaptive Behavior Scales (VABS) assesses the personal and social skills of disabled and nondisabled individuals (Sparrow, Balla, & Cicchetti, 1984). The VABS is a revision of the Vineland Social Maturity Scale published by Doll in 1953. It requires that an informant familiar with the behavior of the referred child either answer behavior-oriented questions posed by an examiner or complete a questionnaire. There are three versions of the VABS: Survey Form, Expanded Form, and Classroom Edition. The Survey and Expanded Forms cover individuals from birth to 18-11 years and older. The Classroom Edition covers individuals from age 3 years to 12-11 years.

The VABS is based on a definition of adaptive behavior as the ability of the individual to perform daily activities required for personal and social sufficiency. Each version of the scale measures adaptive behavior in four domains: Communication, Daily Living Skills, Socialization, and Motor Skills. (The Motor Skills domain covers ages from birth to 5-11 years only.) These four domains combine to form an Adaptive Behavior Composite. The Survey and Expanded Forms also include a Maladaptive Behavior domain.

Table 7-1
Informal Checklist of the 10 AAMR Adaptive Skill Areas

INFORMAL CHECKLIST OF THE 10 AAMR ADAPTIVE SKILL AREAS

Key:

Y (Yes) = Examinee can perform skill at a level appropriate for his or her age.

N (No) = Examinee cannot perform skill at a level appropriate for his or her age.

DK (Don't Know) = Don't know whether examinee can perform skill at a level appropriate for his or her age.

NR (Not Relevant) = This skill is not expected to be performed at the examinee's age level.

Area	Check One			
Communication (Ability to comprehend and express information through symbolic behaviors)				
1. Knows how to comprehend or receive a request.	☐ Y	☐ N	☐ DK	☐ NR
2. Knows how to identify emotions.	☐ Y	☐ N	☐ DK	☐ NR
3. Knows how to write a letter.	☐ Y	☐ N	☐ DK	☐ NR
Other _____	☐ Y	☐ N	☐ DK	☐ NR
Self-Care (Ability to take care of oneself)				
4. Uses utensils properly.	☐ Y	☐ N	☐ DK	☐ NR
5. Dresses self.	☐ Y	☐ N	☐ DK	☐ NR
6. Has adequate grooming.	☐ Y	☐ N	☐ DK	☐ NR
Other _____	☐ Y	☐ N	☐ DK	☐ NR
Home Living (Ability to take care of daily functioning within a home)				
7. Helps with household tasks.	☐ Y	☐ N	☐ DK	☐ NR
8. Communicates needs and choices.	☐ Y	☐ N	☐ DK	☐ NR
9. Is aware of home safety precautions.	☐ Y	☐ N	☐ DK	☐ NR
Other _____	☐ Y	☐ N	☐ DK	☐ NR
Social Skills (Ability to engage in socially appropriate behavior)				
10. Has friends.	☐ Y	☐ N	☐ DK	☐ NR
11. Takes turns in interactions.	☐ Y	☐ N	☐ DK	☐ NR
12. Demonstrates honesty, trustworthiness, and appropriate play.	☐ Y	☐ N	☐ DK	☐ NR
Other _____	☐ Y	☐ N	☐ DK	☐ NR
Community Use (Ability to make use of appropriate community resources)				
13. Uses community facilities.	☐ Y	☐ N	☐ DK	☐ NR
14. Goes shopping.	☐ Y	☐ N	☐ DK	☐ NR
15. Uses public transportation.	☐ Y	☐ N	☐ DK	☐ NR
Other _____	☐ Y	☐ N	☐ DK	☐ NR
Self-Direction (Ability to make choices)				
16. Knows how to follow a schedule.	☐ Y	☐ N	☐ DK	☐ NR
17. Initiates appropriate activities.	☐ Y	☐ N	☐ DK	☐ NR
18. Demonstrates appropriate assertiveness and self-advocacy.	☐ Y	☐ N	☐ DK	☐ NR
Other _____	☐ Y	☐ N	☐ DK	☐ NR

(Continued)

Table 7-1 *(Continued)*

Area	Check One			

Health and Safety (Ability to maintain one's well-being)

19. Eats an appropriate diet.	□ Y	□ N	□ DK	□ NR
20. Identifies illness.	□ Y	□ N	□ DK	□ NR
21. Keeps physically fit.	□ Y	□ N	□ DK	□ NR
Other _____	□ Y	□ N	□ DK	□ NR

Functional Academics (Ability to learn at school)

22. Knows how to read.	□ Y	□ N	□ DK	□ NR
23. Knows how to write.	□ Y	□ N	□ DK	□ NR
24. Knows basic math.	□ Y	□ N	□ DK	□ NR
Other _____	□ Y	□ N	□ DK	□ NR

Leisure (Ability to pursue leisure and recreational activities related to personal preferences)

25. Chooses and initiates activities.	□ Y	□ N	□ DK	□ NR
26. Engages in and enjoys home and community leisure and recreational activities.	□ Y	□ N	□ DK	□ NR
27. Plays socially with others.	□ Y	□ N	□ DK	□ NR
Other _____	□ Y	□ N	□ DK	□ NR

Work (Ability to hold a part- or full-time job or participate in voluntary activity in the community)

28. Is competent on the job.	□ Y	□ N	□ DK	□ NR
29. Has appropriate work skills.	□ Y	□ N	□ DK	□ NR
30. Has appropriate skills related to working and going to work.	□ Y	□ N	□ DK	□ NR
Other _____	□ Y	□ N	□ DK	□ NR

Source: Adapted from AAMR (1992).

Each domain evaluates various adaptive skills (see Table 7-2).

- The Communication domain samples receptive, expressive, and written communication skills.
- The Daily Living Skills domain evaluates personal living habits, domestic task performance, and behavior in the community.
- The Socialization domain focuses on interactions with others, including play, use of free time, and responsibility and sensitivity to others.
- The Motor Skills domain evaluates gross- and fine-motor coordination for children under the age of 6 years.
- The Maladaptive Behavior domain deals with undesirable behaviors that may interfere with adaptive behavior.

The Survey Form contains 297 items administered over a 20- to 60-minute period. The Expanded Form, which takes approximately 60 to 90 minutes to administer, contains 577 items, including the 297 items on the Survey Form. The Ex-panded Form provides a comprehensive measure of adaptive behavior and aids in designing educational, rehabilitative, and treatment programs. The Classroom Edition contains 244 items and provides an assessment of adaptive behavior in the classroom. The child's teacher can complete this form in approximately 20 minutes.

Scores

Items are scored using five categories: 2 = yes, usually, 1 = sometimes, partially, 0 = no, never, N = no opportunity, and DK = don't know. Raw scores are converted to standard scores ($M = 100$, $SD = 15$) for the four adaptive behavior domains and for the Adaptive Behavior Composite, percentile ranks, and age-equivalent scores.

The standard scores for the four adaptive behavior domains range from below 20 to above 160 on all three forms. However, this range is not possible at all ages. For example, at the lowest age levels of the Survey Form (0-0-0 to 0-0-3),

the highest possible standard score is 160+ for all domains, whereas the lowest possible scores are 85 (Communication), 99 (Daily Living Skills), 77 (Socialization), and 85 (Motor Skills). At age 5-0-0, the highest possible standard score is 160+ for Communication, Daily Living Skills, and Socialization, but only 122 for Motor Skills; the lowest possible standard scores are 37 (Communication), 22 (Daily Living), 40 (Socialization), and below 20 (Motor Skills). Finally, at age 18-0-0, the highest possible standard scores are 111 (Communication), 124 (Daily Living), and 116 (Socialization). Uneven ranges of standard scores across the age levels are also found on the Expanded Form and Classroom Edition.

Table B.10 in the Survey Form Manual shows that the distribution of age equivalents for raw scores, while generally uniform, has gaps in the upper ages of the Communication domain. For example, a change of 1 raw-score point from 131 to 132 on Communication represents a change in age-equivalent scores of 15 months (16-6 to 17-9). At the early ages, a change of 1 raw-score point (e.g., from 73 to 74) represents a change in age-equivalent scores of 1 month (4-0 to 4-1). In addition, age equivalents for raw scores for Motor Skills reach a ceiling at age 5-11 years.

Table B.10 in the Expanded Form Manual reveals a similar picture. For example, a change of 1 raw-score point from 262 to 263 on Communication represents a change in age-equivalent scores of 15 months (16-6 to 17-9). At the early ages, a change of 1 raw-score point (e.g., from 166 to 167) represents a change in age-equivalent scores of 1 month (3-5 to 3-6). In addition, age equivalents for raw scores for Motor Skills reach a ceiling at age 5-11 years.

Table B.7 in the Classroom Edition Manual shows that the distribution of age equivalents for raw scores has gaps in the upper age levels of both the Communication and the Socialization domain. For example, a change of 1 raw-score point

from 121 to 122 on Communication represents a change in age-equivalent scores of 15 months (14-9 to 16-0). At the early ages, a change of 1 raw-score point (e.g., from 54 to 55) represents a change in age-equivalent scores of 1 month (3-0 to 3-1). In addition, age equivalents for raw scores for Motor Skills reach a ceiling at age 5-11 years.

Standardization

The standardization sample for the Survey and Expanded Forms generally matched the population as described by the 1980 U.S. Census data. The ages of the 3,000 individuals in the sample ranged from newborn to 18 years. Stratification variables included sex, race or ethnic group, geographical region, community size, and parents' educational level. Norms are provided for ages birth to 18 years. From birth through 1 year, the norms are broken down into 1-month increments; from 2 to 5 years, into 2-month increments; from 6 to 8 years, into 3-month increments; and from 9 to 18 years, into 4-month increments. Supplemental norms are provided for children with mental retardation, emotional disturbance, or physical disabilities who are in residential facilities and for adults with mental retardation who are in nonresidential facilities.

The normative sample for the Classroom Edition consisted of 3,000 students, ages 3 to 12 years, selected to conform to the 1980 U.S. Census data, using the same stratification variables as for the other forms. However, the attempt to obtain a representative sample for the Classroom Edition was not entirely successful (Baily-Richardson, 1988). First, children whose parents were at the lower levels of educational attainment (which was used to measure SES) were seriously underrepresented in the standardization sample. For example, although the U.S. Census data indicated that 20% of adults

Table 7-2
Vineland Adaptive Behavior Scales
Domains and Subdomains

Domain	Subdomain
Communication	Receptive
	Expressive
	Written
Daily Living Skills	Personal
	Domestic
	Community
Socialization	Interpersonal Relationships
	Play and Leisure Time
	Coping Skills
Motor Skills	Gross
	Fine
Maladaptive Behavior	—

Source: Adapted from Sparrow, Balla, and Cicchetti (1984).

had less than a high school education, the standardization sample contained only 9% with this level of education. High school graduates were also underrepresented (33% instead of 40%), and those with some college education were overrepresented (57% instead of 39%). Second, Hispanics were underrepresented. The U.S. Census indicated that Hispanics made up about 9% of the population, but they made up only 4.6% of the norm group. Third, the proportions of urban and rural participants were not in keeping with the U.S. Census data, with urban participants overrepresented (54% to 28%) and rural participants underrepresented (7% instead of 29%).

Reliability

Median internal consistency reliabilities for the five domains on the Survey Form range from .83 to .90 (*Mdn* r_{xx} = .86). Internal consistency reliabilities for the Adaptive Behavior Composite range from .89 to .98 (*Mdn* r_{xx} = .94). Median test-retest reliabilities for a sample of 484 individuals retested over 2 to 4 weeks ranged from r_{tt} = .81 to .88 (*Mdn* r_{tt} = .85) for the five domains. For the Adaptive Behavior Composite, *Mdn* r_{tt} = .88. Interrater reliabilities for 160 parents reinterviewed over 1 to 14 days ranged from r_{rr} = .62 to .78 (*Mdn* r_{rr} = .74) for the five domains. The median interrater reliability for the Adaptive Behavior Composite is .74.

Internal consistency reliabilities for the Expanded Form were estimated based on the Survey Form and adjusted by the Spearman-Brown formula. Median internal consistency reliabilities for the five domains on the Expanded Form range from .83 to .90 (*Mdn* r_{xx} = .86). Internal consistency reliabilities for the Adaptive Behavior Composite, again estimated

based on the Survey Form, range from .89 to .98 (*Mdn* r_{xx} = .94). The Manual indicates that test-retest reliability and interrater reliability studies were not conducted for the Expanded Form.

Median internal consistency reliabilities for the four domains on the Classroom Edition range from .80 to .95 (*Mdn* r_{xx} = .93). Internal consistency reliabilities for the Adaptive Behavior Composite range from .96 to .98 (*Mdn* r_{xx} = .98). The Manual for the Classroom Edition does not report any test-retest reliability or interrater reliability studies for the Classroom Edition.

Validity

The three forms of the VABS have satisfactory construct, content, and criterion-related validity. For example, the Manual reports that scores increase with age, a factor analysis generally supports the various domains, the items measure adaptive behavior, and the forms have satisfactory correlations with other measures of adaptive behavior. Other research, however, indicates that the VABS has only a single factor (Personal Responsibility) for children between 4-0 and 6-11 years (Roberts, McCoy, Reidy, & Crucitti, 1993).

Comment on the VABS

The three forms of the Vineland Adaptive Behavior Scales are useful tools for the assessment of adaptive behavior. The structured interview format is valuable, but takes some effort to learn. The publisher offers a helpful training tape. However, in using the VABS, attention must be given to the following issues.

First, the standardization procedures resulted in serious underrepresentation of Hispanic students, rural students, and students whose parents attained a minimal level of education.

Second, there are difficulties associated with framing questions, eliciting appropriate responses, and scoring responses (Oakland & Houchins, 1985). Some items require knowledge that informants may not possess. For example, in the Communication domain, informants must tell whether the child says at least 100 recognizable words, uses irregular plurals, and prints or writes at least 10 words from memory.

Third, the Manuals fail to report test-retest and interrater reliability studies for the Expanded Form and Classroom Edition.

Fourth, the standard scores are not normally distributed, and the range of standard scores is not the same at all ages or across all domains. Therefore, you must know the available standard-score ranges if you are to make appropriate interpretations. For example, *a child who obtains a Communication standard score of 160 at the age of 5 years and a Communication standard score of 111 at the age of 18 years has not lost 49 points. This is purely an artifact of the instrument—* the highest Communication standard score possible at the age of 18 years is 111. The skewed and uneven distribution of standard scores means that, when individuals have above-average adaptive behavior skills, it will be difficult to evaluate them over time or to evaluate their differential performance in adaptive skill areas.

Fifth, caution must be used in comparing age-equivalent scores among the four adaptive behavior domains.

Finally, only three (Communication, Daily Living Skills, and Socialization) of the 10 adaptive behavior skills specified by the AAMR are measured by the VABS.

AAMR ADAPTIVE BEHAVIOR SCALE–SCHOOL: SECOND EDITION

The AAMR Adaptive Behavior Scale–School: Second Edition (ABS–S:2; Nihira, Leland, & Lambert, 1993) is an adaptive behavior scale designed to measure children's personal and community independence and social skills and adjustment. It is for use with children ages 3 to 21 years who may have mental retardation. The ABS–S:2 assesses two types of competencies: behavioral and affective (see Table 7-3). The 1993 version is a revision of a scale first published in 1975.

Part I of the ABS–S:2 covers 9 behavioral domains and 18 subdomains and has three factors. It is organized along developmental lines and measures behaviors and habits needed to maintain personal independence in daily living. Part II covers 7 domains and has two factors. It focuses primarily on maladaptive behavior related to personality and behavior disorders.

The five factors are as follows:

Part I

- *Personal Self-Sufficiency* (items from Independent Functioning and Physical Development domains)
- *Community Self-Sufficiency* (items from Independent Functioning, Economic Activity, Language Development, Numbers and Time, and Prevocational/Vocational Activity domains)
- *Personal-Social Responsibility* (items from Prevocational/ Vocational Activity, Self-Direction, Responsibility, and Socialization domains)

Part II

- *Social Adjustment* (items from Social Behavior, Conformity, and Trustworthiness domains)
- *Personal Adjustment* (items from Stereotyped and Hyperactive Behavior and Self-Abusive Behavior domains)

The ABS–S:2 takes approximately 15 to 30 minutes to administer; according to the Manual, persons with minimal training can administer it. Two methods can be used to administer the scale. In the *first-person assessment method,* an informant completes the scale by himself or herself. The informant must be familiar with the referred individual and have had enough professional training to make appropriate

Table 7-3
AAMR Adaptive Behavior Scale–School: Second Edition Domains and Subdomains

Domain	Subdomain
Part I Independent Functioning	Eating Toilet Use Cleanliness Appearance Care of Clothing Dressing and Undressing Travel Other Independent Functioning
Physical Development	Sensory Development Motor Development
Economic Activity	Money Handling and Budgeting Shopping Skills
Language Development	Expression Verbal Comprehension Social Language Development
Numbers and Time	—
Prevocational/Vocational Activity	—
Self-Direction	Initiative Perseverance Leisure Time
Responsibility	—
Socialization	—
Part II Social Behavior	—
Conformity	—
Trustworthiness	—
Stereotyped and Hyperactive Behavior	—
Self-Abusive Behavior	—
Social Engagement	—
Disturbing Interpersonal Behavior	—

Source: Adapted from Lambert, Nihira, and Leland (1993).

ratings. In the *interview method,* which is most useful with caregivers, the examiner completes the scale based on information provided by the caregiver.

In evaluating the adaptive behavior levels of deaf-blind children, give credit for any alternative methods of communication the children use—such as sign language, Braille, or finger spelling—when you score language development items on the scale. If you do not give credit for alternative forms of communication, you will penalize children with severe sensory impairments for their inability to use normal modes of communication.

Scores

In Part I, items are scored in one of two ways. Some items have the statements arranged in order of increasing difficulty, and the score corresponds to the statement that best describes the most difficult or highest level the person can usually manage (e.g., 3, 2, 1, or 0). Other items are scored yes or no. In Part II, items are scored using four categories: N (never occurs), O (occasionally occurs), F (frequently occurs), and Other (specific example is recorded).

Raw scores are converted into standard scores for the 16 domains ($M = 10$, $SD = 3$) and for the five factors ($M = 100$, $SD = 15$). Percentile ranks are available for both parts, but age-equivalent scores are available only on Part I because the maladaptive behaviors covered in Part II are *not* age related.

The range of scaled scores on the domains in Parts I and II is not uniform throughout the ages covered by the scale. For example, on Part I, Socialization has a scaled-score range of 1 to 16 for 3-year-olds, whereas Numbers and Time has a scaled-score range of 7 to 17. On Part II, Social Behavior has a scaled-score range of 1 to 16 for 3-year-olds, whereas Self-Abusive Behavior has a scale-score range of 1 to 11. In fact, there is no age at which all the domains in Parts I and II have scaled scores that range from 1 to 20.

The range of scaled scores on the factors also is not uniform throughout the ages covered by the scale. For example, Personal Self-Sufficiency has a scaled-score range of 60 to 141 for 3-year-olds, but a scaled-score range of 60 to 102 for 17-year-olds. On Part II, Social Adjustment has a scaled-score range of 59 to 126 for 3-year-olds, but a scaled-score range of 59 to 120 for 17-year-olds.

Table 7-4 shows the range of age-equivalent scores for the nine domains and three factors in Part I. The age-equivalent scores range from < 3-0 to > 16-0, but this range is not possible for all domains or factors. For example, Independent Functioning has an age-equivalent score range of < 3-0 to > 16-0, whereas Responsibility has a range of < 3-0 to 8-6. Community Self-Sufficiency has an age-equivalent score range of < 3-0 to > 15-9, whereas Personal-Social Responsibility has a range of < 3-0 to 12-9.

Inspection of Table C-1 in the Manual shows that the distribution of age equivalents for raw scores is not uniform. In fact, in some cases the distribution shows large gaps. For example, in Independent Functioning, a change of 1 raw-score point from 82 to 83 represents a change in age-equivalent scores of 3 months (5-6 to 5-9), whereas in Physical Development, a change of 1 raw-score point from 19 to 20 represents a change in age-equivalent scores of 24 months (5-6 to 7-6). Thus, the distribution of item gradients (in this case, conversion of raw scores to age-equivalent scores) is not smooth.

Standardization

The ABS–S:2 was standardized on 2,074 individuals with mental retardation and 1,254 individuals without mental retardation. The samples came from 40 states and were stratified on the basis of race/ethnic group status, gender, residence, and geographic region. The sample was similar to the school-aged population, but the comparison U.S. Census year was not given in the Manual.

Table 7-4
Range of Age-Equivalent Scores on Part I of the Adaptive Behavior Scale–School: Second Edition

Range	Domain									Factor		
	IF	PD	EA	LD	N/T	PA	SD	RE	SO	PSS	CSS	PSR
Lowest	< 3-0	< 3-0	< 3-0	< 3-0	< 3-0	< 3-0	< 3-0	< 3-0	< 3-0	< 3-0	< 3-0	< 3-0
Highest	16-0	14-6	>16-0	13-3	11-3	10-9	10-0	8-6	10-9	14-9	15-9	12-9

Note. Abbreviations are as follows: IF = Independent Functioning; PD = Physical Development; EA = Economic Activity; LD = Language Development; N/T = Numbers and Time; PA = Prevocational/Vocational Activity; SD = Self-Direction; RE = Responsibility; SO = Socialization; PSS = Personal Self-Sufficiency; CSS = Community Self-Sufficiency; PSR = Personal-Social Responsibility.
Source: Adapted from Lambert, Nihira, and Leland (1993).

Reliability

Average internal consistency reliabilities in the sample with mental retardation are as follows: In Part I, they range from .82 to .98 (*Mdn* r_{xx} = .93) for the domains and from .97 to .98 (*Mdn* r_{xx} = .98) for the factors. In Part II, they range from .84 to .94 (*Mdn* r_{xx} = .90) for the domains and from .93 to .97 (*Mdn* r_{xx} = .95) for the factors.

Average internal consistency reliabilities in the sample without mental retardation in Part I range from .82 to .92 (*Mdn* r_{xx} = .88) for the domains and from .88 to .93 (*Mdn* r_{xx} = .93) for the factors. In Part II, they range from .87 to .97 (*Mdn* r_{xx} = .88) for the domains and from .92 to .96 (*Mdn* r_{xx} = .94) for the factors.

Test-retest reliabilities in Part I for a sample of 45 adolescents with emotional disturbance retested over 2 weeks ranged from .42 to .79 (*Mdn* r_{tt} = .61) for the domains and from .61 to .72 (*Mdn* r_{tt} = .66) for the factors. Interrater reliabilities for two professionals completing 15 protocols were .97 and above for the domains and factors in each part.

Validity

Content validity is satisfactory for Part I, as noted by acceptable correlations between items and the total score. However, in Part II, correlations between items and the total score were less satisfactory. Criterion-related validity is acceptable for Part I, as noted by satisfactory correlations with other measures of adaptive behavior, including the Vineland Adaptive Behavior Scales and the Adaptive Behavior Inventory. Construct validity is satisfactory. Correlations between Part I and the WISC–R range from .28 to .59 (*Mdn* r_{xx} = .41) for the domains and from .41 to .61 (*Mdn* r_{xx} = .59) for the factors. Correlations between Part II and the WISC–R were not significant or were very low (–.14 to –.18). As noted earlier, according to the Manual, the ABS–S:2 has three factors in Part I and two factors in Part II, derived from a factor analysis. However, an independent factor analysis reported only two factors in the ABS–S:2 (Stinnett, Fuqua, & Coombs, 1999). Discriminant validity is satisfactory, as the ABS–S:2 discriminates between children with mental retardation and those without mental retardation.

Comment on the ABS–S:2

The ABS–S:2 is a useful measure of adaptive behavior for children who are being assessed for possible mental retardation. Both parts of the scale provide information useful for assessing behavior and for monitoring progress. Reliability and validity are satisfactory. However, because the range of standard scores is not uniform, it will be difficult to evaluate differential performance among the domains. In retest situations, it will be important that you study the available scaled-score ranges in order to make appropriate interpretations of score changes. Gradients of raw scores to age-equivalent scores also show dramatic differences on Part I. You must be thoroughly familiar with these differences if you use age-equivalent scores. (See Chapter 4 in *Assessment of Children: Cognitive Applications* for a discussion of problems associated with the use of age-equivalent scores.) Because the range of age-equivalent scores is restricted in several domains, you must use caution in making comparisons among the domains and factors when you use these scores. Part II must be used cautiously because items are given equal weighting regardless of the severity of the behavior (e.g., stomping one's feet versus choking others; Perry & Factor, 1989). Stinnett (1997) pointed out that *only* the social skills and self-care domains provide a good match with the areas listed in the AAMR (1992) definition of adaptive behavior. Therefore, you will need to supplement the ABS–S:2 with additional procedures to obtain a more adequate assessment of the other eight adaptive skill areas listed by the AAMR.

AAMR ADAPTIVE BEHAVIOR SCALE— RESIDENTIAL AND COMMUNITY: SECOND EDITION

The AAMR Adaptive Behavior Scale–Residential and Community: Second Edition (ABS–RC:2; Nihira, Leland, & Lambert, 1993) is an adaptive behavior scaled designed to measure personal independence and responsibility in daily living and social behavior in adults ages 18 to 79 years. It is for use with individuals who may have mental retardation, and it assesses two types of competencies: behavioral and affective (see Table 7-5). The 1993 version is a revision of the scale first published in 1969.

Part I of the ABS–RC:2 covers 10 behavioral domains and 21 subdomains and has three factors. It measures behaviors and habits needed to maintain personal independence in daily living. Part II covers 8 domains and has two factors. It focuses primarily on maladaptive behavior related to personality and behavior disorders.

The five factors are as follows:

Part I

- *Personal Self-Sufficiency* (items from Independent Functioning and Physical Development domains)
- *Community Self-Sufficiency* (items from Independent Functioning, Economic Activity, Language Development, Numbers and Time, and Domestic Activity domains)
- *Personal-Social Responsibility* (items from Prevocational/ Vocational Activity, Self-Direction, Responsibility, and Socialization domains)

Part II

- *Social Adjustment* (items from Social Behavior, Conformity, and Trustworthiness domains)
- *Personal Adjustment* (items from Stereotyped and Hyperactive Behavior, Sexual Behavior, and Self-Abusive Behavior domains)

Table 7-5
AAMR Adaptive Behavior Scale–Residential and Community: Second Edition Domains and Subdomains

Domain	Subdomain
Part I Independent Functioning	Eating Toilet Use Cleanliness Appearance Care of Clothing Dressing and Undressing Travel Other Independent Functioning
Physical Development	Sensory Development Motor Development
Economic Activity	Money Handling and Budgeting Shopping Skills
Language Development	Expression Verbal Comprehension Social Language Development
Numbers and Time	—
Domestic Activity	Cleaning Kitchen Other Domestic Duties
Prevocational/Vocational Activity	—
Self-Direction	Initiative Perseverance Leisure Time
Responsibility	—
Socialization	—
Part II Social Behavior	—
Conformity	—
Trustworthiness	—
Stereotyped and Hyperactive Behavior	—
Sexual Behavior	—
Self-Abusive Behavior	—
Social Engagement	—
Disturbing Interpersonal Behavior	—

Source: Adapted from Nihira, Leland, and Lambert (1993).

The ABS–RC:2 takes approximately 15 to 30 minutes to administer, and persons with minimal training can administer it. Two methods can be used to administer the scale. In the *first-person assessment method,* an informant completes the scale by himself or herself. The informant must be familiar with the individual and have had enough professional training to make appropriate ratings. In the *interview method,* which is most useful with caregivers, the examiner completes the scale based on information provided by the caregiver.

In evaluating the adaptive behavior levels of severely disabled individuals, give credit for any alternative method of communication the individuals use—such as sign language, Braille, or finger spelling—when you score language development items on the scale. If you do not give credit for alternative forms of communication, you will penalize individuals with severe sensory impairments for their inability to use typical modes of communication.

Scores

In Part I, items are scored in one of two ways. Some items have statements arranged in order of increasing difficulty, and the score corresponds to the statement that best describes the most difficult or highest level the person can usually manage (e.g., 3, 2, 1, 0). Other items are scored yes or no. In Part II, items are scored using four categories: N (never occurs), O (occasionally occurs), F (frequently occurs), and Other (specific example is recorded).

Raw scores are converted into standard scores for the 18 domains ($M = 10$, $SD = 3$) and for the five factors ($M = 100$, $SD = 15$). Percentile ranks are available for both parts, but age-equivalent scores are available only on Part I because the maladaptive behaviors covered in Part II are *not* age related.

The range of scaled scores on the domains in Parts I and II is not uniform throughout the ages covered by the scale. For example, on Part I, Independent Functioning has a scaled-score range of 1 to 19 for 18-year-olds, whereas Responsibility has a scaled-score range of 5 to 15. On Part II, Stereotyped and Hyperactive Behavior has a scaled-score range of 1 to 16 for 18-year-olds, whereas Sexual Behavior has a scaled-score range of 1 to 12. In fact, on Part II, the longest scaled-score range is only 1 to 16.

The range of scaled scores on the factors also is not uniform throughout the ages covered by the scale. For example, Personal Self-Sufficiency has a scaled-score range of 60 to 144 for 18-year-olds, but a scaled-score range of 63 to 142 for 60-year-olds. On Part II, Personal Adjustment has a scaled-score range of 56 to 122 for 18-year-olds, but a scaled-score range of 58 to 125 for 60-year-olds.

Table B-1 in the Manual shows age-equivalent scores for the 10 domains and three factors on Part I. Although the ABS–RC:2 is designed for adults, the Manual provides the same age-equivalent scores (ranging from 3-0 to 16-0) that are in the ABS–S:2 Manual. The Manual provides no rationale for presenting age-equivalent scores for adults. *I recommend that they not be used on the ABS–RC:2.*

Standardization

The ABS–RC:2 was standardized on 4,103 individuals with developmental disabilities who resided in their communities or in residential facilities. The sample came from 46 states and was stratified on the basis of race/ethnicity, gender, and urban/rural status. The distribution of the sample was similar to that of the adult population, but the comparison U.S. Census year was not provided in the Manual.

Reliability

Average internal consistency reliabilities in Part I range from .82 to .98 ($Mdn\ r_{xx} = .94$) for the domains and from .97 to .99 ($Mdn\ r_{xx} = .98$) for the factors. In Part II, they range from .81 to .94 ($Mdn\ r_{xx} = .87$) for the domains and from .96 to .97 ($Mdn\ r_{xx} = .96$) for the factors.

Test-retest reliabilities for a sample of 45 individuals ages 24 to 65 retested over 2 weeks is satisfactory. On Part I, they ranged from .88 to .99 ($Mdn\ r_{tt} = .96$) for the domains and from .93 to .98 ($Mdn\ r_{tt} = .94$) for the factors. On Part II, they ranged from .96 to .99 ($Mdn\ r_{tt} = .96$) for the domains and from .85 to .98 ($Mdn\ r_{tt} = .92$) for the factors.

Interrater reliabilities for two graduate students completing 16 protocols were .96 and above for the domains and factors in Parts I and II, except for Prevocational/Vocational Activity, which had a correlation of .83.

Validity

Content validity is satisfactory for Part I, as noted by acceptable correlations between items and the total score. However, in Part II, correlations between items and the total score were less satisfactory. Criterion-related validity is acceptable for Part I, as noted by satisfactory correlations with other measures of adaptive behavior, including the Vineland Adaptive Behavior Scales and the Adaptive Behavior Inventory. Construct validity is satisfactory. Correlations between Part I and the WAIS–R range from .27 to .73 ($Mdn\ r_{xx} = .51$) for the domains and from .49 to .72 ($Mdn\ r_{xx} = .62$) for the factors. Correlations between Part II and the WAIS–R were not significant or were very low (−.09 to .15). As noted earlier, the ABS–RD:2 has three factors in Part I and two factors in Part II, derived from a factor analysis. Discriminant validity is satisfactory, as the ABS–RC:2 discriminates between adults with mental retardation and those without mental retardation.

Comment on the ABS–RC:2

The ABS–RC:2 is a useful measure of adaptive behavior for adults who are being assessed for possible mental retardation. Both parts of the scale provide information useful for assessing behavior and for monitoring progress. Reliability and validity are satisfactory. However, because the range of standard scores is not uniform, it will be difficult to evaluate differential performance among the domains. In retest situations, it will be important that you study the available scaled-score ranges in order to make appropriate interpretations of score changes. *Use of age-equivalent scores is not recommended for any clinical or diagnostic purpose.* Stinnett's (1997) observation on the ABS–S:2 generally holds for the ABS–RC:2—that is, only a few domains provide a good match with the 10 areas listed in the AAMR (1992) definition of adaptive behavior. Therefore, you will need to supplement the ABS–RC:2 with additional procedures to obtain a more adequate assessment of the adaptive skill areas listed by the AAMR.

SCALES OF INDEPENDENT BEHAVIOR–REVISED

The Scales of Independent Behavior–Revised (SIB–R; Bruininks, Woodcock, Weatherman, & Hill, 1996) is an individually administered measure of skills needed to function independently in home, social, and community settings. The SIB–R covers an age span from infancy to mature adult (age 80 years and older). The SIB–R has the following composition (see Table 7-6):

- The Full Scale contains 14 subscales organized into four adaptive behavior clusters (Motor Skills, Social Interaction and Communication Skills, Personal Living Skills, and Community Living Skills).
- The Problem Behavior Scale contains 8 problem area scales organized into three Maladaptive Behavior indices (Internalized Maladaptive Behavior, Asocial Maladaptive Behavior, and Externalized Maladaptive Behavior).
- The Short Form contains 40 items that can be administered to persons at any developmental level.
- The Early Development Scale contains 40 items designed for children from infancy through about 6 years of age or for older individuals whose developmental levels are below 8 years of age.

The SIB–R Full Scale takes approximately 60 minutes to administer, and the Short Form and the Early Development Form each take about 15 to 20 minutes to administer. Although an informant usually completes the scale, in some cases the individual herself or himself can provide the information needed to complete the scale.

Scores

The adaptive behavior items are scored on a 4-point scale: 0 (never or rarely performs the task or activity), 1 (does the task, but not well, or about ¼ of the time), 2 (does the task fairly well, or about ¾ of the time), 3 (does the task very well, or always or almost always). Raw scores are converted into standard scores ($M = 100$, $SD = 15$), percentile ranks, stanines, normal-curve equivalents, or age-equivalent scores. The standard score for the Full Scale is called "Broad Independence," while the standard score for the Problem Behavior Scale is called "General Maladaptive Index." The Manual

Table 7-6
Scales of Independent Behavior–Revised Clusters and Skills/Areas

Cluster	Skills/Areas
Adaptive Behavior Skills Motor Skills	Gross Motor Fine Motor
Social Interaction and Communication Skills	Social Interaction Language Comprehension Language Expression
Personal Living Skills	Eating and Meal Preparation Toileting Dressing Personal Self-Care Domestic Skills
Community Living Skills	Time and Punctuality Money and Value Work Skills Home/Community Orientation
Problem Behavior Areas Internalized Maladaptive Behavior	Hurtful to Self Unusual or Repetitive Habits Withdrawal or Inattentive Behavior
Asocial Maladaptive Behavior	Socially Offensive Behavior Uncooperative Behavior
Externalized Maladaptive Behavior	Hurtful to Others Destructive to Property Disruptive Behavior

includes instructional range scores, a Support Score based on an individual's adaptive behavior and problem behavior scores, and an adjusted behavior score associated with the Woodcock-Johnson–R Broad Cognitive Ability cluster score. Because the Woodcock-Johnson has been revised (see Chapter 16 in *Assessment of Children: Cognitive Applications*), this procedure does not use the latest norms available on the Woodcock-Johnson.

The problem behavior items are scored on two 5-point scales. The five ratings on the frequency scale are 1 (less than once a month), 2 (1 to 3 times a month), 3 (1 to 6 times a week), 4 (1 to 10 times a day), and 5 (1 or more times an hour). The five ratings on the severity scale are 0 (not serious), 1 (slightly serious), 2 (moderately serious), 3 (very serious), and 4 (extremely serious).

Standardization

The norm sample for the SIB–R consisted of 2,182 individuals ages 3 months to 60–90 years. Individuals were chosen to conform to the 1990 U.S. Census data on gender, race, Hispanic origin, occupational status, occupational level, geographic region, and type of community. Of the 2,182 individuals in the sample, 1,817 were between 3 months and 19 years of age, and 365 were between 20 and 90 years of age. The Manual does not give the numbers of people at the individual ages from 20 to 90 years.

The distribution of the norm group does not match the distribution in the four nationwide census regions. For example, in the 1990 U.S. Census data, the Northwest region comprised 20.4% of the population and the Midwest region comprised 24.0% of the population. In the norm group, these two regions comprised 12.2% and 50.5%, respectively. Thus, there are disparities of 8.3% and 26.5%, respectively, between the norm group and the U.S. Census data for these two regions. Disparities are 11.7% for the South region and 6.4% for the West region.

Reliability

Median corrected split-half reliabilities for all age levels range from .70 to .88 (*Mdn* r_{xx} = .81) for the 14 adaptive subscales and from .88 to .94 (*Mdn* r_{xx} = .90) for the four cluster scores. The median corrected split-half reliabilities are .98 for Broad Independence and .76 for the Short Form. Standard errors of measurement are reported in *W* scale units, not in the more popular standard score distribution with $M = 100$ and $SD = 15$. Further, median corrected split-half reliabilities are not presented for the Problem Behavior Scale.

Test-retest reliability was assessed on a sample of 31 children without disabilities, ages 6 to 13 years, who were retested within 4 weeks. Median stability coefficients were r_{tt} = .93 for the 14 adaptive subscales, r_{tt} = .96 for the four clusters, r_{tt} = .98 for Broad Independence, r_{tt} = .83 for the General Maladaptive Index, and r_{tt} = .96 for the Support Score. Other test-retest studies reported in the Manual for the Maladaptive Behavior Index and Early Development Form generally show test-retest reliability coefficients in the .70s and .80s.

Interrater reliabilities are reported in the Manual for four different samples. They range from the .70s to the .90s for the 14 adaptive subscales, from the .80s to the .90s for the four adaptive clusters and Broad Independence, in the .90s for the Support Score, from the .60s to the .80s for the Maladaptive Behavior Index, and from the .60s to the .90s for the Early Development Form.

Validity

The Manual reports several indices of construct validity. First, correlations between SIB–R adaptive behavior scores and chronological age were high (ranging from .54 to .73 for the four clusters and Broad Independence). Second, based on the prior version of the scale, adaptive behavior scores were lower for individuals with disabilities than for those without disabilities. Third, the pattern of subscale intercorrelations provides support for construct validity. Criterion-related validity is satisfactory, as seen, for example, by a .82 correlation between the Broad Independence and the Woodcock-Johnson Broad Cognitive Ability Scale in a sample of 312 individuals without disabilities. Finally, the Manual presents other evidence of construct validity and criterion validity based on the former version of the scale.

Comment on the SIB–R

The SIB–R is useful in assessing adaptive behavior over a wide age range. However, the Manual and scale have several limitations. First, the numerous scores complicate use of the scale. Second, the procedure that compares the scale with the Woodcock-Johnson Broad Cognitive Ability cluster score is out of date. Third, the distribution of the norm sample by region does not match U.S. Census data. Fourth, additional test-retest reliability studies are needed over the entire age span covered by the scale and with both individuals with disabilities and individuals without disabilities. Fifth, the Manual does not provide a factor analysis of the SIB–R or criterion-related validity studies using the SIB–R. Sixth, the SIB–R does not measure all of the adaptive skill areas proposed by the AAMR. Finally, research is needed to evaluate the usefulness of the support scores and other special scores provided in the Manual.

ADAPTIVE BEHAVIOR ASSESSMENT SYSTEM

The Adaptive Behavior Assessment System (ABAS; Harrison & Oakland, 2000) is designed to measure adaptive behavior skills of children and adults ages 5 to 89 years. It has three forms, each of which takes about 15 to 20 minutes to complete:

- The Teacher Form covers individuals ages 5 to 21 years, contains 193 items, and can be completed by a teacher or teacher's aide.
- The Parent Form covers ages 5 to 21 years, contains 232 items, and can be completed by a parent or other primary caregiver.
- The Adult Form covers adolescents and adults ages 16 to 89 years and contains 239 items. The "Others" version can be completed by a family member or another adult familiar with the referred individual; the "Self" version can be completed by a referred individual who has adequate reading comprehension.

The ABAS covers the 10 adaptive skill areas proposed by the AAMR. The Work adaptive skill area is designed only for individuals who have a part- or full-time job. Table 7-7 shows the 10 adaptive skill areas, the number of items in each area, and sample items.

Informants completing the forms need to have a thorough knowledge of the child's or adult's daily activities. If not, the results will be unreliable or invalid.

The Manual states that the ABAS items were written at a fifth-grade or lower reading level, but does not state the system used to arrive at this reading level. However, the Flesch-Kincaid reading level system (included in Microsoft Word '97) indicates that reading levels above the fifth grade are required on all three forms (also see Table 7-8):

- 7.1 grade level on the Teacher Form (range of 2.7 to 10.6 grade level over the 10 adaptive skill areas)
- 6.7 grade level on the Parent Form (range of 3.7 to 8.9 grade level over the 10 adaptive skill areas)
- 6.8 grade level on the Adult Form (range of 3.7 to 8.7 grade level over the 10 adaptive skill areas)

In addition, several individual items require a twelfth-grade reading level.

The Flesch Reading Ease Score (also included in Microsoft Word '97) for each form is as follows (preferred scores are between 60 and 70, with higher numbers indicating greater ease of reading):

- 61.7 on the Teacher Form (range of 42.6 to 86.7)
- 63.4 on the Parent Form (range of 53.2 to 78.8)
- 62.8 on the Adult Form (range of 54.4 to 79.9)

Although the overall reading ease score on each form is within acceptable limits, several areas have reading ease scores below 60 (see Table 7-8). Over all three forms, the Leisure adaptive skill area has the most difficult reading level, while the Self-Care adaptive skill area has the easiest reading level.

The Manual states that if informants cannot read at a fifth-grade level, then the items can be read to them. However, the analysis presented above indicates that *items on the ABAS may have to be read to informants who cannot read at least at the seventh-grade level.*

Scores

Each item is rated on a 4-point scale: 0 = is not able, 1 = never when needed, 2 = sometimes when needed, and 3 = always when needed. An option is provided after each item for guessing (Check if you Guessed). Raw scores are converted into standard scores for the 10 adaptive skill areas ($M = 10$, $SD = 3$), to a General Adaptive Composite (GAC) for the total score ($M = 100$, $SD = 15$), and to age-equivalent scores. The Manual provides confidence intervals and percentile ranks for the GAC. The following classifications are used for the adaptive skill areas and the GAC: Extremely Low, Borderline, Below Average, Average, Above Average, and Superior.

GAC scores range from 40 to 130 on both the Teacher Form (see Table 7-9) and the Parent Form (see Table 7-10). However, a score of 130 is available only at ages 5, 6, and 7 years on both forms; at ages 8 to 21 years, the highest GAC available is 120. The lowest score is either 40 or 41 on both forms, depending on the individual's age. The distribution of GAC scores is truncated, with scores ranging from 4 standard deviations *below* the mean to 2 standard deviations *above* the

Table 7-7
Description of and Sample Items from the Adaptive Skill Areas Measured by the Adaptive Behavior Assessment System

Adaptive skill area	Number of items			Description	Sample items
	Teacher Form	Parent Form	Adult Form		
Communication	22	24	25	Speech, language, and listening skills needed for communication with other people, including vocabulary, responding to questions, conversation skills, etc.	Names 20 or more familiar objects. Ends conversation appropriately. Uses up-to-date information to discuss current events.
Community Use	15	23	24	Skills needed for functioning in the community, including use of community resources, shopping skills, getting around in the community, etc.	Mails letters at the postal box or local post office. Finds and uses pay phone. Orders his/her own meals when eating out.
Functional Academics	22	23	27	Basic reading, writing, mathematics, and other academic skills needed for daily, independent functioning, including telling time, measurement, writing notes and letters, etc.	Reads his/her own written name. Finds somebody's telephone number in the phone book. Makes reminder notes or lists.
Home/School Living[a]	20	25	23	Skills needed for basic care of a home or living setting (or, for the teacher form, school and classroom setting), including cleaning, straightening, property maintenance and repairs, food preparation, performing chores, etc.	Wipes up spills at home/school. Takes out trash when can is full. Keeps toys, games, or other belongings neat and clean.
Health and Safety	16	22	20	Skills needed for protection of health and to respond to illness and injury, including following safety rules, using medicines, showing caution, etc.	Carries scissors safely. Follows general safety rules at home/school. Tests hot foods before eating them.
Leisure	17	22	23	Skills needed for engaging in and planning leisure and recreational activities, including playing with others, engaging in recreation at home, following rules in games, etc.	Plays alone with toys, games, or other fun activities. Waits for his/her turn in games and other fun activities. Tries a new activity to learn about something new.
Self-Care	19	24	25	Skills needed for personal care, including eating, dressing, bathing, using the toilet, grooming, hygiene, etc.	Buttons his/her own clothing. Uses public restroom alone. Keeps hair neat during the day by brushing or combing.
Self-Direction	21	25	25	Skills needed for independence, responsibility, and self-control, including starting and completing tasks, keeping a schedule, following time limits, following directions, making choices, etc.	Stops a fun activity, without complaints, when told that time is up. Controls temper when disagreeing with friends. Completes large home or school projects on time.

(Continued)

Table 7-7 (Continued)

Adaptive skill area	Number of items			Description	Sample items
	Teacher Form	Parent Form	Adult Form		
Social	20	23	23	Skills needed to interact socially and get along with other people, including having friends, showing and recognizing emotions, assisting others, and using manners.	Says "thank you" when given a gift. Laughs in response to funny comments or jokes. Listens to friends or family members who need to talk about problems.
Work[b]	21	21	24	Skills needed for successful functioning and holding a part- or full-time job in a work setting, including completing work tasks, working with supervisors, and following a work schedule.	Shows positive attitude toward jobs. Starts back to work willingly after taking a break or lunch. Cares properly for work supplies and equipment.
Total Items	193	232	239	—	—

[a]On the Parent Form and Adult Form, the adaptive skill area is titled Home Living. On the Teacher Form, the adaptive skill area is titled School Living.
[b]The Work skill area is completed only when individuals have a part- or full-time job.
Source: From the Manual of the *Adaptive Behavior Assessment System.* Copyright © 2000 by The Psychological Corporation, a Harcourt Assessment Company. Reproduced by permission. All rights reserved. "Adaptive Behavior Assessment System" and "ABAS" are trademarks of The Psychological Corporation.

mean. On the two Adult Forms (Self and Others), the GAC scores range from 40 to 120 at all ages.

Scaled scores range from 1 to 17 on the Teacher Form; however, this range is not possible for all adaptive skill areas or at all ages. Of the nine adaptive skill areas on the Teacher Form (Work is not included), Functional Academics has the largest scaled-score range (1 to 17), whereas Self-Care has the smallest scaled-score range (1 to 13). The largest ranges are at the earliest ages of the scale. For example, Communication has a range of 1 to 15 at age 5 years, but a range of only 1 to 11 at ages 13 to 17–21 years. Functional Academics has a range of 1 to 17 at ages 5 and 6 years, but a range of only 1 to 11 at ages 15 to 21 years.

Scaled scores range from 1 to 18 on the Parent Form; however, this range is not possible for all adaptive skill areas or at all ages. Of the nine adaptive skill areas on the Parent Form (Work is not included), School Living, Leisure, and Self-Direction have the largest scaled-score range (1 to 18), whereas Self-Care and Social have the smallest scaled-score range (1 to 16). The largest ranges are at the earliest ages of the scale. For example, School Living has a range of 1 to 18 at age 5 years, but a range of only 1 to 13 at ages 17–21 years. Communication has a range of 1 to 17 at ages 5-0 and 5-4 years, but a range of only 1 to 12 at ages 17–21 years.

Scaled scores range from 1 to 15 on the Adult Form (Self); however, this range is not possible for all adaptive skill areas or at all ages. For the 10 adaptive skill areas on the Adult Form (Self), Functional Academics has the largest scaled-score range (1 to 15), whereas Self-Care has the smallest scaled-score range (1 to 12). The upper limits of the

scaled-score range differ, at most, by 3 scaled-score points across all ages and adaptive skill areas.

Scaled scores range from 1 to 15 on the Adult Form (Others); however, this range is not possible for all adaptive skill areas or at all ages. For the 10 adaptive skill areas on the Adult Form (Others), Home Living has the largest scaled-score range (1 to 15), whereas Communication, Health and Safety, Self-Care, and Work have the smallest scaled-score range (1 to 13). The upper limits of the scaled-score range differ, at most, by 2 scaled-score points across all ages and adaptive skill areas.

Table 7-11 shows the age-equivalent scores on the Teacher and Parent Forms for the nine adaptive skill areas that have age-equivalent scores. On the Teacher Form, age-equivalent scores range from 5-0 to 17-0 years, but this range is not possible for all adaptive skill areas. For example, Functional Academics has an age-equivalent score range of 5-0 to 16-0 years, whereas Self-Care has an age-equivalent score range of 5-4 to 12-4 years. On the Parent Form, the range of age-equivalent scores is more uniform, 5-0 to 17-0 in seven of nine adaptive skill areas (Work is not included). Social has an age-equivalent score range of 5-4 to 17-0, whereas Self-Care has an age-equivalent score range of 5-0 to 12-8 years.

Inspection of Table A.4 in the Manual shows that the distribution of age equivalents for raw scores is not uniform. In fact, in some cases the distribution shows large gaps. For example, on Functional Academics, a raw score of 51 yields an age-equivalent score of 7-8 years, while a raw score of 52 yields an age-equivalent score of 8-4 years. However, on School Living, a raw score of 51 yields an age-equivalent

Table 7-8
Flesch Reading Ease Score and Flesch-Kincaid Grade Level Reading Score on the Adaptive Behavior Assessment System

Readability index	Adaptive skill area										
	COM	CU	FA	HL/SL[c]	HS	LS	SC	SD	SOC	WK	Total
Teacher Form											
Flesch Reading Ease Score[a]	56.4	42.6	62.0	67.6	63.8	55.7	86.7	60.9	70.7	59.4	61.7
Flesch-Kincaid Grade Level[b]	7.7	10.6	6.8	6.5	7.3	8.8	2.7	7.2	5.5	7.3	7.1
Parent Form											
Flesch Reading Ease Score[a]	55.8	61.3	64.4	73.8	64.4	53.2	78.8	61.9	67.2	59.0	63.4
Flesch-Kincaid Grade Level[b]	7.6	7.6	6.3	5.0	6.4	8.9	3.7	6.9	6.1	7.3	6.7
Adult Form											
Flesch Reading Ease Score[a]	57.1	61.7	61.5	71.4	59.6	54.4	79.9	60.6	66.9	59.8	62.8
Flesch-Kincaid Grade Level[b]	7.5	7.5	6.7	5.5	7.1	8.7	3.7	7.1	6.2	7.1	6.8

[a]Rates text on a 100-point scale; the higher the score, the easier it is to understand the document. For most standard documents, a score of approximately 60 to 70 is satisfactory.
[b]Rates text on a U.S. grade-school level. For example, a score of 8.0 means that an eighth grader can understand the document.
[c]On the Parent Form and Adult Form, the adaptive skill area is titled Home Living. On the Teacher Form, the adaptive skill area is titled School Living.
Note. Readability indices and definitions of indices obtained from Microsoft Word in Windows '97.
Abbreviations are as follows: COM = Communication, CU = Community Use, FA = Functional Academics, HL = Home Living, SL = School Living, HS = Health and Safety, LS = Leisure, SC = Self-Care, SD = Self-Direction, SOC = Social, WK = Work.

Table 7-9
Range of GACs by Age on the Adaptive Behavior Assessment System, Teacher Form

Age	Range of GACs
5	40–130
6	40–130
7	41–130
8	40–120
9	40–120
10	40–120
11	41–120
12	41–120
13–14	40–120
15–16	40–120
17–21	41–120

Source: Adapted from Harrison and Oakland (2000, pp. 112–122).

Table 7-10
Range of GACs by Age on Adaptive Behavior Assessment System, Parent Form

Age	Range of GACs
5	40–130
6	40–130
7	40–130
8	40–120
9	40–120
10	40–120
11	40–120
12	40–120
13–14	40–120
15–16	40–120
17–21	41–120

Source: Adapted from Harrison and Oakland (2000, pp. 132–142).

Table 7-11
Lowest and Highest Test-Age Equivalents in the Teacher and Parent Forms of the Adaptive Behavior Assessment System

Form	Adaptive skill area								
	COM	CU	FA	HL/SL[a]	HS	LS	SC	SD	SOC
Teacher Form									
Lowest	5-4	5-0	5-0	5-4	5-4	5-8	5-4	5-4	5-8
Highest	17-0	14-0	16-0	12-8	12-8	17-0	12-4	15-0	17-0
Parent Form									
Lowest	5-0	5-0	5-0	5-0	5-0	5-0	5-0	5-0	5-4
Highest	17-0	17-0	17-0	17-0	17-0	17-0	12-8	17-0	17-0

[a]On the Parent Form, the adaptive skill area is titled Home Living. On the Teacher Form, the adaptive skill area is titled School Living.

Note. There are no test-age equivalents for the Work adaptive skill area.

Abbreviations are as follows: COM = Communication, CU = Community Use, FA = Functional Academics, HL = Home Living, SL = School Living, HS = Health and Safety, LS = Leisure, SC = Self-Care, SD = Self-Direction, SOC = Social.

Source: From the Manual of the *Adaptive Behavior Assessment System.* Copyright © 2000 by The Psychological Corporation, a Harcourt Assessment Company. Adapted and reproduced by permission. All rights reserved. "Adaptive Behavior Assessment System" and "ABAS" are trademarks of The Psychological Corporation.

score of 8-4 years, while a raw score of 52 yields an age-equivalent score of 10-8 years. In the former case, a change of 1 raw-score point reflects a change of 8 months in age-equivalent scores, whereas in the latter case, a change of 1 raw-score point reflects a change of 2-4 years in age-equivalent scores. Thus, the distribution of item gradients (in this case, conversion of raw scores to age-equivalent scores) is not smooth on the Teacher Form; it is somewhat smoother, although still with some gaps, on the Parent Form.

Standardization

The standardization sample consisted of 5,270 individuals stratified by gender, race/ethnicity, geographic region, and parent educational level, following the 1999 U.S. Census data.

Reliability

On the Teacher Form, average internal consistency reliabilities range from .89 to .96 (*Mdn* r_{xx} = .94) for the adaptive skill areas; the average GAC internal consistency reliability is .99. For the individual ages, the internal consistency reliabilities range from .79 to .98. Average SEMs range from .60 to 1.00 (*Mdn* SEM = .70) over the 10 adaptive skill areas. Test-retest reliabilities based on a sample of 143 children evaluated over 11 days range from .88 to .97 (*Mdn* r_{tt} = .92) for nine adaptive skill areas (Work not included); the test-retest reliability for the GAC is .97. Interrater reliabilities on a sample of 84 children rated by two informants range from

.72 to .88 (*Mdn* r_{rr} = .82) for the nine skill areas; the interrater reliability for the GAC is .94.

On the Parent Form, average internal consistency reliabilities range from .86 to .93 (*Mdn* r_{xx} = .92) for the adaptive skill areas; the average GAC internal consistency reliability is .98. For the individual ages, the internal consistency reliabilities range from .79 to .96. Average SEMs range from .80 to 1.10 (*Mdn* SEM = .80) over the 10 adaptive skill areas. Test-retest reliabilities based on a sample of 102 children evaluated over 11 days range from .79 to .94 (*Mdn* r_{tt} = .92) for nine adaptive skill areas (Work not included); the test-retest reliability for the GAC is .96. Interrater reliabilities on a sample of 81 children rated by two informants range from .61 to .81 (*Mdn* r_{rr} = .70) for the nine skill areas; the interrater reliability for the GAC is .83.

On the Adult Form (Self), average internal consistency reliabilities range from .88 to .94 (*Mdn* r_{xx} = .92) for the adaptive skill areas; the average GAC internal consistency reliability is .99. For the individual ages, the internal consistency reliabilities range from .82 to .97. Average SEMs range from .67 to 1.04 (*Mdn* SEM = .85) over the 10 adaptive skill areas. Test-retest reliabilities based on a sample of 65 adults evaluated over 11 days range from .91 to .97 (*Mdn* r_{tt} = .96) for the 10 adaptive skill areas; the test-retest reliability for the GAC is .99.

On the Adult Form (Others), average internal consistency reliabilities range from .93 to .97 (*Mdn* r_{xx} = .95) for the adaptive skill areas; the average GAC internal consistency reliability is .99. For the individual ages, the internal consistency reliabilities range from .86 to .99. Average SEMs range from .52 to .79 (*Mdn* SEM = .67) over the 10 adaptive skill areas.

Test-retest reliabilities based on a sample of 51 adults evaluated over 11 days range from .86 to .96 ($Mdn\ r_{tt} = .92$) for the 10 adaptive skill areas. The test-retest reliability for the GAC is .97. Interrater reliabilities on a sample of 47 adults rated by two informants range from .71 to .83 ($Mdn\ r_{rr} = .77$) for the nine skill areas; the interrater reliability for the GAC is .87.

The consistency between teacher and parent ratings was studied in a sample of 30 children. Interrater reliabilities range from .51 to .84 ($Mdn\ r_{rr} = .67$) for nine adaptive skill areas (Work not included); the interrater reliability for the GAC is .81.

Validity

The ABAS has satisfactory content and concurrent validity and differentiates between clinical and nonclinical samples. For example, the correlation between the ABAS GAC and Vineland Adaptive Behavior Scale–Classroom Edition Composite is $r_{xx} = .82$. Correlations between the ABAS GAC and measures of intelligence range from .42 to .55 ($Mdn\ r_{xx} = .49$; see Table 7-12). Correlations between the ABAS GAC and WIAT range from .56 to .79 ($Mdn\ r_{xx} = .67$). A factor analysis of the ABAS indicates that one factor (Adaptive Skill) best describes the scale.

Comment on the ABAS

The ABAS is a valid and reliable instrument for assessing adaptive behavior of children and adults. Overall, the Manual provides valuable information about the ABAS. However, in using the scale, attention must be given to the following issues.

Table 7-12
Correlations Between the Adaptive Behavior Assessment System and Wechsler Intelligence Tests and the Stanford-Binet: IV

ABAS form	Intelligence test	Sample	N	r
Teacher Form	WISC–III	Mixed clinical sample	116	.50
Parent Form	WISC–III	Nonclinical sample	49	.44
Teacher Form	WISC–III	Nonclinical sample	21	.55
Adult Form (Self)	WAIS–III	Nonclinical sample	37	.48
Parent Form	WASI	Nonclinical sample	72	.42
Teacher Form	SB: IV	Mixed clinical sample	20	.50

Source: Adapted from Harrison and Oakland (2000).

First, a seventh-grade (not fifth-grade) reading level (according to the Flesch-Kincaid system) is required, overall, on each form. This should not pose a problem for teachers, but it may be a problem for some informants and for adult clients who do not read at least at the seventh-grade level.

Second, several items appear to require a high level of comprehension. For example, how many informants know what a noun and a verb are, what irregular plural nouns are, what "personal identification" means, and what "routine household task" means? Some items appear to be abstract, such as "Follows safety rules for fire or weather alarms at home," "Maintains safety of bike or car," "Makes plans for home projects in logical steps," and "Places reasonable demands on friends." And some items appear confusing. For example, an item inquiring about playing baseball gives only the option of being part of an organized program. A child can play baseball without being in an organized program.

Third, a "Don't know" or "Does not apply" option would be useful, in addition to or instead of the "Check if you Guessed" option.

Fourth, the standard scores are not normally distributed, and the range of scaled scores is not the same at all ages. Therefore, you must know the available scaled-score ranges if you are to use the scores to make interpretations. For example, *a child who obtains a GAC of 130 at the age of 7 years and a GAC of 120 at the age of 8 years has not lost 10 points. This is purely an artifact of the instrument*—the highest GAC possible at the age of 8 years is 120. The skewed and uneven distribution of scaled scores means that, when individuals have above-average adaptive behavior skills, it will be difficult to evaluate them over time or to evaluate their differential performance in the adaptive skill areas.

Fifth, the ABAS has a limited ceiling (scores run 2 standard deviations or less above the mean). However, this should not be a problem in evaluating most children with developmental disabilities. Also, some adaptive skill areas may reach a ceiling by early adolescence and therefore cannot be reliably measured beyond these years.

Sixth, the gradients of raw scores to age-equivalent scores show dramatic differences on the Teacher Form. You must be thoroughly familiar with these differences if you use the age-equivalent scores. (See Chapter 4 in *Assessment of Children: Cognitive Applications* for a discussion of problems associated with the use of age-equivalent scores.) Similarly, because the range of age-equivalent scores is restricted in some adaptive skill areas, you must use caution in making comparisons among the adaptive skill areas when using age-equivalent scores.

Finally, because the ABAS has one factor only, the 10 adaptive skill areas do not receive factorial support. What this means for the use of the scale in meeting the AAMR requirements (see Chapter 13) remains to be determined.

More research is needed to evaluate the usefulness of the ABAS as a measure of adaptive behavior. Research is especially needed on how the ABAS compares with other measures of adaptive behavior in clinical groups.

BATTELLE DEVELOPMENTAL INVENTORY

The Battelle Developmental Inventory (BDI; Newborg, Stock, & Wnek, 1984) measures developmental skills in children from birth to age 8 years. The BDI has 341 items grouped into five domains: Personal-Social, Adaptive, Motor, Communication, and Cognitive. Items within each domain are clustered into subdomains, or specific skill areas (see Table 7-13). Additionally, there is a Screening Test composed of 96 of the 341 items. The complete BDI takes approximately 60 minutes to administer, while the Screening Test takes about 10 to 15 minutes to administer to children under 3 years and about 20 to 30 minutes to administer to children over 3 years of age.

Following are descriptions of the five domains.

- The Personal-Social domain has 85 items that center on the child's ability to engage in meaningful social interactions. Items involve the quality and frequency of the child's interactions with adults, ability to express emotions such as affection or anger, development of self-awareness and personal knowledge, quality of interactions with other children of the same age, ability to deal with the environment, and adequacy of social-interpersonal development.
- The Adaptive domain has 59 items related to self-help skills and task-related skills. The focus is on behaviors that will enable the child to become increasingly independent. Items relate to visual and auditory attention skills and skills involved in eating, dressing, assuming personal responsibilities, and toileting.
- The Motor domain has 82 items assessing gross- and fine-motor development. Abilities measured include control over large muscles used in sitting, standing, and transferring objects from one hand to the other; physical coordination; locomotion skills; and fine-motor control and visual-motor coordination involved in turning pages, stringing beads, building towers, printing, and other similar activities.
- The Communication domain has 59 items assessing receptive and expressive communication skills. Receptive communication skills involve the ability to discriminate, recognize, and understand sounds, words, nonverbal signs, and gestures. The expressive communication skills involve the ability to produce and use sounds, words, and gestures to relate information to others.
- The Cognitive domain has 56 items assessing conceptual skills. The abilities measured include perceptual discrimination, memory, reasoning and academic skills, and grasping concepts and drawing relationships among objects.

The information needed to evaluate each item is obtained by one of three methods: (a) a structured test format, (b) interviews with parents, or (c) observations of the child in natural settings. Items can be modified for use with children with disabilities. Items are arranged in order of increasing difficulty and are grouped by 6-month intervals from birth to 2 years and by 1-year intervals from 2 to 8 years.

Scores

A 3-point system is used to score the items: 2 points for behavior meeting the specified criterion, 1 point for behavior attempted but not meeting the specified criterion, and no points for behavior failed or not attempted. Raw scores are converted into T scores, standard scores ($M = 100$, $SD = 15$), and age-equivalent scores. The norms were recalibrated in 1987, using medians instead of means to develop the age norms.

Standardization

Stratified quota sampling was used to match the norming sample to the 1981 U.S. Census data, with the stratification variables being geographical region, race, and sex. A total of 800 children participated nationally. Although socioeconomic status was not used as a stratification variable, the SES spectrum was wide, but with a middle-class emphasis. The

Table 7-13
Battelle Developmental Inventory Domains and Subdomains

Domain	Subdomain
Personal-Social	Adult Interaction Expression of Feelings/Affect Self-Concept Peer Interaction Coping Social Role
Adaptive	Attention Eating Dressing Personal Responsibility Toileting
Motor	Muscle Control Body Coordination Locomotion Fine Muscle Perceptual Motor
Communication	Receptive Expressive
Cognitive	Perceptual Discrimination Memory Reasoning and Academic Skills Conceptual Development

Source: Newborg, Stock, and Wnek (1984).

test sites controlled, to some extent, the urban/rural and SES characteristics of the sample.

Reliability

Internal consistency reliabilities are not presented in the Manual. Test-retest reliabilities for the five domains for a sample of 183 children in the norming and clinical samples retested within 1 month of their original test ranged from .76 to .99 (*Mdn* r_{tt} = .95).

Validity

Content validity is acceptable, as judged by experts who evaluated the item content. Construct validity is also satisfactory, as indicated by high intercorrelations among the subdomains and the increasing percentage of items passed by older children. Additionally, the nonclinical standardization sample obtained higher scores than did the clinical sample.

Correlations between the BDI and the Vineland Social Maturity Scale, Developmental Activities Screening Inventory, Stanford-Binet Intelligence Scale: Form L-M, WISC–R, and PPVT were usually significant. The highest correlations were obtained with the Vineland (*r*'s from .79 to .93). With the WISC–R Full Scale IQ, the highest correlations were with the Expressive and Fine Motor subdomains (*r*'s of .79 and .75, respectively), and the lowest correlations were with the Personal-Social and Cognitive subdomains (*r*'s of .42 and .44, respectively). The low correlation between the Cognitive subdomain and the WISC–R is not easy to explain. The Manual did not report a factor analysis for the BDI.

Comment on the BDI

The Battelle Developmental Inventory provides helpful information about important areas of development in young children. Useful features include the mixture of structured test items with interview and observational data and the provisions for evaluating children with physical disabilities. However, in using the BDI, attention must be given to the following issues. First, the norms are over 15 years old. Second, the Manual fails to provide SES information about the norm group. Third, the Manual fails to provide internal consistency reliabilities. Fourth, the age groupings in the norms are too broad—namely, 6-month intervals up to 23 months and 12-month intervals after 23 months (McLinden, 1989). These age groupings fail to take into account the rapid changes that occur during the first 5 to 6 years of development. The broad age ranges may result in a lack of precision in determining standard scores. Fifth, in the first printing of the Manual, the SEMs in the manual are incorrect—they are reported as standard errors of the mean instead of standard errors of measurement (McLinden, 1989). Sixth, more information is needed

about the factor structure of the BDI. McLinden (1989) suggests that the BDI be used as a criterion-referenced instrument rather than as a standardized norm-referenced instrument.

THINKING THROUGH THE ISSUES

1. What are some differences and similarities between adaptive behavior and intelligence?
2. What are some differences and similarities among children with the following three profiles: Profile 1: IQ = 65, Adaptive Behavior Composite = 65; Profile 2: IQ = 65, Adaptive Behavior Composite = 90; Profile 3: IQ = 90, Adaptive Behavior Composite = 65?
3. What uses, if any, might adaptive behavior scales have for individuals other than those with mental retardation?

SUMMARY

1. Adaptive behavior scales assist clinicians in making diagnoses, formulating discharge plans, and developing interventions.
2. Adaptive behavior scales play an important role in the assessment of children with developmental disabilities and children with mental retardation in particular.

Definition of Adaptive Behavior

3. The American Association on Mental Retardation (AAMR, 1992) defines adaptive behavior as the effectiveness with which individuals meet the standards of personal independence and social responsibility expected of individuals of their age and cultural group.
4. Adaptive behavior is best viewed as having a multifactorial structure.
5. Adaptive behavior is not independent of intelligence.
6. The number of dimensions associated with adaptive behavior is unknown.
7. What is accepted as adaptive behavior at one age may not be acceptable at another age.
8. What constitutes adaptive behavior depends on the demands of a given environment.
9. Different measures of adaptive behavior may give different results.
10. An assessment of adaptive behavior must consider the child's physical skills, cognitive ability, affect, motivation, culture, socioeconomic status, family, and environment.

Psychometric Considerations

11. The measurement of adaptive behavior usually depends on information obtained from a parent, a teacher, or another informant.
12. Differences among informants may yield invalid scores, especially when informants lack appropriate information or distort their responses.
13. Research shows that informants have higher levels of agreement when rating externalizing behaviors than when rating internalizing behaviors.

14. Informants who occupy similar roles in relation to the child have higher levels of agreement ($M\ r = .60$) than those who occupy different roles ($M\ r = .28$).

15. Children's self-ratings correlate poorly with ratings made by others ($M\ r = .22$).

16. In evaluating measures of adaptive behavior, use the same criteria as you would for any psychometric measure.

17. Jenkinson (1996) proposed that a needs-based assessment be used to evaluate adaptive behavior because the concept does not lend itself to adequate psychometric measurement.

Informal Assessment of Adaptive Behavior

18. An informal assessment of the 10 adaptive skill areas in the AAMR definition of adaptive behavior may be useful.

Vineland Adaptive Behavior Scales

19. The VABS contains three forms that measure the personal and social skills of disabled and nondisabled individuals. The Survey and Expanded Forms cover individuals from birth to 18-11 years, while the Classroom Edition covers ages 3 to 12-11 years. The standardization sample for the Survey and Expanded Forms generally matched the U.S. Census data, but the standardization sample for the Classroom Edition did not. Reliability and validity are acceptable. The standard scores are not normally distributed throughout all age levels. Caution must be used in comparing age-equivalent scores among the four adaptive behavior domains. The VABS does not measure all of the adaptive behavior areas proposed by the AAMR.

AAMR Adaptive Behavior Scale–School: Second Edition

20. The ABS–S:2 is an adaptive behavior scale designed to measure children's personal and community independence and social skills and adjustment. It is for use with individuals ages 3 to 21 years who may have mental retardation. Standardization, reliability, and validity are satisfactory. The nonuniform range of standard scores makes it difficult to evaluate differential performance among the domains. Caution must be used in comparing age-equivalent scores among the domains. The ABS–S:2 does not measure all of the adaptive behavior areas proposed by the AAMR.

AAMR Adaptive Behavior Scale–Residential and Community: Second Edition

21. The ABS–RC:2 is an adaptive behavior scale designed to measure personal independence and responsibility in daily living and social behavior in adults ages 18 to 79 years. It is for use with individuals who may have mental retardation. Standardization, reliability, and validity are satisfactory. The nonuniform range of standard scores makes it difficult to evaluate differential performance among the domains. The ABS–RC:2 does not measure all of the adaptive behavior areas proposed by the AAMR.

Scales of Independent Behavior–Revised

22. The SIB–R is an individually administered measure of skills needed to function independently in home, social, and community settings. It covers an age span from infancy to mature adult (ages 60 to 90 years). The distribution of the standardization sample by region does not match U.S. Census data. Reliability and validity are satisfactory. The numerous scores provided complicate the use of the scale. The SIB–R does not measure all of the adaptive skill areas proposed by the AAMR. Additional reliability and validity studies are needed.

Adaptive Behavior Assessment System

23. The ABAS has three forms and is designed to measure adaptive behavior skills of children and adults ages 5 to 89 years. Standardization, reliability, and validity are satisfactory. A seventh-grade (not fifth-grade) reading level is required by the scales. The standard scores are not normally distributed. The ABAS has a limited ceiling. Gradients of raw scores to age-equivalent scores show dramatic differences on the Teacher Form; therefore, age-equivalent scores must be carefully interpreted.

Battelle Developmental Inventory

24. The BDI measures developmental skills in children from birth to age 8 years. The norms are over 15 years old. The Manual fails to provide SES information about the norm group or internal consistency reliabilities. The age groupings are too broad, resulting in a failure to take into account the rapid changes that occur during the first 5 to 6 years of development. More information is needed about the factor structure of the BDI. The instrument serves better as a criterion-referenced instrument than as a standardized norm-referenced instrument.

KEY TERMS, CONCEPTS, AND NAMES

Adaptive behavior (p. 190)
Difficulties in defining adaptive behavior (p. 190)
Psychometric considerations in the measurement of adaptive behavior (p. 190)
Informal assessment of adaptive behavior (p. 191)
Vineland Adaptive Behavior Scales (p. 191)
AAMR Adaptive Behavior Scale–School: Second Edition (p. 196)
AAMR Adaptive Behavior Scale–Residential and Community: Second Edition (p. 198)
Scales of Independent Behavior–Revised (p. 200)
Adaptive Behavior Assessment System (p. 202)
Battelle Developmental Inventory (p. 208)

STUDY QUESTIONS

1. Define adaptive behavior. Include in your definition the AAMR definition, the multifactorial structure of adaptive behavior, and difficulties in defining adaptive behavior.

2. Discuss several psychometric considerations involved in the measurement of adaptive behavior.

3. Discuss the strengths and weaknesses of each of the following measures of adaptive behavior:

   Vineland Adaptive Behavior Scales
   AAMR Adaptive Behavior Scale–School: Second Edition

AAMR Adaptive Behavior Scale–Residential and Community: Second Edition

Scales of Independent Behavior–Revised

Adaptive Behavior Assessment System

Battelle Developmental Inventory

Include in your discussion of each measure a description, domains or skill areas, scores, standardization, reliability, validity, and an overall evaluation.

4. Imagine you were going to create a new measure of adaptive behavior for infants and adults to age 90 years. Given the knowledge that you have acquired from this chapter, what type of information would you include in the measure and why? Discuss whether any measure of adaptive behavior can meet the rigorous psychometric requirements of a norm-referenced measure.

8

ASSESSMENT OF VISUAL-MOTOR PERCEPTION AND MOTOR PROFICIENCY

What should be remembered is that many less than perfect measures have proven to be useful in psychology.
—Edward F. Zigler

Bender Visual Motor Gestalt Test

Beery-Buktenica Developmental Test of Visual-Motor Integration–Fourth Edition

Bruininks-Oseretsky Test of Motor Proficiency

Comment on Tests of Visual-Motor Perception and Motor Proficiency

Thinking Through the Issues

Summary

Goals and Objectives

This chapter is designed to enable you to do the following:

• Describe and evaluate two individually administered measures of visual-motor ability

• Describe and evaluate an individually administered measure of motor proficiency

The tests reviewed in this chapter focus on visual-motor perception and integration, visual perception, and motor proficiency. These expressive and receptive functions are an important link in the processing of information, and measuring them is useful in evaluating examinees with possible learning disabilities or neurological deficits. Tests of visual-motor integration and fine- and gross-motor ability are helpful in determining the intactness of the examinee's sensory and motor modalities and in developing remediation programs.

BENDER VISUAL MOTOR GESTALT TEST

The Bender Visual Motor Gestalt Test (Bender-Gestalt; Bender, 1938) is a widely used visual-motor test. The test was developed by Lauretta Bender in 1938 for use with adult clinical populations and with children. It was derived from Gestalt configurations devised by Wertheimer in 1923 to demonstrate the perceptual principles of Gestalt psychology.

The Bender-Gestalt is an individually administered paper-and-pencil test based on nine geometric figures drawn in black (see Figure 8-1) on 4-by-6-inch white cards. The designs are presented one at a time, and the examinee is instructed to copy them on a blank sheet of paper. The test can serve as a good icebreaker at the beginning of an evaluation—the task is innocuous, nonthreatening, interesting, and usually appealing to examinees.

Administrative Suggestions

Give the examinee a No. 2 pencil with an eraser, and place a single sheet of unlined blank 8½-by-11-inch paper vertically in front of the examinee on the table. Also on the table have extra sheets of paper (usually equal to the number of cards) and an extra pencil (in case of breakage).

Place the stack of nine Bender-Gestalt cards face down in the correct position (card A on the top and card 8 on the bottom) on the table and then do one of the following:

Say, "I have nine cards here with designs on them for you to copy." Point to the stack of cards. "Here is the first one." Turn over the first card. "Now go ahead and make one just like it."

or

Say, "Now I would like you to draw some designs for me. There are nine cards here and each card has a drawing on it." Point to the stack of cards. "I want you to copy each drawing. Make each drawing the best you can." Turn over the first card.

If the examinee raises any questions, give a noncommittal reply such as "Make it look as much like the picture on the card as you can," "Do it the way you think best," or "Do the best job you can."

Present each card individually, beginning with card A and following with cards 1 through 8 in numerical order. Be sure to orient the cards correctly. The cards are numbered sequen-

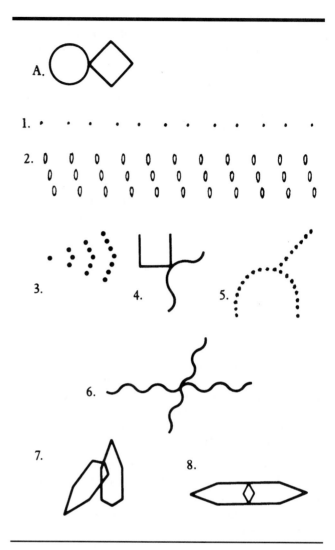

Figure 8-1. Designs on the Bender Visual Motor Gestalt Test.

tially in approximate order of difficulty. Permit the examinee to erase, but do not allow the use of any mechanical aids such as rulers; the examinee must complete or execute the drawings freehand.

The nine designs take approximately 5 minutes to complete. Observe the examinee as he or she draws each design, and record the starting and ending time for each design. Note any large deviation in the time required by the examinee to complete the designs, as a large time deviation (in either direction) suggests how the examinee approaches novel situations. For example, an examinee who requires 15 minutes to copy the designs might have a slow, methodical approach to situations, compulsive tendencies, or depressive features, whereas one who finishes in 2 or 3 minutes or less might have an impulsive style. If the examinee rotates any cards, note the letter or number of each card that is rotated and the amount and direction of the rotation. If the examinee uses more than one sheet of paper, place a caret (∧) at the top of each design that the examinee rotates. The caret will help you recall at a later time the extent of the examinee's rotations. Also, note the examinee's approach to the task, such as his or her degree of impulsiveness or compulsiveness, ability to cope with frustration, and attitude toward the task. Obviously, you should not administer visual-motor tests to examinees with severe visual impairments, unless their vision has been sufficiently corrected with glasses, or to examinees with severe motor impairments.

Variations in Administration

Several other procedures that can be used in administering the Bender-Gestalt are the tachistoscopic procedure, the memory phase procedure, and the group-test procedure. Note that these procedures were not part of the original test.

In the *tachistoscopic procedure,* you show each card for 5 seconds and then remove the card and ask the examinee to draw the design from memory. For the tachistoscopic procedure, use the following directions:

Say, "I am going to show some cards with designs on them. After I show you each card, I will take the card away. Then I want you to draw the design from memory. Do not begin to draw the design until I say, 'Go ahead and draw the design.' Here is the first card. Look at the design." Show the card for 5 seconds, take the card away, and say, "Go ahead and draw the design." Introduce each of the following cards by saying "Here is the next card. Look at the design." Use the same procedure as for the first card.

In the *memory phase procedure,* the examinee draws the nine designs following the standard procedure. After the examinee has drawn the designs, you take away the sheet of paper the examinee used, present a fresh sheet, and ask him or her to draw as many of the designs as he or she can remember: "Now, draw as many of the designs as you can from memory."

For the *group-test procedure,* you need to do one of the following:

- Make enlarged copies of the designs and present the enlarged cards at the front of the room.
- Reproduce the designs in a booklet, with a blank space under each design. Instruct the examinees to copy each design in the blank space under the design.
- Show the designs on an overhead projector or on a slide projector.
- Present individual decks of Bender-Gestalt cards to the examinees.

The most successful method with large numbers of examinees is the first method, the presentation of enlarged Bender-Gestalt cards. The projector methods require special equipment and leave the examinees to draw their designs in semi-darkness. Individual decks have been successful with hyperactive or immature examinees who require extra attention, but you should test only two or three examinees at once using this method. Overall, studies indicate that group administration of the Bender-Gestalt yields reliable protocols, comparable to those obtained under individual administration (Koppitz, 1975).

Observing Performance

In observing an examinee's performance on the Bender-Gestalt (or any other) visual-motor test, consider the following:

1. How does the examinee hold the pencil?
2. In which hand does the examinee hold the pencil?
3. Are the examinee's drawings done with extreme care and deliberation, or are they done impulsively and haphazardly?
4. Does the examinee trace the design with a finger before she or he draws it?
5. Does the examinee count the dots, loops, or sides of figures before drawing a design?
6. Does the examinee glance at the design briefly and then draw it from memory?
7. Does the examinee rotate the card or paper (or both)?
8. Does the examinee make frequent erasures? If so, on what figures or parts of figures (e.g., curves, angulations, overlapping parts, open figures)?
9. What part of a design does the examinee draw first?
10. In what direction does the examinee copy the designs? For example, does the examinee draw the designs from top down or bottom up, from inside out or outside in? Does the examinee change direction of movement from design to design?
11. Does the examinee sketch the designs?
12. Does the examinee have particular difficulty drawing one or more designs? If so, which one or ones?
13. How much space does the examinee use to draw the design? For example, is the drawing approximately the same size as the original or greatly reduced or greatly expanded?
14. How does the examinee arrange the designs on the page? For example, are they laid out in an organized manner or in a random fashion? Is sufficient space allowed between the designs, or are they cramped?
15. How accurate are the examinee's drawings?
16. Do the examinee's drawings show any gross distortions?
17. Does the examinee spend approximately the same amount of time on each design? If not, how much time does she or he spend on the different designs?
18. Does the examinee recognize her or his errors? If so, how does the examinee handle errors? What does she or he say about poorly executed drawings?
19. Does the examinee make comments about each design? If so, what are they?
20. Does the examinee show signs of fatigue? If so, what signs of fatigue does she or he show and when does she or he show them (e.g., at the beginning, middle, or end of the task)?
21. Does the examinee need encouragement to complete the drawings? If so, how does the examinee respond to encouragement?
22. How long does the examinee take to complete the task?
23. Is the amount of time taken by the examinee to draw the designs excessively long or unusually short?

24. What is the examinee's overall reaction to the task? For example, does the examinee express satisfaction or dissatisfaction with the end product?

25. Is there anything unusual or atypical about how the examinee responds to or carries out the task?

Answers to these questions will help you evaluate the examinee's maturation level, visual-motor integration skills, style of responding, reaction to frustration, ability to correct errors, planning and organizational ability, and motivation. The informal observations you make will complement the information you obtain from a formal scoring system. Both informal and formal evaluations will aid you in developing hypotheses about the examinee's perceptual-motor functioning.

Testing-of-Limits

In testing-of-limits on visual-motor tests, you can ask the examinee to compare his or her drawing with the model drawing. For example, you might say, "Look at your drawing and the one on the card. How are they alike and how are they different?" You can then give the examinee another chance to draw one or more of the designs. You might say, "Draw this design again. Do your very best." Your inquiries should help you answer such questions as the following:

- Does the examinee recognize differences between her or his drawing and the model drawing?
- Does the examinee draw the figures correctly after you give her or him another chance?
- Were the examinee's failures due to poor attention to detail, carelessness, impulsiveness, poor organization, fear of completing a difficult task, fatigue, lack of interest, or some other factor(s)?

Some examinees are aware of their errors and can correct them, others are aware of their errors but cannot correct them, and still others are not aware of their errors. Testing-of-limits procedures can help you to (a) pinpoint whether the problem is perceptual, motor, or perceptual-motor integration, (b) develop and test hypotheses about the examinee's performance, and (c) develop recommendations.

Developmental Bender Test Scoring System

The Developmental Bender Test Scoring System (Koppitz, 1964, 1975) is a popular objective scoring system for evaluating the Bender-Gestalt drawings of young examinees. It is composed of two parts: (a) developmental scoring and (b) optional scoring of emotional indicators. The first part has the most relevance for the evaluation of visual-motor perception. There are 30 developmental scoring items; each item receives 1 or 0 points, depending on whether an error occurs (see Table 8-1).

The Developmental Bender Test Scoring System uses four categories to classify errors: distortion of shape, rotation, in-

tegration difficulties, and perseveration. On a scoring sheet, record 1 point for each distortion made by the examinee. Then sum the points to obtain a total error score, and convert this score to a percentile rank. Percentile norms are available for examinees ages 5-0 to 11-11 years (Koppitz, 1975). Table F-4 in Appendix F shows standard scores ($M = 100$, $SD = 15$) for the total error raw score based on the Koppitz data. These scores are most suitable for ages 5-0 through 8-0 and should not be used above age 11-11. Since the norms are over 25 years old, they should be used cautiously; we do not know how representative they are at present.

Error classifications.   Let's examine examples of the four types of errors in the Developmental Bender Test Scoring System.

1. *Distortion of shape.* This error involves destruction of the Gestalt, such as a misshapen figure, disproportionate sizing of the parts of a figure, substitution of circles or dashes for dots, substitution of distinct angles for curves, total lack of curves where they should exist, extra angles, or missing angles. Score distortion of shape for Figures A, 1, 3, 5, 6, 7, and 8, for a possible total error score of 10 points.

2. *Rotation.* This error involves rotation of a figure or any part thereof by 45° or more. Score rotation when the examinee rotates a Bender-Gestalt card, even if the examinee copies the design correctly as shown on the rotated card. Score this error for Figures A, 1, 2, 3, 4, 5, 7, and 8, for a possible total error score of 8 points.

3. *Integration.* This error involves (a) failure to connect the two parts of a figure properly, either by leaving more than ⅛ inch between the parts or by causing them to overlap, (b) failure to cross two lines or crossing them in an incorrect place, or (c) omission or addition of rows of dots or loss of the overall shape in the case of figures composed of dots or circles. Score integration difficulties for Figures A, 2, 3, 4, 5, 6, and 7, for a possible total error score of 9 points.

4. *Perseveration.* This error involves increase, continuation, or prolongation of the number of units in the design. Score this error for three of the designs: (a) when there are more than 15 dots in a row in Figure 1, (b) when there are more than 14 columns of circles in Figure 2, and (c) when there are 6 or more complete curves in either direction in Fig-

Table 8-1
Developmental Bender Test Scoring System

Figure	Error	Description of error
A	Distortion of shape	(a) Square, circle, or both excessively flattened or misshapen, with one axis of circle or square being twice as long as the other one; (b) disproportionate sizing of square and circle, with one being twice as large as the other one.
	Rotation	(a) Rotation of figure or any part of it by 45° or more; (b) rotation of stimulus card, even if figure is then copied correctly as shown on the rotated card.
	Integration	Failure to join circle and square, with curve and adjacent corner of square being more than ⅛ inch apart (applies also to overlap).
1	Distortion of shape	Five or more dots converted into circles.
	Rotation	(a) Rotation of figure by 45° or more; (b) rotation of stimulus card, even if figure is then copied correctly as shown on the rotated card.
	Perseveration	More than 15 dots in a row.
2	Rotation	(a) Rotation of figure by 45° or more; (b) rotation of stimulus card, even if figure is then copied correctly as shown on the rotated card.
	Integration	(a) Omission of one or two rows of circles; (b) use of row of dots for Figure 1 as first row for Figure 2; (c) four or more circles in the majority of columns; (d) addition of row of circles.
	Perseveration	More than 14 columns of circles in a row.
3	Distortion of shape	Five or more dots converted into circles.
	Rotation	(a) Rotation of axis of figure by 45° or more; (b) rotation of stimulus card, even if figure is then copied correctly as shown on the rotated card.
	Integration	(a) Shape of design lost, as noted by failure to increase each successive row of dots, unrecognizable or reversed shape of arrow head, conglomeration of dots, or single row of dots; (b) continuous line instead of row of dots.
4	Rotation	(a) Rotation of figure or part of it by 45° or more; (b) rotation of stimulus card, even if figure is then copied correctly as shown on the rotated card.
	Integration	(a) Curve and adjacent corner more than ⅛ inch apart (applies also to overlap); (b) curve touching both corners.
5	Distortion of shape	Five or more dots converted into circles.
	Rotation	Rotation of total figure by 45° or more.
	Integration	(a) Shape of design lost, as noted by conglomeration of dots, straight line, or circle of dots instead of an arc; (b) continuous line instead of dots in either arc, extension, or both.
6	Distortion of shape	(a) Substitution of three or more distinct angles for curves; (b) no curve at all in one or both lines.
	Integration	(a) Two lines not crossing or crossing at the extreme end of one or both lines; (b) two wavy lines interwoven.
	Perseveration	Six or more complete sinusoidal curves in either direction.
7	Distortion of shape	(a) Disproportionate sizing of two hexagons, with one being at least twice as large as the other one; (b) hexagons excessively misshapen, as noted by extra or missing angles in one or both.
	Rotation	(a) Rotation of figure or any part of it by 45° or more; (b) rotation of stimulus card, even if figure is then copied correctly as shown on the rotated card.
	Integration	Lack of overlap or excessive overlap of hexagons.
8	Distortion of shape	Hexagon or diamond excessively misshapen, as noted by extra angles, missing angles, or omission of diamond.
	Rotation	(a) Rotation of figure by 45° or more; (b) rotation of stimulus card, even if figure is then copied correctly as shown on the rotated card.

Source: From Elizabeth Munsterberg Koppitz, THE BENDER GESTALT TEST FOR YOUNG CHILDREN. Copyright © 1975 by Allyn & Bacon. Reprinted/adapted by permission.

ure 6. A total error score of 3 points is possible. (This type of perseveration is referred to as *within-card perseveration.* There is a second, much rarer type of perseveration called *card-to-card perseveration,* which occurs when a preceding design or parts of it influence succeeding designs. You do not score card-to-card perseveration in the Developmental Bender Test Scoring System.)

Emotional indicators. There are 12 emotional indicators in the Developmental Bender Test Scoring System. These indicators purport to evaluate the examinee's emotional stability, based on a qualitative analysis of his or her visual-motor performance. Little is known about the validity of these indicators. Consequently, they are not further discussed in this chapter and *are not recommended for use.*

Standardization. The 1975 Koppitz norms are based on a sample of 975 elementary school examinees, ages 5-0 to 11-11 years, living in rural areas, small towns, suburbs, and large metropolitan centers in the West, South, and Northeast. The composition of the sample was 86% Euro American, 8.5% African American, 4.5% Hispanic American, and 1% Asian American. The sample was not representative of the country, as its geographic distribution was highly skewed in favor of the Northeast. The socioeconomic characteristics of the sample were not reported.

Reliability. Test-retest reliabilities for the Developmental Bender Test Scoring System total score range from $r_{tt} = .50$ to .90 (*Mdn* $r_{tt} = .77$), with intervals ranging from the same day to 8 months for samples of 19 to 193 examinees in kindergarten to sixth grade (Koppitz, 1975). These reliabilities are not sufficiently high to warrant the making of diagnostic decisions. They do appear adequate for formulating hypotheses about an examinee's visual-motor ability, however.

Interexaminer reliabilities are high, ranging from $r = .79$ to .99 (*Mdn* $r = .91$; Koppitz, 1975). Other studies report high interexaminer reliabilities (r ranges from .93 to .97; Bolen, Hewett, Hall, & Mitchell, 1992; McIntosh, Belter, Saylor, & Finch, 1988; Neale & McKay, 1985).

The test-retest reliabilities of the four separate error scores (distortion, rotation, integration, and perseveration) are much lower than those of the total score ($r_{tt} = .83$ for total score, $r_{tt} = .29$ to .62 for error scores; Wallbrown & Fremont, 1980). Therefore, your focus in interpreting the Bender-Gestalt should be on the total score, not on the individual sources of error.

Validity. The validity of the Developmental Bender Test Scoring System depends on how the test is used. When the Bender-Gestalt is used as a test of perceptual-motor development in examinees, the Developmental Bender Test Scoring System has acceptable validity, provided research shows that the norms are representative. Copying errors decrease

steadily between the ages of 5 and 9 years, suggesting that the test is sensitive to maturational changes. For examinees over 8 years of age, however, the Developmental Bender Test Scoring System distinguishes only those with below-average perceptual-motor development from those with normal development, because most examinees obtain near-perfect performance (Koppitz, 1964). Mean errors were also found to decrease in a sample of 1,165 Italian children between the ages of 3-6 and 11-5 years (Mazzeschi & Lis, 1999).

Concurrent validity of the Developmental Bender Test Scoring System has been established by correlating it with several tests of visual-motor perception (Koppitz, 1975). Correlations with the Frostig Developmental Test of Visual Perception range from $r = .39$ to .56 (*Mdn* $r = .47$), and correlations with the Developmental Test of Visual-Motor Integration range from $r = .51$ to .77 (*Mdn* $r = .65$; Breen, 1982; Breen, Carlson, & Lehman, 1985; DeMers, Wright, & Dappen, 1981; Krauft & Krauft, 1972; Lehman & Breen, 1982; Porter & Binder, 1981; Shapiro & Simpson, 1994; Skeen, Strong, & Book, 1982; Spirito, 1980; Wesson & Kispert, 1986; Wright & DeMers, 1982).

Correlations with several intelligence tests range from $r = -.19$ to $-.66$ (*Mdn* $r = -.48$; Koppitz, 1975). (The negative correlations occur because the Developmental Bender Test Scoring System yields error scores—higher error scores are associated with lower intelligence test scores.) Other studies also report low to moderate correlations between the Developmental Bender Test Scoring System and measures of intelligence (Aylward & Schmidt, 1986; Breen et al., 1985; Nielson & Sapp, 1991; Shapiro & Simpson, 1994; Yousefi, Shahim, Razavieh, Mehryar, Hosseini, & Alborzi, 1992).

Research supports the validity of error scores as a general measure of visual-motor integration (Snow & Desch, 1989). Studies also indicate that the Bender-Gestalt has low to moderate correlations with measures of reading and arithmetic and school grades for elementary school examinees (Blaha, Fawaz, & Wallbrown, 1979; Brannigan, Aabye, Baker, & Ryan, 1995; Caskey & Larson, 1980; Fuller & Vance, 1993; Fuller & Wallbrown, 1983; Koppitz, 1975; Lesiak, 1984; Nielson & Sapp, 1991; Smith & Smith, 1988; Vance, Fuller, & Lester, 1986). These findings suggest that the relationship between the Bender-Gestalt and academic skills is *too weak to warrant the use of the Bender-Gestalt for predicting school achievement for any individual examinee.* Successful academic achievement depends on many factors, including cognitive ability, level of maturity, experience, school atmosphere, pedagogy, perceptual-motor development, motivational variables, and familial factors; perceptual-motor skills, therefore, comprise only one part of the total picture.

Qualitative Scoring System

The Qualitative Scoring System for the Modified Version of the Bender-Gestalt (Brannigan & Brunner, 1989, 1996) is designed to measure visual-motor skills in children ages 4-6 to

You see—at this age they can't copy a diamond properly.

From *OF CHILDREN, 3rd edition*, by G. R. Lefrancois © 1980. Reprinted with permission of Wadsworth, a division of Thomson Learning. Fax 800 730-2215.

8-5 years. In the 1996 revision, a minor change was made in the scoring system and a new norm group was used.

The system uses six cards from the Bender-Gestalt (A, 1, 2, 4, 6, and 8) and the following 6-point scoring system to judge the overall quality of each design.

- 0 is given for random drawing, scribbling, no concept of the design, or no attempt at copying the design.
- 1 is given for a drawing that reflects an attempt to create a design that resembles the original, although omissions and severe distortions may be present.
- 2 is given for a drawing that has all the major elements present, although major distortions may be present.
- 3 is given for a drawing that has all the major elements present and is recognizable, although minor distortions may be present.
- 4 is given for a design that is clearly recognizable and is drawn with only slight inconsistencies.
- 5 is given for a design that represents an accurate representation.

The norms are based on a sample of 1,160 children ages 4-6 to 8-5 years, drawn from all four geographic regions of the United States. Although no U.S. Census data are presented, the sample generally matched the 1990 U.S. Census data with respect to sex, urban/suburban area, and ethnicity (G. Brannigan, personal communication, July 2001).

T scores and percentile ranks are provided for six-month age intervals and for grade levels. Studies based on the 1989 and 1996 versions suggest that the test generally has satisfactory interrater, test-retest, and split-half reliability, as well as satisfactory concurrent and predictive validity (Brannigan

& Brunner, 1989, 1991, 1993; Brannigan, Aabye, Baker, & Ryan, 1995; Chan, 2000; Fuller & Vance, 1995; Moose & Brannigan, 1997; Parsons & Weinberg, 1993; Schachter, Brannigan, & Tooke, 1991).

Other Scoring Systems

Other scoring systems available for the Bender-Gestalt include those by Hutt (1969), Mercer and Lewis (1978), Pascal and Suttell (1951), and Watkins (1976); however, these systems are not reviewed in this chapter. You should carefully evaluate the norming sample, reliability, and validity of any system that you use to score the Bender-Gestalt.

Interpreting Performance on the Bender-Gestalt (and Other Visual-Motor Tests)

Copying designs requires fine-motor development, perceptual discrimination ability, the ability to integrate perceptual and motor processes, and the ability to shift attention between the original design and the design that is being drawn. Inadequate visual-motor performance may result from misperception (faulty interpretation of input information), execution difficulties (faulty fine-motor response output), or integrative or central processing difficulties (faulty memory storage or retrieval systems). (Note that you do not have to use any scoring system to interpret performance on the Bender-Gestalt.)

Sometimes it is possible to discern whether the difficulty lies in the output process (motor or expressive functions) or the input process (perceptual or receptive functions).

- If the examinee struggles to reproduce the designs, the difficulty is likely to be motor or expressive.
- If the examinee draws the designs quickly and easily but with errors that he or she does not recognize, the difficulty may be perceptual or receptive and not entirely motor.
- If the examinee cannot see his or her errors, the trouble may lie in input mechanisms.
- If the examinee can acknowledge his or her errors but cannot correct them, the difficulty may be with faulty output mechanisms.

Factors that may lead to poor perceptual-motor functioning include the following:

- Visual problems
- Physiological limitations associated with illness, injury, fatigue, or muscular weakness
- Physically disabling conditions, such as low birth weight, cerebral palsy, or sickle cell anemia
- Environmental stresses
- Impulsiveness
- Inadequate motivation
- Emotional problems

- Mental retardation
- Social or cultural deprivation
- Limited experiences

Clinicians sometimes use the Bender-Gestalt to assess brain injury. However, there are no specific pathognomonic signs (i.e., signs indicative of a disease) on the Bender-Gestalt that are definitely associated with brain injury, mental retardation, or any other physical or psychological disorder. *Never use the Bender-Gestalt alone to make a diagnosis of brain injury.* It is a tool for evaluating visual-motor ability, and inadequate visual-motor ability may or may not reflect brain injury. For the assessment of brain injury, use the Bender-Gestalt in conjunction with a battery of neuropsychological tests (see Chapter 19).

Following are some indications of poor visual-motor ability on the Bender-Gestalt (Marley, 1982). You will need to evaluate these indications in the context of medical, developmental, educational, psychological, and neuropsychological information in order to develop hypotheses to account for a child's performance on the Bender-Gestalt.

1. *Sequence confusion*—changing direction three or more times (a directional change occurs when the order in which the designs are drawn differs from the expected or logical progression). Example:

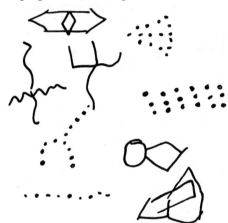

2. *Collision*—crowding the designs or allowing the end of one design to touch or overlap a part of another design. Example:

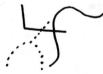

3. *Superimposition of design*—drawing one design (or more) directly on top of another design. Example:

4. *Workover*—reinforcing a line or lines in a whole design or a part thereof. Example:

5. *Irregular line quality*—drawing irregular lines, particularly when the examinee shows tremor during the drawing of the lines. Example:

6. *Angulation difficulty*—increasing, decreasing, distorting, or omitting the angulation on any figure in a design. Example:

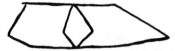

7. *Perseveration*—redrawing an entire design or a part thereof, thereby increasing, continuing, or prolonging the number of units in the design. Example:

8. *Line extension*—extending a line or adding lines that were not present in the stimulus figure. Example:

9. *Contamination*—combining parts of two different Bender-Gestalt figures. Example:

10. *Rotation*—rotating a figure 45° or more from its standard position. Example:

11. *Omission*—leaving a gap in a figure, reproducing only part of a figure, separating or fragmenting parts of a design, or omitting elements of a design. Example:

12. *Retrogression*—substituting solid lines or loops for circles; substituting dashes for dots, dots for circles, or circles for dots; and/or filling in circles. Example:

• . • • • • . • • •
• . • • . . . • • •
. • . • • • • • • •

13. *Bizarre doodling*—adding peculiar elements that have no relationship to the stimulus design. Example:

14. *Scribbling*—drawing primitive lines that have no relationship to the stimulus design. Example:

Comment on the Bender-Gestalt

The Bender-Gestalt is useful for developing hypotheses about an examinee's perceptual-motor ability. Alone, however, it is not a sufficient basis for making definitive diagnoses. It provides indices of the perceptual-motor development of examinees, particularly those between 5 and 8 years of age, and of perceptual-motor deficits in older examinees and adults. It continues to be a popular instrument (Piotrowski, 1995).

Exercise 8.1.
Evaluating Statements Made on the Basis
of the Bender-Gestalt

Each of the following statements contains an error. Critically evaluate each statement, and then compare your evaluations with those in the Comment section.

Poor Writing

1. "Her perceptual-motor skill fell in her age level."
2. "She drew quickly and carefully during the Bender-Gestalt test, but rarely inspected the cards. She positioned her face very close to each card and was very precise by counting the dots."
3. "The Bender-Gestalt determines whether or not the person is suffering from distortion in the visual-motor process."

Technical Errors

4. "The Bender-Gestalt results are invalid because the Developmental Bender Test Scoring System does not permit one to score the Bender-Gestalt for a 14-year-old."
5. "On the Bender-Gestalt she had two errors."

Inaccurate or Incomplete Interpretations

6. "All of the errors Tom made on the Bender-Gestalt are significant indicators of brain injury."
7. "Two figures collided, which possibly indicates some peripheral neurological impairment."
8. "The Bender-Gestalt results suggest good reading ability."
9. "Her small Bender-Gestalt drawings suggest that she was anxious during the test session."
10. "Alice, a 14-year-old, scored a 1 on the Koppitz developmental scoring system for the Bender-Gestalt. Therefore, a slight perceptual-motor problem may exist."
11. "Her completion of the designs in less than 3 minutes may indicate an impulsive style."
12. This statement was written about a 16-year-old: "Bill's performance on the Bender-Gestalt suggests a slightly abnormal level of perceptual-motor maturation."
13. "Karla's generally quiet behavior during testing was supported by indications of passivity in her Bender-Gestalt drawings."
14. "Her variable use of space on the Bender-Gestalt—constricting and expanding in the same protocol—may indicate ambivalent modes of approach-avoidance behavior and wide mood fluctuations."
15. "Susan's Bender-Gestalt drawings showed no score, and suggest no obvious personality characteristics."
16. "His methodical sequencing may indicate rigidity in cognitive style."

Inappropriate Recommendations

17. "The existence of emotional indicators on the Bender-Gestalt suggests that Joanne should participate in counseling."
18. "His performance on the Bender-Gestalt indicates that Frank should have visual-motor training to assist with his handwriting skills."

Comment

1. This sentence is awkward. *Suggestion:* "Her perceptual-motor skills appear to be adequate for her age."
2. This description is contradictory and confusing. If she rarely inspected the cards, how could she have been very precise by counting the dots?
3. This is an awkward way of describing the abilities required by the Bender-Gestalt. A better way is to describe the child's performance on the Bender-Gestalt: "On the Bender-Gestalt, which is a measure of visual-motor ability, the child's performance was in the normal range (at the 55th percentile)."
4. "Invalid" means that the test instrument does not measure what is purports to measure. Therefore, you should not criticize the validity of the Bender-Gestalt based on the absence of norms for 14-year-olds in the Developmental Bender Test Scoring System. In addition, it is possible to interpret the Bender-Gestalt without using the Developmental Bender Test Scoring System norms. There are

other scoring systems, and the drawings can be evaluated for visual-motor difficulties using the Koppitz framework.

5. This sentence fails to give the name of the scoring system or the standard score and percentile rank associated with the two errors. A list of the number of errors is of limited, if any, use. *Suggestion:* "Under the Developmental Bender Test Scoring System, her standard score on the Bender-Gestalt was _____, which is at the _____ percentile rank."

6. This statement is misleading. Errors on the Bender-Gestalt may have no relationship to brain injury. Errors may simply be indicators of maturational difficulties, developmental delays, perceptual difficulties, integration difficulties, and so forth. Do not suggest a possible brain disorder on the basis of Bender-Gestalt errors exclusively. A diagnosis of brain injury should be arrived at by considering the neurological evaluation and clinical history, as well as a neuropsychological evaluation where appropriate (see Chapters 18 and 19).

7. Do not interpret collision as indicating "peripheral neurological impairment." This interpretation is not supported by research. Collision may be due to poor planning, carelessness, impulsiveness, or other factors; it may have nothing to do with peripheral neurological impairment. As noted in item 6, a statement indicating possible neurological impairment should never be made solely on the basis of Bender-Gestalt performance.

8. Results from the Bender-Gestalt should not be used to assess reading ability. Reading ability should be evaluated with valid measures of reading.

9. Small Bender-Gestalt drawings may have nothing to do with anxiety. Small drawings may simply reflect the examinee's response style.

10. The Koppitz norms are primarily applicable for ages 5 through 8 and somewhat applicable for ages 9, 10, and 11 years. Although the norms do not apply after 11 years, the method of analyzing errors is applicable for any age. One minor error at any age is not likely to reflect a perceptual problem.

11. Drawing or copying rapidly is not necessarily an indication of impulsivity. Although completing designs rapidly is a possible indication of impulsivity, the quality of performance is also important in determining impulsivity. Before suggesting impulsivity, the examiner should look for corroborating signs.

12. "Abnormal" is a powerful term, and it may be misinterpreted. Do not use this term unless there is clear evidence of severe perceptual-motor difficulties. *Suggestion:* "Bill's performance on the Bender-Gestalt suggests that he has some perceptual-motor difficulties." Follow this statement by a discussion of the aspects of the child's performance that led to this conclusion.

13. There is little, if any, research to indicate that the Bender-Gestalt provides valid indices of passivity in children. Therefore, delete this statement.

14. "Variable use of space" may indicate organizational difficulties, subtle loss of efficiency of judgment or planning, or some other type of difficulty and may have little to do with personality or mood. Therefore, delete this statement.

15. This is a poor way of saying that her performance was excellent or that no errors were made. Also, the interpretation is misleading because the reader is led to believe that (a) the test measures personality rather than perceptual-motor skills and (b) the child has no personality. *Suggestion:* "Susan's visual-motor perceptual skills appear appropriate for her age."

16. Being methodical could also indicate a well-organized and careful style. The hypothesis given is fraught with problems and should be deleted. It is permissible, however, to say that the child approached the task in a careful and methodical manner.

17. Emotional indicators on the Bender-Gestalt are not well supported by research. The clinical history, observations, interview, and other test results should be considered in evaluating a child's affective reactions. The Bender-Gestalt alone should *never* be used to make a recommendation for counseling.

18. This recommendation is vague because it does not specify what type of visual-motor training is needed. Furthermore, because the Bender-Gestalt does not assess handwriting skills, this recommendation is inappropriate. Handwriting should be assessed with handwriting samples.

BEERY-BUKTENICA DEVELOPMENTAL TEST OF VISUAL-MOTOR INTEGRATION–FOURTH EDITION

The Beery-Buktenica Developmental Test of Visual-Motor Integration–Fourth Edition (VMI–4; Beery, 1997) is a test of perceptual-motor ability for examinees ages 3 to 17 years. There are 27 items arranged in order of increasing difficulty. The first three items, for examinees who are under the age of 6 years or who have difficulty copying designs, require examinees to imitate the examiner's drawings of vertical, horizontal, and circular lines. The remaining 24 items require all examinees to copy designs printed in a test booklet. The examinee draws each design in a square directly below the model. No erasing or rotating of the booklet is permitted. The test is discontinued after three consecutive failures. The VMI–4 can be either individually or group administered in about 15 minutes. There is also a short form consisting of 18 items. New supplemental tests of visual perception and motor coordination are described in the Manual, but these tests are not covered in this review.

Scores

Each design is scored 1 or 0. Each of several criteria must be met to obtain a score of 1. Raw scores are converted into standard scores ($M = 100$, $SD = 15$), percentile ranks, and age-equivalent scores. Norms are in 1-month intervals from ages 3-0 to 17-11 years.

The range of standard scores on the VMI–4 differs at different ages (see Table 8-2). The highest standard score is 155, but this score is available only at ages 3-0 to 9-3. Beginning at age 9-4, the highest scaled score available drops by about 1 additional point for each age group. By age 17-10, the highest standard score is 106. Similarly, the lowest standard score is

Table 8-2
Range of VMI–4 Standard Scores

Age	VMI	Age	VMI	Age	VMI
3-0 to 3-1	73–155	8-0 to 8-1	45–155	13-0 to 13-1	45–128
3-2 to 3-3	71–155	8-2 to 8-3	45–155	13-2 to 13-3	45–127
3-4 to 3-5	69–155	8-4 to 8-5	45–155	13-4 to 13-5	45–126
3-6 to 3-7	67–155	8-6 to 8-7	45–155	13-6 to 13-7	45–125
3-8 to 3-9	65–155	8-8 to 8-9	45–155	13-8 to 13-9	45–124
3-10 to 3-11	63–155	8-10 to 8-11	45–155	13-10 to 13-11	45–124
4-0 to 4-1	62–155	9-0 to 9-1	45–155	14-0 to 14-1	45–123
4-2 to 4-3	60–155	9-2 to 9-3	45–155	14-2 to 14-3	45–122
4-4 to 4-5	57–155	9-4 to 9-5	45–154	14-4 to 14-5	45–122
4-6 to 4-7	56–155	9-6 to 9-7	45–153	14-6 to 14-7	45–121
4-8 to 4-9	54–155	9-8 to 9-9	45–152	14-8 to 14-9	45–120
4-10 to 4-11	52–155	9-10 to 9-11	45–150	14-10 to 14-11	45–119
5-0 to 5-1	51–155	10-0 to 10-1	45–149	15-0 to 15-1	45–119
5-2 to 5-3	49–155	10-2 to 10-3	45–148	15-2 to 15-3	45–118
5-4 to 5-5	46–155	10-4 to 10-5	45–146	15-4 to 15-5	45–117
5-6 to 5-7	45–155	10-6 to 10-7	45–145	15-6 to 15-7	45–116
5-8 to 5-9	45–155	10-8 to 10-9	45–144	15-8 to 15-9	45–115
5-10 to 5-11	45–155	10-10 to 10-11	45–143	15-10 to 15-11	45–114
6-0 to 6-1	45–155	11-0 to 11-1	45–142	16-0 to 16-1	45–113
6-2 to 6-3	45–155	11-2 to 11-3	45–141	16-2 to 16-3	45–112
6-4 to 6-5	45–155	11-4 to 11-5	45–140	16-4 to 16-5	45–111
6-6 to 6-7	45–155	11-6 to 11-7	45–139	16-6 to 16-7	45–110
6-8 to 6-9	45–155	11-8 to 11-9	45–138	16-8 to 16-9	45–110
6-10 to 6-11	45–155	11-10 to 11-11	45–136	16-10 to 16-11	45–109
7-0 to 7-1	45–155	12-0 to 12-1	45–135	17-0 to 17-1	45–109
7-2 to 7-3	45–155	12-2 to 12-3	45–133	17-2 to 17-3	45–108
7-4 to 7-5	45–155	12-4 to 12-5	45–132	17-4 to 17-5	45–108
7-6 to 7-7	45–155	12-6 to 12-7	45–130	17-6 to 17-7	45–107
7-8 to 7-9	45–155	12-8 to 12-9	45–129	17-8 to 17-9	45–107
7-10 to 7-11	45–155	12-10 to 12-11	45–128	17-10 to 17-11	45–106

45, but this score is not available at ages 3-0 to 5-4. In fact, the lowest standard score available at age 3-0 is 73.

and socioeconomic status following the 1996 U.S. Census data.

Standardization

The standardization sample consisted of 2,614 children stratified by gender, ethnicity, region, geographical residence,

Reliability

Internal consistency reliabilities range from .79 to .89 ($M\ r_{xx} =$ .82) for the 24 items that are directly copied. SEMs range from

4 to 6 points. Test-retest reliability with a sample of 122 children in a regular school is $r_{tt} = .87$. Interrater reliability, assessed by having two raters score 100 protocols, is $r_{rr} = .94$.

Validity

Content validity, concurrent validity, and construct validity are satisfactory. The content of the VMI–4 reflects visual-motor ability. Acceptable correlations between the VMI–4 and other tests of visual-motor ability are reported in the Manual. Construct validity is supported by an increase in raw scores with age and by acceptable correlations with intelligence test scores and achievement test scores. In a sample of 17 children between the ages of 6 and 12 years who had learning disabilities, correlations with the WISC–R were as follows: .48 with the Verbal Scale IQ, .66 with the Performance Scale IQ, and .62 with the Full Scale IQ. In a sample of 44 fourth- and fifth-grade students from regular classrooms, correlations between the VMI–4 and the California Test of Basic Skills were as follows: .58 with Reading, .68 with Language, .42 with Mathematics, and .63 with Overall Total. Mayes and Calhoun (1998) reported a correlation of .99 between the VMI–3 and the VMI–4 in a sample of 120 children ages 4 to 17 years. The mean difference between the two forms was 1.5 points.

Comment on the VMI–4

The VMI–4 is a useful measure of visual-motor ability. The initial designs are especially helpful with young children. In spite of the high interexaminer reliability reported in the Manual, however, several subjective scoring judgments are required. A protractor is needed for accurate scoring. At ages above 12-6 years, the norms are skewed in that standard scores range three standard deviations below the mean but only two standard deviations (or less) above the mean. Thus, you must be careful in interpreting retest scores. For example, a change in standard scores from 142 at age 11 years to 128 at age 13 years does not reflect a decline in visual-motor abilities. At both ages, these are the highest possible standard scores available on the VMI–4. Many of the observation guidelines and interpretive rationales described for the Bender-Gestalt (see earlier in this chapter) also apply to the VMI–4. However, the VMI–4 does not require the examinee to organize drawings on a blank page. Abbatiello and Kpo (1988) advise that use of the VMI be restricted to children under the age of 12 years because the test has a marked ceiling effect.

BRUININKS-OSERETSKY TEST OF MOTOR PROFICIENCY

The Bruininks-Oseretsky Test of Motor Proficiency (Bruininks, 1978) is an individually administered test of gross- and fine-motor functioning for examinees ages 4½ to 14½ years. The test contains 46 items grouped into eight subtests (see Table 8-3); four measure gross-motor skills (subtests 1, 2, 3, and 4), three measure fine-motor skills (subtests 6, 7, and 8), and one measures both gross- and fine-motor skills (subtest 5). In addition to individual subtest scores, composite scores are obtained for the gross-motor subtests, fine-motor subtests, and total battery. A short form of 14 items can be used as a brief survey of motor proficiency. The complete test takes between 45 and 60 minutes to administer.

The Bruininks-Oseretsky is based on the United States adaptation of the Oseretsky Tests of Motor Proficiency (Doll, 1946). About 60% of the items are new; the remainder are

---

Table 8-3
Description of Subtests in the Bruininks-Oseretsky Test of Motor Proficiency

Test	Description
1. Running Speed and Agility (one item)	Running speed
2. Balance (eight items)	Static balance and maintaining balance while executing various walking movements
3. Bilateral Coordination (eight items)	Sequential and simultaneous coordination of upper with lower limbs and of upper limbs only
4. Strength (three items)	Arm and shoulder strength, abdominal strength, and leg strength
5. Upper Limb Coordination (nine items)	Visual tracking with movements of arms and hands and precise movements of arms, hands, and fingers
6. Response Speed (one item)	Ability to respond quickly to a moving visual stimulus
7. Visual-Motor Control (eight items)	Ability to coordinate precise hand and visual movements
8. Upper Limb Speed and Dexterity (eight items)	Hand and finger dexterity, hand speed, and arm speed

from the Oseretsky Tests of Motor Proficiency. The Bruininks-Oseretsky reflects advances in content, structure, and technical qualities over former versions of the tests.

Scores

The test provides subtest scores ($M = 15$, $SD = 5$), a Gross Motor Composite score, a Fine Motor Composite score, and a Battery Composite score ($M = 50$, $SD = 10$ for all composite scores). For each of these areas, the Manual provides standard scores, percentile ranks, and stanines; in addition, it provides age equivalents for the subtest scores.

Standardization

The Bruininks-Oseretsky was standardized on 765 boys and girls selected from several schools, day-care centers, nursery schools, and kindergartens in the United States and Canada. A stratified sampling procedure, based on 1970 U.S. Census data, was used to select the examinees. Stratification variables included age, sex, race, community size, and geographic region.

Reliability

Test-retest reliabilities over a period of 7 to 12 days for the Battery Composite were $r_{tt} = .89$ both for a sample of 63 second-graders and for a sample of 63 sixth-graders. For the Fine Motor Composite, they were $r_{tt} = .88$ and .68 for the second- and sixth-graders, respectively; and for the Gross Motor Composite, they were $r_{tt} = .77$ and .85 for the second- and sixth-graders, respectively. Average subtest test-retest reliabilities range from $r_{tt} = .56$ to .86 ($Mdn = .74$). Subtest reliabilities indicate that caution is needed in using subtest scores as a basis for clinical interpretation. Average standard errors of measurement are 4.0 for the Battery Composite, 4.6 for the Gross Motor Composite, and 4.7 for the Fine Motor Composite.

Validity

The construct validity of the Bruininks-Oseretsky was examined in terms of (a) the relationship between test scores and chronological age, (b) the internal consistency of the subtests, and (c) the factor structure of the items in each subtest. Product-moment correlations between subtest scores and chronological age for the standardization sample range from $r = .57$ to .86 ($Mdn\ r = .78$). These correlations indicate a close relationship between subtest scores and chronological age. Subtest scores show the expected increase from one age group to the next. Internal consistency measures indicate that the correlations between items and their respective subtest scores are closer than between items and total test scores.

A factor analysis performed on the standardization sample provides limited support for the grouping of items into sub-tests. The Manual reports five factors, with one factor (general motor ability) accounting for approximately 70% of the total variance. Thus, only 30% of the variance was associated with the individual subtests. Most of the items measuring fine-motor ability (14 out of 17) loaded on the general motor ability factor. The fine-motor subtests did not cluster on clearly identifiable factors the way the gross-motor subtests did.

Some research suggests that the 14-item short form of the test is not reliable for children age 5 years (Moore, Reeve, & Boan, 1986). In a study of 5- to 9-year-old children, the short form produced significantly higher scores than did the full scale (Verderber & Payne, 1987). More research is needed on the validity of the short form of the test.

Comment on the Bruininks-Oseretsky Test of Motor Proficiency

The Bruininks-Oseretsky Test is useful in assessing examinees' gross- and fine-motor skills, in developing and evaluating motor training programs, and in screening for special purposes. It is a refinement of the previous scale and is helpful in the clinical evaluation of motor skills. The Manual and materials are attractive and well designed. The variety of scores available facilitates the use and interpretation of the results. However, the structure of the test is not supported by factor analysis, and reliability coefficients are lower than desirable (Hattie & Edwards, 1987).

GUILFORD PONDERS WHETHER TIM'S MOTOR SKILLS ARE 'GROSS' OR 'FINE'

Courtesy of Herman Zilinski.

COMMENT ON TESTS OF VISUAL-MOTOR PERCEPTION AND MOTOR PROFICIENCY

Although the Bender-Gestalt and the Developmental Test of Visual-Motor Integration are similar tests of visual-motor integration skills, the scores derived from the two tests are not interchangeable (Breen, 1982; Breen, Carlson, & Lehman, 1985; DeMers et al., 1981; Knoff & Sperling, 1986; Lehman & Breen, 1982; Skeen et al., 1982). For example, in a study of the 1982 VMI norms, 11 of 32 comparisons between the VMI and the Bender-Gestalt revealed differences of at least 18 months (Breen, 1982). The two tests have different formats, which may subtly affect the examinee's performance. For example, the VMI is more structured than the Bender-Gestalt. On the VMI the examinee copies each design within a designated area on the page, whereas on the Bender-Gestalt the examinee can draw the designs anywhere on the page with minimal size restraints. Also, erasing is allowed on the Bender-Gestalt but not on the VMI. Finally, the scoring system on the Bender-Gestalt is based on errors, whereas the scoring system on the VMI is based on correct performance. Thus, the Bender-Gestalt and the VMI may measure different aspects of visual-motor development.

THINKING THROUGH THE ISSUES

1. When would you include a visual-motor test or a test of fine- and gross-motor proficiency in an assessment battery?
2. How are tests of visual-motor perception different from tests of cognitive ability?
3. When an examinee makes an error on a visual-motor test, how might you investigate the source of the error?

SUMMARY

1. The assessment of visual-motor perception and integration, visual perception, and motor proficiency can aid in the evaluation of examinees with possible learning disabilities or neurological deficits.

Bender Visual Motor Gestalt Test

2. The Bender Visual Motor Gestalt Test is a widely used visual-motor test.
3. The test was derived from Gestalt configurations devised by Wertheimer in 1923 to demonstrate the perceptual principles of Gestalt psychology.
4. Procedures that can be used in administering the Bender-Gestalt include the tachistoscopic procedure, the memory phase procedure, and the group-test procedure.
5. Observation of an examinee's visual-motor performance complements the more formal scoring procedures and aids in developing hypotheses about the examinee's perceptual-motor functioning.
6. Testing-of-limits procedures can help to pinpoint areas of possible visual-motor deficits.

7. The Developmental Bender Test Scoring System is a popular objective scoring system for evaluating the drawings of young examinees.
8. The four types of errors studied in the Developmental Bender Test Scoring System are distortion of shape, rotation, integration, and perseveration.
9. Little is known about the reliability and validity of the emotional indicators in the Developmental Bender Test Scoring System.
10. The reliability of the Developmental Bender Test Scoring System is not adequate for making diagnostic decisions, but is adequate for formulating hypotheses about an examinee's visual-motor ability.
11. The Developmental Bender Test Scoring System has acceptable validity when used to assess perceptual-motor development, but concurrent and predictive validities are too low for predicting school achievement.
12. The Qualitative Scoring System appears to be useful in evaluating visual-motor functioning.
13. Copying designs requires fine-motor development, perceptual discrimination ability, the ability to integrate perceptual and motor processes, and the ability to shift attention between the original design and the design that is being drawn.
14. Inadequate visual-motor performance may result from misperception, execution difficulties, or integrative or central processing difficulties.
15. There are no specific pathognomonic signs on the Bender-Gestalt that are definitively associated with brain injury, mental retardation, or any other physical or psychological disorder.
16. Never use the Bender-Gestalt alone to make a diagnosis of brain injury.
17. Errors on the Bender-Gestalt include sequence confusion, collision, superimposition of design, workover, irregular line quality, angulation difficulty, perseveration, line extension, contamination, rotation, omission, retrogression, bizarre doodling, and scribbling.

Beery-Buktenica Developmental Test of Visual-Motor Integration–Fourth Edition

18. The Developmental Test of Visual Motor Integration–Fourth Edition is a test of perceptual-motor ability for examinees ages 3 to 17 years. However, at ages above 12-6, the norms are skewed, and thus norms above this age should be used with caution.

Bruininks-Oseretsky Test of Motor Proficiency

19. The Bruininks-Oseretsky Test is useful in assessing examinees' gross- and fine-motor skills, in developing and evaluating motor training programs, and in screening for special purposes. However, the structure of the test is not supported by factor analysis, and reliability coefficients are lower than desirable.

Comment on Tests of Visual-Motor Perception and Motor Proficiency

20. Although the Bender-Gestalt and the Developmental Test of Visual-Motor Integration are similar tests of visual-motor integration skills, the scores derived from the two tests are not interchangeable.
21. The Bender-Gestalt and the VMI may measure different aspects of visual-motor development.

KEY TERMS, CONCEPTS, AND NAMES

Bender Visual Motor Gestalt Test (p. 213)

Bender-Gestalt tachistoscopic procedure (p. 214)

Bender-Gestalt memory phase procedure (p. 214)

Bender-Gestalt group test procedure (p. 214)

Observing performance on the Bender-Gestalt (and other visual-motor tests) (p. 214)

Testing-of-limits on visual-motor tests (p. 215)

Developmental Bender Test Scoring System (p. 215)

Distortion of shape on the Bender-Gestalt (p. 215)

Rotation on the Bender-Gestalt (p. 215)

Integration difficulties on the Bender-Gestalt (p. 215)

Perseveration on the Bender-Gestalt (p. 215)

Within-card perseveration (p. 217)

Card-to-card perseveration (p. 217)

Qualitative Scoring System (p. 217)

Interpreting performance on the Bender-Gestalt (and other visual-motor tests) (p. 218)

Sequence confusion on the Bender-Gestalt (p. 219)

Collision on the Bender-Gestalt (p. 219)

Superimposition of design on the Bender-Gestalt (p. 219)

Workover on the Bender-Gestalt (p. 219)

Irregular line quality on the Bender-Gestalt (p. 219)

Angulation difficulty on the Bender-Gestalt (p. 219)

Line extension on the Bender-Gestalt (p. 219)

Contamination on the Bender-Gestalt (p. 219)

Omission on the Bender-Gestalt (p. 219)

Retrogression on the Bender-Gestalt (p. 220)

Bizarre doodling on the Bender-Gestalt (p. 220)

Scribbling on the Bender-Gestalt (p. 220)

Beery-Buktenica Developmental Test of Visual-Motor Integration–Fourth Edition (p. 221)

Bruininks-Oseretsky Test of Motor Proficiency (p. 223)

STUDY QUESTIONS

1. Discuss the assets and limitations of the Bender Visual Motor Gestalt Test.
2. What method would you use to observe performance on the Bender-Gestalt and other visual-motor tests?
3. How would you conduct testing-of-limits on the Bender-Gestalt and other visual-motor tests?
4. Discuss how to interpret the Bender-Gestalt and other visual-motor tests.
5. Discuss the assets and limitations of the Developmental Test of Visual Motor Integration–Fourth Edition.
6. Discuss the assets and limitations of the Bruininks-Oseretsky Test of Motor Proficiency.

9

FUNCTIONAL BEHAVIORAL ASSESSMENT

It is the close observation of little things which is the secret of success in business, in art, in science, and in every pursuit in life.

—Samuel Smiles

The unfortunate thing about this world is that good habits are so much easier to give up than bad ones.

—W. Somerset Maugham

Goals and Objectives

This chapter is designed to enable you to do the following:

- Understand when and how to conduct a functional behavioral assessment

- Understand how to design interventions stemming from a functional behavioral assessment

A *functional behavioral assessment* is designed to arrive at an understanding of a student's problem behavior and develop a behavioral intervention plan. To conduct a functional behavioral assessment, you will need to consider (a) the type of problem behavior, (b) conditions under which the problem behavior occurs (including the events that trigger the problem behavior), and (c) probable reasons for or causes of the problem behavior (including biological, social, cognitive, affective, and environmental factors).

WHEN IS A FUNCTIONAL BEHAVIORAL ASSESSMENT REQUIRED?

A functional behavioral assessment is needed when children who have been classified as having a disability under the Individuals with Disabilities Education Act (IDEA; see Chapter 3 in *Assessment of Children: Cognitive Applications*) behave in ways that *interfere* with their education or with the education of others. Under the IDEA, a functional behavioral assessment is required when a student with a disability is suspended or will be suspended for more than 10 days during a school year. The assessment must be conducted either before or not later than 10 days after either the first removal beyond 10 cumulative days or any removal resulting in a change of placement for the student.

A functional behavioral assessment usually is required when the student's behavior is characterized as one or more of the following:

• Aggressive (e.g., fighting)
• Destructive (e.g., breaking windows)
• Noncompliant (e.g., consistently failing to follow directions)
• Self-injurious (e.g., banging his or her head)
• Dangerous (e.g., bringing weapons to school, destroying property, making threats, placing himself/herself or others at risk of injury)

Other reasons for conducting a functional behavioral assessment may include the following (Florida Department of Education, 1999):

• Behavioral concerns are excluding the student from participating in activities with peers.
• The educational team is considering a more restrictive placement because of behavioral concerns.
• A current intervention involves excessively intrusive procedures (e.g., restraint, isolation).
• The student's behavioral difficulties persist despite consistently implemented behavior management strategies based on a less comprehensive assessment.

A functional behavioral assessment, of course, can be used to evaluate any problem behavior in any setting. In fact, it is better to conduct a functional behavioral assessment when the student first begins to display a potentially serious problem behavior, rather than waiting until she or he is removed from the setting in which the problem behavior occurred (OSEP Technical Assistance Center, 2001).

Several members of the interdisciplinary team contribute to a functional behavioral assessment. Psychologists, counselors, and behavior specialists (who also may be psychologists or counselors) have special skills in assessing behavior and in dealing with challenging behavior. Social workers have special skills in family relations. Nurses have special skills in assessing children with physical illnesses and evaluating effects of medication. General education teachers have special skills in teaching and classroom management. Special education teachers have expertise in working with students with disabilities. And speech and language pathologists have special skills with regard to communication.

A functional behavioral assessment is *not* required for a manifestation determination. According to the IDEA '97, a manifestation determination is carried out by the IEP team to determine whether there is a relationship between a child's disability and the behavior subject to disciplinary action (see Chapter 3 in *Assessment of Children: Cognitive Applications*). Thus, a manifestation determination serves to establish how a problem behavior relates to the student's disability—that is, whether the student's disability impairs his or her (a) understanding of the consequences of his or her problem behavior and (b) ability to control the problem behavior (OSEP Technical Assistance Center, 2001). A functional behavioral assessment, on the other hand, helps the IEP team design and implement effective strategies to reduce, change, or eliminate the problem behavior. The information obtained from a functional behavioral assessment, along with other assessment information, is useful in conducting a manifestation determination, however.

FUNCTIONS OF CHALLENGING BEHAVIOR

Before you conduct a functional behavioral assessment, it is important to understand why children exhibit challenging behavior (OSEP Technical Assistance Center, 2001).

The motivation underlying human behavior is complex, varied, and sometimes difficult to ascertain. However, identifying the functions of behavior provides straightforward explanations of how a particular behavior "works" for an individual in a given context. By examining the outcomes or consequences of human behavior, including challenging behavior, we can describe two main functions: (a) to get something (e.g., social attention, a tangible object) (positive reinforcement) or (b) to escape or avoid something (e.g., an undesired activity or person) (negative reinforcement).

Examples of behavioral functions are observed daily in classrooms. For example, students learn to raise their hand in class to gain access to adult social attention, extra assistance on a difficult task, or indicate that they are done with a task. Similarly, students learn to use their words to tell another student to leave them alone or stop teasing. Unfortunately, some students use socially inappropriate behaviors to achieve the same outcomes. Some students push other students to gain access to the first place in line, close their textbooks to get the teacher to assist them with difficult work, or display noncompliant behavior with their teachers to enhance their social status with peers. Finally, some students disrupt lessons so that the teacher will ask them to leave the classroom, and yet other students display self-injurious or aggressive behavior to avoid having to comply with adult requests. In each of these examples, both appropriate and inappropriate behaviors are maintained because the outcomes (consequences) provide opportunities for the student to gain or get something (positive reinforcement) or to escape something (negative reinforcement).

When examining the function of behavior, it is important to consider three additional things. First, more than one behavior may serve a similar function for a student. For example, a student might talk out, leave the classroom, or touch other people's property to gain teacher attention. Second, one behavior might serve different functions in different contexts. For example, a student might use profanity to gain peer attention in the hallway, but also use the same behavior to be removed from a difficult lesson. Third, students usually do not display individual behaviors, but strings or chains of behavior that are occasioned by social interactions. For example, the first talkout displayed by a student might function to gain adult attention, but as the interaction escalates, talkouts might function to escape the confrontation. (pp. 3–4)

GUIDELINES FOR CONDUCTING A FUNCTIONAL BEHAVIORAL ASSESSMENT

The following seven steps are useful in conducting a functional behavioral assessment in a school setting (Miller, Tansy, & Hughes, 1998).

Step 1. *Consider what data you want to collect.* The goal is to describe the problem behavior in observable and measurable terms.

Step 2. *Perform the assessment activities.* These include the following:

- Review the student's records (e.g., results from prior psychological or psychoeducational evaluations, teachers' comments on report cards, disciplinary records, anecdotal home notes, medical reports, descriptions of prior interventions and their results).
- Conduct systematic behavioral observations, focusing on those behaviors most disruptive to the learning environment (see Chapters 4 and 5).
- Interview the student, teacher, parents, and other individuals as needed (see Chapters 1 and 2).
- Conduct other formal and informal assessments as needed (see Chapters 8 to 18 in *Assessment of Children: Cognitive Applications*).

Step 3. *Evaluate the data you have gathered.* This process includes identifying patterns in the data that may indicate the purpose or cause of the problem behavior.

Step 4. *Systematically consider plausible hypotheses to account for the problem behavior.* The hypotheses should attempt to explain the relationship between the problem behavior and the situations in which the problem behavior occurs and explain the function of the behavior. The hypotheses should contain (a) a description of the problem behavior, (b) possible antecedents, (c) possible consequences, and (d) possible *setting events* (e.g., any event that predisposes the student to engage in the problem behavior, such as not taking medication or arguing with parents before school).

Step 5. *Propose a behavioral intervention plan to improve the problem behavior.* In school settings, the IEP team carries out this function.

Step 6. *Implement the behavioral intervention plan.*

Step 7. *Evaluate the behavioral intervention plan, and modify it as needed.*

ASSESSING BEHAVIOR THROUGH OBSERVATIONS AND INTERVIEWS

Observations

After defining the problem behavior and identifying the situations in which that behavior occurs, you will want to observe the student (a) in several different settings (e.g., classroom, gym, cafeteria, playground), (b) during different types of activities (e.g., lectures, study periods, group activities, sports), and (c) at different times during the day (e.g., morning, afternoon; Gable, Quinn, Rutherford, & Howell, 1998). Design the behavioral observation using the procedures described in Chapters 4 and 5. In addition to the recording forms shown in Chapters 4 and 5, you can use the self-monitoring form shown in Table 9-1, which focuses on the location and frequency of the problem behavior.

Observation may have either an *interindividual focus,* in which a child's performance is compared with that of a norm group or a peer, or an *intraindividual focus,* in which a child's own performance is compared across different environments and across different tasks (Alessi, 1988). When a teacher refers a student for a problem behavior, you will want to determine whether the student's behavior is considerably different from that of his or her classroom peers. If you determine that the behavior is considerably different, you then will want to identify the (a) settings, (b) tasks, (c) reward contingencies (e.g., positive reinforcement, such as attention, extra playtime, playing with toys, and watching TV), and (d) relief contingencies (e.g., negative reinforcement, such as escaping from tasks and responsibilities) that influence the student's problem behaviors. In essence, an interindividual focus is used for screening, while an intraindividual focus is used for a more comprehensive individual assessment.

A functional behavioral assessment may also involve manipulating environmental events (e.g., type of activity, consequences) and then observing the effects of the manipulations; this approach is referred to as a *functional analysis.* For example, to support the hypothesis that the student engages in off-task behavior when she or he is playing on a team, you might ask the teacher to have the student engage in a solitary play activity, in addition to playing on a team. There are ethical

Table 9-1
Student Daily Schedule

STUDENT DAILY SCHEDULE

Name: _____ Date: _____

Directions: Fill in the name of each subject and the name of each teacher. Then place an X in each column to show whether you always, frequently, sometimes, seldom, or never have difficulty during this time, period, or place.

If you **always** have difficulty during this time, period, or place, put an X in the box opposite number 5.

If you **frequently** have difficulty during this time, period, or place, put an X in the box opposite number 4.

If you **sometimes** have difficulty during this time, period, or place, put an X in the box opposite number 3.

If you **seldom** have difficulty during this time, period, or place, put an X in the box opposite number 2.

If you almost **never** have difficulty during this time, period, or place, put an X in the box opposite number 1.

Time, Period, or Place

	Before school	1st period	Hall	2nd period	Hall	3rd period	Hall	4th period	Lunch	5th period	Hall	6th period	Hall	7th period	Hall	8th period	After school
Subject																	
Teacher																	
Rating																	
5																	
4																	
3																	
2																	
1																	

Source: Adapted from Reed, Thomas, Sprague, and Horner (1997).

issues, however, associated with manipulating environmental events. For example, if you hypothesize that off-task behavior occurs when the student faces difficult material, is it ethical to arrange for the student to be given difficult material in order to see whether the behavior occurs under this condition? Doing so might increase the student's anxiety level. In such situations, consider whether you should use another method to support or explore your hypothesis. However, if the teacher is fairly certain that the student can do the task and simply does not want to do it, there should be no breach of ethics in manipulating environmental events.

Interview Questions

The following questions may be useful in interviewing a student about a problem behavior (Gable et al., 1998; also see the questions in Table B-1 in Appendix B):

1. Tell me what happened.
2. How often does [name of problem behavior] occur?
3. How long does [name of problem behavior] last?
4. What do you think triggers [name of problem behavior]?
5. What were you thinking just before you [description of problem behavior]?
6. How did you feel just before you [description of problem behavior]?
7. What was happening to you before [name of problem behavior] began?
8. When you [description of problem behavior], what usually happens afterward?
9. What changes could be made so that [name of problem behavior] wouldn't happen again?

The following questions are useful for interviewing a teacher or a parent about the student's problem behavior:

1. Tell me about [name of child]'s problem behavior.
2. When does the problem behavior typically occur?

(Ask questions 3 to 6 as needed.)

3. (If the problem behavior is associated with activities that the child is asked to do) For example, does it happen when [name of child] is asked to clean [his/her] room, pick up toys, do homework, or complete tasks in school?
4. (If the problem behavior is associated with activities that the child is asked to stop doing) For example, does it happen when [name of child] is asked to stop watching TV, stop talking in class, stop teasing peers, or stop playing video games?
5. (If the problem behavior is associated with activities in which the child presses someone else to do something that person doesn't want to do) For example, does it happen when [name of child] is trying to get you to play games, to buy toys or clothes, to give [him/her] money, or to drive [him/her] someplace?
6. (If the problem behavior is associated with activities in which the child presses someone else to stop doing something that person wants to do) For example, does it

happen when [name of child] is trying to get you to stop watching TV, to stop talking on the phone, or to stop putting rules into effect?
7. When does the problem behavior typically not occur?
8. Where does the problem behavior typically occur?
9. How often does the problem behavior occur?
10. How long does the problem behavior last?
11. If there are other students or adults present, how do they react to [name of child]'s problem behavior?
12. What do you think triggers the problem behavior?
13. What do you do when the problem behavior occurs?
14. How does [name of child] react to what you do?
15. If there are other children or adults present, how do they react to what you do?
16. What happens to the task or project that is going on when [name of child] engages in the problem behavior?
17. Why do you think [name of child] acts this way? (If needed) What does [name of child] get out of it or avoid?
18. Tell me what you have done in the past that has helped reduce the problem behavior.
19. Tell me what you have done in the past that has not been successful in reducing the problem behavior.
20. What are [name of child]'s strengths or positive attributes?
21. Tell me anything else that you believe may be important in understanding [name of child].

In interviewing a student's teacher and parents about the student's problem behavior, you also can use the interview questions shown in Tables B-11 and B-5, respectively, in Appendix B. Three questionnaires also will be useful in obtaining information that will help you assess the problem behavior. These are the Background Questionnaire (Table A-1 in Appendix A), the Personal Data Questionnaire (Table A-2 in Appendix A), and the School Referral Questionnaire (Table A-3 in Appendix A).

DESCRIBING THE PROBLEM BEHAVIOR

Table 9-2 shows an extensive form for recording behavior, antecedents, consequences, and interventions. Answering the questions in Table 9-2 will help you describe the problem behavior. The questions focus on events that occur during, before, and after the problem behavior. Table 9-3 shows a brief form for recording behavior, antecedents, and consequences in ABC order.

FORMULATING HYPOTHESES TO ACCOUNT FOR THE PROBLEM BEHAVIOR

Hypotheses serve to summarize the assessment results, offer explanations for the student's problem behavior, and guide the development of the behavioral intervention plan (Knoster & Llewellyn, 1998a). Following are some questions designed

Table 9-2
Functional Behavioral Assessment Recording Form

FUNCTIONAL BEHAVIORAL ASSESSMENT RECORDING FORM

Name of student: _____   Date: _____

Sex: _____   Age: _____   School: _____

Date of birth: _____   Examiner: _____

Problem Behavior

1. Describe the problem behavior (e.g., refusing to follow instructions, disrupting class, making verbal threats, hurting self, destroying property, screaming or yelling, biting, throwing things, kicking, running away, grabbing or pulling, crying): _____ _____

2. When does it begin? _____ _____

3. When does it stop? _____ _____

4. Does it escalate gradually or quickly? _____ _____

5. How intense is the problem behavior (i.e., magnitude, such as degree of dangerousness)? _____ _____

6. How often does the problem behavior occur (i.e., frequency)? _____ _____

7. How long does the problem behavior last (i.e., duration)? _____ _____

8. When did the problem behavior first start? _____ _____

9. Has the frequency of the problem behavior increased or decreased recently? _____ _____

10. When was the last time the problem behavior occurred? _____ _____

11. Have there been any significant medical problems that may have affected the problem behavior? _____ _____

12. What internal characteristics of the student may have affected the problem behavior (e.g., lack of sleep, health, irritability, concern about a problem at home, boredom)? _____ _____

13. What events in the life of the student might have affected his or her behavior (e.g., divorce in family, death of family member, recent move, traumatic event in school, natural disaster)? _____ _____

(Continued)

Table 9-2 *(Continued)*

Events Before the Problem Behavior (Antecedent Events)

1. What usually happens before the problem behavior begins? For example, is the student arguing with a peer, being teased, being reprimanded, being ignored, taking a test, being intimidated or harassed, being told not to do something, being given a warning, engaged in horseplay, or being asked to perform a task? Are others in conflict or being reprimanded? Has there been a change in activity or in the environment, a delay between one task and another, a change in the time or order of task performance, or a change in the type of material used? _____

_____

2. Where does the problem behavior usually take place (e.g., classroom, playground, gym, hallway, bus)?_____

_____

3. What are the setting characteristics where the problem behavior takes place (e.g., nature of materials, type of activity, length of activity, type of instruction, number of other students and adults present, classroom rules and routines involved, reward system, lighting, noise level, temperature, seating arrangement, room location)? _____

_____

4. At what times of day does the problem behavior usually occur? _____

_____

5. Who usually is present when the problem behavior takes place (e.g., peers, teachers, teacher's aides, parents, other adults)?

_____

6. When the problem behavior takes place, is anyone absent who is usually in the setting?_____

_____

7. What activities usually take place prior to the problem behavior (e.g., teacher lecture on a specific topic, individual seat work, large-group activity, small-group activity, play activity, unstructured time)? _____

_____

8. What is the pace of the classroom activity before the problem behavior takes place (i.e., slow, moderate, or fast)? _____

_____

9. What is the student's affect before the problem behavior takes place (e.g., bored, angry, depressed, anxious, happy)? _____

_____

10. What is happening in the student's home and life in general on days when the problem behavior occurs? _____

_____

Events After the Problem Behavior (Consequent Events)

1. How does the teacher react to the problem behavior? _____

_____

2. How do other students react to the problem behavior (e.g., leave student alone, criticize student, laugh at student)? _____

_____

3. How does the administrator react to the problem behavior? _____

_____

(Continued)

Table 9-2 (Continued)

4. What are the consequences associated with the problem behavior (e.g., student is removed from task, given another activity, reprimanded, punished, ignored, placed in time-out, sent to office, asked to write sentences, threatened by consequences, denied privileges, physically managed, or suspended; parent is called; note is sent home; family is asked to pay for damages; student obtains a desired outcome)? _____

5. How do other adults usually respond to the problem behavior (e.g., reinforce the behavior; pay no attention to the behavior; punish the student; accept the behavior; become angry, puzzled, confused, or frightened by the behavior)? _____

6. What purposes are served by the problem behavior (e.g., what does the student obtain or avoid by the problem behavior)?_____

7. How much time elapses between when the student engages in the problem behavior and when others respond? _____

8. How does the student usually react after the problem behavior takes place (e.g., anxious, defiant, depressed, confused, happy, remorseful, apologetic)? _____

9. What actions seem to decrease the problem behavior once it begins? _____

10. How long does it usually take to get the student back to the scheduled activity? _____

11. How do the intensity, duration, and frequency of the problem behavior interfere with the student's learning? _____

Interventions

1. Are crisis intervention procedures needed to ensure safety and deescalation of the student's behavior, and, if so, what procedures should be used? _____

2. What potential cognitive and motivational resources does the student have for coping with the problem behavior? _____

3. What are the student's attitudes about the class, the teacher, and the school? _____

4. What are the student's attitudes about his or her parents, siblings, and other relatives? _____

5. What are the teachers', parents', and other concerned individuals' levels of understanding of the problem behavior? _____

6. What are the student's, family's, school's, and community's strengths and resources for change? _____

7. What are some positive strategies for diminishing the problem behavior and promoting skills the student needs to function more effectively? _____

(Continued)

Table 9-2 *(Continued)*

8. What are some positive strategies for changing the environment to prevent the problem behavior from occurring? _____

_____

9. What other factors should be considered in designing the behavioral intervention plan? _____

_____

10. What strategies should be used to facilitate the transfer of behavior changes across environments? _____

_____

11. Describe previous interventions, if any, and how successful they were. _____

_____

12. How should the intervention strategies be structured? _____

_____

Table 9-3
Functional Behavioral Assessment Brief Recording Form

FUNCTIONAL BEHAVIORAL ASSESSMENT BRIEF RECORDING FORM

Name of student: _____   Date: _____

Sex: _____   Age: _____   School: _____

Date of birth: _____   Examiner: _____

A—Antecedents (Describe what happened before the problem behavior occurred)	B—Behavior (Describe what the child did)	C—Consequences (Describe what happened after the problem behavior occurred)

SCHOOLIES © 1999 by John P. Wood

Sorry I was absent. My school parking permit expired yesterday, so I had to keep driving.

to help you develop hypotheses to account for the problem behavior.

1. *What are the relevant background factors associated with the problem behavior?* Examples include the following:

Individual Student Factors

- Age
- Sex
- Ethnicity
- Cultural background
- Socioeconomic status
- Personal appearance (including height, weight, physical anomalies)
- Health history (including prescribed medications)
- Physiological factors (e.g., sleep patterns, physical pain, hunger)
- Academic history
- Psychological/emotional history
- Interpersonal relations
- Previous responses to interventions and their effectiveness

Environmental Factors

- School system (e.g., classroom seating, school rules and code of conduct, noise level, length of bus rides)
- Family (e.g., how the family has dealt with the problem, family structure, family disciplinary practices, parental expectations, parent/child relationships, child maltreatment, domestic violence, divorce)
- Environmental events (e.g., stressors such as death or illness in the family, moving)
- Peer group (e.g., type of peer group, gender and age of peer group members)
- Neighborhood (e.g., lower, middle, or upper income; presence of violence; ethnic tensions)
- Community (e.g., community tolerance for violence, prevalence of gangs and drug and alcohol abuse)
- Nation (e.g., approval of violence and violence-related behaviors)

2. *Where does the problem behavior occur, and where does it not occur?* Examples include the following:

- Classroom
- Hallway

MR. WOODHEAD © 1998 by John P. Wood

Usually all I get in music class is criticism.

But today, I got a compliment from my teacher.

She told me that I take criticism very well.

- Gym
- Locker room
- Playground
- Cafeteria
- Walkways
- Restroom
- Auditorium
- Special classrooms
- Library
- Computer room
- Workshop
- Bus stop
- Bus

3. *When does the problem behavior occur, and when does it not occur?* Consider such factors as the following:

- Time of day when the problem behavior occurs (e.g., before school, in the morning, at noon, in the afternoon)
- Subjects being taught or activity taking place when the problem behavior occurs (e.g., reading, math, English, social studies, gym, lunch, changing classes)
- Type of instructional activity taking place when the problem behavior occurs (e.g., individual assignments, small-group work, lecture, independent work)
- Setting events related to the problem behavior
- Interpersonal conditions under which the problem behavior occurs (e.g., when certain persons such as a teacher, aide, or staff member are present; when others do not respond to the student in a certain way; or when others act in ways that increase the problem behavior, decrease the problem behavior, or trigger the problem behavior)
- Situations that might induce the problem behavior (e.g., making a transition from one class period to another class period; performing a disliked activity, a difficult assignment, a long assignment, or a boring assignment; taking a test; changing from one assignment to another; not knowing what is required on an assignment; fearing failure; fearing ridicule by a teacher or peers)

4. *How does the problem behavior affect the student's ability to learn and the student's school grades?* Consider what impact the problem behavior has on the student's academic performance and which subjects, in particular, are affected.

5. *What purposes appear to be served by the problem behavior?* Various purposes can be served by the problem behavior, such as the following:

- Escaping or avoiding an activity (e.g., mathematics), person (e.g., peer who teases), internal discomfort (e.g., hunger), or some combination thereof (e.g., having to work on a difficult task with other children in a group)
- Obtaining something desirable
- Obtaining stimulation
- Obtaining verbal attention
- Obtaining physical attention
- Communicating that the work is too hard or too demanding
- Reducing anxiety

- Signaling hunger, thirst, or pain
- Gaining a sense of control over others
- Obtaining a tangible item
- Obtaining assistance with a task

6. *What potential cognitive and motivational resources does the student have for coping with the problem behavior?* Following are some examples of potential cognitive and motivational resources:

- Understanding why the behavior occurs
- Understanding that some behaviors are appropriate in one situation but not in another (e.g., shouting at a sporting event but not during a spelling bee)
- Wanting to behave in an appropriate manner
- Knowing the situations in which he or she does not engage in the problem behavior

7. *What are the student's attitudes about the class, the teacher, and the school?* Consider the student's attitudes toward school in general, classroom rules, teacher expectations, the amount of time spent studying, the amount of help received, the difficulty level of the material, and so forth.

8. *What are the student's attitudes about his or her parents, siblings, and other relatives?* Consider whether the student's attitudes are positive, negative, or indifferent; whether the student accepts or questions rules; and whether the student believes the parents' expectations are too high or too low.

9. *What factors not considered above might be contributing to the student's problem behavior?*

10. *What are the teachers', parents', and other concerned individuals' levels of understanding of the problem behavior?* Consider whether they have little or no understanding, some understanding, or in-depth understanding of the problem behavior and what reasons they give to explain the problem behavior.

11. *What are the student's, family's, school's, and community's strengths and resources for change?* First consider the student's resources. Then consider whether the family, school, and community have adequate resources to help the student and, if so, the nature of these resources.

Following are four examples of hypotheses developed on the basis of a functional behavioral assessment.

When Selena is not engaged with others or activities for 15 minutes or longer (especially during lunch or free time), or when she did not get to sleep before 10:00 P.M. the previous evening or does not feel well, she screams, slaps her face, and pulls her hair to gain access to teacher attention. (Knoster & Llewellyn, 1998a, p. 4, with changes in notation)

When David is presented with academic work (in large- or small-group settings) requiring writing, multiple worksheets, or work that he perceives to be too difficult, he mumbles derogatory comments about the teacher, refuses to complete his work, destroys his assignment sheet, and/or pushes/kicks his desk or chair over in order to escape demonstrating academic failure in front of his peers. (Knoster & Llewellyn, 1998a, p. 4, with changes in notation)

When Juan is unclear about what is expected of him on an assignment or what is going to happen next in the daily schedule, or when unexpected changes in his typical routine or transition activities occur, Juan will make loud guttural sounds, grind his teeth, and scratch, bite, or hit others in order to gain teacher attention in the form of reassurance or clarification as to what is to occur next. (Knoster & Llewellyn, 1998a, p. 4, with changes in notation)

Karen enjoys interacting with others and keeping busy with activities. She seems happiest when she is interacting one-to-one with an adult (e.g., teacher) or participating in adult-led activities. She will occasionally sit alone for 15 minutes when listening to music of her choice, although she seems to grow bored in such situations. Karen currently has limited means of formal communication. While she enjoys interacting with others, she has never been observed to independently initiate appropriate interactions with her teacher or other students. Her independent initiation skills are very limited. Karen has limited access to non-disabled peers during her day at school (e.g., afternoon recess) and has a history of colds and viral infections which, in turn, adversely affect her sleep patterns. Karen's self-injury appears to signal her desire for social interaction, something to do, teacher assistance, or comfort when she is tired and/or not feeling well. Given her current situation, Karen's self-injury appears to be her most viable means to communicate these basic needs. (Knoster & Llewellyn, 1998b, p. 7)

Now let's look at some examples of hypotheses and possible interventions based on functional behavioral assessments.

Matt's problem behavior takes place when he is asked to write, read, or use higher-order thinking skills. He talks with peers when he is not supposed to, leaves his seat without permission, yells, and refuses to do assigned activities in order to get out of tasks that are challenging and frustrating. He should be required to complete writing, reading, and higher-order thinking assignments (escape responses should be blocked). Then he should be rewarded (e.g., complimented by his teacher, given passes, or given free time on the computer) when the required task is completed. (Lohrmann-O'Rourke, Knoster, & Llewellyn, 1999, p. 40, with changes in notation)

In the cafeteria, between classes, before and after school, or in the locker room, Henry teases other students, curses them, pushes them, hits them, or puts them in a headlock in order to draw attention from other peers and also to gain control over situations in which he feels inferior. He needs to be disciplined for his problem behavior (e.g., given time-outs, kept after school, or sent to the principal's office) and rewarded (e.g., complimented by the teacher, given passes or free time on the computer, or appointed to assist the teacher or be a peer tutor to a younger child) when he performs acceptable behaviors. (Lohrmann-O'Rourke, Knoster, & Llewellyn, 1999)

When other children play with Jacob's toys, he bangs his head, whines, and throws things. When he does this, the children return his toys. Jacob needs to be taught to ask children to return his toys when they take them (e.g., teach him sign language). When he exhibits aggressive behavior, he should not get his toys back. (Miltenberger, 1997)

Jamie, who does not talk, becomes aggressive whenever she is asked to sit and complete a sorting task. Her nonverbal actions suggest that she does not like the sorting task. When she becomes aggressive, the staff moves her to a chair in the corner of the room. Her actions appear to be getting her relief because she is removed from a disliked task. Jamie should be taught a means to signal when tasks are too hard

or when they are disliked. If the sorting task is deemed to be useful, it might be changed in some way (e.g., made easier or more difficult) to better meet her needs. If, in spite of these changes, she is still aggressive, she should not be allowed to escape from the task. (Snell, 1988)

BEHAVIORAL INTERVENTION PLANS

The information you obtain from a functional behavioral assessment will help you design a behavioral intervention plan (Miltenberger, 1997). The behavioral intervention plan aims to help the student develop more appropriate behaviors and to reduce the frequency and severity of the problem behavior. The key is to replace undesirable behavior with desirable behavior that serves the same function for the student (OSEP Technical Assistance Center, 2001). This may be done in part by arranging the setting and antecedent events so that the *replacement behaviors* (appropriate behaviors) are more likely to be encouraged and by arranging consequent events so that the replacement behaviors are more likely to be reinforced and the problem behavior is less likely to be reinforced.

In designing the behavioral intervention plan, you need to consider the following:

- Alternative desirable behaviors that are in the student's repertoire
- Reinforcers and punishers, including items, activities, and the reactions of others
- Environmental changes needed to prevent the problem behavior from occurring and to promote positive behaviors
- Ways to make changes in the antecedent variables
- Skills needed by the student to replace problem behaviors

Developing the Behavioral Intervention Plan

The behavioral intervention plan should be practical, workable, and reasonable, and it should help the student benefit from classroom instruction. The plan should be tailored to the student's needs. It generally should have incremental improvement goals designed to reduce the problem behavior, rather than one large-scale improvement goal.

Consider the following questions in developing a behavioral intervention plan (Gable et al., 1998).

1. *What are some positive strategies for diminishing the problem behavior and increasing appropriate replacement behaviors?* Strategies might include the following:

- Provide the student with skill training, including training in more appropriate ways (such as acceptable replacement behaviors) to obtain desired goals without engaging in the problem behavior
- Provide extra assistance
- Make a written behavioral contract
- Modify assignments to match the student's skills
- Arrange for easier access to desired items or activities

- Arrange for the student to receive counseling
- Have the student use self-monitoring forms under the guidance of a counselor or psychologist (see Chapter 5)
- Suggest to teachers ways to maximize reinforcements for positive behavior and minimize reinforcements for negative behavior

2. *What are some positive strategies for changing the environment to prevent the problem behavior from occurring?* Strategies could include the following:

- Make changes in the student's class schedule—change classes or teachers or reschedule classes
- Change seating arrangements
- Clarify rules and expected behavior for the whole class
- Provide for more effective use of reinforcers
- Teach replacement behaviors that are not in the student's repertoire
- Use adult or peer tutors
- Use resource rooms
- Remove existing unintended consequences that may be reinforcing the problem behavior (e.g., prevent the student from escaping or avoiding required classroom tasks through misbehavior)

3. *What other factors should be considered in designing the behavioral intervention plan?* Questions to consider include the following:

- Can the same behavioral intervention plan be used when there is more than one problem behavior?
- What behaviors or items (e.g., objects, free time, computer time, privilege of assisting teacher) are reinforcing to the student?
- Can the student perform the behaviors recommended in the intervention plan?
- How can the consequences be managed to ensure that the student receives reinforcement for positive behavior and not for the problem behavior?
- What strategies are needed to ensure that behavior changes transfer across environments?
- Are crisis management procedures needed to ensure safety and deescalation of the student's problem behavior?

4. *How should the intervention strategies be structured?* Consider the following variables:

- Time and duration of the interventions
- Setting in which the interventions should take place
- Individual roles and responsibilities of staff members

5. *How should the plan's effectiveness by evaluated?* Ways to evaluate the plan's effectiveness include the following:

- Evaluate whether short- and long-term goals have been reached
- Monitor activities
- Review intervention outcomes periodically at specified times
- Note completion of the behavioral contract

- Record points earned
- Review self-monitoring forms
- Monitor grades
- Monitor teachers' anecdotal notes

Monitoring the Behavioral Intervention Plan

In monitoring the behavioral intervention plan, consider the following questions (Tilly, Knoster, Kovaleski, Bambara, Dunlap, & Kincaid, 1998):

- Is the plan being implemented as proposed?
- Is the student acquiring new skills?
- Is the student using the new skills in different situations?
- Has the problem behavior decreased to an acceptable rate?
- What barriers hinder the student's learning?
- Is the student's academic performance improving?
- Does the student understand the consequences of her or his actions?
- Is the student able to control her or his behavior?
- Are the student, teacher, and parents satisfied with the plan and its outcomes?
- Do the student, teacher, and parents have any suggestions for improving the plan?
- What modifications in the plan are needed, if any?

A behavioral intervention plan needs to foster interdisciplinary cooperation and efforts among teachers, related service providers, administrators, family members, and outside agency

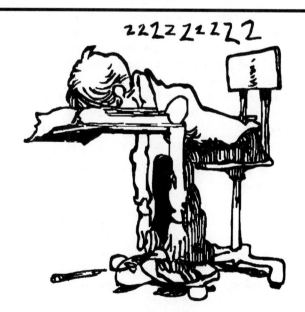

This was not quite what the school psychologist had in mind as an intervention for Timmy's out-of-seat behavior.

Courtesy of Daniel Miller.

personnel (in cases where the student and family are involved with an outside agency).

Examples of Behavioral Intervention Plans

Here are two examples of behavioral intervention plans.

Example 1. *Positive reinforcement hypothesis and intervention plan* (Repp, 1999).

ASSESSMENT

Setting: Henry's problem behavior takes place during a large-group instructional session.

Setting event: Henry did not take his medication.

Antecedents: The teacher attends to peers, Henry needs to wait his turn, and he has few turns.

Problem behavior: He lies down on the floor, shouts, and kicks his feet.

Consequences: The teacher reprimands Henry, and his peers laugh at him.

Function: Henry obtains attention from others.

Setting where problem behavior does not occur: The problem behavior does not take place during small-group instruction, during which the teacher gives Henry attention and each student has several turns.

INTERVENTION

Change setting: Use small-group instruction or 1:1 instruction when possible.

Change setting event: Ensure that Henry takes his medication.

Change antecedents: Ask teacher to try to give both Henry and his peers attention during large-group instruction.

Replacement behaviors: The teacher (a) has the group respond in unison, (b) has students raise their hands, (c) has students follow instructions, and (d) has students wait their turn.

Change consequences: The teacher praises Henry (and other students) for listening and waiting.

Function of replacement behavior: Henry obtains attention for enacting new behaviors.

Example 2. *Negative reinforcement hypothesis and intervention plan.*

ASSESSMENT

Setting: Amanda's problem behavior takes place when she is working individually on assignments in class.

Setting event: Amanda arrived at school hungry.

Antecedents: The assignments require that Amanda work quietly and independently.

Problem behavior: She slams materials and makes noises (e.g., bird calls) about 10 to 15 times in a 45-minute class period. This behavior interferes with other students' learning.

Consequences: The teacher checks Amanda's work, reminds her to be quiet, and, if the behavior does not improve, sends her to time-out.

Function: Amanda escapes doing the task.

Setting where problem behavior does not occur: The problem does not occur during music or during cooperative learning activities.

INTERVENTION

Change setting: Use peer learning activities when possible.

Change setting event: Try to ensure that Amanda does not come to school hungry by offering to enroll her in the school breakfast program.

Change antecedents: Ask the teacher to try to use more group learning activities in the classroom.

Replacement behaviors: The teacher encourages Amanda to (a) use a keyboard for typing when she works on lengthy written assignments, (b) raise her hand when she needs help, when she is ready to have her work checked, and when she needs a break, and (c) join the band to develop friendships.

Change consequences: The teacher gives Amanda attention whenever she raises her hand, even if it is to say, "I'll be there in a minute." The teacher also ignores all the noises Amanda makes and instructs other students to do the same, minimizes the use of time-outs, and allows Amanda to earn homework passes for the assignments she completes.

Function of replacement behavior: Amanda achieves success, obtains attention from the teacher, and discontinues the disruptive behaviors.

Exhibit 9-1 shows an in-depth behavioral intervention plan for a 10-year-old girl who was uncooperative and engaged in disruptive behavior. For more information about functional behavioral assessment, see O'Neill, Horner, Albin, Sprague, Storey, and Newton (1997); Repp and Horner (1999); and Sturmey (1996).

THINKING THROUGH THE ISSUES

1. How does a functional behavioral assessment differ from a psychological or psychoeducational assessment?
2. In what ways can a functional behavioral assessment be useful for conditions other than behavioral problems?

SUMMARY

1. A functional behavioral assessment is designed to arrive at an understanding of a student's problem behavior and develop a behavioral intervention plan.
2. To conduct a functional behavioral assessment, you will need to consider (a) the type of problem behavior, (b) conditions under which the problem behavior occurs (including the events that trigger the problem behavior), and (c) probable reasons for or

Exhibit 9-1
Behavioral Intervention Plan

BEHAVIORAL INTERVENTION PLAN

Name of student: Marisa Springfield

Date: April 15, 2001

Sex: Female

Grade: 4th

Date of birth: April 12, 1991   Age: 10-0

School: Harper Elementary

Behaviors in Need of Change

1. Leaves assigned area without permission
2. Refuses to go to designated area
3. Disruptive behavior, such as slamming lockers, screaming, and banging desks

Perceived Functions of Behaviors

1. Attention
2. To gain control or power
3. To avoid nonpreferred activities
4. To express anger or frustration

Target Replacement Behaviors

1. Remain in assigned area unless given permission to leave
2. Go to designated area when directed to do so
3. Use an appropriate voice to communicate to others when upset
4. Respect property

Strategies to Prevent the Problem Behavior(s)

1. *Pre-kindergarten helper*
   To provide Marisa with additional attention in a positive way, the following are recommended:

   a. When Marisa comes to school each morning, she will assist the pre-kindergarten teacher.

   b. Marisa's time in the pre-kindergarten classroom should be 10 to 15 minutes daily. Marisa can help set up the class, assist children with the morning transition, and do other jobs as requested by the teacher.

   c. Marisa's morning job in the pre-kindergarten classroom is not contingent upon her behavior. Therefore, it is not something she must earn. However, Marisa's classroom teacher and the pre-kindergarten teacher should communicate frequently to monitor Marisa's ability to handle the responsibilities of the job.

   d. Both the classroom teacher and the pre-kindergarten teacher should provide Marisa with verbal praise for a job well done.

2. *Library assistant*
   To provide Marisa with opportunities for additional attention, the following are recommended:

   a. Marisa should report to the library at the end of every day to assist the librarian.

   b. Marisa should spend 10 to 15 minutes helping put books away, cleaning up the library, and assisting with other duties as assigned.

   c. Marisa's time in the library is not contingent upon her behavior. If, however, Marisa is having a problem at the time she is to report to the library, she should not go until she is calm and has completed what she needed to do in class.

   d. The librarian and the classroom teacher should maintain communication to make sure that the job is working well for everyone. They should also provide Marisa with verbal praise for doing her job well.

3. *Morning snack break*
   To provide Marisa with a break from the classroom, as well as an opportunity for adult attention and time to discuss any concerns she may have, the following are recommended:

   a. Marisa should be given the opportunity daily at 11:30 a.m. to eat a snack in the guidance office or school office.

   b. This snack time is not contingent upon good behavior, nor is it mandatory. Marisa may choose not to go if she wishes.

   c. This snack time should last about 10 minutes, and it is a good time to play games or talk if Marisa wants to.

   d. Verbal praise should be provided for any appropriate behaviors that Marisa demonstrates while in the office.

4. *Increased opportunities for choice*
   To meet Marisa's need for control, the following are recommended:

   a. Provide Marisa with daily opportunities to make choices. Opportunities for choice may include which work to do first, whether to do odd or even problems, where to sit in a group, whom to pick first for a group, and when in the period to complete an assignment.

   b. Provide verbal praise for good choices made.

(Continued)

Exhibit 9-1 (Continued)

5. *Skill-building sessions*

   To provide Marisa with social skills and anger management training and to help her develop coping skills, the following are recommended:

   a. Marisa will have 2 sessions weekly with the school guidance counselor.

   b. Sessions will last 20–30 minutes each. The tentative schedule for Marisa is Tuesdays 11:10–11:30 a.m. and Thursdays 1:15–1:45 p.m.

   c. The guidance counselor initially will work on establishing rapport with Marisa. Once Marisa feels comfortable with the guidance counselor, they will work on anger identification and management skills, social skills, and coping skills (to assist with handling disappointment, noise in the cafeteria, etc.). There will also be ongoing work to assist Marisa in learning how to communicate her feelings appropriately when there is a problem.

6. *Daily reinforcement system*

   To provide Marisa with the incentive to remain in class, as well as feedback regarding her behavior, the following are recommended:

   a. Marisa will be provided with a daily sheet and will be awarded a sticker or stamp or initial every time she goes to and remains in the assigned area for an entire class period.

   b. Marisa will be provided with a list of reinforcers she can buy with her stickers. *The reinforcer list will be developed with Marisa* and will include things like lunch with a chosen adult, pencils, and other school supplies, and having her fingernails painted.

   c. Marisa will choose when and how to spend her stickers.

   d. Marisa's daily sheet will go home every afternoon for her mother to review and sign. Marisa will earn a bonus sticker for returning the sheet to school with her mother's signature on it.

   e. Verbal praise should be provided when Marisa earns stickers. Positive daily sheets should be shared with administrators to provide her with positive attention from them.

Strategies to Deal with the Problem Behavior(s)

1. *Leaves assigned area without permission or refuses to go to designated area*

   To correct Marisa's leaving an area without permission or refusing to go to a designated area, the following are recommended:

   a. Always use a calm, matter-of-fact tone of voice when giving Marisa directions.

   b. State directions positively. Tell Marisa exactly what she needs to do (e.g., "Go to reading").

   c. Only one person should deal with Marisa, to minimize the amount of attention she receives for her behavior. If the person who originally gave the direction is unable to stay with Marisa, another person should be called to step in.

   d. Marisa should be told that a staff member will talk to her only after she follows directions. No other verbal interactions should occur until she follows directions. This is not the time to play games or have fun with Marisa. Positive attention should occur only when Marisa is doing well.

   e. When Marisa finally follows directions, the staff member should review with her better choices she can make in the future if a similar situation arises. No further mention of the incident should be made, to avoid reinforcing the behavior accidentally. Get Marisa back on task as quickly as possible.

2. *Disruptive behavior*

   To address the occurrence of disruptive behavior, the following are recommended:

   a. Give Marisa clear and concise directions, using a calm tone of voice.

   b. Do not address specific behaviors. Simply tell her what she needs to do.

   c. Keep verbal interactions to a minimum. Let Marisa know you will talk to her when she is calm and following directions.

   d. Only one staff member should be involved, if possible, to minimize the attention Marisa receives for negative behavior.

   e. If Marisa becomes a danger to herself or others, staff may, as a last resort, physically intervene to keep her and others safe.

   f. Once calm, Marisa may need 20–30 minutes of quiet time out of the classroom to get herself together.

   g. Follow-up problem solving should occur after her quiet time to determine her ability to get back to work.

   h. The goal is to get Marisa back on task and in a regular routine as quickly as possible with as little attention as possible. It is important to remember that attention and time out of class are reinforcing to Marisa, and we do not want to reinforce her challenging behaviors—we want to reinforce positive behaviors.

"This last step in Timmy's behavior management plan seems a bit extreme."

Courtesy of Daniel Miller.

causes of the problem behavior (including biological, social, cognitive, affective, and environmental factors).

When Is a Functional Behavioral Assessment Required?

3. A functional behavioral assessment is needed when children who have been classified as having a disability under the Individuals with Disabilities Education Act (IDEA) behave in ways that *interfere* with their education or with the education of others.

4. A functional behavioral assessment usually is required when the student's behavior is aggressive, destructive, noncompliant, self-injurious, or dangerous.

5. Several members of the interdisciplinary team contribute to a functional behavioral assessment, including psychologists, social workers, nurses, general education teachers, special education teachers, and speech and language pathologists.

6. A functional behavioral assessment is *not* required for a manifestation determination, according to the IDEA '97.

Functions of Challenging Behavior

7. Two main functions of challenging behavior are to get something (positive reinforcement) and to escape or avoid something (negative reinforcement).

8. More than one behavior may serve a similar function for a student.

9. A behavior might serve different functions in different contexts.

10. Students usually do not display individual behaviors, but strings or chains of behavior that are occasioned by social interactions.

Guidelines for Conducting a Functional Behavioral Assessment

11. The following seven steps are useful in conducting a functional behavioral assessment in a school setting: (1) Consider what data you want to collect. (2) Perform the assessment activities. (3) Evaluate the data you have gathered. (4) Systematically consider plausible hypotheses to account for the problem behavior. (5) Propose a behavioral intervention plan to improve the problem behavior. (6) Implement the behavioral intervention plan. (7) Evaluate the behavioral intervention plan, and modify it as needed.

Assessing Behavior Through Observation and Interviews

12. After defining the problem behavior and identifying the situations in which that behavior occurs, you will want to observe the student in several different settings, during different types of activities, and at different times during the day.

13. Students, teachers, and parents should be interviewed about the problem behavior.

Describing the Problem Behavior

14. In describing the student's problem behavior, focus on events that occur during, before, and after the problem behavior.

Formulating Hypotheses to Account for the Problem Behavior

15. Hypotheses serve to summarize the assessment results, offer explanations for the student's problem behavior, and guide the development of the behavioral intervention plan.

16. In developing hypotheses to account for the problem behavior, consider the relevant background factors; where the problem behavior occurs and does not occur; when the problem behavior occurs and does not occur; how the problem behavior affects the student's ability to learn and the student's school grades; the purposes served by the problem behavior; the potential cognitive and motivational resources the student has for coping with the problem behavior; the student's attitudes about the class, the teacher, and the school; the student's attitudes about his or her parents, siblings, and other relatives; the teachers', parents', and other concerned individuals' levels of understanding of the problem behavior; and the student's, family's, school's, and community's strengths and resources for change.

Behavioral Intervention Plans

17. Information obtained from a functional behavioral assessment will help you design a behavioral intervention plan that includes (a) alternative desirable behaviors that are in the student's repertoire, (b) reinforcers and punishers, including items, activities, and the reactions of others, (c) environmental changes needed to prevent the problem behavior from occurring and to promote positive behaviors, (d) ways to make changes in the antecedent variables, and (e) skills needed by the student to replace problem behaviors with appropriate behaviors (referred to as *replacement behaviors*).

18. In developing a behavioral intervention plan, also consider (a) positive strategies for diminishing the problem behavior and increasing appropriate replacement behaviors, (b) positive strategies for changing the environment to prevent the problem behavior from occurring, (c) other factors that should be considered, (d) how the intervention strategies should be structured, and (e) how the plan's effectiveness should be evaluated.

19. A behavioral intervention plan needs to foster interdisciplinary cooperation and efforts among teachers, related service providers, administrators, families, and outside agency personnel.

KEY TERMS, CONCEPTS, AND NAMES

Functional behavioral assessment (p. 228)
Setting events (p. 229)
Observations (p. 229)
Interindividual focus (p. 229)
Intraindividual focus (p. 229)
Functional analysis (p. 229)
Interview questions (p. 231)
Formulating hypotheses (p. 231)
Behavioral intervention plan (p. 238)
Replacement behaviors (p. 238)

STUDY QUESTION

Describe functional behavioral assessment. Include in your discussion guidelines for conducting a functional behavioral assessment, assessing behavior through observations and interviews, describing the problem behavior, formulating hypotheses to account for the problem behavior, and developing a behavioral intervention plan.

10

CHILDREN WITH SPECIAL NEEDS: AN INTRODUCTION

All children need:
To be free from discrimination
To develop physically and mentally in freedom and dignity
To have a name and nationality
To have adequate nutrition, housing, recreation, and medical
*   services*
To receive special treatment if handicapped
To receive love, understanding, and material security
To receive an education and develop [their] abilities
To be the first to receive protection in disaster
To be protected from neglect, cruelty, and exploitation
To be brought up in a spirit of friendship among people
—United Nations' Declaration of the Rights of the Child

Goals and Objectives

This chapter is designed to enable you to do the following:

- Understand how psychological problems develop in children

- Become familiar with general assessment issues

- Understand instructional strategies for children with special needs

This chapter provides an overview of the assessment of children with special needs. The following chapters cover the major forms of childhood disorders or exceptionalities, including attention-deficit/hyperactivity disorder, learning disabilities, mental retardation, giftedness, visual impairments, hearing impairments, autistic disorder, and brain injuries.

Children with special needs are a heterogeneous group. They may have problems involving cognitive functions (such as impaired ability to reason or learn), affect (such as anxiety or depressive reactions), or behavior (such as socially inappropriate behavior, hyperactivity, or violence toward self or others). In addition, they may have physical disabilities, medical problems, or other conditions.

Generalizations about children with special needs must be made with caution because each child has unique temperament and personality characteristics, cognitive skills, social skills, adaptive-behavior skills, and support systems. *Approach each child as a unique individual and never only as representing a particular disorder.* If you stereotype the child, your ability to obtain accurate information will be impaired. Your goal is to learn as much about the child's positive coping strategies and accomplishments and the protective factors in her or his life—including those provided by the immediate and extended family—as you do about the symptoms, negative coping strategies, and other factors that hinder her or his development.

Children who have special needs may have more than one disorder, a phenomenon referred to as *co-occurring disorders* or *comorbid disorders.* Examples of disorders that commonly occur together are conduct disorder and attention-deficit/hyperactivity disorder, autistic disorder and mental retardation, and childhood depression and anxiety (Mash & Dozois, 1996). Children with co-occurring disorders are likely to have more complex and longer-lasting psychological problems than children with only a single disorder. Nottelmann and Jensen (1995), for example, found that sixth-grade boys with both conduct problems and depressive symptoms were more likely to continue to have problems in eighth grade than boys with only one disorder. Always consider whether children have more than one type of disorder, because disorders in childhood may not be "pure."

Children with special needs *usually* go through the same developmental sequences as typically developing children, although sometimes at a different rate. For example, some may be delayed in reaching developmental milestones (see the table on the inside front cover), and some—particularly those with severe behavioral or developmental problems such as autistic disorder or mental retardation—may never reach more mature stages of language development or conceptual thinking. Advise parents to obtain a detailed assessment if their children have significant developmental delays. For example, children may have a significant motor delay if they are not walking by 18 months of age or a significant language delay if they are not speaking by 3 years of age.

Children with special needs form their self-concepts in ways similar to those used by other children. Parents are the primary source of feedback, followed by siblings and other relatives, friends and neighbors, and teachers and other professionals. You will want to learn about children's self-concepts, how their self-concepts affect their relationships with others, their feelings about having problems, and their aspirations. You also will want to learn about how the parents perceive their children and their children's disorders and about the parents' aspirations for their children. Children with special needs are likely to have more negative self-concepts and to experience more frustration, rejection, teasing, prejudice, depression, anxiety, and motivational deficiencies than children without special needs (Cobb, 1989).

Children with special needs who also have physical impairments may be limited in their ability to obtain a full range of sensory information, to socialize, and to engage in sports and other physical activities and may not reach expected height and weight. These limitations may interfere with the development of cognitive, affective, and interpersonal skills. Physical impairments, in conjunction with behavioral disorders, pose considerable challenges for children's care and development. The following section examines some factors that contribute to the development of psychological problems in children.

HOW PSYCHOLOGICAL PROBLEMS DEVELOP IN CHILDREN

Psychological problems in children develop from the interaction among (a) genetic and biological factors, (b) environmental factors (such as inadequate caregiving, parents with psychological problems or drug habits, stress, and exposure to violence), and (c) individual characteristics (such as personality, emotional reactions, self-concept, coping strategies, motivations, and beliefs). Genetic and biological factors and environmental factors are discussed below. Individual characteristics will be addressed when we discuss specific types of special needs.

Genetic and Biological Factors

Several hereditary disorders, as well as prenatal factors, can affect both physical and psychological development. Examples include the following (see Table 10-1 for definitions of the disorders):

- *Chromosomal abnormalities,* such as the translocations found in Down syndrome (Trisomy 21) and fragile X syndrome
- *Inborn errors of metabolism,* such as phenylketonuria (PKU) and Tay-Sachs disease
- *Infections,* such as rubella, toxoplasmosis, cytomegalovirus (CMV), syphilis, and human immunodeficiency virus (HIV)
- *Placental dysfunction*

Table 10-1
Definitions of Hereditary Disorders and Prenatal Factors That Can Affect Both Physical and Psychological Development

Cytomegalovirus (CMV). Systemic illness that may be transmitted prenatally, as the baby passes through an infected birth canal, or postnatally, through infected urine, saliva, breast milk, feces, tears, or blood. Although some carriers are completely asymptomatic, in its most severe form CMV causes global central nervous system infection involving the cerebral cortex, brain stem, cochlear nuclei, cranial nerves, and inner ear.

Down syndrome, or Trisomy 21. Chromosomal abnormality characterized by the presence of an extra chromosome 21. Many children with Down syndrome are mentally retarded, with delays in physical, psychomotor, and language development. Children usually have a flat skull, thickened skin on the eyelids, stubby fingers, and a short, stocky body.

Fragile X syndrome. Condition characterized by a physical abnormality on the X chromosome. It is one of the more common genetic causes of mental retardation, especially in males.

Phenylketonuria (PKU). Chromosomal abnormality that causes a child to be unable to metabolize the protein phenylalanine. Because the gene for PKU is recessive, it must come from both parents. Untreated PKU results in severe mental retardation; it also may cause convulsions, behavioral problems, severe skin rash, and a musty odor of the body and urine.

Placental dysfunction. Improper functioning of the placenta, an organ that develops in mothers during pregnancy. The placenta may fail to supply adequate oxygen, nutrients, and antibodies to the fetus, or it may fail to adequately remove waste products.

Rubella, or German measles. Infectious disease that, if contracted by the mother during the first three months of pregnancy, has a high risk of causing congenital anomalies, including deafness, cataracts, cardiac malformation, learning disabilities, and mental retardation. On reaching adulthood, children with congenital rubella syndrome may have diabetes, glaucoma, endocrine pathology, and central nervous system infections.

Tay-Sachs disease. Progressive degenerative disease resulting from a disorder of lipid metabolism. Caused by a recessive gene, it is characterized by severe mental retardation, seizures, paralysis, and death.

Teratogens. Agents in the environment of a developing embryo and fetus that can cause structural and functional abnormalities. Examples include alcohol, radiation, pathogens causing intrauterine infection, drugs and environmental chemicals, and untreated maternal metabolic imbalances like PKU.

Toxoplasmosis, maternal. Parasitic infection transmitted by pregnant women to developing fetuses. Symptoms include blindness, central nervous system damage, jaundice, hydrocephalus, and mental retardation.

- *Teratogens,* such as alcohol, cocaine, radiation, and maternal PKU
- *Toxins,* such as lead

Genetic or biological vulnerabilities may limit children's development and may make it more difficult for them to acquire needed competencies and cope with stress.

A critical factor affecting children's development is whether their mothers used or abused drugs or alcohol during pregnancy. Children born to mothers who abuse substances are at risk for birth defects, as well as for motor, cognitive, language, social, and emotional deficits (Cunningham, 1992; Phelps & Cox, 1993). As infants, they may tremble; be agitated, restless, hyperactive, or rigid; have sleep and respiratory difficulties; or be difficult to console. As toddlers and preschoolers, they may have subtle cognitive delays and show deficits in fine-motor control, self-organization and initiation, activity level, attention, speech, and language. As school-aged children and adolescents, they may exhibit mild mental retardation, developmental learning disorders, attention difficulties, hyperactivity, and conduct disorders. Children born to drug- or alcohol-abusing mothers will need a comprehensive assessment of their physical and psychological functioning.

Environmental Factors

The primary way in which infants and young children learn about themselves and others is through familial experiences. These experiences may be encoded in memory as a set of beliefs about themselves and others and expectations about future relationships with others.

Inadequate caregiving. Children's adjustment likely will be adversely affected if their parents have one or more of the following characteristics (Bagley & Shewchuk-Dann, 1991; Cunningham, 1992; Kendziora & O'Leary, 1992):

- Are cold and insensitive
- Are rejecting or neglectful (e.g., fail to meet their basic needs for adequate food, clothing, attention)
- Have inappropriate developmental expectations for them
- Inadvertently encourage their inappropriate behavior
- Are vague in communicating
- Are unable to establish reasonable expectations and limits for them
- Are inconsistent with them and have difficulty handling situations that call for discipline
- Delay dealing with their misbehavior
- Use overly harsh or overly lax disciplinary procedures
- Physically, psychologically, or sexually abuse them
- Have psychological problems (e.g., are anxious or depressed; show unexpected changes in mood, energy, or self-esteem; or have deficient reality testing—that is, difficulty determining their relationships with the external world and with social environments)
- Are substance abusers
- Are experiencing chaotic living arrangements
- Are lacking in social supports
- Are under considerable stress (e.g., from domestic violence, work pressures, financial pressures, low socioeconomic status, legal matters, or criminal matters)

Children whose caregivers are insensitive or rejecting may come to think of themselves as incompetent or unworthy, to think of others as hostile or unresponsive, and to think of relationships with others as aversive or unpredictable. These negative thoughts about self and others may interfere with the development of their emotions and behavior-regulation skills. Children may find it particularly difficult to cope with parental rejection, which can arise when a parent is absent physically or emotionally from the child. Children may experience loss of love, care, protection, guidance, and a model to emulate. Under such conditions, children are at risk for depression and other forms of behavior disorders (LaRoche, 1986).

Parents with psychological problems or drug habits.
Parents with psychological problems may have difficulty helping their children feel emotionally secure, gain an understanding of social causes and effects, develop planning ability, learn the importance of delayed gratification, and learn to take responsibility for their own actions (Clarke & Clarke, 1994). They also may have difficulty coping with developmental changes in their children and will be more likely to be thrown into a crisis by stressful events (Frude, 1991).

Although children whose parents become addicted to drugs *after* the children are born are not considered "drug exposed," this kind of exposure to drugs or alcohol nevertheless places them at risk for developing psychological difficulties. Preoccupation with alcohol or drugs or organic deficits sustained as a result of excessive use of substances can interfere with the parents' ability to raise their children (Cunningham, 1992). Parents who are substance abusers may have various psychological problems—such as depression, anxiety, somatoform disorders, temper tantrums, aggressiveness, and hyperactivity—and be at risk for neglecting their children or for physically, sexually, or emotionally maltreating their children.

Other environmental stresses faced by children.
Children may face stresses associated with any of several events or conditions, such as the following:

- The birth of a sibling
- Moving to a new home or apartment
- Changing schools
- Failing classes
- Being suspended
- Having poor proficiency in English
- Being exposed to cultural clashes
- Being a victim of violence (such as maltreatment, mugging, or sexual assault)
- Becoming involved with drugs or alcohol
- Being overweight or underweight
- Being rejected by peers
- Being poor at sports
- Going to jail
- Attempting suicide

- Running away from home
- Having a best friend move
- Losing a job
- Having a parent lose a job
- Having a relative or close friend die
- Having parents divorce
- Becoming pregnant or impregnating someone

Stress is a key factor in the development of behavior disorders in children. Stress can exacerbate problems that children face and bring about new problems—by, for example, leading to acting-out behavior or a breakdown in behavior and producing changes in various neurochemicals in the body.

Exposure to violence.
Direct *exposure to violence* may affect children's psychological adjustment. In a national survey of a representative sample of 2,000 American children (1,042 boys and 958 girls) aged 10 to 16 years, one-third of the children reported having been the victim of an assault (Boney-McCoy & Finkelhor, 1995). Assaults were characterized as aggravated assault (12.3%), simple assault (11.5%), sexual assault (10.5%), genital violence (7.5%), attempted kidnapping (6.1%), nonparental family assault (5.1%), parental assault (2.2%), and other (44.8%). Extrapolating these results to the entire nation suggests that over 6.1 million youths ages 10 to 16 have suffered some form of assault. The *victimized children* reported more psychological and behavioral symptoms than did the nonvictimized children. The victimized children experienced (a) more symptoms of *posttraumatic stress disorder* during the past week, (b) increased sadness during the past month, and (c) more trouble with teachers during the past year. (Posttraumatic stress disorder, or PTSD, is a psychological reaction to a highly distressing event, such as a natural disaster, an accident, war, or rape; symptoms include frightening thoughts and images, trouble falling asleep, and uncontrollable temper outbursts.)

Boney-McCoy and Finkelhor (1995) concluded:

Evidence suggests that violent victimization is a major traumagenic [trauma-causing] influence in child development, and it may account for a substantial portion of mental health morbidity in both childhood and later adult life. These are powerful arguments for the need to quell the tide of violence in society and to protect children from its consequences. (p. 735)

They noted that the experience of being victimized and its associated trauma may interfere with or distort several developmental tasks of childhood. For example, victimized children may have impaired attachment to a caregiver or impaired self-esteem, adopt highly sexualized or highly aggressive modes of relating to others, fail to acquire competence in peer relations, or deal with anxiety in dysfunctional ways, such as by using drugs, dissociating, or engaging in self-injurious behavior (Finkelhor, 1995). The developmental effects of being victimized are likely to be more severe when the victimization is repetitive and ongoing; changes the nature of the child's relationship with her or his caregivers;

adds to other serious stressors, such as when a child is simultaneously victimized and suffering from bereavement, parental divorce, or racial discrimination; and interrupts a crucial developmental transition, such as when an adolescent is sexually abused.

Comment on the Development of Psychological Problems in Children

Psychological problems may lead children to experience a diminished sense of mastery and control, affecting family interactions as well as biological functioning. By disrupting important social bonds, undermining their existing competencies, inducing stress, and reaffirming their negative views of themselves and the world, psychological problems may compromise children's future development (Hammen & Rudolph, 1996).

GENERAL ASSESSMENT ISSUES

Before you evaluate children who may have special needs, their vision, hearing, physical condition, and health status should be examined. If you know before you evaluate a child that he or she has communication difficulties, ask parents and teachers about the signs, signals, or gestures that the child understands or uses to communicate.

The following suggestions should help you evaluate children with behavior disorders, cognitive/affective disorders, or physical disorders (Ramirez, 1978; Shontz, 1977; Wright, 1983):

- Do not allow a disorder in one area to bias your perception of how a child functions in other areas. For example, children who are mentally retarded may have excellent motor skills.
- Keep the session short because children may become fatigued easily if they are unaccustomed to concentrating for long periods. If you need to, schedule more than one session.
- Be prepared to work hard to establish rapport and to ensure that the children understand your questions.
- Think about how you can best position the children in your office so as to make them comfortable and accommodate any physical disabilities.
- Be sure that, during the evaluation, children use any adaptive equipment they routinely use (e.g., eyeglasses or hearing aids).
- Ask children who may need assistance, "Do you need help?" or "How should I help you?"
- Do not "talk over" or provide words for children who have difficulty speaking. Be patient, listen, and let them speak for themselves. Do not try to outguess them or assume that you know what they are trying to express.
- Do not direct your conversation to an attendant, assistant, or nearby companion as though the child were not present.

PERSONAL DOCUMENTS

A personal document written by a student—such as an autobiography, a diary, a journal, letters, essays, compositions, or poems—may be useful in evaluating the student's behavioral, social, and emotional competencies. Information obtained from these documents can be explored further during an interview.

Before you read any personal document, ask the student and a parent for permission to do so and have the student and parent sign a form granting you permission. Personal documents may give you insight about the student's home, school, friends, activities, attitudes and feelings (including self-concept), and related matters. If possible, evaluate whether the information in the personal document reflects what has happened in the student's life. Personal documents contain intimate information, and a trusting relationship between you and the student is needed if you are to make use of them. Be sure that the student understands your duty to report information about danger to self or others (see Chapter 3 in *Assessment of Children: Cognitive Applications*). You should also check with the school administration concerning district policy about examining personal documents.

CUMULATIVE SCHOOL RECORDS

Cumulative school records provide a summary of the student's academic performance and school behavior. Study the records and note the child's academic grades, attendance, work habits, behavior, and degree of cooperativeness. Be sure to note any trends in the records. Be aware that you may need to review several different school records, including a cumulative file, a health file, and a special education file.

Following are some areas to consider:

- Grades obtained by the student in each subject
- Citizenship ratings
- Changes in the child's grades and behavior as he or she progressed from grade to grade
- Relationship between the student's academic grades and behavior
- Retention in grade
- Number of absences and latenesses, if excessive, and reasons for them
- Disciplinary problems, reasons for them, and disciplinary actions taken
- Results of any psychoeducational or other assessments that were performed
- Any interventions and their results

It may be helpful to make a chart of the child's grades, with rows for subjects and columns for years. Related subjects (e.g., language arts and English) might be placed in adjacent rows. Information from cumulative school records should be compared with other information that you have about the student and his or her family.

ASSESSMENT OF INFANTS AND PRESCHOOL CHILDREN

Most people find infants and young children inherently attractive. They are spontaneous, open, and direct in expressing their ideas, likes, dislikes, and desires. Although they are less predictable and may move through many more moods than older children, they remain more responsive to how you handle a situation. Less restricted by social rules, they will give you candid feedback about your appearance and behavior and their feelings. Simultaneously, infants and young children permit you to be more spontaneous and joyful than you would be with older children. (Some material in this part of the chapter was adapted from Robinson and Harris, 1980.)

Nevertheless, assessing infants and young children may be demanding. For example, infants who withdraw from or are slow to adapt to new situations will be difficult to evaluate. Fearful or shy children, particularly those who are not accustomed to being with strangers, will frequently need special help. They may show inconsistent performance in unfamiliar environments. You must guide young children, maintaining their attention and cooperation. Often you must not only tell but also show them what you want them to do. The younger the child, the more clear and precise your gestures and use of materials must be. With babies, exaggerate your movements a little so that they see what you want—for example, if you want the child to imitate your actions, pat a doll rather firmly and then motion for the baby to do the same. Through the tone of your voice and your actions—such as handing material to the child—make clear to the child when you expect a response.

Young children's attention spans are short, and their moods are variable. Hedonism prevails—the younger the child, the more likely it is that he or she will do only what seems attractive at the moment. Thus, they may be distractible. Young children also are prone to being overwhelmed by primary physiological needs. Although an attractive task might override mildly unmet needs in older infants or preschoolers, you cannot do much with crying, hungry, or sleepy infants other than comfort them, feed them, or put them down for a nap. Watch for early signs of boredom, fatigue, physical discomfort, or emotional distress, and take appropriate action before such conditions become acute. Consider rescheduling the evaluation if the infant does not calm down. If the parent is present, the young child may prefer that the parent—rather than you—wipe his or her nose or take him or her to the bathroom. This is perfectly okay. But do not take too many breaks, because this will lengthen the overall time and possibly fatigue the child. *Thus, behavioral state and temperament will play a much larger role in assessing infants and preschoolers than in assessing older children.*

Positive reinforcement is one of the most potent tools for working with infants and young children. Attend to behavior you appreciate. Nodding, smiling, and other appreciative gestures may be more effective than words. As with children of all ages, reinforce effort, whether or not success follows.

Do not, however, say "good" or "great" excessively. You want to build an image of yourself as a kind but firm, fairly exciting but predictable adult who likes infants and young children and will be pleased by their efforts.

Additional considerations are important in evaluating infants. First, because infant instruments draw so heavily on motor items, you will have difficulty evaluating infants with severe motor impairments. Second, with some infants, you may have difficulty judging whether their responses are representative of their capabilities. Third, tests based exclusively on the mother's or other informant's report are completely dependent on the informant's accuracy; consequently, you will need to judge the reliability of the informant. In addition to conducting formal testing, you will want to observe the infant in her or his natural environment (e.g., at home) and see how the infant interacts with the parents (see Chapters 4 and 5). The guidelines in Table 10-2 will help you observe several facets of an infant's behavior: interactions with play materials and involvement in play, affect in play, attention span in play, temperament and motivation, auditory responsiveness, expressive language, motor behavior, eating patterns, and general behavior.

When meeting infants and young children for the first time, approach them with confidence. If you are tense or apprehensive, they may sense your feelings and become resistant or negative, especially if you try too hard to gain their cooperation. At the opposite extreme, if you prolong the preliminary getting-acquainted time with overstimulating or entertaining play, you may interfere with the assessment process. Sometimes, you may need to ignore or circumvent the behaviors that you do not like, and instead distract or redirect the child. If a parent is present, she or he may be able to help you get the child on track, but some parents interfere more than they help. Generally, handle problems by trying to foresee and forestall them. Consider these guidelines as you establish rapport:

- In speaking with a young child, listen carefully to what she or he says.
- Be patient, do not overpower the child with many requests, and allow some time for pauses.
- Reflect the child's feelings and periodically paraphrase what she or he has said.
- Follow the child's leads and maintain the child's pace. However, control the pace so as not to prolong the evaluation and cause fatigue.
- Recognize that the child's comments are important and require your undivided attention.
- Be warm and friendly in your conversation, consider the child's perspective, and keep in mind the child's age and level of cognitive development. (The table on the inside front cover provides landmarks for the first five years of development.)

An infant's temperament can be classified based on the following nine dimensions (Laucht, Esser, & Schmidt, 1993; Medoff-Cooper, Carey, & McDevitt, 1993; Chess & Thomas,

Table 10-2
Guidelines for Observing Infants

Guideline 1. Observe the infant's interactions with play materials and involvement in play.

Note, for example:

- How does the infant examine, touch, and manipulate objects (e.g., actively, passively)?
- What objects hold special interest for the infant (e.g., those that make sounds; those made of wood, plastic, or cloth; those that can be used as containers)?
- How does the infant play with toys that can be used in several ways (e.g., small boxes with tops; nesting toys; cubes and containers with lids, including pots and pans)?
- How does the infant approach new situations or objects (e.g., with anticipation, fearfully)?
- How much encouragement does the infant require to become involved in play (e.g., little encouragement, much encouragement)?
- How does the infant show interest in a toy (e.g., looks at the toy, makes grasping movements toward the toy)?
- How does the infant's interest vary with different activities?
- How intense is the infant's play?
- How much time does it take the infant to become involved in playing with a toy?
- How does the infant's behavior change when he or she is given time to explore an object or use materials?
- How often does the infant achieve goals in play?
- What does the infant do after being interrupted in an activity (e.g., goes back to the activity, goes to a new activity)?

Guideline 2. Observe the infant's affect in play.

Note, for example:

- What emotions does the infant show during play (e.g., happiness, anger, tension, irritability, sadness)?
- How does the infant express likes and dislikes (e.g., smiles, whines, laughs, cries)?
- How does the infant react when he or she is given a new object, discovers a new way to use a toy, or is given just enough help to succeed in an activity?
- What activities frustrate the infant?
- What does the infant do when frustrated (e.g., cries, reacts stoically, looks for caregiver)?

Guideline 3. Observe the infant's attention span in play.

Note, for example:

- What activities hold the infant's attention the longest?
- How does the infant explore objects (e.g., attends briefly, attends for a long period of time, turns object frequently)?
- How long does the infant play with an object?
- What toys does the infant select (e.g., those that keep him or her involved and interested for a reasonable time, those that are nearest)?

Guideline 4. Observe the infant's temperament and motivation.

Note, for example:

- What is the infant's temperament (e.g., active or passive, content or fussy, relaxed or tense, engaging or unfocused,

sleepy or alert, cuddly or rigid, easy to comfort or difficult to comfort)?
- What distresses the infant, and how does the infant show distress (e.g., frowns, turns away, makes sounds, kicks)?
- What cues does the infant give that she or he is overstimulated, bored, frustrated, happy, or involved?
- How consistent is the infant's tempo across several activities?
- How persistent is the infant in pursuing a goal in play in the face of obstacles?
- How interested is the infant in activities?
- How does the infant's tempo compare with that of the infant's parent(s)?
- What changes in temperament does the infant show during the observation?

Guideline 5. Observe the infant's auditory responsiveness.

Note, for example:

- How does the infant respond to the spoken language of others (e.g., becomes attentive, animated, quiet)?
- What does the infant do when someone calls his or her name (e.g., looks up, attends to the face of the person talking, does not look up, does not attend)?
- What does the infant do when adults talk to each other in his or her presence?
- How does the infant seem to understand and attend to words (e.g., looks at a ball when it is mentioned, touches his or her nose when it is named, attends to words or phrases contingent on his or her activity)?
- What cues does the infant give that indicate some interest in spoken language (e.g., looks at a speaker when language is not directed to him or her, turns toward a speaker)?
- What is required to get the infant's attention (e.g., clapping hands, talking loudly, using dramatic gestures)?
- How does the infant attend to language when there is background noise?

Guideline 6. Observe the infant's expressive language.

Note, for example:

- What sounds does the infant make?
- Does the infant babble or use jargon (e.g., as if participating in others' conversation, making playful sounds without semblance of participation in others' conversation)?
- What vocalizations does the infant make in various situations (e.g., when excited, when a parent is on the telephone, when a parent watches, when engaged in solitary play)?
- How does the infant react to his or her vocalizing (e.g., becomes more animated, shows no particular reaction)?
- What does the infant do when making certain sounds (e.g., looks consistently at the same object when making a specific sound, such as "baba" for blanket or "ga" for cracker; makes sounds without specific referents)?
- How does the infant express wants or needs (e.g., makes sounds, kicks feet, points, crawls to place)?
- How does the infant communicate without using vocal language?

(Continued)

Table 10-2 (Continued)

- How does the infant react when he or she continues making a certain sound and does not get a response?

Guideline 7. Observe the infant's motor behavior.

Note, for example:

- What fine- and gross-motor behaviors does the infant show (e.g., ability to handle various objects of different sizes and shapes, ability to throw a ball, ability to move)?
- What is the quality of the infant's motor behaviors (e.g., normal motor development, delayed motor development, disturbed motor development)?
- How does the infant react when staying in one place for long periods?
- How does the infant's motor behavior change in different situations?
- How does the infant show newly acquired or emerging skills (e.g., persists in repeating skills, performs skill only once or a few times)?
- What does the infant do when encouraged to perform a motor movement for which he or she is not developmentally ready?

Guideline 8. Observe the infant's eating patterns.

Note, for example:

- What cues does the infant give indicating a readiness to eat (e.g., reaches for bottle, spoon, or food; opens mouth eagerly)?
- How is the infant fed (e.g., breast fed, bottle fed, breast and bottle fed, fed with solid food and finger foods)?

- How does the infant feed himself or herself (e.g., with fingers, with utensils)?
- What foods does the infant eat (e.g., liquids, solids, soft foods, chewable foods)?
- How does the infant react to being fed and to feeding (e.g., sucks, swallows, or chews food eagerly; pushes food or bottle away; holds food in mouth without chewing or swallowing; vocalizes to avoid eating; becomes easily distracted from feeding)?

Guideline 9. Observe the infant's general behavior.

Note, for example:

- What are the infant's best-developed skills?
- How does the infant's behavior vary in different activities (e.g., when engaged in play, in social behavior, in language, in motor activities)?
- How does the infant react to people (e.g., familiar adults, children, strangers)?
- What atypical behaviors are displayed by the infant (e.g., fails to cuddle, cries excessively, rocks constantly, bangs head)?
- In what situations are the atypical behaviors displayed (e.g., with mother, with father, with both parents, with babysitter, with stranger present along with caregiver, with siblings, with other relative)?
- How does the infant indicate readiness for some independence (e.g., plays alone, sits on floor alone)?

Note. Record specific instances of each behavior, where appropriate, and the conditions under which the behavior occurred.

1986; Willis & Walker, 1989). Most of the information needed to classify an infant's temperament will come from a caregiver.

1. *Activity level*—the amount of physical motion during sleeping, eating, playing, dressing, bathing, and so forth. An active infant is characterized by much movement and fitful sleep; the caregiver is likely to feel that he or she cannot leave the infant alone for even a few seconds for fear that the infant will move or fall. Note, for example, whether the infant has a normal activity level or is hyperactive or hypoactive.

2. *Rhythmicity*—the regularity of physiological functions, such as hunger, sleep, and elimination. An infant with rhythmicity has regular feeding times, sleeping times, and times for bowel movements. Note, for example, whether the infant has predictable rhythmicity or is dysrhythmic.

3. *Approach or withdrawal*—the nature of initial responses to new stimuli, including people, situations, places, foods, toys, and procedures. An infant with an approach tendency approaches people eagerly and reacts well to new people and new surroundings. Note, for example, whether the infant has a normal approach or shows resistance to change.

4. *Adaptability*—the ease or difficulty with which reactions to stimuli can be modified in an appropriate way. An

adaptable infant adjusts easily to unexpected company, new people, new foods, and unfamiliar settings. Note, for example, whether the infant has normal adaptability or is slow to adapt.

5. *Threshold of responsiveness*—the amount of stimulation, such as sound or light, necessary to evoke discernable responses in the infant. An infant with a good threshold of responsiveness adjusts well to noises, textures of clothing, heat, cold, and environmental sounds, such as the ring of a telephone and a siren. Note, for example, whether the infant has a normal threshold of responsiveness or is hypersensitive or hyposensitive.

6. *Intensity of reaction*—the energy level of responses, as well as the direction (high or low) when intensity is unusual. An infant with a high level of intensity displays pleasure or displeasure vigorously. Note, for example, whether the infant has a normal intensity of reaction or is irritable or apathetic.

7. *Quality of mood*—whether behavior tends to be pleasant, joyful, and friendly or unpleasant, crying, and unfriendly. An infant with a joyful mood is happy and content overall and displays this mood in varied situations. Note, for example, whether the infant's mood is happy or dysphoric.

8. *Distractibility*—the ability of extraneous environmental stimuli to interfere with or alter the direction of ongo-

ing behavior. An infant who is not distractible can carry out her or his activities, such as eating, despite some noise or people entering the room. Note, for example, whether the infant is minimally, moderately, or highly distractible.

9. *Attention span and persistence*—the length of time particular activities are pursued by the child and the extent to which activities are continued in the face of obstacles. An infant with a good attention span and persistence can stay with an activity for a period—when the child drops a toy, for instance, he or she looks for the toy and then persists at trying to retrieve it. Note, for example, whether the infant shows a good, moderate, or poor attention span.

These nine dimensions, in turn, lead to three temperamental types (Willis & Walker, 1989, p. 35, with changes in notation):

- The easy child is one who is mild, predominantly positive in mood, approachable, adaptable, and rhythmic.
- The difficult child is one who is predominantly negative and intense in mood, not very adaptable, and arrhythmic.
- The slow-to-warm-up child is one who is low in activity and adaptability, withdrawn, and variable in rhythm.

To work with young children, you need to recognize when they are ready to interact, to communicate, and to cooperate with you. If you are not accustomed to spending much time with infants or preschoolers, observe several experienced examiners as they work with them. You will eventually develop your own style of interacting with young children. Table F-5 in Appendix F shows a brief rating scale useful in rating the competencies of kindergarten-age children.

SCHOOLIES © 1999 by John P. Wood

I've mastered the ABC's. I'm just having a little trouble with the other 23 letters . . .

DYNAMIC ASSESSMENT

Dynamic assessment—also referred to as learning potential assessment, interactive assessment, testing-of-limits, mediated assessment, and assisted learning and transfer—is designed to evaluate an examinee's ability to improve performance following a systematic learning experience (Budoff & Hamilton, 1976; Campione & Brown, 1987; Feuerstein, 1979; Guthke, 1982; Hegarty & Lucas, 1978). The focus is on (a) processes that underlie successful performance, (b) assessment of specific areas of functioning rather than general ability per se, (c) dynamics of change in the learning process, and (d) continuous assessment of the examinee's level of ability and processing style (Campione & Brown, 1987).

In dynamic assessment, the examinee is taught principles that can be used to help solve problems. For example, the examinee might be taught the principles underlying the construction of a particular block pattern on a block design task. Measuring the examinee's ability to solve additional block design problems yields an estimate of his or her ability to learn and to apply this learning to similar problems. Progressively more complex tasks are used, with continual teaching and feedback.

Dynamic assessment focuses on what the examinee can learn, how readily she or he acquires strategies and problem-solving skills, and whether the strategies and skills are generalizable. The procedures may incorporate mini–learning situations that permit the systematic observation and evaluation of the examinee's responses to structured teaching. An enrichment program—which stresses the acquisition of learning strategies rather than the acquisition of specific subject-area content—may also be tied to the evaluation procedure. Dynamic assessment developed because traditional assessment practices purportedly (a) rely too much on static, product-based tests, (b) provide inappropriate descriptions of cognitive abilities, (c) fail to focus on the processes that underlie the competence being measured, and (d) fail to reveal how the examinee arrived at her or his answers (Campione, 1989).

Dynamic Assessment Procedures

Let's look at three dynamic assessment procedures.

Test-train-test paradigm.   The test-train-test paradigm involves a pretest, a training procedure, and a posttest.

1. *Pretest (initial testing).* The examinee is assessed in standard fashion with culture-fair test stimuli. The stimuli may be unfamiliar to the examinee, particularly when they are incorporated into the teaching procedure. Nonverbal reasoning tasks frequently are used, such as variations of Kohs Block Design (e.g., those found on the WISC–III) or Raven's Progressive Matrices. This step gives baseline information—that is, how the examinee performed without assistance.

2. *Training procedure (teaching of principles).* The examinee receives instruction in solving the task. Instructional

principles include attending to all choices and applying analytic skills. Techniques include giving feedback, prompts, and extended teaching with practice in item-solving strategies. Training varies depending on the task. The goal is to help the examinee develop appropriate problem-solving strategies. This step gives information about the amount and type of help the examinee needs to solve the problems.

3. *Posttest (retesting).* The examinee is retested on the original task or on an alternative form of it. This step gives information about how much the examinee improved as a result of the training, including whether he or she learned the principles and strategies that were taught and can apply them to new problems.

In some cases, the test-train-test sequence is standardized and consistent across examinees. In other cases, an informal clinical assessment approach is used in which the examiner has considerable latitude in the selection of tasks and training procedures.

Within-test procedure. In the within-test paradigm, modifications are made during the test proper (Cormier, Carlson, & Das, 1990). Examinees are encouraged to engage in concurrent or retrospective verbalizations about their performance. A four-step procedure is used.

1. *Description phase.* The examinee is asked to describe the task.

2. *Think-aloud phase.* The examinee is asked to think aloud as he or she solves the problem.

3. *Explanation-of-answer-chosen phase.* The examinee is asked to explain why the answer she or he selected is correct.

4. *Explanation-of-answer-rejected phase.* The examinee is asked to explain why the alternatives that were not chosen are incorrect.

Although the examiner does not provide feedback concerning the correctness of a solution during the four phases, she or he interacts actively with the examinee, stimulating the examinee to explain his or her responses.

Dynamic assessment in conjunction with a standardized test. When dynamic assessment is used in conjunction with a standardized test, a six-step procedure may be followed (Haywood, 1997):

1. *Administering the test.* A standardized test is administered without assistance.

2. *Identifying deficits.* Cognitive functions that lead to poor performance are identified.

3. *Providing help.* Assistance is given to improve performance, and the examinee tries again.

4. *Evaluating responses.* The responses to help are evaluated, including (a) the magnitude of the improvement in performance following intervention and (b) the degree of generalization of concepts and principles of thinking, learning, and problem solving to new problems.

5. *Identifying noncognitive factors.* Noncognitive factors that may affect performance are identified.

6. *Interventions.* Conditions needed to improve the examinee's performance are specified.

In this approach, dynamic assessment complements standardized testing and attempts to explain why children perform poorly on standardized tests.

Aims of Dynamic Assessment

Dynamic assessment evaluates the examinee's ability to acquire new information and problem-solving strategies. Its aims are to help the examinee link new information to prior information and to restructure thought processes by directing the examinee's attention to newly discovered ways to solve problems. In dynamic assessment, scores reflect not only the number of correct solutions, but also the number of helping steps needed to solve the problem.

In dynamic assessment, it is necessary to consider such factors as the following:

1. The stimuli used for teaching (e.g., spatial-visual and other concept formation tasks, number seriation tasks, pictorial series tasks, geometric series tasks, paired-associate learning tasks, auditory-rote learning tasks)
2. The teaching methods used (e.g., feedback linked to each step, open-ended feedback, social or monetary reinforcement)
3. The extent to which the examinee knew the correct responses before teaching began
4. The extent to which the tasks and activities involved in the tasks were unfamiliar to the examinee

Ideally, the examinee should neither know the correct responses before teaching starts nor be familiar with the test stimuli. If these two conditions are not met, it will be difficult to evaluate the effectiveness of dynamic assessment because scores will be confounded—that is, they will reflect both present learning *and* prior learning. In practice, these two assumptions may never be fully met.

As a result of training, some examinees will improve their performance and others will not. Those examinees who do not learn under one type of teaching strategy may learn more efficiently under another. Similarly, those examinees who perform poorly on some tasks may learn more rapidly on others. Consequently, every dynamic assessment should include several teaching strategies and tasks.

According to Haywood (1997), dynamic assessment should be used in the following situations:

1. The examinee performs poorly on standardized tests.
2. The examinee's standard scores are 2 to 3 standard deviations below the mean (e.g., IQs in the 60s or 50s).
3. The examinee has large discrepancies between performance on achievement tests and performance on intelligence tests.

4. The examinee is from a culturally and linguistically different background.
5. The examinee is from a low socioeconomic group.
6. The examinee has an emotional disturbance or a learning disability, is extremely shy or unmotivated, or has a history of chronic failure.

Dynamic Assessment and Traditional Intelligence Assessment

Dynamic assessment differs from traditional intelligence assessment in several ways (see Table 10-3). Dynamic assessment attempts to measure the *process* of learning rather than the *content* of learning. Traditional intelligence assessment focuses on the examinee's present level of cognitive development (what and how much has been mastered or learned); dynamic assessment focuses on the examinee's present learning process (why and how the material has been mastered). The former emphasizes description; the latter, explanation.

The two procedures, however, overlap considerably. For example, both focus on cognitive processes and provide information useful in describing and explaining the examinee's present level of functioning. An examinee enters both an intelligence assessment and a dynamic assessment with the same learning history. The two procedures measure current achievement, but in different ways. And although there is not a one-to-one correspondence between intelligence and learning ability (as defined by a dynamic assessment), intelligence *is* related to the ability to learn. Intelligence and learning ability are complex multidimensional concepts, with the former more easily defined and measured than the latter.

Comment on Dynamic Assessment

Dynamic assessment aims to obtain information about the examinee's potential. However, an examinee's potential for learning is based primarily on present and past learnings. Because intelligence tests are useful in making judgments about an examinee's learning potential, attempts to equate dynamic assessment *exclusively* with the measurement of learning potential are inappropriate. For example, an examinee with an IQ of 130 has a much better potential for learning in school than does an examinee with an IQ of 70. Research indicates that dynamic assessment tests do *not* have better predictive validity than do intelligence tests (Glutting & McDermott, 1990; Grigorenko & Sternberg, 1998).

Sternberg (1991, 1992) notes some difficulties with dynamic assessment. Assigning a number that indicates how much "potential" a child has pigeonholes the child just as much as assigning an IQ to the child. Does a number derived from a dynamic assessment then place the final limit on the child's learning ability? In dynamic assessment, individual differences and the way the material is taught need to be taken into account (Sternberg, 1992). What works well with one child may not work well with another child, because no one form of instruction is equally suitable for all children. In addition, instructions that work well for some types of learning situations may not work well for other types of situations.

Still, dynamic assessment can be useful, particularly when the results improve understanding of the examinee's abilities and aid in the design of remedial programs. Of course, evidence is always needed about how the results obtained from dynamic assessment correlate with results from other measures. As with all assessment procedures, the reliability and validity of dynamic assessment must be evaluated. Dynamic assessment may complement—but should not replace—standardized assessments (Frisby & Braden, 1992). As of 1997, Grigorenko and Sternberg (1998) concluded "that dynamic testing has great potential for helping to understand people's potentials but that its potential has yet to be realized fully" (p. 75). For more information about dynamic assessment, see Brown, Campione, Webber, and McGilly (1992), Grigorenko and Sternberg (1998), and Lidz (1991, 1997).

Table 10-3
Comparison of Traditional Intelligence Assessment with Dynamic Assessment

Intelligence testing	Dynamic assessment
1. Focuses on the content of learning	1. Focuses on the process of learning
2. Attempts to determine what has been learned	2. Attempts to determine why learning takes place
3. Gives no feedback to examinee	3. Gives feedback to examinee
4. Establishes a neutral but supportive relationship	4. Establishes an atmosphere of teaching and helping
5. Attempts to determine how much material has been mastered	5. Attempts to determine how material is mastered
6. Focuses on a description of the child's performance	6. Focuses on an explanation of how the child learns
7. Attempts to predict future performance	7. Attempts to prescribe appropriate remedial interventions

---

SCHOOL VIOLENCE

The U.S. Secret Service National Threat Assessment Center studied 37 school shootings involving 41 attackers who were current or recent students at the schools. The cases spanned a period from 1974 to 1999 and took place in 26 states. Incidents were *not* included if the shootings were clearly related to gang or drug activity or if there was an interpersonal or relationship

SCHOOLIES © 1998 by John P. Wood

I'm not a very good self-directed learner. Isn't there some way you could force me to learn this material?

dispute that just happened to occur at the school. The preliminary findings were as follows (Vossekuil, Reddy, Fein, Borum, & Modzeleski, 2000; adapted from pp. 3–8).

INCIDENT CHARACTERISTICS

1. Boys or young men committed all of the attacks.
2. In over half the incidents, a school administrator, faculty member, or staff member was the target.
3. In more than two-thirds of the incidents, the attacker killed one or more students, faculty, or others at the school.

PRELIMINARY FINDINGS

1. Incidents of targeted violence at school are rarely impulsive.

- In almost all of the incidents, the attacker developed the idea to harm the target before the attack.
- In well over three-quarters of the incidents, the attacker planned the attack.
- Over half of the attackers had a revenge motive.
- More than three-quarters of the attackers were known to have a grievance at the time of the attack.

2. Prior to most incidents, the attacker told someone about his idea or plan.

- In over three-quarters of the cases, the attacker told someone before the attack of his interest in mounting an attack at school.
- In virtually all of those cases, the attacker told a friend, schoolmate, or sibling.

3. There is no profile of "the school shooter."

- Attackers ranged from 11 to 21 years of age.
- They came from a variety of racial and ethnic backgrounds.
- They came from a range of family situations.
- Their academic performance ranged from excellent to failing.
- They had a range of friendship patterns, from socially isolated to popular.
- Their behavioral histories varied, with some showing no observed behavioral problems and others showing multiple behaviors warranting reprimand or discipline.
- Few attackers showed any marked change in academic performance, friendship status, interest in school, or disciplinary problems at school prior to the attack.
- Few of the attackers had been diagnosed with any mental disorder prior to the incident. Additionally, less than one-third of the attackers had a history of drug or alcohol abuse.

4. Most attackers had previously used guns and had access to them.

- Over half of the attackers had a history of gun use.
- In nearly two-thirds of the incidents, the attackers got the gun(s) used in the attack from their own home or that of a relative.

5. Most shooting incidents were not resolved by law enforcement intervention.

- Over half of the attacks were resolved or ended before law enforcement responded to the scene.
- In only three cases did law enforcement personnel discharge any weapons during the incident.
- Most incidents lasted about 20 minutes or less.

6. In many cases, other students were involved in some capacity.

- In almost half of the cases, the attackers were influenced or encouraged by others.
- In over three-quarters of the incidents, other students knew about the attack before it occurred.

7. In a number of cases, having been bullied played a key role in the attack.

- In over two-thirds of the cases, the attackers felt persecuted, bullied, threatened, attacked, or injured by others prior to the incident.
- Several attackers had experienced bullying and harassment that was longstanding and severe.

8. Most attackers engaged in some behavior, prior to the incident, that caused others concern or indicated a need for help.

- In almost every incident, the attacker had engaged in behavior that caused others (e.g., school officials, police, fellow students) to be concerned about the attacker.
- Behaviors that led others to be concerned about the attacker prior to the attack included behaviors related to the

attack, such as efforts to get a gun, as well as other disturbing behaviors not related to the subsequent attack.

- In well over three-quarters of the incidents, the attackers had difficulty coping with a major change in a significant relationship or loss of status (e.g., personal failure) prior to their school attack.
- Prior to the incident, nearly three-quarters of the attackers either threatened to kill themselves, made suicidal gestures, or tried to kill themselves.

The following guidelines will assist in implementing interventions in cases of threats of school violence (O'Toole, 2000):

A school cannot ignore any threat of violence. Plausible or not, every threat must be taken seriously, investigated, and responded to. A clear, vigorous response is essential for three reasons: first and most important, to make sure that students, teachers, and staff *are* safe (that is, that a threat will not be carried out); second, to assure that they will *feel* safe; and third, to assure that the person making the threat will be supervised and given the treatment that is appropriate and necessary to avoid future danger to others or himself. (p. 25)

Schools should have appropriate policies and procedures in place to handle targeted threats of violence. A threat management program should be established in every school, using the following guidelines (O'Toole, 2000).

1. *Have the threat management policies written down, with clear guidelines about how to handle potentially violent situations.* The guidelines should include a safety plan in the event that a violent act occurs.

2. *Inform students and parents of school policies.* At the beginning of each year, the school should inform all students and parents about what is expected of them. Students should be told that they are expected to inform school authorities any time they know of a threat. Parents should be told that they will be contacted if their child makes a threat of any kind and asked to provide information to evaluate the threat. When new students enter the school, they and their parents should be similarly informed.

3. *Designate a school threat assessment coordinator.* A threat assessment coordinator should be appointed at each school to oversee that school's response to threats. This individual should be knowledgeable about the school's policies on targeted school violence, be able to assess the seriousness of the threat of targeted violence (or refer to another member of the staff who has this skill), and be capable of working with law enforcement personnel. Whoever receives the threat initially should then refer the threat to the threat assessment coordinator. The threat assessment coordinator should be given the authority to make decisions on how to respond to the threat. The threat assessment coordinator should establish a close working relationship with local law enforcement personnel. The threat assessment coordinator can have several responsibilities, including the following:

- Developing a threat management system
- Maintaining consistency in the school's threat response procedures

- Arranging for an initial assessment to determine the level of threat
- Making a decision about what to do in case of an attack
- Arranging for an evaluation of the student or students who made the threat
- Monitoring all interventions
- Acting as a liaison with outside experts

4. *Form a multidisciplinary team.* In addition to appointing a threat assessment coordinator, the school can form a multidisciplinary team, usually including a law enforcement representative as well as the threat assessment coordinator, to "review threats, consult with outside experts, and provide recommendations and advice to the coordinator and to the school administration" (O'Toole, 2000, p. 26).

5. *Evaluate the threat or the student's intent in each case.* Schools "should not deal with threats by simply kicking the problem out the door. Expelling or suspending a student for making a threat must not be a substitute for careful threat assessment and a considered policy of intervention. Disciplinary action alone, unaccompanied by any effort to evaluate the threat or the student's intent, may actually exacerbate the danger…" (O'Toole, 2000, p. 26). Suspended or even expelled students eventually come back to school. It is important to be prepared for their reentry.

6. *Provide training to school administrators and staff in the fundamentals of threat assessment, adolescent development and violence, and other mental health issues.*

7. *Educate and sensitize students about cues indicating potential violence.* "Students are often in the best position to see and hear signs or cues of potential violence, and training should stress that ignoring those cues or remaining silent can be dangerous for themselves as well as others" (O'Toole, 2000, p. 32). Schools should strive to develop an atmosphere in which students feel free to report information to adults. Students need to understand and believe that everyone is responsible for safety in the school.

8. *Provide intervention services to the threatener.* Counseling should be offered to students who have made threats. For example, efforts should be directed to understanding why the student made the threat in the first place (e.g., uncovering unmet needs) and helping the student work through conflict areas.

INSTRUCTIONAL STRATEGIES FOR CHILDREN WITH SPECIAL NEEDS

Children with special needs may require services in schools or modifications in classroom procedures. For example, they may need (a) additional instructional help, such as resource teachers, consultants, specialists, therapists, and aides, (b) flexible classrooms that are "open" and provide direct instruction in small, self-contained areas, (c) assignment to specific teachers whose teaching styles match their learning styles, or (d) placement in small classes (Johnson, 1987).

MR. WOODHEAD © 1998 by John P. Wood

Because I've been failing so miserably in school, my mom signed me up for a self-esteem class.

And has it helped?

Yeah.

Now I'm failing fabulously.

Instructional strategies and other types of interventions for specific disorders are discussed in other chapters of the book. Following are some general instructional strategies that may be useful in consulting with teachers of children with special needs (Scruggs & Mastropieri, 1992).

1. *Ensure that presented information is understood by all students.* Teachers should be certain that students with special needs (as well as other students) understand new material. If the material is not understood, the teacher should provide concrete examples or analogies to link the content to the students' experience.

2. *Provide additional help.* Teachers should give additional help to students who cannot master material in the allotted time. Student teachers, aides, peers, or parents can be asked to help students master material.

3. *Attend to the developmental requirements of the content.* Teachers should know the age or grade level to which materials are geared and the age or grade level at which students can master material, and then select appropriate materials for students.

4. *Intensify instruction for later recall.* Teachers can highlight important points on the board or on an overhead projector and have students repeat the information several times.

5. *Promote effective encoding.* Teachers can enhance the meaningfulness, familiarity, and concreteness of the content being taught by questioning students often, having students relate information to their prior knowledge, and having students attend to the acoustic properties of new words (e.g., what word the new word sounds like).

6. *Allow sufficient time for responding.* After addressing questions to students, teachers should wait a sufficient amount of time for them to answer.

7. *Assist students in developing listening skills.* Teachers should cue students about the important items that need to be attended to and then check for understanding by asking students to repeat what was said. Other useful techniques include asking the entire class to repeat the assignment or directions, asking some students to write important points about the assignment on the board, or pairing students and having one student in the pair check to see whether her or his companion understands the assignment.

8. *Integrate language activities into regular instruction.* Various ways to integrate language activities should be attempted. One way is to have the entire class practice using vocabulary words in speaking and writing in several subjects outside the language lesson.

9. *Reinforce positive classroom behavior.* Teachers should show students that they care about them. Teachers should praise students when they display appropriate affect and motivation. After students show positive behavior for a while, they should be encouraged to self-monitor their behavior (see Chapter 5).

10. *Teach social skills.* Teachers should help students learn social skills if their social skills are deficient. If time does not permit such instruction, these skills can be taught in another school setting (e.g., special education class or counseling). In the classroom, teachers can model, prompt, and reinforce the social skills taught in other settings.

11. *Use attribution training.* Teachers should help students understand that academic success occurs because of the students' effort, perseverance, and task-appropriate academic strategies, such as using good study habits.

12. *Consult support personnel when necessary.* Teachers should consult the school counselor, school psychologist, or other support personnel when severe behavioral, cognitive, affective, or motivational problems are present.

13. *Employ a parent as tutor.* Teachers should ask parents whether they are interested in tutoring students at home. If so, students can be tutored in their areas of deficit. Parents should keep a record of students' progress, keep sessions to about 30 to 45 minutes, and reward students for effort and improvement.

14. *Employ peer tutoring.* Teachers can assign peers to help students. Teachers should assign a peer to a student with whom he or she gets along, give the peer appropriate instructional materials, carefully sequence and structure the sessions, and monitor the sessions, at least indirectly. A peer can provide prompts, models, and positive alternatives to inappropriate behavior. Teachers should help peers understand that tutoring is a privilege rather than an obligation.

15. *Formulate appropriate organizational structure.* Teachers should incorporate effective teaching strategies into their instruction. These strategies include teaching to clearly specified objectives, providing clear directions and guided independent practice activities, monitoring students' progress, allocating instructional time wisely, and providing timely feedback on performance.

16. *Teach cognitive strategies.* Teachers should help students use more effective cognitive strategies to master academic material. These strategies include self-questioning, self-monitoring, predicting, generating questions, and task analysis.

17. *Increase proximity.* Teachers may need to move certain students closer to their desks and give them more attention—asking them more questions about the material, for example.

18. *Provide structure; be explicit with all assignments.* Teachers should give clear, explicit directions for all assignments. Directions should include models of appropriately completed assignments, time lines for completion (with dates for drafts of papers, suggested completion, and extra-help sessions), and criteria for acceptable performance on projects.

19. *Teach general study techniques.* Teachers should conduct study sessions on how students can succeed in class. The focus might be on best ways to (a) review and study a particular textbook, (b) take class notes, (c) highlight or outline, (d) prepare for tests, (e) organize class notebooks, (f) keep assignment books, and (g) prepare for the class.

20. *Measure achievement at later, rather than earlier, stages of acquisition.* Teachers should wait to grade students until after they all have had a chance to become familiar with the material.

21. *Make use of external memory systems when appropriate.* Teachers should instruct students to write down important facts—such as social security number, home address, and telephone number—and keep this information in a wallet or purse. Similarly, students should be instructed to write down their class schedule and keep it in a notebook.

22. *Use mnemonic instruction.* Teachers can help students recall technical terms by associating them with easier terms or incorporating them into the lyrics of a song.

23. *Establish goals for learning.* Teachers should first help students set short-term and long-term goals for learning and then help them monitor progress toward meeting these goals. Teachers should reward students for quick, efficient task completion.

RESOURCES

Two excellent resources that provide useful information for parents and professionals about children with special needs

MR. WOODHEAD © 1997 by John P. Wood

This assignment has been scientifically designed just for me. It's based on my personality type, my cognitive profile and my learning preference inventory.

I hate it.

are *Clinical and Forensic Interviewing of Children and Families: Guidelines for the Mental Health, Education, Pediatric, and Child Maltreatment Fields* by Sattler (1998) and *The Special Needs Reading List: An Annotated Guide to the Best Publications for Parents and Professionals* by Sweeney (1998). The Sattler text has a list of recommended readings, a list of organizations for parents, a cross-disciplinary glossary, and several forms useful in evaluating children with special needs. The Sweeny text covers 700 authors and 200 organizations that provide information about children with disabilities. In addition, *Assessment of Children: Cognitive Applications* has a list of useful web sites (Table F-7 in Appendix F, pages 887–890).

For more information about school violence, a good book to consult is *Youth Aggression and Violence: A Psychological Approach* (Moeller, 2001). The following web sites are also useful resources:

National Threat Assessment Center of the Secret Service
http://www.treas.gov/usss/index.htm?ntac.htm&1

National School Safety Center
http://www.nssc1.org/savd/savd.pdf

U.S. Office of Education (Timely Response site)
http://www.keepschoolssafe.org/school.html

Center for Effective Collaboration and Practice
http://www.air-dc.org/cecp/guide

The School Shooter: A Threat Assessment Perspective (FBI)
http://www.fbi.gov/publications.htm

THINKING THROUGH THE ISSUES

1. Do you think that you can evaluate children with special needs?
2. How will an understanding of psychological disorders help you assess children who may have special needs?
3. With which type of children with special needs do you think you will have the most difficulty establishing rapport?
4. How will your expectations about psychological disorders affect how you evaluate children who may have special needs?
5. When do you think you would use a dynamic assessment procedure and why?
6. What would you do if you were a threat coordinator in a school?

SUMMARY

1. Children with special needs are a heterogeneous group.
2. Generalizations about children with special needs must be made with caution because each child has unique temperament and personality characteristics, cognitive skills, social skills, adaptive-behavior skills, and support systems.
3. Approach each child as a unique individual and never only as representing a particular disorder.
4. Children who have special needs may have more than one disorder, a phenomenon referred to as co-occurring disorders or comorbid disorders.

5. Children with special needs usually go through the same developmental sequences as typically developing children, although sometimes at a different rate.
6. Children with special needs form their self-concepts in ways similar to those used by other children.
7. Children with special needs who also have physical impairments may be limited in their ability to obtain a full range of sensory information, to socialize, and to engage in sports and other physical activities and may not reach expected height and weight.

How Psychological Problems Develop in Children

8. Psychological problems in children develop from the interaction among (a) genetic and biological factors, (b) environmental factors (such as inadequate caregiving, parents with psychological problems or drug habits, stress, and exposure to violence), and (c) individual characteristics (such as personality, emotional reactions, self-concept, coping strategies, motivations, and beliefs).
9. A critical factor affecting children's development is whether their mothers used or abused drugs or alcohol during pregnancy.
10. The primary way in which infants and young children learn about themselves and others is through familial experiences.
11. Children whose caregivers are insensitive or rejecting may come to think of themselves as incompetent or unworthy, to think of others as hostile or unresponsive, and to think of relationships with others as aversive or unpredictable.
12. Parents with psychological problems may have difficulty helping their children feel emotionally secure, gain an understanding of social causes and effects, develop planning ability, learn the importance of delayed gratification, and learn to take responsibility for their own actions.
13. Although children whose parents become addicted to drugs *after* the children are born are not considered "drug exposed," this exposure to drugs or alcohol nevertheless places them at risk for developing psychological difficulties.
14. Children may face stresses associated with other environmental conditions as well, such as the birth of a sibling, moving, changing schools, and failing classes.
15. Stress is a key factor in the development of behavior disorders in children.
16. Direct exposure to violence may affect children's psychological adjustment.
17. Children who have been victimized report more psychological and behavioral symptoms than do nonvictimized children.
18. Being a victim of violence can lead to mental health problems.
19. Psychological problems may lead children to experience a diminished sense of mastery and control, affecting family interactions as well as biological functioning, and compromise children's future development by disrupting important social bonds, undermining their existing competencies, inducing stress, and reaffirming their negative views of themselves and the world.

General Assessment Issues

20. Before you evaluate children who may have special needs, their vision, hearing, physical condition, and health status should be examined.

Personal Documents

21. Personal documents may be useful in evaluating behavioral, social, and emotional competencies. Before you read any personal document, ask the student and a parent for permission to do so and have the student and parent sign a form granting you permission.

Cumulative School Records

22. A study of the student's cumulative school records will give you information about his or her academic grades, attendance, work habits, behavior, and degree of cooperativeness.

Assessment of Infants and Preschool Children

23. Although infants and young children permit you to be more spontaneous and joyful than you would be with older children, assessing infants and young children may be demanding.
24. The younger the child, the more clear and precise your gestures and use of materials must be.
25. Young children's attention spans are short, and their moods are variable.
26. Behavioral state and temperament will play a much larger role in assessing infants and preschoolers than in assessing older children.
27. Positive reinforcement is one of the most potent tools for working with infants and young children.
28. In addition to conducting formal testing, you will want to observe the infant in her or his natural environment and see how the infant interacts with the parents.
29. When meeting infants and young children for the first time, approach them with confidence.
30. An infant's temperament can be classified based on the following nine dimensions: activity level, rhythmicity, approach or withdrawal, adaptability, threshold of responsiveness, intensity of reaction, quality of mood, distractibility, attention span, and persistence.
31. The nine dimensions of temperament, in turn, lead to three temperamental types: the easy child, the difficult child, and the slow-to-warm-up child.
32. To work with young children, you need to recognize when they are ready to interact, to communicate, and to cooperate with you.

Dynamic Assessment

33. Dynamic assessment—also referred to as learning potential assessment, interactive assessment, testing-of-limits, mediated assessment, and assisted learning and transfer—is designed to evaluate an examinee's ability to improve performance following a systematic learning experience.
34. The focus of dynamic assessment is on (a) processes that underlie successful performance, (b) assessment of specific areas of functioning rather than general ability per se, (c) dynamics of change in the learning process, and (d) continuous assessment of the examinee's level of ability and processing style.
35. In dynamic assessment, the examinee is taught principles that can be used to help solve problems.
36. Dynamic assessment focuses on what the examinee can learn, how readily she or he acquires strategies and problem-solving skills, and whether the strategies and skills are transferable.
37. Three dynamic assessment procedures are a test-train-test paradigm, a within-test procedure, and dynamic assessment in conjunction with a standardized test.
38. Dynamic assessment aims to help the examinee link new information to prior information and to restructure thought processes by directing the examinee's attention to newly discovered ways to solve problems.
39. Traditional intelligence assessment focuses on the examinee's present level of cognitive development (what and how much has been mastered or learned); dynamic assessment focuses on the examinee's present learning process (why and how the material has been mastered). The former emphasizes description; the latter, explanation.
40. Traditional intelligence assessment and dynamic assessment overlap considerably.
41. Intelligence and learning ability are complex multidimensional concepts, with the former more easily defined and measured than the latter.
42. Dynamic assessment may complement—but should not replace—standardized assessments.

School Violence

43. The U.S. Secret Service National Threat Assessment Center studied 37 school shootings involving 41 attackers who were current or recent students at the schools. The findings showed that (a) boys or young men committed all of the attacks, (b) in over half the incidents, a school administrator, faculty member, or staff member was the target, and (c) in more than two-thirds of the incidents, the attacker killed one or more students, faculty, or others at the school.
44. Incidents of targeted violence at school are rarely impulsive.
45. Prior to most incidents, the attacker told someone about his idea or plan.
46. There is no profile of "the school shooter."
47. Most attackers had previously used guns and had access to them.
48. Most shooting incidents were not resolved by law enforcement intervention.
49. In many cases, other students were involved in some capacity.
50. In a number of cases, having been bullied played a key role in the attack.
51. Most attackers engaged in some behavior, prior to the incident, that caused others concern or indicated a need for help.
52. Schools should have appropriate policies and procedures in place to handle targeted threats of violence.
53. The threat management policies should be written down, with clear guidelines about how to handle potentially violent situations.
54. Students and parents should be informed of school policies about threatening acts of violence.
55. A school threat assessment coordinator should be designated.
56. A multidisciplinary team should be formed.
57. The threat or the student's intent should be evaluated in each case.
58. Training should be provided to school administrators and staff in the fundamentals of threat assessment, adolescent development and violence, and other mental health issues.
59. Students should be educated and sensitized about cues indicating potential violence.
60. Intervention services should be provided to the threatener.

Instructional Strategies for Children with Special Needs

61. Children with special needs may require services in schools or modifications in classroom procedures.

Resources

62. Two resources that provide useful information for parents and professionals about children with special needs are *Clinical and Forensic Interviewing of Children and Families* (Sattler, 1998) and *The Special Needs Reading List* (Sweeney, 1998). For information about school violence, a good book to consult is *Youth Aggression and Violence: A Psychological Approach* (Moeller, 2001).

KEY TERMS, CONCEPTS, AND NAMES

Co-occurring disorders (p. 246)
Comorbid disorders (p. 246)
Chromosomal abnormalities (p. 246)
Inborn errors of metabolism (p. 246)
Infections (p. 246)
Placental dysfunction (p. 246)
Teratogens (p. 247)
Toxins (p. 247)
Inadequate caregiving (p. 247)
Parents with psychological problems or drug habits (p. 248)
Other environmental stresses (p. 248)
Stress (p. 248)
Exposure to violence (p. 248)
Victimized children (p. 248)
Posttraumatic stress disorder (PTSD) (p. 248)
Personal documents (p. 249)
Cumulative school records (p. 249)
Activity level (p. 252)
Rhythmicity (p. 252)
Approach or withdrawal (p. 252)
Adaptability (p. 252)
Threshold of responsiveness (p. 252)
Intensity of reaction (p. 252)
Quality of mood (p. 252)
Distractibility (p. 252)
Attention span and persistence (p. 253)
Easy child (p. 253)
Difficult child (p. 253)
Slow-to-warm-up child (p. 253)
Dynamic assessment (p. 253)
Test-train-test paradigm (p. 253)
Within-test procedure (p. 254)
Dynamic assessment in conjunction with a standardized test (p. 254)
School violence (p. 255)
Instructional strategies (p. 257)

STUDY QUESTIONS

1. Discuss children with special needs. Include in your discussion why children with special needs are a heterogeneous group, making generalizations about children with special needs, co-occurring disorders, developmental sequences, development of self-concepts, and physical impairments.
2. Discuss how psychological problems develop in children. Include in your discussion genetic and biological factors and environmental factors (such as inadequate caregiving, parents with psychological problems or drug habits, other environmental stresses faced by children, and exposure to violence).
3. Discuss some general assessment issues in evaluating children with special needs.
4. Discuss the use of personal documents and cumulative school records in evaluating children with special needs.
5. Discuss some general considerations in the assessment of infants and preschool children. Include in your discussion dimensions of infant temperament.
6. Discuss dynamic assessment. Include in your discussion dynamic assessment procedures, aims of dynamic assessment, dynamic assessment compared to traditional intelligence assessment, and an evaluation of dynamic assessment.
7. Discuss school violence.
8. Discuss instructional strategies for children with special needs.

11

ATTENTION-DEFICIT/HYPERACTIVITY DISORDER

by Jerome M. Sattler, Lisa Weyandt, and Mary Ann Roberts

In all our efforts to provide "advantages" we have actually produced the busiest, most competitive, highly pressured and over-organized generation of youngsters in our history—and possibly the unhappiest. We seem hell-bent on eliminating much of childhood.

—Eda J. Le Shan

Etiology

Assessment Issues

Interviews

Behavioral Observations

Rating Scales

Psychological Tests

Comment on Assessment Issues

Interventions

Thinking Through the Issues

Summary

Goals and Objectives

This chapter is designed to enable you to do the following:

- Become familiar with methods for assessing children who have attention-deficit/hyperactivity disorder

- Understand interventions for children with attention-deficit/hyperactivity disorder

Attention-deficit/hyperactivity disorder (ADHD) is a neuro-behavioral syndrome characterized by inattention, hyperactivity, and impulsivity (American Psychiatric Association, 2000). Historically, the disorder has been identified as minimal brain damage, minimal brain dysfunction, hyperkinesis, hyperkinetic reaction of childhood, and attention deficit disorder with or without hyperactivity. According to *DSM-IV–TR,* in order for a diagnosis of ADHD to be made, the symptoms of the disorder must be present before age 7 years, for at least 6 months, and to a degree that is maladaptive and inconsistent with an individual's developmental level; must occur in two or more settings; and must significantly affect the child's social or academic functioning. Three types of ADHD are cited in *DSM-IV–TR:* (a) *attention-deficit/hyperactivity disorder: combined type,* (b) *attention-deficit/hyperactivity disorder: predominantly inattentive type,* and (c) *attention-deficit/hyperactivity disorder: predominantly hyperactive-impulsive type.*

DSM-IV–TR symptoms associated with ADHD are as follows:

Inattention

a. Often fails to give close attention to details or makes careless mistakes in schoolwork, work, or other activities
b. Often has difficulty sustaining attention in tasks or play activities
c. Often does not seem to listen when spoken to directly
d. Often does not follow through on instructions and fails to finish schoolwork, chores, or duties in the workplace
e. Often has difficulty organizing tasks and activities
f. Often avoids, dislikes, or is reluctant to engage in tasks that require sustained mental effort (such as schoolwork or homework)
g. Often loses things necessary for tasks or activities such as toys, school assignments, pencils, or books
h. Often is easily distracted by extraneous stimuli
i. Often is forgetful in daily activities

Hyperactivity

a. Often fidgets with hands or feet or squirms in seat
b. Often leaves seat in classroom or in other situations in which remaining seated is expected
c. Often runs about or climbs excessively in situations in which it is inappropriate
d. Often has difficulty playing or engaging in leisure activities quietly
e. Often is "on the go" or acts as if "driven by a motor"
f. Often talks excessively

Impulsivity

g. Often blurts out answers before questions have been completed
h. Often has difficulty awaiting turn
i. Often interrupts or intrudes on others (e.g., butts into conversations or games)

Following are major psychological and behavioral components of attention, which can pose a key problem for children with ADHD (Shelton & Barkley, 1994):

- *Arousal or alertness* (overall level of activity or responsivity)
- *Impulsivity* (taking an action, drawing a conclusion, or making a statement before the pros and cons of the behavior are considered)
- *Selectivity* (ability to focus on important features in the environment)
- *Persistence* (ability to sustain effort on a task)
- *Ability to shift* (ability to move from one event to another)
- *Ability to divide attention* (ability to pay attention to two or more events simultaneously)
- *Ability to search* (ability to employ strategies to inspect and evaluate events)
- *Encoding capacity* (capacity to retain information in working or short-term memory)

Children with ADHD may exhibit behaviors and symptoms associated with other disorders. Following are estimated prevalence rates for selected coexisting conditions (Green, Wong, Atkins, Taylor, & Feinlieb, 1999; Shelton & Barkley, 1994):

- Learning disorders, 25% to 50%
- Oppositional defiant disorder, 35%
- Conduct disorder, 26%
- Depressive disorder, 18%
- Anxiety disorder, 26%

DSM-IV–TR notes that approximately 50% of clinic-referred children with ADHD also have oppositional defiant disorder or conduct disorder.

The ADHD population is heterogeneous, displaying a diversity of associated behavior problems in addition to the underlying attention problems. Children diagnosed with ADHD at an early age may be at risk for later learning problems, including reading problems. They also may have low self-esteem, lability of mood (i.e., quickly shifting from one emotion to another), low tolerance for frustration, and temper outbursts. The disorder becomes most evident when children enter school, where the demands of the classroom require sustained attention and in-seat, independent work. Overactivity is a common hallmark of ADHD in early childhood, but overactivity decreases with age. Boys with ADHD tend to display more aggressive and oppositional behaviors than do girls with ADHD (Gaub & Carlson, 1997).

Children with a dual diagnosis of ADHD and conduct disorder are likely to have more problems during adolescence and adulthood than those who have either diagnosis alone. Those with a dual diagnosis are likely to have more severe symptoms, increased risk for later antisocial behavior disorders, more peer rejection, and more deficient processing of social information (Abikoff & Klein, 1992; Moffitt, 1990; Paternite, Loney, Salisbury, & Whaley, 1999). Their parents may also face increased parenting stress, frustration, and de-

" Your principal called. He said you won't do your homework in your English class, you refuse to bring your sneakers to your gym class, and you keep changing his bank statement in your computer class."

Reprinted with permission from Michael Shapiro.

spair. Similarly, children with both ADHD and a learning disability may have more problems with controlling impulses, working independently, and functioning adequately in a classroom than do children who have a learning disability only (Robins, 1992).

Approximately 3 to 7% of the school-aged population has ADHD (American Psychiatric Association, 2000; *DSM-IV–TR*). Estimates of ADHD in clinical populations of children range from 23% to 50% (Whalen, 1989). ADHD is more common in boys than in girls, with estimates ranging from 3:1 in non-referred samples to 6:1 in clinic-referred samples (Rapport, 1994). ADHD is the most frequent reason for referral to child mental health clinics (Barkley, 1998).

Research suggests that children with ADHD, in addition to having problems with inattention, impulsivity, and overactivity, may have the following types of deficits: cognitive deficits, adaptive functioning deficits, language deficits, task performance deficits, motor and physical deficits, emotional deficits, school performance deficits, and health and accidental injury deficits (see Table 11-1).

Underlying the difficulties of children with ADHD may be a deficit of *self-regulation;* that is, they may have difficulty with organization and planning, with the mobilization and maintenance of effortful attention, and with the inhibition of inappropriate responding. Consequently, they may show considerable variability across situations. Their behavior depends on the task requirements, the quantity and type of environmental distractors, the support they receive from others, and their ability to regulate their behavior. Overall, ADHD is characterized by deficits in (a) behavioral inhibition, (b) working memory, (c) regulation of motivation, and (d) motor control (Barkley, 1997). Adults with ADHD have the best prognosis when they have average to above-average intelligence, do not display aggressive behavior, are able to

obtain post-secondary education, and have a supportive, nurturing family (Barkley, 1998).

ETIOLOGY

Given the heterogeneity of its symptoms, ADHD most likely has no single cause; multiple factors likely contribute to its development.

1. *Genetic component.* Genetic studies indicate that ADHD tends to run in families and is more likely to occur in identical twins than in fraternal twins (Stevenson, Pennington, Gilger, DeFries, & Gillis, 1993). However, the mode of inheritance and the types of specific genetic abnormalities have not been discovered (Hechtman, 1994; Weyandt, 2001).

2. *Brain functioning.* Individuals with ADHD have been reported to have (a) brain structures that differ anatomically from those of individuals without ADHD (Semrud-Clikeman, Filipek, Biederman, Steingard, Kennedy, Renshaw, & Bekken, 1994); (b) an imbalance of or deficiency in one or more brain neurotransmitters, with involvement of several areas of the brain, particularly the frontal lobes (Hechtman, 1994); and (c) difficulty on neuropsychological tasks that reflect executive functioning (Barkley, Grodzinsky, & DuPaul, 1992; Weyandt & Willis, 1994).

3. *Environmental toxins.* Exposure to environmental toxins—such as lead in the child's surroundings and cigarette smoking or alcohol consumption by the mother during

Copyright © 2000 by John P. Wood.

Table 11-1
Possible Deficits (in Addition to Inattention, Impulsivity, and Overactivity) Associated with ADHD

Type	Example
Cognitive Deficits	
Information-processing deficits involving task analysis, strategic planning, and executive behavior	• Inefficient use of time • Underestimating the amount of work and time needed to complete assignments • Failing to pace work evenly throughout the time allotted for assignments or failing to begin assignments in a timely manner • Superficial analysis of written or spoken material • Inadequate evaluation of promising strategies to help with learning or recalling information • Poor rehearsal strategies • Limited awareness of problem-solving and organizational strategies
Mild deficits in intelligence test scores, primarily in verbal areas associated with working memory	• Verbal IQs in the 90s • Lower than average memory span scores • Difficulty with internalized speech
Poor academic performance and poor scores on standardized achievement tests	• Below average scores in reading comprehension, mathematics, and problem solving
Learning disabilities	• Problems in reading • Problems in math • Problems in spelling • Problems in written expression
Memory difficulties	• Forgetting to write down homework assignments • Neglecting to bring home materials needed to complete homework assignments • Forgetting to check assignment books when doing homework • Forgetting to bring completed homework to school
Impaired behavioral and verbal creativity	• Impaired flexibility • Impaired originality
Adaptive Functioning Deficits	
Deficits involving social and adaptive functioning	• Poor self-help skills • Difficulty assuming personal responsibility and independence • Lack of insight into or recognition of their contribution to problems that arise • Externalizing blame and becoming defensive when criticized • Difficulty behaving in a socially acceptable manner (e.g., displaying aggression) • Tantrums • Silliness • Bossiness • Impulsivity
Difficulties with adherence to rules and instructions	• Frequent arguments with parents • Needing to have instructions repeated • Failing to comply with instructions and follow directions • Irresponsibility • Laziness
Difficulties in getting along with other children	• Alienating friends through aggressive or unintentionally rough play • Bossiness • Intrusive behavior • Inflexibility • Unwillingness to take turns

(Continued)

Table 11-1 *(Continued)*

Type	*Example*
Language Deficits	
Impaired language development	• Poor expressive language skill, such as producing less information in story narratives
Delayed or inadequate internalization of language	• Difficulty in using self-guidance to solve problems
Task Performance Deficits	
Variable task performance	• Variability in completing homework assignments • Variability in taking tests • Variability in completing in-class assignments
Motivational difficulties	• Limited interest in achieving
Lack of persistence	• Tendency to give up easily
Motor and Physical Developmental Deficits	
Poor fine-motor and gross-motor coordination	• Difficulty drawing designs • Poor handwriting
Minor physical anomalies	• Greater than normal head circumference • Index finger longer than middle finger
Emotional Deficits	
Emotional reactivity	• Difficulty modulating emotional responses (on occasion, they may explode in anger when they encounter a disappointment, or they may become so happy and joyously out of control when something pleasant occurs that the effort needed to contain their behavior detracts from the pleasure of the event)
School Performance Deficits	
Disruptive school performance	• Suspensions and expulsions for disruptive behavior
Underachievement in school relative to ability	• Need for academic tutoring • Repeating grades • Failing to graduate from high school
Health and Accidental Injury Deficits	
General health problems and possible delay in growth during childhood	• Not as tall as peers • More illnesses than peers
Sleep problems	• Difficulty falling and staying asleep
Proneness to accidental injuries	• Falling off objects more frequently than peers
Greater risk for automobile accidents as adolescents and young adults	• Not as careful an automobile driver as peers

Source: Adapted from Barkley and Murphy (1998), Weyandt and Willis (1994), and Whalen (1989).

pregnancy—may contribute to ADHD. However, theories focusing on environmental toxins remain speculative because none have received wide-ranging support (Rapport, 1994). Several empirical studies have demonstrated that food additives, sugar, and fluorescent lighting do not cause ADHD (Barkley, 1998).

4. *Classroom organization and parenting styles.* Poor classroom organization and ineffective parenting styles may exacerbate ADHD symptoms.

In summary, although the precise cause of ADHD is unknown, research across several disciplines suggests that neurological and genetic factors underlie the disorder (Barkley & Murphy, 1998). Advances in genetic and brain imaging technology should help clarify the etiology of ADHD. Whatever the etiology, problems with behavioral inhibition comprise the core of ADHD; these problems, in turn, may express themselves as behavioral deficits in executive functions, working memory, internalized speech, and self-regulation (Barkley, 1998).

Compared with parents of normally functioning children, parents of children with ADHD tend to be more depressed and have lower self-esteem (because they believe that they have diminished parenting skills and experience), feel more guilt, and enjoy less marital satisfaction (Blakemore, Shindler, & Conte, 1993). No listing of symptoms of ADHD can capture the hardships faced by the parents of children with ADHD. Here is a description by one mother (Richard, 1993):

I'm the mother of nine-year-old twin boys who have (finally) been diagnosed with ADD [attention-deficit disorder] through our school. It has been a rough nine years. They were out of their cribs before they could even crawl. They could open any childproof lock ever made and slept less than any human beings I have ever known. No baby-sitter has ever been willing to come more than twice. No child care center or after-school program has even been willing to keep them, so I quit my part-time teaching job and have stayed home with them since they were three. My husband has to work a second job, so most of the supervision of the boys falls on me. I almost never have any relief. Their grandparents work full-time and live in another state. Over the last few years my health has begun to fail. Although my doctor cannot find anything wrong with me, I am constantly catching colds [and am] exhausted, and have frequent headaches. I'm losing weight. I sleep very poorly. Are there other mothers of children with ADD who feel this way? Is there anything I can do about it? (p. 10)

ASSESSMENT ISSUES

As is true for all childhood disorders, assessment of ADHD requires a comprehensive and thorough evaluation. The focus is on the following (McKinney, Montague, & Hocutt, 1993):

1. *Core symptoms.* Assess the degree to which symptoms of inattention, hyperactivity, and impulsivity are present.

2. *Co-occurring disorders.* Assess the presence of co-occurring disorders. These include, as noted earlier, learning disorders, oppositional defiant disorder, conduct disorder, depressive disorder, and anxiety disorder. *DSM-IV–TR* also lists mood disorders and communication disorders as co-occurring disorders. If ADHD symptoms are severe, it is easy to overlook one or more specific learning disabilities.

3. *Severity.* Assess the severity of the symptoms, including the number and type of symptoms.

4. *Duration.* Assess the duration of the symptoms.

5. *Pervasiveness.* Assess the situations in which the symptoms are displayed and the length of time the symptoms have been present.

6. *Social adjustment.* Assess the child's social competence and adaptiveness.

7. *Educational needs.* Assess the child's educational and instructional needs.

8. *Cognitive abilities.* Assess the child's verbal, nonverbal, short- and long-term memory, and other cognitive abilities.

Assessment procedures include interviews, behavioral observations, rating scales, and psychological tests. The assessment may take several sessions. Schedule the assessment carefully so that it does not come after a stressful situation, such as a test in the classroom. Group intelligence or achievement tests may underestimate the ability level of children with ADHD if the tests are administered without accommodations—for example, if the tests are given with fixed time limits. Consequently, you should use caution when interpreting scores on tests administered in this manner. You will also want to review the child's cumulative school records (see Chapter 10).

INTERVIEWS

Parent Interview

An interview with the child's primary caregiver(s) will provide information about the age at which the problems began and the pervasiveness of the child's difficulties. Parents often report behavior concerns preceding the child's school years, including a difficult temperament, irregular sleeping and feeding routines, proneness to accidents as a toddler, and excessive motor activity (Sanson, Smart, Prior, & Oberklaid, 1993). You may use the interview shown in Table B-5 in Appendix B or the Background Questionnaire in Table A-1 in Appendix A to gather this information from the parent. As is true for any assessment, an interview with a parent is crucial for obtaining information about the child's family, the parent's view of the child's problems, parenting styles and disciplinary techniques, environmental factors that may be contributing to the child's problems, and resources available to the family, as well as information about the child's prenatal and postnatal development and medical, social, and academic history. Parents can also complete one or more rating scales, as discussed later in the chapter.

The child's medical history provides information useful in understanding the impact of comorbid conditions (Blackman, Westervelt, Stevenson, & Welch, 1991). For example, chronic illness or intermittent hearing loss from otitis media can lead to attention difficulties; drugs such as phenobarbital or decongestants can exacerbate hyperactive behavior; and children with conditions involving the central nervous system (e.g., seizure disorder, autistic disorder, fetal alcohol syndrome, or brain injury) may exhibit symptoms of ADHD.

Teacher Interview

Teachers can provide valuable information about the severity of the child's symptoms, situations in which symptoms oc-

SCHOOLIES

I wanted to talk about your son's inability to stay on-task.

© 1996 by John P. Wood

Copyright © 1996 by John P. Wood.

cur, specific behaviors that interfere with the child's school functioning, factors that may exacerbate the child's undesired behavior, academic strengths and weaknesses, social skill strengths and weaknesses, and the quality of the child's peer relationships. Children with ADHD are typically more off-task, disruptive, and impulsive than their classmates and have more difficulty following through on tasks. Teachers may complete the School Referral Questionnaire (see Table A-3 in Appendix A) and a rating scale, discussed later in the chapter. Differences among ratings from several teachers may illuminate effects of different environments, subjects, or teaching styles.

Child Interview

Children often provide valuable information about themselves. The questions shown in Table B-1 in Appendix B may be helpful in obtaining information from children. Children who can read and write may complete the Personal Data Questionnaire (see Table A-2 in Appendix A).

BEHAVIORAL OBSERVATIONS

Observation of the child's behavior will provide (a) information on the antecedents and consequences of the behaviors, as well as the intensity, duration, and rate of the behaviors, (b) information that will help you compare the behavior of the referred child to that of a nonreferred child in the same classroom, and (c) information that will be useful to the child's primary care provider. As noted previously, a com-

mon complaint of teachers is that children with ADHD are frequently off-task. Observation will enable you to identify factors that may be contributing to and sustaining the problem behavior and help you develop interventions. Ideally, as with all behavioral observations, you should conduct observations across multiple settings and at different times of the day. This is especially true for ADHD assessments, as the *DSM-IV–TR* criteria require that the symptoms be present in multiple settings.

Observation of the following behaviors during the assessment should raise suspicions of possible ADHD (Schworm & Birnbaum, 1989). Note, however, that children with ADHD may not show any of these behaviors during the assessment and that children without ADHD may display some of these behaviors.

Overactivity

- Excessive verbalizations that may or may not be related to the ongoing task
- Lower extremity movements, such as swinging, tapping, or shaking of legs and feet
- Upper extremity movements, such as shaking hands, tapping or drumming fingers, playing with hands, or twirling thumbs
- Whole body movements, such as rocking movements of the whole body or changing seating position or posture frequently
- Odd noises, such as humming, clicking teeth, or whistling, during a task

Impulsivity

- Fast, incorrect responding, such as quickly responding without first scanning or surveying choices or responding randomly
- Unsystematic searching, such as looking in the middle of the stimulus first without scanning or surveying in a left-to-right direction
- Responding before directions are given or completed
- Failing to look at possible alternatives or stopping searching prematurely

Distractibility

- Playing with own clothing, such as fiddling with shirt collars, threads, zippers, buttons, pockets, pants, or socks
- Touching things in near vicinity, such as playing with a pencil or edges of a paper, trailing hands on or along the desk or table top, or rubbing pant legs
- Attending to an irrelevant part of the visual task, such as pointing to or commenting in an irrelevant manner on a part of the stimulus during the task
- Attending to an irrelevant part of the environment, such as looking out the window or around the room or simply gazing or staring, during the task
- Attending to background noises, such as footsteps, voices, or buzzers, that are coming from outside the room

Three formal systems for classroom observation of children who may have ADHD are the following:

- *Classroom Observation Code* (Abikoff & Gittelman, 1985; see Table D-1 in Appendix D)
- *Revised ADHD Behavior Coding System* (DuPaul & Stoner, 1994)
- *ADHD School Observation Code* (Gadow, Sprafkin, & Nolan, 1996)

The *Structured Observation of Academic and Play Settings* (Roberts, Milich, & Loney, 1984; see Table D-2 in Appendix D) is useful for observing children in a clinic playroom, because it allows you to simulate a classroom environment and observe the child's behavior while he or she works on a school-related assignment. The procedure is particulary useful in evaluating the effects of medication.

After you complete an observation, remember to check the child's work for accuracy, because the child can be on-task but still not complete the assignment or complete it inaccurately. When you observe a child, note whether she or he is able to remain focused on a task and how she or he responds to distractions in the classroom. Also be aware of repetitive purposeless motion (e.g., playing with things on the desk), inability to remain seated, vocalizations, and aggressive, noncompliant behavior.

RATING SCALES

Ratings scales are useful in obtaining information from parents, teachers, and children. Both broad-band and narrow-band rating scales can help to identify appropriate and inappropriate behaviors, including those specifically related to ADHD. Broad-band scales include questions that survey a wide spectrum of symptoms and behaviors (e.g., externalizing disorder, internalizing disorder), whereas narrow-band scales include questions that are designed to measure behaviors associated with a specific disorder (e.g., ADHD or depression only). Broad-band scales that may be useful in ADHD assessments include the following (see Chapter 6 for a review of these scales):

- Child Behavior Checklist, Teacher Report Form, and Youth Self-Report Form (Achenbach, 1991a, 1991b, 1991c)
- Behavior Assessment System for Children (Reynolds & Kamphaus, 1992)
- Personality Inventory for Children–Second Edition (Wirt, Lachar, Seat, & Broen, 2001)

Narrow-band scales include the following (note that many of these scales contain both parent and teacher versions):

- Conners' Rating Scales–Revised (Conners, 1997)
- ADHD Rating Scales IV (DuPaul, Power, McGoey, Ikeda, & Anastopoulos, 1998)
- Attention Deficit Disorders Evaluation Scale–Second Edition (McCarney, 1989)
- Child Symptom Inventory (Gadow & Sprafkin, 1997)
- Brown Attention Deficit Disorder Scales (Brown, 1996)
- ACTeRS–2nd Edition (Ullman, Sleator, & Sprague, 1991)
- Home Situations Questionnaire (Barkley, 1990)
- School Situations Questionnaire (DuPaul & Barkley, 1992)
- ADHD Questionnaire (see Table D-3 in Appendix D)

Depending on the information collected from the child, parents, and teachers, you may want to include additional narrow-band scales to help evaluate the presence of comorbid disorders. For example, adolescents with ADHD often have coexisting problems such as depression, and younger children may have anxiety or other types of problems. In these situations, the Children's Depression Inventory (Kovacs, 1992), Reynolds Child Depression Scale and Reynolds

MR. WOODHEAD © 1998 by John P. Wood

You just can't seem to sit still today. What's the problem?

Well, people keep calling me.

And my pager is set on "Vibrate."

Adolescent Depression Scale (Reynolds, 1987, 1989), and the Revised Children's Manifest Anxiety Scale (Reynolds & Richmond, 1985) may be helpful. Barkley (1998) has several forms useful for the assessment of ADHD.

PSYCHOLOGICAL TESTS

Although there is no specific test or test battery for establishing a diagnosis of ADHD, several different types of tests are useful in the assessment of children referred for possible ADHD, including intelligence tests, achievement tests, memory tests, and one or more neuropsychological tests (see *Assessment of Children: Cognitive Applications* and Chapter 19 in this book). You may also want to include a computerized continuous performance test such as the Continuous Performance Test (Gordon, 1988), Conners' Continuous Performance Test II (Conners & MHS Staff, 2000), or Test of Variable Attention (TOVA; Greenberg, 1990). These tests purport to measure sustained attention and/or impulsivity. Most involve presenting a visual or auditory stimulus to the child at variable intervals for approximately 20 minutes. The child's task is to indicate (usually by pressing a button) when the stimulus is presented. A record is kept of the number of times the child correctly identifies the stimulus, fails to identify the stimulus, or identifies the stimulus incorrectly. Although the information provided by the various tests varies, most give attention, impulsivity, and reaction-time scores. Scores indicate how the child's degrees of attention and impulsivity compare to those of a norm group of the child's age and gender. If used, continuous performance tests should be only one part of the assessment, as their sensitivity and specificity are not sufficiently high for them to be used exclusively (Green, Wong, Atkins, Taylor, & Feinlieb, 1999). In addition, scores from continuous performance tests can be misleading if used in isolation. For example, a child's score profile could look like an ADHD profile just because the child was taking cold medication, was suffering from anxiety, was fatigued, or was experiencing problems that interfered with his or her concentration.

Intelligence tests should be administered as one component in the diagnostic assessment of a child, to obtain information about cognitive strengths and limitations. Intelligence tests are not sufficiently sensitive to be used exclusively in making a diagnosis of ADHD or discriminating among various subtypes of ADHD (Schwean & Saklofske, 1998). For example, specialized scores—such as the Wechsler Freedom from Distractibility and Processing Speed factor scores—are not useful for identifying ADHD (Anastopoulos, Spisto, & Maher, 1994; Cohen, Becker, & Campbell, 1990; Mayes, Calhoun, & Crowell, 1998; Reinecke, Beebe, & Stein, 1999; Riccio, Cohen, Hall, & Ross, 1997; Semrud-Clikeman, Hynd, Lorys, & Lahey, 1993). However, patterns of strengths and weaknesses revealed by tests such as the Stanford-Binet–IV, DAS, and WISC–III may help you understand the child's intellectual functioning (see *Assessment of Children: Cognitive Applications*).

COMMENT ON ASSESSMENT ISSUES

Arriving at a diagnosis of ADHD is not easy. Restlessness, inattention, and overactive behavior are common in children between the ages of 2 and 12 years. Some "problem" children are never referred for hyperactive behavior because they have parents who are tolerant of their behavior, teachers who do not perceive their behavior as a problem, or parents and teachers who provide environments that are structured to manage problem behavior. Conversely, normal but active children are sometimes referred for an evaluation because of less tolerant environments either at home or at school, inadequate parenting skills, or ineffective classroom management techniques.

The following comparisons point out just how subjective the labeling of behavior can be.

BEHAVIOR LABELING

If an adult is reinforced for behaving appropriately we call it *recognition.*
If a child is reinforced for behaving appropriately we call it *bribery.*

If an adult laughs we call it *socializing.*
If a child laughs we call it *misbehaving.*

If an adult writes in a book we call it *doodling.*
If a child writes in a book we call it *destroying property.*

If an adult sticks to something we call it *perseverance.*
If a child sticks to something we call it *stubbornness.*

If an adult seeks help we call it *consulting.*
If a child seeks help we call it *whining.*

If an adult is not paying attention we call it *preoccupation.*
If a child is not paying attention we call it *distractibility.*

If an adult forgets something we call it *absentmindedness.*
If a child forgets something we call it *attention deficit.*

If an adult tells his side of a story we call it *clarification.*
If a child tells his side of a story we call it *talking back.*

If an adult raises his voice in anger we call it *maintaining control.*
If a child raises his voice in anger we call it *a temper tantrum.*

If an adult hits a child we call it *discipline.*
If a child hits a child we call it *fighting.*

If an adult behaves in an unusual way we call him *unique.*
If a child behaves in an unusual way we refer him for a PSYCHOLOGICAL EVALUATION.

—Author Unknown

The fact that symptoms associated with ADHD also may accompany other childhood problems—such as learning disability, behavior problems, substance use or abuse, anxiety or emotional problems, and medical disorders—compounds diagnostic difficulties. For a diagnosis of ADHD, the symptoms should (a) be present early in the child's life (by the age of 7 years), (b) have caused significant impairment, and (c) not be attributable to some other problem.

The major difficulties of children with ADHD, as we have seen, lie in their inability to inhibit impulsive responding and to organize, focus, and sustain attention. These difficulties are likely to be reflected in their performance in some but not all situations and on some but not all psychological tests. Novel, structured, one-on-one situations (as in an individual assessment) or situations that are highly stimulating and provide frequent feedback about performance (e.g., video games) are not likely to elicit the same degree of ADHD symptomatology as does the child's classroom. Although a child or adolescent with ADHD may have variable scores on individual intelligence tests, no particular pattern of scores on the Wechsler tests or any other intelligence tests has been found to be diagnostic of ADHD. Children with ADHD usually obtain IQs in the Normal range, but their scores tend to be 7 to 14 points lower than those of their peers (Faraone, Biederman, Lehman, Spencer, Norman, Seidman, Kraus, Perrin, Chen, & Tsuang, 1993; Fischer, Barkley, Fletcher, & Smallish, 1990; Whalen, 1989).

The questions in Table 21-2 in Chapter 21 of *Assessment of Children: Cognitive Applications* will help you evaluate the information you obtain from the child, parents, and teachers. In addition, consider the questions in Table 11-2. After you have finished your evaluation, complete Table D-4 in Appendix D to assist you in arriving at a diagnosis.

INTERVENTIONS

Pharmacological, behavioral, cognitive-behavioral, instructional, and familial interventions can be used in the treatment of children with ADHD.

Pharmacological Interventions

A common form of treatment for children with ADHD involves the use of stimulant medications such as *Ritalin (methylphenidate), Dexedrine* (d-amphetamine), and *Cylert (pemoline;* Barkley, 1998; Swanson, McBurnett, Christian, & Wigal, 1995). Methylphenidate or d-amphetamine may also be useful in the treatment of hyperactivity in preschoolers (Musten, Firestone, Pisterman, Bennett, & Mercer, 1997). These medications are short-acting (approximately 3½ to 4 hours for most children); both behavioral benefits (e.g., improved attention) and some side effects (e.g., appetite suppression) are observed only during the effective period of the medication. Longer-acting stimulant medications (e.g., *Dexedrine-SR, Adderall, Concerta, Metadate*) may be preferable for adolescents and young adults when sustained attention beyond school hours is often desirable for homework and other activities. *Tricyclic antidepressants* also have been used with some success, particularly when children have coexisting depression

(Spencer, Biederman, Wilens, Harding, O'Donnell, & Griffin, 1996). Many, but not all, children with ADHD who take stimulant medication show dramatic behavioral changes, with noticeable improvement in motor behavior, attention, and impulse control; in addition, they may show, to a lesser degree, better compliance and more positive social behaviors (Crenshaw, Kavale, Forness, & Reeve, 1999).

Stimulant medications may restore central nervous system arousal levels and inhibitory levels to normal, thereby giving children with ADHD better control and allowing for a wider range of focused behaviors. Thus—in what is commonly, but mistakenly, called a "paradoxical effect"—stimulant pharmacotherapy *decreases* behavioral excesses or disruptive behaviors. However, stimulant pharmacotherapy usually does not correct social or academic deficits. Stimulant medication improves adolescents' performance on study hall assignments and quizzes, although more research is needed to explore the long-term effects of stimulant medication on academic performance (DuPaul & Stoner, 1994). As the effectiveness of stimulant medications is relatively short-lived, some children will benefit from an additional dose for activities outside of school hours (e.g., homework, family activities, club meetings, and team sports).

Approximately 60% to 90% of children with ADHD respond positively to stimulant medication (Whalen, 1989). Stimulant medication may have adverse side effects, however, including appetite suppression, sleep disturbance, headaches, and stomachaches (Hinshaw, 1994; Voeller, 1991). Nutritional counseling is often successful in addressing appetite suppression (e.g., encouraging supplementary calorie consumption when medication is not in effect, such as at breakfast and evening snacks). Side effects such as headaches and stomachaches may be reduced by dosage adjustments; adjusting the timing of the medications may help with sleep disturbance.

Behavioral Interventions

The use of stimulant medication is not a panacea—it does not do away with the need for other interventions. *All children who have serious behavioral or academic deficiencies need remediation.* Behavioral interventions may consist of positive reinforcement to increase appropriate behavior and withdrawal of reinforcement (e.g., time out, response cost) to reduce inappropriate behavior. Teacher attention in the classroom—verbal (e.g., praise) or nonverbal (e.g., eye contact)—may also improve classroom behavior. Verbal praise or correction that is brief and immediately follows the child's behavior is more effective at changing behavior than is verbal feedback that is lengthy or delayed (Abramowitz, O'Leary, & Futtersak, 1988). Interventions that involve a point system (token economy) also have been found to be effective at reducing inappropriate behaviors, especially when used over short periods of time in conjunction with a response-cost program. A response-cost program incorporates a loss of points or privileges if a child displays inappropriate or problem behavior.

Table 11-2
Guidelines for Evaluating a Child for a Possible Attention-Deficit/Hyperactivity Disorder

The Child

Problem
1. How does the child view the referral?
2. What are the child's concerns?
3. Does the child believe that he or she has a problem?
4. If so, how does the child describe his or her problem?
5. How do the child's descriptions of his or her behavior, feelings, and problems agree with the parents' and teacher's descriptions?
6. Can the child control his or her behavior?
7. If so, in what situations and how does the child control his or her behavior?

Learning Style
8. Does the child seek information before undertaking an assignment?
9. Does the child keep notes of class lectures?
10. Does the child review test results?
11. Does the child have a place to study at home that is free from distractions?
12. Does the child study material by reviewing it several times and rehearsing the answers?
13. Does the child seek help with his or her school work from peers, teachers, siblings, parents, or other adults?
14. Does the child read the textbook, study it, reread notes, or review prior tests in preparing for a new test?
15. Does the child receive rewards from parents if performance in school is good?

School
16. How does the child perceive his or her relations with teachers and other school personnel?
17. If interventions were tried at school, what is the child's opinion of them?
18. How does the child feel about his or her present class placement?
19. What changes in the family and at school might lead the child to experience greater happiness?
20. What services would the child like to receive?

Health
21. What is the child's health history?
22. Are there any indications of visual or auditory difficulties?
23. If the child has visual or auditory difficulties, have glasses or hearing aids been prescribed?
24. If so, does the child have these appliances and wear them?
25. Does the child take any medicine that might affect school performance?
26. If so, what medications is the child taking?

Social Skills and Interests
27. How does the child perceive his or her relations with other family members?
28. How does the child get along with other children?
29. Have the child's interpersonal relations changed as he or she has developed?

30. If so, in what way?
31. What responsibilities does the child have at home, and how does he or she fulfill these responsibilities?
32. Has the child shown any aggressive behavior during development?
33. If so, what type of behavior and during what ages?
34. What are the child's general interests, academic interests, and hobbies?

Assessment Findings
35. What were the child's appearance, behavior, motor skills, attention level, activity level, and degree of cooperativeness during the evaluation?
36. What is the quality of the child's expressive and receptive language? For example, did the child understand the questions, make appropriate and coherent replies, seem to understand nonverbal messages, use correct grammar, listen appropriately, and understand idioms presented in the conversation?
37. What social skills did the child exhibit in interacting with the examiner?
38. Can the child take in information from conversation or reading without becoming distracted?
39. Does the child need to work slowly or hear or see one thing at a time in order to stay focused?
40. Can the child sustain attention or concentration when mental processing is required, such as when reading or doing mental arithmetic?
41. Can the child shift back and forth between two or more tasks without becoming overwhelmed or confused?
42. Does the child return to the task at hand spontaneously after being distracted or interrupted?
43. What environmental factors promote optimal attention for the child?
44. If the child has attention deficits, are they associated with excessive motor activity such as restlessness, squirminess, or fidgetiness?
45. How does the child feel about himself or herself?
46. In what situations does the child act impulsively?
47. In what situations does the child seem to have control and not act impulsively?
48. In what situations does the child become angry easily?
49. How often is the child angry?
50. What is the child's response to frustration?
51. Can the child bring his or her emotions under control if they get out of hand?
52. Can the child inhibit inappropriate behaviors or comments?
53. Does the child show rapid fluctuation in mood without environmental cause, frequent tearfulness, or situationally inappropriate affect (such as laughing at serious subjects or lacking emotional reactions to events to which others react)?
54. What factors precipitate, alleviate, or aggravate the child's affect or cause changes in the child's affect?
55. What were other results of the psychological or psychoeducational evaluation?

(Continued)

Table 11-2 *(Continued)*

The Parents

Problem

1. How do the parents describe the child's problems?
2. What are the frequency, duration, and magnitude of the child's problems?
3. Where does the child display her or his problems (e.g., at home, at school, at other places)?
4. How old was the child when the parents became aware of the child's problems?
5. How do the parents handle the child's problems?
6. Which interventions have been successful and which unsuccessful in helping the child?
7. What was the child's temperament as an infant?
8. Were there any signs of irritability?
9. As a toddler, did the child overreact to stimuli and have difficulty settling down?
10. Did the child's behavior problems emerge only after she or he entered school?
11. Does the child have frequent temper tantrums?
12. How do the parents describe the child's strengths and weaknesses?
13. What do the parents believe might contribute to the child's problems (e.g., biological predispositions, deficiencies or delays in basic skill areas, personality and temperament, familial influences, environmental influences, the interaction of any of these factors)?
14. What are the parents' greatest concerns?
15. How do the parents' reports differ from the child's and the teacher's reports?
16. Do the parents agree with each other about the child's problems?
17. If not, in what areas do they disagree?
18. What information have the parents been given by teachers, psychologists, or physicians about the child's problems?

Developmental Considerations

19. How did the mother's pregnancy progress, and was there any unusual exposure to drugs or any unusual event?
20. Did the child have hypoxia, neonatal jaundice, head trauma, meningitis, epilepsy, or any other illnesses or conditions at birth or shortly thereafter?
21. If so, what did the child have, what treatment did the child receive, and what was the outcome of treatment, including any residual symptoms?
22. Did the child reach developmental milestones at the ages expected, or were there delays?
23. If there were delays, in what areas did they occur?
24. Has the child had any problems in fine- and gross-motor development (e.g., mixed dominance—right-handed, right-footed, and left-eyed, or another such combination), in sensory functions (e.g., hearing, vision), in language development, in thinking, in affective or emotional expression, in social adjustment, in academic functioning, or in family relations? For example, with respect to motor and cognitive functions, did the child have difficulty learning to ride a bicycle, skate, tie shoes, remember addresses, recognize familiar routines, tell time, recite the alphabet, count to more than five, or follow single instructions?
25. If so, what problems did the child have, what treatments did the child receive, and what was the outcome of the treatments?

Social Skills

26. How do the parents perceive the child's relationships with other family members?
27. How does the child get along with other children?
28. Have the child's interpersonal relations changed as he or she developed?
29. If so, in what way?
30. What responsibilities does the child have at home, and how does he or she fulfill these responsibilities?
31. Has the child shown any aggressive behavior during development?
32. If so, what type of behavior and at what ages?
33. What are the child's general interests, academic interests, and hobbies?

School

34. How do the parents describe the child's schooling?
35. How do the parents describe the child's teachers?
36. What schools has the child attended?
37. If the child has attended more than one school, what were the reasons for the changes?
38. What has been the child's attendance record at school?
39. Has the child repeated any grades and, if so, what grades?
40. What letter grades has the child received for her or his schoolwork since she or he began elementary school?
41. Has the child shown a consistent pattern in letter grades, and, if so, what is the pattern?
42. Have the letter grades changed and, if so, in what way?
43. Has the child received any special education services?
44. If so, what were the services, what was the individualized educational plan, and what do the parents think about the services?
45. Has the child ever been suspended or expelled from school?
46. If so, when did this take place and for what reason?
47. What, if any, interventions have been attempted?
48. If interventions have been attempted, which have been successful and which unsuccessful in helping the child?
49. What suggestions do the parents have for needed interventions?

Family History

50. Have any family members had a history of learning disabilities, attention-deficit/hyperactivity disorder, or other developmental disorders?
51. If so, who had the disorders, and what disorders did they have?
52. Are there any factors in the family that might affect the child's ability to learn (e.g., dysfunctional family environment, limited economic resources, hunger, lack of privacy for studying, health problems)?

(Continued)

Table 11-2 *(Continued)*

The Teacher

Problem

1. How does the teacher describe the child's problems?
2. How does the teacher describe the child's strengths and weaknesses?
3. What does the teacher believe is the cause of the child's problems?
4. How does the teacher describe the child's family?
5. How well does the teacher's description of the child agree with those of the child and the parents?
6. If there are disagreements, in what areas are they?
7. What is the child's current level of academic functioning (including letter grades and test scores), social functioning, and general classroom behavior?
8. How does the teacher describe the child's ability to sit still, make friends, get along with other children, listen to stories, follow oral and written directions, skim reading selections, locate information in a textbook, take notes from a discussion, sustain attention over a protracted period, understand age-appropriate rule-governed behavior, take turns when playing with other children, understand and manipulate symbols, count, spell, read, carry through a series of goal-oriented moves, maintain appropriate spatial direction, understand the complexities of a short story, and understand the complexities of a long story?
9. If the child has a reading problem, how does the teacher describe the problem? For example, does the child have difficulty reading new words or nonsense syllables (phonological problem), have difficulty in comprehension, show reluctance in trying to read different words, have a tendency to lose his or her place while reading, read quickly without close inspection, have a tendency to repeat words, hold a book close to his or her face, become bored or distracted while reading, become easily tired or fatigued,

become restless and fidget, follow word by word with his or her finger, or use an aid (such as a ruler) to underline what is being read?
10. If the child has a writing problem, how does the teacher describe the problem? For example, does the child have problems in capitalization, punctuation, and syntax; write in an incomprehensible manner with poor sentence structure or poor word choice; fail to use notes; fail to outline; fail to use a dictionary or use other resources; or fail to rewrite or revise?
11. If the child has a spelling problem, how does the teacher describe the problem? For example, does the child reverse letters, substitute incorrect letters, omit letters, add letters, spell the wrong word, or make incomprehensible errors, or does the child not even try to spell the word?
12. What specific examples does the teacher give of the child's attention to tasks, impulse control in various situations, and activity level?
13. Does the child's behavior change as a function of the academic subject, teacher, class size, time of day, or other factors?
14. How well does the child obey the classroom rules?
15. What is the quality of the assignments completed by the child in the classroom and at home?
16. What is the child's current attendance record?
17. What is the frustration level of the teacher when interacting with the child?
18. If the child was given psychological tests, what were the results of the evaluation?
19. What teaching methods are used in the classroom?

Interventions

20. What interventions have been tried?
21. How successful have these interventions been?
22. What suggestions does the teacher have for needed interventions?

Note. These questions also can be used in evaluating the assessment findings in cases of other types of disabilities.
Source: Adapted, in part, from Barkley (1991) and Voeller (1991).

Positive reinforcement should be used whenever possible to increase desirable behavior; withdrawal of reinforcement should be used more sparingly.

Cognitive-Behavioral Interventions

Cognitive-behavioral interventions are based on the premise that the child's behavior is mediated by cognitions (see Chapter 2 in *Assessment of Children: Cognitive Applications*). The aim is to increase the child's ability to think before acting or to delay gratification. An example is the use of self-directed speech and problem-solving skills to enable the child to self-guide behavior. However, studies, overall, have not supported the efficacy of cognitive-behavioral interventions used in isolation with children with ADHD (Gittelman & Abikoff, 1989). More promising are self-monitoring programs in which children and

adolescents are trained to monitor their own behavior and keep track of the frequency of inappropriate and appropriate behavior (see Chapter 5). Research suggests that, in school-based programs, behavior management and instructional interventions are more effective at changing behavior than are cognitive-behavioral interventions (DuPaul & Eckert, 1997).

Instructional Interventions

Instructional interventions include (a) using special teaching techniques, (b) accommodating academic assignments to the student's strengths, and (c) altering the structure of the learning environment. Following are some examples of what teachers and schools might do (also see Fadely and Hosler, 1992, for additional suggestions). *Recognize that not all students with ADHD will respond favorably to the same interventions.*

COMMITTED reprinted by permission of United Feature Syndicate, Inc.

Therefore, it is important to determine what works for each student.

Teaching Techniques

- Provide individual attention involving directed teaching. Use highly structured, step-by-step methods, with ample opportunities for practice, targeting of goals, and regular monitoring of performance (Busch, 1993).
- Employ multi-sensory approaches and colorful, stimulating tasks. For example, supplement traditional lectures with visual aids, video clips, demonstrations, and small-group activities, and allow for physical movement and a hands-on approach (Weyandt, Stein, Rice, & Wermus, 1994). Also use computers, calculators, and tape recorders to increase students' motivation (Lerner, 1997).
- Modify work demands to increase students' success rate (e.g., assign fewer problems during class and for homework, or permit students to do 50% of an assignment if they meet a specified criterion such as 90% accuracy on that part), break tasks into manageable segments, set task priorities, establish fixed work periods, intersperse routine work with high-interest activities to maintain motivation, use novel tasks, alternate activities involving sitting and moving, promote consistent study habits, and promote a

sense of responsibility for completing tasks (Busch, 1993; Lerner, 1997).

- Use short and simple instructions, slow the rate of presentation of materials, present directions in parts, demonstrate and model what is to be done, alert students to critical information by using key phrases (e.g., "this is important" and "listen carefully"), monitor frequently for understanding by asking students to repeat instructions and by looking at samples of work, and ensure mastery of initial elements before proceeding to a new task (Lerner, 1997; Rich & Taylor, 1993). Encourage students to ask for repetition of instructions if they do not understand, rather than guessing. Be careful to reinforce, not discourage, such requests by your tone of voice and facial expressions.
- Use peer tutoring programs, pairing a student with ADHD with another student who has well-developed social, behavior, or academic skills (DuPaul & Hennington, 1993). Pair other students as well, in order to create an environment where students are treated equally.
- Motivate the student by speaking to him or her alone, pointing out that his or her learning is important to you, and emphasizing the importance of paying attention in class.
- With students over age 7 years, use behavioral contracts that specify desired classroom behaviors and consequences for noncompliant behaviors (Lerner, 1997; Rich & Taylor, 1993). Work with students to develop a list of potential reinforcers.
- Allow and even encourage participation in high-interest activities and appropriate social interactions.
- Encourage students to use assignment logs, memory and study strategies, and other organizational aids (Rich & Taylor, 1993). For example, have students use a notebook with dividers to separate sections for lecture notes, assignments, appointments, phone numbers, and so forth. Or, suggest that students use color-coded folders to organize assignments for different subjects such as reading, mathematics, social studies, and science.
- Provide students with concrete aids (e.g., a checklist placed on the top of the desk, oral directions provided in written form) and self-monitoring procedures (see Chapter 5) that they can use to develop their self-monitoring skills.
- Reinforce attending. For example, set an egg timer, alarm clock, or tape recorder to sound at random intervals; if the student is attending when the sound occurs, give her or him reinforcement, such as verbal praise, points, or tokens (Scruggs & Mastropieri, 1992).
- Make sure students know what the assigned homework is before they leave school. Give students a homework assignment sheet, or write assignments on the board and have students copy them in their notebooks (Lerner, 1997). Consider having students complete at least one item of each different homework task before leaving school. Where email is available, allow students to send assignments home from the classroom, to ensure accuracy

and completeness. Consider posting assignments on a classroom web site or on the school's web site.

Scheduling

- Provide a schedule so that students know what will be done during each class period (Lerner, 1997).
- Schedule academic subjects in the morning and nonacademic subjects in the afternoon, as the attention span of students with ADHD tends to worsen across the course of the day (Barkley, 1998).
- Incorporate as much routine as possible into the school environment and establish clear guidelines—by providing clear classroom rules and structure and limits for behavior (Lerner, 1997; Rich & Taylor, 1993). Try to adhere to established routines. When a change is needed, explain in advance, whenever possible, what will be done and why. Also, have students follow routines such as placing books, assignments, and outdoor clothes in designated places so that they can be found easily (Lerner, 1997).

Testing

- Devise alternative ways to test students' knowledge. Consider (a) permitting students to complete a project or make a poster instead of taking a test, (b) modifying examinations (e.g., using multiple-choice questions instead of short-answer questions or using oral examinations instead of written examinations), and (c) modifying the examination process (e.g., testing in a quiet environment or under untimed conditions; Rich & Taylor, 1993).

Room Arrangements

- Reduce distractions by seating the student toward the front of the classroom (preferably with quiet students), where you can better monitor the student's behavior and apply behavior management techniques. Another possibility is to use a study carrel (a small enclosure for individual study; Rich & Taylor, 1993).

Counseling

- Arrange for students to participate in programs tailored to their individual needs—for example, counseling to deal with emotional issues, a social skills training program, an anger management and conflict management training program, an organizational skills training group, or a study skills training program.

Case Manager

- "Have a special staff member at school serve as a case manager to help troubleshoot, provide counseling and support, check work, serve as a liaison between teachers and between school and home, and help in the carrying out and overseeing of any behavioral interventions" (Rich & Taylor, 1993, p. 362).

Family Interventions

Parent training programs can help parents increase the child's compliant behaviors and reduce the child's noncompliant behaviors (Barkley, 2000). For example, parents need to understand what factors lead to noncompliant behavior, how to attend to and reinforce the positive behaviors in and out of the home, and how to use time-outs. Home–school communication strategies can be effective in improving the behavior and academic progress of children with ADHD. For example, teachers and parents can agree to use the same or similar behavior management programs and to keep each other informed about the child's behavior and performance. Communication between home and school may be daily or less frequent, depending on the specific needs of the child. Parents with children who have ADHD may also benefit from participating in a local support group or belonging to a national organization such as Children and Adults with Attention-Deficit/Hyperactivity Disorder (CHADD). Encourage parents' participation in support groups and the

involvement of the student and the family in counseling or therapy, as indicated.

Comment on Interventions

Research has clearly demonstrated that the most effective treatment for ADHD is multi-faceted (DuPaul & Stoner, 1994). Depending on the situation, a child or adolescent with ADHD may require medication, behavior management, social skills training, and/or special academic accommodations to best meet his or her needs. In addition, teachers and parents may need additional training in behavior management, and parents may need to learn effective parenting skills. The principal aim in treating children with ADHD or similar problems is to help them focus and sustain their attention and keep impulsive responding to a minimum so that they can learn and realize their potential. A structured and predictable environment with clear, consistent expectations and immediate feedback is helpful. Psychological interventions with children with ADHD should also be designed to address their interpersonal problems and other adjustment difficulties (Weiss, 1991).

THINKING THROUGH THE ISSUES

1. Do you know children with attention-deficit/hyperactivity disorder? What have you observed?
2. Do you know of any families that have a child with attention-deficit/hyperactivity disorder? If so, what has it been like for the family to raise the child?
3. What is your position with regard to children receiving medication for their disorders?

SUMMARY

1. Attention-deficit/hyperactivity disorder (ADHD) is a neuro-behavioral syndrome marked by inattention, hyperactivity, and impulsivity.
2. Three types of ADHD are cited in *DSM-IV–TR:* (a) attention-deficit/hyperactivity disorder: combined type, (b) attention-deficit/hyperactivity disorder: predominantly inattentive type,

and (c) attention-deficit/hyperactivity disorder: predominantly hyperactive-impulsive type.
3. Children with ADHD may have coexisting conditions such as learning disorders, oppositional defiant disorder, conduct disorder, depressive disorder, and anxiety disorder.
4. The ADHD population is heterogeneous, displaying a diversity of associated behavior problems in addition to the underlying attention problems.
5. Children with a dual diagnosis of ADHD and conduct disorder are likely to have more problems during adolescence and adulthood than those who have either diagnosis alone.
6. Approximately 3% to 7% of the school-aged population has ADHD.
7. Estimates of ADHD in clinical populations of children range from 23% to 50%.
8. ADHD is more common in boys than in girls, with estimates ranging from 3:1 in nonreferred samples to 6:1 in clinic-referred samples.
9. Research suggests that children with ADHD, in addition to having problems with inattention, impulsivity, and overactivity, may have the following types of deficits: cognitive deficits, adaptive functioning deficits, language deficits, task performance deficits, motor and physical developmental deficits, emotional deficits, school performance deficits, and health and accidental injury deficits.
10. Underlying the difficulties of children with ADHD may be a deficit of self-regulation; that is, they may have difficulty with organization and planning, with the mobilization and maintenance of effortful attention, and with the inhibition of inappropriate responding.
11. Overall, ADHD is characterized by deficits in (a) behavioral inhibition, (b) working memory, (c) regulation of motivation, and (d) motor control.

Etiology

12. Given the heterogeneity of ADHD symptoms, ADHD probably has no single cause; multiple factors—such as a genetic component, brain functioning, environmental toxins, and classroom organization and parenting styles—likely contribute to its development.
13. Compared with parents of normally functioning children, parents of children with ADHD tend to be more depressed, have lower self-esteem (because they believe that they have diminished parenting skills), feel more guilt, and enjoy less marital satisfaction.

Assessment Issues

14. As is true for all childhood disorders, assessment of ADHD requires a comprehensive and thorough evaluation. The focus is on core symptoms, co-occurring disorders, severity, duration, pervasiveness, social adjustment, educational needs, and cognitive abilities.
15. Assessment procedures include interviews, behavioral observations, rating scales, and psychological tests.

Interviews

16. An interview with a parent is crucial for obtaining information about the child's family, the parent's view of the child's problems, parenting styles and disciplinary techniques, environmen-

Courtesy of Jerome M. Sattler and Jeff Bryson.

tal factors that may be contributing to the child's problems, and resources available to the family, as well as information about the child's prenatal and postnatal development and medical, social, and academic history.

17. Teachers can provide valuable information about the severity of the child's symptoms, situations in which symptoms occur, specific behaviors that interfere with the child's school functioning, factors that may exacerbate the child's undesired behavior, academic strengths and weaknesses, social skill strengths and weaknesses, and the quality of the child's peer relationships.

18. Children often provide valuable information about themselves.

Behavioral Observations

19. Observation of the child's behavior will provide (a) information on the antecedents and consequences of the behaviors, as well as the intensity, duration, and rate of the behaviors, (b) information that will help you compare the behavior of the referred child to that of a nonreferred child in the same classroom, and (c) information that will be useful to the child's primary care provider.

Rating Scales

20. Ratings scales are useful in obtaining information from parents, teachers, and children.

Psychological Tests

21. Although there is no specific test or test battery for establishing a diagnosis of ADHD, several different types of tests are useful in the assessment of children referred for possible ADHD, including intelligence tests, achievement tests, memory tests, and one or more neuropsychological tests.

22. Intelligence tests should be administered as one component in the diagnostic assessment of a child, to obtain information about cognitive strengths and limitations.

23. Intelligence tests are not sufficiently sensitive to be used exclusively in making a diagnosis of ADHD or discriminating among various subtypes of ADHD.

Comment on Assessment Issues

24. Arriving at a diagnosis of ADHD is not easy, because restlessness, inattention, and overactive behavior are common in children between the ages of 2 and 12 years.

Interventions

25. Pharmacological, behavioral, cognitive-behavioral, instructional, and familial interventions can be used in the treatment of children with ADHD.

26. A common form of treatment for children with ADHD involves the use of stimulant medications such as Ritalin (methylphenidate), Dexedrine (d-amphetamine), and Cylert (pemoline).

27. All children who have serious behavioral or academic deficiencies need remediation.

28. Studies, overall, have not supported the efficacy of cognitive-behavioral interventions used in isolation.

29. Instructional interventions include (a) using special teaching techniques, (b) accommodating academic assignments to the student's strengths, and (c) altering the structure of the learning environment.

30. Parent training programs can help parents increase the child's compliant behaviors and reduce the child's noncompliant behaviors.

31. Research has clearly demonstrated that the most effective treatment for ADHD is multi-faceted, involving some combination of medication, behavior management, social skills training, and special academic accommodations.

32. The principal aim in treating children with ADHD or similar problems is to help them focus and sustain their attention and keep impulsive responding to a minimum so that they can learn and realize their potential.

KEY TERMS, CONCEPTS, AND NAMES

Attention-deficit/hyperactivity disorder (ADHD) (p. 264)
Attention-deficit/hyperactivity disorder: combined type (p. 264)
Attention-deficit/hyperactivity disorder: predominantly inattentive type (p. 264)
Attention-deficit/hyperactivity disorder: predominantly hyperactive-impulsive type (p. 264)
Arousal (p. 264)
Alertness (p. 264)
Impulsivity (p. 264)
Selectivity (p. 264)
Persistence (p. 264)
Ability to shift (p. 264)
Ability to divide attention (p. 264)
Ability to search (p. 264)
Encoding capacity (p. 264)
Cognitive deficits (p. 265)
Adaptive functioning deficits (p. 265)
Language deficits (p. 265)
Task performance deficits (p. 265)
Motor and physical development deficits (p. 265)
Emotional deficits (p. 265)
School performance deficits (p. 265)
Health and accidental injury deficits (p. 265)
Self-regulation (p. 265)
Etiology of ADHD (p. 265)
Genetic component (p. 265)
Brain functioning (p. 265)
Environmental toxins (p. 265)
Classroom organization and parenting styles (p. 267)
Assessment issues in ADHD (p. 268)
Core symptoms in ADHD (p. 268)
Co-occurring disorders in ADHD (p. 268)
Severity of ADHD (p. 268)
Duration of ADHD (p. 268)
Pervasiveness of ADHD (p. 268)
Social adjustment in ADHD (p. 268)
Educational needs in ADHD (p. 268)
Cognitive abilities in ADHD (p. 268)
Parent interview in ADHD (p. 268)
Teacher interview in ADHD (p. 268)
Child interview in ADHD (p. 269)
Behavioral observations in ADHD (p. 269)
Overactivity (p. 269)

STUDY QUESTION

Discuss attention-deficit/hyperactivity disorder. Include in your discussion a description of the disorder, its etiology, assessment issues and procedures, and interventions.

12

SPECIFIC LEARNING DISABILITIES

by Jerome M. Sattler and Lisa Weyandt

The most turbulent, the most restless child has, amidst all his faults, something true, ingenious and natural, which is of infinite value, and merits every respect.

—Fliex A. Dupanlowp

Goals and Objectives

This chapter is designed to enable you to do the following:

- Become familiar with several definitions of learning disability

- Identify subtypes of learning disabilities

- Become familiar with the etiological theories of learning disabilities

- Understand the information-processing models of learning disabilities

- Understand the procedures for conducting formal and informal assessments of learning disabilities

- Become familiar with the research findings concerning intelligence tests and learning disabilities

- Understand intervention methods for children with learning disabilities

It is estimated that approximately 10% to 15% of children in the United States struggle with some form of learning disability, although prevalence rates are difficult to establish because reporting sources use different definitions and diagnostic criteria (Silver, 1991). Children with learning disabilities have difficulty "processing information in a manner that allows them to comprehend, remember, and generalize concepts relevant to the development of oral language, written language, and mathematical skills" (Lyon & Moats, 1988, p. 830). The most common type of learning disability is reading disorder, followed by mathematics disorder and then disorder of written expression (which includes spelling). The reported prevalence rate of learning disability is higher for boys than for girls by a ratio of about 3 to 1 (DeFries, 1989). Learning disabilities may hinder children's educational progress and adversely affect their self-esteem, social status, interpersonal relations, and occupational choices. Early identification and effective interventions are needed to help children with learning disabilities succeed, both academically and socially, in and out of the classroom.

DEFINITIONS OF LEARNING DISABILITY

The term *learning disability* can be used in both a broad and a narrow sense. In the broadest sense, it refers to any form of learning difficulty. In the narrow sense, it refers to a specific learning disability, as defined in the Individuals with Disabilities Education Act (IDEA)'99 (*Federal Register,* March 12, 1999):

(i) General. The term means a disorder in one or more of the basic psychological processes involved in understanding or in using language, spoken or written, that may manifest itself in an imperfect ability to listen, think, speak, read, write, spell, or to do mathematical calculations, including conditions such as perceptual disabilities, brain injury, minimal brain dysfunction, dyslexia, and developmental aphasia.

(ii) Disorders not included. The term does not include learning problems that are primarily the result of visual, hearing, or motor disabilities, of mental retardation, of emotional disturbance, or of environmental, cultural, or economic disadvantage. (p. 12422)

This chapter refers to learning disability in the narrow sense. The IDEA '99 provides the following guidelines for determining the presence of a specific learning disability (*Federal Register,* March 12, 1999):

Sec. 300.541

(a) A team may determine that a child has a specific learning disability if—
   (1) The child does not achieve commensurate with his or her age and ability levels in one or more of the areas listed in paragraph (a)(2) of this section, if provided with learning experiences appropriate for the child's age and ability levels; and
   (2) The team finds that a child has a severe discrepancy between achievement and intellectual ability in one or more of the following areas:
      (i) Oral expression.
      (ii) Listening comprehension.
      (iii) Written expression.
      (iv) Basic reading skill.
      (v) Reading comprehension.
      (vi) Mathematics calculation.
      (vii) Mathematics reasoning.
(b) The team may not identify a child as having a specific learning disability if the severe discrepancy between ability and achievement is primarily the result of—
   (1) A visual, hearing, or motor impairment;
   (2) Mental retardation;
   (3) Emotional disturbance; or
   (4) Environmental, cultural or economic disadvantage.
(Authority: Sec. 5(b), Pub. L. 94-142)

Sec. 300.542 Observation.
(a) At least one team member other than the child's regular teacher shall observe the child's academic performance in the regular classroom setting.
(b) In the case of a child of less than school age or out of school, a team member shall observe the child in an environment appropriate for a child of that age.
(Authority: Sec. 5(b), Pub. L. 94-142)

Sec. 300.543 Written report.
(a) For a child suspected of having a specific learning disability, the documentation of the team's determination of eligibility, as required by Sec. 300.534(a)(2), must include a statement of—
   (1) Whether the child has a specific learning disability;
   (2) The basis for making the determination;
   (3) The relevant behavior noted during the observation of the child;
   (4) The relationship of that behavior to the child's academic functioning;
   (5) The educationally relevant medical findings, if any;
   (6) Whether there is a severe discrepancy between achievement and ability that is not correctable without special education and related services; and
   (7) The determination of the team concerning the effects of environmental, cultural, or economic disadvantage.
(b) Each team member shall certify in writing whether the report reflects his or her conclusion. If it does not reflect his or her conclusion, the team member must submit a separate statement presenting his or her conclusions.
(Authority: Sec. 5(b), Pub. L. 94-142)

Exhibit 12-1 shows a worksheet for determining whether a child is eligible for services under the IDEA because of a learning disability, and Figure 12-1 illustrates the decision-making process for identifying a learning disability under the IDEA.

The definition of learning disability in the IDEA '99 (which is based on the original Public Law 94-142) has been criticized for the following reasons:

1. The discrepancy criterion—that is, the idea that a diagnosis of specific learning disability should be given only when children have a "severe discrepancy" between achievement and intellectual ability in one or more expressive or receptive skills, such as written expression, listening and reading comprehension, or mathematics—may not be valid. Several writers maintain that intellectual ability, as established by a score on an intelligence test, should not be used to decide

Exhibit 12-1
Worksheet to Determine Eligibility for Services Because of a Learning Disability

WORKSHEET TO DETERMINE ELIGIBILITY FOR SERVICES BECAUSE OF A LEARNING DISABILITY

Name: _____   Date: _____

Sex: _____   Grade: _____   School: _____

Birthdate: _____   Teacher: _____

Note: The student *must* meet all criteria listed in the chart to be eligible for special education services because of a learning disability.

Criteria		Criteria met	
		Yes	No
1. Does a severe discrepancy exist between ability and achievement? If yes, indicate which area(s) below. *(Note: At least one area must be identified.)* ☐ listening comprehension ☐ reading comprehension ☐ basic reading skills ☐ oral expression ☐ written expression ☐ mathematics calculation ☐ mathematics reasoning		*	
2. Has a disorder in one of the basic psychological processes involved in understanding or in using spoken or written language been identified?		**	
3. Severe discrepancy is *primarily* caused by:	Yes / No		
a. Lack of instruction in reading and mathematics			
b. Visual, hearing, or motor impairments		*Note: If all of the checks are in the No column, then the student meets Criterion #3.*	
c. Mental retardation			
d. Emotional disturbance			
e. Environmental, cultural, or economic disadvantage			
f. Limited English proficiency			
g. Motivation			
h. Situational trauma			
Has *No* been checked for items a through h?			
4. Are special education and related services required to correct the severe discrepancy identified in #1?			

*Criterion #1: If a severe discrepancy exists but is not evident in the standardized tests, provide the rationale for using clinical judgment: _____
_____
_____

**Criterion #2: If a processing disorder exists, how does it relate to the area of academic concern?
_____
_____
_____

Source: Adapted from Connecticut State Department of Education (1999), p. 27.

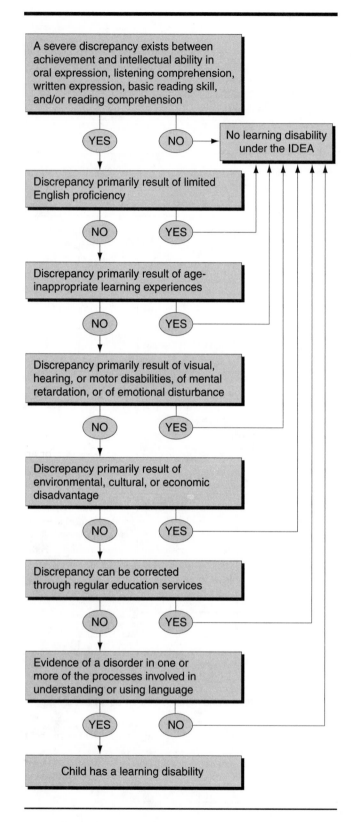

Figure 12-1. Decision-making process for the identification of a learning disability under the IDEA.

whether children have a learning disability, because the same factors that lead to a learning disability could also affect the development of intelligence (see *Journal of Learning Disabilities, 22* [8], 1989).

2. The term *severe discrepancy* usually refers to the difference between a standard score obtained on a general cognitive ability test and a standard score obtained on one or more achievement tests that measure oral expression, listening comprehension, written expression, reading, or mathematics. The discrepancy is often referred to as an ability-achievement difference. We believe, however, that the discrepancy is more accurately called an achievement-achievement difference because cognitive ability tests, like academic achievement tests, primarily measure achievement. Furthermore, the discrepancy definition is open to interpretation, which varies from state to state. For example, some state departments of education focus on the magnitude of the difference between the two scores and the statistical significance of the difference; these education departments advocate the use of discrepancy formulas. Other education departments focus on deficits in specific cognitive processes such as phonological processing (Ackerman & Dykman, 1993; Moats & Lyon, 1993). In addition, the discrepancy definition and the tests used to determine a discrepancy will influence which children are identified as learning disabled. Thus, whether a child is identified as learning disabled depends on a state's definition, how *severe discrepancy* is defined, and the tests used to conduct the assessment.

3. Several statements in the federal definition are ambiguous. For example, the term *basic psychological processes* is vague, subjective, and open to interpretation. The statement "The term does not include learning problems that are *primarily* [italics added] the result of visual..." assumes that one can distinguish primary from secondary causes. In practice, however, it is often difficult to decide which condition is primary and which is secondary. For instance, are the emotional problems of some children with learning disabilities a result of prolonged poor achievement, or are children with emotional problems at greater risk for developing learning disabilities?

4. The exclusionary criteria in the federal definition of learning disability make it difficult for children with sensory problems, emotional problems, or environmental disadvantages to be identified as learning disabled (Morris, 1988). Neither the definition of learning disability nor the accompanying provisions of the IDEA provide any operational criteria for identifying children who have sensory problems, emotional problems, or environmental disadvantages. What degree of sensory loss, for example, is required to exclude a child? Similarly, what criteria are used to identify children as having emotional disturbance or cultural disadvantage?

Furthermore, the exclusionary criteria—such as social, cultural, or economic disadvantage and emotional disturbance—are criteria that influence the development of learning disabilities because they shape "the central nervous system and the child's cognitive and linguistic repertoire" (Lyon, Fletcher, Shaywitz, Shaywitz, Torgesen, Wood, Schulte, & Olson, 2001, p. 268). Consequently, it is poor policy to have an exclusionary element as part of the definition of learning disabilities.

5. The federal definition does not discuss the heterogeneity of the condition or appropriate interventions.
6. The federal definition does not explain that learning disabilities may exist concurrently with other conditions.
7. The federal definition implies but does not explain the causes of learning disability.

Another definition of learning disability, proposed by the National Joint Committee on Learning Disabilities (1987), is generally consistent with the IDEA. The National Joint Committee on Learning Disabilities, however, deletes the term *basic psychological processes* and specifies difficulties in reasoning, in addition to the possible academic and spoken language problems listed in the IDEA. This definition also recognizes the heterogeneity of the condition. The committee's definition is as follows:

Learning disabilities is a general term that refers to a heterogeneous group of disorders manifested by significant difficulties in the acquisition and use of listening, speaking, reading, writing, reasoning, or mathematical abilities. These disorders are intrinsic to the individual, presumed to be due to central nervous system dysfunction, and may occur across the life span. Problems in self-regulatory behaviors, social perception, and social interaction may exist with learning disabilities but do not by themselves constitute a learning disability. Although learning disabilities may occur concomitantly with other handicapping conditions (for example, sensory impairment, mental retardation, serious emotional disturbance) or with extrinsic influences (such as cultural differences, insufficient or inappropriate instruction), they are not the result of those conditions or influences. (p. 1)

This definition also is somewhat vague and ambiguous, fails to operationalize the procedures needed for the determination of a learning disability, and lacks empirical validation (Lyon, 1996a).

DSM-IV–TR provides the following guidelines for defining *learning disorders* (American Psychiatric Association, 2000):

Learning Disorders are diagnosed when the individual's achievement on individually administered, standardized tests in reading, mathematics, or written expression is substantially below that expected for age, schooling, and level of intelligence. The learning problems significantly interfere with academic achievement or activities of daily living that require reading, mathematical, or writing skills. A variety of statistical approaches can be used to establish that a discrepancy is significant. *Substantially below* is usually defined as a discrepancy of more than 2 standard deviations between achievement and IQ. A smaller discrepancy between achievement and IQ (i.e., between 1 and 2 standard deviations) is sometimes used, especially in cases where an individual's performance on an IQ test may have been compromised by an associated disorder in cognitive processing, a comorbid mental disorder or general medical condition, or the individual's ethnic or cultural background. If a sensory deficit is present, the learning difficulties must be in excess of those usually associated with the deficit. Learning Disorders may persist into adulthood. (pp. 49–50)

The *DSM-IV–TR* guidelines essentially follow those of IDEA '99.

Lyon et al. (2001, p. 279) make the following recommendations for improving the federal definition of learning disabilities:

First, replace the current generic exclusionary definition of LD with evidence-based definitions that specify precise characteristics necessary to identify children with LD in reading, mathematics, written expression, and oral language....

Second, jettison the IQ-achievement criterion as a primary marker for LD....

Third, stop excluding children because of inadequate instruction, cultural and social factors, and emotional disturbance....

Fourth, include consideration of a student's response to well-designed and well-implemented early intervention as well as remediation programs as part of the identification of LD.

Lyon et al. (2001) also recommend that the primary method for identifying student underachievement be based on "performance on tasks assessing skills directly related to the academic domain in question. Further, underachievement can be documented by direct comparisons of students' age and grade with their academic functioning in oral language, reading, mathematics, and written language" (p. 279). Finally, they recommend that a multidisciplinary school-support team—with input from teachers, parents, and others responsible for the child's education—be responsible for arriving at a diagnosis of learning disabilities. It is the team, and not solely the test scores, that should be given the final decision-making authority.

Although the definition of learning disability continues to be elusive and children with this label represent an extraordinarily heterogeneous population, *the common characteristic usually shared by children with learning disabilities is academic underachievement.* Our real task is to determine which children need assistance, regardless of legal definitions that specify what constitutes a learning disability. Children with learning disabilities are especially vulnerable to the development of severe academic and perhaps social-emotional difficulties if they fall behind academically and are unable to catch up with their peers.

ETIOLOGY OF LEARNING DISABILITIES

Learning disabilities likely have multiple etiologies, including genetic, biological, and environmental bases. These factors presumably result in an altered or dysfunctional central nervous system (Bigler, Lajiness-O'Neill, & Howes, 1998).

Genetic Basis

Some evidence suggests that learning disabilities have a genetic basis. Specifically, children with learning disabilities have a greater than expected incidence of (a) family histories of learning problems, (b) prenatal and perinatal complications, (c) electrophysiological abnormalities, and (d) learning difficulties despite good behavioral adjustment and environmental support (DeFries & Gillis, 1993; Taylor, 1988b). Although evidence of a genetic basis for learning disabilities is at best suggestive—demonstrable brain disease has not been shown consistently in children with learning disabilities—evidence is accumulating that "phonologically based disabilities are linked to neurobiological and genetic factors…[and] the phonological deficits observed in reading disability are heritable" (Lyon, 1996b, p. 65). There are genetic influences on a broad range of components of literacy development, including phonological awareness and general language ability (Hohnen & Stevenson, 1999). Preliminary evidence linking reading disorder and attention-deficit/hyperactivity disorder also offers support for a shared genetic etiology (Gilger, Pennington, & DeFries, 1992).

Biological Basis

Attempts have been made to isolate a central nervous system dysfunction as a possible etiological factor in learning disabilities. Although the findings are not consistent, researchers using computed tomography (CT; see Chapter 18) report that some children with learning disabilities have enlarged ventricles of the brain (Ackerman, McPherson, Oglesby, & Dykman, 1998; Denckla, LeMay, & Chapman, 1985), as well as reversed cerebral asymmetry (Rosenberger & Hier, 1980). Studies using magnetic resonance imaging and computerized EEGs also indicate anatomical and electrophysiological differences between the brains of some children with learning disabilities and those of children without learning disabilities (Ackerman et al., 1998; Mattson, Sheer, & Fletcher, 1992).

Research using positron emission tomography (PET; see Chapter 18), which measures brain glucose metabolism and cerebral blood flow, suggests that adults with learning disabilities have more irregularities in cerebral blood flow and glucose metabolism than do adults without learning disabilities

(Hinton, Plaut, & Shallice, 1993). Most PET scans are conducted with adults rather than children, because the procedure is invasive and involves exposure to radioactive substances; it requires the injection (or inhalation) of a radioactive isotope to identify the areas of brain activation.

Although this body of research suggests a neurophysiological basis for learning disabilities, the work has limitations. First, many of the samples included in the studies are small, so the generalizability of the findings is in question. Second, the criteria for the learning-disabled designation differed across the studies, as did the techniques employed in the studies. Third, studies of nondisabled individuals might produce similar anatomical and neuroimaging findings. Fourth, some results have not been replicated, and inconsistencies remain. Last, because many of the studies lumped together disparate participants as "learning disabled," neurophysiological differences in subtypes of learning disabilities may be difficult to detect.

Environmental Basis

Although genetic and biological factors may be involved in the development of learning disabilities, environmental factors also need to be considered. Some research suggests that learning disabilities may result from children's use of ineffective learning strategies (Lyon & Moats, 1988). These include ineffective ways of (a) analyzing problems, (b) relating the nature of the problem to previous experience, (c) developing a strategic plan for operating on the information, and (d) monitoring and adjusting performance. Some researchers have argued that learning disabilities are pedagogically induced, especially among students who are linguistically and culturally diverse (Cummins, 1984). Additional environmental variables that influence children's learning and skill acquisition include parental attitudes toward learning, a family's socioeconomic status (SES), child management techniques, family verbal interaction patterns, early reading experiences, children's temperament, and children's level of motivation (Stevenson & Fredman, 1990; Whitehurst & Fischel, 1994).

"KEVIN DOESN'T HAVE A LEARNING DISORDER, MISS HOUSTON..... HE HAS A TEST-TAKING DISORDER!"

© 1988 King Features Syndicate, Inc. World rights reserved

PROBLEMS ASSOCIATED WITH CHILDREN WITH LEARNING DISABILITIES

Children with learning disabilities have deficient academic skills. They also may have deficits in information-processing abilities, neuropsychological skills, and social-behavioral adjustment (Taylor, 1988a). According to the results of a meta-analysis across 152 studies, approximately 75% of students with learning disabilities have social-skill deficits (Kavale & Forness, 1996). These deficits may occur in part because children who experience prolonged failure in school may develop a diminished self-concept, low achievement expectations, and feelings of helplessness. The presence of a learning disability, however, should not in itself be used as a predictor of any one child's social adjustment. Factors such as the nature of the learning disability, the child's self-concept, the quality of the parent-child relationship, and family functioning should also be considered. Children with learning disabilities also may have problems that are characteristic of children who have attention-deficit/hyperactivity disorder (ADHD; see Chapter 11).

Following are some possible problems that may be encountered by children with learning disabilities. Note, however, that some of the same problems may be exhibited by children without learning disabilities.

DEFICITS IN ACADEMIC SKILLS, INFORMATION-PROCESSING ABILITIES, AND NEUROLOGICAL SKILLS

- Difficulty with verbal material, including poor phonological awareness, poor reading recognition (e.g., confusion in identifying or printing certain letters and numerals), losing one's place frequently when reading printed materials, slow reading rate or lack of fluency, poor reading comprehension, deficient oral vocabulary, poor grammatical understanding, poor verbal expression, poor written expression, and poor transfer of learning
- Difficulty with nonverbal material, including poor visual perception, poor spatial perception, poor visual organization, poor revisualization, difficulty with perception of figure-ground relationships, difficulty in temporal sequencing, and difficulty interpreting facial expressions
- Deficient information-processing skills, deficient self-monitoring skills, and deficient self-regulation skills, including poor cognitive strategies, inadequate study skills, difficulty recognizing whether tasks have been performed correctly, difficulty identifying critical information needed to solve problems, and difficulty recognizing whether more information is needed to solve problems
- Poor independent work habits
- Poor organizational and planning skills, including carelessness in paperwork and a disorganized approach to tasks that involve a sequence of actions
- A tendency to be slow to complete work
- Difficulty working under time constraints
- Auditory memory difficulties
- Visual memory difficulties
- Limited attention span
- Poor retrieval of encoded information

- Poor fine-motor coordination, including poor writing and drawing
- Visual perceptual difficulties
- Auditory perceptual deficits
- Cross-modal sensory integration difficulties, such as problems integrating visual and auditory information presented simultaneously
- Speech articulation problems
- Delayed development of consistent hand preference

DEFICITS IN SOCIAL-BEHAVIORAL ADJUSTMENT

- Immaturity
- Disruptiveness
- Impulsiveness
- Destructiveness
- Hyperactivity
- Disorganization
- Irritability
- Mischievousness
- Acting-out behavior
- Poor self-image and low self-esteem
- Minimal confidence in one's ability to influence learning outcomes
- Low expectations for future achievement outcomes
- Anxiety
- Depression
- A tendency to relate better to younger children

Because children with learning disabilities are such a heterogeneous group, it is unlikely that any one child will exhibit all of the above problems. For example, (a) some will have difficulty with verbal material and others with nonverbal material, (b) some will have adequate information-processing and interpersonal skills whereas others will not, (c) some will have behavioral problems whereas others will not, and (d) some will have impairments in one specific area of functioning—such as reading, mathematics, or writing—whereas others will have impairments in several areas. Behavioral problems may stem from learning problems, learning problems may stem from behavioral problems, or both learning and behavioral problems may be associated with a common etiology. Each child with a learning disability is unique.

AN INFORMATION-PROCESSING MODEL OF LEARNING DISABILITIES

Information-processing approaches to the study of cognition, which are discussed in Chapter 5 of *Assessment of Children: Cognitive Applications,* also are helpful in the study of children with learning disabilities.

Four-Stage Model

The information-processing model shown in Figure 12-2 emphasizes the importance of memory in the intervening stages

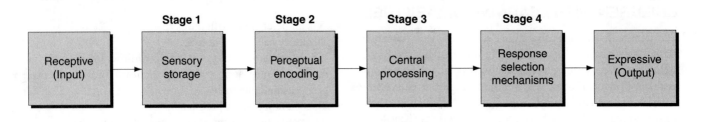

Figure 12-2. Diagram of a four-stage information-processing model.

between the reception of information and the output of a response. The model has four stages (Stanovich, 1978, adapted from p. 31):

Stage 1. *Sensory storage.* In the first stage, the short-term sensory store briefly preserves an intact representation of the incoming information.

Stage 2. *Perceptual encoding.* In the second stage, the intact representation of the information is encoded into a more permanent representation, probably a name code, which can be held in the short-term memory store. The short-term memory store is a temporary holding area where information is maintained for immediate use or for transfer to the long-term memory store.

Stage 3. *Central processing.* In the third stage, encoded information is manipulated and decisions are made about it. For example, the encoded stimulus may be compared with other stimuli held in short-term memory, associates of the encoded stimulus may be retrieved from long-term memory, or response codes of the stimulus may be accessed. The long-term memory store has a large capacity and is relatively permanent in nature.

Stage 4. *Response selection mechanisms.* In the fourth stage, relevant information is retrieved and a response program or processing strategy is selected based on decisions made in the previous stage—for example, a decision might be made to provide an oral response or to use subtraction.

Various control processes—such as selective attention, coding, organization, rehearsal, and retrieval—facilitate memory functions and help to regulate the flow of information through the various stages (Hagen, Barclay, & Schwethelm, 1982). The control processes direct the child toward sources of relevant information, arrange material to be remembered in meaningful chunks, store information in short-term memory, and mediate the transfer of information to long-term memory. The stages of the model are discrete; incoming stimuli are transformed and the transformed (or recoded) stimuli serve as input to subsequent stages.

Deficits Associated with Learning Disabilities

Children with learning disabilities usually perform poorly on tasks requiring active information processing and verbal working memory (Torgesen, 1981; Webster, Plante, & Couvillion, 1997). They typically make little use of such mnemonic aids as labeling, verbal rehearsal, clustering, chunking, and selective attention and thus fail to remember important information. Their difficulty in focusing attention may reflect inadequate executive control functions; they may have difficulty generalizing and flexibly deploying strategies used to understand, remember, and solve problems. If they have a reading disorder, they may be unable to (a) detect inadequacies, confusions, and inconsistencies in the material they read, (b) identify the critical content of what they read, and (c) encode phonological information in long-term memory (Jorm & Share, 1983; Simmons, Kameenui, & Darch, 1988).

The major problem of children with learning disabilities may not be so much an inability to attend selectively to materials as an inability to analyze tasks in ways that will result in the best performance strategy. Difficulty in applying efficient task strategies is not unique to children with learning disabilities, however; children with mental retardation and young nondisabled children also have such difficulties. From an information-processing perspective, learning disabilities may be viewed as "the result of insufficient maturity in the development of the executive or regulatory system" (Borkowski & Burke, 1996, p. 241; also see Chapter 5 in *Assessment of Children: Cognitive Applications*).

Several explanations have been offered to account for the difficulty experienced by children with learning disabilities in using active, organized strategies (Torgesen, 1980):

- They have deficits in memory and attention that underlie their verbal language processing difficulties (e.g., difficulty encoding speech or written symbols).
- They use strategies, but more slowly than children without learning disabilities (developmental-lag hypothesis).
- They come to school unprepared to assume the role of an active, organized learner—they may never have been successfully taught how to participate actively in the teaching-learning process.

The effects of early academic failure in school also must be considered. Delayed development of efficient task strategies may be a response, in part, to early school failure and to the development of a negative self-concept. Children with learning disabilities can be taught to use more efficient learning strategies, as described later in the chapter. Children with effective learning strategies are likely to discover or make use of the organization present in the material being learned. In contrast, poor learners may have the necessary knowledge and strategies at their disposal, but fail to use them effectively.

Learning Disabilities and Mental Retardation

Children with learning disabilities, as well as those with mental retardation, have deficiencies in academic skills and information processing, including limitations in strategic behavior and in working memory (Torgesen, Kistner, & Morgan, 1987). However, children with learning disabilities have different deficiencies in these areas than children with mental retardation. The limitations of children with learning disabilities are likely to be more narrowly focused—involving, for example, primarily the processing of phonological information—than those of children with mental retardation. In the latter case, limitations in coding and storing information in working memory may be pervasive and affect a broad range of complex tasks, depending on the level of mental retardation. In addition, children with learning disabilities usually can learn appropriate compensatory strategies (such as how to study) more quickly than can those with mental retardation.

COMMUNICATION DISORDERS

Communication disorders include expressive language disorder, mixed receptive-expressive language disorder, and phonological disorder (*DSM-IV–TR,* American Psychiatric Association, 2000).

Expressive Language Disorder

DSM-IV–TR provides the following guidelines for defining *expressive language disorder* (American Psychiatric Association, 2000):

The essential feature of Expressive Language Disorder is an impairment in expressive language development as demonstrated by scores on standardized individually administered measures of expressive language development substantially below those obtained from standardized measures of both nonverbal intellectual capacity and receptive language development.... When standardized instruments are not available or appropriate, the diagnosis may be based on a thorough functional assessment of the individual's language ability. The difficulties may occur in communication involving both verbal language and sign language. The language difficulties interfere with academic or occupational achievement or with social communication.... (p. 58)

Children with expressive language disorder may have the following difficulties (Baker & Cantwell, 1989; Damico, 1991):

1. *Problems with vocabulary,* such as
   - Persistent use of only a "core" set of words (e.g., "you know," "thing")
   - Word-finding difficulties
   - Substitution errors (e.g., *chair* for *table*)
   - Use of functional descriptions (e.g., using "thing you drink out of " for *glass*)
   - Overgeneralization (e.g., saying *thing* for *hammer*)
2. *Problems with expressive grammar,* such as
   - Simplification or omission of grammatical structures (e.g., "Daddy go," "Me eat")
   - Limited varieties of grammatical structures (e.g., verbs limited to present tense)
   - Inappropriate word order (e.g., "Sock Daddy has")
   - Inappropriate combinations of grammatical forms (e.g., "He were gone," "Three foots")
3. *Problems with pragmatic use of language,* such as
   - Tangential or inappropriate responses
   - Failure to provide significant information to listeners
   - Limitations in the range of speech content
   - Difficulty in maintaining or changing topics
   - Difficulty in initiating interactions
   - Lack of assertiveness in conversation
   - Failure to ask relevant questions
   - Repetitions or unusual pauses in conversation
   - Many false starts and self-interruptions
   - Difficulty in taking turns during conversation
   - Difficulty in using gestures and facial expressions
   - Difficulty in making eye contact
   - Difficulty in telling a story (e.g., poor sequencing, excessive pauses, vague cohesion, obscuring main points)

Mixed Receptive-Expressive Language Disorder

DSM-IV–TR provides the following guidelines for defining *mixed receptive-expressive language disorder* (American Psychiatric Association, 2000):

The essential feature of Mixed Receptive-Expressive Language Disorder is an impairment in both receptive and expressive language development as demonstrated by scores on standardized individually administered measures of both receptive and expressive language development that are substantially below those obtained from standardized measures of nonverbal intellectual capacity.... When standardized instruments are not available or appropriate, the diagnosis may be based on a thorough functional assessment of the individual's language ability. The difficulties may occur in communication involving both verbal language and sign language. The language difficulties interfere with academic or occupational achievement or with social communication.... (p. 62)

Children with mixed receptive-expressive language disorder may have the following difficulties (Baker & Cantwell, 1989):

1. *Problems with vocabulary,* such as interpreting *elbow* as *knee, down* as *up, this* as *here,* or *glasses* as *spectacles* only.
2. *Problems in comprehending grammatical units,* such as interpreting *pencils* as *pencil* or *had* as *has* or failing to recognize differences among *large, larger,* and *largest.*

3. *Problems in comprehending word-ordering rules (syntax),* such as failing to distinguish between "The rat chased the mouse" and "The rat was chased by the mouse" or misinterpreting "Is this yours?" as "This is yours."

4. *Problems in recognizing multiple meanings,* such as failing to understand that "smoking grass" can refer to a smoldering lawn or inhaling marijuana or that "The fly flew through the air" can refer to an insect or a fishing lure.

5. *Problems in comprehending the meaning of subtle aspects of language usage,* including facial expressions, intonation patterns, tone of voice, sarcasm, innuendo, puns, metaphors, and figures of speech—for example, not knowing whether the statement "Can you get the can opener?" is a question or an imperative.

Phonological Disorder

DSM-IV–TR provides the following guidelines for defining *phonological disorder* (American Psychiatric Association, 2000):

The essential feature of Phonological Disorder is a failure to use developmentally expected speech sounds that are appropriate for the individual's age and dialect.... This may involve errors in sound production, use, representation, or organization such as, but not limited to, substitutions of one sound for another (use of /t/ for target /k/ sound) or omission of sounds (e.g., final consonants). The difficulties in speech sound production interfere with academic or occupational achievement or with social communication.... (p. 65)

Early phonological awareness skills—such as sensitivity to rhyme and the ability to break words into their constituent sounds and blend sounds into words—are especially helpful to young children who are beginning to read (Barnes & Dennis, 1992). Phonemic awareness helps young children acquire spelling-to-sound knowledge on the basis of sound, permitting the decoding of words when they are learning to read. Even at later stages of reading, phonological decoding skills (a) contribute to fluent reading, (b) aid in the recognition of new and less frequently seen words, and (c) foster the recognition of meaningful word clauses. When phonological information is readily available, it may help children recall preceding words and thus increase comprehension by aiding word integration.

Children with phonological disorder often fail to use or perceive speech sounds at a level appropriate for their age and cultural background. An intriguing hypothesis to account for specific language impairment centers on the rate of information processing (Bishop, 1992):

The fundamental deficit in specific language impairment is a slowed rate of information processing that leads to impairment in any task requiring integration of rapidly presented information. Processing of auditory information will normally be much more impaired than processing of visual information because auditory stimuli are typically brief and sequential, whereas visual stimuli usually persist. Language development will suffer disproportionately relative to other aspects of mental development because language entails rapid processing of auditory information. The underlying deficit is not restricted to auditory perception, but it has disproportionately more severe consequences for the processing of auditory stimuli than stimuli in other modalities. (pp. 60–61, with changes in notation)

Bishop's (1992) hypothesis has received support from recent work on neurological correlates of reading disorders (Hotz, 1998, pp. A38–A39, with changes in notation):

- Reading depends on two separate but equally important neural systems involving sound and pictures. The brain reads primarily by translating written characters into the phonological building blocks of spoken language. But the brain also links a memorized picture of a complete written word to its meaning, recalling it in a way that bypasses the need to sound out the word.
- To read well, the brain has only a few thousandths of a second to translate each symbol into its proper sound. Most children can process such sounds in less than 40 milliseconds, but language-impaired children may need up to 500 milliseconds—fast enough to speak fluently, but too slow to read well.
- Minor differences in how the brain handles the visual processing of images, color, fast motion, and contrast can impede reading. Again, the speed of the visual processing may be crucial.
- Men do not use their brains the same way to read as women do; yet both sexes are equally afflicted with reading troubles. Nonetheless, boys may be diagnosed more often with reading disorders than girls.
- Everyone has some trouble adjusting to the written word because it makes such taxing demands on so many different parts of the brain.

The *DSM-IV–TR* definitions of expressive language, mixed receptive-expressive language, and phonological disorders have not been internally or externally validated (Lyon, 1996a). Furthermore, we do not know whether the diagnostic procedures for establishing these conditions (such as discrepancy between nonverbal IQ and expressive and receptive language test scores) differentiate among different disorders or among different types within a disorder (Lyon, 1996b).

READING DISORDER

The Process of Reading

Every language has a basic set of elementary sounds called *phonemes* (Harris & Coltheart, 1986); spoken words are formed by combining these sounds into meaningful sequences. The way written language is expressed, in contrast, differs greatly across languages. The main kinds of writing systems are those in which (a) individual characters generally stand for whole words (referred to as *pictographic* or *logographic*) and (b) individual characters stand for individual sounds within a word (referred to as *syllabic* or *alphabetic*).

Following is a description of the alphabetic system used in English, which was developed by the Greeks about 3,000 years ago (adapted from Harris & Colheart, 1986, pp. 22–24):

1. *Mapping of letters onto phonemes.* In the English writing system, a letter may stand for a phoneme or, as is often the case, a phoneme may be represented by a sequence of two or more letters. The work *thick* has five letters but only three phonemes; the word *thatcher* has eight letters for its four phonemes. A useful concept here is the *grapheme,* which is a written representation of a phoneme. The word *thatcher,* for example, is composed of four graphemes: <th>, <a>, <tch>, and <er>. In English, there is by definition a one-to-one relationship between graphemes and phonemes, but not between letters and phonemes.

2. *Homophones.* Homophones are words that differ in spelling and meaning but have the same pronunciation, such as *knows/nose* or *eye/I.* In English, homophones occur because one phoneme can be written in various ways—*f* and *ph,* for example.

3. *Regularity of spelling-to-sound correspondences.* Although the alphabetic system in English maps each grapheme in the written form of a word onto a single phoneme in the spoken form, the correspondences between graphemes and phonemes are not uniform across all words. For example, in *splint, hint, mint,* and many other words, the grapheme *i* (in *int*) maps onto a short i sound, but there is one word, *pint,* for which this is not true. If one drew up a table of all the graphemes in English and specified what phoneme normally corresponded to each grapheme, there would be a set of words that disobeyed these normal correspondences. Such words are known as exception words or irregular words; examples are *sew, yacht, gauge,* and *colonel.*

Reading is a highly complex process that involves many cognitive and sensory functions. These include (a) attention and concentration, (b) phonological awareness, (c) orthographic awareness, (d) word awareness, (e) form or semantic or syntactic awareness, (f) rapid decoding, (g) verbal comprehension and pragmatic awareness, and (h) general intelligence (Bryen & Gerber, 1987; Stanovich, Cunningham, & Feeman, 1984).

- *Attention and concentration* are necessary to focus on the printed material and retain the material in short-term memory.
- *Phonological awareness* (awareness of the sound characteristics of a word) includes the abilities to segment words into their constituent syllables and phonemes, recognize rhyme, blend phonemic elements, delete and substitute phonemes, and appreciate puns. Phonological awareness likely underlies the ability to segment and analyze speech, an ability particularly important in decoding unknown words.
- *Orthographic awareness* refers to being aware of how words look.
- *Word awareness* includes the abilities to segment sentences or phrases into words, separate words from their referents, appreciate jokes involving lexical ambiguity, match words with other words, recognize synonyms and antonyms, and substitute words.
- *Form or semantic or syntactic awareness* includes the abilities to detect the structural ambiguity in sentences, correct word order violations, and complete sentences when words are missing.
- *Rapid decoding,* which refers to the ability to recognize words quickly and automatically, allows a reader to process information rapidly and thereby focus on comprehending the material's content rather than decoding (or recognizing) the words.
- *Verbal comprehension and pragmatic awareness* are necessary for understanding words and word order, crucial skills underlying reading. Pragmatic awareness includes the abilities to detect inconsistencies between sentences, recognize message inadequacy, understand and repair communication failures, and be aware of the overall message.
- *General intelligence* is associated with overall reading ability.

Phonological awareness and word awareness are probably more closely related to the early stages of reading, syntactic awareness to the later stages of reading, and pragmatic awareness to the advanced stages of reading. Deficient phonological development will impede the learning of phonetic decoding skills and code acquisition in general, while deficient semantic or syntactic development will impede the learning of the skills needed to identify whole words. Research suggests that the ability to retain phonological material in working memory directly influences vocabulary acquisition and reading comprehension (Gathercole & Adams, 1993). Furthermore, impaired phonological memory skills in early childhood are linked with poor "language development in middle childhood and may even play a causal role in specific developmental language impairments" (Gathercole & Adams, 1993, p. 770).

Reading involves primarily two processes: decoding (i.e., word recognition) and linguistic comprehension (i.e., the ability to take information obtained from word recognition and assign it meaning). Both processes need to be evaluated when a child's reading ability is assessed.

Word features.   Five types of word features are important in the acquisition of decoding ability (Vellutino & Shub, 1982):

1. *Graphic features* are the particular visual patterns of a word, formed by the unique array of letters that comprise the word (*bad* vs. *dad* or *hot* vs. *not*). In learning to read, children must store graphic (or featural) information in order to distinguish accurately among printed words.

2. *Orthographic features* are the internal structural features of a word. They include structural regularities, such as sequential dependencies (*sta* is acceptable whereas *xtz* is unacceptable), and letter-sound correspondences (*at* in *fat, cat,* and *rat*). The child who discovers the regularities and redundancies of orthography is developing efficient

processing strategies for making fine-grained discriminations among visually similar words (e.g., *fat/rat, was/saw*) and reducing the amount of visual information that must be processed.

3. *Semantic features* relate to the particular concept or entity symbolized by a word. Semantic features are dynamic—they change as a result of the child's experience. It is these properties that make the word a linguistic unit that can be easily remembered. For example, seeing the word *ball* in close proximity to a picture of a ball helps establish a linguistic unit.

4. *Syntactic features* are the more abstract qualities of a word—those features a word has in common with other words by virtue of rules of grammar. Syntactic classes include nouns, verbs, adjectives, and adverbs. Children use syntactic clues to determine whether words make sense in a given location. Implicit knowledge of such markers helps make words memorable.

5. *Phonological features* are the particular sound characteristics of a word, defined by the unique ordering of vowels and consonants (i.e., phonemes) in a given word.

Dimensions of comprehension. Linguistic comprehension has the following dimensions:

- *Literal comprehension*—understanding the information that is directly contained in the selection
- *Inferential comprehension*—using the information contained in the selection to formulate inferences and hypotheses, including cause-and-effect relationships, comparisons, and sequences
- *Critical comprehension*—evaluating the quality of the selection, including its adequacy, worth, appropriateness, and desirability

Good readers have developed the following skills (Erickson, Stahl, & Rinehart, 1985):

- They perceive in a single fixation chunks of information that can be held in short-term memory.
- They can rapidly retrieve information from long-term memory.
- They are aware of the purposes for reading.
- They adjust their performance to different purposes and tasks.
- They exert control over their reading.
- They monitor ongoing comprehension, regulate the process of reading, and correct comprehension failures when they occur.
- They have a clear notion of what good reading entails.
- They accurately estimate the likelihood of their own comprehension.
- They judge the importance of different idea units to the meaning of a text as a whole.
- They are flexible in adapting their reading rate and style to different tasks and purposes.
- They can detect ambiguous, inconsistent, or otherwise anomalous information.

The following poem (author unknown) illustrates our changing language and the need for flexibility in understanding communications.

Remember When ...

A computer was something on TV
From a science fiction show of note.
A window was something you hated to clean
And ram was the cousin of a goat.

Meg was the name of my girlfriend
And gig was a job for the night.
Now they all mean different things
And that really mega bytes!

An application was for employment
And a program was a TV show.
A cursor used profanity
And a keyboard was a piano.

Memory was something that you lost with age
And a cd was a bank account.
And if you had a 3½" floppy
You surely hoped nobody found out.

Compress was something you did to the garbage
Not something you did to a file.
And if you unzipped anything in public
You'd be in jail for a while.

Log on was adding wood to the fire
And a hard drive was a long trip on the road.
A mouse pad was where a mouse lived
And a backup happened to your commode.

Cut you did with a pocket knife
And paste you did with glue.
A web was a spider's home
And a virus was the flu.

I guess I'll stick to my pad and paper
And the memory in my head.
I hear nobody's been killed in a computer crash
But when it happens they wish they were dead!

Definition of Reading Disorder

DSM-IV-TR provides the following guidelines for defining *reading disorder* (American Psychiatric Association, 2000):

The essential feature of Reading Disorder is reading achievement (i.e., reading accuracy, speed, or comprehension as measured by individually administered standardized tests) that falls substantially below that expected given the individual's chronological age, measured intelligence, and age-appropriate education.... The disturbance in reading significantly interferes with academic achievement or with activities of daily living that require reading skills.... If a sensory deficit is present, the reading difficulties are in excess of those usually associated with it.... In individuals with Reading Disorder (which has also been called "dyslexia"), oral reading is characterized by distortions, substitutions, or omissions; both oral and silent reading are characterized by slowness and errors in comprehension. (pp. 51–52)

Reading disorder also is defined in the literature as a type of learning disability in which children fail to master basic processes such as letter recognition and sound blending, despite adequate intelligence and educational opportunities. The definition suggests that the term *reading disorder* does not refer to children who are of below-average intelligence (unless their reading ability is well below the level expected for their below-average level of intelligence), who have had poor educational experiences, or who have not participated in schooling. Children in these latter categories may be poor readers, but they are not usually considered to have a reading disorder. Children with reading disorder may have *developmental dyslexia,* which refers to difficulty learning to read, or *acquired dyslexia,* which refers to loss of reading ability that has been already acquired, usually as a result of a traumatic brain injury or a disease that affects the brain (see Chapter 18).

Still another definition of dyslexia was proposed by The Orton Dyslexia Society Research Committee (April 1994; cited in Lyon, 1995, p. 9). The Committee calls the definition a *working* definition, recognizing the need for possible alterations in the future. The definition is as follows:

Dyslexia is one of several distinct learning disabilities. It is a specific language-based disorder of constitutional origin characterized by difficulties in single word decoding, usually reflecting insufficient phonological processing. These difficulties in single word decoding are often unexpected in relation to age and other cognitive and academic abilities; they are not the result of generalized development disability or sensory impairment. Dyslexia is manifest by variable difficulty with different forms of language, often including, in addition to problems with reading, a conspicuous problem with acquiring proficiency in writing and spelling.

Reading disorder is the most common type of learning disability—approximately 80% of children in learning disability programs have a diagnosis of reading disorder (Aaron, 1997). Like obesity, reading disorder is best thought of as a continuum that extends from mild to severe, with somewhat arbitrary divisions (Stanovich, 1988). Unlike obesity, however, which has one critical dimension (weight), dyslexia has at least two important dimensions: *phonetic decoding* (i.e., the ability to phonetically read visually presented words) and *orthographic coding* (i.e., the ability to recognize letter sequences or words based on their visual features).

Some children have phonological processing deficits, others have visual processing deficits, and still others have deficits in both dimensions. Finally, some children with reading disorder have no deficits in either dimension, but have deficits in comprehension.

Reading disorder is most likely to be associated with difficulties in the phonological coding of written language, particularly phoneme segmentation (Pennington & Welsh, 1995). These difficulties may be related to genetic factors, sociocultural factors, or both. For example, genetic factors may alter the neurological structures that underlie phonolog-

ical processing, and lack of sociocultural stimulation and failure to provide reading materials can lead to problems in phoneme segmentation skills. Children who have phonological difficulty usually have "slow reading speed, errors in oral reading, poor spelling, errors of syntax in written language, and excessive dependence on context for reading" (Aaron & Simurdak, 1991, p. 525). The primary deficit associated with poor reading may be a "linguistic deficit that interferes with the reader's ability to grasp the concept that words have parts—phonemes, syllables, and morphemes—and that these parts are represented abstractly by the alphabetic code" (Lyon & Moats, 1988, p. 833).

The following are problems that poor readers may have in reading and writing:

Reading

- Difficulty recognizing whole words (e.g., *south* is read as "sug," *circuit* as "kircute," *bowl* as "bowel," *sour* as "sowl")
- Need to sound out even simple words to obtain their pronunciation and meaning
- Difficulty reading multisyllabic words
- Difficulty reading words that have irregular spelling-to-sound patterns
- Difficulty reading words that have homophone confusions (e.g., *sail/sale*)
- Difficulty sounding out words (e.g., *circuit* is read as "circle," *bowl* as "barrel," *children* as "child," *high* as "height")
- Difficulty using phonic analysis and synthesis skills (e.g., difficulty reading nonwords such as *dek, lem, git*)

Writing

- Difficulty writing letters, numbers, or shapes with regularity or precision
- Reversing numbers or letters in manuscript writing
- Transposing letters in spelling
- Confusing upper- and lower-case letters in writing

Some students with reading disorder struggle so much with decoding that they cannot comprehend material they try to read aloud, whereas other students have difficulty paying attention unless they read aloud. It is prudent, therefore, to assess children's reading comprehension both with material that they read aloud and with material that they read silently. Later in the chapter we discuss writing difficulties in more detail.

Research findings. Following are some major findings from research studies related to children with reading disorder (Lyon, 1996b, adapted from p. 64):

1. Children who have reading disorder—with and without an IQ-achievement discrepancy—show similar information-processing, genetic, and neurophysiological profiles. This suggests that an ability-achievement discrepancy is not sufficient to establish a diagnosis of reading disorder.

2. Epidemiological studies indicate that as many females as males manifest dyslexia; however, schools identify three to four times more boys than girls with this disorder.

3. Reading disorder reflects a persistent deficit rather than a developmental lag that will be remedied with time. Longitudinal studies show that, of children with reading disorder in the third grade, approximately 74% continue to read significantly below grade level in the ninth grade.

4. Children with reading disorder differ from one another and from other readers along a continuous distribution. They do *not* aggregate to form a distinct "hump" separate from the normal distribution of readers.

5. The ability to read and comprehend depends on rapid and automatic recognition and decoding of single words. Slow and inaccurate decoding (i.e., poor phonemic awareness) is the best predictor of a deficit in reading comprehension.

6. The ability to decode single words accurately and fluently is dependent on the ability to segment words and syllables into phonemes. A deficit in phonological awareness is the core deficit in dyslexia.

7. The best predictor of reading ability from kindergarten and first-grade performance is phonological awareness.

Subtypes of children with reading disorder.   The three major subtypes of reading disorder, based on patterns of reading errors, are as follows:

- *Dysphonetic reading disorder* (or auditory type of disorder), in which there is a deficiency in phonological decoding

"No, Timmy, not 'I sawed the chair.' It's 'I saw the chair' or 'I have seen the chair.'"

Courtesy of Glenn Bernhardt.

- *Dyseidetic reading disorder* (or visual type of disorder), in which there is a deficiency in whole-word recognition
- *Alexic reading disorder* (or mixed type of disorder), in which there is a deficiency in both phonological decoding and whole-word recognition

Children with dysphonetic reading disorder show greater reliance on a whole-word method in reading, while those with dyseidetic reading disorder show greater reliance on a phonological decoding or alphabetic method. Unfortunately, there is no one-to-one relationship between specific intervention techniques and specific types of reading disorder. In addition, many children do not fall clearly into one subtype (Prior, 1989).

A Progression of Reading Skills

Children usually learn to read aloud by one of two methods (Harris & Colheart, 1986). In the *whole-word procedure* (or *direct procedure*), the child learns direct correspondences between the letter string and the spoken representation. For example, the child might be shown the word *cat* and be told that this word (letter string) says "cat." In the *phonics procedure,* the child uses a system of spelling-to-sound rules. For example, the child can read the word *cat* if he or she knows that *c* is pronounced /k/, *a* is pronounced /a/, and *t* is pronounced /t/. "By applying the three rules to the letter string cat, the child can transform it into the spoken form 'cat.' This is an indirect procedure in the sense that the child links print to pronunciation via an intermediate step (the use of spelling-to-sound rules) rather than using previously learned direct correspondences between individual printed words and their spoken forms" (Harris & Coltheart, 1986, pp. 83–84).

Learning to read likely involves the successive acquisition and integration of several hierarchically organized skills. The following four-phase model illustrates the process of learning to read (Ehri, 1998; & Harris & Coltheart, 1986). Note that the term *alphabetic* used in the model "indicates not simply that words consist of letters, but also that the letters function as symbols for phonemes and phoneme blends in the words" (Ehri, 1998, p. 18).

Phase 1. *Prealphabetic phase.* In the prealphabetic phase (also referred to as the sight-vocabulary phase), which develops at about 4 to 5 years of age, children form connections between selected visual attributes of words and their pronunciations or meanings and store these associations in memory. It is a process of paired-associated learning, or visual cue reading. In this phase, letter-sound relations are not involved in the connections. Children in this phase remember visual cues that accompany print rather than the written words themselves.

Phase 2. *Partial alphabetic phase.* In the partial alphabetic phase (also referred to as the discrimination-net phase), children "remember how to read sight words by forming partial alphabetic connections between only some of the letters in written words and sounds detected in their pronunciations" (Ehri, 1998, p. 19). First and final letters are often selected as the cues to be remembered. Children need to know the relevant letter-sound correspondences and how to segment initial and final sounds in words. In reading single words aloud, children seem to select words in their vocabulary that most resemble the item they see. Novel or unfamiliar words cannot be read aloud in this phase.

Phase 3. *Full alphabetic phase.* In the full alphabetic phase (also referred to as the phonological-recoding phase), children "remember how to read sight words by forming complete connections between letters seen in the written form of words and phonemes detected in their pronunciations" (Ehri, 1998, p. 21). Children now "understand how most graphemes symbolize phonemes in the conventional spelling system…and spellings become…bonded to pronunciations of words in memory" (Ehri, 1998, p. 21). Children in this phase have the ability to decode new words by blending letters into a pronunciation.

Phase 4. *Consolidated alphabetic phase.* In the consolidated alphabetic phase (also referred to as the orthographic phase), children develop skills in using orthographic (i.e., visual) recoding principles—recognizing words on the basis of the way they are spelled rather than the way they sound. These skills allow children to read homophonic words and exception words. Specifically, children in this phase are able

to retain complete information about the spellings of sight words in memory [, which] makes it possible for their print lexicons to grow rapidly as they encounter many different words in their reading. As fully connected spellings of more and more words are retained in memory, letter patterns that recur across different words become consolidated. Repeated experience reading a letter sequence that symbolizes the same phoneme blend across different words yields a consolidated unit. Consolidation allows readers to operate with multiletter units that may be morphemes, syllables, or subsyllabic units.… (Ehri, 1998, p. 22)

Children with reading difficulties may be stuck at different phases in the reading process, as reading difficulties can be associated with deficiencies in information-processing skills connected with any of the phases. The processes most often affected are (a) analyzing complex perceptual patterns, (b) attending to and extracting their significant characteristic details, (c) organizing these details, and (d) generalizing these organizations conceptually. As reading progresses, these processes are applied to more complex material, and word meanings must be integrated in the reading process.

Research (Siegel & Linder, 1984) suggests that younger children with reading disorder (8 to 9 years of age) have a deficiency in phonological coding, while older children with reading disorder (10 to 13 years of age) may use a phonemic code but have a more general deficit in short-term memory, particularly in the context of language processing. These findings are important because they suggest that a phonemic code develops in the short-term memory of children with reading disorder, albeit more slowly.

The following poem (author unknown) illustrates some of the complexities involved in learning how to read English:

Our Incredible Language

When the English tongue we speak
Why is "break" not rhymed with "freak"?
Will you tell me why it's true
We say "sew" but likewise "few"?
And the maker of a verse
Cannot cap his "horse" with "worse."
"Beard" sounds not the same as "heard."
"Cord" is different from "word."
Cow is "cow," but low is "low."
"Shoe" is never rhymed with "roe."
Think of "hose" and "dose" and "lose."
And think of "goose" and yet of "choose."
Think of "comb" and "tomb" and "bomb,"
"Doll" and "roll" and "home" and "come."
And since "pay" is rhymed with "say,"
Why not "paid" with "said," I pray?
We have "blood" and "food" and "good,"
"Mould" is not pronounced like "could."
Wherefore "done" but "gone" and "lone."
Is there any reason known?
And, in short, it seems to me
Sounds and letters disagree.

Individual Differences in Perceptual-Cognitive Processes Related to Reading Ability

Research on the relationship between perceptual-cognitive processes and reading ability suggests the following (items 1–8 from Stanovich, 1985):

1. Deficient eye movement patterns do not appear to cause reading problems.
2. Visual processing abilities—such as iconic memory (brief initial representation of an external stimulus), feature extraction (identification of relevant features of an external stimulus), and visual segmentation (isolation of relevant aspects of the visual field)—are at best weakly related to reading ability and fluency.
3. Phonological awareness and phonological coding skills are strongly linked with early acquisition and development of reading ability.
4. Difficulty in accessing the name code of a symbolic stimulus is weakly linked to reading deficits.
5. "The ability to recognize words automatically is related to reading skill, but a strong relationship is only present in the early stages of reading acquisition" (Stanovich, 1985, p. 200).
6. "Skilled readers are adept at using contextual strategies to facilitate comprehension, but skilled and less skilled readers are equally adept at using context to facilitate word

recognition.... Poor readers are handicapped in using contextual strategies in situations where their deficient word recognition skills have rendered the context functionally useless" (Stanovich, 1985, p. 193, with changes in notation).

7. Short-term memory is related to reading ability. Less skilled "readers are less adept at employing the active, planful memorization strategies (e.g., verbal rehearsal, elaboration) known to facilitate memory performance" (Stanovich, 1985, p. 195). Strategy deficiency, however, cannot explain all of the memory difficulties experienced by poor readers. Some memory problems may be caused by inadequate phonological coding.

8. Less skilled readers have comprehension deficits that are independent of their decoding skills, such as depressed listening comprehension and poor use of general comprehension strategies (e.g., inefficient comprehension monitoring, inefficient manner of approaching text, inefficient text-scanning strategies, less sensitivity to text structure, and less elaborate encoding of text).

9. Less skilled readers have impaired ability to discriminate rapid speech (Kraus, McGee, Carrell, Zecker, Nicol, & Koch, 1996; Miller & Tallal, 1995).

Intelligence and Reading Ability

Scores on reading tests are significantly related to scores on intelligence tests (Stanovich et al., 1984). The relationship between intelligence and reading strengthens with age; typical correlation coefficients are in the .30 to .50 range for early elementary grade children, the .45 to .65 range for middle grade children, and the .60 to .75 range for adults. The verbal portions of intelligence tests such as the WISC–III and Stanford-Binet: Fourth Edition tap many subskills critical for reading, such as use of real-world knowledge, inferential skills, memory strategies, and vocabulary. Future reading performance, however, is more accurately predicted by current reading achievement scores than by intelligence test scores (Stanovich, 1985).

Hyperlexia

Children who have a precocious ability to recognize written words, beyond what would be expected at their general level of intellectual development, are said to be hyperlexic. Although the cause is unknown, hyperlexic children may have accelerated neurological development that results in a precocious ability to recognize written words as linguistic symbols. Hyperlexic children, however, also may demonstrate a delay or disability in receptive or expressive language development. It is important that parents and teachers not develop unrealistic expectations of these children's educational abilities. Although they have superior word-naming ability, many do not have commensurate reading comprehension ability.

Courtesy of Herman Zilinski.

MATHEMATICS DISORDER

DSM-IV–TR provides the following guidelines for defining *mathematics disorder* (American Psychiatric Association, 2000):

The essential feature of Mathematics Disorder is mathematical ability (as measured by individually administered standardized tests of mathematical calculation or reasoning) that falls substantially below that expected for the individual's chronological age, measured intelligence, and age-appropriate education.... The disturbance in mathematics significantly interferes with academic achievement or with activities of daily living that require mathematical skills.... If a sensory deficit is present, the difficulties in mathematical ability are in excess of those usually associated with it.... (p. 53)

Children with mathematics disorder (also called *dyscalculia*) may have one or more of the following difficulties (American Psychiatric Association, 2000; Rourke, 1993):

- *Basic mathematical skill difficulties,* such as difficulty following sequences of mathematical steps, counting objects, and learning multiplication tables
- *Language difficulties,* such as difficulty understanding or naming mathematical terms, operations, or concepts and difficulty decoding written problems into mathematical symbols
- *Perceptual or spatial difficulties,* such as difficulty recognizing or reading numerical symbols or mathematical

signs (e.g., confusing 6 with 9, 2 with 5, or 17 with 71), clustering objects into groups, aligning numbers in columns, and using a number line

- *Attentional skill difficulties,* such as difficulty copying numbers or figures correctly, adding "carried" numbers, and observing operational signs
- *Shifting difficulties,* such as difficulty shifting from one mathematical operation to another
- *Writing difficulties,* such as difficulty writing numbers clearly or writing across the paper in a straight line
- *Verbal memory difficulties,* such as difficulty remembering facts, steps, and procedures necessary to solve math problems

Mathematics disorder is a heterogeneous condition that may or may not occur in conjunction with reading disorder or another disorder (Garnett, 1987). It may be that poor mathematics achievement is attributable to the same language-based deficits that underlie poor reading achievement (Share, Moffitt, & Silva, 1988). Support for this hypothesis comes from research indicating that (a) children with poor mathematics achievement tend to be poor readers, (b) the letter recognition ability of kindergarten children correlates equally well with later reading achievement and mathematics achievement, (c) the ability of kindergarten children to count dots also correlates equally well with reading achievement and mathematics achievement, and (d) early cognitive and neuropsychological predictors of reading and mathematics achievement are strikingly similar (Share et al., 1988). Still, some children have adequate reading skills but relatively isolated difficulties in mathematics, and other children have adequate mathematical skills but difficulties in reading.

Like reading disorder, mathematics disorder ranges from mild to severe. Some children have good conceptual understanding of mathematics but poor understanding of rote aspects of mathematics (e.g., mathematics facts, placement of numbers, attention to signs). Other children have difficulty at the conceptual level but not at the rote level. And still other children have difficulty with the expressive language skills used to talk about mathematics. For example, some children have difficulty recognizing Arabic numerals (e.g., for the number 372, they say, "three seven hundred two") but no difficulty in calculation, whereas others have difficulty in calculation (e.g., $4 \times 5 = 50$ or $56 \div 7 = 6$) but no difficulty in recognizing Arabic numerals. These two mathematics tasks involve different cognitive processes (Macaruso & Sokol, 1999). The cognitive requirements of mathematics also change with time. Computation-focused activities are stressed during the early school years, followed by an emphasis on conceptual and abstract mathematical concepts in later years. The incidence of mathematics disorder is approximately 6% of the school-aged population of children who are of average intelligence, do not have sensory deficits, and are not economically deprived (Lyon, 1996b).

DISORDER OF WRITTEN EXPRESSION

DSM-IV–TR provides the following guidelines for defining *disorder of written expression* (American Psychiatric Association, 2000):

The essential feature of Disorder of Written Expression is writing skills (as measured by an individually administered standardized test of functional assessment of writing skills) that fall substantially below those expected given the individual's chronological age, measured intelligence, and age-appropriate education.... The disturbance in written expression significantly interferes with academic achievement or with activities of daily living that require writing skills.... If a sensory deficit is present, the difficulties in writing skills are in excess of those usually associated with it.... There is generally a combination of difficulties in the individual's ability to compose written texts evidenced by grammatical or punctuation errors within sentences, poor paragraph organization, multiple spelling errors, and excessively poor handwriting. This diagnosis is generally not given if there are only spelling errors or poor handwriting in the absence of other impairment in written expression.... Tasks in which the child is asked to copy, write to dictation, and write spontaneously may all be necessary to establish the presence and extent of this disorder. (pp. 54–55)

Disorder of written expression is commonly found in combination with reading disorder and mathematics disorder.

Children who have reading disorder most often have difficulty with spelling, although the processes involved in reading and spelling appear to be different. Spelling requires knowledge of sound-symbol correspondence (phonological skills), as well as linguistic competence, such as an understanding that the way words are spelled may depend on how they are used. Reading, as discussed previously, likely involves phonetic decoding and whole-word reading ability. Some children can memorize the spelling of individual words but have difficulty spelling the words correctly when they are used in sentences. Achieving skill in spelling also requires knowledge of the correct spelling of irregular words. Children can usually master spelling by focusing on the sound elements or the meaning and structure of the word. Children who have both reading and writing difficulties tend to have a more generalized language disability than those who have either reading disorder or disorder of written expression alone (Harris, 1995a). Children who are good readers but poor spellers tend to have more difficulty manipulating sounds than do good readers who also are good spellers (Goswami, 1992).

Writing involves language, visual-motor processes, and the motor control needed to form letters. It is useful to distinguish between writing and handwriting. Spreen, Tupper, Risser, Tuokko, and Edgell (1984) make the distinction as follows:

Writing refers to the commitment of one's thoughts to a written idea; it involves the ideational (or propositional) use of language, as well as the auditory and visual systems. Disturbances of any of these systems may interfere with the writing process. Handwriting, in contrast, refers to the motor aspects of writing. (p. 349)

Disorder of written expression may be associated with (a) fine-motor deficits, (b) linguistic deficits, (c) visual-spatial deficits, (d) attention and memory deficits, and (e) sequencing deficits (Sandler, Footo, Levine, Coleman, & Hooper, 1992). Estimates of written language deficits range from 8% to 15% of the school-aged population, with girls and boys diagnosed equally often (Lyon, 1996b).

In the beginning stages of learning to write, children must be able to (a) produce alphabet letters rapidly and automatically, (b) retrieve letters from long-term memory, (c) have sufficient finger dexterity and fine-motor coordination, and (d) integrate visual and motor skills (Berninger, Mizokawa, & Bragg, 1991). In the later stages of learning to write, children must be able to (a) connect orthographic codes (words, letters, and letter clusters) with the corresponding phonological codes (phonetic/semantic, phonemic, and syllabic/rhyme, respectively), (b) construct meaningful sentences and paragraphs, (c) plan, and (d) revise their writings. Thus, early writing skills are primarily related to fine-motor coordination and word-level skills, such as decoding and spelling, whereas later writing skills require the generation of ideas and ability to organize. If language is not well established and if its use has not been fully automatized, the process of composing and producing written text likely will be difficult.

When children have *handwriting difficulties* (referred to as *dysgraphia*), they "may have difficulty tracing shapes, using efficient strokes for forming letters, forming letters of appropriate size, or using a comfortable pressure in grasping.... Some children may be able to produce well-formed letters but are extremely slow. Others may have difficulty in beginning to write or in completing a word" (Spreen et al., 1984, p. 349).

Good penmanship has the following characteristics (Phelps, Stempel, & Speck, 1985):

- *Letter forms* are recognizable out of context, of good proportion, consistent in size, and appropriately capitalized.
- *Slant* is generally consistent.
- *Rhythm* is easy, flowing, and even pressured (not too heavy or light).
- *Space* is characterized by lines that are reasonably straight; uncrowded letters, words, and lines; and relatively balanced margins.
- *General appearance* of the page is one that is free of excessive strikeovers.

Inefficiencies in early writing skills "may contribute to future writing disabilities either directly (because of the enormous amount of sustained effort needed to produce written words) or indirectly (owing to an aversion to writing that generalizes from early frustration with production of alphabet letters)" (Berninger et al., 1991, p. 61). Research suggests that handwriting problems tend to be associated with academic difficulties in school-aged children (Graham & Weintraub, 1996). Early identification of inefficiencies in writing skills, coupled with appropriate intervention efforts,

may prevent severe writing problems from emerging later. Writing may be especially taxing for students with attention and concentration problems, including those with attention-deficit/hyperactivity disorder. For students who have a short attention span or poor organizational skills, writing is tedious, as they have difficulty paying attention to several issues at once—for example, content, grammar, style, spelling, and punctuation.

NONVERBAL LEARNING DISABILITY

There is also a syndrome of learning disabilities referred to as nonverbal learning disability (Rourke, Young, Leenaars, 1989). Children with this syndrome may have difficulty with tactile perception, psychomotor coordination, visual-spatial organization, nonverbal problem solving, reading comprehension, mathematics, and social relations but not with rote memory, word decoding, and writing. Their difficulties usually become apparent at around 8 to 9 years of age. It is estimated that about 0.1% to 1.0% of those with learning disabilities have nonverbal learning disability (Pennington, 1991). Note, however, that nonverbal learning disability is not a separate type of disability listed in the IDEA (see Chapter 3 in *Assessment of Children: Cognitive Applications*).

THE FAMILY CIRCUS®   **By Bil Keane**

"Why do I have to keep writin' in these K's when they don't make any noise anyway?"

Reprinted with special permission of King Features Syndicate.

ASSESSMENT OF LEARNING DISABILITIES

The assessment of learning disabilities serves several purposes:

- To obtain an estimate of the child's general intelligence, in order to determine whether the child has the ability for higher achievement despite past or present performance
- To determine the child's areas of impaired functioning, including those associated with reading, mathematics, and written expression
- To determine whether the child has deficits in basic psychological processes
- To find the child's areas of strength that may prove helpful in developing interventions
- To arrive at possible explanations for the child's poor achievement
- To determine possible interventions

Children who come from cultural and linguistic backgrounds that differ from those of the majority group may perform poorly in school because of, for example, experiential differences, family expectations, limited English proficiency, stresses associated with acculturation and discrimination, and cognitive styles and learning strategies that differ from those of the majority group. Consequently, a minority child whose achievement is below average may not have a learning disability per se; rather, her or his achievement level may be related to cultural and linguistic factors. In such a case, it would be improper to label the child as having a "learning disability." Chapters 19 and 20 in *Assessment of Children: Cognitive Applications* review issues and challenges involved in working with culturally and linguistically different children.

Approaches to Determining Whether a Learning Disability Exists

Establishing whether a child has a learning disability is not a simple task. You need to consider all relevant factors, including the child's age, problems, sensory functioning (e.g., visual, auditory, motor), health history, educational history, and cultural background. As noted earlier in the chapter, the criteria in the IDEA for establishing a diagnosis of learning disability include (a) a severe ability-achievement discrepancy, (b) a disorder in one or more of the basic psychological processes, (c) a need for special education services, and (d) the ruling out of physical disabilities and cultural factors as primary causes of the child's impaired achievement. Note that the guidelines do not specify what a severe discrepancy between achievement and intellectual ability is or how to document that a severe discrepancy exists. Although various proposals have been offered to help clinicians determine whether a child's performance is significantly below expectation for his or her age level and intelligence, these proposals,

as discussed below, should be viewed simply as useful guidelines. At present, you will need to consider both clinical and psychoeducational factors in arriving at a diagnosis of learning disability.

Defining a severe discrepancy. The major classification problem centers on how to define a severe discrepancy between *ability,* usually defined by an intelligence test score, and *achievement,* usually defined by a reading, mathematics, or written expression test score or by an overall achievement test score. Note that the federal guidelines do not provide a separate classification for spelling disorder; it is subsumed under disorder of written expression.

Children are sometimes classified as having a learning disability when they have (a) low achievement (regardless of level of intelligence) and (b) a discrepancy between their verbal and performance abilities, as noted by their scores on sections of an intelligence test. *These latter two methods, however, are inappropriate and, if used, could result in the overidentification of children with learning disabilities.* Low achievement may result from factors that are not related to learning per se, such as low motivation, boredom, absenteeism, emotional problems, a mismatch between the child's skills and the curriculum, and poor teaching. A Verbal Scale IQ-Performance Scale IQ discrepancy should never be used as the *only* means of classification because it does not take into account achievement in school tasks. Similarly, a learning disability may be present even if there is no significant difference between the Verbal Scale IQ and the Performance Scale IQ. It is poor practice to rely on patterns on an intelligence test *exclusively* to arrive at a diagnosis of learning disability.

Academic underachievement has been variously defined in terms of a deviation from grade level, an expectancy formula, a difference between standard scores, and a regression equation. *Recognize, however, that none of these discrepancy procedures tell us about the possible reasons for any underlying difficulties.*

Deviation from grade or age level. Underachievement is most simply defined as a discrepancy between the child's grade-equivalent score on an achievement test and his or her grade placement. For example, a fifth-grade child who obtains a grade-equivalent score that is at the third-grade level would be considered to be 2 years below grade placement. Definitions based on a constant deviation criterion specify a particular value the discrepancy must equal or exceed in order to be considered severe. The use of a constant deviation criterion fails to take into account, however, that the same discrepancy means different things at different grade levels. Performance at 2 years below grade level reflects a much greater deficit for a fourth-grader than for an eighth-grader. For the fourth-grader the deficit represents about 50% of her or his years in school, while for the eighth-grader the deficit represents about 25% of her or his years in school. Consequently, some definitions use a graduated deviation criterion in which the amount of deviation required between grade placement and achievement varies as a function of the current grade placement. For example, the discrepancy may be 1 year in first and second grades, 1½ years in third and fourth grades, 2 years in fifth through eighth grades, and 3 years in ninth through twelfth grades. *The deviation-from-grade-level procedure is inadequate, however, because the grade-equivalent scores used in the procedure have few acceptable psychometric properties* (see Chapter 4 in *Assessment of Children: Cognitive Applications*). Any procedure that uses differences between a grade-level score on an achievement test and actual grade level, chronological age level, or mental age level is fraught with problems and will likely lead to invalid interpretations and diagnoses.

Expectancy formulas. Expected grade equivalent, rather than actual grade placement, may be used in the computation of an ability-achievement discrepancy. Expectancy formulas are based on the child's mental age (MA) and chronological age (CA). An example of an expectancy formula is

$$\text{Expected grade equivalent} = \frac{2\text{MA} + \text{CA}}{3} - 5$$

For example, the expected grade equivalent for a 6-year-old child with an MA of 6 would be

$$\text{Expected grade equivalent} = \frac{(2 \times 6) + 6}{3} - 5 = \frac{12 + 6}{3} - 5$$
$$= \frac{18}{3} - 5 = 6 - 5$$
$$= 1$$

or first grade. One problem with expectancy formulas is that they assume a correlation of 1.0 between scores on the ability test (where the MA was obtained) and scores on achievement tests (which are predicted), which is virtually never the case. Furthermore, such formulas rely heavily on the MA concept, which has serious limitations (see Chapter 4 in *Assessment of Children: Cognitive Applications*). Any formula that arbitrarily weights mental age or chronological age has limited theoretical or empirical support.

Difference between standard scores. Another procedure is to compare standard scores on two appropriate tests. A criterion level is set for a severe discrepancy, such as a difference of 1 standard deviation between an academic achievement test score and an intelligence test score. This procedure does not take into account the regression of IQ on achievement, however; and, like the expectancy formula, it implicitly assumes a near-perfect correlation between ability and achievement. It also requires that each test be based on the same standard score distribution. If the standard score distributions are not the same, one of the distributions must be changed to the other's scale or both can be changed to *z* scores (see Chapter 4 in *Assessment of Children: Cognitive Applications*).

Regression equation. A method that is better, although not without problems, is to compare scores on two appropriate tests, using a regression equation to determine expected scores on the second test (see Chapter 4 of *Assessment of Children: Cognitive Applications*). The equation takes into account regression-to-the-mean effects, which occur when the correlation between two measures is less than perfect. The regression-to-the-mean effect predicts that children who score above the mean on the first measure will tend to score somewhat lower on the second measure, whereas those who score below the mean on the first measure will tend to score somewhat higher on the second measure. A regression equation requires knowledge of the correlation between the two tests. Ideally, the correlation should be based on a large representative sample. Table F-6 in Appendix F provides expected scores on academic achievement tests predicted from intelligence test scores for correlations between .30 and .80. A criterion level is set for a severe discrepancy, such as a difference of 1 standard deviation between the academic achievement test score and the intelligence test score. However, the criterion level may be set at different points, depending on the preference of those who establish the guidelines.

Comment on discrepancy formulas. Whenever discrepancy formulas are used, their limitations should be kept in mind.

1. *Clinicians using the same discrepancy formula, but different tests, are likely to arrive at different classifications, as tests differ in their degree of reliability and validity and consequently typically yield different scores.* This is especially true if the reading test is a measure of word recognition only, word comprehension only, or both word recognition and comprehension. In addition, different methods of determining a severe discrepancy cannot be used interchangeably; they produce different rates at which children who may have learning disabilities are identified. For example, the regression approach and the simple difference approach differ in the number of students classified as learning disabled, although there is overlap in the children so classified (Bennett & Clarizio, 1988; Schuerholz, Harris, Baumgardner, Reiss, Freund, Church, Mohr, & Denckla, 1995; Valus, 1986). The United States Department of Special Education, Special Education Programs Work Group on Measurement Issues in the Assessment of Learning Disabilities (Reynolds, 1984) recommended, as did Gaskill (1995), that regression procedures be used to arrive at a significant discrepancy.

2. *Using discrepancy formulas without regard to the absolute level of the child's performance may result in serious misinterpretations and misclassifications.* A discrepancy formula should never be applied without considering the child's actual scores—that is, the level at which the child is functioning. For example, consider the case of a student who obtains an IQ of 150 on the WISC–III and standard scores of 132 on the WRAT–3 Reading, Spelling, and Arithmetic subtests. This student is clearly superior in the achievement areas mea-

sured by both tests. To identify this child as learning disabled because of these discrepant scores would be inappropriate. This student is functioning in the 99th percentile on both tests! A learning disability label indicates that a student needs special help to remediate a disability—clearly not the case in this example. Furthermore, we are not in favor of schools' providing remedial services when children are functioning at or above grade level.

3. *Discrepancy formulas are based on the assumption that the tests used to evaluate a child's intelligence and achievement measure independent constructs, when actually reading and intelligence tests to some extent measure the same constructs (e.g., vocabulary, comprehension, factual information).* Furthermore, the same processing difficulties that impair achievement test scores may impair intelligence test scores. We also need to consider which IQ to use when there is a large discrepancy between the Verbal Scale IQ and the Performance Scale IQ of the Wechsler tests, for example. In cases in which examinees have no physical impairments (e.g., visual, auditory, or motor), choosing the Verbal Scale for one child and the Performance Scale for another child would mean that different measures would be used to determine a discrepancy. Decisions concerning eligibility will change depending on whether the Full Scale, Verbal Scale, or Performance Scale is used (MacMillan, Gresham, & Bocian, 1998). Choosing either the Verbal Scale IQ or the Performance Scale IQ alone is fraught with danger. Unless there is some compelling reason to use the Verbal Scale IQ only or the Performance Scale IQ only (e.g., the child has a hearing deficit or a visual deficit or a severe language problem), we do not recommend that you use one part of an intelligence test alone for measuring a child's intelligence level.

Individual ability patterns and the variability inherent in growth and development also are not taken into account by formulas. Formulas should not be applied in a mechanical fashion. A formula that uses only two test scores cannot substitute for skilled clinical judgment and a synthesis of all relevant information available about the child.

4. *Discrepancy formulas may prevent some lower SES students from receiving services when they exhibit the same reading problems as students from higher socioeconomic backgrounds.* Because, for example, lower SES students tend to obtain lower scores on intelligence tests than do higher SES students (Siegel, 1999), the former may not have a severe discrepancy between their intelligence and academic achievement test scores and thus may be denied services.

5. *Discrepancy formulas fail to identify those children with learning disabilities who show no discrepancy between achievement and intelligence test scores.* A learning disability may interfere with performance on both achievement and intelligence tests. Currently, there is no foolproof system for classifying children as learning disabled. We know little about the distribution of discrepancies in the general population, which makes the use of any discrepancy procedure problematic.

6. *"All professional and legal definitions of LD in reading highlight the same salient features—that is, the child with a reading disability manifests an 'unexpected' difficulty in decoding, word recognition, or comprehension that is not predicted by general intellectual competence"* (Lyon, 1996a, p. 407). The discrepancy criterion tacitly assumes that children with average or above-average IQs who are poor readers (a) are cognitively and neurologically different from poor readers with low IQs, (b) can reliably be differentiated from nondisabled readers and "slow learning" children or children who do not have discrepancies between achievement and intelligence, and (c) can improve their reading skills if assessed and taught properly. Unfortunately, "the concept of discrepancy and the definitions that employ it as a diagnostic criterion have never been empirically validated" (Lyon, 1996a, p. 407).

7. *The discrepancy formula approach to classification lacks validity on both theoretical and empirical grounds.* Aaron (1997) maintains that all children who have difficulty reading (or difficulty with mathematics or written expression) should be classified as having a learning disability. That is, our task is to identify the sources of children's reading problems—such as inadequate phoneme awareness, poor decoding skills, limited vocabulary knowledge, or inadequate use of comprehension strategies—and then tailor instructional strategies to fit specific weaknesses.

8. *The discrepancy formula approach prevents children from receiving services during their early school years.* Because children's achievement abilities cannot be reliably measured before the age of 9 years, children will not receive services when they need them the most (e.g., at ages 6 to 8 years; Lyon et al., 2001).

Despite their limitations, discrepancy formulas do serve a useful purpose. Discrepancy formulas (a) rely on reliable and valid assessment instruments, (b) allow us to provide services even when we do not know the specific causes of learning disability, (c) help us to focus on academic achievement as an integral part of the assessment process, and (d) provide a consistent, objective, and accountable identification procedure (Ashton, 1996; Scruggs, 1987). Doing away with discrepancy formulas might reintroduce subjectivity into the classification process and deprive us of the ability to (a) distinguish between general and specific learning difficulties and (b) show that one child's specific learning difficulties are more serious than another child's difficulties (Ashton, 1996).

Relying only on academic achievement measures would mean that everyone with low scores would be eligible for special education services (Meyen, 1989). Since funding is limited, the discrepancy model does serve a useful purpose in channeling special education services to those who have a particular pattern of scores. However, all children who are not functioning at grade level should be given remedial instruction.

The use of a discrepancy criterion for identification of learning disability is defensible. "It is entirely reasonable to propose a class that has as a defining attribute a difference or discrepancy between intellectual aptitude and actual achievement of performance. The problems come when we attempt to operationalize and measure this difference" (Keogh, 1987, p. 6). Efforts should be directed to developing a comprehensive and useful classification system, together with appropriate techniques for identification.

Low scores on an achievement test may simply represent the lower end of a distribution of scores and not reflect a unique disability. Therefore, the designation "learning disability" should be used only to indicate underachievement related to specific processing deficits whose presumed origin is neurological dysfunction. The problem, of course, is that neurological tests do not measure the biochemical, electrophysiological, and structural integrity of the brain and nervous system; nor do they measure the functional output of the brain (e.g., ability to calculate mathematical problems).

Substituting listening comprehension for intelligence in discrepancy formulas might be a more useful approach (Badian, 1999; Stanovich, 1991). Children showing a significant discrepancy between listening comprehension and reading comprehension would likely be diagnosed as having a decoding problem. However, listening comprehension measures also have limitations. First, they may not be suitable for children whose primary language is not English. Second, phonological memory or attention difficulties may interfere with tasks involving listening comprehension, as well as with tasks involving reading comprehension. Finally, children may have difficulty comprehending oral language, as well as written language; the federal definition recognizes a deficit in listening comprehension as a form of learning disability. According to Stanovich (1991), children who have poor ability in both listening and reading should not be considered dyslexic because they do not have *unexpectedly* low achievement, which, in his opinion, is the key to defining learning disabilities. However, we believe that it is premature to preclude children from receiving an LD diagnosis when both listening comprehension and reading comprehension are low.

More research is needed to help us to determine the most valid predictors of children's reading potential and to find the best methods for identifying children with learning disabilities (Lyon, 1996a). We may find that, although it has limitations, the traditional discrepancy model—that is, comparing an intelligence test score with an achievement test score—is useful when applied in conjunction with other assessment procedures. Examples of other procedures include evaluating for a discrepancy between listening comprehension and reading comprehension, evaluating phonological ability, and evaluating visual identification of letters.

Guidelines for the Assessment of Learning Disabilities

When you evaluate a child for a possible learning disability, consider the following:

- The child's academic, intellectual, perceptual, and motor functioning (e.g., verbal-linguistic ability, visual-spatial-constructional ability, sequential-analytic ability, planning ability, listening ability)
- Neurobehavioral factors that may contribute to poor classroom performance (e.g., short attention span)
- Motivational factors that may relate to the child's learning problems
- Possible contributions of the family, peer group, teachers, and school to the child's learning problems
- Biological correlates that may be associated with the child's learning problems
- The interaction of the above factors over time and the effects they may have had on the child's performance and adjustment

In school settings, you will often work as a member of a multidisciplinary team to evaluate children who are referred for a possible learning disability.

Assessment questions. Here are some useful questions related to the assessment of learning disabilities (Barkley, 1981b; Taylor, 1988a):

1. What are the characteristics of the child's specific academic difficulties, such as in reading, mathematics, and written expression?
2. What specific types of errors does the child make in various academic tasks?
3. What cognitive deficits does the child have that are important to academic achievement?
4. Do the child's learning problems reflect general deficiencies in cognitive processes?
5. Are the child's learning problems task or situation specific?
6. How do environmental and sociocultural factors—such as learning history, social-cultural milieu, learning incentives, child management practices, educational methods, conformity, competitiveness, and achievement orientation—relate to the child's school performance?
7. How do biological factors—such as neurological disorders, other medical disorders, family history of learning problems, developmental delays, and prenatal and perinatal complications—relate to the child's school performance?
8. How likely is it that the child's deficits in one skill area have affected the development of the child's skills in other areas?
9. What emotional factors relate to the child's learning difficulties? '
10. Are parental expectations realistic?
11. How do the child's learning difficulties affect his or her interactions with teachers, parents, siblings, and peers?
12. If the child has interpersonal problems, in what settings are the problems most likely to occur?
13. What seems to be the primary cause of the child's learning disability?
14. What are the child's strengths and how can they be used to develop an intervention program?

15. What is the quality of the teaching that the student is receiving?

16. What resources within the family, school, and community can be used to assist the child in an intervention program?

During the evaluation, pay close attention to how the child responds to your questions and to the child's expressive language, receptive language, motor skills, activity level, and degree of cooperativeness. Note, for example, whether the child easily understood the questions, replied in an appropriate and coherent manner, seemed to understand nonverbal messages, used correct grammar, listened appropriately, and understood colloquialisms used in conversation. (See Chapter 7 in *Assessment of Children: Cognitive Applications* for more information about how to conduct observations during the assessment.)

Assessment battery. The most important tools in the assessment of children who may have a learning disability are good clinical skills in conjunction with reliable and valid intelligence tests, achievement tests, and other relevant tests and procedures. The tests should assess major content areas such as reading, mathematics, and written language (which includes spelling). Although there is no one standard battery for the assessment of learning disability, many of the tests reviewed in *Assessment of Children: Cognitive Applications* are useful. In addition to standardized instruments, informal reading inventories (IRI) and curriculum-based measures can provide helpful information about the child's academic skills. The Comprehensive Test of Phonological Processing (Wagner, Torgesen, & Rashotte, 1999) is a useful measure of phonological processing as are the informal phonological awareness tests discussed later in the chapter.

The assessment of a child with a suspected reading disorder should focus on the child's skills in reading—such as repertoire of words identified on sight; phonemic awareness; knowledge of letter-sound correspondences of vowels, consonants, and blends; oral and silent reading rate; and comprehension skills. Ideally, the assessment should incorporate trial remediation procedures.

As always, the selection of tests should be based partly on the referral question. Consider including in the assessment battery a measure of (a) intelligence, (b) achievement, (c) auditory processing skills, (d) visual-perceptual processing skills, and (e) behavior (e.g., behavior checklists, formal observations). Ideally, diagnostic procedures should be part of the classroom routine, both before and after the psychoeducational evaluation is completed.

Because the teacher plays an important role in evaluating for learning disability, you should interview the teacher and ask her or him to complete a questionnaire or checklist describing the child's academic skills, deficits, and progress, as well as the child's classroom behavior. You should ask the teacher to describe interventions that have been attempted and their degree of success. The School Referral Questionnaire, shown in Table A-3 in Appendix A, is an example of a questionnaire that teachers may be asked to complete. The assessment of behavior is important in cases of suspected learning disability because there is evidence, as noted earlier in the chapter, that children with learning disabilities are more likely to behave inappropriately in school than are children without learning disabilities (Bender & Smith, 1990). This information will be useful in planning interventions.

Learning Disabilities and the WISC–III

Attempts have been made to determine whether various WISC–III patterns—such as discrepancies between the Verbal Scale IQ and the Performance Scale IQ, patterns of subtest scores, and range of subtest scores—can distinguish children with learning disabilities from children who do not have learning disabilities, from children with behavior problems, and from children with mental retardation. *The attempts to find unique WISC–III test patterns among children with learning disabilities have not been successful* (Daley & Nagle, 1996; Mayes, Calhoun, & Crowell, 1998; Prifetera & Dersh, 1993; Ward, Ward, Hatt, Young, & Mollner, 1995; Watkins, 1996; Watkins, Kush, & Glutting, 1997a; Watkins, Kush, & Glutting, 1997b). There is no evidence that Verbal-Performance discrepancies can identify learning disabilities. Similarly, there is no evidence that a cluster of low scores on a subtest profile—such as (a) ACID (Arithmetic, Coding, Information, and Digit Span) or (b) SCAD (Symbol Search, Coding, Arithmetic, and Digit Span), or (c) the profile proposed by Bannatyne (1974), in which Spatial Ability (Picture Completion, Block Design, and Object Assembly) is greater than Conceptual Ability (Similarities, Vocabulary, Comprehension), which is greater than Sequencing Ability (Arithmetic, Digit Span, and Coding)—can reliably distinguish children with learning disabilities from those who do not have learning disabilities. (Bannatyne also proposed a fourth category termed Acquired Knowledge, composed of Information, Arithmetic, and Vocabulary.) These findings suggest that the presence of an ACID, SCAD, or Bannatyne profile does not mean that the child has a learning disability, nor does the absence of such a profile preclude the possibility that the child has a learning disability.

One of these studies was based on the subtest scores of 99 children with learning disabilities and 65 children with attention-deficit/hyperactivity disorder (ADHD) who were in the WISC–III standardization sample (Prifetera & Dersh, 1993). Among the group with learning disabilities, 5% had their lowest scores on all four subtests in the ACID profile and 21% had their lowest scores on three of the subtests in the ACID profile; thus, 74% of the group did *not* show the ACID profile. Among the group with ADHD, 12% had their lowest scores on the four subtests in the ACID profile and 29% had their lowest scores on three of the subtests in the ACID profile; thus, 59% of the group did *not* show the ACID profile.

This same study also looked at the Bannatyne (1974) profile in children with learning disabilities and children with an attention-deficit/hyperactivity disorder (Prifetera & Dersh,

1993). This profile too failed to distinguish children with learning disabilities from normal children and children with ADHD from normal children. Among the group with learning disabilities, 33% showed the Bannatyne profile; among the group with ADHD, 47% showed the profile. Thus, most of the children in these two clinical groups did *not* show the Bannatyne profile.

Similarly unimpressive results have been reported for the WISC–R. For example, in an extensive investigation of 94 WISC–R studies with children with learning disabilities, Kavale and Forness (1984) concluded that no recategorization of WISC–R scores, profiles, factor clusters, or patterns revealed a significant difference between the children with learning disabilities and the children without disabilities. Even within the group of children who were learning disabled, no regrouping scheme was found to be useful in differential diagnosis. Children with learning disabilities do not differ from children without learning disabilities in the variability of their subtest scores (Watkins & Worrell, 2000). For both groups, the mean number of subtests deviating by 3 or more points from the mean of a 10-subtest battery was less than one subtest on the Verbal Scale, about one subtest on the Performance Scale, and about two subtests on the Full Scale.

The failure to find a unique Wechsler test pattern for children with learning disabilities is not surprising. Children with learning disabilities are too heterogeneous a group for one type of Wechsler test profile to be typical of a majority of its members. Because there is no unique WISC–III profile that is reliably diagnostic of learning disability, the WISC–III should be used *only* to assess the child's intelligence and pattern of cognitive efficiency.

Informal Assessment of Learning Disabilities

Because well-normed standardized tests are not available for all types of school readiness, written and oral expression, and listening comprehension skills, informal tests and curriculum-based measures are sometimes needed to evaluate a child's abilities. In addition to using test scores, you should evaluate the child's behavior at home and at school, the types of errors the child makes both on formal and informal tests and on classroom tests, and the factors that facilitate the child's learning.

Informal assessment of reading skills. Note the following:

- Type and extent of the child's reading deficit
- Child's reading fluency (e.g., hesitations, smooth transitions during oral reading)
- Type of inflection the child uses during oral reading (e.g., appropriate or inappropriate)
- Child's ability to make use of the linguistic context to identify words in sentences
- Child's ability to comprehend what is read

Recording oral reading errors. You might record a child's oral reading errors by using the notations shown in Table 12-1. After recording the errors, evaluate the types of errors made by the child and how the errors affected the child's reading (Rupley & Blair, 1979). Following are some questions to consider:

1. What types of errors occurred most frequently?
2. Did the child's omissions change the meaning of the text, occur with any specific types of words, or interfere with the child's ability to respond to comprehension questions?
3. What types of substitutions were most common?
4. Did the child's insertions change the meaning of the text?
5. Was there a pattern to the insertions?
6. Did the child's mispronunciations occur with a particular type of word, such as names or multisyllabic words?
7. Were any reading errors associated with the dialect the child speaks?

Table 12-1
Recording Word-Recognition Miscues and Errors

Miscue	Marking
External assistance	time
Functional attribute	*sit on* chair
Hesitation	✓ time
Insertion	*new* time ^ to
Losing place	*lp* time
Mispronunciation	*door* dog
Omission	time ⟨to⟩
Phonemic substitution	*stool* spool
Refusal to pronounce	*rp* time
Repetition	*r* time
Reversal	time⟨to⟩go
Self-correction	time
Semantic substitution	*leap* jump
Synonym substitution	*big* large
Verb substitution	*beat* heart
Visual misidentification	*ball* balloon

Table 12-2
List of Regular Words, Irregular Words, and Nonsense Words

Regular words		Irregular words		Nonsense words	
Grade 2	Grade 3	Grade 2	Grade 3	Grade 2	Grade 3
up	best	was	glisten	lopeb	fidot
it	nostril	does	pleasure	pilk	peb
am	napkin	learn	prove	sut	ipcrot
crop	rid	one	doubtful	nintred	kaxin
went	scalpel	gone	honest	noxtof	stum
at	spun	lawn	lawn	skep	polt
ran	disc	work	shove	sopog	fisc
hand	drank	among	realm	id	glin
silk	complex	early	gentle	sifton	cospim
tax	demanded	flood	cough	lemp	lemp
top	piano	there	pigeon	ig	hintred
dog	rustic	right	cupboard	tipik	gix
man	hundred	any	fought	flontel	yentop
pen	colt	sugar	rough	marpi	oxitac
get	custom	nothing	hour	lut	pontflact

Source: Adapted from Freebody and Byrne (1988).

Word reading strategies. To evaluate second- and third-grade children's ability to read regular words, irregular words, and nonsense words, you might use lists like the ones shown in Table 12-2; the lists are also useful for evaluating children in other grades who are having problems in reading (Freebody & Byrne, 1988). A child's ability to read these words may help you to determine which of the following reading strategies the child uses:

1. *Memory-based reading strategy.* Children who use a memory-based strategy read irregular words better than they read nonsense words. They attempt to memorize associations between printed words and their pronunciations and have sight word recognition skills.

2. *Decoding strategy.* Children using a decoding strategy read nonsense words better than they read irregular words. They laboriously plod through the task of sounding out grapheme by grapheme, declining to use vocabulary knowledge to solve the problem of the word's identity. These children may be said to have analytic decoding skills.

3. *No strategy.* Children may not use any strategy or may not have one dominant strategy.

Word prediction abilities (or cloze procedures). By administering informal tests of word prediction abilities, you can study the way a child uses semantic and syntactic cues to identify words; these tests supplement standardized reading tests. *Cloze procedures,* illustrated in Table 12-3, require the child to complete sentences. You can administer six items of each type, but you should stop testing earlier if the child becomes frustrated. Score the child's responses as (a) correct (i.e., the exact word deleted from the passage; a synonym of the deleted word; or a word that, when inserted, forms a text that is correct), (b) no response, (c) incorrect but related to

the theme, or (d) incorrect and not related to the theme. Cloze assessment results may be useful in developing instructional recommendations.

Phonological awareness evaluation. Measures of phonological awareness are good predictors of the speed with which children will acquire reading fluency in the early grades (Stanovich, Cunningham, & Cramer, 1984). A child's degree of phonological awareness can be assessed via the following informal tasks:

1. *Strip Initial Consonant Task* (see Table 12-4). In this task, two words are used on the practice trials and nine additional words are presented on the test trials. The child is asked to say the new word that results when the first sound is taken away.

2. *Phonology Oddity Task* (see Table 12-5). In this task, each of the three tests contains eight sets of four words. Within each set of four words in Test 1, three begin with a common sound (e.g., *n, b,* or *g*). The child is asked to name the odd word in the set. In Tests 2 and 3, the common sound is the middle sound and the ending sound, respectively.

3. *Phonological Memory Test* (see Table 12-6). In this task, which is designed for use with preschool children (although children of any age can be given the test), children are asked to repeat 15 words and 15 nonwords. Each set contains 5 one-syllable words, 5 two-syllable words, and 5 three-syllable words.

4. *Auditory Analysis Test* (see Table 12-7). In this task, the child is asked to say the word that results after a specified syllable or phoneme is removed (e.g., "Say *smile* without the /s/").

5. *Yopp-Singer Test of Phoneme Segmentation* (see Table 12-8). In this task, the child is asked to articulate separately, in order, the sounds of spoken words (Yopp, 1995).

Table 12-3
Informal Tests of Word Prediction Abilities

Task	Procedure and examples
Auditory Cloze Child is required to complete a spoken sentence or phrase orally with a word that is both semantically and syntactically correct. This is a good beginning task for children, regardless of age, because it defines the prediction abilities necessary for the subsequent tasks.	Orally present the child with an incomplete sentence. Have the child complete the sentence orally. 1. Maria went to the lake to _____. (fish, swim, relax, etc.) 2. John used his money to buy some _____. (candy, clothes, food, etc.) 3. A horse can run very _____. (fast, quickly, slowly, etc.) 4. On a lonely farm in the country lived a man and his _____. (wife, child, donkey, etc.) 5. Mr. Cook was going to the _____ to get some eggs. (store, market, shop, etc.) 6. Ray finished picking up the trash and walked back to the ____. (house, store, barn, etc.)
Auditory Cloze and Initial Grapheme Child is presented with a spoken phrase or sentence with a single word omitted and is given the initial grapheme of the missing word. The prediction now involves an added constraint; not only must the response be semantically and syntactically acceptable, but it must also begin with the indicated grapheme. This task, unlike auditory cloze, requires familiarity with letters, words, and the reading act.	Orally present the child with an incomplete sentence. Then present the initial letter of the missing word, printed on a card. Have the child complete the sentence orally with a word that begins with the grapheme indicated. 1. My kitten drinks m_____. (milk) 2. Today, the mailman brought a l_____. (letter) 3. Sandy put the small rock in his p_____. (pocket, pack) 4. Last night for supper we had potatoes and b_____. (bread, beef, bacon, etc.) 5. The alligator was hiding in the w_____ of the swamp. (water, weeds) 6. When the car stopped, the old man got out and k_____ it. (kicked)
Visual Cloze with Alternatives Child selects, from two alternatives, the more appropriate word to complete the written sentence. This task, which assesses use of semantic and syntactic cues, relies heavily on a child's ability to read the target sentence and the alternatives. A child may err on this task even though he or she has adequate word prediction ability. The chance factor is much higher on this task than on the others.	Present the child with a printed sentence, one part of which is in parentheses (the correct word and an alternative incorrect word). Have the child choose the correct word orally. 1. Mary can hit the (dill/ball). 2. Sam picked some (fingers/flowers) from his garden. 3. An old lady was in her (house/horse). 4. Kim will (come/came) home after the ballgame. 5. Because she was mad, Mom said, "Go to your room and don't come (out/our)." 6. On the way to school Tim stopped to pick up a (life/leaf).
Visual Cloze with Word Supplied Orally Child is required to complete a written sentence orally with a word that is both semantically and syntactically correct. Odd responses may be based on a miscue of one of the words in the item, not on a misapplication of semantic and syntactic constraints. Scoring should be based on semantic and syntactic acceptability.	Present the child with a printed sentence with one word omitted. Have the child read the sentence silently and supply an appropriate word orally. Record the child's response. 1. Run as fast as you _____. (can, want, etc.) 2. The baby was very _____. (happy, sad, etc.) 3. At breakfast Max spilled milk all over the _____. (table, floor, kitchen, etc.) 4. A red bird built a nest in the _____. (tree, chimney, etc.) 5. The dog is old but he still _____. (runs, eats, etc.) 6. Every day I eat a big bowl of cereal _____ breakfast. (for, at)
Visual Cloze Child is presented with a written phrase or sentence with a word omitted and is required to write an appropriate word in the space provided. Scoring should be based primarily on semantic and syntactic acceptability.	Present the child with a printed sentence with one word omitted. Have the child print an appropriate word in the blank space. 1. The boy kicked the _____. (ball, dog, car, etc.) 2. One day a _____ ran off the road. (car, bike, motorcycle, etc.) 3. I wanted to see if I could _____ fudge. (make, cook, etc.) 4. The duck flew over the water and soon we could not _____ him. (see, find, etc.) 5. Once upon a time there was a king who was so _____ they called him King Fatso. (fat, big, heavy, etc.) 6. Texas Dan was the best cowboy around and he could _____ a bucking bronco. (ride)

(Continued)

Table 12-3 *(Continued)*

Task	Procedure and examples
Visual Cloze with Initial Grapheme Child is presented with a written sentence with a word omitted and is required to provide an appropriate word using the grapheme shown. Providing the initial grapheme limits the range of acceptable responses. Some children seem to become bound to the grapheme, giving responses that meet the initial grapheme criterion but that do not follow the semantic and syntactic cues.	Present the child with a printed sentence with one word omitted but for the initial letter. Have the child, either orally or in writing, complete the sentence with a word that begins with the grapheme indicated. 1. The girl eats the h_____. (hotdog, hamburger, etc.) 2. Peter named his dog B_____. (Bill, Boy, Ben, etc.) 3. My bike is r_____ and white. (red) 4. Mary didn't want her little brother playing w_____ her toys. (with) 5. Where could I go if I wanted t_____ hide? (to) 6. The artist could draw the most beautiful p_____ of flowers. (picture)

Source: Adapted from Allington (1979). The six items for each procedure were obtained from R. L. Allington, personal communication, April 1982.

Table 12-4
Strip Initial Consonant Task

STRIP INITIAL CONSONANT TASK

Name: _____   Date: _____

Sex: _____ Grade: _____   School: _____

Birthdate: _____   Teacher: _____

Score (number correct): _____

As you present each sample and item, speak clearly and distinctly and emphasize the key word.

Say: "Listen carefully. I am going to say a word. If you take away the first sound of the word I say, you will find a new word. First, I'll show you how to do it: *ball*. If you take away the first sound, the new word is *all*. Now let's try another." Give Sample Item 1.

Sample Item 1

Say: "Tell me what the new word is when you take away the first sound in *cat*. What is the new word when you take away the first sound?"

If the child succeeds, go to Sample Item 2. If the child fails, say: "If you take away the first sound from the word *cat*, the new word is *at*."

Repeat Sample Item 1. Say: "*Cat*. What is the new word when you take away the first sound?"

If the child succeeds, go to Sample Item 2. If the child fails, say: "If you take away the first sound from the word *cat*, the new word is *at*." Proceed to Sample Item 2.

Sample Item 2

Say: "Let's try another. What is the new word when you take away the first sound from the word *task*?"

If the child succeeds, go to Test Item 1. If the child fails, say: "If you take away the first sound from the word *task*, the new word is *ask*."

Repeat Sample Item 2. Say: "What is the new word when you take away the first sound from the word *task*?"

If the child succeeds, go to Test Item 1. If the child fails, say: "If you take away the first sound from the word *task*, the new word is *ask*." Proceed to Test Item 1.

Test Items

Give Test Items 1 through 9. Say the word. Then say: "If you take away the first sound, what is the new word?" If necessary, repeat these instructions before each word is said. Do not correct any answers. Give all nine items.

1. pink
2. man
3. nice
4. win
5. bus
6. pitch
7. call
8. hit
9. pout

Source: Adapted from Stanovich, Cunningham, and Cramer (1984).

Table 12-5
Phonology Oddity Task

PHONOLOGY ODDITY TASK

Name: _____ Date: _____

Sex: _____ Grade: _____ School: _____

Birthdate: _____ Teacher: _____

Score (number correct): Test 1 _____ Test 2 _____ Test 3 _____

Speak clearly and distinctly, at an even pace, and emphasize the four key words in each item or example.

TEST 1. FIRST SOUND DIFFERENT

Say: "Listen carefully. I am going to say four words. One of the words begins with a different sound than the other words. Here is an example. If I say *bag, nine, beach, bike*, the word that begins with a different sound is *nine*. Now you try one." Give Sample Item 1.

Sample Item 1

Say: "Which word begins with a different sound than the other words: *rat, roll, ring, pop*?"

If the child succeeds, go to Sample Item 2. If the child fails, say: "*rat, roll, ring, pop*. The word that has a different beginning sound is *pop*."

Repeat Sample Item 1. Say: "Which word begins with a different sound than the other words: *rat, roll, ring, pop*?"

If the child succeeds, go to Sample Item 2. If the child fails, say: "*rat, roll, ring, pop*. The word that has a different beginning sound is *pop*." Go to Sample Item 2.

Sample Item 2

Say: "Let's try another one. Which word has a different beginning sound: *nut, sun, sing, sort*?"

If the child succeeds, go to Test Item 1. If the child fails, say: "*nut, sun, sing, sort*. The word that has a different beginning sound is *nut*."

Repeat Sample Item 2. Say: "Which word has a different beginning sound: *nut, sun, sing, sort*?"

If the child passes, proceed to Test Item 1. If the child fails, say: "*nut, sun, sing, sort*. The word that has a different beginning sound is *nut*." Proceed to Test Item 1.

Test Items

Give Test Items 1 through 8. Say the four words. Then say: "Which word has a different beginning sound?" If necessary, repeat these instructions before each item. Do not correct any answers. Give all eight items.

1. not no nice *son*
2. ball bite *dog* beet
3. girl *pat* give go
4. *yes* run rose round
5. cap *jar* coat come
6. hand hut *fun* here
7. *cat* tan time ton
8. luck like look *arm*

TEST 2. MIDDLE SOUND DIFFERENT

Say: "Listen carefully. I am going to say four words. One of the words has a different sound in the middle than the other words. Here is an example. If I say *tap, cap, tell, hat*, the word that has a different sound in the middle is *tell*. Now you try one." Give Sample Item 1.

Sample Item 1

Say: "Which word has a different sound in the middle than the other words: *mop, hop, tap, pop*?"

If the child succeeds, go to Sample Item 2. If the child fails, say: "*mop, hop, tap, pop*. The word that has a different sound in the middle is *tap*."

Repeat Sample Item 1. Say: "Which word has a different sound in the middle than the other words: *mop, hop, tap, pop*?"

If the child succeeds, go to Sample Item 2. If the child fails, say: "*mop, hop, tap, pop*. The word that has a different sound in the middle is *tap*." Go to Sample Item 2.

Sample Item 2

Say: "Let's try another one. Which word has a different middle sound: *pat, fit, bat, cat*?"

If the child succeeds, go to Test Item 1. If the child fails, say: "*pat, fit, bat, cat*. The word that has a different middle sound is *fit*."

Repeat Sample Item 2. Say: "Which word has a different middle sound: *pat, fit, bat, cat*?"

If the child passes, proceed to Test Item 1. If the child fails, say: "*pat, fit, bat, cat*. The word that has a different middle sound is *fit*." Proceed to Test Item 1.

Test Items

Give Test Items 1 through 8. Say the four words. Then say: "Which word has a different middle sound?" If necessary, repeat these instructions before each item. Do not correct any answers. Give all eight items.

1. lot cot pot *hat*
2. fun *pin* bun gun
3. *hug* dig pig wig
4. red fed *lid* bed
5. wag rag bag *leg*
6. fell *doll* well bell
7. dog fog *jug* log
8. fish dish wish *mash*

(Continued)

Table 12-5 (*Continued*)

TEST 3. LAST SOUND DIFFERENT

Say: "Listen carefully. I am going to say four words. One of the words has a different sound at the end than the other words. Here is an example. If I say *fog, tag, pig, let*, the word that ends with a different sound is *let*. Now you try one." Give Sample Item 1.

Sample Item 1

Say: "Which word has a different sound at the end than the other words: *hat, mat, fan, cat*?"

If the child succeeds, go to Sample Item 2. If the child fails, say: "*hat, mat, fan, cat*. The word that has a different ending sound is *fan*."

Repeat Sample Item 1. Say: "Which word has a different sound at the end than the other words: *hat, mat, fan, cat*?"

If the child succeeds, go to Sample Item 2. If the child fails, say: "*hat, mat, fan, cat*. The word that has a different ending sound is *fan*." Go to Sample Item 2.

Sample Item 2

Say: "Let's try another one. Which word has a different ending sound: *doll, hop, pop, top*?"

If the child succeeds, go to Test Item 1. If the child fails, say: "*doll, hop, pop, top*. The word that has a different ending sound is *doll*."

Repeat Sample Item 2. Say: "Which word has a different ending sound: *doll, hop, pop, top*?"

If the child passes, proceed to Test Item 1. If the child fails, say: "*doll, hop, pop, top*. The word that has a different ending sound is *doll*." Proceed to Test Item 1.

Test Items

Give Test Items 1 through 8. Say the four words. Then say: "Which word has a different ending sound?" If necessary, repeat these instructions before each item. Do not correct any answers. Give all eight items.

1. sun run *tub* fun
2. *hen* peg leg beg
3. fin *sit* pin win
4. map cap gap *jam*
5. cot hot *fox* pot
6. fill *pig* hill mill
7. *peel* weed seed feed
8. pack lack *sad* bac

Source: Adapted from Bradley (1980) and Stanovich, Cunningham, and Cramer (1984).

Table 12-6
Phonological Memory Test

PHONOLOGICAL MEMORY TEST

Name: _____   Date: _____

Sex: _____   Grade: _____   School: _____

Birthdate: _____   Teacher: _____

Score (number correct): Words _____   Nonwords _____

Directions

Word directions: "I am going to say some words. After I say each word, you say it. Let's try one for practice: *big*. Now you say it. . . . OK. Here is the first word. . . . Now you say it."

Scoring: 1 point for each word and nonword repeated correctly.

Nonword directions: "I am going to say some made-up words. After I say each made-up word, you say it. Let's try one for practice: *kek*. Now you say it. . . . OK. Here is the first made-up word. . . . Now you say it."

Words

1. Arm _____
2. Hate _____
3. Pot _____
4. Bird _____
5. Pull _____
6. Rabbit _____
7. Letter _____
8. Driver _____
9. Picture _____
10. Button _____
11. Newspaper _____
12. Alphabet _____
13. Holiday _____
14. Elephant _____
15. Potato _____

Nonwords

16. Grall _____
17. Nate _____
18. Mot _____
19. Plurd _____
20. Tull _____
21. Rubid _____
22. Diller _____
23. Grindle _____
24. Bannock _____
25. Pennet _____
26. Brastering _____
27. Dopelate _____
28. Kannifer _____
29. Tumperine _____
30. Parrazon _____

Source: Adapted from Gathercole and Adams (1993).

Table 12-7
Auditory Analysis Test

AUDITORY ANALYSIS TEST

Name: _____   Date: _____

Sex: _____ Grade: _____   School: _____

Birthdate: _____   Teacher: _____

Score (number correct): _____

Directions: Show the child the top half of a sheet of 8½ × 11-inch paper on which pictures of a cow and a boy's head are drawn side by side. Say: "Say *cowboy.*" After the child responds, cover the picture of the boy and say, "Now say it again, but without *boy.*" If the response is correct (*cow*), expose the bottom half of the sheet and show drawings of a tooth and a brush Say: "Say *toothbrush.*" After the child responds, say: "Say it again, but without *tooth.*"

If the child fails either demonstration item, teach the task by repeating the demonstration procedures with the pictures. If the child again fails to make correct responses to both items, discontinue testing.

If both responses are correct, withdraw the picture sheet and proceed with the test. Say: "Say *birthday.*" Wait for a response, and then say: "Now say it again, but without *day.*" Continue with the test. Always pronounce the specific sound (*not the letter name*) of the item to be omitted. If the child has a speech articulation problem, take this into consideration when you assess the accuracy of the response in which a portion of the word was omitted. If the child fails an item, repeat the item. If there is still no response, record a score of 0 and give the next item. *Discontinue after four consecutive failures.*

(Circle the items that the examinee correctly segments; record incorrect responses on the blank line following the item.)

Items

A. cow(boy) _____
B. (tooth)brush _____
1. birth(day) _____
2. (car)pet _____
3. bel(t) _____
4. (m)an _____
5. (b)lock _____
6. to(ne) _____
7. (s)our _____
8. (p)ray _____
9. stea(k) _____
10. (l)end _____
11. (s)mile _____
12. plea(se) _____
13. (g)ate _____
14. (c)lip _____
15. ti(me) _____
16. (sc)old _____
17. (b)reak _____
18. ro(de) _____
19. (w)ill _____
20. (t)rail _____
21. (sh)rug _____
22. g(l)ow _____
23. cr(e)ate _____
24. (st)rain _____
25. s(m)ell _____
26. Es(ki)mo _____
27. de(s)k _____
28. Ger(ma)ny _____
29. st(r)eam _____
30. auto(mo)bile _____
31. re(pro)duce _____
32. s(m)ack _____
33. phi(lo)sophy _____
34. s(k)in _____
35. lo(ca)tion _____
36. cont(in)ent _____
37. s(w)ing _____
38. car(pen)ter _____
39. c(l)utter _____
40. off(er)ing _____

Source: Adapted from Rosner and Simon (1971).

Table 12-8
Yopp-Singer Test of Phoneme Segmentation

YOPP-SINGER TEST OF PHONEME SEGMENTATION

Name: _____

Date: _____

Sex: _____ Grade: _____

School: _____

Birthdate: _____

Teacher: _____

Score (number correct): _____

Directions: "Today we're going to play a word game. I'm going to say a word and I want you to break the word apart. You are going to tell me each sound in the word in order. For example, if I say *old*, you should say /o/-/l/-/d/. (Be sure to say the sounds, not the letters, in the word.) Let's try a few together."

Practice items: *ride* [pause], *go* [pause], *man* (*Assist the examinee in segmenting these items as necessary.*)

(*Circle the items that the examinee correctly segments. Record incorrect responses on the blank line following the item.*)

Items

1. dog _____
2. keep _____
3. fine _____
4. no _____
5. she _____
6. wave _____
7. grew _____
8. that _____
9. red _____
10. me _____
11. sat _____

12. lay _____
13. race _____
14. zoo _____
15. three _____
16. job _____
17. in _____
18. ice _____
19. at _____
20. top _____
21. by _____
22. do _____

Source: Adapted from Yopp (1995).

Informal assessment of written expression, including spelling skills. Suggestions that may be helpful in informal assessment of a child's written expression follow (State of Iowa, 1981):

- Evaluate the child's classroom writing assignments, especially successive drafts of the same paper. (Verify, if possible, the conditions under which each draft was written—such as the amount of help received—and whether the child used grammar- and spell-check programs.)
- Compare what the child wrote with what was written by a random sample of other children in his or her class.
- Evaluate how the child copies letters, words, sentences, and short paragraphs presented in cursive and printed form from near point (placed on the desk) and far point (placed on the blackboard).
- Evaluate how the child writes letters, words, or sentences (using both uppercase and lowercase cursive or print or both).
- Present 10 different pictures, and evaluate the child's written description of each picture.
- Evaluate the child's behavior during classroom writing assignments.

During the assessment, you can ask the child to write her or his name, write words and sentences from dictation, and write a story. These tasks will provide information about the child's writing skills and ability to express ideas in writing. In addition, note any specific handwriting difficulties such as the following:

- Parts of letters not connected
- Distortion or unequal spacing of letters
- Unequal size of letters
- Letters not on the line
- Heavy use of pencil
- Light use of pencil
- Tense grip while working
- Pencil held in fist or other inefficient grip
- Wavering line
- Progressive deterioration of letters
- Letters copied out of sequence
- Letters omitted or inserted
- Words combined inappropriately

Table 12-9 shows an informal writing inventory that provides guidelines for evaluating the content, grammar, and mechanics of a child's writing sample.

Table 12-9
Informal Writing Inventory

INFORMAL WRITING INVENTORY

Name: _____   Date: _____

Sex: _____ Grade: _____   School: _____

Birthdate: _____   Teacher: _____

Type of Writing: _____

Guidelines

A. Content

1. Development of Ideas—Does the writer have a theme or message to convey? Does the entire composition relate to these basic ideas?
2. Overall Organization—Are paragraphs and sentences logically ordered?
3. Comprehensibility—Is the message clear? Is the writing easy to understand? Will the reader have questions? Are gaps present?
4. Paragraph Development—Does each paragraph have a main idea? Do the sentences in the paragraphs relate to each other? Are sentences logically ordered?
5. Sentence Construction—Are all of the sentences complete (absence of fragments)? Are the sentences well constructed (absence of run-on sentences)?
6. Types of Sentences—What kinds of sentences are included (compound, complex, simple, declarative, interrogative)? Do sentences contain too few or too many words?
7. Use of Words—Are the words descriptive/vague, complex/simple, appropriate/inappropriate, formal/informal? Are words or word parts omitted/added?
8. Length—Is the passage too long or too short? Is the length acceptable? Does the length reflect a reasonable effort?

B. Grammar

9. Subject-Verb Agreement—Do subjects and verbs agree?
10. Verb Tense—Is the correct verb tense used?
11. Pronoun Antecedents—Do pronouns and antecedents agree?
12. Use of Adjectives/Adverbs—Are adjectives and adverbs used properly?
13. Syntax—Is the sentence structure correct (e.g., parallelism, use of modifiers)?
14. Consistency of Tense—Is the tense appropriate and consistent across sentences and paragraphs?

C. Mechanics

15. Capitalization—Are capital letters used appropriately? If not, what types of words need to be capitalized (e.g., proper nouns, first word in a sentence)?
16. Punctuation—Is correct punctuation used? If not, what types of punctuation are needed (e.g., periods, commas, apostrophes)?
17. Spelling—Is the spelling generally correct? What types of spelling problems occurred? Did problems occur with difficult or easy words?

Evaluation Form

Area	Excellent	Adequate	Fair	Poor	Comments
A. Content					
1. Development of Ideas					
2. Overall Organization					
3. Comprehensibility					
4. Paragraph Development					
5. Sentence Construction					
6. Types of Sentences					
7. Use of Words					
8. Length					
B. Grammar					
9. Subject-Verb Agreement					
10. Verb Tense					
11. Pronoun Antecedents					
12. Use of Adjectives/Adverbs					
13. Syntax					
14. Consistency of Tense					
C. Mechanics					
15. Capitalization					
16. Punctuation					
17. Spelling					

Source: Adapted from Billingsley (1988).

The following case illustrates an informal assessment of written expression for a fifth-grade girl, aged 10 years 11 months (State of Iowa, 1981).

Mary's ability to express herself in writing was evaluated by analyzing five classroom writing assignments completed since the beginning of the school year, comparing the five samples with a random sample of 10 writing assignments from classmates, administering the Capitalization and Punctuation subtests of the Brigance Diagnostic Inventory of Basic Skills, and evaluating her ability to copy short paragraphs (in cursive). Mary made numerous spelling and writing errors on each assignment. High-frequency words were misspelled, sentences were incomplete, and capitalization and punctuation errors were frequent. She mixed cursive and printing style, letter formation was awkward and frequently illegible, and she varied spacing between words. Mary's sentences were simple sentences, with limited use of adjectives and adverbs.

Mary's written samples differed from those of her classmates. Her classmates consistently used cursive style; showed lower frequency of capitalization, punctuation, and spelling errors; demonstrated more accurate letter formation and more consistency in spacing; more frequently used adjectives and adverbs; demonstrated the use of paragraph development; and used compound sentences, questions, quotations, and complex sentences.

Mary's performance on the two Brigance subtests indicates that she understands the correct use of capitalization (Capitalization subtest = 80% accuracy) and punctuation (Punctuation subtest = 70% accuracy), even though she does not apply this knowledge when writing.

Mary's copying was laborious. She copied word by word and, with some words, letter by letter, mixing cursive and printing style. Before proceeding to the next copying sample, she elected to use printing. After questioning, Mary said that she did not like to use cursive writing ("I don't know how to make all the letters"). The general appearance of her writing (legibility, spacing, and letter formation) improved significantly when she used printing only. She is the only student in her class who does not use cursive style.

In summary, Mary demonstrates significant problems in using correct spelling, capitalization, punctuation, and paragraph development in her writing. Her use of complex language structures in writing is considerably more limited than that of her classmates. Also, the quality of Mary's handwriting is below that of her classmates. The evaluation results suggest that Mary may have a severe disability in written expression. Further assessment with standardized tests is recommended. Specialized remedial efforts will be needed for her to improve her skills in written expression.

Tables 12-10, 12-11, and 12-12 provide information useful for evaluating spelling ability. Table 12-10 presents an informal test of spelling; List 1 is appropriate for second- and third-grade children and List 2 for third- to sixth-grade children. Table 12-11 gives the critical elements tested by the words in the two lists. Table 12-12 provides guidelines for classifying spelling errors.

Informal assessment of mathematics ability.
Here are some questions for observing a child's performance on tests of mathematics:

1. Does the child use concrete counting aids (e.g., fingers, pencil marks)?

2. Does the child confuse place values when writing numbers?
3. Does the child line up answers in the correct place?
4. Does the child carry the right number?
5. Does the child confuse arithmetic processes (e.g., add when subtraction is required)?
6. Does the child understand the written instructions?
7. Does the child attend to details?
8. Does the child reverse, invert, or transpose numbers?
9. Does the child use an appropriate amount of the working space on the sheet?
10. Can the child easily shift from addition to subtraction problems?
11. Does the child give the same answer to different problems (referred to as perseveration)?
12. Does the child exhibit directional confusion by adding columns from left to right?

Table 12-13 provides an informal list of mathematics problems, and Table 12-14 shows examples of errors children make in multiplication and division.

An assessment of mathematical skills should include assessment of computational skills, knowledge of the language of mathematics (e.g., special words such as *together* and *less,* symbols, and operation signs), and the ability to solve mathematics application problems presented orally and in writing (see Chapter 17 in *Assessment of Children: Cognitive Applications*). You can use testing-of-limits after a mathematics test has been administered by having the examinee, for example, (a) redo problems in which she or he misread the operation signs (e.g., adding instead of subtracting or multiplying), (b) use a calculator to solve failed items, or (c) use paper and pencil to solve orally presented problems.

Informal assessment of meaningful memory.
Table 12-15 (see page 318) contains stories for evaluating a child's ability to remember the meaning of a paragraph. The stories are divided into 44, 34, and 37 logical units, respectively. You can use the following instructions: "I am going to read a story. Listen carefully. When I am through, tell me the story that I read to you." Give the child 1 point for each unit recalled correctly; exact wording is not important. Also consider how the child organizes various elements in the story, what particular features the child recalls in the story, and what features the child distorts in the story.

Informal assessment of social and environmental influences.
Interviews with the child, parents, and teachers (see Chapters 1, 2, and 3), together with questionnaires or checklists they complete (see Tables A-1, A-2, and A-3 in Appendix A), can give you information about the following areas:

- Demographic characteristics (e.g., socioeconomic class, size of family, birth order, ethnicity)
- Cultural values
- Degree of acculturation
- Family interaction patterns

Table 12-10
Diagnostic Spelling Test

DIAGNOSTIC SPELLING TEST

General directions:
Give List 1 to second- or third-graders.
Give List 2 to any child who is above Grade 3.

Directions to child:
"I am going to say some words, and then I want you to spell each one. I will say the word first and then use it in a sentence. Here is the first word." Say the first word in List 1 or List 2, as appropriate; then follow the word with its corresponding sentence.

List 1		List 2	
Word	*Illustrative sentence*	*Word*	*Illustrative sentence*
1. not	He is *not* here.	1. flower	A rose is a *flower*.
2. but	Mary is here, *but* Joe is not.	2. mouth	Open your *mouth*.
3. get	*Get* the wagon, John.	3. shoot	John wants to *shoot* his toy gun.
4. sit	*Sit* down, please.	4. stood	We *stood* under the roof.
5. man	Father is a tall *man*.	5. while	We sang *while* we marched.
6. boat	We sailed our *boat* on the lake.	6. third	We are in the *third* grade.
7. train	Tom has a new toy *train*.	7. each	*Each* child has a pencil.
8. time	It is *time* to come home.	8. class	Our *class* is reading.
9. like	We *like* ice cream.	9. jump	We like to *jump* rope.
10. found	We *found* our lost ball.	10. jumps	Mary *jumps* rope.
11. down	Do not fall *down*.	11. jumped	We *jumped* rope yesterday.
12. soon	Our teacher will *soon* be here.	12. jumping	The girls are *jumping* rope now.
13. good	He is a *good* boy.	13. hit	*Hit* the ball hard.
14. very	We are *very* happy to be here.	14. hitting	John is *hitting* the ball.
15. happy	Jane is a *happy* girl.	15. bite	Our dog does not *bite*.
16. kept	We *kept* our shoes dry.	16. biting	The dog is *biting* on the bone.
17. come	*Come* to our party.	17. study	*Study* your lesson.
18. what	*What* is your name?	18. studies	He *studies* each day.
19. those	*Those* are our toys.	19. dark	The sky is *dark* and cloudy.
20. show	*Show* us the way.	20. darker	This color is *darker* than that one.
21. much	I feel *much* better.	21. darkest	This color is the *darkest* of three.
22. sing	We will *sing* a new song.	22. afternoon	We may play this *afternoon*.
23. will	Who *will* help us?	23. grandmother	Our *grandmother* will visit us.
24. doll	Make a dress for the *doll*.	24. can't	We *can't* go with you.
25. after	We play *after* school.	25. doesn't	Mary *doesn't* like to play.
26. sister	My *sister* is older than I.	26. night	We read to Mother last *night*.
27. toy	I have a new *toy* train.	27. brought	Joe *brought* his lunch to school.
28. say	*Say* your name clearly.	28. apple	An *apple* fell from the tree.
29. little	Tom is a *little* boy.	29. again	We must come back *again*.
30. one	I have only *one* book.	30. laugh	Do not *laugh* at other children.
31. would	*Would* you come with us?	31. because	We cannot play *because* of the rain.
32. pretty	She is a *pretty* girl.	32. through	We ran *through* the yard.

Note. See Table 12-11 for the elements tested in the Diagnostic Spelling Test.
Source: Reprinted from *Teacher's Guide for Remedial Reading* by William Kottmeyer, © 1959, with permission of The McGraw-Hill Companies, pp. 88–89.

Table 12-11
Elements Tested in the Diagnostic Spelling Test

List 1		List 2	
Word	Element tested	Word	Element tested
1. not 2. but 3. get 4. sit 5. man	Short vowels	1. flower 2. mouth	ow-ou spellings of ou sound, er ending, th spelling
6. boat 7. train	Two vowels together	3. shoot 4. stood	Long and short oo, sh spelling
8. time 9. like	Vowel-consonant-e	5. while	wh spelling vowel-consonant
		6. third	th spelling vowel before r
10. found 11. down	ow-ou spelling of ou sound	7. each	ch spelling, two vowels together
12. soon 13. good	Long and short oo	8. class	Double final consonant, c spelling of k sound
14. very 15. happy	Final y as short i	9. jump 10. jumps 11. jumped 12. jumping	Addition of s, ed, ing; j spelling of soft g sound
16. kept 17. come	c and k spellings of the k sound	13. hit 14. hitting	Doubling final consonant before adding ing
18. what 19. those 20. show 21. much 22. sing	wh, th, sh, ch, and ng spellings and ow spelling of long o	15. bite 16. biting	Dropping final e before ing
		17. study 18. studies	Changing final y to i before ending
23. will 24. doll	Doubled final consonant	19. dark 20. darker 21. darkest	er, est endings
25. after 26. sister	er spelling	22. afternoon 23. grandmother	Compound words
27. toy	oy spelling of oi sound	24. can't 25. doesn't	Contractions
28. say	ay spelling of long a sound	26. night 27. brought	Silent gh
29. little	le ending	28. apple	le ending
30. one 31. would 32. pretty	Nonphonetic spellings	29. again 30. laugh 31. because 32. through	Nonphonetic spellings

Note. See Table 12-10 for the list of sentences.
Source: Reprinted and adapted from *Teacher's Guide for Remedial Reading* by William Kottmeyer, © 1959, with permission of The McGraw-Hill Companies, p. 90.

Table 12-12
An Example of a System for Classifying Spelling Errors

Type of error	Test word	Response
1. Omission of a silent letter—a silent consonant or vowel is omitted from the test word.	Weather Remain	Wether Reman
2. Omission of a sounded letter—a letter that is sounded in the ordinary pronunciation of the test word is omitted.	Request Pleasure	Requst Plasure
3. Omission of a double letter—one of a pair of successive, identical letters is omitted from the test word.	Sudden Address	Suden Adress
4. Addition—a letter or letters are added to the test word.	Until Basket	Untill Baskest
5. Transposition or reversal—the correct sequence of the letters of the test word is disturbed.	Saw Test	Was Tset
6. Phonetic substitution for a vowel sound—a vowel or a vowel and a consonant are substituted for a vowel of the test word.	Prison Calendar	Prisin Calender
7. Phonetic substitution for a consonant sound—a consonant that is an alternative sound for a consonant of the test word is substituted.	Second Vacation	Cecond Vakation
8. Phonetic substitution for a syllable—a similarly sounding syllable is substituted for a syllable of the test word or a single letter is substituted for a syllable.	Purchased Neighborhood	Purchest Naborhood
9. Phonetic substitution for a word—an actual word that is generally similar in sound to the test word is substituted.	Very Chamber	Weary Painter
10. Nonphonetic substitution for a vowel—a vowel or vowel and consonant are substituted for the vowel of the test word.	Station Struck	Stition Strick
11. Nonphonetic substitution for a consonant—a consonant or vowel and consonant are substituted for a consonant of the test word.	Washing Importance	Watching Inportance
12. Semantic substitution—a synonym or word from a similar category is substituted for the test word.	Jolt Pencil	Shock Pen
13. Letter misorientation—one or more letters of the test word are reversed.	Job Hop	Jod Hog
14. Unrecognizable or incomplete—the spelled word is unrecognizable as the test word.	Cotton Liberty	Cano Libt

Source: Adapted from Spache (1981).

- Parental attitudes toward learning
- Child management practices in the family
- Peer pressures related to schooling
- Conditions in the home conducive (and not conducive) to studying
- Settings in which the child's problems are likely to occur
- Neighborhood attitudes toward education

Informal assessment of personality and temperament. Information about the child's personality and temperament can be obtained from formal methods of personality assessment, such as structured interviews, behavior checklists, rating scales, story completion techniques, and personality tests (see Chapter 6)—as well as from informal methods, including semistructured or unstructured interviews with parents, teachers, and the child (see Tables B-5, B-11, and B-1 in Appendix B). Table 12-16 contains questions that may be useful in learning about a child's attitude toward reading and writing. You can also use a specialized sentence-completion technique to obtain information about the child's thoughts and feelings regarding reading, mathematics, and writing (see Table 12-17 on page 319). If you use the sentence-completion technique, give the sentences orally and follow up with questions based on the child's answers.

Table 12-13
Informal Assessment of Arithmetic

Number System

Say: "I am going to say some numbers, and I want you to tell me what number comes next. Here is the first one." (Say "Here is the next one" before you give items 2 through 5.)

1. 1, 2, 3, 4, 5,
2. 2, 4, 6, 8,
3. 1, 5, 9, 13,
4. 63, 65, 67,
5. 100, 200, 300,

Counting

6. Say: "Count by tens starting with 10 and stop when I tell you. Go ahead, count by tens starting with 10." (Stop examinee after the fifth one.)

7. Say: "Count by tens starting with 14 and stop when I tell you. Go ahead, count by tens starting with 14." (Stop examinee after the fifth one.)

Writing Numbers from Oral Presentation

Say: "Write these numbers. Use this pencil to write your answers. Here is the first number." (Say one number at a time. Give examinee a blank sheet of paper on which to write the numbers.)

8. 39
9. 400
10. 658
11. 303
12. 550

Reading Numbers

Say: "I am going to show you some numbers, and I want you to tell me what the numbers are. Here is the first one." (Point to the number on this page, or make a 3 x 5 inch card with the number on it and show the card to the examinee.)

13. 18
14. 40
15. 300
16. 509
17. 842

Addition

Say: "I would like you to do the following problems. Use this pencil to write your answers. Go ahead." (Give examinee a blank sheet of paper on which to do the problems.)

18.	4 + 45	22.	17 + 22
19.	6 + 2	23.	23 + 3
20.	8 + 9	24.	47 + 36
21.	6 + 7	25.	439 + 596

Subtraction

Say: "Now, I would like you to do the following problems. Use this pencil to write your answers. Go ahead." (Give examinee a blank sheet of paper on which to do the problems.)

26.	8 − 5	31.	46 − 12
27.	9 − 2	32.	87 − 49
28.	16 − 8	33.	65 − 17
29.	14 − 3	34.	504 − 383
30.	34 − 13	35.	300 − 177

Multiplication

Say: "Now, I would like you to do the following problems. Use this pencil to write your answers. Go ahead." (Give examinee a blank sheet of paper on which to do the problems.)

36.	6 × 4	40.	43 × 2
37.	9 × 0	41.	28 × 49
38.	4 × 1	42.	56 × 22
39.	7 × 6	43.	19 × 10

Division

Say: "Now, I would like you to do the following problems. Use this pencil to write your answers. Go ahead." (Give examinee a blank sheet of paper on which to do the problems.)

44.	$8 \div 4$	48.	$64 \div 7$
45.	$9 \div 3$	49.	$109 \div 5$
46.	$54 \div 6$	50.	$78 \div 46$
47.	$100 \div 2$		

Table 12-14
Examples of Multiplication and Division Errors

Multiplication errors		Division errors	
1. Does not know multiplication facts	**Addition Step**	1. Omits remainder from quotient	9. Brings down wrong number
2. Does not complete problem	13. Does not know addition facts	2. Estimates quotient incorrectly	10. Omits part of remainder from quotient
3. Does not regroup	14. Fails to add and regroup	3. Fails to bring down all numbers	11. Guesses
4. Does not align properly	15. Is careless	4. Fails to recognize that difference is greater than divisor	12. Is careless
5. Shifts multipliers	16. Adds wrong partial product		**Multiplication Step**
6. Does not add in regrouped number		5. Fails to record part of quotient	13. Does not know multiplication facts
7. Guesses		6. Fails to use complete divisor	14. Fails to regroup
8. Regroups with wrong number		7. Records quotient digits in wrong place	15. Is careless
9. Multiplies vertically		8. Divides into remainder	**Subtraction Step**
10. Adds instead of multiplies			16. Does not know subtraction facts
11. Is careless			17. Fails to regroup
12. Multiplies left to right			18. Subtracts up

Source: Adapted from Miller and Milam (1987).

Table 12-15
Stories for Meaningful Memory Recall

Bozo Story

1) Once there were three 2) thieves 3) named 4) Bozo, 5) Tommy, and 6) Frank. 7) Bozo 8) was their leader. 9) They were good 10) friends and 11) went everywhere 12) together. 13) One night the 14) three of them 15) sneaked 16) through 17) a window 18) into 19) a house 20) on a hill. 21) There were trees 22) around the house. 23) Suddenly a 24) light 25) came on 26) in another 27) room. 28) They quickly 29) climbed 30) out 31) of the window. 32) Bozo and 33) Tommy 34) ran 35) down 36) the hill. 37) The other thief 38) climbed 39) a tree. 40) When a man 41) came 42) to the door of the house, 43) he could see 44) no one.

Airplane Story

1) The airplane 2) was coming in 3) for a landing. 4) It was 5) full 6) of people. 7) Suddenly, 8) the airplane 9) leaned 10) far to 11) the left 12) side. 13) All of the passengers 14) were afraid. 15) The pilot 16) did not know 17) what was wrong 18) so he landed the plane 19) very carefully. 20) As he landed, 21) one wing of the plane 22) scraped 23) the ground. 24) The passengers 25) and the pilot 26) climbed out 27) and looked 28) at the plane. 29) To their surprise, 30) a large 31) group 32) of birds 33) was sitting 34) on the wing of the plane.

Linda Story

1) Linda 2) was playing 3) with her new 4) doll 5) in front 6) of her house. 7) Suddenly, 8) she heard 9) a strange 10) sound 11) coming from under 12) the porch. 13) It was the flapping 14) of wings. 15) Linda ran 16) inside 17) the house and 18) grabbed 19) a shoe 20) box 21) from the closet. 22) She found 23) some sheets 24) of paper 25) and cut 26) the paper 27) into pieces 28) and put them 29) in the box. Linda 30) gently 31) picked up 32) the helpless 33) animal 34) and took it 35) with her. 36) Her teacher 37) knew what to do.

Source: Reprinted with permission of E. H. Bacon and D. C. Rubin, unpublished material; used in research by Bacon and Rubin (1983).

Table 12-16
Questions to Help You Learn About Child's Attitude Toward Reading and Writing

Reading
1. How did you learn to read?
2. Who helped you learn to read?
3. What did they do to help you?
4. Who is the best reader you know?
5. Why do you think he or she is the best?
6. Are you a good reader?
7. How do you know?
8. Do you like to read?
9. When do you read?
10. What is your favorite book?
11. What is the last book you read?
12. When did you read it?
13. When you are reading alone and you come to a word you don't know, what do you do?
14. Why do you read?
15. Tell me three words that describe how you feel about reading.
16. How do you decide what you will read?
17. Who is your favorite author?
18. Do you like to be read to?
19. How many books have you read over the past 6 months?

Writing
20. Tell me three words that describe how you feel about writing.
21. How did you learn to write?
22. Why do you write?
23. Are you a good writer?
24. What makes a good writer?
25. When do you write?
26. What do you like to write about?
27. How much have you written over the past 6 months?

Source: Adapted from Farnan and Kelly (1991).

Table 12-17
Sentence Completion Technique for Children Who May Have Learning Problems

SENTENCE COMPLETION TECHNIQUE FOR CHILDREN WHO MAY HAVE LEARNING PROBLEMS

Name: _____   Date: _____

Sex: _____ Grade: _____   School: _____

Birthdate: _____   Teacher: _____

Directions: Say: "I am going to start a sentence. Then I'd like you to finish it any way you want. Here is an example. If I say, 'When I am tired . . . ,' you can say, 'I go to bed,' 'I take a nap,' 'I sit down,' or anything else that you can think of. OK? Let's try the first one."

Reading

1. When reading in class, I become nervous if _____ .
2. Reading is easiest when _____ .
3. Jobs that require reading are _____ .
4. My favorite reading activity is _____ .
5. If I couldn't read, _____ .
6. My favorite place to read is _____ .
7. If I could do any type of reading, I would _____ .
8. Reading reminds me of _____ .
9. The worst place to read is _____ .
10. Jobs that do not require reading are _____ .
11. If you asked people what they thought of reading, most would say _____ .
12. I would be less nervous about reading if _____ .
13. The person with whom I would like to read is _____ .

Mathematics

14. When doing mathematics in class, I become nervous if _____ .
15. Mathematics is easiest when _____ .
16. Jobs that require mathematics are _____ .
17. My favorite mathematics activity is _____ .
18. If I couldn't do mathematics, _____ .
19. My favorite place to do mathematics is _____ .
20. If I could do any type of mathematics, I would _____ .
21. Mathematics reminds me of _____ .
22. The worst place to do mathematics is _____ .
23. Jobs that do not require mathematics are _____ .
24. If you asked people what they thought of mathematics, most would say _____ .
25. I would be less nervous about mathematics if _____ .
26. The person with whom I would like to do mathematics is _____ .

Spelling

27. When doing spelling in class, I become nervous if _____ .
28. Spelling is easiest when _____ .
29. Jobs that require spelling are _____ .
30. My favorite spelling activity is _____ .
31. If I couldn't spell, _____ .
32. My favorite place to do spelling is _____ .
33. If I could do any type of spelling, I would _____ .
34. Spelling reminds me of _____ .

(Continued)

Table 12-17 *(Continued)*

35. The worst place to do spelling is _____ .
36. Jobs that do not require spelling are _____ .
37. If you asked people what they thought of spelling, most would say _____ .
38. I would be less nervous about spelling if _____ .
39. The person with whom I would like to do spelling is _____ .

Writing

40. When doing writing in class, I become nervous if _____ .
41. Writing is easiest when _____ .
42. Jobs that require writing are _____ .
43. My favorite writing activity is _____ .
44. If I couldn't write, _____ .
45. My favorite place to do writing is _____ .
46. If I could do any type of writing, I would _____ .
47. Writing reminds me of _____ .
48. The worst place to do writing is _____ .
49. Jobs that do not require writing are _____ .
50. If you asked people what they thought of writing, most would say _____ .
51. I would be less nervous about writing if _____ .
52. The person with whom I would like to do writing is _____ .

Source: Adapted from Giordano (1987).

PROGNOSIS FOR CHILDREN WITH LEARNING DISABILITIES

We do not have definitive answers about whether children with learning disabilities continue to have problems with reading, mathematics, or written expression after they leave school. However, there is some evidence that, although learning disabilities often persist into adulthood (Spreen, 1988; Taylor, 1988a), the majority of individuals with learning disabilities function well in society (Morrison & Cosden, 1997). A child's prognosis is dependent on such factors as the following:

- Severity of the child's learning disability
- Age at which the child's disability is recognized
- Types of learning problems the child has
- Child's general level of cognitive ability
- Types of interventions attempted with the child
- Child's responses to intervention efforts
- Child's self-concept, level of motivation, expectations, and coping skills
- Family's attitude toward the child's disability
- Teachers' expectations about the child
- Peer group's attitude toward the child

More favorable outcomes tend to be associated with children who have milder forms of learning disability, who have above-average intelligence, who are in the middle or upper socioeconomic class, and who have no identifiable neurolog-ical dysfunction. The prognosis for any individual child, however, cannot be predicted with certainty.

EVALUATING INFORMATION IN CASES OF LEARNING DISABILITY

A thorough assessment should provide you with information about the child's developmental history and family background; medical history; educational history, including current educational performance; level of intelligence; language abilities; mathematical abilities; written expression abilities; motor abilities; and behavioral and social skills. Table 21-2 in Chapter 21 of *Assessment of Children: Cognitive Applications* provides a list of questions to help you evaluate the information you obtained from the assessment. Table 12-18 lists additional questions that focus on learning disabilities. Always try to account for any inconsistencies between the formal results of the psychoeducational evaluation and other information that you have obtained.

COMMENT ON THE ASSESSMENT OF LEARNING DISABILITIES

Reading, mathematics, and written expression are complex cognitive activities influenced by (a) biological factors (including intellectual ability, auditory and visual processing, and memory), (b) affective and nonintellectual factors (including motivation, self-concept, and degree of confidence in

Table 12-18
Additional Questions to Consider in Cases of Learning Disability

Language and Cognition

1. How does the child's expressive language compare with his or her receptive language?
2. Does the child know who he or she is (i.e., oriented to person)?
3. Does the child know where he or she is (i.e., oriented to place)?
4. Does the child know the day and time (i.e., oriented to time)?
5. Does the child think clearly and identify and label thoughts and feelings accurately?
6. Does the child show awareness of any deficits?
7. Does the child set a goal, formulate a realistic plan of action given his or her limits and capacities, and carry out the practical steps in completing the plan?
8. Can the child distinguish relevant from irrelevant facts?
9. Does the child follow the appropriate sequence in completing tasks of daily living, such as dressing, eating, brushing teeth, going to the bathroom, and getting ready for sleep?

Information-Processing Skills

10. Does the child respond effectively when confronted with problems or circumstances that are unfamiliar?
11. Does the child ask for clarification of instructions when needed?
12. Does the child function in unstructured situations by assessing what is needed, bringing order and organization, and initiating an appropriate plan of action?
13. Does the child demonstrate a capacity to engage in productive activities on a regular basis (especially at home) when these are not planned or initiated for him or her by others?
14. Can the child accurately assess the situation at hand?
15. Can the child identify the roles of others in his or her environment?
16. Can the child generalize from one situation to another?
17. Can the child take in information from conversation or reading without losing track of the information?
18. Does the child need to work more slowly or to hear or see one thing at a time in order to stay on track?
19. Can the child sustain attention or concentration when mental processing is required, such as when reading or doing mental arithmetic?
20. Can the child shift back and forth between two or more tasks without becoming overwhelmed or confused?
21. Does the child return to the task at hand spontaneously, without losing track, when he or she is distracted or interrupted?
22. What environmental factors promote optimal attention for the child?
23. If the child has attention deficits, are they associated with any excessive motor activity (e.g., restlessness, squirming, fidgeting, impulsiveness)?

Memory

24. Does the child find it difficult to remember names of either new or familiar people?
25. Does the child fail to keep appointments or do things because he or she forgets?
26. Does the child lose his or her way going to familiar places?

27. Does the child tend to forget things to which he or she does not pay conscious attention?
28. Does the child become confused if there are too many things to remember?
29. Is the child aware of memory problems, and does he or she compensate by consciously increasing attention or writing things down?
30. How do the child's verbal and visual memory compare?
31. How do the child's immediate and delayed memory compare?

Interventions

32. Does it seem likely that the child will benefit from training in specific areas of deficit?
33. Could the child benefit from cuing, invoking and executing routines when cued?
34. What are the child's reward preferences?
35. Does it seem likely that the child will benefit from incentives?

Study Habits

36. Does the child seek information before undertaking an assignment?
37. Does the child keep notes of lectures?
38. Does the child write down homework assignments and refer to these notes later?
39. Does the child review his or her test results?
40. Does the child study material by reviewing it several times and rehearsing the answers?
41. Does the child seek help with school work from peers, teachers, siblings, parents, or other adults?
42. Does the child read textbooks, study them, reread notes, or review prior tests in preparing for upcoming tests?

Social and Interpersonal Skills

43. What is the child's ability to understand facial expressions and other nonverbal forms of communications?
44. What is the child's ability to profit from experience in social situations?
45. Can the child place himself or herself in the position of others and see another's point of view?
46. What is the overall quality of the child's interpersonal behavior (e.g., relationships with family members, peers, teachers, relatives, professionals)?
47. Does the child engage in prosocial behavior (e.g., cooperative behavior, mature behavior, age-appropriate behavior, harmonious behavior, pleasant behavior)?
48. Does the child engage in asocial behavior (e.g., passive behavior, withdrawn behavior, defensive behavior, immature behavior, age-inappropriate behavior)?
49. Does the child engage in antisocial behavior (e.g., aggressive behavior, disruptive behavior, hostility, dishonesty)?
50. Can the child perceive and interpret the actions, intentions, and feelings of others?
51. How does the child respond to feedback and correction from others?
52. Does the child respond to subtle interpersonal cues (e.g., facial expressions, tone of voice, volume, vocal inflections)?

(Continued)

Table 12-18 *(Continued)*

53. Can the child work in groups and conform to changing roles in group situations?
54. Have the child's interpersonal relations changed as he or she has developed? If so, in what way?

Personality and Temperament

55. How does the child feel about himself or herself (e.g., makes remarks that indicate a positive or negative self-concept, makes apologetic statements)?
56. Does the child act impulsively? If so, in what situations?
57. Does the child become angry easily? If so, in what situations?
58. Does the child irritate others? If so, whom does the child irritate and when does it happen?

59. What is the child's response to frustration?
60. Does the child engage in anomalous behavior (e.g., making loud vocalizations, grunting, displaying tics or facial twitches, engaging in repetitive or compulsive behaviors, picking at or playing with body)?
61. How does the child respond if he or she becomes exceedingly upset or angry?
62. Does the child show rapid fluctuation in mood without environmental cause, frequent tearfulness, or situationally inappropriate affect (e.g., laughing at serious subjects, lacking emotional reactions to events that others react to)?
63. What factors precipitate, alleviate, or aggravate the child's affect or cause changes in the child's affect?

Note. These questions supplement those in Table 21-2 (page 683) in Chapter 21 of *Assessment of Children: Cognitive Applications.*

one's ability to influence learning outcomes), and (c) environmental factors (including early literacy experiences and other language and cultural experiences). When you evaluate a child for suspected learning disability, you must consider all of these factors in order to properly identify any disability and develop effective interventions. Unfortunately, the diagnosis of learning disability remains problematic because of the ambiguity of the federal definition (and other definitions as well), variability in the interpretation of the federal definition at state and local levels, the heterogeneity of the nature and manifestation of learning disabilities, co-occurrence with other disabilities, and problems with current assessment tools.

Despite these difficulties, the available techniques for the assessment of learning disabilities provide valuable information about important areas of cognitive and academic functioning. There is much wisdom in Christensen's (1992) observation that "the way ahead does not lie in the continued search for the 'true' child with a learning disability, but rather in a search for specific instructional solutions to reading failure and other learning difficulties regardless of whether the child is developmentally delayed, economically disadvantaged, from a racial or cultural minority, or a Euro American, middle-class male" (p. 278, with changes in notation).

INTERVENTIONS FOR LEARNING DISABILITIES

Although learning disabilities may have a biological basis, this does not mean that improvement is not possible. In addition to biological factors, other factors involved in the development of learning disabilities may include poor early language development, poor phonics instruction, poor mathematics instruction, poor written expression instruction, and poor spelling instruction. Inadequate or inappropriate instruction will likely increase the number of students with potential learning disabilities who actually develop learning disabilities.

A study (Kavale & Reese, 1992) of initial individualized educational programs (IEPs) indicated the following:

- About 75% included reading goals.
- About 40% included mathematics and written expression goals.
- About 15% included spelling and learning skills goals.
- About 10% or less included other goals (e.g., oral expression, social, handwriting, behavioral, listening, fine-motor, visual perception, gross motor, auditory perception, sensori-motor integration, career/vocational, and independent living skills).

When IEPs of the same children were examined in later years, the same emphasis was found on reading and mathematics, but there was increased attention to spelling (about 25% of the cases), written expression (about 60% of the cases), and study/learning skills (about 25% of the cases) and the incidence of career/vocational education goals had risen from about 1% to 9% of the cases. The change in IEPs over time reflects an increasing focus on language arts activities and personal development options.

According to the IDEA '99 (see Chapter 3 in *Assessment of Children: Cognitive Applications*), before a child can receive special education services for a learning disability, classroom interventions must have been attempted. Table 12-19 provides examples of reading and mathematics interventions that are used in regular classrooms.

The most effective interventions for children with learning disabilities are multifaceted. They involve the use of cognitive, linguistic, and behavioral-cognitive methods.

Cognitive Methods

Metacognition refers to awareness of one's own cognitive processes and of one's own self-regulation, or what may be termed "knowing about knowing." Teaching children with learning disabilities to use strategies—such as planning, monitoring, self-pacing, approaching tasks in alternative ways, and checking their work—can increase their awareness

---

Table 12-19
Examples of Reading and Math Interventions in General Education

General Reading Weakness
- Whole-group reading/language arts instruction by the regular teacher
- Small-group reading instruction by the regular teacher, using materials at the student's level

Decoding Skills Weaknesses
- Small-group phonemic awareness instruction
- Small-group or individualized multisensory code-based instruction
- Synthetic phonics instruction (part-to-whole)
- Analytic phonics instruction (whole-to-part)
- Small-group or individualized literature-based instruction that includes semantic and syntactic cues
- Daily fluency practice provided in decodable texts, as well as rich and interesting texts at the student's independent reading level
- Daily opportunities to write, using skills emphasized in lessons

Comprehension Weaknesses
- Using texts of interest to students for instruction
- Small-group instruction in active reading and comprehension strategies—including semantic, graphophonic, and syntactic cue systems
- Vocabulary building
- Daily opportunities to write, using higher-order thinking skills

Mathematics Weaknesses
- Making appropriate technology (e.g., calculator, computer) available, as needed
- Regular opportunities for both guided and independent practice
- Classroom instruction that incorporates real-world examples as well as the student's personal experiences and language
- Using manipulative materials to foster the development of abstract concepts
- Individual or small-group direct instruction to re-teach weak skills

---

Source: Adapted from the Connecticut State Department of Education (1999).

- Go back and read things over again, as needed, to understand the material
- Stop while reading and try to guess what will happen next
- Take notes, underline words, or try to imagine themselves in the story while they read
- Think about what the sentences mean and how they go together
- Recognize that a memory failure occurred (e.g., "I'll have to go back to find the names of the first four presidents")
- Recognize when there is a discrepancy between a heading in the text and the information they obtained (e.g., "I only found two descriptions of countries when the text heading indicated that there were three")
- Recognize when the material was not completely mastered (e.g., "I think I'll reread the last paragraph")
- Determine when some parts of the text are more difficult to read than others (e.g., "I'll have to read this part more slowly than that part")
- Recognize that there is a need to evaluate what was learned (e.g., "I'm going to quiz myself when I finish reading this section")
- Recognize when the environment is distracting (e.g., "I'll have to move to another location because I can't read too well with so much noise")

Children who acquire these metacognitive skills should become more effective learners. Children must come to believe that effort, ability, and choice of strategy—not just luck—are responsible for their success.

Linguistic Methods

In their areas of weaknesses, children may be given special help, tied to a content-based curriculum. If they have a reading disorder, for example, they may be given "highly structured programs that explicitly teach application of phonological rules to print.... [Research shows that] systematic phonics

---

of task demands, their use of appropriate strategies to ease task completion, and their ability to monitor the success of their efforts (Borkowski, Day, Saenz, Dietmeyer, Estrada, & Groteluschen, 1992; Lyon & Moats, 1988; Taylor, 1988a).

Learning to do the following will help children master metacognitive strategies (Billingsley & Wildman, 1990; Garner, 1987):

- Understand that information in a text is of varying importance
- Recognize that text organization can affect comprehension
- Be aware of clues or signals during the task that tell them that they may not be understanding the material
- Understand that prior knowledge affects their comprehension of material

"Your feelings of insecurity seem to have started when Mary Lou Gurnblatt said, 'Maybe I don't have a learning disability—maybe you have a teaching disability.'"

Courtesy of Tony Saltzman.

Table 12-20
Guidelines for Designing Instructional Programs for Children with Learning Disabilities

1. Break large tasks into subtasks and subskills, and organize the subtasks into teachable units.
2. Arrange the tasks in a hierarchy from simple to more complex skills.
3. Obtain a base-line level of performance before the intervention takes place, using explicit step-by-step instructions to ensure that children understand what is required.
4. Use performance incentives to increase the rate and consistency with which children apply strategies already in their repertoire. Do not expect incentives to alter the way children process information.
5. Use orienting procedures—such as telling children to recall words or pictures by categories—to help children retain information or concepts.
6. Teach children strategies that will improve their performance, including the following:

   • Highly specific strategies that apply to one type of task only
   • Mnemonic strategies—such as verbal rehearsal, self-testing, and the generation of meaningful or vivid associations between items—to aid retention in memory
   • Other school-related strategies, such as strategies for note-taking, planning, and test-taking
   • Broad control processes involved in problem solving, such as (a) awareness of one's own cognitive processes or reflective problem-solving activities (e.g., attacking the problem in an orderly fashion with a question such as "Where do I begin?" or "Is there a problem that needs solving?"), (b) self-monitoring of results ("Does this outcome make sense?" or "What past solution efforts were effective or ineffective?"), and (c) searching for alternative procedures ("What should I try now?").

7. Teach phoneme awareness, including the connections between sound segments and letters, to children with reading disabilities. Procedures include learning to (a) count the number of syllables in words ("Say the word *telephone* and then tap the number of syllables in it") (b) recognize syllables in words ("Raise your hand when you hear *er* in a word— *apartment, singer*"), and (c) recognize phonemes ("Raise your hand when you hear a word that has an \a\ sound in it—*sit, hat, flap*"). These tasks can be repeated several times with different words, syllables, and phonemes.
8. Teach children word awareness skills. Procedures include (a) activities that stress word-referent differentiation ("Is train [toe, crocodile] a long or short word?"), (b) word counts ("Say and then count the words in this sentence: *The fire alarm rang and everyone left the building*"), (c) word recognition ("Raise your hand when you hear the word *the* in this sentence: *The boy ran quickly away from the barking dog*"), (d) and word deletion and/or substitution ("Change the word *happy* in this sentence: *The happy child ran to see her friend*").
9. Teach children form or syntactic/semantic awareness skills. Procedures include learning to (a) make judgments about the adequacy of sentences ("Is this a good sentence or a bad sentence: *She is my older brother?*"), (b) detect ambiguity ("Tell me what this sentence means: *They are eating apples*"), and (c) complete sentences ("Fill in the missing word: *John buys milk at the _____* [or] *The thief is stealing computers; these are the computers that he _____*").

10. Teach children pragmatic awareness skills. Procedures include having to (a) role play, (b) retell a story to a very young child or to a blind child, (c) judge whether someone's story is "good" (logically consistent) or "silly" (logically inconsistent) when playing story-telling games with other students, and (d) judge whether a reading passage is difficult or easy.
11. Teach children to recognize how a text is organized into main and subordinate parts. Procedures include having to find and explain the role of the chapter title, major and minor headings, boldface words or terms, words in italics, the summary, appendixes, references, the glossary, etc.
12. Allow children to use a computer or type or dictate their writing assignments if they have trouble writing, and encourage the use of a word-processing program; work on penmanship separately.
13. Give children teacher-prepared worksheets, rather than asking them to copy material from the board or textbook.
14. Teach children note-taking skills if they are having problems listening or taking notes.
15. Help children identify the steps needed to complete a long-term assignment and to estimate accurately how much time each step must be given. Ask the children to create a schedule for completion of each step, breaking work down into night-by-night assignments.
16. Teach children organizational skills (e.g., organizing papers in separate folders by subject; making "to do" lists, including homework; creating an uncluttered work space) and basic principles of completing homework in a timely manner. Work on budgeting time and managing both short-term and long-term assignments.
17. Teach test-taking strategies (e.g., narrowing down possibilities in multiple-choice tests, deciding what and how to study, and going over sample questions in advance).
18. Provide children with explicit feedback on their performance.
19. Measure the children's performance regularly, and compare the results to base-line data in order to assess the effectiveness of the teaching techniques and materials.
20. Ask children what has helped them in the past or what they think might help them in the future.
21. Set a tone that helps children view themselves as competent learners with special academic needs. This includes helping them overcome fear of failure, develop confidence in their ability to do tasks that are at their current level of performance, and cultivate the ability to approach tasks in a planful and reflective manner while looking for meaning in the task. Also, provide experiences that give children an opportunity to succeed.
22. Provide emotional support when children become frustrated.
23. Use multisensory techniques. For example, if directions are given verbally, also provide a written handout.
24. Try to link new ideas and concepts with those children already understand.
25. Provide praise and reinforcement for even small amounts of success. Consider developing a token economy system for children with learning disabilities who also have behavior problems.
26. Help children to recognize that their teachers and parents are their allies and educational partners.
27. Use the results of the assessment as a guide in selecting new teaching techniques and materials.

Source: Adapted from Ball (1993), Borkowski, Schneider, and Pressley (1989), Bryen and Gerber (1987), Busch (1993), Hagen et al. (1982), and Torgesen (1982a, b).

instruction results in more favorable outcomes for disabled readers than does a context-emphasis (whole language) approach" (Lyon, 1996b, p. 65).

Behavioral-Cognitive Methods

Behavioral-cognitive interventions may be needed to improve the social and behavioral adjustment of children with learning disabilities, because they may be more anxious and unhappy, be less liked, and have lower expectations for academic success than their peers who do not have learning disabilities (Casey, Levy, Brown, & Brooks-Gunn, 1992). Interventions should be designed to reduce their frustrations both at school and at home. Children with learning disabilities also may be taught to recognize their strengths and weaknesses, to adjust their expectations accordingly, and to use their strengths to compensate for their weaknesses.

Instructional Programs

Instructional programs should be designed to help children with learning disabilities acquire problem-solving skills, mnemonic strategies, and effective study habits. These strategies should be made part of their repertoire of learning skills through step-by-step instruction and generalization training. Instructional programs must begin with a careful analysis of task functions. Table 12-20 (see page 324) provides guidelines for designing and evaluating instructional programs.

Children with learning disabilities need to understand the implications of failure and that they can learn from their failures (Borkowski, Estrada, Milstead, & Hale, 1989):

Rarely in our classrooms do we emphasize that failure can result in something constructive—that failure can be a unique opportunity to obtain feedback about the appropriateness and effectiveness of strategic-based efforts. We praise successful performance without acknowledging that success is often the result of a series of failures. In intervention programs, therefore, children with a learning disability need to (a) encounter carefully monitored success as well as failure situations; (b) be explicitly shown how information gathered from unsuccessful outcomes can be used to enhance success on subsequent tasks; and (c) learn to "depersonalize" failure experiences as much as possible.

Training children with a learning disability to become spontaneous, strategic, and planful learners is a complex and challenging task that requires instruction at both cognitive and motivational levels. In addition to stressing the role of effort, intervention programs must also provide the child with a learning disability with strategically oriented metacognitive skills that, when applied to academic situations, will result in successful outcomes and enhanced feelings of self-efficacy and self-esteem. (p. 68, with changes in notation)

Preparation for the World of College and Work

Older adolescents with learning disabilities who are entering colleges and universities may need help first in finding schools that meet their needs and have appropriate support services and then in filling out applications. And adolescents entering the work force need to learn how to obtain and maintain a job. They may need guidance in the following areas:

- Getting job training
- Finding a job
- Reading employment ads
- Filling out job applications
- Interviewing
- Following directions on the job
- Learning job skills
- Taking criticism
- Finishing work on time
- Paying attention on the job
- Working carefully

Role playing, tutorials, supervised job training, and other similar interventions may help them improve their chances of success in the world of work. The IDEA requires that future concerns of adolescents with learning disabilities be addressed when the adolescents reach the age of 14 years and that a transition plan be developed when they reach 16 years (see Chapter 3 in *Assessment of Children: Cognitive Applications*). Table 12-21 presents definitions of terms associated with learning disabilities.

PEANUTS reprinted by permission of United Feature Syndicate, Inc.

Table 12-21
Terms Related to Learning Disabilities

Accommodations. Techniques and materials that allow individuals with learning disabilities to complete school or work tasks with greater ease and effectiveness. Examples include spell-check programs, tape recorders, and expanded time for completing assignments.

Achievement test. An examination that measures educationally relevant skills or knowledge in such subjects as reading, spelling, or mathematics.

Acquired dyslexia. Loss of previously acquired reading ability, usually as a result of a traumatic brain injury or a disease that affects the brain.

Age norms. Values representing typical or average performance of people in certain age groups.

Alexia. A mixed type of reading disability involving deficits in both phonological decoding and whole-word recognition.

Assistive technology. Equipment used to maintain or improve the functional capabilities of individuals with disabilities.

Attention span. The length of time an individual can concentrate on a task without being distracted or losing interest.

Auditory comprehension. Ability to understand what is heard.

Auditory discrimination. Ability to detect differences among sounds, such as differences between the sounds made by a cat and a dog or differences between the sounds of the letters *m* and *n*.

Auditory memory. Ability to retain information that has been presented orally. Short-term auditory memory is used to recall information presented several seconds before, long-term auditory memory is used to recall information presented more than a minute before, and sequential auditory memory is used to recall a series of items in proper order.

Auditory perception. Hearing and interpretation of sounds.

Augmentative communication. Any procedure by which people with severe expressive difficulties compensate for their communication limitations, including use of sign language, gestures, fingerspelling, or a computer or keyboard. Also known as *alternative communication*.

Basic skill area. A subject such as reading, writing, spelling, or mathematics.

Battery. A group of tests administered to an individual or group.

Behavior modification. A technique intended to change behavior by rewarding desirable behavior and ignoring undesirable behavior.

Channel. The route through which the content of a communication flows, such as the auditory-vocal channel. A channel includes both expressive and receptive components.

Cloze procedure. A type of reading assessment procedure requiring the examinee to fill in missing words in sentences.

Cognitive ability. Intellectual ability; thinking and reasoning skills.

Cognitive style. A person's typical approach to learning and problem solving.

Compensation. Process by which a person is taught to cope with his or her learning problems and to develop alternative ways of learning and solving problems.

Conceptual disorder. Disturbances in thinking, reasoning, generalizing, or memorizing.

Conceptualization. The process of forming a general idea from what is observed—for example, seeing apples, bananas, and oranges and recognizing that they are all fruit.

Confidential file. In education, a record maintained by a school to which access is limited, usually containing evaluations conducted to determine whether a student is disabled and other information related to the student's school performance. Parents have a right to inspect this file and have copies of any information contained in it.

Configuration. The visual shape or form of words. The configuration may be used as a cue in word attack skills.

Congenital. Existing at birth or before birth.

Co-occurring disorder. A psychological disorder that tends to occur with another psychological disorder. Also called a *comorbid disorder*.

Coordination. The harmonious functioning of muscles in the body to perform complex movements.

Criterion-referenced test. A test designed to provide information on specific knowledge or skills possessed by a student. Such a test usually covers a relatively small unit of content and is closely related to instruction. Scores on criterion-referenced tests are interpreted in terms of what the student knows or can do, rather than in relation to a reference group.

Critical comprehension. Evaluating the quality of a reading selection, including its adequacy, worth, appropriateness, and desirability.

Cross-categorical. Refers to a system in which a teacher addresses more than one handicapping condition within one instructional period.

Cross dominance. A condition in which the preferred eye, hand, and foot are not all on the same side of the body. For example, a person may be right-footed and right-eyed but left-handed. Also called *mixed dominance*.

Cross-modality perception. Process by which a certain stimulus acquires meaning through the use of more than one sensory modality.

Cumulative file. In education, a general file maintained by the school for any student enrolled in the school. Parents have a right to inspect the file and have copies of any information contained in it.

Decoding. Process of getting meaning from written or spoken symbols.

Developmental delay. Lag in the development of cognitive, physical, communicative, social/emotional, or adaptive behavior. Also called *developmental lag*.

Developmental disability. Chronic, severe disability that (a) results from a mental or physical impairment, (b) begins before age 22, (c) is likely to be lifelong, (d) results in major limitations in everyday functioning, such as self-care, language, learning, mobility, self-direction, capacity for independent living, and economic self-sufficiency, and (e) reflects a need for special services that are individually planned and coordinated. Examples of developmental disabilities are cerebral palsy, mental retardation, Down syndrome, autism, epilepsy, deafness, blindness, serious learning disabilities, and spina bifida.

Developmental dyslexia. Difficulty learning to read.

Developmental language disorder. Disorder in children in which language development is late in onset.

Diagnostic test. A test designed to determine the specific learning needs of an individual.

(Continued)

Table 12-21 *(Continued)*

Direct instruction. An approach to instruction in academic subjects that emphasizes carefully sequenced steps, including demonstration, modeling, guided practice, and independent application.

Directional confusion. Tendency to make reversals and substitutions because of left-right confusion.

Directionality. Ability to distinguish direction and orientation, such as right from left, up from down, and forward from backward.

Disability. A mental or physical condition that restricts an individual's ability to engage in substantial gainful activity.

Discrepancy criterion. The requirement that a student must have a severe discrepancy between achievement and intellectual ability in one or more expressive or receptive skills—such as written expression, listening and reading comprehension, or mathematics—in order to receive a diagnosis of learning disability.

Discrimination. Process of detecting differences between stimuli.

Disfluency. Incomplete phrases or other speech difficulties that impair conversational speech.

Disinhibition. Lack of restraint in responding to a situation.

Distractibility. The shifting of attention from the task at hand to sounds, sights, and other stimuli that normally occur in the environment.

Domain-referenced test. A test in which performance is measured against a well-defined set of tasks or body of knowledge (domain). Domain-referenced tests are a specific subset of criterion-referenced tests that have a similar purpose.

Dysarthria. A disorder of the speech muscles that affects the ability to pronounce words.

Dyscalculia. Difficulty in understanding or using mathematical symbols or functions. A child with dyscalculia may be able to read and write but have difficulty performing mathematical calculations.

Dyseidetic reading disability. A visual type of reading disability in which there is a deficiency in whole-word recognition.

Dysfunction. Any disturbance or impairment in the normal functioning of an organ or body part.

Dysgraphia. Difficulty in producing legible handwriting with age-appropriate speed.

Dyslalia. Impaired speech ability.

Dyslexia. Impaired ability to read or to understand what one reads, either silently or aloud.

Dysnomia. Difficulty in remembering names or recalling appropriate words to use in a given context.

Dysphonetic reading disability. An auditory type of reading disability in which there is a deficiency in phonological decoding.

Dyspraxia. Difficulty in performing fine motor acts such as drawing and buttoning. A person with dyspraxia has difficulty producing and sequencing the movements necessary to perform these kinds of tasks.

Early intervention. An attempt to locate, identify, and evaluate young children with developmental disabilities or developmental delays and provide needed services.

Encoding process. Registering of events in memory.

Etiology. Source of origin of a disorder.

Expressive language. Communication through writing, speaking, or gestures.

Expressive language disability. A disability characterized by limited vocabulary, deficits in expressive grammar, and deficits in pragmatic use of language.

Eye-hand coordination. Ability of the eyes and hands to work together to complete a task such as drawing or writing.

Far-point copying. Writing while copying from a model some distance away—for example, copying from the blackboard.

Figure-ground discrimination. Ability to sort out information from the surrounding environment—for example, to listen to a teacher's voice while ignoring noises or to locate a figure in a group of figures.

Fine-motor skills. Use of small muscles for precision tasks, such as writing, tying bows, zipping a zipper, typing, and doing puzzles.

Grade equivalent. The estimated grade level corresponding to a given score.

Grapheme. Written representation of a phoneme.

Graphesthesia. Sense through which outlines, numbers, words, or symbols traced or written on the skin are recognized.

Graphic word features. Particular visual patterns of words that are formed by the unique array of letters that comprise words.

Gross motor skills. Use of large muscles for activities requiring strength and balance, such as walking, running, and jumping.

Handicapped. Describes any person with a physical or mental disability who has difficulty in performing certain tasks such as walking, seeing, hearing, speaking, learning, or working. Federal law defines children with handicaps as those who are mentally retarded, hard of hearing, deaf, speech impaired, visually handicapped, seriously emotionally disturbed, orthopedically impaired, other health impaired, blind, or multihandicapped or have specific learning disabilities and require special educational services because of these disabilities.

Haptic sense. Combined kinesthetic and tactile sense.

Homophones. Words that have different spellings and meanings but the same pronunciation.

Hyperlexia. A precocious ability to recognize written words, beyond what would be expected given the individual's general level of intellectual development.

Impulsivity. Reacting to a situation without considering the consequences.

Inclusion. The set of practices designed to implement the belief that all children should be educated, regardless of disability, in their neighborhood school and in age-appropriate general education settings with appropriate supports and services.

Individualized education plan (IEP). Written plan that identifies a student's strengths, weaknesses, educational needs, and needs for related services. The Individuals with Disabilities Education Act (IDEA) mandates that an IEP be developed for each school-aged child (beginning at age 3) who is eligible for special education and related services and that the plan be reviewed at least annually.

Individuals with Disabilities Education Act (IDEA). Federal law designed to provide assistance to children with disabilities in school.

Inferential comprehension. Using the information directly contained in a reading selection to formulate inferences and hypotheses, including cause-and-effect relationships, comparisons, and sequences.

Informal test. A nonstandardized test designed to give an approximate index of an individual's level of ability.

Insertion. The addition of letters or numbers that do not belong in a word or numeral—for example, writing *sinceare* for *sincere*.

(Continued)

Table 12-21 *(Continued)*

Intelligence. Ability to deal with abstractions, to learn, and to cope with novel situations.

Intelligence test. Psychological test designed to measure cognitive functions, such as reasoning, comprehension, and judgment.

Inversion. Confusion of up-down directionality of letters or numbers—for example, writing *m* for *w* or *6* for *9*.

Itinerant teacher. Teacher who is shared by more than one school.

Kinesthetic. Pertaining to the muscles.

Kinesthetic method. Approach to treating reading disorder in which visual and auditory stimuli are supplemented by the systematic incorporation of muscle movement (as by tracing the outlines of words).

Language. System that gives meaning to speech sounds or written configurations. Understanding, thinking, talking, reading, and writing all involve language.

Language and speech program. Program for students who have articulation, voice, fluency, or language disorders.

Lateral confusion. Inability to distinguish left from right.

Lateral dominance. Preferential dominance of one side of the body. Also called *laterality.*

Learned helplessness. A tendency to be a passive learner who depends on others for decisions and guidance.

Learning disability. Disorder in one or more of the basic psychological processes involved in understanding or using spoken or written language. A learning disability may manifest itself in an impaired ability to listen, think, speak, read, write, spell, or do mathematical calculations. Students with learning disabilities have a severe discrepancy between intellectual ability and achievement in one or more academic areas.

Learning strategy approaches. Techniques for organizing, interacting with, memorizing, and monitoring material.

Learning style. The channels—such as vision, hearing, movement, touching, or any combination of these—through which a person best understands and retains learning; also, temperament, as in an active or passive learning style or a reflective or impulsive learning style.

Least restrictive environment (LRE). Educational setting that gives the student as much involvement in regular education as is appropriate to his or her abilities.

Literal comprehension. Understanding the information that is directly contained in the reading selection.

Locus of control. How a person tends to attribute successes and difficulties—either internally to factors such as effort or externally to factors such as chance.

Mainstreaming. The practice of placing students with disabilities who have special educational needs into regular classrooms for at least a part of their school program.

Maturation lag. Delayed maturity in one or several skills or areas of development.

Mental age. The age at which a given score on an ability test is average or normal. The term is most appropriately used at ages at which mental growth is most rapid, usually from birth to about age 13 to 15 years.

Mental status interview. Interview conducted to evaluate appearance and behavior, speech and communications, content of thought, sensory and motor functioning, cognitive functioning, temperament and emotional functioning, and insight and judgment. It may be part of the intake interview.

Metacognition. Awareness of one's own cognitive processes and of one's own self-regulation, or what may be termed "knowing about knowing."

Metacognitive learning. Instructional approaches emphasizing awareness of the cognitive processes that facilitate one's own learning and application of these processes to academic and work assignments.

Mild learning disabilities. Slight perceptual-conceptual deviations that impair the ability of children to process information effectively.

Mixed dominance theory. Hypothesis that language disorders may be due to the fact that one cerebral hemisphere does not consistently lead the other in the control of sensorimotor functioning, perception, or body movements.

Mixed laterality. Tendency to perform some acts with a right-side preference and others with a left-side preference.

Mixed receptive-expressive language disability. A language disability characterized by problems with both receptive language (e.g., understanding language) and expressive language (e.g., writing or speaking).

Modality. The sensory channel used to acquire information—for example, the visual, auditory, tactile, kinesthetic, olfactory (odors), or gustatory (taste) channel.

Modified self-contained class. A self-contained class in which students receive instruction from a regular education teacher for some part of the school day.

Motor. Pertaining to the origin or execution of muscular activity.

Multi-categorical class. A special education classroom in which students with more than one disability are assigned to a special education teacher.

Multidisciplinary team. In education, a group, made up of a student's classroom teacher and several educational specialists, that evaluates the student's disability and prepares an individualized education plan (IEP) for the student.

Multisensory. Involving most or all of the senses.

Multisensory learning. An instructional approach in which auditory, visual, and tactile elements are used in learning a task. For example, students might trace sandpaper numbers while saying a number fact aloud.

Near-point copying. Writing while copying from a model close at hand—for example, copying from a textbook.

Neurobehavioral. Related to neurological functioning and behavior.

Neurocognitive. Related to neurological functioning and cognitive processing.

Neurological examination. Assessment of sensory and motor responses, especially reflexes, to determine whether the nervous system is impaired.

Neurologically based communication disorders. Speech, language, or voice disorders caused by injury or illness affecting the brain or other portions of the nervous system.

Neuropsychological evaluation. Assessment designed to draw inferences about the functioning of the cerebral hemispheres and to identify the adaptive strengths and weaknesses of children with brain injuries. It complements a neurological examination by providing a profile of cognitive ability, sensorimotor functioning, and affective reactions.

Noncategorical. Refers to a system of grouping students with disabilities together, without reference to a particular label or category of exceptionality.

(Continued)

Table 12-21 *(Continued)*

Nonverbal learning disabilities. Syndrome in which children may have difficulty with tactile perception, psychomotor coordination, visual-spatial organization, nonverbal problem solving, reading comprehension, mathematics, and social relations but not with rote memory, word decoding, and writing.

Norm. Performance standard established by a reference group. Usually norms are determined by testing a representative group and then calculating standard scores for the group's test performance.

Norm-referenced test. An objective test standardized on a group of individuals whose performance is evaluated in relation to the performance of others. Contrasts with *criterion-referenced test*.

Orthographic decoding. Recognizing letter sequences or words based on their visual features.

Orthographic word features. Internal features of a word, including structural regularities and letter-sound correspondences.

Perception. Process whereby sensory stimuli are organized, interpreted, and imbued with a meaning dependent on the past experiences of the individual.

Perceptual abilities. The abilities to process, organize, and interpret information obtained by the five senses.

Perceptual disorder. Difficulty in accurately processing, organizing, and discriminating among visual, auditory, or tactile information. A person with a perceptual handicap may say that *cap* and *cup* sound the same or that *b* and *d* look the same.

Perceptual-motor. Relating to the interaction of the various channels of perception with motor activity.

Perceptual speed. The rate at which an individual performs acts involving vision. It may refer to how fast something is copied or manipulated (motor speed) or how quickly identical items in a given series are identified (visual discrimination).

Perseveration. The repeating of words, motions, or tasks. A child who perseverates often has difficulty shifting to a new task and continues working on an old task long after classmates have stopped.

Phonetic decoding. Reading visually presented words.

Phonetics. Study of articulatory and acoustic specification of speech sounds.

Phonics approach. Method for teaching reading and spelling in which the emphasis is on learning the sounds that letters and their combinations make. In decoding a word, the child sounds out individual letters or letter combinations and then blends them to form a word.

Phonologic word features. The particular sound characteristics of words, defined by the unique ordering of vowels and consonants (i.e., phonemes) that comprise given words.

Phonological processing. Detecting and interpreting the phonemes (or speech sounds) that comprise oral language.

Pictographic system. A writing system in which individual characters generally stand for whole words.

Pragmatic awareness. The ability to detect inconsistencies between sentences, recognize message inadequacy, understand and repair communication failures, and be aware of the overall message.

Pre-referral process. A procedure in which special and regular teachers develop trial strategies to help a student who is having difficulty learning, so that the student can remain in the regular classroom.

Psychoeducational diagnostician. Specialist in education who diagnoses and evaluates children who are having difficulty learning.

Psychological evaluation. Assessment of an individual, usually consisting of the administration of a battery of psychological tests, an interview, and a behavioral observation.

Psychomotor. Pertaining to the motor effects of psychological processes. Performance on psychomotor tests may depend on perceptual-motor coordination.

Rapid decoding. Recognizing words quickly and automatically.

Raw score. The number of items answered correctly on a test.

Readiness. The degree to which an individual has acquired the skills considered prerequisite for academic learning.

Reading comprehension. Ability to understand the printed or written word.

Reading disorder. The most frequent form of learning disability, characterized by difficulty in reading.

Reasoning ability. Generally, nonverbal, deductive, inductive, analytical thinking.

Reauditorization. Ability to recall the names or sounds of visual symbols (letters).

Receptive language. Language that is spoken or written by others and received by the individual. The receptive language skills are listening and reading.

Regrouping. In arithmetic, the process known as carrying in addition or borrowing in subtraction.

Regular education. All education not included under special education.

Remediation. Process by which an individual is provided with instruction and practice in skills that are weak or nonexistent in an effort to strengthen or develop these skills.

Resource program. An instructional program in which a student with a learning disability is enrolled in a regular classroom for most of each day, but also receives regularly scheduled individual services in a specialized resource classroom.

Resource room. An instructional setting where a special education student goes for specified periods of time on a regularly scheduled basis.

Resource teacher. A specialist who works with students with disabilities and who may also act as a consultant to other teachers.

Reversal. Difficulty in reading or reproducing letters alone, letters in words, or words in sentences in their proper position in space or in proper order; also, reversal of mathematical concepts and symbols.

Self-concept. How a person feels and thinks about himself or herself. Also called *self-image*.

Self-contained classroom. Special class for specific types of students with disabilities who spend all or the largest portion of the school day in this setting.

Self-monitoring. Procedure in which an individual systematically observes and records aspects of his or her behavior over a specified period of time. Self-monitoring procedures may involve diaries, rating scales, counters, daily charting, or portable monitoring devices.

Semantic word features. The particular concepts or entities symbolized by words.

Semantics. The meaning or understanding given to oral or written language.

Sensorimotor. Pertaining to the relationship between sensation and movement.

(Continued)

Table 12-21 *(Continued)*

Sensory. Relating to the reception of sensation.

Sensory acuity. The ability to respond to sensation at normal levels of intensity.

Sequence. A consecutive ordering of events, numbers, or other information in some fashion, usually in time or space, or with respect to some dimension like size or magnitude.

Sight-word approach. Method of teaching reading that relies on a student's visual memory skills, with minimal emphasis on sounding out words. The student is instructed to memorize the word based on its overall configuration. Also called *whole-word approach.*

Sight words. Words a child can recognize on sight without aid of phonics or other word attack skills.

Sign language. Natural or formal hand-signing system through which units of thought can be communicated.

Slow learner. Child who is performing below grade level.

Soft neurological signs. Symptoms associated with deficiencies in complex behaviors that are considered uncertain indicators of brain damage. Representative soft neurological signs are poor balance, impaired fine motor coordination, clumsiness, slight reflex asymmetries, and choreiform (irregular, jerky) limb movements.

Sound blending. Smoothly combining all the sounds or parts of a word into a whole.

Spatial orientation. An individual's awareness of space around him or her in terms of distance, form, direction, and position.

Spatial relationships. Relationships between the self and two or more objects, as well as relationships of the objects to each other.

Special class approach. Intervention alternative that involves placing children with disabilities who have similar instructional needs in a special class.

Special education. Education provided to students who, because of their abilities (physical, mental, and social) and learning styles, require alternative teaching methods or related support services in order to benefit from the education program.

Specific language disability. A severe difficulty in some aspect of listening, speaking, reading, writing, or spelling, while skills in the other areas are age-appropriate.

Specific learning disability. Disorder in one or more of the basic psychological processes involved in understanding or using language, spoken or written. It may manifest itself in an imperfect ability to listen, think, speak, read, write, spell, or do mathematical calculations.

Speech impairments. Disorders that impair an individual's ability to verbally communicate. This could include the inability to speak, the inability to maintain a flow or rhythm of speech (e.g., dysfluency or stuttering), or the inability to pronounce certain sounds. Speech impairments can be caused by hearing impairments, neurological disorders, mental retardation, or physical impairments such as cleft palate.

Standardized test. A form of measurement that has been normed against a specific population. Standardization is obtained by administering the test to a given population and then calculating means, standard deviation, standardized scores, and percentiles. Equivalent scores are then produced to permit comparison of an individual score to the norm group's performance.

Structural analysis. Using such word features as syllabication, prefix, suffix, and root word clues to read or spell a word.

Structure. Consistent use of rules, limits, and routines in the classroom or at home.

Substitution. Interchanging a given letter, number, or word for another, such as *sereal* for *cereal.*

Subtype. Within the larger population of individuals identified as having the disability, a specific group with common characteristics.

Survival skills. Minimal skills needed to cope with everyday society.

Syndrome. A set of symptoms that indicates a specific disorder.

Syntactic. Pertaining to grammar and the rules governing sentence structure and sequence.

Syntactic errors. Unconventional ordering of words—for example, "My house, well, I live in, well, my house, uh, I live in" for "I live in my house."

Syntactic or semantic awareness. Ability to detect the structural ambiguity in sentences, to correct word order violation, to complete sentences when words are missing, etc.

Syntactic word features. The more abstract qualities of words—those features a word has in common with other words by virtue of grammatical rules. Syntactic classes include nouns, verbs, adjectives, and adverbs.

Syntax. System of rules defining the ways in which different parts of speech may be legitimately combined to form sentences.

Tactile sense. Sense of touch.

Task analysis. Examining a task to discover the elements that comprise it and the processes required to perform it.

Thematic maturity. Ability to write in a logical, organized, efficient, and meaningful manner.

Thinking skills. Skills related to interpreting, organizing, storing, retrieving, and using knowledge.

Transition. A major change, such as from secondary school to a postsecondary program, work, or independent living; from early childhood to school; or from a more specialized to a mainstreamed setting.

Transposition. Confusion of the order of letters in a word or of numerals in a number—for example, writing *sliver* for *silver* or *432 for 423.*

Underachievement. Performance below that predicted by a test.

Visual association. Relating concepts presented visually through pictures or written words.

Visual closure. Identification of a visual stimulus from an incomplete visual presentation.

Visual discrimination. Ability to detect similarities and differences in materials presented visually—for example, to discriminate *h* from *n* or *b* from *d.*

Visual memory. Ability to retain information presented visually.

Visual-motor skills. Ability to translate information received visually into a motor response.

Visual perception. Ability to correctly interpret what is seen.

Visual sequential memory. Ability to reproduce from memory sequences of items that have been presented visually.

Whole-word procedure. Process of learning to read by noting correspondences between a letter string and the spoken representation. Also called *direct procedure.*

Word attack skills. Ability to analyze unfamiliar words visually and phonetically.

Word recognition. Ability to read or pronounce a word by sight.

Working memory. Ability to hold a small amount of material in memory for a short time while simultaneously processing the same or other material.

Written language. All facets of written expression, including handwriting, capitalization, punctuation, spelling, format, and ability to express one's thoughts in sentences.

THINKING THROUGH THE ISSUES

1. What role do you think psychological factors have in the etiology of learning disabilities?
2. Do you think learning disabilities can be easily overcome? Why or why not?
3. Do you think phonological processing is an important skill in learning how to read? Why or why not?
4. Explain why we have not been able to isolate patterns on intelligence tests that differentiate individuals with learning disabilities from other individuals.

SUMMARY

1. It is estimated that approximately 10% to 15% of children in the United States struggle with some form of learning disability.
2. Children with learning disabilities have difficulty processing information in a manner that allows them to comprehend, remember, and generalize concepts relevant to the development of oral language, written language, and mathematical skills.
3. The most common type of learning disability is reading disorder, followed by mathematics disorder and then disorder of written expression (which includes spelling).

Definitions of Learning Disability

4. In the broadest sense, *learning disability* refers to any form of learning difficulty.
5. In the narrow sense, *learning disability* refers to a specific learning disability as defined in the IDEA '99.
6. The IDEA '99 defines learning disability as "a disorder in one or more of the basic psychological processes involved in understanding or in using language, spoken or written, that may manifest itself in an imperfect ability to listen, think, speak, read, write, spell, or to do mathematical calculations, including conditions such as perceptual disabilities, brain injury, minimal brain dysfunction, dyslexia, and developmental aphasia."
7. The definition of learning disability in the IDEA '99 has been criticized for the following reasons: (a) The discrepancy criterion for establishing a learning disability may not be valid, (b) the discrepancy criterion is open to interpretation, which varies from state to state, as do the tests used use to conduct the assessment, (c) the definition includes several ambiguous terms, such as *basic psychological processes,* (d) it is difficult to distinguish between primary and secondary causes, (e) the definition makes it difficult for children with sensory problems, emotional problems, or environmental disadvantages to be identified as learning disabled, (f) the definition does not discuss the heterogeneity of the condition or appropriate interventions, (g) the definition does not explain that learning disabilities may exist concurrently with other conditions, and (h) the definition implies but does not explain the causes of learning disability.
8. The National Joint Committee on Learning Disabilities defines learning disability in the following way: "*Learning disabilities* is a general term that refers to a heterogeneous group of disorders manifested by significant difficulties in the acquisition and use of listening, speaking, reading, writing, reasoning, or mathematical abilities. These disorders are intrinsic to the individual, presumed to be due to central nervous system dysfunction, and may occur across the life span. Problems in self-regulatory behaviors, social perception, and social interaction may exist with learning disabilities but do not by themselves constitute a learning disability. Although learning disabilities may occur concomitantly with other handicapping conditions (for example, sensory impairment, mental retardation, serious emotional disturbance) or with extrinsic influences (such as cultural differences, insufficient or inappropriate instruction), they are not the result of those conditions or influences."

Etiology of Learning Disabilities

9. Learning disabilities likely have multiple etiologies, including genetic, biological, and environmental bases, although no firm evidence supports any single etiology conclusively.

Problems Associated with Children with Learning Disabilities

10. Children with learning disabilities have deficient academic skills and also may have deficits in information-processing abilities, neuropsychological skills, and social-behavioral adjustment.
11. Children with learning disabilities are a heterogeneous group.

An Information-Processing Model of Learning Disabilities

12. An information-processing model with four stages—sensory storage, perceptual encoding, central processing, and response selection mechanisms—is helpful in the study of children with learning disabilities.
13. Children with learning disabilities usually perform poorly on tasks requiring active information processing and verbal working memory. They typically make little use of such mnemonic aids as labeling, verbal rehearsal, clustering, chunking, and selective attention and thus fail to remember important information.
14. The major problem of children with learning disabilities may not be so much an inability to attend selectively to materials as an inability to analyze tasks in ways that will result in the best performance strategy.
15. Children with learning disabilities have different deficiencies than children with mental retardation in academic skills and information processing.

Communication Disorders

16. Communication disorders include expressive language disorder, mixed receptive-expressive language disorder, and phonological disorder.
17. Children with expressive language disorder may have problems with vocabulary, expressive grammar, and pragmatic use of language.
18. Children with mixed receptive-expressive language disorder may have problems with vocabulary, comprehending grammatical units, comprehending word-ordering rules (syntax), recognizing multiple meanings, and comprehending the meaning of subtle aspects of language usage.
19. Early phonological awareness skills—such as sensitivity to rhyme and the ability to break words into their constituent sounds and blend sounds into words—are especially helpful to young children who are beginning to read.
20. Children with phonological disorder often fail to use or perceive speech sounds at a level appropriate for their age and cultural background. They may have a slowed rate of information

processing that leads to impairment in any task requiring integration of rapidly presented information.

Reading Disorder

21. Every language has a basic set of elementary sounds called phonemes; spoken words are formed by combining these sounds into meaningful sequences.
22. Reading is a highly complex process that involves many cognitive and sensory functions, including (a) attention and concentration, (b) phonological awareness, (c) orthographic awareness, (d) word awareness, (e) form or semantic or syntactic awareness, (f) rapid decoding, (g) verbal comprehension and pragmatic awareness, and (h) general intelligence.
23. Phonological awareness and word awareness are probably more closely related to the early stages of reading, syntactic awareness to the later stages of reading, and pragmatic awareness to the advanced stages of reading.
24. Reading involves two processes primarily: decoding (i.e., word recognition) and linguistic comprehension (i.e., the ability to take information obtained from word recognition and assign it meaning).
25. Word features important in the acquisition of decoding ability include graphic, orthographic, semantic, syntactic and phonological features.
26. Reading disorder (also called dyslexia) is defined as a type of learning disability in which children fail to master basic processes such as letter recognition and sound blending, despite adequate intelligence and educational opportunities.
27. Children with reading disorder may have developmental dyslexia, which refers to difficulty learning to read, or acquired dyslexia, which refers to loss of reading ability that has been already acquired, usually as a result of a traumatic brain injury or a disease that affects the brain.
28. Reading disorder is the most common type of learning disability—approximately 80% of children in learning disability programs have a diagnosis of reading disorder.
29. Dyslexia has at least two important dimensions: phonetic decoding (i.e., the ability to phonetically read visually presented words) and orthographic coding (i.e., the ability to recognize letter sequences or words based on their visual features).
30. Reading disorder is most likely to be associated with difficulties in the phonological coding of written language, particularly phoneme segmentation.
31. Reading disorder may be related to genetic factors that alter the neurological structures underlying phonological processing; with sociocultural factors, such as lack of sociocultural stimulation or failure to provide reading materials; or with both types of factors.
32. Research studies indicate that children who have reading disorder—with and without an IQ-achievement discrepancy—show similar information-processing, genetic, and neurophysiological profiles.
33. Epidemiological studies indicate that as many females as males manifest dyslexia; however, schools identify three to four times more boys than girls with this disorder.
34. Reading disorder reflects a persistent deficit rather than a developmental lag that will be remedied with time.
35. Children with reading disorder differ from one another and from other readers along a continuous distribution.
36. The ability to read and comprehend depends on rapid and automatic recognition and decoding of single words. Slow and inac-curate decoding (i.e., poor phonemic awareness) is the best predictor of a deficit in reading comprehension.
37. The ability to decode single words accurately and fluently is dependent on the ability to segment words and syllables into phonemes.
38. The best predictor of reading ability from kindergarten and first-grade performance is phonological awareness.
39. The three major subtypes of reading disorder, based on patterns of reading errors, are dysphonetic reading disorder, dyseidetic reading disorder, and alexic reading disorder.
40. Children usually learn to read aloud by either the whole-word procedure or the phonics procedure.
41. The four phases in learning to read are the prealphabetic phase, the partial alphabetic phase, the full alphabetic phase, and the consolidated alphabetic phase.
42. Children with reading difficulties may be stuck at different phases in the reading process, as reading difficulties can be associated with deficiencies in information-processing skills connected with any of the phases.
43. Research suggests that younger children with reading disorder (8 to 9 years of age) have a deficiency in phonological coding, while older children with reading disorder (10 to 13 years of age) may use a phonemic code but have a more general deficit in short-term memory, particularly in the context of language processing.
44. The relationship between intelligence and reading strengthens with age; typical correlation coefficients are in the .30 to .50 range for early elementary grade children, the .45 to .65 range for middle grade children, and the .60 to .75 range for adults.
45. Children who have a precocious ability to recognize written words, beyond what would be expected at their general level of intellectual development, are said to be hyperlexic.

Mathematics Disorder

46. Children with mathematics disorder (also called dyscalculia) may have difficulty with basic mathematical skills, the language of mathematical concepts, perceptual or spatial skills, attentional skills, shifting, writing, or verbal memory.
47. Mathematics disorder is a heterogeneous condition that may or may not occur in conjunction with reading disorder or another disorder.
48. Like reading disorder, mathematics disorder ranges from mild to severe.

Disorder of Written Expression

49. Children who have disorder of written expression have a disturbance that significantly interferes with their academic achievement or with activities of daily living that require writing skills.
50. Spelling requires knowledge of sound-symbol correspondence (phonological skills), as well as linguistic competence, such as an understanding that the way words are spelled may depend on how they are used.
51. Disorder of written expression may be associated with (a) fine-motor deficits, (b) linguistic deficits, (c) visual-spatial deficits, (d) attention and memory deficits, and (e) sequencing deficits.
52. Estimates of written language deficits range from 8% to 15% of the school-aged population, with girls and boys diagnosed equally often.

Nonverbal Learning Disability

53. Children with nonverbal learning disability syndrome may have difficulty with tactile perception, psychomotor coordination, visual-spatial organization, nonverbal problem solving, reading comprehension, mathematics, and social relations but not with rote memory, word decoding, and writing.

Assessment of Learning Disabilities

54. The assessment of learning disabilities serves several purposes, including obtaining an estimate of the child's general intelligence, determining the child's areas of impaired functioning, determining whether the child has deficits in basic psychological processes, finding the child's areas of strength that may prove helpful in developing interventions, arriving at possible explanations for the child's poor achievement, and determining possible interventions.

55. A minority child whose achievement is below average may not have a learning disability per se; rather, her or his achievement level may be related to cultural and linguistic factors.

56. In establishing whether a child has a learning disability, you need to consider all relevant factors, including the child's age, problem, sensory functioning, health history, educational history, and cultural background.

57. The criteria in the IDEA for establishing a diagnosis of learning disability include (a) a severe ability-achievement discrepancy, (b) a demonstrated processing disorder, (c) a need for special education services, and (d) the ruling out of physical disabilities and cultural factors as primary causes of the child's impaired achievement.

58. The major classification problem centers on how to define a severe discrepancy between ability, usually defined by an intelligence test score, and achievement, usually defined by a reading, mathematics, or written expression test score or by an overall achievement test score.

59. It is inappropriate to classify children as having a learning disability when they have only (a) low achievement (regardless of level of intelligence) and (b) a discrepancy between their verbal and performance abilities, as noted by their scores on sections of an intelligence test.

60. None of the discrepancy procedures used to identify learning disabilities tell us about the possible reasons for any underlying difficulties.

61. Using a regression equation is the best method of comparing scores on two appropriate tests because it takes into account regression-to-the-mean effects, which occur when the correlation between two measures is less than perfect.

62. Clinicians using the same discrepancy formula, but different tests, are likely to arrive at different classifications.

63. Using discrepancy formulas without regard to the absolute level of the child's performance may result in serious misinterpretations and misclassifications.

64. Discrepancy formulas are based on the assumption that the tests used to evaluate a child's intelligence and achievement measure independent constructs, when actually reading and intelligence tests to some extent measure the same constructs (e.g., vocabulary, comprehension, factual information).

65. Discrepancy formulas may prevent some lower SES students from receiving services when they exhibit the same reading problems as students from higher SES backgrounds.

66. Discrepancy formulas fail to identify those children with learning disabilities who show no discrepancy between achievement and intelligence test scores.

67. "All professional and legal definitions of LD in reading highlight the same salient features—that is, the child with a reading disability manifests an 'unexpected' difficulty in decoding, word recognition, or comprehension that is not predicted by general intellectual competence" (Lyon, 1996a, p. 407).

68. The discrepancy formula approach to classification lacks validity on both theoretical and empirical grounds.

69. The discrepancy formula approach prevents children from receiving services during their early school years.

70. Discrepancy formulas serve a useful purpose.

71. Substituting listening comprehension for intelligence in discrepancy formulas might be a more useful approach.

72. When you evaluate a child for a possible learning disability, consider (a) the child's academic, intellectual, perceptual, and motor functioning (e.g., verbal-linguistic ability, visual-spatial-constructional ability, sequential-analytic ability, planning ability, and listening ability), and neurobehavioral factors that may contribute to poor classroom performance (e.g., short attention span), (b) motivational factors that may relate to the child's learning problems, (c) possible contributions of the family, peer group, teachers, and school to the child's learning problems, (d) biological correlates that may be associated with the child's learning problems, (e) the interaction of the above factors over time and the effects they may have had on the child's performance and adjustment.

73. During the evaluation, pay close attention to how the child responds to your questions and to the child's expressive language, receptive language, motor skills, activity level, and degree of cooperativeness.

74. The most important tools in the assessment of children who may have a learning disability are good clinical skills in conjunction with reliable and valid intelligence tests, achievement tests, and other relevant tests and procedures.

75. The assessment of a child with a suspected reading disorder should focus on the child's skills in reading—such as repertoire of words identified on sight; phonemic awareness; knowledge of letter-sound correspondences of vowels, consonants, and blends; oral and silent reading rate; and comprehension skills. Ideally, the assessment should incorporate trial remediation procedures.

76. Consider including in the assessment battery a measure of (a) intelligence, (b) achievement, (c) auditory processing skills, (d) visual-perceptual processing skills, and (e) behavior (e.g., behavior checklists, formal observations).

77. Because the teacher plays an important role in evaluating for learning disability, you should interview the teacher and ask her or him to complete a questionnaire or checklist describing the child's academic skills, deficits, and progress, as well as the child's classroom behavior.

78. The attempts to find unique WISC–III test patterns among children with learning disabilities have not been successful.

79. Because well-normed standardized tests are not available for all types of school readiness, written and oral expression, and listening comprehension skills, informal tests and curriculum-based measures are sometimes needed to evaluate a child's abilities.

80. In addition to using test scores, you should evaluate the child's behavior at home and at school, the types of errors the child makes both on formal and informal tests and on classroom tests, and the factors that facilitate the child's learning.

81. There are many good informal measures of achievement that are useful in the assessment of children referred for a possible learning disability.

Prognosis for Children with Learning Disabilities

82. We do not have definitive answers about whether children with learning disabilities continue to have problems with reading, mathematics, or written expression after they leave school. However, there is some evidence that, although learning disabilities often persist into adulthood, the majority of individuals with learning disabilities function well in society.

83. More favorable outcomes tend to be associated with children who have milder forms of learning disability, who have above-average intelligence, who are in the middle or upper socioeconomic class, and who have no identifiable neurological dysfunction.

84. The prognosis for any individual child, however, cannot be predicted with any certainty.

Evaluating Information in Cases of Learning Disability

85. A thorough assessment should provide you with information about the child's developmental history and family background; medical history; educational history, including current educational performance; level of intelligence; language abilities; mathematical abilities; written expression abilities; motor abilities; and behavioral and social skills.

Comment on the Assessment of Learning Disabilities

86. Reading, mathematics, and written expression are complex cognitive activities influenced by (a) biological factors (including intellectual ability, auditory and visual processing, and memory), (b) affective and nonintellectual factors (including motivation, self-concept, and degree of confidence in one's ability to influence learning outcomes), and (c) environmental factors (including early literacy experiences and other language and cultural experiences).

87. When you evaluate a child for suspected learning disability, you must consider all of these factors in order to properly identify any disability and develop effective interventions.

Interventions for Learning Disabilities

88. The most effective interventions for children with learning disabilities are multifaceted. They involve the use of cognitive, linguistic, and behavioral-cognitive methods.

89. Cognitive methods emphasize teaching children with learning disabilities to use strategies—such as planning, monitoring, self-pacing, approaching tasks in alternative ways, and checking their work—in order to increase their awareness of task demands, their use of appropriate strategies to ease task completion, and their ability to monitor the success of their efforts.

90. Linguistic methods emphasize teaching children with learning disabilities how to improve their academic skills and phonological skills.

91. Behavioral-cognitive methods emphasize teaching children with learning disabilities social-psychological and emotional skills.

92. Instructional programs should be designed to help children with learning disabilities acquire problem-solving skills, mnemonic strategies, and effective study habits.

93. "Training children with a learning disability to become spontaneous, strategic, and planful learners is a complex and challenging task that requires instruction at both cognitive and motivational levels" (Borkowski et al., 1989, p. 68).

94. Older adolescents with learning disabilities who are entering colleges and universities may need help first in finding schools that meet their needs and have appropriate support services and then in filling out applications. And adolescents entering the work force need to learn how to obtain and maintain a job.

KEY TERMS, CONCEPTS, AND NAMES

Learning disability (p. 282)
Severe discrepancy (p. 284)
Basic psychological processes (p. 284)
Exclusionary criteria (p. 284)
Etiology of learning disabilities (p. 285)
Genetic basis of learning disabilities (p. 285)
Biological basis of learning disabilities (p. 286)
Environmental basis of learning disabilities (p. 286)
Problems associated with children with learning disabilities (p. 287)
An information-processing model of learning disabilities (p. 287)
Sensory storage stage of information processing (p. 288)
Perceptual encoding stage of information processing (p. 288)
Central processing stage of information processing (p. 288)
Response selection mechanisms stage of information processing (p. 288)
Deficits associated with learning disabilities (p. 288)
Learning disability and mental retardation (p. 289)
Communication disorders (p. 289)
Expressive language disorder (p. 289)
Mixed receptive-expressive language disorder (p. 289)
Phonological disorder (p. 290)
The process of reading (p. 290)
Phonemes (p. 290)
Pictographic or logographic (p. 290)
Syllabic or alphabetic (p. 290)
Mapping of letters to phonemes (p. 291)
Homophones (p. 291)
Regularity of spelling-to-sound correspondences (p. 291)
Attention and concentration (p. 291)
Phonological awareness (p. 291)
Orthographic awareness (p. 291)
Word awareness (p. 291)
Form or semantic or syntactic awareness (p. 291)
Rapid decoding (p. 291)
Verbal comprehension and pragmatic awareness (p. 291)
General intelligence (p. 291)
Word features (p. 291)
Graphic features (p. 291)
Orthographic features (p. 291)
Semantic features (p. 292)
Syntactic features (p. 292)
Phonologic features (p. 292)
Literal comprehension (p. 292)
Inferential comprehension (p. 292)
Critical comprehension (p. 292)
Skills of good readers (p. 292)
Reading disorder (p. 292)

Dyslexia (p. 292)
Developmental dyslexia (p. 293)
Acquired dyslexia (p. 293)
Phonetic decoding (p. 293)
Orthographic coding (p. 293)
Dysphonetic reading disability (p. 294)
Dyseidetic reading disability (p. 294)
Alexic reading disorder (p. 294)
A progression of reading skills (p. 294)
Whole-word procedure or direct procedure (p. 294)
Phonics procedure (p. 294)
Prealphabetic phase (p. 294)
Partial alphabetic phase (p. 294)
Full alphabetic phase (p. 295)
Consolidated alphabetic phase (p. 295)
Individual differences in perceptual-cognitive processes related to
    reading ability (p. 295)
Intelligence and reading ability (p. 296)
Hyperlexia (p. 296)
Mathematics disorder (dyscalculia) (p. 296)
Disorder of written expression (p. 297)
Handwriting difficulties (dysgraphia) (p. 298)
Nonverbal learning disabilities (p. 298)
Discrepancy based on deviation from grade or age level (p. 299)
Discrepancy based on expectancy formulas (p. 300)
Discrepancy based on difference between standard scores (p. 300)
Discrepancy based on regression equation (p. 300)
Guidelines for the assessment of learning disabilities (p. 302)
Learning disabilities and the WISC–III (p. 303)
Informal assessment of learning disabilities (p. 304)
Cloze procedures (p. 305)
Prognosis for children with learning disabilities (p. 320)
Interventions for learning disabilities (p. 322)
Cognitive methods (p. 322)
Metacognition (p. 322)
Linguistic methods (p. 323)
Behavioral-cognitive methods (p. 325)
Instructional programs (p. 325)
Preparation for the world of college and work (p. 325)

STUDY QUESTIONS

1. Discuss definitions of learning disabilities. Include in your discussion the definition included in the IDEA. Also, critically evaluate the strengths and weaknesses of the definitions.

2. Discuss etiological theories of learning disabilities.
3. Describe some of the problems associated with children who have learning disabilities.
4. Describe an information-processing model of learning disabilities.
5. What are oral language disabilities? Include in your discussion types of oral language disabilities and diagnostic problems.
6. Describe the process of reading.
7. Discuss reading disorder. Include in your discussion (a) phonological processing, (b) word features important in the acquisition of reading, (c) dimensions of reading comprehension, (d) skills of good readers, (e) types of reading disorder, (f) difficulties that poor readers may have, (g) research findings related to children with reading disorder, (h) subtypes of reading disorder, (i) the progression of reading skills, (j) individual differences in perceptual-cognitive processes related to reading ability, (k) intelligence and reading disorder, and (l) hyperlexia.
8. Discuss mathematics disorder.
9. Discuss disorder of written expression.
10. Discuss nonverbal learning disabilities.
11. Discuss the assessment of learning disabilities. Include in your discussion (a) approaches for determining whether a learning disability exists, including the concept and types of discrepancies, (b) guidelines for the assessment of learning disabilities, (c) a preferred assessment battery, (d) learning disabilities and the WISC–III, and (e) informal assessment of learning disabilities.
12. Discuss the prognosis for children with learning disabilities.
13. Describe how you would go about evaluating information if you were performing an assessment of a child with a possible learning disability.
14. Discuss intervention methods for children with learning disabilities. Include in your discussion (a) the IDEA and interventions, (b) cognitive methods, (c) linguistic methods, (d) behavioral-cognitive methods, (e) instructional programs, and (f) preparation for the world of college and work.

13

MENTAL RETARDATION

Some measure of genius is the rightful inheritance of every man.

—Alfred North Whitehead

Etiology of Mental Retardation

Relationship Between Measured Intelligence
and Adaptive Behavior

Some General Considerations in Understanding
Mental Retardation

Mental Retardation and Intelligence Testing

Assessment of Maladaptive Behavior

Functional Assessment

Guidelines for Evaluating Assessment Information

Distinguishing Between Mental Retardation and
Developmental Delay

Assessment of Children with Severe or Profound
Mental Retardation

Interventions for Individuals with Mental Retardation

Concluding Comment

Thinking Through the Issues

Summary

Goals and Objectives

This chapter is designed to enable you to do the following:

• Understand the definition of mental retardation

• Understand how to assess children with mental retardation

• Understand interventions for children with mental retardation

The term *mental retardation* applies to a heterogeneous group of conditions characterized by low or very low intelligence *and* deficits in adaptive behavior. Two leading professional organizations offer somewhat different definitions of mental retardation. The American Association on Mental Retardation (AAMR, 1992) defines mental retardation in the following way:

Mental retardation refers to substantial limitations in present functioning. It is characterized by significantly subaverage intellectual functioning, existing concurrently with related limitations in two or more of the following applicable adaptive skill areas: communication, self-care, home living, social skills, community use, self-direction, health and safety, functional academics, leisure, and work. Mental retardation manifests before age 18. (p. 5)

Significantly subaverage intellectual functioning is defined as a score of approximately 70 to 75 or below on an individually administered intelligence test (see *Assessment of Children: Cognitive Applications* for a description of intelligence tests). Adaptive skills preferably are measured through use of an appropriately normed and standardized adaptive behavior scale (see Chapter 7). The current AAMR classification system does not use categories, such as mild, moderate, severe, and profound, to classify degrees of mental retardation.

The AAMR cautions that the definition of mental retardation must be applied with four assumptions in mind (AAMR, 1992, adapted from pp. 6–7):

1. Valid assessment considers cultural and linguistic diversity, as well as differences in communication and behavioral factors.
2. The existence of limitations in adaptive skills occurs within the context of community environments typical of the individual's age peers and is indexed to the person's individualized needs for support.
3. Specific adaptive limitations often coexist with strengths in other adaptive skills or other personal capabilities.
4. With appropriate supports over a sustained period, the life functioning of the person with mental retardation will generally improve.

The 1992 AAMR definition has been criticized for (a) being based more on political and social values than on the scientific research, (b) potentially increasing the number of persons diagnosed with mild mental retardation (the upper limit of intellectual functioning was raised from 70 in the 1983 definition to 75 in the 1992 definition), and (c) changing the definition of adaptive behavior in a way that is potentially problematic because few tests of adaptive behavior measure the 10 specific domains reliably (Greenspan, 1995; Jacobson & Mulick, 1994; MacMillan, Gresham, & Siperstein, 1993; Smith, 1997). The 1992 definition, however, has also been characterized as more dynamic, more attentive to the individual's context, more holistic, less deficit-oriented, and more flexible than the former definition (Fredericks & Williams, 1998; Reiss, 1994).

The American Psychiatric Association (2000), in *DSM-IV–TR,* defines mental retardation as

significantly subaverage intellectual functioning…that is accompanied by significant limitations in adaptive functioning in at least two of the following skill areas: communication, self-care, home living, social/interpersonal skills, use of community resources, self-direction, functional academic skills, work, leisure, health, and safety.… The onset must occur before age 18 years. (p. 41)

Subaverage intellectual functioning is defined as an IQ at least 2 standard deviations below the mean on an individually administered intelligence test. This generally corresponds to an IQ of about 70 or below, although the IQ can be as high as 75. Information about adaptive behavior can be obtained from informants, individuals' developmental and medical histories, and scales that measure adaptive behavior. Finally, *DSM-IV–TR* specifies four degrees of severity of mental retardation (also see Table 13-1):

- *Mild mental retardation* (IQ level of 50–55 to approximately 70)
- *Moderate mental retardation* (IQ level of 35–40 to 50–55)
- *Severe mental retardation* (IQ level of 20–25 to 35–40)
- *Profound mental retardation* (IQ level below 20 or 25)

Table 13-1
Classification of Mental Retardation

Level of mental retardation	Educational equivalent description	Range in standard deviation	Range in IQ for any test with SD = 16	Range in IQ for any test with SD = 15	Approximate mental age at adulthood	Approximate % of persons with mental retardation at this level
Mild	Educable	–2.01 to –3.00	67–52	69–55	8-3 to 10-9	85.0
Moderate	Trainable	–3.01 to –4.00	51–36	54–40	5-7 to 8-2	10.0
Severe	Trainable (dependent)	–4.01 to –5.00	35–20	39–25	3-2 to 5-6	3.5
Profound	Custodial (life support)	< –5.00	< 20	< 25	< 3-2	1.5

One of these four degrees of severity must be included in the diagnosis of mental retardation, except when there is a strong presumption of mental retardation but the child's intelligence is untestable by standard tests. In the latter case, the diagnosis according to *DSM-IV–TR* is "Mental Retardation, Severity Unspecified."

In using the *DSM-IV–TR* classification system, remember that the level of retardation described by an intelligence test is dependent on the standard deviation (*SD*) of the test. For example, if a –2 *SD* criterion is used to establish the beginning of the level of mental retardation, then the IQ just below the –2 *SD* point is 69 for the WISC–III, WPPSI–R, WAIS–III, and other tests that use an *SD* of 15. For the Stanford-Binet: IV, however, the IQ is 67 because the Stanford-Binet: IV has an *SD* of 16. Still other cutoff points may be appropriate for other instruments, depending on the *SD*. Always evaluate the psychometric properties of each test carefully (see Chapter 4 in *Assessment of Children: Cognitive Applications*) before you use the test to assess a child for mental retardation.

The two definitions of mental retardation overlap considerably. In fact, *DSM-IV–TR* follows the 1983 AAMR formulation (Grossman, 1983). Both approaches emphasize the importance of administering (a) an individual intelligence test to determine a child's level of intelligence and (b) an adaptive behavior scale to evaluate a child's level of adaptive behavior. The *DSM-IV–TR* approach is preferable because it provides for levels of intellectual functioning. These levels are valuable for discussing assessment results with parents, teachers, and health care providers; for formulating intervention programs; for estimating an individual's future potential; and for research and data-analysis purposes. There is considerable difference between a child with an IQ of 20 and a child with an IQ of 69, even though both may receive a diagnosis of mental retardation.

The AAMR and *DSM-IV–TR* definitions both refer to a level of behavioral performance *without* reference to etiology. Key aspects of both definitions bear closer inspection.

- *Significantly subaverage* refers to performance that is approximately 2 or more standard deviations below the population mean.
- *Intellectual functioning* refers to performance on a standardized intelligence test that measures, as far as is possible, general cognitive ability rather than one limited facet of ability, such as receptive vocabulary or spatial-analytic skills.
- *Adaptive skill areas* or *adaptive functioning* refers to the effectiveness with which individuals meet the standards of personal independence and social responsibility expected of individuals of their age and cultural group. Children's developmental ages are used to evaluate deficits in adaptive behavior. During infancy and early childhood, adaptive behavior is evaluated in terms of sensorimotor skills, communication skills, self-help skills, and socialization skills. During childhood and early adolescence, the focus is on the application of (a) basic academic skills in daily life activities, (b) appropriate reasoning and judgment in interacting with the environment, and (c) social skills.

During late adolescence and adult life, the assessment of adaptive behavior centers on vocational and social responsibilities and behavioral performances.

- The *onset* of the condition must occur during the developmental period, which is between birth and age 18.

Both definitions indicate that two criteria—level of intelligence and level of adaptive behavior—are considered jointly in arriving at a diagnosis. A diagnosis of mental retardation should be made only when an individual falls into the mentally retarded category in both intellectual functioning *and* adaptive behavior functioning. Intelligence is assessed by objective measurement; adaptive behavior is assessed by clinical or objective measurement (e.g., behavioral ratings).

Both definitions have several implications.

- The assessment must focus on a description of *present* behavior (prediction of future intelligence or behavior is a separate process that is fraught with difficulties).
- Both definitions specifically recognize the contribution of individually administered intelligence tests.
- The diagnosis of mental retardation is tied to the developmental process, with behavioral descriptions anchored to the individual's own age level.
- A diagnosis of mental retardation does not rule out the coexistence of other forms of childhood disorders.
- Both definitions avoid the implication that mental retardation is irreversible.
- A diagnosis of mental retardation is inappropriate when an individual is adequately meeting the demands of his or her environment.

Table 13-2 shows a classification system for adaptive behavior that parallels the classification system for measured intelligence. The system coordinates developmental stages and levels of retardation, emphasizing sensorimotor skills, language and communication, learning, degree of self-sufficiency, and vocational potential. A child's adaptive behavior classification may differ from her or his intelligence classification. For instance, a child may receive a mildly retarded adaptive behavior classification, but a moderately retarded intelligence classification.

Intelligence can be assessed more precisely than can adaptive behavior. The Stanford-Binet: IV and Wechsler tests are well-normed instruments for the assessment of intelligence, with excellent reliability and validity. In contrast, there are few nationally standardized instruments for the assessment of adaptive behavior during the developmental period that meet acceptable psychometric standards. Instruments such as the AAMD Adaptive Behavior Scale and the Vineland Adaptive Behavior Scales (see Chapter 7) can be helpful in assessing adaptive behavior, but they are highly dependent on the reliability of the informant (e.g., parent, teacher, primary caregiver). The informant's ability to observe and reliably report the child's skills, behavior, and temperament will determine the accuracy of the adaptive behavior ratings. In addition, social adaptation is an elusive concept that is difficult to

Table 13-2
Levels of Adaptive Behavior for the Mentally Retarded

Level	Preschool age: birth to 5 years	School age: 6 to 21 years	Adult: over 21 years
Mild retardation	Can develop social and communication skills; minimal retardation in sensorimotor areas; rarely distinguished from normal until later age.	Can learn academic skills to approximately sixth-grade level by late teens; generally cannot learn general high school subjects; needs special education, particularly at secondary-school age levels.	Capable of social and vocational adequacy with proper education and training; frequently needs guidance when under serious social and economic stress.
Moderate retardation	Can speak or learn to communicate; poor social awareness; fair motor development; may profit from training in self-help; can be managed with moderate supervision.	Can learn functional academic skills to approximately fourth-grade level by late teens if given special education.	Capable of self-maintenance in unskilled or semi-skilled occupation; needs supervision and guidance when under mild social or economic stress.
Severe retardation	Poor motor development; minimal speech; generally unable to profit from training in self-help; few or no communication skills.	Can learn to speak or communicate; can be trained in elementary health habits; cannot learn functional academic skills; can profit from systematic habit training.	Can contribute partially to self-support under complete supervision; can develop self-protection skills to a minimal useful level in a controlled environment.
Profound retardation	Gross retardation; minimal capacity for functioning in sensorimotor areas; needs nursing care.	Some motor development; cannot profit from training in self-help; needs total care.	Some motor and speech development; totally incapable of self-maintenance; needs complete care and supervision.

Note. States may differ in their definitions of these levels.
Source: Adapted from Sloan and Birch (1955).

define and measure. With an intelligence test, the child is assessed directly—no intermediary is necessary. Present guidelines suggest that a diagnosis of mental retardation must rest in part on clinical judgment; you must therefore consider all relevant factors in arriving at a diagnosis.

ETIOLOGY OF MENTAL RETARDATION

Mental retardation can be a primary diagnosis, occur as a part of a syndrome (fetal alcohol syndrome, fragile X syndrome; see below), or co-occur with other developmental disabilities (autism, attention-deficit/hyperactivity disorder), neurological disorders (epilepsy, cerebral palsy), or psychiatric disorders (challenging behavior, anxiety disorder; Hatton, 1998). Mental retardation can result from a diverse set of factors (American Psychiatric Association, 2000). Following are the major types of predisposing factors:

1. *Heredity.* These factors include inborn errors of metabolism inherited mostly through autosomal recessive mechanisms (e.g., Tay-Sachs disease, a disorder of lipoid metabolism,

caused by a recessive gene, that results in a progressive degenerative disease characterized by severe mental retardation, seizures, paralysis, and death), other single-gene abnormalities (e.g., tuberous sclerosis, a congenital familial disease characterized by tumors on the surfaces of parts of the brain and marked by progressive mental deterioration and seizures), and chromosomal aberrations (e.g., fragile X syndrome, a condition that is characterized by a physical abnormality on the X chromosome and is one of the more common genetic causes of mental retardation, especially in males).

2. *Early alterations of embryonic development.* These factors include chromosomal changes (e.g., Down syndrome, also known as mongolism or Trisomy 21, which is associated with a chromosomal abnormality that arises from the presence of an extra chromosome 21 and usually causes children to have a flat skull, thickened skin on the eyelids, stubby fingers, and a short, stocky body), and prenatal changes due to toxins (e.g., maternal alcohol consumption or infections).

3. *Pregnancy and perinatal problems.* These factors include fetal malnutrition, maternal use of drugs (e.g., alcohol, cocaine), prematurity, hypoxia (deficiency of oxygen reaching the tissues of the body), viral and other infections, and trauma.

4. *General medical conditions acquired in infancy or childhood.* These factors include infections (e.g., meningitis, a brain infection involving acute inflammation of the membranes that cover the brain and spinal cord, characterized by drowsiness, confusion, irritability, and sensory impairments; roseola, a virus characterized by high fever and a rubella-like rash; encephalitis, an acute inflammation of the brain or its meninges, resulting from any of a wide variety of infections and toxins; and rabies), trauma (e.g., head injuries), and poisoning (e.g., lead poisoning).

5. *Environmental influences.* These factors include severe neglect and deprivation of social-linguistic stimulation and other forms of social and cognitive stimulation.

Physical Disabilities

Children who function in the mentally retarded range may also have physical disabilities. For example, infants born to women who abuse alcohol may have *fetal alcohol syndrome*. This syndrome develops when a sufficient amount of alcohol consumed by the mother crosses the placenta and interferes with neurotransmitter production, cell development, cell migration, and brain growth of the fetus. The main characteristics of this syndrome are low birth weight, growth retardation, organic anomalies (including cleft palate; neural tube defect, which is a defect caused by the failure of the neural folds to fuse and form a neural tube; hearing loss; and heart defects), and neurobehavioral deficits (including mental retardation, speech and language disorders, and attention-deficit/hyperactivity disorder). Fetal alcohol syndrome is a leading cause of mental retardation in the western world (Abel & Sokol, 1991).

Effects of Developmental Periods

Abnormalities in different developmental periods may produce different forms of mental retardation (Todd, Swarzenski, Rossi, & Visconti, 1995). For example, abnormalities during the first half of pregnancy, when cells and structures that will become the mature brain are being developed, can result in microencephaly (abnormally small head size), macroencephaly (abnormal enlargement of the head), and disturbances of neural tissues. During the second half of pregnancy, when growth and differentiation are defining the structural detail of the fully developed brain, abnormalities can result in damage to axons and dendrites, difficulties with myelination of axons, and interference with individual cell functioning. Prenatal processes that may lead to mental retardation include ischemic infarction (when tissue is destroyed because of reduced blood flow), chromosomal aberrations, genetic mutations, and fetal intoxication syndromes caused by alcohol or other drugs.

Distribution in the Population

Approximately 1% of the population would be classified as mentally retarded. Of people with mental retardation, approximately 85% are in the mild classification, 10% in the moderate classification, 3% to 4% in the severe classification, and 1% to 2% in the profound classification (American Psychiatric Association, 2000).

Mental Retardation from a Familial Origin or from Brain Injury

Persons with mental retardation can be broadly grouped into two categories: (a) those with mental retardation from a familial origin and (b) those with mental retardation from brain injury (Hodapp & Zigler, 1999).

People with mental retardation from a familial origin.

The group with mental retardation from a familial origin includes individuals with mild mental retardation, in the IQ range of 50 to 69. Individuals with mental retardation from a familial origin usually are simply in the lower portion of the normal distribution of intelligence, with their lower intelligence only a reflection of normal intellectual variability. Intellectual variability is an expected result of normal polygenic variation—that is, the combined action of many genes. Performance in this range, however, can also be associated with (a) pathological factors that interfere with brain functioning (such as subclinical brain damage that has yet to be discovered) or (b) the combined effect of below-average heredity and a markedly below-average environment. In most cases, however, there is no demonstrable organic etiology (Zigler & Hodapp, 1986). Individuals with mental retardation from a familial origin tend to come from low socioeconomic status (SES) groups, and their siblings often function at low levels of intelligence.

Children with mental retardation from a familial origin tend to exhibit the following behaviors (Zigler & Balla, 1981): (a) they are more responsive to social reinforcement than their nonretarded peers, (b) they perform better on tasks when the reward is tangible, (c) they are outer-directed (e.g., they are sensitive to cues provided by adults and are highly imitative), and (d) they have a low expectancy of success and a high expectancy of failure. The different experiences of children with mental retardation and those without mental retardation likely account for the differences in their behavior.

Adults with mental retardation from a familial origin seldom come to the attention of the professional community. One possible reason is that intellectual limitations are more obvious in school settings than in employment settings. A second possibility is that persons with mental retardation from a familial origin gradually acquire adequate adaptive skills. A third reason is that the intellectual ability of individuals with familial mental retardation may improve during adolescence and early adulthood.

Individuals with mental retardation from brain injury.
Individuals with mental retardation from brain injury include primarily those in the IQ range below 50, although organic etiologies are sometimes found in milder forms of mental retardation. The cause of this type of mental retardation, as noted above, may be a genetic component linked to

single gene effects, chromosomal abnormalities, or brain damage. Children with mental retardation from brain injury usually have severe and diffuse brain damage or malformations, commonly originating during the prenatal period. They typically show a severe lag in behavioral development, sometimes accompanied by an abnormal appearance. Those who are functioning at the profound level of mental retardation show poorer language, communication, and motor skills than those who are functioning at the mild level of mental retardation. Identification of the more severe forms of retardation is relatively easy because the children fail to reach normal motor and language developmental milestones. Adults with severe forms of mental retardation will require supervision and life-long care. Mental retardation from brain injury is found at all SES levels; the intellectual level of siblings of children with brain injury is usually average.

The following approaches have been successful in reducing the occurrence of mental retardation (Szymanski & Crocker, 1985):

- Screening and treating infants for metabolic disorders
- Using a low-phenylalanine diet for pregnant women who have *phenylketonuria* (*PKU*) and for infants born with PKU. When a child receives a recessive gene for this chromosomal abnormality from both parents, she or he is unable to metabolize the amino acid phenylalanine. Untreated, PKU results in severe mental retardation; it also may cause convulsions, behavioral problems, severe skin rash, and a musty odor of the body and urine.
- Immunizing children
- Providing education to adults about the effects of alcohol and drug use during pregnancy
- Reducing children's exposure to lead
- Constructing safer automobiles
- Providing public education about the need to use infant seats and seat belts in automobiles
- Using *amniocentesis,* a surgical procedure in which a small sample of amniotic fluid is drawn out of the uterus through a needle inserted in the abdomen of the mother, for prenatal diagnosis of chromosomal disorders. The results of this procedure give the mother (and father) the opportunity to decide whether to continue the pregnancy.
- Screening to identify whether individuals have genetic conditions or metabolic disorders that could result in mental retardation in their offspring and then providing genetic counseling as appropriate

RELATIONSHIP BETWEEN MEASURED INTELLIGENCE AND ADAPTIVE BEHAVIOR

The *DSM-IV–TR*'s definition of mental retardation requires that a child be below the population average by approximately 2 standard deviations on (a) a measure of intelligence and (b) a measure of adaptive behavior. Because intelligence and adaptive behavior are not perfectly correlated, children

who fall below –2 *SD* on an intelligence test may have adaptive behavior skills that do not fall within this range. Thus, the number of children classified as mentally retarded is likely to be lower when both criteria are used than when a single criterion is applied. As you can see in Table 13-3, hypothetical prevalence rates decrease markedly as one moves from a correlation of 1.00 (reflecting the hypothetical case in which all children whose intelligence test scores fell in the mentally retarded range also had adaptive behavior scores in this range) to a correlation of .00 (reflecting the hypothetical case in which there was no relationship between children's scores on an intelligence test and their scores on a measure of adaptive behavior; Silverstein, 1973). Nationwide estimated prevalence rates, using –2 *SD* as the cutting score on each measure, range from 120,000 to over 5,400,000, depending on the correlation assumed between the two measures.

We know that there is a relationship between measures of adaptive behavior and measures of intelligence, but the precise relationship is unknown. An estimate in the .30s to .40s would appear reasonable (Editorial Board, 1996; Harrison & Oakland, 2000). Correlations between the two variables tend to be higher in populations of individuals with severe mental retardation than in those of individuals who are less intellectually impaired. Research suggests that approximately one-third of children who have IQs –2 *SD* below the mean do not have adaptive behavior scores that are within the mentally retarded range (Childs, 1982; Mastenbrook, 1978).

SOME GENERAL CONSIDERATIONS IN UNDERSTANDING MENTAL RETARDATION

Mental retardation is not a disease; rather, it is a symptom of a variety of conditions that interfere with the normal development of the brain, and intellectual impairment is a functional

Table 13-3
Hypothetical Prevalence Rates of Mental Retardation

Correlation	Hypothetical prevalence rate per 1,000	Hypothetical prevalence nationwide
.00	.5	140,000
.20	1.4	392,000
.40	2.9	1,102,000
.60	5.5	1,540,000
.80	9.8	2,744,000
1.00	22.8	6,384,000

Note. These data are based on an assumed population of 280,000,000 and a cutoff of –2 standard deviations for estimates of the correlation between measured intelligence and adaptive behavior in the population.
Source: Adapted from Silverstein (1973).

expression of these conditions. As with children who do not have mental retardation, there is considerable variability in the personality and behavior of children with mental retardation. They may exhibit symptoms of mental illness and have emotional disorders similar to those found in children without mental retardation. During all periods of their lives, however, children with mental retardation are more vulnerable to the development of maladaptive behavior than are children without mental retardation. The label "mental retardation" should not prevent us from seeing that children with mental retardation differ among themselves, as do all children. Mental retardation is complex, and making generalizations about cognitive processes and personality is as difficult among children with mental retardation as among any other group of children.

Chronological age (CA) affects many traits and should be considered in evaluating individuals with mental retardation. Although chronological age per se may have little impact on intelligence test performance, it does relate to less cognitively demanding social behaviors and interests (Zigler et al., 1984). For example, a 25-year-old who has a mental age of 7 years would be expected to catch a bus and go downtown, an activity that one would be hesitant to expect of a 7-year-old with average intelligence. Similarly, learning to skate, starting to date, and marrying and starting a career are activities usually tied to chronological age. In making recommendations, consider behaviors that are CA-sensitive. Many individuals with mental retardation are highly motivated to perform age-appropriate tasks whenever possible.

The following list highlights findings from research concerning the cognitive development and social adaptation skills of children with mental retardation (Landesman-Dwyer & Butterfield, 1983, adapted from pp. 492–493, 495, 498–499, 502–504, and 507).

Learning and Cognition

1. The principles governing the acquisition, maintenance, and extinction of simple responses and basic memory functions are the same for children with and without mental retardation, unless the children have co-existing neurological impairment.
2. Mental age exerts a powerful influence on many aspects of learning and cognition.
3. Noncognitive factors—such as temperament or personality, motivation, and sensory and motor capacities—affect learning and thinking.
4. The intellectual deficiencies of children with mental retardation are more closely related to higher-order cognitive processes than to subordinate processes. Higher-order cognitive processes include efficient problem-solving strategies, generalization, and abstraction. Subordinate cognitive processes include attention, rehearsal, ability to inhibit responses, and discrimination of elements of a problem.
5. Even with cognitive training and supportive environments, children with mental retardation continue to differ from children without mental retardation. No combination of sophisticated prosthetic aids, instructional approaches,

and supportive social environments has made children with mental retardation function the same as children without mental retardation.
6. The behavior of children with mental retardation is similar in many ways to that of children without mental retardation, especially younger children of like mental age. The disparity between the mental and chronological ages of children with mental retardation often creates an atypical pattern of life experiences that contributes to differences found between children with and without mental retardation. Noncognitive factors such as low motivation and poor self-concept sometimes further reduce the cognitive performance of children with mental retardation. In other words, mental retardation represents nonoptimal functioning across many domains.

The Social Ecology of the Lives of Children with Mental Retardation

1. The quality of environments cannot be judged without reference to the specific characteristics and needs of children with mental retardation in those environments. Adjustment is best facilitated when there is a match between environmental expectations and children's abilities.
2. It is important to consider a child's social environment when evaluating his or her mental or developmental age. A caregiver's behavior may be a direct function of the child's capabilities, such as ability to produce speech; consequently, the child's social environment must be considered in relationship to the child's age, physical condition, and functional abilities.
3. Environmental variables account for much of the behavior of children with mental retardation. Environmental variables are highly correlated with behavioral patterns, and social behavior is modifiable by altering environmental conditions.
4. To assess the impact of environmental variables, you should consider the child's social repertoire and behavior in many situations.
5. Children with mental retardation show a variety of deficits and delays in their social development relative to children without mental retardation of the same chronological age. At least some of the differences are due to a mismatch between the social and learning environments of children with mental retardation and their cognitive capabilities. Theoretically, successful social adaptation is influenced by many personal qualities such as self-confidence, physical attractiveness, communication style, consideration of others, and willingness to change. Many of these attributes can be modified by a combination of environmental manipulation, direct instruction, and provision of prosthetic aids.

MENTAL RETARDATION AND INTELLIGENCE TESTING

As early as the first decade of the twentieth century, the National Education Association described the proper use of intelligence tests in the study of children with mental retardation. The policy formulated by a committee of the association concerning the use of tests is as appropriate today as it was when it was first issued (Bruner, Barnes, & Dearborn, 1909): *"Tests of mental deficiency are chiefly useful in the hands of the skilled examiner. No sets of tests have been devised that will give a categorical answer as to the mental status of any individual. In nearly every instance in which they are used, tests need to be interpreted"* (p. 905, with changes in notation). The committee noted that the tests proposed by De-Sanctis and by Binet and Simon were of considerable value as tests of general capacity. Currently, the assessment of intelligence is still a critical component in arriving at a diagnosis of mental retardation.

As previously noted, different levels of mental retardation exist. Useful instruments for the evaluation of mild mental retardation include the Stanford-Binet: IV and the WISC–III, WPPSI–R, and WAIS–III. The Stanford-Binet: IV has a somewhat lower floor than the Wechsler scales, but not at all age levels. Neither the Stanford-Binet: IV nor the Wechsler tests were designed for the assessment of children with severe or profound mental retardation.

Children with mental retardation usually have a slow rate of cognitive development, limited expressive and receptive language abilities, limited adaptive skills, limited experiential background, short attention span, distractibility, and a concrete and literal style in approaching tasks (Cobb, 1989). They tend to show less change in IQ when reevaluated than do children without mental retardation (Silverstein, 1982). Rapport may be difficult to establish because of their "limited verbal abilities, frequent fear of strangers, and distrust of their own ability to communicate effectively" (Ollendick, Oswald, & Ollendick, 1993, p. 49). You must adjust your assessment techniques accordingly if you find these qualities present in children suspected of having mental retardation. Instead of asking open-ended questions, which may be extremely difficult for them to answer in an interview, you may need to simplify questions, provide examples, ask structured questions, and use frequent prompts. Be prepared to repeat or rephrase your interview questions. These strategies will require skill and patience. In addition, children with mental retardation may be hesitant to ask for breaks in the assessment session. Therefore, if you see signs of fatigue—such as changes in attentiveness, restlessness, fidgeting, drooping of head, or yawning—take a break; if necessary, schedule several short sessions.

Children with mental retardation may have higher rates of acquiescence than children who are not mentally retarded; thus, do not rely primarily on yes-no questions. In fact, uncritical acceptance of their responses to yes-no questions may lead you to draw invalid inferences. Children with mental retardation may have difficulty recalling when their problems began and other important details of their lives. To help improve their recall, link problems to events such as birthdays, holidays, school projects, or summer vacations.

Children with mental retardation may have emotional problems unrelated to their intellectual retardation. If they are uncooperative during the assessment, evaluate the possible adaptive significance of the uncooperative behavior. As with all children, developing a warm, accepting relationship may help to reduce unacceptable behavior.

The test age or mental age (MA) obtained from a test of intelligence can be used as a rough index of mental ability. Children of different chronological ages who obtain the same mental age score generally have similar levels of intellectual development. Thus, a 6-year-old with an MA of 9 is probably functioning at roughly the same level of development as a 16-year-old with an MA of 9. The younger child (viewed as being bright) has reached the same level of functioning as the older child (viewed as being less able) at a much earlier age. There may be differences, however, in the qualitative aspects of their intellectual functioning.

ASSESSMENT OF MALADAPTIVE BEHAVIOR

Several procedures are useful for the assessment of maladaptive behaviors in children and adults with mental retardation. These include the (a) Reiss Screen for Maladaptive Behavior (Reiss, 1988), (b) Aberrant Behavior Checklist (Aman, Singh, Stewart, & Field, 1985), (c) Behavior Problems Inventory, the Diagnostic Assessment for the Severely Handicapped–II (Matson, Baglio, Smiroldo, Hamilton, Paclawskyj, Williams, & Kirkpatrick-Sanchez, 1996), (d) Psychopathology Inventory for Mentally Retarded Adults (Matson, 1988), (e) Reiss Scales for Children's Dual Diagnosis (Reiss & Valenti-Hein, 1994), and (f) Nisonger Child Behavior Rating Form (Tasse, Aman, Hammer, & Rojahn, 1996). These checklists complement intelligence tests, adaptive behavior scales, interviews, and observations.

FUNCTIONAL ASSESSMENT

As part of the evaluation, you may want to conduct a functional assessment. A *functional assessment* provides information about which environmental factors might be modified to improve functioning. Functional assessment procedures link assessment and intervention. They focus on the child's survival skills—for example, her or his ability to ask directions, identify police officers, make change, and recognize monetary values. You can use functional assessment procedures to supplement traditional assessments. Whatever assessment procedures you use, you must determine whether a child's failures on tests or in school subjects are caused by physical disabilities, motivational deficits, or knowledge deficits. You will want to observe the child in more than one setting (see Chapters 4 and 5) and obtain information from different informants about how the child behaves in various settings (see Chapter 2). This is important, because the contextual variables that affect behavior may differ in different environments.

Adaptive Behavior Questionnaires, Checklists, and Interviews

You can use the adaptive behavior questionnaires and developmental checklists described in Chapter 7 for evaluating children with mental retardation. The semi-structured interview shown in Table B-5 in Appendix B is useful for obtaining information from parents about their children's problem behavior, home environment, neighborhood, sibling relations, peer relations, relations with parents and other adults, interests and hobbies, routine daily activities, cognitive functioning, academic functioning, behavior, affect, motor skills, health history, and family. You can use Table B-5 in Appendix B in conjunction with the semi-structured developmental history interview shown in Table B-6 in Appendix B.

Following are several procedures that are helpful in evaluating the daily living skills of children with mental retardation (Fredericks & Brodsky, 1994; Hawkins & Hawkins, 1981; Neel & Billingsly, 1990).

1. Instruct the parents to keep a daily diary or checklist (or both) for a week at a time, observing their child's daily activities and performance and noting skills needing development. Role playing and other procedures can help parents learn good observation and recording skills. Also obtain from the teacher a list of the life skills needed by the examinee. Interview both parents and teacher, as needed, to learn about the child's skills, especially if the parents or teacher has not completed a checklist.
2. Ask the teacher and parents to communicate daily about how the child is performing, especially when they have made changes in teaching methods or the procedures used at home.
3. When possible, observe the child at home and in the community, because parents may fail to observe important behaviors or environmental contingencies.
4. Help the teacher make the school environment approximate that of the home. For example, closely matching eating utensils, toys, clothing items, and other stimuli to those found at home will give you information about how the examinee functions at home.
5. Compare the list of life skills needed by the examinee with those that the examinee possesses, and use this information to develop interventions.

Task Analysis

Task analysis focuses on subdividing a skill into its component parts. You can then assess the number of steps in the task that the child performs independently. For example, washing hands can be subdivided into 22 specific steps (see Table 13-4). If you wanted to evaluate a child's ability to wash her hands, you might say, "Bridgette, show me how you would wash your hands" and then observe how adequately she performs the task. Depending on where she had difficulty, you could determine the appropriate entry level skill with which to begin in-

Table 13-4
Task Analysis for Washing Hands

Component Skills

1. Walks to front of sink (soap bar on sink).
2. Directs hand toward water faucet handle (cold, then hot).
3. Touches water faucet handle.
4. Grasps water faucet handle.
5. Turns on water.
6. Discriminates for adequate temperature (not too hot or too cold).
7. Wets hands under running water.
8. Removes hands from water.
9. Directs hand toward soap dish.
10. Touches soap.
11. Picks up soap.
12. Rubs soap between hands.
13. Puts soap back into soap dish.
14. Rubs palms of hands together (creating lather).
15. Rubs back of right hand.
16. Rubs back of left hand.
17. Places hands under running water.
18. Rinses all soap off hands.
19. Turns off running water.
20. Picks up towel.
21. Dries hands.
22. Puts down towel.

Source: Adapted from Van Etten, Arkell, and Van Etten (1980), p. 178.

struction. See Wehman (1979) and Van Etten, Arkell, and Van Etten (1980) for information about task-analysis procedures.

Systematic Observation and Controlled Teaching Trials

The goal of *systematic observation and controlled teaching trials* is to determine which elements of a child's behavior interfere with instruction, how these interfering elements can be reduced, and what motivates the child to attend and respond. Ideally, you should observe the child in the settings in which he or she is expected to function (e.g., school, home, bus, and a sheltered workshop). If possible, have teachers and parents observe the child's daily functional needs and, when appropriate, evaluate the child's skills over an extended period.

The following examples illustrate how you might implement systematic observation and controlled teaching trials (Strain, Sainto, & Maheady, 1984):

1. Determine which behavior patterns interfere with instruction—such as self-stimulating behavior, attention difficulties, or destructive behavior—and the conditions under which they occur.
2. Determine the motivational mechanism that supports the deviant behavior—such as desire to obtain positive reinforcement, terminate an unpleasant task, or obtain sensory feedback—and then use this information to develop

interventions. You can determine the child's preferences for either visual or auditory stimulation by observation or by asking teachers and parents to identify the child's preferences.

The school environment is suited for assessing some, but not all, of the learning needs of children with severe developmental delays. For instance, you can evaluate how a child functions in the cafeteria, locates the bathroom, interacts with schoolmates, places forms on a formboard, or performs other school-related activities. However, you usually will not be able to evaluate how adequately the child uses the bathtub, the refrigerator, or a stove and how the child spends leisure time.

GUIDELINES FOR EVALUATING ASSESSMENT INFORMATION

After you complete the assessment, consider the following questions in formulating the psychological report and in developing recommendations:

History

1. Is there a history of mental retardation in the family?
2. Were there medical complications during the pregnancy? If so, what were the complications?
3. Did the mother have amniocentesis or ultrasound during the pregnancy? If so, what did the tests indicate?
4. Were the pregnancy and delivery normal?

Developmental Considerations

5. When did the child reach specific developmental milestones, such as smiling, sitting, crawling, walking, saying single words, making simple word combinations, reacting to strangers, becoming toilet trained, and acquiring dressing skills? Were there delays in the child's reaching developmental landmarks? If so, in what areas were the delays, and how long were they?
6. Did the parents suspect that something was wrong with the child's rate of development? If so, when did they first suspect that something was wrong?

Medical Findings

7. If a current medical evaluation was conducted, what were the results? In particular, how are the child's vision, hearing, motor skills, and general health?
8. If the child received any medical treatment, what was the child treated for, what was the treatment, and how effective was the treatment?
9. Is there any history of brain injury, including seizures or illnesses such as meningitis or encephalitis, that may have affected the child's development?

Parental Descriptions

10. How do the parents describe the child's cognitive level?
11. How do the parents describe the child's behavior?
12. What are the parents' plans for the child?

School

13. If the child is attending school, how is the child doing at school? What grades is the child receiving? How does the child get along with other children? If the child is receiving special education services, what are the services?
14. How does the teacher describe the child's behavior and academic performance?
15. According to the teacher, which of the child's social and interpersonal skills are adequately developed, and which are not?

Previous Psychological Evaluations

16. If psychological evaluations were performed in the past, what were the results and recommendations?
17. How do the current assessment results compare with any previous results?
18. Do the results of the present assessment indicate that a classification of mental retardation is warranted?

Services

19. Is the child eligible for special services?
20. What is the least restrictive program that will facilitate the child's cognitive development?
21. Is full inclusion a viable option, or is a special class necessary?

Transition Considerations

22. What skills does the adolescent have that can be used for productive employment?
23. Would the adolescent benefit from a sheltered workshop focusing on job training?
24. Can the individual live independently, or will he or she need special facilities (e.g., transition group home, community-based home, or residential setting)?
25. What services are needed by the family?

DISTINGUISHING BETWEEN MENTAL RETARDATION AND DEVELOPMENTAL DELAY

When you suspect that a child may have mental retardation, also consider a possible diagnosis of *developmental delay*, especially with infants or preschool children. Make a diagnosis of mental retardation *only* when the child shows significantly below average general intellectual functioning in conjunction with significant deficits in adaptive behavior.

There are three reasons for distinguishing between mental retardation and developmental delay during infancy and the preschool years (Fotheringhan, 1983). First, although an infant or young child may meet the criteria for a diagnosis of mental retardation, the measure of intelligence may not be reliable because intelligence test scores of infants reflect primarily developmental progress (see Chapter 6 in *Assessment of Children: Cognitive Applications*). Thus, with infants and young children, it is important to conduct repeated assessments to check for changes in the rate of development and to arrive at a valid diagnosis (see the case of *Daniel Hoffman* in Chapter 1 of *Assessment of Children: Cognitive Applications*). Second, other conditions in infancy and preschool years may mimic mental retardation. For example, aphasia or cerebral palsy may reduce a young child's ability to communicate, thus making the assessment of intellectual ability difficult. Third, there may be home circumstances, such as child abuse and neglect, that impair a child's adaptive functioning. Altering these conditions may improve the child's adaptive and cognitive functioning.

When a child shows impaired functioning and you cannot reliably make a diagnosis of mental retardation, consider developmental delay as a tentative diagnosis. A diagnosis of developmental delay alerts the child's parents and professionals to the possibility that (a) the basis for the cognitive deficit is ambiguous, (b) the deficiency may be transitory, (c) the reduced functioning in adaptive behavior may not be sufficient to warrant a diagnosis of mental retardation, or (d) the problems in adaptive behavior may be temporary. In contrast, a diagnosis of mental retardation is more definitive and implies a significant general reduction in cognitive ability and adaptive behavior, determined on the basis of reliable and valid assessment findings.

ASSESSMENT OF CHILDREN WITH SEVERE OR PROFOUND MENTAL RETARDATION

Children with severe or profound mental retardation may be especially difficult to evaluate because of self-stimulating behavior, self-injurious behavior, limited attention span, destructive behavior, temper tantrums, seizures, noncompliance with requests, or inability to understand the test questions. They often have accompanying physical defects (e.g., impaired vision, hearing, and motor coordination), difficulty in attaining an upright posture, undeveloped speech, poor feeding and toileting skills, and difficulty in guarding against physical dangers. Children with profound retardation, in particular, have a high incidence of devastating motor, sensory, and physical handicaps and a high mortality rate. Compared to children with severe retardation, they tend to have a higher incidence of delayed puberty, seizures, enuresis, communication difficulties, pica (a strong craving to eat nonnutritive objects, such as paint, gravel, or hair), self-biting, fecal smearing, mutism, echopraxia (a tendency toward automatic imitation of the movements and gestures of others), abnormal EEGs, encopresis (involuntary defecation not due to a local organic defect or illness), difficulty in self-recognition, inadequate socialization skills, and high pain thresholds (Switzky, Haywood, & Rotatori, 1982). They also have a higher rate of placement in institutions than do children with severe retardation.

As a result of the Individuals with Disabilities Education Act (IDEA; see Chapter 3 in *Assessment of Children: Cognitive Applications*) and the movement toward deinstitutionalization, public schools and community agencies are serving more children with severe handicaps, and fewer children are being placed in residential facilities. Additionally, children with moderate or severe mental retardation now tend to be in school for more years and, consequently, require more frequent assessments.

Traditional assessment approaches may not be useful with children with severe or profound mental retardation. Standardized norm-referenced tests are of limited use because (a) the instructions may be too difficult, (b) the administrative procedures may be too inflexible to permit the children to display their knowledge by unconventional means, and (c) the items may be too difficult to allow the children to demonstrate their knowledge. Extrapolated scores are not

appropriate for individual diagnosis because their reliability and validity are unknown. Norm-referenced tests are also relatively insensitive to the developmental changes that occur in children with severe or profound mental retardation (White & Haring, 1978). To maintain their relative standing on an intelligence test, children with severe or profound mental retardation would need to develop their abilities as rapidly as children without mental retardation, which is highly unlikely. Thus, it may be better to use raw scores rather than standard scores for estimating the progress of children with severe or profound mental retardation.

Curriculum-based assessment, which usually follows standard curriculum guidelines, also may be inappropriate for children with severe or profound mental retardation, because the children are rarely candidates for instruction in the school's standard curriculum. Curriculum-based assessment may fail to consider the children's handicapping conditions, as children without mental retardation form the standardization groups for most curriculum-based assessment tests (White & Haring, 1978). Although children with severe or profound mental retardation may obtain low scores on curriculum-based assessment measures, the skills they do possess may enable them to function at a minimal level of competency. For example, some children with limited vocabulary may still be able to express their needs. In other cases, children with severe or profound mental retardation may need to develop proficiency in a specific skill to overcome a disability, as in the case of deaf children who must develop skills needed for communicating in sign language.

The use of normal developmental scales with severely and profoundly mentally handicapped children is also problematic (White & Haring, 1978). These scales do not consider the limited opportunities available to children with severe or profound mental retardation to develop and refine concepts—their development does not proceed like that of normal young children. If you use normal developmental models for curriculum planning, be sure to adjust them as appropriate.

Although standardized norm-referenced tests, curriculum-based assessment measures, and development-based tests and scales have shortcomings for the assessment of children with severe or profound mental retardation, they play a role. Mental-age, test-age, and developmental-age scores from these scales provide indices of the child's approximate developmental level. Individual items provide information about what the child can and cannot accomplish.

INTERVENTIONS FOR INDIVIDUALS WITH MENTAL RETARDATION

After a diagnosis of mental retardation is made, it is useful to determine the level of support that the individual may need. Here are four such levels (AAMR, 1992, adapted from p. 26):

Level 1. *Intermittent.* Supports are provided on an as-needed basis (e.g., during transitions and crises).

Level 2. *Limited.* Supports are provided more consistently than on an as-needed basis (e.g., during training for employment or transitions from school to work).

Level 3. *Extensive.* Supports are provided at least daily in one or more environments and are not time limited (e.g., long-term home living support).

Level 4. *Pervasive.* Supports are consistently provided across many or all environments, at high intensity, and are potentially of a life-sustaining nature (e.g., full-time medical care).

Services for children with mental retardation may begin shortly after the child's birth or during preschool years and continue throughout the developmental period. These services include medical and dental care, special education programs, in-home living assistance programs, employment assistance, sheltered workshops, and placement in facilities where individuals with mental retardation can lead as normal lives as possible when they reach adulthood (Tanguay & Russell, 1991).

Here are 13 recommendations made by parents of children with mental retardation for helping the children and assisting parents in caring for their children (Westling, 1996):

1. Provide individually determined meaningful instruction, services, and supports appropriate for the child's age and disability, either in regular education or in special classes, as needed.

2. Include in the curriculum socialization and friendship development.

3. Provide opportunities for parents to participate in school activities, especially the planning process involving their child.

4. Make parent education programs available in different formats, such as printed material, workshops, and small-group meetings.

5. Provide other forms of support for parents, such as information about respite care, parent and advocacy groups, and public and private community agencies.

6. Provide family-focused services, including family planning and help in obtaining financial aid and better housing, as needed.

7. Realize that the time of initial entry into programs for children with disabilities is a stressful period for both children and parents. Provide emotional support for the family and any requested information such as medical or developmental information.

8. Provide home-based early intervention services for infants and toddlers and integrated preschool and after-school programs for older children.

9. Designate a staff person to be responsible for helping the family coordinate services and deal with community agencies.

10. Encourage agencies to collaborate with each other when children move from one program or school to another.

11. Encourage professionals, parents, and advocates to work together to increase funding for both individuals with disabilities and their families.

12. Formulate and carry out transition services for adolescents who are leaving school and entering adulthood. These services include providing information about residential placement, if appropriate; discussing employment opportunities; and offering training that focuses on the needs of young adults, which might include developing functional skills, social and interpersonal skills, vocational skills, leisure skills, and domestic living skills.
13. Give parents information during the developmental period about (a) possible positive lifestyles for their child, (b) their child's potentials, and (c) their child's possibilities when she or he reaches maturity.

Therapeutic interventions for children with mental retardation include environmental changes, behavioral treatments, individual psychotherapy, group psychotherapy, family therapy, and pharmacotherapy (under a health care provider's guidance). In designing therapeutic interventions, consider the child's level of cognitive, social, and physical functioning. For example, therapeutic sessions may need to be short and frequent, and therapeutic interventions may need to incorporate extensive structure, reassurance, problem solving, and constructive feedback (Bregman, 1991).

Interventions usually will not lead to significant improvements in the intelligence test scores of children with mental retardation. For example, an examination of the Milwaukee Project (an environmental enrichment project designed to prevent mental retardation from a familial origin in high-risk children between 6 months and 6 years of age) failed to produce evidence that early intervention for children at risk for mental retardation results in meaningful and lasting changes in intelligence (Gilhousen, Allen, Lasater, Farrell, & Reynolds, 1990). These and similar results, however, do not mean that interventions are not needed. The interventions discussed previously focus on the entire child and family, not just on raising the child's intelligence test scores.

All children need the opportunity to learn academic skills, regardless of their IQ and level of adaptive behavior. Test scores should not be used to deny children with mental retardation access to programs that may help them learn valuable skills. Many children whose test scores fall into the mentally retarded range can develop into self-sufficient and productive adults. They need education and training regimens that encourage the full use of their potentials. They need help in bolstering their self-esteem and expectancy of success (Zigler, 1995).

Persons with mental retardation need to be integrated into society, to have their rights to individualization recognized, and to be given opportunities for growth and development. Here are some strategies that will help us meet these goals:

1. Emphasize the similarities, rather than the differences, between people with and without mental retardation.
2. Recognize that people with mental retardation can improve their level of functioning, given a proper opportunity.
3. De-emphasize labeling.
4. Increase individualization.
5. Expand legal rights for people with mental retardation.
6. Increase society's tolerance for individual differences.
7. Recognize that some mental retardation arises out of conditions in society.
8. Emphasize prevention.
9. Plan and coordinate services.

CONCLUDING COMMENT

The assessment of mental retardation requires the use of a reliable, valid, and comprehensive individual measure of intellectual functioning and a reliable, valid, and comprehensive measure of adaptive behavior. In addition, the entire evaluation needs to be comprehensive, because mental retardation may exist concurrently with other disabling conditions (Editorial Board, 1996).

Research on intelligence and mental retardation has changed our view of persons with mental retardation (Detterman, Gabriel, & Ruthsatz, 2000).

People who, at one time, were viewed as unsalvageable are now regarded as people who can learn and accomplish. This is quite a radical change to occur in less than 100 years.... Over the next century, there is reason to hope that the connection between intelligence and mental retardation will be more fully, and perhaps even completely, explicated. Advances in genetics, brain imaging and recording, and neuroscience may allow the connection of behavioral data collected over the last 50 years with underlying biological processes. (p. 155)

Intelligence tests, originally designed to evaluate and help children and adults, currently are used in ways that were never intended by the early psychologists and test developers. For example, intelligence test scores are used by the Social Security Administration to determine whether individuals are eligible for disability benefits under certain programs. In criminal cases, intelligence tests are used to determine whether individuals are competent to stand trial (i.e., whether they have diminished capacity). Finally, in cases of capital punishment, intelligence test results may determine whether individuals live or die—they may be spared the death penalty if they are found to have diminished capacity. Thus, the assessment of individuals referred for evaluation of mental retardation has extremely far-reaching consequences.

THINKING THROUGH THE ISSUES

1. What data obtained from a psychological evaluation would you consider in formulating a response to this question from a parent: "Is my child going to be mentally retarded forever?"
2. In what ways might the following three children differ in their ability to function in school and in society: (a) a child with a WISC–III IQ of 60 and a Vineland Adaptive Behavior Scale Composite score of 90, (b) a child with a WISC–III Full Scale IQ of 90 and a Vineland Adaptive Behavior Scale Composite score of 60, and (c) a child with a WISC–III Full Scale IQ of 60 and a Vineland Adaptive Behavior Scale Composite score of 60?

3. Why should you *not* expect to see similar WISC–III patterns in different children who are classified as mentally retarded?

4. Of what value are informal and functional assessment procedures with children who have severe handicaps? Why do you suppose we don't have better tests to assess low-incidence handicapping conditions?

SUMMARY

1. The most widely used definition of mental retardation is as follows: "*Mental retardation* refers to substantial limitations in present functioning. It is characterized by significantly subaverage intellectual functioning, existing concurrently with related limitations in two or more of the following applicable adaptive skill areas: communication, self-care, home living, social skills, community use, self-direction, health and safety, functional academics, leisure, and work. Mental retardation manifests before age 18" (AAMR, 1992, p. 5).

2. Significantly subaverage intellectual functioning is defined as a score of approximately 70 to 75 or below on an individually administered intelligence test.

3. Adaptive skills preferably are measured through use of an appropriately normed and standardized adaptive behavior scale.

4. Four assumptions underly classification efforts: (a) assessment must consider cultural and linguistic diversity, (b) adaptive skills must be evaluated in reference to the community, (c) adaptive limitations often coexist with strengths in other adaptive skills, and (d) the life functioning of individuals with mental retardation can improve with appropriate supports.

5. The 1992 AAMR definition has been criticized for being too political, potentially increasing the number of persons diagnosed with mild mental retardation, and making the assessment of adaptive behavior problematic by increasing the number of adaptive behavior domains to 10.

6. The *DSM-IV–TR* definition of mental retardation is similar to the AAMR definition but specifies four degrees of severity: (a) mild mental retardation (IQ level of 50–55 to approximately 70), moderate mental retardation (IQ level of 35–40 to 50–55), severe mental retardation (IQ level of 20–25 to 35–40), and profound mental retardation (IQ level below 20 or 25).

7. The AAMR and *DSM-IV–TR* definitions both refer to a level of behavioral performance without reference to etiology.

8. The AAMR and *DSM-IV–TR* definitions both imply that the diagnosis is only a description of present behavior, recognize the contribution of intelligence tests, tie the diagnosis to the developmental process, recognize the possible coexistence of other forms of childhood disorders, and avoid the implication that mental retardation is irreversible.

Etiology of Mental Retardation

9. Mental retardation can be a primary diagnosis, occur as a part of a syndrome, or co-occur with other developmental disabilities, neurological disorders, or psychiatric disorders.

10. Mental retardation can result from a diverse set of predisposing factors, including heredity, early alterations of embryonic development, pregnancy and perinatal problems, general medical conditions acquired in infancy or childhood, and environmental influences.

11. Children with mental retardation may also have physical disabilities.

12. Approximately 1% of the population would be classified as mentally retarded.

13. Of people with mental retardation, approximately 85% are in the mild classification, 10% in the moderate classification, 3% to 4% in the severe classification, and 1% to 2% in the profound classification.

14. Persons with mental retardation can be broadly grouped into two categories: (a) those with mental retardation from a familial origin and (b) those with mental retardation from brain injury.

15. The group with mental retardation from a familial origin includes individuals with mild mental retardation, in the IQ range of 50 to 69.

16. Individuals with mental retardation from brain injury include primarily those in the IQ range below 50, although organic etiologies are sometimes found in milder forms of mental retardation.

17. Approaches successful in reducing the occurrence of mental retardation include (a) screening and treating infants for metabolic disorders, (b) using a low-phenylalanine diet for pregnant women who have PKU and for infants born with PKU, (c) immunizing children, (d) providing education to adults about the effects of alcohol and drug use during pregnancy, (e) reducing children's exposure to lead, (f) constructing safer automobiles, (g) providing public education about the need to use infant seats and seat belts in automobiles, (h) using amniocentesis, (i) and screening to identify whether individuals have genetic conditions or metabolic disorders that could result in mental retardation in their offspring and then providing genetic counseling.

Relationship Between Measured Intelligence and Adaptive Behavior

18. Although the precise relationship between measures of intelligence and adaptive behavior is unknown, an estimate in the .30s would appear reasonable.

Some General Considerations in Understanding Mental Retardation

19. Children with mental retardation show a variety of deficits and delays in their social development relative to children without mental retardation of the same chronological age. At least some of the differences are due to a mismatch between the social and learning environments of children with mental retardation and their cognitive capabilities.

Mental Retardation and Intelligence Testing

20. As early as the first decade of the twentieth century, the National Education Association described the proper use of intelligence tests in the study of children with mental retardation.

21. Useful instruments for the evaluation of mild mental retardation include the Stanford-Binet: IV and the WISC–III, WPPSI–R, and WAIS–III.

22. The Stanford-Binet: IV has a somewhat lower floor than the Wechsler scales, but not at all age levels.

23. Neither the Stanford-Binet: IV nor the Wechsler tests were designed for the assessment of children with severe or profound mental retardation.

24. Children with mental retardation usually have a slow rate of cognitive development, limited expressive and receptive language abilities, limited adaptive skills, limited experiential background, short attention span, distractibility, and a concrete and literal style in approaching tasks.

25. Children with mental retardation may have higher rates of acquiescence than children who are not mentally retarded; thus, do not rely primarily on yes-no questions.

26. Children with mental retardation may have emotional problems unrelated to their intellectual retardation.

27. The test age or mental age obtained from a test of intelligence can be used as a rough index of mental ability.

Assessment of Maladaptive Behavior

28. Several procedures are useful for the assesment of maldaptive behaviors in children and adults with mental retardation.

Functional Assessment

29. As part of an evaluation, you may want to conduct a functional assessment to help you evaluate which environmental factors might be modified to improve the functioning of a child with mental retardation.

30. Functional assessment procedures include (a) adaptive behavior questionnaires, checklists, and interviews; (b) task analysis; and (c) systematic observation and controlled teaching trials.

Guidelines for Evaluating Assessment Information

31. In formulating the psychological report and in developing recommendations, consider the family history, child's development, medical findings, parental descriptions, school records, previous psychological evaluations, needed services, and transition services.

Distinguishing Between Mental Retardation and Developmental Delay

32. When you suspect that a child may have mental retardation, also consider a possible diagnosis of developmental delay, especially with infants or preschool children.

33. Make a diagnosis of mental retardation only when the child shows significantly below average general intellectual functioning in conjunction with significant deficits in adaptive behavior.

Assessment of Children with Severe or Profound Mental Retardation

34. Children with severe or profound mental retardation may be especially difficult to evaluate because of behavioral difficulties or inability to understand the test questions.

35. As a result of the Individuals with Disabilities Education Act and the movement toward deinstitutionalization, public schools and community agencies are serving more children with severe handicaps, and fewer children are being placed in residential facilities.

36. Traditional assessment approaches may not be useful with children with severe or profound mental retardation.

37. Curriculum-based assessment, which usually follows standard curriculum guidelines, may be inappropriate for children with severe or profound mental retardation, because the children are rarely candidates for instruction in the school's standard curriculum.

38. The use of normal developmental scales with severely and profoundly handicapped children is problematic.

Interventions for Individuals with Mental Retardation

39. An individual with mental retardation may need an intermittent, limited, extensive, or pervasive level of support.

40. Services for children with mental retardation may begin shortly after the child's birth or during preschool years and continue throughout the developmental period.

41. These services include medical and dental care, special education programs, in-home living assistance programs, employment assistance, sheltered workshops, and placement in facilities where individuals with mental retardation can lead as normal lives as possible when they reach adulthood.

42. Be prepared to assist parents in caring for their children with mental retardation.

43. Therapeutic interventions for children with mental retardation include environmental changes, behavioral treatments, individual psychotherapy, group psychotherapy, family therapy, and pharmacotherapy (under a health care provider's guidance).

44. Interventions usually will not lead to significant improvement in the intelligence test scores of children with mental retardation.

45. All children need the opportunity to learn academic skills, regardless of their IQ and level of adaptive behavior.

46. Persons with mental retardation need to be integrated into society, to have their rights to individualization recognized, and to be given opportunities for growth and development.

47. The assessment of mental retardation requires the use of a reliable, valid, and comprehensive individual measure of intellectual functioning and a reliable, valid, and comprehensive measure of adaptive behavior.

Concluding Comment

48. The entire evaluation needs to be comprehensive, because mental retardation may exist concurrently with other disabling conditions.

49. The assessment of individuals referred for evaluation of mental retardation has extremely far reaching consequences.

KEY TERMS, CONCEPTS, AND NAMES

Mental retardation (p. 337)
American Association on Mental Retardation (AAMR) (p. 337)
Significantly subaverage intellectual functioning (p. 337)
Adaptive skill areas (p. 337)
Mild mental retardation (p. 337)
Moderate mental retardation (p. 337)
Severe mental retardation (p. 337)
Profound mental retardation (p. 337)
Etiology of mental retardation (p. 339)
Fetal alcohol syndrome (p. 340)
Mental retardation from a familial origin (p. 340)
Mental retardation associated with brain injury (p. 340)
Phenylketonuria (PKU) (p. 341)
Amniocentesis (p. 341)
Prevalence rates of mental retardation (p. 341)

STUDY QUESTIONS

1. Define mental retardation and discuss the implications of the definition and related classification issues. Include in your discussion the AAMR and *DSM-IV–TR* definitions and criticisms associated with the AAMR definition.

2. Discuss the etiology of mental retardation.

3. How are prevalence rates for mental retardation a function of the relationship between measured intelligence and adaptive behavior?

4. Discuss some general considerations in understanding mental retardation.

5. Discuss mental retardation and intelligence testing.

6. Discuss functional assessment in relationship to mental retardation.

7. Discuss some guidelines for evaluating assessment information in the area of mental retardation.

8. How do you distinguish between mental retardation and developmental delay?

9. Discuss the assessment of children with severe or profound mental retardation, and in your discussion address problems with standardized tests and scales.

10. Discuss interventions for individuals with mental retardation.

14

GIFTEDNESS

A great society not only searches out excellence but rewards it when it is found.

—Anonymous

Goals and Objectives

This chapter is designed to enable you to do the following:

- Become familiar with methods for assessing children who are gifted

- Understand how creativity is defined and measured

Children are generally referred to as gifted and talented if they have outstanding prominence in an area, such as an extremely high IQ (above 130, which represents the 98th percentile rank), excellence in art or music, or high scores on tests of creativity. Such children require differentiated educational programs and services beyond those normally provided by the regular program if they are to make contributions to society and maximize their potential (Marland, 1972).

Children who are gifted and talented include those with demonstrated achievement or potential ability in any of the following areas.

1. General intellectual ability
2. Specific academic aptitude
3. Creative or productive thinking
4. Leadership ability
5. Visual and performing arts

A federal definition of children who are gifted and talented follows:

The term "children who are gifted and talented" means children who are identified at the preschool, elementary, or secondary level as possessing demonstrated or potential abilities that give evidence of high performance capability in areas such as intellectual, creative, specific academic, or leadership ability, or in the performing and visual arts, and who, by reason thereof, require services or activities not ordinarily provided by the school. (Gifted and Talented Children's Education Act of 1978, Section 902, with changes in notation)

Essentially, the term *gifted* is used to describe children with exceptionally high IQs, those who have creative talents, and those who are high on both dimensions. This definition applies to approximately 3% to 5% of the population of children in the United States. Table 14-1 gives expected prevalence rates, based solely on IQ, for scores at 0 to 6 standard deviations above the mean. The table shows, for example,

that approximately 2 in 100 individuals have IQs of 130 or above, whereas approximately 3 in 100,000 individuals have IQs of 160 or higher.

INTELLECTUAL AND PERSONALITY CHARACTERISTICS OF CHILDREN WHO ARE GIFTED

Factors that influence the development of gifted intellectual performance include (a) genetics, (b) ability to master symbol systems, (c) opportunities to develop talent, (d) parental encouragement of talent, (e) approval of intellectual activities, and (f) positive peer influences for intellectual activities (Gallagher, 1991). The following list gives some intellectual and personality characteristics associated with children who are gifted (reprinted and adapted with permission of the publisher and author from L. K. Silverman, "Family Counseling with the Gifted," in N. Colangelo and G. A. David, *Handbook of Gifted Education,* p. 390, copyright 1997 by Allyn and Bacon).

Intellectual Characteristics

- Exceptional reasoning ability
- Intellectual curiosity
- Rapid learning rate
- Facility with abstraction
- Complex thought processes
- Keen sense of justice
- Early moral concern
- Passion for learning
- Analytical thinking
- Vivid imagination
- Divergent thinking
- Creativity
- Powers of concentration
- Capacity for reflection

Personality Characteristics

- Insightfulness
- Need to understand
- Need for mental stimulation
- Perfectionism
- Need for precision
- Need for logic
- Questioning of rules
- Questioning of authority
- Sensitivity and empathy
- Intensity
- Acute self-awareness
- Excellent sense of humor
- Nonconformity
- Perseverance
- Tendency toward introversion

Table 14-1
Expected Occurrence of IQs at or Above Each Standard Deviation Above the Mean

Standard deviation above the mean	IQ		Approximate expected occurrence
	SD = 15	SD = 16	
0	100	100	50 in 100
1	115	116	16 in 100
2	130	132	2 in 100
3	145	148	1 in 1,000
4	160	164	3 in 100,000
5	175	180	3 in 10,000,000
6	190	196	1 in 1,000,000,000

Note, however, that children who are gifted usually (a) will not display all these characteristics; (b) will vary with respect to these characteristics; (c) will display these characteristics at different ages, with some children displaying them at earlier ages than others; and (d) will have different clusters of these characteristics (Baska, 1989). Also note that these characteristics are not exclusive to children who are gifted; rather, children who are gifted tend have more of these characteristics than children who are not gifted.

Studies conducted in the 1980s and 1990s on the psychological characteristics of gifted children point to the following conclusions (Robinson & Clinkenbeard, 1998):

Gifted elementary or secondary age children…show some advantages over other students particularly in quantity, speed, and complexity of cognition. They know more about metacognition and can use strategies better in new contexts, but they may not use a wider variety of metacognitive strategies than other students…. both creativity and motivation probably influence the results of research on cognitive and metacognitive characteristics. (p. 125)

Gifted students … tend to have better psychosocial adjustment than other students. They are at least as popular, though they may have different friendship styles. Their self-concepts, while heavily weighted with their academic abilities, are generally high, and they tend to score at normal or above levels on personality measures. They tend to be more internally motivated and have more positive attributions for success and failures; however, they may have more trouble coping when they do encounter failures.

These positive findings may not be true for various subgroups of the gifted. Sex differences have been found such that through adolescence, females tend to decrease and males tend to increase on several positive emotional characteristics. In addition, these psychological advantages may start to disappear as the level of giftedness increases. Students who are extremely far from the norm intellectually seem to have more trouble fitting in socially and emotionally as well. Gifted students who are underachievers may demonstrate considerably different psychological profiles. Finally, students from cultural or ethnic groups where the identification of giftedness has not been traditional have not been thoroughly investigated. (pp. 129–130)

IDENTIFYING CHILDREN WHO ARE GIFTED

There is no one best system for identifying children who are gifted. Any means of identification is in part dependent on the goals of the program. A program that emphasizes cognitive skills needs different identification procedures than one focusing on art or music. Identification procedures include standardized tests, parent and teacher nominations, direct observation of the child's behavior, and review of the child's creative work. The most effective means of identification combines the results from *several* procedures, including the following:

- Group intelligence tests
- Individual intelligence tests
- Achievement tests
- Teacher nominations
- Parent nominations
- Peer nominations
- Self-nominations

In actual practice, schools may give a group intelligence test (such as the Raven Progressive Matrices), rather than individual intelligence tests, to identify children eligible for a gifted program, because group tests are less costly to administer. For many school districts, it would not be economically feasible to administer an individual intelligence test to every child who might be eligible for a gifted program. Table 14-2 shows a recommendation form that teachers and parents can complete for a child being considered for a gifted program.

Because giftedness is not a unitary concept, students should not be selected for a gifted program solely on the

FOXTROT © 1993 Bill Amend. Reprinted with permission of UNIVERSAL SYNDICATE. All rights reserved.

Table 14-2
Teacher/Parent Recommendation Form for Academically Gifted and Talented Program

ACADEMICALLY GIFTED AND TALENTED PROGRAM
TEACHER/PARENT RECOMMENDATION FORM

Child's name: _____ Date: _____ Grade: _____

School: _____ Name of person filling out form: _____

Directions: Please check the box that represents your rating of each characteristic. Use the scale below. Thank you!

Generally yes—Child generally has this characteristic.

Generally no—Child generally does not have this characteristic.

Don't know—Don't know whether child has this characteristic.

Characteristics	Rating		
	Generally yes	*Generally no*	*Don't know*
Learning Characteristics			
1. Has excellent reasoning ability.	☐	☐	☐
2. Is intellectually curious.	☐	☐	☐
3. Learns things rapidly.	☐	☐	☐
4. Is good with abstract concepts.	☐	☐	☐
5. Shows complex thought processes.	☐	☐	☐
6. Has an advanced vocabulary.	☐	☐	☐
7. Achieves well above grade level in several academic areas.	☐	☐	☐
Motivational Characteristics			
8. Is persistent when faced with difficult tasks.	☐	☐	☐
9. Is resourceful in finding answers to questions.	☐	☐	☐
10. Becomes absorbed in tasks when he or she is interested in the tasks.	☐	☐	☐
11. Requires little external motivation to follow through in work that initially excites him or her.	☐	☐	☐
12. Strives toward perfection.	☐	☐	☐
13. Enjoys intellectual pursuits.	☐	☐	☐
14. Is concerned about social and moral issues.	☐	☐	☐
Leadership Characteristics			
15. Is self-confident with other children and adults.	☐	☐	☐
16. Enjoys taking on responsibility.	☐	☐	☐
17. Expresses self well.	☐	☐	☐
Creativity Characteristics			
18. Shows emotional sensitivity.	☐	☐	☐
19. Is nonconforming (or an independent thinker).	☐	☐	☐
20. Is curious about many things.	☐	☐	☐
21. Generates a large number of ideas and solutions to problems.	☐	☐	☐
22. Is independent in thought.	☐	☐	☐
23. Is imaginative.	☐	☐	☐
24. Asks many questions.	☐	☐	☐
25. Has a sense of humor and can laugh at himself or herself.	☐	☐	☐
26. Is a high risk taker and adventurous.	☐	☐	☐

basis of high scores on a test that measures only one specific ability, such as receptive vocabulary or perceptual reasoning ability. A multidimensional cognitive ability test should be used as one component of the identification process.

The single best method available for identifying children with superior cognitive abilities is a standardized, individually administered, multidimensional test of intelligence, such as the Stanford-Binet: IV or a Wechsler test (Zigler & Farber, 1985). Other areas related to giftedness, such as creativity, task commitment, and talent, are more difficult to reliably measure. Children who are identified as gifted should also be appraised in several academic areas, because not all children who are gifted are equally talented in all academic areas. Some children who are gifted have exceptional talent in either mathematics or language arts but not both, whereas others are gifted in both mathematics and language arts.

UNDERACHIEVING CHILDREN WHO ARE GIFTED

Intellectual giftedness does not ensure success in school (Rimm, 1997). The academic success of children who are gifted is determined by the same environmental forces that affect the success of all children—namely, motivation, interests, self-concept, family and home, teachers and school, peers, and society. When the needs of children who are gifted are not recognized and met, their potential may not be reached.

Children who are gifted may underachieve and rebel when (a) they experience excessive parental pressure to succeed in school, (b) schools do not value high achievement in children, require children to reach excessively high goals, or provide curricula that do not challenge children, or (c) there is peer pressure to conform to the average, play it "cool" by not studying, or not put out much effort to learn the course material.

Underachieving children who are gifted may exhibit one or more of the following characteristics (Clark, 1988; Rimm, 1997):

- Low self-esteem
- Low sense of personal control over their lives or inability to assume responsibility for their actions
- Feelings of being rejected by their family
- Marked hostility toward adult authority
- Resistance to guidance from teachers and parents
- Feelings of victimization
- Dislike of school and teachers
- Rebelliousness
- Weak motivation for academic achievement
- Poor study habits
- Limited intellectual adaptiveness
- Limited persistence in completing classroom assignments
- Limited leadership qualities
- Immaturity
- Poor personal adjustment
- Few hobbies

- Phobia about tests
- Low aspirations
- Poor planning for the future
- Goals that do not match their interests or abilities
- Preference for careers that involve manual activities, business, or sales rather than socially concerned or professional occupations

The characteristics most frequently found among underachieving students who are gifted are *low self-esteem* and *a low sense of personal control over their own lives* (Rimm, 1997).

Underachieving students who are gifted may have complex behavior patterns that are not easily amenable to intervention (Gallagher, 1997), especially if their behavior patterns have been established over a long period of childhood. When teachers and parents see a pattern of underachievement, they may assume that a student who was once gifted is no longer gifted. To reverse longstanding patterns of underachievement, the following steps are recommended (Rimm, 1997):

1. Assess the child.
2. Obtain information from the parents and teachers about the child.
3. Change the expectations of the child, parents, teachers, peers, and siblings about the child's ability to succeed in school.
4. Provide role models for the child.
5. Correct skill deficiencies.
6. Modify reinforcements used at home and at school.

CHILDREN WHO ARE GIFTED AND HAVE LEARNING DISABILITIES

Some children who are gifted have specific learning disabilities that interfere with their ability to learn in school. They may have poor penmanship, difficulty following directions, poor spelling, reversal of letters, or problems with numeric transpositions. Their test results may show uneven patterns of strengths and weaknesses. For example, they may obtain high scores on vocabulary tests and give fluent and in-depth definitions of words, while obtaining low scores on arithmetic or spelling tests. They may have emotional problems and be frustrated because they have been told that they are gifted, yet they are doing poorly in school. A case of a child who is gifted and has a learning disability follows.

Paul, aged 13 years 2 months, was referred because of a severe spelling disability (1st percentile on the Stanford Achievement Test). His teachers indicated that his specific deficits in spelling and writing were interfering with his academic performance. His test scores in other areas indicated average to above-average reading skills (44th to 88th percentiles) and average to above-average arithmetic skills (54th to 94th percentiles). Reading comprehension scores were better than word recognition scores. On the WISC–III Paul obtained a Verbal Scale IQ of 135, a Performance Scale IQ of 127, and a Full Scale IQ of 134. The results suggested that Paul is a gifted youngster with a specific learning disability in the area of written expression.

CHILDREN WHO ARE GIFTED AND HAVE EMOTIONAL PROBLEMS

The incidence of emotional problems is likely to be about the same among children who are gifted and children who are not gifted (Pendarvis, Howley, & Howley, 1990). However, when children who are gifted challenge authority, respond in unconventional ways, or have limited tolerance for frustration, they may be classified by teachers as emotionally disturbed. As Grossberg and Cornell (1988) noted, "High IQ may place some children at risk due to others' jealousy, fear, negative attitudes, absence of an appropriate school program, or lack of intellectual peers. Not high intelligence but rather its consequences may have a negative effect" (pp. 270–271, with changes in notation).

PRESCHOOL CHILDREN WHO ARE GIFTED

Infants and preschool children who are gifted may show their superior ability or talents in the following ways (Roedell, 1980b; Silverman, 1997):

- Show unusual alertness in infancy
- Demonstrate a preference for novelty
- Show advanced progression through the developmental milestones
- Display a long attention span
- Show curiosity and ask many questions
- Have an advanced vocabulary
- Show early interest in time
- Use metaphors or analogies
- Make up songs or stories spontaneously
- Make interesting shapes or patterns with blocks, board shapes, playdough, or drawing materials
- Modify language when talking to less mature children
- Put together difficult puzzles
- Have a sense of humor
- Understand abstract or complex concepts
- Master a new skill, concept, song, or rhyme with unusual speed
- Use language to exchange ideas
- Become absorbed in one kind of activity
- Display great interest or skill in ordering or grouping objects
- Take apart and reassemble things with unusual skill
- Understand directions, such as right and left, at an early age
- Remember and make mental connections between past and present experiences
- Show sensitivity to the needs or feelings of other children or adults

- Carry out complex instructions to do several things in succession
- Show unusual attentiveness to features of the preschool environment
- Use verbal skills to handle conflict or to influence other children's behavior

Table 14-3 shows a checklist, based on the above list, that parents can use to identify preschool children who are gifted.

Preschool children who are gifted tend to be more precocious in memory than in general intelligence, reading achievement, or spatial reasoning. The following profile is from the case of a remarkably gifted preschool girl (Roedell, 1980a):

This preschool girl obtained an estimated Stanford-Binet Intelligence Scale: Form L-M IQ of 177. Her highest performance was on verbal reasoning items; she showed less extraordinary spatial reasoning skills. Although she was not remarkably proficient in map-making or design-copying, she read at the fourth grade level by the age of 4. Her favorite books then were The Little House series by Laura Ingalls Wilder. She also enjoyed making up elaborate fantasy dramas involving several characters and complicated plots. Her daily language skills were also excellent.

The academic abilities of preschool children who are gifted show diverse skill patterns (Roedell, 1980a). However, the early acquisition of advanced academic skills may not be related to level of intelligence. Some preschool children with IQs above 160 have not mastered reading or arithmetic, whereas others with IQs of 116 are fluent readers by the age of 3. Preschool children who are gifted may show highly differentiated abilities in various cognitive areas, such as highly developed spatial reasoning ability and vocabulary, exceptional memory ability, unusual mathematical skills, or unusual early reading skills. Young children who are exceptionally adept in one area are not necessarily advanced in other areas, as "intraindividual differences among abilities are the rule, not the exception" (Robinson, 1981, p. 72). For example, children with extraordinary spatial reasoning ability may have only moderately advanced verbal skills; those who have remarkable skills in memory may be ordinary in other respects. It is highly unlikely, however, that children who are extraordinary in one area of mental functioning will be average or below average in all other areas of functioning.

The following sketch describes some personality and adjustment patterns of preschool children who are gifted (Roedell, 1980a):

Preschool children who are gifted show a wide range of personality characteristics and levels of social maturity. While children with moderately advanced intellectual abilities often show good overall adjustment, children with extremely advanced intellectual skills may have more difficulty. Adjustment problems may, in some cases, result from the uneven development that occurs when intellectual capabilities far outstrip the child's levels of physical or social development. Children with advanced intellectual skills sometimes tend to show advanced understanding of social situations and to be better able to judge other people's feelings. Intellectually advanced preschool children, however, may need guided social experience to

Table 14-3
Parent Recommendation Form for Preschool Children Who Are Gifted

CHECKLIST FOR PRESCHOOL CHILDREN WHO ARE GIFTED
PARENT RECOMMENDATION FORM

Child's name: _____ Date: _____ Age: _____

School: _____ Name of person filling out form: _____

Directions: Please check the box that represents your rating of each characteristic. Use the scale below. Thank you!

Generally yes—Child generally has this characteristic.
Generally no—Child generally does not have this characteristic.
Don't know—Don't know whether child has this characteristic.

Characteristics	Rating		
	Generally yes	*Generally no*	*Don't know*
Developmental Characteristics			
1. Showed unusual alertness in infancy.	☐	☐	☐
2. Showed advanced progression through the early developmental milestones.	☐	☐	☐
3. Understood directions, such as right and left, at an early age.	☐	☐	☐
Learning Characteristics			
4. Has an advanced vocabulary.	☐	☐	☐
5. Showed early interest in time.	☐	☐	☐
6. Uses metaphors or analogies.	☐	☐	☐
7. Makes up songs or stories spontaneously.	☐	☐	☐
8. Makes interesting shapes or patterns with blocks, board shapes, or other materials.	☐	☐	☐
9. Puts together difficult puzzles.	☐	☐	☐
10. Understands abstract or complex concepts.	☐	☐	☐
11. Masters a new skill, concept, song, or rhyme with unusual speed.	☐	☐	☐
12. Uses language to exchange ideas.	☐	☐	☐
13. Takes apart and reassembles things with unusual skill.	☐	☐	☐
14. Remembers and makes mental connections between past and present experiences.	☐	☐	☐
15. Carries out complex instructions to do several things in succession.	☐	☐	☐
Personality Characteristics			
16. Demonstrates a preference for novelty.	☐	☐	☐
17. Displays a long attention span.	☐	☐	☐
18. Shows curiosity and asks many questions.	☐	☐	☐
19. Modifies language when talking to less mature children.	☐	☐	☐
20. Has a sense of humor.	☐	☐	☐
21. Becomes absorbed in one kind of activity.	☐	☐	☐
22. Displays great interest or skill in ordering or grouping objects.	☐	☐	☐
23. Shows sensitivity to the needs or feelings of other children or adults.	☐	☐	☐
24. Shows unusual attentiveness to features of the home or preschool environment.	☐	☐	☐
25. Uses verbal skills to handle conflict or to influence other children's behavior.	☐	☐	☐

Source: Adapted from Roedell (1980b) and Silverman (1997).

help them make use of their advanced social understanding. (p. 26, with changes in notation)

In identifying the abilities of preschool children who are gifted, you may need to use tests that did not include their age range in the standardization group. For example, if a young child obtains scores at the highest level on one or more of the WPPSI–R subtests, you can administer similar WISC–III subtests, though the WISC–III was not standardized on preschool children. In such cases, you can use test-age equivalents to estimate the child's performance. For example, the test-age equivalent for a 4-year-old who obtains a raw score of 30 on the WISC–III Block Design subtest is 11-2 (11 years 2 months).

You can also use the WPPSI–R, WISC–III, Stanford-Binet: IV, and other similar tests (see *Assessment of Children: Cognitive Applications*) to obtain test-age equivalents for children younger than age 4. The test-age equivalents that accompany each subtest are helpful for this purpose. Do not use group tests of general intelligence with preschool children, because the children usually are not sufficiently attentive, compliant, and persistent in a group situation.

TERMAN'S AND LOVELL AND SHIELDS'S STUDIES OF INDIVIDUALS WHO ARE GIFTED

An extensive longitudinal study by Terman (1925; Terman & Oden, 1959) followed a sample of 1,528 children who were gifted (857 males and 671 females), from the time they were approximately 11 years old through adulthood. The children's IQs on the Stanford-Binet Intelligence Scale: 1916 Form ranged from 135 to 200, and their IQs on group tests were 135 and above. In comparison with a control group of unselected children, the children who were gifted were physically healthier; superior in reading, arithmetical reasoning, and information, but not computation and spelling; more interested in abstract subjects (literature, debating, dramatics, and history); and less interested in practical subjects (penmanship, manual training, drawing, and painting). Teachers rated this sample of children who were gifted as above the mean of the control group on intellectual, volitional, emotional, aesthetic, moral, physical, and social traits. In only one area—mechanical ingenuity—were the children who were gifted rated slightly below the children in the control group.

On follow-up in middle age (Terman & Oden, 1959), members of the group who were gifted were found to have more education, higher incomes, more desirable and prestigious occupations, more entries in *Who's Who,* better physical and mental health, a lower suicide rate, a lower mortality rate, a lower divorce rate, and brighter spouses and children than a random sample of the population. This sample of children who were gifted "evolved into productive professionals with good mental health and stable interpersonal relationships" (Subotnik, Karp, & Morgan, 1989, p. 143). The

follow-up study demonstrates that measured intelligence does relate to accomplishments outside of school. As Brody and Brody (1976) observed, "It is doubtful that the attempt to select children scoring in the top 1% of any other single characteristic would be as predictive of future accomplishment" (p. 109).

A similar but less extensive study was carried out in England with a sample of 55 English boys and girls, ages 8 to 12 years, who had WISC Verbal Scale IQs above 140 (Lovell & Shields, 1967). Teachers rated the children outstandingly high in general intelligence and desire to know; very high in originality, desire to excel, truthfulness, common sense, will power, perseverance, and conscientiousness; rather high in prudence and forethought, self-confidence, and sense of humor; and close to average in freedom from vanity and egotism. There were few sex differences. The mean ratings given by the British teachers to their sample of children were close to those given by the American teachers to the children in Terman's sample over 40 years earlier. The ordering of the traits in the two studies was highly correlated ($r = .90$). Thus, despite changes over time and between countries in education and in life generally, teachers in the United States in the 1920s and in England in the 1960s rated children who were gifted in similar ways. The results also indicated that tests of creativity did not measure any intellectual functions independent of those measured by the WISC or by tests of logical thought.

PROMOTING PSYCHOSOCIAL ADJUSTMENT IN CHILDREN WHO ARE GIFTED

Following are some guidelines for promoting the psychosocial adjustment of children who are gifted (Blackburn & Erickson, 1986; Robinson & Noble, 1991):

1. Recognize that there is a wide range of individual differences among children who are gifted.
2. Establish a good working relationship with the parents of children who are gifted, who themselves may be bright and verbal and who are likely to be highly child-centered and effective advocates for their children.
3. Reach out to parents of children who are culturally and linguistically diverse. These parents may be less sophisticated than parents from the majority group in working with the school system.
4. Recognize that, although many families of children who are gifted function well, some may not. In such cases, children who are gifted need help in coping with less than optimal family situations.
5. Recognize the potential of children who are gifted for maturity in other realms besides the academic, and strive to allow them to express these potentials.
6. Help children who are gifted at an early age to meet and master academic challenges so that they develop a strong sense that achievement comes only with effort.

7. Encourage children who are gifted to pursue traditional as well as nontraditional goals, and help them to select from an entire range of available options.

8. Help children who are gifted to develop healthy, realistic self-esteem, based on a clear understanding of their strengths and weaknesses.

9. Help children who are gifted to learn internal motivation and evaluation through a deemphasis on competition and an emphasis on personal goal-setting and self-evaluation.

10. Help children who are gifted to learn to accept their mistakes, to learn to reduce their fear of failure (if present), and to recognize that they can learn from their errors.

11. Help children who are gifted to learn to accept help from others and learn from others.

12. Help children who are gifted to learn how to help others.

13. Help children who are gifted to develop a sense of humor about themselves and the events outside their control, thus avoiding the problem of taking everything so seriously that their interest becomes debilitating and self-defeating.

EDUCATING CHILDREN WHO ARE GIFTED

Children who are gifted need instructional programs commensurate with their abilities. Ideally, the programs would include the following (VanTassel, 1979):

- Activities that enable them to operate cognitively and affectively at complex levels of thought and feeling
- Opportunities for divergent production
- Opportunities to talk to intellectual peers
- Experiences that promote understanding of human value systems
- Opportunities to see interrelationships among bodies of knowledge
- Courses in their areas of strength and interest that accelerate the pace and depth of content
- Exposure to new areas of learning within the school and community
- Opportunities to apply their abilities to problems in the world of work and in the community
- Opportunities to learn skills in critical thinking, creative thinking, research methodology, problem solving, coping with exceptionality, decision making, and leadership

Schools can meet these goals by providing programs such as the following (Pendarvis et al., 1990):

- Enriched programs in regular classes (including additional grade-level activities on topics related to the curriculum)
- Advanced programs in regular classes (offering instruction at a higher grade level)
- Resource rooms (rooms where students can attend advanced classes or study independently and use special resources)
- Special classes (such as honors classes or advanced placement [AP] classes)
- Acceleration in classes (such as early entrance into kindergarten or college, grade skipping, grade acceleration for part of the school day to receive advanced instruction in one or more school subjects, or taking classes at institutions of higher learning)
- Accelerated curriculum (such as speeding up the pace at which material is presented or expected to be mastered in a regular classroom, resource room, or special class)
- Special school (a school that offers advanced classes or rapidly paced classes)
- Individually paced instruction in an area of strength
- Examinations to obtain course credit without attending classes
- Internship programs with community sponsors
- Enrichment opportunities such as independent projects or after-school or weekend enrichment classes
- Competitions and contests

Inappropriate placements may be harmful to students who are gifted and result in frustration and disappointment (this, of course, is true for any student). A special placement should not be made without the approval of the child, the child's family, and the teacher. The child and her or his family should be appraised of the special placement and why it is recommended. Keeping children who are gifted in regular classes with an unmodified curriculum may be acceptable if the children are not bored and can work on individual projects or do other activities to enhance their skills. This, however, should be a last resort, considered only when (a) the school district has no resources to offer special classes for the gifted and talented or other educational opportunities or (b) there are personal family reasons (e.g., difficulty in getting the child to a special school or a need for the child to leave school at a certain time). However, we are doing a disservice to children who are gifted if we let them become bored and turned off by an unchallenging curriculum. As a nation, we cannot afford to lose our brightest and most talented youngsters because of inadequate school curricula.

The simplest way to educate academically advanced children is to place them in existing classes at more advanced grade levels. *The principle is placement according to competence* (Robinson, 1980). Following this procedure ensures many children an appropriate education. Correct placement also may enhance their zest for learning, reduce boredom in school, and enhance feelings of self-worth and accomplishment. Arguments that acceleration is harmful to children have proven to be without empirical foundation. The following case illustrates the application of the placement principle to a mathematically gifted adolescent (Robinson, 1980):

A month after his tenth birthday, CB took the SAT in a regular administration and scored 600 Verbal and 680 Mathematical; a year later he raised these scores to 710 and 750, respectively. His IQ was

estimated to be about 200. A Chinese-American youngster whose father is a professor of physics and whose mother has a master's degree in psychology, CB has two younger siblings who are also bright. He attended a private school in Baltimore, where he was given special educational opportunities. Although CB had only taken first-year high-school algebra (as a fifth grader), he had acquired by age 11 the subject matter of algebra II, algebra III, and plane geometry. Trigonometry took him a few weeks to learn, as did analytic geometry. At age 12, while his father was doing research using the linear accelerator at Stanford University, CB completed his high school career in Palo Alto while simultaneously taking a demanding calculus course at Stanford. When he was still 12 years old, CB entered Johns Hopkins with sophomore standing. He had been accepted at Harvard and Cal Tech as well. He received his baccalaureate at age 15, with a major in physics. (pp. 11–12, with changes in notation)

CREATIVITY

Creativity is a loosely defined, broad, complex, and multifaceted concept; it involves the creative process (i.e., the production of novel and original content) and the creative product (i.e., what stems from the creative process). The relationship between creativity and intelligence is complicated by problems of measurement and definition. A reasonable hypothesis is that creativity is minimal at low levels of intelligence, whereas all levels of creativity are found at high levels of intelligence, with only some bright children (e.g., with IQs above 120) performing in a creative manner (Amabile, 1983; Runco, 1992). Intelligence appears to be a component of creativity—a necessary but not sufficient contributing factor. Some minimum level of intelligence is probably required for creative performance. Most traditional intelligence tests do not assess creativity.

The following three types of variables interact to produce creative products (Eysenck, 1994; Rossman & Horn, 1972; also see Figure 14-1):

1. *Cognitive variables* such as intelligence, originality, flexibility, fluency, knowledge, technical skills, and special talents
2. *Personality variables* such as internal motivation, confidence, nonconformity, striving for novelty, striving to test self or risk-taking, preference for complexity, independence of judgment, tendency to dominate, attitudinal openness, minimal anxiety, affective or aesthetic sensitivity, playfulness, and creativity
3. *Environmental variables* such as politico-religious factors, cultural factors, socioeconomic factors, and educational factors

Creative achievement requires special talents—such as musical, numerative, verbal, or visuospatial talents—that are focused on a specific area; acquiring the knowledge to develop the talent may take several years (Eysenck, 1994).

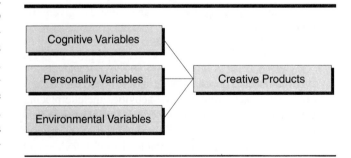

Figure 14-1. Three variables that interact to produce creative products.

Because of the highly specialized knowledge and the amount of factual information needed to make a creative contribution, it would be difficult for any person in the twenty-first century to be creative in more than one field.

Students who are creative have been found to have both positive and negative traits (Davis, 1997; Welsh, 1975). On the positive side, they may be original, independent, adventurous, attracted to complexity, open-minded, intuitive, spontaneous, energetic, curious, flexible, and artistic and have a sense of humor. On the negative side, they may be unstable, irresponsible, careless, disorderly, rebellious, uncontrolled, self-seeking, tactless, temperamental, emotional, unwilling to follow rules, uncooperative, impulsive, argumentative, and overactive physically and mentally.

IDENTIFYING CREATIVITY

Creativity is difficult to identify for the following reasons (Boden, 1994):

Creativity is a puzzle, a paradox, some say a mystery. Inventors, scientists, and artists rarely know how their original ideas arise. They mention intuition, but cannot say how it works. Most psychologists cannot tell us much about it, either. What's more, many people assume that there will never be a scientific theory of creativity—for how could science possibly explain fundamental novelties? As if all this were not daunting enough, the apparent unpredictability of creativity seems to outlaw any systematic explanation, whether scientific or historical. (p. 75)

Still, psychologists and educators attempt to measure and assess creativity. Representative procedures used to measure creativity include the following:

- Torrance Tests of Creativity (Torrance, 1966)
- Wallach and Kogan tests, which include Instances, Alternate Uses, Pattern Meanings, and Line Meanings (Wallach & Kogan, 1965)
- Attitude and interest inventories
- Personality inventories
- Biographical inventories
- Ratings of creativity by teachers, peers, supervisors, and parents
- Actual achievements or judgments of products, including publications, patent awards, and awards given by organizations

The simplest and most straightforward method for identifying creativity is listed last: *an inventory of past and current creative achievements and activities* (Hocevar, 1981). Examples of creative achievements and activities include placing first, second, or third in a science contest; exhibiting or performing a work of art; publishing poems, stories, or articles in a newspaper; inventing a patentable or useful device; and acting in plays. Table 14-4 shows a checklist for rating creative traits in children.

Measures of ideational fluency, which are included in the Torrance tests and the Wallach and Kogan tests, also are useful in identifying creativity (see Chapter 19, Table 19-13, for measures of ideational fluency). Ideational fluency tests, which involve coming up with imaginative verbal or nonverbal responses or productive ideas, measure divergent thinking (Eysenck, 1994). Divergent-thinking problems—for example, "What are some uses for a rock?"—have several possible answers. Scoring for divergent-thinking problems can be both quantitative (the number of responses; also referred to as *ideational fluency*) and qualitative (the unusualness or usefulness of the responses). In contrast, convergent-thinking problems—for example, "What number comes after 1, 4, 7, 10, 13?"—usually have only one correct answer and can be scored only quantitatively.

Tests designed to measure creativity have several potential shortcomings (Eysenck, 1994):

- They may be influenced by extraneous factors such as boredom or the type of classroom instruction received by the examinee.
- They may fail to measure the quality of the responses.
- They may have limited construct validity, failing to predict creative production.
- They may have subjective scoring procedures that rely on the test constructor's criteria rather than on more meaningful criteria such as novelty, appropriateness, or satisfyingness.
- They may fail to correlate with other measures of creativity.
- They may restrict the meaning of originality because of the heavy influence of verbal fluency on originality scores.

What little common variance tests of creativity have with each other may be accounted for by *g*, the general intelligence factor. Some tests of creativity measure cognitive abilities not reliably distinguished from intelligence, whereas others measure attributes different from those measured on intelligence tests. Although many creativity tests do measure abilities and dispositions probably important for creative performance, it is inappropriate to label the results of creativity tests "as directly indicative of some global quality that can be called creativity...such judgments can ultimately only be subjective" (Amabile, 1983, p. 26).

SUGGESTIONS FOR MAINTAINING AND ENHANCING CREATIVITY IN CHILDREN

The following suggestions are useful for encouraging creativity in children (Amabile, 1983):

1. Create a stimulating teaching environment.
2. Teach children to scan the environment for cues that might be relevant to problem solving.
3. Provide children with special teachers, special materials, and the time and freedom to develop their talents when they show special aptitudes.
4. Train children to identify and use the positive aspects of their own work and the work of others.

Table 14-4
Checklist for Identifying Children Who Are Creative

CHECKLIST FOR IDENTIFYING CHILDREN WHO ARE CREATIVE

Child's name: _____   Rater: _____

Sex: _____   Grade: _____   Class: _____   Date: _____

Rating scale:	1	2	3	4	5
	Not present	Minimally present	Somewhat present	Moderately present	Strongly present

Characteristic	Rating (Circle one number)	Characteristic	Rating (Circle one number)
1. Ability to concentrate	1 2 3 4 5	19. Imagination, insight	1 2 3 4 5
2. Ability to defer judgment	1 2 3 4 5	20. Independence	1 2 3 4 5
3. Ability to see that solutions generate new problems	1 2 3 4 5	21. Internal locus of control and evaluation	1 2 3 4 5
4. Above-average IQ	1 2 3 4 5	22. Inventiveness	1 2 3 4 5
5. Adaptability	1 2 3 4 5	23. Lack of tolerance for boredom	1 2 3 4 5
6. Aesthetic appreciation	1 2 3 4 5	24. Need for supportive climate	1 2 3 4 5
7. Attraction to the complex and mysterious	1 2 3 4 5	25. Nonconformism	1 2 3 4 5
8. Commitment to task	1 2 3 4 5	26. Openness to experience	1 2 3 4 5
9. Curiosity	1 2 3 4 5	27. Playfulness	1 2 3 4 5
10. Delight in beauty of theory	1 2 3 4 5	28. Self-confidence	1 2 3 4 5
11. Delight in invention for its own sake	1 2 3 4 5	29. Sense of identity as originator	1 2 3 4 5
12. Desire to share products and ideas	1 2 3 4 5	30. Sense of mission	1 2 3 4 5
13. Eagerness to resolve disorder	1 2 3 4 5	31. Sensitivity	1 2 3 4 5
14. Extensive knowledge background	1 2 3 4 5	32. Spontaneity	1 2 3 4 5
15. Flexibility	1 2 3 4 5	33. Tolerance for ambiguity and conflict	1 2 3 4 5
16. Good memory, attention to detail	1 2 3 4 5	34. Willingness to face social ostracism	1 2 3 4 5
17. High energy level, enthusiasm	1 2 3 4 5	35. Willingness to daydream and fantasize	1 2 3 4 5
18. Humor (perhaps bizarre)	1 2 3 4 5	36. Willingness to take risks	1 2 3 4 5

Source: Characteristics obtained from Ford and Ford (1981).

5. Encourage teachers and parents to be enthusiastic and supportive and to nurture creative processes in children who are nonconforming and unpredictable.

6. Diminish peer influences for conformity by teaching highly talented children in special classes.

7. Teach *all* children to resist peer pressure to conform, in order to increase their creativity.

8. Be aware of the dangers of formal education—recognize that an excessively extended formal education can be detrimental, particularly if it provides no opportunities for independent projects and leads to overreliance on established ways of thinking.

9. Endorse appropriate socialization experiences, encouraging parents to provide nurturance and affectional bonds, as well as to display low levels of authoritarianism.

10. Encourage parents to show respect for and confidence in their children, providing secure affection but allowing their children some independence from parental evaluation.

11. Expose children to models of creative achievement, and encourage them to go beyond the observed modeled behavior.

12. Expose children to cultural diversity throughout their development—through travel and other means—so as to enrich and elevate their capacity for creative behavior.

13. Encourage appropriate work attitudes by helping children appreciate the enjoyable aspects of their work, the inherent satisfaction in engaging in work activities, and the pleasure of watching their own work unfold.

14. Encourage children to eliminate the strict dichotomy between work and play.

15. Allow children the freedom to decide on the problems to approach, materials and methods to use, and subgoals, and give them as much choice as possible in their activities.

16. Teach children to be self-observant and to engage in self-evaluation, in order to limit their dependence on external evaluation.

17. Encourage high levels of self-determination and self-control.

18. Encourage teachers to allow some time in the classroom for individualized and self-directed learning in an informal atmosphere.

19. Tailor reinforcements to the individual child's levels of interest and ability at both home and school.

20. Encourage parents and teachers to use tangible rewards sparingly, especially if they are given explicitly as payment for some activity; however, unusually high rewards, given as bonuses for performance, may enhance creativity.

21. Stimulate interest level, particularly when a high level of intrinsic interest is not present initially. In such cases, it may be necessary to offer a reward to encourage the child to engage in the activity. As interest develops, rewards can be withdrawn or made less salient.

CONCLUDING COMMENT

In her review of research on intelligence and giftedness, Callahan (2000) observed the following:

It is most significant that the categorization of children has taken a back seat to attempts to understand the instructional and psychological needs of the individuals who are highly able or who have the potential for displaying gifted behaviors in specific and general domains of performance. Increasingly, researchers have shifted concerns from the process of finding the "right test" to finding ways to match the capabilities of children to the instructional program and support systems necessary to translate intellectual potential into adult accomplishment. (p. 173)

THINKING THROUGH THE ISSUES

Develop a procedure that you believe would be useful in identifying children who are gifted, and compare it to the procedures used in your state. How would your procedure be useful in identifying children who are gifted and who also are underachievers, physically or neurologically handicapped, or culturally different? How can we increase children's creativity at home and at school?

> *Great achievers have high IQs, but high IQ does not guarantee creative achievement.*
>
> —Hans J. Eysenck

SUMMARY

1. Children are generally referred to as gifted and talented if they have outstanding prominence in an area, such as an extremely high IQ (above 130, which represents the 98th percentile rank), excellence in art or music, or high scores on tests of creativity.

2. Children who are gifted and talented require differentiated educational programs and services beyond those normally provided by the regular program if they are to make a contribution to society and maximize their potential.

3. Children who are gifted and talented include those with demonstrated achievement or potential ability in any of the following areas: general intellectual ability, specific academic aptitude, creative or productive thinking, leadership ability, visual and performing arts.

4. Approximately 3% to 5% of the population of children in the United States have exceptionally high IQs, creative talents, or both.

Intellectual and Personality Characteristics of Children Who Are Gifted

5. Factors that influence the development of gifted intellectual performance include (a) genetics, (b) ability to master symbol systems, (c) opportunities to develop talent, (d) parental encouragement of talent, (e) approval of intellectual activities, and (f) positive peer influences for intellectual activities.

6. Intellectual and personality characteristics associated with children who are gifted include exceptional reasoning ability, intellectual curiosity, rapid learning rate, insightfulness, questioning of authority, and tendency toward introversion.

Identifying Children Who Are Gifted

7. There is no one best system for identifying children who are gifted. Any means of identification is in part dependent on the goals of the program.

8. The most effective means of identification combines the results from several procedures, including group intelligence tests, individual intelligence tests, achievement tests, teacher nominations, parent nominations, peer nominations, and self-nominations.

9. In actual practice, schools may give a group intelligence test, rather than individual intelligence tests, to identify children eligible for a gifted program, because group tests are less costly to administer.

10. Because giftedness is not a unitary concept, students should not be selected for a gifted program solely on the basis of high scores on a test that measures only one specific ability, such as receptive vocabulary or perceptual reasoning ability.

11. The single best method available for identifying children with superior cognitive abilities is a standardized, individually administered, multidimensional test of intelligence, such as the Stanford-Binet: IV or a Wechsler test.

Underachieving Children Who Are Gifted

12. Intellectual giftedness does not ensure success in school.
13. The academic success of children who are gifted is determined by the same environmental forces that affect the success of all children—namely, motivation, interests, self-concept, family and home, teachers and school, peers, and society.
14. Children who are gifted may underachieve and rebel when (a) they experience excessive parental pressure to succeed in school, (b) schools do not provide adequate programs, and (c) there is peer pressure to conform to the average.
15. The characteristics most frequently found among underachieving students who are gifted are low self-esteem and a low sense of personal control over their own lives.
16. Underachieving students who are gifted may have complex behavior patterns that are not easily amenable to intervention.

Children Who Are Gifted and Have Learning Disabilities

17. Some children who are gifted have specific learning disabilities that interfere with their ability to learn in school.

Children Who Are Gifted and Have Emotional Problems

18. The incidence of emotional problems is likely to be about the same among children who are gifted and children who are not gifted.

Preschool Children Who Are Gifted

19. Infants and preschool children who are gifted may show unusual alertness in infancy, show advanced progression through developmental milestones, understand abstract or complex concepts, use language to exchange ideas, and show sensitivity to the needs or feelings of other children or adults.
20. Preschool children who are gifted tend to be more precocious in memory than in general intelligence or reading achievement or spatial reasoning.
21. The academic abilities of preschool children who are gifted show diverse skill patterns.
22. In identifying the abilities of preschool children who are gifted, you may need to use tests that did not include their age range in the standardization group.

Terman's and Lovell and Shields's Studies of Individuals Who Are Gifted

23. An extensive longitudinal study by Terman showed that the children who were gifted not only were brighter than the general population of children but also tended to have better physical health. In later life, they evolved into productive professionals with good mental health and stable interpersonal relationships. Lovell and Shields's study had similar findings.

Promoting Psychosocial Adjustment in Children Who Are Gifted

24. Be aware that children who are gifted may need help in their psychosocial adjustment.

Educating Children Who Are Gifted

25. Children who are gifted need instructional programs commensurate with their abilities.

26. School programs for children who are gifted can include enriched programs, advanced programs, resource rooms, special classes, acceleration in classes, an accelerated curriculum, a special school, individually paced instruction, examinations to obtain course credit without attending classes, internship programs, enrichment opportunities, and competitions and contests.
27. Inappropriate placements may be harmful to students who are gifted and result in frustration and disappointment.
28. The simplest way to educate academically advanced children is to place them in existing classes at more advanced grade levels. The principle is placement according to competence.

Creativity

29. Creativity is a loosely defined, broad, complex, and multifaceted concept; it involves the creative process and the creative product.
30. A reasonable hypothesis is that creativity is minimal at low levels of intelligence, whereas all levels of creativity are found at high levels of intelligence, with only some bright children (e.g., with IQs above 120) performing in a creative manner.
31. Intelligence appears to be a component of creativity—a necessary but not sufficient contributing factor.
32. Most traditional intelligence tests do not assess creativity.
33. Three types of variables interact to produce creative products: cognitive variables, personality variables, and environmental variables.
34. On the positive side, students who are creative may be original, independent, adventurous, attracted to complexity, open-minded, intuitive, spontaneous, energetic, curious, flexible, and artistic and have a sense of humor.
35. On the negative side, students who are creative may be unstable, irresponsible, careless, disorderly, rebellious, uncontrolled, self-seeking, tactless, temperamental, emotional, unwilling to follow rules, uncooperative, impulsive, argumentative, and overactive physically and mentally.

Identifying Creativity

36. Creativity is difficult to identify.
37. Tests designed to measure creativity have several potential shortcomings.
38. What little common variance tests of creativity have with each other may be accounted for by g, the general intelligence factor.

Suggestions for Maintaining and Enhancing Creativity in Children

39. Creativity in children can be enhanced many ways, including creating a stimulating teaching environment, using effective teaching methods, diminishing peer influences for conformity, reducing formal education, endorsing appropriate socialization experiences, encouraging appropriate work attitudes, minimizing control, using rewards sparingly, and stimulating interest level.

KEY TERMS, CONCEPTS, AND NAMES

Children who are gifted and talented (p. 353)
Intellectual and personality characteristics of children who are gifted (p. 353)

STUDY QUESTIONS

1. Discuss the following issues as they pertain to gifted and talented children: (a) definition of gifted and talented, (b) intellectual and personality characteristics of children who are gifted, and (c) means of identifying children who are gifted.

2. Discuss (a) underachieving children who are gifted, (b) children who are gifted and have learning disabilities, and (c) children who are gifted and have emotional problems.

3. Discuss preschool children who are gifted.

4. Discuss Terman's and Lovell and Shields's studies of the gifted.

5. Explain how you would go about promoting adjustment in children who are gifted.

6. Discuss educating children who are gifted.

7. Discuss the concept of creativity. Include in your discussion variables associated with creativity, means of identification, and ways to maintain and enhance creativity in children.

15

VISUAL IMPAIRMENTS

by Jerome M. Sattler and Carol Anne Evans

Like most of the truly important inventions in human history, the braille code is elegantly simple. The braille cell is made up of six raised dots, arranged like the six in dominos, two vertical columns of three. All the letters of the alphabet, plus special symbols for certain common words, consist of from one to six of these dots. Each character is the right size to fit even a child's fingertip, so the reader moves the finger smoothly from left to right. The braille alphabet is easy to memorize, and it's hard to mistake one letter for another....

When I learned all the letters of the alphabet I read this: "Congratulations! You have now mastered the entire braille alphabet." I was startled, then enthralled. I read it again. For the first time in decades I felt in absolute and stable contact with the text. This had nothing to do with the precarious guesswork I'd called reading since I lost my visual acuity. This was certain, unequivocal. I touched the words. Meaning flowed into my brain. Suddenly my mind rushed ahead to imagine the thousands of texts I wanted to read and reread in this way.

—Georgina Kleege

Goals and Objectives

This chapter is designed to enable you to do the following:

- Understand how to assess children with visual impairments

- Understand how to design interventions for children with visual impairments

Children with *visual impairments* have conditions that range from limited vision to no vision at all (blind). Any type of serious vision loss can affect a child's ability to process information. Vision helps the individual to (a) identify the qualities, attributes, colors, shapes, and other features of objects, (b) acquire concepts related to space, distance, sizes, and other attributes of spatial relations, and (c) integrate disparate elements into a more coherent whole, or gestalt. Key variables in understanding visual impairments are the type, severity, etiology, and age of onset of the impairment. Several disorders that affect vision have a congenital basis, while others are acquired through injury or illness. Congenital etiologies account for over 50% of the cases of blindness in children (Freedman, Feinstein, & Berger, 1988).

Children who have recently lost all or part of their vision will need to adjust to their visual loss and learn to use adaptive strategies and compensatory devices. A child should be referred to an optometrist or ophthalmologist for a visual examination if there are any signs of a visual impairment. Chapter 7 in *Assessment of Children: Cognitive Applications* (pages 200–201) points out indicators of a possible visual impairment. In the 1998–1999 school year, the prevalence rate of individuals aged 6 to 21 years with visual impairments served under the IDEA (see Chapter 3 in *Assessment of Children: Cognitive Applications*) was .5% (26,132; U.S. Department of Education, 2000). About 90% of children with visual impairments retain some vision (Kelley, Sanspree, & Davidson, 2000).

DISORDERS THAT AFFECT VISION

Refractive Errors

The following three conditions all result from refractive errors. They are most often correctable with glasses or contact lenses.

- In *myopia,* or nearsightedness, the eyeball is too large or the shape of the lens or cornea of the eye is such that the focal point for light entering the eye is in front of the retina rather than directly on it.
- In *hyperopia,* or farsightedness, the eyeball is too short or the shape of the lens or cornea of the eye is such that the focal point for light entering the eye is behind the retina rather than directly on it.
- In *astigmatism,* irregular curvature of the cornea or lens causes distorted or blurred vision.

Children with these conditions should wear their glasses or lenses during the assessment. Modifications in the assessment procedures should not be required, other than normal precautions to minimize glare.

Central Visual Field Defects

The central portion of the retina (macula and fovea) contains mostly cone cells. Cone cells are a type of specialized light-sensitive cells (called photoreceptors) that provide sharp central vision and color vision. Three conditions that result in vision loss in the central visual field are juvenile macular degeneration, diabetic retinopathy, and achromatopsia.

- *Juvenile macular degeneration* refers to a group of genetically transmitted disorders, occurring during mid to late childhood, that affect the cones at the center of the retina. The photoreceptors of the macula malfunction and eventually die, causing gradual decline and loss of central vision but leaving peripheral vision intact. Currently, there is no cure for the condition, but visual function can be improved through optical aids and teaching more effective use of low-vision abilities.
- *Diabetic retinopathy* is an acquired disease associated with diabetes. In nonproliferative retinopathy, small capillaries in the retina break and leak, resulting in distortion of parts of the field of vision; if the hemorrhages are near the macula, vision may be blurred. In proliferative retinopathy, damage to the retina stimulates the abnormal growth of new blood vessels, leading to scarring and sometimes to retinal detachment; total or near total blindness can result. Laser surgery can prevent and reduce loss of vision, and visual function may be improved through optical aids and teaching more effective use of low-vision abilities.
- *Achromatopsia* is a genetically transmitted disorder that impairs the cones at the center of the retina, causing color blindness, poor visual acuity, and extreme sensitivity to bright light. Measures that reduce the intensity of visual stimulation (e.g., visors and sunglasses) are useful, along with optical aids and teaching more effective use of low-vision abilities.

Peripheral Visual Field Defects

The peripheral portion of the retina contains mostly rod cells. Rod cells are another type of photoreceptor that provide peripheral vision and the ability to see objects in dim light. Retinitis pigmentosa and glaucoma are two disorders that result in loss of vision in the peripheral portion of the visual field, causing mobility problems; in their initial stages, they leave reading vision intact.

- *Retinitis pigmentosa* is a genetically transmitted progressive disorder, resulting in degeneration of the rods at the periphery of the retina. First comes loss of night vision. Following are several stages of "tunnel vision" as the peripheral field vision decreases. Eventually the entire retina becomes involved and the individual becomes blind. Vitamin A may help to slow the progress of the disease. Visual functioning may be improved through optical aids and teaching more effective use of low-vision abilities.
- *Glaucoma* is a progressive condition in which the pressure inside the eye increases because of excessive production of or inability to drain aqueous humor (fluid), causing damage to the optic nerve. Glaucoma may be congenital

(caused by a recessive gene) or acquired (caused by any of several illnesses). Some types of glaucoma can be treated and controlled with surgery or medication, but not cured. People with glaucoma are at risk for blindness. Visual functioning may be improved through optical aids and teaching more effective use of low-vision abilities.

Whole Visual Field Defects

The following disorders cause general visual loss across the whole visual field.

- *Retinopathy of prematurity* is a disorder in which blood vessels in the back of the eye develop abnormally in premature infants. In severe cases, the blood vessels may bleed and lead to a detached retina, causing vision loss. "The main risk factor for developing retinopathy of prematurity is extreme prematurity; high oxygen levels in the blood from the treatment of breathing problems may increase the risk" (Berkow, 1997, p. 1207). Treatments include freezing the peripheral portions of the retina and the use of lasers. Visual functioning may be improved through optical aids and teaching more effective use of low-vision abilities.
- *Cataracts* are opacities of the crystalline lens that prevent light and images from entering the eye. Following removal of the cataracts, intraocular lenses may be implanted and bifocal lenses prescribed, but individuals may still need vision services, optical aids, and instruction in effective use of low-vision abilities.
- *Aniridia* is a congenital absence of the iris that prevents regulation of the amount of light entering the eye, causing extreme sensitivity to bright light and a significant reduction in visual acuity. Children with aniridia are at risk for developing glaucoma. Visual functioning may be improved through optical aids, pinhole contact lenses, and teaching more effective use of low-vision abilities.
- *Albinism* is a deficiency of pigmentation (i.e., no melanin is formed). Lack of pigmentation in the iris and retina causes extreme sensitivity to bright light and significant reduction in visual acuity. Treatment consists of reducing illumination (e.g., through use of visors, tinted lenses or sunglasses, or pinhole contact lenses). Visual functioning may be improved through optical aids, and teaching more effective use of low-vision abilities.
- *Retinoblastoma* is a rare, but life-threatening, malignant tumor of the retina. The condition may be transmitted genetically or result from a spontaneous mutation. Most cases are diagnosed before the age of 4 years. Large tumors are treated by removal of the more severely affected eye; smaller tumors are treated by radiation, cryotherapy (freezing), or laser therapy. Visual functioning in the remaining eye may be improved through optical aids and teaching more effective use of low-vision abilities.

Other Conditions That May Affect Vision

Following are examples of other conditions that may affect vision.

- *Cortical visual impairment* refers to damage to the visual cortex of the brain. The damage can occur in conjunction with neurological insults, such as hypoxic (insufficient oxygen) or anoxic (no oxygen) events, premature birth, cerebral palsy, or injury to the occipital lobe. The effect on visual functioning is variable, and thus confusion can result. Treatment consists of vision stimulation activities, optical aids, and teaching more effective use of low-vision abilities.
- *Fetal alcohol syndrome* is associated with several neurological and learning deficits, which sometimes include vision loss. Treatment consists of vision stimulation activities, optical aids, and teaching more effective use of low-vision abilities.
- *Congenital optic nerve disorders* are often associated with developmental disabilities. Some children benefit from vision stimulation activities, optical aids, and teaching more effective use of low-vision abilities.
- *Multiple sclerosis* is a slowly progressive disease in which the nerves of the eye, brain, and spinal cord lose patches of myelin. Movement, speech, and vision may be affected. Treatment consists of optical aids and teaching more effective use of low-vision abilities.
- *Amblyopia* refers to vision loss in one eye leading to impaired binocular vision and depth perception. Strabismus (misalignment of the eyes) is a major cause of amblyopia. Medical, surgical, and optical treatments are available.

Many eye conditions (as well as a central nervous system disorder) may be accompanied by *nystagmus,* which involves rapid involuntary repeated oscillations of one or both eyes in any or all fields of vision. The eyes may move together or separately, reducing the ability to maintain steady fixation on a visual target. Individuals with nystagmus may require more time to complete visual tasks. To increase their ability to focus, they may turn their heads and tilt their faces to find a gaze position that reduces movements.

CHILDREN WITH MILD, MODERATE, OR SEVERE VISUAL IMPAIRMENTS

Although they may see with altered visual acuity or with a diminished visual field, children with visual impairments usually have some useful vision. Most children are visual learners despite their vision loss. Children with mild or moderate visual loss still may use vision as their primary learning channel. Some rely solely on their low residual vision, with varying results. Children with severe to profound vision loss, however, need to use tactile and auditory sensory input to obtain information, in addition to using whatever residual vision, if any, is available to them.

Clarity of vision is defined in terms of *visual acuity*. Berkow (1997) explains the system as follows:

As acuity decreases, vision becomes progressively blurred. Acuity is usually measured on a scale that compares a person's vision at 20 feet with that of someone who has full acuity. Thus, a person who has 20/20 vision sees objects 20 feet away with complete clarity, but a person who has 20/200 vision sees at 20 feet what a person with full acuity sees at 200 feet. (p. 1027)

Visual acuity is represented by a continuum from normal vision to total blindness.

- Normal vision is acuity of 20/20.
- Mild low vision is acuity of 20/70.
- Moderate low vision is acuity of 20/200.
- Severe low vision is acuity of 20/800.
- Profound low vision is acuity lower than 20/800.
- Total blindness refers to no light perception at all.

Profound low vision is designated by the following terms:

- CF (counts fingers at a specified distance)
- HM (perceives hand movement at a specified distance)
- LP (light perception)

Individuals with profound vision loss can still access some objects in the environment and have some vision for use in daily living and travel. For example, a person with directional light perception (LP) is essentially blind and likely uses Braille for reading and writing and mobility devices for travel in the environment, but he or she may be able to maintain orientation in travel through a corridor when there are windows on one side. The medical report of a person with no light perception may indicate that vision is NLP or nil.

Blindness refers to vision loss that is total or sight that is so impaired that the individual primarily uses senses other than vision for obtaining information and for interacting with the environment. Blindness occurs when "(a) light can't reach the retina, (b) light rays don't focus properly on the retina, (c) the retina can't sense light rays normally, (d) the nerve impulses from the retina aren't transmitted to the brain normally, and (e) the brain can't interpret information sent by the eye" (Berkow, 1997, p. 1028, with changes in notation). People who are blind may still be able to distinguish shapes and shadows, but not normal visual detail. Reading is accomplished by using Braille and auditory materials (e.g., recorded speech or speech synthesized by a computer). Travel in the environment is managed by the use of a long cane or guide dog. Children who are blind need training by qualified teachers to master these specialized aids and skills.

The legal definition of blindness is used to determine eligibility for benefits. *Legal blindness* is defined as corrected visual acuity of less than 20/200 in the better eye or a visual field of 20° or less (a normal field is close to 180°) in the bet-ter eye. Children who are legally blind usually have some useful vision.

DEVELOPMENT OF CHILDREN WHO ARE BLIND OR PROFOUNDLY VISUALLY IMPAIRED

Children who become blind before 5 years of age face more developmental challenges than those who become blind after 5 years of age. For example, children who are born blind will be hampered in exploring their environment independently and may have difficulty learning concepts commonly achieved through visual experience.

Children who become blind after infancy face the struggles associated with having to expend more energy to accomplish routine tasks. They will need help in travel and with written communication, and they usually will not be invited to participate fully in many recreational activities, thus increasing their dependency on their parents (Freedman et al., 1988). Physical movement may be somewhat restricted, sensory input is reduced, and many cues obtained from nonverbal visual communications are not available. However, children who become blind after the age of 5 years may remember the shapes and colors of objects in their environment, and these memories may assist them in their interactions with others and in their schooling (Bradley-Johnson, 1994).

The language ability of children with visual impairments shows relatively normal development (Hodapp, 1998). Children with normal vision usually learn the meanings of words in the context of their visual experience, while children who are blind usually learn the meanings of words—particularly words relating to objects outside of their immediate experience—through verbal explanations. Thus, children who are blind may be hampered in their understanding of words that are based on visual experiences (Elbers & Van Loon-Vervoorn, 1999). It is therefore essential that children who are blind receive instruction to help them understand words and concepts. Such instruction can be carried out in part by placing blind children in physical contact with objects that appeal to their remaining senses, such as hearing, taste, and touch. An example would be placing food in the child's hands and then directing the child to put the food in his or her mouth.

Children with congenital blindness develop concepts of space in a sequence similar to that followed by sighted children, but at a slower rate; those who are congenitally blind and were born prematurely are at higher risk for spatial impairments (Stuart, 1995). Spatial understanding is essential to emerging skills in learning Braille and in learning orientation and mobility. Knowledge of spatial concepts will facilitate children's abilities to understand directions given by others, to cross safely at light-controlled intersections, and to use optical aids such as telescopes (Hill, Guth, & Hill, 1985). Overall, children who are totally blind have more developmental variability and are more likely to show regressions in development than those with even a small degree of vision.

Children with visual impairments are at higher risk for impaired social functioning than their normally sighted counterparts. They have difficulty acquiring meaningful physical gestures and facial expressions, using assertiveness skills, using visual cues to assist them in interpersonal relations, receiving adequate feedback about their actions, and receiving positive feedback from others (Sisson & Van Hasselt, 1987). Also, those who are severely visually impaired have difficulty joining in sports and other activities that help form social bonds. Similarly, children with visual impairments may have more behavioral and social problems than children with normal sight. Children who are suddenly blinded by trauma or who are experiencing a progressive type of vision loss will require considerable support (as in other life-changing events and processes) as they adjust to these changes.

Just as there is enormous variability among children with normal vision, there is also enormous variability among children with visual impairments. Visual impairment or blindness does not exclude conditions from giftedness to mental retardation, nor does it preclude the presence of learning, physical, mental, or developmental strengths or disabilities.

CHILDREN WITH VISUAL IMPAIRMENTS AND THE IDEA

The IDEA of 1997 provides the following guidelines for working with children with visual impairments:

Sec. 300.7 Child with a disability.
  (13) Visual impairment including blindness means an impairment in vision that, even with correction, adversely affects a child's educational performance. The term includes both partial sight and blindness.

Sec. 300.19 Native language.
  (a) As used in this part, the term native language, if used with reference to an individual of limited English proficiency, means the following:
  (b) For an individual with deafness or blindness, or for an individual with no written language, the mode of communication is that normally used by the individual (such as sign language, Braille, or oral communication).

Sec. 300.24 Related services.
  (6) Orientation and mobility services—
    (i) Means services provided to blind or visually impaired students by qualified personnel to enable those students to attain systematic orientation to and safe movement within their environments in school, home, and community; and
    (ii) Includes teaching students the following, as appropriate:
      (A) Spatial and environmental concepts and use of information received by the senses (such as sound,

temperature and vibrations) to establish, maintain, or regain orientation and line of travel (e.g., using sound at a traffic light to cross the street);
      (B) To use the long cane to supplement visual travel skills or as a tool for safely negotiating the environment for students with no available travel vision;
      (C) To understand and use remaining vision and distance low vision aids; and
      (D) Other concepts, techniques, and tools.

Sec. 300.346 Development, review, and revision of IEP.
  (2) Consideration of special factors. The IEP team also shall—
    (iii) In the case of a child who is blind or visually impaired, provide for instruction in Braille and the use of Braille unless the IEP team determines, after an evaluation of the child's reading and writing skills, needs, and appropriate reading and writing media (including an evaluation of the child's future needs for instruction in Braille or the use of Braille), that instruction in Braille or the use of Braille is not appropriate for the child.
    (v) Consider whether the child requires assistive technology devices and services.

Assistive technology devices for children with visual impairments include the following:

Enhancement of Print

- Large print
- Colored overlays
- Optical aids: Portable magnifiers, used to improve ability to read print and see small objects; portable telescopes, used to locate distant targets (e.g., scan a shopping center to find a particular store)
- Video magnifiers: Closed-circuit televisions with adjustable print size, color combinations, brightness, and contrast
- Screen magnification: Computer software that enlarges text and graphics for word processing and other applications

Auditory Access

- Cassette and CD players
- Speech synthesizers: Hardware (either an external unit that connects to a computer or an internal chip or circuit card) that produces speech output
- Speech output software: Software (often integrated into a specific application, such as a word-processing program) that translates standard text into a phonetic code that can be "spoken" by a speech synthesizer
- Screenreaders: Software that works in conjunction with other applications to convert the text on screen into speech output
- Scanners that convert printed text to speech on speech synthesizers or computer sound cards

Braille Access

- Braille keyboard: A nine-key device that enables users to "Braille in" text

- Braille keyboard conversion software: Software that converts nine specified keys on the standard keyboard into a Braille keyboard
- Braille keyboard labels/overlays: Labels with Braille letters that can be placed on individual keys. (Alternatively, Braille dots can be placed directly on keys by means of a liquid substance that hardens after application.)
- Tactile locators: Tactile stickers or other materials that can be strategically placed on the keyboard to identify important keys and facilitate positioning for touch typing
- "Refreshable" or "paperless" Braille display: A hardware template (either a separate component or part of an integrated system) that displays Braille as it is being written. As each letter is typed, round-tip plastic pins corresponding to Braille dots pop up on the template to form Braille letters. The Braille display is refreshable because it can be altered as the text is changed and advanced letter by letter or line by line.
- Braille software translators: Devices that enable users to print high-quality Braille documents from a computer. Software converts the screen display to Braille before it is sent to the Braille embosser to be printed. Reading systems perform optical character recognition to convert printed text into speech or computer files.
- Braille embossers: Devices that emboss documents in Braille. Braille embossers typically have blunt pins that punch dots into special heavy (100-pound basis weight) paper.

ASSESSMENT CONSIDERATIONS

As part of the assessment, note any information relevant to visual impairment, such as the following:

- Type and extent of the visual impairment (including the ophthalmologic findings and quality of usable vision)
- Etiology of the visual loss
- Age of onset of the visual loss
- Findings from a functional vision evaluation (see below)
- Information about the sensory channels and media (e.g., print, Braille, or auditory medium) that best help the child learn
- Other health-related information

If a functional vision evaluation is required, conduct detailed observation of the child's use of vision in everyday settings—such as the classroom, hallways, lunchroom, and playground—to gather information about how the child functions. Consider the following questions, as applicable (Bishop, 1996):

Task Performance

1. How well does the child reach for objects?
2. How well does the child pick up objects?
3. How well does the child locate objects?

4. How well does the child place objects in a specific location?
5. How well does the child find food on a table or tray?
6. How well does the child use utensils?
7. How well does the child imitate gestures?
8. How well does the child copy shapes, designs, letters, numbers, words, and sentences?
9. How well does the child identify details in a picture?
10. How well does the child use a computer or typewriter?
11. How well does the child color within lines, fill in missing parts, trace, cut, string beads, and draw from memory?
12. How does the child's reading fluency compare to that of the norm group?
13. How does the length of time the child spends on reading passages compare to the times for the norm group?
14. What is the child's apparent level of visual discomfort while reading?
15. What does the child say about her or his ability to read and level of comfort while reading?
16. How well does the child use a zipper, tie shoes, button clothes?
17. How well does the child use a screwdriver, use a hammer, and thread a needle (depending on the age of the child)?
18. How well does the child find locations, such as the classroom, main office, restroom, and cafeteria?
19. How well does the child walk on the sidewalk, cross streets, read street signs, and avoid obstacles?
20. How does the child compare with her or his sighted peers in terms of time required to complete tasks?

Qualitative Features

1. Which activities does the child participate in during physical education and at recess?
2. Which activities does the child prefer?
3. Which activities does the child avoid?
4. Does the child use low-vision aids in class?
5. If low-vision aids are used, what aids are used, and when does the child use them? Does the teacher need to tell the child to use them?
6. What is the quality of the child's social relationships?
7. What materials can the child read?
8. How do lighting and quality of materials affect the child's performance?

Children with mildly or moderately low vision often can see the test materials with or without some means of magnification. You might begin by using the standard test materials in the usual way. If the child has difficulty seeing the test materials, modify the materials as needed. Recognize that any modifications in the test stimuli or other test procedures represent a violation of standard procedures and may affect the validity of the test results (see Chapter 7 in *Assessment of Children: Cognitive Applications*). The critical consideration is the extent to which the modifications give additional cues to the child. If the modifications do not give the child additional cues, there is less chance that the modified procedures will invalidate the results. If you do modify the procedures, note in the report precisely what you did. For example, you might write, "These results should be interpreted with caution inasmuch as accommodations were made to allow the student to take the test. These accommodations included _____."

The following suggestions can help you evaluate children with visual impairments.

- Before you administer any tests, ask the child's teacher and parents about how to make the environment visually comfortable for the child (e.g., whether to increase or decrease lighting, what the child's position should be relative to the window) and how to present the materials (e.g., using enlarged print, the child's prescribed optical magnifier, or video magnification in the form of a closed-circuit television device).

- Ask the parents and teacher for suggestions about interacting with the child, including the child's preferred manner of navigating in the environment. A child who is familiar with the school may be able to walk beside you to your office while engaged in conversation. The child who is blind and uses a cane will be able to walk with you to your office with little more assistance than some verbal instructions about the direction of turns in the corridor. Blind children who have not yet mastered cane travel techniques may appreciate an offer of assistance, particularly when in unfamiliar environments such as a clinic. Do this by offering your upper arm, elbow, or wrist (depending on the height of the child), not by taking the child's arm. You should be about a half-step ahead. As you approach obstacles, hesitate briefly, giving a verbal direction (e.g., say, "Stairs going up" before going up the stairs). When entering a narrow space, say so, and extend your arm behind you as a signal to the child to walk behind, rather than next to you. You can offer your hand to a young child who is blind.

- Be sure that the child is wearing his or her prescribed glasses or contact lenses and uses his or her prescribed low-vision device.

- Inform the child about the general layout of the room and other details, such as the presence of a tape recorder if you are using one.

- If your stopwatch or other equipment makes any sound, let the child know what to expect.

- Providing verbal descriptions as needed, allow the child to explore your office, and then guide him or her to a chair. If necessary, place the child's hand on the top of the back of the chair to orient the child to its location.

- In the examination room, reduce glare, use a supplementary light source if needed (such as an adjustable high/low intensity or full-spectrum compact fluorescent lamp), eliminate flickering light, and offer the use of a book stand, which will free the child's hands and may reduce the fatigue associated with reading (Bradley-Johnson, 1994). Also, use a contrasting background for all testing materials (e.g., dark for light materials and light for dark materials). Examinees with visual impairments can usually see things better when there is a good contrast between the testing materials and the table or blackboard.

- Speak in a normal tone of voice to the child. It is all too easy to slip into a louder voice.

- Do not avoid common expressions that might seem awkward at first, such as asking a child who is blind whether he or she has *seen* a specific event. The English language is filled with these terms, and you are likely to be more sensitive to them than the children you are evaluating. Moreover, children who are blind commonly use the terms *see* and *look* freely themselves.

- Use descriptive language when directing older children who are blind. Say, for example, "From where you are standing now, the chair is about 3 feet straight ahead," instead of saying "The chair is right over there."

- Encourage the child to let you know about his or her concerns and to ask you questions at any time.

- As you administer the tests, talk about what you are doing.

- Give the child every opportunity to know what is going on during the evaluation and to explore the materials.

Selecting Tests

Although cognitive tests designed for children with visual impairments would be useful, there currently are no nationally standardized tests available for use with this population. Therefore, you will need to select portions of currently available instruments. You should be able to administer some parts of intelligence tests—such as the WISC–III, WPPSI–R, WAIS–III, Stanford-Binet: Fourth Edition, and Differential Abilities Scale (DAS)—to children with visual impairments, depending on their degree of useful vision (see *Assessment of Children: Cognitive Applications*). On any test that has separate scores for verbal and performance items, for example, you can administer just the verbal subtests to a child who is blind or severely visually impaired.

The ability of children who are congenitally blind to answer items on cognitive ability tests may be limited if the information depends wholly or in part on visual experiences. The same may be true of children with severe visual impairments who have not had life experiences similar to those of sighted children.

The Verbal subtests of the Wechsler tests are very useful in evaluating children with visual impairments. A valuable feature of the Stanford-Binet: Fourth Edition for children with low vision is the absence of bonuses for speed on the Pattern Analysis subtest. The early items on the Vocabulary (Routing) subtest, however, do use pictures.

The DAS also has some useful features. The Pattern Construction subtest has an optional untimed scoring procedure that eliminates time bonuses but retains time limits. Also, the blocks used for items 3 through 6 of the subtest are flat rather than cube-shaped, making the surface easier to recognize.

However, the other school-age spatial subtest—Recall of Designs—requires the child to draw from memory copies of relatively small geometric designs. If you want to administer this subtest, consider enlarging the stimuli. Finally, the Speed of Information Processing subtest is supplementary and not part of the core cognitive subtests. Disadvantages of the DAS for children with visual impairments are that the Verbal subtests for preschool children use pictures and objects and there are not enough subtests at this level that tap verbal ability.

Modifying Standard Procedures

For children who are blind, you can omit subtests requiring vision, obtain materials in Braille, and substitute verbal descriptions for pictures, where applicable. For children who have low vision, you can read printed items aloud, enlarge text material and pictures, and use optical, non-optical, or electronic low-vision devices (Erin & Koenig, 1997). Also, you can provide additional lighting, reduce glare, increase contrast by using a lighter or darker background, use a reading stand to position reading material close to the child, and adapt seating as needed (Bishop, 1996). For a child who is totally blind, you can use Lego blocks for counting tasks, a Braille ruler for measuring tasks, and a Braille teaching clock for clock-reading tasks.

As mentioned earlier, modifications may change the nature of the task and make it difficult to use the norms, especially in the case of timed tests. Enlarged print, for example, takes more time to read than ordinary print (Bradley-Johnson, 1994). Carefully evaluate the requirements needed to perform timed tests before you use them, because these tests may lead to lower scores for children with visual impairments (Groenveld & Jan, 1992). *In the psychological or psychoeducational report, always report the modifications you use.*

Some examiners simply do not give performance subtests to students with low vision. Leaving out performance items, however, deprives you of information about children who may use their vision to learn. Therefore, we recommend that performance-type tests be administered to children with low vision, and *the results used for qualitative purposes only.* The results may also be useful in recommending appropriate modifications of classroom materials and instructional methods.

Following are examples of qualitative information that you might include in psychological reports of children who have visual impairments:

• Samantha correctly completed some of the more difficult items on the WISC–III Block Design subtest, but she required about 50% more time than fully sighted children of her age usually do. These results suggest that she is able to do some types of visual work accurately when given adequate time to complete the work. Therefore, when she is given visual tasks to perform, she should be given extra time if necessary.
• Franklin had difficulty seeing the pictures on the WISC–III Picture Arrangement subtest because the features were too

small and of low contrast. Visual materials that he is given will need to be evaluated with regard to size and contrast and may need to be enlarged and to have the background modified.
• José performed more slowly on the WISC–III Object Assembly subtest than sighted children of his age because of his spotty visual field loss associated with cerebral palsy. He turned and tilted his head in order to see the full array of pieces. He also said that he was more comfortable when the array was placed on a dark background. José's visual limitations indicate that he should have extended time to perform visual tasks and that the contrast of the visual material should be enhanced.
• Although Lynne was successful on the WISC–III Symbol Search and Coding subtests, she worked slowly. This is likely a result of the nystagmus (rapid involuntary movement of the eyes) and photophobia (extreme response to light) associated with albinism. Lynne requires extended time to perform visual tasks accurately. In addition, a low-intensity portable lamp directed at the task could be useful.
• On the Stanford-Binet: Fourth Edition, Maureen accurately but slowly assembled abstract geometric designs with cubes. She drew fairly accurate copies of abstract designs on the Copying subtest, she reproduced the bead constructions on the Bead Memory subtest, and she correctly solved some of the abstract visual Matrices puzzles. However, she had difficulty making sense of the pictures on the Absurdities subtest. Maureen has useful functional vision in some, but not all, areas. Meaningful illustrations, such as pictures of people and places, will need to be explained to her.
• On the Stanford-Binet: Fourth Edition Absurdities subtest, Cordella completed many of the items wearing her glasses only, but she had difficulty on items requiring an ability to see small critical details (such as teeth on a saw). When the stimuli were placed on a video magnification system, however, she was able to appreciate these finer details. Cordella should be encouraged to use a video magnification system for work requiring perception of fine details.

INTERVENTIONS

Interventions should be designed to help children with visual impairments become independent, self-sufficient, competent individuals. Specialized services for children with visual impairments include instruction in (a) using appropriate methods for reading and writing, (b) orientation and mobility, (c) using assistive technologies to access information, (d) personal and home care, (e) functioning within the community, (f) recreational skills and activities, and (g) selecting appropriate careers.

Decisions on how to teach reading to a child with a visual impairment should be based on a study of each case. Braille is usually the best choice for children with severe to total vision loss. For children with less severe losses, consider (a) the type and severity of the vision loss, (b) the portions of the visual field affected, (c) the prognosis with respect to further deterioration of vision, and (d) the length of time the child can comfortably read print. Some children with moderately to severely low vision who are not taught Braille may have difficulty learning to read because they cannot easily distinguish some letters and are confused by the vast number of type styles.

IDEA (Section 300.346) emphasizes teaching Braille unless it is not appropriate to do so. The nationwide shortage of qualified teachers of Braille means that this provision may be difficult to implement. Technologies for accessing print, including video magnification and auditory materials, blur the distinction between those who should use Braille and those who should use print. Some children with visual impairments may use both Braille and print for different tasks and under different circumstances. Whether Braille or print is selected as the primary reading medium, children with visual impairments often will benefit from the use of auditory materials. Auditory materials should supplement, not substitute for, the reading of Braille or print, because Braille and print provide students with a better appreciation of the structure of language (Martelle, 1999).

Children with visual impairments and with no other significant disabilities should achieve at levels comparable to those of sighted children with similar advantages, provided they receive early intervention. This early intervention should include instruction in assistive technologies; high-quality teaching, preferably with a qualified teacher of the visually impaired; provision of materials in appropriate formats, including auditory materials as needed; direct experiences geared to their remaining senses; and the support of family members.

THINKING THROUGH THE ISSUES

1. What do you think it must be like to be born with total blindness?
2. What do you think it must be like to become blind after 5 years of age or older?
3. Which condition do you believe has a more profound effect on a child's ability to function—a visual impairment or a hearing impairment? What is the basis for your answer?

SUMMARY

1. Children with visual impairments have conditions that range from limited vision to no vision at all (blind).
2. Key variables in understanding visual impairments are the type, severity, etiology, and age of onset of the impairment.
3. Several disorders that affect vision have a congenital basis, while others are acquired through injury or illness.
4. Congenital etiologies account for over 50% of the cases of blindness in children.

Disorders That Affect Vision

5. Vision may be affected by refractive errors, central visual field defects, peripheral visual field defects, whole visual field defects, and other conditions.

Courtesy of Herman Zilinski and Carol Evans.

Children with Mild, Moderate, or Severe Visual Impairments

6. Children with mild or moderate visual loss usually employ vision as their primary learning channel. Children with severe to profound vision loss, however, need to use tactile and auditory sensory input to obtain information, in addition to using whatever residual vision, if any, is available to them.
7. Blindness refers to vision loss that is total or sight that is so impaired that the individual primarily uses senses other than vision for obtaining information and for interacting with the environment.

Development of Children Who Are Blind or Profoundly Visually Impaired

8. Children who become blind before 5 years of age face more developmental challenges than those who become blind after 5 years of age.
9. Children who become blind after infancy face the struggles associated with having to expend more energy to accomplish routine tasks.
10. Children with normal vision usually learn the meanings of words in the context of their visual experience, while children who are blind usually learn the meanings of words—particularly words relating to objects outside of their immediate experience—through verbal explanations.
11. Children with congenital blindness develop concepts of space in a sequence similar to that followed by sighted children, but at a slower rate; those who are congenitally blind and were born prematurely are at higher risk for spatial impairments.

12. Children with visual impairments are at higher risk for impaired social functioning than their normally sighted counterparts.

13. Just as there is enormous variability among children with normal vision, there is also enormous variability among children with visual impairments.

Children with Visual Impairments and the IDEA

14. The IDEA of 1997 provides guidelines for working with children with visual impairments.

15. Assistive technology devices can help children with visual impairments.

Assessment Considerations

16. Children with mildly or moderately low vision often can see the test materials with or without some means of magnification.

17. Recognize that any modifications in the test stimuli or other test procedures represent a violation of standard procedures and may affect the validity of the test results.

18. Although cognitive tests designed for children with visual impairments would be useful, there currently are no nationally standardized tests available for use with this population. Therefore, you will need to select portions of currently available instruments.

19. For children who are blind, you can omit subtests requiring vision, obtain materials in Braille, and substitute verbal descriptions for pictures, where applicable.

Interventions

20. Children with visual impairments and no other significant disabilities should achieve at levels comparable to those of sighted children with similar advantages, provided they receive early intervention—including instruction in assistive technologies; high-quality teaching, preferably by with a qualified teacher of the visually impaired; provision of materials in appropriate formats, including auditory materials as needed; direct experiences geared to their remaining senses; and the support of family members.

KEY TERMS, CONCEPTS, AND NAMES

Visual impairments (p. 368)
Disorders that affect vision (p. 368)

Myopia (p. 368)
Hyperopia (p. 368)
Astigmatism (p. 368)
Juvenile macular degeneration (p. 368)
Diabetic retinopathy (p. 368)
Achromatopsia (p. 368)
Retinitis pigmentosa (p. 368)
Glaucoma (p. 368)
Retinopathy of prematurity (p. 369)
Cataracts (p. 369)
Aniridia (p. 369)
Albinism (p. 369)
Retinoblastoma (p. 369)
Cortical visual impairment (p. 369)
Fetal alcohol syndrome (p. 369)
Congenital optic nerve disorders (p. 369)
Multiple sclerosis (p. 369)
Amblyopia (p. 369)
Nystagmus (p. 369)
Visual acuity (p. 370)
CF (p. 370)
HM (p. 370)
LP (p. 370)
NLP (p. 370)
Legal blindness (p. 370)
Children with visual impairments and the IDEA (p. 371)
Assistive technology devices (p. 371)
Enhancement of print (p. 371)
Auditory access (p. 371)
Braille access (p. 371)
Assessment considerations for children with visual impairments (p. 372)
Selecting tests (p. 373)
Modifying standard procedures (p. 374)
Interventions with children with visual impairments (p. 374)

STUDY QUESTION

Discuss children with visual impairments. Include in your discussion disorders that affect vision; mild, moderate, and severe visual impairments; development of children who are visually impaired; children with visual impairments and the IDEA; assessment considerations, including selecting tests and modifying standard procedures; and interventions.

16

HEARING IMPAIRMENTS

by Jerome M. Sattler and Steven T. Hardy-Braz

[Sign language] is, in the hands of its masters, a most beautiful and expressive language, for which, in their intercourse with each other and as a means of easily and quickly reaching the minds of the deaf, neither nature nor art has given them a satisfactory substitute.

It is impossible for those who do not understand it to comprehend its possibilities with the deaf, its powerful influence on the moral and social happiness of those deprived of hearing, and its wonderful power of carrying thought to intellects which would otherwise be in perpetual darkness. Nor can they appreciate the hold it has upon the deaf. So long as there are two deaf people upon the face of the earth and they get together, so long will signs be with us.

—J. Schuyler Long
Head teacher, Iowa School for the Deaf (1910)

Goals and Objectives

This chapter is designed to enable you to do the following:

- Understand how to assess children with hearing impairments

- Understand how to design interventions for children with hearing impairments

Inability to hear clearly can adversely affect the speech and communication, linguistic, and academic abilities of children. Acquiring fluency in a spoken language is a major developmental task facing children with hearing impairments. (Note that in this chapter we use the phrase "children with hearing impairments" to refer to those who are deaf, are hard-of-hearing, have a hearing impairment, or have a hearing loss.) Infants born with hearing impairments follow a normal pattern of vocalization until about 7 months of age (Marschark, 1993). After this age, the rate of development of spoken productions is often reduced. The frequent failure of such infants to learn to speak clearly is not the result of a vocal problem; it is because they cannot hear speech clearly, if at all.

Hearing impairments may also affect children's behavior, self-concept, identity, and social and emotional development. Some children who have severe hearing losses tend to be somewhat more impulsive, dependent, and rigid and less motivated and accepting of personal responsibility than children with normal hearing (Keane, 1987). A high percentage of children with hearing impairments also have conduct problems and anxiety disorders (Hodapp, 1998). Those with multiple handicaps usually show higher levels of academic difficulties than those with only hearing impairments. Therefore, it is important to conduct a comprehensive assessment of children with hearing impairments. If you suspect that a child has an undiagnosed hearing loss, refer the child to an audiologist for a hearing evaluation. Chapter 7 in *Assessment of Children: Cognitive Applications* (pages 201–202) describes indicators of a possible hearing impairment.

Children with hearing impairments also may have difficulties with balance, equilibrium, and other motor skills related to the vestibular system. Thus, delays in early developmental milestones (e.g., walking) may also be observed. In the 1998–1999 school year, the prevalence rate of individuals aged 6 to 21 years with hearing impairments served under the IDEA (see Chapter 3 in *Assessment of Children: Cognitive Applications*) was 1.3% (70,888; U.S. Department of Education, 2000).

Hearing impairment is a general term that refers to hearing losses ranging from mild to profound.

- A child who is *deaf* has a hearing disability that prevents successful processing of linguistic information through audition.
- A child who is *hard-of-hearing* has residual hearing sufficient for successful processing of linguistic information through audition, generally with the use of an assistive technology device (discussion to follow).
- A child who is *prelingually deaf* (i.e., a child whose deafness was present at birth or occurred before the child developed speech and language) is usually unable to acquire speech in a normal fashion.
- A child who is *postlingually deaf* (i.e., a child who became deaf after speech and language had been developed) has significant difficulties in acquiring or maintaining ad-

ditional spoken language proficiency, but usually not to the same extent as children who are prelingually deaf.

ETIOLOGY

Hearing impairments occur because of disease, accidents, or congenital or hereditary conditions. It is estimated that heredity accounts for 50% of early childhood hearing impairments with known etiology (Marschark, 1993). Following are examples of high-risk conditions in infancy and later life that may lead to hearing impairments, as well as other disabilities.

Infancy

- *Asphyxia* is a lack of oxygen or excess of carbon dioxide in the body. It may lead to unconsciousness, seizures, damage to various sensory systems, and death.
- *Cytomegalovirus* (CMV) is a systemic illness that may be transmitted prenatally, as the baby passes through the infected birth canal, or postnatally, through infected urine, saliva, breast milk, feces, tears, or blood. Although some carriers of the virus are asymptomatic, in its most severe form CMV causes global central nervous system infection involving the cerebral cortex, brain stem, cochlear nuclei, cranial nerves, and inner ear.
- *Herpes simplex virus* is a virus that may be transmitted to the fetus during the birth process if the mother is actively infected. It may cause a severe generalized disease in the neonate, with high risk of mortality and devastating sequelae, including brain infections, respiratory difficulties, convulsions, hepatitis, and hearing impairments.
- *Hyperbilirubinemia,* also known as elevated bilirubin, is a condition that occurs when the blood contains an excessive amount of bilirubin (formed from the metabolism of red blood cells). High levels of bilirubin can cause jaundice, and very high levels can lead to kernicterus, causing brain and spinal cord damage and hearing impairment. Initial treatment of hyperbilirubinemia is by light (photo) therapy; exchange transfusions may be needed in severe cases.
- *Premature birth* is defined as birth before 36 weeks' gestation. Low birthweight is defined to be a birthweight of less than approximately 5 lb 8 oz, or 2,500 grams.
- *Meningitis* is a brain infection involving acute inflammation of the membranes that cover the brain and spinal cord. It is characterized by drowsiness, confusion, irritability, and sensory impairments.
- *Rh incompatibility* is a condition that arises when the mother has Rh negative blood and the fetus has Rh positive blood. When blood from the fetus mixes in the placenta with the mother's blood, antibodies may be produced that will destroy the red blood cells of the fetus in any subsequent pregnancy. If this condition is not treated, it can cause such conditions as abortion, stillbirth, jaundice, deafness, and mental retardation.

- *Rubella,* or German measles, is an infectious disease that, if contracted by the mother during the first three months of pregnancy, has a high risk of causing congenital anomalies, including deafness, deaf-blindness, visual impairments, cataracts, cardiac malformation, and mental retardation. On reaching adulthood, children with congenital rubella syndrome may have diabetes, glaucoma, endocrine pathology, and central nervous system infections.
- *Syphilis* is a sexually transmitted bacterial infection that may result in central nervous system abnormalities, including hearing loss; vestibular dysfunction; and heart conditions. Mental retardation also may result, depending on the severity of the neurologic damage.
- *Toxoplasmosis* is a parasitic infection transmitted by pregnant women to developing fetuses. Symptoms include blindness, central nervous system damage, jaundice, hydrocephalus, and mental retardation.
- *Down syndrome* is a chromosomal abnormality that may lead to a conductive hearing loss resulting from narrow ear canals and frequent middle ear infections.
- *Usher syndrome* is an autosomal recessive gene defect that may result in a hearing loss as well as visual loss and severe balance problems associated with neurological impairments.
- *Waardenburg syndrome* is an autosomal dominant gene defect that may result in a hearing loss because of abnormalities of the inner ear.
- *Treacher Collins syndrome* is either an autosomal dominant gene defect (in 40% of the cases) or the product of a mutated genetic change (in 60% of the cases) that may result in a hearing loss associated with physical defects and abnormalities of the ears and mouth.
- *Intrauterine exposure to drugs through maternal drug abuse.*

Later Life

- Severe blow to the head
- Exposure to very loud noise that results in acoustic trauma
- Childhood diseases such as measles, mumps, and chicken pox
- Inner ear infections (otitis media)
- Other infections accompanied by high fever
- Reactions to certain prescription medications

Adequate prenatal care and efficient obstetrical procedures, as well as early treatment of ear infections and high fevers, may prevent auditory problems.

CLASSIFICATION OF HEARING IMPAIRMENT

Hearing ability is represented by a continuum ranging from very acute perception, such as that of a gifted musical conductor who can detect an out-of-tune instrument in an orchestra, to total deafness, such as that of an individual who can detect only strong vibrations through tactile sensations. An inability to hear may be either unilateral (just one ear) or bilateral (both ears).

Hearing ability is evaluated on two dimensions: sound frequency and sound intensity. *Sound frequency* is measured in cycles per second; the unit of measure is the Hertz (Hz). Hearing loss can be confined to low or high frequencies, or it can be across all frequencies. *Sound intensity,* or the loudness of sound, is measured in decibels (dB). A decibel is $\frac{1}{10}$ of a bel—hence the prefix *deci.* The bel is a logarithmic unit; a sound that is 10 decibels louder than another is ten times as loud.

The following classification scheme is used by audiologists to evaluate hearing ability. It is based on the extent to which the individual needs a higher-than-average intensity of sound to hear.

1. *Normal range* is 0–15 dB.
2. *Slight hearing loss* is a loss of 15–20 dB. Children with a loss of less than 20 dB are the least hard-of-hearing. They hear vowel sounds clearly, but they may miss unvoiced consonant sounds. You should have no difficulty evaluating these children.
3. *Mild hearing loss* is a loss of 20–40 dB. Children with a mild hearing loss may not be recognized as having a problem unless communication problems develop, in which case they may be referred for an audiological evaluation. They may miss soft or whispered speech, and they may have mild speech problems. You should have little difficulty evaluating these children unless they exhibit communication problems. Still, you should be aware of any testing conditions that may impede the children's ability to perceive information accurately.
4. *Moderate hearing loss* is a loss of 41–60 dB. Children with a moderate hearing loss may have difficulty hearing most speech sounds at normal conversational levels when there is background noise. They usually have moderate speech problems. You may have difficulty evaluating these children—you may have to speak loudly and use special communication procedures (discussion to follow).
5. *Severe hearing loss* is a loss of 61–90 dB. Children with a severe hearing loss hear only the loudest speech sounds; they cannot detect any speech sounds at normal conversational levels. If they have oral speech, their articulation, vocabulary, and voice quality will differ from those of children with normal hearing. They usually have severe speech problems. You will need to use special communication procedures (discussion to follow) to evaluate most, if not all, children in this group.
6. *Profound hearing loss* is a loss greater than 90 dB. Children with a profound hearing loss usually hear no speech or other sounds. Many have no oral speech at all. This degree of hearing loss has a profound impact on communication. You will need to use special communication procedures (discussion to follow) to evaluate children in this group.

When a child is evaluated for a hearing loss, her or his classification may depend on whether an assistive listening device is used. Thus, for example, a child may have a severe hearing loss when unaided, but only a moderate loss when wearing a hearing aid. However, a child with a mild to moderate hearing loss when aided still may not have fluent speech or speech perception.

There are two major types of hearing loss (Berkow, 1997):

- A *conductive hearing loss* occurs when a mechanical problem in the ear canal or middle ear blocks the conduction of sound.
- A *sensorineural hearing loss* occurs when there is damage to the inner ear, auditory nerve, or auditory nerve pathways in the brain.

Children with hearing impairments are a heterogenous group. Two children with the same degree of loss may have different abilities to hear sound or produce speech and may benefit differently from assistive listening devices. The distinction between deaf and hard-of-hearing may be difficult to specify. Because IDEA does not provide a definition of deafness, eligibility criteria are not consistent across states (Bienenstock & Vernon, 1994). Thus, what one state considers to be "deaf" might be considered "hard-of-hearing" in another state.

ASSISTIVE TECHNOLOGY DEVICES

Assistive technology devices for children with hearing impairments include the following (Abledata, 1999):

Computer-Assisted Devices

- Speech recognition software: Software that converts spoken language into written text.

Pre-Recorded Live Captioning

- Closed-captioning decoders: Devices that allow a person to view the dialogue and sound effects of any television program that has been encoded into text. The text appears at the bottom of the screen, much like the subtitles on foreign motion pictures.

Telephone Communication Systems

- Telecommunication devices for the deaf (TDDs): Visual telephones that allow users to converse by typing. The devices come with many options, including printers, large-print displays, announcers, and voice-carrying capability.
- Amplified telephones: Telephones that enhance the clarity and loudness of spoken words. One type of device has a built-in sound equalizer that selectively increases the volume of high-frequency sounds. Another type of device has an in-line amplifier that, when connected to a telephone, receives the incoming signals intended for the handset, increases the volume of these signals, and sends the boosted signals out to the handset.

Environmental Alert Devices

- Visual alert signalers and remote receivers: Devices that use an electrical connection to alert people to signals from doorbells, telephones, or smoke detectors. The signal triggers a warning, such as a flashing light, a loud horn, or vibrations.
- Wake-up alarm systems: Systems that use a combination of visual, auditory, and tactile stimulation to wake people with hearing disabilities. When connected to a lamp or bed shaker, these systems provide the user with the option of waking up to a flashing light, a horn, or a gentle shaking.
- Hearing ear dogs: Dogs who have been trained to alert their owners to significant sounds
- Car alert systems: Systems that emit a high-pitched sound to enhance a person's residual ability to detect unusual or sudden noises
- Visual beep indicator programs: Programs that add visual indicators to audible computer beeps that signal an error or another message. These programs are particularly useful to computer users with little or no residual hearing ability.

Cochlear Implants

- Cochlear implants: Devices that transmit sound directly to the auditory nerve, bypassing the ear. Used primarily for individuals with severe to profound nerve deafness that is not helped by conventional hearing aids, they do not restore normal hearing, and their effectiveness varies with the recipient.
- Auditory brainstem implants: Implants that use the same technology as cochlear implants, but are placed on the area of the brainstem that ordinarily receives neural impulses from the cochlea through the auditory nerve

Assistive Listening Devices (ALDs)

- Infrared systems: Systems that transmit sounds by means of invisible light beams. The receiver must be within direct line of sight of the transmitter of the light beam. Infrared systems are useful for TV listening and small-group meetings. The transmitters connect directly to TVs, audio output jacks, or microphones. The infrared system does not work well outdoors because of interference from sunlight.
- FM systems: Systems that transmit sounds via radio waves. The speaker wears a compact transmitter and microphone, while the listener uses a portable receiver with headphones or earphones. FM systems are useful for classrooms or meetings and work well both indoors and outdoors.
- Loop systems: Systems in which a special microphone and amplifier are used by the primary speaker and the am-

plified speech signals are circulated through a loop wire in a telecoil circuit placed within the listener's hearing aid.

- Hearing aids: A variety of small devices that amplify sounds. Several different types are available, including in-the-ear hearing aids, in-the-canal hearing aids, completely-in-the-canal hearing aids, and behind-the-ear hearing aids.

EVALUATION OF HEARING LOSS

When you evaluate a child who has a hearing impairment or is suspected of having a hearing impairment, consider the following:

- Type of hearing loss
- Etiology of hearing loss
- Degree of hearing loss
- Age of onset of hearing loss
- Stability of hearing
- Range of frequencies affected
- Use of assistive listening devices
- Ability to benefit from assistive listening devices
- Age of identification
- Education history
- Communication ability and communication preference (e.g., sign, speech and sign, or speech only)
- Visual acuity (see Chapter 15)
- Ability to use fine-motor skills for fingerspelling or cued speech
- Degree of residual hearing
- Auditory processing capability
- Comorbid disabilities
- Communication patterns within the family, school, and other environments, including use of spoken language and sign language and availability of assistive listening devices

Let's look at four of these factors in more detail.

1. *Etiology of hearing loss.* Consider the origin of the hearing loss. Some etiologies not only lead to a hearing loss but also have other adverse effects. For example, 17% of children who are born deaf as a result of genetic transmission also have an additional disability (Braden, 1994). If the hearing loss was a result of a neurological disorder (such as meningitis or CMV), there may be concomitant dysfunctions.

2. *Degree of hearing loss.* Children with mild to moderate hearing loss may be able to be evaluated orally if they have an assistive listening device. In addition, room lighting should be adequate, and they should be positioned to see you easily. In some cases, children with mild to moderate hearing loss may prefer using sign language. Children with severe hearing loss will need to be administered tests in their preferred language or communication modality.

3. *Age of onset of hearing loss.* Children who had the opportunity to hear oral language before the hearing loss was

sustained may understand verbal communications better than those who sustained the hearing loss earlier. Onset of deafness prior to the age of 5 years is likely to have a negative effect on development of language, particularly spoken language.

4. *Stability of hearing.* The ability to hear may fluctuate from day to day, month to month, or year to year. For example, some etiologies result in a decline in residual hearing ability, and illnesses, ear infections, ear wax, and other conditions can affect an individual's hearing in various ways.

Determine from the parents, an audiologist, or a speech and language therapist whether the child's hearing loss affects his or her ability to understand speech sounds. Become familiar with the child's receptive and expressive skills—that is, the methods by which the child receives and communicates information—by interviewing his or her parents and teachers and by observing the child in a classroom and other settings. During the evaluation, encourage the child to respond in the way with which he or she is most comfortable. The tests you select and the ways you present the materials should suit the child's abilities and limitations.

Following are some key questions that you should ask the parents of an examinee who may have a hearing deficit:

1. When did you first suspect that [child's name] had a hearing problem?
2. What led you to believe that [child's name] had a hearing problem?
3. What professional did you see first to help you determine whether [child's name] had a hearing problem?
4. How long did it take to confirm or rule out your suspicions that [child's name] had a hearing problem?

If the child has a hearing loss, ask the following questions:

5. What interventions occurred when the hearing loss was diagnosed?
6. Did the interventions help your child?
7. How do you and others communicate with your child?
8. Do you have concerns about any other aspects of your child's development?

Deafness is an invisible, as well as a low-incidence, disability; it usually represents a static and irreversible condition (Danek, 1988). According to Marschark (1993),

About 90% of children with congenital or early onset deafness are born into families in which both parents are hearing. Another 7% of such children have one deaf parent, leaving only about 3% who have two deaf parents. Most deaf children therefore are raised almost entirely in the hearing world, at least during infancy. (p. 5)

Parents are often unprepared to recognize a hearing impairment in their infant. At first, they may believe that their child is slow, mentally retarded, or learning disabled or that something is not quite right. There may be a considerable delay between when the parents first suspect some difficulty and when a conclusive diagnosis is reached. In some cases, the child may not be identified as having a hearing loss until she or he is 1 or 2 years of age or older (Yoshinaga-Itano, Sedey, Coulter, & Mehl, 1998); as of May 2001, only 65% of American newborns were routinely tested for a hearing loss (Manning, 2001).

COMMUNICATION MODALITIES AND LANGUAGE

Three types of communication modalities are particularly useful with children with hearing impairments.

1. *Oral methods of communication.* Oral communication methods (or auditory-verbal methods) emphasize the use of residual hearing, speech development, and speech reading. Children can use hearing aids, cochlear implants, or FM systems to amplify sounds. They should receive intensive speech therapy to help them learn to speak English or other spoken languages. The primarily auditory approach stresses residual hearing and the development of discrimination and sound perception ability. The cued speech approach combines an auditory emphasis with visual cues. The cues are eight hand shapes that are used in four positions near the face to supplement spoken language. Each hand shape represents a group of consonant sounds, and the positions represent vowel sounds.

2. *Artificial manual sign methods of communication.* There are several artificial manual sign methods to help children with hearing impairments communicate; they differ primarily in the language used as a base. Signed English, Seeing Essential English, and Signing Exact English are all forms of a signed system based on the English language and developed for teaching.

3. *Native manual sign languages.* A native manual sign language such as *American Sign Language (ASL)* is a recognized language with its own grammar and syntax. ASL is widely used in the deaf community in the United States, while other sign languages are used in some other countries. Movement, handshape, facial expressions, and location of signs are all used to convey complex grammatical structures. Children born to parents who are deaf usually can hear, but their first language may be a native sign language such as ASL.

Several methods combine two of the above modalities. The Rochester method involves the simultaneous use of fingerspelling and speech. In the Total Communication method, which is commonly used in programs for children who are deaf, speech may be used in conjunction with English-based signs, signs used in English order, or American Sign Language.

Children using ASL or any other method of communication still must learn to read and write in English (Hodapp, 1998):

Yet the grammar of written English is much more closely allied to the grammar of spoken English than to ASL, whose grammar is loosely associated with the French from which it arose. Similarly, although the correspondence between English speech sounds and writing is not perfect (compare the words "to," "too," and "two"), written phonology also generally conforms to the sound system of spoken English. Even fluent, native ASL signers, then, must learn to read and write in an English that is very different from ASL. (pp. 100–101)

Research reviewed by Hodapp (1998) indicates that "Deaf children with higher levels of language perform better on high-level cognitive tasks than do deaf children with lower language skills.... [And] the language of children who are deaf develops best when their parents are ASL signers who are deaf. These children develop language from their earliest years, in a natural way" (p. 168).

The study of children with hearing impairments gives us insights into the process of cognitive development (Mayberry, 1992):

Children who are deaf have taught us that the human mind is characterized by enormous linguistic creativity. When language is unavailable, the child invents the beginnings of one (home sign). When a group of people is cut off from acoustic language, they evolve a visual language (sign). (pp. 65–66, with changes in notation)

CHILDREN WITH HEARING IMPAIRMENTS AND THE IDEA

The IDEA of 1997 (see Chapter 3 in *Assessment of Children: Cognitive Applications*) provides the following guidelines for working with children with hearing impairments.

Sec. 300.7 Child with a disability.
(3) Deafness means a hearing impairment that is so severe that the child is impaired in processing linguistic information through hearing, with or without amplification, that adversely affects a child's educational performance.
(5) Hearing impairment means an impairment in hearing, whether permanent or fluctuating, that adversely affects a child's educational performance but that is not included under the definition of deafness in this section.

Sec. 300.19 Native language.
(a) As used in this part, the term native language, if used with reference to an individual of limited English proficiency, means the following:
(b) For an individual with deafness or blindness, or for an individual with no written language, the mode of communication is that normally used by the individual (such as sign language, braille, or oral communication).

Sec. 300.24 Related services.
(1) Audiology includes—
    (i) Identification of children with hearing loss;
    (ii) Determination of the range, nature, and degree of hearing loss, including referral for medical or other professional attention for the habilitation of hearing;
    (iii) Provision of habilitative activities, such as language habilitation, auditory training, speech reading (lipreading), hearing evaluation, and speech conservation;

(iv) Creation and administration of programs for prevention of hearing loss;

(v) Counseling and guidance of children, parents, and teachers regarding hearing loss; and

(vi) Determination of children's needs for group and individual amplification, selecting and fitting an appropriate aid, and evaluating the effectiveness of amplification.

Sec. 300.303 Proper functioning of hearing aids.

Each public agency shall ensure that the hearing aids worn in school by children with hearing impairments, including deafness, are functioning properly.

Sec. 300.346 Development, review, and revision of IEP.

(2) Consideration of special factors. The IEP team also shall—

(iv) Consider the communication needs of the child, and in the case of a child who is deaf or hard of hearing, consider the child's language and communication needs, opportunities for direct communications with peers and professional personnel in the child's language and communication mode, academic level, and full range of needs, including opportunities for direct instruction in the child's language and communication mode; and

(v) Consider whether the child requires assistive technology devices and services.

ASSESSMENT CONSIDERATIONS

The IDEA of 1997 mandates that tests and other evaluation materials normally be administered in the student's native language or other mode of communication. You need to have special communication skills to evaluate children with hearing impairments. If you have not received special training in administering tests to children with hearing impairments, observe classes for the hearing impaired and note how the teachers communicate with students. If you are to obtain accurate responses from children with hearing impairments, they must understand your instructions and questions. (This is true, of course, for all children who are being evaluated.) Furthermore, you must be able to make instructions understood without giving leading cues in the process.

If you use pantomime, recognize that children may not interpret your actions as you intend. Pantomime and visual aids are inferior administration procedures for the majority of standardized tests. The Universal Nonverbal Intelligence Test (UNIT) and the Leiter International Performance Test–Revised (Leiter–R), however, are exceptions because both of these tests have been standardized, for the most part, using pantomime procedures (see Chapter 16 in *Assessment of Children: Cognitive Applications*). Unless you are administering tests standardized using pantomime procedures, use pantomime and visual aids only when you cannot communicate fluently in sign language, cued speech, or written language or when the children are not versed in sign language or other special communication modalities. Pantomime and visual aids are, however, preferable to a verbal-only administration.

In reviewing a child's case history, note the following (Kirk, Gallagher, & Anastosiow, 1997):

- Complaints of earaches, discomfort of the ears, or hearing strange ringing or buzzing noises
- Discharges from the ears or excessively heavy wax buildup in the ear canal
- Turning up the volume of the radio, television, or records so loud that others complain
- Being unresponsive or inattentive when spoken to in a normal voice
- Reluctance to participate in oral activities

Evaluating children with hearing impairments may be more fatiguing, demand greater attention and concentration, and require more time and flexibility than evaluating children with normal hearing. Both you and the children may be self-conscious because a premium is placed on observation. With proper preparation, you should be able to meet the challenges of evaluating children with hearing impairments. If you routinely evaluate children with hearing impairments, learn sign language and other means of communicating with them. If you believe that you are not qualified to evaluate children with hearing impairments, refer them to a more qualified professional.

Suggestions for Test Administration

The following suggestions for evaluating a child with a hearing impairment take into account the mandates of the IDEA (Braden & Hannah, 1998):

Preferred Communication

1. Determine the child's preferred mode of communication.
2. Administer the tests in the child's preferred communication modality or language.
3. Arrange for a psychologist who knows how to communicate in the child's preferred communication modality or language to administer the tests if you cannot do so.

Interpreter

1. Use a qualified interpreter/transliterator skilled in the child's preferred communication modality or language if you cannot obtain the services of a psychologist who knows how to communicate in the child's preferred modality or language.
2. Do not use a parent, another family member, or the child's teacher as the interpreter, because the child may not discuss his or her feelings openly in the presence of a family member or teacher.
3. Maintain eye contact and speak directly to the child, using a normal conversational tone and pace.
4. Do not speak to the interpreter about the child as if the child weren't there.
5. You and the interpreter should sit near each other and across from the child, with the interpreter slightly to your rear and to one side, within the child's line of sight.

6. Only one of you should speak at a time.

7. Coordinate your activities with the interpreter so that the child can look at your demonstration either before or after looking at the interpreter. Remember that, during instructions that require directions and demonstrations, the child will not be able to visually attend simultaneously to the interpreter's signs *and* your demonstrations.

8. Be sensitive to the child's ability to watch you and the interpreter.

9. Use an interpreter to evaluate the child even if you administer nonverbal tests in which gestures and demonstrations are used.

10. Prepare and train the interpreter prior to the evaluation, and after the evaluation discuss with the interpreter any issues pertaining to the translation of the test stimuli or the interpretation of the child's responses.

11. Recognize that some concepts have different levels of difficulty in English and ASL (or other spoken languages and native sign languages). (See Chapter 19 in *Assessment of Children: Cognitive Applications* for more information about using an interpreter and problems involved in translations. Also see the Web site *www.rid.org* for more information about interpreters/transliterators who work with individuals who are hearing impaired.)

12. Recognize that some test items may be difficult to administer in ASL. Test items that require recall of numbers and letters (e.g., Letter-Number Sequencing on the WAIS–III) are one example. Because some letters and numbers are signed in similar ways (e.g., the letter F and the numeral 9, the letter D and the numeral 1, the letter W and the numeral 6), items using these letters or numbers together in noncontextual strings (e.g., 6D9W1) may not be administered clearly in sign language. In assessing a child in ASL, consider the accuracy of hand-shape responses in light of the task stimuli (letters, numbers, or both)—if the stimuli are numbers only, you do not have to question whether the child means 6 or W. Another example is a test item that asks the child to point to his or her nose or eye. Because the signs for these terms demonstrate the item, the task in ASL is very different from the task in spoken English.

13. Recognize that when instructions on performance tests are signed, children with hearing impairments may be at a disadvantage. Children with hearing impairments must process the instructions visually and then shift their attention to the test items, whereas children with normal hearing can view the test materials while the instructions are being given.

14. Recognize that using an interpreter will increase the time needed to conduct the evaluation.

Variety of Techniques

1. Use a combination of techniques—speech, gesture, pantomime, writing, signing, fingerspelling, and drawing—if the child has no preferred mode of communication. Where feasible, a total communication approach, such as sign language with speech, is preferred.

2. Use one or more of the following methods to give directions, depending on your skills and the child's abilities (Braden & Hannah, 1998, pp. 177–178, with changes in notation):

   - Careful oral enunciation without exaggerated lip movements
   - Supplementing oral directions with a written transcript of the directions
   - Fingerspelling directions
   - Signing directions in English signs
   - Concurrently saying directions orally and signing them in an English-type sign dialect
   - Translating directions into ASL without concurrent voice
   - Gestures
   - Providing supplementary examples/demonstrations of similar test items (e.g., demonstrating the task requirements with items below the starting point from easier tests [such as the WPPSI–R or the WISC–III])

Condition of the Room

1. Be sure that the room is illuminated adequately, so that your face and hands (and the hands and face of the interpreter, if there is one) can be clearly seen, and that you are in close physical proximity to the child.

2. Do not sit with the sun or a bright light behind you, because this can create shadows and eyestrain for the child.

3. Be sure that the light does not shine in the child's eyes or create a glare on the materials.

4. Be sure that the room is free of noise and visual distractions.

Facial Expressions and Speech

1. Make sure that you look at the child when you speak to him or her and that the child, in turn, is watching you or the interpreter/transliterator, if there is one.

2. Maintain a pleasant facial expression.

3. Speak clearly, distinctly, and naturally, at a reduced rate, without exaggerating or distorting your lip movements, particularly if the child has some hearing ability or speech-reading ability.

4. Use short, simple sentences.

5. Do not turn away from the child in the middle of a sentence.

6. Be sure that there are no obstructions blocking the child's view of your lips.

7. Do not chew gum, smoke a cigarette, put your hand on your chin, or do anything else that might impede speech reading.

Additional Administrative Suggestions

1. Be sure that the child who has an assistive listening device has it turned on, that it is working, and that she or he brings extra hearing-aid batteries to the examination.

2. Touch the child gently on the arm or wave your hand in the child's line of vision if the child is looking away.

3. Rephrase misunderstood concepts into simpler, more visible forms rather than repeating them in the same way.
4. Consider presenting some questions in written form if the child can read.
5. Observe the child's nonverbal behavior.
6. Give credit to pantomimed responses only when you have no doubt about the accuracy of the response.
7. Do not accept a nod or a smile when you are trying to determine whether the child understands the task; instead, ask the child to tell you in her or his own words.
8. Take breaks as needed.
9. State in your report how communication was established and what means were used to check the examinee's comprehension of instructions and test items.

False Impressions

Although children with hearing impairments may give the impression of being able to understand your questions, they may be feigning comprehension in order to obtain your approval. For example, they may have learned to pretend that they understand to avoid being embarrassed. In turn, you may have difficulty understanding their answers, particularly if they have accents or speech or motor difficulties. Do *not* interpret the difficulties children with hearing impairments have with expressive language, receptive language, or both as indications of limited intelligence.

Cues

Because sight is the chief means by which children who are hearing impaired receive stimuli, they are particularly likely to seek to gain understanding from visual cues—such as facial expressions and hand movements. Recognize that any movements you make, including eye movements, may cue a child. Facial expressions, rather than the tone of your voice, will convey your mood. Children with hearing impairments may quickly notice if you frown or grimace in impatience and may unfavorably interpret such gestures. Smile to reward their efforts, but not to reward their responses. Avoid smiling when they say something that is not comprehensible; you do not want to encourage them to think that they are communicating effectively. Being aware of your facial expressions and gestures is especially important when you administer multiple-choice tests or subtests such as TONI–3, Leiter–R, UNIT, Finger Windows (from the WRAML), or Spatial Span (from the WISC–III PI). You must avoid looking at the correct response—or any response, for that matter.

Confidentiality

Children who have hearing impairments have the same concerns about confidentiality as children who are not hearing impaired and should be given the same information (see Chapter 3 in *Assessment of Children: Cognitive Applica-*

tions). If a professional interpreter is used, children need to be reassured that the interpreter also will respect confidentiality, and the need for confidentiality must be explained to the interpreter before the assessment.

Establishing Rapport

Particularly if their primary language involves signing, children who have hearing impairments may have a poorer command of standard English grammar, use different idioms, or use more concrete expressions than children with normal hearing. These difficulties can affect rapport. Children with hearing impairments also may be uncooperative. If they are uncooperative, they may sign too rapidly, look away from you, turn off their assistive listening device, close their eyes, or seem to have only selective understanding of what you say. They also may have difficulty handling silence, as they may view silence as a breakdown in communication rather than a simple pause. If rapport problems develop, use the same techniques with children with hearing impairments as you would use with other children (see Chapter 7 in *Assessment of Children: Cognitive Applications*).

Use of Standardized Tests

In assessing children with hearing impairments, consider first the way the test is administered. Tests should be administered in the children's preferred mode of communication. If they are not administered in this way, the results are likely to be invalid. Also, consider how much importance should be placed on the results of verbally oriented tests. Traditionally, verbal cognitive tests have been viewed as not giving an accurate picture of the mental ability of children with hearing impairments; instead, they have been viewed as a measure of the extent of the children's verbal or English language achievement. This may still be true in many cases, especially when children have not been exposed to signing or other methods of communication.

Sullivan and Montoya (1997), however, maintain that verbal cognitive tests *should* be used to estimate the intelligence level of children with hearing impairments:

The historic taboo against the use of verbal intelligence tests with children who are hearing impaired needs to be reexamined for several reasons. The majority of children with hearing impairments are educated in settings where they must compete with hearing peers in academic subjects that are language based. The Verbal Scale IQ is a better predictor than the Performance Scale IQ of reading and math achievement among children with hearing impairments. Finally, in order for children and youth with hearing impairments to obtain higher paying jobs in adulthood, higher levels of numeracy, English literacy, and face-to-face communication skills with hearing peers are required. (p. 320, with changes in notation)

We recommend that when you evaluate a child with a hearing impairment, you select only the most appropriate tests and use at least one well-standardized nonverbal measure of cognitive ability. Use verbal tests or portions of tests cautiously to arrive at an estimate of the cognitive ability of children with hearing impairments. Verbal ability measures are certainly important, but they may not accurately assess intelligence in children with hearing impairments.

The performance tests you select for children with hearing impairments should not depend on verbal directions, unless the tests are administered in the child's preferred mode of communication. Timed tests may be less valid for children with hearing impairments because the added stress of being timed may interfere more with their performance than it does with the performance of children with normal hearing. Representative nonverbal tests include the Performance Scale subtests of the WISC–III, WPPSI–R, and WAIS–III; the Abstract/Visual Reasoning subtests of the Stanford-Binet: Fourth Edition; the Leiter–R; the UNIT; the Spatial, Nonverbal, and Nonverbal Reasoning clusters of the DAS; the nonverbal subtests of the K-ABC; Raven's Progressive Matrices; the Comprehensive Test of Nonverbal Intelligence; and the Test of Nonverbal Intelligence–Third Edition. These tests differ with respect to reliability, validity, norming samples, date of publication, and types of cognitive ability measured; it is important to select the most valid one(s) to obtain a measure of the cognitive ability of children with hearing impairments. (See *Assessment of Children: Cognitive Applications* for reviews of tests of intelligence.)

Research is needed concerning the reliability and validity of any tests used to estimate the cognitive ability and achievement scores of children with hearing impairments. Although reliability studies are limited, more information is available about the validity of the WISC–III. In three studies that reported WISC–III Verbal Scale IQs, Performance Scale IQs, and Full Scale IQs for samples of children who are deaf, Performance Scale IQs were higher than Verbal IQs by about 14 to 26 points (VS IQ = 81.63 vs. PS IQ = 102.32; VS IQ = 75.35 vs. PS IQ = 100.63; VS IQ = 81.10 vs. PS IQ = 105.80; Braden et al., 1994; Sullivan & Montoya, 1997; Wechsler, 1991). In reviewing these studies, Braden and Hannah (1998) noted that there is no characteristic profile for children who are deaf. Factor analysis supports a language comprehension factor and a visual-spatial organization factor on the WISC–III (Sullivan & Montoya, 1997). Correlations between the WISC–III and achievement tests with samples of children who are deaf are moderately high; *r*s range from .43 to .81 for the Full Scale, from −.04 to .64 for the Performance Scale, and from .48 to .85 for the Verbal Scale (Braden et al., 1994; Maller & Braden, 1993; Slate & Fawcett, 1995). Even though correlations between the WISC–III Verbal Scale and achievement tests are satisfactory, items on the WISC–III Verbal Scale have a different rank order of difficulty for children with hearing impairments than they do for children with normal hearing (Maller, 1996). When you use the WISC–III (or other Wechsler tests), we recommend that you consider the WISC–III Performance Scale IQ as the best estimate of the cognitive ability of children with hearing impairments. The Verbal Scale IQ can be considered as an estimate of their English language learning (Maller & Braden, 1993).

A review of 324 studies of the intelligence test scores of individuals with hearing impairments found a mean nonverbal IQ of 97.14 (Braden, 1994). Thus, individuals with hearing impairments have nonverbal IQs similar to those of individuals without hearing impairments. However, the academic achievement test scores of individuals with hearing impairments are well below those reported for individuals without hearing impairments (Braden, 1994). Prelingually deaf children, in particular, may be as much as 50% or more behind children with normal hearing in reading (Morgan & Vernon, 1994).

The Meadow-Kendall Social Emotional Inventory for Deaf and Hearing Impaired Students (Meadow, 1983) provides useful information about how the behavior of a child with a hearing impairment compares to that of other children who are hearing impaired.

Modifying Standard Procedures

Ways of modifying test administration for children with hearing impairments include omitting verbal tests, adding printed or signed words, and using pantomime, demonstration, and manual communication. To obtain additional information, you can test limits, reinforce responses, use test-type items for practice, drop time limits, or demonstrate task strategies. Table A-15 in Appendix A (pp. 767–770) in *Assessment of Children: Cognitive Applications* presents special instructions for administering the WISC–III Performance Scale to children with hearing impairments. *Obviously, when standard procedures are modified, standardized norms can be used only as a rough guide and the results used qualitatively or as an approximation of the child's level of cognitive ability. Any modifications that you use need to be noted in the report.*

Observation Guidelines

Although the audiologist and speech-language pathologist are the specialists in determining the communication skills of children with hearing impairments, you, as a psychologist, will be making observations, both formal and informal, of the child's communication skills. Record where your observations occurred (e.g., your office, a classroom, the playground, the child's home, a job or social setting), because the child's communication skills may differ across settings. Also note how the child and the other individuals in each setting communicated with one another (e.g., spoken language or sign language). Assess the child's skills in reading and writing, speech (intelligibility and pleasantness), and speech reading. Notice the extent to which the child was able to understand conversation during the evaluation.

Here are some questions for you to consider:

1. Are the volume and pitch of the child's voice appropriate to the situation?
2. Is the child's pronunciation intelligible, consistent, and age appropriate?
3. Are the size and rate of the child's signs appropriate to the situation?

4. Is the child's speech or signing fluent, or are there unusual pauses?
5. Does the child grope for words or signs?
6. Are the child's replies timely, or are there unusual delays?
7. Does the child respond once to a sound and not respond again?
8. Does the child understand your speech or signs?
9. Does the child ask you to repeat what you have just said?
10. Does the child turn to you in an effort to hear you better?
11. Does the child confuse similar-sounding words or similar-looking signs?
12. If the child does not speak or sign, how does he or she communicate (e.g., pointing, gesturing, shifting eye gaze)?
13. How does the child react when you do not understand him or her?
14. How does the child behave when he or she is frustrated (e.g., withdraws, acts out, tries a new approach such as drawing)?
15. How well does the child understand questions that are out of context or that are unexpected?

As noted earlier, do not assume that the communication difficulties of children with hearing impairments indicate that they have limited intelligence. A congenital hearing loss, for example, can interfere with the development of skills that may *not* be related to cognitive ability (e.g, ability to speak clearly). The case of *Daniel Hoffman v. the Board of Education of the City of New York* (Exhibit 1-1 in Chapter 1 of *Assessment of Children: Cognitive Applications*) illustrates the tragic consequences that can occur when psychologists fail to consider or inform themselves about a child's hearing impairment.

INTERVENTIONS

Interventions for children who are hearing impaired should focus on helping the children become independent and succeed academically. This may require instruction in sign language and speech. Hearing aids (or other assistive devices) should be prescribed when appropriate. If a child is a good candidate for a cochlear implant, it may be helpful because it may permit the child to become aware of speech.

Three factors are critical in helping children with hearing impairments develop competencies in dealing with the world (Marschark, 1993). One is to provide extensive early language experiences, regardless of their mode. A second is to provide a diversity of experiences that allow children with hearing impairments to explore their environment actively and interact with people (both hearing and deaf) and things. A third is to foster social interactions to enhance the self-concept, achievement motivation, and moral development of children with hearing impairments. The overriding aims are to identify hearing losses early, begin appropriate interventions as soon as possible, and establish supportive home and school environments. Implementing these goals will allow children with hearing impairments to develop to their fullest potentials.

THINKING THROUGH THE ISSUES

1. What do you think it must be like to be born deaf?
2. What do you think it would be like to become deaf after 5 years of age?
3. When would you use a verbal cognitive test with children with hearing impairments? And how would you interpret the results?

SUMMARY

1. Inability to hear clearly can adversely affect the speech and communication, linguistic, and academic abilities of children.
2. Acquiring fluency in a spoken language is a major developmental task facing children with hearing impairments.
3. Infants born with hearing impairments follow a normal pattern of vocalization until about 7 months of age. After this age, rate of development of spoken productions is reduced. The frequent failure of such infants to learn to speak clearly is not the result of a vocal problem; it is because they cannot hear speech clearly, if at all.
4. Hearing impairments may also affect children's behavior, self-concept, identity, and social and emotional development.
5. Children with hearing impairments also may have difficulties with balance, equilibrium, and other motor skills related to the vestibular system. Thus, delays in early developmental milestones (e.g., walking) may also be observed.
6. Hearing impairment is a general term that refers to hearing losses ranging from mild to profound.
7. A child who is deaf has a hearing disability that prevents successful processing of linguistic information through audition.
8. A child who is hard-of-hearing has residual hearing sufficient for successful processing of linguistic information through audition, generally with the use of an assistive technology device.
9. A child who is prelingually deaf (i.e., a child whose deafness was present at birth or occurred before the child developed speech and language) is usually unable to acquire speech in normal fashion.
10. A child who is postlingually deaf (i.e., a child who became deaf after speech and language had been developed) has significant difficulties in acquiring or maintaining additional spoken language proficiency, but usually not to the same extent as children who are prelingually deaf.

Etiology

11. Hearing impairments occur because of disease, accidents, or congenital or hereditary conditions.
12. It is estimated that heredity accounts for 50% of early childhood hearing impairments with known etiology.

Classification of Hearing Impairment

13. Hearing ability is represented by a continuum ranging from very acute perception, such as that of a gifted musical conductor who can detect an out-of-tune instrument in an orchestra, to total deafness, such as that of an individual who can detect only strong vibrations through tactile sensations.
14. Hearing ability is evaluated on two dimensions: sound frequency and sound intensity.
15. Sound frequency is measured in cycles per second; the unit of measure is the Hertz (Hz). Hearing loss can be confined to low or high frequencies, or it can be across all frequencies.

16. Sound intensity, or the loudness of sound, is measured in decibels (dB).

17. The two major types of hearing loss are a conductive hearing loss (which occurs when a mechanical problem in the ear canal or middle ear blocks the conduction of sound) and a sensorineural hearing loss (which occurs when there is damage to the inner ear, auditory nerve, or auditory nerve pathways in the brain).

18. Children with hearing impairments are a heterogenous group.

Assistive Technology Devices

19. Assistive technology devices include computer-assisted devices, pre-recorded live captioning, telephone communication systems, environmental alert devices, cochlear implants, and assistive listening devices (ALDs).

Evaluation of Hearing Loss

20. When you evaluate a child who has a hearing impairment or is suspected of having a hearing impairment, consider factors such as the type of hearing loss, etiology of hearing loss, degree of hearing loss, age of onset of hearing loss, and stability of hearing.

21. Determine from the parents, an audiologist, or a speech and language therapist whether the child's hearing loss affects his or her ability to understand speech sounds.

22. Become familiar with the child's receptive and expressive skills—that is, the methods by which the child receives and communicates information—by interviewing his or her parents and teachers and by observing the child in a classroom and other settings.

Communication Modalities and Language

23. Three types of communication modalities particularly useful with children with hearing impairments are oral methods of communication, artificial manual sign methods, and native manual sign languages.

24. Children using ASL or any other method of communication still must learn to read and write in English.

Children with Hearing Impairments and the IDEA

25. The IDEA of 1997 provides guidelines for working with children with hearing impairments.

Assessment Considerations

26. You need to have special communication skills to evaluate children with hearing impairments.

27. If you are to obtain accurate responses from children with hearing impairments, they must understand your instructions and questions.

28. If you use pantomime, recognize that children may not interpret your actions as you intend.

29. Unless you are administering tests standardized using pantomime procedures, use pantomime and visual aids only when you cannot communicate fluently in sign language, cued speech, or written language or when the children are not versed in sign language or other special communication modalities.

30. Evaluating children with hearing impairments may be more fatiguing, demand greater attention and concentration, and require more time and flexibility than evaluating children with normal hearing.

31. In administering tests to children with hearing impairments, determine their preferred mode of communication, use a qualified interpreter if needed, use a variety of techniques if needed, prepare the room to accommodate the children's needs, and use appropriate facial expressions and speech.

32. Tests should be administered in a child's preferred mode of communication.

33. We recommend that when you evaluate a child with a hearing impairment, you select only the most appropriate tests and use at least one well-standardized nonverbal measure of cognitive ability.

34. Use verbal tests or portions of tests cautiously to arrive at an estimate of the cognitive ability of children with hearing impairments.

35. The performance tests you select for children with hearing impairments should not depend on verbal directions, unless the tests are administered in the child's preferred mode of communication.

36. A review of 324 studies of the intelligence test scores of individuals with hearing impairments found a mean nonverbal IQ of 97.14.

37. Ways of modifying test administration for children with hearing impairments include omitting verbal tests, adding printed or signed words, and using pantomime, demonstration, and manual communication.

38. To obtain additional information, you can test limits, reinforce responses, use test-type items for practice, drop time limits, or demonstrate task strategies.

39. Observe children with hearing impairments carefully during the evaluation.

Interventions

40. Interventions for children who are hearing impaired should focus on helping the children become independent and succeed academically.

KEY TERMS, CONCEPTS, AND NAMES

Hearing impairment (p. 378)
Deaf (p. 378)
Hard-of-hearing (p. 378)
Prelingually deaf (p. 378)
Postlingually deaf (p. 378)
Asphyxia (p. 378)
Cytomegalovirus (CMV) (p. 378)
Herpes simplex virus (p. 378)
Hyperbilirubinemia (p. 378)
Meningitis (p. 378)
Rh incompatibility (p. 378)
Rubella (p. 379)
Syphilis (p. 379)
Toxoplasmosis (p. 379)
Down syndrome (p. 379)
Usher syndrome (p. 379)
Waardenburg syndrome (p. 379)
Treacher Collins syndrome (p. 379)
Sound frequency (p. 379)
Sound intensity (p. 379)
Normal range (p. 379)
Slight hearing loss (p. 379)

Mild hearing loss (p. 379)
Moderate hearing loss (p. 379)
Severe hearing loss (p. 379)
Profound hearing loss (p. 379)
Conductive hearing loss (p. 380)
Sensorineural hearing loss (p. 380)
Assistive technology devices (p. 380)
Computer-assisted devices (p. 380)
Pre-recorded live captioning (p. 380)
Telephone communication systems (p. 380)
Environmental alert devices (p. 380)
Cochlear implants (p. 380)
Assistive listening devices (ALDs) (p. 380)
Etiology of hearing loss (p. 381)
Degree of hearing loss (p. 381)
Onset of hearing loss (p. 381)
Stability of hearing (p. 381)
Oral methods of communication (p. 382)
Artificial manual sign methods of communication (p. 382)
Native manual sign languages (p. 382)
American Sign Language (ASL) (p. 382)

Children with hearing impairments and the IDEA (p. 382)
False impressions of children with hearing impairments (p. 385)
Cues used by children with hearing impairments (p. 385)
Confidentiality with children with hearing impairments (p. 385)
Establishing rapport with children with hearing impairments (p. 385)
Use of standard tests with children with hearing impairments (p. 385)
Modifying standard procedures with children with hearing impairments (p. 386)
Observation guidelines with children with hearing impairments (p. 386)

STUDY QUESTION

Discuss children with hearing impairments. Include in your discussion a description of the different types of hearing impairments; etiology; classification; evaluation of hearing loss; communication modalities and language; children with hearing impairments and the IDEA; assessment considerations; and interventions.

17

AUTISTIC DISORDER

Children are ever the future of a society. Every child who does not function at a level commensurate with his or her possibilities, every child who is destined to make fewer contributions to society than society needs, and every child who does not take his or her place as a productive adult diminishes the power of that society's future.
—Degen Horowitz and Marion O'Brien

Symptoms of Autistic Disorder

Intelligence and Autistic Disorder

Assessment Considerations

Interventions

Thinking Through the Issues

Summary

Goals and Objectives

This chapter is designed to enable you to do the following:

- Become familiar with the symptoms of autistic disorder

- Understand how to assess children who may have autistic disorder

- Understand interventions with children who have autistic disorder

Autistic disorder is classified in *DSM-IV–TR* (American Psychiatric Association, 2000) as a pervasive developmental disorder, along with Asperger's disorder, Rett's disorder, childhood disintegrative disorder, and pervasive developmental disorder not otherwise specified. This chapter discusses autistic disorder and briefly comments on Asperger's disorder, Rett's disorder, and childhood disintegrative disorder.

Autistic disorder is a neurodevelopmental disorder, with genetic factors playing a predominant role in its etiology (Jordan, 1999). It is a lifelong disorder that is evenly distributed across socioeconomic and educational levels. There are no biological markers or laboratory tests that can be used to diagnose the disorder. Similarly, there is no widely accepted theory that can explain the characteristic symptoms of autistic disorder (such as difficulties in language usage, imitation, affective expression and sharing, attention, and comprehension of the mental states of others), which can vary from mild to severe. A minority of children with autistic disorder have special skills such as the ability to dismantle and reassemble a complicated mechanical apparatus or the ability to memorize mathematical tables, bus schedules, and calendars. The prevalence of autistic disorder is about 5 in 10,000, with a male to female ratio of about 3.7 to 1 (American Psychiatric Association, 2000; Fombonne, 1998). In the 1998–1999 school year, the prevalence rate of individuals aged 6 through 21 years with autistic disorder served under the IDEA (see Chapter 3 in *Assessment of Children: Cognitive Applications*) was 1.0% (53,576; U.S. Department of Education, 2000).

Asperger's disorder is diagnosed in individuals who function at the higher levels of the autistic continuum (Trevarthen, Aitken, Papoudi, & Robarts, 1998). Children with Asperger's disorder show social impairment and all-absorbing circumscribed interests, but do not have the speech delay or cognitive delay present in children with autistic disorder. The essential features of Asperger's disorder are (a) severe and sustained impairment in social interactions and (b) the development of restricted, repetitive patterns of behavior and interests (American Psychiatric Association, 2000). Some individuals with Asperger's disorder also are clumsy and lack an appreciation of humor. Although speech is not delayed, language is used in a stilted and stereotyped manner. The disorder occurs in both males and females. Individuals with Asperger's disorder share many features with those with autistic disorder; the distinctions between the two conditions are a matter of degree. In fact, some researchers believe that Asperger's disorder is not distinct from autistic disorder (Jordan, 1999).

Rett's disorder involves the loss of several functions after normal development during the first 5 months of life (American Psychiatric Association, 2000). The primary symptoms include (a) deceleration of head growth between 5 and 48 months of age, (b) loss of previously acquired purposeful hand skills between 5 and 30 months of age, with subsequent development of stereotyped hand movements, (c) loss of social engagement, (d) poorly coordinated gait or trunk movements, and (e) severely impaired expressive and receptive language, with severe psychomotor retardation. This disorder occurs only in females.

Childhood disintegrative disorder involves the loss of previously acquired skills after the age of 2 years (but before the age of 10 years) in two or more of the prescribed areas, which include expressive or receptive language, social skills or adaptive behavior, bowel or bladder control, play, and motor skills. Symptoms include qualitative impairments in social interaction and communication and restricted, repetitive, and stereotyped patterns of behavior, interests, and activities. The latter social and communicative deficits also are observed in autistic disorder. Childhood disintegrative disorder is more common in males than in females.

SYMPTOMS OF AUTISTIC DISORDER

A diagnosis of autistic disorder is arrived at when a child has impairments in each of three areas: social interaction, communication, and behavior. A delay or abnormal functioning in at least one of these areas must occur before the age of 3 years (American Psychiatric Association, 2000). Specific impairments in each of these areas are listed below (American Psychiatric Association, 2000; Filipek, Accardo, Baranek, Cook, Dawson, Gordon, Gravel, Johnson, Kallen, Levy, Minshew, Prizant, Rapin, Rogers, Stone, Teplin, Tuchman, & Volkmar, 1999; Prior & Ozonoff, 1998; Trevarthen et al., 1998).

Impairments in Social Interaction

1. *Marked impairment in the use of nonverbal behaviors.* Children with autistic disorder are impaired in their ability to perceive and process social and emotional cues from people and the environment. Primary impairments are in imagination, communication, and socialization. As infants, they may not lift their arms or change posture in anticipation of being held, they may not cuddle, they may be stiff and resistant to contact, and their bodies may be passive and floppy. "Some appear placid and undemanding of human attention and are described as exceptionally 'good' babies; others are difficult to manage, their needs cannot be identified and satisfied, and they are impossible to comfort" (Prior & Ozonoff, 1998, p. 81).

Some children with autistic disorder engage in unacceptable social behavior, such as rocking, head banging, self-stimulatory and self-injurious behavior (e.g., hand biting, punching themselves), screaming, temper tantrums, aggressive behavior, hyperactive behavior, taking objects that do not belong to them, and engaging in socially embarrassing eating, toileting, and verbal behavior.

2. *Failure to develop peer relationships.* Their interactions with peers are impaired: They have extreme difficulty interacting spontaneously with other children of their age. If they do make friends, the focus may be on only one specific activity. They may gravitate to adults or to older peers.

3. *Lack of spontaneous seeking to share enjoyment, interests, or achievements with other people.* "The characteristic give-and-take in lap play that is seen in typically developing children by the end of the first year is often missing. They often do not point things out or use eye contact to share the pleasure of seeing something with another person..." (Filipek et al., 1999, p. 444).

4. *Lack of social and emotional reciprocity.* Later in life, they make minimal mutual eye contact, pay minimal attention to people and events, and exhibit much avoidant behavior. Key qualities are "aloofness, indifference, passivity, distractibility, noncompliance, along with lack of cooperation and engagement in the activities of others,...although they may vary on a continuum from almost totally withdrawn to occasional or 'active but odd' contact" (Prior & Ozonoff, 1998, p. 82). *The hallmark of autistic disorder is a lack of reciprocal social interaction: Children with autistic disorder have great difficulty empathizing with others—there is a lack of insight into the thoughts, feelings, plans, and wishes of others.*

Impairments in Communication

1. *Delay in or lack of development of spoken language, not accompanied by compensation via other modes of communication.* Children with autistic disorder usually do not develop communicative language. It is rare for them to acquire language if they have not done so by the age of 6 years. As infants and toddlers, they often do not (a) babble, (b) attend to human speech, (c) show comprehension of language, (d) speak their first words when they are expected to, or (e) imitate sounds and speech. They may use another person's hand to indicate a desired object (i.e., "hand-over-hand pointing").

2. *Marked impairment in the ability to initiate or sustain conversation with others. The most universal language deficit in children with autistic disorder is the failure to use language to communicate socially.* Children with autistic disorder "have difficulty adapting their discourse to the listener's response, in perceiving what the listener might be wanting or thinking, and in imagining where to go next in the conversation" (Prior & Ozonoff, 1998, p. 88). Language impairments "include comprehension deficits, literal interpretations of messages, perseveration, deficits in turn taking and problems with maintaining conversational topics" (Prior & Ozonoff, 1998, p. 89).

3. *Stereotyped and repetitive use of language or idiosyncratic language.* Language difficulties, which exist on a continuum and vary among individuals with autistic disorder, include "concreteness, literalness, pronominal reversal [reversal of pronouns—referring to self as 'he' and others as 'I'], deviant or monotonous prosodic features, metaphorical language, inability to initiate or sustain a conversation, ritualistic and inflexible language, and insensitivity to the listener's response" (Prior & Ozonoff, 1998, p. 87). Children with autistic disorder may regress after initial speech development, show echolalia (both immediate and delayed), and repeat rhymes or jingles without any apparent communicative function.

4. *Lack of varied, spontaneous make-believe play or social imitative play appropriate to developmental level.* Children with autistic disorder may have no interest in using toys in pretend play, or they may use toys in a mechanical fashion. If they are verbal, they "may invent a fantasy world which becomes the sole focus of repetitive play" (Filipek et al., 1999, p. 445).

Impairments in Behavior

1. *Stereotyped and restricted patterns of interest.* Children with autistic disorder may ask the same question repeatedly (if verbal), engage in highly repetitive perseverative play, or be preoccupied with unusual interests.

2. *Inflexible adherence to specific nonfunctional routines or rituals.* Some children "are so preoccupied with 'sameness' in their home and school environments or with routines, that little can be changed without prompting a tantrum or other emotional disturbance" (Filipek et al., 1999, p. 446).

3. *Stereotyped and repetitive motor movements.* Some children display stereotypic motor movements, such as hand clapping, arm flapping, aimless running, rocking, spinning, toe-walking, or other odd movements.

4. *Persistent preoccupation with parts of objects or things that move.* Some children engage in repetitive actions involving particular objects. For example, they may (a) open and close doors, drawers, or flip-top trash cans, (b) turn light switches on and off, (c) flick strings, elastic bands, measuring tapes, or electric cords, (d) transfer water back and forth from one vessel to another, or (e) spin objects for long periods of time.

Additional features associated with children with autistic disorder include the following (Prior & Ozonoff, 1998; Trevarthen et al., 1998):

- Difficulty coordinating and integrating varying kinds of sensory input
- Difficulty forming a coherent functional picture of the world
- Abnormal sensitivity to sounds, light, or touch
- Obsession with sensory effects
- Awkward and clumsy fine- and gross-motor development
- Difficulty with attention
- Obliviousness to environmental stimuli
- Avoidance of environmental stimuli
- Response to only a subset of environmental cues
- Difficulty shifting attention
- Difficulty selecting the salient attributes of stimuli to be processed
- Susceptibility to distraction by irrelevant stimuli
- Limited curiosity
- Little desire to obtain information
- Failure to ask "wh" questions (what, when, where, and why)
- Better performance in scholastic areas requiring primarily rote, mechanical, or procedural abilities than in those requiring abstract, conceptual, or interpretive abilities (e.g., better at reading single words and nonwords and at spelling than at reading comprehension)

- Difficulty in encoding and organizing material, but not in acquiring, storing, and retaining information
- Selective memory deficits rather than widespread and all-encompassing ones
- Inability to recognize emotions at a level commensurate with their level of intelligence
- Inability to develop emotional attachments and have affective reactions to others

INTELLIGENCE AND AUTISTIC DISORDER

In the past, IQs obtained from children with autistic disorder were often considered to be invalid. The hope was that with the right intervention, intellectual ability would develop to a normal level. Unfortunately, however, interventions with children with autistic disorder usually do not result in significantly improved levels of intellectual performance.

Research on the intellectual functioning of children with autistic disorder suggests the following findings (see Freeman, Rahbar, Ritvo, Bice, Yokota, & Ritvo, 1991; Harris, Handleman, & Burton, 1990; Lord & Schopler, 1989; Prior & Ozonoff, 1998; Sattler, 1992; Siegel, Minshew, & Goldstein, 1996; Trevarthen et al., 1998; Venter, Lord, & Schopler, 1992).

1. About 75–80% of children with autistic disorder fall into the mentally retarded range.
2. The IQs obtained by children with autistic disorder have the same properties as do those obtained by other children. For example, (a) IQs show moderate stability throughout childhood and adolescence (test-retest correlations for periods of 2 to 15 years range from .63 to .90), especially if the children are tested after 5 years of age, and (b) IQs are a reasonable predictor of later educational attainment.
3. Children's IQs fail to change markedly, even after their social responsiveness greatly improves. Poor motivation does not account for their below-average performance on intelligence tests.
4. Those who were untestable at a young age were later found to perform in much the same manner as severely retarded children. In addition, those who appear to be untestable may be testable when given items at sufficiently low mental age levels.
5. Those children who have adequate conversational speech or adequate social relationships obtain higher IQs than do other children with autistic disorder.
6. Cognitive skills are variable (see Table 17-1; also see Chapter 9 in *Assessment of Children: Cognitive Applications* for descriptions of the Wechsler subtests and Chapter 14 for a description of the Stanford-Binet: IV subtests). Children with autistic disorder tend to have difficulty (a) with tasks involving language, imitation, abstract or conceptual reasoning, sequencing, organization, planning, and flexibility (e.g., low scores on the Wechsler Comprehension subtest and the Stanford-Binet: IV Absurdities sub-

Table 17-1
Mean Scaled Scores on Wechsler Subtests from 11 Studies of Children with Autistic Disorder

Scale and subtest	N	Mean	Rank
Verbal Scale			
Information	207	5.48	7
Similarities	278	6.14	5
Arithmetic	278	5.39	8
Vocabulary	278	4.68	10
Comprehension	278	3.57	11
Digit Span	254	7.28	3
Performance Scale			
Picture Arrangement	278	5.80	6
Picture Completion	278	6.78	4
Object Assembly	278	8.53	2
Block Design	278	9.61	1
Coding	223	5.04	9

Source: Adapted from Happé (1994).

test), (b) in seeing relations between pieces of information, identifying central patterns or themes, distinguishing relevant from irrelevant information, and deriving meaning from the bigger picture (e.g., low scores on the Wechsler Picture Arrangement and Coding subtests), and (c) in appreciating subtleties of thought. Skills that tend to be relatively well developed include (a) visual-spatial processing (e.g., relatively average scores on the Wechsler Block Design and Object Assembly subtests and the Stanford-Binet: IV Pattern Analysis subtest), (b) eye-hand coordination (e.g., ability to solve tasks that involve manipulating concrete materials), and (c) attention to detail and rote memory (e.g., ability to solve tasks in which the stimulus materials themselves suggest what is required, such as tasks on the Wechsler Digit Span subtest and the Stanford-Binet: IV Memory for Sentences subtest).
7. Given that children with autistic disorder have relatively good visual-spatial and memory abilities but poor sequencing and language skills, a specific cognitive defect involving the use of language seems likely.
8. Wechsler profiles should not be used to establish a differential diagnosis of autistic disorder.

ASSESSMENT CONSIDERATIONS

A child who may have autistic disorder should be evaluated in the same manner as any other child with a disability.

Assessment should include administering a battery of formal and informal tests (see *Assessment of Children: Cognitive Applications*); conducting interviews with the child, parents, and teachers; and making observations. The tests, depending on the child's age, should include a developmental scale or an intelligence test, an achievement test, a perceptual-motor test, and a language test. Receptive language tests with multiple-choice picture responses, such as the OWLS Listening Comprehension Scale or some of the CASL tests, may be valuable. Also consider administering a nonverbal test with minimal verbal instructions, such as the LIPS–R Visualization and Reasoning and Attention and Memory Scales (see *Assessment of Children: Cognitive Applications*). Parents should complete the Background Questionnaire (see Table A-1 in Appendix A) and an adaptive behavior scale (see Chapter 7). Teachers should complete the School Referral Questionnaire (see Table A-3 in Appendix A) and an adaptive behavior scale (see Chapter 7). In addition, one or more of the special instruments discussed later in this section may be useful.

Interviewing Issues

The inherent disabilities of children with autistic disorder—such as difficulty establishing social relationships, impaired communication skills, and unusual responses to sensory stimuli—may tax your resources as an examiner. As many as 50% of individuals with autistic disorder remain mute or nonverbal (Wetherby & Prizant, 1992). In addition, children with autistic disorder may show little or no desire to interact with you, and your normal methods of encouragement, such as smiling, may be ineffective. If the child can speak and attend to your questions, use the semistructured interview shown in Table B-1 in Appendix B. For a guide to interviewing parents, see Table B-5 in Appendix B.

Before you interview a child who may have autistic disorder, find out as much as possible about the child's communication skills from the parents and teachers; also observe how the child talks and behaves in the classroom. Consider the following:

- Can the child follow simple directions?
- Can the child answer "yes" or "no"?
- Does the child understand gestures or signing?
- Can the child read?
- Can the child speak?
- Does the child have any idiosyncrasies, such as using code words or phrases ("bye-bye" for "no" or "look, look" for a favorite toy)?
- Does the child have sufficient attention to perform the assessment tasks?

In interviewing a child with autistic disorder, talk slowly and simply, use short sentences, be concrete, and omit unnecessary words and complex grammatical forms. Be prepared to repeat sentences as needed or rephrase sentences to make them simpler. Make sure you have the child's visual attention when you speak; visual cues will help her or him attend to and process your speech.

Under no conditions should you use *facilitated communication* to interview a child with autistic disorder. In facilitated communication, a facilitator guides an individual's hand, wrist, or arm across a keyboard or keyboard facsimile to help the individual type a message or point to letters. The theoretical justification for facilitated communication is the belief that people with autistic disorder do not have cognitive impairments but, instead, have motor apraxia, or the "neurologically determined inability to voluntarily initiate behavior or movement" (Mulick, Jacobson, & Kobe, 1993, p. 277). This impairment supposedly prevents individuals with autistic disorder from communicating via oral or written expression without the aid of a facilitator (Biklen, Morton, Gold, Berrigan, & Swaminathan, 1992). Biklen et al. (1992) believe that this is the explanation for the surprisingly advanced communication skills and general knowledge of individuals who, before using facilitated communication, could barely communicate and were considered developmentally delayed. Because experimental results fail to support the validity of facilitated communication, Shane (1993) concluded that *facilitated communication appears to be a pseudoscientific procedure and a hoax.*

Why is facilitated communication used when children with autistic disorder or other severe communication disorders have the motor skills needed to type or point? Why can't the children simply type out their responses or point to letters without help if they can spell, however poorly? Why can't they use the reliable and valid augmentative communication procedures that do not require a facilitator (Sattler, 1998)? And if they can't spell, how can they spell when a facilitator merely guides their hand?

If you are reviewing a report based on information obtained by means of facilitated communication, ignore the information. The information is likely contaminated and probably reflects the facilitator's communications rather than those of the child. Facilitated communication is no longer a harmless tool used to create the illusion of intelligence and normalcy in individuals with autistic disorder or other severe developmental disabilities. *It is a dangerous, ineffective procedure that is inadvertently being used to disrupt families, ruin reputations, and waste the time, energy, and money of all those involved in helping communicatively handicapped individuals.* "If the rhetoric and media hype boosting 'facilitated communication' without research accountability continues, it may succeed in setting autism back 40 years" (Schopler, 1992, p. 6). The American Psychological Association (APA) at its Spring 1995 council meeting approved the following resolution: "*Therefore, be it resolved that APA adopts the position that facilitated communication is a controversial and unproved communicative procedure with no scientifically demonstrated support for its efficacy.*" For more information about facilitated communication, see Sattler (1998).

Observational Guidelines

When you observe a child who may have autistic disorder, use the following guidelines (Schopler, Reichler, & Renner, 1986; Schreibman, 1988):

1. *Observe the child's ability to make eye contact.* Does the child engage in eye contact either spontaneously or upon a request to do so?

2. *Observe the child's interaction with toys.* Does the child interact with toys? If so, does the child engage in appropriate play or self-stimulation? Are there restricted repertoires of toy play, long delays in approaching toys, or repetitive manipulations of toys?

3. *Observe the child's interaction with her or his parents.* Does the child notice her or his parents? Does the child interact with them or avoid them? Is the child cooperative or uncooperative with her or his parents? Does the child initiate any affectionate contact with the parents, such as sitting on a parent's lap or hugging or kissing a parent? If a parent has to ask the child for a hug, does the child respond appropriately or does she or he fuss or turn away and back into the parent's arms? How much discipline do the parents need to exert to get the child to comply with their requests?

4. *Observe the child's speech.* Does the child have speech? If so, what is the nature of the speech? Is it age appropriate? Is it peculiar, bizarre, or unrecognizable? Does the child name toys when asked to do so?

5. *Observe the child's affect.* What are the child's facial expressions, postures, and manners? Is the child's affect appropriate or inappropriate? Is the child's affect inhibited, moderate, or excessive? Does the child show pleasure and displeasure? If so, how?

6. *Observe the child's motor patterns and activity level.* Are the child's motor patterns age appropriate? Does the child seem driven or apathetic? Is it difficult to get the child to respond to anything? Does the child engage in self-stimulation? If so, what type? Is it easy or difficult to redirect the child to a different activity?

7. *Observe the child's interactions with you.* Is the child cooperative or uncooperative? Does the child seem intensely aloof or oblivious to you? Does the child have tantrums?

You can use the procedures described in Chapters 4 and 5 to observe the child in a play setting. Following is a specific procedure for observing children with autistic disorder (Adrien, Ornitz, Barthelemy, Sauvage, & Lelord, 1987): Present the child with the following toys, each for a 2-minute period: (1) a toy that produces musical sounds when a handle is turned, (2) a toy helicopter, (3) a toy that produces music when a string is pulled, (4) a flashlight, (5) a telephone that rings when dialed, (6) a textured ball, (7) a spinning top, (8) 10 blocks, and (9) a doll, a toy cup, a toy pot, and a toy stove. Other toys can be used as appropriate. During all periods except the sixth period, allow the child to play by himself or herself. During the sixth period, actively interact with the child and attempt to engage in ball play. Use a whole-interval procedure (see Chapter 4) to record the behaviors you observe during each period (see the recording form in Table E-1 in Appendix E).

Special Instruments Designed to Evaluate Autistic Disorder

Brief descriptions of some instruments specifically designed to evaluate autistic disorder follow.

- The Autism Diagnostic Observation Schedule–WPS (ADOS–WPS; Lord, Rutter, DiLavore, & Risi, 1999) is a standardized, semistructured instrument for assessment of social interactions, communication, play, and imaginative use of materials in individuals with autistic disorder or related disorders. It consists of four modules designed for children of different ages and language levels.

- The Childhood Autism Rating Scale (CARS; Schopler, Reichler, DeVellis, & Daly, 1980) evaluates 15 dimensions of behavior related to autistic disorder (see Table E-2 in Appendix E). The examiner uses a 4-point scale to rate each behavior.

- The Screening Tool for Autism in Two-Year-Olds (STAT; Stone, 1998) contains 12 activities involving play (both pretend play and reciprocal social play), motor imitation, and nonverbal and verbal communication development.

- The Autism Screening Instrument for Educational Planning (ASIEP; Krug, Arick, & Almond, 1980) is a battery of five procedures useful in evaluating children with autistic disorder. The procedures are Autism Behavior Checklist, Sample of Vocal Behavior, Interaction Assessment, Educational Assessment of Functional Skills, and Prognosis of Learning Rate. Scores and percentile ranks are provided for each procedure.

- The Checklist of Autism in Toddlers (CHAT; Baron-Cohen, Allen, & Gillberg, 1992) is a screening measure designed to evaluate the presence of autistic disorder in children 18 months of age (see Table E-3 in Appendix E). It has two parts. One part involves asking the parent nine questions about the toddler's behavior, and the other part involves observing the toddler in various types of play.

- The AD Questionnaire (see Table E-4 in Appendix E) has 34 items associated with behaviors found in autistic disorder. It is designed to be completed by a caregiver.

Evaluating Assessment Information

The questions in Table 17-2 will help you evaluate the information you obtain from parents and teachers (and the child, where possible). Table E-5 in Appendix E shows some signs, obtained from the case history, that place a child at risk for having autistic disorder. Table E-6 in Appendix E is a checklist for autistic disorder, based on *DSM-IV–TR*.

Table 17-2
Guidelines for Evaluating a Child for Possible Autistic Disorder

Developmental History
1. Were there any prenatal or perinatal difficulties? If so, what were they?
2. Were there any suspicions of sensory deficits, such as deafness or blindness? If so, what were the suspicions based on?
3. Did the child reach developmental language milestones, such as babbling by 12 months, gesturing (pointing, waving bye-bye) by 12 months, using single words by 16 months, and using two-word spontaneous phrases by 24 months?

Social Behavior as an Infant
1. Was the infant responsive to people?
2. How did the infant react when he or she was held (e.g., was the infant overly rigid or flaccid, resistant to being held, indifferent to being held)?
3. Did the infant make eye contact with others?
4. Was the infant content to be alone, or did he or she cry or demand attention?
5. Did the infant reciprocate in lap play (e.g., engage in give-and-take lap play)?

Social Behavior as a Toddler or Older Child
1. Does the child seem to tune out the parents?
2. Does the child seem to be in her or his own world?
3. Does the child make eye contact with the parents?
4. Do the parents think that their child is truly "attached" to them?
5. Is the child affectionate with the parents?
6. Does the child seek out the parents if she or he is hurt or frightened?
7. What is the child's interest in other children (i.e., does the child want to be with other children or does the child prefer to play alone)?
8. Does the child interact with other children? If so, what is the quality of the child's interactions?
9. Does the child appear to be isolated from her or his surroundings? If so, in what way?
10. Does the child smile when expected to?

Speech Development and Communication
1. Does the child have speech? If not, has the child ever spoken in the past? If so, when and for how long?
2. If the child speaks, what is the quality of the speech (e.g., does the child display echolalia, pronominal reversals, or extreme literalness in comprehension and expression)?
3. Does the child respond to his or her name?
4. Was there a loss of language at any age? If so, at what age?
5. Does the child point or wave bye-bye?
6. Does the child understand what other people say? If so, how does the child show his or her understanding?
7. Does the child indicate his or her own wishes? If so, how does the child do this?
8. In the parents' estimation, what is the extent of the child's language abilities?

Self-Stimulation or Self-Injury
1. Does the child engage in self-stimulation? If so, what kind of self-stimulation?
2. Does the child engage in self-injurious behavior? If so, what kind of self-injurious behavior?
3. If the child currently does not engage in self-stimulation or self-injurious behavior, has she or he ever done so? If so, when and what kind of behavior?

Affect
1. Does the child have any irrational fears? If so, what are they?
2. Does the child have appropriate fears (e.g., fear of moving vehicles on a busy street)?
3. Does the child seem to laugh or cry at unusual times or for no apparent reason? If so, at what times?
4. Does the child show rapid, typically inexplicable mood swings? If so, what kind of mood swings and when do they happen?

Perception
1. Does the child have an empty gaze?
2. Does the child have a strange gaze?
3. Is the child interested in only certain parts of objects? If so, what parts?
4. Is the child exceptionally interested in things that move? If so, what things?
5. Does the child seem not to listen when spoken to?
6. Does the child have strange reactions to sound? If so, what kind of reactions?
7. How does the child react to cold?
8. Does the child look at objects, patterns, or movements in bizarre ways? If so, in what ways?

Insistence on Maintenance of Sameness
1. Does the child become upset if the environment is altered (e.g., if the furniture is rearranged)?
2. Does the child become upset at changes in routine?
3. Does the child have any compulsive rituals? If so, what are they?
4. Does the child have any unusual food demands (e.g., eats only one or two foods, demands to eat out of a particular bowl, refuses to eat crackers or cookies if they are broken)? If so, what are they?
5. Is the child unusually attached to an object (e.g., always demands to carry a certain object, refuses to relinquish an outgrown garment)? If so, what is the object and how long has the attachment existed?

Isolated Skills
1. Does the child show particular skill at a certain task? If so, what is the skill?
2. Is the child a whiz at assembling puzzles? If so, what kind of puzzles?
3. Does the child demonstrate unusual ability in music? If so, what kind of ability?
4. Does the child have an exceptional memory in one or more areas? If so, in what areas?

Behavior and Behavior Problems
1. What is the child's behavior at home?
2. What is the child's behavior at school?
3. Does the child have behavior problems (e.g., has severe tantrums, is hyperactive, is uncooperative, is aggressive, toe walks, lines things up frequently, is oversensitive to certain textures or sounds, performs odd movements)?
4. Is the child toilet trained? If so, at what age was the child toilet trained?
5. Does the child eat without assistance?
6. Does the child dress herself or himself?

Source: Adapted from Filipek et al. (1999); Gillberg, Nordin, and Ehlers (1996); and Schreibman (1988).

INTERVENTIONS

Interventions for children with autistic disorder include social and behavioral therapies designed to improve their social communicative skills and to reduce stereotypic and bizarre behaviors. Interventions should begin early in life, with parents actively involved in the treatment. Behavioral techniques are often used with children with autistic disorder to (a) reduce their maladaptive behaviors, such as self-stimulation (e.g., rocking and twirling) and self-injurious behaviors (e.g., head banging and biting hands or wrists), and (b) teach them skills (e.g., sitting and establishing eye contact). If the self-injurious behaviors are life-threatening, physical restraints also may be used. There are no cures for autistic disorder; the focus usually is on reducing symptoms and encouraging desirable behaviors. In some cases, early and intense interventions have enabled children with autistic disorder to perform at normal levels and to appear normal to all but the most expert observers.

One such program, called TEACCH, emphasizes five components (Mesibov, Adams, & Klinger, 1997, p. 85, with changes in notation):

1. Organizing and simplifying the physical environment to be more consistent with the ways in which people with autism process sensory information
2. Developing meaningful schedules to make each day more predictable
3. Developing individual work systems for independent functioning so that students always understand how long they will be working on tasks and when they will be finished
4. Using visually clear and meticulously organized materials and teaching students to identify and use visual cues that facilitate generalization
5. Establishing positive and productive routines

Following are some ways these objectives can be carried out (Saskatchewan Education, 1998):

Visual Supports

- Adopt strategies for organizing the environment. For example, label objects and containers; post signs, mini-schedules, lists, charts, calendars, and outlines; and use choice boards.
- Use visual aids in giving directions, such as cards with classroom rules, file cards with directions for specific tasks and activities, and pictographs and written instructions to convey new information.
- Use visual aids to encourage social development. For example, post rules and routines, and teach social skills through the use of stories.
- Use visual aids in managing challenging behaviors and developing self-control. For example, use pictographs to provide cues for expected behavior.
- Use concrete examples and hands-on visual activities when teaching abstract ideas and conceptual thinking.

- Teach an augmentative communication system (e.g., a sign language) to students who are nonverbal.

Classroom Environment

- Structure the environment with consistency and clarity. For example, students should know where things belong, what is expected of them in a specific situation, and what to anticipate.
- Vary tasks to prevent boredom, and alternate familiar successful experiences with less preferred activities to reduce anxiety and prevent inappropriate behaviors.
- Use reinforcers that are meaningful to the student, such as being left alone for a time, getting time to talk to a favorite staff member, making a trip to the cafeteria, going for a walk, playing with a favorite object, playing in water, getting to perform a favorite routine, spending time with objects that provide specific sensory stimulation, or sitting at the window.
- Use modeling, physical prompts, visual cues, and reinforcement to encourage attention, imitation, communication, and interaction.
- Eliminate visual distractions such as excessive light, movement, reflection, or background patterns.
- Eliminate auditory distractions such as noisy fans and loudspeakers.
- Eliminate textures that seem to be aversive.
- Check to be sure that the temperature in the room is appropriate.
- Provide a quiet designated area where the student can go to relax.
- Introduce unfamiliar tasks in a familiar environment when possible.

Social Skills

- Provide opportunities for meaningful contact with peers who have appropriate social behavior.
- Involve the student in shared learning arrangements.
- Pair the student with a buddy for walking down the hall, playing on the playground, and other unstructured times.
- Vary peer buddies across time and activities to prevent dependence on one peer.
- Provide opportunities for the student to interact in a variety of natural environments where appropriate models, natural cues and stimuli, and functional reinforcers are available.
- Teach self-management procedures in order to increase independence. One strategy is to (a) define the target behavior, (b) identify reinforcers, (c) choose or design an appropriate self-monitoring method such as a wrist counter or stickers, (d) teach the student to use the self-monitoring device, and (e) facilitate independence by gradually reducing prompts and increasing the time the student spends self-managing his or her behavior.

Following are some goals and objectives that might be included in an IEP for a 4-year-old male with autistic disorder (Schreck, 2000):

- The child's ability to shift attention will improve (e.g., he will inspect an object placed in his hands, look at an object placed in his line of vision, interrupt an activity when his name is called).
- The child's ability to imitate adults will improve (e.g., he will look at an adult, imitate actions after a 1- to 2-minute delay, engage in play for 30 seconds to 1 minute).
- The child's receptive language ability will improve (e.g., he will pick up an object from a choice of three; pick up a picture of an object from a choice of two; respond to a simple direction; point to one of two objects, indicating choice).
- The child's expressive language will improve (e.g., he will label people, objects, body parts, actions, colors, shapes, letters, numbers).
- The child's self-help skills will improve (e.g., he will use utensils to feed himself, dress independently, use the toilet independently).
- The child's motor skills will improve (e.g., he will draw lines and shapes, color in a shape, open and close scissors, cut a line, reposition paper while cutting, string beads, wind a toy, unbutton one button).

Mesibov et al. (1997) summarize the role of interventions in autistic disorder in the following way:

Behavioral interventions have been the most effective to date in helping people with autistic disorder. Early behavioral efforts emphasized operant conditioning techniques and have been very effective. More recently, cognitive approaches are making experiences more meaningful for people with autistic disorder, leading to better generalization and more flexibility in their skill development. Social learning theory is also becoming an effective framework for developing social skills through structured activities with nonhandicapped peers. (p. 91)

Pharmacological interventions are useful in reducing impulsivity, overactivity, short attention span, and obsessive preoccupations. However, medications are usually not effective in treating impairments in social interaction and communication (Tanguay, 2000).

Here are some suggestions for working with parents of children with autistic disorder (Morgan, 1984):

1. *Explaining the child's condition.* Give parents a realistic and cautious interpretation of autistic disorder, presenting the child as a unique individual with a special set of problems. Parents may have misconceptions about the disorder, perhaps stemming from a stereotypic image of autistic disorder derived from television or magazine articles. Help them recognize that symptoms such as bizarre responses to the environment, insistence on sameness, attachment to objects, and deficient and unusual language are part of the syndrome of autistic disorder.

2. *Explaining the child's level of functioning.* Help parents to understand their child's level of functioning in cognitive and adaptive areas and the possibilities for improvement. Often, parents want to believe that their child's cognitive impairment is only temporary and that their child will return to normal when her or his behavioral and emotional problems are resolved. Caution parents that they should not equate the child's isolated abilities—such as early motor development or good rote memory—with general intelligence. Convey to the parents their child's strengths and weaknesses. By interpreting the child's relative skills, you may help the parents feel less threatened; as a result, they may become more receptive to your suggestions.

3. *Reassuring parents.* Assure parents that they are not responsible for the child's refusal to interact with the world. Parents of a child with autistic disorder often blame themselves for their child's condition because autistic disorder has social and emotional overtones. A prime feature of autistic disorder that distinguishes it from other disorders is the child's inability to form affectionate and social relationships. This is most disturbing to parents. You can best deal with any feelings of guilt by presenting parents with information about the diagnosis and the causes of autistic disorder. Knowing that they did not cause their child's disorder will enable parents to move past their guilt and participate in intervention programs.

4. *Dealing with parental reactions.* Prepare yourself to deal with other reactions, such as anger and denial, that may occur when parents learn that their child has a severe disorder.

5. *Discussing prognoses.* Phrase statements about prognosis cautiously. Most cases of autistic disorder are severe and long term. Parents can play an active role in intervention programs, however.

6. *Helping the family to accept the child.* Prepare yourself to work with the child's siblings to help them understand their brother's or sister's disorder. Families that gain an understanding of autistic disorder will be in a better position to accept and help the children who have the disorder. For more information about interventions and other issues related to autistic disorder, see Schopler, Van Bourgondien, and Bristol (1993).

THINKING THROUGH THE ISSUES

1. Do you know a child with autistic disorder? If so, what have you observed?
2. Do you know of any families that have a child with autistic disorder? If so, what has it been like for the family to raise the child?
3. What pressure might parents face from relatives, spouses, and members of the community in raising a child with autistic disorder? In what way might raising a child with autistic disorder be different from raising one with attention-deficit/hyperactivity disorder?

SUMMARY

1. Autistic disorder is a neurodevelopmental disorder, with genetic factors playing a predominant role in its etiology.
2. It is a lifelong disorder that is evenly distributed across socioeconomic and educational levels.
3. There are no biological markers or laboratory tests that can be used to diagnose the disorder.
4. Similarly, there is no widely accepted theory that can explain the characteristic symptoms of autistic disorder (such as difficulties in language usage, imitation, affective expression and sharing, attention, and comprehension of the mental states of others), which can vary from mild to severe.
5. Asperger's disorder is diagnosed in individuals who function at the higher levels of the autistic continuum. Children with Asperger's disorder show social impairment and all-absorbing circumscribed interests, but do not have the speech delay or cognitive delay present in children with autistic disorder.
6. Rett's disorder involves the loss of several functions after normal development during the first 5 months of life. The primary symptoms include (a) deceleration of head growth between 5 and 48 months of age, (b) loss of previously acquired purposeful hand skills between 5 and 30 months of age, with subsequent development of stereotyped hand movements, (c) loss of social engagement, (d) poorly coordinated gait or trunk movements, and (e) severely impaired expressive and receptive language, with severe psychomotor retardation.
7. Childhood disintegrative disorder involves the loss of previously acquired skills after the age of 2 years (but before the age of 10 years) in two or more of the prescribed areas, which include expressive or receptive language, social skills or adaptive behavior, bowel or bladder control, play, and motor skills. Symptoms include qualitative impairments in social interaction and communication and restricted, repetitive, and stereotyped patterns of behavior, interests, and activities.

Symptoms of Autistic Disorder

8. A diagnosis of autistic disorder is arrived at when a child has impairments in each of three areas: social interaction, communication, and behavior; a delay or abnormal functioning in at least one of these areas must occur before the age of 3 years.
9. The hallmark of autistic disorder is a lack of reciprocal social interaction: Children with autistic disorder have great difficulty empathizing with others—there is a lack of insight into the thoughts, feelings, plans, and wishes of others.

Intelligence and Autistic Disorder

10. About 75–80% of children with autistic disorder fall into the mentally retarded range.
11. The visual-spatial and memory abilities of children with autistic disorder are better developed than their sequencing and language skills.

Assessment Considerations

12. A child who may have autistic disorder should be evaluated in the same manner as any other child with a disability. Assessment should include administering a battery of formal and informal tests; conducting interviews with the child, parents, and teachers; and making observations.

13. Under no conditions should you use facilitated communication to interview a child with autistic disorder.
14. Facilitated communication appears to be a pseudoscientific procedure and a hoax.
15. If you are reviewing a report based on information obtained by means of facilitated communication, ignore the information.
16. When you observe a child who may have autistic disorder, observe her or his ability to make eye contact, interaction with toys, interactions with her or his parents, speech, affect, motor patterns and activity level, and interactions with you.
17. Also, use one or more instruments that have been specially designed to evaluate autistic disorder.

Interventions

18. Interventions for children with autistic disorder include social and behavioral therapies designed to improve their social communicative skills and to reduce stereotypic and bizarre behaviors.
19. Behavioral interventions have been the most effective in helping children with autistic disorder.
20. Pharmacological interventions are useful in reducing impulsivity, overactivity, short attention span, and obsessive preoccupations. However, medications are usually not effective in treating impairments in social interaction and communication.

KEY TERMS, CONCEPTS, AND NAMES

Autistic disorder (p. 391)
Asperger's disorder (p. 391)
Rett's disorder (p. 391)
Childhood disintegrative disorder (p. 391)
Marked impairment in the use of nonverbal behaviors (p. 391)
Failure to develop peer relationships (p. 391)
Lack of spontaneous seeking to share enjoyment, interests, or achievements with other people (p. 392)
Lack of social and emotional reciprocity (p. 392)
Delay in or lack of development of spoken language, not accompanied by compensation via other modes of communication (p. 392)
Marked impairment in the ability to initiate or sustain conversation with others (p. 392)
Stereotyped and repetitive use of language or idiosyncratic language (p. 392)
Lack of varied, spontaneous make-believe play or social imitative play appropriate to developmental level (p. 392)
Stereotyped and restricted patterns of interest (p. 392)
Inflexible adherence to specific nonfunctional routines or rituals (p. 392)
Stereotyped and repetitive motor movements (p. 392)
Persistent preoccupation with parts of objects or things that move (p. 392)
Intelligence and autistic disorder (p. 393)
Assessment considerations in autistic disorder (p. 393)
Interviewing issues in autistic disorder (p. 394)
Facilitated communication (p. 394)
Observational guidelines in autistic disorder (p. 395)
Autism Diagnostic Observation Schedule–WPS (ADOS–WPS) (p. 395)
Childhood Autism Rating Scale (CARS) (p. 395)

vasive developmental disorders; symptoms; intelligence; assessment considerations, including interviewing issues, observational guidelines, and special instruments; and interventions.

STUDY QUESTION

Discuss children with autistic disorder. Include in your discussion a description of the disorder; how the disorder differs from other per-

18

BRAIN INJURIES: THEORY AND REHABILITATION PROGRAMS

by Jerome M. Sattler and Rik D'Amato

Do not mistake a child for his symptom.

—Erik H. Erikson

Goals and Objectives

This chapter is designed to enable you to do the following:

- Understand recent findings in neuroscience

- Describe lateralization of cognitive, perceptual, motor, and sensory activities

- Describe common causes of brain injury in children

- Describe the cognitive, behavioral, and emotional effects of brain injury on children and their families

- Give examples of neurological and neuropsychological diagnostic techniques

- Recognize the symptoms of brain injuries in children

- Assess children with brain injuries

- Interview children with brain injuries and their parents

- Identify rehabilitation strategies for children with brain injuries

- Work effectively with families of children with brain injuries

This is the first of two chapters covering the assessment of children with brain injuries and brain dysfunctions. *Brain injury* refers to any disruption in brain structure (anatomy) or physiology (function). *Brain dysfunction* refers to symptoms that are associated with cerebral processing difficulties, but not necessarily with brain injury. Evaluating children with brain injuries requires (a) knowing the types and causes of brain injuries and their effects on children's cognitive, behavioral, social, and affective processes, (b) knowing how to communicate with children with brain injuries and how to recognize their cognitive, social, and behavioral limitations, as well as their intact abilities, (c) knowing how to administer, score, and interpret neuropsychological tests and procedures, (d) understanding the various ways families relate to their children with brain injuries, (e) being familiar with rehabilitation strategies useful for children with brain injuries, and (f) knowing which interventions are useful for families of children with brain injuries. These two chapters provide a general introduction to neuropsychological assessment and rehabilitation; you will need to read or review texts in biological psychology and neuropsychology to gain a fuller appreciation of neuropsychological assessment.

The assessment of brain injury is a complex and exacting process. It requires extensive specialized knowledge and interdisciplinary cooperation. A multidisciplinary team is usually involved in the assessment of a child with brain injury and in the formulation of rehabilitation programs. Multidisciplinary teams in various settings may include neurologists, neurosurgeons, orthopedists, neuropsychologists, speech/language pathologists, educators, physical therapists, occupational therapists, school psychologists, and social workers.

Psychologists can help children with brain injuries, as well as their parents, families, and teachers, in several ways. For example, they can explain how brain injury may affect a child's cognitive functioning, affective reactions, personality, and temperament. Psychologists also can help parents, teachers, and the child carry out the rehabilitation efforts necessary to deal with changes in the child's functioning. An important part of consultation is to delineate the cognitive strengths and deficits of the child with brain injury in order to help others understand the child's neurobehavioral competencies. Although the behaviors of children with brain injuries vary greatly, there are similarities in the ways these children function, particularly in their patterns of neuropsychological deficits. Although this and the following chapter focus on traumatic brain injury (which is the most common cause of brain injury in young children and adolescents), other types of brain injury are covered as well.

BACKGROUND CONSIDERATIONS IN UNDERSTANDING BRAIN FUNCTIONS

Recent developments in the neurosciences indicate the following about the human brain and its development (adapted from Hotz, 1996a, pp. A20, A22, and 1996b, p. 10):

1. There is no center of consciousness, no single clearinghouse for memory, no one place where information is processed, emotions generated, or language stored. Instead, the human brain is a constantly changing constellation of connections among billions of cells. Complex networks of neurons are linked by forged pathways, then continually revised, in response to interactions with the environment.

2. There is no way to separate the development of the brain's neural structure from the influence of the environment that nurtures it. During growth and development, the feedback between the brain and its environment is so intimate that the two are essentially inseparable.

3. There is no single, predetermined blueprint for the brain. More than half of all human genes—about 15,000—are somehow involved in laying the brain's foundation. And collectively they exert a powerful influence over temperament, learning ability, and personality.

4. No two brains are identical. The complex connections of each brain are so individual that it is unlikely that any two people perceive the world in quite the same way.

5. Subtle differences in brain anatomy appear to affect the ways men and women process information, even when thinking about the same things, hearing the same words, or solving similar problems.

6. The most efficient brains—that is, those that use the least energy—appear also to be the most intelligent. Learning and practice appear to improve brain efficiency.

7. Small structural abnormalities appear to develop in the brains of people with Alzheimer's disease and Huntington's disease long before any noticeable behavioral symptoms can be diagnosed. Structural abnormalities, however, do not always result in cognitive or behavioral symptoms or deficits.

8. Minor alterations in neural circuits for vision and hearing (and perhaps other areas) may be responsible for dyslexia; abnormalities in regions of the brain involved in inhibiting mental and behavioral activity could be the cause of attention-deficit/hyperactivity disorder.

LATERALIZATION

Although the brain tends to behave as a unified whole, injuries to various parts of the brain tend to produce different results. These differences are related to the normal functions of the part that is disrupted by the injury. The two hemispheres of the brain differ somewhat in their normal functioning; thus, injuries to the left hemisphere may have different effects than injuries to the right hemisphere.

Lateralization refers to the specialization of the two hemispheres of the cerebral cortex for cognitive, perceptual, motor, and sensory activities. In general, the side of the brain that controls a *sensorimotor activity* (an activity that combines the functions of the sensory and motor portions of the brain) is opposite to the side of the body that carries out the activity. Consequently, damage on the right cerebral hemisphere may result in deficits on the left side of the body, whereas damage on the left cerebral hemisphere may produce deficits on the right side of the body. Examples of sensorimotor deficits are limb weakness, poor coordination, and insensitivity to stimulation. Subcortical (below the cortex) damage, especially damage to the cerebellum, may produce deficits on the same side of the body where the damage occurred.

Lateral specialization (also referred to as cerebral or hemispheric specialization) for all cognitive, sensory, and motor functions cannot be clearly established for several reasons. First, the role of lateralization is less clear for visuo-constructional skills (skills related to visual and motor integration) than it is for language skills. Second, some tasks whose components are encoded both verbally *and* perceptually, such as tasks involving easily recognizable figures with familiar names, are bilaterally represented. Third, although the evidence for lateralized cerebral specialization is strong in adults, it is weaker in young children because young children show language disorders with right-sided brain damage as well as with left-sided brain damage (Hécaen, 1983). Fourth, there are individual variations in lateral specialization, including those related to left- and right-hand dominance. Finally, although language and speech may be lateralized at birth (in the sense that the left hemisphere more readily supports these functions), complex changes in the direction and strength of hemispheric specialization occur as development proceeds (Lewkowicz & Turkewitz, 1982).

Hemispheric Higher-Level Functions

The two cerebral hemispheres—known as the left hemisphere and right hemisphere—are specialized to varying degrees for higher-level functions, such as language and memory (Lezak, 1995).

1. Left cerebral hemisphere. The left hemisphere in most people is specialized for verbal functions—including reading, writing, speaking, verbal ideation, verbal memory, and certain aspects of arithmetic ability (such as skilled math analysis and computation). Left hemisphere processing has been described as analytic, temporal, sequential, serial, logical, and differential.

2. Right cerebral hemisphere. The right hemisphere in most people is specialized for nonverbal, perceptual, and spatial functions—including spatial visualization, visual learning and memory, arithmetical calculations involving spatial organization of the problem elements, vocal inflection nuances, complex visual-motor organization, and nonverbal sequencing. Right hemisphere processing is considered holistic (i.e., emphasizing the importance of the whole and the interdependence of its parts), simultaneous, gestalt-like, intuitive, parallel, and integrative.

For simple tasks, nonverbal stimuli can be processed holistically by either hemisphere. The right hemisphere is generally inferior to the left hemisphere in the expressive functions of speech and writing, but is not as inferior in the comprehension of language.

Specialized Functions of the Cerebral Hemispheres

Within each hemisphere there are four lobes, or areas (see Figure 18-1):

1. The *frontal lobes* are associated with planning, initiation, and modulation of behavior (including self-control) and with expressive verbal fluency, control of motor functions, and motor planning.
2. The *temporal lobes* are associated with auditory perception, auditory comprehension, verbal memory, visual memory, and some forms of visual processing.
3. The *parietal lobes* are associated with somatosensory functions, visual-spatial ability, and the integration of visual, somatosensory, and auditory stimuli.

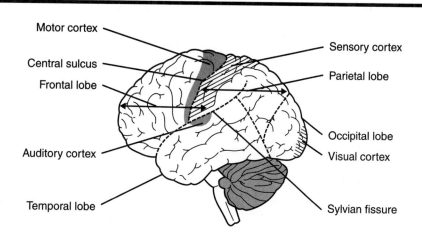

Figure 18-1. Drawing of the surface of the left hemisphere of the cerebrum.

4. The *occipital lobes* are associated with visual perception, elaboration and synthesis of visual information, and the integration of visual information with information gathered by the auditory and other sensory systems.

Injuries to the frontal, temporal, parietal, and occipital lobes and to subcortical centers (such as the basal ganglia and hippocampal structures) may lead to disorders in cognition, memory, affect, motor output, and motivation. Following are examples of symptoms associated with injury to the cerebral lobes (adapted from Hickey, 1992, p. 493).

Frontal Lobes

- Inappropriate behavior
- Inattentiveness
- Inability to concentrate
- Emotional lability
- Indifference
- Loss of self-restraint
- Inappropriate social behavior
- Impairment of recent memory
- Difficulty with abstraction
- Difficulty correcting mistakes or optimizing performance
- A quiet, flat affect

Parietal Lobes

- *Hypoesthesia*—impaired sensation in which there is decreased tactile sensitivity
- *Paresthesia*—abnormal sensation involving tingling, crawling, or burning of the skin
- *Loss of two-point discrimination*—inability to determine by feeling whether the skin is touched at one point or at two points simultaneously
- *Astereognosis*—inability to locate or recognize an object by feeling its size or shape
- *Autotopagnosia*—inability to locate or recognize parts of the body
- *Anosognosia*—loss of awareness of or denial of a motor and sensory defect in the affected part(s) of the body
- *Disorientation of external environmental space*—a tendency to ignore that part of the environment opposite to the cerebral damage
- *Finger agnosia*—inability to identify or select specific fingers of the hands
- *Loss of right-left discrimination*—inability to discriminate which side of the body is touched
- *Agraphia*—loss of the ability to write
- *Acalculia*—difficulty in calculating numbers
- *Constructional apraxia*—inability to draw the part of an object—such as the section of the face of a clock—that is on the side opposite to the cerebral damage
- *Homonymous hemianopia*—blindness affecting the right halves or the left halves of the visual fields of the two eyes

Temporal Lobes

- Disturbance of auditory sensation and perception
- Disturbance of selective attention to auditory and visual input
- Disturbance of visual perception
- Impaired organization and categorization of verbal material
- Disturbance of language comprehension
- Impaired long-term memory
- Altered personality and affective behavior
- Altered sexual behavior
- Psychomotor seizures
- Loss of use of the upper quadrant of the body opposite to the damage

Occipital Lobes

- *Contralateral homonymous hemianopia*—blindness affecting the right halves or the left halves of the visual fields of the two eyes, with the half affected being the half opposite to the location of the brain injury
- Visual hallucinations
- Inability to recognize objects, faces, and drawings

Development of Lateralization

Lateralization develops gradually, as bilateral (i.e., both sides) movements are replaced with unilateral (i.e., one side) movements. Lateralization begins in utero and continues through childhood into adulthood (Spreen, Risser, & Edgell, 1995). For most children of both sexes, linguistic functions are localized in the left hemisphere at birth (Hahn, 1987; Paquier & Van Dongen, 1993). Functions lateralized in the right hemisphere are less straightforward—certain abilities are lateralized at birth, whereas others become lateralized with age. For example, the right hemisphere appears to be specialized at birth for processing nonlinguistic stimuli, but its ability to process spatial information develops over time. Research on cerebral lateralization in childhood is continuing.

Comment on Lateralization

Once language develops, the left hemisphere is dominant for language in most individuals; the right hemisphere has limited potential for language functions. Language disorders in children, as in adults, are associated more frequently with left hemisphere damage than with right hemisphere damage. There may be some recovery of the functions mediated by the right hemisphere; deficits may continue to exist in grammar, reading, and writing skills when there is left hemisphere damage (Moscovitch, 1981; Whitten, D'Amato, & Chittooran, 1992).

Although right hemisphere functions are less well understood than left hemisphere functions, a primary right hemisphere function may be to integrate information into meaningful wholes. The right hemisphere does not have the specific analytic skills required to process linguistic input phonetically or to decode complex syntax, but it does support communication (Moscovitch, 1981). Impairments of the right hemisphere may interfere with communication, conceptual skills, memory, and other cognitive functions, especially when a task requires the integration of multiple sources of information or the comprehension of nonliteral language, such as metaphor or sarcasm. Additionally, the right hemisphere appears to be important in prosody, allowing for the recognition of emotional expression in one's own speech and that of others.

TYPES OF MEMORY

Memory is critical for processing information. Before the age of 6 years, children infrequently use mnemonic (memory) strategies such as rehearsal and chunking. Between the ages of 7 and 10 years, mnemonic strategies begin to emerge. And after the age of 10 years, mnemonic strategies mature and become increasingly refined, flexible, and effective. Thus, as children develop, they are better able to use strategies to aid them in the encoding and retrieval of information (Boyd, 1988). Strategic competence in memory appears to be a key source of individual differences as children grow. The development of memory span involves changes in children's knowledge bases, efficiency of basic processes, and use of strategies.

There are at least ten different types of memory. Children with brain injuries may have difficulty with one type of memory but not with another, depending on their injury (Baddeley, 1992; Gianutsos, 1987).

Sensory Memory

1. *Iconic memory* is for storage of visual images for the short term—as briefly as half a second. "It is this system that makes cinematography possible. A series of separate and discrete still pictures, each separated by a blank period, is perceived as a single moving figure since the information is stored during the blank interval and integrated into a single percept" (Baddeley, 1992, p. 6).
2. *Echoic memory* is for short-term auditory storage; it allows us to perceive speech sounds. A literal representation of the initial stimulus is stored in echoic memory for

3 to 4 seconds. Persons can usually recall verbatim the last five or six words of a communication, which is roughly the number of words we speak in 3 to 4 seconds.

Short-Term Working Memory

3. *Primary memory* (also termed intermediate memory or working memory) is for temporary storage of information acquired while learning, reading, reasoning, or thinking. Information is lost from this store when new information comes into it. It is assumed that the longer information is maintained in short-term memory, the more likely it is to be transferred to long-term memory. Rehearsal may be important in transferring information to long-term memory.

Long-Term Memory

4. *Visual memory* is for storage of visual objects, such as pictures and faces.
5. *Verbal memory* is for storage of verbal terms, such as words and sentences.
6. *Semantic memory* is for storage of information not associated with a time sequence, such as the name of the president of the country, a telephone number, or the population of a city. Semantic memory requires access to general knowledge.
7. *Episodic memory* is for storage of autobiographical events that happened at a particular time—for example, what you had for breakfast or an incident that occurred at a birthday party last year. Episodic memory requires access to recall of the specific past incident.
8. *Declarative memory* (also termed declarative knowledge) allows us to describe how to perform an action, such as how to get to the library or how to operate a VCR.
9. *Procedural memory* (also termed procedural knowledge) allows us to perform an action, such as going to the library, riding a bicycle, or operating a device.

Frank and Ernest

10. *Prospective memory* allows us to remember to do something at a later point in time, such as go to the library after school or call a friend about an assignment.

CAUSES OF BRAIN INJURY

Brain injuries can result from factors present before birth or from injuries sustained during the birth process, immediately after birth, or at any point in life after birth. Let's briefly examine the factors that may contribute to brain injuries during each of these periods.

Prenatal Period

Prenatal environmental factors (factors existing or occurring before birth) that contribute to brain injury include the following:

- Severe maternal malnutrition
- Maternal use of alcohol, drugs (prescription or illegal), or tobacco
- Maternal exposure to toxic substances such as lead, asbestos, chlorines, fluorides, nickel, or mercury
- Maternal infections caused by viruses or bacteria, such as rubella or syphilis or other sexually transmitted diseases
- Maternal illnesses such as hypertension or diabetes
- Radiation
- Congenital disorders such as cerebral palsy or spina bifida
- Physical injury to the uterus

Perinatal Period

Conditions associated with the period shortly before and after birth (the *perinatal period*) that may lead to brain injury include the following (note, however, that these conditions or events do not always lead to brain injury):

- Prematurity or very low birthweight
- Physical trauma associated with labor and delivery
- *Asphyxia,* which is caused by a lack of oxygen or an excess of carbon dioxide in the body and may lead to unconsciousness, seizures, or damage to various sensory systems
- *Hypoglycemia,* or low blood sugar
- *Meningitis,* which is a brain infection involving an acute inflammation of the membranes (meninges) that cover the brain and spinal cord and is characterized by fever, headache, vomiting, weakness, and stiff neck
- *Encephalitis,* an acute inflammation of the brain or its meninges, which may result from any of several different infections or toxins and is characterized by changes in personality, seizures, body weakness, confusion, sleepiness that can progress into a coma, and the symptoms of meningitis
- *Kernicterus,* or *severe jaundice,* which produces severe neurological symptoms and is accompanied by high levels

of bilirubin (a yellow pigment resulting from the normal breakdown of red blood cells) in the blood
- *Rh incompatibility,* a condition that occurs when the mother has Rh-negative blood and the fetus has Rh-positive blood; if the mother has had a previous Rh-incompatible pregnancy, the mother has antibodies against the fetus's blood that destroy the fetus's red blood cells and may cause pathologies such as jaundice, anemia, or mental retardation

Postnatal Period

During the *postnatal period* (period after birth), conditions that may result in brain injury include the following:

- *Hydrocephaly,* a condition marked by increased accumulation of fluid within the ventricles of the brain
- *Hypothyroidism,* a metabolic disorder in which the child has difficulty producing enough thyroid hormone; if untreated, it can cause delays in brain development
- *Tay-Sachs disease,* a hereditary disorder in which gangliosides (products of fat metabolism) accumulate in the tissues; it usually results in blindness, paralysis, dementia, severe mental retardation, and death by the age of 3 or 4 years
- *Niemann-Pick disease,* a hereditary disorder in which a deficiency of a specific enzyme results in the accumulation of sphingomyelin, a product of fat metabolism; it may result in mental retardation, anemia, dark pigmentation of the skin, and enlarged liver, spleen, and lymph nodes
- *Phenylketonuria* (*PKU*), a hereditary disorder in which the enzyme that processes the amino acid phenylalanine is missing, leading to a dangerously high level of phenylalanine in the blood; if untreated, it may result in seizures, aggressive and/or self-injurious behavior, hyperactivity, body odors, and mental retardation
- *Galactosemia,* a high blood level of galactose caused by a genetically related metabolic condition involving lack of an enzyme necessary to metabolize milk and milk products (sources of galactose); symptoms include mental retardation, jaundice, cataracts, short stature, and poor weight gain

Infancy, Early Childhood, and Adolescence

During infancy, early childhood, and adolescence, brain injury may be caused by the following:

- Trauma such as that associated with automobile or bicycle accidents, falls, or physical abuse
- Infections such as scarlet fever, rabies, Rocky Mountain spotted fever, encephalitis, or meningitis
- Radiation
- Drug and alcohol abuse
- Exposure to *neurotoxins* such as lead, arsenic, mercury, carbon disulfide, or manganese
- Deficiency of nutrients such as iodine, protein, or vitamin A, B_1, B_2, or D

TRAUMATIC BRAIN INJURY

Each year approximately 1 million children in the United States sustain head injuries from falls, physical abuse, recreational accidents, or motor vehicle accidents (Savage, 1993). It has been estimated that brain injuries to children annually result in "7,000 deaths of children, 150,000 hospitalizations, hospital care costing over $1 billion, and 30,000 children becoming permanently disabled" (Savage, 1993, p. 4). Overall, approximately 81% of children with traumatic brain injury have mild brain injuries, 14% have moderate to severe brain injuries, and 5% die as a result of their brain injuries (Yablon, Cabrera, Yudofsky, & Silver, 1994).

Although most children survive head injuries, thanks to advances in medical treatment, they often have cognitive, language, somatic, and behavioral difficulties. Traumatic brain injury is a threat to a child's quality of life—including life style, education, social and recreational activities, interpersonal relationships, freedom to make changes, and control over his or her self and destiny (Hickey, 1992). Approximately 70% of children with severe traumatic brain injury continue to receive special education services 5 years after the injury (Massagli, Michaud, & Rivara, 1996). Trauma to the head, however, does not always lead to brain injury.

Developmentally, traumatic brain injury is associated primarily with physical abuse (shaken baby syndrome or thrown infant syndrome) in infants under the age of 1 year; with falls and physical abuse in toddlers and preschoolers; with bicycle, motor vehicle, and sports-related accidents and injuries in children over the age of 5 years; and with motor vehicle accidents (including reckless driving, driving while intoxicated, and being struck by intoxicated drivers) or with accidents involving risk-taking behaviors in adolescents. Motor vehicle accidents, bicycle accidents, and falls account for between 75% and 80% of brain injuries in children (Yeates, 2000).

The incidence of traumatic brain injuries varies with sex and age (Yeates, 2000).

Boys are at considerably higher risk for closed-head trauma than are girls.... the ratio of boys to girls rises from approximately 1.5:1 for preschool children to approximately 2:1 for school-age children and adolescents.... The change appears to reflect a sharp increase in head injuries among males and a gradual decrease among females....

The incidence is relatively stable from birth to age 5, with injuries occurring in about 160 per 100,000 children in this age group. After age 5, the overall incidence gradually increases until early adolescence and then shows rapid growth, reaching a peak incidence of approximately 290 per 100,000 by age 18.... (p. 94)

Focal Head Injuries and Diffuse Head Injuries

The two general types of traumatic brain injuries are *focal head injuries* (also referred to as open-head injuries or penetrating head injuries; *focal* refers to effects of brain injury that are in a circumscribed area) and *diffuse head injuries*

(also referred to as closed-head injuries, nonpenetrating head injuries, bilateral injuries, or multifocal injuries). In both types of injuries, multiple areas of the brain may be involved.

In a focal head injury, the skull is usually penetrated by a high-velocity projectile, such as a bullet, and contact occurs between the brain tissue and the outside environment. The damage is usually confined to the site of the injury. The following primary and secondary effects may be present (Fennell & Mickle, 1992):

EFFECTS OF FOCAL HEAD INJURIES

Primary Effects

- Lacerations of various layers of brain tissue
- Intracranial hemorrhage
- Focal compression of brain tissue
- Damage arising from skull fragments penetrating brain tissue
- Contusion (bruising) of the brain tissue at the site opposite where the impact occurred (because the impact forces the brain to rebound against the opposite side of the skull, causing an injury called a *contrecoup*), which can cause tissue damage and bleeding
- Neuronal stretching and shearing

Secondary Effects

- Cerebral edema (swelling in the cerebrum)
- Diffuse brain swelling
- Increased intracranial pressure
- Degeneration of nerve tissue
- Posttraumatic hydrocephalus

Trauma produced by closed-head injuries may lead to alterations in brain tissue as well as disruptions in brain function at a cellular level. A diffuse head injury may damage the brain severely, even though the skull is not penetrated. The force of the trauma affects the brain within the closed, bony space of the skull (Yeates, 2000).

The primary injuries that arise from head trauma reflect biomechanical forces, which can involve either impression or acceleration–deceleration. *Impression* occurs when there is direct contact between a stationary head and some physical force, as when a person sustains a blow to the head from a moving object. *Acceleration–deceleration* occurs when there is an impact with a moving head. Most of the common causes of head injuries in children, including falls and transportation-related, give rise to acceleration–deceleration injuries. (pp. 95–96)

Brain tissue may be bruised at the point of impact or in an area opposite to the point of impact. The *coup-contrecoup effect* occurs because the brain, which is enclosed in a fluid sac inside the skull, moves with the impact of the injury. The brain is bruised when it hits against the skull at the point of impact (referred to as the *coup*) and then again when it hits the skull on the opposite side (the *contrecoup*). If an *intracranial hematoma* (a collection of blood within the brain or between the brain and the skull) is present, there may be damage to adjacent areas as well. Diffuse head injuries—particularly those caused by motor vehicle accidents—also may result in micro shearing of the nerve fibers, especially in vulnerable areas of the brain such as the inferior (underside) frontal lobes and the mesial (middle) temporal lobes.

Research on the neurochemistry of brain injury suggests that head trauma can result in a variety of neurochemical events that can disrupt cell functioning and lead to diffuse axonal injury (Yeates, 2000). These neurochemical events include excessive production of free radicals (by-products of metabolism), excessive production of excitatory amino acids (a type of neurotransmittor), and disruption of the calcium balance inside cells.

Motor vehicle accidents are the most frequent cause of diffuse head injuries in adolescents. These injuries produce a range of physical symptoms, depending on the type and severity of the injury.

Following are examples of primary and secondary effects of diffuse head injuries (Fennell & Mickle, 1992; Kolb & Whishaw, 1990):

EFFECTS OF DIFFUSE HEAD INJURIES

Primary Effects

- Contusion of the brain tissue at the site of impact
- Contusion of the brain tissue at the site opposite where the impact occurred
- Microscopic damage formed by a twisting or shearing of the nerve fibers (because of the violent movement of the brain within the skull)
- Hemorrhage associated with the bruises and strains (which may form a hematoma that places pressure on the surrounding tissue and structures)

Secondary Effects

- Hypoxia (deficiency of oxygen reaching the tissues of the body)
- Shock
- Seizures
- Elevated intracranial pressure (because of diffuse brain swelling or cerebral edema in response to intracranial hematomas or contused brain tissue)
- Posttraumatic hydrocephalus

Children with diffuse head injuries usually have more cognitive difficulties than those with focal head injuries (Aram & Eisele, 1992). The greater or the more widespread the damage, the more limited are the possibilities for neural reallocation of functions. Focal head injuries, however, may impair not only the functions associated with the specific site of injury, but also the acquisition of new cognitive skills. Even when alternative brain regions take over impaired functions, the "alternative brain regions may not be as effective or efficient as the regions initially destined to serve specific functions" (Aram & Eisele, 1992, p. 85).

Outcomes of Traumatic Brain Injuries

Children with a traumatic brain injury may experience the following outcomes (Jennett & Bond, 1975):

1. *Good recovery.* The child is able to resume activities and schooling with minimal neurological deficits.
2. *Mild disability.* The child is able to resume most activities and schooling but still experiences cognitive, behavioral, physical, or social problems.
3. *Moderate disability.* The child is able to function independently, but at a reduced level relative to his or her pre-injury status. Special education or rehabilitation services are required.
4. *Severe disability.* The child is unable to function independently and requires substantial assistance with self-care.
5. *Persistent vegetative state.* The child is unable to function without a life-care support system.
6. *Death.* The child dies as a result of the brain injury.

Of children with closed-head injuries, about 75% to 95% have a good recovery (but still may show neurobehavioral impairments or functional disabilities), about 10% have moderate disabilities, about 1% to 3% have severe disabilities, and fewer than 1% remain in a persistent vegetative state (Yeates, 2000). Research on outcomes associated with mild brain injury is not clear (Yeates, 2000). Some studies find few persistent cognitive deficits resulting from mild brain injury, whereas other studies report cognitive, somatic, and behavioral deficits. We need more research, with better designed studies, to evaluate the short- and long-term effects of mild brain injuries in children.

One study of 6- to 12-year-old children with moderate or severe traumatic brain injury indicated that 6 months after injury over 25% of the children were still having the following problems (from most to least often): fatiguability, headaches or dizziness, over- or under-activity, sleeping problems, eating problems, moodiness, anger, memory problems, concentration problems, confusion, coordination problems and clumsiness, anxiety, problems following directions, aggressiveness, and visual problems (Barry, Taylor, Klein, & Yeates, 1996). Other research suggests that children with severe traumatic brain injury also may have limited verbal learning skills, poor verbal memory, impaired verbal fluency, and slow speed of information processing 2 years after returning to school (Kinsella, Prior, Sawyer, Ong, Murtagh, Eisenmajer, Bryan, Anderson, & Klug, 1997).

SPECIFIC EFFECTS OF BRAIN INJURY IN CHILDREN

Brain injury may have the following effects:

- General deterioration in all or most aspects of functioning
- Differential symptoms, depending on (a) the location, extent, and type of injury, (b) the child's age, (c) the child's

premorbid cognitive, temperament, personality, and psychosocial functioning, (d) the child's familial and environmental supports, and (e) the promptness and quality of treatment
- Highly specific symptoms when the injury is in specialized locations
- Subtle symptoms that can be detected only by careful study of the child's behavior and performance
- Symptoms not seen until several years after the injury
- No observable symptoms

Symptoms of brain injury are usually directly related to the functions mediated by the area where the damage occurred. For example, if the damage is in the occipital lobe, the symptoms will likely include difficulty with visual perception. Occasionally, symptoms arising after brain injury disappear quickly; however, subtle impairments may remain (Kolb & Whishaw, 1990). Because the most common area of brain injury is the frontal-temporal area, the most commonly seen symptoms of brain injury are behavior problems (e.g., disinhibition) and memory deficits. Damage to the frontal-temporal area has a profound impact on school success and daily functioning.

Physical, Cognitive, and Behavioral Symptoms of Brain Injury

Brain injuries may produce physical and cognitive disturbances, in addition to changes in temperament, personality, and psychosocial functioning.

Physical symptoms. The physical symptoms associated with mild to severe brain injuries include the following (Mild Traumatic Brain Injury Committee, 1993):

Mild Brain Injuries

- Nausea
- Vomiting
- Dizziness
- Headache
- Blurred vision
- Sleep disturbance
- Premature fatigue
- Lethargy
- Abnormal smelling and hearing
- Other sensory losses that cannot be accounted for by peripheral injury or other causes

Severe Brain Injuries (in addition to the above)

- Skull fracture
- Bruises on the brain
- Cerebral laceration
- Intracranial hematoma
- Seizures

- Paralysis
- Inability to maintain balance and other coordination problems
- Cerebrospinal fluid draining from the nose to the mouth
- Blood collecting behind the eardrum or in the sinuses

Cognitive disturbances. Cognitive disturbances after brain injury include the following:

- Disorders of attention and concentration
- Disorders of planning, initiating, and maintaining goal-directed activities (executive functions)
- Disorders of judgment and perception
- Disorders of learning and memory
- Disorders of language and communication
- Disorders in the speed of information processing

In school, children with cognitive disturbances may have the following troubles:

1. Difficulty completing their work and understanding tasks (poor attention and concentration)
2. Difficulty locating classrooms, getting to classes on time, and following schedules (poor orientation to time and place, particularly in severe cases)
3. Difficulty remembering what they have learned in class or what they have studied at home (poor retention and retrieval of information)
4. Difficulty staying on task, communicating and interacting with others, and staying out of potentially dangerous situations (impulsivity)
5. Difficulty organizing thoughts, planning, and processing information
6. Difficulty changing routines or activities (inflexibility)
7. Difficulty taking initiative or acting independently
8. Difficulty applying information learned to the correct situation at the appropriate time, connecting old and new information, and identifying patterns (inability to generalize)
9. Difficulty recognizing that their abilities have changed, which causes children to resist academic, social, or behavioral supports (denial of the brain injury or poor awareness of the effects of the brain injury)

Following are examples of communication difficulties (Adamovich, 1991, p. 79):

1. Inability to understand the point of view of others
2. Rigidity in modifying an opinion
3. Difficulty recognizing the main point of a conversation and sticking to the topic
4. Difficulty joining an ongoing conversation appropriately
5. Inability to question or clarify in an attempt to gain additional information necessary to form an appropriate conclusion
6. Difficulty taking turns
7. Difficulty giving and receiving feedback

8. Concern for self-goals, which causes difficulty in accepting group decisions
9. Presentation of too little or too much information
10. Difficulty switching from one topic to another
11. Lack of self-esteem and self-appraisal
12. Inability to connect short-term goals and long-term goals, which leads to failure to see the relationship between therapy tasks or group activities and her or his life in general
13. Establishment of unrealistic individual goals and aspirations because of a denial of deficits

Some cognitive impairments diminish with time, others are permanent, and still others remain hidden until later in life, when more advanced cognitive skills are needed (Prigatano, Fordyce, Zeiner, Roueche, Pepping, & Wood, 1986). The correlation between severity of initial injury and neurodevelopmental outcome is far from perfect; however, if severe damage results in a coma of long duration, there is greater probability of impaired cognitive functioning. In addition, some children with only mild traumatic brain injury still have significant neurobehavioral symptoms.

Often, you will want to estimate the child's *premorbid level*—that is, the level at which the child was functioning before his or her brain injury. Premorbid level can best be estimated from the following types of information: (a) scores obtained on nationally standardized measures of intellectual ability, (b) measures of achievement found on grade school or high school transcripts, (c) Scholastic Aptitude Test scores, (d) information from a child's social history, (e) information from an older adolescent's occupational history, and (f) estimates based on the mean of the parents' levels of education. However, a pre- and post-injury comparison of specific test scores will not give a true picture of the child's deficits if the test does not assess the areas of the child's impairments. A child may have behavioral problems, memory deficits, or perceptual-motor problems, for example, that are not measured by the test.

If there are no past test scores available, consider using scores on the WISC–III obtained by the child *after* the injury to estimate her or his premorbid functioning. Regression equations that use demographic variables and subtest scaled scores to predict premorbid IQs are provided by Vanderploeg et al. (1998). These equations result in predicted IQs that are highly correlated with the actual IQs obtained by the standardization sample ($r = .82$ for the Full Scale IQ, $r = .81$ for the Verbal Scale IQ, and $r = .71$ for the Performance Scale IQ). Differences between the predicted IQs and actual premorbid IQs are about 2 to 4 IQ points.

Some symptoms present during the early stages of recovery—such as delusions, irritability, hallucinations, and suspiciousness—may impair cognitive processes (Wood, 1987). These symptoms frequently reflect difficulty in regulating behavior in response to environmental stimuli. Thus, if present, the symptoms will probably reduce the child's ability to think adaptively or flexibly and will hamper his or her

control over mental processes. Frequently, however, these symptoms are resolved prior to discharge from a rehabilitation center.

Some symptoms may be associated with medications. For example, antiseizure medication can produce or exacerbate learning or memory disturbances, antipsychotic medication may produce blunted affect, and both types of medications may produce psychomotor retardation (Lezak, 1995).

Brain injury may lead to losses in automatic processing—such as ability to button clothing, dial a telephone, or brush one's teeth (Wood, 1987). Previously overlearned and automatic sequential activities that were carried out quickly and effortlessly before an injury may require concentration and deliberation after the injury. With the loss of automatic processing, children with brain injuries have less flexibility and less ability to adjust rapidly to environmental changes. Thus, they are placed at a disadvantage in novel situations. In addition, deficits in one area of functioning may impair their performance in other areas. Changes in cognitive efficiency, vigilance, reaction time, and temperament may make children with brain injuries more vulnerable to sustaining subsequent head injuries (Levin, Ewing-Cobbs, & Fletcher, 1989).

Children with brain injuries may have cognitive impairments that are not evident in an evaluation. For example, they may have little difficulty during a mental status evaluation but show attentional deficits when left to their own resources. Similarly, although they may be able to converse adequately during the evaluation, they may easily become distracted when several people are talking.

As you read about the following language and symbolic disorders, recognize that neuropsychological examination findings for children with various types of brain injuries (e.g., those associated with a motor vehicle accident, cranial irradiation, or hydrocephalus) are seldom localized; the injury usually has diffuse effects. That is, children with brain injuries only rarely totally lose or fail to develop a particular skill or function; rather, the severity of deficits varies over a broad range.

The major symbolic and language disturbances associated with brain injuries are agnosia, apraxia, and aphasia.

Agnosia.   Agnosia is a central nervous system disorder manifested through impaired ability to recognize familiar stimuli. Agnosia is not caused by sensory or intellectual impairment. Following are several forms of agnosia:

- *Visual agnosia* is impaired ability to name or recognize objects.
- *Prosopagnosia* is impaired ability to recognize familiar faces.
- *Auditory agnosia* is impaired ability to identify sounds.
- *Tactile agnosia* is impaired ability to identify familiar objects by touch, with the eyes closed.
- *Visual-spatial agnosia* is impaired ability to follow directions, to find one's way in familiar surroundings, to understand spatial details such as left-right positions or the

layout of a classroom, and to understand other types of visual-spatial characteristics.

Apraxia. Apraxia is impaired ability to execute learned movements or to carry out purposeful or skilled acts. Apraxia is not caused by muscle weakness, sensory defects, poor comprehension, or intellectual deterioration. Some forms of apraxia follow:

- *Ideomotor apraxia* is impaired ability to carry out an action on verbal command, although the action can be performed automatically (e.g., to brush teeth).
- *Ideational apraxia* is impaired ability to execute a series of acts, although each step can be performed separately (e.g., to fold a letter, place it in an envelope, seal it, and stamp it).
- *Bucco-facial apraxia* is impaired ability to perform facial movements in response to commands, although the movements can be executed spontaneously (e.g., to whistle, pucker lips, protrude tongue, cough, sniff).
- *Limb-kinetic apraxia* is impaired ability to use a single limb, resulting in clumsiness or the inability to carry out fine motor acts with the affected limb (e.g., to grasp an object or to carry out simple manipulations).
- *Constructional apraxia* is impaired ability to construct objects (e.g., to construct a pattern with blocks or to draw from a copy).
- *Dressing apraxia* is impaired ability to dress (e.g., to put on clothing correctly).

Aphasia. Aphasia is a deficit in the perception, production, or symbolic use of language. The following three subgroups of childhood aphasia differ from one another mainly in the severity and age of onset of the language difficulty:

- *Congenital aphasia* is a language deficit present at birth, marked by an almost complete failure to acquire language.
- *Developmental language disorder* is a less pervasive cognitive and developmental impairment, in which language is late in onset and fails to develop fully.
- *Acquired aphasia* is a language deficit resulting from brain injury following normal language development.

Aphasia may involve expressive components, receptive components, or both. *Expressive aphasia* (also referred to as *nonfluent aphasia*) is impaired ability to use spoken and/or written language. The effects of the disability range from completely losing the ability to speak to simply having difficulty finding the appropriate word (i.e., problems with word finding or word retrieval). Children with expressive aphasia may have a restricted vocabulary, may use words repetitively, and may pause for long periods between words or phrases. Expressive aphasia primarily affects the symbolic use of language, with some aphasic disturbances involving word usage and order. Following are some forms of expressive aphasia.

- *Agrammatism* refers to using a paucity of connecting and modifying words in speech, which gives it a telegraphic quality (e.g., "I work factory make steel").

- *Paragrammatism* refers to employing an incoherent and aimless syntactic structure in speech, with nouns appearing in verb slots and vice versa (e.g., "Runs he fast").
- *Anomia* is impaired access to vocabulary or word knowledge. Types of anomia include the following:
  1. *Verbal paraphasia* (also termed *semantic paraphasia*) refers to the unintentional use of another word in lieu of the target word (e.g., "I went to the store…no, the school"). For an error to be classified as an example of verbal paraphasia, the target words must have been present in the child's repertoire.
  2. *Phonemic paraphasia* refers to the production of unintended sounds or syllables in the utterance of a partially recognizable word (e.g., "paker" for "paper" or "sisperos" for "rhinoceros").
  3. *Phonosemantic blending* refers to phonemic sound substitution in the target word that creates another real word, related in sound but not in meaning (e.g., "cable" for "table" or "television" for "telephone").
  4. *Neologistic paraphasia* refers to the production of a nonsense word or words, usually without recognition of the error (e.g., "tilto" for "table").
- *Acalculia* is an inability to carry out simple mathematical calculations.
- *Agraphia* is loss or impairment of the ability to express language in written or printed form.

You can help a child who has word or sound retrieval difficulties by giving the child the first sounds of the word that she or he is having difficulty with (referred to as phonemic priming). If the child is successful in producing the word, it is a positive sign that there is some integrity of function in the processes under evaluation.

Writing has "a special place within the repertoire of learned motor skills.… Writing is a complex function that requires the coordinated activity of linguistic, motor, spatial, and perceptual systems for optimum performance. Considering the sheer number and diversity of cognitive operations involved, it is perhaps not altogether surprising that writing takes a long time to master and that it remains a fragile skill highly susceptible to disruption by brain damage" (Rapcsak, 1997, pp. 149, 166).

Repetition of what someone says requires the auditory perception of speech and the ability to articulate the sounds that are heard. Children with aphasia respond to repetition tasks in a manner "similar in quality and degree of impairment to their spontaneous or conversational speech" (Goodglass, 1993, pp. 138–139). Examples of repetition errors include saying "Come bin" for "Come in" and saying "He park…he came with the car" for "He parks the car." In some cases, children with aphasia may be aware of the inaccuracy of their production and make repeated attempts to correct it. In other cases, they may be unaware of the source of their poor understanding and act out behaviorally.

Receptive aphasia (also referred to as *fluent aphasia*) is impaired ability to understand spoken and/or written language.

Speech may be relatively intact, although disfluencies—that is, use of incomplete sentences or phrase repetitions—may be present. Forms of receptive aphasia include the following:

- *Auditory aphasia* is impaired ability to comprehend the meaning of spoken words, although the ability to hear remains intact.
- *Alexia* is loss of the ability to comprehend written or printed language, despite adequate vision and intelligence.

Auditory comprehension may be disturbed in children with aphasia for several reasons. First, focal brain damage may impair speech-sound and word-meaning recognition. Second, attentional and short-term auditory memory problems may be present. Third, situational variables—such as personal relevance and emotional significance of the subject matter of the communication—may affect comprehension. Finally, all of these factors may interact to affect comprehension.

Disorders of auditory comprehension can involve problems with the comprehension of individual words, certain categories of words such as body parts or letters of the alphabet, and sentences. Pure word-deafness is a rare disorder of auditory comprehension involving an inability to perceive speech sounds, while other language processes such as speaking, writing, and reading remain intact.

When children have impaired abilities in both expressive and receptive domains, the condition is called *global aphasia* or *mixed-type aphasia*. Children with receptive deficits also are likely to have expressive disturbances, but those with expressive disturbances do not necessarily have receptive problems. Table 18-1 illustrates procedures used to evaluate agnosia, apraxia, and aphasia.

Comment on children with aphasia.   Children with aphasia who are older than 8 to 10 years have symptoms similar to those of adults, whereas younger children do not (Aram & Eisele, 1992; Paquier & Van Dongen, 1993). Instead, infants and very young children show "delays in gestural development (i.e., pointing), prelexical expression (i.e., babbling), lexical comprehension and production, and early word combinations" (Aram & Eisele, 1992, p. 82). Acquired aphasia occurs in children for the same reasons that it does in adults—as a result of trauma, vascular damage, tumors, infection, or seizure disorders. However, the distribution of etiologies in children is somewhat different from that in adults. In children, for instance, brain injury from a traumatic event is the main cause of aphasia, whereas in adults the main cause of aphasia is a cerebrovascular accident (CVA; i.e., stroke). Traumatic events are more likely than cerebrovascular accidents to produce diffuse injuries and thus lead to fewer clear-cut aphasic symptoms.

Children with aphasia who are under the age of 10 years are usually alert, attentive, and eager to communicate their thoughts and reactions. The prognosis for recovery from aphasia is more favorable for children than for adults. When recovery is not complete, children with brain injuries may have long-term deficits, including naming disorders, impaired use of syntax, and writing disorders, all of which can disrupt academic performance. The type of aphasic disturbance exhibited and the prognosis for recovery are clearly related to the severity of the injury, including the etiology of the injury and the size and nature of the damage. The presence of seizures can impede recovery. Sometimes children will recover from aphasia, but still perform poorly in school or have deficits in verbal skills (Martins & Ferro, 1992; Woods & Carey, 1979).

Exercise 18-1.
Identifying Language and Symbolic Disorders

Read each statement and identify the type of language or symbolic disorder it illustrates. Each statement reflects one of the following disorders: acalculia, agraphia, agrammatism, auditory aphasia, alexia, visual agnosia, prosopagnosia, auditory agnosia, tactile agnosia, visual-spatial agnosia, constructional apraxia, facial apraxia, ideational apraxia, ideomotor apraxia, or dressing apraxia.

1. A child age 9 years with a brain injury is shown a baseball bat, and she calls it "a piece of wood."
2. An adolescent age 16 years with a brain injury is asked to touch a doll's right ear, and he says, "I don't know where to touch it."
3. A child age 8 years with a brain injury is asked to put her hands in the air, and she stares out the window.
4. A child age 9 years with a brain injury is asked to put on a sweater, and he fails in his attempt to do so. However, he can clap his hands when he is asked to do so.
5. A child age 8 years with a brain injury is shown a picture of three blocks that are stacked in a tower from largest to smallest. She is asked to build the same tower. The child puts her three blocks in a row, thus failing to duplicate the pattern shown in the picture.
6. An adolescent age 13 with a brain injury is shown a picture of his brother, and he calls it "a picture of someone."
7. When asked to write his name, a child age 10 years with a brain injury makes random marks.
8. An adolescent age 15 years with a brain injury is asked to identify a coin placed in her hand without looking at it, and she says, "It is something."
9. An adolescent age 16 years with a brain injury and with adequate vision, speech, and intelligence is asked to read aloud a paragraph from a third-grade reader, and he is unable to do so.
10. A child age 10 years with a brain injury is asked to drink out of a cup filled with water, and she complies with the request. The child is shown another cup, but this time it is empty. When the child is asked to show how she would drink out of it, she simply looks puzzled at the request and does not perform any actions.
11. A child age 8 years with a brain injury is asked to identify the sound of a drum, and he says, "I don't know what it is."
12. An adolescent age 12 years with a brain injury says, "I go store buy candy."   *(Continued on page 414)*

Table 18-1
Procedures Used in Testing for Agnosia, Apraxia, and Aphasia

Disorder	Ability	Procedure
Agnosia	Sound recognition	Ask the child, with eyes closed, to identify familiar sounds, such as a ringing bell or a whistling sound.
	Auditory perception	Ask the child to repeat what you say.
	Auditory-verbal comprehension	Ask the child to answer questions and carry out instructions.
	Recognition of body parts and sidedness	Ask the child to point to her or his left and right sides and to name body parts.
	Visual object recognition	Ask the child to identify familiar objects placed in front of her or him, such as a pen or a wristwatch.
	Color recognition	Ask the child to name colors.
	Facial recognition	Observe whether the child recognizes familiar faces.
	Tactile recognition	Ask the child, with eyes closed, to identify familiar objects placed in her or his hand, such as keys, comb, and pencil.
	Visual-spatial recognition	(For older child) Ask the child to walk to the left side of the room.
Apraxia	Bucco-facial movement	Ask the child to show you how to drink through a straw, blow out a match, cough, yawn, and stick out his or her tongue.
	Limb movement	Ask the child to wave good-bye, show you how to comb his or her hair, make a fist, throw a ball, and kick a ball.
	Bilateral limb movement	Ask the child to show you how to play a piano and file his or her fingernails.
	Whole-body movement	Ask the child to show you how to stand like a boxer, take a bow, and shovel dirt (or snow).
	Integrated skilled motor act (as well as memory)	Say to the child: "Here are three papers: a big one, a middle-sized one, and a little one. Take the biggest one, rumple it up, and throw it on the ground. Give me the middle-sized one. Put the smallest one in your pocket."
Aphasia	Verbal comprehension	Ask the child to name articles of clothing that she or he is wearing and to touch her or his nose, leg, mouth, eyes, and ears.
	Visual comprehension	Ask the child to tell you what you are doing. Pantomime such activities as writing, drinking, hammering a nail, combing hair, cutting, and waving.
	Visual-verbal comprehension	Ask the child to read a sentence from the newspaper and explain its meaning. If the child is unable to speak, print instructions on a sheet of paper and note whether the child can carry them out.
	Motor speech	Ask the child to imitate several sounds and phrases: "la-la," "me-me," "this is a good book," and others of increasing difficulty. Note abnormal word usage in conversation.
	Automatic speech	Ask the child to repeat one or two series of words that she or he has learned in the past, such as the days of the week or the months of the year.
	Volitional speech	Ask the child to answer questions. Note whether the answers are relevant.
	Writing	Ask the child to write (a) her or his name and address, (b) a simple sentence, and (c) the name of an object that you show her or him.

Note. All activities in the table pertain only to children who would be expected, based on their age, to have mastered the skill.

13. A child age 9 years with a brain injury is asked to add 4 + 3 + 2, and she says, "432."
14. An adolescent age 13 years with a brain injury is asked to show his tongue, and he simply stares ahead.
15. A child age 10 years with a brain injury is asked to open the door, pick up a pencil from the table, and then put it on the chair. The child says, "I don't know."

Answers

1. Visual agnosia
2. Visual-spatial agnosia
3. Auditory aphasia
4. Dressing apraxia
5. Constructional apraxia
6. Prosopagnosia
7. Agraphia
8. Tactile agnosia
9. Alexia
10. Ideomotor apraxia
11. Auditory agnosia
12. Agrammatism
13. Acalculia
14. Facial apraxia or auditory aphasia
15. Ideational apraxia (if a comprehension deficit has been ruled out as the cause)

To acquire aphasia is to suddenly lose both an important part of oneself and one's attachment to reality with no readily available means of compensation.

—Pierre Y. Létourneau

Temperament, personality, and psychosocial functioning changes. The changes in temperament, personality, and psychosocial functioning that children with brain injuries exhibit relate both to their brain injury and to their preexisting personality and temperament. Unfortunately, there is no simple way to interpret the behavioral symptoms of children with brain injuries, because behavioral symptoms may (a) be neurologically based, reflecting, in part, impairment of cognitive, emotional, or psychosocial functions directly associated with the neurological insult, (b) be emotional reactions to failures or performance difficulties, (c) reflect preexisting personality patterns or exaggerations of these patterns, or (d) combine elements of the above in various degrees and in varying ways over time (Asarnow, Satz, Light, Lewis, & Neumann, 1991). You will need to study the complete case history carefully to arrive at an understanding of the behavioral symptom patterns.

Following are some symptoms, associated with temperament, personality, and psychosocial functioning, that children with brain injuries may exhibit (Prigatano et al., 1986):

1. *Emotional lability.* Symptoms include a lowered tolerance for frustration, rapid mood shifts, temper outbursts, demanding behavior, excessive dependence on others, and talkativeness. Emotional lability may be a reaction to failure, may be neurologically based, or may reflect preexisting personality characteristics.

2. *Anxiety.* Symptoms include restlessness, fatigue, concentration problems, irritability, and sleep disturbances. Anxiety may come about because of difficulties coping with the environment or because of a decrease in emotional control associated with neurological injury.

3. *Denial of illness* (or *anosognosia*). Symptoms include unwillingness to recognize existing deficits or failure to recognize physical or psychological changes that have resulted in reduced ability. Denial of illness may be an attempt to protect oneself from an environment that is difficult to cope with, or it may reflect injury-related neurological disturbances in awareness and attention.

4. *Paranoid ideation.* Symptoms include suspiciousness, hypervigilance, and distrust of others. Paranoid ideation may be related to preexisting personality difficulties, or it may reflect disturbances in neurological functioning.

5. *Psychomotor agitation.* Symptoms include restlessness, excessive motor movements, fear, and tension. Psychomotor agitation may be related to preexisting personality difficulties, or it may reflect disturbances in neurological functioning.

6. *Depression and amotivational states.* Symptoms include feelings of worthlessness, helplessness, or guilt; loss of interest in school, work, or family activities; decreased interest in social activities; and decreased sexual drive in adolescents. Depression and amotivational states may reflect an attempt to reduce the demands of an insensitive or overwhelming environment, may be neurologically based, or may reflect preexisting personality characteristics.

7. *Psychosocial disturbances and difficulty carrying through on accepted social rules.* Symptoms include socially inappropriate behavior (such as saying embarrassing things and performing actions that embarrass others), reduced awareness of personal impact on others, insensitivity to others, difficulty making friends, social withdrawal, and forgetting school responsibilities. Psychosocial disturbances and difficulty carrying through on accepted rules may reflect an attempt to reduce the demands of an insensitive or overwhelming environment, may be neurologically based, or may reflect preexisting personality and behavior characteristics.

Note that many behavioral symptoms, such as depression, emotional lability, limited motivation, and paranoid ideation, may—like language and motor symptoms, such as aphasia and hemiplegia—be neurologically based (Prigatano et al., 1986). Whatever the relationship between the behavior problems and the brain injury, of particular importance are (a) how the child perceives her or his limitations, (b) the significance of these limitations, and (c) what interventions are needed. These considerations, in turn, are related to the child's age, cognitive ability, social skills, family and environmental supports, schooling, ethnicity, and social status.

Some children with brain injuries show a pattern of behavior associated with *overarousal* (such as inattentiveness, irritability, distractibility, hyperactivity, impulsivity, inappropriate behavior, aggressiveness, and, for adolescents, increased sexual drive), whereas others show a pattern of behavior associated with *underarousal* (such as apathy, poor motivation, and social withdrawal) (Filley, Cranberg, Alexander, & Hart, 1987). Overall, behavior problems are more likely to follow a severe brain injury than one that is mild or moderate (Fennell & Mickle, 1992).

Differential Effects of Brain Injury in Young Children and in Adults

The effects of brain injury in children under 5 years old are different from those in adults, because young children's brains are still developing. When adults sustain a brain injury, there may be a loss or dissolution of previously acquired functions, manifested in impairment of language, memory, perceptual-motor functions, social relations, or general intelligence. In contrast, when children sustain a brain injury, there is likely to be interference with development in many areas, rather than a striking loss of function in one area. If brain injury is global, mental retardation may be the result; if it is region-specific, specific difficulties may result, such as difficulty with speech or difficulty with the recognition of shapes.

Acquired brain injuries usually produce less specific effects in young children than in adults. In young children, brain injury may have more than a simple depressing effect on cognitive skills; it may alter the basic pattern of cognitive development. Large unilateral injuries in infants usually produce a more widespread deficit in intellectual functions than do similar injuries in adults.

To understand brain injury in children, it is helpful to consider the principles of behavior development and the relationship between neural structures and behavior (Shaheen, 1984). The first 5 years of life constitute the period of greatest cortical development. The process of myelination in various brain regions affects behavioral and cognitive development. *Myelination* is the process of insulating, or coating, the axon of a neuron, and it increases the speed with which messages are transmitted among neurons. Myelination occurs in different areas at different times (Harris, 1995b):

1. At 40 weeks' gestation, in the spinal tract areas involved in postural control
2. At ages 2 to 3 months, in the midbrain areas involved in smiling
3. At the end of the first year of life, in the spinal tract areas involved in fine-motor control
4. During the second year of life, in the brain areas involved in motor control and coordination
5. During school years and later in life, in the brain areas involved in learning motor programs and higher mental processing

Conceivably, the behavioral difficulties that occur among children with brain injuries could be related to the neurostructural components undergoing the most rapid development at the time of the injury. For example, from a cognitive developmental perspective, diffuse brain injuries may affect the development of the following neurostructural components:

1. During the second year of life, speech and language
2. During the third year of life, spatial-symbolic processing
3. During the preschool years, expressive and receptive language functions
4. During middle childhood (particularly between ages 6 and 8 years), written language
5. During adolescence, verbal processing, nonverbal processing, and visuospatial processing

> *Dear, dear! How queer everything is today! And yesterday things went on just as usual. I wonder if I've been changed in the night? Let me think: Was I the same when I got up this morning? I almost think I can remember feeling a little different. But if I'm not the same, the next question is, "Who am I?" Ah, that's the great puzzle.*
>
> —Lewis Carroll

Cerebral Plasticity and Recovery of Function

Cerebral plasticity is the ability of the brain to change in order to compensate for loss of function. The change may involve (a) the taking over, by one part of the brain, of functions impaired by damage in another part of the brain or (b) the functional reorganization of the central nervous system to restore impaired functions. The brain has much plasticity and is capable of extensive reorganization and modification in response to injury, but there are limits to the degree of neuroanatomical plasticity attainable following brain injury. Although cerebral plasticity operates at any age, it is more extensive at younger ages than at older ages. We need to consider (a) how permanent the effects of brain injuries are in children, (b) how easy it is for children to recover from brain injury, and (c) how the effects of early brain injuries compare with those of later brain injuries. Recovery of function depends in part on the ability of the neurons in the damaged area to regenerate terminals and produce new terminals (see Figure 18-2). Reorganization is beneficial when the sprouting of intact axon collaterals facilitates the processing of information, but it is harmful when anomalous neuronal connections are made that interfere with the processing of information (Rutter, 1982; Taylor, 1991). Exhibit 18-1 describes how the brain may repair itself.

The following are tentative generalizations, based on research studies, about age of injury and recoverability (Taylor & Alden, 1997).

1. Traumatic brain injuries in infancy or early childhood are likely to result in more impaired cognitive and academic functioning than brain injures sustained during middle childhood or adolescence.
2. Early traumatic brain injuries impair perceptual-motor and spatial skills, global intellectual functioning, verbal

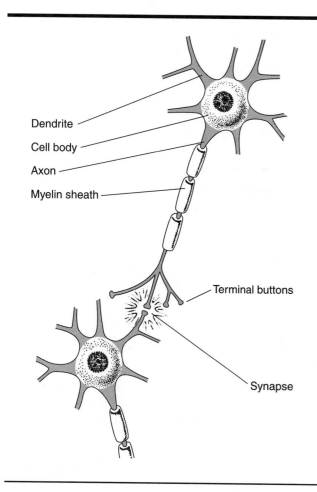

Figure 18-2. Typical structure of a neuron.

and written language abilities, attention, and metacognitive functioning.

3. Among children who sustain early brain injuries, cognitive impairments become more prominent as the children age. This is because the effects of brain injury on young children may not be fully recognized until several years after the injury, when children are expected to master complex, higher-level cognitive and behavioral processes. Skills relatively undeveloped at the time of injury may seem to have been spared, but later in life these skills may not develop fully or their expression may be impaired.

4. Children who sustain early brain injuries tend to develop cognitive and academic skills at a slower rate than those who sustain brain injuries at school age or during adult years.

5. It is not known whether the slower rate of development of cognitive and academic skills after early brain injury reflects deterioration in skills related to learning, failure of children to develop at the expected rate, or inability of children to cope with tasks that have become too complex.

6. Deficits that appear several years after the brain injury was sustained often include verbal memory impairment,

adaptive behavior deficits, behavior problems, impaired advanced memory strategies, and poor executive and self-regulatory processes.

7. Skills undergoing active development at the time the brain injury was sustained are likely to be more susceptible to disruption than previously established skills.

Overall, studies show that children do not necessarily completely recover all of their functions after brain injury (Johnson, 1992; St. James-Roberts, 1981; Taylor & Alden, 1997). Thus, there is little reason to believe that young children with brain injuries *always* or *usually* make a better recovery than older children with brain injuries. In fact, early brain injury may result in greater impairment than brain injury sustained later in life. Generally, however, recovery is variable within each age group, depending on the child's age at the time of the brain injury, premorbid status, experiential history, preexisting problems, education, type and severity of the brain injury (including the nature, locus, extent, and progression of the brain damage), promptness and quality of treatment, age at the time of treatment, and time since treatment. In addition, after injury, some functions may improve more than others, and some anatomical areas may be more susceptible to permanent deficits than others. Changes in cognitive development after brain injury may best be viewed as involving cumulative interactions among etiological variables, recovery-period variables, and experiential variables.

Children sustaining brain injury early in life should be reassessed during early adolescence because it is during these years that more complex and higher-level cognitive and behavioral processes emerge. More research is needed to examine the long-term effects of brain injuries on cognitive, academic, and psychosocial functions. Until we learn more about the relationship among brain, behavior, and development, the best position to take with regard to plasticity is the following: *"In short, it is impossible to formulate any general principle regarding age-related change in plasticity [in relation to brain injury in children]"* (Segalowitz & Hiscock, 1992, p. 57, italics added). *Furthermore, there is little support for unlimited potential for neural reorganization in the immature brain* (Aram & Eisele, 1992).

When 159 children with brain injuries (sustained at a mean age of 8 years) were evaluated 23 years later, the severity of the brain injury was the best predictor of long-term outcome; the IQ obtained shortly after the brain injury also was a reliable predictor of long-term outcome (Klonoff, Clark, & Klonoff, 1993). Prognostic statements about a child's ability to recover from brain injury should be made carefully; it is more difficult to evaluate language, speech, and other cognitive functions in children than in adults because young children have only relatively rudimentary skills in these areas. The effects of brain injury on a skill yet to be developed will be different from those on an established skill (Rutter, 1982). It is necessary to study not only the child's *degree of recovery* following brain injury but also his or her *ability to learn and relearn* cognitive skills.

Exhibit 18-1
Scott LaFee on When the Brain Takes a Bump

To understand how the brain may repair itself, it's necessary to know how brain injury typically occurs. Usually, it's a consequence of several events. The first event is the actual trauma, such as a hard blow to the skull that ruptures the blood-brain barrier. The latter is the network of vessels carrying oxygen and fuel to the brain. These arteries and capillaries, unlike those found elsewhere in the body, are tightly constructed of endothelial cells that permit only select substances such as glucose (sugar) to pass through their walls and into the brain itself. If the blood-brain barrier is breached by injury, whole blood, proteins, and other materials that normally circulate throughout the rest of the body can pour into the brain's cellular spaces, where neurons and supporting glial cells reside. These substances, which probably also include charged particles of oxygen and iron called free radicals, are poison to neurons. Direct contact with ordinary blood kills nerve cells. The blood flood causes swelling, or edema. Glial cells attempt to counteract the growing damage by absorbing unwanted chemicals, but if the blood flow is too great, the glial cells quickly become overloaded, rupture, and re-release their toxic contents into the brain, where the neuron-killing can begin anew.

At the same time that glial cells are struggling to clear away killer debris, injured, dying, or traumatized nerve cells are releasing their stores of neurotransmitters—the chemicals used to communicate with other nerve cells—and the calcium ions needed to activate them. This sudden, massive release of neurotransmitters can decimate nearby neurons, corroding their membranes or overstimulating them to the point of fatal burn out, a phenomenon called excitotoxicity. It can also activate enzymes within neurons, effectively signaling them to kill their makers.

The scene in a newly injured brain is, in some ways, like that of a major traffic accident. Some neurons die immediately; others suffer grave wounds that will kill them shortly. Yet other neurons seem to escape with only minor injuries or a simple case of shock. These latter neurons can appear normal, but many never fully regain their original functions. Some, for example, are permanently weakened, vulnerable to stress, or prone to failure at inappropriate times. On the whole, the brain adapts to trauma as best it can, re-establishing as quickly as possible its vital biochemical stability. The blood-brain barrier is repaired post-haste. All able neurons are called upon to resume ordinary duties without delay.

The architecture of a typical, living, healthy neuron resembles a bush. From the central cell body, an axon extends like a taproot. The axon's job is to carry messages away from the body of the cell toward neighboring cells. Branchy dendrites elsewhere on the cell stretch out to receive incoming communications. The axon is usually covered with smaller rootlets. If some, perhaps even most, of these rootlets are damaged or destroyed, the neuron will probably still be OK. Repairs can be made. But if too much of the axon is damaged by trauma, the remaining section retreats back into the body of the cell, a process called retrograde degeneration. The neuron, unable to draw sustenance, isolated from its neighbors, withers and dies, not unlike a tree chopped away from its root system.

Many variables, of course, affect whether a neuron successfully overcomes trauma or not, among them the age of the person injured (old cells don't fare as well as young ones), the type of cell damaged (neuron varieties with short axons tend to be more vulnerable), the distance between the brain lesion or injury and the cell body (the farther away the injury, the better), and the presence of healthy, neighboring cells capable of providing vital nutrients, called trophic factors.

Source: Adapted from LaFee (1999).

Absence of evidence is not evidence of absence.
—Hans L. Teuber

DIAGNOSTIC TECHNIQUES

Children with brain injury should be assessed by both a neurological examination, which may include brain scanning and electrodiagnostic procedures, and a neuropsychological examination, which may include an interview, administration of intelligence and personality measures, and administration of a battery of specialized neuropsychological tests.

Neurological Examination

A *neurological examination* includes a clinical history, a mental status examination, and a study of cranial nerves, motor functions (including tone, strength, and reflexes), coordination, sensory functions, and gait. Several laboratory procedures augment the neurological examination. These include computed tomography (CT scans), magnetic resonance imaging (MRI scans), electroencephalography (EEGs), positron emission tomography (PET scans), single photon emission computed tomography (SPECT), skull x-rays, lumbar punctures, and cerebral angiography.

In the neurological examination, *lower-level functions* (basic biological processes such as motor system functions and reflexes) can be evaluated on the two sides of the body by (a) *motor functioning tests* (measuring such factors as finger-tapping rate, strength of grip, and motor dexterity), (b) *standard neurological techniques* (assessing reflexes and tactile, visual, and auditory senses), (c) *bilateral simultaneous stimulation* (stimulating both sides of the body at the same time), and (d) *dichotic listening* (stimulating both ears with distinctly different stimuli).

Scanning and radiography methods. A brief description of six scanning and radiography methods follows.

1. *Computed tomography (CT or CAT scan).* This x-ray technique uses a computer to sequentially scan the organ under evaluation and produce radiologic images, creating a high-resolution image of the organ for analysis. CT scans are useful in locating focal pathologies—such as tumors and hemorrhages—and in showing changes in brain structure. However, there are disadvantages to CT scans: (a) they expose children to radiation, (b) the contrast material injected into the bloodstream may cause an allergic reaction, and (c) the contrast between grey matter and white matter of the brain may be poor.

2. *Magnetic resonance imaging (MRI scan).* In this procedure, a scan "of the brain or spinal cord is performed by placing a person's head or entire body in a confined space and generating a very powerful magnetic field that produces exquisitely detailed anatomic images. No x-rays are involved, and MRI is extremely safe" (Berkow, 1997, p. 286). Although MRI in itself is noninvasive and involves no potentially harmful radiation, a contrast agent is sometimes injected into the person's veins to further enhance the image. An advantage of MRI over CT is the ability to show better contrast in soft tissue, a feature that makes it particularly suitable for the investigation of tumors, edema, tissue pathology, and small lesions. MRI is not as widely available as CT, and it is more expensive.

3. *Electroencephalography (EEG).* In this procedure, electrodes are placed on the scalp to record the electrical activity of the brain. When a computer is used to collect and analyze data, the procedure is called *computerized electroencephalography* (CEEG) or *quantitative electroencephalography* (QEEG). Electroencephalography is easy to perform, is relatively inexpensive, involves no radiation, and is noninvasive. An advantage of EEG is the ability to record subtle brain activity changes in real time. Disadvantages are that the recordings (a) do not necessarily bear a specific relation to any brain structure, (b) may pick up artificial signals of noncerebral activity, and (c) may fail to identify abnormal signals that occur in lower brain structures because they are made at the surface of the brain.

4. *Positron emission tomography (PET scan).* This scanning method produces a cross-sectional image of cellular activity or blood flow in the brain, following the intravenous injection of a radioactive substance. PET scans provide information about regional metabolic activity by measuring regional cerebral glucose utilization. PET scans monitor a broad range of biochemical processes and indicate changes in brain activity during behavioral and cognitive tasks. Disadvantages of PET are that the technique is expensive and that it exposes children to radioactive substances that must be inhaled or injected. Also, the normative standards and clinical correlations are not as well established as they are for structural neuroimaging techniques (such as CT and MRI). During the 1990s, PET scans were used mainly in research.

5. *Single photon emission computed tomography (SPECT).* This procedure provides a three-dimensional representation of regional cerebral blood flow. SPECT brings together tomographic techniques for imaging brain structure with methods for measuring brain blood flow. Radioisotopes are inhaled or injected, and the radioactivity produced is monitored. Like PET scans, SPECT scans monitor a broad range of biochemical processes and indicate changes in brain activity during behavioral and cognitive tasks. The measurement of cerebral blood flow by SPECT is noninvasive, painless, and relatively safe. SPECT has some disadvantages,

Frank and Ernest

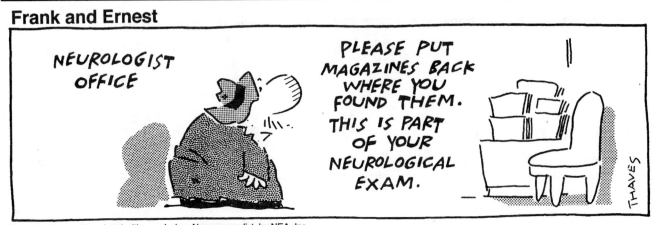

though: (a) its use per year must be limited because of radiation exposure, (b) spatial resolution is limited, (c) the representation may be contaminated by background radiation, and (d) detecting lesions in white matter is difficult. However, progress is being made in addressing these limitations. SPECT scans are generally not as accurate or as specific as PET scans. Also, normative standards and clinical correlations are not well established for SPECT.

6. *Cerebral angiography.* In this procedure, a radiopaque (visible on x-ray) dye is injected into an artery so that the flow of blood through the brain can be followed via x-ray. This allows blood vessel abnormalities in the brain to be visualized. The dye may cause an allergic reaction.

Scanning techniques, in general, provide excellent detail about the gross anatomy of the brain and excel in depicting major structural anomalies, including hydrocephalus and the degenerative effects of infectious disorders, tumors, congenital mishaps, and other childhood disorders. Electrodiagnostic procedures provide information about the electrical activity of the brain and can help differentiate seizure types (e.g., petit mal vs. grand mal epileptic seizures). Neither scanning techniques nor electrodiagnostic procedures, however, provide reliable information about levels of cognitive functioning or about functional levels of performance—that is, how the child functions in everyday activities and situations.

Neurological signs. The neurological examination may reveal hard neurological signs or soft neurological signs. *Hard neurological signs* are those that are fairly definitive indicators of cerebral injury, such as abnormalities in reflexes, cranial nerves, and motor organization, as well as asymmetrical failures in sensory and motor responses. Hard neurological signs usually correlate with other independent evidence of brain injury, such as the results of CT scans or EEGs.

Soft neurological signs are mild and equivocal neurological irregularities in primarily sensorimotor functions. Representative soft neurological signs are as follows:

- Poor balance
- Impaired fine motor coordination
- Clumsiness
- Slight reflex asymmetries
- *Choreiform* (irregular, jerky) *limb movements*
- Tremor
- Inability to perform rapid, alternating movements of hands and feet in a smooth, fluid, and rhythmic fashion (*dysdiadochokinesia*)
- Inability to detect predisplayed symbols traced on the palmar surface when blindfolded (*dysgraphesthesia*)
- Inability to identify three-dimensional objects in the outstretched hand when blindfolded (astereognosis)
- Awkwardness
- Impaired auditory integration
- Atypical sleep patterns
- Visual-motor difficulties
- Mild word-finding difficulties

- Labile affect
- Dysarthria (disturbance in articulation)

The term *soft neurological signs* applies to behavioral and motor indicators that may not have any systematic relationship to demonstrated neuropathology but may suggest neurological impairment, immaturity of development, or the milder part of a continuum of injury. There is *no* direct relationship between soft neurological signs and specific neuropsychological impairments. Table 19-9 in Chapter 19 shows useful procedures for assessing soft neurological signs.

Neuropsychological Examination

The aims of the *neuropsychological examination* are to draw inferences about the global functioning of the cerebral hemispheres, specify the adaptive strengths and weaknesses of the child (including formulating a profile of cognitive ability, sensorimotor functions, and affective reactions), and plan an appropriate rehabilitation. An adequate assessment of brain-behavior relationships requires a thorough developmental history, reports from parents and teachers, and the administration of several tests, as no single test can adequately assess the behavioral effects of widely variable cerebral lesions or other causes of cerebral impairments. Both quantitative and qualitative approaches are used in a comprehensive neuropsychological evaluation.

Quantitative approaches use standard neuropsychological batteries that provide normative data. Qualitative approaches evaluate cognitive functions, language, and behavior and may include (a) examination procedures for which there are only preliminary norms or (b) testing-of-limits procedures (see Chapter 7 in *Assessment of Children: Cognitive Applications*). Testing-of-limits includes (a) modifying instructions to involve more or fewer cues, (b) adjusting the pace at which information is presented, (c) modifying the modality of presentation or response, (d) modifying the starting or discontinuance procedure by administering additional items, (e) adjusting memory demands (e.g., using recognition instead of recall procedures), (f) modifying the response format (e.g., allowing pointing instead of oral responses), (g) adjusting task complexity (e.g., making tasks more concrete), and (h) asking for explanations of responses. Here are some examples of testing-of-limits:

- On a memory test, you might compare the child's spoken responses with his or her written responses to determine which response modality is more adequate.
- After orally requesting the child to draw a circle, you might have the child copy a circle from a stimulus figure or, failing that, imitate your drawing of a circle.
- When the child cannot recall a word, you might give him or her a choice of several words. For example, although a child with brain injuries may not give the right answer to a question about who invented the light bulb, the child may select the correct answer when given four choices (Morse, Edison, Wright Brothers, Marconi).

Neuropsychological assessment of children differs from that of adults (Tramontana & Hooper, 1988). First, very young children have difficulty reporting their symptoms because their language ability has not yet fully developed. Thus, parents or other caregivers must be relied on for information about children's functioning. Second, environmental factors—particularly those related to the family—play a significant role in shaping outcomes. Third, in cases of early brain injury, it is difficult to evaluate children's premorbid levels of functioning. Fourth, deficits may be "silent" until later in life. Finally, it is sometimes difficult to distinguish between developmental delays and deficits in performance.

A neuropsychological examination complements a neurological examination. It typically includes measures of the following areas and functions (Mapou, 1995):

- *General intellectual skills and academic achievement,* including evaluation of reasoning, problem solving, reading, writing, and mathematics abilities
- *Arousal and attention,* including evaluation of level of alertness, focused attention, sustained attention, span of attention, and resistance to interference
- *Sensory and motor functions,* including evaluation of visual functions, auditory functions, somatosensory functions (pertaining to bodily sensations, including those of touch, pain, pressure, and temperature), functional laterality (side of the body preferred for sensory and motor tasks), motor strength, fine-motor skills (such as speed and dexterity), and sensorimotor integration
- *Executive functions and problem-solving abilities,* including evaluation of planning, flexibility of thinking, sequencing and organizational skills, and verbal and nonverbal reasoning abilities
- *Language functions,* including evaluation of comprehension and production
- *Visuospatial functions,* including evaluation of perceptual skills, constructional skills, and spatial awareness
- *Learning and memory,* including ability to learn new information, immediate and delayed recall, recognition, working memory, sequential memory, visual memory, and auditory memory
- *Personality,* including evaluation of motivation, interests, impulsiveness, ability to tolerate changes in activities, compulsions, and phobias
- *Emotional functioning,* including evaluation of range of expressed affect, lability of affect, and modulation of emotional reactivity

The results of the neuropsychological examination can be useful in the following ways:

- Identifying areas of brain injury that impair a child's ability to perform successfully
- Localizing hemispheric involvement
- Helping to differentiate static tumors from rapidly growing tumors (by revealing changes over repeated evaluations)

- Evaluating the effects of progressive diseases of the central nervous system on adaptive abilities (by documenting rate and quality of change with the passage of time)
- Differentiating behavioral disturbances that may stem from brain injury from those that may stem from other causes
- Planning for rehabilitation—estimating potential for recovery and improvement, describing management implications of the assessment findings, and designing interventions
- Providing information regarding changes in children's capabilities and limitations in their everyday functioning
- Providing teachers with information on modifying the curriculum and on using teaching methods designed for children with brain injuries
- Helping courts determine levels of loss and compensation

Neuropsychological examinations may also help in evaluating children who have relatively isolated reading or other academic problems, learning disabilities, or ADHD by providing (a) objective behavioral information about their adaptive functioning, (b) base-line measures for evaluating the course of various neuropathological processes, and (c) indices of the effects of different therapeutic programs on cerebral functions. *Base-line measures* are those obtained when children are initially evaluated before any treatment begins. Performance on base-line measures is used to assess changes in cognitive processes or behavior over time, including those resulting from treatment.

Neuropsychological assessment increases our understanding of the psychological effects of brain injury and, more generally, of brain-behavior relations. A battery of neuropsychological tests provides a comprehensive, objective, and quantified series of measures useful in assessing initial and later effects of various neuropathological conditions, neurosurgical procedures, and drug therapies.

Neuropsychological assessment has shifted from assisting in the diagnosis of cerebral damage to assisting in the assessment of the functional capacities of children with brain injuries and the development of rehabilitation programs to help them develop better adaptive capacities and make better progress in school (D'Amato, Dean, & Rhodes, 1998; Lyon, Moats, & Flynn, 1988). This shift has taken place because brain-imaging techniques that provide accurate information about the location of brain damage have become more widely available.

No matter how many improvements are made in brain-imaging techniques, though, the functional capacities of children with brain injuries will always need to be evaluated. Questions to explore during a neuropsychological assessment include the following:

- Which areas are intact, and which ones show a deficit?
- What changes in ability and personality can be expected of the child, and when might these changes occur?
- What can the teacher do to help the child learn better?
- What medical problems does the child have that will necessitate changes in the classroom?

- What type of rehabilitation program or special education services does the child need?
- How has the family been affected by the child's condition?
- What services does the family need?

Comment on Diagnostic Techniques

The goal of both the neurological and the neuropsychological examination is to assess brain injury accurately. However, the neurological examination focuses primarily on evaluating lower-level functions (e.g., motor system and reflexes), whereas the neuropsychological examination deals more extensively with evaluating higher-level cognitive processes (e.g., language and memory).

A standard neurological examination—coupled with an EEG and other ancillary diagnostic studies—usually establishes the presence and locus of intracranial disease or damage. Because these procedures are not designed to evaluate functional impairment, they should be supplemented with a neuropsychological examination. A neuropsychological examination can help to confirm a diagnosis of brain injury and define the nature and the severity of defects in higher-level (cognitive) and lower-level (motor and perceptual) brain functions. Thus, a complete assessment of a child with brain injury includes a neurological examination, use of brain-imaging techniques when recommended by a neurologist, and a neuropsychological examination.

We are at the brink of enormous breakthroughs in this area—developmental neurobiology—and there is no longer a boundary between biology, psychology, culture and education.

—Bennett L. Laventhal

ASSESSMENT CONSIDERATIONS

During the neuropsychological evaluation, be alert to the child's language, attention, memory, intellectual and cognitive functioning, emotions, executive functions, rate of information processing, and sensorimotor functioning. Children who have sustained severe head injuries may be difficult to evaluate, especially if their speech is impaired, if they have aphasic disturbances, or if they have not fully regained consciousness. In the latter case, the child is likely to be hospitalized. A child who is confused and disoriented cannot participate fully in a formal assessment and therefore should not be evaluated with standardized tests. Consequently, stage of recovery is important to consider in evaluating the deficits of children with brain injuries. The semi-comatose child observed immediately after a blunt head injury, for example, bears little resemblance to the same child who has had partial recovery of function 2 months after injury.

Some children have *posttraumatic amnesia*—that is, severe memory difficulties for a period of time after the injury.

During this period, the child may not be able to recall whether she or he saw a certain movie or what she or he ate for lunch. Two forms of posttraumatic amnesia are (a) *anterograde amnesia* (inability to remember events that occurred *after* the onset of the disorder) and (b) *retrograde amnesia* (inability to remember events that occurred *before* the onset of the disorder). Posttraumatic amnesia may be categorized on the following continuum, depending on its duration (Jennett & Teasdale, 1981):

1. Very mild—less than 5 minutes
2. Mild—5 to 60 minutes
3. Moderate—1 to 24 hours
4. Severe—1 to 7 days
5. Very severe—1 to 4 weeks
6. Extremely severe—more than 4 weeks

The semistructured interview for older school-aged children in Table B-1 in Appendix B is useful for interviewing children with brain injuries. It will help you determine what the child sees as the problem, the child's understanding of the onset and progression of the problem, when the child first noticed the problem, how the problem developed, what aggravates and diminishes the problem, and what type of help has been received.

You also may want to conduct a mental status interview (see Table B-2 in Appendix B) to determine the child's general orientation to time, place, and person; ability to concentrate; alertness; ability to perform simple tasks; and ability to draw or write. The following norms, based on a sample of 227 normal children between the ages of 8 and 13 years, may be useful (Iverson, Iverson, & Barton, 1994): (a) 100% knew their name, age, birthday, school, and grade; (b) 88% estimated the time of day within 1 hour of the correct time; (c) 98% knew the day of the week; (d) 97% knew the month; (e) 77% knew the day of the month; and (f) 99% knew the year.

You may want to use the questions in Table B-4 in Appendix B to find out about (a) the accident (if one occurred), (b) specific problem areas often associated with brain injury, and (c) any changes in the child's behavior or relationships since the injury. The questions that focus on the accident will be useful in cases of traumatic brain injury; the other questions will be useful for children with any type of brain injury. Thus, you can use three tables in Appendix B—Tables B-1, B-2, and B-4—to interview children with brain injuries. Although it may be difficult to evaluate children younger than 8 or 9 years with brain injuries, you can ask some general orientation questions and questions designed to elicit how they are feeling about and coping with the brain injury.

Assessment of children with brain injuries needs to focus on interpersonal skills and social judgment, as well as on cognitive, academic, and behavioral skills. Problems with impulse control and self-monitoring—areas that represent executive functioning—may be responsible for some of the interpersonal and social difficulties characteristic of children with brain injuries (Papero, Prigatano, Snyder, & Johnson, 1993).

Establishing Rapport

Before beginning the evaluation, arrange to have a quiet room and reduce all potential sources of distraction. Some children respond to the test questions without difficulty, whereas others are fearful, reticent, or emotionally labile, becoming easily aroused and shifting quickly from one emotion to another. They may also *perseverate* (persistently repeat the same thought or response), display inappropriate anger and hostility, withdraw from the situation, or give irrelevant responses, such as saying "I go to school" when asked to give their home address. Such behavior often is not under their willful control; rather, it reflects the effects of the brain injury. Still, these behaviors need to be reported, evaluated, and interpreted.

Seemingly irrelevant or disconnected responses may in fact be meaningful to the child. For example, a child may say "George Washington" in response to a query about whether he or she likes school if George Washington is the name of the child's school. In this case, consider the response as tangential rather than irrelevant.

If the child is anxious about the evaluation, deal with her or his anxieties *before* you begin the formal evaluation. You can do this, for example, by working together on simple gamelike materials; by increasing your use of praise, encouragement, and constructive comments; by keeping interview questions simple; and by beginning the assessment with relatively easy tasks to help the child experience initial successes.

Occasionally, a child may take a long time to answer a question. He or she may sit quietly or make a tentative, hesitant response. In such cases, do not pressure the child; allow the child to proceed at his or her own pace. However, when the delay is excessive (say, over 30 seconds), repeat the question or instructions because the child may not remember what you said. If the child does not answer an important question, ask it again later in the examination, perhaps rephrasing it in a simpler form.

You need to be especially attentive to the reactions of children with brain injuries in order to minimize their frustration and fatigue. When they seem to be frustrated or fatigued, change the pace or content of the assessment, take a break, and make supportive comments. If necessary, schedule another session.

Other Techniques for Working with Children with Brain Injuries

Experiment with different communication methods, rates of communication, and types of content to find the most effective way to communicate. Here are some helpful guidelines (DePompei, Blosser, & Zarski, 1989; Lubinski, 1981):

1. Face the child when speaking with her or him. Eye contact promotes attention and helps the child take advantage of nonverbal cues.

2. Alert the child that communication is about to occur. For example, say the child's name and a few words of greeting before introducing a topic, question, or instruction.

3. Speak slowly and clearly.

4. Introduce questions slowly and casually.

5. Avoid sudden movements or noises.

6. Talk about concrete topics, such as objects and people in the immediate environment.

7. Keep related topics together; do not jump from topic to topic.

8. Use short, grammatically correct, complete sentences.

9. Pause between comments to give the child time to comprehend and interpret the message.

10. Verify that the child understood your communication before proceeding. You might ask a question based on the information presented or have the child show her or his understanding of the information by pointing to an object or a picture.

11. Repeat important ideas several ways; redundancy helps comprehension.

12. Use nonverbal cues to augment spoken communication.

13. Ask questions that require short responses or pointing responses.

14. Allow the child to use any means to communicate, including speaking, writing, typing, using a computer or another augmentative communication device, pointing to letters, signing, or gesturing. Before the evaluation begins, find out the communication method used by the child.

15. Use a multiple-choice array of responses if needed.

16. Ask the child to repeat an unintelligible word or statement.

17. Encourage the child to express ideas in several ways when communications are not clear. Say, for example, "Tell me about that in another way so I can understand it better" or "Give me an example of...." Occasionally, a child may be able to sing an answer when she or he cannot express it in any other way.

18. Be prepared to discuss communication difficulties openly. However, avoid pointing out any inadequacies in the child's responses. Recognize difficulties and proceed to an easier topic, if possible, or to a nonverbal activity.

19. Redirect the child to the topic at hand if perseveration occurs.

20. Repeat what the child has said at various intervals to help focus the conversation.

21. Recognize that the child may know what she or he wants to say but be unable to say it because of difficulty in recall or in initiating a task or for some other reason.

22. Recognize that the child may have difficulty in generalizing from one situation to another.

23. Recognize that inappropriate language, self-centeredness, and poor personal hygiene, for example, may be related to the brain injury and be difficult for the child to control.

24. Know what nonverbal cues you are giving the child, because the cues may tell the child how you feel about the

effectiveness of her or his communications. Do not show signs of impatience or annoyance. Instead, show that you are interested in and accepting of the child, even though there may be communication difficulties.

25. Stop the evaluation if the emotional lability becomes too severe, and then sit quietly until the child seems ready to continue. Whatever happens, remain calm and take your time.

26. Understand that an in-depth assessment is a lengthy and sometimes tiring process. Therefore, consider several short sessions rather than one long session.

OBSERVATION GUIDELINES

Ideally, you should observe the child in several settings—for example, during the administration of tests, in an interview, and in natural settings across different times of day (see Chapters 1 and 7 in *Assessment of Children: Cognitive Applications* and Chapters 4 and 5 in this book). Observations will give you information about the child's developmental level and capabilities, including language skills, motor skills, social skills, compensatory skills and strategies, temperament, personality, motivation, and interpersonal skills.

INTERVIEWING PARENTS

Interview one or both parents to obtain a detailed clinical and developmental history of the child (see Chapter 2). Table B-6 in Appendix B provides a semistructured interview useful for obtaining an in-depth developmental history. In addition, it will be useful to have a parent complete the Background Questionnaire (see Table A-1 in Appendix A) and the Pediatric Inventory of Neurobehavioral Symptoms (PINS; Roberts & Furuseth, 1997; see Table 19-14 in Chapter 19). If needed, you also can use Table B-5 in Appendix B to obtain information about problem areas.

With minor modifications, you can use the questions in Table B-4 in Appendix B to interview parents about the functioning of their child. You especially want to give parents an opportunity to describe their concerns about the child since the injury, including their concerns about the child's physical status, personality, temperament, behavior, and learning ability. If you ask the child the questions in Table B-4 in Appendix B and then ask the parents the same questions about the child, you can compare the responses.

When you interview the child's parents, recognize that they may not always be objective. They may describe the child's premorbid behavior and ability in an overly favorable light. And they may selectively disclose historical information or fail to disclose the child's problems. This may happen for several reasons. For example, they may have forgotten important details, they may have vague recollections, they may be experiencing emotional distress, or they may be involved in litigation associated with the child's brain injury.

When possible, it is helpful to interview persons outside the immediate family to document the consistency of the history. Again, recognize that friends and others may not be objective for similar reasons.

In the history, pay particular attention to events or signs that have etiological importance for brain injury, including the following:

- Occasions of prolonged high fever, nausea, and vomiting that are not related to common illnesses
- Blurred vision, loss of consciousness, or dilated pupils
- Visual or olfactory hallucinations
- Injuries to the head
- Use of anesthetics during surgery
- Poisoning associated with foods, chemicals, or medications
- Changes in appearance, hygiene, social behavior, temperament, personality, energy level, work habits, or performance of daily routines
- Sudden or progressive declines in cognitive, language, speech, memory, or motor functioning or school performance
- Disruptive, aggressive, or confused behavior that interferes with daily living activities, interpersonal relations, or school performance
- Significant delays in achieving developmental milestones
- Unexplained instability, irritability, or lethargy

Sudden and inadequately explained changes in behavior are likely to be associated with acute, as opposed to chronic, brain disorders. Also recognize that many of the above symptoms (e.g., prolonged nausea and vomiting and changes in behavior or school performance) that occur without the presence of head trauma may be associated with drug use, depression, or other conditions.

REHABILITATION PROGRAMS

Rehabilitation programs are designed to help children with brain injuries become more independent by increasing their functional and daily living skills. Rehabilitation aims to improve children's general adjustment and help them achieve success in school, in social relationships, and in work. Recognize that children's post-injury behavior is related to the type of brain injury sustained, their pre-injury development, their post-injury environment, and the treatment and rehabilitation program (see Figure 18-3). As noted earlier in the chapter, you usually will be working with a multidisciplinary health care team to develop and carry out the rehabilitation program.

Rehabilitation programs for children with brain injuries should have the following goals:

1. Reducing cognitive confusion by improving attention, concentration, learning, and memory skills and by gradually helping children process information more efficiently
2. Increasing children's awareness of their residual strengths and deficits, helping them accept their limitations, and

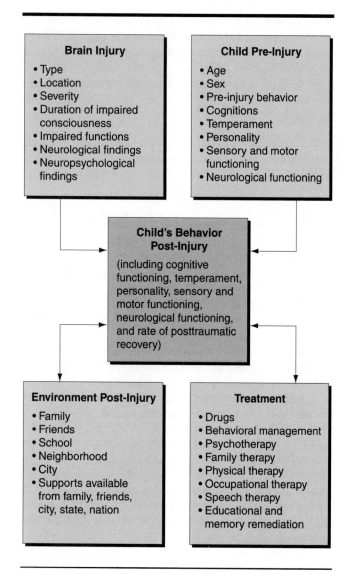

Brain Injury
- Type
- Location
- Severity
- Duration of impaired consciousness
- Impaired functions
- Neurological findings
- Neuropsychological findings

Child Pre-Injury
- Age
- Sex
- Pre-injury behavior
- Cognitions
- Temperament
- Personality
- Sensory and motor functioning
- Neurological functioning

Child's Behavior Post-Injury

(including cognitive functioning, temperament, personality, sensory and motor functioning, neurological functioning, and rate of posttraumatic recovery)

Environment Post-Injury
- Family
- Friends
- School
- Neighborhood
- City
- Supports available from family, friends, city, state, nation

Treatment
- Drugs
- Behavioral management
- Psychotherapy
- Family therapy
- Physical therapy
- Occupational therapy
- Speech therapy
- Educational and memory remediation

Figure 18-3. Factors that may affect the child's post-injury behavior.

teaching them to apply compensatory strategies to solve problems, using their remaining intact functions and learning new skills to compensate for lost or impaired abilities

3. Improving cognitive deficits in children's interpersonal relations by reducing social withdrawal, interpersonal isolation, paranoid ideation, hyperactivity, and emotionality

4. Restoring impaired areas of functioning through application of educational and other intervention procedures, including speech therapy, occupational therapy, and physical therapy

5. Altering the physical environment to help children with physical disabilities become more mobile and independent

6. Creating for children an environment that is highly organized, contains few distracting stimuli, and provides methods of improving their ability to function, such as the use of timers and lists as reminders

7. Helping children gradually make the transition back to their natural environments, where things are less struc-

tured and more demanding, if they are being discharged from a hospital or rehabilitation center

8. Helping family members understand, accept, and learn to cope with their child's disabilities by (a) providing them with information about brain-behavior relationships and the child's assets and limitations and (b) suggesting strategies for handling the increased demands of raising a child with disabilities

The following propositions provide a useful underpinning for rehabilitation efforts in cases of traumatic brain injury (Alfano & Finlayson, 1987; Cicerone & Tupper, 1986; Jacobs, 1993; Milton, 1988):

1. Rehabilitation goals for children with brain injuries should be appropriate to the child's physical and neuropsychological status, as well as his or her specific injury, and be geared to each child's readiness and motivation to reach the goals.

2. Goals may change, depending on the progress made by the child. For example, the initial focus of speech-language therapy may be on structured sensorimotor stimulation and improvement of oral motor skills, whereas later therapy may focus on more practical areas, such as the integration of functional language skills (e.g., using the telephone and developing strategies to cope with residual memory impairments).

3. In setting up a rehabilitation program, consider such factors as (a) the best time to begin the program, (b) whether, once the program is begun, there is a critical period when rehabilitation efforts would be maximally effective, and (c) how improvement on assessment measures relates to improvement in daily living activities.

4. Cognitive functions are differentially affected by traumatic brain injury.

5. Each affected cognitive function may exhibit a different potential for recovery or remediation.

6. Traumatic brain injury may lead to deficits in some areas of functioning, but not in others.

7. The child can be taught to use intact skills and processes to develop compensatory mechanisms, master new strategies, and transfer and generalize skills to new situations and contexts.

8. Strategies used for cognitive remediation may include repetitive vocabulary-like exercises, visual imagery, and development of alternative ways of responding. These strategies are designed to improve minimally functioning skills or establish alternative means of carrying out functions.

9. In carrying out the rehabilitation efforts, consider (a) how much the child will benefit from the training, (b) how explicit the training must be to raise performance, (c) how much additional training the child needs to maintain his or her skills, and (d) how quickly the child acquires skills.

10. In evaluating rehabilitation efforts, consider whether the child can (a) maintain improvement and effectively use problem-solving strategies (e.g., re-use a strategy that

formerly was effective in solving the same problem), (b) transfer the learning to a related task (e.g., use the same strategy on a different but related problem), and (c) generalize the new knowledge to new situations (e.g., use strategies in situations that differ from the ones encountered in training).

11. Some rehabilitation goals may be difficult to achieve because children with acquired brain injury may have limited understanding of their condition. They may be poorly informed about (a) basic brain functioning, (b) how their injuries were sustained, (c) how their problems developed, and (d) how their injuries affect their cognitive processes and social interactions. They may show confusion about the passage of time, and they may believe that their difficulties are primarily physical.

12. To make sense of their injury, children may hold contradictory ideas about their normality. For example, a child may recognize that he loses his temper easily, but attribute the behavior to being tired or to the actions of others.

13. Holding contradictory ideas may be a way for children with brain injuries to avoid stigmatization and believe they are like their peers. However, some may avoid participating in activities with their peer group, particularly in adolescence, because they are aware of their deficits.

Effects of Alcohol on Rehabilitation Efforts

Consumption of alcohol can complicate both physical and cognitive recovery from a brain injury (Miller, 1989). Adolescents admitted to hospitals with a positive blood alcohol level have lower levels of consciousness, remain in a coma longer, and have longer hospital stays than those who have not consumed alcohol. In addition, excessive blood alcohol can lead to fluid and electrolyte abnormalities that exacerbate cerebral edema. Excessive alcohol has other effects, such as altering blood-clotting mechanisms and increasing the risk of brain hypoxia, respiratory depression, and infection.

Chronic abuse of alcohol can produce cognitive deficits that interact with those produced by the traumatic brain injury. This interaction may interfere with the recovery process. Adolescents who have a history of alcohol abuse may be less able to compensate for the effects of a head injury and may have fewer intact abilities to assist in their rehabilitation than those without such a history. Perhaps even more important is their increased potential for resuming the abuse of alcohol and illegal drugs because of the stresses inherent in coping with a brain injury. Obviously, drug and alcohol abuse will interfere with the effectiveness of any rehabilitation and recovery program.

Designing a Rehabilitation Program

The rehabilitation program should be based on the results of the assessment. In addition, you will need to consider such factors as the following:

1. *Length of time since injury.* Consider the length of time between the injury and the start of the rehabilitation ef-

fort. Neuropsychological deficits usually are most prominent during the first 6 months after a head injury. Although most of the recovery occurs within the first 12 to 18 months after the brain injury, subtle changes may still occur several years after the injury, and changes in temperament and personality may persist even after recovery of neurological functions.

2. *Differential rate of improvement in cognitive, motor, affective, and interpersonal areas.* Remember that different neuropsychological functions improve at different rates; therefore, do not generalize from one area to another.

3. *Need for re-examination.* Consider recommending relatively frequent neuropsychological re-examinations to chart progress and changes. However, interpretation of changes may be complicated by practice effects, especially when alternative forms of neuropsychological tests are not available. If a child improves on repeated testing, it will be difficult to determine whether the improvement is because of practice or because of actual improvement in skills (see Chapter 4 in *Assessment of Children: Cognitive Applications*).

The following example shows how cognitive-behavioral deficits can interfere with activities of daily living and why it may be necessary to focus on each step of the retraining activity (Kay & Silver, 1989).

The child with a brain injury is likely to have the physical ability to perform activities of daily living. The child is able to pick up a toothbrush, squeeze the toothpaste tube, execute the requisite motor movements, rinse, and put things away; yet, the spontaneous integrated sequencing of these activities into a smooth continuity from beginning to end may not be possible. The toothbrush cannot be located. Enormous amounts of toothpaste are squeezed out; the behavior is not terminated at the appropriate point. Brushing is done in a cursory, repetitive, incomplete fashion. Rinsing is forgotten. The brush and toothpaste are left on the sink. And even if brushing one's teeth can be carried out in a reasonable fashion, it does not occur to the child to do so each morning unless prompted. When questioned, the child dutifully reports having brushed, with possibly no recollection of (or concern for) whether the activity was actually performed that day or not. (adapted from p. 146)

Now let's look at examples of specific difficulties encountered during interventions, together with suggestions for handling these difficulties (Blosser & DePompei, 1989; Deaton, 1987).

1. *Child does not understand the task demands.* Provide clear, concrete instructions, or do the task yourself to show the child how it should be done.

2. *Child does not begin the task.* Give the child prompts, and reinforce each instance of initiative that the child shows, however minor.

3. *Child is unable to do the task.* Simplify the task, and provide training for the child in the underlying skills required for successful performance. Teach each step of the task separately, and use "reverse chaining" to integrate the steps one at a time, beginning with the last step and working toward the first.

4. *Child of preschool or elementary age cannot find the right words to express herself or himself.* Use structured play and manipulative activities to help the child develop concrete

verbal strategies to compensate for any word retrieval difficulties.

5. *Child of adolescent age cannot find the right words to express herself or himself.* Teach the adolescent to understand and appraise the effects of her or his deficits, involve the adolescent actively in the design of the treatment plan, and focus efforts on realistic goals. Adolescents with mild traumatic brain injuries who can read and comprehend material will likely benefit from reading the treatment manual authored by Mittenberg, Zielinski, and Fichera (1993).

6. *Child is not motivated.* Make the task more interesting, and give the child rewards when she or he completes the task.

7. *Child tries to avoid failure by not complying with the task instructions.* Alternate difficult tasks with easy and enjoyable tasks, and provide tasks at which the child may succeed.

8. *Child avoids doing a task by complaining.* Inform the child that she or he must complete the task before she or he can go on to other activities. Also inform the child that she or he can take as much time as needed to complete the task.

9. *Child receives attention for not doing a task.* Use a time-out procedure when the child is noncompliant, or ignore the child's behavior. Reinforce the child with attention for cooperation. Reinforce other children in the room for their cooperation.

10. *Child is careless about safety.* Set firm limits on the child's behavior. Establish specific rules for behavior in certain places and at certain times of the day. Work with the child on the activity before allowing her or him to do it independently.

11. *Child argues and fights with peers on the playground.* Set firm limits on the child's behavior. Select a buddy with whom the child gets along. Encourage the buddy to be with the child with the brain injury during recess. Work with the child with the brain injury in small groups to encourage sharing.

12. *Child forgets to do homework.* Develop with the child a daily written assignment sheet indicating dates and times that assignments are due.

The following rehabilitation program was designed to help children with brain injuries who have a limited attention span (Wilson, 1991). The program uses principles of behavioral treatment, including reinforcement and feedback, and may be implemented by a teacher, an occupational therapist, or other rehabilitation personnel, often in consultation with a psychologist. With proper supervision and support, parents can also assist in carrying out this program.

1. Ask the teacher/clinician to identify tasks that the child can manage on his or her own, such as looking at picture books or baseball or football cards, sorting colors, listening to audiotapes, or coloring in a coloring book.

2. Ask the teacher/clinician to identify tasks that the child has difficulty managing, such as completing a simple puzzle or printing his or her name and address.

3. Have the child work for at least 30 seconds on a task that can be managed on his or her own. Sound a timer after 30 seconds to let the child know that he or she was successful in reaching the goal.

4. Increase the interval by 5 seconds every time the child succeeds in reaching the goal.

5. Each time the child achieves the goal, praise the child, give the child feedback, allow the child to get up and walk around for up to 3 minutes, and encourage the child to appraise his or her progress by putting a sticker on a wall chart (see Number 9).

6. Once the child can work on his or her own for 5 to 15 minutes, alternate the original task with more difficult ones. Use shorter intervals for a younger child.

7. Have the child work on the more difficult tasks for about 2 to 3 minutes at a time.

8. Teach the child the more difficult tasks one step at a time, using prompts, demonstrations, and reinforcement.

9. Monitor the child's progress with record sheets or wall charts. Record (a) the date and time of the session, (b) the duration of the interval set for each session, (c) the child's successes and failures, and (d) incidents of appropriate and inappropriate behavior. Show the child what you have recorded, and encourage the child to help record his or her progress.

> *"...because life after head injury may never be the same."*
> —New York State Head Injury Association

Rehabilitation Programs in School Settings

When children with traumatic brain injuries return to school, they may have processing difficulties, memory difficulties, emotional difficulties, and physical difficulties. Here are some examples of these difficulties and symptoms that they may have in school (Roberts, 1999):

Difficulties

- Difficulty taking notes because the lectures go too fast
- Difficulty catching on to new concepts and newly presented information
- Difficulty finishing assignments or tests on time
- Difficulty beginning and completing projects
- Difficulty coping with changes in the daily schedule
- Difficulty performing tasks that have multiple components
- Difficulty retrieving previously learned facts
- Difficulty giving detailed and meaningful responses to questions
- Difficulty maintaining friendships or the give-and-take of conversations with peers

Symptoms

- Brief staring spells
- Unexplained emotional outbursts
- Headaches
- Feelings of irritability in noisy environments

- Feelings of being confused by "too much going on at once"
- Feeling distressed by word-finding difficulties
- Feeling distressed about taking too long to process information

You will also need to work with school personnel to meet the rehabilitation goals. Recognize that particularly in cases of mild traumatic brain injury, teachers, peers, and school personnel may fail to understand or believe the magnitude of the student's struggles (Roberts, 1999). Help them understand that such symptoms as memory deficits, staring spells, and emotional outbursts are not a result of poor motivation or attention problems and do not require disciplinary action. Even "the student him-herself may be unable to account for recent onset memory deficits, word-finding problems, and periodic confusion, further exacerbating the frustration encountered" (Roberts, 1999, p. 505). Before the child returns to her or his classroom, visit the classroom and decide, in consultation with the school staff, what modifications are needed to facilitate the child's learning and adjustment. (Chapter 4 presents useful guidelines for observing the classroom.) Finally, help the teacher carry out appropriate strategies for (a) modifying, eliminating, and reducing barriers to learning, (b) reintegrating the child in the classroom, and (c) establishing objectives. Review the child's educational placement periodically, especially during the early stages of recovery, because her or his needs are likely to change (Savage & Carter, 1988).

Exhibit 18-2 describes 11 strategies that teachers can use to help children with brain injuries function better in school. These strategies focus on involvement, structure, adequate presentation, flexibility, consistency, repetition, specificity, practicality, reward, meaningfulness, and communication.

Exercise 18-2.
Evaluating a School's Understanding of a Child with a Brain Injury

Read the following case, answer the questions that follow, and then compare your answers with those in the Suggested Answers section. The material in this exercise was adapted from Savage (1987).

James was 15 years old when he sustained a closed-head injury from a motorcycle accident. He was comatose for 6 days and suffered injury to the right frontal and temporal lobe areas of his brain. After 36 days in the regional medical center, James returned home while still experiencing problems in attention, memory, impulsiveness, and appropriate social and personal behaviors.

Upon reentering school 44 days after his accident, James, who had previously been a "C" to "B" student, was unable to keep up in his previous academic subjects, failed to complete homework assignments, and started to act out aggressively in class. His friends soon began to avoid him because of his weird actions. After an extremely violent fight with a younger student, James was suspended from school for 10 days. Following the suspension period, a special education resource specialist tested James and found that his academic skills were 4 years below grade level and that his emotional stability was below the norm for his age group. Because he looked good to his teachers, they could not see any reason for his inability to keep up with his school work, if he would only just try harder.

The school's staffing team, consisting of a special educator, his primary room teacher, and the assistant principal, decided to place James in a classroom for emotionally impaired students within the school's special education program. However, James continued his outbursts and aggressive acts to the point where residential placement in a school for emotionally disturbed adolescents was initiated. After 2 weeks in the residential school, James attempted suicide with a drug overdose.

1. After James left the hospital, what plans were made for his rehabilitation or for his return to school?
2. How was the school prepared to cope with James's return?
3. How did James perform when he first reentered school?
4. Did placement in a class for emotionally disturbed children meet James's needs?
5. Assuming the basic staffing team was inadequate, who was needed on the team?
6. What were some possible reasons for James's poor school performance?
7. How did the school treat James's aggressive and impulsive behavior?
8. How should the school have treated James?

Suggested Answers
1. As far as can be determined from the case study, no plans were made for James's rehabilitation or for his return to school.
2. As far as can be determined, the school staff was not familiar with children who have traumatic brain injuries and the resulting possible cognitive-behavioral disorders.
3. James could not meet the requirements of a regular classroom. Both his academic work and his social functioning were seriously impaired.
4. No.
5. Besides the three educators, the staffing team should have had, ideally, other teachers, James's parents, the school nurse, the school psychologist, the school counselor, the social worker from the hospital medical team (or a school social worker), the speech and language therapist, and the vocational rehabilitation counselor. Also, a neuropsychologist trained in rehabilitation should have been consulted and asked to serve on the team.
6. His failure to perform well in school may have been associated with difficulty in integrating new learning with previous learning, memory and organizational problems, language disabilities, concentration difficulties, inappropriate psychosocial behaviors, and fatigue. Because of his right frontal and temporal lobe injuries, he may have had difficulty in organization, in developing study habits, and in controlling his impulsiveness and emotions.
7. The school failed to recognize that James's higher-level functions were impaired. They treated his actions as intentional misbehavior rather than as inappropriate behavioral sequelae of his head injury; therefore, the school used a

traditional discipline model and suspended him from school.

8. The school should have begun a special program that considered his cognitive impairments and behavioral difficulties. Such a program would include structured cuing to initiate tasks and to complete assignments, a reduced course load, a shorter day, work with a resource specialist, and provision of a peer tutor.

Families' Role in a Rehabilitation Program

The recovery of a child with a brain injury depends, in part, on family support and on the family's ability to manage the child's day-to-day problems. You will need to evaluate how the family members function and assess their ability to care for the physical, emotional, and behavioral needs of the child. You should also evaluate their communication patterns, cohesion, adaptability, and adjustment (e.g., whether

---

Exhibit 18-2
Strategies to Help Teachers Work with Children with Brain Injuries

Involvement

Involve children with brain injuries directly in the program to increase their motivation, interest, and self-control; doing so will help them reduce their stress level. When feasible, allow them to decide which activities to work on, how much time they want to spend on an activity, whether they want to share the products of their work with others, where they would like to do the activity, and so forth. Encourage them to reduce their course load in school if the work becomes overwhelming. Find ways to help them calm down when they are frustrated, such as by giving them extra time to respond or by having them take a deep breath. Avoid having them perform in front of the class, unless they want to do so. Plan many small-group activities to facilitate learning of appropriate interaction skills. Select classroom buddies to keep children with brain injuries aware of instructions, transitions, and assignments. Plan extracurricular activities tailored to the children's physical and emotional capabilities and their interests.

Structure

Carefully structure the environment for children with brain injuries, especially in the early stages of recovery, to reduce confusion. They may be confused about where to start in solving a problem, have difficulty ordering or sequencing information, and be unsure about when, where, and how to ask for help. Insufficient structure is probably the most common reason for failure of intervention plans. Children with brain injuries typically do not do well with nebulous situations; it is better to overstructure than to understructure the program in the early stages of recovery. Avoid overstimulation or overloading the children with information, and keep the immediate environment understandable. Structure the physical environment of the classroom to decrease distractions and permit ease of movement by carefully planning seating and furniture arrangements. Help children identify when the environment is distracting (e.g., too stimulating or confusing), and aid them in doing something about the situation. Children with brain injuries may become confused when confronted with changes in activities. Help them formulate and use a system for maintaining organization. Require them to carry a written log of activities, a schedule of classes, a list of assignments and their due dates, and a list of room locations. Encourage children with brain injuries to use a self-monitoring system (see Chapter 5). Frequently monitor their use of the organizational system.

Adequate Presentation

A careful presentation of information will help children with brain injuries deal with their various problems in the areas of attention, processing information (e.g., poor language comprehension when information is given too quickly or difficulty handling multiple bits of information at one time), tangential thought and speech (e.g., problems in word selection, loose connection of thought and ideas, impaired abstract thinking, and straying from the core message or topic), staying on task, and comprehension. In presenting information, observe the following guidelines:

- Take base-line measures of the child's performance in the areas of interest.
- Slow down the pace at which you present information. Use pauses when giving classroom instructions, to allow the child time to process the information.
- Present information in a controlled and manageable fashion, and space learning over time.
- Determine the optimum rate and level of reception of information for the child.
- Provide clear, concrete instructions. Clarify verbal and written instructions by (a) accompanying verbal instructions with written instructions, (b) repeating instructions and redefining words and terms, and (c) alerting the child to the important topic or concept being taught ("I'm going to tell a story and then we'll discuss where it takes place").
- Keep the child's choices to a minimum.
- Use orientation and memory cues liberally.
- Break complex behaviors down into small, well-defined steps to reduce confusion and to help the child compensate for organizational and memory deficits.
- Simplify communicative interactions. Avoid figurative, idiomatic, ambiguous, ironic, and sarcastic language when presenting lessons (e.g., "You're a handful").
- Increase communication activities gradually and systematically.
- Guide the child to listen for specific information in sentences or paragraphs, and gradually increase the amount of information to be processed.
- Focus on activities that the child has a chance of completing successfully, that are neither too easy nor too boring, and that the child likes.

(Continued)

Exhibit 18-2 *(Continued)*

- Keep assignments to a reasonable level, fitted to the child's ability.
- Use frequent rest periods, select simple tasks, present tasks one at a time, and be prepared for delays in the child's responses.
- Use multimodal cuing (i.e., more than one sensory modality), as needed, to help the child learn and consolidate new information.
- Establish, if needed, a system of verbal or nonverbal signals to cue the student to attend, respond, or alter behavior. Examples include calling the child's name, touching the child's shoulder (if touching is comfortable for the child), using written signs, and using hand signals.
- Develop resources to accompany textbook assignments. For example, use pictures and written cues to illustrate important information and concepts. Assign review questions at the end of the chapter. Write new vocabulary. Present a summary of the chapter on audiotape or on paper. Go over errors made on tests to let the child know where and why errors occurred.
- Select times of the day at which the child will be most alert, keep distractions to a minimum, and limit the length of the sessions to keep the child from becoming too fatigued.
- Allow as much time as needed for the child to complete tasks.

Flexibility
Permit the child with a brain injury to use devices such as calculators, tape recorders, computers, and other augmentative communication devices. Allow a child who cannot write to use a typewriter, computer, plastic magnetic letters, or other types of letters, or allow the child to ask a classmate to write for him or her. Modify and individualize the child's assignments and tests to accommodate his or her special needs. Examples of modifications include reducing the number of questions to be answered or the amount of material to be read, enlarging printed matter, and permitting the child to tape-record lectures or his or her responses to test questions. Change the format of tasks—for example, allow additional time to complete assignments, give homework assignments in written form to the child who has difficulty with oral comprehension, use oral presentations for the child with a visual impairment or a visual processing problem, and duplicate class notes for the child who cannot take notes rapidly. Reduce stressful experiences, such as pop quizzes.

Consistency
Have the child with a brain injury do the same tasks at the same time each day with the same people to establish a familiar routine. Consistent scheduling helps make the world predictable and reduces confusion and agitation caused by changes in the environment. Provide the child with advance notice when schedule changes (e.g., special assemblies) are to occur.

Repetition
Use repetition and drilling on important tasks because children with brain injuries usually have attention deficits and difficulties with recent memory. Repetition and drilling will help children with brain injuries consolidate previously learned material. However, do not overdo the amount of repetition. Privately ask the child to repeat information or answer a few key questions to be sure that he or she understood important information presented. Take care, however, not to cause stress in the child who has difficulty responding to direct questions.

Specificity
Focus your intervention program on specific goals relevant for a particular child. Because the child with a brain injury will usually have difficulty mastering generalized problem-solving strategies, focus on the exact behavior that you want in the exact situation in which it will be performed. Do not depend on the child with a brain injury to generalize from one learning situation to another. The child may have problems connecting previously learned and new information or seeing patterns in the information presented.

Practicality
Select goals for rehabilitation that will meet the basic needs of the child with a brain injury, will be pragmatic and comprehensible to the child, and will be relevant to the long-term outcome goals.

Reward
Use positive reinforcement to increase desired behavior from children with brain injuries; however, make sure that the rewards are appropriate. Reinforce children for cooperation. You are likely to increase motivation and foster independence by establishing a caring, nurturing environment.

Meaningfulness
Set goals that are meaningful to children, their families, and the staff. Children with brain injuries probably will try harder to achieve goals pertinent to their needs when they have support from their families and the staff. They need to recognize that their abilities may have changed, and they should be encouraged to participate in new programs that may help them overcome some of their limitations.

Communication
Clarify for the family the goals you are attempting to reach and the methods you are using. Update the family about their child's progress and problems. Monitor the progress of the child closely so that revisions in the curriculum or the rehabilitation plan can be made as improvements in functioning occur. Make sure that knowledgeable staff members are available to answer the family's questions. Whenever possible, directly involve the family in the rehabilitation program.

Source: Adapted from Cohen (1991); DePompei and Blosser (1987); Howard (1988); Martin (1988); Prigatano et al. (1986); Roberts (1999); and Ylvisaker (1986).

the family has a history of accidents, domestic violence, psychiatric disturbances, substance abuse, or child maltreatment). A family that was dysfunctional before the injury is likely to have a more difficult time coping with a child's injuries than is a family that was not dysfunctional. (See Sattler, 1998, for ways to assess family functioning.)

When a child sustains a brain injury, family patterns may change. There may be disruption of family relationships, shifting of social roles and responsibilities within the family, and adjustment problems among family members. Sometimes, latent family strengths or weaknesses come to the surface.

The degree of physical disability of children with brain injuries typically is *not* the crucial factor causing stress in families; rather, the behavioral, cognitive, and affective deficits that accompany the injury often are the most distressing factors. Families may be concerned about the children's irritability, inattentiveness, difficulties with social interaction, violence, aggression, immaturity, and dependency—characteristics that, in turn, are likely to diminish family harmony. Overall, families of children who sustain severe traumatic brain injury experience more stress than do families of children who sustain moderate traumatic brain injury (Wade, Taylor, Drotar, Stancin, & Yeates, 1998).

Family stressors.   Families of children with traumatic brain injuries confront several types of stressors, including the following:

1. Coping with the shock (in cases of sudden onset) of a traumatic brain injury to their child
2. Facing uncertainty about their child's degree of recovery
3. Coping with dramatic changes in their child's cognitive abilities, personality, and temperament—such as diminished memory, problems with decision making, mood swings, limited motivation, and decreased academic performance
4. Coping with their child's increased dependency and the constant struggle with dependence/independence issues
5. Coping with their child's symptoms—such as flashbacks, sleeping difficulties, anxiety reactions—associated with a possible posttraumatic stress disorder
6. Facing the dilemma of wanting to foster their child's independence and speedy recovery, yet also wanting to provide control and structure to maintain their child's safety
7. Coping with siblings' possible jealousy, resentment about increased responsibilities, or anger at having a changed family structure (e.g., they may not be able to bring friends home or participate in activities because the parents must take care of the sibling with a brain injury)
8. Working through possible feelings of blame or guilt and personal responsibility for their child's injury
9. Working through grief reactions associated with loss of a normal life for their child
10. Working out possible disagreements or misunderstandings with professionals about what actions to take to help their child

11. Coping with the financial, time, and energy demands of a long-term rehabilitation program
12. Facing the possibility that the community has poor rehabilitation and educational programs
13. Facing the possibility that their child may need to be placed in a long-term residential care facility

> *The uninjured sibling can become a potent source of help and support for the patient, or a target for clinical intervention [because of the stress of dealing with the patient]. It is the responsibility of the rehabilitation team to ensure that the former happens and not the latter.*
>
> —D. Neil Brooks

Suggestions for working with families.   Helping families of children with brain injuries may take years, not just weeks or months (Brooks, 1991). Rehabilitation is best conceived of as a process involving three stages:

1. *Stage of acute crisis.* Your goal is to help family members accept information about their child. If they are in a state of shock, despair, or denial, they may not listen or understand what they hear. Gauge their ability to receive and understand the information, and, if necessary, delay the discussion until they appear able to listen.

2. *Stage of prolonged rehabilitation.* Families need information to help them make realistic plans. When possible, involve them in the treatment decisions.

3. *Stage of disengagement.* Families need to disengage from active professional intervention, but maintain access to professional help for crises and guidance.

Following are suggestions for helping families of children with brain injuries (DePompei, Zarski, & Hall, 1988; Lezak, 1978; Miller, 1993; Rollin, 1987; Sachs, 1991).

EDUCATION

1. Give the family accurate information about the nature of the trauma, the strengths and weaknesses of their child, the types of problems their child may display, and the possible prognosis. Be sure that the information you give is consistent with that provided by other members of the health care team.
2. Explain that there may be advances and setbacks during recovery.
3. Explain why their child may have behavioral problems during the recovery period, and explain the relationship between behavioral problems and their child's brain injury.
4. Explain the principles of behavioral interventions that they will need to use.

COGNITIVE AND BEHAVIORAL LIMITATIONS

1. Encourage the family to (a) learn to read the nonverbal cues their child gives when he or she wants to speak, (b) regain

the conversational lead if their child does not relinquish it, and (c) return their child to the topic of conversation.

2. Encourage the family to (a) allow their child to communicate on his or her own, (b) wait out conversational pauses with patience, and (c) use cues to assist, but not to speak *for,* their child.

3. Encourage the family to allow their child a choice about participation in social activities and to recognize that their child's behavior is not intended to embarrass them.

4. Encourage the family to (a) read behavioral signs that their child is reaching his or her frustration level, (b) recognize that their child's outbursts are not deliberate, and (c) decrease stimulation in their child's environment.

5. Encourage the family to allow their child to share thoughts and feelings with them at his or her own pace.

6. Encourage the family to focus on the remaining strengths of their child, and help them accept that their child may not be able to do things that he or she did before the injury.

PROBLEM SOLVING

1. Identify the child's problems and the possible effects of the problems on the family.

2. Help the family become involved in the education and treatment of their child.

3. Help the family establish goals consistent with their child's potential and with their own values and expectations.

4. Encourage the family to allow their child to become independent, as much as this is possible.

5. Encourage the family to allow their child to progress at her or his own pace.

6. Elicit from the family their suggestions for positive reinforcers that can be used with their child.

7. Help the family adjust to their child and to their changed roles.

8. Encourage the family to approach seemingly insurmountable problems that they are having with their child by breaking the problems into manageable parts and by rehearsing and role-playing potentially stressful activities with their child.

9. Help the family resolve their own differences over how to handle their child's problems.

SUPPORT

1. Help the family work through their grief, anxiety, guilt, depression, and sense of hopelessness. They need to recognize that anger, frustration, and sorrow are natural emotions under the circumstances.

2. Help the family become organized and focused on the tasks needed to help their child.

3. Enhance the parents' self-esteem by pointing out that they have control over their own lives. Recognize, however, that this will be difficult to accomplish if their child's behavior is extremely difficult to manage.

4. Help the family develop realistic expectations about the length of time needed for their child to show improvements.

5. Support the parents' efforts to set limits on their child's behavior.

6. Encourage the parents to continue to pursue activities that they enjoy; they must take care of themselves if they are going to provide their child with good care. They will need to find respite care so that they can have some time alone, with each other, and with other family members.

7. Help the family accept their child at the level at which he or she is functioning.

8. Recognize that some parents may resist your efforts to foster independence in their child. Caring for a child with a disability may give their lives added purpose. In such cases, you will need to work even harder to assist the parents in carrying out the rehabilitation program.

9. Recommend that the parents seek drop-in counseling; brief, limited therapy to work through specific problems; support groups; parent training; or family therapy, as needed. Provide telephone numbers and addresses of local services.

10. Help the family contact appropriate agencies.

Comment on Rehabilitation Programs

Rehabilitation efforts should be monitored closely to determine children's progress and to ensure that programs are not creating undue stress on them or their families. If the rehabilitation goals are met, children will be better able to cope with the brain injury and improve the quality of their lives. Improved functioning would include having a more positive attitude toward school, achieving better grades in school, carrying out assignments with minimal help, participating in extracurricular activities, resuming and maintaining friendships, being cooperative and dependable, and assuming increased responsibility at home for personal and household chores. Many children with brain injuries can make significant progress even though they may not become fully independent or regain their former level of skills. Rehabilitation efforts will improve as we learn more about how brain injury affects cognitive, linguistic, affective, and behavioral processes. Table 18-2 presents definitions of terms associated with brain injury that are referred to in the chapter.

THINKING THROUGH THE ISSUES

1. Do you know a child or an adult who has had a brain injury? If so, what is the child or adult like? In what way has the brain injury affected him or her?

2. Why is it difficult to evaluate aphasic disturbances in young children?

3. What behavioral observations are particularly important when evaluating children with brain injuries?

4. After you completed an evaluation of a child who was referred to you for psychological problems, under what circumstances would you refer the child to a neuropsychologist or to a neurologist?

Table 18-2
Terms Associated with Brain Injury

Acalculia. Impaired ability to perform arithmetical operations.

Acquired aphasia. Language deficit resulting from brain injury following normal language development.

Agrammatism. Omission of connecting and modifying words in speech, giving it a telegraphic quality.

Agraphia. Loss or impairment, associated with brain injury, of the ability to express language in written or printed form.

Alexia. Disturbance of the ability to read or interpret written symbols, despite adequate vision and intelligence; also known as word blindness.

Anomia. Difficulty in naming objects, finding the right word, or recalling names; also known as anomic aphasia or nominal aphasia.

Anosognosia. Failure or refusal to recognize that one has a deficit or a disease.

Anterograde amnesia. Inability to remember events that occur subsequent to some trauma to the brain.

Aphasia. Deficit in the perception, production, and symbolic use of language.

Asphyxia. Lack of oxygen or excess of carbon dioxide in the body. It may lead to unconsciousness, seizures, damage to various sensory systems, and death.

Astereognosis. Form of agnosia thought to be caused by lesions in the central parietal lobe and characterized by an inability to recognize objects or geometric forms by touch.

Auditory agnosia. Impaired ability to identify sounds.

Autotopagnosia. Disturbance in recognition of body parts; also known as body-image agnosia.

Bilateral simultaneous stimulation. A neurological procedure in which both sides of the body are stimulated at the same time.

Bucco-facial apraxia. Impaired ability to perform facial movements in response to commands, although the movements can be executed spontaneously (e.g., to whistle, pucker lips, protrude tongue, cough, sniff).

Cerebral angiography. Procedure involving radiographic recording of internal structures of the vascular system of the brain. A contrast material (e.g., iodinated compound) is injected into the arterial blood system, and its progress is followed via x-rays.

Cerebral edema. Swelling in the cerebrum.

Cerebral plasticity. Ability of the brain to change in various ways to compensate for loss of function caused by brain injury.

Cerebrum. The largest area of the brain, occupying the uppermost part of the skull. It consists of two hemispheres; each hemisphere is further divided into four lobes: frontal, temporal, parietal, and occipital.

Computed tomography (CT). Imaging technique in which an array of detectors is used to collect information from an x-ray beam that has passed through a portion of the brain or another body part. The beam is rotated to produce the equivalent of a "slice" through the area of interest. A computer reconstructs the internal structure from the information collected and displays it on a screen.

Computerized electroencephalography (CEEG). A technique in which a computer is used to collect and analyze data from electroencephalography; also known as quantitative electroencephalography.

Congenital aphasia. Language deficit marked by almost complete failure to acquire language.

Constructional apraxia. Impaired ability to construct objects, manifested, for example, through an inability to construct a pattern with blocks.

Contralateral homonymous hemianopia. Blindness affecting the right halves or the left halves of the visual fields of the two eyes opposite to the location of the brain injury.

Contusion. A bruise. When it occurs on the brain, it can cause tissue damage and bleeding.

Coup. Bruising of brain tissue at the point of impact.

Coup-contrecoup effect. Bruising of brain tissue at the point of impact and then again in an area opposite to the point of impact (contrecoup).

Declarative knowledge. See *Declarative memory*.

Declarative memory. Memory that allows us to describe how to perform actions—for example, to explain to someone how to get to a library or how to operate a VCR; also known as declarative knowledge.

Developmental language disorder. Late development of language in children.

Dichotic listening. A procedure in which both ears are stimulated with distinctly different stimuli.

Disorientation of external environmental space. A tendency to ignore that part of the environment opposite to the cerebral damage.

Dressing apraxia. Impaired ability to dress oneself.

Dysarthria. A disturbance in articulation.

Echoic memory. Short-term auditory memory that allows us to perceive speech sounds.

Electroencephalogram (EEG). Recording of the electrical potentials from the brain, created by placing electrodes on the scalp or in the brain.

Encephalitis. Acute inflammation of the brain or its meninges, resulting from any of a wide variety of infections and toxins; also known as encephalopathy.

Episodic memory. Memory for autobiographical events—that is, events that happened at a particular time.

Expressive aphasia. Inability, caused by brain injury, to remember the pattern of movement required to speak, write, or use signs, even though the individual knows what she or he wants to say; also known as nonfluent aphasia.

Finger agnosia. Inability, usually associated with brain injury, to identify or select the individual fingers of one's own hand or the hands of others.

Fluent aphasia. See *Receptive aphasia*.

Focal. Focused. It is applied to brain injury in a circumscribed area.

Focal head injury. A brain injury in which the skull is usually penetrated by a high-velocity projectile, such as a bullet, and contact occurs between the brain tissue and the outside environment.

Galactosemia. A high blood level of galactose, caused by a genetically related metabolic condition involving lack of an enzyme necessary to metabolize milk and milk products (sources of galactose). Symptoms include mental retardation, jaundice, cataracts, short stature, and poor weight gain.

Global aphasia. Impaired language abilities in both expressive and receptive domains; also known as mixed-type aphasia.

Hard neurological signs. Fairly definitive indicators of cerebral injury, such as abnormalities in reflexes, cranial nerves, and

(Continued)

Table 18-2 *(Continued)*

motor organization, as well as asymmetrical failures in sensory and motor responses.

Higher-level functions. Cognitive processes such as reasoning, thinking, planning, language, reading, and memory.

Homonymous hemianopia. Blindness affecting the right halves or the left halves of the visual fields of the two eyes.

Hydrocephalus. Increased accumulation of fluid within the ventricles of the brain.

Hyperesthesia. Extreme sensitivity to touch.

Hypoglycemia. Low blood sugar, which may cause a person to feel jittery, weak, or sweaty and have a headache, blurred vision, and hunger. If it occurs during the perinatal period, it may lead to brain injury.

Hypothyroidism. A metabolic disorder in which the child has difficulty producing sufficient levels of the thyroid hormone. If untreated, it can cause delays in brain development.

Hypoxia. Deficiency of oxygen reaching the tissues of the body.

Iconic memory. Very short-term, image-like memory.

Ideational apraxia. Impaired ability to execute a series of acts, although the steps can be performed separately.

Ideomotor apraxia. Impaired ability to carry out an action on verbal command, although the action can be performed automatically.

Intermediate memory. See *Primary memory.*

Intracranial hematoma. Collection of blood within the brain or between the brain and the skull.

Kernicterus. Condition with severe neurological symptoms characterized by high levels of bile secretion in the blood, often associated with jaundice.

Limb-kinetic apraxia. Apraxia localized to a single limb, resulting in clumsiness or inability to carry out fine motor acts with the affected limb.

Loss of right-left discrimination. Inability to determine which side of the body is being touched.

Loss of two-point discrimination. Inability to determine by feeling whether the skin is being touched at one point or at two points simultaneously.

Lower-level functions. Basic biological processes such as motor system functions and reflexes.

Magnetic resonance imaging (MRI). Diagnostic tool that provides a two-dimensional intensity plot of a cross-sectional slice of any part of the body. The plot is an image of the anatomy at the cross section.

Meningitis. An infection that causes acute inflammation of the membranes covering the brain and spinal cord and is characterized by drowsiness, confusion, irritability, and sensory impairments.

Mixed-type aphasia. See *Global aphasia.*

Myelination. Process of insulating, or coating, the axon of a neuron with myelin

Neologistic paraphasia. The production of a nonsense word or words, such as "tilto" for "table," usually without recognition of the error.

Niemann-Pick disease. A hereditary disorder in which a deficiency of a specific enzyme results in the accumulation of sphingomyelin, a product of fat metabolism. It may cause mental retardation, anemia, dark pigmentation of the skin, and enlarged liver, spleen, and lymph nodes.

Nonfluent aphasia. See *Expressive aphasia.*

Paragrammatism. Incorrect use of verbs, clauses, or prepositional phrases.

Paresthesia. Abnormal sensation involving tingling, crawling, or burning of the skin.

Perseveration. Persistent repetition of the same thought or response.

Phenylketonuria (PKU). Chromosomal abnormality that arises from a recessive gene coming from both parents and causes a child to be unable to metabolize the protein phenylalanine. Untreated, it results in severe mental retardation; it also may cause convulsions, behavioral problems, severe skin rash, and a musty odor of the body and urine.

Phonemic paraphasia. Recognizable mispronunciation of a word in which sounds or syllables are out of sequence—for example, "psghetti" for "spaghetti."

Phonosemantic blend. Phonemic sound substitution in the target word that creates another real word, related in sound but not in meaning, such as "cable" for "table" or "television" for "telephone."

Positron emission tomography (PET). Scanning procedure that produces a cross-sectional image of cellular activity or blood flow in the brain, following intravenous injection of a radioactive substance.

Premorbid level. Level at which an individual was functioning before the brain injury.

Prenatal environmental factors. Environmental factors existing or occurring before birth.

Primary memory. Temporary memory for holding information during learning, reading, reasoning, or thinking; also known as intermediate memory.

Procedural knowledge. See *Procedural memory.*

Procedural memory. Memory that allows us to perform an action, such as going to the library, riding a bicycle, or operating a device; also known as procedural knowledge.

Prosopagnosia. Impaired ability to recognize familiar faces.

Prospective memory. Memory that one needs to do something at a later point in time.

Quantitative electroencephalograhy. See *Computerized electroencephalography.*

Receptive aphasia. Impaired ability to understand spoken and/or written language; also known as fluent aphasia.

Retrograde amnesia. Inability to remember events that occurred prior to the trauma or disease that caused the amnesia.

Rh incompatibility. Condition in which the mother has Rh-negative blood and the fetus has Rh-positive blood. When blood from the fetus mixes in the placenta with the mother's blood, antibodies may be produced that will destroy the red blood cells of the fetus in subsequent pregnancies. If this condition is not treated, it can cause pathologies such as jaundice, anemia, or mental retardation.

Semantic memory. Memory for information not associated with a time sequence, such as the name of the president of the country, a telephone number, or the population of a city.

Semantic paraphasia. See *Verbal paraphasia.*

Shearing. Tearing of nerve fibers in the brain at the microscopic level because of movement of the brain during a head injury.

Single photon emission computed tomography (SPECT). Scanning procedure that provides a three-dimensional representation of regional cerebral blood flow. It brings together

(Continued)

Table 18-2 *(Continued)*

tomographic techniques for imaging brain structure with methods for measuring brain blood flow.

Soft neurological signs. Mild and equivocal neurological irregularities in primarily sensorimotor functions.

Tactile agnosia. Impaired ability to identify, without looking, familiar objects placed in the hand.

Tay-Sachs disease. A disorder of lipoid metabolism, caused by a recessive gene, that results in a progressive degenerative disease characterized by severe mental retardation, seizures, paralysis, and death.

Verbal memory. Memory for verbal terms, such as words and sentences.

Verbal paraphasia. The unintended use of another word in lieu of the target word (e.g., "I went to the store...no, the school");

also known as semantic paraphasia. For an error to be classified as a verbal paraphasia, the words must have been present in the child's repertoire before the brain injury.

Visual agnosia. Impaired ability to recognize familiar objects by sight.

Visual memory. Memory for visual objects, such as pictures and faces.

Visual-spatial agnosia. Impaired ability to follow directions, to understand spatial details such as left-right positions or the floor plan of a house, and to understand other types of visual-spatial factors.

Working memory. See *Primary memory.*

---

5. Why is it preferable to have a child receive both a neuropsychological evaluation and a neurological evaluation in cases of suspected brain injury?

6. What can you do to educate teachers and others who work with children with brain injuries about the relationship between brain injury and behavior?

7. Do you think that you have the patience to work with children with brain injuries? Why or why not?

8. Why do you think mental health professionals can play an important role in the rehabilitation of children with brain injuries?

9. Do you believe that it will be possible to reduce the incidence of brain injuries in children in the future? What is the basis for your answer?

SUMMARY

1. Brain injury refers to any disruption in brain structure (anatomy) or physiology (function). The assessment of brain injury is a complex and exacting process requiring extensive specialized knowledge and interdisciplinary cooperation.

2. Psychologists can help children with brain injuries, as well as their parents, families, and teachers, by explaining how brain injury may affect a child's cognitive functioning, affective reactions, personality, and temperament. Psychologists can also help parents, teachers, and the child carry out the rehabilitation efforts necessary to deal with changes in the child's functioning.

Background Considerations in Understanding Brain Functions

3. The human brain is a constantly changing constellation of connections among billions of cells. Complex networks of neurons are linked by forged pathways, then continually revised, in response to interactions with the environment.

4. There is no way to separate the development of the brain's neural structure from the influence of the environment that nurtures it.

5. No two brains are identical, and the complex connections of each brain are so individual that it is unlikely that any two people perceive the world in quite the same way.

6. The most efficient brains—those that use the least energy—appear also to be the most intelligent.

7. Small structural abnormalities appear to develop in the brains of people with Alzheimer's disease and Huntington's disease long before any noticeable behavioral symptoms can be diagnosed.

8. Minor alterations in neural circuits for vision and hearing (and perhaps other areas) may be responsible for dyslexia; abnormalities in regions of the brain involved in inhibiting mental and behavioral activity could be the cause of attention-deficit/hyperactivity disorder.

Lateralization

9. Lateralization refers to the specialization of the two hemispheres of the cerebral cortex for cognitive, perceptual, motor, and sensory activities.

10. In general, the side of the brain that controls a sensorimotor activity is opposite to the side of the body that carries out the activity.

11. The left hemisphere in most people is specialized for verbal functions—including reading, writing, speaking, verbal ideation, verbal memory, and certain aspects of arithmetic ability.

12. Left hemispheric processing has been described as analytic, temoral, sequential, serial, logical, and differential.

13. The right hemisphere in most people is specialized for nonverbal, perceptual, and spatial functions—including spatial visualization, visual learning and memory, arithmetical calculations involving spatial organization of the problem elements, vocal inflection nuances, complex visual-motor organization, and nonverbal sequencing.

14. Right hemispheric processing is considered holistic, simultaneous, gestalt-like, intuitive, parallel, and integrative.

15. The frontal lobes are associated with planning, initiation, and modulation of behavior and with expressive verbal fluency, control of motor functions, and motor planning.

16. The temporal lobes are associated with auditory perception, auditory comprehension, verbal memory, visual memory, and some forms of visual processing.

17. The parietal lobes are associated with somatosensory functions, visual-spatial ability, and the integration of visual, somatosensory, and auditory stimuli.

18. The occipital lobes are associated with visual perception, elaboration and synthesis of visual information, and the integration of visual information with information gathered by the auditory and other sensory systems.

19. Injuries to the frontal, temporal, parietal, and occipital lobes and to subcortical centers (such as the basal ganglia and hippocampal structures) may lead to disorders in cognition, memory, affect, motor output, and motivation.

20. Lateralization develops gradually, as bilateral movements are replaced with unilateral movements.

21. For most children of both sexes, linguistic functions are localized in the left hemisphere at birth.

22. Functions lateralized in the right hemisphere are less straightforward—certain abilities are lateralized at birth, whereas others become lateralized with age.

23. The left hemisphere is dominant for language in most individuals; the right hemisphere has limited potential for language functions.

24. A primary function of the right hemisphere may be to integrate information into meaningful wholes.

Types of Memory

25. There are at least 10 different types of memory: iconic memory, echoic memory, primary memory, visual memory, verbal memory, semantic memory, episodic memory, declarative memory, procedural memory, and prospective memory.

Causes of Brain Injury

26. Brain injuries can result from factors present before birth or from injuries sustained during the birth process, immediately after birth, or at any point in life after birth.

27. Prenatal environmental factors (factors existing or occurring before birth) that contribute to brain injury include severe maternal malnutrition; maternal use of substances such as alcohol, drugs, or tobacco; maternal exposure to toxic substances; maternal infections caused by viruses or bacteria; maternal illnesses; radiation; congenital disorders, and physical injury to the uterus.

28. In the perinatal period (the period shortly before and after birth), conditions that may lead to brain injury include prematurity, physical trauma associated with labor and delivery, asphyxia, hypoglycemia, meningitis, encephalitis, kernicterus, and Rh incompatibility.

29. During the postnatal period (period after birth), conditions that may result in brain injury include hydrocephaly, hypothyroidism, Tay-Sachs disease, Niemann-Pick disease, phenylketonuria (PKU), and galactosemia.

30. During infancy, early childhood, and adolescence, brain injury may be caused by trauma, infections, radiation, drug and alcohol abuse, exposure to neurotoxins, and deficiency of nutrients.

Traumatic Brain Injury

31. Each year approximately 1 million children in the United States sustain head injuries from falls, physical abuse, recreational accidents, or motor vehicle accidents.

32. Traumatic brain injury is a threat to a child's quality of life—including life style, education, social and recreational activities, interpersonal relationships, freedom to make changes, and control over his or her self and destiny.

33. In a focal head injury, the skull is usually penetrated by a high-velocity projectile, such as a bullet, and contact occurs between the brain tissue and the outside environment.

34. A diffuse head injury may damage the brain severely, even though the skull is not penetrated.

35. Motor vehicle accidents are the most frequent cause of diffuse head injuries in adolescents.

36. Children who sustain a traumatic brain injury may have a good recovery, a mild disability, a moderate disability, or a severe disability. They also may become vegetative or die.

Specific Effects of Brain Injury in Children

37. Brain injury may produce a general deterioration in all or most aspects of functioning, differential symptoms, highly specific symptoms, subtle symptoms, symptoms not seen until several years later, or no observable symptoms.

38. Some cognitive impairments diminish with time, others are permanent, and still others remain hidden until later in life, when more advanced cognitive skills are needed.

39. Some symptoms present during the early stages of recovery—such as delusions, irritability, hallucinations, and suspiciousness—may impair cognitive processes.

40. Brain injury may lead to losses in automatic processing.

41. Children with brain injuries may have cognitive impairments that are not evident in the interview portion of an evaluation.

42. Agnosia is a central nervous system disorder manifested through impaired ability to recognize familiar stimuli.

43. Apraxia is impaired ability to execute learned movements or to carry out purposeful or skilled acts.

44. Aphasia is a deficit in the perception, production, or symbolic use of language.

45. Aphasia may involve expressive components, receptive components, or both.

46. Expressive aphasia is impaired ability to use spoken and/or written language.

47. Receptive aphasia is impaired ability to understand spoken and/or written language.

48. Global aphasia, or mixed-type aphasia, involves impaired abilities in both expressive and receptive domains.

49. In children, brain injury from a traumatic event is the main cause of aphasia; in adults, the main cause of aphasia is a cerebrovascular accident (CVA; i.e., stroke).

50. Traumatic events are more likely than cerebrovascular accidents to produce diffuse injuries and thus lead to fewer clearcut aphasic symptoms.

51. The changes in temperament, personality, and psychosocial functioning that children with brain injuries may exhibit relate both to their brain injury and to their pre-existing personality and temperament.

52. Symptoms that children with brain injuries may exhibit include emotional lability, anxiety, denial of illness, paranoid ideation, psychomotor agitation, depression and amotivational states, and psychosocial disturbances.

53. Behavioral symptoms, like language and motor symptoms, may be neurologically based.

54. Some children with brain injuries show a pattern of behavior associated with overarousal, whereas others show a pattern of behavior associated with underarousal.

55. When children sustain a brain injury, there is likely to be interference with development in many areas, rather than a striking loss of function in one area.

56. If brain injury is global, mental retardation may be the result; if it is region-specific, specific difficulties may result, such as difficulty with speech or difficulty with the recognition of shapes.

57. In young children, brain injury may have more than a simple depressing effect on cognitive skills; it may alter the basic pattern of cognitive development.

58. Large unilateral injuries in infants usually produce a more widespread deficit in intellectual functions than do similar injuries in adults.

59. The process of myelination in various brain regions affects behavioral and cognitive development.

60. Myelination is the process of insulating, or coating, the axon of a neuron.

61. Myelination is essential if an impulse is to be passed along an axon at high speed.

62. The behavioral difficulties that occur among children with brain injuries could be related to the neurostructural components undergoing the most rapid development at the time of the injury.

63. Cerebral plasticity is the ability of the brain to change in order to compensate for loss of function. The change may involve (a) the taking over, by one part of the brain, of functions impaired by damage in another part of the brain or (b) the functional reorganization of the central nervous system to restore impaired functions.

64. Cerebral plasticity operates at any age, but it is more extensive at younger ages than at older ages.

65. Studies show that children do not necessarily completely recover all of their functions after brain injury.

66. Changes in cognitive development after brain injury may best be viewed as involving cumulative interactions among etiological variables, recovery-period variables, and experiential variables.

67. It is more difficult to evaluate language, speech, and other cognitive functions in children than in adults because young children have only relatively rudimentary skills in these areas.

Diagnostic Techniques

68. A neurological examination includes a clinical history, a mental status examination, and a study of cranial nerves, motor functions, coordination, sensory functions, and gait. Several laboratory procedures augment the neurological examination.

69. Computed tomography (CT or CAT scan) is an x-ray technique that uses a computer to sequentially scan the organ under evaluation and produce radiologic images.

70. Magnetic resonance imaging (MRI scan) is a procedure in which a scan "of the brain or spinal cord is performed by placing a person's head or entire body in a confined space and generating a very powerful magnetic field that produces exquisitely detailed anatomic images" (Berkow, 1997, p. 286).

71. Electroencephalography (EEG) is a procedure in which electrodes are placed on the scalp to record the electrical activity of the brain.

72. Positron emission tomography (PET scan) is a scanning method that produces a cross-sectional image of cellular activity or blood flow in the brain, following the intravenous injection of a radioactive substance.

73. Single photon emission computed tomography (SPECT) is a procedure that provides a three-dimensional representation of regional cerebral blood flow.

74. Cerebral angiography is a procedure in which a radiopaque dye is injected into an artery so that the flow of blood through the brain can be followed via x-ray.

75. Hard neurological signs are fairly definitive indicators of cerebral injury.

76. Soft neurological signs are mild and equivocal neurological irregularities in primarily sensorimotor functions.

77. The aims of the neuropsychological examination are to draw inferences about the global functioning of the cerebral hemispheres, specify the adaptive strengths and weaknesses of the child, and plan an appropriate rehabilitation.

78. Quantitative neuropsychological approaches use standard neuropsychological batteries that provide normative data.

79. Qualitative neuropsychological approaches evaluate cognitive functions, language, and behavior and may include (a) examination procedures for which there are only preliminary norms or (b) testing-of-limits procedures.

80. A neuropsychological examination complements a neurological examination.

81. No matter how many improvements are made in brain-imaging techniques, the functional capacities of children with brain injuries will always need to be evaluated.

Assessment Considerations

82. Children who have sustained severe head injuries may be difficult to evaluate, especially if their speech is impaired, if they have aphasic disturbances, or if they have not fully regained consciousness.

83. Assessment of children with brain injuries needs to focus on interpersonal skills and social judgment, as well as on cognitive, academic, and behavioral skills.

84. Before beginning the evaluation, arrange to have a quiet room and reduce all potential sources of distraction.

85. If the child is anxious about the evaluation, deal with his or her anxieties *before* you begin the formal evaluation.

86. You need to be especially attentive to the reactions of children with brain injuries in order to minimize their frustration and fatigue.

87. Experiment with different communication methods, rates of communication, and types of content to find the most effective way to communicate.

Observation Guidelines

88. Ideally, you should observe the child in several settings.

89. Observations will give you information about the child's developmental level and capabilities, including language skills, motor skills, social skills, compensatory skills and strategies, temperament, personality, motivation, and interpersonal skills.

Interviewing Parents

90. Interview one or both parents to obtain a detailed clinical and developmental history of the child.

91. When you interview the child's parents, recognize that they may not always be objective.

92. In the history, pay particular attention to events or signs that have etiological importance for brain injury.

93. Sudden and inadequately explained changes in behavior are likely to be associated with acute, as opposed to chronic, brain disorders.

Rehabilitation Programs

94. Rehabilitation programs are designed to help children with brain injuries become more independent by increasing their functional and daily living skills.

95. Rehabilitation aims to improve children's general adjustment and help them achieve success in school, in social relationships, and in work.

96. Usually, you will be working with a multidisciplinary health care team to develop and carry out the rehabilitation program.

97. Rehabilitation goals for a child with brain injuries should be appropriate to the child's physical and neuropsychological status, as well as his or her specific injury, and be geared to the child's readiness and motivation to reach the goals.

98. Consumption of alcohol can complicate both physical and cognitive recovery from a brain injury.

99. Chronic abuse of alcohol can produce cognitive deficits that interact with those produced by the traumatic brain injury.

100. The rehabilitation program should be based on the results of the assessment.

101. In addition, you will need to consider such factors as (a) the length of time since injury, (b) the differential rate of improvement in cognitive, motor, affective, and interpersonal areas, and (c) the need for re-examination.

102. When children with traumatic brain injuries return to school, they may have processing difficulties, memory difficulties, emotional difficulties, and physical difficulties.

103. You will need to work with school personnel to meet the rehabilitation goals.

104. Review the child's educational placement periodically, especially during the early stages of recovery, because his or her needs are likely to change.

105. The recovery of a child with a brain injury depends, in part, on family support and on the family's ability to manage the child's day-to-day problems.

106. When a child sustains a brain injury, family patterns may change.

107. The degree of physical disability of children with brain injuries typically is *not* the crucial factor causing stress in families; rather, the behavioral, cognitive, and affective deficits that accompany the injury often are the most distressing factors.

108. Helping families of children with brain injuries may take several years, not just a few weeks or months.

109. Rehabilitation is best conceived of as a process involving three stages: stage of acute crisis, stage of prolonged rehabilitation, and stage of disengagement.

110. Families of children with brain injuries need to be educated about brain injury, encouraged to help their child overcome cognitive and behavioral limitations, helped to solve problems associated with their child's brain injury, and provided with the support they need to help their child.

111. Rehabilitation efforts should be monitored closely to determine children's progress and to ensure that programs are not creating undue stress on them or their families.

KEY TERMS, CONCEPTS, AND NAMES

Brain injury (p. 402)
Brain dysfunction (p. 402)
Lateralization (p. 402)
Sensorimotor activities (p. 402)
Left cerebral hemisphere (p. 403)
Right cerebral hemisphere (p. 403)
Frontal lobes (p. 403)
Temporal lobes (p. 403)
Parietal lobes (p. 403)
Occipital lobes (p. 404)
Hyperesthesia (p. 404)
Paresthesia (p. 404)
Loss of two-point discrimination (p. 404)
Astereognosis (p. 404)
Autotopagnosia (p. 404)
Anosognosia (p. 404)
Disorientation of external environmental space (p. 404)
Finger agnosia (p. 404)
Loss of right-left discrimination (p. 404)
Agraphia (p. 404)
Acalculia (p. 404)
Constructional apraxia (p. 404)
Homonymous hemianopia (p. 404)
Contralateral homonymous hemianopia (p. 404)
Iconic memory (p. 405)
Echoic memory (p. 405)
Primary memory (p. 405)
Visual memory (p. 405)
Verbal memory (p. 405)
Semantic memory (p. 405)
Episodic memory (p. 405)
Declarative memory (p. 405)
Procedural memory (p. 405)
Prospective memory (p. 406)
Prenatal period (p. 406)
Prenatal environmental factors (p. 406)
Perinatal period (p. 406)
Asphyxia (p. 406)
Hypoglycemia (p. 406)
Meningitis (p. 406)
Encephalitis (p. 406)
Kernicterus (p. 406)
Severe jaundice (p. 406)
Rh incompatibility (p. 406)
Postnatal period (p. 406)
Hydrocephaly (p. 406)
Hypothyroidism (p. 406)
Tay-Sachs disease (p. 406)
Niemann-Pick disease (p. 406)
Phenylketonuria (PKU) (p. 406)
Galactosemia (p. 406)
Neurotoxins (p. 406)
Traumatic brain injury (p. 407)
Focal head injuries (p. 407)
Diffuse head injuries (p. 407)
Contrecoup (p. 407)
Coup-contrecoup effect (p. 407)
Coup (p. 407)
Intracranial hematoma (p. 407)

STUDY QUESTIONS

1. Discuss recent developments in the neurosciences concerning brain functioning.
2. Discuss different types of memory.
3. Discuss the causes of brain injury, using a developmental perspective. Include in your discussion factors that may cause brain injury during the prenatal period, the perinatal period, the postnatal period, infancy, early childhood, and adolescence.
4. Discuss traumatic brain injury. Include in your discussion the incidence of traumatic brain injury, types of traumatic brain injuries, and types of recovery.
5. Discuss the lateralization of cognitive, perceptual, and motor activities.
6. Brain injury produces specific as well as diverse effects. Describe some cognitive and behavioral symptoms of brain injury. Include in your discussion (a) symptoms associated with aphasia, agnosia, and apraxia and (b) possible interpretations of behavioral symptoms of brain injury.
7. Discuss how brain injury may affect children and adults in different ways.
8. Discuss why the assumption of complete recovery of brain functioning in children with brain injuries has been questioned. What position does the text advocate with respect to recovery of functions in children with brain injuries, and what reasons does it offer for this position?
9. Describe a neurological examination. Include in your discussion (a) the components of the examination, (b) a brief description of several scanning and radiography methods, and (c) examples of several hard and soft signs of possible brain injury that may be found during the neurological examination.
10. Describe a neuropsychological examination. In what way does a neuropsychological examination complement a neurological examination? Include in your discussion how a neuropsychological examination contributes to the assessment process.
11. Discuss some techniques for interviewing children with brain injuries. Include in your discussion the areas to cover in the interview, how to establish rapport, handling perseverative and avoidance behaviors, and techniques for working with children with language impairments and brain injuries.

12. Discuss several difficulties in establishing rapport with children with brain injuries. Include in your discussion how you would handle these difficulties. In addition, describe some useful techniques for working with language-impaired children with brain injuries.

13. What are some important areas to observe when interviewing a child with a brain injury? Include in your discussion what you should observe in the child's language, listening behaviors, and motor movements.

14. What are some key areas to focus on in interviewing a child with a brain injury for a rehabilitation program?

15. When you interview parents of a child with a brain injury, what areas are important to inquire about?

16. After you have interviewed a child with a brain injury and her or his parents and have read the neurological and neuropsychological reports, what information would you want to include in your report?

17. What areas are particularly important to cover when you are evaluating the ability of a child with a brain injury to perform daily living activities?

18. What factors should you consider in offering a prognosis for a child with a brain injury?

19. Explain several goals of a rehabilitation program for children with brain injuries. Use a developmental framework, in part, in your discussion. Also discuss some important factors in designing a rehabilitation program.

20. If you were a consultant to a school, how would you advise school personnel about working with children with brain injuries?

21. Discuss the following proposition: "The recovery of a child with a brain injury will, in part, depend on the level of family support and on the family's ability to manage the child's day-to-day activities." Include in your discussion ways to help family members cope both with their child with a brain injury and with the changes within the family.

19

BRAIN INJURIES: FORMAL BATTERIES AND INFORMAL MEASURES

by Jerome M. Sattler and Rik D'Amato

If the brain were so simple we could understand it, we would be so simple we couldn't.

—Lyall Watson

Neuropsychological Test Batteries for Children

Additional Procedures for the Assessment of Children with Brain Injuries

Evaluating the Assessment Findings

Concluding Comment on the Assessment of Children with Brain Injuries

Thinking Through the Issues

Summary

Goals and Objectives

This chapter is designed to enable you to do the following:

- Understand the major neuropsychological test batteries
- Use informal techniques when assessing children with brain injuries

NEUROPSYCHOLOGICAL TEST BATTERIES FOR CHILDREN

Halstead-Reitan Neuropsychological Test Battery for Older Children and Reitan-Indiana Neuropsychological Test Battery for Children

Two batteries useful for evaluating children suspected of having brain injury are the Halstead-Reitan Neuropsychological Test Battery for Older Children, designed for children ages 9 to 14 years, and the Reitan-Indiana Neuropsychological Test Battery for Children, designed for children ages 5 to 8 years (Reitan & Davison, 1974; Reitan & Wolfson, 1985, 1992; Selz, 1981). Both batteries contain cognitive and perceptual-motor tests, a few of which appear in the adult battery and a few of which were especially designed for young children. (See Table 19-1 for a description of the batteries.) Table 19-2 gives the instructions for the Reitan-Indiana Aphasia Screening Test, and Figure 19-1 shows the stimulus figures for the test. The complete Halstead battery also includes an intelligence test and a measure of personality.

Information about the reliability and validity of both batteries is limited. A review indicates, first, that clear developmental trends appear on the Halstead-Reitan Neuropsychological Battery for Older Children for all tests except the Tactual Performance Test–Memory, Tactual Performance Test–Localization, and Seashore Rhythm Test (Leckliter, Forster, Klonoff, & Knights, 1992). Second, it indicates that four tests may be unreliable: Tactual Performance Test (all timed measures and memory and localization tasks), Trail Making Test (Part B among younger children), Speech Sounds Perception Test, and Seashore Rhythm Test. Leckliter et al. suggest that clinicians may want to exclude the Speech Sounds Perception Test from the battery or at least interpret it with extreme caution. Other research indicates that internal consistency reliabilities on the battery for older children are relatively low for the Seashore Rhythm Test, moderate for the Aphasia Screening Test, and relatively good for the Speech Sounds Perception Test (Livingston, Gray, & Haak, 1999). Finally, the battery for older children appears to have seven factors: Spatial Processing, Motor Strength, Nonverbal Memory/Learning, Sensory-Perceptual, Auditory Processing, Motor Speed, and Visual Attention (Livingston, Gray, Haak, & Jennings, 1997).

Research indicates that the batteries are useful in discriminating children with brain injuries from other groups (Dalby & Obrzut, 1991) and that the Reitan-Indiana Aphasia Screening Test is useful as a screening procedure for identifying children with brain injuries (Dodrill, Farwell, & Batzel, 1987; Reitan & Wolfson, 1992). Note, however, that the batteries cannot localize brain injury or predict recovery from brain injury (Hynd, 1992). A short form of the intermediate version of the Halstead Category Test, based on the first 15 items of every subtest, appears to be useful (Donders, 1996). Normative data are available for children ages 5 to 14 years on several of the tests (unpublished norms provided by Findeis and Weight

and reprinted in Nussbaum and Bigler, 1997) and for adolescents and adults (Yeudall, Reddon, Gill, & Stefanyk, 1987). Overall, the batteries offer unique information not tapped by the Wechsler tests or by pediatric neurological examinations (Yi, Johnstone, Doan, & Townes, 1990) and can be useful for diagnosis and treatment planning (D'Amato, Gray, & Dean, 1988; Leckliter et al., 1992; Russell, 1998).

Luria-Nebraska Neuropsychological Battery–Children's Revision

The Luria-Nebraska Neuropsychological Battery–Children's Revision (LNNB–C) is designed to assess a broad range of neuropsychological functions in children ages 8 to 12 years (Golden, 1987). It can be considered a downward extension of the adult version, although items are not necessarily interpreted in the same manner on the two versions. The LNNB–C is designed to assess cognitive deficits and aid in planning rehabilitation programs.

The LNNB–C is individually administered. It contains 149 items, grouped into 11 clinical scales (see Table 19-3) and 2 optional scales. Additionally, the items are regrouped into 3 summary scales and 11 factor scales. The clinical scales are designed to assess sensorimotor, perceptual, and cognitive abilities. The summary scales provide information for discriminating between children with and without brain injury. Golden (1987) noted that the factor scales are helpful in assessing specific neuropsychological functions, although they must be interpreted cautiously. The LNNB–C takes approximately 2½ hours to administer.

Scoring. All items are scored 0, 1, or 2. A score of 0 indicates normal functioning, 1 indicates weak evidence of brain injury, and 2 indicates strong evidence of brain injury. Note that higher raw scores indicate a poorer response. Raw scores are transformed into T scores ($M = 50$, $SD = 10$), with higher T scores indicating poorer performance. The manual provides qualitative scoring that has 57 individual categories—such as attention difficulties, fatigue, jargon, perseveration, sequence errors, and tremors—for classifying errors.

Standardization sample. The normal group in the standardization sample consisted of 125 children (65 females, 60 males) between the ages of 8 and 12 years. An additional sample of 719 children, many of whom were disabled, was used in the development and validation of the scales. Unfortunately, demographic information is scarce, and the manual gives no information about the representativeness of the normal group.

Reliability. Internal consistency reliability coefficients, based on 714 children (240 nonimpaired, 474 impaired), range from $r_{xx} = .67$ to $.90$ (Mdn $r_{xx} = .82$) for the 11 clinical scales. Reliability coefficients are much higher for the group with brain injuries than for the group without brain injuries. Golden

Table 19-1
Description of the Halstead-Reitan Neuropsychological Test Battery for Older Children and the Reitan-Indiana Neuropsychological Test Battery for Children

Test	Description	H-R	R-I
Category Test	Measures concept formation; requires child to find a reason (or rule) for comparing or sorting objects	■	■
Tactual Performance Test	Measures somatosensory and sensorimotor ability; requires child, while blindfolded, to place blocks in appropriate hole using dominant hand alone, nondominant hand alone, and both hands	■	■
Finger Tapping Test	Measures fine motor speed; requires child to press and release a lever, like a telegraph key, as fast as possible	■	■
Aphasia Screening Test	Measures expressive and receptive language functions and laterality; requires child to name common objects, spell, identify numbers and letters, read, write, calculate, understand spoken language, identify body parts, and differentiate between right and left	■	■
Matching Pictures Test	Measures perceptual recognition; requires child to match figures at the top of a page with figures at the bottom of the page	■	■
Individual Performance tests			
Matching Figures	Measures perception; requires child to match complex figures		■
Star	Measures visual-motor ability; requires child to copy a star		■
Matching V's	Measures perception; requires child to match letter V's		■
Concentric Squares	Measures visual-motor ability; requires child to copy a series of concentric squares		■
Marching Test	Measures gross motor control; requires child to (a) use a crayon to connect a series of circles in a given order, first with right hand alone and then with left hand alone, and (b) reproduce examiner's finger and arm movements		■
Progressive Figures Test	Measures flexibility and abstraction; requires child to connect several figures, each consisting of a small shape contained within a large shape		■
Color Form Test	Measures flexibility and abstraction; requires child to connect colored shapes, first by color and then by shape		■
Target Test	Measures memory for figures; requires child to reproduce a visually presented pattern after a 3-second delay		■
Seashore Rhythm Test	Measures alertness, sustained attention, and auditory perception; requires child to indicate whether two rhythms are the same or different	■	
Speech Sounds Perception Test	Measures auditory perception and auditory-visual integration; requires child to indicate, after listening to a word on tape, which of four spellings represents the word	■	
Trail Making Test (Parts A and B)	Measures appreciation of symbolic significance of numbers and letters, scanning ability, flexibility, and speed; requires child to connect circles that are numbered or lettered	■	
Sensory-Perceptual Examination	Measures sensory-perceptual ability; requires child to perceive bilateral simultaneous sensory stimulation of tactile, auditory, and visual modalities in separate tests	■	■
Tactile Finger Recognition	Measures sensory-perceptual ability; requires child, while blindfolded, to recognize which finger is touched	■	■
Fingertip Number Writing	Measures sensory-perceptual ability; requires child, while blindfolded, to recognize numbers written on fingertips	■	■
Tactile Form Recognition	Measures sensory-perceptual ability; requires child to identify various coins through touch alone, with each hand separately	■	■
Strength of Grip	Measures motor strength of upper extremities; requires child to use Smedley Hand Dynamometer with preferred hand and nonpreferred hand	■	■

Note. H-R = Halstead-Reitan Neuropsychological Test Battery for Older Children, R-I = Reitan-Indiana Neuropsychological Test Battery for Children. The WISC–III (or WAIS–III) is often administered as part of the complete battery.

Table 19-2
Instructions for the Reitan-Indiana Aphasia Screening Test

Task	Instructions
1. Copy *square*	*First, draw this* (point to the square) *on your paper. I want you to do it without lifting your pencil from the paper. Make it about the same size* (pointing to the square).
2. Name *square*	*What is that shape called?* (or) *What is the name for that figure?*
3. Spell *square*	*Would you spell that word for me?*
4. Copy *cross*	*Draw this* (point to the cross) *on your paper. Go around the outside like this* (quickly draw a finger-line around the edge of the stimulus figure) *until you get back to where you started. Make it about the same size* (point to the cross).
5. Name *cross*	*What is that shape called?*
6. Spell *cross*	*Would you spell the name of it?*
7. Copy *triangle*	*Now I want you to draw this figure.* (Point to the triangle.)
8. Name *triangle*	*What would you call that figure?*
9. Spell *triangle*	*Would you spell the name of it for me?*
10. Name *baby*	*What is this?* (Show item 10.)
11. Write *clock*	*Now I am going to show you another picture, but do NOT tell me the name of it. I don't want you to say anything out loud. Just WRITE the name of the picture on your paper.* (Show item 11.)
12. Name *fork*	*What is this?* (Show item 12.)
13. Read *7 six 2*	*I want you to read this.* (Show item 13.)
14. Read *M G W*	*Read this.* (Show item 14.)
15. Reading I	*Now I want you to read this.* (Show item 15.)
16. Reading II	*Can you read this?* (Show item 16.)
17. Repeat *triangle*	*Now I am going to say some words. I want you to listen carefully and say them after me as carefully as you can. Say this word: "triangle."*
18. Repeat *Massachusetts*	*The next one is a little harder, but do your best. Say this word: "Massachusetts."*
19. Repeat *Methodist Episcopal*	*Now repeat this one: "Methodist Episcopal."*
20. Write *square*	*Don't say this word out loud.* (Point to the stimulus word "square.") *Just write it on your paper.*
21. Read *seven*	*Would you read this word?* (Show item 21.)
21A. Repeat *seven*	Remove the stimulus card and say: *Now, I want you to say this after me: "seven."*
22. Repeat-explain *He shouted the warning*	*I am going to say something that I want you to say after me, so listen carefully: "He shouted the warning." Now you say it. Tell me in your own words what that means.*
23. Write *He shouted the warning*	*Now I want you to write that sentence on the paper.*
24. Compute *85 – 27 =*	*Here is an arithmetic problem. Copy it down on your paper any way you like and try to work it out.* (Show item 24.)
25. Compute *17 × 3 =*	*Now do this one in your head. Write down only the answer.*
26. Name *key*	*What is this?* (Show item 26.)
27. Demonstrate use of *key*	(Still presenting the picture of the key) *If you had one of these in your hand, show me how you would use it.*
28. Draw *key*	*Now I want you to draw a picture that looks just like this* (pointing to the picture of the key). *Try to make your key look enough like this one* (still pointing to the picture of the key) *so that I would know it was the same key from your drawing. Make it about the same size.*
29. Read	*Would you read this?* (Show item 29.)
30. Place *left hand to right ear*	*Now, would you do what it said?* Be sure to note any false starts or even mild expressions of confusion.
31. Place *left hand to left elbow*	*Now I want you to put your left hand to your left elbow.*

Note. See Figure 19-1 for stimulus figures. The Reitan-Indiana Aphasia Screening Test is part of the Reitan-Indiana Neuropsychological Test Battery for Children. Considerable clinical experience is needed to administer and interpret the test or the battery. Two books that can assist you in interpreting the battery are *Aphasia and Sensory-Perceptual Deficits in Adults* by Reitan (1984) and *Aphasia and Sensory-Perceptual Deficits in Children* by Reitan (1985). Additionally, Reitan and Wolfson's (1985) *Halstead-Reitan Neuropsychological Test Battery: Theory and Clinical Interpretation* is an excellent source for information on how to integrate the findings of the Reitan-Indiana Aphasia Screening Test with the rest of the results of the Halstead-Reitan Neuropsychological Test Battery for a complete neuropsychological assessment. Separate kits for adults and children, which include the appropriate book, recording forms, and test booklet, are available from the Reitan Neuropsychology Lab, P.O. Box 66080, Tucson, AZ 85728-6080.

Source: Reprinted, with changes in notation and with permission of the publisher and authors, from R. M. Reitan and D. Wolfson, *The Halstead-Reitan Neuropsychological Test Battery* (Tucson, AZ: Neuropsychology Press, 1985), pp. 75–78. Copyright 1985 by Neuropsychology Press.

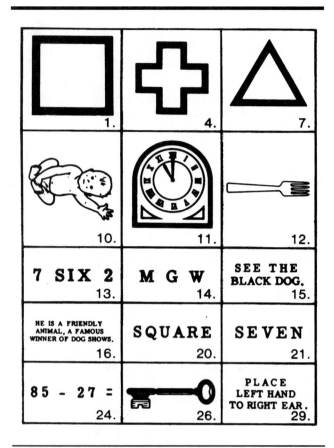

Figure 19-1. Stimulus figures for the Reitan-Indiana Aphasia Screening Test.

(1987) attributes this difference to the restriction in the range of scores in the group without brain injuries—children in this group made few errors. The manual provides standard errors of measurement for both the nonimpaired sample (SEM from 1.2 to 3.2) and the impaired sample (SEM from 1.4 to 3.6). Internal consistency reliability coefficients for the summary scales are similar to those for the clinical scales.

Validity.   The manual, as well as a research review (Dalby & Obrzut, 1991), indicates that the LNNB–C is useful in distinguishing children with brain injuries from other groups. However, the accuracy with which the LNNB–C classifies subjects as nonimpaired or brain injured depends on the number of scales used in the classification, the type of disorder the children have, and the critical level of the cutoff scores.

Comment on the LNNB–C.   Overall, the LNNB–C may be a useful addition to the field of neuropsychological assessment; however, we need more research to evaluate its contribution. Caution is needed in using the LNNB–C because the manual fails to describe the standardization sample adequately and reliability is less than adequate. Each scale likely measures a heterogeneous group of skills, making interpreta-

tion difficult. Additionally, the test fails to consider maturational variables in assessing children and instead offers a downsized version of the adult battery with the adult items made easier (Williams & Boll, 1997). Also, it is unclear whether the LNNB–C makes a distinct contribution to an assessment or whether a battery composed of the WISC–III, WRAT–3, and other special ability tests would serve the same purpose. However, some LNNB–C scales, such as Motor Functions, Rhythm, and Tactile Functions, appear to make a unique contribution to an assessment battery (Hynd, 1992).

NEPSY—A Developmental Neuropsychological Assessment

NEPSY—A Developmental Neuropsychological Assessment is a neuropsychological test designed for children ages 3 to 12 years (Korkman, Kirk, & Kemp, 1998). It is an American adaptation of a Finnish test called the NEPSU (Korkman, 1990). There are two batteries: a core battery and a full battery. The core battery contains 11 subtests for children ages 3 to 4 years and 14 subtests for children ages 5 to 12 years. The full battery contains 14 subtests for children ages 3 to 4 years and 26 subtests for children ages 5 to 12 years. There are a total of 27 subtests. The subtests (see Table 19-4) comprise five domains: Attention/Executive Functions, Language, Sensorimotor Functions, Visuospatial Processing, and Memory and Learning. The NEPSY provides quantitative and qualitative information about neuropsychological processes.

Administration of the core battery takes approximately 45 minutes for preschoolers and about an hour for school-age children, whereas the full battery takes about 1 hour for preschoolers and about 2 hours for school-age children. The manual includes directions for administration, psychometric data, a sample clinical history form, a handedness inventory (with norms), an orientation questionnaire that focuses on the child's knowledge of self and place (with norms), and a table for suggested subtest usage with different disability populations.

Scoring.   The NEPSY yields several types of scores. First, there are standard scores for the five domains ($M = 100$, $SD = 15$) and 27 subtests ($M = 10$, $SD = 3$). Second, there are supplementary standard scores for the Auditory Attention and Response Set, Memory for Faces, and Memory for Names subtests. The supplementary scores break down the child's performance into Attention vs. Response Set components and Immediate vs. Delayed Memory components. Third, information is provided about the number of times examinees in the standardized group engaged in several behaviors—such as articulation, hand tremors, type of pencil grip (mature, intermediate, immature), and off-task behavior—during the administration of 19 of the 27 subtests.

Standardization sample.   The standardization sample consisted of 1,000 children ages 3 to 12 years, with 100 children in each of the 10 age groups, stratified according to the

Table 19-3
Clinical Scales of the Luria-Nebraska Neuropsychological Battery–Children's Revision (LNNB–C)

Scale	Number of items	Description
C1: Motor Functions	34	Measures various motor functions, such as motor speed, kinesthetic movement, coordination, construction skills, motor imitation skills, and verbal control of simple motor behaviors; requires child to perform various motor movements
C2: Rhythm	8	Measures auditory perception; requires child to hum, sing, report number of beeps heard, and reproduce a series by tapping
C3: Tactile Functions	16	Measures various aspects of tactile sensitivity; requires child to report cutaneous sensation, discriminate the point of a pin, discriminate pressure differentials, report direction of pressure, recognize various objects, discriminate a number written on wrist, and recognize objects placed in hand
C4: Visual Functions	7	Measures perceptual skills without involving motor movements; requires child to recognize objects visually and detect spatial positions of objects
C5: Receptive Speech	18	Measures ability to understand spoken speech; requires child to repeat spoken sounds and letters, discriminate phonemic sounds, comprehend words, understand simple sentences, and understand logical grammatical structures
C6: Expressive Speech	21	Measures fluency and articulatory speech skills; requires child to repeat spoken sounds and words, pronounce sounds and words that are read, repeat sentences from memory, count, and engage in spontaneous speech
C7: Writing	7	Measures ability to communicate in writing; requires child to spell, copy letters and syllables, and write from dictation
C8: Reading	7	Measures ability to read; requires child to read letters, syllables, words, phrases, and sentences
C9: Arithmetic	9	Measures arithmetic ability; requires child to write and read numbers; tell which number is larger; perform simple multiplication, addition, and subtraction; and count backwards
C10: Memory	8	Measures verbal and nonverbal memory; requires child to recall orally presented words, pictures, visually presented words, and a meaningful paragraph
C11: Intellectual Processes	14	Measures complex reasoning and problem-solving skills; requires child to describe pictures and put them in a meaningful order, indicate what is foolish about a picture, interpret a story, define words, identify the similarity and difference between two things, and answer arithmetic reasoning problems

Note. The optional scales are Spelling and Motor Writing; the summary scales group items into Pathognomonic, Left Sensorimotor, and Right Sensorimotor Scales; the factor scales group items into Academic Achievement, Integrative Functions, Spatial-Based Movement, Motor Speed and Accuracy, Drawing Quality, Drawing Speed, Rhythm Perception and Production, Tactile Sensations, Receptive Language, Expressive Language, and Word and Phrase Repetition Scales.

Source: Adapted from Golden (1987).

1995 U.S. Census data by age, gender, race/ethnicity, geographic region, and education of parents. Standardization data from an additional 500 children were collected for validation purposes.

Reliability. Average internal reliability coefficients in the five core domains for children ages 5 to 12 years range from a high of .87 on the Language and Memory and Learning Domains to a low of .79 on the Sensorimotor Domain. For children ages 3 to 4 years, average internal reliability coefficients range from a high of .91 on the Memory and Learning Domain to a low of .70 on the Attention/Executive Domain.

However, 13 of the 50 internal reliability coefficients in the five domains are below .80. Generally, the domain reliabilities are lowest at the upper age levels of the test, mainly at ages 10 to 12 years.

The subtest average internal consistency reliabilities for children ages 5 to 12 years range from a high of .91 on List Learning and Phonological Processing to a low of .59 on Design Fluency. For children ages 3 to 4 years, average internal consistency reliabilities range from a high of .91 on Sentence Repetition to a low of .50 on Statue.

Although there are 27 subtests, internal reliability coefficients are reported for only 22 of the subtests (the exceptions

Table 19-4
Description of NEPSY Subtests by Domain

Subtest	Description
Attention/Executive Functions	
Tower	Measures the executive functions of planning, monitoring, self-regulation, and problem solving; requires child to move three colored rings to target positions on three pegs in a prescribed number of moves
Auditory Attention and Response Set	Measures vigilance, selective auditory attention, and ability to shift set, to maintain a complex mental set, and to regulate responses to contrasting and matching stimuli; requires child to shift set and respond to contrasting stimuli
Visual Attention	Measures the speed and accuracy with which child can scan an array and locate a target; requires child to scan an array of pictures and mark the targets as quickly and accurately as possible
Statue	Measures inhibition and motor persistence; requires child to stand still in a set position over a 75-second period and inhibit a response (eyes opening, body movement, vocalization) to distractors
Design Fluency	Measures ability to generate novel designs as quickly as possible on structured and unstructured arrays of dots; requires child to make as many different designs as possible by connecting two or more dots
Knock and Tap	Measures self-regulation and ability to inhibit immediate impulses evoked by visual stimuli that conflict with a verbal direction; requires child to learn a pattern of motor responses, maintain that cognitive set, and inhibit the impulse to imitate the examiner's action
Language	
Body Part Naming	Measures naming, a basic component of expressive language; requires child to name the parts of the body
Phonological Processing	(a) Measures ability to identify words from segments and form an auditory gestalt; requires child to identify a picture from an orally presented word segment (b) Measures phonological segmentation at the level of letter sounds and word segments; requires child to create a new word by omitting a word segment (syllable) or letter sound (phoneme) or by substituting one phoneme for another
Speed Naming	Measures ability to access and produce familiar words rapidly; requires child to name items by size, color, and shape
Comprehension of Instructions	Measures ability to process and respond to verbal instructions of increasing syntactic complexity; requires child to point to objects and shapes of different sizes, colors, and positions
Repetition of Nonsense Words	Measures phonological encoding and decoding of a sound pattern, as well as articulation of complex nonwords; requires child to listen to nonsense words and repeat each word
Verbal Fluency	Measures ability to generate words according to semantic and phonemic categories; requires child to produce as many animal names as possible in 1 minute and then name as many things to eat and drink as possible in 1 minute—older children produce words beginning with the letters *F* and *S* in 1-minute trials
Oromotor Sequence	Measures rhythmic oromotor coordination; requires child to repeat sound sequences and tongue twisters
Sensorimotor Functions	
Fingertip Tapping	Measures finger dexterity; requires child to tap index finger against thumb 32 times as quickly as possible and tap fingers sequentially against the thumb from index finger to little finger as quickly as possible
Imitating Hand Positions	Measures ability to imitate a hand position from a model; requires child to reproduce hand positions modeled by examiner
Visuomotor Precision	Measures fine motor skills and hand-eye coordination; requires child to draw a line inside a track as quickly as possible
Manual Motor Sequences	Measures ability to imitate a series of rhythmic movements; requires child to produce hand movement sequences demonstrated by examiner
Finger Discrimination	Measures ability to perceive tactile input without the aid of vision; requires child to indicate which finger or fingers were touched by examiner (with the child's hand shielded from view)

(Continued)

Table 19-4 *(Continued)*	
Subtest	Description
Visuospatial Processing	
Design Copying	Measures visuomotor integration; requires child to copy two-dimensional geometric figures on paper
Arrows	Measures ability to judge line orientation; requires child to look at an array of arrows around a target and indicate the two arrows that point to the center of the target
Block Construction	Measures spatial-visual ability; requires child to reproduce, from models and from pictures, three-dimensional block constructions
Route Finding	Measures understanding of visuospatial relationships and directionality, as well as ability to transfer this knowledge from a simple schematic map to a more complex one; requires child to find a target in a schematic map
Memory and Learning	
Memory for Faces	Measures memory for faces; requires child to identify the gender of a series of faces, select the faces from three-face arrays, and, after a 30-minute delay, select the same faces from new three-face arrays
Memory for Names	Measures memory for names; requires child to learn over three trials, the name of each of six or eight children depicted in line drawings and then, after a 30-minute delay, name the six or eight children
Narrative Memory	Measures narrative memory; requires child to listen to a story and recall it under free recall and cued conditions
Sentence Repetition	Measures memory of verbal material; requires child to recall sentences of increasing length and complexity
List Learning	Measures supraspan memory and ability to recall a list after interference; requires child to learn a list of 15 words and repeat the list after a new list is introduced, and again after 30 minutes

Source: Adapted from Korkman, Kirk, and Kemp (1998).

are Oromotor Sequence, Knock and Tap, Manual Motor Sequences, Finger Discrimination, and Route Finding). Of the 182 reliability coefficients reported for these 22 subtests, 105 are below .80. The subtests exhibiting the highest reliability coefficients are Phonological Processing, Memory for Names, and List Learning. Generally, the subtest internal reliabilities are lowest at the middle to upper age levels of the test, mainly ages 7 to 12 years.

Average standard errors of measurement (SEM) in the five domains for children ages 3 to 4 years range from a low of 4.43 on the Memory and Learning Domain to a high of 8.22 on the Attention/Executive Domain. For children ages 5 to 12 years, the average standard errors of measurement range from a low of 5.43 on the Language Domain to a high of 7.14 on the Sensorimotor Domain. The subtest average standard errors of measurement for children ages 3 to 4 years range from a low of .90 on Sentence Repetition to a high of 2.12 on Statue. For children ages 5 to 12 years, the subtest average standard errors of measurement range from a low of .92 on List Learning to a high of 1.94 on Design Fluency.

Test-retest reliability coefficients were obtained from a sample of 168 children who were retested over a period of 2 to 10 weeks, with an average retest interval of 38 days. The 30 children ages 3 to 4 years had test-retest reliability coefficients that ranged from .63 on the Attention/Executive Domain to .90 on the Memory and Learning Domain. The

median test-retest change was 3.76 points. The largest mean score change was 5.67 points on the Sensorimotor Domain ($M = 98.27$ on the first administration and $M = 103.93$ on the second administration), whereas the lowest mean score change was 3.13 points on the Memory and Learning Domain ($M = 103.70$ on the first administration and $M = 106.83$ on the second administration).

The 138 children ages 5 to 12 years had test-retest reliability coefficients that ranged from .47 on the Attention/Executive Domain to .84 on the Memory and Learning Domain. The median test-retest change was 6.81. The largest mean score change was 17.35 points on the Memory and Learning Domain ($M = 100.94$ on the first administration and $M = 118.29$ on the second administration, for children ages 7 to 8 years), whereas the lowest mean score change was –.42 point on the Visuospatial Domain ($M = 99.12$ on the first administration and $M = 98.70$ on the second administration, for children ages 11 to 12 years).

The largest test-retest changes were at ages 5 to 6 years (range of 6.36 to 15.98) and in the Memory and Learning Domain (11.78 to 17.35). The test-retest changes for the Attention/Executive Domain also were large (4.01 to 15.19).

Validity. The manual cites several studies that appear to support the content and construct validity of the NEPSY. However, fewer than 30 children were sampled in many of the studies.

Therefore, more work is needed to evaluate the validity of the NEPSY. The validity studies indicate that three domains—Language, Memory and Learning, and Visuospatial—are moderately related to intelligence test scores and to school grades, whereas two domains—Sensorimotor and Attention/Executive—are not.

Correlations between the NEPSY and various neuropsychological tests provide a mixed pattern of results. Generally, NEPSY subtests correlated moderately with other neuropsychological tests when the content was similar in the two tests. More research is needed to evaluate the relationship between the NEPSY and other neuropsychological instruments.

The clinical utility and sensitivity of the NEPSY were studied in several clinical groups—ADHD, ADHD and learning disability, reading disability, language disorder, autistic, fetal alcohol syndrome, traumatic brain injury, and hearing impaired. Overall, the results indicate that NEPSY domain scores differentiate clinical groups from matched controls. However, some findings of interest were noted. First, children with a combined diagnosis of ADHD and learning disability were not significantly different from the control group on the Visuospatial Domain. Second, children with a reading disability were not significantly different from the control group on three domains: Attention/Executive, Sensorimotor, and Visuospatial. Third, children with autism were not significantly different from the control group on two domains: Sensorimotor and Visuospatial. Thus, the Visuospatial Domain least discriminates clinical groups from matched control groups.

Comment on the NEPSY. The NEPSY is a complex multidimensional instrument that provides useful information about neurodevelopmental functioning of children with brain injuries. However, much time is needed to learn how to administer the test and to interpret the results. Although it is well standardized, the stability of the NEPSY is questionable, particularly for the Memory and Learning and Attention/Executive Domains and for children ages 5 to 6 years. It may be, however, that these traits are unstable and that the NEPSY just reflects the instability of the traits. Reliability is problematic because 13 out of 50 coefficients are below .80 and test-retest changes surpass 1 standard deviation in 4 of 25 instances. The NEPSY appears to have adequate content and construct validity, although a factor analysis is needed. In addition, research is needed to determine how well the NEPSY differentiates among clinical groups. The different levels of scoring and interpretation, particularly the supplemental scores and qualitative analyses, are useful. The test must be used with caution, and additional research is needed.

Contributions to Neuropsychological Assessment Battery

The Contributions to Neuropsychological Assessment Battery (Benton, Hamsher, Varney, & Spreen, 1983) contains 12 individual tests designed to measure orientation, learning, percep-

tion, and motor ability. Five of the tests have norms for children (see Table 19-5). Although the manual does not give reliability data for any of the tests, the tests have a long history of use in neuropsychological assessment and should prove useful in the assessment process. More research is needed, however, to examine the reliability and validity of the battery.

Wechsler Tests as Part of a Neuropsychological Test Battery

Cornerstones of most neuropsychological test batteries, the Wechsler tests provide a standardized series of tasks for evaluating the cognitive and visual-motor skills of children and adults with brain injuries. For individuals of any age, brain injury can impair the ability to learn, to solve unfamiliar prob-

Table 19-5
Description of Tests with Children's Norms in the Contributions to Neuropsychological Assessment Battery

Test	Description
Facial Recognition	Measures sensory-perceptual ability; requires child to identify and discriminate photographs of unfamiliar human faces (norms for ages 6 to 14 years)
Judgment of Line Orientation	Measures spatial perception and orientation; requires child to select, from a stimulus array, a line that points in the same direction as the stimulus line (norms for ages 7 to 14 years)
Tactile Form Perception	Measures nonverbal tactile discrimination and recognition; requires child to touch concealed geometric figures made of fine-grade sandpaper and then visually identify the figures on a card containing ink-line drawings of the figures (norms for ages 8 to 14 years)
Finger Localization	Measures sensory-perceptual ability; requires child to identify fingers touched when hand is visible and then not visible (norms for ages 3 to 12 years)
Three-Dimensional Block Construction	Measures visuoconstructive ability; requires child to construct an exact replica of three block models (a pyramid, an 8-block four-level construction, a 15-block four-level construction) (norms for ages 6 to 12 years)

Note. The total battery consists of 12 tests: Temporal Orientation, Right-Left Orientation, Serial Digit Learning, Facial Recognition, Judgment of Line Orientation, Visual Form Discrimination, Pantomime Recognition, Tactile Form Perception, Finger Localization, Phoneme Discrimination, Three-Dimensional Block Construction, and Motor Impersistence.
Source: Benton, Hamsher, Varney, and Spreen (1983).

lems, to remember, to perform subtle visual-motor activities, and to think abstractly. The Wechsler tests are sensitive to some of these areas, but they do not provide a thorough measure of each area.

The Verbal Scale subtests on the Wechsler tests rely heavily on retrieval of information acquired *before* the injury. However, the Verbal Scale subtests fail to sample important abilities such as verbal learning, rapid and efficient processing and integration of large amounts of verbal information, verbal organization, and use and understanding of metaphors, verbal absurdities, synonyms, and antonyms. Also, the Wechsler tests do not adequately probe for subtle memory deficits and subtle visual-motor impairments that may occur as a result of brain injury. Overall, higher-level verbally mediated thinking—such as detecting and clearly stating main ideas in an essay, drawing appropriate inferences, and interpreting complex events correctly—is not measured by any current individually administered intelligence test. Thus, a comprehensive assessment of language ability must go beyond the administration of the Wechsler tests (or other individually administered intelligence tests) if language functioning and other functions are to be fully assessed.

There is no single pattern of subtest scores on Wechsler tests that reveals brain injury. In some cases, Wechsler scores may show extreme variability (e.g., as much as a 30-point difference between Verbal Scale and Performance Scale IQs), and in other cases, little—if any—variability. An overall reduction in level of intelligence is a key finding in some cases of brain injury.

Wechsler Verbal Scale–Performance Scale discrepancies. Do WISC–III Verbal Scale–Performance Scale discrepancies distinguish between right- and left-sided brain damage? The answer is likely "no." Studies with the prior version of the tests reported that the relationship between laterality of damage and Verbal Scale–Performance Scale IQs is tenuous (Aram & Ekelman, 1986; Aram, Ekelman, Rose, & Whitaker, 1985; Hynd, Obrzut, & Obrzut, 1981). Even among adults, discrepancies between Wechsler Verbal Scale and Performance Scale IQs do not occur regularly enough in patients with either right- or left-hemisphere damage to be clinically reliable (Bornstein, 1983; Kljajic & Berry, 1984; Larrabee, 1986; Lezak, 1983). These findings do not mean that the Verbal Scale–Performance Scale IQ relationship has no importance in assessing neurobehavioral deficits. The relationship can still provide important information about the behavioral consequences of brain injury for individual children, particularly when a Wechsler test is used along with tests of sensorimotor, language, and visual-spatial ability.

When brain injury has been documented (by history, CT, PET, MRI, or surgery), you can use the Wechsler tests to assess the cognitive sequelae of the neurological disorder and to identify adaptive deficits requiring more detailed analysis. If the Verbal Scale IQ is 12 or more points lower than the Performance Scale IQ, you should consider investigating linguistic abilities in more depth. (This discrepancy has less meaning for Verbal Scale IQs above 120.) Carefully analyze

the child's verbal responses to questions on the Comprehension, Similarities, and Vocabulary subtests. You may need to administer specialized tests of naming, verbal fluency, and language comprehension if the child demonstrates word-finding difficulties, paraphasias, or inability to grasp the intent of the instructions or questions. The child's responses to the Arithmetic and Digit Span subtests will provide information about his or her ability to attend, concentrate, and deal effectively with numerical stimuli. Poor performance in these areas may suggest the need for additional tests and procedures to evaluate the extent of impairment.

If the Performance Scale IQ is 12 or more points below the Verbal Scale IQ, you should consider the possibility of impaired visual-spatial, constructional, or perceptual organization skills. An examination of the quantitative and qualitative features of performance on the Block Design, Object Assembly, Picture Arrangement, and Picture Completion subtests may reveal a need for further assessment focusing on graphomotor, spatial, and visual scanning abilities.

You should not consider discrepancies of even 15 or more points between the Verbal and Performance Scale IQs on the Wechsler tests pathognomonic of brain injury, because approximately 12% to 14% of normal children in the WISC–III standardization group and approximately 9% of normal adults in the WAIS–III standardization group had differences of this magnitude or greater in either direction (see Tables A-4 and A-5 on pages 745 and 746 for the WISC–III and Tables C-4 and C-5 on pages 818 and 819 for the WAIS–III in *Assessment of Children: Cognitive Applications*). A large Verbal Scale–Performance Scale IQ discrepancy is not evidence of brain injury; rather, it is an index of test performance that you should use to generate hypotheses for further investigation. In addition to the Verbal Scale–Performance Scale discrepancy, you must consider individual subtest scores, qualitative features of subtest performance, behavioral observations, and the results of additional neuropsychological and neurological assessment procedures in evaluating cognitive performance.

Wechsler subtest interpretation. Chapters 9 and 13 in *Assessment of Children: Cognitive Applications* provide detailed descriptions of the WISC–III and WAIS–III subtests, respectively. Much of this material has neuropsychological implications. The following interpretive suggestions are for developing and testing clinical hypotheses; they are not meant to be diagnostic rules. Integrate the hypotheses you formulate about subtest scores (and all Wechsler scores) with the hypotheses you develop based on qualitative features of a child's performance, the results of specialized neuropsychological measures, the clinical history and background information, and the findings of the neurological evaluation.

1. *Information.* This subtest may be minimally affected by brain injury, except in cases of lesions involving the cortical or subcortical language areas. Scores on Information may provide an estimate of the examinee's premorbid level of functioning, particularly for older adolescents and adults. A pattern of failure on easy items and success on more difficult

items suggests possible retrieval difficulties associated with long-term memory (Milberg, Hebben, & Kaplan, 1996). Retrieval difficulties may arise because the information was never learned, because the information is not accessible, or because there is a deficit in recalling specific types of information (e.g., history, geography, science).

2. *Comprehension.* This subtest may be minimally affected by brain injury, except in cases of lesions involving the cortical or subcortical language areas. However, in some cases, Comprehension may reveal difficulties with impulsivity, inattention, poor judgment, concrete thinking, perseveration, and disturbed associations. Examinees with brain injuries may fail the two proverb questions on the WAIS–III because they cannot understand the abstract nature of the proverbs; instead, they may offer a concrete example (e.g., "If the stone keeps rolling, moss will not stick to it").

3. *Similarities.* This subtest may reveal difficulties with verbal abstraction. In some cases, examinees with brain injuries may show extremely concrete reasoning (e.g., "Orange and banana are not alike because one is long and one is round"). Examinees also may be able to define each word but not integrate the pairs. And some may give differences between the words, but not their similarities.

4. *Digit Span.* This subtest may reveal attention problems. Additionally, large differences between Digits Forward and Digits Backward (differences of 3 or more digits correctly recalled) may suggest a loss of flexibility or impaired attention (especially in more complex situations demanding the kind of attention associated with Digits Backward). Note whether the examinee begins the series before you are finished or repeats the digits at a rapid rate. Examine where the errors occurred: at the beginning, at the end, or in the middle. If there is a pattern of errors, it may suggest proactive interference (digits early in the series interfere with recall of later ones) or retroactive interference (digits later in the series interfere with recall of earlier ones).

5. *Arithmetic.* This subtest is good for evaluating attention, concentration, and cognitive reasoning processes. An examinee's anxiety about her or his arithmetical ability may result in low scores on this subtest. When you use testing-of-limits procedures on this subtest, you may obtain valuable information about the examinee's writing skills, sequencing, and mastery of basic arithmetical processes. Note whether the examinee was impulsive in giving responses. Consider the possible reasons for any failures.

6. *Vocabulary.* This subtest may be minimally affected by brain injury, except in cases of lesions directly involving the cortical or subcortical language areas. Scores on Vocabulary (as well as Information and Comprehension) may provide an estimate of the examinee's premorbid level of functioning, particularly for older adolescents and adults. The subtest may reveal expressive difficulties, perseveration, distractibility, or association difficulties. If the examinee cannot define a word, you can ask him or her, after the test is completed, to use the word in a sentence.

7. *Letter–Number Sequencing.* This subtest may reveal information about attention and memory, visuospatial func-

tions, and processing speed. Note, for example, possible short-term memory deficits, anxiety, inattention, distractibility, impulsivity, or auditory sequencing problems.

8. *Picture Completion.* This subtest can be sensitive to visual difficulties. For example, an examinee may give a response such as "nothing is missing" when his or her visual field is restricted. Examinees with visual agnosia may completely misidentify the stimulus picture, whereas those with expressive language difficulties may give an incorrect verbal response but correctly point to the missing part. Note whether the examinee has difficulty when the missing part is from the central portion of the figure but not when it is from the contour of the figure. Also note whether the difficulty is associated with "items requiring inferences about symmetry, inferences based on the knowledge of the object, or inferences based on knowledge of natural events" (Milberg et al., 1996, p. 66). If the examinee has difficulty naming the missing parts, provide a pointed dowel to help him or her point to the missing parts.

9. *Picture Arrangement.* This subtest can be sensitive to disturbances in serial ordering or sequencing. Some examinees with brain injuries may leave the cards in the order in which they were placed or only minimally move the cards. This behavior may indicate attentional deficits or impaired conceptual skills.

10. *Block Design.* This subtest may reveal visual-spatial difficulties. Carefully observe the examinee's performance. Note whether the examinee has difficulty in bringing the parts together to form a whole or has fumbling or angulation difficulties. Are the reproductions grossly inaccurate? Breaks in a 2 × 2 or 3 × 3 block configuration may suggest visual-spatial difficulties. Some children with brain injuries who have constructional apraxia may fail to produce the designs and yet be able to accurately describe the designs or the differences between the designs and their copies. This indicates intact perceptual ability, but impaired ability to carry out purposeful movements.

11. *Object Assembly.* This subtest also may reveal visual organization problems. Note which items are passed and which ones are failed. Did the failed items require appreciation of contour and edge alignment or appreciation of internal details? What kind of test-taking strategies did the examinee use? Can the examinee say what the object is supposed to be even though she or he cannot assemble the pieces accurately?

12. *Coding or Digit Symbol—Coding.* This subtest may reveal information about sequencing, speed, visual-motor functioning, new learning, scanning, and other related processes. Carefully observe the examinee's performance. Note, for example, the presence of perseveration, rotation of figures, transformation of figures (e.g., to perceptually similar letters), anxiety, extreme caution, slowness, or skipping of boxes.

13. *Matrix Reasoning.* This subtest may reveal information about perceptual reasoning ability, attention to detail, concentration, and spatial ability. Carefully observe the examinee's performance. Note, for example, possible reasoning difficulties, perseveration, anxiety, inattention, distractibility, impulsivity, or slow responding.

14. *Symbol Search.* This subtest may reveal information about perceptual discrimination, speed and accuracy, attention and concentration, short-term memory, and cognitive flexibility. Carefully observe the examinee's performance. Note, for example, the presence of perseveration, anxiety, confusion, visual-motor difficulties, extreme caution, slowness, or skipping of rows.

As noted in Chapter 10 of *Assessment of Children: Cognitive Applications,* performance on intelligence tests (and other tests as well) is likely to be multidetermined. For example, the written responses to the WISC–III Coding subtest are the end product of the integration of visual, perceptual, oculomotor (i.e., pertaining to eye movements), fine-motor, and mental functions. Disturbances in any or all of these functions may result in poor performance. Consequently, to account for the observed deficits, you will need to identify the abilities related to performance on each subtest and evaluate each ability separately.

Comment on the Wechsler tests. Effects of brain injury on intelligence test performance may be general (i.e., a global reduction in intelligence) or specific (i.e., impairment of selective areas of cognitive functioning). Because of this variability, there are no patterns on the WISC–III (such as Verbal Scale–Performance Scale discrepancies, subtest patterns, or specific subtest scores) that reliably distinguish children with brain injuries from children who are emotionally disturbed or normal. Children with brain injuries may obtain lower IQs than normal children. Perhaps the best single indicator of brain injury on the Wechsler tests (and on other measures of intelligence as well) is a lower than expected total score (such as the Full Scale IQ), taking into consideration the child's age, education, socioeconomic status, and related factors.

The Wechsler Intelligence Scale for Children–III as a Process Instrument (WISC–III PI; Kaplan, Fein, Kramer, Delis, & Morris, 1999) is also useful in the assessment of brain injury for children (see Chapter 16 in *Assessment of Children: Cognitive Applications,* pages 569 to 571, for a review). The test is particularly helpful for determining which processes are deficient when examinees perform poorly on the test.

ADDITIONAL PROCEDURES FOR THE ASSESSMENT OF CHILDREN WITH BRAIN INJURIES

This section describes additional procedures useful for assessing children with brain injuries. For information on other neuropsychological tests, see Spreen and Strauss (1998).

Scales for Assessing Coma

The Glasgow Coma Scale (GCS; Teasdale & Jennett, 1974) is widely used in hospitals for assessing levels of consciousness in children and adults with brain injuries. The scale is useful for monitoring changes during the first few days after injury, but it can also be used to describe posttraumatic states of altered consciousness. The GCS has three parts: Eye Opening, Best Motor Response, and Best Verbal Response or Best Behavior Response (see Table 19-6). When estimating level of consciousness, consider scores on each part of the GCS separately, and supplement the scores with other clinical data. The Children's Orientation and Amnesia Test (COAT) is also used to evaluate cognition in children and adolescents during the early stages of recovery from traumatic brain injury (Ewing-Cobbs, Levin, Fletcher, Miner, & Eisenberg, 1991), as is the Westmead PTA Scale (Marosszeky, Batchelor, Shores, Marosszeky, Klein-Boonschate, & Fahey, 1993). Age norms for the COAT have been published (Iverson, Woodward, & Iverson, in press).

Self-Perceptions of Ability

The Pediatric Inventory of Neurobehavioral Symptoms–Self-Report (PINS–SR), shown in Table 19-7, is useful for obtaining information about how adolescents perceive their abilities. If they have difficulty in reading the questionnaire, you can read the items to them. Compare their responses with results obtained from neuropsychological tests and with information provided by their parents and teachers on the Pediatric Inventory of Neurobehavioral Symptoms, which is covered later in the chapter.

Questions for Determining Lateral Preference

Several questions are helpful in determining lateral preference. The expectation is that there will be a 10% superiority in the preferred (or most utilized) side. With a young child, make the following requests:

- Pick up this ball and throw it to me.
- Point to your nose.
- Pick up a crayon and draw a circle.
- Touch your nose with a finger.
- Pick up this tissue and wipe your face.

With a child age 8 years and older, ask the following questions:

- Which hand do you use to throw a ball?
- Which hand do you use to draw?
- Which hand do you use to write with?
- Which hand do you use to hold a toothbrush when you brush your teeth?
- Which hand do you use to hold an eraser when you erase a pencil mark?

You can classify their responses using the following scheme: 0 = never performed, 1 = always left, 2 = usually left, 3 = both equally, 4 = usually right, 5 = always right. Higher scores are associated with a right-hand preference (i.e., left hemisphere dominance). A standardized inventory with norms is also available for measuring lateral preference (Dean & Anderson, 1997).

Table 19-6
Glasgow Coma Scale

Eye Opening (for all ages)

4 Spontaneously—opens eyes spontaneously when approached

3 To speech—opens eyes in response to speech, normal or shout

2 To pain—opens eyes only to painful stimuli

1 Not at all—does not open eyes, even to painful stimuli

Best Motor Response

6 Follows simple commands—obeys command to raise a hand or move lips or blink eyes (this is the best motor response for children age 2 years and older)

5 Localizes pain—pulls examiner's hand away on painful stimuli (this is the best motor response for infants and children ages 6 to 24 months)

4 Purposeful movement in response to pain—pulls part of his or her body away on painful stimuli

3 Flexion to pain—flexes body inappropriately to pain (this is the best motor response for infants from birth to 6 months)

2 Extends upper and lower extremities to pain—painful stimulation results in extension of the limb

1 None—no motor response to a painful stimulus

Best Verbal Response

5 Oriented—oriented to time, place, and person (this is the best verbal response for children age 5 years and older)

4 Confused—converses, although seemingly confused or disoriented (this is the best verbal response for infants and young children ages 1 to 5 years)

3 Inappropriate—speaks only in words or phrases that make little or no sense (this is the best verbal response for infants ages 6 to 12 months)

2 Incomprehensible—responds with incomprehensible sounds, such as groans (this is the best verbal response for infants from birth to 6 months)

1 None—no verbal response

Best Behavior Response (for children under age 3 years)

5 Smiles, is oriented to sound, interacts, follows objects

4 Consolable crying, but inappropriate interactions

3 Inconsistently consolable, moaning

2 Inconsolable, restless, and irritable

1 No response

Note. You can substitute Best Behavior Response for Best Verbal Response for children under age 3 years. If you use only the first three categories that are in the Glasgow Coma Scale (Eye Opening, Best Motor Response, and Best Verbal Response) for children under age 5 years, the highest possible scores are as follows: birth to 6 months, 9; 6 to 12 months, 12; 12 to 24 months, 13; 2 to 5 years, 14; older than 5 years, 15.

Scores range from 3 to 15. A score of 15 indicates a fully alert child, while a score of 3 indicates a child in a deep coma. Scores between 13 and 15 indicate mild brain injury in individuals who are generally alert, who have spontaneous eye opening, and whose verbal responses vary from confused to oriented; scores between 9 and 12 suggest moderate brain injury; and scores 8 or lower suggest severe brain injury in individuals who cannot open their eyes, are unable to obey commands, and fail to utter recognizable words. Two parts of the Glasgow Coma Scale—Eye Opening and Best Motor Response—also can be used for children under the age of 3 years. For the third part, substitute Best Behavior Response for Best Verbal Response. The Best Verbal Response is not valid for children who do not yet speak or for children with a hearing deficit or who are mute.

Source: Adapted from Hahn, Chyung, Barthel, Bailes, Flannery, and McLone (1988); Reilly, Simpson, Sprod, and Thomas (1988); and Teasdale and Jennett (1974).

Bender Visual Motor Gestalt Test

A child's performance on the Bender Visual Motor Gestalt Test may reveal visual-motor difficulties associated with brain injury (see Chapter 8). You can administer the Bender-Gestalt twice—first as a memory test and then as a copying test—to screen different mental functions, including short-term visual memory and visual perception. The Bender-Gestalt gives information about visual-motor functioning; it should not be used exclusively as a diagnostic test for brain injury. Children with no known brain injury may also display visual-motor difficulties on the Bender-Gestalt.

Ray-Osterrieth Complex Figure Test

The Ray-Osterrieth Complex Figure Test (ROCFT) is a measure of children's visual-motor ability (see Figure 19-2). Detailed scoring systems are available (Bernstein & Waber, 1996; Loring, Martin, Meador, & Lee, 1990; Spreen & Strauss, 1998; Stern, Singer, Duke, Singer, Morey, Daughtrey, & Kaplan, 1994; Taylor, 1959). The ROCFT also can be used as a memory test, with the memory phase administered *after* the copying phase. A comparison of the initial drawing and the drawing recalled from memory may provide useful information. Children with brain injuries may do poorly on the test because of their difficulties in organizing perceptual material. However, children with similar difficulties and no known brain injury may also do poorly on the ROCFT.

Benton Visual Retention Test–Revised

The Benton Visual Retention Test–Revised (Benton, 1963) assesses visual memory, visual perception, and visuoconstructive abilities. It has three forms, with 10 designs in each form. The child copies the designs directly from the cards and also draws them from memory. You score the test by counting

Table 19-7
Pediatric Inventory of Neurobehavioral Symptoms–Self-Report (PINS–SR)

PINS–SELF-REPORT

Name:_____   Date: _____

Sex: (Circle one)   Male   Female   Birthdate: _____   Age: _____

Directions: Please circle one—T (True), F (False), or DK (Don't Know)—for each item.

Circle One

T	F	DK	1. I get confused a lot.
T	F	DK	2. It is hard for me to keep friends.
T	F	DK	3. Other people get upset with the way I talk or with what I say.
T	F	DK	4. I get headaches that keep me from doing things I enjoy.
T	F	DK	5. Sometimes food just tastes blah to me.
T	F	DK	6. I have a tough time coming up with ideas for things to do.
T	F	DK	7. I get in trouble for not paying attention in school.
T	F	DK	8. I often do or say the wrong thing when I am with other kids.
T	F	DK	9. People tell me about having conversations with me that I don't remember at all.
T	F	DK	10. I am always hungry.
T	F	DK	11. I can do my best when other people show me exactly what to do.
T	F	DK	12. Sometimes I do things that other people think are dangerous.
T	F	DK	13. I don't get many phone calls from friends.
T	F	DK	14. I sometimes get really upset over little things.
T	F	DK	15. I just don't know why I get into trouble all the time.
T	F	DK	16. People tell me I rush through my school work.
T	F	DK	17. Other kids make fun of me.
T	F	DK	18. I sometimes hear ringing, buzzing, or tapping noises.

Note. The PINS–SR is based on the PINS (see Table 19-14). Items are classified into the following five scales:

- Mental Inertia Scale: 1, 6, 11, 15
- Social Inappropriateness Scale: 2, 7, 12, 16
- Dissociation of Affect and Behavior Scale: 3, 8, 13, 17
- Episodic Scale: 4, 9, 14, 18
- Biologic Scale: 5, 10

The note in Table 19-14 describes each scale and relevant intervention guidelines.
Source: The PINS–SR was developed by Mary Ann Roberts and Jerome M. Sattler.

---

the number of correct responses or the number of errors. The Benton Visual Retention Test–Revised is similar to the Bender-Gestalt, but it contains more complex stimuli. See Spreen and Strauss (1998) for normative data on adolescents.

Bruininks-Oseretsky Test of Motor Proficiency

The Bruininks-Oseretsky Test of Motor Proficiency (see Chapter 8) contributes to the assessment of brain injury because it reliably measures fine- and gross-motor functions.

Purdue Pegboard

The Purdue Pegboard measures sensorimotor functions, particularly fine-motor coordination, that are essentially independent of educational achievement. In the first three 30-second parts of the test, the child places pegs in a pegboard with the preferred hand, then with the nonpreferred hand, and finally with both hands. In the fourth part of the test, which takes 60 seconds, the child forms "assemblies" out of a peg, a washer, a collar, and another washer. This test is a quick, simple instrument that has value for predicting the presence and laterality of cerebral injury. Norms are

Courtesy of Herman Zilinski.

available for preschool children ages 2-6 to 5-11 years (Wilson, Iacoviello, Wilson, & Risucci, 1982), for school-age children ages 5-0 to 16-11 years (Gardner, 1979; Spreen & Strauss, 1998), and for adolescents ages 14-0 to 18-11 years (Mathiowetz, Rogers, Dowe-Keval, Donahoe, & Rennells,

1986). The Purdue Pegboard permits comparison of lower-level sensorimotor functions with higher-level cognitive functions, and it provides information about lateralized or bilateral deficits.

Test of Right-Left Discrimination

Table 19-8 shows a useful procedure for obtaining information about the child's understanding of right and left. You must consider the child's age when you interpret the results.

Informal Measures of Soft Neurological Signs

Table 19-9 shows several motor-movement procedures for assessing soft neurological signs in children age 3 years and older.

Finger Localization Test

Another procedure for evaluating soft neurological signs is the Finger Localization Test (see Table 19-10). Again, always consider the results with the child's age in mind.

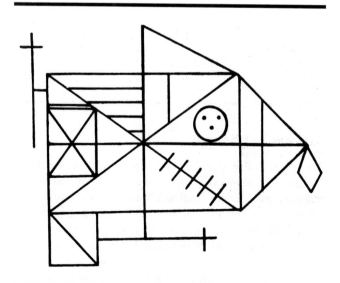

Figure 19-2. Ray-Osterrieth Complex Figure Test.

Table 19-8
Right-Left Discrimination Test

1. Raise your right hand.
2. Touch your left ear.
3. Point to your right eye.
4. Raise your left hand.
5. Show me your right leg.
6. Show me your left leg.
7. Point to your left ear with your right hand.
8. Point to the wall on your right.
9. Examiner touches the child's left hand: "Which hand is this?"
10. Examiner touches his or her own right eye: "Which eye is this?"
11. Examiner touches his or her own right hand: "Which hand is this?"
12. Examiner touches his or her own left ear: "Which ear is this?"
13. With the child's eyes closed, the examiner touches the child's left ear: "Which ear is this?"
14. Examiner touches his or her own left hand: "Which hand is this?"
15. Examiner touches his or her own left eye: "Which eye is this?"
16. Examiner touches child's right hand: "Which hand is this?"

Scoring: Give 1 point for each correct response.

Source: Adapted from Belmont and Birch (1965) and Croxen and Lytton (1971).

Table 19-9
Assessment of Soft Neurological Signs

Task	Description	Scoring	Ages 3 to 4 years	Ages 5 years and over
Walk on toes	Ask the child to walk across the room on his or her toes after you demonstrate the task.	The child must walk on his or her toes with both feet.	■	■
Walk on heels	Ask the child to walk across the room on his or her heels after you demonstrate the task.	The child must walk on his or her heels with both feet.	■	■
Tandem gait forward	Ask the child to walk forward, heel to toe, on a taped line after you demonstrate the task.	The child must walk forward with sufficient balance to avoid stepping off the line.	■	■
Tandem gait backward	Ask the child to walk backward, heel to toe, on a taped line after you demonstrate the task.	The child must walk backward with sufficient balance to avoid stepping off the line.		■
Touch localization	Ask the child to close his or her eyes and point to or report where he or she is touched. First touch the back of the child's right hand; second, the back of the child's left hand; third, the back of both of the child's hands.	The child must report all localizations correctly, either verbally or nonverbally.	■	■
Restless movements	Ask the child to sit on a chair with feet off the floor and hands in lap for 1 minute (timed).	The child must remain seated for 1 minute and motionless for at least 30 seconds.	■	■
Downward drift	Ask the child to stand with outstretched hands for 20 seconds, with eyes closed.	The child must not have a downward drift of either arm.		■
Hand coordination	Ask the child to initiate rapid alternating movements of each hand (palms up and palms down), one hand at a time.	The child must perform smooth palms up–palms down for at least three cycles with each hand.	■	■
Hopping	Ask the child to hop on one foot at a time. If needed, demonstrate.	The child must hop on each foot.		■
Alternate tapping	Ask the child to imitate three tapping tasks: (1) tap 5 times with right index finger (at a rate of about 2 taps per second); (2) tap 5 times with left index finger; (3) tap alternately with left and right index fingers for four cycles.	The child must perform all three tasks.		■
Complex tapping	Ask the child to imitate two tapping tasks: (1) tap twice with left index finger and then twice with right index finger, repeating the pattern 5 times (at a rate of about 2 taps per second); (2) tap once with left index finger and twice with right index finger, repeating the pattern 5 times.	The child must perform both tasks correctly.		■

Note. Score each item as pass or fail.
Source: Adapted from Huttenlocher, Levine, Huttenlocher, and Gates (1990).

Verbal Fluency Tests

Tests of verbal fluency are useful in assessing word-finding ability in children with brain injuries. Verbal fluency can be defined as the ability to retrieve words that belong to a specified category in a given time period. Factors associated with verbal fluency include the abilities to accumulate and store items and to access the stored information within a limited amount of time. The two different types of verbal fluency tests shown in Table 19-11 require different kinds of semantic processing. The Animal-Naming Test requires retrieval from a narrowly defined category, with words being accessed according to their meaning; this task involves a semantic factor. In contrast, the Controlled Word Association Test (naming as

Table 19-10
Finger Localization Test

Subtest	Instructions[a]
I. Visual Subtest	Ask the child to extend her or his arm with the palm of the hand up. With the child's hand visible to her or him, ask the child to localize single fingers that have been tactually stimulated. Give 10 stimulations to each hand. Touch each finger twice in a randomized order.
II. Tactual Subtest	Ask the child to extend her or his arm with the palm of the hand up. Use a card as a shield to prevent the child from seeing her or his hand. With the child's hand hidden from her or his view, ask the child to localize single fingers that have been tactually stimulated. Give 10 stimulations to each hand. Touch each finger twice in a randomized order.
III. Tactual Pairs Subtest	This subtest is like the Tactual Subtest, but the child localizes two fingers that have been tactually stimulated simultaneously. Give 10 stimulations to each hand. Touch every possible combination on each hand.

Scoring: Give 1 point for each correct response. For the Tactual Pairs Subtest, a misidentification of either one or both of the fingers is counted as a single error. Maximum score = 20 for each part. Maximum score = 60 for the three parts.

[a]In administering the three subtests in the Finger Localization Test, numbered diagrams of a right hand and a left hand are shown to the child. The child "localizes" by indicating the finger touched, either by pointing to it on the diagram, indicating its number, or naming it. A paperclip may be used to touch the child's fingertips.
Source: Adapted from Benton (1959) and Croxen and Lytton (1971).

Table 19-11
Verbal Fluency Tests

Test	Directions
1. Animal-Naming Test	"Give the names of as many animals as you can think of. Begin." Allow 60 seconds.
2. Controlled Word Association Test	"Give as many words as you can think of that begin with the letter *F.* Do not give names of persons—like Frank or Florence—or names of states or cities—like Florida or Fresno—or other proper names. Begin." Allow 60 seconds. Then say, "Now give as many words as you can think of that begin with the letter *A.* Again do not give proper names. Begin." Allow 60 seconds. Then say, "Now give as many words as you can think of that begin with the letter *S.* Again do not give proper names. Begin." Allow 60 seconds.

Scoring: Give 1 point for each correct response. Do not count repetitions, proper nouns, or different forms of the same word.

Note. Verbal fluency tests can be administered in either an oral or a written format. For children younger than 7 or 8 years of age, the written format generally is not appropriate. With older children, it may be valuable occasionally to compare oral and written performances on the same tests. The directions above are for the oral version. For the written version, substitute the word *write* for *give.* Tentative norms for the Animal-Naming Test, with a 1-minute time interval, are as follows (Levin, Culhane, Hartmann, Evankovich, Mattson, Harward, Ringholz, Ewing-Cobbs, & Fletcher, 1991): 7 to 8 years, $M = 14.4$ ($SD = 4.7$); 9 to 12 years, $M = 18.2$ ($SD = 4.5$); 13 to 15 years, $M = 21.1$ ($SD = 5.0$).

many words as possible that begin with a certain letter) requires retrieval from different logical categories, with word meanings becoming irrelevant or being suppressed; this task involves a symbolic factor. When you give both tests, you can make comparisons between the child's semantic and symbolic word-finding abilities. If a child cannot speak, the responses can be written. You must consider the child's age and intelligence when evaluating the results of verbal fluency tests.

Picture Naming

You can measure *dysnomia* (difficulty in naming objects) with the WISC–III Picture Completion subtest. Use the

following procedure to screen for dysnomia. Point to a part of a picture on each card and ask, "What is this called?" Table 19-12 shows what parts you should point to. You can use a similar procedure with the WAIS–III and WPPSI–R Picture Completion subtests. The Boston Naming Test is another procedure useful for evaluating naming ability (Kaplan, Goodglass, & Weintraub, 1983; Yeates, 1994). The Peabody Picture Vocabulary Test–III and the Expressive Vocabulary Test (see Chapter 18 in *Assessment of Children: Cognitive Applications*) allow comparison of performance on a receptive vocabulary test with that on a picture naming (i.e., expressive vocabulary) test normed on the same standardization group.

Informal Measures of Spatial Orientation

To informally evaluate a child's spatial orientation, you can ask the child to do the following (the age at which the ability

Table 19-12
WISC–III Picture Completion Stimulus Cards for Assessing Dysnomia

	Stimulus card	Examiner points to	Correct response
1.	Sample	pencil	pencil
2.	Card 2	box	box, carton
3.	Card 3	cat	cat, kitten
4.	Card 4	hand	hand
5.	Card 5	elephant	elephant
6.	Card 7	man	man, person, adult
7.	Card 8	door	door
8.	Card 9	ladder	ladder, stepladder, stepstool
9.	Card 10	clock	clock
10.	Card 11	belt	belt
11.	Card 15	leaf	leaf, leaves
12.	Card 16	light bulb	light bulb, bulb
13.	Card 17	piano	piano, player piano
14.	Card 18	scissors	scissors
15.	Card 19	whistle	whistle
16.	Card 20	bathtub	bathtub
17.	Card 23	telephone	telephone, phone
18.	Card 24	fish	fish, goldfish, koi
19.	Card 29	umbrella	umbrella, parasol
20.	Card 30	shoe	shoe, sneaker, tennis shoe

emerges is shown in parentheses): (a) draw a person (about 5 years), (b) print numbers 3, 5, 6, 7, 9 (5 to 6 years), (c) print lower-case letters b, d, q, w, z, m, n (5½ to 6½ years), (d) draw a clock that shows 9 a.m. (7½ to 8½ years), and (e) print or write three sentences saying what he or she did last night (about 7½ years).

Informal Measures of Writing Ability

A child's writing ability can be assessed in several ways (Rapcsak, 1997). You can ask her or him to (a) write individual letters, (b) write her or his name, (c) write a sentence, (d) write a paragraph that tells a story, (e) spell orally, type, and spell using blocks with letters, (f) write in a different case or style and transcribe from upper- to lowercase and from print to script, and (g) copy letters, words, nonwords, and nonlinguistic visual patterns (e.g., Bender-Gestalt designs). These informal measures will help you clarify the relationships among the various output modalities and determine more precisely the nature of the child's functional im-

pairment. For example, in certain cases a child with a brain injury cannot write letters from dictation, but can copy letters. This, of course, also has implications for the child's educational program.

Informal Measures of Divergent Thinking

The assessment of divergent thinking provides information about the child's ability to formulate new ideas and produce a variety of responses. Supplementing standardized cognitive measures, which usually assess mainly convergent thinking, with informal measures of divergent thinking may provide additional information about a child's thinking style. These measures may be of special value in the assessment of children with brain injuries and culturally and linguistically diverse children, as well as in the general assessment of creativity. Table 19-13 illustrates a variety of informal divergent thinking tasks.

Raven's Progressive Matrices

The Raven's Progressive Matrices provides an estimate of a child's nonverbal cognitive ability. A child suspected of having a brain injury who performs more poorly on the Raven's Progressive Matrices (see Chapter 16 in *Assessment of Children: Cognitive Applications*) than on verbal intelligence tests may have nonverbal reasoning difficulties. The child may be able to concentrate on only one aspect of the stimulus array and thus may be unable to integrate the necessary spatial relationships to arrive at a correct response. In such cases, do not use the child's performance on the Raven's Progressive Matrices to estimate his or her general intelligence. The strategies needed to solve Raven's Progressive Matrices are not unique to either hemisphere (Zaidel, Zaidel, & Sperry, 1981). For example, a child could solve the matrices either with an analytic strategy (i.e., sampling one element at a time) or with a synthetic strategy (i.e., grouping patterns into larger units or wholes). Consequently, do not assess lateralization of injury based on performance on the Raven's Progressive Matrices. Note that the SB:IV, DAS, WAIS–III, and K–BIT (see *Assessment of Children: Cognitive Applications*), for example, allow comparison of performance on a matrix subtest with that on verbal subtests normed on the same standardization group.

Token Test for Children

The Token Test for Children (DiSimoni, 1978) is useful as a screening test of receptive language (auditory comprehension) for children between 3-0 and 12-5 years. Other versions are available for older adolescents and adults (De Renzi, 1980; De Renzi & Faglioni, 1978). The test requires children to manipulate tokens in response to commands given by the examiner, such as, "Touch the red circle." The commands

Table 19-13
Informal Measures of Divergent Thinking Tasks

Test	Description	Example
Unusual Uses	Child is asked to identify novel ways to use specific common objects.	Use the following instructions (Price-Williams & Ramirez, 1977, p. 7): "Let's see how clever you can be about using things. For instance, if I asked you how many ways an old tire could be used, you might say to fix up an old car, for a swing, to roll around and run with, to cut up for shoe soles, and so on. Now if I asked you 'How many ways can you use a pebble?' what would you say?" After you give these instructions, ask the child to give uses for a newspaper, a table knife, a coffee cup, a clock, and money. Two scores are obtained: an ideational fluency score (the uses mentioned for all five objects are summed) and an ideational flexibility score (the different categories of usage for each object are summed). The following example illustrates the scoring: As a response to "newspaper," "to read, to make a mat, and to use as an umbrella" receives a fluency score of 3 and a flexibility score of 3. As a response to "table knife," "cut your meat and cut other things" receives a fluency score of 2 and a flexibility score of 1. The two scores also form an efficiency index (ratio of flexibility score to fluency score).
Common Situations	Child is asked to list problems inherent in a common situation.	"Tell me some problems that someone might have while walking with a crutch."
Product Improvement	Child is asked to suggest ways to improve an object.	"Think of different ways to improve a toy car so that you would have more fun playing with it."
Consequences	Child is asked to list the effects of a new and unusual event.	"Just suppose that people no longer needed or wanted automobiles. What would happen? Tell me your ideas and guesses."
Object Naming	Child is asked to list objects that belong to a broad class of objects.	"Name as many objects as you can that cut."
Differences	Child is asked to suggest ways in which two objects are different.	"Tell me the ways in which a spoon and ball are different."
Similarities	Child is asked to suggest ways in which two objects are alike.	"Tell me the ways in which cheese and vegetables are alike."
Word Arrangements	Child is asked to produce sentences containing specified words.	"Make up a sentence containing the words 'dog' and 'walked.'"
Word Fluency	Child is asked to say words that contain a specified word or letter.	"What words have the /b/ sound in them?"
Possibilities	Child is asked to list objects that can be used to perform a certain task.	"Tell me as many different things as you can that can be used to write with."
Quick Response	Child is asked to say the first word that he or she can think of in response to words read aloud.	"What is the first word you think of when I say 'run'?"
Associational Fluency	Child is asked to list synonyms for a given word.	"What words mean the same as 'big'?"
Social Institutions	Child is asked to list two improvements for a social institution.	"Tell me two ways that you could improve or change marriage."
Planning Elaboration	Child is asked to detail the steps needed to make a briefly outlined plan work.	"Your club is planning to have a party. You are in charge of the arrangements. What will you do?"
Ask and Guess	Child is encouraged to ask questions about a particular picture or to guess possible consequences of actions presented in the picture.	Show the child a picture of a boat. "Here is a picture of a boat. What are some questions that you can ask about the picture?"

(Continued)

Table 19-13 *(Continued)*

Test	Description	Example
What Would	Child is asked to think of items that could be improved if changed in a particular way.	"What would taste better if it were sweeter?"
Criteria	Child is asked to tell the criteria that might be used in judging an event or object.	"Tell me some reasons why people might like to eat apple pie."
Questions	Child is asked to list questions related to specified words.	"What questions could you ask about the word 'city'?"

Source: The tasks are from Guilford and Hoepfner (1971), Parnes (1966), and Torrance and Myers (1970).

vary in length and syntactic complexity. The 20 tokens vary along the dimensions of color, shape, and size. The Token Test is a sensitive indicator of mild receptive disturbances in aphasic children who have passed other auditory tests. Although the test is only a screening device because its psychometric properties or norms are not well established, it is a useful instrument for the assessment of receptive aphasia. See Spreen and Strauss (1998) for normative data for children ages 6 to 13 years.

Reporter's Test

The Reporter's Test is a useful screening test for examining expressive language (De Renzi & Ferrari, 1978). You administer the test by performing various actions on an array of 20 tokens. The child reports the performance verbally in a way that would enable a hypothetical third person to replicate your actions. For example, if you touch the large yellow square, the child must state the relevant information so that the imaginary third person can perform the action. A correct response would be "Touch the large yellow square." The child must produce an accurate connected sequence of words. Research suggests that the Reporter's Test provides useful information for assessing expressive language (Ballantyne & Sattler, 1991; Feldman, 1984; Hall & Jordan, 1985; Jordan & Hall, 1985). The Reporter's Test complements the Token Test and usually is administered after the Token Test.

Memory and Learning Tests

The following tests are useful measures of memory and learning:

- California Verbal Learning Test–Children's Version (CVLT–C; Delis, Kramer, Kaplan, & Ober, 1994)
- Children's Auditory Verbal Learning Test–Second Edition (CAVLT–2; Talley, 1993)
- Children's Memory Scale (CMS; Cohen, 1997)
- Rey Auditory-Verbal Learning Test (RAVLT; Forrester & Geffen, 1991; Savage & Gouvier, 1992; Taylor, 1959)
- Tests of Memory and Learning (TOMAL; Reynolds & Bigler, 1994)
- Wide Range Assessment of Memory and Learning (WRAML; Adams & Sheslow, 1990)

Computerized Test Batteries

Kane and Kay (1992) provide a useful review of 13 computerized neuropsychological and performance test batteries and several computer-administered tests for the assessment of brain injury.

SCHOOLIES

You mean to tell me that you forgot the note to get the pass to get the slip that you exchange for the note that serves as the pass that gets you back into class?!!

© 1997 by John P. Wood

Pediatric Inventory of Neurobehavioral Symptoms

The Pediatric Inventory of Neurobehavioral Symptoms (PINS; Roberts, 1992; Roberts & Furuseth, 1997) is a rating scale completed by parents or teachers for children who have sustained a traumatic brain injury. (Table 19-14 shows a preliminary version of the PINS.) Items are scored on a 0- to 3-point scale. Norms are being developed. Contact Dr. Mary Ann Roberts, University of Iowa Hospital, Department of Pediatrics, Iowa City, IW 52242 for further information about the PINS.

Norms for Neuropsychological Tests

Yeudall, Fromm, Reddon, and Stefanyk (1986) published normative data for 12 neuropsychological tests, stratified for age and sex (ages 15 to 40 years). The tests are the Language Modalities Test for Aphasia, Memory-for-Designs, Raven's Coloured Progressive Matrices, Symbol-Gestalt, Minute Estimation, Controlled Word Association, Written Word Fluency, Purdue Pegboard, Williams Clinical Memory, Symbol Digit Modalities, L. J. Tactile Recognition, and Wisconsin Card Sorting. Schum, Sivan, and Benton (1989) published norms for the Multilingual Aphasia Examination for children between 6 and 12 years. Consult these norms whenever you give any of these tests to individuals in the age groups covered by the tests.

EVALUATING THE ASSESSMENT FINDINGS

A comprehensive neuropsychological evaluation may reveal disturbances in the child's motor, sensory, affective, cognitive, social, temperament, and personality domains. For example, intellectual deficits may be revealed by a global reduction of IQ or by reduced efficiency in specific performance or verbal areas. During the early stages of brain injury, symptoms such as hallucinations may mimic the symptoms of psychiatric disorders. Brain injury itself may play a major role in predisposing children to severe forms of psychopathology, as well as to subtle changes in personality. Brain injury also may exacerbate a subclinical psychiatric condition that was present before the injury.

Inferential Methods of Test Analysis

You can use several inferential methods to analyze the data you obtain from a neuropsychological test battery.

1. *Level of performance.* This approach compares the child's test scores with cutoff points based on a normative sample. The level-of-performance approach gives explicit recognition to the quantification of behavioral data. However, establishing cutoff points is not easy because the performances of normal children vary greatly. Additionally, poor scores might be caused by factors unrelated to the brain injury, such as motivational deficiency, attention problems, sensory difficulties, and testing conditions. The level-of-performance approach, if used exclusively, may generate high false-positive rates—some children will be identified as brain injured when in fact they are not. However, the approach is useful in comparing a child's present performance with past performance and in noting changes in a child's performance. When you do not have pre-injury scores, estimates of a child's premorbid level can be made from the child's school grades, teachers' and parents' reports, and special class placements and work products. For example, a 10-year-old child in the fourth grade with a 3.5 average probably had at least average or high-average ability before the brain injury was sustained. If an intelligence test administered after the brain injury indicates an IQ in the 70 to 80 range (or below), there is a strong possibility that the child's ability has decreased considerably.

2. *Pattern of performance.* The aim of this approach is to obtain information about functional deficits and strengths by considering the pattern of results (a) among several tests and (b) within each test.

3. *Pathognomonic signs of brain injury.* This approach focuses on signs of pathology in the test performance (such as aphasic or apractic disturbances, visual field defects, or severe memory disturbances) and on neurological tests (such as EEG abnormalities). The pathognomonic approach assumes that certain indices on neuropsychological tests and on the neurological examination reflect brain impairment. However, the pathognomonic approach, if used exclusively, may generate high false-negatives rates—some children will be identified as not brain injured when in fact they are. This is because the absence of signs is not necessarily an indication of health. The pathognomonic approach may also lead to false positives. For example, EEG abnormalities may not necessarily indicate the presence of brain injury.

4. *Comparison of performance on the two sides of the body.* This approach attempts to determine lateralization of deficits—the relative efficiency of the right versus the left side of the body. The focus, therefore, is primarily on tests of lower-level motor, sensory, and sensorimotor functioning. Although the child serves as his or her own control (one side of the body versus the other side), you will find that normative data are useful. The normative data, which should be age standardized, provide information about the absolute level of performance for each side of the body. Do not use this approach exclusively in the assessment, because unilateral injury may not always produce lateralized motor or sensory difficulties. Also, this approach tells only about lower-level brain functions, not about higher-level brain functions that are particularly important for learning and everyday functioning.

You should compare the findings resulting from each approach to arrive at a diagnostic impression; do not use one method exclusively.

Table 19-14
Pediatric Inventory of Neurobehavioral Symptoms

PEDIATRIC INVENTORY OF NEUROBEHAVIORAL SYMPTOMS

Child's name: _____   Date: _____

Sex: ☐ Male   ☐ Female   Birthdate: _____ Age: _____

Name of person filling out form: _____

Directions:

Please rate your child's (student's) behavior over the past two months using the following rating scale:

0	1	2	3
Almost never or not at all	Sometimes or just a little	Often or pretty much	Very often or very much

Items	Circle One
1. Has difficulty developing plans or setting a goal	0 1 2 3
2. Reacts to minor events as if they were catastrophes	0 1 2 3
3. Does not anticipate the consequences or outcomes of his or her actions	0 1 2 3
4. Swears or uses vulgar gestures	0 1 2 3
5. Complains of headaches or sharp head pains	0 1 2 3
6. Has difficulty accepting unexpected changes in schedule	0 1 2 3
7. Has difficulty with transitions from one activity to another	0 1 2 3
8. Does not perceive others' feelings accurately (for example, keeps talking when the other person is giving clear signals that it is time to be quiet)	0 1 2 3
9. Makes comments that are frequently irrelevant or off the topic being discussed	0 1 2 3
10. Blurts out tactless statements about others (for example, says aloud, "That person is fat")	0 1 2 3
11. Often moves too fast; seldom slows down	0 1 2 3
12. Has difficulty sustaining friendships; loses friendships after a short time	0 1 2 3
13. Has very little confidence in his or her own judgment	0 1 2 3
14. Lacks initiative (waits for directions before starting something)	0 1 2 3
15. Is unable to focus or stay on task without constant redirection	0 1 2 3
16. Smells or licks objects	0 1 2 3
17. Responds to changes in temperature differently from others at home (for example, is always cold when others are okay or warm)	0 1 2 3
18. Prefers spicier foods or asks for more seasoning on foods (compared to preferences in his or her younger years)	0 1 2 3
19. Complains of hearing ringing, buzzing, or tapping noises	0 1 2 3
20. Is impatient to have his or her needs met	0 1 2 3
21. Has a facial expression that seldom changes, even when he or she is mad, sad, or happy	0 1 2 3
22. Has difficulty memorizing even simple information	0 1 2 3
23. Is too easily led by other children or adolescents	0 1 2 3
24. Says or does things unexpectedly, or "out of the blue," that are unrelated to what is going on	0 1 2 3
25. Complains of food tasting or smelling bad or rotten when the food is *not* bad or rotten	0 1 2 3
26. Has difficulty applying intelligence in practical ways	0 1 2 3
27. Misreads social situations	0 1 2 3
28. Puts non-food items (for example, small toys) in mouth	0 1 2 3

(Continued)

Table 19-14 *(Continued)*

Items	Circle One
29. Completes work appropriately only if the task is highly structured and predictable	0 1 2 3
30. Sometimes stares off, unaware of what's going on around him or her	0 1 2 3
31. Has temper tantrums for no real reason over things that usually are "not a big deal"	0 1 2 3
32. Is restless or fidgety	0 1 2 3
33. Has decreased appreciation of dangerous situations	0 1 2 3
34. Tends to be withdrawn	0 1 2 3
35. Behaves like a child several years younger than he or she is	0 1 2 3
36. Complains of seeing things that other people cannot see	0 1 2 3
37. Is into the refrigerator or cupboards just a few minutes after eating a meal (never seems to be full)	0 1 2 3
38. Is puzzled when social situations do not go well	0 1 2 3
39. Is confused concerning time sequences	0 1 2 3
40. Has difficulty acting spontaneously; would prefer to just sit and do nothing	0 1 2 3
41. Sometimes seems confused, but confusion lasts only a short time	0 1 2 3
42. Seems unaware of others' feelings (for example, does not realize that someone is upset; does not understand why)	0 1 2 3
43. Completes school work too quickly	0 1 2 3
44. Has expressions of emotion that are overdone, exaggerated, or inappropriate to the situation (for example, says "I love you" to a stranger)	0 1 2 3
45. Complains that food is tasteless	0 1 2 3
46. Feels sad or cries for no reason; has no explanation for the sad feelings	0 1 2 3
47. Is inflexible; insists on doing what he or she wants to do	0 1 2 3
48. Has difficulty modulating tone of voice appropriately (for example, may shout or use harsh tone when only mildly irritated)	0 1 2 3
49. Has quick and dramatic mood changes (extremely happy one minute, extremely sad the next)	0 1 2 3
50. Fails to learn from positive or negative consequences	0 1 2 3
51. Seems to forget having had conversations with people	0 1 2 3
52. Repeats the same behavior over and over	0 1 2 3
53. Responds only to what is right here and now; does not think about what happened yesterday or what could happen tomorrow	0 1 2 3
54. Breaks into conversation abruptly or awkwardly	0 1 2 3

Note. Items are classified into the following five scales:

- Mental Inertia Scale: 1, 3, 13, 14, 22, 23, 26, 29, 34, 39, 40, 53
- Social Inappropriateness Scale: 4, 9, 10, 11, 12, 15, 20, 32, 33, 35, 43, 54
- Dissociation of Affect and Behavior Scale: 6, 7, 8, 21, 27, 38, 42, 44, 47, 48, 50, 52
- Episodic Scale: 2, 5, 19, 24, 25, 30, 31, 36, 41, 46, 49, 51
- Biologic Scale: 16, 17, 18, 28, 37, 45

The Mental Inertia Scale is defined as reduced initiation of appropriate behavior. A student with problems on the Mental Inertia Scale would benefit from increased environmental structure and coaching or prompting. The Social Inappropriate Scale is defined as failure to inhibit inappropriate behavior. A student with problems on the Social Inappropriate Scale would benefit from referral to a physician for consideration of stimulant trial. Implementing positive daily routines also would be helpful. The Dissociation of Affect and Behavior Scale is defined as inability to modulate emotional responses as well as reduced capacity to read other people's emotions or behavior. A student with problems on the Dissociation of Affect and Behavior Scale would benefit from structured social experiences. The Episodic Scale is defined as sensory, cognitive, and emotional symptoms that come and go for no apparent reason or with minimal provocation. A student with problems on the Episodic Scale would benefit from a neurobehavioral evaluation for consideration of anticonvulsants or mood stabilizers. The Biologic Scale is defined as alterations in basic biological functions. A student with problems on the Biologic Scale has a high probability of deficits in executive function and would benefit from the setting up of a structured and safe environment. A functional academic program (e.g., practicing math skills in the real-world environment of the grocery store) is often beneficial, particularly as the student reaches junior high grades.

Source: Reprinted, with adaptations and with permission of the author, from M. A. Roberts, "Pediatric Inventory of Neurobehavioral Symptoms," unpublished manuscript, University Hospital School, University of Iowa, Iowa City, Iowa 52242. Copyright © 1992.

Diagnostic Considerations

The diagnostic effort should be based on a comprehensive assessment of information from (a) a neuropsychological evaluation (which includes formal tests, informal tests, a mental status evaluation, and an interview), (b) interviews with the child's parents, relatives, friends, and teachers about how the child is currently functioning, how the child functioned *before* the injury, and how the family and school are coping with the child's disability, and (c) evaluations conducted by neurologists, speech/language pathologists, and other professionals.

You will want to consider the following:

1. What are the relevant background characteristics of the child? These include age at the time of the injury; gender; overall adjustment before the injury; level of cognitive, perceptual-motor, and affective functioning before the injury; behavior, temperament, personality, and interpersonal skills before the injury; medical history; and educational history.

2. What are the neurological/medical findings? These encompass the type of brain injury the child sustained, lateralization of the injury, location of the injury, duration of the injury, immediate effects of the injury (including loss of consciousness and duration of coma, if relevant), diaschisis effects (injury in one part of the brain that affects other parts of the brain via connections between the parts), treatment (including any hospitalization), and prognosis.

3. What are the results of the neuropsychological evaluation? (See Table 19-15 for symptoms associated with brain injuries.) Consider such factors as the following (Kay & Silver, 1989):

   • *Arousal level*—ability to initiate activities, including behaviors that are purposeful, thoughtful, consistent, and independent

Table 19-15
Possible Symptoms Associated with Brain Injury

Physical	Sensory	Affective	Cognitive	Social/Personality
Headaches	Problems with vision	Depression	Alterations in consciousness	Impaired social skills, including misperception of the intentions of others, unusual remarks, or inappropriate actions
Vomiting	Problems with hearing	Blunted affect	Confusion	
Seizures	Problems with speech	Anxiety	Decreased intellectual efficiency	
Drowsiness	Problems with taste	Apathy	Problems following directions	
Psychomotor slowing	Problems with smell	Elation or euphoria	Impaired orientation	Subtle changes in personality (as when a previously fastidious child becomes unkempt and careless)
Extreme slowness in reaction time and in processing information	Hallucinations and other unusual episodic sensory experiences (for example, smelling odd odors or seeing visions of lights)	Emotional lability	Impaired judgment	
Hyperactivity		Talkativeness (or verbal expansiveness)	Poor planning	
Muscle weakness		Restlessness	Concentration and attention difficulties	
Stiffness	Pain	Poor frustration tolerance	Memory difficulties	Regression to a more immature level of functioning
Paralysis	Paresthesias (abnormal sensations)	Guilt feelings	Distractibility	
Dizziness		Moodiness	Failure to learn from experience	Hypochondriacal preoccupations
Vertigo		Anger	Problems in communication	
Head buzzing		Hostility	Difficulties in understanding	Antisocial behavior (lying, stealing, truancy, sexual offenses)
Head tingling		Indifference		
Bowel problems		Impulsivity	Rigid and inflexible thinking	
Bladder problems		Difficulty inhibiting actions	Difficulty in shifting cognitive set	Uncooperativeness
Genital problems		Agitation	Deterioration of academic performance	Suspiciousness
Tremors		Withdrawal		Impolite speech or coarse language
Jerking		Aggression		
Tics		Difficulty modulating emotions	Overly concrete thinking	Diminished sensitivity to others
Grimaces		Rage reactions	Unusual thought content	Limited initiative
Problems with balance and coordination		Boastfulness	Difficulties with spatial relationships	Inaccurate insight and self-appraisal
Fatigue				Denial of difficulties
Problems with sleep				
Problems with eating				
Problems with swallowing				
Somatic concerns				

Note. Symptoms of brain injury will vary as a function of lesion type, location, and rate of tumor growth. Additionally, not all symptoms will be present in any individual case.

- *Motor skills*—ability to perform fine- and gross-motor movements
- *Complex attention and speed of information processing*—ability to focus, sustain, shift, and divide attention
- *Learning and memory*—ability to learn and retain new information and recall previously learned information
- *Higher complex cognitive functions*—ability to use words to convey the desired meanings adequately; ability to think abstractly, integrate new information, and generalize and apply it flexibly across changing situations
- *Executive functioning*—ability to plan, organize, monitor, modulate, and adjust behavior; ability to perceive task elements accurately, select a strategy, integrate information, and reach a solution; awareness of behavior, including degree of orientation and awareness of deficits
- *Affect, temperament, motivation, and behavior modulation*—ability to display the appropriate affect for the situation, display appropriate motivation, and behave in a planned, good-natured, and calm manner
- *Interpersonal skills*—ability to interact with others in a meaningful way
- *Self-care skills*—ability to take care of personal needs, including dressing, feeding, bathing, and other aspects of personal hygiene
- *Compensatory functions*—awareness of and ability to compensate for deficits

Also consider how the child's current level of functioning compares to her or his previous level of functioning. Information about the child's prior functioning is critical in evaluating the assessment results. For example, if a 6-year-old could not read *before* the accident, it's not surprising that the child cannot read *after* the accident. *You do not want to report a loss of functioning when the competency was never established in the first place.*

4. What resources do the family and community have to assist the child in the rehabilitation? This includes the family history, support systems available to the family, and the home, school, and community environment. Does the family have adequate transportation, insurance, and finances?

When you evaluate the information from the child's case history, use a normative-developmental framework (see Chapter 2 in *Assessment of Children: Cognitive Applications*). For example, recognize that children usually crawl before they walk, babble before they say meaningful words, draw lines before they draw circles, and identify individual alphabet letters before they read whole words. A normative-developmental approach encourages you to consider, for example, that most children begin to use individual words by 18 months, draw circles by 3 years, and learn to read by 6 to 8 years (see Tables C-1 through C-7 in Appendix C). Answers to the questions in Table 21-2 on page 683 in *Assessment of Children: Cognitive Applications* will help you review the information obtained by the multidisciplinary health care team and work with them to plan a rehabilitation program.

There is evidence to suggest that "the brain is an interactive system whose two hemispheres participate conjointly in the production of behavior, and that damage in one component inevitably affects other components" (Sergent, 1984, p. 99). Thus, even with unilateral brain injury, changes in brain-behavior functioning must be understood in the context of the whole neural system. Study each case thoroughly to identify the factors responsible for the behavioral effects shown by the child.

Brain injuries produce highly complex behavioral effects that lead to diagnostic difficulties. Here are some reasons for the diagnostic difficulties.

1. Similar forms of brain injury do not always produce the same behavioral effects, nor do behavioral differences among children with brain injuries always relate directly to the severity of the injury or to their premorbid personality characteristics.
2. Some children with brain injuries are able to compensate for deficits and may not show markedly impaired performance on psychological or neuropsychological tests.
3. Conversely, because complex human behavior is multidetermined (e.g., by the integrity of the individual's brain, emotions, and motivational factors), impaired performance on psychological or neuropsychological tests does not necessarily mean that the individual has brain injury.
4. Low test scores may be related to motivational difficulties, anxiety, educational deficits, physical handicaps, cultural factors, developmental delays, or cerebral impairment. Thus, you cannot rely on level of performance as a key diagnostic sign in evaluating brain injury; you also must consider other factors.
5. Positive neurological findings may be present without observable behavioral correlates. Examples are when the brain injury (a) affects specific deep reflexes or superficial reflexes only, (b) affects cranial nerves or other subcortical structures only, or (c) leads to transient epileptiform activity (brain waves that resemble those of an epileptic disorder but are not associated with any directly observable clinical indication of seizures).
6. Neuropsychological tests may be insensitive to some subtle signs of behavioral disturbance.
7. Neuropsychological tests may reveal marked impairment in some areas of functioning, even though the neurological examination indicates intact functioning.
8. With evolving cerebral injury, there may be an interval when pathological brain processes develop without affecting the functions assessed by either the neurological or the neuropsychological examination.
9. Early in the development of pathology, the child's compensation for deficits may mask clinical manifestations of progressive injury.
10. It is difficult to pinpoint the reasons for vague complaints, such as loss of memory, dizziness, or irritability.
11. Children with a hearing deficit, learning disability, mild mental retardation without brain injury, autistic disorder,

emotional instability, or delayed speech may display symptoms similar to those of children with a brain injury, thus making a differential diagnosis difficult. For example, the emotionally disturbed behavior of a child with aphasia who has a brain injury, which stems from the frustrating inability to communicate and understand language, may be difficult to distinguish from that of the child with an emotional disturbance but no brain injury. Children with aphasia and children with autism share abnormal responses to sounds, delay in language acquisition, and problems in articulation. Children with aphasia, however, usually do not manifest the perceptual or motor disturbances characteristic of children with autism. Furthermore, children with aphasia, in contrast with children with autism, relate to others through nonverbal gestures and expressions, are sensitive to gestures and expressions of others, learn to point toward desired objects, and show communicative intent and emotion when they acquire speech.

12. Deficits associated with a brain injury incurred at an early age may not become evident until several years later.

Qualitative analysis and testing-of-limits are primarily useful for generating, but not proving, hypotheses. These approaches are not standardized and do not have norms or validated guidelines for interpretation. Making interpretations from these approaches requires much experience. You must take care not to confuse an interesting hypothesis based on qualitative analysis with a finding that has received substantial empirical support. Nevertheless, qualitative analysis and testing-of-limits are important components of the neuropsychological assessment.

Reliability of Information

Corroborate any information obtained from the child—such as the nature of the trauma, length of unconsciousness, perceived changes in functioning, and seizure history—with information obtained from the parents and from the child's medical records. Compare what the child tells you about himself or herself with what the parents tell you about the child. The extent of agreement between the child's and parents' reports is a useful measure of the validity of the child's report. Children with brain injuries sometimes cannot recognize that they are having problems. They tend to underestimate the severity of their problems and may even deny having any. Because children with brain injuries may be unreliable reporters as a result of memory and attention problems, the interview with the parents takes on added importance. Information from parents may allow you to compare the child's pre-injury level of functioning with his or her post-injury level of functioning.

Prognosis

The severity of children's head injuries is the best predictor of long-term outcome (Klonoff, Clark, & Klonoff, 1993).

The poorest prognosis is associated with a long period of unconsciousness, skull fracture, poor neurological status, and the presence of posttraumatic seizures. Severe impairments caused by brain injuries, such as hemiplegia (paralysis of one side of the body) and visual field defects (difficulty in seeing parts of the visual field), may show little or no improvement after several years, whereas milder impairments of sensorimotor functions may show improvement. Mental processes, which are more complex than sensory or motor processes and are not as circumscribed or anatomically restricted, may recover gradually. The rate of recovery is most rapid in the months immediately following injury. Severe cases of brain injury in childhood may limit future learning and subsequent development of higher-level cognitive and behavioral skills; in fact, measured intelligence may decline over time.

Children with traumatic brain injury are at greater risk for incurring subsequent head injury than children without brain injury (Annegers, 1983). It is not clear, however, whether the increased risk is related to nonspecific accident proneness or is a consequence of the initial head injury (e.g., related to changes in cognitive efficiency, vigilance, or temperament).

As noted previously, the factors that affect prognosis are complex. Some children with severe brain injuries recover functions, whereas others with seemingly minor injuries show considerable lifelong deficits. Therefore, recoverability of impaired functions should not be expected automatically in every case. You must make prognostic statements tentatively and with caution, subject to revision based on the results of periodic reassessments (Tramontana & Hooper, 1988).

Report Writing

Chapter 21 in *Assessment of Children: Cognitive Applications* presents detailed guidelines for report writing. There may be occasions, however, when you will want to use a standardized format for reporting assessment results. Table 19-16 shows a general worksheet that you can modify to suit your needs. The worksheet outlines several standard procedures, with appropriate spaces for recording the findings. Some items call for a checkmark (e.g., tests administered) or a number (IQ or percentile rank), whereas others require detailed comments (e.g., behavioral observations). You can type the final report directly from the worksheet.

CONCLUDING COMMENT ON THE ASSESSMENT OF CHILDREN WITH BRAIN INJURIES

As in all clinical cases, you will want to base your interpretations, conclusions, and recommendations on a careful analysis of all available information. Focus on children's deficits and strengths; their awareness and acceptance of their deficits; their motivation; the environmental supports available to them; the degree of accommodation they (and their parents)

Table 19-16
Neuropsychological Report Writing Worksheet for Children of School Age

NEUROPSYCHOLOGICAL REPORT WRITING WORKSHEET

Instructions: Insert applicable information in the spaces and cross out inapplicable phrases.

Reason for Referral

_____ is a _____ -year-old male/female who was born on _____ . He/She was referred for a neuropsychological evaluation after a _____ on _____ .

Tests Administered

The following records, tests, and assessment procedures were used [check appropriate ones]:

1. School records
2. Medical records
3. Interview with parents
4. Interview with child
5. Wechsler Intelligence Scale for Children–III
6. Wechsler Adult Intelligence Scale–III
7. Stanford-Binet: Fourth Edition
8. Bender Visual Motor Gestalt Test
9. Benton Visual Retention Test–Revised
10. Wide Range Achievement Test–Third Edition
11. Halstead-Reitan Neuropsychological Test Battery for Older Children
12. Reitan-Indiana Neuropsychological Test Battery for Children
13. Luria-Nebraska Neuropsychological Battery–Children's Revision
14. Contributions to Neuropsychological Assessment Battery
15. NEPSY—A Developmental Neuropsychological Assessment
16. Bruininks-Oseretsky Test of Motor Proficiency
17. Purdue Pegboard
18. Token Test for Children
19. Reporter's Test
20. Raven's Progressive Matrices
21. California Verbal Learning Test–Children Version (CVLT–C)
22. Children's Auditory Verbal Learning Test–Second Edition (CAVLT–2)
23. Children's Memory Scale (CMS)
24. Rey Auditory-Verbal Learning Test (RAVLT)
25. Test of Memory and Learning (TOMAL)
26. Wide Range Assessment of Memory and Learning (WRAML)
27. Informal tests
28. Other tests: _____

_____

History

The child has noticed/parents have reported the following problems since the accident/onset of symptoms:

1. _____
2. _____

3. _____
4. _____
5. _____
6. _____
7. _____

These problems appear to be improving/getting worse/remaining the same.

The child is in the _____ grade and was performing at a satisfactory/an unsatisfactory level before the injury/onset of symptoms. Behavioral problems were/were not present before the brain injury. [If present, describe the behavioral problems: The child had difficulties in _____ .]

Birth was normal/abnormal. [If abnormal, describe what was abnormal: _____ .]

Achievement of developmental milestones was satisfactory/ delayed. [If delayed, describe what milestones were delayed _____ .]

Behavioral Observations

When seen for testing, _____ was/was not alert and well oriented. There were/were not any difficulties observed during the evaluation. [If present, describe the difficulties: These difficulties included _____ .]

Intellectual Functioning

The child achieved a Verbal Scale IQ of _____ (_____ percentile), a Performance Scale IQ of _____ (_____ percentile), and a Full Scale IQ of _____ + _____ on the Wechsler Intelligence Scale for Children–III/Wechsler Adult Intelligence Scale–III. His/Her overall score suggests that current intellectual functioning falls within the _____ range and at the _____ percentile. The chances that the range of scores from _____ to _____ includes his/her true IQ are about _____ out of 100. The results appear/do not appear to be reliable.

The Full Scale IQ appears/does not appear to reflect the child's level of functioning before the injury/onset of symptoms. This estimate is based on parents' and teacher's reports/prior psychological tests. Thus, there is/is no evidence of a general loss of intellectual functioning. [If present, describe the estimated loss: The loss appears to be of approximately _____ IQ points.]

Marked intellectual impairments were/were not noted on the subtests of the WISC–III/WAIS–III. There was/was no evidence of clinically significant scaled score deviations. [If present, describe which subtest scores deviated significantly from the mean of each scale: Strengths were shown in _____

_____

(Continued)

Table 19-16 *(Continued)*

Weaknesses were shown in _____
_____.]

Higher cognitive functions (comprehension, abstract thinking, and problem solving) appeared to be generally intact/impaired.

Educational Achievement

Reading skills are at the _____ grade level and the _____ percentile (standard score of _____); spelling skills are at the _____ grade level and the _____ percentile (standard score of _____); and arithmetic skills are at the _____ grade level and the _____ percentile (standard score of _____), as measured by the _____.

These standard achievement scores are consistent/discrepant with _____'s level of scholastic attainment before injury/onset of symptoms. Writing ability was adequate/impaired and thus not indicative/indicative of dysgraphia. There is/is no evidence of a learning disability. [If present, describe the learning disability: The learning disability involves the child's reading/spelling/arithmetic, with difficulties in _____
_____
_____.]

Motor Functioning

_____ demonstrated consistent right/left/mixed hand dominance. Gross motor coordination was intact/impaired. Fine motor coordination was adequate/impaired. [Additional comments: _____
_____.]

Auditory Perceptual Functioning

Auditory perceptual functioning was intact/impaired. _____
had no/had difficulty in differentiating between pairs of words. [Additional comments: _____
_____
_____.]

Tactile Perceptual Functioning

Tactile perceptual functioning was relatively intact/impaired. There were no/some errors indicating finger agnosia, no/some errors in graphesthesia, and no/some errors in stereognosis. [Additional comments: _____
_____
_____.]

Visuo-Spatial Functioning

Visuo-spatial functioning appeared to be adequate/impaired. Visuomotor speed was adequate/impaired. [Additional comments: _____
_____
_____.]

Oral Language Ability

Language ability was intact/impaired with respect to reading, writing, listening, and talking. There was no/was evidence of dysarthria. Motor aspects of speech were intact/impaired, as there was no/was evidence of disturbance in articulation and repetition. Comprehension of speech was adequate/inadequate and thus not indicative/indicative of a receptive disorder. Word-finding fluency was intact/impaired and thus not indicative/indicative of an expressive disorder. [Additional comments:
_____
_____
_____.]

Memory Processes and Attentional Processes

_____'s immediate memory was intact/impaired. Recent memory, including the ability to learn both new verbal and visual information, was adequate/impaired. Remote memory was satisfactory/impaired. Attentional processes were intact/impaired. There was no/was evidence of an impairment of concentration or attention. [Additional comments:
_____
_____
_____.]

Behavior

Parental reports indicate that _____ has satisfactory/unsatisfactory behavior patterns. [If unsatisfactory, include additional comments here: Parents report that _____
_____.]
School reports indicate that his/her behavior in school is satisfactory/unsatisfactory. [If unsatisfactory, include additional comments here: Teachers report that _____
_____
_____.]

Comments

[Include additional comments and recommendations here:
_____
_____
_____
_____
_____
_____
_____
_____
_____
_____
_____
_____
_____.]

Source: Adapted from Gilandas, Touyz, Beumont, and Greenberg (1984). Permission was obtained from the publisher and authors to adapt this form from *Handbook of Neuropsychological Assessment,* pp. 256–259, copyright by Grune & Stratton.

have made to any changes in their personality, temperament, cognitive abilities, and social skills; and their goals and future plans (Kay & Silver, 1989). The behavior of children with brain injuries must be understood in relation to their organically based neuropsychological deficits—do not conclude, for example, that children with brain injuries are lazy, apathetic, and lacking in initiative when, in fact, their behavior may be directly related to their organic impairment. Also, remember that physical recovery does not guarantee cognitive recovery. Although a child's physical appearance may have returned to normal (e.g., scars healed, orthotic devices no longer needed), cognitive and neurobehavioral deficits may remain for years.

In follow-up assessments and reevaluations, learn whether children with mild traumatic brain injuries still experience occasional physical, emotional, and cognitive symptoms (also referred to as "episodic symptoms"), such as staring spells, temper outbursts, memory gaps, episodic tinnitus, and severe headaches (Roberts, 1999). Inquire about these symptoms, because rating scales may miss mood changes and emotional variability. It is important to reiterate that some problems may not show up until several years later, when increasing cognitive and organizational demands are placed on the child.

THINKING THROUGH THE ISSUES

1. Defend the proposition that the WISC–III is a neuropsychological instrument.
2. Why is it difficult, if not impossible, to find uniform neuropsychological test profiles in children with brain injuries?
3. When would you use both formal and informal neuropsychological measures?

SUMMARY

Neuropsychological Test Batteries for Children

1. The Halstead-Reitan Neuropsychological Test Battery for Older Children is designed for children ages 9 to 14 years.
2. The Reitan-Indiana Neuropsychological Test Battery for Children is designed for children ages 5 to 8 years.
3. Although information about the reliability and validity of both batteries is limited, research indicates that both batteries are useful in discriminating children with brain injuries from other groups.
4. The Luria-Nebraska Neuropsychological Battery–Children's Revision (LNNB–C) is designed to assess a broad range of neuropsychological functions in children ages 8 to 12 years. Caution is needed in using the LNNB–C because the manual fails to describe the standardization sample adequately and reliability is less than adequate.
5. The NEPSY—A Developmental Neuropsychological Assessment is a neuropsychological test designed for children ages 3 to 12 years. The reliability of the NEPSY is problematic, and the test must be used with caution.
6. The Contributions to Neuropsychological Assessment Battery contains 12 individual tests designed to measure orientation,

learning, perception, and motor ability in children. More research is needed to examine the reliability and validity of the battery.
7. Cornerstones of most neuropsychological test batteries, the Wechsler tests provide a standardized series of tasks for evaluating the cognitive and visual-motor skills of children and adults with brain injuries.
8. The Verbal Scale subtests on the Wechsler tests rely heavily on retrieval of information acquired *before* the injury.
9. There is no single pattern of subtest scores on Wechsler tests that reveals brain injury.
10. Verbal Scale–Performance Scale discrepancies on the Wechsler tests do not distinguish between right- and left-sided brain damage. Therefore, you should not consider discrepancies of even 15 or more points between the Verbal and Performance Scale IQs on the Wechsler tests pathognomonic of brain injury.
11. Perhaps the best single indicator of brain injury on the Wechsler tests (and on other measures of intelligence as well) is a lower than expected total score (such as the Full Scale IQ), taking into consideration the child's age, education, socioeconomic status, and related factors.

Additional Procedures for the Assessment of Children with Brain Injuries

12. Additional procedures useful in the assessment of brain injury in children include scales for assessing coma, self-perceptions of ability, questions for determining lateral preference, Bender Visual Motor Gestalt Test, Ray-Osterrieth Complex Figure Test, Benton Visual Retention Test–Revised, Bruininks-Oseretsky Test of Motor Proficiency, Purdue Pegboard, Test of Right-Left Discrimination, informal measures of soft neurological signs, Finger Localization Test, verbal fluency tests, picture naming, informal measures of spatial orientation, informal measures of writing ability, informal measures of divergent thinking, Raven's Progressive Matrices, Token Test for Children, Reporter's Test, memory and learning tests, computerized test batteries, and Pediatric Inventory of Neurobehavioral Symptoms.

Evaluating the Assessment Findings

13. A comprehensive neuropsychological evaluation may reveal disturbances in the child's motor, sensory, affective, cognitive, social, temperament, and personality domains.
14. Several inferential methods are used to interpret the results of a neuropsychological test battery, including (a) analysis of level of performance, (b) analysis of pattern of performance, (c) analysis of pathognomonic signs of brain injury, and (d) comparison of performance on the two sides of the body.
15. The diagnostic effort should be based on a comprehensive assessment of information from (a) a neuropsychological evaluation (which includes formal tests, informal tests, a mental status evaluation, and an interview), (b) interviews with the child's parents, relatives, friends, and teachers about how the child is currently functioning, how the child functioned *before* the injury, and how the family and school are coping with the child's disability, and (c) evaluations conducted by neurologists, speech/language pathologists, and other professionals.
16. In arriving at a diagnosis, you will want to consider the relevant background characteristics of the child, the neurological/medical findings, the neuropsychological findings, and the resources of the family and community.

17. Use a normative-developmental framework in evaluating the information you obtain.
18. Brain injuries produce highly complex behavioral effects that lead to diagnostic difficulties.
19. Qualitative analysis and testing-of-limits are primarily useful for generating, but not proving, hypotheses.
20. Corroborate any information obtained from the child—such as the nature of the trauma, length of unconsciousness, perceived changes in functioning, and seizure history—with information obtained from the parents and from the child's medical records.
21. The severity of children's head injuries is the best predictor of long-term outcome.
22. The rate of recovery is most rapid in the months immediately following injury.
23. Children with traumatic brain injury are at greater risk for incurring subsequent head injury than children without brain injury.

Concluding Comment on the Assessment of Children with Brain Injuries

24. As in all clinical cases, you will want to base your interpretations, conclusions, and recommendations on a careful analysis of all available information.
25. Focus on children's deficits and strengths; their awareness and acceptance of their deficits; their motivation; the environmental supports available to them; the degree of accommodation they (and their parents) have made to any changes in their personality, temperament, cognitive abilities, and social skills; and their goals and future plans.
26. The behavior of children with brain injuries must be understood in relation to their organically based neuropsychological deficits.
27. Remember that physical recovery does not guarantee cognitive recovery.
28. It is important to reiterate that some problems may not show up until several years later, when increasing cognitive and organizational demands are placed on the child.

KEY TERMS, CONCEPTS, AND NAMES

Halstead-Reitan Neuropsychological Test Battery for Older Children (p. 441)
Reitan-Indiana Neuropsychological Test Battery for Children (p. 441)
Luria-Nebraska Neuropsychological Battery–Children's Revision (p. 441)
NEPSY—A Developmental Neuropsychological Assessment (p. 444)
Contributions to Neuropsychological Assessment Battery (p. 448)
Wechsler Tests as part of a neuropsychological test battery (p. 448)
Glasgow Coma Scale (GCS) (p. 451)
Children's Orientation and Amnesia Test (COAT) (p. 451)
Westmead PTA Scale (p. 451)
Self-perceptions of ability (p. 451)
Questions for determining lateral preference (p. 451)
Bender Visual Motor Gestalt Test (p. 452)
Ray-Osterrieth Complex Figure Test (ROCFT) (p. 452)

Benton Visual Retention Test–Revised (p. 452)
Bruininks-Oseretsky Test of Motor Proficiency (p. 453)
Purdue Pegboard (p. 453)
Test of Right-Left Discrimination (p. 454)
Informal measures of soft neurological signs (p. 454)
Finger Localization Test (p. 454)
Verbal fluency tests (p. 455)
Animal-Naming Test (p. 455)
Controlled Word Association Test (p. 455)
Picture naming (p. 456)
Dysnomia (p. 456)
Informal measures of spatial orientation (p. 456)
Informal measures of writing ability (p. 457)
Raven's Progressive Matrices (p. 457)
Token Test for Children (p. 457)
Reporter's Test (p. 459)
Memory and learning tests (p. 459)
Computerized test batteries (p. 459)
Pediatric Inventory of Neurobehavioral Symptoms (PINS) (p. 460)
Norms for neuropsychological tests (p. 460)
Inferential methods of test analysis (p. 460)
Level of performance (p. 460)
Pattern of performance (p. 460)
Pathognomonic signs of brain injury (p. 460)
Comparison of performance on the two sides of the body (p. 460)
Arousal level (p. 463)
Motor skills (p. 464)
Complex attention and speed of information processing (p. 464)
Learning and memory (p. 464)
Higher complex cognitive functions (p. 464)
Executive functioning (p. 464)
Affect, temperament, motivation, and behavior modulation (p. 464)
Interpersonal skills (p. 464)
Self-care skills (p. 464)
Compensatory functions (p. 464)
Reliability of information (p. 465)
Prognosis (p. 465)
Report writing (p. 465)

STUDY QUESTIONS

1. Discuss the place of neuropsychological test batteries in the assessment of children with brain injuries.
2. Discuss the role of the Wechsler batteries in the assessment of children with brain injuries.
3. Describe assessment procedures—other than neuropsychological test batteries and the Wechsler tests—useful in the assessment of brain injury in children.
4. Discuss the inferential methods used to analyze the findings from a neuropsychological assessment.
5. Discuss some diagnostic considerations in the assessment of children with brain injuries. Include in your discussion (a) major areas to consider in the diagnostic process, (b) reasons for diagnostic difficulties, (c) reliability of information, and (d) prognosis.

APPENDIX A

QUESTIONNAIRES

Table A-1
Sample Background Questionnaire Used in a Child Guidance Clinic or School

BACKGROUND QUESTIONNAIRE

FAMILY DATA

Child's name _____ Today's date _____

Birthdate _____ Age _____ Sex: ☐ Male ☐ Female

Home address _____

_____

School _____ Teacher _____

Person(s) filling out this form: ☐ Mother ☐ Father ☐ Stepmother ☐ Stepfather ☐ Caregiver

☐ Other (please explain) _____

Mother's name _____ Age _____ Education _____

Occupation _____ Phone: Home _____ Business _____

Father's name _____ Age _____ Education _____

Occupation _____ Phone: Home _____ Business _____

Stepmother's name _____ Age _____ Education _____

Occupation _____ Phone: Home _____ Business _____

Stepfather's name _____ Age _____ Education _____

Occupation _____ Phone: Home _____ Business _____

Marital status of parents _____ If separated or divorced, how old was the child when the separation occurred? _____

If remarried, how old was the child when the stepparent entered the family? _____

List all people living in the household (please list additional people on a separate sheet if necessary):

Name	*Sex*	*Relationship to Child*	*Age*

List the name, sex, relationship to child, and age of any brothers, sisters, or other significant people living outside the home: _____

_____

_____

Dominant language spoken in the home _____ Other languages spoken in the home _____

What language does the child use to speak to you? _____

What language does the child use to speak with friends? _____

Was the child adopted? ☐ Yes ☐ No If yes, at what age? _____ Does the child know? ☐ Yes ☐ No

Name of medical coverage group or insurance company (If none, write "none") _____

Name of medical provider _____

If insured, insured's name _____

If referred, who referred you here? _____

(Continued)

Table A-1 *(Continued)*

PRESENTING PROBLEM

Briefly describe the child's current difficulties: _____

_____

_____

_____

How long has this problem been of concern to you? _____

When was the problem first noticed? _____

What seems to help the problem? _____

What seems to make the problem worse? _____

Have you noticed changes in the child's abilities? ☐ Yes   ☐ No

If yes, please describe: _____

Have you noticed changes in the child's behavior? ☐ Yes   ☐ No

If yes, please describe: _____

Has the child received evaluation or treatment for the current problem or similar problems? ☐ Yes   ☐ No

If yes, when and with whom? _____

Is the child being treated for a medical illness? ☐ Yes   ☐ No

If yes, for what condition is the child being treated? _____

Is the child on any medication at this time? ☐ Yes   ☐ No

If yes, please note the kind of medication: _____

SOCIAL AND BEHAVIORAL CHECKLIST

Place a check next to any behavior or problem that the child *currently* exhibits.

☐ Has difficulty with hearing
☐ Has difficulty with vision
☐ Has difficulty with coordination
☐ Has difficulty with balance
☐ Has difficulty making friends
☐ Has difficulty keeping friends
☐ Refuses to share
☐ Prefers to be alone
☐ Does not get along well with brothers/sisters
☐ Does not get along well with adults
☐ Fights verbally with adults
☐ Fights physically with adults
☐ Yells and calls children names
☐ Shows wide mood swings
☐ Is aggressive (describe)
_____
☐ Is withdrawn (describe)
_____
☐ Is shy or timid
☐ Clings to others
☐ Tires easily, has little energy
☐ Is more interested in things (objects) than in people
☐ Engages in behavior that could be dangerous to self or others (describe)
_____
_____

☐ Breaks objects deliberately
☐ Lies (describe)
_____
☐ Steals (describe)
_____
☐ Injures self often
☐ Runs away
☐ Has low self-esteem
☐ Blames others for his or her troubles
☐ Is argumentative
☐ Does not get along well with other children
☐ Fights verbally with other children
☐ Fights physically with other children
☐ Does not show feelings
☐ Has frequent crying spells
☐ Has unusual or special fears, habits, or mannerisms (describe)
_____
☐ Wets bed
☐ Bites nails
☐ Sucks thumb
☐ Has frequent temper tantrums
☐ Has trouble sleeping (describe)
_____
☐ Rocks back and forth
☐ Bangs head
☐ Holds breath

☐ Eats poorly
☐ Is stubborn
☐ Has poor bowel control (soils self)
☐ Is much too active
☐ Is fidgety
☐ Is easily distracted
☐ Is disorganized
☐ Is clumsy
☐ Is unusually talkative
☐ Is forgetful
☐ Has blank spells
☐ Daydreams too much
☐ Worries a lot
☐ Is impulsive
☐ Takes unnecessary risks
☐ Gets hurt frequently
☐ Has too many accidents
☐ Doesn't learn from experience
☐ Feels that he or she is bad
☐ Is slow to learn
☐ Moves slowly
☐ Stares into space for long periods
☐ Engages in stereotyped behavior (describe) _____
☐ Does not understand other people's feelings
☐ Has difficulty following directions
☐ Gives up easily

(Continued)

Table A-1 *(Continued)*

- ☐ Complains of aches or pains
- ☐ Is disobedient
- ☐ Gets into trouble with the law
- ☐ Constantly seeks attention
- ☐ Is restless
- ☐ Has periods of confusion or disorientation
- ☐ Is jealous (describe)
  _____
- ☐ Is extremely selfish
- ☐ Feels hopeless
- ☐ Is nervous or anxious

- ☐ Is immature
- ☐ Is easily frustrated
- ☐ Has difficulty learning when there are distractors
- ☐ Is suspicious of other people
- ☐ Requires constant supervision
- ☐ Has difficulty resisting peer pressure
- ☐ Shows anger easily
- ☐ Has difficulty accepting criticism
- ☐ Feels sad or unhappy often
- ☐ Talks about wanting to die
- ☐ Has poor attention span

- ☐ Has poor memory
- ☐ Sets fires
- ☐ Is afraid of new situations
- ☐ Has trouble making plans
- ☐ Eats inedible objects
- ☐ Is not toilet trained
- ☐ Uses illegal drugs (describe)
  _____
- ☐ Drinks alcohol
- ☐ Other problems (describe)
  _____
  _____

Place a check next to any behavior or problem that the child has shown *within the last three months.*

- ☐ Shows sexually provocative behavior
- ☐ Has extreme fear of bathroom or bathing
- ☐ Has anxiety when separated from parents
- ☐ Has extreme anxiety about going to school
- ☐ Has fear at bedtime
- ☐ Is wary of any physical contact with adults in general

- ☐ Refuses to sleep alone
- ☐ Refuses to go to bed
- ☐ Has loss of bladder control
- ☐ Is fearful of strangers
- ☐ (In cases of divorce) Is fearful of visiting a parent or caregiver
- ☐ Overeats
- ☐ Is very eager to please others
- ☐ Refuses to undress for physical education classes at school

- ☐ Has compulsion about cleanliness— wanting to wash or feeling dirty all the time
- ☐ Appears dazed, drugged, or groggy upon return from visiting a divorced or separated parent
- ☐ Other recent behaviors or problems (describe) _____
  _____

LANGUAGE/SPEECH CHECKLIST

Place a check next to any language or speech problem that the child *currently* exhibits.

- ☐ Speaks in shorter sentences than expected for age
- ☐ Does not know names of common objects
- ☐ Has difficulty recalling familiar words
- ☐ Substitutes vague words (e.g., "thing") for specific words
- ☐ Responds better to gestures than to words
- ☐ Does not make appropriate gestures to communicate

- ☐ Uses gestures instead of words to express ideas
- ☐ Has difficulty making speech understood
- ☐ Speaks very slowly
- ☐ Speaks too fast
- ☐ Is often hoarse
- ☐ Has unusually loud speech
- ☐ Has unusually soft speech
- ☐ Makes sounds but no words
- ☐ Mixes up the order of events

- ☐ Seems uninterested in communicating
- ☐ Prefers to speak to adults only
- ☐ Prefers to speak to children only
- ☐ Prefers to speak to family members only
- ☐ Speaks in a monotone or exaggerated manner

EDUCATIONAL CHECKLIST

Place a check next to any educational problem that the child *currently* exhibits.

- ☐ Has difficulty with reading
- ☐ Has difficulty with arithmetic
- ☐ Has difficulty with spelling
- ☐ Has difficulty with handwriting
- ☐ Has difficulty with other subjects (please list) _____
  _____

- ☐ Has difficulty paying attention in class
- ☐ Has difficulty sitting still in class
- ☐ Has difficulty waiting turn in school
- ☐ Has difficulty taking notes in class
- ☐ Has difficulty respecting others' rights
- ☐ Has difficulty remembering things
- ☐ Forgets homework

- ☐ Has difficulty getting along with teacher
- ☐ Has difficulty getting along with other children
- ☐ Dislikes school
- ☐ Resists going to school
- ☐ Refuses to do homework

Did the child attend preschool? ☐ Yes ☐ No

If yes, at what ages? _____ How often? _____

At what age did the child begin kindergarten? _____ What is his or her current grade? _____

Is the child in a special education class? ☐ Yes ☐ No

If yes, what type of class? _____

(Continued)

Has the child been held back in a grade? ☐ Yes ☐ No

If yes, what grade and why? _____

Has the child ever received special tutoring or therapy in school? ☐ Yes ☐ No

If yes, please describe: _____

Has the child's school performance become poorer recently? ☐ Yes ☐ No

If yes, please describe: _____

Has the child missed a lot of school? ☐ Yes ☐ No

If yes, please indicate reasons: _____

DEVELOPMENTAL HISTORY

Pregnancy

Did the mother have any problems during pregnancy? ☐ Yes ☐ No ☐ Don't know

If yes, what kind? _____

How old was the mother when she became pregnant? _____ Was this a first pregnancy? ☐ Yes ☐ No

If no, how many times was the mother previously pregnant? _____

During pregnancy, did the mother smoke? ☐ Yes ☐ No ☐ Don't know

If yes, how many cigarettes each day? _____

During pregnancy, did the mother drink alcoholic beverages? ☐ Yes ☐ No ☐ Don't know

If yes, what did she drink? _____ Approximately how much alcohol was consumed each day? _____

During which part of pregnancy—1st trimester, 2nd trimester, 3rd trimester—was the alcohol consumed? _____

Were there times when 5 or more drinks were consumed? ☐ Yes ☐ No ☐ Don't know

If yes, during which trimester—1st trimester, 2nd trimester, 3rd trimester? _____

During pregnancy, did the mother use drugs (including prescription, over-the-counter, and recreational)? ☐ Yes ☐ No ☐ Don't know

If yes, what kind? _____

During pregnancy, was the mother exposed to any x-rays or chemicals? ☐ Yes ☐ No ☐ Don't know

If yes, what kind? _____

During pregnancy, was the mother exposed to any infectious disease? ☐ Yes ☐ No ☐ Don't know

If yes, what disease? _____

During pregnancy, did the mother receive prenatal care? ☐ Yes ☐ No ☐ Don't know

Was delivery induced? ☐ Yes ☐ No ☐ Don't know

How long was labor? _____ Were forceps used during delivery? ☐ Yes ☐ No ☐ Don't know

Was a cesarean section performed? ☐ Yes ☐ No ☐ Don't know

If yes, for what reason? _____

Were there any complications associated with the delivery? ☐ Yes ☐ No ☐ Don't know

If yes, what kind? _____

Was the child premature? ☐ Yes ☐ No ☐ Don't know

If yes, by how many weeks? _____

Was neonatal care needed? ☐ Yes ☐ No ☐ Don't know

If yes, what kind of care and how long was it needed? _____

Table A-1 *(Continued)*

Infancy

What was the child's birthweight? _____ Were there any birth defects or complications? ☐ Yes   ☐ No

If yes, please describe: _____

Were there any feeding problems? ☐ Yes   ☐ No

If yes, please describe: _____

Were there any sleeping problems? ☐ Yes   ☐ No

If yes, please describe: _____

Were there any other problems? ☐ Yes   ☐ No

If yes, please describe: _____

As an infant, was the child quiet? ☐ Yes   ☐ No   As an infant, did the child like to be held? ☐ Yes   ☐ No

As an infant, was the child alert? ☐ Yes   ☐ No   As an infant, did the child grow normally? ☐ Yes   ☐ No

If no, please describe: _____

As an infant, was the child different in any way from siblings? ☐ Yes   ☐ No   ☐ Not applicable

If yes, please describe: _____

First Years

During the child's first years, did he or she show any of the following behaviors? Place a check next to each one that he or she showed.

☐ Did not enjoy cuddling
☐ Was not calmed by being held
☐ Was colicky
☐ Was excessively restless
☐ Had poor sleep patterns
☐ Banged head frequently
☐ Was constantly into everything
☐ Had an excessive number of accidents
☐ Was exposed to lead

☐ Had fine-motor problems
☐ Had gross-motor problems
☐ Did not babble
☐ Did not speak
☐ Had excessive fears
☐ Ignored toys
☐ Was attached to an unusual object (describe) _____
☐ Was unaware of painful bumps or falls

☐ Had peculiar patterns of speech
☐ Preferred to play alone
☐ Had poor eye contact
☐ Was not interested in other children
☐ Did not smile socially
☐ Was insensitive to cold or pain
☐ Did not wave bye-bye

Were there any other special problems in the growth and development of the child during the first few years? ☐ Yes   ☐ No

If yes, please describe: _____

The following is a list of infant and preschool behaviors. Please indicate the age at which the child first demonstrated each behavior. If you are not certain of the age but have some idea, write the age followed by a question mark. If you don't remember or don't know the age at which the behavior occurred, please write a question mark. If the child has not yet demonstrated the behavior, write an X.

Behavior	Age	Behavior	Age	Behavior	Age
Showed response to mother	_____	Babbled	_____	Played pat-a-cake or peek-a-boo	_____
Held head erect	_____	Spoke first word	_____	Took off clothing alone	_____
Rolled over	_____	Showed fear of strangers	_____	Put on clothing alone	_____
Sat alone	_____	Put several words together	_____	Tied shoelaces	_____
Crawled	_____	Become toilet trained during day	_____	Rode tricycle	_____
Stood alone	_____	Stayed dry at night	_____	Named colors	_____
Walked alone	_____	Drank from cup	_____	Said alphabet in order	_____
Ran with good control	_____	Fed self	_____		

(Continued)

Table A-1 (Continued)

CHILD'S MEDICAL HISTORY

Place a check next to any illness or condition that the child has had. When you check an item, also note the approximate age of the child when he or she had the illness or condition.

Illness or condition	*Age*	*Illness or condition*	*Age*	*Illness or condition*	*Age*
☐ Measles	_____	☐ Seizures	_____	☐ Bone or joint disease	_____
☐ German measles	_____	☐ Broken bones	_____	☐ Gonorrhea or syphilis	_____
☐ Mumps	_____	☐ Hearing problems	_____	☐ Anemia	_____
☐ Chicken pox	_____	☐ Ear infections	_____	☐ Jaundice/hepatitis	_____
☐ Whooping cough	_____	☐ Seeing problems	_____	☐ Diabetes	_____
☐ Diphtheria	_____	☐ Fainting spells	_____	☐ Cancer	_____
☐ Polio	_____	☐ Loss of consciousness	_____	(list type) _____	
☐ Scarlet fever	_____	☐ Paralysis	_____	☐ High blood pressure	_____
☐ Meningitis	_____	☐ Dizziness	_____	☐ Heart disease	_____
☐ Encephalitis	_____	☐ Frequent headaches	_____	☐ Asthma	_____
☐ High fever	_____	☐ Difficulty concentrating	_____	☐ Bleeding problems	_____
☐ Convulsions	_____	☐ Memory problems	_____	☐ Eczema or hives	_____
☐ Allergies	_____	☐ Extreme tiredness	_____	☐ Suicide attempt(s)	_____
(please list) _____		☐ Rheumatic fever	_____	☐ Sleeping problems	_____
☐ Hay fever	_____	☐ Epilepsy	_____	☐ HIV	_____
☐ Injuries to head	_____	☐ Tuberculosis	_____	☐ AIDS	_____

Does the child have any disabilities? ☐ Yes ☐ No   If yes, please describe: _____

Has the child had any serious illnesses? ☐ Yes ☐ No   If yes, what illnesses? _____

Has the child been hospitalized? ☐ Yes ☐ No   If yes, please list reasons: _____

Has the child had any operations? ☐ Yes ☐ No   If yes, please list reasons: _____

Has the child had any accidents? ☐ Yes ☐ No   If yes, please describe: _____

Are the child's immunizations up to date? ☐ Yes ☐ No   Child's height _____ Child's weight _____

FAMILY MEDICAL HISTORY

Place a check next to any illness or condition that any member of the immediate family has had. When you check an item, please note the family member's relationship to the child.

	Relationship of family member to child		*Relationship of family member to child*
☐ Academic problem	_____	☐ Emotional problem	_____
☐ Alcoholism	_____	☐ Epilepsy	_____
☐ Cancer	_____	☐ Heart trouble	_____
☐ Depression	_____	☐ Neurological disease	_____
☐ Developmental problem	_____	☐ Suicide attempt	_____
☐ Diabetes	_____	☐ Other problems (please list)	_____
☐ Drug problem	_____		_____

(Continued)

Table A-1 *(Continued)*

OTHER INFORMATION

Child's Activities

What are the child's favorite activities?

1. _____ 2. _____ 3. _____
4. _____ 5. _____ 6. _____

What activities would the child like to engage in more often than he or she does at present?

1. _____ 2. _____ 3. _____

What activities does the child like least?

1. _____ 2. _____ 3. _____

What chores does the child do around the house? _____

Has there been any recent change in his or her ability to carry out these chores? ☐ Yes ☐ No

If yes, please describe the change: _____

What time does the child usually go to bed on weekdays? _____ On weekends? _____

Trouble with the Law

Has the child ever been in trouble with the law? ☐ Yes ☐ No

If yes, please describe briefly: _____

Referral to Child Protective Services or Similar Agency

Has the child ever been referred to Child Protective Services or another similar agency for having been maltreated? ☐ Yes ☐ No

If yes, please describe briefly: _____

Your Use of Disciplinary Techniques

Place a check next to each technique that you commonly use when the child behaves inappropriately. There also is space for writing in any other disciplinary techniques that you use.

☐ Ignore problem behavior   ☐ Reason with child   ☐ Take away some activity or food
☐ Scold child   ☐ Redirect child's interest   ☐ Other technique (describe)
☐ Spank child   ☐ Tell child to sit on chair   _____
☐ Threaten child   ☐ Send child to his or her room ☐ Don't use any technique

Which disciplinary techniques are usually effective? _____

_____

With what types of problems? _____

_____

Which disciplinary techniques are usually ineffective? _____

_____

With what types of problems? _____

_____

Which parent (caregiver) usually administers discipline? _____

Activities Checklist

Place a check next to each activity that the child can do by himself or herself (even if the child does not do the activity regularly).

☐ Sets table   ☐ Helps with grocery shopping   ☐ Puts clothes away
☐ Cooks meals   ☐ Unpacks groceries   ☐ Sews
☐ Cleans table   ☐ Does laundry   ☐ Empties garbage
☐ Washes dishes   ☐ Does ironing   ☐ Does homework alone

(Continued)

Table A-1 *(Continued)*

Child's Responsibilities

Can the child be trusted to care for a pet? ☐ Yes ☐ No

If no, why not? _____

Does the child handle his or her personal finances? ☐ Yes ☐ No

If no, why not? _____

Does the child take responsibility for his or her personal hygiene? ☐ Yes ☐ No

If no, why not? _____

Is the child's behavior generally age appropriate? ☐ Yes ☐ No

If no, please describe in what ways it is not age appropriate: _____

_____

Other Areas

What do you enjoy doing with the child? _____

_____

What have you found to be the most satisfactory ways of helping the child? _____

_____

What are the child's assets or strengths? _____

_____

Is there any other information that you think may help us in working with the child? _____

_____

_____

_____

What prompted you to seek help at this time? _____

_____

Family Stress Survey

Every family sometimes experiences some form of stress. Please put a check next to each event that your family has experienced *in the last 12 months*. There also is a place for listing other types of stresses that your family experienced in the last 12 months.

☐ Child's mother died.
☐ Child's father died.
☐ Child's brother died.
☐ Child's sister died.
☐ Parents divorced.
☐ Parents separated.
☐ Grandparent died.
☐ Someone in family was seriously injured or became ill (list person):
_____
☐ Parent remarried.
☐ Father lost job.
☐ Mother lost job.
☐ Family moved to another city.

☐ Family moved to another part of town.
☐ Someone in family was in trouble with the law or police (list person):
_____
☐ Family's financial condition changed.
☐ Member of family was accused of child abuse or neglect (list person):
_____
☐ Neighborhood was changing for the worse.
☐ Child was a victim of violence.
☐ Family experienced a natural disaster (list): _____

☐ Child started having trouble with parents (caregiver).
☐ Child started having trouble with sisters/brothers.
☐ Child started having trouble in school.
☐ Child changed schools.
☐ Child's close friend moved away.
☐ Child's pet died.
☐ Other types of stresses (list): _____
_____
_____
_____
_____

Table A-1 *(Continued)*

Parent Needs Survey[a]

Listed below are some needs commonly expressed by parents (caregivers). Please put a check next to each item if you need help in that area.

- ☐ More information about the child's abilities.
- ☐ Someone who can help me feel better about myself.
- ☐ Help with child care.
- ☐ More money/financial help.
- ☐ Someone who can babysit for a day or evening so that I can get away.
- ☐ Better medical care for the child.
- ☐ Better dental care for the child.
- ☐ More information about child development.
- ☐ More information about behavior problems.
- ☐ More information about programs that can help the child.
- ☐ Help communicating with the child's school.
- ☐ Someone to help with household chores.
- ☐ Counseling to help me cope with my situation.

- ☐ Better therapy services for the child.
- ☐ Day care so that I can get a job.
- ☐ A bigger or better house or apartment.
- ☐ More information about how I can help the child.
- ☐ More information about nutrition or feeding.
- ☐ Assistance in handling other children's jealousy of their brother or sister.
- ☐ Health insurance.
- ☐ Vocational training for me.
- ☐ Assistance in dealing with problems with in-laws or other relatives.
- ☐ Assistance in dealing with problems with friends or neighbors.
- ☐ Special equipment to meet the child's needs.
- ☐ Opportunities to meet people who have a child like mine.
- ☐ Someone to talk to about my problems.
- ☐ Assistance in dealing with problems with my husband/wife/partner.

- ☐ A car or other form of transportation.
- ☐ Medical care for myself.
- ☐ More time for myself.
- ☐ More time to be with the child.
- ☐ More time to be with my spouse/partner.
- ☐ More time to be with other adults.
- ☐ A vacation.
- ☐ Other needs (list)

_____

_____

_____

_____

_____

_____

_____

_____

Thank you.

[a]These items are modifications of items included in the Parent Needs Survey by M. Seligman and R. B. Darling in *Ordinary Families, Special Children: A Systems Approach to Childhood Disability* (New York: Guilford Press, 1989). The Parent Needs Survey is an instrument designed to identify the priorities and concerns of parents of young children with disabilities. Reprinted and adapted with permission of the publisher and author.

Table A-2
Sample Personal Data Questionnaire

PERSONAL DATA QUESTIONNAIRE

Please complete this questionnaire as carefully as you can. All information will be treated confidentially. Please print clearly.

Name _____

              First   Middle   Last

Address _____

                    Street

_____

          City   State   Zip code

School _____ Grade _____ Age _____ Sex _____ Birthdate _____

Phone number _____ Email _____ Today's date _____

SCHOOL INFORMATION

	Name of school	Grades attended	Years attended	Course of study or special classes
Elementary				
Middle school				
High school				
College				
Other				

Best-liked subjects _____

Least-liked subjects _____

Easiest subjects _____

Hardest subjects _____

Leisure-time (or free-time) activities _____

Hobbies _____

Favorite music group _____

Do you read magazines? ☐ Yes ☐ No If yes, which ones? _____

Do you read books? ☐ Yes ☐ No If yes, what types? _____

(If you read books) Approximately how many books have you read in the last month? _____

Do you participate in sports or athletic activities? ☐ Yes ☐ No If yes, which ones? _____

_____

(Continued)

Table A-2 (Continued)

SCHOOL ACTIVITIES

School activity	Number of years of participation	Positions held	Describe activity

Please note any awards received or class offices held: _____

WORK EXPERIENCE

Job held	When	What did you like best about your job?	What did you like least about your job?

FAMILY AND HOME

Name	Does this person live at your home? (yes or no)	Age	Occupation	Years of school
Father				
Mother				
Brother/Sister				

HEALTH

Current height _____ Current weight _____

Do you have normal eyesight? ☐ Yes ☐ No If no, do you wear glasses or contacts? ☐ Yes ☐ No

Normal hearing? ☐ Yes ☐ No If no, do you wear a hearing aid? ☐ Yes ☐ No

Do you eat a healthy diet? ☐ Yes ☐ No If no, briefly indicate in what way your diet is not healthy: _____

_____

Briefly list important factors in your health history, including any serious illnesses or times in the hospital: _____

_____

List any health problems you have now: _____

_____

Are you taking any medications? ☐ Yes ☐ No If yes, list the medications and what you are taking them for: _____

_____

Table A-2 *(Continued)*

PERSONAL CHARACTERISTICS

Circle Y (yes) if the item describes you fairly well, or circle N (no) if the item does not describe you fairly well.

Y N 1. Active	Y N 11. Imaginative	Y N 21. Submissive	Y N 31. Jittery
Y N 2. Ambitious	Y N 12. Original	Y N 22. Absentminded	Y N 32. Likeable
Y N 3. Self-confident	Y N 13. Witty	Y N 23. Methodical	Y N 33. Leader
Y N 4. Persistent	Y N 14. Calm	Y N 24. Timid	Y N 34. Sociable
Y N 5. Hard working	Y N 15. Easily discouraged	Y N 25. Lazy	Y N 35. Quiet
Y N 6. Nervous	Y N 16. Serious	Y N 26. Frequently gloomy	Y N 36. Shy
Y N 7. Impatient	Y N 17. Easy-going	Y N 27. Tough	Y N 37. Self-conscious
Y N 8. Impulsive	Y N 18. Good-natured	Y N 28. Dependable	Y N 38. Lonely
Y N 9. Quick-tempered	Y N 19. Unemotional	Y N 29. Cheerful	Y N 39. Fearful
Y N 10. Excitable	Y N 20. Shy	Y N 30. Sarcastic	Y N 40. Intelligent

What do you like best about yourself? _____

What do you like least about yourself? _____

Do you use drugs? _____ If yes, what kinds? _____

How often? _____

Do you use alcohol? _____ If yes, what kinds? _____

How often? _____

Do you smoke? _____ If yes, how many cigarettes per day do you smoke? _____

List the stressful events that you have experienced in the past year: _____

HOW I DO THINGS

Circle Y (yes) if the item generally describes how you do things, or circle N (no) if the item does not generally describe how you do things.

Y N 1. I usually can find my school supplies when I need them.
Y N 2. I usually remember to do my jobs at home.
Y N 3. I put my books in the same place every day when I come home from school.
Y N 4. I usually get to classes on time.
Y N 5. I usually finish a project I start.
Y N 6. I usually think about something before I do it.
Y N 7. My clothes are usually clean and acceptable.

STRESS

Circle Y (yes) if the item generally causes you stress now, or circle N (no) if the item does not generally cause you stress now.

Y N 1. Examinations and tests	Y N 11. Cost of books and equipment	Y N 22. Not knowing how to study properly
Y N 2. Parents who don't understand what it's like to be a student today	Y N 12. Cost of clothes I need	Y N 23. No time for leisure activities
	Y N 13. Wishing my parents were richer	Y N 24. Being asked to read aloud or talk in front of the class
Y N 3. Having too much work to prepare for class	Y N 14. Appearing foolish to others	Y N 25. Teachers who talk to other students rather than to me
Y N 4. Poor relations with other students	Y N 15. Difficulty with a boy/girl relationship	Y N 26. Sexual problems
Y N 5. Being picked out by the teacher for poor work	Y N 16. No place to study at home	Y N 27. Watching so much TV that it affects my homework
Y N 6. Being disciplined in school for doing things wrong	Y N 17. No time to relax between classes	Y N 28. Being neglected or abused emotionally at home
Y N 7. Being teased by other students	Y N 18. Nobody to talk to about personal problems	Y N 29. Being abused physically or subjected to excessive physical punishment at home
Y N 8. Being ignored by other students	Y N 19. Difficulties in travel to school	
Y N 9. Shortage of money	Y N 20. Being unable to really talk to my mother	Y N 30. Being abused sexually by an older person
Y N 10. Having too many things to study	Y N 21. Being unable to really talk to my father	

Table A-2 *(Continued)*

Y N 31. Being unable to relate to people my own age
Y N 32. Fear of asking teachers about school work
Y N 33. Worry about part-time employment
Y N 34. Worry about finding a job after leaving school
Y N 35. Worry about entering senior high school
Y N 36. Worry about entering junior high school
Y N 37. Adults who treat me like a child
Y N 38. Pressure to behave in a way my parents won't approve of
Y N 39. Feelings of loneliness
Y N 40. What others think of me
Y N 41. Mother's drinking habit
Y N 42. Father's drinking habit
Y N 43. My own drinking habit

Y N 44. Worry that I may not get a good job when I leave school
Y N 45. Unemployment generally
Y N 46. Pressure to smoke cigarettes
Y N 47. Pressure to have sex
Y N 48. Pressure to take alcoholic drinks
Y N 49. Being unable to keep up with others in school work
Y N 50. Pressure to use drugs
Y N 51. Parents being divorced or separated
Y N 52. My smoking habit
Y N 53. Experience with drugs
Y N 54. School classes that are too large
Y N 55. Classmates jealous of my success in school
Y N 56. Problems of self-concept

Y N 57. Demands by parents on after-school time
Y N 58. Shyness in social situations
Y N 59. Being abused sexually by someone close in age
Y N 60. Adults who don't listen when I talk about problems
Y N 61. Uncertainty about what values are the correct ones
Y N 62. Lack of self-confidence
Y N 63. Rejection by a group I want to belong to
Y N 64. Doubts about my religious beliefs
Y N 65. Lack of privacy at home
Y N 66. Arguments between my parents
Y N 67. Concern about my health
Y N 68. Pressure from my parents to get on in life

RELATIONSHIP WITH PARENTS

Circle Y (yes) if the item generally describes your parents, or circle N (no) if the item does not generally describe your parents.

Y N 1. My parents are very affectionate with me.
Y N 2. My parents enjoy talking things over with me.
Y N 3. My parents comfort me and help me when I have troubles.
Y N 4. My parents are happy when they are with me.
Y N 5. My parents smile at me very often.
Y N 6. My parents punish me by making me do extra work.
Y N 7. My parents scold and yell at me.
Y N 8. My parents threaten to spank me.

Y N 9. My parents lose their temper with me when I don't help around the house.
Y N 10. When I am bad, my parents forbid me to do things I especially enjoy.
Y N 11. My parents won't let me roam around because something might happen to me.
Y N 12. My parents worry that I can't take care of myself.
Y N 13. My parents worry about me when I am away.
Y N 14. My parents do not approve of my spending a lot of time away from home.

Y N 15. My parents ask me to tell them everything that happens when I am away from home.
Y N 16. My parents let me off easy when I misbehave.
Y N 17. My parents are consistent about punishing me when they feel I deserve it.
Y N 18. My parents let me get away without doing work they tell me to do.
Y N 19. My parents find it difficult to punish me.
Y N 20. My parents excuse my bad conduct.

FAMILY

Circle Y (yes) if the item generally describes your family, or circle N (no) if the item does not generally describe your family.

Y N 1. Family members pay attention to each other's feelings.
Y N 2. Our family would rather do things together than with other people.
Y N 3. We all have a say in family plans.
Y N 4. Grownups in the family understand and agree on family decisions.
Y N 5. Grownups in the family compete and fight with each other.
Y N 6. There is closeness in my family, but each person is allowed to be special and different.

Y N 7. We accept each other's friends.
Y N 8. There is confusion in our family because there is no leader.
Y N 9. Family members touch and hug each other.
Y N 10. Family members put each other down.
Y N 11. We speak our minds, no matter what.
Y N 12. In our home, we feel loved.
Y N 13. Even when we feel close, our family is embarrassed to admit it.
Y N 14. We argue a lot and never solve problems.

Y N 15. Our happiest times are at home.
Y N 16. The grownups in my family are strong leaders.
Y N 17. The future looks good to our family.
Y N 18. We usually blame one person in our family when things aren't going right.
Y N 19. Family members go their own way most of the time.
Y N 20. Our family is proud of being close.
Y N 21. Our family is good at solving problems together.

(Continued)

Table A-2 *(Continued)*

Y N 22. Family members easily express warmth and caring toward each other.

Y N 23. It's okay to fight and yell in our family.

Y N 24. One of the adults in my family has a favorite child.

Y N 25. When things go wrong, we blame each other.

Y N 26. We say what we think and feel.

Y N 27. Family members would rather do things with other people than together.

Y N 28. Family members pay attention to each other and listen to what is said.

Y N 29. We worry about hurting each other's feelings.

Y N 30. The mood in my family is usually sad and blue.

Y N 31. We argue a lot.

Y N 32. One person controls and leads our family.

Y N 33. My family is happy most of the time.

Y N 34. Each person takes responsibility for his/her behavior.

PLANS

What are your plans for the future? _____

_____

What occupation would you like to have? _____

_____

Are there issues bothering you that you would like to discuss with a professional? ☐ Yes ☐ No If yes, what are they? _____

_____

ANY OTHER COMMENTS?

_____

_____

_____

_____

Thank you!

Table A-3
Sample School Referral Questionnaire

SCHOOL REFERRAL QUESTIONNAIRE

Student's name _____ Grade _____ Sex _____ Date _____

School _____ Teacher's name _____

PRESENTING PROBLEM

Briefly describe student's current problem: _____

_____

_____

How long has this problem been of concern to you? _____

When did you first notice the problem? _____

What seems to help the problem? _____

What seems to make the problem worse? _____

Have you noticed changes in the student's abilities? ☐ Yes ☐ No

If yes, please describe: _____

Have you noticed changes in the student's behavior? ☐ Yes ☐ No

If yes, please describe: _____

Has the student received evaluation or treatment for the current problem or similar problems? ☐ Yes ☐ No

If yes, when and with whom? _____

What are the student's current school grades? _____

_____

What do you want to learn from this evaluation? _____

_____

CHECKLIST

Directions: Place a check mark next to each item that accurately describes the student. If you can't evaluate an item, please write a question mark next to the box by the item number.

Cognitive
- ☐ 1. Has poor comprehension of material
- ☐ 2. Has poor short-term memory for verbal stimuli
- ☐ 3. Has poor short-term memory for nonverbal stimuli
- ☐ 4. Has limited attention span
- ☐ 5. Has difficulty understanding oral directions
- ☐ 6. Has difficulty understanding written directions
- ☐ 7. Has difficulty following a sequence of directions
- ☐ 8. Misunderstands material presented at a fast rate
- ☐ 9. Has difficulty recalling story sequences
- ☐ 10. Has difficulty understanding teacher when he or she moves around the room
- ☐ 11. Has difficulty shifting ways of looking at or doing things
- ☐ 12. Has difficulty reasoning abstractly
- ☐ 13. Has difficulty conceptualizing material
- ☐ 14. Uses problem-solving strategies inefficiently
- ☐ 15. Learns very slowly
- ☐ 16. Has poor long-term memory
- ☐ 17. Forgets newly learned skills

Language/Academic
- ☐ 18. Has difficulty decoding words
- ☐ 19. Has poor reading comprehension
- ☐ 20. Has poor expressive language
- ☐ 21. Has poor listening comprehension
- ☐ 22. Uses gestures instead of words
- ☐ 23. Has difficulty rapidly naming objects
- ☐ 24. Has difficulty rapidly reading words
- ☐ 25. Has speech impairment
- ☐ 26. Has difficulty producing rhymes
- ☐ 27. Has difficulty recognizing similar phonemes
- ☐ 28. Has difficulty arranging phonemes into words
- ☐ 29. Has difficulty using verbal coding as an aid in memory
- ☐ 30. Has difficulty using verbal coding as an aid in rehearsal
- ☐ 31. Has poor grammar
- ☐ 32. Has poor math computation skills
- ☐ 33. Has limited math problem-solving skills
- ☐ 34. Does not retain math facts
- ☐ 35. Has poor spelling

(Continued)

Table A-3 *(Continued)*

- ☐ 36. Has fluctuating performance
- ☐ 37. Has difficulty writing compositions
- ☐ 38. Does not know names of common objects

Perceptual/Motor
- ☐ 39. Has poor auditory perception
- ☐ 40. Has poor visual perception
- ☐ 41. Has poor tactile discrimination
- ☐ 42. Has poor handwriting
- ☐ 43. Has clumsy and awkward movements
- ☐ 44. Has poor speech communication
- ☐ 45. Has difficulty putting objects in correct sequence
- ☐ 46. Has difficulty remembering sequence of objects
- ☐ 47. Has right-left confusion
- ☐ 48. Has poor gross-motor coordination
- ☐ 49. Has poor fine-motor coordination
- ☐ 50. Moves slowly

Behavioral
- ☐ 51. Avoids doing work in class
- ☐ 52. Gives up easily
- ☐ 53. Has difficulty beginning tasks on time
- ☐ 54. Has difficulty completing tasks on time
- ☐ 55. Asks questions constantly
- ☐ 56. Is impulsive
- ☐ 57. Has trouble starting and continuing tasks
- ☐ 58. Has difficulty changing from one assignment to another
- ☐ 59. Shifts often to other activities
- ☐ 60. Has difficulty working independently
- ☐ 61. Has difficulty playing quietly
- ☐ 62. Is easily distracted
- ☐ 63. Doesn't seem to listen
- ☐ 64. Shows aggressive behavior
- ☐ 65. Shows disruptive behavior
- ☐ 66. Talks excessively
- ☐ 67. Interrupts others often
- ☐ 68. Speaks out of turn (often blurts out answers)
- ☐ 69. Makes comments not related to topic being discussed
- ☐ 70. Has difficulty remaining seated
- ☐ 71. Fidgets often when seated
- ☐ 72. Does not arrive on time for class
- ☐ 73. Fails to return on time to class
- ☐ 74. Has limited persistence
- ☐ 75. Fails to do homework
- ☐ 76. Loses homework
- ☐ 77. Seeks attention constantly
- ☐ 78. Is unorganized
- ☐ 79. Uses immature vocabulary
- ☐ 80. Is slow to complete tasks
- ☐ 81. Behaves inappropriately
- ☐ 82. Uses drugs or alcohol
- ☐ 83. Hurts others
- ☐ 84. Is cruel to animals
- ☐ 85. Talks about suicide
- ☐ 86. Destroys others' property
- ☐ 87. Is out of chair when supposed to be doing work
- ☐ 88. Has constant and repetitive behavior
- ☐ 89. Speaks slowly
- ☐ 90. Shouts or yells for no apparent reason
- ☐ 91. Has hallucinations

- ☐ 92. Stutters
- ☐ 93. Injures self often
- ☐ 94. Bites nails
- ☐ 95. Bangs head
- ☐ 96. Holds breath
- ☐ 97. Does not tolerate changes in routine
- ☐ 98. Wanders aimlessly around room
- ☐ 99. Is a daydreamer
- ☐ 100. Tires easily
- ☐ 101. Tells lies
- ☐ 102. Steals things
- ☐ 103. Has numerous physical complaints
- ☐ 104. Is frequently absent
- ☐ 105. Has poor eye contact
- ☐ 106. Requires constant supervision
- ☐ 107. Engages in dangerous behaviors
- ☐ 108. Prefers not to try new activities

Social
- ☐ 109. Is immature
- ☐ 110. Is stubborn
- ☐ 111. Has low self-esteem
- ☐ 112. Is socially isolated
- ☐ 113. Has low popularity
- ☐ 114. Has difficulty communicating interests
- ☐ 115. Has difficulty accepting criticism
- ☐ 116. Has limited social perceptiveness
- ☐ 117. Gives in to peer pressure
- ☐ 118. Is uncooperative
- ☐ 119. Has poor skills on playground
- ☐ 120. Is overly compliant
- ☐ 121. Is selfish
- ☐ 122. Seems suspicious of other people
- ☐ 123. Refuses to share
- ☐ 124. Shows sexually provocative behavior
- ☐ 125. Blames others for problems
- ☐ 126. Has difficulty seeking help
- ☐ 127. Has difficulty accepting help from teacher
- ☐ 128. Has difficulty accepting help from peers
- ☐ 129. Does not get along with other children
- ☐ 130. Does not offer opinions and answers when asked
- ☐ 131. Does not enjoy group activities
- ☐ 132. Does not show concern for others' feelings and property
- ☐ 133. Solves conflicts by shouting, fighting, or intimidating others
- ☐ 134. Has difficulty making constructive contributions during group activities
- ☐ 135. Avoids others completely
- ☐ 136. Has anger management problems
- ☐ 137. Displays inappropriate humor
- ☐ 138. Seeks to manipulate others
- ☐ 139. Is rigid and opinionated
- ☐ 140. Has unusual interest in sensational violence
- ☐ 141. Is fascinated with violence-filled entertainment

Affect/Motivation
- ☐ 142. Is easily frustrated
- ☐ 143. Shows anger quickly
- ☐ 144. Has limited motivation

(Continued)

Table A-2 *(Continued)*

□ 145. Is often anxious
□ 146. Is depressed or unhappy
□ 147. Has low interest in school work
□ 148. Is self-critical
□ 149. Is overexcitable
□ 150. Is hyperactive
□ 151. Has temper tantrums
□ 152. Has unusual fears
□ 153. Is easily annoyed
□ 154. Frequently cries
□ 155. Is tense and fearful
□ 156. Seldom shows emotion
□ 157. Is shy or timid
□ 158. Is upset by changes in routine
□ 159. Has wide mood changes
□ 160. Feels hopeless

Self-Care Skills
□ 161. Has poor personal hygiene
□ 162. Has disheveled and unclean personal appearance
□ 163. Fails to dress appropriately for weather
□ 164. Has poor table manners in cafeteria
□ 165. Fails to use free time appropriately
□ 166. Engages in self-stimulating behaviors
□ 167. Has slumped posture
□ 168. Has rigid, tense posture
□ 169. Has atypical, inappropriate posture
Other problems _____
_____
_____

Assets

Please list the child's assets or strengths in each of the following areas.

Cognitive _____

Language/academic _____

Perceptual/motor _____

Social/behavioral _____

Other Comments

Please list anything else about the child that you think may be helpful. _____
_____
_____

Thank you!

APPENDIX B

SEMISTRUCTURED INTERVIEW QUESTIONS

Table B-1
Semistructured Interview Questions for a Child (or Adolescent) of School Age

Introduction

1. Hi! I'm Dr. [Ms., Mr.] _____. And you are [cite child's name]. How are you today?
2. When you don't understand a question that I ask, please say "I don't understand." When you tell me that, I'll try to ask it better. OK?
3. Please tell me how old you are.
4. When is your birthday?
5. What is your address?
6. And what is your telephone number?

Information About Problem

7. Has anyone told you why you are here today? (If yes, go to question 8; if no, go to question 10.)
8. Who told you?
9. What did he [she] tell you?
10. Tell me why you think you are here. (If child mentions a problem or a concern, explore it in detail. Ask questions 11 to 40, as needed. If the child does not mention a problem or concern, go to question 41.)
11. Tell me about [cite problem child mentioned].
12. When did you first notice [cite problem]?
13. How long has it been going on?
14. (If relevant) Where does [cite problem] happen?
15. (If needed) Does it occur at home ... at school ... when you're traveling ... at a friend's house?
16. (If relevant) When does the problem happen?
17. (If needed) Does it happen when you first get up in the morning ... during the day ... at night before bedtime ... at mealtimes? ... Does it happen when you are with your mother ... your father ... brothers and sisters ... other children ... other relatives ... the whole family together ... friends ... at school?
18. (If relevant) How long does the problem last?
19. How often does [cite problem] occur?
20. (If relevant) Do your brothers and sisters also have [cite problem]?
21. (If yes) Is your [cite problem] worse than or not as bad as theirs?
22. In what way?
23. What happens just before [cite problem] begins?
24. What happens just after [cite problem] begins?
25. What makes [cite problem] worse?
26. What makes [cite problem] better?
27. What do you do when you have [cite problem]?
28. What seems to work best?
29. What do you think caused [cite problem]?
30. Was anything happening in your family when [cite problem] first started?
31. (If needed) Did your parents get separated or divorced ... you move to another city or school ... your dad or mom lose a job ... someone in your family go into the hospital?

32. (If some event occurred) How did you feel when [cite event] happened?
33. How do your parents help you with [cite problem]?
34. (If relevant) How do your brothers and sisters help you with [cite problem]?
35. And your friends, do they help in any way?
36. Have you seen anybody for help with [cite problem]? (If yes, go to question 37; if no, go to question 41.)
37. Whom did you see?
38. What kind of help did you get?
39. Has it helped?
40. (If needed) In what way?

School

41. Let's talk about school. What grade are you in?
42. What is your teacher's name [are your teachers' names]?
43. How do you get along with your teacher[s]?
44. Who is your favorite teacher?
45. Tell me about him [her].
46. Who is the teacher you like the least?
47. Tell me about him [her].
48. What subjects do you like best?
49. What is it about these subjects that you like?
50. And what subjects do you like least?
51. What is it about these subjects that you don't like?
52. What grades are you getting?
53. Are you in any activities at school?
54. (If yes) What activities are you in at school?
55. How do you get along with your classmates?
56. Tell me how you spend a usual day at school.

Attention and Concentration at School

57. Do you have any trouble following what your teacher says [teachers say]?
58. (If yes) What kind of trouble do you have?
59. Do you daydream a lot when you are in class?
60. (If yes) Tell me about that.
61. Can you complete your assignments, or are you easily distracted?
62. (If distracted) What seems to distract you?
63. Do you have trouble sitting still or staying in your seat at school?
64. (If yes) Tell me about the trouble you're having.
65. Do you find it hard to sit still for a long time and need a lot of breaks while studying?
66. Do you like to leave your studies to go see what's going on, get a drink, or change rooms or positions?
67. (If yes) Tell me more about that.
68. Do you have any trouble copying what your teacher writes on the blackboard?
69. (If yes) What kind of trouble do you have?

(Continued)

70. Do you have any trouble remembering things?
71. (If yes) Tell me about the trouble you're having.
72. How is your concentration?
73. Do you like to keep at your work until it's done?
74. Tell me more about that.
75. Do you have trouble taking notes in class?
76. (If yes) Tell me about the trouble you're having.
77. Do you have trouble taking tests?
78. (If yes) Tell me about the trouble you're having.

Home

79. Now let's talk about your home. Who lives with you at home?
    (Many questions from 80 to 117 assume that the child lives in a family with two caregivers. Ask those questions that apply to the child or modify them as needed—for example, substituting "stepmother" for "mother" or "sister" for "brothers and sisters.")
80. Tell me a little about [cite persons child mentioned].
81. (If needed) What does your father do for work?
82. (If needed) What does your mother do for work?
83. Tell me what your home is like.
84. Do you have your own room at home?
    (If no, go to question 85; if yes, go to question 87.)
85. Whom do you share it with?
86. How do you get along?
87. What chores do you do at home?
88. How do you get along with your father?
89. What does he do that you like?
90. What does he do that you don't like?
91. How do you get along with your mother?
92. What does she do that you like?
93. What does she do that you don't like?
    (If child has one or more siblings, go to question 94 and modify questions accordingly; if child has no siblings, go to question 101.)
94. How do you get along with your brothers and sisters?
95. What do they do that you like?
96. What do they do that you don't like?
97. What do you argue or fight with your brothers and sisters about?
98. What does your mother or father do when you argue or fight with your brothers and sisters?
99. Do your parents treat you and your brothers and sisters the same?
100. (If no) Tell me about that.
101. Are there rules you must follow at home?
102. Tell me about that.
103. When you get in trouble at home, who disciplines you?
104. Tell me about how your father [mother] disciplines you.
105. How do your parents tell you or show you that they like what you have done?

106. When you have a problem, whom do you talk to about it?
107. How does he [she] help you?
108. Do you think your parents are worried about you?
109. (If yes) What are their worries about you?
110. Is there anyone else in your family whom you are close to, like a grandparent or other relative?
111. (If yes) Tell me about him [her, them].
112. Do you spend much time at home alone?
113. (If yes) Tell me about that.
114. Does your family eat meals together?
115. (If yes) Tell me about the meals you eat together.
116. (If needed) How often do you eat meals together?
117. In general, how would you describe your family?

Interests

118. Now let's talk about what you like to do. What hobbies and interests do you have?
119. What do you do in the afternoons after school?
120. What do you do in the evenings on school days?
121. Tell me what you usually do on Saturdays and Sundays.
122. Do you play any sports?
123. (If yes) Tell me what sports you play.
124. Of all the things you do, what do you like doing best?
125. And what do you like doing least?
126. Do you belong to any group like the Boy Scouts [Girl Scouts] or a church group?
127. (If yes) Tell me about the group you belong to.
128. How much TV do you watch in a day?
129. Would you like to watch more TV?
130. (If yes) About how much more would you like to watch?
131. What are your favorite programs?
132. What do you like about them?
133. Do you play games on a Play Station or some similar system?
    (If yes, go to question 134; if no, go to question 137.)
134. Where do you play these games?
135. How many hours a day do you play them?
136. What are your favorite games?
137. Do you like music?
138. (If yes) What kind of music—what are your favorite groups?

Friends

139. Do you have friends?
    (If yes, go to question 140; if no, go to question 149.)
140. Tell me about your friends.
    (Ask questions 141 to 148, as needed.)
141. (If needed) What do you like to do with your friends?
142. (If needed) Are you spending as much time with your friends now as you used to?
143. (If needed) When you are with your friends, how do you feel?

Table B-1 *(Continued)*

144. (If needed) How are your friends treating you?
145. Who is your best friend?
146. Tell me about him [her].
147. What do you like to do together?
148. How many of your friends do your parents know? (Go to item 150.)
149. Tell me about your not having friends.

Mood/Feelings

150. Tell me about how you've been feeling lately.
151. Do you have different feelings in the same day?
152. (If yes) Tell me about these different feelings.
153. Have you been feeling more nervous over the past couple of days, as though you can't relax?
154. (If yes) Tell me about that.
155. Nearly everybody feels happy at times. What kinds of things make you feel happiest?
156. And sometimes people feel sad. What makes you feel sad?
157. What do you do when you're sad?
158. Sometimes children [teenagers] begin to get less pleasure from things that they used to enjoy. Has this happened to you?
159. (If yes) Tell me about that.
160. Have there been times lasting more than a day when you felt very cheerful in a way that was different from your normal feelings?
161. (If yes) Tell me about these feelings.
162. Almost everybody gets angry at times. What kinds of things make you angriest?
163. What do you do when you are angry?
164. Do you ever get into fights?
165. (If yes) Tell me about the fights.

Fears/Worries

166. Most children [teenagers] get scared sometimes about some things. What do you do when you are scared?
167. Tell me what scares you.
168. Does anything else scare you?
169. Are you startled by noises?
170. (If yes) Tell me more about that.
171. Do you have any special worries?
172. (If yes) Tell me about what you are worried about.

Self-Concept

173. What do you like best about yourself?
174. Anything else?
175. Tell me about the best thing that ever happened to you.
176. What do you like least about yourself?
177. Anything else?
178. Tell me about the worst thing that ever happened to you.

179. If you had a child of the same sex as you, how would you want the child to be like you?
180. How would you want the child to be different from you?

Somatic Concerns

181. Tell me how you feel about your body.
182. How have you been feeling lately?
183. Do you have any problems with not having enough energy to do the things you want to do?
184. (If yes) Tell me what problems you're having.
185. Tell me how you feel about eating.
186. Are you having problems sleeping enough?
187. (If yes) Tell me about your problems getting enough sleep.
188. Are you sleeping too much?
189. (If yes) Tell me about your problems with sleeping too much.
190. Tell me about your health.
191. (If needed) Have you been sick a lot?
192. (If yes) Tell me about that. (Follow up as needed.)
193. Do you ever get headaches?
194. (If yes) Tell me about them.
195. (If needed) How often do you get them?… What do you usually do?
196. Do you get stomachaches?
197. (If yes) Tell me about them.
198. (If needed) How often do you get them?… What do you usually do?
199. Do you get any other kinds of body pains?
200. (If yes) Tell me about them.
201. Do you have any trouble seeing things?
202. (If yes) Tell me about the trouble you're having seeing.
203. Do you have any trouble hearing things?
204. (If yes) Tell me about the trouble you're having hearing.
205. Do you take medicine every day? (If yes, go to question 206; if no, go to question 210.)
206. What do you take the medicine for?
207. What medicine do you take?
208. How often do you take the medicine?
209. How does the medicine make you feel?

Obsessions and Compulsions

210. Some children [teenagers] have thoughts that they think are silly or unpleasant or do not make sense, but these thoughts keep repeating over and over in their minds. Have you had thoughts like this?
211. (If yes) Tell me about these thoughts.
212. Some children [teenagers] are bothered by a feeling that they have to do something over and over even when they don't want to do it. For example, they might keep washing their hands or check over and over again whether the door is locked or the stove is turned off. Is this a problem for you?
213. (If yes) Tell me about it.

(Continued)

Table B-1 *(Continued)*

Thought Disorder

214. Do you ever hear things no one else hears that seem funny or unusual?
215. (If yes) Tell me about them.
216. (If a voice) What does it say?… How often do you hear it?… How do you feel about the voice?… What do you usually do?
217. Do you ever see things no one else sees that seem funny or unreal?
218. (If yes) Tell me about them.
219. (If needed) How often do you see them?… How do you feel about them?… What do you usually do?
220. Do you ever feel as if someone's spying on you or plotting to hurt you?
221. (If yes) Tell me about these feelings.
222. Does your thinking seem to speed up or slow down at times?
223. (If yes) Tell me about it.
224. Is it hard for you to make decisions?
225. (If yes) Tell me about it.
226. Is it hard for you to concentrate on your reading?
227. (If yes) Tell me about it.
228. Is it hard for you to understand people when they talk?
229. (If yes) Tell me about it.
230. Does it seem as if your thoughts are getting more mixed up or jumbled lately?
231. (If yes) Tell me more about that.
232. Have you had experiences that seemed odd or frightening to you?
233. (If yes) Tell me about them.

Memories/Fantasy

234. What's the first thing you can remember from the time you were a little baby?
235. How old were you then?
236. Tell me about your dreams.
237. Do you ever have the same dream over and over again?
238. (If yes) Tell me about that.
239. Who are your favorite television characters?
240. Tell me about them.
241. What animals do you like best?
242. Tell me what you like about these animals.
243. What animals do you like least?
244. Tell me what you don't like about these animals.
245. What is your happiest memory?
246. What is your saddest memory?
247. If you could change places with anyone in the whole world, who would it be?
248. Tell me about that.
249. If you could go anywhere you wanted to right now, where would you go?
250. Tell me about that.

251. If you could have three wishes, what would they be?
252. What things do you think you might need to take with you if you were to go to the moon and stay there for six months?

Aspirations

253. What do you plan on doing when you're grown up?
254. Do you think you will have any problem doing that?
255. If you could do anything you wanted when you became an adult, what would it be?
(If interviewee is an adolescent, go to questions following question 258.)

Concluding Questions

256. Do you have anything else that you would like to tell me about yourself?
257. Do you have any questions that you would like to ask me?
258. Thank you for talking with me. If you have any questions or if you want to talk to me, please call me or ask your teacher to let me know. Here is my card.

FOR ADOLESCENTS
Jobs

1. Do you have an after-school job or a summer job?
2. (If yes) Tell me about your job.

Sexual Relations

3. Do you have a special girlfriend [boyfriend]?
4. (If yes) Tell me about her [him].
5. Have you had any sexual experiences?
6. (If yes) Tell me about them.
7. Do you have any sexual concerns?
8. (If yes) Tell me about them.
9. Are you concerned about getting a sexual disease?
10. Tell me about that.
11. Are you sexually active now?
(If yes, go to question 12; if no, go to directions after question 16.)
12. Tell me about it.
13. Do you use birth control?
(If yes, go to question 14; if no, go to question 16.)
14. What type?
15. (If needed) Do you [Does your partner] use a condom?
(If adolescent is a female, go to question 17; if adolescent is a male, go to question 51.)
16. Tell me about your not using birth control.
(If adolescent is a female, go to question 17; if adolescent is a male, go to question 51.)

Questions for Adolescent Females Only

17. Have you ever been pregnant?
(If yes, go to question 18; if no, go to question 86.)

(Continued)

18. Tell me about it.
    (Ask questions 19 to 50, as needed.)
19. How many times have you been pregnant?
    (Ask questions 20 to 50 for each pregnancy, as needed.)
20. How old were you when you [the first time, the second time, etc.] became pregnant?
21. Did you have the baby?
    (If yes, go to question 22; if no, go to question 44.)
22. When was the baby born?
23. Did you have a boy or a girl?
24. How is the child?
25. Who helped you during the pregnancy?
26. Did you see a doctor for care during your pregnancy?
27. Were there any problems during your pregnancy?
28. And were there any complications while you were in labor?
29. And during delivery, were there any problems?
30. Did you have any problems soon after the baby was born?
31. How did you feel during the pregnancy?
32. How do you feel about your baby?
33. How did your family react to your being pregnant?
34. And how did the baby's father react to your being pregnant?
35. Are you raising the baby?
    (If yes, go to question 36; if no, go to question 40.)
36. What is it like being a mother?
37. What kind of help are you getting?
38. Does the baby's father contribute money?
39. Does the baby's father see the baby?
    (Go to question 86.)
40. Who is raising the baby?
41. How do you feel about that?
42. (If needed) Do you ever see the baby?
43. (If yes) Tell me about that.
    (Go to question 86.)
44. What happened during your pregnancy that you didn't have the baby?
    (If interviewee had an abortion, go to question 45; otherwise, go to question 86.)
45. Tell me about the abortion.
    (Ask questions 46 to 50, as needed.)
46. What were your feelings about the abortion before it was performed?
47. And how did you feel afterwards?
48. What would having a baby have meant for your future?
49. Would your family have helped you if you had had the baby?
50. Tell me about that.
    (Go to question 86.)

Questions for Adolescent Males Only

51. Have you ever gotten anyone pregnant?
    (If yes, go to question 52; if no, go to question 86.)
52. Tell me about it.
    (Ask questions 53 to 55, as needed.)
53. How many times have you gotten someone pregnant? (Ask questions 54 to 80 for each time interviewee got someone pregnant.)

54. How old were you when you [the first time, the second time, etc.] got someone pregnant?
55. Did she have the baby?
    (If yes, go to question 56; if no, go to question 81.)
56. When was the baby born?
57. Did you have a boy or a girl?
58. How is the child?
59. Who helped the mother during the pregnancy?
60. Did she see a doctor for care during her pregnancy?
61. Were there any problems during her pregnancy?
62. And were there any problems while she was in labor?
63. And during her delivery, were there any problems?
64. And were there any problems soon after the baby was born?
65. How did she feel during her pregnancy?
66. How did she feel about the baby?
67. And how did you react to her being pregnant?
68. Do your parents know that you got someone pregnant?
69. (If yes) How did your parents react to her being pregnant?
70. Who is raising the baby?
    (If the baby is being raised by the mother or by someone else the father knows, go to question 71; if the baby is being raised by the father, go to question 76; if the baby was given up for adoption, go to question 78.)
71. How is the baby doing?
72. Do you see the baby?
73. (If yes) Tell me about that.
74. Do you contribute to the baby's support?
75. Tell me about that.
    (Go to question 86.)
76. How is the baby doing?
77. What is it like being a father?
    (Go to question 86.)
78. How do you feel about the baby's being adopted?
79. Is there anything else you want to tell me about your feelings about the adoption?
80. (If yes) Go ahead.
    (Go to question 86.)
81. What happened during her pregnancy that she didn't have the baby?
    (If she had an abortion, go to question 82; otherwise, go to question 86.)
82. Tell me about the abortion.
    (Ask questions 83 to 85, as needed.)
83. What were your feelings about the abortion before it was performed?
84. And how did you feel afterwards?
85. What would having a baby have meant for your future?
    (Go to question 86.)

Eating Habits

86. Now I'm going to ask some questions about your eating habits. Tell me about what you eat.
87. Tell me where you usually eat your meals.
88. Tell me when you usually eat your meals.

(Continued)

Table B-1 *(Continued)*

89. Have you ever gone on eating binges—that is, eaten an abnormally large amount of food over a short period of time?
90. (If yes) Tell me about these eating binges.
91. Has there ever been a time when people gave you a hard time about being too thin or losing too much weight?
92. (If yes) Tell me about that.

Drug/Alcohol Use

93. Do your parents drink alcohol?
94. (If yes) Tell me about their drinking.
95. (If needed) How much do they drink?… How frequently do they drink?… Where do they drink?
96. Do your friends drink alcohol?
97. (If yes) Tell me about their drinking.
98. Do you drink alcohol?
99. (If yes) Tell me about your drinking.
100. Was there ever a time when you drank too much?
101. (If yes) Tell me about the time[s] when you drank too much.
102. Has anyone in your family, a friend, a doctor, or anyone else ever said that you drank too much?
103. (If yes) Tell me about that.
104. Has alcohol ever caused problems for you?
105. (If yes) Tell me about that.
106. Do your parents use drugs?
107. (If yes) Tell me about the drugs they use.
108. (If needed) How much of the drugs do they take?… How frequently do they take them?… Why do they take them?
109. Do your friends use drugs?
110. (If yes) Tell me about the drugs they use.
111. Do you use drugs?
112. (If yes) Tell me about the drugs you use.
113. Have you or has anyone else ever thought that you used drugs too much?
114. (If yes) Tell me about that.
115. Do your friends huff or use aerosols or inhalants?
116. (If yes) Tell me about that.
117. Have you ever huffed or used aerosols or inhalants?
118. (If yes) Tell me about that.
    (Go to question 256 in the main interview.)

Table B-2
Semistructured Interview Questions for an Older Child or Adolescent in a Mental Status Evaluation

1. Hi! I'm Dr. [Ms., Mr.] _____. I'd like to ask you some questions. OK?

General Orientation to Time, Place, and Person

2. What is your name?
3. How old are you?
4. What is today's date?
5. What day of the week is it?
6. What is the season?
7. What time of day is it?
8. Where are you?
9. What is the name of the state we are in?
10. What is the name of this city?
11. What is the name of this place?

Recent and Remote Memory

12. And your telephone number is …?
13. What is your address?
14. What do you do?
15. What is my name?
16. What did you have for breakfast?
17. What did you do in school [at the hospital, at home] yesterday?
18. Who is the president of the United States?
19. Who was the president before him?
20. (If relevant) Where did you live before you moved to [cite city]?
21. Name three major cities in the United States.
22. What are two major news events that happened in the last month?
23. How did you get to this hospital [clinic, office]?
24. What is your father's name?
25. What is your mother's name?
26. When is your birthday?
27. Where were you born?

28. What school do you go to?
29. (If relevant) When did you finish elementary school?
30. (If relevant) When did you finish high school?

Immediate Memory

31. Say these numbers after me: 6-9-5 … 4-3-8-1 … 2-9-8-5-7.
32. Say these numbers backwards: 8-3-7 … 9-4-6-1 … 7-3-2-5-8.
33. Say these words after me: pencil, chair, stone, plate.

Insight and Judgment

34. What does this saying mean: "Too many cooks spoil the broth"?
35. What does this saying mean: "A stitch in time saves nine"?
36. How are a banana, peach, and pear alike?
37. How are a bicycle, wagon, and car alike?

Reading, Writing, and Spelling

38. Read these words. (Give interviewee a piece of paper with the following words on it: pat, father, setting, intervention.)
39. Now write these same words. (Give interviewee a blank piece of paper on which to write; show the same words as in question 38 for child to copy.)
40. Spell these words aloud: spoon … cover … attitude … procedure.

Arithmetical Concentration

41. (For children between 7 and 12 years) Subtract by 3s, starting with 30.
42. (For adolescents) Subtract by 7s, starting with 50.

Concluding Questions

43. Are there any questions that you would like to ask me?
44. (If yes) Go ahead.
45. Thank you for talking with me. If you have any questions or if you want to talk to me, please call me. Here is my card.

Table B-3
Semistructured Interview Questions for a Child (or Adolescent) with a Learning Disability

Introduction

1. Hi! I'm Dr. [Ms., Mr.] _____. I'd like to talk to you about how you are getting along. OK?
2. When you don't understand a question that I ask, please say "I don't understand." When you tell me that, I'll try to ask it better. OK?

Attitude Toward School

3. How are you getting along in school?
4. What do you like about school?
5. What don't you like about school?
6. What are your favorite subjects?
7. What are your least favorite subjects?
8. Which subjects are easiest for you?
9. Which subjects are hardest for you?
10. Now I'd like to talk to you about some specific subjects. OK?

Reading

11. How well do you read?
12. Do you like to read?
13. Tell me about that.
14. When you read, do you make mistakes like skipping words or lines, reading the same lines twice, or reading letters backwards?
15. (If needed) Tell me about the mistakes you make when you read.
16. Do you find that you can read each line of every paragraph, but, when you finish the page or chapter, you don't remember what you've just read?
17. Do you understand and remember better when you read aloud or when you read silently?

Writing

18. How good is your handwriting?
19. Do you find that you cannot write as fast as you think?
20. (If yes) Do you run one word into another when you're writing because you're thinking of the next word rather than the one you're writing?
21. How good is your spelling?
22. Tell me about that.
23. How good is your grammar?
24. Tell me about that.
25. How good is your punctuation?
26. Tell me about that.
27. Do you know how to type on a computer?
28. (If yes) Does using a computer make writing easier for you?
29. Tell me about that.
30. Do you have difficulty copying from the chalkboard?
31. Tell me about that.

32. Do you have difficulty taking notes when the teacher lectures?
33. Tell me about that.

Math

34. Do you know the multiplication tables?
35. (If no) Tell me about that.
36. When you do math, do you make mistakes like writing "21" when you mean to write "12," mixing up columns of numbers, or adding when you mean to subtract?
37. Tell me about the mistakes you make when you do math.
38. Do you sometimes start a math problem but halfway through forget what you are trying to do?

Sequencing

39. When you speak or write, do you sometimes find it hard to get everything in the right order—that is, do you start in the middle, go to the beginning, and then jump to the end?
40. Do you have trouble saying the alphabet in order?
41. (If yes) Tell me about that.
42. Do you have to start from the beginning each time you say the alphabet?
43. Do you have trouble saying the days of the week in order?
44. (If yes) Tell me about that.
45. Do you have trouble saying the months of the year in order?
46. (If yes) Tell me about that.

Abstraction

47. Do you understand jokes when your friends tell them?
48. (If no) Tell me about that.
49. Do you sometimes find that people seem to say one thing yet tell you that they meant something else?
50. (If yes) Tell me about that.

Organization

51. What does your notebook look like?
52. (If needed) Is it pretty neat and organized, or is it a mess, with papers in the wrong place or falling out?
53. Is it hard for you to organize your thoughts or to organize the facts you're learning into the bigger idea that the teacher is trying to teach you?
54. Can you read a chapter and answer the questions at the end of the chapter but still not be sure what the chapter is about?
55. (If yes) Tell me about that.
56. Do you have trouble planning your time so that things get done on time?
57. (If yes) Tell me about that.
58. What does your bedroom at home look like?

(Continued)

Table B-3 *(Continued)*

Memory

59. How is your memory?
60. Has it changed in any way?
    (Ask questions 61 to 64, as needed.)
61. Do you find that you can learn something at night but, when you go to school the next day, you don't remember what you learned?
62. When talking, do you sometimes forget what you are saying halfway through?
63. (If yes) What do you do when this happens?
64. (If needed) Do you cover up by saying things like "Whatever," "Oh, forget it," or "It's not important"?

Language

65. When the teacher is speaking in class, do you have trouble understanding or keeping up?
66. (If yes) Tell me about that.
67. Do you sometimes misunderstand people and, therefore, give the wrong answer?
68. (If yes) Tell me when this happens.
69. Do you sometimes lose track of what people are saying?
70. (If yes) Does this sometimes cause you to lose your concentration in class?
71. Do you sometimes have trouble organizing your thoughts when you speak?
72. (If yes) Tell me about that.
73. Do you often have a problem finding the word you want to use?
74. (If yes) When this happens, what do you do?

Study Habits

75. Now I'd like to ask you about your learning and study habits. Tell me about what happens when you study.
76. Do you learn better alone, with one friend, or in a group?
77. Tell me more about that.
78. When you study, do you like to have adults help you, be available to help you, or leave you alone?
79. Tell me about that.

Time Rhythm

80. At what time of day do you learn best?
81. (If needed) Do you learn best early in the morning, right before lunch, after lunch, after school, or right before bedtime?
82. After you wake up in the morning, how long does it take you to feel really awake?
83. Do you sometimes have trouble staying awake after lunch or dinner?
84. (If yes) Tell me more about that.
85. Do you like to get up early?
86. If you stay up late, do you feel "foggy" the next day—as if your head's in a cloud?
87. What time do you usually go to bed?

88. How long does it usually take you to fall asleep?

Environment

89. Where is the best place for you to study?
90. Tell me more about that.
91. Do you like to study in a room with bright lighting or low lighting?
92. Do you think you feel cold or hot more often than other people?
93. (If yes) Tell me about that.
94. Do you like the room you're in to be warm or cool?

Attention and Concentration

95. Do you prefer noise or silence when you are studying?
96. Can you study if you hear a radio or television in the background?
97. Are you distracted if you hear people talking or children playing?
98. Do you like to study with music playing?
99. (If yes) What kind of music?
100. Do you daydream a lot when you are in class?
101. (If yes) Tell me about that.
102. Do you have trouble sitting still or staying in your seat at school?
103. (If yes) Tell me about the trouble you're having.
104. And at home, do you have trouble sitting still or staying in your seat?
105. (If yes) Tell me about that.
106. How is your concentration?
107. Can you complete your assignments, or are you easily distracted?
108. (If distracted) What seems to distract you?
109. Do you like to leave your studies to go see what's going on, get a drink, or change rooms or positions?
110. (If yes) Tell me more about that.
111. Do you like to keep at your work until it's done?
112. Tell me more about that.

Study Habits

113. Do you like to eat, chew gum, or have a drink while you are studying?
114. (If yes) How does it help?
115. Do you overeat while you are studying?
116. (If yes) How does it help?
117. Do you have any nervous habits while you're studying, such as chewing your fingernails or a pencil?
118. (If yes) Tell me about your habits.

Motivation

119. How important is it for you to get good grades?
120. Tell me about that.

(Continued)

Table B-3 *(Continued)*

121. Do you think your grades are important to your parents?
122. Tell me about that.
123. Do you think your grades are important to your teachers?
124. Tell me about that.
125. When you try to get good grades, is it more to please adults or to please yourself?
126. Tell me about that.
127. Do you think that getting a good education is one of the most important things in life?
128. Tell me about that.
129. Do you think reading is important for more things in life than just school?
130. Tell me about that.
131. Do you let things go until the last minute?
132. Tell me about that.
133. Do you feel responsible for your learning?
134. Tell me about that.
135. How do you feel when you don't do well in school?
136. How do you feel when you turn in an assignment late?
137. How do you feel when you don't finish an assignment?
138. Do you like solving problems on your own, or do you prefer being told exactly what is expected and how to do it?
139. Do you get upset easily when you are learning?
140. (If yes) Tell me about that.

141. Do you like to learn and find out things, even when you aren't in school and don't have to?
142. Tell me about that.
143. How do you feel when someone criticizes your schoolwork?
144. Tell me about that.
145. Do you usually try to do your very best in school?
146. Tell me about that.

Anxiety

147. Do you think that you worry more about school or tests than other kids do?
148. (If yes) Tell me about that.
149. Do you feel shaky when the teacher asks you to read aloud, get up in front of the class, or write on the board?
150. (If yes) Tell me about that.
151. How do you feel about surprise tests?

Concluding Comments

152. Is there anything else you would like to tell me or talk about?
153. Do you have any questions that you would like to ask me?
154. (If yes) Go ahead.
155. Thank you for talking with me. If you have any questions or if you want to talk to me, please call me. Here is my card.

Note. With modifications, these questions also can be used for a parent. You would need to substitute the child's name for "you" or "your" and make the appropriate grammatical changes.
Source: Adapted from Dunn and Dunn (1977) and Silver (1992).

Table B-4
Semistructured Interview Questions for an Older Child or Adolescent with Traumatic Brain Damage

These questions supplement those in Table B-1 in this Appendix.

Introduction

1. Hi, I'm Dr. [Ms., Mr.] _____. And your name is…? I'm going to be asking you some questions. When you don't understand a question that I ask, please say "I don't understand." When you tell me that, I'll try to ask it better. OK?
2. Has anyone told you why you are here today?
   (If yes, go to question 3; if no, go to question 5.)
3. Who told you?
4. What did he [she, they] tell you?
   (Go to question 6.)
5. Tell me why you think you are here. (If interviewee doesn't know, explain to her or him that you want to find out how she or he is getting along or something similar.)

General Problems

6. Please tell me anything you can about how you are getting along.
7. (If needed) Are you having any problems?
   (If child says that he or she is having problems, go to question 8; otherwise, go to question 19.)
8. Tell me about [cite problems mentioned by child].
9. How do you feel about [cite problems]?
10. What changes have you noticed since [cite problems] began?
11. In what situations do you have the most difficulty with [cite problems]?
12. What do you do in these situations?
13. Is there anything that helps?
14. (If yes) How does it help?
15. What kind of help would you like?
16. How do your parents feel about the problems you are having?
17. How do your friends feel about the problems you are having?
18. And how do your teachers feel about the problems you are having?

Specific Current Problems and Complaints

19. I'm going to name some other areas in which you may have problems. If you have problems or complaints in any of these areas, please let me know by saying yes. After we finish the list, we'll go back to the beginning and I'll ask you more about these problems. OK?

    (*If the child previously told you about a problem, do not mention it again now.* Pause after you name each problem or complaint. From time to time, remind the child of the task by prefacing the name of the problem with "Are you having a problem with …?" or "Do you have any complaints about …?")

General Physical Problems
- bowel or bladder control
- seizures
- headaches
- dizziness
- pain
- sleeping
- numbness
- loss of feeling
- blackouts
- muscle strength
- endurance
- coordination

Sensory-Motor Problems
- seeing
- hearing
- smelling
- speaking
- balance
- movements you can't control or stop
- standing
- walking
- running
- drawing
- handwriting
- eating
- dressing
- recognizing objects
- building or constructing things
- hearing ringing sounds
- changes in taste
- tingling in your fingertips or toes

Cognitive Problems
- thinking
- planning
- concentrating
- remembering
- paying attention
- understanding directions
- giving directions
- learning
- judging
- reading
- writing stories, poems, and other things
- spelling
- doing simple arithmetic problems
- understanding what is read to you
- handling money
- finding your way around

(Continued)

Table B-4 *(Continued)*

Psychosocial-Affective Problems

- keeping up with your responsibilities at home
- staying interested in things
- bathing
- organizing things
- getting along with other children
- getting along with friends and family members
- getting along with teachers
- controlling your temper
- feeling sad
- feeling anxious
- showing initiative
- doing things too fast or too slowly
- realizing that another person is upset
- controlling your laughter
- being inconsiderate of others
- being impatient
- being inflexible
- becoming angry without cause
- changing moods easily
- being irritable
- being aggressive
- being uncooperative
- being negative
- lying
- stealing
- having to do things exactly the same way each time
- changes in your personality
- failing to recognize problems in yourself
- being insecure
- changing from one activity to another
- visiting friends
- keeping friends
- going shopping

Language and Communication Problems

- talking too much
- talking too little
- using the right word
- using peculiar words
- saying embarrassing things
- reversing what you hear
- defining words
- naming objects that are shown to you
- counting
- naming the days of the week
- repeating names
- carrying on a conversation
- recognizing mistakes that you make in speaking or writing or reading

- using the telephone
- watching television
- looking up telephone numbers
- remembering telephone numbers

Consciousness Problems

- feeling disoriented
- feeling that you are losing your body
- feeling that some unknown danger is lurking
- doing things that you are unaware of
- starting to do one thing and then finding yourself doing something else
- feeling that the size of your hands or feet or head is changing

(If the child responded "yes" to any area, go to question 20; otherwise, go to question 24.)

20. You told me that you have a problem with [cite area]. Tell me more about your difficulty with [cite area]. (Repeat for each problem.)
21. Which problems bother you most?
22. How do you deal with these problems?
23. How do your parents deal with these problems?

Accident or Injury

24. I'd like to learn about the accident [injury]. Please tell me about it.
    (Ask questions 25 to 36 as needed.)
25. What happened?
26. What were you doing at the time of the accident [injury]?
27. Who else was involved in the accident [injury]?
28. Were you unconscious?
    (If yes, go to question 29; if no, go to question 31.)
29. How long were you unconscious?
30. Where did you wake up?
31. What kind of treatment did you get?
32. How did the treatment help?
33. What kind of treatment are you receiving now?
34. What was your behavior like right after the accident [injury] happened?
35. What was your behavior like several days later?
36. And what is your behavior like now?

Adjustment to Brain Injury and Typical Activities

37. Have you noticed any changes since the accident [injury] in how you are getting along with your parents?
38. (If yes) Tell me what you have noticed.
39. (If relevant) Have you noticed any changes since the accident [injury] in how you are getting along with your brothers and sisters?
40. (If yes) Tell me what you have noticed.
41. Have you noticed any changes since the accident [injury] in how you are getting along with your friends?

(Continued)

Table B-4 *(Continued)*

42. (If yes) Tell me what you have noticed.

43. Have there been any changes in your schoolwork since the accident [injury]?

44. (If yes) Tell me about the changes in your schoolwork.

45. (If relevant) Have there been any changes in your work habits since the accident [injury]?

46. (If yes) Tell me about the changes in your work habits.

Concluding Questions

47. Is there anything else that you want to tell me or that you think I should know?

48. (If yes) Go ahead.

49. Do you have any questions that you would like to ask me?

50. (If yes) Go ahead.

51. Thank you for talking with me. If you have any questions, if you want to talk to me, or if you think of anything else you want to tell me, please call me. Here is my card.

Note. With modifications, these questions also can be used for a parent. You would need to substitute the child's name for "you" or "your" and make the appropriate grammatical changes.

Table B-5
Semistructured Interview Questions for a Parent of a Child Who May Have a Psychological or Educational Problem or Disorder

Some of the questions in this table (for example, those dealing with peer relationships, interests and hobbies, and academic functioning) are not applicable to infants, and other questions (for example, those dealing with academic functioning) may not be applicable to toddlers. Therefore, use your judgment in selecting appropriate questions to use. This table can be used in conjunction with Table B-6 in this Appendix, which contains additional questions concerning specific areas of child development in infancy and the toddler/preschool years. At the end of this table are additional questions that you can use to inquire about adolescents.

Introduction

1. Hi! I'm Dr. [Ms., Mr.] _____. I'd like to talk to you about [cite child's name]'s adjustment and functioning. OK?

Parent's Perception of Problem Behavior

2. Please tell me your concerns about [cite child's name].
3. (If needed) Can you describe these concerns a little more?
4. Is there anything else that you are concerned about?
5. What concerns you most?
6. Let's discuss [cite problem] in more detail. How serious do you consider [cite problem] to be?
7. When did you first notice [cite problem]?
8. How long has [cite problem] been going on?
9. Where does [cite problem] occur?
10. (If needed) Tell me about how [cite child's name] behaves at school … in stores or other public places … in a car … at friends' houses … with visitors at home.
11. When does [cite problem] occur?
12. (If needed) Does it happen in the morning … in the afternoon … at bedtime?… Does it occur when [cite child's name] is with you … his [her] father [mother] … his [her] brothers and sisters … other children … other relatives?
13. How long does [cite problem] last?
14. How often does [cite problem] occur?
15. What happens just before [cite problem] begins?
16. What happens just after [cite problem] begins?
17. What makes [cite problem] worse?
18. What makes [cite problem] better?
19. What do you do when [cite problem] occurs?
20. Has this been successful?
21. What do you think is causing [cite problem]?
22. Was anything significant happening in your family when [cite problem] first started?
23. (If needed) For example, had you recently separated or divorced … moved to another city or school district … had financial problems … dealt with the serious illness of a family member?
24. (If some event occurred) What was [cite child's name]'s reaction to [cite event]?
25. How does [cite child's name] deal with [cite problem]?

26. Do any other children in your family also have [cite problem]?
27. (If yes) How does [cite child's name]'s [cite problem] compare with theirs?
28. Has [cite child's name] been evaluated or received any help for [cite problem]?
    (If yes, go to question 29; if no, go to question 31.)
29. What type of evaluation or help has he [she] received?
30. And what progress has been made?
31. Why do you think [cite child's name] has [cite problem]?
32. How do you deal with [cite problem]?
33. How do family members react to [cite child's name]'s [cite problem]?
34. Are any of the other problems you mentioned, such as [cite problem], of particular concern to you now?
    (If yes, repeat questions 6 to 33 as needed.)

Home Environment

35. Tell me what your home is like.
36. Where does [cite child's name] sleep?
37. Where does [cite child's name] play?
38. Who lives at your home?
39. (If needed) Do you have a husband [wife] or partner?
40. (If relevant) Tell me about your husband [wife, partner].

Neighborhood

41. Tell me about your neighborhood.
42. Do you know your neighbors?
43. (If yes) What do you think of your neighbors?
44. (If needed) How do you get along with them?

Sibling Relations (if relevant)

45. How does [cite child's name] get along with his [her] brothers and sisters?
46. What do they do that [cite child's name] likes?
47. What do they do that [cite child's name] dislikes?
48. How do they get along when you aren't around?
49. Is it different when you are there?

Peer Relations

50. Does [cite child's name] have friends?
    (If yes, go to question 51; if no, go to question 59.)
51. Tell me about [cite child's name]'s friends.
52. (If needed) About how many friends does he [she] have?
53. (If needed) What are their ages?
54. How does he [she] get along with his [her] friends?
55. What does [cite child's name] do with his [her] friends?
56. How does he [she] get along with friends of the opposite sex?

(Continued)

Table B-5 *(Continued)*

57. Do you approve of his [her] friends?
58. Does [cite child's name] usually go along with what his [her] friends want to do, or is [cite child's name] more likely to do what he [she] wants to do?
(Go to question 63.)
59. Tell me about [cite child's name]'s not having friends.
60. Does [cite child's name] have usual opportunities to meet other children?
61. (If needed) Tell me more about that.
62. Does [cite child's name] seem to want to have friends?
63. Does [cite child's name] have a problem keeping friends?
64. (If yes) Tell me about that.
65. How do other children react to [cite child's name]?

Child's Relations with Parents and Other Adults

66. How does [cite child's name] get along with you?
67. What does [cite child's name] do with you on a regular basis?
68. How does [cite child's name] express his [her] affection for you?
69. What are the good times like for [cite child's name] and you?
70. What are the bad times like for [cite child's name] and you?
71. Are there times when both you and [cite child's name] end up feeling angry or frustrated with each other?
72. (If yes) Tell me more about that.
(If there are other adults in the household, repeat questions 66 to 72 for each adult, substituting the adult's name, and then go to question 73; otherwise, go to question 79.)
73. When something is bothering [cite child's name], whom does he [she] confide in most often?
74. Who is responsible for discipline?
75. Who is most protective of [cite child's name]?
76. Do you have any concerns about how other adults interact with [cite child's name]?
77. (If yes) Tell me about your concerns.
78. (If needed) About whom do you have concerns?
79. Does [cite child's name] listen to what he [she] is told to do?
80. How is [cite child's name] disciplined?
81. Which techniques are effective?
82. Which are ineffective?
83. What have you found to be the most satisfactory ways of helping your child?
84. How do you express your affection for [cite child's name]?

Child's Interests and Hobbies

85. What does [cite child's name] like to do in his [her] spare time?
86. What types of games does [cite child's name] like to play?
87. How skilled is [cite child's name] at sports or other games?
88. Is [cite child's name] involved in any extracurricular activities?
89. (If yes) Tell me about that.

90. What does [cite child's name] like to do alone … with friends … with family members?
91. What activities does [cite child's name] like least?
92. How much television does [cite child's name] watch each day?
93. Do you think that is the right amount of television?
94. (If no) Tell me about that.
95. What are his [her] favorite programs?
96. How do you feel about the programs he [she] watches?
97. Does [cite child's name] play video or computer games?
98. (If yes) How much time does [cite child's name] spend each day playing these games?
99. Do you think that is the right amount of time?
100. (If no) Tell me about that.
101. (If needed) And how about listening to music? Does [cite child's name] listen to music?
(If yes, go to question 102; if no, go to question 104.)
102. What kind of music does [cite child's name] listen to?
103. How do you feel about the music [cite child's name] listens to?

Child's Routine Daily Activities

104. How does [cite child's name] behave when he [she] wakes up?
105. What changes occur in [cite child's name]'s behavior during the course of a day?
106. (If needed) Does he [she] become more fidgety or restless as the day proceeds, or does he [she] become more calm and relaxed?
107. Does [cite child's name] do household chores?
108. (If yes) What chores does he [she] do?
109. What does [cite child's name] do before bedtime?
110. How does [cite child's name] behave when he [she] goes to bed?

Child's Cognitive Functioning

111. How well does [cite child's name] learn things?
112. Does [cite child's name] seem to understand things that are said to him [her]?
113. Does [cite child's name] seem to be quick or slow to catch on?
114. Does [cite child's name] stick with tasks that he [she] is trying to learn?

Child's Academic Functioning

115. How is [cite child's name] getting along in school?
116. What does he [she] like best about school?
117. What does he [she] like least about school?
118. What grades does [cite child's name] get?
119. What are [cite child's name]'s best subjects?
120. What are [cite child's name]'s worst subjects?

(Continued)

Table B-5 *(Continued)*

121. Are you generally satisfied with [cite child's name]'s achievement in school?
122. (If no) Tell me what you're not satisfied about?
123. How does [cite child's name] feel about his [her] schoolwork?
124. How does [cite child's name] get along with the other children at school?
125. How does [cite child's name] get along with his [her] teacher[s]?
126. What do you think about [cite child's name]'s school?
127. What do you think about [cite child's name]'s teacher[s]?
128. What do you think about the principal of the school?
129. Has [cite child's name] ever repeated a grade or attended a readiness or transition class?
130. (If yes) Tell me about that.
131. Has any teacher recommended special help or special education services for [cite child's name]?
    (If yes, go to question 132; if no, go to question 135.)
132. Tell me about the help that was recommended.
133. Please describe what help, if any, he [she] has received.
134. Does [cite child's name] attend a special class?
135. Have you needed to attend specially scheduled parent-teacher meetings because of [cite child's name]'s behavior?
136. (If yes) What did you learn at the meeting[s]?

Child's Behavior

137. Tell me about [cite child's name]'s attention span.
138. What kind of self-control does [cite child's name] have?
139. How well does [cite child's name] follow directions?
140. Tell me about [cite child's name]'s activity level.
141. Is [cite child's name] impulsive?
142. (If yes) Tell me about his [her] impulsiveness.

Child's Affective Life

143. What kinds of things make [cite child's name] happy?
144. What makes him [her] sad?
145. What does [cite child's name] do when he [she] is sad?
146. What kinds of things make [cite child's name] angry?
147. What does [cite child's name] do when he [she] is angry?
148. What kinds of things make [cite child's name] afraid?
149. What does [cite child's name] do when he [she] is afraid?
150. What kinds of things does [cite child's name] worry about?
151. What kinds of things does [cite child's name] think about a lot?
152. What sorts of things does [cite child's name] ask questions about?
153. How does [cite child's name] typically react to a painful or uncomfortable event, such as when he [she] gets an injection or has to take pills?
154. How does [cite child's name] feel about himself [herself]?
155. How does [cite child's name] behave when faced with a difficult problem?

156. What makes [cite child's name] frustrated?
157. What does [cite child's name] do when he [she] is frustrated?
158. Does [cite child's name] ever become annoyed when you try to help him [her] with something?
159. (If yes) Tell me about that.
160. What things does [cite child's name] do well?
161. What things does [cite child's name] really enjoy doing?
162. Tell me what [cite child's name] is really willing to work to obtain.
163. What do you do when [cite child's name] is sad … is angry … is afraid … worries a lot … is in pain?

Child's Motor Skills

164. Tell me about [cite child's name]'s ability to do things that require small motor movements, such as turning pages of a book, using scissors, and folding paper.
165. Tell me about [cite child's name]'s general coordination, such as his [her] ability to walk, jump, skip, and roll a ball.

Child's Health History

166. I'd like to ask you about [cite child's name]'s health history. What common childhood illnesses has [cite child's name] had?
167. And has [cite child's name] had any serious illnesses?
168. (If yes) Tell me about them.
169. (As needed) When did the illness start?… What was the treatment?… Was the treatment successful?
170. Has he [she] had any surgical procedures?
171. (If yes) Tell me about them.
172. How would you describe [cite child's name]'s usual state of health?
173. Do you believe that [cite child's name] has been growing adequately?
174. (If no) Tell me more about that.
175. How is [cite child's name]'s hearing?
176. How is [cite child's name]'s vision?
177. Did [cite child's name] ever have any serious accidents or injuries?
178. (If yes) Tell me about them.
179. Did [cite child's name] ever go to an emergency room for an accident or illness?
180. (If yes) Tell me about it.
181. Did [cite child's name] ever need any stitches?
182. (If yes) Tell me about it.
183. Has [cite child's name] ever had any broken bones?
184. (If yes) Tell me about it.
185. Did [cite child's name] ever swallow anything dangerous?
186. (If yes) Tell me about what happened.
187. Does [cite child's name] have any allergies?
188. (If yes) Tell me about them.
189. What immunizations has [cite child's name] had?

(Continued)

Table B-5 (Continued)

190. Does [cite child's name] eat well?
191. (If no) Tell me about that.
192. Does [cite child's name] sleep well?
193. (If no) Tell me about that.
194. Does [cite child's name] have nightmares or other sleep problems?
195. (If yes) Tell me about that.
196. Does [cite child's name] have problems with bowel or bladder control?
197. (If yes) Tell me about that.
198. Does [cite child's name] take any medicine regularly? (If yes, go to question 199; if no, go to question 205.)
199. What medicine does he [she] take regularly?
200. What does [cite child's name] take the medicine for?
201. Does [cite child's name] report any side effects from taking the medicine? (If yes, go to question 202; if no, go to question 205.)
202. What are the side effects?
203. Have you discussed them with your doctor?
204. (If yes) What did the doctor say?

Family

205. Tell me about your family. Does anyone in your immediate or extended family have any major problems?
206. (If yes) Tell me about them.
207. (If relevant) How are you getting along with your husband [wife, partner]?
208. (If relevant) How do you see your relationship with your husband [wife, partner] affecting [cite child's name]'s problem?
209. What kinds of serious medical or psychological difficulties have you or members of your family had?
210. Has anyone in the family that [cite child's name] was close to died?
211. (If yes) Tell me about that.
212. How about a close friend? Have any of [cite child's name]'s friends died?
213. (If yes) Tell me about that.
214. Has the family lost a pet?
215. (If yes) Tell me about the loss.
216. Has anyone in your family been the victim of a crime?
217. (If yes) Please tell me about what happened.
218. Have you recently changed your place of residence?
219. (If yes) Tell me about your move.
220. (If relevant) Has [cite child's name]'s caregiver recently changed?
221. (If yes) Tell me about that.
222. In addition to [cite child's name], is any other family member currently having a problem at school or work?
223. (If yes) Tell me about him [her, them].
224. Have any members of your family had a problem similar to [cite child's name]'s problem?
225. (If yes) Tell me about that.

226. Has anyone in the family shown a major change in behavior within the past year?
227. (If yes) Tell me about that.
228. (If needed) Do any members of your family have a problem with drugs or alcohol?
229. (If yes) Tell me about that.
230. Do you have any concerns about your child's having been physically abused or sexually abused?
231. (If yes) Tell me about your concerns.

Parent's Expectations

232. Do you think that [cite child's name] needs treatment, special education, or special services?
233. What do you expect such services to do for [cite child's name]?
234. What are your goals for [cite child's name]?
235. How would your life be different if [cite child's name]'s problems were resolved?
236. (If relevant) Do you desire treatment for your own difficulties? (If there are other adult members of the household, go to question 237; otherwise, go to instructions following question 242.)
237. Who in the family is most concerned about [cite child's name]'s problem?
238. Who is least concerned?
239. Who is most affected by the problem?
240. Who is least affected?
241. How does your view of [cite child's name]'s problem compare with that of [cite other adult members of household]?
242. How does your view about what should be done to help [cite child's name] compare with that of [cite other adult members of household]?

(Before concluding the interview, ask the questions below about the development of an adolescent or those in Table B-6 in this Appendix about the development of an infant or toddler/preschooler, as needed.)

Concluding Questions

243. Overall, what do you see as [cite child's name]'s strong points?
244. And overall, what do you see as [cite child's name]'s weak points?
245. Is there any other information about [cite child's name] that I should know?
246. Where do you see [cite child's name] five years from now?
247. Thank you for talking with me. If you have any questions or if you want to talk to me, please call me. Here is my card.

Additional Questions About Adolescent's Development

1. Is [cite child's name] involved in any dating activities?
2. (If yes) What kind of dating activities?

(Continued)

Table B-5 *(Continued)*

3. Are there any restrictions on his [her] dating activities?

4. (If yes) How does he [she] feel about them?

5. Have you talked with [cite child's name] about sexual behaviors?
   (If yes, go to question 6; if no, go to question 10.)

6. Tell me what you've talked about.

7. What kinds of sexual concerns does [cite child's name] have?

8. Do you and [cite child's name] agree or disagree about appropriate sexual behavior?

9. Tell me about that.

10. Does [cite child's name] use drugs?
    (If yes, go to question 11; if no, go to question 20.)

11. Tell me about his [her] drug use.
    (Ask questions 12 to 19, as needed.)

12. What kind of drugs does [cite child's name] use?

13. How does [cite child's name] get the drugs?

14. How does [cite child's name] pay for the drugs?

15. Has [cite child's name] ever gotten into trouble because of his [her] drug use?

16. (If yes) Tell me about that.

17. Has [cite child's name] received any treatment for his [her] drug use?

18. (If yes) Tell me about the treatment he [she] has received.

19. Is there anything else you want to tell me about [cite child's name]'s drug use?

20. Does [cite child's name] drink alcohol?
    (If yes, go to question 21; if no, go to question 30.)

21. Tell me about his [her] drinking.
    (Ask questions 22 to 29, as needed.)

22. What kind of alcohol does [cite child's name] drink?

23. How does [cite child's name] get the alcohol?

24. (If relevant) How does [cite child's name] pay for the alcohol?

25. Has [cite child's name] ever gotten into trouble because of his [her] drinking?

26. (If yes) Tell me about that.

27. Has [cite child's name] received any treatment for his [her] use of alcohol?

28. (If yes) Tell me about the treatment he [she] has received.

29. Is there anything else you want to tell me about [cite child's name]'s drinking?

30. Does [cite child's name] get high by using other things besides drugs or alcohol?
    (If yes, go to question 31; if no, go to question 243 in main interview.)

31. What does [cite child's name] use to get high?

32. Tell me about that.
    (Ask questions 33 to 39, as needed.)

33. How does [cite child's name] get [cite substance]?

34. (If relevant) How does [cite child's name] pay for [cite substance]?

35. Has [cite child's name] ever gotten into trouble because of his [her] use of [cite substance]?

36. (If yes) Tell me about that.

37. Has [cite child's name] received any treatment for his [her] use of [cite substance]?

38. (If yes) Tell me about the treatment he [she] has received.

39. Is there anything else you want to tell me about [cite child's name]'s use of [cite substance]?
    (Go to question 243 in main interview.)

Note. If you want to obtain information about other problems, repeat questions 7 through 34 in the main interview. Any responses given to questions in this interview can be probed further. If you want to ask additional questions about maternal obstetric history, pregnancy, or labor and delivery or if you suspect that the parent has minimal parenting skills, see Table B-6 in this Appendix.

Table B-6
Semistructured Interview Questions for a Mother to Obtain a Detailed Developmental History Covering Her Child's Early Years and to Evaluate Her Parenting Skills

The questions in this semistructured interview supplement those in Table B-5 in this Appendix, which should be used first. You then have the choice of following up in areas related to infancy and toddler/preschool years. The questions are designed not only to obtain information about the child but also to evaluate parenting skills. Select the questions that you believe are applicable to the specific case and that complement those in Table B-5. If you want information about the mother's obstetric history, you can say, for example, "I'd now like to get some more information about [cite child's name]'s development. I would first like to learn about the time before [cite child's name] was born." If you decide to begin the semistructured interview with another section, use an appropriate introduction. The questions can be used to inquire about an infant or toddler/preschooler. Sections that pertain specifically to infants or toddlers/preschoolers are so identified in the section headings.

Additional Questions About Maternal Obstetric History

1. How old were you when [cite child's name] was born?
2. Have you had any other pregnancies?
   (If yes, go to question 3; if no, go to question 9.)
3. Tell me about them. (Pay particular attention to miscarriages, abortions, and premature births and their outcomes.)
4. How many living children do you have?
5. (If more than one child) How old are they now?
6. (If any child died) How did your child die?
7. (If needed) Tell me about what happened.
8. (If needed) How old was your child when he [she] died?
9. I'd like to talk to you about your pregnancy with [cite child's name]. What was your pregnancy like?
   (Ask questions 10 to 13, as needed.)
10. Was it planned?
11. (If yes) How long did it take you to become pregnant?
12. Did you have any illnesses or problems during pregnancy? (Pay particular attention to vaginal bleeding, fevers, rashes, hospitalizations, weight gain, weight loss, vomiting, hypertension, proteinuria [the presence of an excess of protein in the urine; also called albuminuria], preeclampsia [a toxemia of late pregnancy characterized by hypertension, albuminuria, and edema], general infections, and urinary tract infections.)
13. Were one or more sonograms performed?
    (If yes, go to question 14; if no, go to question 16.)
14. How many were performed?
15. What did it [they] show?
16. Was your blood type incompatible with that of [cite child's name]?
17. (If yes) Tell me about that.
18. Did you take any medications or street drugs during pregnancy?
19. (If yes) What did you take? (Pay particular attention to prescription drugs; over-the-counter pills; cocaine/crack; marijuana/pot; hallucinogens, such as LSD, PCP, DMT,

mescaline, and mushrooms; stimulants, such as uppers, speed, amphetamines, crystal, crank, and Dexedrine; tranquilizers, such as downers, Valium, Elavil, quaaludes, Stelazine, barbiturates, and thorazine; opiates, such as morphine, Demerol, Percodan, codeine, Darvon, Darvocet, heroin, and methadone; *and other drugs that may affect the development of the fetus.* If the medicine or drug is listed here or if it is any drug that may affect the development of the fetus, go to question 20; if not, go to question 25.)
20. How often did you take it?
21. When during your pregnancy did you take it?
22. How did it make you feel?
23. Did you tell your health care provider that you were taking [cite drug]?
24. (If yes) Tell me about that.
25. Did you drink alcohol during your pregnancy?
    (If yes, go to question 26; if no, go to question 32.)
26. What did you drink?
27. How often did you drink alcohol?
28. And how much did you drink each time?
29. When during your pregnancy did you start drinking?
30. Did you drink throughout your pregnancy?
31. Did you tell your health care provider that you were drinking alcohol during your pregnancy?
32. Did you smoke cigarettes during your pregnancy?
    (If yes, go to question 33; if no, go to question 37.)
33. And how many cigarettes did you smoke each day?
34. When during your pregnancy did you start smoking?
35. Did you smoke throughout your pregnancy?
36. Did you tell your health care provider that you were smoking during your pregnancy?
37. Did you have x-rays taken during your pregnancy?
38. (If yes) Tell me about them.
39. Were you exposed to chemicals or other potentially harmful substances during your pregnancy?
40. (If yes) Tell me about what you were exposed to.
41. Did you see a health care provider during your pregnancy?
    (If yes, go to question 42; if no, go to question 44.)
42. What kind of health care provider did you see during your pregnancy?
43. How many visits did you make?
    (Go to question 45.)
44. What was the reason you did not see a health care provider?
45. Did you see anyone else for care during your pregnancy?
46. (If yes) Tell me about whom you saw.
47. Overall, was your pregnancy with [cite child's name] a good experience or a bad experience?
48. Tell me about your answer.
49. In general, how would you rate your health during your pregnancy with [cite child's name]?
50. Tell me about your answer.

(Continued)

Table B-6 *(Continued)*

Additional Questions About Labor, Delivery, Infant's Condition at Birth, and Immediate Postpartum Period for Mother

1. Now I'd like to talk to you about your labor and delivery. Tell me about your labor and delivery.
   (Ask questions 2 to 14, as needed.)
2. What were your thoughts and feelings during labor?
3. Was [cite child's name] born on time?
4. (If early) How early was [cite child's name] born?
5. (If late) How late was [cite child's name] born?
6. How long did the labor last?
7. What kind of delivery did you have?
8. (If needed) Was it normal … breech … cesarean … forceps … induced?
9. (If delivery was cesarean, forceps, or induced) Why was this type of delivery needed?
10. How did the delivery go?
11. (If needed) Were there any complications at delivery?
12. (If yes) Tell me about them.
13. Were you given anything for pain during labor?
14. (If yes) Tell me about it.
15. Were labor and delivery what you expected?
16. What were your first impressions of your new baby?
17. Was the baby's father present during delivery?
18. (If yes) What were his first impressions of the new baby?
19. How was [cite child's name] right after he [she] was born?
20. What was [cite child's name]'s weight at birth?
21. What was [cite child's name]'s length at birth?
22. What was [cite child's name]'s skin color?
23. Did [cite child's name] cry soon after birth?
24. Do you know [cite child's name]'s Apgar score?
25. (If yes) What was it?
26. Did you want to hold [cite child's name] right away?
27. Were you allowed to hold [cite child's name]?
28. (If father was present) Was the baby's father allowed to hold [cite child's name]?
29. Did you have any physical problems immediately after [cite child's name] was born?
30. (If yes) Tell me about them.
31. Did you have any psychological problems after [cite child's name] was born?
32. (If yes) Tell me about them.
33. Did you have a rooming-in arrangement with the baby?
   (If yes, go to question 34; if no, go to question 35.)
34. What was it like to have the baby in the room with you?
   (Go to question 36.)
35. Tell me your reason for not having a rooming-in arrangement.
36. Did [cite child's name] have any health problems following birth?
37. (If yes) Tell me about them.

38. Was [cite child's name] in a special care nursery in the hospital for observation or treatment?
   (If yes, go to question 39; if no, go to question 47.)
39. Tell me about the reason [cite child's name] was in a special care nursery.
40. Did you visit [cite child's name] when he [she] was in the special care nursery?
41. Did you feed [cite child's name] when he [she] was in the special care nursery?
42. How did you feel about having [cite child's name] stay in the special care nursery?
43. And how many days old was [cite child's name] when he [she] went home from the special care nursery?
   (If the father is in the picture, go to question 44; if not, go to question 47)
44. Did the baby's father visit [cite child's name] when he [she] was in the special care nursery?
45. Did the baby's father feed [cite child's name] when he [she] was in the special care nursery?
46. How did the baby's father feel about having [cite child's name] stay in the special care nursery?
47. How did you spend your time at home with [cite child's name] in the first few days after he [she] was born?
48. After the first few days, how much time did you spend at home with [cite child's name]?
49. Was [cite child's name] breastfed or bottlefed?
50. How did that go?
   (If the father is in the picture, go to question 51; if not, end this section.)
51. Did [cite child's name]'s father also spend time with him [her]?
52. What was their relationship like at this time?
53. (If needed) How did he feel about the baby?
54. Did the baby's father help you during this time?
55. Tell me about that.

Additional Questions About Infant's Attachment

1. When [cite child's name] came home from the hospital, what was it like to have him [her] home?
2. Did you feel you knew the baby?
3. Tell me about that.
4. Did you feel the baby knew you?
5. Tell me about that.
6. How was [cite child's name]'s first few weeks of life at home?
7. Did [cite child's name] have any problems?
8. (If needed) Did [cite child's name] have problems with eating … drinking … sleeping … alertness … irritability?
9. (If yes) Tell me about [cite child's name]'s problems. (Inquire about the types of problems, their severity, what the parent did, treatment, outcomes, and so forth.)
10. Was it easy or difficult to comfort [cite child's name]?

(Continued)

Table B-6 *(Continued)*

11. How did you go about comforting [cite child's name]?
12. Was [cite child's name] too good—that is, did he [she] demand little or no care?
13. (If yes) What did you think about this?
14. Was [cite child's name] alert as a baby?
15. (If no) Tell me about how [cite child's name] reacted.
16. What was [cite child's name]'s mood generally?
17. How well did he [she] adjust to new things or routines?
18. How did he [she] respond to new people?
19. Was he [she] cuddly or rigid?
20. Was he [she] overactive or underactive?
21. Did he [she] engage in any tantrums … rocking behavior … head banging?
22. Did [cite child's name] develop a regular pattern of eating and sleeping?
23. (If no) Tell me about that.
24. Were there any surprises during [cite child's name]'s first weeks of life at home?
25. What was most enjoyable about taking care of [cite child's name]?
26. And what was least enjoyable about taking care of [cite child's name]?
27. What was most difficult about taking care of [cite child's name]?
28. What was easiest about taking care of [cite child's name]?
29. How did you feel about [cite child's name] during his [her] first few weeks of life at home?
30. (If father is in the picture) How did his [her] father feel about [cite child's name] during his [her] first few weeks of life?
31. (If other children in family) How did the other children in the family react to [cite child's name]?
32. (If needed) Did the other children show any signs of jealousy?
33. (If yes) How did they demonstrate their jealousy, and how did you [you and your husband, you and the baby's father] handle the jealousy?
34. Did you have confidence in yourself as a parent during the first six months of [cite child's name]'s life?
35. Tell me about that.
36. What kind of adjustments did you [you and your family] have to make?
37. How did your extended family react to [cite child's name]?

Additional Questions About Infant's Responsiveness (if infant is focus of interview)

1. Does [cite child's name] respond to your voice?
2. When you pick [cite child's name] up, does he [she] become quiet?
3. Does [cite child's name] smile?
4. Does [cite child's name] look at you when you try to talk to or play with him [her]?
5. (If no) What does [cite child's name] do instead?
6. What sounds does [cite child's name] make?

7. Can [cite child's name] reach out and grasp a person's face or finger?
8. Can [cite child's name] tell the difference between strangers and familiar people?
9. Can [cite child's name] play with other people?
10. How does [cite child's name] respond to new people?
11. How does [cite child's name] respond to being in a new place?
12. How often does [cite child's name] want to be held?
13. Does [cite child's name] like physical contact, such as when you gently touch his [her] face, hands, and arms?
14. Is there any physical activity that [cite child's name] seems to enjoy especially?

Additional Questions About Infant's Crying, Adjustment to Caregiving Situation, Behavior in Public, and Unusual Behavior (if infant is focus of interview)

1. When does [cite child's name] cry?
2. What do you do when [cite child's name] cries?
3. Why do you think [cite child's name] cries?
4. (If needed) When [cite child's name] cries, does it usually mean that something is really wrong or is it that something is bothering him [her] only a little bit and he [she] wants attention?
5. Can you tell the difference between the types of crying [cite child's name] does?
6. (If yes) How?
7. (If no) What does he [she] do that makes it difficult to know what his [her] crying means?
8. With whom do you leave [cite child's name] when you go out?
9. How do you feel about leaving [cite child's name]?
10. Do you leave [cite child's name] at a day care center, at somebody's house, or at your house with a sitter during any part of the week?
   (If yes, go to question 11; if no, go to question 28.)
11. Where do you leave him [her]?
12. Tell me about the reason you leave [cite child's name] there.
13. (If day care center or someone's house) How did you find out about [cite place where child is cared for]?
14. Are you satisfied with the way [cite child's name] is cared for there?
15. How is [cite child's name] getting along at [cite place where child is cared for]?
16. (If needed) Is [cite child's name] having any problems there?
17. (If yes) Tell me about them.
18. (If needed) How does [cite child's name] get along with the child care provider[s]?
19. And how does [cite child's name] get along with the other children?
20. Do you have a chance to talk regularly about [cite child's name] with the person[s] taking care of him [her]?

(Continued)

21. How long does it take you to get to [cite place where child is cared for]?

22. How does [cite child's name] act when you leave him [her] at [cite place where child is cared for]?
(If behavior is not satisfactory, go to question 23; if behavior is satisfactory, go to question 27.)

23. How do you feel when [cite child's name] acts this way?

24. Does [cite child's name] always show that he [she] is upset in the same way?

25. What do you do when [cite child's name] is upset to quiet him [her]?

26. How does it help?

27. How does [cite child's name] react when you pick him [her] up from [cite place where child is cared for]?

28. How do you feel about taking [cite child's name] out in public?

29. How does [cite child's name] behave when he [she] is outside the home?

30. How does [cite child's name] react when you take him [her] to a friend's home?
(If there are problems or concerns, go to question 31; otherwise, go to question 33.)

31. How do you handle these problems?

32. What seems to work best?

33. Does [cite child's name] have any unusual behaviors?
(If yes, go to question 34; if no, end this section.)

34. What unusual behaviors does [cite child's name] have?

35. How often does [cite child's name] [cite unusual behavior]?

36. What is most likely to bring on [cite unusual behavior]?

37. What situations seem to make [cite child's name]'s [cite unusual behavior] worse?

38. What do you do at these times?

39. What works best?

40. Is there any connection between what [cite child's name] eats and [cite unusual behavior]?

41. How do you feel about taking care of [cite child's name] when he [she] behaves in this way?

Additional Questions About Infant's Play, Language, Communication, and Problem-Solving Skills (if infant is focus of interview)

1. What does [cite child's name] play?

2. What toys does [cite child's name] like to play with?

3. What is [cite child's name]'s favorite toy?

4. Does [cite child's name] like to do the same activity over and over again?

5. What sounds does [cite child's name] make?

6. How long has he [she] been making these sounds?

7. In which situations does [cite child's name] make sounds?

8. (If needed) Does he [she] makes sounds early in the morning in his [her] crib … while riding in the car … when other children are around … when playing by himself [herself] … when adults are talking … when someone is talking on the phone … when in a quiet room?

9. At what times during the day does [cite child's name] make the most sounds?

10. What is happening at these times?

11. Does [cite child's name] seem to be trying to tell you something as he [she] babbles or makes sounds?

12. Do you have any idea what [cite child's name] is trying to say when he [she] makes sounds?

13. How does [cite child's name] let you know that he [she] wants something?

14. How does [cite child's name] let you know how he [she] feels?

15. (If relevant) About how many words does [cite child's name] understand?

16. (If relevant) Tell me about [cite child's name]'s ability to gesture or point.

17. Do you ever hear [cite child's name] making sounds a few minutes after an adult speaks to him [her]?

18. Was there a time when [cite child's name] made more sounds or babbled more?
(If yes, go to question 19; if no, go to question 21.)

19. When did he [she] babble more?

20. How long has it been since he [she] stopped babbling as much?

21. Has [cite child's name] had any recent illness with fever and earache?

22. Is [cite child's name] exhibiting any other behavior that concerns you?

23. (If yes) What is this behavior?

24. Have there been any changes or stressful events in your home recently?

25. (If yes) Tell me about them.

26. Does [cite child's name] say any words?

27. (If yes) How old was [cite child's name] when he [she] spoke his [her] first words?

28. How does [cite child's name] use his [her] hands, eyes, and body to solve problems?

29. Is [cite child's name] able to transfer small objects from hand to hand?

30. Does [cite child's name] help you hold the bottle?

31. Is [cite child's name] able to follow an object or face with his [her] eyes?

32. Does [cite child's name] use his [her] eyes to examine his [her] hands?

33. Does [cite child's name] reach for objects?

34. Tell me about [cite child's name]'s attention span.

Additional Questions About Infant's Motor Skills (if infant is focus of interview)

(Note that these questions are arranged in developmental sequence. If the child has not mastered a motor skill, it is unlikely that he or she will be able to perform the next motor skill. Therefore, you can stop your inquiry after you find that the child has not mastered a skill.)

1. Can [cite child's name] roll over?

2. (If yes) How old was he [she] when he [she] first rolled over? (Go to question 4.)

3. What progress is [cite child's name] making toward rolling over?

4. Can [cite child's name] crawl?

5. (If yes) How old was he [she] when he [she] began to crawl? (Go to question 7.)

6. What progress is [cite child's name] making toward crawling?

7. Can [cite child's name] sit up?

8. (If yes) How old was he [she] when he [she] first sat up? (Go to question 10.)

9. What progress is [cite child's name] making toward sitting up?

10. Can [cite child's name] pull himself [herself] up to a standing position?
(If yes, go to question 11; if no, go to question 13.)

11. How old was he [she] when he [she] first pulled himself [herself] up to a standing position?

12. Does [cite child's name] sometimes remain standing for a short time after he [she] has pulled himself [herself] up? (Go to question 14.)

13. What progress is he [she] making toward pulling himself [herself] up to a standing position?

14. Can [cite child's name] walk?

15. (If yes) How old was he [she] when he [she] first walked? (Go to question 18.)

16. What progress is he [she] making toward walking?

17. (If needed) Does [cite child's name] seem to want to move and explore on his [her] own?

18. In what situations is [cite child's name] most active physically?

19. (If needed) Is he [she] most active when someone plays with him [her] … when other children are around … when he [she] is outdoors?

20. Tell me about [cite child's name]'s ability to do things that require small-motor movements, such as his [her] ability to grasp things, pick things up, hold onto things, and release things.

Additional Questions About Infant's Temperament and Activity Level (if infant is focus of interview)

1. How would you describe [cite child's name] to someone who did not know him [her] well?

2. What moods does [cite child's name] have?

3. How would you describe [cite child's name]'s activity level?

4. Are there times when [cite child's name] engages in quiet activities?

5. (If yes) Tell me about these times.

6. When does [cite child's name] get overexcited?

7. When [cite child's name] gets overexcited, what do you do to calm him [her] down?

8. What kinds of comforting make [cite child's name] feel better?

9. How does [cite child's name] respond to new situations?

10. How does [cite child's name] respond to separation from you?

11. (If relevant) And how does [cite child's name] respond to separation from his [her] father?

12. (If child has trouble separating) How long does [cite response] last?

13. What do you do to help [cite child's name] with difficult changes?

14. (If responses to questions in this section do not give you the information you want about the child's temperament, ask more direct questions, such as the following.) Would any of the following terms be helpful in describing [cite child's name]—even-tempered … moody … independent … clinging … stubborn … flexible … active … calm … happy … sad … serious … carefree?

15. (If yes to any of the above) Please give me an example of why you would say [cite child's name] is [cite term].

Additional Questions About Infant's Eating (if infant is focus of interview)

1. I'd like to learn about [cite child's name]'s eating. How is [cite child's name] eating?

2. What does [cite child's name] like to eat?

3. Is [cite child's name] a messy eater?

4. (If yes) Tell me about that.

5. How does [cite child's name] let you know that he [she] is hungry?

6. How does [cite child's name] show that he [she] likes certain foods?

7. How does [cite child's name] show his [her] dislike for certain foods?

8. Is [cite child's name] able to tolerate most foods?

9. Does [cite child's name] like warm foods or cold foods?

10. Does [cite child's name] like foods with any special flavors … special smells … special colors?

11. What does [cite child's name] seem to enjoy about being fed?

12. (If needed) Does [cite child's name] enjoy having you pay attention to him [her] … being at eye level with you while he [she] is in the high chair … having you talk to him [her] while he [she] eats … playing with the spoon?

13. What meals does [cite child's name] eat during the day?

14. What snacks does [cite child's name] eat during the day?

15. Are there certain times during the day when [cite child's name] makes excessive demands for food? (If yes, go to question 16; if no, go to question 18.)

16. At what times does this happen?

17. Do you think [cite child's name] is truly hungry, or is he [she] just asking for attention?

18. Does [cite child's name] skip meals and not ask to eat?

19. (If yes) Tell me about that.

20. Does [cite child's name] eat when you do or at different times?

21. (If at different times) Tell me about the reason [cite child's name] eats at different times.
22. How often does [cite child's name] see adults in the family eat?
23. Does [cite child's name] eat what he [she] is given at mealtimes?
24. Does [cite child's name] have any problems with eating?
25. (If yes) What are the problems?
26. Does [cite child's name] drink from a cup or bottle?
27. Does [cite child's name] have any problems with drinking from a cup [bottle]?
28. (If yes) What are the problems?
    (If child has problems with eating, drinking, or both, go to question 29; otherwise, end this section.)
29. How do you handle the problems?
30. Do those methods work?
31. (If father is in the picture) What does [cite child's name]'s father think about how you handle the problems?

Additional Questions About Infant's Sleeping (if infant is the focus of the interview)

1. How is [cite child's name] sleeping at night?
2. About how many hours of sleep does he [she] get at night?
3. Tell me what happens at night before bedtime.
4. (If needed) Does [cite child's name] go to sleep on his [her] own, or does he [she] need to be rocked, patted, or given some other kind of help from you?
5. Does [cite child's name] take a daytime nap or naps?
6. (If yes) Around what time[s] does he [she] nap?
7. And for how long?
8. Do you think that [cite child's name] is tired enough at bedtime to go to sleep easily?
9. (If child naps) Is there any connection between the amount of time he [she] sleeps during the day and his [her] sleeping at night?
10. What kind of routine do you have at night for putting [cite child's name] to bed?
11. What parts of the nighttime routine do you think [cite child's name] likes?
12. What parts of the nighttime routine do you think [cite child's name] dislikes?
13. What parts of the routine do you like?
14. And what parts of the routine do you dislike?
15. Does [cite child's name] wake up during the night?
    (If yes, go to question 16; if no, go to question 23.)
16. How often does [cite child's name] wake up during the night?
17. About what time does [cite child's name] wake up?
18. How does [cite child's name] act when he [she] wakes up?
19. (If needed) Does he [she] moan … scream … whimper occasionally … call you?
20. What do you do when [cite child's name] gets up during the night?

21. What seems to work the best?
22. Have you noticed any changes in [cite child's name]'s behavior during the daytime since he [she] began to wake up at night?
23. Have you noticed any signs of physical discomfort, such as teething, earache, congestion from a cold, or general fussiness, during the day?
24. (If yes) What have you noticed?
25. Have there been any changes recently in your home or in the child's routine related to bedtime?
26. (If yes) Tell me about these changes.
27. Does anyone share [cite child's name]'s bedroom?
28. (If yes) Who shares his [her] bedroom?
29. Does [cite child's name] have any difficulties falling asleep?
30. (If yes) Tell me about them.
31. Does [cite child's name] have his [her] own bed?
32. (If no) With whom does [cite child's name] sleep?
33. When does [cite child's name] usually go to bed?
34. How do you know when [cite child's name] is tired?

Additional Questions About Toddler's/Preschooler's Personal-Social-Affective Behavior (if toddler/preschooler is focus of interview)

1. Does [cite child's name] take turns?
2. Can [cite child's name] point to body parts on a doll?
3. Does [cite child's name] name his [her] own body parts?
4. Can [cite child's name] identify himself [herself] in a mirror?
5. Does [cite child's name] use words like *I, me,* and *them* correctly?
6. Does [cite child's name] feed himself [herself]?
7. Does [cite child's name] use a spoon or a fork?
8. Does [cite child's name] imitate things you do, like sweeping the floor and making a bed?
9. Does [cite child's name] play with a doll and do such things as feed, hug, and scold the doll?
10. How does [cite child's name] handle common dangers?
11. How does [cite child's name] behave when he [she] plays with another child?
12. Does [cite child's name] share his [her] toys?
    (If yes, go to question 13; if no, go to question 15.)
13. What toys does he [she] share?
14. And with whom does he [she] share them?
    (Go to question 16.)
15. What have you done to help him [her] learn how to share?
16. Does [cite child's name] have temper tantrums?
    (If yes, go to question 17; if no, go to question 26.)
17. Tell me about the temper tantrums.
18. What sets off the temper tantrums?
19. Are the temper tantrums more frequent at certain times of the day than at other times?
20. (If yes) Tell me about these times.
21. Where do the temper tantrums occur?

(Continued)

Table B-6 *(Continued)*

22. What happens when [cite child's name] has a temper tantrum?
23. How do you feel about the temper tantrums?
24. How do you deal with [cite child's name]'s temper tantrums?
25. Which methods seem to be most effective?
26. How does [cite child's name] get along with other children?
27. Is [cite child's name] stubborn at times?
    (If yes, go to question 28; if no, go to question 31.)
28. In what way is [cite child's name] stubborn?
29. How do you handle his [her] stubbornness?
30. Has it worked?
31. Does [cite child's name] hit, bite, or try to hurt other children?
    (If yes, go to question 32; if no, go to question 36.)
32. How does he [she] hurt other children?
33. Why do you think he [she] acts this way?
34. How do you handle these situations?
35. What seems to work best?
36. Does [cite child's name] have any fears?
    (If yes, go to question 37; if no, go to question 46.)
37. What fears does he [she] have?
38. What kinds of situations tend to make [cite child's name] fearful?
39. Are these new situations or old ones?
40. What does [cite child's name] do when he [she] is fearful?
41. How long has [cite child's name] been fearful?
42. What do you do when [cite child's name] shows fear?
43. How does it work?
44. Have you found that some methods are more effective than others?
45. (If yes) Tell me about them.
46. How do you handle [cite child's name]'s demands for your attention?
47. What situations seem to cause [cite child's name] to demand your attention?
48. What kinds of things does [cite child's name] seem to want when he [she] asks for attention?
49. Does he [she] demand your attention for a long time, or will a short time do?
50. Have you noticed any changes during the past few months in how much attention [cite child's name] has demanded?
51. (If yes) Tell me about the changes you've noticed.
52. How does [cite child's name] react when he [she] meets new people?
53. How do you feel about [cite child's name]'s behavior when he [she] meets new people?
54. (If needed) Is there anything you can do to make [cite child's name] more comfortable when he [she] meets new people?
55. When does [cite child's name] cry?
56. What do you do when [cite child's name] cries?
57. Why do you think [cite child's name] cries?
58. (If needed) When [cite child's name] cries, does it usually mean that something is really wrong or is it that something

is bothering him [her] only a little bit and he [she] wants attention?
59. How can you tell the difference between the types of crying [cite child's name] does?
60. Does [cite child's name] play with his [her] private parts?
    (If yes, go to question 61; if no, go to question 66.)
61. When does [cite child's name] play with his [her] private parts?
62. (If needed) Does this occur during any particular situations?
63. (If yes) In what situation[s] does he [she] play with his [her] private parts?
64. How do you feel about his [her] doing this?
65. And what do you do when you find [cite child's name] playing with his [her] private parts?
66. What kinds of activities does [cite child's name] seem to be interested in?
67. What does [cite child's name] like to do on his [her] own?
68. What difficulties are you having with [cite child's name] about performing daily routines, such as washing hands … dressing … picking up clothes … putting away toys?
69. Does [cite child's name] let you do things *with* him [her]?
70. Tell me about that.
71. Does [cite child's name] let you do things *for* him [her]?
72. Tell me about that.
73. How does [cite child's name] get along with adults?
74. Is [cite child's name] interested in people?
75. Tell me more about that.
76. How does [cite child's name] spend his [her] time during a typical weekday?
77. And on weekends, how does [cite child's name] spend his [her] time?
78. How does [cite child's name] feel about himself [herself]?
79. (If there are other siblings in family) How does [cite child's name] compare with his [her] sisters and brothers?
80. Is [cite child's name] interested in animals?
81. Tell me more about that.
82. Is [cite child's name] generally interested in things?
83. (If no) Tell me more about that.
84. At what time of the day is [cite child's name] most active?
85. When [cite child's name] needs to do things, like get dressed or put things away, does he [she] do them too fast, too slowly, or at just about the right pace?
    (If too fast, go to question 86; if too slowly, go to question 90; otherwise, go to question 94.)
86. What happens when you try to make [cite child's name] move more slowly?
87. What other things does [cite child's name] do too fast?
88. (If needed) Does [cite child's name] eat too fast … get ready for bed too fast?
89. Are you concerned that [cite child's name] may be hyperactive?
    (Go to question 94.)
90. What happens when you try to make [cite child's name] move faster?

(Continued)

91. What other things does [cite child's name] do slowly?

92. (If needed) Does he [she] eat slowly … get ready for bed slowly?

93. Are you concerned that [cite child's name] may be generally slow?

94. How does [cite child's name] react when his [her] play is interrupted?

95. How does [cite child's name] let you know when he [she] wants to stay with an activity longer than you had planned?

96. Does [cite child's name] have any unusual behaviors? (If yes, go to question 97; if no, end this section.)

97. What unusual behaviors does [cite child's name] have?

98. How often does [cite child's name] [cite unusual behavior]?

99. What is most likely to bring on [cite unusual behavior]?

100. What situations seem to make [cite child's name]'s [cite unusual behavior] worse?

101. What do you do at these times?

102. What works best?

103. Is there any connection between what [cite child's name] eats and [cite unusual behavior]?

104. How do you feel about taking care of [cite child's name] when he [she] behaves in this way?

Additional Questions About Toddler's/Preschooler's Play and Cognitive Ability (if toddler/preschooler is focus of interview)

1. How does [cite child's name] occupy himself [herself] during the day?

2. What does [cite child's name] like to play?

3. How would you describe [cite child's name]'s play?

4. (If needed) Is it quiet play … active play?… Does he [she] build things … color?

5. What toys or other objects does [cite child's name] play with?

6. What kinds of things does [cite child's name] do with the toys or other objects that he [she] plays with?

7. What toys seem to be particularly interesting to [cite child's name]?

8. And how does [cite child's name] play with the toys he [she] especially likes?

9. Is [cite child's name] interested in exploring objects?

10. (If yes) Tell me more about what [cite child's name] does.

11. What happens when [cite child's name] is left on his [her] own to play?

12. How long does [cite child's name] usually stay with an activity?

13. Does [cite child's name] seem to play better at certain times of the day than at others?

14. What is particularly distracting to [cite child's name]?

15. In what situations does [cite child's name] get the most out of his [her] play?

16. How does [cite child's name] let you know what he [she] is interested in?

17. Tell me more about that.

18. (If relevant) Can [cite child's name] find his [her] toys when they are mixed up with those of his [her] brothers and sisters?

19. Is [cite child's name] more interested in watching others play than in playing himself [herself]?

20. Do you think that [cite child's name]'s play is about the same as that of other children of his [her] age?

21. (If no) In what way is it different?

22. What changes have you noticed over the last few months in the way [cite child's name] plays?

23. Where does [cite child's name] play at home?

24. (If needed) Does he [she] play in different rooms?

25. Does he [she] have enough space to play?

26. (If no) What have you done to get more space for [cite child's name] to play in?

27. How long does [cite child's name] stay in his [her] own room to play?

28. Is this amount of time OK with you?

29. Does [cite child's name] prefer playing outside or inside?

30. Does [cite child's name] prefer playing alone or with someone?

31. With whom does he [she] like to play?

32. Does [cite child's name] prefer quiet activities, such as arts and crafts or board games, to more physical games, or does he [she] enjoy both types of activities?

33. Does [cite child's name] engage in any pretend play?

34. (If needed) Does he [she] play house … play school … play doctor?

35. Does [cite child's name] have any imaginary friends?

36. (If yes) Who are they?

37. How does [cite child's name]'s play change when an adult plays with him [her]?

38. What kinds of things does [cite child's name] like to do with you?

39. How does [cite child's name] react when you try to show him [her] how to use a toy?

40. How much fun is [cite child's name] to play with?

41. Have you ever wondered whether [cite child's name] enjoys playing with you?

42. Tell me about that.

43. How much time do you spend playing with [cite child's name]?

44. Does having [cite child's name]'s toys underfoot in the house bother you?

45. (If yes) Tell me about that.

46. Does [cite child's name] look at you when you try to talk to or play with him [her]?

47. (If no) What does he [she] do instead?

48. Is [cite child's name] responsive to you?

49. Is [cite child's name] responsive to other adults?

50. Does [cite child's name] like physical contact, such as when you gently touch his [her] face, hands, and arms?

Table B-6 *(Continued)*

51. (If no) Tell me about that.
52. Is there any physical activity that [cite child's name] seems to enjoy especially?
53. Does [cite child's name] like doing the same activity over and over again?
54. Does [cite child's name] like to spin objects?
55. (If yes) Tell me about that.
56. Does [cite child's name] play outdoors?
    (If yes, go to question 57; if no, go to question 62.)
57. Where does he [she] play outdoors?
58. (If needed) Do you take [cite child's name] to any parks or playgrounds?
59. How does [cite child's name] react when you take him [her] outdoors to play?
60. Does [cite child's name] behave differently outdoors than indoors?
61. (If yes) In what way?
62. Does [cite child's name] seem to be in constant motion?
63. (If yes) How do you handle that?
64. Tell me about [cite child's name]'s ability to pay attention.
65. Does [cite child's name] like to put puzzles together?
66. Tell me about that.
67. Can [cite child's name] construct things out of blocks?
68. Tell me about that.

Additional Questions About Toddler's/Preschooler's Adjustment to Caregiving Situation (if toddler/preschooler is focus of interview)

1. Do you leave [cite child's name] at a day care center, preschool, at somebody's house, or at your house with a sitter during any part of the week?
   (If yes, go to question 2; if no, go to question 20.)
2. Where do you leave him [her]?
3. Tell me about the reason you leave [cite child's name] there.
4. How do you feel about leaving [cite child's name]?
5. (If day care center, preschool, or someone's house) How did you find out about [cite place where child is cared for]?
6. Are you satisfied with the way [cite child's name] is cared for there?
7. How is [cite child's name] getting along at [cite place where child is cared for]?
8. (If needed) Is [cite child's name] having any problems there?
9. (If yes) Tell me about them.
10. (If needed) How does [cite child's name] get along with the caregiver[s]?
11. And how does he [she] get along with the other children?
12. Do you have a chance to talk regularly about [cite child's name] with the person[s] taking care of him [her]?
13. How long does it take you to get to [cite place where child is cared for]?
14. How does [cite child's name] act when you leave him [her] at [cite place where child is cared for]?

(If behavior is not satisfactory, go to question 15; if behavior is satisfactory, go to question 19.)
15. How do you feel when [cite child's name] acts this way?
16. Does [cite child's name] always show that he [she] is upset in the same way?
17. What have you done to try to help him [her]?
18. How does it help?
19. How does [cite child's name] react when you pick him [her] up from [cite place where child is cared for]?
20. How do you feel about taking [cite child's name] out in public?
21. How does [cite child's name] behave when he [she] is outside the home?
22. How does [cite child's name] react when you take him [her] to a friend's home?
    (If there are problems or concerns, go to question 23; otherwise, end section.)
23. How do you handle these problems?
24. What seems to work best?

Additional Questions About Toddler's/Preschooler's Self-Help Skills (if toddler/preschooler is focus of interview)

1. Is [cite child's name] toilet trained?
   (If yes, go to question 2; if no, go to question 5.)
2. How old was [cite child's name] when he [she] was toilet trained?
3. Does [cite child's name] have toilet accidents once in a while?
4. (If yes) Tell me about the toilet accidents [cite child's name] has.
   (Go to question 13.)
5. Have you begun to toilet train [cite child's name]?
6. (If no) At what age do you think [cite child's name] should be toilet trained?
   (Go to question 13.)
7. Tell me how it's going.
   (Ask questions 8 to 10, as needed.)
8. Are you having any problems with the toilet training?
9. (If yes) Tell me about the problems you're having.
10. What training methods are you using?
11. What did [cite child's name] do to make you think that he [she] was ready to be toilet trained?
12. (If needed) Did he [she] come to you to be changed? Was he [she] interested in watching others in the bathroom … imitating others … staying dry?
13. Tell me about how [cite child's name] dresses and undresses himself [herself].
    (Ask questions 14 to 17, as needed.)
14. What clothing can [cite child's name] put on?
15. What clothing can [cite child's name] take off?
16. (If child is older than 4 years) Can [cite child's name] tie his [her] shoes?
17. How much supervision does [cite child's name] need in dressing and undressing?

18. Tell me about [cite child's name]'s bath time.

19. (If needed) Does [cite child's name] wash himself [herself]?

20. Does [cite child's name] wash his [her] hands when necessary, such as when he [she] is dirty or after he [she] goes to the toilet?

21. (If no) Tell me about [cite child's name]'s not washing his [her] hands when necessary.

22. Does [cite child's name] brush his [her] teeth?

23. (If no) Tell me about [cite child's name]'s not brushing his [her] teeth.

24. Does [cite child's name] brush or comb his [her] hair?

25. (If no) Tell me about [cite child's name]'s not brushing his [her] hair.

Additional Questions About Toddler's/Preschooler's Language, Communication, Speech, Comprehension, and Problem-Solving Skills (if toddler/preschooler is focus of interview)

1. Does [cite child's name] talk?
   (If yes, go to question 2; if no, go to question 20.)

2. When did [cite child's name] begin to talk?

3. Does [cite child's name] have any problems with his [her] speech?

4. (If yes) Tell me about [cite child's name]'s problems with speech.

5. (If needed) Is [cite child's name] having problems speaking clearly … forming grammatically correct sentences … saying the right words in order … stuttering?

6. About how many words can [cite child's name] say?

7. What kinds of words does [cite child's name] usually say?

8. Does [cite child's name] have any pet phrases?

9. (If yes) What are they?

10. Does [cite child's name] use action words?

11. Can [cite child's name] speak in sentences?

12. (If yes) How old was [cite child's name] when he [she] first combined words to make sentences?

13. Did [cite child's name] have any problems with speech in the past?

14. (If yes) Tell me about that.

15. Do you understand what [cite child's name] says?

16. (If no) Tell me more about that.

17. Do other people also understand [cite child's name]'s speech?

18. (If no) Tell me more about that.

19. What kinds of things does [cite child's name] talk about? (Go to question 25.)

20. How is [cite child's name] able to tell you about what he [she] needs?

21. (If needed) Does [cite child's name] make any sounds?

22. (If yes) Tell me about the sounds that [cite child's name] makes.

23. Did [cite child's name] ever talk?

24. (If yes) Tell me about when he [she] talked.

25. Does [cite child's name] understand most things?

26. (If no) What problems does [cite child's name] have in understanding things?

27. Can [cite child's name] follow directions?

28. (If no) What problems does [cite child's name] have in following directions?

Additional Questions About Toddler's/Preschooler's Motor Skills (if toddler/preschooler is focus of interview)

1. Tell me about [cite child's name]'s ability to do things that require small motor movements, such as his [her] ability to grasp things, pick up things, hold onto things, and release things.

2. (If needed) Tell me about [cite child's name]'s ability to open doors … turn pages in a book … use scissors to cut paper … fold paper … build objects with blocks … use pencils … use crayons … draw … copy circles or squares … screw things … unscrew things … button … tie shoes … use a zipper … play with Lego-type toys … print letters.

3. What types of toys are most frustrating to [cite child's name]?

4. Tell me about [cite child's name]'s other motor skills, such as his [her] ability to walk, run, jump, skip, and play ball.

5. (If needed) Tell me about [cite child's name]'s ability to walk up steps … walk down steps … hop … roll a ball … throw a ball … climb … ride a tricycle … use a slide … use a jungle gym.

Additional Questions for Pregnant Mother About Toddler's/Preschooler's Acceptance of the Arrival of a New Baby (if toddler/preschooler is focus of interview)

1. How do you think [cite child's name] will handle the coming of the new baby?

2. What do you think will be most difficult for [cite child's name] to handle?

3. What might you do to help [cite child's name] adjust to the new baby?

4. Have you told [cite child's name] about the new baby?
   (If yes, ask questions 5 and 6; if no, end this section.)

5. What did you say to him [her]?

6. And how did he [she] react?

Additional Questions for Mother About the Family Environment and Family Relationships

1. I'd now like to ask you about life at home. OK?

2. How does [cite child's name] get along with you?

3. (For older child) How did [cite child's name] get along with you when he [she] was younger?

4. Who else lives at home?
   (If father or other adult male is in the picture, go to question 5; otherwise, go to question 7.)

5. How does [cite child's name] get along with [cite name of father or other adult male]?

(Continued)

Table B-6 *(Continued)*

6. With whom does [cite child's name] get along better, you or [cite name of father or other adult male]?
7. (If child has siblings) How does [cite child's name] get along with his [her] sisters and brothers?
(Ask questions 8 to 11, as needed.)
8. What situations tend to cause conflict between [cite child's name] and the other children?
9. What do you do when the children argue?
10. What have you found that works?
11. What do you think would happen if you let the children settle their arguments themselves—except when you thought that one child might hurt the other?
12. What relatives live in your home or nearby?
13. (If any relatives mentioned) Where do they live?
14. (If child has grandparents) How does [cite child's name] get along with his [her] grandparents?
15. (If child has other relatives at home or living nearby) How does [cite child's name] get along with his [her] other relatives?
16. How does everyone get along at home?
(If mother has a husband or partner, go to question 17; otherwise, see directions preceding question 19.)
17. How are you getting along with your husband [partner]?
18. (If needed) Is there anything bothering you about your relationship with your husband [partner]?
(If in-laws, relatives, or friends are staying at child's home, go to question 19; otherwise, end this section.)
19. How are things working out with your mother-in-law [father-in-law, mother, father, etc.] staying at your home?
20. Are there any problems with having her [him, them] there?

Additional Questions to Evaluate Parent's Ability to Set Limits and Discipline Child

1. How do you make [cite child's name] mind you?
2. Do you feel that you are spoiling [cite child's name]?
3. Tell me about your answer.
4. Does anyone tell you that you are spoiling [cite child's name]?
5. (If yes) Tell me about that.
6. Do you believe that [cite child's name] acts spoiled?
7. (If yes) In what ways does he [she] act spoiled?
8. Do you ever give in to [cite child's name]?
(If yes, go to question 9; if no, go to question 14.)
9. Give me some examples of how you give in to [cite child's name].
10. How often do you give in to [cite child's name]?
11. How do you feel about giving in?
12. Which things are you sorry you gave in to?
13. Which of the things you gave in to do you feel are disruptive to the family?
14. Do you believe that you are too easy with [cite child's name], too strict, or just about right?
15. Tell me about that.
16. Which of [cite child's name]'s behaviors are particularly irritating to you?

17. In which areas would you most like to set limits?
18. What things won't you let [cite child's name] do?
19. Overall, how satisfied are you with [cite child's name]'s behavior?
20. Are there times when [cite child's name] doesn't mind you or gets into trouble?
(If yes, go to question 21; if no, go to question 32.)
21. Tell me about these times.
22. (If needed) What kind of trouble does [cite child's name] get into?
23. What do you do when [cite child's name] doesn't mind [gets into trouble]?
24. (If relevant) How does [cite child's name] react when he [she] is punished?
25. Which methods of discipline work best?
26. Which methods don't work?
27. How do you feel when you have to discipline [cite child's name]?
28. What problems are you most concerned about?
29. What does [cite child's name] do that makes you most angry?
30. Does [cite child's name] usually understand what is expected of him [her]?
31. How do you expect [cite child's name] to behave?
32. What does [cite child's name] do that leads you to think that he [she] can live up to your expectations?
(If the child's father or stepfather or any other adult male lives at home or has visitation rights, go to question 33, substituting the appropriate name for "father" as necessary; otherwise, end this section.)
33. What about [cite child's name] makes his [her] father most angry?
34. What does his [her] father discipline him [her] for?
35. How does his [her] father discipline him [her]?
36. Does his method work?
37. How does [cite child's name]'s father feel when he has to discipline him [her]?
38. How does [cite child's name] respond to his [her] father's discipline?
39. Do you and [cite child's name]'s father agree about how to discipline him [her]?
40. (If no) How do you handle the disagreements?
41. How do you feel about what [cite child's name]'s father does when he is angry with him [her]?
42. Do you do anything about your feelings?

Additional Questions to Evaluate Environmental Safeguards and Neighborhood

1. What have you done to make the house safe for [cite child's name] and to keep him [her] from getting into things?
2. (If needed) Have you put covers on electric outlets?... Have you put safety latches on any drawers or cupboards that contain cleaning products or other poisons, knives, guns, or other dangerous things?

(Continued)

Table B-6 *(Continued)*

3. Does [cite child's name] get into things at home that he [she] is not supposed to?
   (If yes, go to question 4; if no, go to question 8.)

4. What does he [she] get into?

5. Have you been teaching [cite child's name] not to get into these things?

6. (If yes) How has it been going?

7. How do you feel when [cite child's name] wants to get into everything he [she] sees?

8. Does [cite child's name] ever break things?

9. (If yes) How do you feel when this happens?

10. (If yes) And what do you do when he [she] breaks things?

11. Does [cite child's name] seem to understand when you tell him [her] not to touch objects?

12. (If yes) Do you think that he [she] can remember not to get into things?

13. Which objects seem to be particularly attractive to [cite child's name]?

14. Why do you think [cite child's name] likes them so much?

15. How do you stop [cite child's name] when he [she] is about to do something dangerous?

16. How long have you lived in your present house [apartment]?

17. How do you like living there?

18. (If needed) Tell me about that.

19. How do you get along with your neighbors?

20. (If needed) Tell me about that.

21. Are there any problems in the neighborhood?

22. (If yes) Tell me about them.

Additional Questions to Evaluate Mother's Resources and Occupation

1. Do you have any living relatives?
   (If yes, go to question 2; if no, go to question 8.)

2. Tell me who your living relatives are.

3. How often do you see your relatives?

4. And how do you get along?

5. Do they give you help when you need it?
   (If yes, go to question 6; if no, go to question 8.)

6. Which relatives give you help when you need it?

7. How do they help you?

8. Do you have any close friends?
   (If yes, go to question 9; if no, go to question 12.)

9. Tell me about them.

10. Have you ever turned to them for help?

11. (If yes) And how did they respond?

12. To whom would you turn for help if your family needed it?

13. Do you have someone to talk to when you have a problem or are feeling frustrated and upset?

14. Tell me about it.

15. Do you have medical insurance?

16. (If no) How do you plan to take care of any hospitalizations?

17. Have you been in contact with any social agencies?

18. (If yes) Tell me about your contacts.

19. Are you a member of a religious group?

20. (If yes) Tell me about it.

21. Do you have a job outside of the home?
    (If yes, go to question 22; if no, go to instructions following question 24.)

22. What is your occupation?

23. How do you like your job?

24. (If needed) Tell me more about that.
    (If father is in the picture, go to question 25; otherwise, end this section.)

25. What is [cite child's name]'s father's occupation?

26. And how does [cite child's name]'s father like his job?

27. (If needed) Tell me more about that.

Additional Questions to Evaluate a Mother Who Stays at Home

1. What do you enjoy about being a full-time parent?

2. What do you find most difficult about being a full-time parent?

3. What made you decide to be a full-time parent?

4. (If needed) What were you doing before your child was [children were] born?

5. Are you occasionally able to get out of the house with [cite child's name]?

6. Are you able to get some time for yourself on a regular basis?

7. Tell me about your answer.

8. (If needed) Do you get a babysitter occasionally and go out by yourself or with a friend [with your husband/partner]?

9. Do you know other parents with young children in the neighborhood?

10. (If yes) Have you worked out any cooperative babysitting arrangements with them?

Additional Questions About Spending Time with Child
(for mother who works)

1. How much time do you spend with [cite child's name]?

2. How do you feel about the amount of time you spend with [cite child's name]?

3. How do you spend time with [cite child's name] before you go to work?

4. And when you come home, how do you spend time together?

5. And on weekends, how do you spend time together?

6. Which times seem to be the most enjoyable for you and [cite child's name]?

7. Which times seem to be the most rushed and tense for you and [cite child's name]?

8. How do you feel about taking care of [cite child's name] when you return home from work?

9. What do you usually do when you pick [cite child's name] up after work?

(Continued)

Table B-6 *(Continued)*

10. Do you have any time alone when you come home after work?

11. How do you deal with [cite child's name] if he [she] cries and fusses in the evening?

12. How do you get [cite child's name] to relax when you get home after work?

13. How do you get to relax when you get home after work?

Additional Questions About Family Medical History

1. I'd like to know about your health history. Have you had any serious illnesses, accidents, or diseases?

2. (If yes) Tell me about them.

3. (As needed) How was the diagnosis established?... Tell me about the course of your illness, its treatment, and the prognosis.

4. (If father is in the picture) And how about [cite child's name]'s father—has he had any serious illnesses, accidents, or diseases?

5. (If yes) Tell me about them.

6. (As needed) How was the diagnosis established?... Tell me about the course of his illness, its treatment, and the prognosis.

7. (If child has siblings) And [cite child's name]'s sisters and brothers—have they had any serious illnesses, accidents, or diseases?

8. (If yes) Tell me about them.

9. (As needed) How was the diagnosis established?... Tell me about the course of the illness, its treatment, and the prognosis.

Additional General Questions About Infant or Toddler/ Preschooler and Mother

1. We've covered a lot of areas. Before we finish, I have just a few more questions I'd like to ask you. OK?

2. What experiences did you have with young children before you had a child?

3. What do you like about being a parent?

4. What do you dislike about being a parent?

5. Is being a parent what you expected?

6. Tell me about that.

7. (If needed) What is the same as what you expected? What is different from what you expected?

8. What would it take to make it easier for you to be a parent?

9. What about [cite child's name] gives you the most pleasure?

10. What kinds of things do you do together that are fun?

11. Do you have quiet times when you relax together?

12. (If yes) Tell me about them.

13. (If mother has other children) Do you spend about the same amount of time with [cite child's name] that you do with the other children?

14. (If no) Tell me about that.
(If child's father or stepfather or any other adult male lives at home or has visitation rights, go to question 15, substituting the appropriate name for "father" as necessary; otherwise, go to question 19.)

15. What kinds of things does [cite child's name] do with his [her] father?

16. How much time do they spend together?

17. (If father has other children) Is this about the same amount of time he spends with the other children in the family?

18. (If no) Tell me about that.

19. In general, does [cite child's name] act like other children of his [her] age?

20. (If not) In what way doesn't he [she] act like other children of his [her] age?

21. Is there anything else about [cite child's name] that you would like to tell me?

22. (If yes) Go ahead.

23. Is [cite child's name] having any problems that we didn't discuss?

24. (If yes) What are they?

25. (If not asked previously) Do you have any reason to think that [cite child's name] is under any particular stress at this time?

26. (If yes) Tell me about that.

27. (If not asked previously) Have there been any changes in the home or in the child's routine recently?

28. (If yes) Tell me about that.

29. Have you discussed your concerns about [cite child's name]'s problems with a health care provider?

30. (If yes) What did the health care provider say?

31. Is there anything else about your role as a parent that you would like to tell me?

32. (If yes) Go ahead.

33. Do you have any questions that you would like to ask me?

34. (If yes) Go ahead.

35. Thank you for talking with me. If you have any questions or if you want to talk to me, please call me. Here is my card.

Note. This table is designed for interviewing mothers about their young children. With some alterations, it also can be used to interview fathers or other caregivers. Use Table B-9 in this Appendix to interview a parent who has a child who may have a pervasive developmental disorder.
Source: Adapted from Bromwich (1981) and Ferholt (1980).

Table B-7
Semistructured Interview Questions for a Parent Regarding a Brief Screening of Her or His Preschool-Aged Child

1. Hi! I'm Dr. [Ms., Mr.] _____. I'd like to talk to you about [cite child's name]. Tell me a little bit about him [her].

2. Please tell me what [cite child's name] has been doing and learning lately.

3. How well do you think [cite child's name] is doing now?

4. Do you have any concerns about [cite child's name]'s health?

5. (If yes) What are your concerns?

6. Are you concerned about [cite child's name]'s general physical coordination or his [her] ability to run, climb, or do other motor activities?

7. (If yes) What are your concerns?

8. How well does [cite child's name] seem to understand things that are said to him [her]?

9. How well does [cite child's name] let you know what he [she] needs?

10. How would you describe [cite child's name]'s speech?

11. Does [cite child's name] speak in sentences?

12. Does [cite child's name] have any unusual speech behaviors?
    (If yes, go to question 13; if no, go to question 15.)

13. Tell me what seems to be unusual about his [her] speech.

14. (If needed) Is [cite child's name]'s speech intelligible?

15. Do you have any concerns about [cite child's name]'s behavior?

16. (If yes) What are your concerns?

17. How well does [cite child's name] get along with other children … with adults … with his [her] brothers or sisters … with you [you and your spouse/partner]?

18. How well does [cite child's name] feed himself [herself] … dress himself [herself] … go to the toilet by himself [herself]?

19. Is there anything else about [cite child's name] that you wonder or worry about?

20. Did [cite child's name] have any difficulties during his [her] first two years of life?

21. (If yes) Tell me about that.

22. Does [cite child's name] have any problems that we did not cover?

23. Do you have any questions that you would like to ask me?

24. (If yes) Go ahead.

25. Thank you for talking with me. If you have any questions or if you want to talk to me, please call me. Here is my card.

Note. You can use probing questions to follow up on any problem areas mentioned by the parent.
Source: Adapted from Lichtenstein and Ireton (1984).

Table B-8
Semistructured Interview Questions for a Parent Regarding How Her or His Preschool-Aged or Elementary School–Aged Child Spends a Typical Day

Introduction

1. Hi! I'm Dr. [Ms., Mr.] _____. I'd like to know how [cite child's name] spends a typical day. I'll be asking you about how [cite child's name] spends the morning, afternoon, and evening. OK? Let's begin.

Early Morning

2. What time does [cite child's name] usually wake up?
3. Does [cite child's name] wake up by himself [herself]?
4. How do you know [cite child's name] is awake?
5. What does [cite child's name] do after he [she] wakes up?
6. Where are the other members of the family at that time?
7. What is [cite child's name]'s mood when he [she] wakes up?
8. How does [cite child's name] get along with other members of the family soon after he [she] wakes up?
9. When does [cite child's name] get dressed?
10. Does [cite child's name] dress himself [herself]?
11. (If no) What kind of help does [cite child's name] need?
(Go to question 13.)
12. Can [cite child's name] manage buttons … manage zippers … tie his [her] shoes?
13. Does [cite child's name] choose his [her] own clothes?
14. Are there any conflicts over dressing?
15. (If yes) Tell me about that.

Breakfast

16. Does [cite child's name] usually eat breakfast?
(If yes, go to question 17; if no, go to question 22.)
17. When does [cite child's name] usually eat breakfast?
18. What does [cite child's name] usually have for breakfast?
19. With whom does [cite child's name] eat breakfast?
20. Are there any problems at breakfast?
21. (If yes) Tell me about them.
(Go to question 23.)
22. Tell me about [cite child's name]'s not eating breakfast.

Morning

23. What does [cite child's name] do after breakfast [in the morning]?
24. (If needed) Does [cite child's name] go to a day care center or preschool, a regular school, or a sitter's house, or does he [she] stay at home?
(For children who stay at home, go to question 25; for children who go to a sitter's house, go to question 30; for children who go to a day care center or preschool, go to question 43; for children who go to a regular school, go to question 78.)

Stays at Home

25. Who is at home with [cite child's name]?

26. (If parent stays at home with child) How do you about feel about being at home with him [her] during the day?
27. How does [cite child's name] spend his [her] time at home?
28. Does [cite child's name] have any problems at home during the day?
29. (If yes) Tell me about them.
(Go to question 107.)

Goes to Sitter's House

30. Tell me about the sitter who watches [cite child's name].
31. How long does it take you to get to the sitter's house?
32. What time does [cite child's name] go there?
33. What time does [cite child's name] leave the sitter's?
34. How many other children are at the sitter's house when [cite child's name] is there?
35. (If one or more children) Tell me about the other children.
36. (If needed) How old are the other children at the sitter's?
37. How does [cite child's name] like it at the sitter's?
38. What kinds of things does [cite child's name] do there?
39. How is [cite child's name] doing at the sitter's?
40. Are you satisfied with [cite child's name]'s care at the sitter's?
41. (If no) Tell me about why you're not satisfied.
42. What changes have you noticed in [cite child's name]'s behavior since he [she] has been at the sitter's?
(Go to question 107.)

Goes to Day Care Center or Preschool

43. Tell me about the day care center [preschool] that [cite child's name] goes to.
44. How long does it take you to get there?
45. What time does [cite child's name] go there?
46. What time does [cite child's name] leave the center [preschool]?
47. How old are the other children at the center [preschool]?
48. How many children are in [cite child's name]'s group?
49. And how many caregivers are in [cite child's name]'s group?
50. How does [cite child's name] like it at the center [preschool]?
51. What kinds of things does [cite child's name] do there?
52. How is [cite child's name] doing at the center [preschool]?
53. Are you satisfied with the center [preschool]?
54. (If no) Tell me about why you're not satisfied.
55. What changes have you noticed in [cite child's name]'s behavior since he [she] has been at the center [preschool]?
56. How did you decide to send [cite child's name] to this center [preschool]?
57. Have you met with [cite child's name]'s teacher?
58. (If yes) Tell me what you learned in talking with the teacher.
(Go to question 61.)

(Continued)

59. Do you believe that you need to meet with [cite child's name]'s teacher?
60. (If yes) Tell me about the reason you want to meet with [cite child's name]'s teacher.
61. Do you participate in any activities at the center [preschool]?
62. (If yes) Tell me about them.
63. Is [cite child's name] having any problems at the center [preschool]?
(If yes, go to question 64; if no, go to question 107.)
64. Tell me about [cite child's name]'s problem[s].
65. What is being done about it [them]?
66. Is anything being accomplished?
67. (If needed) Have you discussed the problem[s] with the teacher?
68. (If yes) What did the teacher say?
69. How do you feel about how the center [preschool] is handling the problem[s]?
70. Has [cite child's name] had problems in a center [preschool] before?
(If yes, go to question 71; if no, go to question 74.)
71. Tell me about them.
72. What did you do about the problems then?
73. How did it turn out?
74. (If relevant) Have any of your other children had problems in a center [preschool]?
75. (If yes) Tell me about that.
76. Is there anything you would like to ask me about [cite child's name]'s problem[s] at the center [preschool]?
77. Is there anything you think I might do to help you with [cite child's name]'s problem[s] at the center [preschool]?
(Go to question 107.)

Goes to Regular School

78. Tell me about [cite child's name]'s school.
79. How is [cite child's name] doing at school?
80. What are [cite child's name]'s best subjects?
81. What are his [her] poorest subjects?
82. What activities does [cite child's name] like best at school?
83. How does [cite child's name] get along with the other children?
84. How does [cite child's name] get along with the teachers?
85. Are you satisfied with the school?
86. (If no) Tell me about that.
87. How did you decide to send [cite child's name] to this school?
88. Have you met with [cite child's name]'s teacher?
89. (If yes) Tell me what you learned in talking with the teacher.
(Go to question 92.)
90. Do you believe that you need to meet with [cite child's name]'s teacher?
91. (If yes) Tell me about the reason you want to meet with [cite child's name]'s teacher.

92. Are you involved in any school activities?
93. Tell me about that.
94. Is [cite child's name] having any problems at school?
(If yes, go to question 95; if no, go to question 101.)
95. Tell me about [cite child's name]'s problem[s].
96. What is being done about it [them]?
97. Is anything being accomplished?
98. (If needed) Have you discussed the problem[s] with the teacher?
99. (If yes) What did the teacher say?
100. How do you feel about how the school is handling the problem[s]?
101. Has [cite child's name] had problems in school before?
(If yes, go to question 102; if no, go to question 107.)
102. Tell me about them.
103. What did you do about the problems then?
104. How did it turn out?
105. Is there anything you would like to ask me about [cite child's name]'s problem[s] at school?
106. Is there anything you think I might do to help you with [cite child's name]'s problem[s] at school?

Lunch

107. When does [cite child's name] usually eat lunch?
108. What does [cite child's name] usually have for lunch?
109. Does [cite child's name] usually eat his [her] lunch?
110. Who eats with [cite child's name] at lunchtime?
111. Are there any problems at lunchtime?
112. (If yes) Tell me about the problems.

Afternoon

113. How does [cite child's name] spend his [her] afternoons?
114. Are there any problems in the afternoon?
115. (If yes) Tell me about them.

Related Areas

(Ask about any of the following areas, as needed.)

116. Before we get to supper and the end of the day, I'd like to ask you about [cite child's name]'s eating, friends, play activities, TV watching, and behavior outside the home. Let's first turn to [cite child's name]'s eating. OK?

Eating

117. How is [cite child's name]'s diet in general?
118. What are [cite child's name]'s likes and dislikes in food?
119. What is [cite child's name]'s behavior like when he [she] refuses to eat something?
120. How do you handle that kind of situation?
121. What does [cite child's name] usually have for snacks?
122. Are there any problems about snacks?
123. (If yes) Tell me about that.

(Continued)

Table B-8 *(Continued)*

Friends

124. Tell me about [cite child's name]'s friends.
125. (If needed) How old are they?
126. Where do the children play?
127. What do they do together?
128. How do they get along?
129. Are they able to take turns and share toys?
130. (If no) Tell me about that.
131. Who supervises them?
132. What kind of supervision do they need?

Play Activities

133. Does [cite child's name] ride a tricycle or bicycle?
134. (If yes) How well does [cite child's name] ride the tricycle [bicycle]?
135. Is [cite child's name] reckless in his [her] play?
136. (If yes) Tell me about that.
137. Does [cite child's name] have any fears about climbing?
138. (If yes) Tell me about that.
139. What are some of [cite child's name]'s favorite toys?
140. What does [cite child's name] like to do with them?
141. Is [cite child's name] able to play alone?
142. Tell me about that.

TV Watching

143. Does [cite child's name] watch television?
(If yes, go to question 144; if no, go to question 154.)
144. What TV programs does [cite child's name] watch?
145. How much time does [cite child's name] spend watching television in an average day?
146. Does anyone in the family watch television with him [her]?
147. Does [cite child's name] watch any adult shows?
148. (If yes) Which adult shows does he [she] watch?
149. Has [cite child's name] ever been frightened by any shows?
150. (If yes) Tell me about that.
151. How did you handle his [her] fright?
152. Do you supervise [cite child's name]'s TV viewing?
153. Tell me about that.

Behavior Outside the Home

154. I'd like to know how [cite child's name] gets along when you go out, such as to a store, friend's house, church or synagogue or mosque, or restaurant. First, does [cite child's name] go shopping with you?
(If yes, go to question 155; if no, go to question 159.)
155. How does [cite child's name] behave in the stores?

156. Does [cite child's name] like to choose things to buy?
157. What happens if [cite child's name] wants things he [she] cannot have?
158. How do you handle it?
159. How does [cite child's name] behave at a friend's house?
160. And how does [cite child's name] behave at church or synagogue or mosque, if you go there?
161. And how about at a restaurant—how does [cite child's name] behave there?

Supper

162. When does [cite child's name] usually eat supper?
163. What does [cite child's name] usually have for supper?
164. Does [cite child's name] usually eat all his [her] food?
165. Who eats with [cite child's name] at supper?
166. Are there any problems at suppertime?
167. (If yes) Tell me about them.

Evening

168. What does [cite child's name] usually do in the evening?
169. When does [cite child's name] usually go to bed?
170. Does [cite child's name] have any routines associated with going to bed?
171. (If yes) Tell me about them.
172. Does [cite child's name] have any problems around bedtime?
173. (If yes) Tell me about them.
174. How much sleep does [cite child's name] usually get?
175. Does [cite child's name] sleep through the night?
(If no, go to question 176; if yes, to to question 179.)
176. How often does [cite child's name] wake up?
177. What does [cite child's name] do when he [she] wakes up?
178. How do you handle it?
179. Where does [cite child's name] sleep?
180. Does [cite child's name] share a room with anyone?
181. (If yes) With whom?
182. How does that arrangement work out?

Concluding Questions

183. Is there anything that we have left out about how [cite child's name] spends a typical day?
184. (If yes) Please tell me about that.
185. Is there anything that you would like to ask me?
186. (If yes) Go ahead.
187. Thank you for talking with me. If you have any questions or if you want to talk to me, please call me. Here is my card.

Source: Adapted from Ferholt (1980).

Table B-9
Semistructured Interview Questions for a Parent of a Child Who May Have a Pervasive Developmental Disorder

The questions in this table primarily apply to children who are at least toddler-age. If the child is an infant, use only those questions that are appropriate.

Introduction

1. Hi! I'm Dr. [Ms., Mr.] _____. I'd like to get from you a fairly complete picture of [cite child's name]'s development. OK?

Developmental History

2. Did you [the mother] experience any problems during your [her] pregnancy?
3. (If yes) Tell me about the problems.
4. Did you [the mother] experience any difficulties during labor and delivery?
5. (If yes) Tell me about those difficulties.
6. After [cite child's name] was born, did you sometimes wonder whether he [she] might have problems?
7. (If needed) Did you sometimes wonder whether he [she] might be deaf or blind?
8. (If yes) Tell me what you were concerned about.
9. Do you recall when [cite child's name] sat unassisted for the first time?
10. (If yes) When was that?
11. Do you recall how old [cite child's name] was when he [she] took his [her] first steps?
12. (If yes) When was that?
13. How would you describe [cite child's name]'s emotional responses during infancy?

Social Behavior as Infant

14. Now please tell me how [cite child's name] responded to you when he [she] was an infant.
    (Ask questions 15 to 22, as needed.)
15. Was [cite child's name] overly rigid when you held him [her]?
16. Was [cite child's name] ever overly limp when you held him [her]?
17. Did [cite child's name] seem to resist being held closely?
18. Did [cite child's name] seem indifferent to being held?
19. Did [cite child's name] look at you when you spoke to him [her]?
20. Did [cite child's name] enjoy playing peek-a-boo?
21. Was [cite child's name] content to be alone?
22. (If no) Did [cite child's name] cry and demand attention if he [she] was left alone?
23. And now please tell me how [cite child's name] responded to other adults.
    (Ask questions 24 to 27, as needed.)
24. Was [cite child's name] frightened of other people?
25. (If yes) Tell me more about that.
26. Did [cite child's name] withdraw from people?
27. (If yes) Tell me more about that.

Social Behavior as Toddler, Preschooler, or School-Aged Child

28. How does [cite child's name] interact with you now?
    (Ask questions 29 to 51, as needed.)
29. Does [cite child's name] look at you while you are playing with him [her]?
30. (If no) What does he [she] do?
31. Does [cite child's name] look at you when you are talking to him [her]?
32. (If no) What does he [she] do?
33. Does [cite child's name] make direct eye contact with you?
34. Does [cite child's name] point with his [her] finger to show you things or to ask for them?
35. What does [cite child's name] do when you smile at him [her]?
36. Does [cite child's name] look through you as if you weren't there?
37. Does [cite child's name] seem to be hard to reach or in his [her] own world?
38. (If yes) Give me some examples.
39. Does [cite child's name] bring you things to show you?
40. Does [cite child's name] want you for comfort when he [she] is sick or hurt?
41. (If no) Tell me more about that.
42. Does [cite child's name] enjoy being held or cuddled?
43. Does [cite child's name] enjoy being bounced on your knee or swung?
44. Does [cite child's name] hug or kiss you back when you hug or kiss him [her]?
45. Does [cite child's name] come to you for a kiss or hug on his [her] own, without your asking him [her] to?
46. Does [cite child's name] enjoy being kissed?
47. Is [cite child's name] particular about when or how he [she] likes affection?
48. (If yes) Give me some examples of this.
49. Does [cite child's name] go limp when you hold or hug him [her]?
50. Does [cite child's name] pull away from you when you are being affectionate with him [her]?
51. Does [cite child's name] smile back at you when you smile at him [her]?
52. And how does [cite child's name] interact with adults?
    (Ask questions 53 to 58, as needed.)
53. Does [cite child's name] ignore people who try to interact with him [her]?
54. (If yes) Tell me more about that.
55. Does [cite child's name] actively avoid looking at people during interactions with them?
56. (If yes) Tell me more about that.
57. Does [cite child's name] look at people more when they are far away than when they are interacting with him [her]?
58. Does [cite child's name] make direct eye contact with people other than you?

(Continued)

Table B-9 *(Continued)*

Peer Interactions

59. Now I'd like to talk to you about how [cite child's name] gets along with other children. Please tell me about that. (Ask questions 60 to 69, as needed.)

60. Does [cite child's name] prefer to play alone rather than with other children?

61. Does [cite child's name] like to watch other children while they are playing?

62. Will [cite child's name] ever join in play with other children?

63. Do other children invite [cite child's name] to play with them?

64. Does [cite child's name] play games with other children in which they each take turns?

65. (If yes) What games does he [she] play with other children?

66. Does [cite child's name] enjoy playing with other children?

67. How does [cite child's name] show his [her] feelings toward other children?

68. Does [cite child's name] seem to be interested in making friends with other children?

69. (If yes) How does [cite child's name] show this interest?

Affective Responses

70. Now I'd like to ask you about [cite child's name]'s feelings. Does [cite child's name] seem to understand how others are feeling?

71. Please give me some examples.

72. Does [cite child's name] understand the expressions on people's faces?

73. Is it difficult to tell what [cite child's name] is feeling from his [her] facial expressions?

74. (If yes) What makes it hard to tell?

75. Does [cite child's name] smile during his [her] favorite activities?

76. Does [cite child's name] smile, laugh, and cry when you expect him [her] to?

77. Do [cite child's name]'s moods change quickly, without warning?

78. (If yes) Please give me some examples of these changes.

79. Does [cite child's name] become very frightened of harmless things?

80. (If yes) What does he [she] become frightened of?

81. Does [cite child's name] laugh for no obvious reason?

82. Does [cite child's name] cry for no obvious reason?

83. Does [cite child's name] shed tears when he [she] cries?

84. Does [cite child's name] make unusual facial expressions?

85. (If yes) Please describe them.

Communication Ability

86. Now I'd like to talk to you about [cite child's name]'s language. Does [cite child's name] currently speak or attempt to speak? (If yes, go to question 87; if no, go to question 93.)

87. Tell me about his [her] speech.

88. Does [cite child's name] repeat words or phrases spoken by others?

89. Does [cite child's name] refer to himself [herself] as "you" or by his [her] name?

90. Does [cite child's name] have any problems when he [she] speaks?

91. (If yes) Tell me about that.

92. Overall, how would you describe [cite child's name]'s language abilities? (Go to question 101.)

93. Has he [she] ever spoken in the past? (If yes, go to question 94; if no, go to question 101.)

94. When did [cite child's name] speak in the past?

95. What did he [she] say?

96. How old was [cite child's name] when he [she] stopped speaking?

97. Did anything happen at the time he [she] stopped speaking?

98. (If yes) Tell me about what happened.

99. What did you think when [cite child's name] stopped speaking?

100. Tell me about that.

101. In addition to talking, there are lots of other ways that children can communicate their needs and wants, such as making sounds, pointing, or gesturing. Does [cite child's name] communicate by any other method?

102. (If yes) Tell me about that.

103. Does [cite child's name] have a range of facial expressions?

104. (If yes) Tell me about them.

105. Does [cite child's name] nod or shake his [her] head, clearly meaning yes or no?

106. Does he [she] use other gestures such as "thumbs up" to indicate success or approval?

107. Can you understand what [cite child's name] is trying to communicate?

108. Can other people understand him [her]?

109. Does [cite child's name] become frustrated when he [she] tries to communicate?

110. (If yes) What does [cite child's name] do when he [she] is frustrated?

111. Does [cite child's name] respond when you say his [her] name?

112. Does [cite child's name] understand what you say to him [her]?

113. How can you tell?

114. Does [cite child's name] seem interested in the conversations other people are having?

115. (If yes) Tell me more about that.

116. Does [cite child's name] follow simple directions, such as "Get your coat"?

117. Does [cite child's name] respond to only one word in a sentence rather than to the whole meaning of the sentence?

118. (If yes) Please give me some examples of this.

(Continued)

119. Does [cite child's name] take some speech literally? For example, would [cite child's name] think that the saying "It's raining cats and dogs" literally meant that cats and dogs were falling from the sky?

120. Does [cite child's name] listen to you when you read him [her] short stories?

121. Do you ever send [cite child's name] out of the room to get one object?

122. Could [cite child's name] be sent to get two or three things?

123. Can [cite child's name] follow a sequence of commands, such as "First do this, then this, then this"?

124. Can [cite child's name] understand the past tense ... the future tense ... the present tense?

125. Does [cite child's name] have any problems with spatial words, such as "under," "in," or "above"?

126. Does [cite child's name] understand better if instructions are sung to a tune instead of spoken?

127. Do you have to point or use gestures to help [cite child's name] understand what you say?

128. (If yes) Please give me some examples of what you do.

129. Does [cite child's name] understand that a nod or a shake of the head means yes or no?

130. Does [cite child's name] understand your different tones of voice?

131. Please give me some examples.

132. Does [cite child's name] understand other gestures you use?

133. Please give me some examples.

134. When you point to something, does [cite child's name] look in the direction you point?

Using Senses and Responding to Environment

135. Now I'd like to ask you about the way [cite child's name] uses his [her] senses and how he [she] responds to the environment. First, how does he [she] react to painful events, such as falling down or bumping his [her] head?

136. Is [cite child's name] overly sensitive to being touched?

137. (If yes) How does he [she] show this?

138. Does [cite child's name] examine objects by sniffing or smelling them?

139. (If yes) Please give me some examples of this.

140. Does [cite child's name] put inedible objects in his [her] mouth?

141. (If yes) What are some of the inedible objects he [she] puts in his [her] mouth?

142. Does [cite child's name] examine objects by licking or tasting them?

143. (If yes) Please give me some examples of this.

144. Is [cite child's name] overly interested in the way things feel?

145. (If yes) Tell me about this.

146. Does [cite child's name] enjoy touching or rubbing certain surfaces?

147. (If yes) Give me some examples of this.

148. Is [cite child's name] oversensitive to sounds or noises?

149. (If yes) Give me some examples of his [her] oversensitivity.

150. Does [cite child's name] cover his [her] ears at certain sounds?

151. (If yes) Please give me some examples of when he [she] does this.

152. Does [cite child's name] become agitated or upset at sudden or loud noises?

153. (If yes) Give me some examples of when this happens.

154. Does it seem to you that [cite child's name] does not hear well?

155. (If yes) Tell me more about this.

156. Does [cite child's name] ever ignore loud noises?

157. (If yes) Give me some examples of when he [she] ignores loud noises.

158. Does [cite child's name] stare into space for long periods of time?

159. (If yes) When might he [she] do this?

160. Is [cite child's name] overly interested in looking at small details or parts of objects?

161. (If yes) Please give me some examples of this.

162. Does [cite child's name] hold objects close to his [her] eyes to look at them?

163. Is [cite child's name] overly interested in watching the movements of his [her] hands or fingers?

164. Is [cite child's name] overly interested in watching objects that spin?

165. (If yes) Give me some examples of what he [she] likes to watch spin.

166. Is [cite child's name] overly interested in looking at lights or shiny objects?

167. (If yes) Give me some examples of this.

168. Is [cite child's name] overly sensitive to bright lights?

169. (If yes) Tell me more about this.

170. Does [cite child's name] look at things out of the corners of his [her] eyes?

171. (If yes) Give me some examples of this.

172. Does [cite child's name] do things without looking at what he [she] is doing?

173. (If yes) Give me some examples of what he [she] does without looking.

174. Is [cite child's name] aware of dangers, such as from hot things or sharp things?

175. Tell me about that.

Movement, Gait, and Posture

176. The next topic I'd like to cover is the way [cite child's name] moves and uses his [her] body. First, does [cite child's name] walk?
(If yes, go to question 177; if no, go to question 184.)

177. How does [cite child's name] walk?

178. (If needed) Does he [she] walk with swinging arms ... on tip toe ... oddly and awkwardly ... gracefully?

Table B-9 *(Continued)*

179. Can [cite child's name] walk upstairs without help?
180. Can [cite child's name] walk downstairs without help?
181. Is [cite child's name] able to climb well?
182. Can [cite child's name] pedal a tricycle or a bicycle?
183. Can [cite child's name] run as well as other children of his [her] age?
184. Is [cite child's name]'s posture odd or awkward in any way?
185. (If yes) Tell me in what way his [her] posture is odd or awkward.
186. Can [cite child's name] copy other people's movements?
187. Does [cite child's name] wave goodbye?
188. Does [cite child's name] clap his [her] hands?
189. Are [cite child's name]'s movements easy, or are they stiff and awkward?
190. How easily does he [she] learn gymnastic exercises, dances, or miming games?
191. Does he [she] confuse up/down, back/front, or right/left when trying to imitate others?
192. How does he [she] behave when excited?
193. Does excitement produce movements of his [her] whole body, including face, arms, and legs?
194. Does [cite child's name] spin or whirl himself [herself] around for long periods of time?
195. (If yes) Tell me more about that.
196. Does [cite child's name] rock back and forth for long periods of time?
197. (If yes) Tell me more about that.
198. Does [cite child's name] move his [her] hands or fingers in unusual or repetitive ways, such as flapping or twisting them?
199. (If yes) Please give me some examples.
200. How well does [cite child's name] use his [her] fingers?
201. Tell me about that.
202. Does [cite child's name] move his [her] body in unusual or repetitive ways?
203. (If yes) Please give me some examples.
204. Would you say that [cite child's name] is more active or less active than other children of his [her] age?
205. Tell me about that.

Need for Sameness

206. Now I'd like to talk to you about [cite child's name]'s flexibility in adapting to change. Tell me how [cite child's name] responds when something out of the ordinary happens and his [her] routines must be changed.
207. Does [cite child's name] insist on certain routines or rituals, such as wearing only certain clothes or types of clothing?
208. (If yes) Tell me more about that.
209. Does [cite child's name] become upset if changes are made in his [her] daily routines?
210. (If yes) Please give me some examples of how he [she] becomes upset.

211. Does [cite child's name] become upset if his [her] belongings are moved or disturbed?
212. (If yes) Please give me some examples of how he [she] becomes upset.
213. Does [cite child's name] become upset if changes are made in the household—for example, if furniture is moved?
214. (If yes) Please give me some examples of how he [she] becomes upset.
215. Does [cite child's name] have certain favorite objects or toys that he [she] insists on carrying around?
216. (If yes) Tell me more about that.
217. Does [cite child's name] become upset when things don't look right, such as when the rug has a spot on it or books on a shelf lean to the side?
218. (If yes) Please give me some examples of this.
219. Does [cite child's name] become upset when he [she] is interrupted before he [she] has finished doing something?
220. (If yes) Give me some examples of this.
221. Does [cite child's name] become agitated or upset by new people, places, or activities?
222. (If yes) Please give me some examples of this.
223. Does [cite child's name] insist on performing certain activities over and over again?
224. (If yes) Tell me more about these activities.
225. Does [cite child's name] become upset when he [she] puts on new clothes?
226. (If yes) Tell me more about that.
227. Does [cite child's name] have certain mealtime rituals, such as eating from only one specific plate?
228. (If yes) Tell me about [cite child's name]'s mealtime rituals.
229. Does [cite child's name] have unusual food preferences, such as foods of a certain color or texture?
230. (If yes) Please give me some examples of what foods he [she] prefers.

Play and Amusements

231. Now I'd like to talk to you about [cite child's name]'s play. What kinds of games does [cite child's name] play?
232. Does [cite child's name] ever pretend to do things, such as pretending to feed himself [herself] with pretend food?
233. Does [cite child's name] enjoy playing simple hide-and-seek games with you?
234. Does [cite child's name] like to play with toys?
235. Does [cite child's name] roll things along the floor?
236. How many blocks can [cite child's name] use to build a tower?
237. Can [cite child's name] put puzzles together?
238. (If yes) How large a puzzle—how many pieces—can he [she] put together?
239. Does [cite child's name] make things with Legos, Tinker Toys, or similar toys?
240. (If yes) Can [cite child's name] follow the printed diagrams that come with such toys?

(Continued)

241. Does [cite child's name] use toys in unusual ways, such as spinning them or lining them up over and over again?
242. (If yes) Tell me how he [she] uses toys in unusual ways.
243. Is [cite child's name] destructive with toys?
244. (If yes) Tell me about that.
245. Does [cite child's name] play with toys or other objects in the same exact way each time?
246. Does [cite child's name] imitate what you do when you play with him [her]?
247. (If yes) Tell me about that.
248. Does [cite child's name] imitate what other children do in their play?
249. (If yes) Tell me about that.
250. Does [cite child's name] engage in make-believe play?
251. (If needed) Does he [she] pretend to be a cowboy [cowgirl], policeman [policewoman], or doctor while acting out an imaginary game?
252. (If yes) Tell me about that.
253. Does [cite child's name] play with cars or trains as if they were real, such as by putting cars into a garage or moving trains around on a track?
254. Does [cite child's name] play with toy animals, dolls, or tea sets as if they were real?
255. Does [cite child's name] kiss the toy animals and dolls, put them to bed, hold tea parties for them, or play school with them?
256. Does [cite child's name] engage in imaginative play with other children, such as doctor and nurse, mother and father, or teacher and student?
257. Does [cite child's name] take an active part, or is he [she] always passive and not contributing to the play fantasy?
258. Does [cite child's name] join in cooperative play that does not incorporate fantasy, such as tag, hide-and-seek, ball games, and table games?
259. What types of outings does [cite child's name] enjoy?
260. What does [cite child's name] watch on television?
261. How long does [cite child's name] watch at a time?
262. How much time does [cite child's name] spend watching television each day?
263. What are [cite child's name]'s favorite shows?
264. Does [cite child's name] enjoy listening to music?
265. (If yes) What kind of music does [cite child's name] like?
266. Can [cite child's name] sing in tune?
267. Can [cite child's name] play a musical instrument?
268. (If yes) What instrument?

Special Skills

269. I'd like to learn whether [cite child's name] is especially good at something. Does he [she] have any special skills?
270. (If yes) Tell me about his [her] skills.
271. (If needed) We talked earlier about working with puzzles. Now can you tell me whether [cite child's name] has an unusual talent for assembling puzzles?

272. (If yes) Tell me about that.
273. Does [cite child's name] show any unusual abilities in music?
274. (If yes) Tell me about his [her] unusual abilities in music.
275. Does [cite child's name] have a very good memory?
276. (If yes) Tell me about his [her] memory.

Self-Care

(Modify the following questions based on the child's age.)

277. Now I'd like to talk to you about how [cite child's name] can take care of himself [herself]. First, does [cite child's name] have to be fed, or can he [she] feed himself [herself] with his [her] fingers, a spoon, a spoon and a fork, or a knife and a fork?
278. Does [cite child's name] need a special diet?
279. (If yes) Tell me about his [her] special diet.
280. Can [cite child's name] help himself [herself] to food when at the table?
281. Can [cite child's name] cut a slice of bread from a loaf?
282. How good are [cite child's name]'s table manners?
283. Does [cite child's name] have any problems with chewing?
284. Does [cite child's name] drink from a cup?
285. Does [cite child's name] dribble?
286. Can [cite child's name] wash and dry his [her] hands?
287. Can [cite child's name] bathe himself [herself] without help?
288. Is [cite child's name] aware when his [her] hands or face is dirty?
289. Can [cite child's name] dress himself [herself]?
290. (If yes) Tell me what [cite child's name] can do.
291. Can [cite child's name] undress himself [herself]?
292. (If yes) Tell me what [cite child's name] can do.
293. Can [cite child's name] brush or comb his [her] own hair?
294. Can [cite child's name] brush his [her] own teeth?
295. Is [cite child's name] concerned if his [her] clothes are dirty or untidy?
296. What stage has [cite child's name] reached in his [her] toilet training in the daytime?
297. (If dry during the day) And at nighttime, does [cite child's name] stay dry?
298. (If no) Tell me more about this.
299. Can [cite child's name] get objects that he [she] wants for himself [herself]?
300. Does [cite child's name] look for things that are hidden?
301. Does [cite child's name] climb on a chair to reach things?
302. Can [cite child's name] open doors?
303. Can [cite child's name] open locks?
304. Is [cite child's name] aware of the danger of heights or of deep water?
305. Is [cite child's name] aware that traffic is dangerous?
306. Does [cite child's name] know how to cross a street safely?
307. How much does [cite child's name] have to be supervised?

(Continued)

Table B-9 *(Continued)*

308. Is [cite child's name] allowed to go alone into another room … outside … in the neighborhood … farther away?

309. (If child is older than 11 or 12 years) Can [cite child's name] travel on a bus or train alone?

Sleep

310. Let's now talk about [cite child's name]'s sleeping habits. What are [cite child's name]'s sleeping habits? (Ask questions 311 to 320, as needed.)

311. What time does [cite child's name] go to sleep?

312. Does [cite child's name] have any rituals before going to sleep?

313. (If yes) Tell me about them.

314. Does [cite child's name] have any problems going to sleep?

315. (If yes) Tell me about them.

316. About how many hours of sleep does [cite child's name] get at night?

317. Does [cite child's name] take a daytime nap or naps?

318. (If yes) Around what time[s] does he [she] nap?

319. For how long?

320. What time does [cite child's name] get up?

Behavior Problems

(Modify the following questions based on the child's age.)

321. Let's now talk about [cite child's name]'s behavior. Does [cite child's name] run away or wander?

322. (If yes) Tell me about that.

323. Is [cite child's name] destructive with toys or other things?

324. (If yes) Tell me about that.

325. Does [cite child's name] have severe temper tantrums?

326. (If yes) Tell me about them.

327. (If needed) When do they occur?… Where do they occur? … How long do they last?

328. Does [cite child's name] hurt other children by biting, hitting, or kicking them?

329. (If yes) Give me some examples of how [cite child's name] hurts other children.

330. Does [cite child's name] try to hurt adults by biting, hitting, or kicking them?

331. (If yes) Give me some examples of how [cite child's name] tries to hurt adults.

332. How does [cite child's name] behave in public?

333. (If needed) Does [cite child's name] grab things in shops … scream in the street … make nasty remarks … feel people's clothing, hair, or skin … do anything else that is annoying?

334. Does [cite child's name] resist whatever you try to do for him [her]?

335. Does [cite child's name] automatically say "no" to any suggestion?

336. Is [cite child's name] generally aggressive?

337. (If yes) Tell me about his [her] aggressiveness.

338. Is [cite child's name] generally manipulative?

339. (If yes) Tell me about that.

340. Does [cite child's name] comply with rules or requests?

341. (If no) Tell me about what he [she] does.

342. Does [cite child's name] hurt himself [herself] on purpose, such as by banging his [her] head, biting his [her] hand, or hitting or deeply scratching any part of his [her] body?

343. (If yes) Please give me some examples.

344. How would you describe [cite child's name]'s overall behavior at home?

School and Learning Ability

345. (If relevant) Now I'd like to talk about school. Does [cite child's name] go to school? (If yes, go to question 346; if no, go to question 350. Modify questions 350 to 362 based on the child's age.)

346. Where does [cite child's name] go to school?

347. How is [cite child's name] doing in school?

348. What subjects does [cite child's name] study in school?

349. (If subjects named) Tell me about how [cite child's name] is doing in these subjects.

350. Tell me about [cite child's name]'s ability to recognize objects in pictures.

351. (If needed) What kinds of pictures does [cite child's name] recognize?

352. Tell me about [cite child's name]'s ability to read.

353. (If needed) What kinds of things does [cite child's name] read?

354. Tell me about [cite child's name]'s ability to write.

355. (If needed) What does [cite child's name] write?

356. Tell me about [cite child's name]'s ability to do arithmetic.

357. (If needed) What kind of arithmetic problems can [cite child's name] do?

358. Can [cite child's name] tell time?

359. Does [cite child's name] know the days of the week?

360. Does [cite child's name] know the months of the year?

361. Does [cite child's name] know dates?

362. Can [cite child's name] draw?

Domestic and Practical Skills

(Modify the following questions based on the child's age.)

363. Now let's talk about how [cite child's name] functions at home. Does [cite child's name] have any chores to do around the house?

364. (If yes) Tell me about what [cite child's name] does. (Ask questions 365 and 366, as needed.)

365. Does [cite child's name] help set the table … clean the table?

366. Does [cite child's name] straighten up his [her] room … wash his [her] clothes … help with washing dishes … use a vacuum cleaner … help with shopping … help prepare food … cook … knit or sew … do woodwork … help with gardening … do any other kind of craft work?

(Continued)

Table B-9 *(Continued)*

Concluding Questions

367. Is there anything else you would like to discuss?

368. (If yes) Go ahead.

369. Does [cite child's name] have any problems that we didn't discuss?

370. (If yes) Tell me about them.

371. Do you have any questions that you would like to ask me?

372. (If yes) Go ahead.

373. Thank you for talking with me. If you have any questions later or if you want to talk to me, please call me. Here is my card.

Source: Adapted from Schreibman (1988), Stone and Hogan (1993), and Wing (1976). Permission to use questions from the "Parent Interview for Autism" was obtained from W. L. Stone.

Table B-10
Semistructured Interview Questions for a Family

1. Hi! I'm Dr. [Ms., Mr.] _____. In order to try to work out the problems you're having as a family, I'd like to hear from everyone about what's going on. OK?
2. (Looking at the family members present) Would you like to tell me why you are here today?

Perception of Problem

3. What do you see as the problem? (Obtain each member's view, if possible.)
4. When did the problem start?
5. How did the problem start?
6. What is the problem like now?
7. How has the problem affected all of you? (Obtain each member's view, if possible.)
8. How have you dealt with the problem? (Obtain each member's view, if possible.)
9. To what degree have your attempts been successful?
10. Have you had any previous professional help? (If yes, go to question 11; if no, go to question 15.)
11. What kind of help did you receive?
12. What do you think about the help you received?
13. Was it successful?
14. Tell me in what ways it was successful [unsuccessful].

Description of Family

15. What words would you use to describe your family?
16. How do you think other people would describe your family?
17. What's it like when you are all together?
18. (Looking at the family members) What kind of a person is Mr. [cite father's last name]?
19. (Looking at the family members) What kind of a person is Mrs. [cite mother's last name]?
20. (Looking at the family members) What kind of son is [cite each son's name in turn]?
21. (Looking at the family members) What kind of daughter is [cite each daughter's name in turn]?
22. Do you agree with the description of yourself given by the other family members? (Obtain a response from each member.)
23. Which parent deals more with the children?
24. Do the children have any specific chores to do at home?
25. Are these arrangements satisfactory and fair?
26. (If no) How could they be better?
27. Do you find it easy to talk with others in your family? (Obtain a response from each member; explore any difficulties, including who is involved and what the problem is.)
28. What's it like when you discuss something together as a family?
29. Who talks the most?

30. Who talks the least?
31. Does everybody get a chance to have a say?
32. (Looking at the family members) Do you find you have to be careful about what you say in your family?
33. Who are the good listeners in your family?
34. Is it helpful to talk things over with the family, or does it seem to be a waste of time?
35. Is it easy to express your feelings in your family?
36. Do you generally know how the others in your family are feeling?
37. How can you tell how they are feeling?
38. How much time do you spend together as a family?
39. What sorts of things do you do together?
40. Who does what with whom?
41. Is this okay with everybody?
42. Who is closest to whom in the family?
43. How are decisions made in your family?
44. Is this satisfactory?
45. (If no) What would be preferable?
46. Do you have disagreements in your family? (If yes, go to question 47; if no, go to question 53.)
47. Who has disagreements?
48. What are they about?
49. What are the disagreements like?
50. What happens?
51. How do they end up?
52. Do they get worked out?
53. What kind of work does Mr. [cite father's last name] do?
54. What kind of work does Mrs. [cite mother's last name] do?
55. (Indicating the children) Do any of you have jobs?
56. (If yes) What kind of work do you do?

Extended Family

57. Are there any other relatives or close friends living at home or nearby? (If yes, go to question 58; if no, go to question 60.)
58. Who are they?
59. How do all of you get along with them [him, her]?

Concluding Questions

60. How might each of you change in order to improve the family situation?
61. Is there anything else that you would like to discuss?
62. Are there any questions that any of you would like to ask me?
63. (If yes) Go ahead.
64. Thank you for talking with me. If you have any questions or if you want to talk to me, please call me. Here is my card.

Note. This table is based on the Family Assessment Interview, which was prepared by Dr. Peter Loader for the Family Research Programme at Brunel–The University of West London. Work related to the interview schedule was published by Kinston and Loader (1984).
Source: Adapted from Kinston and Loader, unpublished manuscript, 1984.

Table B-11
Semistructured Interview Questions for a Teacher of a Child Referred for School Difficulties

Introduction

1. Hi! I'm Dr. [Ms., Mr.] _____. Please tell me why you referred [cite child's name].

2. Before we talk about these problems, I'd like to ask you about how [cite child's name] functions in some general areas. Does [cite child's name] have any auditory problems that you have noticed?

3. Does he [she] have any problems in the visual area ... in the motor area ... with speech ... with attention ... with concentration ... in getting along with other children ... in getting along with you or other teachers?

4. How about [cite child's name]'s energy level? Does he [she] tire easily?

5. And how is [cite child's name]'s motivation?

6. How does [cite child's name] handle assignments that require organization ... that require planning ... that require independent effort?

7. Does [cite child's name] attend class regularly?

8. (If no) Tell me about that.

9. Does [cite child's name] arrive in class on time, or is he [she] frequently late?

10. (If late) Do you know why he [she] is late?

11. Tell me about how [cite child's name] does his [her] homework?
(If academic problems are important, go to question 12 and then go to specific sections for problems in reading, mathematics, spelling, use of language, attention and memory, perception, and motor skills. If child has primarily behavioral problems, go to question 134. If needed, ask questions from both the academic and behavioral sections. To conclude the interview after you inquire about the child's academic and/or behavioral problems, go to question 184.)

Academic Problems

12. What types of academic problems is [cite child's name] having in the classroom?

Reading Difficulties

13. What types of reading difficulties does [cite child's name] have?
(Ask questions 14 to 23, as needed.)

14. Does [cite child's name] have any problems with silent reading ... oral reading ... reading comprehension ... reading speed ... endurance ... listening?

15. Does [cite child's name] have difficulty reading single letters ... words ... sentences ... paragraphs ... stories?

16. How accurately does [cite child's name] seem to hear sounds in words?

17. Does [cite child's name] have difficulty with specific parts of words, such as prefixes, suffixes, middle sound units, vowels, or consonants?

18. How does [cite child's name] go about attacking words?

19. Does [cite child's name] have receptive difficulties, such as difficulty in understanding what he [she] reads?

20. Does [cite child's name] have expressive difficulties, such as difficulty in telling you about what he [she] has read?

21. Is there a discrepancy between [cite child's name]'s silent and oral reading?

22. (If yes) Tell me about the discrepancy.

23. What do you think should be done to help [cite child's name] master reading skills?

Mathematics Difficulties

24. What types of mathematical difficulties does [cite child's name] have?

25. Tell me about [cite child's name]'s problem with [cite mathematical difficulty].

26. (Include only relevant items, based on the child's grade level and the information obtained in questions 24 and 25.) Does [cite child's name] have difficulty with addition ... subtraction ... multiplication ... division ... memorization or recall of number facts ... word problems ... oral problems ... fractions ... decimals ... percents ... measurement concepts such as length ... area ... liquid measures ... dry measures ... temperature ... time ... money ... exponents ... numerical reasoning ... numerical application ... story problems ... algebra ... geometry?

27. Is [cite child's name] careless when he [she] does mathematical problems?

28. Is [cite child's name] impulsive when he [she] does mathematical problems?

29. Is [cite child's name] unmotivated when he [she] does mathematical problems?

30. What do you think should be done to help [cite child's name] master mathematical skills?

Spelling Difficulties

31. What types of spelling difficulties does [cite child's name] have?

32. Tell me more about [cite child's name]'s problem with [cite spelling difficulty].

33. (If needed) Does [cite child's name] tend to insert extra letters ... omit letters ... substitute one letter for another one ... spell phonetically ... reverse sequences of letters ... put letters in the wrong order?

34. What do you think should be done to help [cite child's name] master spelling skills?

Language Skill Difficulties

35. What types of language difficulties does [cite child's name] have?

36. Tell me more about [cite child's name]'s problem in [cite language skill difficulty].
(Ask questions 37 to 49, as needed.)

(Continued)

37. Does [cite child's name] have oral expressive language difficulties?

38. (If yes) Tell me about them.

39. Does [cite child's name] have difficulty speaking in complete sentences … using correct words in speaking … writing expressive language?

40. (If yes) Tell me about his [her] difficulties.

41. Does [cite child's name] have difficulty with writing complete sentences … using correct words in writing … generating ideas … grammar … punctuation … writing organized compositions?

42. How would you compare [cite child's name]'s oral and written language?

43. Does [cite child's name] have difficulty using nonverbal gestures or signs?

44. Does [cite child's name] have difficulty speaking?

45. (If yes) What kinds of difficulties does he [she] have speaking?

46. (If needed) Does [cite child's name] have problems with pronunciation … speed of talking … vocal tone … intonation?

47. Does [cite child's name] have receptive language difficulties, such as difficulty understanding what others say … what he [she] reads … gestures?

48. How well does [cite child's name] recognize pictures … environmental sounds … nonverbal signs?

49. What do you think should be done to help [cite child's name] master language skills?

Attention and Memory Difficulties

50. What types of attention and/or memory difficulties does [cite child's name] have?

51. Tell me more about [cite child's name]'s problem with [cite attention and/or memory difficulty].
(Ask questions 52 to 92, as needed.)

General Attention

52. Under what conditions does [cite child's name] have difficulty attending to things?

53. Is [cite child's name] able to concentrate for a time period commensurate with his [her] chronological age?

54. Can [cite child's name] focus on a specific task?

55. Is [cite child's name] able to sustain attention for the duration of a typical assignment?

56. Is [cite child's name] distractible?

57. (If yes) Tell me about that.

58. Does [cite child's name] talk excessively … have difficulty working or playing quietly … often fail to finish things or follow through … often seem to not listen … often act before thinking … excessively shift from one activity to another?

59. Does [cite child's name] have difficulty organizing work … often lose things necessary for activities at school or home, such as toys, pencils, books, or assignments?

60. Does [cite child's name] need a lot of supervision?

61. Does [cite child's name] call out in class or blurt out answers?

62. Is [cite child's name] able to filter out surrounding noises—such as pencil sharpening or noises in the hall—so that he [she] can concentrate on the assigned task?

63. Does [cite child's name] stare into space for relatively long periods of time … doodle frequently?

64. Can [cite child's name] sit still for a long period of time?

65. (If no) Tell me what he [she] does.

66. Can [cite child's name] sit still for a short period of time?

67. (If no) Tell me what he [she] does.

68. Does [cite child's name] repeatedly say "What" or "Huh"?

69. Does [cite child's name] seek quiet places to work … become very upset in noisy, crowded places?

70. Is [cite child's name] constantly in motion?

71. What is [cite child's name]'s tolerance for frustration like?

72. Is [cite child's name] impulsive in his [her] behavior?

Auditory Attention

73. How does [cite child's name] attend to sounds … lectures … class discussions?

74. Can [cite child's name] shift his [her] attention from one sound to another?

75. Does [cite child's name] have difficulty maintaining his [her] focus on sounds?

76. (If yes) Are there any specific types of sounds that he [she] has difficulty focusing on?

77. Is it easier for [cite child's name] to attend to rhythmic sounds, like music, than to spoken language sounds?

78. Does [cite child's name] mistake words he [she] hears, like *rat* for *ran*?

79. Can [cite child's name] attend better when you speak slowly to him [her]?

Auditory Memory

80. Does [cite child's name] have a good memory for things that happened recently … for things that happened in the distant past … for present events?

81. Can [cite child's name] recall the names of people easily?

82. Does [cite child's name] have difficulty learning telephone numbers … addresses … the ABCs?

83. Does [cite child's name] call common objects, such as buttons and zippers, by their correct names?

84. Does [cite child's name] hesitate to name objects when he [she] is asked to do so?

85. Does [cite child's name] often ask to have questions repeated?

Visual Attention

86. How does [cite child's name] attend to visual stimuli?

87. (If needed) How does he [she] attend to pictures … words in print … TV presentations … movie presentations … actions on a computer screen?

(Continued)

Table B-11 *(Continued)*

Visual Memory

88. Does [cite child's name] remember things that he [she] saw recently … things that he [she] saw in the distant past … present events?

89. Can [cite child's name] recall the names of people he [she] has seen?

90. Does [cite child's name] have difficulty associating names with pictures?

91. Does [cite child's name] have difficulty in recognizing letters … numbers … shapes?

92. What do you think should be done to help [cite child's name] master attention and memory skills?

Perceptual Difficulties

93. What types of perceptual difficulties does [cite child's name] have?

94. Tell me more about [cite child's name]'s problem with [cite perceptual difficulties].
(Ask questions 95 to 111, as needed.)

95. Does [cite child's name] have difficulty in auditory perception?

96. Does he [she] have difficulty with localizing sounds … identifying sounds … distinguishing between sounds … auditory sequencing … sound blending … figure-ground identification of sounds—that is, identifying only the most important sounds and ignoring other potentially useful sounds?

97. Does [cite child's name] have difficulty in visual perception?

98. Does he [she] have difficulty with identifying visual stimuli … matching forms … figure-ground discrimination of shapes—that is, identifying only the key letter, shape, or form on a page … recognizing letters or words in different forms, such as lowercase versus uppercase or standard type versus italics?

99. Does [cite child's name] have difficulty in spatial perception?

100. Does he [she] have difficulty recognizing the position or location of an object on a page … in a room … in a building … on the playground?

101. Does [cite child's name] have difficulty with appreciating relative sizes … depth perception … perspective … recognizing whether objects differ in size?

102. Does [cite child's name] have difficulty distinguishing right from left?

103. Which modality—visual or auditory—does [cite child's name] prefer?

104. Does [cite child's name] prefer to look at pictures or at graphs?

105. Does [cite child's name] prefer making oral or written presentations?

106. Does [cite child's name] seem to have difficulty processing visual information … auditory information?

107. Can [cite child's name] copy material from a chalkboard … from an overhead … from dictation?

108. Can [cite child's name] keep his [her] place on a page while reading?

109. Can [cite child's name] find his [her] way around a school building?

110. Can [cite child's name] open his [her] locker?

111. What do you think should be done to help [cite child's name] master perceptual skills?

Motor Skill Difficulties

112. What types of motor difficulties does [cite child's name] have?

113. Tell me more about [cite child's name]'s problem with [cite motor difficulties].
(Ask questions 114 to 133, as needed.)

114. Does [cite child's name] have gross-motor problems?

115. (If yes) Please describe them.

116. Do they involve walking … running … sitting … throwing … balance?

117. Does [cite child's name] have fine-motor problems?

118. (If yes) Tell me about them.

119. Do they involve drawing … handwriting … coloring … tracing … cutting … pencil grip … hand dexterity?

120. Tell me more about these problems.

121. (If there are handwriting problems) Does [cite child's name] have problems in sequencing, such as transposing letters … spatial orientation, such as placing a letter of one word at the end of the preceding word (for example, writing "goh ome" for "go home") … writing letters or words on the same line … writing letters of appropriate size?

122. Does [cite child's name] scrawl?

123. Does [cite child's name] make tiny compressed letters?

124. Are [cite child's name]'s papers messy or neat?

125. How would you compare how [cite child's name] writes on a spelling test with how he [she] writes spontaneously?

126. Is [cite child's name] able to clearly write single letters … uppercase letters … lowercase letters … words … sentences … paragraphs … short stories or themes?

127. Is [cite child's name]'s problem in remembering shapes or in reproducing letter shapes?

128. Does [cite child's name] have visual-motor integration difficulties?

129. (If yes) Tell me about them.

130. What do you think should be done to help [cite child's name] master motor skills?

131. Can [cite child's name] type?

132. (If yes) How well does [cite child's name] type?

133. Does [cite child's name] do better with a word processor than with hand writing?

Behavioral Difficulties

134. Now I'd like to talk with you about [cite child's name]'s behaviors that bother you most. I'd like to discuss these behaviors, when they occur, how often they occur, and what occurs in your classroom that might influence the behaviors. I also would like to discuss some other matters related to [cite child's name] that will help us develop useful interven-

(Continued)

Table B-11 *(Continued)*

tions. Please describe exactly what [cite child's name] does that causes you concern.

135. Which behaviors bother you most?

136. Which of these behaviors are of most pressing concern to you now?

137. Which behaviors, in order of most to least pressing, would you like to work on now?

138. Let's look into the first problem in more detail. How serious is the problem behavior?

139. How long has it been going on?

140. When does the problem behavior occur?

141. (If needed) Does it occur when the children are just arriving at school ... at their desks in the classroom ... in small groups ... at recess ... at lunch ... on a field trip ... at an assembly ... working on a reading assignment ... working on a math assignment ... working on a history assignment ... working on a writing assignment ... working on a spelling assignment ... working on an art assignment ... working on a music assignment ... working on a social studies assignment?... Does it occur on a particular day of the week?

142. What classroom activity is generally taking place at the time the problem behavior occurs?

143. (If needed) Does the problem occur when the child is involved in a lecture ... unstructured play ... independent work ... interaction with you ... interaction with other children?

144. How does the problem behavior affect the other children in the class?

145. How long does the problem behavior last?

146. How often does the problem behavior occur?

147. How many other children in the class also have this problem?

148. How does [cite child's name]'s problem behavior compare with that of other children in the class who show the same behavior?

149. What happens just before the problem behavior begins?

150. What happens just after the problem behavior begins?

151. What makes the problem behavior worse?

152. What makes the problem behavior better?

Teacher's Reactions to Problem Behavior and Child

153. What do you do when the problem behavior occurs?

154. What does [cite child's name] do then?

155. What have you done that has been even partially successful in dealing with the problem behavior?

156. What do you think is causing the problem behavior?

157. What is your reaction to [cite child's name] in general?

Child's Relationship with Peers

158. How does [cite child's name] get along with his [her] classmates?

159. Does [cite child's name] have many friends?

160. Do the children include [cite child's name] in their games and activities?

161. Is [cite child's name] disliked by other children?

162. (If yes) Tell me why other children dislike [cite child's name].

163. How do other children contribute to [cite child's name]'s problem?

164. What do they do when [cite child's name] engages in the problem behavior?

165. How do other children help reduce the problem behavior?

166. How do other children react to [cite child's name] in general?

167. (If relevant) How do other teachers perceive and react to [cite child's name]?

Child's Social-Interpersonal Difficulties

(If social-interpersonal difficulties were not discussed, use this section.)

168. Does [cite child's name] have social and interpersonal problems?

169. (If yes) Tell me more about [cite child's name]'s problem in [cite social-interpersonal difficulties].
(Ask questions 170 to 177, as needed. Whenever there is a yes response, you might say "Please tell me more about that.")

170. Does [cite child's name] cry easily ... give up easily ... fly into a rage with no obvious cause ... fear trying new games or activities ... lie or cheat in games ... have problems with losing ... show overcontrolling tendencies ... prefer the company of younger children ... prefer to be alone?

171. Does [cite child's name] have difficulty waiting for his [her] turn in games or group situations?

172. Does [cite child's name] fight, hit, or punch other children?

173. Does [cite child's name] frequently interrupt other children's activities?

174. Is [cite child's name] bossy, always telling other children what to do?

175. Does [cite child's name] tease other children or call them names?

176. Does [cite child's name] refuse to participate in group activities?

177. Does [cite child's name] lose his [her] temper often and easily?

Teacher's Expectations and Suggestions

178. For what part of the day is [cite child's name]'s behavior acceptable?

179. What do you consider to be an acceptable level of frequency for the problem behavior?

180. What expectations do you have for [cite child's name]?

181. What suggestions do you have for remedying the problem behavior?

182. What would you like to see done?

183. How would your life be different if [cite child's name]'s problems were resolved?

(Continued)

Table B-11 *(Continued)*

Child's Strengths

184. What are [cite child's name]'s strengths?
185. In what situations does [cite child's name] display these strengths?
186. How can these strengths be used in helping [cite child's name]?

Teacher's View of Child's Family

187. How much contact have you had with [cite child's name]'s family?

188. What impressions do you have about [cite child's name]'s family?

Concluding Questions

189. Are there any questions that you would like to ask me?
190. (If yes) Go ahead.
191. Thank you for talking with me. If you have any questions or if you want to talk to me further, please call me. Here is my card.

Note. Questions 138 through 152 can be repeated for additional problem areas.
Source: Some questions in this table were adapted from McMahon and Forehand (1988) and Witt and Elliott (1983).

APPENDIX C

TABLES FOR DEVELOPMENTAL TRENDS

Table C-1
Developmental Trends in Cognitive Development

Age	Developmental trend
Birth to 2 years	Focus on senses and motor abilities Realize that objects exist even when they can't be seen Remember and imagine ideas and experiences
3 to 6 years	Think symbolically, using pretend play and language Focus on one aspect of a problem at a time Think concretely and deal with specific content
7 to 11 years	Assume multiple perspectives Take on the role of another Reason simultaneously about a subclass and the whole class Give relatively more weight to language than to contextual cues Think more logically and objectively Continue to tie thinking to concrete experiences
12 years and on	Engage in abstract thought Develop problem-solving strategies Develop personal characteristics, values, and relationships Consider how several different aspects of a problem might affect other people Separate the real from the impossible Recognize a hypothetical problem Think sequentially Consider events in relation to one another Separate one's own point of view from that of others Recognize how one's opinions affect others See from another's perspective Detect inconsistent logic Understand metaphors Generalize

Source: Adapted, in part, from Hughes (1988) and Worchel (1988).

Table C-2
Developmental Trends in Language Acquisition

Age	Developmental trend
0 to 9 months	Progress from crying to cooing to babbling to patterned speech
9 to 13 months	Use gestures or sounds to communicate Speak first meaningful words
13 to 18 months	Increase use of gesturing for communication (e.g., pointing, waving) Develop vocabulary of approximately 50 words Understand that words represent objects that can be acted upon Overextend word meanings (e.g., call all adult males "Daddy") Underextend word meanings (e.g., call only a red ball "ball")
18 to 30 months	Increase vocabulary from a few dozen to several hundred words Use imitation Engage in conversation Develop syntactical skills needed to create two- or three-word sentences (e.g., "I want milk")
30 months to 5 years	Use strings of sounds that convey meaning (grammatical morphemes), including plurals, prepositions, irregular verb endings, articles, possessives, auxiliary verbs, and verb contractions Develop vocabulary of approximately 900 words by 3 years Use language competently in a meaningful context Use simple sentences
5 to 8 years	Structure language much as adults do, using an awareness of grammar and language structure and meaning Continue to increase vocabulary rapidly, from approximately 10,000 words at 6 years to approximately 20,000 words at 8 years Use concrete word definitions, referring to functions and appearance Improve language awareness
8 to 11 years	Develop vocabulary of approximately 40,000 words by 10 years Use word definitions that emphasize synonyms and categorical relations Understand complex grammatical forms Grasp double meanings of words, as in metaphors and humor Consider needs of listeners in complex communicative situations Refine conversational strategies

Source: Adapted from Anglin (1993), Berk (1993), Hughes (1988), Prizant and Wetherby (1993), and Stone and Lemanek (1990).

Table C-3
Developmental Trends in Concept of Self

Age	Developmental trend
9 to 12 months	Begin to show self-recognition
15 to 18 months	Differentiate between pictures of oneself and pictures of others
18 to 24 months	Refer to oneself by name
28 months	Describe physical states (e.g., thirsty, tired)
3 to 6 years	Conceptualize oneself primarily in physical terms (e.g., "I have black hair") Make distinctions between oneself and others primarily on the basis of observable behaviors and characteristics (e.g., "Bill is tall") Have overly positive perceptions of one's own abilities, despite feedback to the contrary
7 to 8 years	Realize that one has better access to one's own thoughts than others do Use information about one's own performance, as well as that of peers, in evaluating oneself Change from "all or none" thinking to being able to distinguish between one situation and another (e.g., "I'm good in reading but not good in drawing") Distinguish between mental and physical aspects of self Recognize that discrepancies may exist between psychological experiences and physical appearance (e.g., one can act one way and feel another way) Adjust self-perceptions on the basis of feedback and past experiences with success and failure
10 years	Realize that one can be smart and ignorant in the same area (e.g., "I'm good at equations but not good at word problems")
12 years	Realize that one knows oneself better than one's parents do Incorporate abstract conceptions (such as temperament), beliefs, attitudes, and values (e.g., "I'm stubborn," "I'm a liberal") in self-descriptions Engage in self-reflection, self-monitoring, and self-evaluation Exhibit self-consciousness, self-centeredness, and preoccupation with one's own thoughts Imagine that one is the center of attention (or the focus of other people's attention) Overreact to criticism Become susceptible to shame and self-doubt Think that one is special Think that no one else is capable of experiencing similar events or feelings Believe that unfortunate consequences will happen to others but not to oneself

Source: Adapted from Stone and Lemanek (1990).

Table C-4
Developmental Trends in Person Perception

Age	Developmental trend
3½ to 4 years	Differentiate oneself from others but fail to distinguish between one's own social perspective (thoughts, feelings) and those of others Label others' overt feelings but fail to see the cause-and-effect relationship between reasons and social actions Describe others primarily in terms of concrete, observable characteristics, such as clothes, possessions, hair color, and size (e.g., "Lisa has pretty clothes") View others as good or bad (that is, use "all or none" reasoning) Equate effort with ability, regardless of outcome Describe others in global, highly evaluative, egocentric, and subjective terms (e.g., "He is nice because he gave me a toy") Report one's own misdeeds honestly (because of an inability to deceive, which requires taking another's perspective) Exhibit eagerness for adult approval
4 years	Assume that all acts and outcomes are intended (because of an inability to differentiate accidental from intended actions or outcomes)
5 to 6 years	Distinguish accidental from intended acts and outcomes Assume that others in similar situations will have perceptions like one's own Reflect on thoughts and feelings from another's perspective Understand that another's perspective is different
7 to 12 years	Describe others in more differentiated, individualized, and detailed ways, using traits, dispositions, and attitudes (e.g., "Alice is nice," "Henry is stubborn") Describe others in "all or none" fashion (that is, as possessing either desirable or undesirable traits) Understand that effort influences outcome Realize that individuals are aware of others' perspectives and that this awareness influences them Put oneself in another's place as a way of judging the other's intentions, purposes, and actions
12 to 13 years and on	View behavior of others as an interaction between personal characteristics and situational factors Use psychological constructs to reflect consistent traits in describing others ("Bill is smarter than Frank") Understand how personal characteristics relate to each other Differentiate among specific courses of behavior Develop more advanced, less hedonistic concepts of morality Understand that others may have simultaneously both desirable and undesirable traits

Source: Adapted from Selman (1976) and Stone and Lemanek (1990).

Table C-5
Developmental Trends in Moral Judgment

Age	Developmental trend
3 to 6 years	Base judgments of right and wrong on good or bad consequences and not on intentions Base moral choices on wishes that good things would happen to oneself Simply assert choices rather than attempting to justify choices
6 to 8 years	Define morality by resorting to authority figures, whose rules must be obeyed Understand that good actions are based on good intentions Develop a sense of fairness
8 to 10 years	Realize that others have a different point of view and that others are aware that one has one's own particular point of view Recognize that if someone has a mean intention toward one, it may be right to act in a similar way Define right by what one values
10 to 12 years	Focus on conforming to what people believe is the right behavior Define right in terms of the Golden Rule: Do unto others as you would have others do unto you Obey rules to obtain the approval of people one cares about
12 to 15 years and on	View morality from the perspective of the social system and what is necessary to keep it working Consider individual needs less important than maintaining the social order Base morality on protecting each individual's human rights View behavior that harms society as wrong

Note. Not all children reach the highest level of moral development.
Source: Kohlberg (1976) and Selman (1976).

Table C-6
Developmental Trends in Temporal Concepts

Age	Developmental trend
2 to 3½ years	Focus primarily on the present
3½ to 5 years	Understand time in a rudimentary way, but have difficulty distinguishing morning from afternoon and remembering days of the week Measure time by special events or identified routines, such as time to get up instead of morning
6 to 8 years	Master clock time, days of the week, and then months of the year Give temporal information about symptoms and their duration (e.g., how long it takes to fall asleep or how long a headache has been present)
8 to 9 years	Understand temporal concepts, such as temporal order (succession of events) and temporal duration (length of intervals between events)
9 to 11 years	Comprehend years, as well as dates Estimate adults' ages Develop a grasp of historical chronology
12 to 14 years	Develop a more complete sense of personal and historical time, making it possible to report on the duration of one symptom relative to others and on the persistence of symptoms
14 years and on	Develop greater understanding of and preoccupation with the future

Source: Adapted from Clarizio (1994) and Helms and Turner (1976).

Table C-7
Developmental Trends in Recognition of Emotion

Age	Developmental trend
7 months	Distinguish facial expressions
12 months	Use expressive information from mother's face to guide behavior
3 to 5 years	Reliably identify sad, angry, and happy Communicate about simple emotions in everyday situations Deny the presence of simultaneous emotions Identify feelings in stories based on situational cues Base judgments of affect on facial expressions Use idiosyncratic body cues (e.g., a smile) or situational cues (e.g., a birthday party) to identify one's own emotions See feelings as global and "all or none" (either good or bad), rather than mixed Believe that an event causes the same feelings in all people
5 to 6 years	Believe that one is the cause of other people's emotions
6 to 8 years	Identify fear, disgust, and other more difficult emotions Accept the possibility of simultaneous feelings only if they are separated temporally (e.g., feeling happy when eating an ice cream cone and sad when some of the ice cream falls to the ground) Use inner experiences and mental cues to identify emotions Understand that one can change and hide one's feelings See oneself as the primary cause of parental emotions, but at the same time identify causes that are more appropriate Recognize one's own emotions but have difficulty describing them, often associating physiological or behavioral cues with feelings (e.g., saying "I have a stomachache" when feeling bad or "I kicked the door" when feeling angry)
8 to 10 years	Use content cues in judging a story character's feelings Base judgments of affect on situational cues Accept the simultaneous co-occurrence of two emotions (e.g., feeling happy and sad at the same time)
10 to 12 years	Understand that internal emotional experiences and external affective expressions need not correspond Recognize that the sources of one's parents' emotions can include people and events unrelated to oneself Recognize that emotions come from "inner experiences"

Source: Adapted from Hughes (1988) and Stone and Lemanek (1990).

APPENDIX D

TABLES FOR ATTENTION-DEFICIT/HYPERACTIVITY DISORDER

Table D-1
Classroom Observation Code: A Modification of the Stony Brook Code

GENERAL INSTRUCTIONS FOR USING THE CLASSROOM OBSERVATION CODE

1. This observation coding system is used to record behaviors that occur during structured didactic teaching and/or during periods of independent work under teacher supervision. Behaviors that occur during free play periods, snack time, etc., are not recorded. In addition, observers should not code behaviors in the following situations: a) whenever the child is out of seat at the teacher's request to hand out or collect materials, read in front of the class, work at the chalkboard, or wait in line to have work checked; b) whenever the child receives individualized instruction from the teacher; c) whenever there is no assigned task, including instances in which the child is not required to initiate a new task after completion of assigned work; and d) whenever the teacher leaves the room.

2. Observers must be aware of the specific task assigned to the child and must note the particular class activity on the observation sheet. In addition, observers must be familiar with the general rules in each classroom. These rules, obtained from the teacher, are used as guidelines for employing this coding system. For example, a child who leaves his or her seat to sharpen a pencil without asking the teacher will be scored as "Gross Motor–Standing" (*GMs*) only if this behavior requires teacher permission. (*See* the following form: Classroom Observation Code Observer Data Sheet: Classroom Rules.)

3. When a behavior category is observed, *circle* the respective symbols on the coding sheet. If no behavior category is observed, then code "Absence of Behavior" (*AB*); one should slash this particular symbol.

4. In coding a particular category, it is essential that the observer be familiar with the *timing requirements* of each of the behavior categories. That is, non-timed behaviors are coded as soon as they occur within a 15-second interval, with only the first occurrence noted. Timed categories are coded only if the child engages in behavior for *more* than 15 consecutive seconds. For example, a child is scored as "Off-Task" in interval 2 if the behavior began in interval 1 and continued uninterrupted throughout interval 2. Continue coding the behavior in subsequent intervals as long as the behavior continues, uninterrupted, throughout these intervals. Each box on the observation coding sheet corresponds to a 15-second interval.

5. Any time the child leaves the room for more than one full interval without permission, those interval boxes on the coding sheet should be crossed out. (*See* "Non-Compliance" and "Off-Task" for further details.)

6. Each coding sheet is divided into four 2-minute blocks. Observe each child for a total of 16 minutes, alternating 4-minute observations on each child.

I. Interference—Symbol: *I*

Purpose: This category is intended to detect any verbal or physical behaviors or noises that are disturbing to others; the purpose here is to detect a discrete and distinct behavior that does not necessarily persist.

Timing: This category is coded as a Discrete, Non-Timed Behavior.

Description:
A. Interruption of the teacher or another student during a lesson or quiet work period.
Examples:
1. Calling out during a lesson when the teacher or another student has the floor (includes ooh's and ahh's when raising hand).
2. Initiating discussion with another child during a work period.

Note:
1. "Interference" is coded immediately within the interval in which it first occurs.
2. If the child initiates a conversation that overlaps two intervals, code *I* only in the first interval.
3. If conversation stops and then starts anew in the next interval, code that interval as *I* if conversation is initiated by the target child.
4. In most classrooms a child is scored as *I* if he or she calls out an answer to the teacher's question. However, *I* is *not* coded in classrooms where calling out answers is permitted.
5. If the child engages in a conversation overlapping two intervals that is initiated by *another* child, do *not* code *I* in *either* interval.
6. Do *not* score the child as *I* if there is *uncertainty* as to whether the child initiated conversation or is only responding to another child.
7. Do *not* score the child as *I* if there is *uncertainty* as to whether or not a sound (e.g., "ooh") was made by the child.

B. Production of Sounds
Examples:
1. Vocalizations: e.g., screams, whistles, calls across room. Include operant coughs, sneezes, or loud yawns.
2. The child makes noises other than vocalization through the use of materials available: slamming or banging objects, tapping ruler, foot tapping, hand clapping, etc.

Note: Do not code *I* if a sound is made accidentally (e.g., the child drops a book, knocks over a chair, etc.).

C. Annoying Behavior: This behavior refers to non-verbal interruption. The child interrupts *another child* during a teacher-directed or independent work lesson.
Examples:
1. Tapping lightly or making gentle physical movements or gestures toward another child.
2. Sitting on another's desk when that child is present at the desk.
3. Moving or lifting another's desk when the owner is present.

D. Clowning: The following behaviors are to be coded as *I*.
Examples:
1. Mimicking the teacher or another child.
2. Kicking an object across the floor.
3. Engaging in or organizing games and other inappropriate activities during a work period (e.g., playing kickball in the class, throwing and catching a ball).
4. Showing off his cr her own work when not called on by the teacher.
5. Making animal imitations.

(Continued)

Table D-1 *(Continued)*

6. Calling out a wildly inappropriate answer or making an obviously inappropriate public statement.

7. Shooting paper clips, airplanes, spitballs, etc. (If aimed at someone, this behavior is coded as "Aggression," *A*.)

8. Standing on a desk, chair, or table when not requested to do so by the teacher, or in any other inappropriate situation.

9. Posturing (child acts to characterize an action, an object, or another person).

10. Dancing in the classroom.

11. Play-acting.

12. Making mock threats. (If this does not occur in a clowning situation, then it is coded instead as "Threat or Verbal Aggression," *AC*.)

Note: If clowning involving vigorous gross motor movements (e.g., running, dancing) occurs while the child is out of chair, then code both *I* and "Gross Motor–Vigorous" (*GMv*).

II. Off-Task—Symbol: *X*

Purpose: This category is intended to monitor behaviors where the child, *after initiating* the appropriate task-relevant behavior, attends to stimuli other than the assigned work.

Timing: This category is coded as Timed Behavior.

Description:

A. Manipulation and/or attending to objects, people, or parts of the body to the *total exclusion* of the task for one full interval following the interval in which the behavior began.

Examples:

1. The child plays with a pencil for one full interval after the interval in which the behavior was initially seen, without visual orientation toward the assigned task.

2. The child engages in extended conversation when he or she is supposed to be working.

3. The child does a task other than the assigned one (e.g., reads a different book). It is therefore essential that the observer be aware of the classroom situation and the specific assigned task.

Note:

1. When the child is doing something under the desk or where the observer can't see and is not attending to the task, assume the behavior is inappropriate and code *X*.

2. If the teacher is conducting a lesson at the board, such that the task requires the child to *look at* the teacher or the board, score the child as *X* if he or she *does not* look at the teacher and/or the board *at any time* during the interval after the interval in which he or she first looked away.

3. If the teacher or another student is lecturing, reading a story, issuing instructions, etc., such that the child's task is to *listen* to the speaker, then code *X* if the child, by *his or her behavior*, indicates that he or she is not listening (e.g., head down on the desk, doodling in book, looking in book, etc.). Do *not* code *X* if the child *looks at* the speaker at any time during the interval.

4. Do *not* code *X* if the child shows any visual orientation to the task. Do *not* code *X* if there is uncertainty as to his or her visual orientation.

5. Do *not* code *X* if the child, by *his or her behavior*, indicates that he or she is listening (e.g., the child looks at the speaker's subject matter).

6. Do *not* code *X* if the child plays with or manipulates an object while attending to the task.

B. Code as *X* those instances when the child is allowed to leave his or her seat (e.g., to throw refuse away) but remains away from the seat for more than five consecutive intervals following the interval in which he or she first left the seat.

Example:

Leaves Seat	Out of Seat	Out of Seat	Out of Seat	Out of Seat	Out of Seat	Out of Seat
1	2	3	4	5	6	7

Interval 7 is coded as *X* and "Out-of-Chair" (*OC*). Continue coding *X* and *OC* as long as the child remains away from his or her desk. If the child engages in task-relevant behavior while out of seat (e.g., attends to a teacher lesson), then stop coding *X* but continue coding *OC*.

Note:

1. If after initiating the task the child leaves the classroom for more than one full interval without permission, code *X* and indicate that the child is out of the room by crossing out the interval box. Continue coding *X* as long as the child remains out of the room.

2. Do *not* code *X* if the child stops working and there is uncertainty as to whether he or she has *completed* the task. However, put a dot above the interval in which there is uncertainty. If the teacher then confirms that the child was off-task (e.g., she says: "Why aren't you working?"), then go back and code these "dotted" intervals as *X*. If the teacher gives no indication, do not code *X*.

3. Do *not* code *X* in any interval that has been coded as "Solicitation" (*S*).

III. Non-Compliance—Symbol: *NC*

Purpose: This category is intended to monitor behaviors that reflect a failure on the part of the child to follow teacher instructions.

Timing: This category is coded as a Timed Behavior.

Description: The child fails to *initiate* appropriate behavior in response to a command or request from the teacher. It is to be distinguished from "Off-Task" (*X*), which is coded when the child, *after initiating* task-relevant behavior, ceases this task-relevant behavior.

Example: After a command has been given by the teacher (e.g., "Copy the words on the board into your notebook"), the child has one full interval after the interval in which the command was given to initiate the request. If the child has not complied, begin coding *NC* and continue coding *NC* for each full interval in which the child fails to initiate the task.

Note:

1. When the teacher gives a specific command, write "T.C." *above* the interval box in which the teacher *finished* giving the command.

2. If the child indicates that he or she is *carrying out* the teacher's command (e.g., the child looks for his or her notebook), then allow the child *five* full intervals to comply. If after this time period he or she has not initiated task-relevant behavior (e.g., copying words), then begin coding *NC*.

3. If before initiating the task the child leaves the classroom for more than one full interval without permission, code *NC* and cross out the interval box. Continue coding *NC* as long as the child remains out of the room.

4. The teacher will often issue *commands* that are *not task-related*, but are instead related to the *handling of materials* (e.g., "Put down your pencils," "Put away your book"). If the child has not complied by the end of the first full interval following the interval in which the command was given, then code that interval as *NC*. Do *not* continue coding *NC*. If the teacher repeats the same commands, then note "T.C." and begin to time the child to see if he or she complies.

5. A teacher may issue more than one command (e.g., "Put down your pencils and look at the board"). The child should *not* be scored as *NC* if he or she looks at the board but does not put down his or her pencil. Therefore, do not code *NC* if the child follows the more salient, task-related aspect of the teacher's command. The child should be scored as *NC* if he or she does *not* follow the more salient command (i.e., "look at the board").

6. The teacher will often tell the class to take out a textbook and begin working independently on a particular page. Do *not* code *NC* if the child begins working in the book on the wrong page.

7. A child may not have a book in school or may be unable to find it. Give the child *five* full intervals to attempt to find the appropriate materials. If at the end of this time interval the child has not informed the teacher that he or she doesn't have the book (homework, crayons, etc.), then begin coding *NC* until he or she notifies the teacher.

Situations arise in the classroom which make it difficult to decide whether a child is noncompliant or off-task. The following guidelines should be useful in clarifying some of these situations.

8. During a classroom lesson the teacher will often issue commands that are *specific to the ongoing lesson*. In these instances, a child who had been working on the lesson but did not follow the new command should be scored as *X* rather than *NC*. For example, during a math lesson, the children have been working in their math workbooks. They have been following the teacher's directions and have worked on specific math examples. The teacher tells them to "Do example 10." The child has been working all along but does not do example 10. If the required time interval elapses and the child has not begun work on this example, he or she should be scored as *X*.

9. The following situation should be coded as *NC* and not "Off-Task" (*X*). During a classroom lesson, the teacher issues a command such that the children are expected to work on or direct their attention to a task different from the one on which they had been working. For example, during a math lesson, the children have been working in their math *workbooks*. The teacher now shifts the focus of the math lesson and instructs the children to work on set theory using *colored blocks*. If the child does *not* follow these instructions within the required time interval, he or she should be scored as *NC*.

IV. Minor Motor Movement—Symbol: *MM*

Purpose: There are two aspects to this category, both of which are intended to monitor behaviors of the child that are indicative of restlessness and fidgeting.

Timing: This category is coded as Discrete, Non-Timed Behavior.

Description: Minor motor movements refer to *buttock movements* and *rocking movements* of the child while he or she is in the seat and/or to buttock movements while he or she is in *nonerect* positions while out of seat.

A. The child engages in in-seat movements such that there is an *observable* movement of the lower buttock(s)—i.e., that part of the buttock(s) that is in contact with the seat of the chair.

Examples: The following pertain to movements of one or both buttocks.

1. Sliding in seat.
2. Twisting, turning, wiggling, etc.—coded only when accompanied by buttock movement.
3. Lifting one or both buttocks off the seat.
4. Buttock movements while kneeling or squatting in seat.

B. The child produces *rocking* movements of his or her body and/or chair. Body rocking movements are defined as *repetitive* movements (at least two complete back-and-forth movements) where the child moves from the waist up in a back-and-forth manner. Movements of the chair are also coded as *MM* when the child lifts two chair legs off the floor.

Note:

1. Do *not* code *MM* if the child makes *just one* forward leaning movement or *just one* backward leaning movement. However, if this movement is accompanied by an observable buttock movement, then *MM* should be coded.

2. Code as *MM any* movement which takes the child from a seated position into a kneeling, squatting, or crouching position, either in or out of the seat.

3. If the child is kneeling in or out of his or her seat or *leaning* over a desk or table, then code as *MM* any observable movements of the lower and/or upper buttocks—i.e., that area from the upper thigh to the hip.

4. If the child goes from a standing to a kneeling or squatting position, code this as *MM*.

5. Do *not* code *MM* if the *physical* set-up is such that the child *must* move in order to work on a task. There are *two* specific situations where minor motor movements should not be coded.

(a) The position of the child's desk requires that he or she *must* move in order to work on a task—for example, the child faces the side of the room and the chalkboard is in front. In this situation, the child *must* move his or her buttocks in order to copy from the board.

(b) While working on a task that requires his or her visual attention (e.g., copying from the board, watching the teacher), the child's view is obstructed, thereby requiring him or her to move in order to maintain visual contact.

6. Do *not* code *MM* if the child moves from a standing or kneeling position to a sitting position in the chair.

V. Gross Motor Behavior

Purpose: There are two aspects of this category which are intended to monitor motor activity that results in the child's leaving his or her seat and/or engaging in vigorous motor activity.

Timing: This category is coded as a Discrete, Non-Timed Behavior.

A. Gross Motor–Standing—Symbol: *GMs*

Description: GMs refers to motor activity that results in the child's *leaving* his or her seat and *standing* on one or both legs (on the floor, chair, or desk) in an erect or semi-erect position such that the child's body from the waist up is *at least* at a 135-degree angle with the floor.

Note:

1. Do *not* code *GMs* when the child has *permission*, specific or implied, to leave his or her seat (e.g., to sharpen a pencil, throw refuse away, get materials, go to the board, go to the teacher's desk, etc.). If the child leaves his or her seat without permission, then code *GMs*.

2. Do *not* code *GMs* if the *physical* set-up is such that the child *must* move in order to work on a task. For example, while working on a task that requires his or her visual attention (e.g., copying from the board, watching a demonstration), the child's view is *obstructed*, thereby requiring him or her to stand up in order to maintain visual contact.

3. If there is *uncertainty* as to whether or not the child had to stand up, then code *GMs*.

B. Gross Motor–Vigorous—Symbol: *GMv*

Description: This is coded when the child engages in vigorous motor activity *while not seated at his or her desk* or when the child *leaves* his or her seat in a sudden, abrupt, or impulsive manner.

Examples:
1. Jumping up out of seat.
2. Running away from seat.
3. Running in the classroom.
4. Crawling across the floor.
5. Twirling.
6. Acrobatics.
7. Swinging between two seats or desks.

VI. Out-of-Chair Behavior—Symbol: *OC*

Purpose: This category is intended to monitor extended out-of-seat behavior.

Timing: This category is coded as a Timed Behavior.

Description: The child remains out of chair for one full interval after the interval in which he or she first left the seat.

Note:

1. *OC* is coded for each complete interval that the child remains out of chair, irrespective of whether the child is standing, sitting, or kneeling on the floor or roaming around the classroom.

2. If while being coded as *OC* the child kneels or squats (out-of-chair) or sits on the floor, then code this movement as "Minor Motor Movement" (*MM*) and continue to code *OC*. Any buttock movements that occur while the child is seated on the floor are coded as *MM*. *OC* is discontinued only when the child sits or kneels in a chair—be it his or her own or someone else's.

3. If the child is out of a chair getting materials, sharpening a pencil, getting a drink of water, throwing refuse away, etc. (when these are *permitted* behaviors), then allow the child a maximum of five full intervals after the interval in which he or she first left the seat to complete this task. After these five intervals, if the child is still out of chair, then begin coding *OC*. If the child is *not working* during this period, then also score him or her as "Off-Task" (*X*).

4. If less than five intervals have elapsed and the child has obtained his or her goal (e.g., gotten his book, thrown away refuse, etc.), then allow him or her one full interval to return to his or her seat. If at the end of that interval he or she has not returned to the seat, then code that interval as *OC*.

5. It is essential to be familiar with those classroom rules regarding leaving seat with and without permission.

VII. Physical Aggression—Symbol: *A*

Purpose: This category is intended to measure physical aggression directed at another person or destruction of other's property. This behavior is coded regardless of the accuracy of the intended assault.

Timing: This category is coded as a Discrete, Non-Timed Behavior.

Description:

A. The child makes a forceful movement directed at another person, either directly or by utilizing a material object as an extension of the hand.

Examples:
1. Blocking someone with arms or body; tripping, kicking, or hitting another person.
2. Throwing objects at another person.
3. Pinching, biting.

Note:

1. In all of the above examples, even if the child misses his or her goal, the behavior should be coded as *A*.

2. Code *A* even when the physical aggression is initiated by another child and the target child defends himself or herself. However, this should be noted on the coding sheet.

B. Destruction of others' materials or possessions or school property.

Examples:
1. Tearing or crumpling others' work.
2. Breaking crayons, pencils, or pens of others.
3. Misusing others' books (ripping out pages, writing in them, etc.).
4. Writing on another child or on another child's work.
5. Writing on a school desk.
6. Writing in a school textbook.

Note:

1. Code *A* even if the owner of the material is not at his or her desk.

2. If the child engages in *continuous* destructive behavior (e.g., writes on a desk or in a school textbook for several consecutive intervals), then code *A* only in the first interval in which the behavior occurs. If the child *interrupts* this destructive behavior and then returns to it, then code *A* anew.

C. Grabbing material in a sudden manner.

Examples:
1. The child grabs a book out of the hands of another child.
2. The child grabs his or her own material from another child.

Note:

Exclude casually taking material out of another's hand.

Table D-1 *(Continued)*

VIII. Threat of Verbal Aggression—Symbol: to children = *AC*, to Teacher = *AT*

Purpose: This category is intended to monitor verbalizations or physical gestures of children that are abusive or threatening.

Timing: This category is coded as a Discrete, Non-Timed Behavior.

Description:

A. The child uses abusive language and gestures to children.

Examples:

1. The child curses at another, says "shut up" to another.
2. The child sticks out his tongue at another, makes a threatening gesture, etc.
3. The child threatens others.
4. The child teases others, criticizes others.
5. The child bullies others.

B. When asked to do something by the teacher, the child directly states, "No I won't; I'm not going to do that." This should be coded as "Interference" (*I*) and *AT*. Do *not* code "Solicitation" (*S*).

C. The child answers the teacher back when a reply is *not* acceptable.

Example:

The teacher states, "We are not going outside today." The child calls back in a defiant manner, "Why not? I want to."

IX. Solicitation of Teacher—Symbol: *S*

Purpose: This category monitors behaviors directed toward the teacher. It is important to note that this behavior is *target-child initiated.*

Timing: This category is coded as a Discrete, Non-Timed Behavior.

Description: Behaviors directed at obtaining the teacher's attention.

Examples:

1. Leaving seat and going up to the teacher. (This would be coded as *S* and "Gross Motor–Standing" (*GMs*); if the child speaks to the teacher, "Interference" (*I*) is also coded.)

2. Raising hand.
3. Calling out to the teacher.

Note:

1. These behaviors are coded as *S* whether or not the teacher recognizes the child.

2. When a child calls out to the teacher by mentioning the teacher's name or directs a question or statement specifically to the teacher while the teacher is attending to another child or addressing the class, then the behavior is coded as both *S* and "Interference" (*I*).

3. If the child says "ooh," "ahh," etc., while raising his or her hand in response to the teacher's question, code this as "Interference" (*I*) but *not S*.

4. If the observation begins while a teacher-child interaction is taking place, assume that the teacher initiated the interaction and do *not* code *S*.

5. If the child raises his or her hand in order to solicit the teacher and keeps the hand raised for more than one interval, *S* is coded *only* in the first interval in which the behavior occurred.

6. "Solicitation" and "Interference" (*I*) are coded if the child calls out an answer to the teacher when another child has the floor.

7. "Solicitation" is *not* coded if the child raises his or her hand in response to a teacher's question.

8. "Solicitation" is *not* coded if the child calls out in response to a teacher's question. In most classrooms, the child is scored as "Interference" (*I*) if he or she calls out an answer to a teacher's question.

X. Absence of Behavior—Symbol: *AB*

If no inappropriate behaviors as defined by the above categories occur in an interval, then code *AB*.

(Continued)

Table D-1 *(Continued)*

CLASSROOM OBSERVATION CODE
OBSERVER DATA SHEET: CLASSROOM RULES

\#_____ Child A: _____ Seat: _____

B: _____ Seat: _____

School: _____ Teacher: _____ Room #: _____

1. Must a child always raise his or her hand before asking or answering questions?

   a) During a teacher-conducted lesson _____

   b) During independent work _____

   c) Comments _____

2. May a child engage in conversation with other children?

   a) During a teacher-conducted lesson _____

   b) During independent work _____

   c) Comments _____

3. Must a child work after completion of assigned task? _____

   a) On what? _____

   b) Can this be done out of his or her assigned seat? _____

4. May a child leave the room without permission? _____

5. May a child leave his or her seat without permission to:

   a) sharpen a pencil _____   e) get materials _____

   b) throw refuse away _____   f) stand while working _____

   c) get a drink _____   g) other _____

   d) speak to the teacher _____

6. Other classroom rules: _____

_____

(Continued)

Table D-1 *(Continued)*

CLASSROOM OBSERVATION CODE
SCORING SHEET

	1	2	3	4	5	6	7	8
A	X A NC AC MM AT GMs GMv OC S AB	X A NC AC MM AT GMs GMv OC S AB	X A NC AC MM AT GMs GMv OC S AB	X A NC AC MM AT GMs GMv OC S AB	X A NC AC MM AT GMs GMv OC S AB	X A NC AC MM AT GMs GMv OC S AB	X A NC AC MM AT GMs GMv OC S AB	X A NC AC MM AT GMs GMv OC S AB

#
Pg

	1	2	3	4	5	6	7	8
B	X A NC AC MM AT GMs GMv OC S AB	X A NC AC MM AT GMs GMv OC S AB	X A NC AC MM AT GMs GMv OC S AB	X A NC AC MM AT GMs GMv OC S AB	X A NC AC MM AT GMs GMv OC S AB	X A NC AC MM AT GMs GMv OC S AB	X A NC AC MM AT GMs GMv OC S AB	X A NC AC MM AT GMs GMv OC S AB

	1	2	3	4	5	6	7	8
C	X A NC AC MM AT GMs GMv OC S AB	X A NC AC MM AT GMs GMv OC S AB	X A NC AC MM AT GMs GMv OC S AB	X A NC AC MM AT GMs GMv OC S AB	X A NC AC MM AT GMs GMv OC S AB	X A NC AC MM AT GMs GMv OC S AB	X A NC AC MM AT GMs GMv OC S AB	X A NC AC MM AT GMs GMv OC S AB

	1	2	3	4	5	6	7	8
D	X A NC AC MM AT GMs GMv OC S AB	X A NC AC MM AT GMs GMv OC S AB	X A NC AC MM AT GMs GMv OC S AB	X A NC AC MM AT GMs GMv OC S AB	X A NC AC MM AT GMs GMv OC S AB	X A NC AC MM AT GMs GMv OC S AB	X A NC AC MM AT GMs GMv OC S AB	X A NC AC MM AT GMs GMv OC S AB

#
Pg

Abbreviations: I = Interference; A = Physical Aggression; AC = Threat of Verbal Aggression to Children; AT = Threat of Verbal Aggression to Teacher; GMv = Gross-Motor Vigorous; S = Solicitation of Teacher; AB = Absence of Behavior; X = Off-Task; NC = Non-Compliance; MM = Minor Motor Movement; GMs = Gross Motor–Standing; OC = Out-of-Chair.

Observer _____ Date _____ Time _____

Source: Reprinted, with changes in notation, with permission of the authors from H. Abikoff and R. Gittelman, "Classroom Observation Code: A Modification of the Stony Brook Code," *Psychopharmacology Bulletin*, 1985, *21*, pp. 901–909.

Table D-2
Structured Observation of Academic and Play Settings (SOAPS)

INSTRUCTIONS FOR STRUCTURED OBSERVATION OF ACADEMIC AND PLAY SETTINGS

To conduct the observation, you will need two tables (or desks) and chairs, a popular toy (e.g., hand-held videogame), five double-sided worksheets, and three copies of the recording form. Before the child enters the room, place the five double-sided worksheets on one table (or desk) and the toy on a nearby table (or desk). The room should be equipped with a one-way mirror or with a mounted camera for observing the child from an adjacent room.

Bring the child into the room and say, "This is our classroom. Here is your table. Let me show you some worksheets and how to do them." Help the child do a sample item at the top of each worksheet. Then say, "There are too many problems here for you to complete them all. But while I am gone for 15 minutes, I want you to do as many of them as you can. Keep working, don't leave your chair, and don't play with the toy over there. I'll be next-door to make sure you're okay. I'll let you know when the 15 minutes are over." Then leave the room.

Use a 5-second time interval to record five behaviors: attention, sitting, fidgeting, noisy, and toy play. Note that the first two behaviors are appropriate behaviors and the last three are inappropriate behaviors. Make an audiotape that gives you prompts indicating the beginning of each interval. Record the following: "Begin 1 [5 seconds], Begin 2 [5 seconds], Begin 3, ... , Begin 60."

In each of the five behavior code columns on the recording form, circle the code representing the behavior observed during each interval. Three recording forms are needed for each 15-minute session.

After the session, record the number of intervals that the child was on-task. Convert the number of on-task intervals to a percentage (divide by 60). A general rule is that a minimum of 80% on-task behavior is expected for elementary-age children (Roberts, 1990). Also record the number of worksheet items correctly completed.

Definitions of Coded Behaviors

1. *Attention* (Attending = AT; Not Attending = /AT). Code Attention when the child's eyes are focused on one of the assigned worksheets. Momentary shifts in focus away from a worksheet as well as obvious scribbling and clear lack of engagement with the task are coded as Not Attending (off-task).

2. *Sitting* (Sitting = SI; Not Sitting = /SI). Code Sitting when the child is sitting in the chair or when the child's weight is supported by the chair (e.g., when the child is sitting on his or her legs on the chair or when the child stands on the chair).

3. *Fidgeting* (Fidgeting = FI; Not Fidgeting = /FI). Code Fidgeting when the child makes any repetitive movement that is not directed to the completion of worksheet items (e.g., tapping a pencil on the table).

4. *Noisy* (Noisy = NO; Not Noisy = /NO). Code Noisy when the child makes an audible vocalization, even if the vocalization is low in volume or is unintelligible (e.g., whispering, singing, yelling).

5. *Toy Play* (Toy Play = TO; Not Toy Play = /TO). Code Toy Play when the child plays with the toy or when the child is looking at the toy and is within arm's reach of it.

(Continued)

Table D-2 *(Continued)*

RECORDING FORM FOR STRUCTURED OBSERVATION OF ACADEMIC AND PLAY SETTINGS

Name: _____ Date: _____ School: _____

Sex: _____ Grade: _____ Birthdate: _____ Teacher: _____

Intervals on-task: AT____/60 = ____%; SI____/60 = ____%; /FI____/60 = ____%; /NO____/60 = ____%; /TO____/60 = ____%

No. of items completed correctly: 1_____; 2_____; 3_____; 4_____; 5_____; 6_____; 7_____; 8_____; 9_____; 10_____

Interval	Attention		Sitting		Fidgeting		Noisy		Toy Play	
1	AT	/AT	SI	/SI	FI	/FI	NO	/NO	TO	/TO
2	AT	/AT	SI	/SI	FI	/FI	NO	/NO	TO	/TO
3	AT	/AT	SI	/SI	FI	/FI	NO	/NO	TO	/TO
4	AT	/AT	SI	/SI	FI	/FI	NO	/NO	TO	/TO
5	AT	/AT	SI	/SI	FI	/FI	NO	/NO	TO	/TO
6	AT	/AT	SI	/SI	FI	/FI	NO	/NO	TO	/TO
7	AT	/AT	SI	/SI	FI	/FI	NO	/NO	TO	/TO
8	AT	/AT	SI	/SI	FI	/FI	NO	/NO	TO	/TO
9	AT	/AT	SI	/SI	FI	/FI	NO	/NO	TO	/TO
10	AT	/AT	SI	/SI	FI	/FI	NO	/NO	TO	/TO
11	AT	/AT	SI	/SI	FI	/FI	NO	/NO	TO	/TO
12	AT	/AT	SI	/SI	FI	/FI	NO	/NO	TO	/TO
13	AT	/AT	SI	/SI	FI	/FI	NO	/NO	TO	/TO
14	AT	/AT	SI	/SI	FI	/FI	NO	/NO	TO	/TO
15	AT	/AT	SI	/SI	FI	/FI	NO	/NO	TO	/TO
16	AT	/AT	SI	/SI	FI	/FI	NO	/NO	TO	/TO
17	AT	/AT	SI	/SI	FI	/FI	NO	/NO	TO	/TO
18	AT	/AT	SI	/SI	FI	/FI	NO	/NO	TO	/TO
19	AT	/AT	SI	/SI	FI	/FI	NO	/NO	TO	/TO
20	AT	/AT	SI	/SI	FI	/FI	NO	/NO	TO	/TO
21	AT	/AT	SI	/SI	FI	/FI	NO	/NO	TO	/TO
22	AT	/AT	SI	/SI	FI	/FI	NO	/NO	TO	/TO
23	AT	/AT	SI	/SI	FI	/FI	NO	/NO	TO	/TO
24	AT	/AT	SI	/SI	FI	/FI	NO	/NO	TO	/TO
25	AT	/AT	SI	/SI	FI	/FI	NO	/NO	TO	/TO
26	AT	/AT	SI	/SI	FI	/FI	NO	/NO	TO	/TO
27	AT	/AT	SI	/SI	FI	/FI	NO	/NO	TO	/TO
28	AT	/AT	SI	/SI	FI	/FI	NO	/NO	TO	/TO
29	AT	/AT	SI	/SI	FI	/FI	NO	/NO	TO	/TO
30	AT	/AT	SI	/SI	FI	/FI	NO	/NO	TO	/TO
31	AT	/AT	SI	/SI	FI	/FI	NO	/NO	TO	/TO
32	AT	/AT	SI	/SI	FI	/FI	NO	/NO	TO	/TO
33	AT	/AT	SI	/SI	FI	/FI	NO	/NO	TO	/TO
34	AT	/AT	SI	/SI	FI	/FI	NO	/NO	TO	/TO
35	AT	/AT	SI	/SI	FI	/FI	NO	/NO	TO	/TO
36	AT	/AT	SI	/SI	FI	/FI	NO	/NO	TO	/TO
37	AT	/AT	SI	/SI	FI	/FI	NO	/NO	TO	/TO
38	AT	/AT	SI	/SI	FI	/FI	NO	/NO	TO	/TO
39	AT	/AT	SI	/SI	FI	/FI	NO	/NO	TO	/TO
40	AT	/AT	SI	/SI	FI	/FI	NO	/NO	TO	/TO

(Continued)

Table D-2 *(Continued)*

Interval	Attention		Sitting		Fidgeting		Noisy		Toy Play	
41	AT	/AT	SI	/SI	FI	/FI	NO	/NO	TO	/TO
42	AT	/AT	SI	/SI	FI	/FI	NO	/NO	TO	/TO
43	AT	/AT	SI	/SI	FI	/FI	NO	/NO	TO	/TO
44	AT	/AT	SI	/SI	FI	/FI	NO	/NO	TO	/TO
45	AT	/AT	SI	/SI	FI	/FI	NO	/NO	TO	/TO
46	AT	/AT	SI	/SI	FI	/FI	NO	/NO	TO	/TO
47	AT	/AT	SI	/SI	FI	/FI	NO	/NO	TO	/TO
48	AT	/AT	SI	/SI	FI	/FI	NO	/NO	TO	/TO
49	AT	/AT	SI	/SI	FI	/FI	NO	/NO	TO	/TO
50	AT	/AT	SI	/SI	FI	/FI	NO	/NO	TO	/TO
51	AT	/AT	SI	/SI	FI	/FI	NO	/NO	TO	/TO
52	AT	/AT	SI	/SI	FI	/FI	NO	/NO	TO	/TO
53	AT	/AT	SI	/SI	FI	/FI	NO	/NO	TO	/TO
54	AT	/AT	SI	/SI	FI	/FI	NO	/NO	TO	/TO
55	AT	/AT	SI	/SI	FI	/FI	NO	/NO	TO	/TO
56	AT	/AT	SI	/SI	FI	/FI	NO	/NO	TO	/TO
57	AT	/AT	SI	/SI	FI	/FI	NO	/NO	TO	/TO
58	AT	/AT	SI	/SI	FI	/FI	NO	/NO	TO	/TO
59	AT	/AT	SI	/SI	FI	/FI	NO	/NO	TO	/TO
60	AT	/AT	SI	/SI	FI	/FI	NO	/NO	TO	/TO

(Continued)

WORKSHEET FOR STRUCTURED OBSERVATION OF ACADEMIC AND PLAY SETTINGS
Note that each of the following worksheets is a reduced version and needs to be enlarged to fill an 8½-by-11-inch page.

1

Name: _____

Date: _____

FILL IN THE EMPTY BOXES

P	V	R	N	O	Z	B	U	H	X
1	2	3	4	5	6	7	8	9	10

V	P	Z	O	H	R	B	Z	N	X	U	R	Z	V

R	O	B	H	P	V	N	Z	U	X	R	U	Z	X

N	H	O	X	P	Z	R	B	H	P	V	R	U	B

O	X	Z	V	B	U	X	P	O	N	B	R	H	P

Z	P	B	R	U	V	N	Z	H	X	P	O	B	N

B	V	U	N	H	P	R	X	Z	H	U	V	N	X

U	R	H	O	X	P	Z	B	U	X	H	N	O	Z

2

FILL IN THE EMPTY BOXES

@	%	#	*	$	!	¢	=	?	+
1	2	3	4	5	6	7	8	9	10

$	¢	#	@	+	=	!	*	%	?	*	@	+	$

=	%	$	!	¢	#	?	!	@	+	*	?	%	#

$	%	+	¢	@	%	#	!	?	=	!	¢	@	*

=	$	#	*	¢	+	?	=	!	%	+	=	¢	#

@	+	$	*	=	$	#	%	+	?	!	¢	#	@

¢	+	=	%	@	?	!	$	*	#	?	%	@	=

+	¢	#	*	!	$	+	!	%	@	#	=	?	*

3

MARK OUT ALL OF THE A'S THAT YOU SEE

G K A B P L A

T R C A L J V A A L W Q P F

Q W R A N C K A F W T D V P

O E X S H A W Z N L P D A I

K A P T A D W Q L H N B F A

G F A B K Y U S A D A C D F

A J X W N D A N W A C Y S L

T H X A M V D E A H L I A N

F G A D R A U O P Q S A D R

P K T A Y D R A T A W N A A

J A G N U S R T A N C A R U

4

MARK OUT ALL OF THE H'S THAT YOU SEE

K J Y H U P N

U R E C N H T R S U N G A J

H H M W S T R H O Y T H K P

R D H S W P O U H R D G H F

N H I L S H B D V M H X A T

L S Y C H W M H D N S X J A

F D C A D G S Y T J B A F G

A F V N H L Q W D A T P A K

I A D P L N Z W A H S X B O

T Y J H L Y E S E L S N E O

Y U I R F G N M B C V D H H

(Continued)

5

FILL IN THE EMPTY BOXES

R	X	S	U	Z	Q	T	E	G	H
1	2	3	4	5	6	7	8	9	10

U	E	R	G	X	H	G	T	S	Q	E	Z	T	H

X	E	U	Z	R	T	S	X	Q	H	R	G	Z	Q

S	Z	R	H	Q	T	U	X	G	S	E	U	R	T

E	S	X	G	Q	U	H	Z	T	H	U	R	E	Z

S	X	E	Q	G	R	T	Z	U	H	G	X	Q	S

E	T	H	X	R	U	Q	G	S	Z	S	H	E	X

Q	U	R	T	G	Z	X	H	E	S	T	G	R	Z

6

FILL IN THE EMPTY BOXES

Q	W	R	T	Y	P	S	D	F	G
1	2	3	4	5	6	7	8	9	10

T	D	Q	F	W	G	F	S	R	P	D	Y	S	G

W	D	T	Y	Q	S	R	W	P	G	Q	F	Y	P

R	Y	Q	G	P	S	T	W	F	R	D	T	Q	S

D	R	W	F	P	T	G	Y	S	G	T	Q	D	Y

R	W	D	P	F	Q	S	Y	T	G	F	W	P	R

D	S	G	W	Q	T	P	F	R	Y	R	G	D	W

P	T	Q	S	F	Y	W	G	D	R	S	F	Q	Y

7

MARK OUT ALL OF THE 4'S THAT YOU SEE

2 5 6 8 4 3 0 4

4 5 6 8 4 4 9 0 3 1 5 4 6 7

6 7 3 2 4 8 1 4 0 9 8 5 4 4

7 5 4 6 8 4 9 0 7 4 5 7 3 2

4 4 9 8 0 6 4 5 7 3 7 3 7 4

3 7 5 4 8 0 1 2 4 4 4 7 5 4

2 3 7 5 6 8 9 0 7 5 6 8 9 0

5 8 9 4 6 5 2 1 0 3 0 9 8 4

5 7 6 8 9 0 1 2 3 7 5 8 9 0

4 6 5 7 4 8 9 0 3 2 7 1 6 9

0 9 2 3 6 4 7 8 1 4 5 6 2 9

8

MARK OUT ALL OF THE 3'S THAT YOU SEE

3 7 1 9 0 3 2 5

3 2 9 6 4 0 1 3 8 4 3 9 0 2

7 3 5 2 9 7 6 4 5 3 1 2 5 4

0 5 7 8 3 1 4 2 4 6 8 7 3 5

9 5 2 8 0 4 3 7 4 1 3 6 0 5

6 8 3 3 5 1 8 5 3 9 2 9 4 3

9 4 3 5 2 3 6 6 3 9 0 1 9 4

8 4 1 0 6 4 3 2 7 3 9 0 6 4

7 5 2 7 3 9 0 8 3 1 5 3 6 7

6 2 3 1 6 8 9 3 5 7 2 6 0 4

5 3 6 1 7 9 2 5 4 3 0 7 3 8

(Continued)

Table D-2 *(Continued)*

9

FILL IN THE EMPTY BOXES

Y	O	I	C	D	J	T	B	L	S
1	2	3	4	5	6	7	8	9	10

I	D	T	B	L	O	Y	S	J	C	T	L	D	I

B	O	C	L	Y	S	O	J	C	B	J	Y	L	T

I	T	D	Y	L	S	O	J	C	B	J	Y	L	T

Y	D	O	J	I	S	C	T	L	B	I	Y	S	D

J	L	O	B	S	Y	I	L	T	D	C	B	J	O

D	T	S	L	Y	J	I	C	B	O	L	I	Y	S

L	C	Y	D	J	I	B	S	O	T	C	D	O	B

10

FILL IN THE EMPTY BOXES

B	C	N	R	Z	J	P	K	A	G
1	2	3	4	5	6	7	8	9	10

P	J	N	R	C	G	A	B	Z	K	N	C	J	P

R	G	K	C	A	B	J	P	Z	N	G	R	K	B

P	N	J	A	C	B	G	Z	K	R	Z	A	C	N

A	J	B	Z	P	B	K	N	C	R	P	A	G	J

Z	K	G	B	R	P	A	C	N	J	K	R	Z	G

J	N	B	C	A	Z	P	K	R	G	C	P	A	B

C	K	A	J	Z	P	R	B	G	N	K	J	G	R

Source: Adapted from Roberts, Milich, and Loney (1984). Worksheets reproduced, with changes in notation, with permission from Mary Ann Roberts.

Table D-3
ADHD Questionnaire

ADHD QUESTIONNAIRE

Child's name: _____   Name of person filling out form: _____

Age: _____   Grade: _____   School: _____   Date: _____

Directions: Please read each item and check either Y ("Yes") or N ("No"). If you check "Yes," please answer the questions in the last three columns for that item. Be sure to indicate whether you are using years or months for your answers.

Behavior	*Check one*	*How old was the child when you first noticed the behavior?*	*How long has the behavior persisted?*	*In what settings does the child show this behavior (such as home, playground, school, or work)?*
1. Often fails to give close attention to details or makes careless mistakes in schoolwork, work, or other activities	☐ Y ☐ N			
2. Often has difficulty sustaining attention in tasks or play activities	☐ Y ☐ N			
3. Often does not seem to listen when spoken to directly	☐ Y ☐ N			
4. Often does not follow through on instructions and fails to finish schoolwork, chores, or duties in the workplace	☐ Y ☐ N			
5. Often has difficulty organizing tasks and activities	☐ Y ☐ N			
6. Often avoids, dislikes, or is reluctant to engage in tasks that require sustained mental effort (such as schoolwork or homework)	☐ Y ☐ N			
7. Often loses things necessary for tasks or activities, such as toys, school assignments, pencils, or books	☐ Y ☐ N			
8. Often is easily distracted by extraneous stimuli	☐ Y ☐ N			
9. Often is forgetful in daily activities	☐ Y ☐ N			
10. Often fidgets with hands or feet or squirms in seat	☐ Y ☐ N			
11. Often leaves seat in classroom or in other situations in which remaining seated is expected	☐ Y ☐ N			
12. Often runs about or climbs excessively in situations in which it is inappropriate	☐ Y ☐ N			
13. Often has difficulty playing or engaging in leisure activities quietly	☐ Y ☐ N			
14. Often is "on the go" or acts as if "driven by a motor"	☐ Y ☐ N			
15. Often talks excessively	☐ Y ☐ N			
16. Often blurts out answers before questions have been completed	☐ Y ☐ N			
17. Often has difficulty awaiting turn	☐ Y ☐ N			
18. Often interrupts or intrudes on others (e.g., butts into conversations or games)	☐ Y ☐ N			

Source: Adapted from American Psychiatric Association (2000).

Table D-4
***DSM-IV–TR* Checklist for Attention-Deficit/Hyperactivity Disorder**

	Symptoms	Check one

A.

1. Inattention

   a. Often fails to give close attention to details or makes careless mistakes in schoolwork, work, or other activities   ☐ Y   ☐ N

   b. Often has difficulty sustaining attention in tasks or play activities   ☐ Y   ☐ N

   c. Often does not seem to listen when spoken to directly   ☐ Y   ☐ N

   d. Often does not follow through on instructions and fails to finish schoolwork, chores, or duties in the workplace   ☐ Y   ☐ N

   e. Often has difficulty organizing tasks and activities   ☐ Y   ☐ N

   f. Often avoids, dislikes, or is reluctant to engage in tasks that require sustained mental effort (such as schoolwork or homework)   ☐ Y   ☐ N

   g. Often loses things necessary for tasks or activities, such as toys, school assignments, pencils, or books   ☐ Y   ☐ N

   h. Often is easily distracted by extraneous stimuli   ☐ Y   ☐ N

   i. Often is forgetful in daily activities   ☐ Y   ☐ N

2. Hyperactivity-Impulsivity

Hyperactivity

   a. Often fidgets with hands or feet or squirms in seat   ☐ Y   ☐ N

   b. Often leaves seat in classroom or in other situations in which remaining seated is expected   ☐ Y   ☐ N

   c. Often runs about or climbs excessively in situations in which it is inappropriate   ☐ Y   ☐ N

   d. Often has difficulty playing or engaging in leisure activities quietly   ☐ Y   ☐ N

   e. Often is "on the go" or acts as if "driven by a motor"   ☐ Y   ☐ N

   f. Often talks excessively   ☐ Y   ☐ N

Impulsivity

   g. Often blurts out answers before questions have been completed   ☐ Y   ☐ N

   h. Often has difficulty awaiting turn   ☐ Y   ☐ N

   i. Often interrupts or intrudes on others (e.g., butts into conversations or games)   ☐ Y   ☐ N

B. Some hyperactive-impulsive or inattentive symptoms that caused impairment were present before age 7 years.   ☐ Y   ☐ N

C. Some impairment from the symptoms is present in two or more settings (e.g., at school [or work] and at home).   ☐ Y   ☐ N

D. There is clear evidence of clinically significant impairment in social, academic, or occupational functioning.   ☐ Y   ☐ N

E. The symptoms do not occur exclusively during the course of a pervasive developmental disorder, schizophrenia, or other psychotic disorder and are not better accounted for by another mental disorder (e.g., mood disorder, anxiety disorder, dissociative disorder, or personality disorder).   ☐ Y   ☐ N

(Continued)

Table D-4 *(Continued)*		

Diagnostic Criteria	Check one	
Attention-Deficit/Hyperactivity Disorder, Combined Type		
a. Six or more items from numbers 1 and 2 present for at least 6 months to a degree that is maladaptive and inconsistent with developmental level	☐ Y	☐ N
b. Some items from numbers 1 or 2 present before age 7 years	☐ Y	☐ N
c. Some items from numbers 1 or 2 present in two or more settings	☐ Y	☐ N
d. Clear evidence of clinically significant impairment in social, academic, or occupational functioning	☐ Y	☐ N
e. Symptoms not occurring exclusively during the course of a pervasive developmental disorder, schizophrenia, or other psychotic disorder and not better accounted for by another mental disorder	☐ Y	☐ N
f. Items a through e in this part checked *Yes*—criteria fulfilled for a diagnosis of attention-deficit/hyperactivity disorder, combined type	☐ Y	☐ N
Attention-Deficit/Hyperactivity Disorder, Predominantly Inattentive Type		
a. Six or more items from number 1 present for at least 6 months to a degree that is maladaptive and inconsistent with developmental level	☐ Y	☐ N
b. Six or more items from number 2 *not* present for at least 6 months	☐ Y	☐ N
c. Some items from number 1 present before age 7 years	☐ Y	☐ N
d. Some items from number 1 present in two or more settings	☐ Y	☐ N
e. Clear evidence of clinically significant impairment in social, academic, or occupational functioning	☐ Y	☐ N
f. Symptoms not occurring exclusively during the course of a pervasive developmental disorder, schizophrenia, or other psychotic disorder and not better accounted for by another mental disorder	☐ Y	☐ N
g. Items a through f in this part checked *Yes*—criteria fulfilled for a diagnosis of attention-deficit/hyperactivity disorder, predominantly inattentive type	☐ Y	☐ N
Attention-Deficit/Hyperactivity Disorder, Predominantly Hyperactive-Impulsive Type		
a. Six or more items from number 2 present for at least 6 months to a degree that is maladaptive and inconsistent with developmental level	☐ Y	☐ N
b. Six or more items from number 1 *not* present for at least 6 months	☐ Y	☐ N
c. Some items from number 2 present before age 7 years	☐ Y	☐ N
d. Some items from number 2 present in two or more settings	☐ Y	☐ N
e. Clear evidence of clinically significant impairment in social, academic, or occupational functioning	☐ Y	☐ N
f. Symptoms not occurring exclusively during the course of a pervasive developmental disorder, schizophrenia, or other psychotic disorder and not better accounted for by another mental disorder	☐ Y	☐ N
g. Items a through f in this part checked *Yes*—criteria fulfilled for a diagnosis of attention-deficit/hyperactivity disorder, predominantly hyperactive-impulsive type	☐ Y	☐ N

Source: Based on *DSM-IV–TR* (American Psychiatric Association, 2000).

APPENDIX E

TABLES FOR AUTISTIC DISORDER

Table E-1
Observation Form for Recording Symptoms That May Reflect Autistic Disorder and Positive Behaviors

OBSERVATION FORM FOR RECORDING SYMPTOMS
THAT MAY REFLECT AUTISTIC DISORDER AND POSITIVE BEHAVIORS

Child's name: _____   Examiner's name: _____

Age: _____   Grade: _____   School: _____   Date: _____

Direction: Place an X in a box to indicate that the behavior was observed during that period. For "Other," write in the name of the behavior.

				Period						
Sensory Modulation	1	2	3	4	5	6	7	8	9	*Tot.*
1. Bangs ear										
2. Grinds teeth										
3. Looks at hands										
4. Stares										
5. Rubs surfaces										
6. Sniffs objects										
7. Sniffs hands										
8. Switches light on and off										
9. Locks and unlocks door										
10. Spins objects for a long time										
11. Other:										
12. Other:										
Motility										
1. Flaps hands										
2. Turns head often										
3. Flicks or wiggles finger										
4. Grimaces										
5. Whirls or spins										
6. Walks on toes										
7. Darts or lunges										
8. Engages in peculiar postures										
9. Rocks body										
10. Jumps repetitively										
11. Runs aimlessly										
12. Bangs head										
13. Taps back of hand often										
14 Other:										
15. Other:										
General Behavior										
1. Mouths objects										
2. Claps hands										
3. Mouths hands										
4. Lacks appropriate facial expressions										
5. Other:										
6. Other:										
Relation to Examiner										
1. Makes no eye contact										
2. Does not smile										
3. Does not respond to his or her name when called										
4. Turns face away when called										
5. Clings in an infantile way										

(Continued)

Table E-1 (Continued)										
	Period									Tot.
Relation to Examiner (continued)	1	2	3	4	5	6	7	8	9	
6. Insists on being held										
7. Makes inappropriate attempts at contact										
8. Ignores examiner										
9. Asks the same questions repeatedly										
10. Other:										
11. Other:										
Relation to Toys										
1. Uses toys inappropriately										
2. Uses toys ritualistically										
3. Spins toys inappropriately										
4. Orders and reorders toys continuously										
5. Lets toys fall out of hand										
6. Throws toys inappropriately										
7. Ignores toys										
8. Uses toys in a restricted manner with few combinations and in few constructive ways										
9. Other:										
10. Other:										
Language										
1. Is mute										
2. Babbles										
3. Shouts										
4. Shows immediate echolalia										
5. Shows delayed echolalia										
6. Reverses pronouns										
7. Uses words in a peculiar fashion										
8. Has difficulty initiating or sustaining conversation										
9. Gives tangential details when answering questions										
10. Other:										
11. Other:										
Positive Behavior										
1. Shows examiner a toy										
2. Asks examiner to play with him or her										
3. Asks examiner questions										
4. Asks examiner for help										
5. Engages in pretend play[a]										
6. Takes turns rolling or throwing the ball										
7. Other:										
8. Other:										

[a] Examples are pretending to talk on the phone, fly the helicopter, cook, or feed the doll.

Note. Tot. = Total.

Source: Adapted from Adrien et al. (1987) and Filipek et al. (1999).

Table E-2
Childhood Autism Rating Scale (CARS)

Scale	Rating			
	1	*2*	*3*	*4*
	Age appropriate	*Mildly abnormal*	*Moderately abnormal*	*Severely abnormal*
I. Relationships with people	Age-appropriate degrees of shyness, guardedness, negativism	Some lack of eye contact; some negativism or avoidance; excessive shyness; some lack of responsiveness to the examiner	Considerable aloofness; intensive intrusion may be necessary to get a response, contact is not normally initiated by child	Intense aloofness, avoidance, obliviousness, child seldom responds to examiner; only the most intensive intervention produces a response
II. Imitation (verbal and motoric)	Age-appropriate imitation (both verbal and motoric)	Child imitates most of the time; occasionally prodding may be required or imitation may be delayed	Child imitates only part of the time; great persistence is required on the part of the examiner	Child seldom, if ever, imitates either verbally or motorically
III. Affect	Age- and situation-appropriate affective responses—child shows pleasure, displeasure, and interest through changes in facial expression, posture, and manner	Some lack of appropriate responsiveness to changes in affective stimuli; affect may be somewhat inhibited or excessive	Definite signs of inappropriate affect; reactions are quite inhibited or excessive or are often unrelated to the stimulus	Extremely rigid perseveration of affect; responses are seldom appropriate to the situation and are extremely resistant to modification by the examiner
IV. Use of body	Age-appropriate use and awareness of body	Minimal peculiarities in body use and awareness—some stereotyped movements, clumsiness, and lack of coordination	Moderate signs of dysfunction—peculiar finger or body posturing, examination of body, self-directed aggression, rocking, spinning, finger-wiggling, toe-walking	Extreme or pervasive occurrence of those functions listed in third column
V. Relation to non-human objects	Age-appropriate interest in, use of, and exploration of objects	Mild lack of interest in materials or mildly age-inappropriate use of materials—infantile mouthing of objects, banging of materials, fascination with materials that squeak, turning lights on and off	Significant lack of interest in most objects or peculiar and obvious preoccupation with repetitive use of objects—e.g., picking at objects with fingernails, spinning wheels, becoming fascinated with one small part	Severely inappropriate interest in, use of, and exploration of objects—extreme or pervasive occurrence of those functions listed in third column; child is very difficult to distract
VI. Adaptation to environmental change	Age-appropriate responses to change	Some evidence of resistance to environmental changes—staying with an object or activity or persisting in same response pattern; child can be distracted	Active resistance to change in activities, with signs of irritability and frustration; child is difficult to distract when intervention is attempted	Severe reactions to change that are extremely resistant to modification; child may engage in a tantrum if change is insisted upon

(Continued)

Table E-2 *(Continued)*

Scale	Rating			
	1	*2*	*3*	*4*
	Age appropriate	*Mildly abnormal*	*Moderately abnormal*	*Severely abnormal*
VII. Visual responsiveness	Age-appropriate visual responses used in an integrated way with other sensory systems	Child must be reminded occasionally to look at materials; some preoccupation with mirror image; some avoidance of eye contact; some staring into space; some fascination with lights	Child must be reminded frequently to look at what he or she is doing, likes to look at shiny objects, makes little eye contact even when forced, looks "through" people, frequently stares into space	Pervasive visual avoidance of objects and people; bizarre use of visual cues
VIII. Auditory responsiveness	Age-appropriate auditory responses used in an integrated way with other sensory systems	Some lack of response to auditory stimuli or to particular sounds; responses may be delayed; stimuli may occasionally have to be repeated; child is hypersensitive to or distracted by extraneous noises	Inconsistent responses to auditory stimuli; stimuli may have to be repeated several times before child responds; child is hypersensitive to certain sounds (e.g., very easily startled, covers ears)	Pervasive auditory avoidance, regardless of type of stimulus, or extreme hypersensitivity
IX. Near receptor responsiveness	Normal response to pain, appropriate to intensity; normal tactual and olfactory exploration, but not to the exclusion of other forms of exploration	Some lack of appropriate response to pain or evidence of mild preoccupation with tactual exploration, smelling, tasting, etc.; some infantile mouthing of objects	Moderate lack of appropriate response to pain or evidence of moderate preoccupation with tactual exploration, smelling, tasting, etc.	Excessive preoccupation with tactual exploration (mouthing, licking, feeling, or rubbing) for sensory rather than functional experience; pain may be either ignored or met with gross overreaction
X. Anxiety reaction	Age- and situation-appropriate reactions—reactions are not prolonged	Mild anxiety reactions	Moderate anxiety reactions	Severe anxiety reactions—child may not settle down during the entire session or may be obviously fearful, withdrawn, etc.
XI. Verbal communication	Age-appropriate speech	Overall retardation of speech; most speech is meaningful, but it may include remnants of echolalia	Absence of speech or a mixture of some meaningful speech with some inappropriate speech (e.g., echolalia, jargon)	Severely abnormal speech; virtual absence of intelligible words or peculiar and bizarre use of more recognizable language

(Continued)

Table E-2 *(Continued)*

	Rating			
	1	*2*	*3*	*4*
Scale	*Age appropriate*	*Mildly abnormal*	*Moderately abnormal*	*Severely abnormal*
XII. Nonverbal communication	Age-appropriate nonverbal communication	Overall retardation of nonverbal communication; communication may consist of simple or vague responses, such as pointing to or reaching for what is wanted	Absence of nonverbal communication—child does not use or respond to nonverbal communication	Peculiar, bizarre, and generally incomprehensible nonverbal communication
XIII. Activity level (motility patterns)	Normal activity level—child is neither hyperactive nor hypoactive	Child is mildly restless or is somewhat slow to move about, but generally can be controlled; activity level interferes only slightly with performance	Child is quite active and hard to restrain, with a driven quality to activity, or quite inactive and slow-moving; examiner must either exert control frequently or exert a great effort to get a response	Extremely abnormal activity level—child is either driven or apathetic; child is very difficult to manage or to get to respond to anything; almost constant control by an adult is required
XIV. Intellectual functioning	Normal intellectual functioning—no evidence of retardation	Mildly abnormal intellectual functioning—skills appear fairly evenly retarded across all assessed areas	Moderately abnormal intellectual functioning—some skills appear retarded and others are at or very near age level (hints of potential)	Severely abnormal intellectual functioning—some skills appear retarded and others are above age level or are unusual
XV. General impression	No autism	Minimal or mild autism	Moderate signs of autism	Maximum or extreme signs of autism

Source: This table is a condensed tabular presentation of the Childhood Autism Rating Scale, which is described in the unpublished appendix that accompanies Schopler, Reichler, DeVellis, and Daly (1980). See Schopler, Reichler, and Renner (1986) for a more current version of the CARS. Permission to reprint this condensed version of the CARS was given by E. Schopler.

Table E-3
Checklist for Autism in Toddlers (CHAT)

CHECKLIST FOR AUTISM IN TODDLERS

Sections	Check one

Section A: Ask the parent the following questions.

1. Does [name of child] enjoy being swung or bounced on your knee? ☐ Y ☐ N
2. Does [name of child] take an interest in other children? ☐ Y ☐ N
3. Does [name of child] like climbing on things, such as stairs? ☐ Y ☐ N
4. Does [name of child] enjoy playing peek-a-boo or hide-and-seek? ☐ Y ☐ N
5. Does [name of child] ever pretend, for example, to feed [himself or herself] or feed a doll with milk and cookies from an empty cup and plate? ☐ Y ☐ N
6. Does [name of child] ever use [his or her] index finger to point, to ask for something? ☐ Y ☐ N
7. Does [name of child] ever use [his or her] index finger to point, to indicate interest in something? ☐ Y ☐ N
8. Can [name of child] play properly with small toys—such as cars or bricks—without just mouthing, fiddling, or dropping them? ☐ Y ☐ N
9. Does [name of child] ever bring objects over to you to show you something? ☐ Y ☐ N

Section B: Answer the following questions based on your own observation of and interaction with the child.

1. Get the child's attention, then point across the room at an interesting object and say, "Oh look! There's a [name of toy]!" Watch the child's face. Does the child look across to see what you are pointing at?[a] ☐ Y ☐ N
2. Get the child's attention, then give the child a miniature toy cup and teapot and say, "Can you feed the doll or give the doll a drink?" Does the child pretend to feed the doll or give the doll a drink?[b] ☐ Y ☐ N
3. Say to the child, "Where's the light?" or "Show me the light." Does the child point with his or her index finger at the light?[c] ☐ Y ☐ N
4. Get the child's attention, put 8 blocks before the child, and say "See these blocks. I want you to build a tower with as many blocks as you can. Go ahead." Can the child build a tower of blocks? If so, with how many blocks? (Number of blocks: _____) ☐ Y ☐ N
5. During the evaluation, has the child made eye contact with you? ☐ Y ☐ N

[a] Before you record Yes on this item, ensure that the child has not simply looked at your hand, but actually looked at the object you are pointing at.
[b] If you can elicit an example of pretending in some other game, score a Yes on this item.
[c] If child does not understand the word "light," ask about the teddy bear or some other unreachable object. For Yes to be recorded on this item, the child must have looked up at your face around the time of pointing.
Note. The CHAT is designed to be administered to children who are 18 months of age.
Source: Adapted from Baron-Cohen, Allen, and Gillberg (1992).

AD QUESTIONNAIRE

Child's name: _____   Examiner's name: _____

Age: _____   Grade: _____   School: _____   Date: _____

Directions: Please read each item and check either Y ("Yes") or N ("No"). If you check "Yes," please answer the questions in the last two columns for that item. Be sure to indicate whether you are using years or months for your answers.

Behavior	*Check one*	*How old was the child when you first noticed the behavior?*	*How long has the behavior persisted?*
1. Was stiff and rigid when I held or hugged him or her or went limp when I held him or her	☐ Y ☐ N		
2. Did not play games like pat-a-cake or peek-a-boo, or wave bye-bye, or smile when I smiled at him or her	☐ Y ☐ N		
3. Has difficulty making friends	☐ Y ☐ N		
4. Is not interested in making friends	☐ Y ☐ N		
5. Does not spontaneously share experiences with other people	☐ Y ☐ N		
6. Prefers to play alone rather than with other children	☐ Y ☐ N		
7. Ignores people who are trying to interact with him or her or does not participate in cooperative play	☐ Y ☐ N		
8. Does not seem to understand how others are feeling or seems to live in a world of his or her own	☐ Y ☐ N		
9. Did not babble	☐ Y ☐ N		
10. Does not speak	☐ Y ☐ N		
11. Speaks, but has difficulty starting a conversation with people	☐ Y ☐ N		
12. Speaks, but has difficulty taking turns speaking	☐ Y ☐ N		
13. Has peculiar patterns of speech (such as odd tone or volume), repeats other people's phrases over and over again, or speaks in a repetitive and stereotyped way	☐ Y ☐ N		
14. Speaks, but confuses the word "I" with the word "he" or "she" or makes up new words that do not make sense	☐ Y ☐ N		
15. Does not engage in imaginative play or use toys in pretend play	☐ Y ☐ N		
16. Plays with toys in a rigid way	☐ Y ☐ N		
17. Has strong attachments to unusual objects (such as sticks or pieces of paper) rather than to teddy bears or dolls	☐ Y ☐ N		
18. Has a narrow and intense focus on a particular topic (for example, train schedules) or skill (for example, memorizing phone numbers)	☐ Y ☐ N		
19. Is preoccupied with things being done in a certain way (for example, insists on drinking from the same cup or plays with toys in the same way each time) and becomes upset if changes are made in his or her daily routines	☐ Y ☐ N		
20. Becomes upset if things don't look right (such as a stain on a table cloth), or if something is out of place, or if there is a change in the way things are arranged or done	☐ Y ☐ N		
21. Does the same thing over and over again with his or her body (such as rocking, clapping hands, flapping arms, running aimlessly, walking on toes, or doing other odd movements)	☐ Y ☐ N		
22. Does the same thing over and over again with objects (such as opening and closing doors, flipping the tops of trash cans, turning a light switch on and off, flicking strings, transferring water from one container to another, or spinning objects)	☐ Y ☐ N		
23. Is overly interested in looking at small objects or parts of objects	☐ Y ☐ N		
24. Is preoccupied with parts of objects	☐ Y ☐ N		

Table E-5
Checklist of Signs Obtained from the Case History That Indicate a Child May Have an Autistic Disorder

Signs	Check one	
Social Interaction		
1. Child does not smile socially.	☐ Y	☐ N
2. Child is not interested in being held.	☐ Y	☐ N
3. Child is not interested in playing peek-a-boo games.	☐ Y	☐ N
4. Child prefers to play alone.	☐ Y	☐ N
5. Child fails to follow mother around.	☐ Y	☐ N
6. Child has an expressionless face.	☐ Y	☐ N
7. Child has poor eye contact.	☐ Y	☐ N
8. Child is in his or her own world.	☐ Y	☐ N
9. Child tunes parents out.	☐ Y	☐ N
10. Child is not interested in other children.	☐ Y	☐ N
11. Child has lost social skills.	☐ Y	☐ N
Communication		
1. Child does not respond to his or her name.	☐ Y	☐ N
2. Child cannot tell parent what he or she wants.	☐ Y	☐ N
3. Child's language is delayed.	☐ Y	☐ N
4. Child does not follow directions.	☐ Y	☐ N
5. Child does not respond to sounds or names, and deafness is suspected.	☐ Y	☐ N
6. Child seems to hear sometimes but not at other times.	☐ Y	☐ N
7. Child does not point or wave bye-bye.	☐ Y	☐ N
8. Child used to say a few words but does not now.	☐ Y	☐ N
9. Child did not babble by 12 months.	☐ Y	☐ N
10. Child did not gesture (e.g., pointing, waving bye-bye) by 12 months.	☐ Y	☐ N
11. Child had no single words by 16 months.	☐ Y	☐ N
12. Child had no 2-word spontaneous phrases (not just echolalic) by 24 months.	☐ Y	☐ N
13. Child displays immediate echolalia.	☐ Y	☐ N
14. Child displays delayed echolalia.	☐ Y	☐ N
15. Child has stereotyped and repetitive use of language or idiosyncratic language.	☐ Y	☐ N
Restricted Repertoire		
1. Child has tantrums.	☐ Y	☐ N
2. Child is hyperactive.	☐ Y	☐ N
3. Child is uncooperative.	☐ Y	☐ N
4. Child is oppositional.	☐ Y	☐ N
5. Child does not know how to play with toys.	☐ Y	☐ N
6. Child gets stuck on things over and over.	☐ Y	☐ N
7. Child toe-walks.	☐ Y	☐ N
8. Child has unusual attachments to objects.	☐ Y	☐ N
9. Child lines things up obsessively.	☐ Y	☐ N
10. Child has odd movement patterns.	☐ Y	☐ N
11. Child is hypersensitive to taste.	☐ Y	☐ N
12. Child is hyposenstive to cold or pain.	☐ Y	☐ N
13. Child is oversensitive to certain textures or sounds.	☐ Y	☐ N

Source: Adapted from Filipek et al. (1999) and Stone, MacLean, and Hogan (1995).

Table E-6
DSM-IV–TR Checklist for Autistic Disorder

Symptoms	Check one	
A.		
1. Social Interaction		
a. Marked impairment in the use of multiple nonverbal behaviors	☐ Y	☐ N
b. Failure to develop peer relations	☐ Y	☐ N
c. Lack of spontaneous seeking to share enjoyment, interests, or achievements with other people	☐ Y	☐ N
d. Lack of social or emotional reciprocity	☐ Y	☐ N
2. Communication		
a. Delay in or total lack of spoken language	☐ Y	☐ N
b. Impairment in initiating or sustaining a conversation	☐ Y	☐ N
c. Stereotyped and repetitive use of language or idiosyncratic language	☐ Y	☐ N
d. Lack of varied, spontaneous make-believe play or social imitative play	☐ Y	☐ N
3. Restricted Repertoire		
a. Stereotyped and restricted pattern of interests	☐ Y	☐ N
b. Inflexible adherence to specific, nonfunctional routines or rituals	☐ Y	☐ N
c. Stereotyped and repetitive motor mannerisms	☐ Y	☐ N
d. Persistent preoccupation with parts of objects	☐ Y	☐ N
B. Delay or abnormal functioning must be present in at least one of the following three areas, with onset prior to age 3 years:		
a. Social interaction	☐ Y	☐ N
b. Language used in social communications	☐ Y	☐ N
c. Symbolic or imaginative play	☐ Y	☐ N
C. The disturbance is not better accounted for by Rett's disorder or childhood disintegrative disorder.	☐ Y	☐ N
Diagnostic Criteria		
a. Six or more items from numbers 1, 2, and 3	☐ Y	☐ N
b. At least two items from number 1	☐ Y	☐ N
c. At least one item from number 2	☐ Y	☐ N
d. At least one item from number 3	☐ Y	☐ N
e. Delay or abnormal functioning in at least one area covered in numbers 1, 2, and 3, with onset prior to age 3 years	☐ Y	☐ N
f. Not better accounted for by Rett's disorder or childhood disintegrative disorder	☐ Y	☐ N
g. Diagnostic criteria a through f checked *Yes*—criteria fulfilled for a diagnosis of autistic disorder	☐ Y	☐ N

Source: Based on *DSM-IV–TR* (American Psychiatric Association, 2000).

APPENDIX F

MISCELLANEOUS TABLES

Table F-1
Sources for Obtaining Highly Structured Interviews

Child Adolescent Schedule (CAS)[a]

Kay Hodges, Ph.D.
Eastern Michigan University
Department of Psychology
537 Mark Jefferson
Ypsilanti, MI 48197

Child and Adolescent Psychiatric Assessment (CAPA): Version 4.2—Child Version[a]

Adrian Angold, MRC Psych
Developmental Epidemiology Program
Duke Medical Center
P.O. Box 3454
Durham, NC 27710

Diagnostic Interview for Children and Adolescents—Revised (DICA-R) 8.0[a]

Wendy Reich (Ed.), Ph.D.
Washington University
School of Medicine, Department of Psychiatry
4940 Children's Place
St. Louis, MO 63110

Diagnostic Interview Schedule for Children (DISC-IV)[a]

David Shaffer, M.D.
Division of Child Psychiatry
New York State Psychiatric Institute
722 W. 168th Street
New York, NY 10032

Revised Schedule for Affective Disorders and Schizophrenia for School Aged Children: Present and Lifetime Version (K-SADS-PL)

Joan Kaufman, Ph.D.
Western Psychiatric Institute and Clinic
University of Pittsburgh School of Medicine
3811 O'Hara Street
Pittsburgh, PA 15213

Schedule for Affective Disorders & Schizophrenia for School-Age Children (K-SADS-IVR)

Paul Ambrosini, M.D.
Allegheny University of the Health Sciences
2900 Queen Lane
Philadelphia, PA 19129

Schedule for Affective Disorders and Schizophrenia for School-Age Children, Epidemological Version 5 (K-SADS-E5)[b]

Helen Orvaschel, Ph.D.
NOVA Southeastern University
Center for Psychological Studies
3301 College Avenue
Fort Lauderdale, FL 33314

[a] Parent version also available.
[b] Parent and child versions are contained within the same interview.
Source: Adapted and updated from Hodges (1993).

Table F-2
Abbreviated Coding System for Observing Children's Play

I. **Solitary Play:** Target child plays alone, makes no attempt to communicate with other children, and is centered on his or her own activity.

  a. *Functional Play.* Examples: Target child makes faces and dances while watching self in mirror, lies on back in the middle of the floor, spins truck wheels with fingers, or runs around by himself or herself in a circle.

  b. *Constructive Play.* Examples: Target child pushes car alone in middle of floor along a track, plays alone with puzzle pieces of people and places them in cars, plays alone with robot and punches button on robot, builds building using blocks, or constructs an object with Legos.

  c. *Dramatic Play.* Examples: Target child plays alone with puppets, taking on the role of each puppet and making them talk to each other. Target child plays alone in housekeeping area, talks to himself or herself, and takes on role of mother or father while feeding and dressing dolls.

  d. *Games-with-Rules.* Example: Target child sits alone and plays a board game, obviously adhering to the game rules.

II. **Parallel Play:** Target child plays in close proximity to another child, but each child works on his or her own task.

  a. *Functional Play.* Examples: Target child sits at a table with another child; both are drawing, but there is no interaction between the two children. Target child and another child push button, open door, and ring bells on busy box, but they do not attend to each other's actions as they play.

  b. *Constructive Play.* Examples: Target child and another child paint together at a table, target child tells the other child that he or she is making a rainbow, and they trade crayons. Target child and another child sit at a table, and each makes his or her own construction out of Legos. Target child and another child sit at a table working on a puzzle, with no interaction between the two children.

  c. *Dramatic Play.* Examples: Target child and another child are close to one another and play with puppets, but target child takes on the role of the puppet and the other child plays separately by just manipulating the puppet.

  d. *Games-with-Rules.* Examples: Target child and another child play on the same board game, but they do not play together. The target child plays according to the game rules, but the other child moves the board pieces in no organized manner.

III. **Group Play:** Child plays with another child or children. They borrow play things from each other or follow each other's actions.

  a. *Functional Play.* Example: Target child and another child are engaged in imitative behavior involving touching one another, smiling, and laughing.

  b. *Constructive Play.* Examples: (a) Target child and another child play with surprise box type toy. Target child pushes button and looks at the other child and laughs. The other child does the same. They continue to take turns. (b) Target child and the other child exchange objects or offer objects to one another. (c) Target child throws a ball and waits for the other child to retrieve it. (d) Target child and another child shovel sand into a truck and then dump the sand into a large pile.

  c. *Dramatic Play.* Examples: (a) Target child and another child pretend to order pizza. Target child is the customer, and the other child has a puppet who manages the restaurant. Target child gives his or her order. (b) Target child and another child are dressed in pretend clothes. Target child begins to leave area, and the other child says, "Don't go without your hat."

  d. *Games-with-Rules.* Example: Target child and another child play ball under a self-imposed, strict set of rules.

Note. Definitions are as follows:
  Functional Play: Child makes simple repetitive muscle movements with or without objects.
  Constructive Play: Child manipulates objects to construct or create something.
  Dramatic Play: Child uses imagery in play.
  Games-with-Rules: Child accepts prearranged rules to follow in games.
Source: Adapted from Guralnick and Groom (1988).

Table F-3
Social Competence Observation Schedule

Category	Description
Interacting with Peers	
1. Passively accepts aggression or domination from peer	Child allows another to boss, push, hit, or grab things from him or her without retaliation of any kind
2. Communicates in a positive way with peer	Child shows natural communication with peers—appears at ease and comfortable in the situation
3. Is involved in cooperative activity with peer	Child voluntarily becomes involved with one or more children in an activity not required by the teacher
4. Shows successful leadership activity	Child initiates activity and makes suggestions that are followed by peers
5. Bosses or bullies peer—verbal	Child tells others what or what not to do, commands others
6. Exhibits physical aggression against peer	Child engages in aggression involving actual physical contact
Interacting with Teacher	
7. Clings to teacher	Child constantly stays by teacher's side or, for example, holds on to teacher's hand or clothes
8. Tenses or withdraws in response to teacher's approach	Child tenses body or moves farther away when approached by teacher
9. Communicates feelings to teacher in positive way	Child makes a positive statement to the teacher that is not a suggestion related to classroom activities
10. Volunteers ideas or suggestions to teacher	Child makes suggestions or gives ideas during formal, teacher-directed classroom activities
11. Seeks attention of teacher while latter is interacting with another child	Child calls out to teacher, grabs teacher's arm, or performs similar actions when teacher is involved with another child
12. Exhibits physical aggression toward teacher	Child hits, kicks, or bites teacher
13. Seeks teacher attention—negative	Child uses inappropriate behavior to seek teacher's attention
14. Follows teacher request for help	Child follows teacher's directions willingly and immediately
15. Follows teacher suggestion regarding play activity	Child accepts and follows teacher's ideas or suggestions during informal, free activity
16. Exhibits other cooperative interactions with teacher	—
Child Is Alone	
17. Quietly listens to peer or teacher	Child is attentive to teacher while latter is giving instruction, reading a story, or performing a similar activity
18. Daydreams, stares into space, has blank look	Child has tuned out what is happening in the classroom, is unaware of what is going on, and looks sad
19. Puts things away carefully	—
20. Appears alone, confused, and bewildered	Child's face registers confusion; child appears not to understand or know how to organize or carry out an activity
21. Cries or screams—frightened	Child cries or screams from some emotion other than, for example, anger or humiliation
22. Wanders aimlessly	—
23. Engages in task in positive manner	Child is actively involved in carrying out task sanctioned by teacher; he or she is concentrating, alert, and interested
24. Engages in task in negative manner	Child resists instructions, destroys an object, or engages in similar negative behaviors
25. Throws temper tantrum	Child screams, kicks
26. Exhibits inappropriate verbal activity	Child expresses anger or frustration through words or gestures
27. Exhibits inappropriate gross motor activity	Child runs around room, throws objects, jumps, or performs similar inappropriate gross-motor activity
28. Exhibits other isolated negative behavior	—

Note. Item numbers for the factor scores are as follows: Factor I (Interest-Participation vs. Apathy-Withdrawal): 1, 2, 4, 7, 8, 9, 10, 17, 18, 19, 20, 21, 22, 28; Factor II (Cooperation-Compliance vs. Anger-Defiance): 3, 5, 6, 11, 12, 13, 14, 15, 16, 23, 24, 25, 26, 27. The following items are scored in a negative direction: 1, 5, 6, 7, 8, 11, 12, 13, 18, 20, 21, 22, 24, 25, 26, 27, 28.

This schedule was designed to parallel the two teacher-judgment measures developed by Martin Kohn (the Social Competence Scales and the Problem Checklist). For additional information about the schedule, see Ali Khan and R. D. Hoge, "A Teacher-Judgment Measure of Social Competence: Validity Data," *Journal of Consulting and Clinical Psychology*, 1983, *51*, 809–814.

Source: Reprinted, with changes in notation, by permission of R. D. Hoge.

Table F-4
Standard Scores for the Koppitz Developmental Scoring System

	Chronological age												
Errors	5-0 to 5-5	5-6 to 5-11	6-0 to 6-5	6-6 to 6-11	7-0 to 7-5	7-6 to 7-11	8-0 to 8-5	8-6 to 8-11	9-0 to 9-5	9-6 to 9-11	10-0 to 10-5	10-6 to 10-11	11-0 to 11-11
0	160	143	139	131	126	125	125	118	119	116	115	115	115
1	155	138	135	127	122	119	119	112	112	109	107	107	104
2	150	134	130	122	117	114	113	106	105	102	99	98	94
3	146	130	125	118	113	109	107	100	99	95	91	90	83
4	141	125	121	114	108	103	101	94	92	88	83	82	72
5	137	121	116	109	104	98	95	88	85	81	76	73	61
6	132	116	112	105	99	92	89	82	78	74	68	65	51
7	128	112	107	101	95	87	83	76	71	66	60	57	
8	123	108	103	97	90	82	77	70	65	59	52		
9	119	103	98	92	85	76	71	64	58	52			
10	114	99	94	88	81	71	65	58	51	45			
11	110	94	89	84	76	66	59	52					
12	105	90	85	79	72	60	53	46					
13	100	85	80	75	67	55	47						
14	96	81	75	71	63	50							
15	91	77	71	67	58								
16	87	72	66	63	54								
17	82	68	62	58	49								
18	78	63	57	54	45								
19	73	59	53	49									
20	69	55	48	45									
21	64	50											
22	60	46											
23	55												

Note. These standard scores ($M = 100$, $SD = 15$) are based on a linear transformation of the data obtained from E. M. Koppitz's (1975) normative 1974 sample. Standard scores are useful primarily from 5 to 8 years of age. After the age of 8 years, the low ceiling and the skewed distribution of developmental scores reduce the meaningfulness of standard scores.

Table F-5
Rating Scale for Kindergarten Children

RATING SCALE FOR KINDERGARTEN CHILDREN

Name: _____   Rater's name: _____

Age: _____ Sex: _____   Date: _____

Directions:
Use the following 5-point scale for your ratings:

1	2	3	4	5	DK
Very Poor	Poor	Average	Good	Excellent	Don't Know

Items	Rating
1. Academic ability	1 2 3 4 5 DK
2. Attention span	1 2 3 4 5 DK
3. Ability to follow oral directions	1 2 3 4 5 DK
4. Ability to articulate and speak clearly	1 2 3 4 5 DK
5. Ability to describe verbally a sequence of events	1 2 3 4 5 DK
6. Gross-motor ability for movement in physical education	1 2 3 4 5 DK
7. Social participation and play behavior with other children	1 2 3 4 5 DK
8. Ability to recite the alphabet	1 2 3 4 5 DK
9. Ability to name all the letters of the alphabet when they are shown in random order	1 2 3 4 5 DK
10. Ability to correctly name numbers between 1 and 20 shown in random order	1 2 3 4 5 DK
11. Ability to print his or her name correctly without reversals, deletions, additions, or misalignments	1 2 3 4 5 DK
12. Ability to identify primary colors shown in random order	1 2 3 4 5 DK
13. Ability to use scissors to cut paper correctly	1 2 3 4 5 DK

Source: Adapted from Carter and Swanson (1995).

Table F-6
Achievement Scores Necessary to Establish a Significant (p = .10) IQ–Achievement Discrepancy Using Standard Scores with M = 100 and SD = 15

IQ	Correlation																
	.80	.79	.78	.77	.76	.75	.74	.73	.72	.71	.70	.69	.68	.67	.66	.65	.64
	Achievement test score necessary for discrepancy																
150	125	124	123	122	121	121	120	119	118	118	117	116	115	115	114	113	112
149	124	123	122	121	121	120	119	118	118	117	116	115	115	114	113	113	112
148	123	122	121	121	120	119	118	118	117	116	115	115	114	113	113	112	111
147	122	121	121	120	119	118	118	117	116	115	115	114	113	113	112	111	111
146	121	121	120	119	118	118	117	116	115	115	114	113	113	112	111	111	110
145	121	120	119	118	118	117	116	115	115	114	113	113	112	111	111	110	109
144	120	119	118	118	117	116	115	115	114	113	113	112	111	111	110	109	109
143	119	118	118	117	116	115	115	114	113	113	112	111	111	110	109	109	108
142	118	118	117	116	115	115	114	113	113	112	111	111	110	109	109	108	107
141	117	117	116	115	115	114	113	113	112	111	111	110	109	109	108	107	107
140	117	116	115	115	114	113	112	112	111	110	110	109	109	108	107	107	106
139	116	115	114	114	113	112	112	111	110	110	109	108	108	107	107	106	105
138	115	114	114	113	112	112	111	110	110	109	108	108	107	107	106	105	105
137	114	114	113	112	112	111	110	110	109	108	108	107	107	106	105	105	104
136	113	113	112	111	111	110	109	109	108	108	107	106	106	105	105	104	104
135	113	112	111	111	110	109	109	108	108	107	106	106	105	105	104	103	103
134	112	111	111	110	109	109	108	107	107	106	106	105	104	104	103	103	102
133	111	110	110	109	108	108	107	107	106	106	105	104	104	103	103	102	102
132	110	110	109	108	108	107	107	106	105	105	104	104	103	103	102	101	101
131	109	109	108	108	107	106	106	105	105	104	104	103	102	102	101	101	100
130	109	108	107	107	106	106	105	104	104	103	103	102	102	101	101	100	100
129	108	107	107	106	105	105	104	104	103	103	102	102	101	101	100	100	99
128	107	106	106	105	105	104	104	103	102	102	101	101	100	100	99	99	98
127	106	106	105	104	104	103	103	102	102	101	101	100	100	99	99	98	98
126	105	105	104	104	103	103	102	102	101	101	100	100	99	99	98	98	97
125	105	104	104	103	102	102	101	101	100	100	99	99	98	98	97	97	96
124	104	103	103	102	102	101	101	100	100	99	99	98	98	97	97	96	96
123	103	102	102	101	101	100	100	99	99	98	98	97	97	97	96	96	95
122	102	102	101	101	100	100	99	99	98	98	97	97	96	96	95	95	95
121	101	101	100	100	99	99	98	98	97	97	97	96	96	95	95	94	94
120	101	100	100	99	99	98	98	97	97	96	96	95	95	95	94	94	93
119	100	99	99	98	98	97	97	96	96	96	95	95	94	94	93	93	93
118	99	99	98	98	97	97	96	96	95	95	94	94	94	93	93	92	92
117	98	98	97	97	96	96	95	95	95	94	94	93	93	93	92	92	91
116	97	97	96	96	96	95	95	94	94	93	93	93	92	92	91	91	91
115	97	96	96	95	95	94	94	94	93	93	92	92	92	91	91	90	90
114	96	95	95	94	94	94	93	93	92	92	92	91	91	91	90	90	89
113	95	95	94	94	93	93	92	92	92	91	91	91	90	90	89	89	89
112	94	94	93	93	93	92	92	91	91	91	90	90	90	89	89	88	88
111	93	93	93	92	92	91	91	91	90	90	90	89	89	88	88	88	88

(Continued)

Table F-6 *(Continued)*

IQ	\.80	\.79	\.78	\.77	\.76	\.75	\.74	\.73	\.72	\.71	\.70	\.69	\.68	\.67	\.66	\.65	\.64
						Correlation — Achievement test score necessary for discrepancy											
110	93	92	92	91	91	91	90	90	90	89	89	88	88	88	88	87	87
109	92	91	91	91	90	90	90	89	89	88	88	88	87	87	87	87	86
108	91	91	90	90	89	89	89	88	88	88	87	87	87	86	86	86	86
107	90	90	89	89	89	88	88	88	87	87	87	86	86	86	86	85	85
106	89	89	89	88	88	88	87	87	87	86	86	86	85	85	85	85	84
105	89	88	88	88	87	87	87	86	86	86	85	85	85	84	84	84	84
104	88	87	87	87	86	86	86	86	85	85	85	84	84	84	84	83	83
103	87	87	86	86	86	85	85	85	84	84	84	84	83	83	83	83	82
102	86	86	86	85	85	85	84	84	84	83	83	83	83	82	82	82	82
101	85	85	85	84	84	84	84	83	83	83	83	82	82	82	82	81	81
100	85	84	84	84	83	83	83	83	82	82	82	82	81	81	81	81	80
99	84	84	83	83	83	82	82	82	82	81	81	81	81	80	80	80	80
98	83	83	82	82	82	82	81	81	81	81	80	80	80	80	80	79	79
97	82	82	82	81	81	81	81	80	80	80	80	80	79	79	79	79	79
96	81	81	81	81	80	80	80	80	79	79	79	79	79	78	78	78	78
95	81	80	80	80	80	79	79	79	79	79	78	78	78	78	78	77	77
94	80	80	79	79	79	79	78	78	78	78	78	77	77	77	77	77	77
93	79	79	79	78	78	78	78	77	77	77	77	77	77	76	76	76	76
92	78	78	78	78	77	77	77	77	77	76	76	76	76	76	76	75	75
91	77	77	77	77	77	76	76	76	76	76	76	75	75	75	75	75	75
90	77	76	76	76	76	76	75	75	75	75	75	75	75	74	74	74	74
89	76	76	75	75	75	75	75	75	74	74	74	74	74	74	74	74	73
88	75	75	75	74	74	74	74	74	74	74	73	73	73	73	73	73	73
87	74	74	74	74	74	73	73	73	73	73	73	73	73	72	72	72	72
86	73	73	73	73	73	73	72	72	72	72	72	72	72	72	72	72	72
85	73	72	72	72	72	72	72	72	72	71	71	71	71	71	71	71	71
84	72	72	72	71	71	71	71	71	71	71	71	71	70	70	70	70	70
83	71	71	71	71	70	70	70	70	70	70	70	70	70	70	70	70	70
82	70	70	70	70	70	70	70	69	69	69	69	69	69	69	69	69	69
81	69	69	69	69	69	69	69	69	69	69	69	68	68	68	68	68	68
80	69	69	68	68	68	68	68	68	68	68	68	68	68	68	68	68	68
79	68	68	68	68	67	67	67	67	67	67	67	67	67	67	67	67	67
78	67	67	67	67	67	67	67	67	66	66	66	66	66	66	66	66	66
77	66	66	66	66	66	66	66	66	66	66	66	66	66	66	66	66	66
76	65	65	65	65	65	65	65	65	65	65	65	65	65	65	65	65	65
75	65	65	65	64	64	64	64	64	64	64	64	64	64	64	64	64	64
74	64	64	64	64	64	64	64	64	64	64	64	64	64	64	64	64	64
73	63	63	63	63	63	63	63	63	63	63	63	63	63	63	63	63	63
72	62	62	62	62	62	62	62	62	62	62	62	62	62	62	62	62	63
71	61	61	61	61	61	61	61	61	61	61	62	62	62	62	62	62	62
70	61	61	61	61	61	61	61	61	61	61	61	61	61	61	61	61	61
69	60	60	60	60	60	60	60	60	60	60	60	60	60	60	60	61	61
68	59	59	59	59	59	59	59	59	59	59	59	60	60	60	60	60	60
67	58	58	58	58	58	58	58	58	59	59	59	59	59	59	59	59	59
66	57	57	57	58	58	58	58	58	58	58	58	58	58	58	58	59	59

(Continued)

Table F-6 *(Continued)*

IQ	Correlation																
	.80	.79	.78	.77	.76	.75	.74	.73	.72	.71	.70	.69	.68	.67	.66	.65	.64
	Achievement test score necessary for discrepancy																
65	57	57	57	57	57	57	57	57	57	57	57	57	58	58	58	58	58
64	56	56	56	56	56	56	56	56	56	57	57	57	57	57	57	57	57
63	55	55	55	55	55	55	55	56	56	56	56	56	56	56	56	57	57
62	54	54	54	54	55	55	55	55	55	55	55	55	56	56	56	56	56
61	53	54	54	54	54	54	54	54	54	54	55	55	55	55	55	55	56
60	53	53	53	53	53	53	53	53	54	54	54	54	54	54	55	55	55
59	52	52	52	52	52	52	53	53	53	53	53	53	53	54	54	54	54
58	51	51	51	51	51	52	52	52	52	52	52	53	53	53	53	53	54
57	50	50	50	51	51	51	51	51	51	52	52	52	52	52	53	53	53
56	49	50	50	50	50	50	50	50	51	51	51	51	51	52	52	52	52
55	49	49	49	49	49	49	50	50	50	50	50	51	51	51	51	51	52
54	48	48	48	48	48	49	49	49	49	49	50	50	50	50	51	51	51
53	47	47	47	48	48	48	48	48	48	49	49	49	49	50	50	50	50
52	46	46	47	47	47	47	47	48	48	48	48	48	49	49	49	49	50
51	45	46	46	46	46	46	47	47	47	47	48	48	48	48	49	49	49
50	45	45	45	45	45	46	46	46	46	47	47	47	47	48	48	48	48

IQ	Correlation																
	.63	.62	.61	.60	.59	.58	.57	.56	.55	.54	.53	.52	.51	.50	.49	.48	.47
	Achievement test score necessary for discrepancy																
150	112	111	110	110	109	108	108	107	106	106	105	104	104	103	102	102	101
149	111	110	110	109	108	108	107	106	106	105	104	104	103	103	102	101	101
148	111	110	109	109	108	107	107	106	105	105	104	103	103	102	101	101	100
147	110	109	109	108	107	107	106	105	105	104	103	103	102	102	101	100	100
146	109	109	108	107	107	106	105	105	104	104	103	102	102	101	100	100	99
145	109	108	107	107	106	105	105	104	104	103	102	102	101	101	100	99	99
144	108	107	107	106	105	105	104	104	103	102	102	101	101	100	99	99	98
143	107	107	106	106	105	104	104	103	102	102	101	101	100	100	99	98	98
142	107	106	106	105	104	104	103	103	102	101	101	100	100	99	99	98	97
141	106	106	105	104	104	103	103	102	101	101	100	100	99	99	98	97	97
140	105	105	104	104	103	103	102	101	101	100	100	99	99	98	98	97	96
139	105	104	104	103	103	102	101	101	100	100	99	99	98	98	97	97	96
138	104	104	103	103	102	101	101	100	100	99	99	98	98	97	97	96	96
137	104	103	102	102	101	101	100	100	99	99	98	98	97	97	96	96	95
136	103	102	102	101	101	100	100	99	99	98	98	97	97	96	96	95	95
135	102	102	101	101	100	100	99	99	98	98	97	97	96	96	95	95	94
134	102	101	101	100	100	99	99	98	98	97	97	96	96	95	95	94	94
133	101	101	100	100	99	98	98	97	97	96	96	96	95	95	94	94	93
132	100	100	99	99	98	98	97	97	96	96	95	95	95	94	94	93	93
131	100	99	99	98	98	97	97	96	96	95	95	94	94	94	93	93	92

(Continued)

Table F-6 *(Continued)*

IQ	Correlation																
	.63	.62	.61	.60	.59	.58	.57	.56	.55	.54	.53	.52	.51	.50	.49	.48	.47
	Achievement test score necessary for discrepancy																
130	99	99	98	98	97	97	96	96	95	95	94	94	94	93	93	92	92
129	99	98	98	97	97	96	96	95	95	94	94	93	93	93	92	92	91
128	98	97	97	97	96	96	95	95	94	94	93	93	92	92	92	91	91
127	97	97	96	96	95	95	95	94	94	93	93	92	92	92	91	91	90
126	97	96	96	95	95	94	94	94	93	93	92	92	91	91	91	90	90
125	96	96	95	95	94	94	93	93	93	92	92	91	91	91	90	90	89
124	95	95	95	94	94	93	93	92	92	92	91	91	90	90	90	89	89
123	95	94	94	94	93	93	92	92	91	91	91	90	90	90	89	89	88
122	94	94	93	93	92	92	92	91	91	91	90	90	89	89	89	88	88
121	94	93	93	92	92	92	91	91	90	90	90	89	89	89	88	88	88
120	93	92	92	92	91	91	91	90	90	89	89	89	88	88	88	87	87
119	92	92	91	91	91	90	90	90	89	89	89	88	88	88	87	87	87
118	92	91	91	91	90	90	89	89	89	88	88	88	87	87	87	86	86
117	91	91	90	90	90	89	89	89	88	88	88	87	87	87	86	86	86
116	90	90	90	89	89	89	88	88	88	87	87	87	86	86	86	85	85
115	90	89	89	89	88	88	88	87	87	87	86	86	86	86	85	85	85
114	89	89	88	88	88	87	87	87	87	86	86	86	85	85	85	85	84
113	88	88	88	88	87	87	87	86	86	86	85	85	85	85	84	84	84
112	88	88	87	87	87	86	86	86	85	85	85	85	84	84	84	84	83
111	87	87	87	86	86	86	85	85	85	85	84	84	84	84	83	83	83
110	87	86	86	86	85	85	85	85	84	84	84	84	83	83	83	83	82
109	86	86	85	85	85	85	84	84	84	84	83	83	83	83	82	82	82
108	85	85	85	85	84	84	84	83	83	83	83	83	82	82	82	82	81
107	85	84	84	84	84	83	83	83	83	82	82	82	82	82	81	81	81
106	84	84	84	83	83	83	83	82	82	82	82	81	81	81	81	81	80
105	83	83	83	83	82	82	82	82	82	81	81	81	81	81	80	80	80
104	83	83	82	82	82	82	81	81	81	81	81	80	80	80	80	80	80
103	82	82	82	82	81	81	81	81	80	80	80	80	80	80	79	79	79
102	82	81	81	81	81	80	80	80	80	80	80	79	79	79	79	79	79
101	81	81	80	80	80	80	80	80	79	79	79	79	79	79	78	78	78
100	80	80	80	80	80	79	79	79	79	79	79	78	78	78	78	78	78
99	80	79	79	79	79	79	79	78	78	78	78	78	78	78	77	77	77
98	79	79	79	79	78	78	78	78	78	78	77	77	77	77	77	77	77
97	78	78	78	78	78	78	77	77	77	77	77	77	77	77	76	76	76
96	78	78	77	77	77	77	77	77	77	77	76	76	76	76	76	76	76
95	77	77	77	77	77	76	76	76	76	76	76	76	76	76	75	75	75
94	76	76	76	76	76	76	76	76	76	75	75	75	75	75	75	75	75
93	76	76	76	76	75	75	75	75	75	75	75	75	75	75	74	74	74
92	75	75	75	75	75	75	75	75	74	74	74	74	74	74	74	74	74
91	75	75	74	74	74	74	74	74	74	74	74	74	74	74	74	73	73
90	74	74	74	74	74	74	73	73	73	73	73	73	73	73	73	73	73
89	73	73	73	73	73	73	73	73	73	73	73	73	73	73	73	73	72
88	73	73	73	73	72	72	72	72	72	72	72	72	72	72	72	72	72
87	72	72	72	72	72	72	72	72	72	72	72	72	72	72	72	72	72
86	71	71	71	71	71	71	71	71	71	71	71	71	71	71	71	71	71

(Continued)

Table F-6 *(Continued)*

IQ	.63	.62	.61	.60	.59	.58	.57	.56	.55	.54	.53	.52	.51	.50	.49	.48	.47
								Achievement test score necessary for discrepancy									
85	71	71	71	71	71	71	71	71	71	71	71	71	71	71	71	71	71
84	70	70	70	70	70	70	70	70	70	70	70	70	70	70	70	70	70
83	70	70	70	70	69	69	69	69	69	69	70	70	70	70	70	70	70
82	69	69	69	69	69	69	69	69	69	69	69	69	69	69	69	69	69
81	68	68	68	68	68	68	68	68	68	68	68	68	69	69	69	69	69
80	68	68	68	68	68	68	68	68	68	68	68	68	68	68	68	68	68
79	67	67	67	67	67	67	67	67	67	67	67	67	68	68	68	68	68
78	66	66	66	67	67	67	67	67	67	67	67	67	67	67	67	67	67
77	66	66	66	66	66	66	66	66	66	66	66	66	66	67	67	67	67
76	65	65	65	65	65	65	65	66	66	66	66	66	66	66	66	66	66
75	65	65	65	65	65	65	65	65	65	65	65	65	66	66	66	66	66
74	64	64	64	64	64	64	64	64	65	65	65	65	65	65	65	65	65
73	63	63	63	64	64	64	64	64	64	64	64	64	64	65	65	65	65
72	63	63	63	63	63	63	63	63	63	64	64	64	64	64	64	64	64
71	62	62	62	62	62	63	63	63	63	63	63	63	63	64	64	64	64
70	61	61	62	62	62	62	62	62	62	62	63	63	63	63	63	63	64
69	61	61	61	61	61	61	61	62	62	62	62	62	62	63	63	63	63
68	60	60	60	61	61	61	61	61	61	61	62	62	62	62	62	62	63
67	59	60	60	60	60	60	60	61	61	61	61	61	61	62	62	62	62
66	59	59	59	59	59	60	60	60	60	60	60	61	61	61	61	61	62
65	58	58	59	59	59	59	59	59	60	60	60	60	60	61	61	61	61
64	58	58	58	58	58	58	59	59	59	59	59	60	60	60	60	61	61
63	57	57	57	58	58	58	58	58	58	59	59	59	59	60	60	60	60
62	56	57	57	57	57	57	58	58	58	58	58	59	59	59	59	60	60
61	56	56	56	56	57	57	57	57	57	58	58	58	58	59	59	59	59
60	55	55	55	56	56	56	56	57	57	57	57	58	58	58	58	59	59
59	54	55	55	55	55	56	56	56	56	57	57	57	57	58	58	58	58
58	54	54	54	55	55	55	55	55	56	56	56	57	57	57	57	58	58
57	53	53	54	54	54	54	55	55	55	55	56	56	56	57	57	57	57
56	53	53	53	53	54	54	54	54	55	55	55	55	56	56	56	57	57
55	52	52	52	53	53	53	54	54	54	54	55	55	55	56	56	56	57
54	51	52	52	52	52	53	53	53	54	54	54	54	55	55	55	56	56
53	51	51	51	52	52	52	52	53	53	53	54	54	54	55	55	55	56
52	50	50	51	51	51	51	52	52	52	53	53	53	54	54	54	55	55
51	49	50	50	50	51	51	51	52	52	52	53	53	53	54	54	54	55
50	49	49	49	50	50	50	51	51	51	52	52	52	53	53	53	54	54

(Continued)

Table F-6 *(Continued)*

IQ	Correlation																
	.46	.45	.44	.43	.42	.41	.40	.39	.38	.37	.36	.35	.34	.33	.32	.31	.30
	Achievement test score necessary for discrepancy																
150	101	100	99	99	98	97	97	96	96	95	94	94	93	93	92	91	91
149	100	99	99	98	98	97	96	96	95	95	94	93	93	92	92	91	91
148	100	99	98	98	97	97	96	95	95	94	94	93	93	92	91	91	90
147	99	99	98	97	97	96	96	95	94	94	93	93	92	92	91	91	90
146	99	98	98	97	96	96	95	95	94	94	93	92	92	91	91	90	90
145	98	98	97	97	96	95	95	94	94	93	93	92	92	91	90	90	89
144	98	97	97	96	96	95	94	94	93	93	92	92	91	91	90	90	89
143	97	97	96	96	95	95	94	93	93	92	92	91	91	90	90	89	89
142	97	96	96	95	95	94	94	93	93	92	92	91	91	90	89	89	88
141	96	96	95	95	94	94	93	93	92	92	91	91	90	90	89	89	88
140	96	95	95	94	94	93	93	92	92	91	91	90	90	89	89	88	88
139	95	95	94	94	93	93	92	92	91	91	90	90	89	89	89	88	88
138	95	94	94	93	93	93	92	92	91	91	90	90	89	89	88	88	87
137	95	94	94	93	93	92	92	91	91	90	90	89	89	88	88	87	87
136	94	94	93	93	92	92	91	91	90	90	89	89	88	88	88	87	87
135	94	93	93	92	92	91	91	90	90	89	89	89	88	88	87	87	86
134	93	93	92	92	91	91	90	90	90	89	89	88	88	87	87	87	86
133	93	92	92	91	91	90	90	90	89	89	88	88	87	87	87	86	86
132	92	92	91	91	90	90	90	89	89	88	88	88	87	87	86	86	85
131	92	91	91	90	90	90	89	89	88	88	88	87	87	86	86	86	85
130	91	91	90	90	90	89	89	88	88	88	87	87	86	86	86	85	85
129	91	90	90	90	89	89	88	88	88	87	87	86	86	86	85	85	85
128	90	90	90	89	89	88	88	88	87	87	86	86	86	85	85	85	84
127	90	90	89	89	88	88	88	87	87	86	86	86	85	85	85	84	84
126	89	89	89	88	88	88	87	87	86	86	86	85	85	85	84	84	84
125	89	89	88	88	88	87	87	86	86	86	85	85	85	84	84	84	83
124	89	88	88	87	87	87	86	86	86	85	85	85	84	84	84	83	83
123	88	88	87	87	87	86	86	86	85	85	85	84	84	84	83	83	83
122	88	87	87	87	86	86	86	85	85	85	84	84	84	83	83	83	82
121	87	87	87	86	86	86	85	85	85	84	84	84	83	83	83	82	82
120	87	86	86	86	85	85	85	85	84	84	84	83	83	83	82	82	82
119	86	86	86	85	85	85	84	84	84	84	83	83	83	82	82	82	82
118	86	85	85	85	85	84	84	84	83	83	83	83	82	82	82	82	81
117	85	85	85	84	84	84	84	83	83	83	83	82	82	82	81	81	81
116	85	85	84	84	84	83	83	83	83	82	82	82	82	81	81	81	81
115	84	84	84	84	83	83	83	83	82	82	82	82	81	81	81	81	80
114	84	84	83	83	83	83	82	82	82	82	81	81	81	81	81	80	80
113	84	83	83	83	82	82	82	82	82	81	81	81	81	80	80	80	80
112	83	83	83	82	82	82	82	81	81	81	81	81	80	80	80	80	79
111	83	82	82	82	82	81	81	81	81	81	80	80	80	80	80	79	79
110	82	82	82	81	81	81	81	81	80	80	80	80	80	79	79	79	79
109	82	81	81	81	81	81	80	80	80	80	80	79	79	79	79	79	79
108	81	81	81	81	80	80	80	80	80	79	79	79	79	79	79	78	78
107	81	81	80	80	80	80	80	79	79	79	79	79	79	78	78	78	78
106	80	80	80	80	80	79	79	79	79	79	79	78	78	78	78	78	78

(Continued)

Table F-6 *(Continued)*

IQ	.46	.45	.44	.43	.42	.41	.40	.39	.38	.37	.36	.35	.34	.33	.32	.31	.30
							Achievement test score necessary for discrepancy										
105	80	80	79	79	79	79	79	79	79	78	78	78	78	78	78	78	77
104	79	79	79	79	79	79	78	78	78	78	78	78	78	77	77	77	77
103	79	79	79	78	78	78	78	78	78	78	77	77	77	77	77	77	77
102	78	78	78	78	78	78	78	77	77	77	77	77	77	77	77	77	76
101	78	78	78	78	77	77	77	77	77	77	77	77	77	76	76	76	76
100	78	77	77	77	77	77	77	77	77	77	76	76	76	76	76	76	76
99	77	77	77	77	77	77	76	76	76	76	76	76	76	76	76	76	76
98	77	76	76	76	76	76	76	76	76	76	76	76	76	75	75	75	75
97	76	76	76	76	76	76	76	76	75	75	75	75	75	75	75	75	75
96	76	76	76	75	75	75	75	75	75	75	75	75	75	75	75	75	75
95	75	75	75	75	75	75	75	75	75	75	75	75	75	74	74	74	74
94	75	75	75	75	75	74	74	74	74	74	74	74	74	74	74	74	74
93	74	74	74	74	74	74	74	74	74	74	74	74	74	74	74	74	74
92	74	74	74	74	74	74	74	74	74	74	74	74	74	73	73	73	73
91	73	73	73	73	73	73	73	73	73	73	73	73	73	73	73	73	73
90	73	73	73	73	73	73	73	73	73	73	73	73	73	73	73	73	73
89	72	72	72	72	72	72	72	72	72	72	72	72	72	73	73	73	73
88	72	72	72	72	72	72	72	72	72	72	72	72	72	72	72	72	72
87	72	72	72	72	72	72	72	72	72	72	72	72	72	72	72	72	72
86	71	71	71	71	71	71	71	71	71	71	71	71	71	72	72	72	72
85	71	71	71	71	71	71	71	71	71	71	71	71	71	71	71	71	71
84	70	70	70	70	70	70	70	70	71	71	71	71	71	71	71	71	71
83	70	70	70	70	70	70	70	70	70	70	70	70	70	71	71	71	71
82	69	69	69	69	69	70	70	70	70	70	70	70	70	70	70	70	70
81	69	69	69	69	69	69	69	69	69	69	70	70	70	70	70	70	70
80	68	68	68	69	69	69	69	69	69	69	69	69	69	70	70	70	70
79	68	68	68	68	68	68	68	69	69	69	69	69	69	69	69	69	70
78	67	67	68	68	68	68	68	68	68	68	68	69	69	69	69	69	69
77	67	67	67	67	67	67	68	68	68	68	68	68	68	69	69	69	69
76	66	67	67	67	67	67	67	67	67	68	68	68	68	68	68	69	69
75	66	66	66	66	67	67	67	67	67	67	67	68	68	68	68	68	68
74	66	66	66	66	66	66	66	67	67	67	67	67	67	68	68	68	68
73	65	65	65	66	66	66	66	66	66	67	67	67	67	67	67	68	68
72	65	65	65	65	65	65	66	66	66	66	66	67	67	67	67	67	67
71	64	64	65	65	65	65	65	65	66	66	66	66	66	67	67	67	67
70	64	64	64	64	64	65	65	65	65	65	66	66	66	66	66	67	67
69	63	63	64	64	64	64	64	65	65	65	65	65	66	66	66	66	67
68	63	63	63	63	64	64	64	64	64	65	65	65	65	66	66	66	66
67	62	63	63	63	63	63	64	64	64	64	65	65	65	65	65	66	66
66	62	62	62	63	63	63	63	63	64	64	64	64	65	65	65	65	66

(Continued)

Table F-6 *(Continued)*

IQ	.46	.45	.44	.43	.42	.41	.40	.39	.38	.37	.36	.35	.34	.33	.32	.31	.30
	Achievement test score necessary for discrepancy																
65	61	62	62	62	62	63	63	63	63	64	64	64	64	65	65	65	65
64	61	61	61	62	62	62	62	63	63	63	63	64	64	64	65	65	65
63	61	61	61	61	61	62	62	62	63	63	63	63	64	64	64	64	65
62	60	60	61	61	61	61	62	62	62	62	63	63	63	64	64	64	64
61	60	60	60	60	61	61	61	61	62	62	62	63	63	63	64	64	64
60	59	59	60	60	60	61	61	61	61	62	62	62	63	63	63	64	64
59	59	59	59	60	60	60	60	61	61	61	62	62	62	63	63	63	64
58	58	58	59	59	59	60	60	60	61	61	61	62	62	62	63	63	63
57	58	58	58	59	59	59	60	60	60	61	61	61	62	62	62	63	63
56	57	58	58	58	59	59	59	60	60	60	61	61	61	62	62	62	63
55	57	57	57	58	58	58	59	59	60	60	60	61	61	61	62	62	62
54	56	57	57	57	58	58	58	59	59	59	60	60	61	61	61	62	62
53	56	56	57	57	57	58	58	58	59	59	59	60	60	61	61	61	62
52	55	56	56	57	57	57	58	58	58	59	59	60	60	60	61	61	61
51	55	55	56	56	56	57	57	58	58	58	59	59	60	60	60	61	61
50	55	55	55	56	56	56	57	57	58	58	58	59	59	60	60	60	61

Note. This table was constructed following Heath and Kush (1991). For this table to be used, the intelligence test and the achievement test must have $M = 100$ and $SD = 15$. The following procedure was used to obtain the observed achievement levels necessary for a significant IQ–achievement discrepancy.

1. All correlation values between .30 and .80 and all IQ values between 50 and 150 were selected.
2. The standard error of estimate for each correlation value was computed by using the following formula: $SEE = SD\sqrt{1 - r_{xy}^2}$.
3. The predicted achievement scores were then computed by using the following formula: $\hat{y} = r_{xy}(IQ - 100) + 100$.
4. A z value of 1.65 was used to establish confidence intervals about the predicted achievement scores. This z value at $p = .10$ is a reasonable compromise between too stringent and too lax a criterion. The formula used to establish the confidence interval was $15z\sqrt{1 - r_{xy}^2}$.
5. The lower limit of the confidence interval was then subtracted from the predicted achievement scores to obtain the minimal achievement level that represents a discrepancy at the $p = .10$ level.

An example of how the table is read follows: For a child with an IQ of 100 who is administered an achievement test that has a .65 correlation with the intelligence test (see 17th column), an achievement score of 81 or lower represents a significant discrepancy.

REFERENCES

Aaron, P. G. (1997). The impending demise of the discrepancy formula. *Review of Educational Research, 67,* 461–502.

Aaron, P. G., & Simurdak, J. (1991). Reading disorders: Their nature and diagnosis. In J. E. Obrzut & G. W. Hynd (Eds.), *Neuropsychological foundations of learning disabilities: A handbook of issues, methods, and practice* (pp. 519–548). San Diego: Academic Press.

Abbatiello, A., & Kpo, W. (1988). Test of Visual-Motor Integration: Evaluation of test effectiveness for practitioners. *Special Services in the Schools, 5,* 77–88.

Abel, E. L., & Sokol, R. J. (1991). A revised estimate of the economic impact of fetal alcohol syndrome. In M. Galanter, H. Begleiter, R. Deitrich, D. M. Gallant, D. Goodwin, E. Gottheil, A. Paredes, M. Rothschild, D. H. Van Thiel, & D. Cancellare (Eds.), *Recent developments in alcoholism: Vol. 9. Children of alcoholics* (pp. 117–125). New York: Plenum.

Abikoff, H., & Gittelman, R. (1985). Classroom observation code: A modification of the Stony Brook Code. *Psychopharmacology Bulletin, 21,* 901–909.

Abikoff, H., & Klein, R. G. (1992). Attention-deficit hyperactivity and conduct disorder: Comorbidity and implications for treatment. *Journal of Consulting and Clinical Psychology, 60,* 881–892.

Abledata. (1999). *Informed consumer guide to assistive technology for people with hearing disabilities* [On-line]. Available: http://www.abledata.com/text2/icg_hear.htm

Abramowitz, A. J., O'Leary, S. G., & Futtersak, M. W. (1988). The relative impact of long and short reprimands on children's off-task behavior in the classroom. *Behavior Therapy, 19,* 243–247.

Achenbach, T. M. (1991a). *Manual for the Child Behavior Checklist and 1991 Profile.* Burlington, VT: University Associates in Psychiatry.

Achenbach, T. M. (1991b). *Manual for the Teacher's Report Form and 1991 Profile.* Burlington, VT: University Associates in Psychiatry.

Achenbach, T. M. (1991c). *Manual for the Youth Self-Report and 1991 Profile.* Burlington, VT: University Associates in Psychiatry.

Achenbach, T. M. (1993). Implications of multiaxial empirically based assessment for behavior therapy with children. *Behavior Therapy, 24,* 91–116.

Achenbach, T. M., & McConaughy, S. H. (1992). Taxonomy of internalizing disorders of childhood and adolescence. In W. M. Reynolds (Ed.), *Internalizing disorders in children and adolescents* (pp. 19–60). New York: Wiley.

Ackerman, P. T., & Dykman, R. A. (1993). Phonological processes, confrontational naming, and immediate memory in dyslexia. *Journal of Learning Disabilities, 26,* 597–609.

Ackerman, P. T., McPherson, B. D., Oglesby, D. M., & Dykman, R. A. (1998). EEG power spectra of adolescent poor readers. *Journal of Learning Disabilities, 31,* 83–90.

Adamovich, B. L. B. (1991). Cognition, language, attention, and information processing following closed head injury. In J. S. Kreutzer & P. H. Wehman (Eds.), *Cognitive rehabilitation for persons with traumatic brain injury: A functional approach* (pp. 75–86). Baltimore: Paul H. Brookes.

Adams, W., & Sheslow, D. (1990). *Wide Range Assessment of Memory and Learning.* Wilmington, DE: Jastik Associates.

Adrien, J. L., Ornitz, E., Barthelemy, C., Sauvage, D., & Lelord, G. (1987). The presence or absence of certain behaviors associated with infantile autism in severely retarded autistic and non-autistic retarded children and very young normal children. *Journal of Autism and Developmental Disorders, 17,* 407–416.

Alessi, G. J. (1980). Behavioral observation for the school psychologist: Responsive-discrepancy model. *School Psychology Review, 9,* 31–45.

Alessi, G. J. (1988). Direct observation methods for emotional/behavior problems. In E. S. Shapiro & T. R. Kratochwill (Eds.), *Behavioral assessment in schools* (pp. 14–75). New York: Guilford.

Alfano, D. P., & Finlayson, M. A. J. (1987). Clinical neuropsychology in rehabilitation. *Clinical Neuropsychologist, 1,* 105–123.

Allen, K. D., & Matthews, J. R. (1998). Behavior management of recurrent pain in children. In T. S. Watson & F. M. Gresham (Eds.), *Handbook of child behavior therapy* (pp. 263–285). New York: Plenum.

Allington, R. L. (1979). Diagnosis of reading disability: Word prediction ability tests. *Academic Therapy, 14,* 267–274.

Amabile, T. M. (1983). *The social psychology of creativity.* New York: Springer-Verlag.

Aman, M. G., Singh, N. N., Stewart, A. W., & Field, C. J. (1985). Psychometric characteristics of the Aberrant Behavior Checklist. *American Journal of Mental Deficiency, 89,* 492–50l.

Ambrosini, P., & Dixon, J. F. (1996). *Schedule for Affective Disorders & Schizophrenia for School-Age Children (K-SADS–IVR).* Philadelphia: Allegheny University of the Health Sciences.

American Association on Mental Retardation. (1992). *Mental retardation: Definition, classification, and systems of supports* (9th ed.). Washington, DC: Author.

American Psychiatric Association. (2000). *Diagnostic and statistical manual of mental disorders: Text revision (DSM-IV–TR)* (4th ed.). Washington, DC: Author.

Anastopolous, A. D., Spisto, M. A., & Maher, M. C. (1994). The WISC–III Freedom from Distractibility factor: Its utility in identifying children with attention deficit hyperactivity disorder. *Psychological Assessment, 6,* 368–371.

Anderson, C. M., & Stewart, S. (1983). *Mastering resistance: A practical guide to family therapy.* New York: Guilford.

Anglin, J. M. (1993). Vocabulary development: A morphological analysis. *Monographs of the Society for Research in Development, Serial No. 238, 58*(10).

Angold, A., Cox, A., Rutter, M., & Simonoff, E. (1996). *Child and Adolescent Psychiatric Assessment (CAPA): Version 4.2–Child version.* Durham, NC: Duke Medical Center.

Annegers, J. F. (1983). The epidemiology of head trauma in children. In K. Shapiro (Ed.), *Pediatric head trauma* (pp. 1–10). Mount Kisco, NY: Futura.

Aram, D. M., & Eisele, J. A. (1992). Plasticity and recovery of higher cognitive functions following early brain injury. In I. Rapin & S. J. Segalowitz (Eds.), *Handbook of neuropsychology* (Vol. 6, pp. 73–92). Amsterdam, Netherlands: Elsevier Science.

Aram, D. M., & Ekelman, B. L. (1986). Cognitive profiles of children with early onset of unilateral lesions. *Developmental Neuropsychology, 2,* 155–172.

Aram, D. M., Ekelman, B. L., Rose, D. F., & Whitaker, H. A. (1985). Verbal and cognitive sequelae following unilateral lesions acquired in early childhood. *Journal of Clinical and Experimental Neuropsychology, 7,* 55–78.

Archer, R. P. (1997). *MMPI–A: Assessing adolescent psychopathology* (2nd ed.). Mahwah, NJ: Erlbaum.

Archer, R. P.(1999). *MMPI–A Interpretive System Version 2.* Odessa, FL: Psychological Assessment Resources.

Asarnow, R. F., Satz, P., Light, R., Lewis, R., & Neumann, E. (1991). Behavior problems and adaptive functioning in children with mild and severe closed head injury. *Journal of Pediatric Psychology, 16,* 543–555.

Ashton, C. (1996). In defence of discrepancy definitions of specific learning difficulties (A response to Frederickson and Reason). *Educational Psychology in Practice, 12,* 131–140.

Atkins, M. S., Pelham, W. E., & Licht, M. H. (1988). The development and validation of objective classroom measures for conduct and attention deficit disorders. *Advances in Behavioral Assessment of Children and Families, 4,* 3–31.

Aylward, E. H., & Schmidt, S. (1986). An examination of three tests of visual-motor integration. *Journal of Learning Disabilities, 19,* 328–330.

Bacon, E. H., & Rubin, D. C. (1983). Story recall by mentally retarded children. *Psychological Reports, 53,* 791–796.

Baddeley, A. D. (1992). Memory theory and memory therapy. In B. A. Wilson & N. Moffat (Eds.), *Clinical management of memory problems* (2nd ed., pp. 1–31). San Diego: Singular Publishing Group.

Badian, N. A. (1999). Reading disability defined as a discrepancy between listening and reading comprehension: A longitudinal study of stability, gender differences, and prevalence. *Journal of Learning Disabilities, 32,* 138–148.

Bagley, C. (1992). Development of an adolescent stress scale for use by school counsellors: Construct validity in terms of depression, self-esteem and suicidal ideation. *School Psychology International, 13,* 31–49.

Bagley, C., & Shewchuk-Dann, D. (1991). Characteristics of 60 children and adolescents who have a history of sexual assault against others: Evidence from a controlled study. *Journal of Child and Youth Care* (Special Issue), 43–52.

Bailey-Richardson, B. (1988). [Review of the *Vineland Adaptive Behavior Scales, Classroom Edition*]. *Journal of Psychoeducational Assessment, 6,* 87–91.

Baird, S. M., Haas, L., McCormick, K., Carruth, C., & Turner, K. D. (1992). Approaching an objective system for observation and measurement: Infant-Parent Social Interaction Code. *Topics in Early Childhood Special Education, 12,* 544–571.

Bakeman, R., & Gottman, J. M. (1986). *Observing interaction: An introduction to sequential analysis.* New York: Cambridge University Press.

Baker, L., & Cantwell, D. P. (1989). Specific language and learning disorders. In T. H. Ollendick & M. Hersen (Eds.), *Handbook of clinical psychology* (pp. 93–104). New York: Plenum.

Ball, E. W. (1993). Phonological awareness: What's important and to whom? *Reading & Writing, 5,* 141–159.

Ballantyne, A. O., & Sattler, J. M. (1991). Validity and reliability of the Reporter's Test with normally achieving and learning disabled children. *Psychological Assessment, 3,* 60–67.

Bannatyne, A. (1974). Diagnosis: A note on recategorization of the WISC scaled scores. *Journal of Learning Disabilities, 7,* 272–274.

Barker, P. (1990). *Clinical interviews with children and adolescents.* New York: Norton.

Barker, R. G., & Wright, H. F. (1954). *Midwest and its children: The psychological ecology of an American town.* Evanston, IL: Peterson.

Barker, R. G., & Wright, H. F. (1966). *One boy's day: A specimen record of behavior.* New York: Archon.

Barkley, R. A. (1981a). *Hyperactive children: A handbook for diagnosis and treatment.* New York: Guilford.

Barkley, R. A. (1981b). Learning disabilities. In E. Mash & L. Terdal (Eds.), *Behavioral assessment of childhood disorders* (pp. 441–482). New York: Guilford.

Barkley, R. A. (1990). *Attention-deficit hyperactivity disorder: A handbook for diagnosis and treatment.* New York: Guilford.

Barkley, R. A. (1991). *Attention-deficit hyperactivity disorder: A clinical workbook.* New York: Guilford.

Barkley, R. A. (1997). Behavioral inhibition, sustained attention, and executive functions: Constructing a unifying theory of ADHD. *Psychological Bulletin, 121,* 65–94.

Barkley, R. A. (1998). *Attention-deficit hyperactivity disorder: A handbook for diagnosis and treatment* (2nd ed.). New York: Guilford.

Barkley, R. A. (2000). *Taking charge of ADHD* (Rev. ed.). New York: Guilford.

Barkley, R. A., Grodzinsky, G., & DuPaul, G. J. (1992). Frontal lobe functions in attention deficit disorder with and without hyperactivity: A review and research report. *Journal of Abnormal Child Psychology, 20,* 163–188.

Barkley, R. A., & Murphy, K. R. (1998). *Attention-deficit hyperactivity disorder: A clinical work-book.* New York: Guilford.

Barnes, M. A., & Dennis, M. (1992). Reading in children and adolescents after early onset hydrocephalus and in normally developing age peers: Phonological analysis, word recognition, word comprehension, and passage comprehension skill. *Journal of Pediatric Psychology, 17,* 445–465.

Baron-Cohen, S., Allen, J., & Gillberg, C. (1992). Can autism be detected at 18 months? The needle, the haystack, and the CHAT. *British Journal of Psychiatry, 161,* 839–843.

Barry, C. T., Taylor, H. G., Klein, S., & Yeates, K. O. (1996). Validity of neurobehavioral symptoms reported in children with traumatic brain injury. *Child Neuropsychology, 2,* 213–226.

Baska, L. K. (1989). Characteristics and needs of the gifted. In J. F. Feldhusen, J. VanTassel-Baska, & K. Seeley (Eds.), *Excellence in educating the gifted* (pp. 15–28). Denver: Love.

Beavers, W. R., & Hampson, R. B. (1990). *Successful families: Assessment and intervention.* New York: Norton.

Beery, K. E. (1997). *Developmental Test of Visual-Motor Integration–Fourth Edition.* Cleveland: Modern Curriculum.

Bellack, A. S., & Hersen, M. (1980). *Introduction to clinical psychology.* New York: Oxford University Press.

Belmont, L., & Birch, H. G. (1965). Lateral dominance, lateral awareness, and reading disability. *Child Development, 36,* 57–71.

Bender, L. (1938). A Visual Motor Gestalt Test and its clinical use. *American Orthopsychiatric Association Research Monograph No. 3.*

Bender, W. N., & Smith, J. K. (1990). Classroom behavior of children and adolescents with learning disabilities: A meta-analysis. *Journal of Learning Disabilities, 23,* 298–305.

Benjamin, A. (1981). *The helping interview* (3rd ed.). Boston: Houghton Mifflin.

Bennett, D. E., & Clarizio, H. F. (1988). A comparison of methods for calculating a severe discrepancy. *Journal of School Psychology, 26,* 359–369.

Benton, A. L. (1959). *Right-left discrimination and finger localization.* New York: Hoeber-Harper.

Benton, A. L. (1963). *Benton Visual Retention Test* (Rev. ed.). San Antonio, TX: The Psychological Corporation.

Benton, A. L., Hamsher, K. DeS., Varney, N. R., & Spreen, O. (1983). *Contributions to neuropsychological assessment: A clinical manual.* New York: Oxford University Press.

Bergan, J. R. (1977). *Behavioral consultation.* Columbus, OH: Merrill.

Berk, L. E. (1993). *Infants, children, and adolescents.* Needham Heights, MA: Allyn & Bacon.

Berkow, R. (1997). *The Merck manual of medical information.* Whitehouse Station, NJ: Merck Research Laboratories.

Berninger, V. W., Mizokawa, D. T., & Bragg, R. (1991). Theory-based diagnosis and remediation of writing disabilities. *Journal of School Psychology, 29,* 57–59.

Bernstein, J. H., & Waber, D. (1996). *Developmental scoring system for the Rey-Osterrieth Complex Figure.* Odessa, FL: Psychological Assessment Resources.

Besharov, D. J. (1990). *Recognizing child abuse: A guide for the concerned.* New York: Free Press.

Bienenstock, M., & Vernon, M. (1994). Classification by the states of the deaf and hard of hearing students. *American Annals of the Deaf, 139,* 128–131.

Bierman, K. L. (1983). Cognitive development and clinical interviews with children. In B. B. Lahey & A. E. Kazdin (Eds.), *Advances in clinical child psychology* (Vol. 6, pp. 217–250). New York: Plenum.

Bierman, K. L. (1990). Using the clinical interview to assess children's interpersonal reasoning and emotional understanding. In C. R. Reynolds & R. W. Kamphaus (Eds.), *Handbook of psychological and educational assessment of children: Personality, behavior, and context* (pp. 204–219). New York: Guilford.

Bierman, K. L., & Schwartz, L. A. (1986). Clinical child interviews: Approaches and developmental considerations. *Journal of Child and Adolescent Psychotherapy, 3,* 267–278.

Bigler, E. D., Lajiness-O'Neill, R., & Howes, N. (1998). Technology in the assessment of learning disability. *Journal of Learning Disabilities, 31,* 67–82.

Biklen, D., Morton, M. W., Gold, D., Berrigan, C., & Swaminathan, S. (1992). Facilitated communication: Implications for individuals with autism. *Topics in Language Disorders, 12,* 1–28.

Billingsley, B. S. (1988). Writing: Teaching assessment skills. *Academic Therapy, 24,* 27–35.

Billingsley, B. S., & Wildman, T. M. (1990). Facilitating reading comprehension in learning disabled students: Metacognitive goals and instructional strategies. *RASE: Remedial & Special Education, 11,* 18–31.

Bird, H. R., Gould, M. S., Rubio-Stipec, M., & Staghezza, B. M. (1991). Screening for childhood psychopathology in the community using the Child Behavior Checklist. *Journal of the American Academy of Child and Adolescent Psychiatry, 30,* 116–123.

Bishop, D. V. (1992). The underlying nature of specific language impairment. *Journal of Child Psychology and Psychiatry and Allied Disciplines, 33,* 3–66.

Bishop, V. E. (1996). *Teaching visually impaired children* (2nd ed.). Springfield, IL: Charles C Thomas.

Blackburn, A. C., & Erickson, D. B. (1986). Predictable crises of the gifted student. *Journal of Counseling & Development, 64,* 552–555.

Blackman, J. A., Westervelt, V. D., Stevenson, R., & Welch, A. (1991). Management of preschool children with attention deficit–hyperactivity disorder. *Topics in Early Childhood Special Education, 11,* 91–104.

Blaha, J., Fawaz, N., & Wallbrown, F. H. (1979). Information processing components of Koppitz errors on the Bender Visual-Motor Gestalt Test. *Journal of Clinical Psychology, 35,* 784–790.

Blakemore, B., Shindler, S., & Conte, R. (1993). A problem solving training program for parents of children with attention deficit hyperactivity disorder. *Canadian Journal of School Psychology, 9,* 66–85.

Blosser, J. L., & DePompei, R. (1989). The head-injured student returns to school: Recognizing and treating deficits. *Topics in Language Disorders, 9,* 67–77.

Boden, M. A. (1994). Dimensions of creativity. In M. A. Boden (Ed.), *The definition of creativity* (pp. 75–117). Cambridge, MA: MIT Press.

Bogdan, R. C., & Biklen, S. K. (1982). *Qualitative research for education: An introduction to theory and methods.* Needham Heights, MA: Allyn & Bacon.

Boggs, S. R., & Eyberg, S. (1990). Interview techniques and establishing rapport. In A. M. La Greca (Ed.), *Through the eyes of the child: Obtaining self-reports from children and adolescents* (pp. 85–108). Needham Heights, MA: Allyn & Bacon.

Bolen, L. M., Hewett, J. B., Hall, C. W., & Mitchell, C. C. (1992). Expanded Koppitz scoring system of the Bender Gestalt Visual-Motor Test for Adolescents: A pilot study. *Psychology in the Schools, 29,* 113–115.

Boney-McCoy, S., & Finkelhor, D. (1995). Psychosocial sequelae of violent victimization in a national youth sample. *Journal of Consulting and Clinical Psychology, 63,* 726–736.

Borkowski, J. G., & Burke, J. E. (1996). Theories, models, and measurements of executive functioning: An information processing perpective. In G. L. Lyon & N. A. Krasnegor (Eds.), *Attention, memory, and executive function* (pp. 235–261). Baltimore: Paul H. Brookes.

Borkowski, J. G., Day, J. D., Saenz, D., Dietmeyer, D., Estrada, M. T., & Groteluschen, A. (1992). Expanding the boundaries of cognitive interventions. In B. Y. L. Wong (Ed.), *Contemporary intervention research in learning disabilities: An international perspective* (pp. 1–21). New York: Springer-Verlag.

Borkowski, J. G., Estrada, M. T., Milstead, M., & Hale, C. A. (1989). General problem-solving skills: Relations between metacognition and strategic processing. *Learning Disability Quarterly, 12,* 57–70.

Borkowski, J. G., Schneider, W., & Pressley, M. (1989). The challenges of teaching good information processing to learning disabled students. *International Journal of Disability, Development and Education, 36,* 169–185.

Bornstein, P. H., Hamilton, S. B., & Bornstein, M. T. (1986). Self-monitoring procedures. In A. R. Ciminero, K. S. Calhoun, & H. E. Adams (Eds.), *Handbook of behavioral assessment* (2nd ed., pp. 176–222). New York: Wiley.

Bornstein, R. A. (1983). Verbal IQ–Performance IQ discrepancies on the Wechsler Adult Intelligence Scale–Revised in patients with unilateral or bilateral cerebral dysfunction. *Journal of Consulting and Clinical Psychology, 51,* 779–780.

Boxer, R., Challen, M., & McCarthy, M. (1991). Developing an assessment framework: The distinctive contribution of the educational psychologist. *Educational Psychology in Practice, 7,* 30–34.

Boyd, T. A. (1988). Clinical assessment of memory in children. In M. G. Tramontana & S. R. Hooper (Eds.), *Assessment issues in child neuropsychology* (pp. 172–204). New York: Plenum.

Boyer, P., & Chesteen, H. (1992). Professional helpfulness? The experiences of parents of handicapped children with counsellors and social workers. *Journal of Child and Youth Care, 7,* 37–48.

Braden, J. P., & Hannah, J. M. (1998). Assessment of hearing-impaired and deaf children with the WISC–III. In A. Prifitera & D. H. Saklofske (Eds.), *WISC–III clinical use and interpretation* (pp. 177–202). San Diego: Academic Press.

Braden, J. P. (1994). *Deafness, deprivation, and IQ.* New York: Plenum.

Braden, J. P., Kostrubala, C. E., & Reed, J. (1994). Why do deaf children score differently on performance vs. motor-reduced nonverbal intelligence tests? *Journal of Psychoeducational Assessment, 12,* 357–363.

Bradley, L. (1980). *Assessing reading difficulties: A diagnostic and remedial approach.* London: MacMillan.

Bradley, R. H. (1994). The HOME inventory: Review and reflections. *Advances in Child Development and Behavior, 25,* 241–288.

Bradley-Johnson, S. (1994). *Psychoeducational assessment of students who are visually impaired or blind: Infancy through high school* (2nd ed.). Austin, TX: Pro-Ed.

Bramlett, R. K., & Barnett, D. W. (1993). The development of a direct observation code for use in preschool settings. *School Psychology Review, 22,* 49–62.

Brannigan, G. G., Aabye, S. M., Baker, L. A., & Ryan, G. T. (1995). Further validation of the qualitative scoring system for the Modified Bender-Gestalt Test. *Psychology in the Schools, 32,* 24–26.

Brannigan, G. G., & Brunner, N. A. (1989). *The Modified Version of the Bender-Gestalt Test for Preschool and Primary School Children.* Brandon, VT: Clinical Psychology Publishing Company.

Brannigan, G. G., & Brunner, N. A. (1991). Relationship between two scoring systems for the Modified Version of the Bender-Gestalt Test. *Perceptual and Motor Skills, 72,* 286.

Brannigan, G. G., & Brunner, N. A. (1993). Comparison of the qualitative and developmental scoring systems for the Modified Version of the Bender-Gestalt Test. *Journal of School Psychology, 31,* 327–330.

Brannigan, G. G., & Brunner, N. A. (1996). *The Modified Version of the Bender-Gestalt Test for Preschool and Primary School Children–Revised.* Brandon, VT: Clinical Psychology Publishing Company.

Breen, M. J. (1982). Comparison of educationally handicapped students' scores on the Revised Developmental Test of Visual-Motor Integration and Bender-Gestalt. *Perceptual and Motor Skills, 54,* 1227–1230.

Breen, M. J., Carlson, M., & Lehman, J. (1985). The Revised Developmental Test of Visual-Motor Integration: Its relation to the VMI, WISC-R, and Bender Gestalt for a group of elementary aged learning disabled students. *Journal of Learning Disabilities, 18,* 136–138.

Bregman, J. D. (1991). Current developments in the understanding of mental retardation: II—Psychopathology. *Journal of the American Academy of Child and Adolescent Psychiatry, 30,* 861–872.

Breslau, N. (1987). Inquiring about the bizarre: False positives in Diagnostic Interview Schedule for Children (DISC) ascertainment of obsessions, compulsions, and psychotic symptoms. *Journal of the American Academy of Child and Adolescent Psychiatry, 26,* 639–644.

Brockway, B. S. (1978). Evaluating physician competency: What difference does it make? *Evaluation and Program Planning, 1,* 211.

Brody, E. B., & Brody, N. (1976). *Intelligence: Nature, determinants, and consequences.* New York: Academic Press.

Bromwich, R. M. (1981). *Working with parents and infants: An interactional approach.* Baltimore: University Park Press.

Brooks, D. N. (1991). The head-injured family. *Journal of Clinical and Experimental Neuropsychology, 13,* 155–188.

Brown, A. L., Campione, J. C., Webber, L. S., & McGilly, K. (1992). Interactive learning environments: A new look at assessment and instruction. In B. R. Gifford & M. C. O'Connor (Eds.), *Changing assessments: Alternative views of aptitude, achievement and instruction—Evaluation in education and human services* (pp. 121–211). Boston: Kluwer Academic Publishers.

Brown, T. E. (1996). *Brown Attention Deficit Disorder Scales Manual.* San Antonio, TX: The Psychological Corporation.

Bruininks, R. H. (1978). *Bruininks-Oseretsky Test of Motor Proficiency.* Circle Pines, MN: American Guidance Service.

Bruininks, R. H., Woodcock, R., Weatherman, R., & Hill, B. (1996). *Scales of Independent Behavior–Revised.* Chicago, IL: Riverside.

Bruner, F. G., Barnes, E., & Dearborn, W. F. (1909). Report of committee on books and tests pertaining to the study of exceptional and mentally deficient children. *Proceedings of the National Education Association, 47,* 901–914.

Bryen, D. N., & Gerber, A. (1987). Metalinguistic abilities and reading: A focus on phonological awareness. *Journal of Reading, Writing, and Learning Disabilities International, 3,* 357–367.

Budoff, M., & Hamilton, J. L. (1976). Optimizing test performance of moderately and severely mentally retarded adolescents and adults. *American Journal of Mental Deficiency, 81,* 49–57.

Busch, B. (1993). Attention deficits: Current concepts, controversies, management, and approaches to classroom instruction. *Annals of Dyslexia, 43,* 5–25.

Butcher, J. N., & Williams, C. L. (1992). *Essentials of MMPI–2 and MMPI–A interpretation.* Minneapolis, MN: University of Minnesota Press.

Butcher, J. N., Williams, C. L., Graham, J. R., Archer, R. P., Tellegen, A., Ben-Porath, Y. S., & Kaemmer, B. (1992). *MMPI–A (Minnesota Multiphasic Personality Inventory–Adolescent): Manual for administration, scoring, and interpretation.* Minneapolis, MN: University of Minnesota Press.

Callahan, C. M. (2000). Intelligence and giftedness. In R. Sternberg (Ed.), *Handbook of intelligence* (pp. 158–175). New York: Cambridge.

Campione, J. C. (1989). Assisted assessment: A taxonomy of approaches and an outline of strengths and weaknesses. *Journal of Learning Disabilities, 22,* 151–165.

Campione, J. C., & Brown, A. L. (1987). Linking dynamic assessment with school achievement. In C. S. Lidz (Ed.), *Dynamic assessment: An interactional approach to evaluating learning potential* (pp. 82–115). New York: Guilford.

Canino, I. (1985). Taking a history. In D. Shaffer, A. A. Erhardt, & L. L. Greenhill (Eds.), *The clinical guide to child psychiatry* (pp. 393–407). New York: Free Press.

Carter, J. D., & Swanson, H. L. (1995). The relationship between intelligence and vigilance in children at risk. *Journal of Abnormal Child Psychology, 23,* 201–220.

Casat, C. D., Norton, H. J., & Boyle-Whitesel, M. (1999). Identification of elementary school children at risk for disruptive behavioral disturbance: Validation of a combined screening method. *Journal of the American Academy of Child and Adolescent Psychiatry, 38,* 1246–1253.

Casey, R., Levy, S. E., Brown, K., & Brooks-Gunn, J. (1992). Impaired emotional health in children with mild reading disability. *Journal of Developmental and Behavioral Pediatrics, 13,* 256–260.

Cashel, M. L., Rogers, R., Sewell, K. W., & Holliman, N. B. (1998). Preliminary validation of the MMPI–A for a male delinquent sample: An investigation of clinical correlates and discriminant validity. *Journal of Personality Assessment, 71,* 49–69.

Caskey, W. E., Jr., & Larson, G. L. (1980). Scores on group and individually administered Bender-Gestalt Test and Otis-Lennon IQs of kindergarten children. *Perceptual and Motor Skills, 50,* 387–390.

Chan, P. W. (2000). Relationship of visual motor development and academic performance of young children in Hong Kong assessed on the Bender-Gestalt Test. *Perceptual and Motor Skills, 90,* 209–214.

Chess, S., & Thomas, A. (1986). *Temperament in clinical practice.* New York: Guilford.

Childs, R. E. (1982). A study of the adaptive behavior of retarded children and the resultant effects of this use in the diagnosis of mental retardation. *Education and Training of the Mentally Retarded, 17,* 109–113.

Christensen, C. A. (1992). Discrepancy definitions of reading disability: Has the quest led us astray? A response to Stanovich. *Reading Research Quarterly, 27,* 276–278.

Cicerone, K. D., & Tupper, D. E. (1986). Cognitive assessment in the neuropsychological rehabilitation of head-injured adults. In B. P. Uzzell & Y. Gross (Eds.), *Clinical neuropsychology of intervention* (pp. 59–83). Boston: Martinus Nijhoff.

Clarizio, H. F. (1994). *Assessment and treatment of depressions in children and adolescents* (2nd ed.). Brandon, VT: Clinical Psychology Publishing Company.

Clark, C. R. (1988). Sociopathy, malingering, and defensiveness. In R. Rogers (Ed.), *Clinical assessment of malingering and deception* (pp. 54–64). New York: Guilford.

Clark, H. H. (1985). Language use and language users. In G. Lindzey & E. Aronson (Eds.), *Handbook of social psychology* (3rd ed., Vol. 2, pp. 179–232). New York: Random House.

Clarke, A. M., & Clarke, A. D. B. (1994). Variations, deviations, risks, and uncertainties in human development. In W. B. Carey & S. C. McDevitt (Eds.), *Prevention and early intervention: Individual differences as risk factors for the mental health of children: A Festschrift for Stella Chess and Alexander Thomas* (pp. 83–91). New York: Brunner/Mazel.

Cobb, H. C. (1989). Counseling and psychotherapy with handicapped children and adolescents. In D. T. Brown & H. T. Prout (Eds.), *Counseling and psychotherapy with children and adolescents: Theory and practice for school and clinic settings* (2nd ed., pp. 467–501). Brandon, VT: Clinical Psychology Publishing Company.

Cohen, D. H., & Stern, V. (1970). *Observing and recording the behavior of young children.* New York: Teachers College Press.

Cohen, D. H., Stern. V., & Balaban, N. (1997). *Observing and recording the behavior of young children* (4th ed.). New York: Teachers College Press.

Cohen, J. (1960). A coefficient of agreement for nominal scales. *Educational and Psychological Measurement, 20,* 37–46.

Cohen, J. (1968). Weighted kappa: Nominal scale agreement with provision for scaled disagreement or partial credit. *Psychological Bulletin, 70,* 213–220.

Cohen, M. (1997). *Children's Memory Test.* San Antonio, TX: The Psychological Corporation.

Cohen, M., Becker, M. G., & Campbell, R. (1990). Relationships among four methods of assessment of children with attention deficit–hyperactivity disorder. *Journal of School Psychology, 28,* 189–202.

Cohen, S. B. (1991). Adapting educational programs for students with head injuries. *Journal of Head Trauma Rehabilitation, 6,* 56–63.

Cone, J. D., & Foster, S. L. (1982). Direct observation in clinical psychology. In P. C. Kendall & J. N. Butcher (Eds.), *Handbook of research methods in clinical psychology* (pp. 311–354). New York: Wiley.

Conger, A. J. (1980). Integration and generalization of kappas for multiple raters. *Psychological Bulletin, 88,* 322–328.

Connecticut State Department of Education. (1999). *Guidelines for identifying children with learning disabilities* (2nd ed.). Hartford, CT: Author.

Conners, C. K. (1997). *Conners' Rating Scales–Revised: Technical manual.* North Tonawanda, NY: Multi-Health Systems.

Conners, C. K., & MHS Staff. (2000). *Conners' Continuous Performance Test II (CPT II).* Niagara Falls, NY: Multi-Health Systems.

Cormier, L. S., & Cormier, B. (1998). *Interviewing strategies for helpers: Fundamental skills and cognitive behavioral interventions* (4th ed.). Pacific Grove, CA: Brooks/Cole.

Cormier, P., Carlson, J. S., & Das, J. P. (1990). Planning ability and cognitive performance: The compensatory effects of a dynamic assessment approach. *Learning & Individual Differences, 2,* 437–449.

Crenshaw, T. M., Kavale, K. A., Forness, S. R., & Reeve, R. E. (1999). Attention deficit hyperactivity disorder and the efficacy of stimulant medication: A meta-analysis. *Advances in Learning and Behavioral Disabilities, 13,* 135–165.

Croxen, M. E., & Lytton, H. (1971). Reading disability and difficulties in finger localization and right-left discrimination. *Developmental Psychology, 5,* 256–262.

Cummins, J. (1984). *Bilingualism and special education: Issues in assessment and pedagogy.* San Diego: College Hill Press.

Cunningham, R. (1992). Developmentally appropriate psychosocial care for children affected by parental chemical dependence. *Journal of Health Care for the Poor & Underserved, 3,* 208–221.

D'Amato, R. C., Dean, R. S., & Rhodes, R. L. (1998). Subtyping children's learning disabilities with neuropsychological, intellectual, and achievement measures. *International Journal of Neuroscience, 96,* 107–125.

D'Amato, R. C., Gray, J. W., & Dean, R. S. (1988). A comparison between intelligence and neuropsychological functioning. *Journal of School Psychology, 26,* 283–292.

Dadds, M. R., Schwartz, S., & Sanders, M. R. (1987). Marital discord and treatment outcome in the treatment of childhood conduct disorders. *Journal of Consulting and Clinical Psychology, 55,* 396–403.

Dalby, P. R., & Obrzut, J. E. (1991). Epidemiologic characteristics and sequelae of closed head-injured children and adolescents: A review. *Developmental Neuropsychology, 7,* 35–68.

Daley, C. E., & Nagle, R. J. (1996). Relevance of WISC–III indicators for assessment of learning disabilities. *Journal of Psychoeducational Assessment, 14,* 320–333.

Damico, J. S. (1991). Clinical discourse analysis: A functional language assessment technique. In C. S. Simon (Ed.), *Communication skills and classroom success: Assessment and therapy methodologies for language and learning disabled students* (pp. 125–150). Eau Claire, WI: Thinking Publications.

Danek, M. (1988). Deafness and family impact. In P. W. Power, A. E. Dell Orto, & M. B. Gibbons (Eds.), *Family interventions throughout chronic illness and disability* (pp. 120–135). New York: Springer.

Darley, F. L. (1978). A philosophy of appraisal and diagnosis. In F. L. Darley & D. C. Spriestersbach (Eds.), *Diagnostic methods in speech pathology* (pp. 1–60). New York: Harper & Row.

Davis, G. A. (1997). Identifying creative students and measuring creativity. In N. Colangelo & G. A. Davis (Eds.), *Handbook of gifted education* (2nd ed., pp. 269–281). Needham Heights, MA: Allyn & Bacon.

Dean, R. S., & Anderson, J. L. (1997). Lateralization of cerebral functions. In A. M. Horton, D. Wedding, & J. Webster (Eds.), *The neuropsychology handbook: Foundations and assessment* (2nd ed., pp. 139–170). New York: Springer.

Deaton, A. V. (1987). Behavioral change strategies for children and adolescents with severe brain injury. *Journal of Learning Disability, 20,* 581–589.

DeFries, J. C. (1989). Gender ratios in children with reading disability and their affected relatives: A commentary. *Journal of Learning Disabilities, 22,* 544–545.

DeFries, J. C., & Gillis, J. J. (1993). Genetics of reading disability. In R. Plomin & G. E. McClearn (Eds.), *Nature, nurture & psychology* (pp. 121–145). Washington, DC: American Psychological Association.

Delis, D. C., Kramer, J. H., Kaplan, E. F., & Ober, B. A. (1994). *California Verbal Learning Test–Children's Version.* San Antonio, TX: The Psychological Corporation.

DeMers, S. T., Wright, D., & Dappen, L. (1981). Comparison of scores on two visual-motor tests for children referred for learning or adjustment difficulties. *Perceptual and Motor Skills, 53,* 863–867.

Denckla, M. B., LeMay, M., & Chapman, C. A. (1985). Few CT scan abnormalities found even in neurologically impaired learning disabled children. *Journal of Learning Disabilities, 18,* 132–135.

DePompei, R., & Blosser, J. L. (1987). Strategies for helping head-injured children successfully return to school. *Language, Speech, and Hearing Services in Schools, 18,* 292–300.

DePompei, R., Blosser, J. L., & Zarski, J. J. (1989, November). *The path less traveled: Counseling family and friends of T.B.I. survivors.* Paper presented at the American Speech-Language-Hearing Association National Convention, St. Louis, MO.

DePompei, R., Zarski, J. J., & Hall, D. E. (1988). Cognitive communication impairments: A family-focused viewpoint. *Journal of Head Trauma Rehabilitation, 3,* 13–22.

De Renzi, E. (1980). The Token Test and the Reporter's Test: A measure of verbal input and a measure of verbal output. In M. T. Sarno & O. Hook (Eds.), *Aphasia: Assessment and treatment* (pp. 158–169). New York: Masson.

De Renzi, E., & Faglioni, P. (1978). Normative data and screening power of a shortened version of the Token Test. *Cortex, 14,* 41–49.

De Renzi, E., & Ferrari, C. (1978). The Reporter's Test: A sensitive test to detect expressive disturbances in aphasics. *Cortex, 14,* 279–293.

Detterman, D. K., Gabriel, L. T., & Ruthsatz, J. M. (2000). Intelligence and mental retardation. In R. Sternberg (Ed.), *Handbook of intelligence* (pp. 141–158). New York: Cambridge University Press.

DiSimoni, F. G. (1978). *Token Test for Children.* Allen, TX: DLM Teaching Resources.

Dodrill, C. B., Farwell, J., & Batzel, L. W. (1987, September). Validity of the Aphasia Screening Test for Young Children. In J. M. Fletcher (Chair), *Poster session: Child neuropsychology: Innovations and advances.* Symposium conducted at the meeting of the American Psychological Association, New York.

Doll, E. A. (1946). *The Oseretsky Tests of Motor Proficiency: A translation from the Portuguese adaption.* Minneapolis, MN: Educational Test Bureau.

Donaghy, W. C. (1984). *The interview: Skills and applications.* Glenview, IL: Scott, Foresman.

Donders, J. (1996). Validity of short forms of the intermediate Halstead Category Test in children with traumatic brain injury. *Archives of Clinical Neuropsychology, 11,* 131–137.

Downs, C. W., Smeyak, G. P., & Martin, E. (1980). *Professional interviewing.* New York: Harper & Row.

Doyle, A., Ostrander, R., Skare, S., Crosby, R. D., & August, G. J. (1997). Convergent and criterion-related validity of the Behavior Assessment System for Children–Parent Rating Scale. *Journal of Clinical Child Psychology, 26,* 276–284.

Drotar, D., & Crawford, P. (1987). Using home observation in the clinical assessment of children. *Journal of Clinical Child Psychology, 16,* 342–349.

Drotar, D., Stein, R. E., & Perrin, E. C. (1995). Methodological issues in using the Child Behavior Checklist and its related instruments in clinical child psychology research. *Journal of Clinical Child Psychology, 24,* 184–192.

Dumas, J. E. (1987). Interact—A computer-based coding and data management system to assess family interactions. *Advances in Behavioral Assessment of Children and Families, 3,* 177–202.

Dunn, R., & Dunn, K. (1977). *How to raise independent and professionally successful daughters.* Englewood Cliffs, NJ: Prentice-Hall.

DuPaul, G. J., & Barkley, R. A. (1992). Situational variability of attention problems: Psychometric properties of the Revised Home and School Situations Questionnaires. *Journal of Clinical Child Psychology, 21,* 178–188.

DuPaul, G. J., & Eckert, T. L. (1997). The effects of school-based interventions for attention deficit hyperactivity disorder: A meta-analysis. *School Psychology Review, 26,* 5–27.

DuPaul, G. J., & Hennington, P. N. (1993). Peer tutoring effects on the classroom performance of children with ADHD. *School Psychology Review, 22,* 134–143.

DuPaul, G. J., Power, T. J., McGoey, K. E., Ikeda, M. J., & Anastopoulos, A. D. (1998). Reliability and validity of parent and teacher ratings of attention-deficit/hyperactivity disorder symptoms. *Journal of Psychoeducational Assessment, 16,* 55–68.

DuPaul, G. J., & Stoner, G. (1994). *ADHD in the schools: Assessment and intervention strategies.* New York: Guilford.

Edelbrock, C. S., & Costello, A. J. (1988). Structured psychiatric interviews for children. In M. Rutter, A. H. Tuma, & I. Lann

(Eds.), *Assessment diagnosis in child psychopathology* (pp. 87–112). New York: Guilford.

Edelbrock, C. S., Costello, A. J., Dulcan, M. K., Conover, N. C., & Kalas, R. (1986). Parent-child agreement on child psychiatric symptoms assessed via structured interview. *Journal of Child Psychology and Psychiatry, 27,* 181–190.

Edelbrock, C. S., Costello, A. J., Dulcan, M. K., Kalas, R., & Conover, N. C. (1985). Age differences in the reliability of the psychiatric interview of the child. *Child Development, 56,* 265–275.

Editorial Board. (1996). Definition of mental retardation. In J. W. Jacobson & J. A. Mulick (Eds.), *Manual of diagnosis and professional practice in mental retardation* (pp. 13–53). Washington, DC: American Psychological Association.

Ehri, L. C. (1998). Grapheme–phoneme knowledge is essential for learning to read words in English. In J. L. Metsala & L. C. Ehri (Eds.), *Word recognition in beginning literacy* (pp. 3–40). Mahwah, NJ: Erlbaum.

Elbers, N., & Van Loon-Vervoorn, A. (1999). Lexical relationships in children who are blind. *Journal of Visual Impairment & Blindness, 93,* 419–421.

Erickson, L. G., Stahl, S. A., & Rinehart, S. D. (1985). Metacognitive abilities of above and below average readers: Effects of conceptual tempo, passage level, and error type on error detection. *Journal of Reading Behavior, 17,* 235–252.

Erin, J. N., & Koenig, A. J. (1997). The student with a visual disability and a learning disability. *Journal of Learning Disabilities, 30,* 309–320.

Evans, H. L., & Sullivan, M. A. (1993). Children and the use of self-monitoring, self-evaluation, and self-reinforcement. In A. J. Finch, Jr., W. M. Nelson, III, & E. S. Ott (Eds.), *Cognitive-behavioral procedures with children and adolescents: A practical guide* (pp. 67–89). Needham Heights, MA: Allyn & Bacon.

Ewing-Cobbs, L., Levin, H. S., Fletcher, J. M., Miner, M. E., & Eisenberg, H. M. (1991). The Children's Orientation and Amnesia Test: Relationship to severity of acute head injury and to recovery of memory. *Neurosurgery, 27,* 683–691.

Eysenck, H. J. (1994). Dimensions of creativity. In M. A. Boden (Ed.), *The measurement of creativity* (pp. 199–242). Cambridge, MA: MIT Press.

Fadely, J. L., & Hosler, V. N. (1992). *Attentional deficit disorder in children and adolescents.* Springfield, IL: Charles C Thomas.

Faraone, S. V., Biederman, J., Lehman, B. K., Spencer, T., Norman, D., Seidman, L. J., Kraus, I., Perrin, J., Chen, W. J., & Tsuang, M. T. (1993). Intellectual performance and school failure in children with attention deficit hyperactivity disorder and in their siblings. *Journal of Abnormal Psychology, 102,* 616–623.

Farnan, N., & Kelly, P. (1991). Keeping track: Creating assessment portfolios in reading and writing. *Journal of Reading, Writing, and Learning Disabilities International, 7,* 255–269.

Farrell, A. D. (1991). Computers and behavioral assessment: Current applications, future possibilities, and obstacles to routine use. *Behavioral Assessment, 13,* 159–179.

Fassnacht, G. (1982). *Theory and practice of observing behavior.* New York: Academic Press.

Feldman, J. A. (1984). *Performance of learning disabled and normal children on three versions of the Token Test.* Unpublished master's thesis, San Diego State University, San Diego, CA.

Fennell, E. B., & Mickle, J. P. (1992). Behavioral effects of head trauma in children and adolescents. In M. G. Tramontana &

S. R. Hooper (Eds.), *Advances in child neuropsychology* (pp. 24–49). New York: Springer-Verlag.

Ferholt, J. D. L. (1980). *Clinical assessment of children: A comprehensive approach to primary pediatric care.* Philadelphia: Lippincott.

Feuerstein, R. (1979). *The dynamic assessment of retarded performers: The learning potential assessment device, theory, instruments, and techniques.* Baltimore: University Park Press.

Filipek, P. A., Accardo, P. J., Baranek, G. T., Cook, E. H., Jr., Dawson, G., Gordon, B., Gravel, J. S., Johnson, C. P., Kallen, R. J., Levy, S. R., Minshew, N. J., Prizant, B. M., Rapin, I., Rogers, S. J., Stone, W. L., Teplin, S., Tuchman, R. F., & Volkmar, F. R. (1999). The screening and diagnosis of autistic spectrum disorders. *Journal of Autism and Developmental Disorders, 29,* 439–484.

Filley, C. M., Cranberg, L. D., Alexander, M. P., & Hart, E. J. (1987). Neurobehavioral outcome after closed head injury in childhood and adolescence. *Archives of Neurology, 44,* 194–198.

Finkelhor, D. (1995). The victimization of children: A developmental perspective. *American Journal of Orthopsychiatry, 65,* 177–193.

Fischer, M., Barkley, R., Fletcher, K., & Smallish, L. (1990). The adolescent outcome of hyperactivity children diagnosed by research criteria, II: Academic, attentional, and neuropsychological status. *Journal of Consulting and Clinical Psychology, 58,* 580–588.

Florida Department of Education. (1999). *Functional behavioral assessment and behavioral intervention plans* (Technical Assistance Paper, No. FY 1999-3). Tallahassee, FL: Author.

Foddy, W. H. (1993). *Constructing questions for interviews and questionnaires: Theory and practice in social research.* New York: Cambridge University Press.

Fombonne, E. (1998). Epidemiological surveys of autism. In F. R. Volkmar (Ed.), *Autism and pervasive developmental disorders* (pp. 32–63). New York: Cambridge University Press.

Ford, B. G., & Ford, R. D. (1981). Identifying creative potential in handicapped children. *Exceptional Children, 48,* 115–122.

Forrester, G., & Geffen, G. (1991). Performance measure of 7- to 15-year-old children on the Auditory Verbal Learning Test. *Clinical Neuropsychologist, 5,* 345–359.

Foster, S. L., & Cone, J. D. (1986). Design and use of direct observation systems. In A. Ciminero, K. Calhoun, & H. E. Adams (Eds.), *Handbook of behavioral assessment* (2nd ed., pp. 253–324). New York: Wiley.

Fotheringhan, J. B. (1983). Mental retardation and developmental delay. In K. D. Paget & B. A. Bracken (Eds.), *The psychoeducational assessment of preschool children* (pp. 207–223). New York: Grune & Stratton.

Fredericks, B., & Brodsky, M. (1994). Assessment for a functional curriculum. In E. O. Cipani & F. Spooner (Eds.), *Curricular and instructional approaches for persons with severe disabilities* (pp. 31–48). Needham Heights, MA: Allyn & Bacon.

Fredericks, D. W., & Williams, W. L. (1998). New definition of mental retardation for the American Association of Mental Retardation. *Image—The Journal of Nursing Scholarship, 30,* 53–56.

Freebody, P., & Byrne, B. (1988). Word-reading strategies in elementary school children: Relations to comprehension, reading time, and phonemic awareness. *Reading Research Quarterly, 23,* 441–453.

Freedman, D. A., Feinstein, C., & Berger, K. (1988). The blind child and adolescent. In C. J. Kestenbaum & D. T. Williams

(Eds.), *Handbook of clinical assessment of children and adolescents* (Vol. 2, pp. 864–878). New York: New York University Press.

Freeman, B. J., Rahbar, B., Ritvo, E. R., Bice, T. L., Yakota, A., & Ritvo, R. (1991). The stability of cognitive and behavioral parameters in autism: A twelve-year prospective study. *Journal of the American Academy of Child & Adolescent Psychiatry, 30,* 479–482.

Frick, P. J., Silverthorn, P., & Evans, C. (1994). Assessment of childhood anxiety using structured interviews: Patterns of agreement among informants and association with maternal anxiety. *Psychological Assessment, 6,* 372–379.

Frisby, C. L., & Braden, J. P. (1992). Feuerstein's dynamic assessment approach: A semantic, logical, and empirical critique. *Journal of Special Education, 26,* 281–301.

Frude, N. (1991). *Understanding family problems: A psychological approach.* New York: Wiley.

Fuller, G. B., & Vance, B. (1993). Comparison of the Minnesota Percepto-Diagnostic Test–Revised and Bender-Gestalt in predicting achievement. *Psychology in the Schools, 30,* 220–226.

Fuller, G. B., & Vance, B. (1995). Interscorer reliability of the Modified Version of the Bender-Gestalt Test for preschool and primary school children. *Psychology in the Schools, 32,* 264–266.

Fuller, G. B., & Wallbrown, F. H. (1983). Comparison of the Minnesota Percepto-Diagnostic Test and Bender-Gestalt: Relationship with achievement criteria. *Journal of Clinical Psychology, 39,* 985–988.

Gable, R. A., Quinn, M. M., Rutherford, R. B., Jr., & Howell, K. (1998). *Addressing problem behaviors in schools: Use of functional assessments and behavior intervention plans* [On-line]. Available: http://www.ldonline.org/ld_indepth/special_education/quinn_behavior.html

Gadow, K. D., & Sprafkin, J. (1997). *Child Symptom Inventory–4.* Stony Brook, NY: Checkmate Plus.

Gadow, K. D., Sprafkin, J., & Nolan, E. E. (1996). *ADHD School Observation Code.* Stony Brook, NY: Checkmate Plus.

Gallagher, J. J. (1991). Editorial: The gifted: A term with surplus meaning. *Journal for the Education of the Gifted, 14,* 353–365.

Gallagher, J. J. (1997). Issues in the education of gifted children. In N. Colangelo & G. A. Davis (Eds.), *Handbook of gifted education* (pp. 10–23). Needham Heights, MA: Allyn & Bacon.

Garbarino, J., & Stott, F. M. (1989). *What children can tell us: Eliciting, interpreting, and evaluating information from children.* San Francisco: Jossey-Bass.

Garbarino, J. K., Guttman, E., & Seeley, J. W. (1987). *The psychologically battered child: Strategies for identification, assessment, and intervention.* San Francisco: Jossey-Bass.

Gardner, R. A. (1979). *The objective diagnosis of minimal brain dysfunction.* Cresskill, NJ: Creative Therapeutics.

Garner, R. (1987). *Metacognition and reading comprehension.* Norwood, NJ: Ablex.

Garnett, K. (1987). Math learning disabilities: Teaching and learners. *Journal of Reading, Writing, & Learning Disabilities International, 3,* 1–8.

Gaskill, F. W. (1995, March). *Drop in ability scores using the WISC–III: Implications for ability achievement discrepancy analysis.* Paper presented at the 27th Annual NASP Convention, Chicago, IL.

Gathercole, S. E., & Adams, A. (1993). Phonological working memory in very young children. *Developmental Psychology, 29,* 770–778.

Gaub, M., & Carlson, C. L. (1997). Meta-analysis of gender differences in ADHD. *Attention, 2,* 25–30.

George, E. L., & Bloom, B. L. (1997). A brief scale for assessing parental child-rearing practice: Psychometric properties and psychosocial correlates. *Family Process, 36,* 63–80.

Gianutsos, R. (1987). A neuropsychologist's primer on memory for educators. *Neuropsychology, 1,* 51–58.

Gilandas, A., Touyz, S., Beumont, P. J. V., & Greenberg, H. P. (1984). *Handbook of neuropsychological assessment.* New York: Grune & Stratton.

Gilbert, R. K., & Christensen, A. (1988). The assessment of family alliances. *Advances in Behavioral Assessment of Children and Families, 4,* 219–252.

Gilger, J. W., Pennington, B. F., & DeFries, J. C. (1992). A twin study of the etiology of comorbidity: Attention-deficit hyperactivity disorder and dyslexia. *Journal of the American Academy of Child & Adolescent Psychiatry, 31,* 343–348.

Gilhousen, M. R., Allen, L. F., Lasater, L. M., Farrell, D. M., & Reynolds, C. R. (1990). Veracity and vicissitude: A critical look at the Milwaukee Project. *Journal of School Psychology, 28,* 285–299.

Gillberg, C., Nordin, V., & Ehlers, S. (1996). Early detection of autism: Diagnostic instruments for clinicians. *European Child & Adolescent Psychiatry, 5,* 67–74.

Gilmore, S. K. (1973). *The counselor-in-training.* New York: Appleton-Century-Crofts.

Giordano, G. (1987). Diagnosing specific math disabilities. *Academic Therapy, 23,* 69–74.

Gittelman, R., & Abikoff, H. (1989). The role of psychostimulants and psychosocial treatments in hyperkinesis. In T. Sagvolden & T. Archer (Eds.), *Attention deficit disorder: Clinical and basic research* (pp. 167–180). Hillsdale, NJ: Erlbaum.

Glutting, J. J., & McDermott, P. A. (1990). Principles and problems in learning potential. In C. R. Reynolds & R. W. Kamphaus (Eds.), *Handbook of psychological and educational assessment of children: Intelligence and achievement* (pp. 296–347). New York: Guilford.

Golden, C. J. (1987). Screening batteries for the adult and children's versions of the Luria Nebraska Neuropsychological Batteries. *Neuropsychology, 1,* 63–66.

Goldenberg, H. (1983). *Contemporary clinical psychology* (2nd ed.). Monterey, CA: Brooks/Cole.

Goldstein, D. J., Smith, K. B., Waldrep, E. L., & Inderbitzen, H. (1987). Comparison of the Woodcock-Johnson Scales of Independent Behavior and Vineland Adaptive Behavior Scales in infant assessment. *Journal of Psychoeducational Assessment, 5,* 1–6.

Goodglass, H. (1993). *Understanding aphasia. Foundations of neuropsychology.* San Diego: Academic Press.

Goodman, J. D., & Sours, J. A. (1967). *The child mental status examination.* New York: Basic Books.

Gorden, R. L. (1975). *Interviewing: Strategy, techniques, and tactics* (Rev. ed.). Homewood, IL: Dorsey.

Gordon, M. (1988). *The Gordon Diagnostic System.* Dewitt, NY: Gordon Systems.

Goswami, U. (1992). Phonological factors in spelling development. *Journal of Child Psychology and Psychiatry, 33,* 967–975.

Graham, S., & Weintraub, N. (1996). A review of handwriting research: Progress and prospects from 1980 to 1994. *Educational Psychology Review, 8,* 7–87.

Gratus, J. (1988). *Successful interviewing.* Harmondsworth, Middlesex, England: Penguin Books.

Green, M., Wong, M., Atkins, D., Taylor, J., & Feinlieb, M. (1999). *Diagnosis of attention deficit/hyperactivity disorder: Technical review 3.* Rockville, MD: U.S. Department of Health and Human Services, Agencies for Health Care Policy and Research Publication 99-0050.

Greenbaum, A. (1982). Conducting effective parent conferences. *Communique, 10,* 4–5.

Greenberg, L. M. (1990). *Test of Variable of Attention (TOVA).* Los Alamitos, CA: Universal Attention Disorders.

Greenspan, S. (1995). Selling DSM: The rhetoric of science in psychiatry. *American Journal on Mental Retardation, 99,* 683–685.

Greenwood, C. R., Hops, H., Walker, H. M., Guild, J. J., Stokes, J., Young, K. R., Keleman, K. S., & Willardson, M. (1979). Standardized classroom management program: Social validation and replication studies in Utah and Oregon. *Journal of Applied Behavior Analysis, 12,* 235–253.

Gresham, F. M. (1983). Social skills assessment as a component of mainstreaming placement decisions. *Exceptional Children, 49,* 331–336.

Gresham, F. M. (1984). Behavioral interviews in school psychology: Issues in psychometric adequacy and research. *School Psychology Review, 13,* 17–25.

Gresham, F. M., & Elliott, S. N. (1990). *The Social Skills Rating System.* Circle Pines, MN: American Guidance Services.

Grigorenko, E. L., & Sternberg, R. J. (1998). Dynamic testing. *Psychological Bulletin, 124,* 75–111.

Groenveld, M., & Jan, J. E. (1992). Intelligence profiles of low vision and blind children. *Journal of Visual Impairment & Blindness, 86,* 68–71.

Grossberg, I. N., & Cornell, D. G. (1988). Relationship between personality adjustment and high intelligence: Terman versus Hollingworth. *Exceptional Children, 55,* 266–272.

Grossman, H. (Ed.). (1983). *Classification in mental retardation.* Washington, DC: American Association on Mental Deficiency.

Guida, F. V. (1987). Naturalistic Observation of Academic Anxiety Scale. *Journal of Classroom Interaction, 22,* 13–18.

Guilford, J. P., & Hoepfner, R. (1971). *The analysis of intelligence.* New York: McGraw-Hill.

Guralnick, M. J., & Groom, J. M. (1988). Friendships of preschool children in mainstreamed playgroups. *Developmental Psychology, 24,* 595–604.

Guthke, J. (1982). The learning test concept—an alternative to the traditional static intelligence test. *German Journal of Psychology, 6,* 306–324.

Hagen, J. W., Barclay, C. R., & Schwethelm, B. (1982). Cognitive development of the learning-disabled child. In N. R. Ellis (Ed.), *International review of research in mental retardation* (Vol. 11, pp. 1–41). New York: Academic Press.

Hahn, W. K. (1987). Cerebral lateralization of function: From infancy through childhood. *Psychological Bulletin, 101,* 376–392.

Hahn, Y. S., Chyung, C., Barthel, M. J., Bailes, J., Flannery, A. M., & McLone, D. G. (1988). Head injuries in children under 36 months of age: Demography and outcome. *Child's Nervous System, 4,* 34–40.

Hall, P. K., & Jordan, L. S. (1985). The Token and Reporter's Test: Use with 123 language-disordered students. *Language, Speech, and Hearing Services in Schools, 16,* 244–255.

Hammen, C., & Rudolph, K. D. (1996). Childhood depression. In E. J. Mash & R. A. Barkley (Eds.), *Child psychopathology* (pp. 153–195). New York: Guilford.

Handwerk, M. L., Larzelere, R. E., Friman, P. C., & Soper, S. H. (1999). Parent and child discrepancies in reporting severity of problem behaviors in three out-of-home settings. *Psychological Assessment, 11,* 14–23.

Happé, F. G. E. (1994). Wechsler IQ profile and theory of mind in autism: A research note. *Journal of Child Psychology and Psychiatry, 35,* 1461–1471.

Harms, T., & Clifford, R. (1998). *Early Childhood Environment Rating Scale* (rev. ed.). New York: Teacher College Press.

Harris, F. C., & Lahey, B. B. (1982). Subject reactivity in direct observational assessment: A review and critical analysis. *Clinical Psychology Review, 2,* 523–538.

Harris, J. C. (1995a). *Developmental neuropsychiatry: Vol. 1. Fundamentals.* Cary, NC: Oxford University Press.

Harris, J. C. (1995b). *Developmental neuropsychiatry: Vol. 2. Assessment, diagnosis, and treatment of developmental disorders.* Cary, NC: Oxford University Press.

Harris, M., & Coltheart, M. K. (1986). *Language processing in children and adults: An introduction.* London, England: Routledge & Kegan Paul.

Harris, S. L., Handleman, J. S., & Burton, J. B. (1990). The Stanford-Binet profiles of young children with autism. *Special Services in the School, 6,* 135–143.

Harrison, P. L., & Oakland, T. (2000). *Adaptive Behavior Assessment System.* San Antonio, TX: The Psychological Corporation.

Harter, S. (1988). *Manual for the Self-Perception Profile for Adolescents.* Denver: University of Denver.

Hattie, J., & Edwards, H. (1987). A review of the Bruininks-Oseretsky Test of Motor Proficiency. *British Journal of Educational Psychology, 57,* 104–113.

Hatton, C. (1998). Intellectual disabilities—Epidemiology and causes. In E. Emerson, C. Hatton, & J. Bromley (Eds.), *Clinical psychology and people with intellectual disabilities* (pp. 20–38). New York: Wiley.

Hawkins, R. P., & Hawkins, K. K. (1981). Parental observations on the education of severely retarded children: Can it be done in the classroom? *Analysis and Intervention in Developmental Disabilities, 1,* 13–22.

Haynes, S. N. (1998). The changing nature of behavioral assessment. In A. S. Bellack & M. Hersen (Eds.), *Behavioral assessment: A practical handbook* (4th ed., pp. 1–21). Needham Heights, MA: Allyn & Bacon.

Haynes, S. N., & Horn, W. F. (1982). Reactivity in behavioral observation: A review. *Behavioral Assessment, 4,* 369–385.

Haywood, H. C. (1997). Interactive assessment. In R. L. Taylor (Ed.), *Assessment of individuals with mental retardation* (pp. 103–121). San Diego: Singular.

Heath, C. P., & Kush, J. C. (1991). Use of discrepancy formulas in assessment of learning disabilities. In J. E. Obzurt & G. W. Hynd, (Eds.), *Neuropsychological foundations of learning disabilities: A handbook of issues, methods, and practice* (pp. 287–307). San Diego: Academic Press.

Hécaen, H. (1983). Acquired aphasia in children: Revisited. *Neuropsychologia, 21,* 581–587.

Hechtman, L. (1994). Genetic and neurobiological aspects of attention hyperactive disorder: A review. *Journal of Psychiatry & Neuroscience, 19,* 193–201.

Hegarty, S., & Lucas, D. (1978). *Ability to learn? The pursuit of culture-fair assessment.* Windsor Banks, England: NFER Publishing.

Helms, D. B., & Turner, J. S. (1976). *Exploring child behavior.* Philadelphia: Saunders.

Hickey, J. V. (1992). *The clinical practice of neurological and neurosurgical nursing* (3rd ed.). Philadelphia: J. B. Lippincott.

Hill, E. W., Guth, D. A., & Hill, M. M. (1985). Spatial concept instruction for children with low vision. *Education of the Visually Handicapped, 16,* 152–161.

Hiltonsmith, R. W., & Keller, H. R. (1983). What happened to the setting in person-setting assessment? *Professional Psychology: Research and Practice, 14,* 419–434.

Hinshaw, S. P. (1994). *Attention deficits and hyperactivity in children.* Newbury Park, CA: Sage.

Hinton, G. E., Plaut, D. C., & Shallice, T. (1993). Simulating brain damage. *Scientific American, 269,* 76–82.

Hirshberg, L. M. (1993). Clinical interviews with infants and their families. In C. H. Zeanah, Jr. (Ed.), *Handbook of infant mental health* (pp. 173–190). New York: Guilford.

Hocevar, D. (1981). Measurement of creativity: Review and critique. *Journal of Personality Assessment, 45,* 450–464.

Hodapp, R. M. (1998). *Development and disabilities: Intellectual, sensory, and motor impairments.* New York: Cambridge University Press.

Hodapp, R. M., & Zigler, E. (1999). Intellectual development and mental retardation—some continuing controversies. In M. Anderson (Ed.), *The development of intelligence* (pp. 295–308). Hove, England: Psychology Press.

Hodges, K. (1993). Structured interviews for assessing children. *Journal of Child Psychology & Psychiatry & Allied Disciplines, 34,* 49–68.

Hodges, K. (1997). *Child Adolescent Schedule (CAS).* Ypsilanti, MI: Eastern Michigan University.

Hohnen, B., & Stevenson, J. (1999). The structure of genetic influences on general cognitive, language, phonological, and reading abilities. *Developmental Psychology, 35,* 590–603.

Hops, H., Biglan, A., Sherman, L., Arthur, J., Friedman, L., & Osteen, V. (1987). Home observations of family interactions of depressed women. *Journal of Consulting and Clinical Psychology, 55,* 341–346.

Horton, C. B., & Kochurka, K. A. (1995). The assessment of children with disabilities who report sexual abuse: A special look at those most vulnerable. In T. Ney (Ed.), *True and false allegations of child sexual abuse: Assessment and case management* (pp. 275–289). New York: Brunner/Mazel.

Hotz, R. L. (1996a, October 13). Deciphering the miracles of the mind. *Los Angeles Times,* pp. A1, A20–A22.

Hotz, R. L. (1996b, October 16). Unraveling the riddle of identity. *Los Angeles Times,* pp. A1, A10–A11.

Hotz, R. L. (1998, October 18). In art of language, the brain matters. *Los Angeles Times,* pp. A1, A38–A39.

Howard, M. E. (1988). Behavior management in the acute care rehabilitation setting. *Journal of Head Trauma Rehabilitation, 3,* 14–22.

Hughes, J. N. (1988). Interviewing children. In J. M. Dillard & R. R. Reilly (Eds.), *Systematic interviewing: Communication skills for professional effectiveness* (pp. 90–113). Columbus, OH: Merrill.

Hutt, M. L. (1969). *The Hutt adaptation of the Bender-Gestalt Test* (2nd ed.). New York: Grune & Stratton.

Huttenlocher, P. R., Levine, S. C., Huttenlocher, J., & Gates, J. (1990). Discrimination of normal and at-risk preschool children on the basis of neurological tests. *Developmental Medicine & Child Neurology, 32,* 394–402.

Hynd, G. W. (1992). *Neuropsychological assessment in clinical child psychology.* Newbury Park, CA: Sage.

Hynd, G. W., Obrzut, J. E., & Obrzut, A. (1981). Are lateral and perceptual asymmetries related to WISC–R and achievement test performance in normal and learning-disabled children? *Journal of Consulting and Clinical Psychology, 49,* 977–979.

Iverson, G. L., Iverson, A. M., & Barton, E. A. (1994). The Children's Orientation and Amnesia Test: Educational status is a moderator variable in tracking recovery from TBI. *Brain Injury, 8,* 685–688.

Iverson, G. L., Woodward, T. S., & Iverson, A. M. (In press). Regression-predicted age norms for the Children's Orientation and Amnesia Test. *Archives of Clinical Neuropsychology.*

Iverson, T. J., & Segal, M. (1992). Social behavior of maltreated children: Exploring links to parent behavior and beliefs. In I. E. Sigel (Ed.), *Parental belief systems: The psychological consequences for children* (2nd ed., pp. 267–289). Hillsdale, NJ: Erlbaum.

Jacobs, M. P. (1993). Limited understanding of deficit in children with brain dysfunction. *Neuropsychological Rehabilitation, 3,* 341–365.

Jacobson, J. W., & Mulick, J. A. (1994). Facilitated communication: Better education through applied ideology. *Journal of Behavioral Education, 4,* 95–107.

Jenkinson, J. C. (1996). Identifying intellectual disability: Some problems in the measurement of intelligence and adaptive behavior. *Australian Psychologist, 31,* 97–102.

Jennett, B., & Bond, M. R. (1975). Assessment of outcome after severe brain damage. *Lancet, 1,* 480–484.

Jennett, B., & Teasdale, G. (1981). *Management of head injuries.* Philadelphia: F. A. Davis.

Jennings, R. L. (1982). *Handbook for basic considerations in interviewing children.* Unpublished manuscript, Counseling and Assessment Service, Independence, IA.

Jensen, P. S., Salzberg, A. D., Richter, J. E., & Watanabe, H. K. (1993). Scales, diagnoses, and child psychopathology, I: Child Behavior Checklist and DISC relationships. *Journal of the American Academy of Child and Adolescent Psychiatry, 38,* 700–707.

Jensen, P. S., & Watanabe, H. K. (1999). Sherlock Holmes and child psychopathology assessment approaches: The case of the false-positive. *Journal of the American Academy of Child and Adolescent Psychiatry, 38,* 138–146.

Johnson, A. B. (1987). Attitudes toward mainstreaming: Implications for inservice training and teaching the handicapped. *Education, 107,* 229–233.

Johnson, C., Archer, R. P., Sheaffer, C. I., & Miller, D. (1992). Relationships between the MAPI and the MMPI in the assessment of adolescent psychopathology. *Journal of Personality Assessment, 58,* 277–286.

Johnson, D. A. (1992). Head injured children and education: A need for greater delineation and understanding. *British Journal of Educational Psychology, 62,* 404–409.

Jordan, L. S., & Hall, P. K. (1985). The Token and Reporter's Tests using two scoring conventions: A normative study with 286 grade and junior high students. *Language, Speech, and Hearing Services in Schools, 16,* 227–243.

Jordan, R. (1999). *Autistic spectrum disorders: An introductory handbook for practitioners.* London, England: David Fulton.

Jorm, A. F., & Share, D. L. (1983). Phonological recording and reading acquisition. *Applied Psycholinguistics, 4,* 103–147.

Kadushin, A. (1983). *The social work interview* (2nd ed.). New York: Columbia University Press.

Kahng, S. W., & Iwata, B. A. (1998). Computerized systems for collecting real-time observational data. *Journal of Applied Behavior Analysis, 2,* 253–261.

Kane, R. L., & Kay, G. G. (1992). Computerized assessment in neuropsychology: A review of tests and test batteries. *Neuropsychology Review, 3,* 1–117.

Kanfer, R., Eyberg, S. M., & Krahn, G. L. (1983). Interviewing strategies in child assessment. In C. E. Walker & M. C. Roberts (Eds.), *Handbook of clinical child psychology* (pp. 95–108). New York: Wiley.

Kanfer, R., Eyberg, S. M., & Krahn, G. L. (1992). Interviewing strategies in child assessment. In C. E. Walker & M. C. Roberts (Eds.), *Handbook of clinical child psychology* (2nd ed., pp. 49–62). New York: Wiley.

Kaplan, E. F., Fein, D., Kramer, J., Delis, D., & Morris, R. (1999). *WISC–III PI.* San Antonio, TX: The Psychological Corporation.

Kaplan, E. F., Goodglass, H., & Weintraub, S. (1983). *The Boston Naming Test* (2nd ed.). Philadelphia: Lea & Febiger.

Karoly, P. (1981). Self-management problems in children. In E. J. Mash & L. G. Terdal (Eds.), *Behavioral assessment of childhood disorders* (pp. 79–126). New York: Guilford.

Karpel, M. A., & Strauss, E. S. (1983). *Family evaluation.* New York: Gardner.

Katz, E. R., Kellerman, J., & Siegel, S. E. (1980). Behavioral distress in children with cancer undergoing medical procedures: Developmental considerations. *Journal of Consulting and Clinical Psychology, 48,* 356–365.

Kaufman, J., Birmaher, B., Brent, D. A., Rao, U., & Ryan N. (1996). *Revised Schedule for Affective Disorders and Schizophrenia for School Aged Children: Present and Lifetime version (K-SADS–PL).* Pittsburgh: Western Psychiatric Institute and Clinic.

Kavale, K. A., & Forness, S. R. (1984). A meta-analysis of the validity of Wechsler Scale profiles and recategorizations: Patterns or parodies? *Learning Disability Quarterly, 7,* 136–156.

Kavale, K. A., & Forness, S. R. (1996). Social skill deficits and learning disabilities: A meta-analysis. *Journal of Learning Disabilities, 3,* 226–237.

Kavale, K. A., & Reese, J. H. (1992). The character of learning disabilities: An Iowa profile. *Learning Disability Quarterly, 15,* 74–94.

Kay, T., & Silver, S. M. (1989). Closed head trauma: Assessment for rehabilitation. In M. D. Lezak (Ed.), *Assessment of the behavioral consequences of head trauma* (pp. 145–170). New York: Liss.

Kazdin, A. E. (1981). Behavioral observation. In M. Hersen & A. S. Bellack (Eds.), *Behavioral assessment: A practical handbook* (2nd ed., pp. 101–124). New York: Pergamon.

Keane, K. J. (1987). Assessing deaf children. In C. S. Lidz (Ed.), *Dynamic assessment: An interactional approach to evaluating learning potential* (pp. 360–376). New York: Guilford.

Kearns, K., Edwards, R., & Tingstrom, D. H. (1990). Accuracy of long momentary time-sampling intervals: Implications for classroom data collection. *Journal of Psychoeducational Assessment, 8,* 74–85.

Kelley, P. A., Sanspree, M. J., & Davidson, R. C. (2001). Visual impairment in children and youth. In B. Silverstone, M. A. Lang, B. Rosenthal, & E. E. Faye (Eds.), *The Lighthouse handbook on visual impairment and vision rehabilitation* (pp. 1137–1151). New York: Oxford University Press.

Kendziora, K. T., & O'Leary, S. G. (1992). Dysfunctional parenting as a focus for prevention and treatment of child behavior problems. *Advances in Clinical Child Psychology, 15,* 175–206.

Keogh, B. K. (1987). A shared attribute model of learning disabilities. In S. Vaughn & C. S. Bos (Eds.), *Research in learning disabilities: Issues and future directions* (pp. 3–18). Boston: College-Hill.

Khan, N. A., & Hoge, R. D. (1983). A teacher-judgment measure of social competence: Validity data. *Journal of Consulting and Clinical Psychology, 51,* 809–814.

Kinsbourne, M., & Caplan, P. J. (1979). *Children's learning and attention problems.* Boston: Little, Brown.

Kinsella, G. J., Prior, M., Sawyer, M., Ong, B., Murtagh, D., Eisenmajer, R., Bryan, D., Anderson, V., & Klug, G. (1997). Predictors and indicators of academic outcome in children 2 years following traumatic brain injury. *Journal of the International Neuropsychology Society, 3,* 608–616.

Kinston, W., & Loader, P. (1984). Eliciting whole-family interaction with a standardized clinical interview. *Journal of Family Therapy, 6,* 347–363.

Kirk, S. A., Gallagher, J. J., & Anastasiow, N. J. (1997). *Educating exceptional children* (8th ed.). Boston: Houghton Mifflin.

Klein, R. G. (1991). Parent-child agreement in clinical assessment of anxiety and other psychopathology: A review. *Journal of Anxiety Disorders, 5,* 187–198.

Kleinmuntz, B. (1982). *Personality and psychological assessment.* New York: St. Martin's.

Kljajic, I., & Berry, D. (1984). Brain syndrome and WAIS PIQ VIQ difference scores corrected for test artifact. *Journal of Clinical Psychology, 40,* 271–277.

Klonoff, H., Clark, C., & Klonoff, P. S. (1993). Long-term outcome of head injuries: A 23 year follow up study of children with head injuries. *Journal of Neurology, Neurosurgery and Psychiatry, 56,* 410–415.

Knoff, H. M., & Sperling, B. L. (1986). Gifted children and visual-motor development: A comparison of Bender-Gestalt and VMI test performance. *Psychology in the Schools, 23,* 247–251.

Knoster, T., & Llewellyn, G. (1998a). *Functional behavioral assessment for students with individualized educational programs.* Harrisburg: Instructional Support System of Pennsylvania, Pennsylvania Department of Education.

Knoster, T., & Llewellyn, G. (1998b). *Screening for an understanding of student problem behavior: An initial line of inquiry* (2nd ed.). Harrisburg: Instructional Support System of Pennsylvania, Pennsylvania Department of Education.

Kohlberg, L. (1976). Moral stages and moralization: The cognitive-developmental approach. In T. Lickona (Ed.), *Moral development and behavior: Theory, research, and social issues* (pp. 31–53). New York: Holt, Rinehart and Winston.

Kolb, B., & Whishaw, I. Q. (1990). *Fundamentals of human neuropsychology* (3rd ed.). New York: Freeman.

Koppitz, E. M. (1964). *The Bender Gestalt Test for young children.* New York: Grune & Stratton.

Koppitz, E. M. (1975). *The Bender Gestalt Test for young children: Vol. 2. Research and application, 1963–1973.* New York: Grune & Stratton.

Korkman, M. (1990). *NEPSY, Neuropsychologisk underskoning: 4–7 ar, Svensk version [NEPSY, Neuropsychological assessment:*

4–7 years, Swedish version]. Stockholm, Sweden: Psykologi-Forlaget AB.

Korkman, M., Kirk, U., & Kemp, S. (1998). *NEPSY: A developmental neuropsychological assessment.* San Antonio, TX: The Psychological Corporation.

Korotitsch, W. J., & Nelson-Gray, R. O. (1999). An overview of self-monitoring research in assessment and treatment. *Psychological Assessment, 11,* 415–425.

Kovacs, M. (1992). *Children's Depression Inventory (CDI).* North Tonawanda, NY: Multi-Health Systems.

Krauft, V. R., & Krauft, C. C. (1972). Structured vs. unstructured visual-motor tests for educable retarded children. *Perceptual and Motor Skills, 34,* 691–694.

Kraus, N., McGee, T. J., Carrell, T. D., Zecker, S. G., Nicol, T. G., & Koch, D. B. (1996). Auditory neurophysiologic responses and discrimination deficits in children with learning problems. *Science, 273,* 971–973.

Krehbiel, R., & Kroth, R. L. (1991). Communicating with families of children with disabilities or chronic illness. In M. J. Fine (Ed.), *Collaboration with parents of exceptional children* (pp. 103–127). Brandon, VT: Clinical Psychology Publishing Company.

Kropenske, V., & Howard, J. (1994). *Protecting children in substance-abusing families.* Washington, DC: U.S. Department of Health and Human Services.

Krug, D. A., Arick, J. R., & Almond, P. J. (1980). *Autism Screening Instrument for Educational Planning.* Portland, OR: ASIEP Educational Company.

Lachar, D., & Gruber, C. P. (1995a). *Personality Inventory for Youth (PIY) manual: Technical guide.* Los Angeles: Western Psychological Services.

Lachar, D., & Gruber, C. P. (1995b). *Personality Inventory for Youth (PIY) manual: Administration and interpretation guide.* Los Angeles: Western Psychological Services.

Lachar, D., Wingenfeld, S. A., Kline, R. B., & Gruber, C. P. (2000). *Student Behavior Survey.* Los Angeles: Western Psychological Services.

LaFee, S. (1999, September 29). When the brain takes a bump. *San Diego Union Tribune,* pp. E1, E5.

La Greca, A. M. (1983). Interviewing and behavioral observations. In C. E. Walker & M. C. Roberts (Eds.), *Handbook of clinical child psychology* (pp. 109–131). New York: Wiley.

Lambert, N., Nihira, K., & Leland, H. (1993). *AAMR Adaptive Behavior Scale–School* (2nd ed.). Austin, TX: Pro-Ed.

Landesman, S. (1987). The changing structure and function of institutions: A search for optimal group care environments. In S. Landesman, P. M. Vietze, & M. J. Begab (Eds.), *Living environments and mental retardation* (pp. 79–126). Washington, DC: American Association on Mental Retardation.

Landesman-Dwyer, S., & Butterfield, E. C. (1983). Mental retardation: Developmental issues in cognitive and social adaptation. In M. Lewis (Ed.), *Origins of intelligence: Infancy and early childhood* (2nd ed., pp. 479–519). New York: Plenum.

LaRoche, C. (1986). Prevention in high risk children of depressed parents. *Canadian Journal of Psychiatry, 31,* 161–165.

Larrabee, G. J. (1986). Another look at VIQ-PIQ scores and unilateral brain damage. *International Journal of Neuroscience, 29,* 141–148.

Laucht, M., Esser, G., & Schmidt, M. H. (1993). Adverse temperamental characteristics and early behaviour problems in 3-month-old infants born with different psychosocial and biological risks. *Acta Paedopsychiatrica: International Journal of Child & Adolescent Psychiatry, 56,* 19–24.

LeBaron, S., & Zeltzer, L. (1984). Assessment of acute pain and anxiety in children and adolescents by self-reports, observer reports, and a behavior checklist. *Journal of Consulting and Clinical Psychology, 52,* 729–738.

Leckliter, I. N., Forster, A. A., Klonoff, H., & Knights, R. M. (1992). A review of reference group data from normal children for the Halstead-Reitan Neuropsychological Test Battery for Older Children. *Clinical Neuropsychologist, 6,* 201–229.

Lehman, J., & Breen, M. J. (1982). A comparative analysis of the Bender-Gestalt and Beery-Buktenica Tests of Visual-Motor Integration as a function of grade level for regular education students. *Psychology in the Schools, 19,* 52–54.

Lerner, J. W. (1997). Attention deficit disorder. In J. W. Lloyd, D. J. Kameenui, & D. Chard (Eds.), *Issues in educating students with disabilities* (pp. 27–44). Mahwah, NJ: Erlbaum.

Lesiak, J. (1984). The Bender Visual Motor Gestalt Test: Implications for the diagnosis and prediction of reading achievement. *Journal of School Psychology, 22,* 391–405.

Levin, H. S., Culhane, K. A., Hartmann, J., Evankovich, K., Mattson, A. J., Harward, H., Ringholz, G., Ewing-Cobbs, L., & Fletcher, J. M. (1991). Developmental changes in performance on tests of purported frontal lobe functioning. *Developmental Neuropsychology, 7,* 377–395.

Levin, H. S., Ewing-Cobbs, L., & Fletcher, J. M. (1989). Neurobehavioral outcome of mild head injury in children. In H. S. Levin, H. M. Eisenberg, & A. L. Benton (Eds.), *Mild head injury* (pp. 189–213). New York: Oxford University Press.

Lewis, M. (1991). Psychiatric assessment of infants, children, and adolescents. In M. Lewis (Ed.), *Child and adolescent psychiatry: A comprehensive textbook* (pp. 447–463). Baltimore: Williams & Wilkins.

Lewkowicz, D. J., & Turkewitz, G. (1982). Influence of hemispheric specialization in sensory processing on reaching in infants: Age and gender related effects. *Developmental Psychology, 18,* 301–308.

Lezak, M. D. (1978). Living with the characterologically altered brain-injured patient. *Journal of Clinical Psychiatry, 39,* 592–598.

Lezak, M. D. (1983). *Neuropsychological assessment* (2nd ed.). New York: Oxford University Press.

Lezak, M. D. (1995). *Neuropsychological assessment* (3rd ed.). New York: Oxford University Press.

Lichtenstein, R., & Ireton, H. (1984). *Preschool screening: Identifying young children with developmental and educational problems.* New York: Grune & Stratton.

Lidz, C. S. (1991). *Practitioner's guide to dynamic assessment.* New York: Guilford.

Lidz, C. S. (1997). Dynamic assessment approaches. In D. P. Flanagan, J. L. Genshaft, & P. L. Harrison (Eds.), *Contemporary intellectual assessment: Theories, tests, and issues* (pp. 281–296). New York: Guilford.

Livingston, R. B., Gray, R. M., & Haak, R. A. (1999). Internal consistency of three tests from the Halstead-Reitan Neuropsychological Battery for Older Children. *Assessment, 6,* 93–99.

Livingston, R. B., Gray, R. M., Haak, R. A., & Jennings, E. (1997). Factor structure of the Halstead-Reitan Neuropsychological Test Battery for Older Children. *Child Neuropsychology, 3,* 176–191.

Lohrmann-O'Rourke, S., Knoster, T., & Llewellyn, G. (1999). Screening for understanding: An initial line of inquiry for school-based settings. *Journal of Positive Behavior Interventions, 1,* 35–42.

Lord, C., Rutter, M., DiLavore, P. C., & Risi, S. (1999). *Autism Diagnostic Observation Schedule–WPS (ADOS–WPS).* Los Angeles: Western Psychological Services.

Lord, C., & Schopler, E. (1989). Stability of assessment results of autistic and non-autistic language-impaired children from preschool years to early school age. *Journal of Child Psychology & Psychiatry & Allied Disciplines, 30,* 575–590.

Lord, R. G. (1985). Accuracy in behavioral measurement: An alternative definition based on raters' cognitive schema and signal detection theory. *Journal of Applied Psychology, 70,* 66–71.

Loring, D. W., Martin, R. C., Meador, K. J., & Lee, G. P. (1990). Psychometric construction of the Rey-Osterrieth Complex Figure: Methodological considerations and interrater reliability. *Archives of Clinical Neuropsychology, 5,* 1–14.

Lovell, K., & Shields, J. B. (1967). Some aspects of a study of the gifted child. *British Journal of Educational Psychology, 37,* 201–208.

Lubinski, R. (1981). Environmental language intervention. In R. Chapey (Ed.), *Language intervention strategies in adult aphasia* (pp. 223–245). Baltimore: Williams & Wilkins.

Lyon, G. R. (1995). Toward a definition of dyslexia. *Annals of Dyslexia, 45,* 3–27.

Lyon, G. R. (1996a). Learning disabilities. In E. J. Mash & R. A. Barkley (Eds.), *Child psychopathology* (pp. 390–435). New York: Guilford.

Lyon, G. R. (1996b). Learning disabilities. *Future of Children, 6,* 54–76.

Lyon, G. R., Fletcher, J. M., Shaywitz, S. E., Shaywitz, B. A., Torgesen, J. K., Wood, F. B., Schulte, A., & Olson, R. (2001). Rethinking learning disabilities. In C. E. Finn, Jr., A. J. Rotherham, & C. R. Hokanson, Jr. (Eds.), *Rethinking special education for a new century* (pp. 259–287). Washington, DC: Thomas B. Fordham Foundation and the Progressive Policy Institute.

Lyon, G. R., & Moats, L. C. (1988). Critical issues in the instruction of the learning disabled. *Journal of Consulting and Clinical Psychology, 56,* 830–835.

Lyon, G. R., Moats, L., & Flynn, J. M. (1988). From assessment to treatment: Linkage to intervention with children. In M. G. Tramontana & S. R. Hooper (Eds.), *Assessment issues in child neuropsychology* (pp. 113–142). New York: Plenum.

Macaruso, P., & Sokol, S. M. (1999). Cognitive neuropsychology and developmental dyscalculia. In C. Dolan (Ed.), *The development of mathematical skills* (pp. 201–225). Hove, England: Psychology Press.

Mace, F. C., & Kratochwill, T. R. (1988). Self-monitoring. In J. C. Witt, S. N. Elliott, & F. M. Gresham. (Eds.), *Handbook of behavior therapy in education* (pp. 489–522). New York: Plenum.

MacMillan, D. L., Gresham, F. M., & Bocian K. M. (1998). Curing mental retardation and causing learning disabilities: Consequences of using various WISC–III IQs to estimate aptitude of Hispanic students. *Journal of Psychoeducational Assessment, 16,* 36–54.

MacMillan, D. L., Gresham, F. M., & Siperstein, G. N. (1993). Conceptual and psychometric concerns about the 1992 definition of mental retardation. *American Journal on Mental Retardation, 98,* 325–335.

Mahoney, G., Powell, A., & Finger, I. (1986). The Maternal Behavior Rating Scale. *Topics in Early Childhood Special Education, 6,* 44–56.

Maller, S. J. (1996). WISC–III verbal item invariance across samples of deaf and hearing children of similar measured ability. *Journal of Psychoeducational Assessment, 14,* 152–165.

Maller, S. J., & Braden, J. P. (1993). The construct and criterion-related validity of the WISC–III with deaf adolescents. In B. A. Bracken and R. S. McCallum (Eds.), *Wechsler Intelligence Scale for Children: Third Edition.* Journal of Psychoeducational Assessment Monograph Series—Advances in psychoeducational assessment (pp. 105–113). Brandon, VT: Clinical Psychology Publishing.

Manning, A. (2001, May 22). More babies given tests for hearing loss: Painless test leads to early correction; campaign assesses states' efforts. *USA Today,* p. 1D.

Mannuzza, S., Fyer, A. J., & Klein, D. F. (1993). Assessing psychopathology. *International Journal of Methods in Psychiatric Research, 3,* 157–165.

Mapou, R. L. (1995). A cognitive framework for neuropsychological assessment. In R. L. Mapou & J. Spector (Eds.), *Clinical neuropsychological assessment: A cognitive approach* (pp. 295–337). New York: Plenum.

Marland, S. P., Jr. (1972). *Education of the gifted and talented: Report to the Congress of the United States by the Commissioner of Education.* Washington, DC: U.S. Government Printing Office.

Marley, M. L. (1982). *Organic brain pathology and the Bender-Gestalt Test: A differential diagnostic scoring system.* New York: Grune & Stratton.

Marosszeky, N. E., Batchelor, J., Shores, E. A., Marosszeky, J. E., Klein-Boonschate, M., & Fahey, P. P. (1993). The performance of hospitalized, non head-injured children on the Westmead PTA Scale. *Clinical Neuropsychologist, 7,* 85–95.

Marschark, M. (1993). *Psychological development of deaf children.* New York: Oxford University Press.

Martelle, S. (1999, July 28). Technology replacing braille. *The Los Angeles Times,* pp. A1, A15.

Martin, D. A. (1988). Children and adolescents with traumatic brain injury: Impact on the family. *Journal of Learning Disabilities, 21,* 464–470.

Martins, I. P., & Ferro, J. M. (1992). Recovery of acquired aphasia in children. *Aphasiology, 6,* 431–438.

Mash, E. J., & Barkley, R. A. (1986). Assessment of family interaction with the Response-Class Matrix. *Advances in the Behavioral Assessment of Children and Families, 2,* 29–67.

Mash, E. J., & Dozois, D. J. A. (1996). Child psychopathology: A developmental-systems perspective. In E. J. Mash & R. A. Barkley (Eds.), *Child psychopathology* (pp. 3–60). New York: Guilford.

Mash, E. J., & Terdal, L. G. (1981). Behavioral assessment of childhood disturbance. In E. J. Mash and L. G. Terdal (Eds.), *Behavioral assessment of childhood disorders* (pp. 3–76). New York: Guilford.

Mash, E. J., & Terdal, L. G. (1988). Behavioral assessment of child and family disturbance. In E. J. Mash & L. G. Terdal (Eds.), *Behavioral assessment of childhood disorders* (2nd ed., pp. 3–65). New York: Guilford.

Massagli, T. L., Michaud, L. J., & Rivara, F. P. (1996). Association between injury indices and outcome after severe traumatic brain injury in children. *Archives of Physical Medicine and Rehabilitation, 3,* 13–25.

Mastenbrook, J. (1978, August). Future directions in adaptive behavior assessment: Environmental adaptation measure. In A. T. Fisher (Chair), *Impact of adaptive behavior: ABIC and the environmental adaptation measure.* Symposium presented at the meeting of the American Psychological Association, Toronto, Canada.

Mathiowetz, V., Rogers, S. L., Dowe-Keval, M., Donahoe, L., & Rennells, C. (1986). The Purdue Pegboard: Norms for 14- to 19-year-olds. *American Journal of Occupational Therapy, 40,* 174–179.

Matson, J. L. (1988). *The PIMRA manual.* Orland Park, IL: International Diagnostic System.

Matson, J. L., Baglio, C. S., Smiroldo, B. B., Hamilton, M., Paclawskyj, T. R., Williams, D., & Kirkpatrick-Sanchez, S. (1996). Characteristics of autism as assessed by the Diagnostic Assessment for the Severely Handicapped–II (DASH–II). *Research in Developmental Disabilities, 17,* 135–143.

Mattes, L. J., & Omark, D. R. (1984). *Speech and language assessment for the bilingual handicapped.* San Diego: College-Hill Press.

Mattson, A. J., Sheer, D. E., & Fletcher, J. M. (1992). Electrophysiological evidence of lateralized disturbances in children with learning disabilities. *Journal of Clinical and Experimental Neuropsychology, 14,* 707–716.

Mayberry, R. I. (1992). The cognitive development of deaf children: Recent insights. In S. J. Segalowitz & I. Rapin (Eds.), *Handbook of neuropsychology: Vol. 7. Child neuropsychology* (pp. 51–68). Amsterdam, Netherlands: Elsevier Science.

Mayes, S. D. (1991). Play assessment of preschool hyperactivity. In C. S. Schaefer, K. Gitlin, & A. Sandgrund (Eds.), *Play diagnosis and assessment* (pp. 249–272). New York: Wiley.

Mayes, S. D., & Calhoun, S. L. (1998). Comparison of scores on two recent editions of the Development Test of Visual-Motor Integration. *Perceptual and Motor Skills, 87,* 1324–1326.

Mayes, S. D., Calhoun, S. L., & Crowell, E. W. (1998). WISC–III Freedom from Distractibility as a measure of attention in children with and without attention deficit hyperactivity disorder. *Journal of Attention Disorders, 2,* 217–227.

Mazzeschi, C., & Lis, A. (1999). The Bender-Gestalt Test: Koppitz's Developmental Scoring System administered to two samples of Italian preschool and primary school children. *Perceptual and Motor Skills, 88,* 1235–1244.

McCarney, S. B. (1989). *Attention Deficit Disorders Evaluation Scale.* Columbia, MO: Hawthorne Educational Services.

McConaughy, S. H. (1996). The interview process. In M. Breen & C. Fiedler (Eds.), *Behavioral approach to the assessment of emotionally/behaviorally disordered youth: A handbook for school-based practitioners* (pp. 181–223). Austin, TX: Pro-Ed.

McConaughy, S. H., & Achenbach, T. M. (1994). *Manual for the Semistructured Clinical Interview for Children and Adolescents.* Burlington, VT: University Associates in Psychiatry.

McGraw, K. O., & Wong, S. P. (1996). Forming inferences about some intraclass correlation coefficients. *Psychological Methods, 4,* 390.

McIntosh, J. A., Belter, R. W., Saylor, C. F., & Finch, A. J. (1988). The Bender-Gestalt with adolescents: Comparison of two scoring systems. *Journal of Clinical Psychology, 44,* 226–230.

McKinney, J. D., Montague, M., & Hocutt, A. M. (1993). Educational assessment of students with attention deficit disorder. *Exceptional Children, 60,* 125–131.

McLinden, S. E. (1989). An evaluation of the Battelle Developmental Inventory for determining special education eligibility. *Journal of Psychoeducational Assessment, 7,* 66–73.

McMahon, R. J., & Forehand, R. (1988). Conduct disorders. In E. J. Mash & L. G. Terdal (Eds.), *Behavioral assessment of childhood disorders* (2nd ed., pp. 105–153). New York: Guilford.

Meadow, K. P. (1983). An instrument for assessment of social-emotional adjustment in hearing impaired preschoolers. *American Annals of the Deaf, 128,* 826–834.

Medoff-Cooper, B., Carey, W. B., & McDevitt, S. C. (1993). The Early Infancy Temperament Questionnaire. *Journal of Developmental and Behavioral Pediatrics, 14,* 230–235.

Mercer, J. R., & Lewis, J. F. (1978). *System of Multicultural Pluralistic Assessment.* San Antonio: The Psychological Corporation.

Mesibov, G. B., Adams, L. W., & Klinger, L. G. (1997). *Autism: Understanding the disorder.* New York: Plenum.

Meyen, E. (1989). Let's not confuse test scores with the substance of the discrepancy model. *Journal of Learning Disabilities, 22,* 482–483.

Middleton, H. A., Keene, R. G., & Brown, G. W. (1990). Convergent and discriminant validities of the Scales of Independent Behavior and the revised Vineland Adaptive Behavior Scales. *American Journal on Mental Retardation, 94,* 669–673.

Milberg, W. P., Hebben, N., & Kaplan, E. (1996). The Boston process approach to neuropsychological assessment. In I. Grant & K. M. Adams (Eds.), *Neuropsychological assessment of neuropsychiatric disorders* (2nd ed., pp. 58–80). New York: Oxford University Press.

Mild Traumatic Brain Injury Committee. (1993). Definition of mild traumatic brain injury. *Journal of Head Trauma Rehabilitation, 8,* 86–87.

Miller, J. A., Tansy, M., & Hughes, T. L. (1998). Functional behavioral assessment: The link between problem behavior and effective intervention in schools. *Current Issues in Education* [On-line], *1(5).* Available: http://cie.ed.asu/volume1/number5

Miller, J. H., & Milam, C. P. (1987). Multiplication and division errors committed by learning disabled students. *Learning Disabilities Research, 2,* 119–122.

Miller, L. (1989). Neuropsychology, personality and substance abuse: Implications for head injury rehabilitation. *Cognitive Rehabilitation, 7,* 26–31.

Miller, L. (1993). Family therapy of brain injury: Syndromes, strategies, and solutions. *American Journal of Family Therapy, 21,* 111–121.

Miller, S. L., & Tallal, P. (1995). A behavioral neuroscience approach to developmental language disorders: Evidence for a rapid temporal processing deficit. In D. Cicchetti & D. J. Cohen (Eds.), *Developmental psychopathology: Vol. 2. Risk, disorder, and adaptation* (pp. 274–298). New York: Wiley.

Millon, T., Green, C. J., & Meagher, R. B. (1982). *Millon Adolescent Personality Inventory.* Minneapolis, MN: National Computer Systems.

Miltenberger, R. G. (1997). *Behavior modification: Principles and procedures.* Pacific Grove, CA: Brooks/Cole.

Milton, S. B. (1988). Management of subtle cognitive communication deficits. *Journal of Head Trauma Rehabilitation, 3,* 1–11.

Mittenberg, W., Zielinski, R., & Fichera, S. (1993). Recovery from mild head injury: A treatment manual for patients. *Psychotherapy in Private Practice, 12,* 37–52.

Moats, L. C., & Lyon, G. R. (1993). Learning disabilities in the United States: Advocacy, science, and the future of the field. *Journal of Learning Disabilities, 26,* 282–294.

Moeller, T. G. (2001). *Youth aggression and violence: A psychological approach.* Mahwah, NJ: Erlbaum.

Moffitt, T. E. (1990). Juvenile delinquency and attention deficit disorder: Boys' developmental trajectories from age 3 to age 15. *Child Development, 61,* 893–910.

Moore, J. B., Reeve, T. G., & Boan, T. (1986). Reliability of the short form of the Bruininks-Oseretsky Test of Motor Proficiency with five-year-old children. *Perceptual and Motor Skills, 62,* 223–226.

Moore, M. (1987). Inter-judge reliability expressed as percent of agreement between observers. *Archivio di Psicologia, Neurologia e Psichiatria, 48,* 124–129.

Moose, D., & Brannigan, G. G. (1997). Comparison of preschool children's scores on the Modified Version of the Bender-Gestalt Test and the Developmental Test of Visual-Motor Integration. *Perceptual and Motor Skills, 85,* 766.

Morgan, A., & Vernon, M. (1994). A guide to diagnosis of learning disabilities in deaf and hard-of-hearing children and adults. *American Annals of the Deaf, 139,* 358–370.

Morgan, C. J., & Cauce, A. M. (1999). Predicting DSM-III–R disorders from the Youth Self-Report: Analysis of data from a field study. *Journal of the American Academy of Child and Adolescent Psychiatry, 38,* 1237–1245.

Morgan, S. B. (1984). Helping parents understand the diagnosis of autism. *Developmental and Behavioral Pediatrics, 5,* 78–85.

Morris, R. D. (1988). Classification of learning disabilities: Old problems and new approaches. *Journal of Consulting and Clinical Psychology, 56,* 789–794.

Morrison, G. M., & Cosden, M. A. (1997). Risk, resilience, and adjustment of individuals with learning disabilities. *Learning Disability Quarterly, 20,* 43–60.

Moscovitch, M. (1981). Right-hemisphere language. *Topics in Language Disorders, 1,* 41–61.

Mulick, J. A., Jacobson, J. W., & Kobe, F. H. (1993). Anguished silence and helping hands: Autism and facilitated communication. *Skeptical Inquirer, 17,* 270–280.

Murphy, H. A., Hutchison, J. M., & Bailey, J. S. (1983). Behavioral school psychology goes outdoors: The effects of organized games on playground aggression. *Journal of Applied Behavior Analysis, 16,* 29–35.

Musten, L. M., Firestone, P., Pisterman, S., Bennett, S., & Mercer, J. (1997). Effects of methylphenidate on preschool children with ADHD: Cognitive and behavioral functions. *Journal of the American Academy of Child and Adolescent Psychiatry, 36,* 1407–1416.

Naglieri, J. A., LeBuffe, P. A., & Pfeiffer, S. I. (1994). *Devereux Scales of Mental Disorders.* San Antonio, TX: The Psychological Corporation.

National Joint Committee on Learning Disabilities. (1987). Learning disabilities: Issues on definition. *Journal of Learning Disabilities, 20,* 107–108.

Nay, W. R. (1979). *Multimethod clinical assessment.* New York: Gardner.

Neale, M. D., & McKay, M. F. (1985). Scoring the Bender-Gestalt Test using the Koppitz developmental system: Interrater reliability, item difficulty, and scoring implications. *Perceptual and Motor Skills, 60,* 627–636.

Neel, R., & Billingsly, R. (1990). *IMPACT: A functional curriculum handbook for students with moderate to severe disabilities.* Baltimore: Paul H. Brooks.

Newborg, J., Stock, J. R., & Wnek, L. (1984). *Battelle Developmental Inventory.* Chicago: Riverside.

Nihira, K., Leland, H., & Lambert, N. (1993). *AAMR Adaptive Behavior Scale–Residential and Community* (2nd ed.). Austin, TX: Pro-Ed.

Northern, J. L., & Downs, M. P. (1991). *Hearing in children* (4th ed.). Baltimore: Williams & Wilkins.

Nottelmann, E. D., & Jensen, P. S. (1995). Comorbidity of disorders in children and adolescents: Developmental perspectives. *Advances in Clinical Child Psychology, 17,* 109–155.

Nussbaum, N. L., & Bigler, E. D. (1997). Halstead-Reitan Neuropsychological Test Batteries for Children. In C. R. Reynolds & E. Fletcher-Janzen (Eds.), *Handbook of clinical child neuropsychology* (2nd ed., pp. 219–236). New York: Plenum.

Oakland, T. D., & Houchins, S. (1985). Testing the test: A review of the Vineland Adaptive Behavior Scales, Survey Form. *Journal of Counseling and Development, 63,* 585–586.

Ollendick, T. H., Oswald, D. P., & Ollendick, D. G. (1993). Anxiety disorders in mentally retarded persons. In J. L. Matson & R. P. Barrett (Eds.), *Psychopathology in the mentally retarded* (2nd ed., pp. 41–85). Needham Heights, MA: Allyn & Bacon.

Olson, D. H., & Portner, J. (1983). Family Adaptability and Cohesion Evaluation Scales. In E. E. Filsinger (Ed.), *Marriage and family assessment: A source book for family therapy* (pp. 299–315). Newbury Park, CA: Sage.

O'Neill, R. E., Horner, R. H., Albin, R. W., Sprague, J. R., Storey, K., & Newton, J. S. (1997). *Functional assessment and program development for problem behavior: A practical handbook* (2nd ed.). Pacific Grove, CA: Brooks/Cole.

Orvaschel, H. (1995). *Schedule for Affective Disorders and Schizophrenia for School-Age Children–Epidemiological version 5 (K-SADS-E5).* Ft. Lauderdale, FL: NOVA Southeastern University.

OSEP Technical Assistance Center. (2001). *Functional assessment* [On-line]. Available: http://www.pbis.org

Oster, G. D., Caro, J. E., Eagen, D. R., & Lillo, M. A. (1988). *Assessing adolescents.* New York: Pergamon.

O'Toole, M. E. (2000). *The school shooter: A threat assessment perspective.* Quantico, VA: National Center for the Analysis of Violent Crime, FBI Academy.

Oud, J. H., & Sattler, J. M. (1984). Generalized kappa coefficient: A microsoft BASIC program. *Behavior Research Methods, Instruments, & Computers, 16,* 481.

Papero, P. H., Prigatano, G. P., Snyder, H. M., & Johnson, D. L. (1993). Children's adaptive behavioural competence after head injury. *Neuropsychological Rehabilitation, 3,* 321–340.

Paquier, P., & Van Dongen, H. R. (1993). Current trends in acquired childhood aphasia: An introduction. *Aphasiology, 7,* 421–440.

Parnes, S. (1966). *Workshop for creative problem solving institutes and courses.* Buffalo, NY: Creative Educational Foundation.

Parsons, L., & Weinberg, L. (1993). The Sugar scoring system for the Bender-Gestalt Test: An objective approach that reflects clinical judgment. *Perceptual and Motor Skills, 77,* 883–893.

Pascal, G. R., & Suttell, B. J. (1951). *The Bender-Gestalt Test: Quantification and validity for adults.* New York: Grune & Stratton.

Paternite, C. E., Loney, J., Salisbury, H., & Whaley, M. A. (1999). Childhood inattention-overactivity, aggression, and stimulant medication history as predictors of young adult outcomes. *Journal of Child and Adolescent Psychopharmacology, 9,* 169–184.

Paulsen J. S., & Altmaier, E. M. (1995). The effects of perceived versus enacted social support on the discriminative cue function of spouses for pain behaviors. *Pain, 60,* 103–110.

Pendarvis, E. D., Howley, C. B., & Howley, A. A. (1990). *The abilities of gifted children.* Englewood Cliffs, NJ: Prentice Hall.

Pennington, B. F. (1991). *Diagnosing learning disorders: A neuro-psychological framework.* New York: Guilford.

Pennington, B. F., & Welsh, M. (1995). Neuropsychology and developmental psychopathology. In D. Cicchetti & D. J. Cohen (Eds.), *Developmental psychopathology: Vol. 1. Theory and methods* (pp. 254–290). New York: Wiley.

Perrin, E. C., Stein, R. E. K., & Drotar, D. (1991). Cautions in using the Child Behavior Checklist: Observations based on research about children with a chronic illness. *Journal of Pediatric Psychology, 16,* 411–421.

Perry, A., & Factor, D. C. (1989). Psychometric validity and clinical usefulness of the Vineland Adaptive Behavior Scales and the AAMD Adaptive Behavior Scale for an autistic sample. *Journal of Autism and Developmental Disorders, 19,* 41–55.

Peterson, L., & Tremblay, G. (1999). Self-monitoring in behavioral medicine: Children. *Psychological Assessment, 11,* 458–465.

Phelps, J., Stempel, L., & Speck, G. (1985). The Children's Handwriting Scale: A new diagnostic tool. *Journal of Educational Research, 79,* 46–50.

Phelps, L., & Cox, D. (1993). Children with prenatal cocaine exposure: Resilient or handicapped? *School Psychology Review, 22,* 710–724.

Pianta, R. C., Smith, N., & Reeve R. E. (1991). Observing mother and child behavior in a problem solving situation at school entry: Relations with classroom adjustment. *School Psychology Quarterly, 6,* 1–15.

Piers, E. V. (1984). *Piers-Harris Children's Self-Concept Scale.* Los Angeles: Western Psychological Services.

Piotrowski, C. (1995). A review of the clinical and research use of the Bender-Gestalt Test. *Perceptual and Motor Skills, 81,* 1272–1274.

Polansky, N. A., Borgman, R. D., & De Saix, C. (1972). *Roots of futility.* San Francisco: Jossey-Bass.

Porter, G. L., & Binder, D. M. (1981). A pilot study of visual-motor development inter-test reliability: The Beery Developmental Test of Visual-Motor Integration and the Bender Visual Motor Gestalt Test. *Journal of Learning Disabilities, 14,* 124–127.

Price-Williams, D. R., & Ramirez, M., III. (1977). Divergent thinking, cultural differences, and bilingualism. *Journal of Social Psychology, 103,* 3–11.

Prifitera, A., & Dersh, J. (1993). Base rates of WISC–III diagnostic subtest patterns among normal, learning-disabled, and ADHD samples. In B. A. Bracken & R. S. McCallum (Eds.), *Wechsler Intelligence Scale for Children: Third Edition.* Journal of Psychoeducational Assessment Monograph Series—Advances in psychoeducational assessment (pp. 43–55). Brandon, VT: Clinical Psychology Publishing.

Prigatano, G. P., Fordyce, D. J., Zeiner, H. K., Roueche, J. R., Pepping, M., & Wood, B. C. (1986). *Neuropsychological rehabilitation after brain injury.* Baltimore: Johns Hopkins University Press.

Prior, M. R. (1989). Reading disability: "Normative" or "pathological." *Australian Journal of Psychology, 41,* 135–158.

Prior, M. R., & Ozonoff, S. (1998). Psychological factors in autism. In F. R. Volkmar (Ed.), *Autism and pervasive developmental disorders* (pp. 64–108). New York: Cambridge University Press.

Prizant, B. M., & Wetherby, A. M. (1993). Communication in preschool autistic children. In E. Schopler, M. E. Van Bourgondien, & M. M. Bristol (Eds.), *Preschool issues in autism* (pp. 95–128). New York: Plenum.

Quay, H. C., & Peterson, D. R. (1996). *Revised Behavior Problem Checklist, PAR Edition.* Odessa, FL: Psychological Assessment Resources.

Ramirez, D. N. (1978). *College of the Desert guide: Education of handicapped adults.* Palm Desert, CA: College of the Desert.

Rapcsak, S. Z. (1997). Disorder of writing. In L. J. G. Rothi & K. M. Heilman (Eds.), *Apraxia: The neuropsychology of action* (pp. 149–172). Hove, England: Psychology Press.

Rapport, M. D. (1994). Attention-deficit/hyperactivity disorder. In V. B. Van Hasselt & M. Hersen (Eds.), *Advance abnormal psychology* (pp. 189–206). New York: Plenum.

Reed, H., Thomas, E., Sprague, J. R., & Horner, R. H. (1997). Student guided functional assessment interview: An analysis of student and teacher agreement. *Journal of Behavioral Education, 7,* 33–49.

Reich, W. (Ed.). (1996). *Diagnostic Interview for Children and Adolescents–Revised (DICA–R) 8.0.* St. Louis: Washington University.

Reilly, P. L., Simpson, D. A., Sprod, R., & Thomas, L. (1988). Assessing the conscious level in infants and young children: A paediatric version of the Glasgow Coma Scale. *Child's Nervous System, 4,* 30–33.

Reinecke, M. A., Beebe, D. W., & Stein, M. A. (1999). The third factor of the WISC–III: It's (probably) not freedom from distractibility. *Journal of the American Academy of Child & Adolescent Psychiatry, 38,* 322–328.

Reisman, J. M. (1973). *Principles of psychotherapy with children.* New York: Wiley.

Reiss, S. (1988). *Test manual for the Reiss Screen for Maladaptive Behavior.* Orland Park, IL: International Diagnostic Systems.

Reiss, S. (1994). Issues in defining mental retardation. *American Journal on Mental Retardation, 99,* 1–7.

Reiss, S., & Valenti-Hein, D. (1994). Development of a psychopathology rating scale for children with mental retardation. *Journal of Consulting and Clinical Psychology, 62,* 28–33.

Reitan, R. M. (1984). *Aphasia and sensory-perceptual deficits in adults.* Tucson, AZ: Neuropsychology Press.

Reitan, R. M. (1985). *Aphasia and sensory perceptual deficits in children.* Tucson, AZ: Neuropsychology Press.

Reitan, R. M., & Davison, L. A. (Eds.). (1974). *Clinical neuropsychology: Current status and applications.* Washington, DC: Winston.

Reitan, R. M., & Wolfson, D. (1985). *The Halstead-Reitan Neuropsychological Test Battery.* Tucson, AZ: Neuropsychology Press.

Reitan, R. M., & Wolfson, D. (1992). *Neuropsychological evaluation of young children.* Tucson, AZ: Neuropsychology Press.

Repp, A. C. (1999). Naturalistic functional assessment of regular and special education students in classroom settings. In A. C. Repp & R. H. Horner (Eds.), *Functional analysis of problem behavior: From effective assessment to effective support* (pp. 238–258). Belmont, CA: Wadsworth.

Repp, A. C., & Barton, L. E. (1980). Naturalistic observations of institutionalized retarded persons: A comparison of licensure decisions and behavioral observations. *Journal of Applied Behavior Analysis, 13,* 333–341.

Repp, A. C., & Horner, R. H. (Eds.). (1999). *Functional analysis of problem behavior: From effective assessment to effective support.* Belmont, CA: Wadsworth.

Reynolds, C. R. (1984). Critical measurement issues in learning disabilities. *Journal of Special Education, 18,* 451–476.

Reynolds, C. R., & Bigler, E. D. (1994). *Test of Memory and Learning.* Austin, TX: Pro-Ed.

Reynolds, C. R., & Kamphaus, R. W. (1992). *Behavior Assessment System for Children.* Circle Pines, MN: American Guidance Service.

Reynolds, C. R., & Richmond, B. O. (1985). *Revised Children's Manifest Anxiety Scale.* Los Angeles: Western Psychological Services.

Reynolds, W. M. (1987). *Reynolds Adolescent Depression Scale.* Odessa, FL: Psychological Assessment Resources.

Reynolds, W. M. (1989). *Reynolds Child Depression Scale.* Odessa, FL: Psychological Assessment Resources.

Reynolds, W. M. (1998a). *Adolescent Psychopathology Scale: Administration and interpretive manual.* Odessa, FL: Psychological Assessment Resources.

Reynolds, W. M. (1998b). *Adolescent Psychopathology Scale: Psychometric and technical manual.* Odessa, FL: Psychological Assessment Resources.

Reynolds, W. M. (2000). *Adolescent Psychopathology Scale–Short Form: Professional manual.* Odessa, FL: Psychological Assessment Resources.

Reynolds, W. M. (2001). *Reynolds Adolescent Adjustment Screening Inventory: Professional manual.* Odessa, FL: Psychological Assessment Resources.

Riccio, C. A., Cohen, M. J., Hall, J., & Ross, C. M. (1997). The third and fourth factors of the WISC–III: What they don't measure. *Journal of Psychoeducational Assessment, 15,* 27–39.

Rich, D., & Taylor, H. G. (1993). Attention deficit hyperactivity disorder. In M. Singer, L. Singer, & T. Anglin (Eds.), *Handbook for screening adolescents at psychosocial risk* (pp. 333–374). New York: Lexington Books.

Richard, M. (1993, December). Ask CH.A.D.D. *CH.A.D.D.er,* p. 10.

Rimm, S. B. (1997). Underachievement syndrome: A national epidemic. In N. Colangelo & G. A. Davis (Eds.), *Handbook of gifted education* (pp. 416–434). Needham Heights, MA: Allyn & Bacon.

Roberts, C., McCoy, M., Reidy, D., & Crucitti, F. (1993). A comparison of methods of assessing adaptive behavior in pre-school children with developmental disabilities. *Australia & New Zealand Journal of Developmental Disabilities, 18,* 261–272.

Roberts, M. A. (1992). *Pediatric Inventory of Neurobehavioral Symptoms.* Unpublished manuscript, University of Iowa at Iowa City.

Roberts, M. A. (1999). Mild traumatic brain injury in children and adolescents. In W. R. Varney & R. J. Roberts (Eds.), *Mild head injury: Causes, evaluation, and treatment* (pp. 493–512). Hillsdale, NJ: Erlbaum.

Roberts, M. A., & Furuseth, A. (1997). Eliciting parental report following pediatric traumatic brain injury: Preliminary findings on the Pediatric Inventory of Neurobehavioral Symptoms. *Archives of Clinical Neuropsychology, 12,* 449–457.

Roberts, M. A., Milich, R., & Loney, J. (1984). *Structured Observation of Academic and Play Settings (SOAPS).* Unpublished manuscript, University of Iowa at Iowa City.

Robins, P. M. (1992). A comparison of behavioral and attentional functioning in children diagnosed as hyperactive or learning-disabled. *Journal of Abnormal Child Psychology, 20,* 65–82.

Robinson, A., & Clinkenbeard, P. R. (1998). Giftedness: An exceptionality examined. *Annual Review of Psychology, 49,* 117–139.

Robinson, H. B. (1980, November). *A case for radical acceleration: Programs of the Johns Hopkins University and the University of Washington.* Paper presented at the meeting of the 1980 Symposium of the Study of Mathematically Precocious Youth, Baltimore.

Robinson, H. B. (1981). The uncommonly bright child. In M. Lewis & L. A. Rosenblum (Eds.), *The uncommon child: Genesis of behavior* (Vol. 3, pp. 57–81). New York: Plenum.

Robinson, N., & Harris, S. R. (1980). *Tricks of the trade: Testing infants and preschoolers.* Unpublished manuscript, University of Washington, Child Development and Mental Retardation Center at Seattle.

Robinson, N. M., & Noble, K. D. (1991). Social-emotional development and adjustment of gifted children. In M. C. Wang, M. C. Reynolds, & H. J. Walberg (Eds.), *Handbook of special education: Research and practice: Vol. 4. Emerging programs—Advances in education* (pp. 57–76). Oxford, England: Pergamon.

Roedell, W. C. (1980a). Characteristics of gifted young children. In W. C. Roedell, N. E. Jackson, & H. B. Robinson (Eds.), *Gifted young children* (pp. 7–26). New York: Teachers College Press.

Roedell, W. C. (1980b). Programs for gifted young children. In W. C. Roedell, N. E. Jackson, & H. B. Robinson (Eds.), *Gifted young children* (pp. 66–89). New York: Teachers College Press.

Rogers, R. (1988). Current status of clinical methods. In R. Rogers (Ed.), *Clinical assessment of malingering and deception* (pp. 293–308). New York: Guilford.

Rollin, W. J. (1987). *The psychology of communication disorders in individuals and their families.* Englewood Cliffs, NJ: Prentice-Hall.

Rosenberger, P. B., & Hier, D. B. (1980). Cerebral asymmetry and verbal intellectual deficits. *Annals of Neurology, 8,* 300–304.

Rosner, J., & Simon, D. P. (1971). The Auditory Analysis Test: An initial report. *Journal of Learning Disabilities, 4,* 40–48.

Rossman, B. B., & Horn, J. L. (1972). Cognitive, motivational and temperamental indicants of creativity and intelligence. *Journal of Educational Measurement, 9,* 265–286.

Rourke, B. P. (1993). Arithmetic disabilities, specific and otherwise: A neuropsychological perspective. *Journal of Learning Disabilities, 26,* 214–226.

Rourke, B. P., Young, G. C., & Leenaars, A. A. (1989). A childhood learning disability that predisposes those afflicted to adolescent and adult depression and suicide risk. *Journal of Learning Disabilities, 22,* 169–175.

Rudel, R. G. (1988). *Assessment of developmental learning disorders: A neuropsychological approach.* New York: Basic Books.

Runco, M. A. (1992). Children's divergent thinking and creative ideation. *Developmental Review, 12,* 233–264.

Rupley, W. H., & Blair, T. R. (1979). *Reading diagnosis and remediation: A primer for classroom and clinic.* Chicago: Rand McNally.

Russell, E. W. (1998). In defense of the Halstead Reitan Battery: A critique of Lezak's review. *Archives of Clinical Neuropsychology, 13,* 365–381.

Rutter, M. (1982). Developmental neuropsychiatry: Concepts, issues, and prospects. *Journal of Clinical Neuropsychology, 4,* 91–115.

Sachs, P. R. (1991). *Treating families of brain-injury survivors. Springer series on rehabilitation: Vol. 9.* New York: Springer.

Sandler, A. D., Footo, M., Levine, M. D., Coleman, W. L., & Hooper, S. R. (1992). Neurodevelopmental study of writing disorders in middle childhood. *Developmental and Behavioral Pediatrics, 13,* 17–23.

Sandoval, J., & Echandia, A. (1994). Review of the Behavioral Assessment System for Children. *Journal of School Psychology, 32,* 419–425.

Sanson, A., Smart, D., Prior, M., & Oberklaid, F. (1993). Precursors of hyperactivity and aggression. *Journal of the American Academy of Child and Adolescent Psychiatry, 32,* 1207–1216.

Saskatchewan Education. (1998). *Teaching students with autism: A guide for educators, 1998* [On-line]. Available: http://www.sasked.gov.sk.ca/curr_inst/speced/hero.html

Sattler, J. M. (1992). *Assessment of children* (revised and updated 3rd ed.). San Diego: Sattler.

Sattler, J. M. (1998). *Clinical and forensic interviewing of children and families: Guidelines for the mental health, education, pediatric, and child maltreatment fields.* San Diego: Sattler.

Saudargas, R. A., & Lentz, F. E. (1986). Estimating percent of time and rate via direct observation: A suggested observational procedure and format. *School Psychology Review, 15,* 36–48.

Savage, R., & Carter, R. (1988). Transitioning pediatric patients into educational systems: Guidelines for rehabilitation professionals. *Cognitive Rehabilitation, 6,* 10–14.

Savage, R. C. (1987). Educational issues for the head-injured adolescent and young adult. *Journal of Head Trauma Rehabilitation, 2,* 1–10.

Savage, R. C. (1993). Children with traumatic brain injury. *TBI Challenge, 1,* 4–5.

Savage, R. M., & Gouvier, W. D. (1992). Rey Auditory-Verbal Learning Test: The effects of age and gender, and norms for delayed recall and story recognition trials. *Archives of Clinical Neuropsychology, 7,* 407–414.

Schachter, S., Brannigan, G. G., & Tooke, W. (1991). Comparison of two scoring systems for the Modified Version of the Bender-Gestalt Test. *Journal of School Psychology, 29,* 265–269.

Schalock, R. L. (1999). The merging of adaptive behavior and intelligence: Implications for the field of mental retardation. In R. L. Schalock (Ed.), *Adaptive behavior and its measurements* (pp. 43–59). Washington, DC: American Association on Mental Retardation.

Schopler, E. (1992). Facilitated communication—Hope or hype? *Autism Society of North Carolina, 8,* 6.

Schopler, E., Reichler, R. J., DeVellis, R. F., & Daly, K. (1980). Toward objective classification of childhood autism: Childhood Autism Rating Scale (CARS). *Journal of Autism and Developmental Disorders, 10,* 91–103.

Schopler, E., Reichler, R. J., & Renner, B. R. (1986). *The Childhood Autism Rating Scale* (CARS). New York: Irvington.

Schopler, E., Van Bourgondien, M. E., & Bristol, M. M. (Eds.). (1993). *Preschool issues in autism: Current issues in autism.* New York: Plenum.

Schreck, K. A. (2000). It can be done: An example of a behavioral individualized education program (IEP) for a child with autism. *Behavioral Interventions, 15,* 279–300.

Schreibman, L. E. (1988). *Autism.* Newbury Park, CA: Sage.

Schuerholz, L. J., Harris, E. L., Baumgardner, T. L., Reiss, A. L., Freund, L. S., Church, R. P., Mohr, J., & Denckla, M. B. (1995). An analysis of two discrepancy-based models and a processing-deficit approach in identifying learning disabilities. *Journal of Learning Disabilities, 28,* 18–29.

Schum, R. L., Sivan, A. B., & Benton, A. (1989). Multilingual Aphasia Examination: Norms for children. *Clinical Neuropsychologist, 3,* 375–383.

Schwab-Stone, M., Fallon, T., Briggs, M., & Crowther, B. (1994). Reliability of diagnostic reporting for children aged 6–11 years: A test-retest study of the Diagnostic Interview Schedule for Children–Revised. *American Journal of Psychiatry, 151,* 1048–1054.

Schwab-Stone, M., Fisher, P., Piacentini, J., Shaffer, D., Davies, M., & Briggs, M. (1993). The Diagnostic Interview Schedule for Children–Revised version (DISC–R): II. Test-retest reliability. *Journal of the American Academy of Child and Adolescent Psychiatry, 32,* 651–657.

Schwean, V. L., & Saklofske, D. H. (1998). WISC–III assessment of children with attention deficit/hyperactivity disorder. In A. Prifitera & D. H. Saklofske (Eds.), *WISC–III clinical use and interpretation* (pp. 91–118). San Diego: Academic Press.

Schworm, R. W., & Birnbaum, R. (1989). Symptom expression in hyperactive children: An analysis of observations. *Journal of Learning Disabilities, 22,* 35–40.

Scruggs, T. E. (1987). Theoretical issues surrounding severe discrepancy: A discussion. *Learning Disabilities Research, 3,* 21–23.

Scruggs, T. E., & Mastropieri, M. A. (1992). Effective mainstreaming strategies for mildly handicapped students. *Elementary School Journal, 92,* 389–409.

Segalowitz, S. J., & Hiscock, M. (1992). The emergence of a neuropsychology of normal development: Rapprochement between neuroscience and developmental psychology. In I. Rapin & S. J. Segalowitz (Eds.), *Handbook of neuropsychology* (Vol. 6, pp. 45–71). Amsterdam, Netherlands: Elsevier Science.

Seligman, M., & Darling, R. B. (1989). *Ordinary families, special children: A systems approach to childhood disability.* New York: Guilford.

Selman, R. L. (1976). Social-cognitive understanding: A guide to educational and clinical practice. In T. Lickona (Ed.), *Moral development and behavior: Theory, research, and social issues* (pp. 299–316). New York: Holt, Rinehart and Winston.

Selz, M. (1981). Halstead-Reitan Neuropsychological Test Battery for Children. In G. W. Hynd & J. E. Obrzut (Eds.), *Neuropsychological assessment and the school-age child: Issues and procedures* (pp. 195–235). New York: Grune & Stratton.

Semrud-Clikeman, M., Filipek, P. A., Biederman, J., Steingard, R., Kennedy, D., Renshaw, P., & Bekken, K. (1994). Attention-deficit hyperactivity disorder: Magnetic resonance imaging morphometric analysis of the corpus callosum. *Journal of the American Academy of Child and Adolescent Psychiatry, 33,* 875–881.

Semrud-Clikeman, M., Hynd, G. W., Lorys, A. R., & Lahey, B. B. (1993). Differential diagnosis of children with ADHD and ADHD/with co-occurring conduct disorder. *School Psychology International, 14,* 361–370.

Sergent, J. (1984). Inferences from unilateral brain damage about normal hemispheric functions in visual pattern recognition. *Psychological Bulletin, 96,* 99–115.

Shaffer, D. (1996). *Diagnostic Interview Schedule for Children (DISC–IV).* New York: New York State Psychiatric Institute.

Shaheen, S. J. (1984). Neuromaturation and behavior development: The case of childhood lead poisoning. *Developmental Psychology, 20,* 542–550.

Shane, H. C. (1993). The dark side of facilitated communication. *Topics in Language Disorders, 13,* ix–xv.

Shapiro, B. K. (1991). The pediatric neurodevelopmental assessment of infants and young children. In A. J. Capute & P. J. Accardo (Eds.), *Developmental disabilities in infancy and childhood* (pp. 139–164). Baltimore: Brookes.

Shapiro, E. S. (1984). Self-monitoring procedures. In T. H. Ollendick & M. Hersen (Eds.), *Child behavioral assessment: Principles and procedures* (pp. 148–165). New York: Pergamon.

Shapiro, E. S. (1996). *Academic skills problems workbook.* New York: Guilford.

Shapiro, E. S., & Cole, C. L. (1994). *Behavior change in the classroom: Self-management intervention.* New York: Guilford.

Shapiro, E. S., & Cole, C. L. (1999). Self-monitoring in assessing children's problems. *Psychological Assessment, 11,* 448–457.

Shapiro, S. K., & Simpson, R. G. (1994). Patterns and predictors of performance on the Bender-Gestalt and the Developmental Test of Visual Motor Integration in a sample of behaviorally and emotionally disturbed adolescents. *Journal of Psychoeducational Assessment, 12,* 254–263.

Share, D. L., Moffitt, R. E., & Silva, P. A. (1988). Factors associated with arithmetic-and-reading disability and specific arithmetic disability. *Journal of Learning Disabilities, 21,* 313–320.

Shea, S. C. (1988). *Psychiatric interviewing: The art of understanding.* Philadelphia: Saunders.

Shelton, T. L., & Barkley, R. A. (1994). Critical issues in the assessment of attention deficit disorders in children. *Topics in Language Disorders, 14,* 26–41.

Sholle-Martin, S., & Alessi, N. E. (1988). Adaptive functioning in children hospitalized for psychiatric disturbances. *Journal of the American Academy of Child and Adolescent Psychiatry, 27,* 636–641.

Shontz, F. C. (1977). Six principles relating disability and psychological adjustment. *Rehabilitation Psychology, 24,* 207–210.

Shrout, P. E., & Fleiss, J. L. (1979). Intraclass correlations: Uses in assessing rater reliability. *Psychological Bulletin, 86,* 420–428.

Shrout, P. E., Spitzer, R. L., & Fleiss, J. L. (1987). Quantification in psychiatric diagnosis revisited. *Archives of General Psychiatry, 44,* 172–177.

Siegel, D. J., Minshew, N. J., & Goldstein, G. (1996). Wechsler IQ profiles in diagnosis of high-functioning autism. *Journal of Autism and Developmental Disorders, 26,* 389–406.

Siegel, L. S. (1999). Issues in the definition and diagnosis of learning disabilities: A perspective on Guckenberger v. Boston University. *Journal of Learning Disabilities, 32,* 304–319.

Siegel, L. S., & Linder, B. A. (1984). Short-term memory processes in children with reading and arithmetic learning disabilities. *Developmental Psychology, 20,* 200–207.

Silver, L. B. (1991). Developmental learning disorders. In M. Lewis (Ed.), *Child and adolescent psychiatry: A comprehensive textbook* (pp. 522–528). Baltimore: Williams & Wilkins.

Silver, L. B. (1992). *Attention-deficit hyperactivity disorder: A clinical guide to diagnosis and treatment.* Washington, DC: American Psychiatric Press.

Silverman, L. K. (1997). Family counseling with the gifted. In N. Colangelo & G. A. Davis (Eds.), *Handbook of gifted education* (pp. 382–397). Needham Heights, MA: Allyn & Bacon.

Silverstein, A. B. (1973). Note on prevalence. *American Journal of Mental Deficiency, 77,* 380–382.

Silverstein, A. B. (1982). Note on the constancy of the IQ. *American Journal of Mental Deficiency, 87,* 227–228.

Simmons, D. C., Kameenui, E. J., & Darch, C. B (1988). The effect of textual proximity on fourth- and fifth-grade LD students' megacognitive awareness and strategic comprehension behavior. *Learning Disability Quarterly, 11,* 380–395.

Sisson, L. A., & Van Hasselt, V. B. (1987). Visual impairment. In V. B. Van Hasselt & M. Hersen (Eds.), *Psychological evaluation of the developmentally and physically disabled* (pp. 115–153). New York: Plenum.

Skeen, J. A., Strong, V. N., & Book, R. M. (1982). Comparison of learning disabled children's performance on Bender Visual-Motor Gestalt Test and Beery's Developmental Test of Visual-Motor Integration. *Perceptual and Motor Skills, 55,* 1257–1258.

Slate, J. R., & Fawcett, J. (1995). Validity of the WISC–III for deaf and hard of hearing persons. *American Annals of the Deaf, 140,* 250–254.

Slate, J. R., & Saudargas, R. A. (1987). Classroom behaviors of LD, seriously emotionally disturbed, and average children: A sequential analysis. *Learning Disability Quarterly, 10,* 125–134.

Sloan, W., & Birch, W. R. (1955). A rationale for degrees of retardation. *American Journal of Mental Deficiency, 60,* 258–264.

Smith, J. D. (1997). Mental retardation: Defining a social invention. In R. L. Taylor (Ed.), *Assessment of individuals with mental retardation* (pp. 103–121). San Diego: Singular Publishing Group.

Smith, T. C., & Smith, B. L. (1988). The Visual Aural Digit Span and Bender Gestalt Test as predictors of Wide Range Achievement Test–Revised scores. *Psychology in the Schools, 25,* 264–269.

Snell, M. E. (1988). Curriculum and methodology for individuals with severe disabilities. *Education & Training in Mental Retardation, 23,* 302–314.

Snow, J. H., & Desch, L. W. (1989). Subgroups based on medical, developmental, and growth variables with a sample of children and adolescents referred for learning difficulties. *International Journal of Clinical Neuropsychology, 11,* 71–79.

Song, L., Singh, J., & Singer, M. (1994). The Youth Self-Report Inventory: A study of its measurement fidelity. *Psychological Assessment, 6,* 236–245.

Spache, G. D. (1981). *Diagnosing and correcting reading disabilities* (2nd ed.). Needham Heights, MA: Allyn & Bacon.

Sparrow, S. S., Balla, D. A., & Cicchetti, D. V. (1984). *Vineland Adaptive Behavior Scales.* Circle Pines, MN: American Guidance Service.

Spencer, T., Biederman, J., Wilens, T., Harding, M., O'Donnell, D., & Griffin, S. (1996). Pharmacotherapy of attention-deficit hyperactivity disorder across the life cycle. *Journal of the American Academy of Child and Adolescent Psychiatry, 35,* 409–432.

Spielberger, C. D. (1973). *State-Trait Anxiety Inventory for Children.* Palo Alto, CA: Consulting Psychologists Press.

Spirito, A. (1980). Scores on Bender-Gestalt and Developmental Test of Visual-Motor Integration of learning-disabled children. *Perceptual and Motor Skills, 50,* 1214.

Spreen, O. (1988). Prognosis of learning disability. *Journal of Consulting and Clinical Psychology, 56,* 836–842.

Spreen, O., & Risser, A. H. (1981). Assessment of aphasia. In M. T. Sarno (Ed.), *Acquired aphasia* (pp. 67–127). New York: Academic Press.

Spreen, O., Risser, A. H., & Edgell, D. (1995). *Developmental neuropsychology.* New York: Oxford University Press.

Spreen, O., & Strauss, E. (1998). *A compendium of neuropsychological tests: Administration, norms, and commentary* (2nd ed.). New York: Oxford University Press.

Spreen, O., Tupper, D., Risser, A., Tuokko, H., & Edgell, D. (1984). *Human developmental neuropsychology.* New York: Oxford University Press.

Stanovich, K. E. (1978). Information processing in mentally retarded individuals. *International Review of Research in Mental Retardation, 9,* 29–60.

Stanovich, K. E. (1985). Cognitive determinants of reading in mentally retarded individuals. *International Review of Research in Mental Retardation, 13,* 181–214.

Stanovich, K. E. (1988). Explaining the differences between the dyslexic and the garden-variety poor reader: The phonological-core variable-difference model. *Journal of Learning Disabilities, 21,* 590–604, 612.

Stanovich, K. E. (1991). Discrepancy definitions of reading disability: Has intelligence led us astray? *Reading Research Quarterly, 26,* 7–29.

Stanovich, K. E., Cunningham, A. E., & Cramer, B. B. (1984). Assessing phonological awareness in kindergarten children: Issues of task comparability. *Journal of Experimental Child Psychology, 38,* 175–190.

Stanovich, K. E., Cunningham, A. E., & Feeman, D. J. (1984). Intelligence, cognitive skills, and early reading progress. *Reading Research Quarterly, 19,* 278–303.

State of Iowa, Department of Public Instruction. (1981). *The identification of pupils with learning disabilities.* Des Moines, IA: Author.

Stein, T. J., Gambrill, E. D., & Wiltse, K. T. (1978). *Children in foster homes: Achieving continuity of care.* New York: Praeger.

Stern, D. N., MacKain, K., Raduns, K., Hopper, P., Kaminsky, C., Evans, S., Shilling, N., Giraldo, L., Kaplan, M., Nachman, P., Trad, P., Polan, J., Barnard, K., & Spieker, S. (1992). The Kiddie-Infant Descriptive Instrument for Emotional States (KIDIES): An instrument for the measurement of affective state in infancy and early childhood. *Infant Mental Health Journal, 13,* 107–118.

Stern, R. A., Singer, E. A., Duke, L. M., Singer, N. G., Morey, C. E., Daughtrey. E. W., & Kaplan, E. F. (1994). The Boston qualitative scoring system for the Rey-Osterrieth Complex Figure: Description and interrater reliability. *Clinical Neuropsychologist, 8,* 309–322.

Sternberg, R. J. (1991). Death, taxes, and bad intelligence tests. *Intelligence, 15,* 257–269.

Sternberg, R. J. (1992). Metaphors of mind underlying the testing of intelligence. In J. C. Rosen & P. McReynolds (Eds.), *Advances in psychological assessment* (Vol. 8, pp. 1–39). New York: Plenum.

Stevenson, I. (1960). *Medical history-taking.* New York: Hoeber.

Stevenson, I. (1974). The psychiatric interview. In S. Arieti (Ed.), *American handbook of psychiatry* (2nd ed., Vol. 1, pp. 1138–1156). New York: Basic Books.

Stevenson, J., & Fredman, G. (1990). The social environmental correlates of reading ability. *Journal of Child Psychology and Psychiatry, 31,* 681–689.

Stevenson, J., Pennington, B. F., Gilger, J. W., DeFries, J. C., & Gillis, J. J. (1993). Hyperactivity and spelling disability: Testing for shared genetic aetiology. *Journal of Child Psychology and Psychiatry, 34,* 1137–1152.

Stinnett, T. A. (1997). [Review of the *AAMR Adaptive Behavior Scale–School*]. *Journal of Psychoeducational Assessment, 15,* 361–372.

Stinnett, T. A., Fuqua, D. R., & Coombs, W. T. (1999). Construct validity of the AAMR Adaptive Behavior Scale–School: 2. *School Psychology Review, 28,* 31–43.

St. James-Roberts, I. (1981). A reinterpretation of hemispherectomy data without functional plasticity of the brain. *Brain and Language, 13,* 31–53.

Stone, W. L. (1998, June). *Descriptive information about the Screening Tool for Autism in two-year-olds (STAT).* Paper presented at the NIH State of the Science in Autism: Screening and Diagnosis Working Conference, Bethesda, MD.

Stone, W. L., & Hogan, K. L. (1993). A structured parent interview for identifying young children with autism. *Journal of Autism & Developmental Disorders, 23,* 639–652.

Stone, W. L., & Lemanek, K. L. (1990). Developmental issues in children's self-reports. In A. M. La Greca (Ed.), *Through the eyes of the child: Obtaining self-reports from children and adolescents* (pp. 18–56). Needham Heights, MA: Allyn & Bacon.

Stone, W. L., MacLean, W. E., Jr., & Hogan, K. L. (1995) Autism and mental retardation. In M. C. Roberts (Ed.), *Handbook of pediatric psychology* (2nd ed., pp. 655–675). New York: Guilford.

Strain, P. S., Sainto, D. M., & Maheady, L. (1984). Toward a functional assessment of severely handicapped learners. *Educational Psychologist, 19,* 180–187.

Strube, M. J. (1985). A BASIC program for the calculation of intraclass correlations based on fixed effects and random effects models. *Behavior Research Methods, Instruments, & Computers, 17,* 578.

Stuart, I. (1995). Spatial orientation and congenital blindness: A neuropsychological approach. *Journal of Visual Impairment & Blindness, 89,* 129–141.

Sturmey, P. (1996). *Functional analysis in clinical psychology.* New York: Wiley.

Subotnik, R. F., Karp, D. E., & Morgan, E. R. (1989). High IQ children at midlife: An investigation into the generalizability of Terman's genetic studies of genius. *Roeper Review, 11,* 139–144.

Sullivan, P. M., & Montoya, L. A. (1997). Factor analysis of the WISC–III with deaf and hard-of-hearing children. *Psychological Assessment, 9,* 317–321.

Sulzer-Azaroff, B., & Reese, E. P. (1982). *Applying behavioral analysis: A program for developing professional competence.* New York: Holt, Rinehart and Winston.

Swanson, J., McBurnett, K., Christian, D., & Wigal, J. (1995). Stimulant medication and the treatment of children with ADHD. *Advances in Clinical Child Psychology, 17,* 265–322.

Sweeney, W. K. (1998). *The special-needs reading list: An annotated guide to the best publications for parents and professionals.* Bethesda, MD: Woodbine House.

Switzky, H. N., Haywood, H. C., & Rotatori, A. F. (1982). Who are the severely and profoundly mentally retarded? *Education and Training of the Mentally Retarded, 17,* 268–272.

Szapocznik, J., & Kurtines, W. M. (1989). *Breakthroughs in family therapy with drug abusing and problem youth.* New York: Springer.

Szymanski, L. S., & Crocker, A. C. (1985). Mental retardation. In H. I. Kaplan & B. J. Sadock (Eds.), *Comprehensive book of psychiatry* (Vol. 2, 4th ed., pp. 1635–1671). Baltimore: Williams & Wilkins.

Talley, J. L. (1993). *Children's Auditory Verbal Learning Test–2.* Odessa, FL: Psychological Assessment Resources.

Tanguay, P. E. (2000). Pervasive developmental disorders: A 10-year review. *Journal of the American Academy of Child and Adolescent Psychiatry, 39,* 1079–1095.

Tanguay, P. E., & Russell, A. T. (1991). Mental retardation. In M. Lewis (Ed.), *Child and adolescent psychiatry: A comprehensive textbook* (pp. 508–516). Baltimore: Williams & Wilkins.

Tarbell, S. E., Cohen, I. T., & Marsh, J. L. (1992). The Toddler-Preschooler Postoperative Pain Scale: An observational scale for measuring postoperative pain in children aged 1–5: Preliminary report. *Pain, 50,* 273–280.

Tasse, M. J., Aman, M. G., Hammer, D., & Rojahn, J. (1996). The Nisonger Child Behavior Rating Form: Age and gender effects and norms. *Research in Developmental Disabilities, 17,* 59–75.

Taylor, E. (1991). Developmental neuropsychiatry. *Journal of Child Psychology and Psychiatry and Allied Disciplines, 32,* 3–47.

Taylor, E. M. (1959). *The appraisal of children with cerebral defects.* Cambridge, MA: Harvard University Press.

Taylor, H. G. (1988a). Learning disabilities. In E. J. Mash & L. G. Terdal (Eds.), *Behavioral assessment of childhood disorders* (2nd ed., pp. 402–450). New York: Guilford.

Taylor, H. G. (1988b). Neuropsychological testing: Relevance for assessing children's learning disabilities. *Journal of Consulting and Clinical Psychology, 56,* 795–800.

Taylor, H. G., & Alden, J. (1997). Age-related differences in outcomes following childhood brain insults: An introduction and overview. *Journal of the International Neuropsychological Society, 3,* 555–567.

Teasdale, G., & Jennett, B. (1974). Assessment of coma and impaired consciousness. *Lancet, 11,* 81–84.

Terman, L. M. (1925). *Genetic studies of genius* (Vol. 1). Stanford, CA: Stanford University Press.

Terman, L. M., & Oden, M. H. (1959). *The gifted group at midlife.* Stanford, CA: Stanford University Press.

Tharp, R. G., & Wetzel, R. J. (1969). *Behavior modification in the natural environment.* New York: Academic Press.

Thompson, R. J., Merritt, K. A., Keith, B. R., Murphy, L. B., & Johndrow, D. A. (1993). Mother-child agreement on the Child Assessment Schedule with nonreferred children: A research note. *Journal of Child Psychology and Psychiatry, 34,* 813–820.

Thurber, S., & Hollingsworth, D. K. (1992). Validity of the Achenbach and Edelbrock Youth Self-Report with hospitalized adolescents. *Journal of Clinical Child Psychology, 21,* 249–254.

Tilly, W. D., III, Knoster, T. P., Kovaleski, J., Bambara, L., Dunlap, G., & Kincaid, D. (1998). *Functional behavioral assessment: Policy development in light of emerging research and practice.* Alexandria, VA: National Association of State Directors of Special Education (NASDSE).

Todd, R. D., Swarzenski, B., Rossi, P. G., & Visconti, P. (1995). Structural and functional development of the human brain. In D. Cicchetti & D. J. Cohen (Eds.), *Developmental psychopathology: Vol. 1. Theory and methods* (pp. 161–194). New York: Wiley.

Torgesen, J. K. (1980). Conceptual and educational implications of the use of efficient task strategies by learning disabled children. *Journal of Learning Disabilities, 13,* 364–371.

Torgesen, J. K. (1981). The relationship between memory and attention in learning disabilities. *Exceptional Education Quarterly, 2,* 51–59.

Torgesen, J. K. (1982a). The learning disabled child as an inactive learner: Educational implications. *Topics in Learning and Learning Disabilities, 2,* 45–52.

Torgesen, J. K. (1982b). The study of short-term memory in learning disabled children: Goals, methods, and conclusions. *Advances in Learning and Behavioral Disabilities, 1,* 117–149.

Torgesen, J. K., Kistner, J. A., & Morgan, S. (1987). Component processes in working memory. In J. G. Borkowski & J. D. Day (Eds.), *Cognition in special children: Comparative approaches to retardation, learning disabilities, and giftedness* (pp. 49–85). Norwood, NJ: Ablex.

Torrance, E. P. (1966). *Torrance Tests of Creative Thinking: Norms technical manual.* Princeton, NJ: Personnel.

Torrance, E. P., & Myers, R. E. (1970). *Creative learning and teaching.* New York: Dodd, Mead.

Tramontana, M. G., & Hooper, S. R. (1988). Child neuropsychological assessment: Overview of current status. In M. G. Tramontana & S. R. Hooper (Eds.), *Assessment issues in child neuropsychology* (pp. 3–38). New York: Plenum.

Trapani, C., & Gettinger, M. (1996). Treatment of students with learning disabilities: Case conceptualization and program design. In M. A. Reinecke, F. M. Dattilio, & A. Freeman (Eds.), *Cognitive therapy with children and adolescents: A casebook for clinical practice* (pp. 251–277). New York: Guilford.

Trevarthen, C., Aitken, K., Papoudi, D., & Robarts, J. (1998). *Children with autism: Diagnosis and interventions to meet their needs* (2nd ed.). Philadelphia: Jessica Kingsley.

Tunks, E., & Billissimo, A. (1991). *Behavioral medicine: Concepts and procedures.* New York: Pergamon.

Turk, D. C., & Kerns, R. D. (1985). The family in health and illness. In D. C. Turk & R. D. Kerns (Eds.), *Health, illness, and families: A life-span perspective* (pp. 1–22). New York: Wiley.

Uebersax, J. S. (1982). A design-independent method for measuring the reliability of psychiatric diagnosis. *Journal of Psychiatric Research, 17,* 335–342.

Ullman, R. K., Sleator, E. K., & Sprague, R. L. (1991). *ACTeRS Teacher Form–Second Edition (ACTeRS–2nd Ed.).* Champaign, IL: MetriTech.

U.S. Department of Education. (2000). *To assure the free appropriate public education of all children with disabilities: Twenty-second annual report to Congress on the implementation of the Individuals with Disabilities Education Act.* Washington, DC: Author.

U.S. Department of Health and Human Services. (1999). *Mental health: A report of the Surgeon General–Executive summary.* Rockville, MD: U.S. Department of Health and Human Services, Substance Abuse and Mental Health Services Administration, Center for Mental Health Services, National Institutes of Health, National Institute of Mental Health.

Valus, A. (1986). Achievement-potential discrepancy status of students in LD programs. *Learning Disability Quarterly, 9,* 200–205.

Vance, H. B., Fuller, G. B., & Lester, M. L. (1986). A comparison of the Minnesota Perceptual Diagnostic Test Revised and the Bender Gestalt. *Journal of Learning Disabilities, 19,* 211–214.

Vanderploeg, R. D., Schinka, J. A., Baum, K. M., Tremont, G., & Mittenberg, W. (1998). WISC–III premorbid prediction strategies: Demographic and best performance approaches. *Psychological Assessment, 10,* 277–284.

Van Etten, G., Arkell, C., & Van Etten, C. (1980). *The severely and profoundly handicapped: Programs, methods, and materials.* St. Louis: C. V. Mosby.

VanTassel, J. (1979). A needs assessment for gifted education. *Journal of the Education of the Gifted, 2,* 141–148.

Vaughn, M. L., Riccio, C. A., Hynd, G. W., & Hall, J. (1997). Diagnosing ADHD (predominantly inattentive and combined type subtypes): Discriminant validity of the Behavior Assessment System for Children and the Achenbach Parent and Teacher Rating Scales. *Journal of Clinical Child Psychology, 26,* 349–357.

Vellutino, F. R., & Shub, M. J. (1982). Assessment of disorders in formal school language: Disorders in reading. *Topics in Language Disorders, 2,* 20–33.

Venter, A., Lord, C., & Schopler, E. (1992). A follow-up study of high functioning autistic children. *Journal of Child Psychology and Psychiatry, 33,* 489–507.

Verderber, J. M., & Payne, V. G. (1987). A comparison of the long and short forms of the Bruininks-Oseretsky Test of Motor Proficiency. *Adapted Physical Activity Quarterly, 4,* 51–59.

Voeller, K. K. (1991). Clinical management of attention deficit hyperactivity disorder. *Journal of Child Neurology, 6,* S51–S67.

Vossekuil, B., Reddy, M., Fein, R., Borum, R., & Modzeleski, W. (2000). *U.S.S.S. safe school initiative: An interim report on the prevention of targeted violence in schools.* Washington, DC: U.S. Secret Service, National Threat Assessment Center.

Wade, S. L., Taylor, H. G., Drotar, D., Stancin, T., & Yeates, K. O. (1998). Family burden and adaptation during the initial year after traumatic brain injury in children. *Pediatrics, 102,* 110–116.

Wagner, R., Torgesen, J. K., & Rashotte, C. (1999). *Comprehensive Test of Phonological Processing.* Austin, TX: Pro-Ed.

Wallbrown, F. H., & Fremont, T. S. (1980). The stability of Koppitz scores on the Bender-Gestalt for reading disabled children. *Psychology in the Schools, 17,* 181–184.

Wallach, M., & Kogan, N. (1965). *Modes of thinking in young children.* New York: Holt, Rinehart, & Winston.

Ward, S. B., Ward, T. J., Jr., Hatt, C. V., Young, D. L., & Mollner, N. R. (1995). The incidence and utility of the ACID, ACIDS, and SCAD profiles in a referred population. *Psychology in the Schools, 32,* 267–276.

Watkins, E. O. (1976). *The Watkins Bender-Gestalt scoring system.* Novato, CA: Academic Therapy.

Watkins, M. W. (1996). Diagnostic utility of the WISC–III development index as a predictor of learning disabilities. *Journal of Learning Disabilities, 29,* 305–312.

Watkins, M. W., Kush, J. C., & Glutting, J. J. (1997a). Discriminant and predictive validity of the WISC–III ACID profile among children with learning disabilities. *Psychology in the Schools, 34,* 309–319.

Watkins, M. W., Kush, J. C., & Glutting, J. J. (1997b). Prevalence and diagnostic utility of the WISC–III SCAD profile among children with disabilities. *School Psychology Quarterly, 12,* 235–248.

Watkins, M. W., & Worrell, F. C. (2000). Diagnostic utility of the number of WISC–III subtests deviating from mean performance among students with learning disabilities. *Psychology in the Schools, 37,* 303–309.

Webster, P. E., Plante, A. S., & Couvillion, M. L. (1997). Phonological impairment and prereading: Update on a longitudinal study. *Journal of Learning Disabilities, 4,* 365–375.

Wechsler, D. (1991). *Wechsler Intelligence Scale for Children–Third Edition.* San Antonio, TX: The Psychological Corporation.

Wehman, P. (1979). *Curriculum design for the severely and profoundly handicapped.* New York: Human Sciences Press.

Weiss, G. (1991). Attention deficit hyperactivity disorder. In M. Lewis (Ed.), *Child and adolescent psychiatry: A comprehensive textbook* (pp. 544–561). Baltimore: Williams & Wilkins.

Welsh, G. (1975). *Creativity of intelligence: A personality approach.* Chapel Hill, NC: University of North Carolina Press.

Wesson, M. D., & Kispert, K. (1986). The relationship between the Test for Visual Analysis Skills (TVAS) and standardized visual-motor tests in children with visual perception difficulty. *Journal of the American Optometric Association, 57,* 844–849.

Westling, D. L. (1996). What do parents of children with moderate and severe mental disabilities want? *Education & Training in Mental Retardation, 31,* 86–114.

Wetherby, A. M., & Prizant, B. M. (1992). Facilitating language and communication development in autism: Assessment and intervention guidelines. In D. E. Berkell (Ed.), *Autism: Identification, education, and treatment* (pp. 107–134). Hillsdale, NJ: Erlbaum.

Weyandt, L. L. (2001). *An ADHD primer.* Needham Heights, MA: Allyn & Bacon.

Weyandt, L. L., Stein, S., Rice, J. A., & Wermus, C. (1994). Classroom interventions for children with attention-deficit hyperactivity disorder. *The Oregon Conference Monograph, 6,* 137–143.

Weyandt, L. L., & Willis, W. G. (1994). Executive functions in school-aged children: Potential efficacy of tasks in discriminating clinical groups. *Developmental Neuropsychology, 10,* 27–38.

Whalen, C. K. (1989). Attention deficit and hyperactivity disorders. In T. H. Ollendick & M. Hersen (Eds.), *Handbook of child psychopathology* (pp. 131–169). New York: Plenum.

Whalen, C. K., Henker, B., Swanson, J. M., Granger, D., Kliewer, W., & Spencer, J. (1987). Natural social behaviors in hyperactive children: Dose effects of methylphenidate. *Journal of Consulting and Clinical Psychology, 55,* 187–193.

White, O. R., & Haring, N. G. (1978). Evaluating educational programs serving the severely and profoundly handicapped. In N. G. Haring & D. D. Bricker (Eds.), *Teaching the severely handicapped* (Vol. 3, pp. 153–200). Seattle: American Association for the Education of the Severely/Profoundly Handicapped.

Whitehurst, G. J., & Fischel, J. E. (1994). Early developmental language delay: What, if anything, should the clinician be doing about it? *Journal of Child Psychology and Psychiatry, 35,* 613–648.

Whitman, T. L., Scibak, J. W., Butler, K. M., Richter, R., & Johnson, M. R. (1982). Improving classroom behavior in mentally retarded children through correspondence training. *Journal of Applied Behavior Analysis, 15,* 545–564.

Whitten, C. J., D'Amato, R. C., & Chittooran, M. M. (1992). The neuropsychological approach to intervention. In R. C. D'Amato & B. A. Rothlisberg (Eds.), *Psychological perspectives on intervention: A case study approach to prescriptions for change* (pp. 112–136). New York: Longman.

Williams, C. L., Butcher, J. N., Ben-Porath, Y. S., & Graham, J. R. (1992). *MMPI–A: Assessing psychopathology in adolescents.* Minneapolis, MN: University of Minnesota Press.

Williams, M. A., & Boll, T. J. (1997). Recent advances in neuropsychological assessment of children. In G. Goldstein & T. M. Incagnoli (Eds.), *Contemporary approaches to neuropsychological assessment* (pp. 231–276). New York: Plenum.

Willis, D. J., & Walker, C. E. (1989). Etiology. In T. H. Ollendick & M. Hersen (Eds.), *Handbook of child psychopathology* (2nd ed., pp. 29–51). New York: Plenum.

Wilson, B. (1991). Theory, assessment, and treatment in neuropsychological rehabilitation. *Neuropsychology, 5,* 281–291.

Wilson, B. C., Iacoviello, J. M., Wilson, J. J., & Risucci, D. (1982). Purdue Pegboard performance of normal preschool children. *Journal of Clinical Neuropsychology, 4,* 19–26.

Wing, L. (1976). Assessment: The role of the teacher. In M. P. Everard (Ed.), *An approach to teaching autistic children* (pp. 15–30). New York: Pergamon.

Wirt, R. D., Lachar, D., Seat, P. D., & Broen, W. E., Jr. (2001). *Personality Inventory for Children–Second Edition.* Los Angeles: Western Psychological Services.

Wistedt, B., Rasmussen, A., Pedersen, L., Malm, U., Traskman-Bendz, L., Wakelin, J., & Bech, P. (1990). The development of an observer-scale for measuring social dysfunction and aggression. *Pharmacopsychiatry, 23,* 249–252.

Witt, J. C., & Elliott, S. N. (1983). Assessment in behavioral consultation: The initial interview. *School Psychology Review, 12,* 42–49.

Wong, S. P., & McGraw, K. O. (1999). Confidence intervals and F tests for intraclass correlations based on three-way random effects models. *Educational & Psychological Measurement, 59,* 270–288.

Wood, R. L. (1987). *Brain injury rehabilitation: A neurobehavioral approach.* London: Croom Helm.

Woods, B. T., & Carey, S. (1979). Language deficits after apparent clinical recovery from childhood aphasia. *Annals of Neurology, 6,* 405–409.

Worchel, F. F. (1988). Interviewing adolescents. In J. M. Dillard & R. R. Reilly (Eds.), *Systematic interviewing: Communication skills for professional effectiveness* (pp. 114–138). Columbus, OH: Merrill.

Wright, B. A. P. (1983). *Physical disability—A psychosocial approach* (2nd ed.). New York: Harper & Row.

Wright, D., & DeMers, S. T. (1982). Comparison of the relationship between two measures of visual-motor coordination and academic achievement. *Psychology in the Schools, 19,* 473–477.

Yablon, S. A., Cabrera, M., Yudofsky, S. C., & Silver, J. M. (1994). Prevention. In J. M. Silver, S. C. Yudofsky, & R. E. Hales (Eds.), *Neuropsychiatry of traumatic brain injury* (pp. 805–834). Washington, DC: American Psychiatric Press.

Yarrow, L. J. (1960). Interviewing children. In P. H. Mussen (Ed.), *Handbook of research methods in child development* (pp. 561–602). New York: Wiley.

Yeates, K. O. (1994). Comparison of developmental norms for the Boston Naming Test. *Clinical Neuropsychologist, 8,* 91–98.

Yeates, K. O. (2000). Closed-head injury. In K. O. Yeates, M. D. Ris, & H. G. Taylor (Eds.), *Pediatric neuropsychology: Research, theory, and practice* (pp. 92–116). New York: Guilford.

Yeudall, L. T., Fromm, D., Reddon, J. R., & Stefanyk, W. O. (1986). Normative data stratified by age and sex for 12 neuropsychological tests. *Journal of Clinical Psychology, 42,* 918–946.

Yeudall, L. T., Reddon, J. R., Gill, D. M., & Stefanyk, W. O. (1987). Normative data for the Halstead-Reitan neuropsychological tests stratified by age and sex. *Journal of Clinical Psychology, 43,* 346–367.

Yi, S., Johnstone, B., Doan, R., & Townes, B. D. (1990). The relationship between the pediatric neurological examination and neuropsychological assessment measures for young children. *International Journal of Neuroscience, 50,* 73–81.

Ylvisaker, M. (1986). Language and communication disorders following pediatric head injury. *Journal of Head Trauma Rehabilitation, 1,* 48–56.

Ylvisaker, M., Hartwick, P., & Stevens, M. (1991). School reentry following head injury: Managing the transition from hospital to school. *Journal of Head Trauma Rehabilitation, 6,* 10–22.

Yopp, H. K. (1995). A test for assessing phonemic awareness in young children. *The Reading Teacher, 49,* 20–29.

Yoshinaga-Itano, C., Sedey, A. L., Coulter, D. K., & Mehl, A. L. (1998). Language of early- and later-identified children with hearing loss. *Pediatrics, 102,* 1161–1171.

Yousefi, F., Shahim, S., Razavieh, A., Mehryar, A. H., Hosseini, A. A., & Alborzi, S. (1992). Some normative data on the Bender Gestalt Test performance of Iranian children. *British Journal of Educational Psychology, 62,* 410–416.

Zahn-Waxler, C., Iannotti, R. J., Cummings, E. M., & Denham, S. (1990). Antecedents of problem behaviors in children of depressed mothers. *Development & Psychopathology, 2,* 271–291.

Zahn-Waxler, C., McKnew, D. H., Cummings, E. M., Davenport, Y. B., & Radke-Yarrow, M. (1984). Problem behaviors and peer interactions of young children with a manic-depressive parent. *American Journal of Psychiatry, 141,* 236–240.

Zaidel, E., Zaidel, D. W., & Sperry, R. W. (1981). Left and right intelligence: Case studies of Raven's Progressive Matrices following brain bisection and hemidecortication. *Cortex, 17,* 167–186.

Zigler, E. (1995). Can we "cure" mild mental retardation among individuals in the lower socioeconomic stratum? *American Journal of Public Health, 85,* 302–304.

Zigler, E., & Balla, D. (1981). Recent issues in developmental approach to mental retardation. In M. P. Friedman, J. P. Das, & N. O'Connor (Eds.), *Intelligence and learning* (pp. 25–38). New York: Plenum.

Zigler, E., Balla, D., & Hodapp, R. M. (1984). On the definition and classification of mental retardation. *American Journal of Mental Deficiency, 89,* 215–230.

Zigler, E., & Farber, E. A. (1985). Commonalities between the intellectual extremes: Giftedness and mental retardation. In F. D. Horowitz & M. O'Brien (Eds.), *The gifted and talented: Developmental perspectives* (pp. 387–408). Washington, DC: American Psychological Association.

Zigler, E., & Hodapp, R. M. (1986). *Understanding mental retardation.* New York: Cambridge University Press.

Zima, J. P. (1983). *Interviewing: Key to effective management.* Chicago: Science Research Associates.

NAME INDEX

List of Tables in Appendixes A to F